Frommer's

Southeast Asia

3rd Edition

by Charles Agar,
Jennifer Eveland, and Beth Reiber

Here's what the critics say about Frommer's:

"Amazingly easy to use. Very portable, very complete."
—*Booklist*

"Detailed, accurate, and easy-to-read information for all price ranges."
—*Glamour Magazine*

"Hotel information is close to encyclopedic."
—*Des Moines Sunday Register*

"Frommer's Guides have a way of giving you a real feel for a place."
—*Knight Ridder Newspapers*

WILEY
Wiley Publishing, Inc.

Published by:

Wiley Publishing, Inc.

111 River St.
Hoboken, NJ 07030

ISBN 0-7645-2540-9
ISSN 1098-9455

Editor: Amy Lyons
Production Editor: M. Faunette Johnston
Cartographer: Nick Trotter
Photo Editor: Richard Fox
Production by Wiley Indianapolis Composition Services

For information on our other products and services or to obtain technical support, please contact our Customer Care Department within the U.S. at 800-762-2974, outside the U.S. at 317-572-3993 or fax 317-572-4002.

Wiley also publishes its books in a variety of electronic formats. Some content that appears in print may not be available in electronic formats.

Manufactured in the United States of America

5 4 3 2 1

Contents

List of Maps   viii

What's New in Southeast Asia   1

Regional Safety &
Health Concerns 2

1   The Best of Southeast Asia   6

1 The Most Unforgettable
Travel Experiences 6
2 The Best Small Towns
& Villages 10
3 The Best Beaches 11
4 The Best Outdoor Adventures . . .11
5 The Most Intriguing Temples,
Shrines, Palaces
& Archaeological Sites 13
6 The Best Museums 14
7 The Best Festivals
& Celebrations 15
8 The Biggest Cultural No-Nos . . .16
9 The Best Resorts
& Luxury Hotels 17
10 The Best Hotel Bargains 18
11 The Best Local Dining
Experiences 19
12 The Best Markets 20
13 The Best Shopping Bargains 21
14 The Hottest Nightlife Spots 22

2   Introducing Southeast Asia   23

1 The Region Today 23
Get Lost to Get Found 25
2 A Southeast Asian
Cultural Primer 29
Buddha and Buddhism
in Southeast Asia 30
Understanding Feng Shui 35
Everything Has a Price:
Haggling 36

3   Planning Your Trip to Southeast Asia   37

1 Visitor Information 37
Southeast Asia: Red Alert
Checklist 37
2 Entry Requirements
& Customs 38
3 Money 41
4 When to Go 44
Packing Sensibly 45
5 Travel Insurance 46
6 Health & Safety 47
7 Specialized Travel Resources 51
8 Planning Your Trip Online 56
Frommers.com: The Complete
Travel Resource 57
9 The 21st-Century Traveler 57
Online Traveler's Toolbox 59
10 Getting There 60

11 Packages for the Independent
  Traveler 64

12 Escorted General-Interest
  Tours 65

13 Getting Around
  Southeast Asia 68

14 Suggested Itineraries 69

  Fast Facts: Southeast Asia 70

4 Hong Kong   74

by Beth Reiber

1 Getting to Know Hong Kong . . .74

2 Planning Your Trip to
  Hong Kong 75

  Fast Facts: Hong Kong 80

3 Where to Stay 82

4 Where to Dine 91

5 Exploring Hong Kong 96

6 Shopping 100

7 Nightlife 100

5 Thailand   104

by Jennifer Eveland

1 Getting to Know Thailand 104

  Wats 101 111

2 Planning Your Trip
  to Thailand 114

  The Thai Sex Industry & AIDS . . .116

  Fast Facts: Thailand 120

3 Bangkok 124

  *Telephone Dialing Info
  at a Glance* 126

  Fast Facts: Bangkok 129

4 The Eastern Seaboard 160

5 Pattaya 162

  Fast Facts: Pattaya 164

6 Ko Samet 172

  Fast Facts: Ko Samet 175

7 The Southern Peninsula 176

8 Southern Peninsula: Hua Hin
  & Cha-Am 177

  *Fast Facts: Hua Hin
  & Cha-Am* 178

9 Ko Samui 187

  Fast Facts: Ko Samui 191

10 Phuket 199

  Fast Facts: Phuket 203

11 An Introduction to
  Northern Thailand 218

12 Chiang Mai 222

  Fast Facts: Chiang Mai 225

13 Chiang Rai 237

  Fast Facts: Chiang Rai 238

14 Chiang Saen & the
  Golden Triangle 242

6 Vietnam   246

by Charles Agar

1 Getting to Know Vietnam 247

2 Planning Your Trip
  to Vietnam 253

  Tours for Vietnam Veterans . . .254

  *Have You Hugged Your
  Taxi Driver Today?* 260

  Fast Facts: Vietnam 261

3 Hanoi 264

Telephone Dialing Information at a Glance 265

Fast Facts: Hanoi 269

Have You Tried the Snake? . . .280

4 The Far North 289

5 Sapa 289

6 An Introduction to the Central Coast 294

7 Hue 294

Fast Facts: Hue 297

8 Danang & China Beach 304

9 Hoi An 308

Fast Facts: Hoi An 310

10 An Introduction to South Central Vietnam 321

11 Nha Trang 321

Fast Facts: Nha Trang 324

12 Dalat 332

Fast Facts: Dalat 333

13 Phan Thiet Town & Mui Ne Beach 341

14 Ho Chi Minh City (Saigon) 346

Fast Facts: Ho Chi Minh City . . .350

15 The Mekong Delta 369

16 Chau Doc 370

⑦ **Laos** 372

by Charles Agar

Travel Advisory 373

1 Getting to Know Laos 374

Baci Ceremony 376

2 Planning Your Trip to Laos 378

Fast Facts: Laos 388

3 Vientiane 390

Telephone Dialing Info at a Glance 391

Fast Facts: Vientiane 394

4 Vang Vieng 406

5 Luang Prabang 407

Fast Facts: Luang Prabang 410

Going to Refuge: Making Friends at the Temple 420

6 Luang Namtha & the Far North 421

7 Xieng Khouang Province: Phonsavan 423

⑧ **Singapore** 427

by Jennifer Eveland

1 Getting to Know Singapore . . .427

2 Planning Your Trip to Singapore 431

Fast Facts: Singapore 444

Telephone Dialing Info at a Glance 447

3 Where to Stay 448

4 Where to Dine 463

5 Attractions 480

6 Sports & Recreation 506

7 Shopping 508

8 Singapore After Dark 512

⑨ **Malaysia** 520

by Jennifer Eveland

1 Getting to Know Malaysia 521

2 Planning Your Trip to Malaysia 522

Fast Facts: Malaysia 533

3 Kuala Lumpur 535

4 Johor Bahru 553

5 Malacca 558

6 Penang 565

7 Langkawi 575

10 Bali (Indonesia)   581

updated by Charles Agar

1 Getting to Know Bali 581

2 Planning Your Trip to Bali 587

Telephone Dialing Info at a Glance 592

Fast Facts: Bali 592

3 Kuta 594

Fast Facts: Kuta 594

4 Nusa Dua 601

5 Ubud 603

Fast Facts: Ubud 604

6 Candi Dasa 613

Fast Facts: Candi Dasa 614

7 Lovina 617

Fast Facts: Lovina 617

8 Lombok 620

Fast Facts: Lombok 622

9 Senggigi 622

10 Kuta 624

11 Cambodia   625

by Charles Agar

1 Getting to Know Cambodia . . .626

2 Planning Your Trip to Cambodia 630

3 Phnom Penh 635

Fast Facts: Phnom Penh 636

4 Siem Reap and Angkor Wat . . .650

Fast Facts: Siem Reap 653

The Magic Hours at Angkor Wat 660

12 The Philippines   663

updated by Charles Agar

1 Getting to Know the Philippines 663

Travel Warning: The Philippines 664

2 Planning Your Trip to the Philippines 666

Fast Facts: The Philippines 669

Telephone Dialing Info at a Glance 671

3 Manila 671

Fast Facts: Manila 674

4 Excursions from Manila 679

5 Boracay Island 680

6 Palawan 683

Amanpulo Resort 684

7 Cebu and the South 685

13   Myanmar (Burma)   686

by Charles Agar

1 Getting to Know Myanmar 686

2 Planning Your Trip
to Myanmar 691

3 Yangon 693

4 Mandalay 693

5 Bagan 694

Index   695

General Index 695

Accommodations Index 710

List of Maps

Southeast Asia   8

Hong Kong Region   76

Kowloon   83

Central District   87

Thailand   105

Skytrain   127

Bangkok Accommodations
   & Dining   130

Exploring Bangkok   148

The East Coast Beaches   161

Pattaya   163

Ko Samet   173

Southern Peninsula:
   East Coast   179

Southern Peninsula:
   West Coast   186

Ko Samui   189

Phuket   201

Northern Thailand   219

Chiang Mai   223

Vietnam   249

Hanoi Accommodations
   & Dining   266

Hanoi: The Old City   283

Hue   295

Hoi An   309

Nha Trang   323

Ho Chi Minh City (Saigon)   348

Laos   375

Vientiane   392

Luang Prabang   409

Singapore   429

Urban Singapore
   Neighborhoods   432

MRT Transit Map   441

Urban Singapore
   Accommodations   450

Urban Singapore Dining   464

Urban Singapore Attractions   482

Sentosa Island Attractions   503

Peninsular Malaysia   523

East Malaysia   525

Kuala Lumpur   537

Johor Bahru   555

Malacca   559

Penang Island   567

Georgetown   569

Langkawi   577

Bali   582

Lombok   621

Cambodia   627

Phnom Penh   639

Siem Reap   651

The Philippines   665

Manila   672

Myanmar   687

About the Authors

Charles Agar (Vietnam, Laos, Bali, the Philippines, Cambodia, and Myanmar) After completing a Masters in English Literature at the University of Rochester, work as an English teacher in Japan first brought Charles to Asia. The years since have found him in the region whenever possible, practicing Buddhism, teaching and studying language. This is his first assignment with Frommer's and he'd like to thank the many people who helped him, among them: Rick Tuggey and Tim Miner for teaching him how to work, Bill Indick for being at the airport rain or shine, Eunice Agar for the tea, sympathy, and editing, Annette Monreal for sharing the roads of Laos, Mr. Abhay, Mr. Sousath, Kerry Howley, Tony Tran, and Ms. Phuoc. A special thanks to Connell McGrath for his help and encouragement, Keith Cahalan, Chaula Hopefisher, the Mandels for all the groovy dinners and above all his loving family as well as the many kind expats and fellow travelers he met while trudging along the happy road.

Jennifer Eveland (Thailand, Singapore, and Malaysia) She was a child when she and her family first moved to Singapore, and after returning to the United States, she was drawn again and again to the magic of Singapore, East Asia, and Southeast Asia. She is the author of *Frommer's Singapore & Malaysia* and currently lives in Singapore.

Beth Reiber (Hong Kong) She worked for several years in Germany as a freelance travel writer for major U.S. newspapers and in Tokyo as the editor of *Far East Traveler.* Now a freelancer again and residing in Lawrence, Kansas, with her husband and two children, she is the author of several Frommer's guides including *Frommer's Hong Kong, Frommer's Portable Hong Kong, Frommer's Japan,* and *Frommer's Tokyo,* and is a contributor to *Frommer's Europe from $70 a Day.*

An Invitation to the Reader

In researching this book, we discovered many wonderful places—hotels, restaurants, shops, and more. We're sure you'll find others. Please tell us about them, so we can share the information with your fellow travelers in upcoming editions. If you were disappointed with a recommendation, we'd love to know that, too. Please write to:

Frommer's Southeast Asia, 3rd Edition
Wiley Publishing, Inc. • 111 River St. • Hoboken, NJ 07030

An Additional Note

Please be advised that travel information is subject to change at any time—and this is especially true of prices. We therefore suggest that you write or call ahead for confirmation when making your travel plans. The authors, editors, and publisher cannot be held responsible for the experiences of readers while traveling. Your safety is important to us, however, so we encourage you to stay alert and be aware of your surroundings. Keep a close eye on cameras, purses, and wallets, all favorite targets of thieves and pickpockets.

Other Great Guides for Your Trip:

Frommer's Hong Kong
Frommer's Singapore & Malaysia
Frommer's Thailand

Frommer's Star Ratings, Icons & Abbreviations

Every hotel, restaurant, and attraction listing in this guide has been ranked for quality, value, service, amenities, and special features using a **star-rating system.** In country, state, and regional guides, we also rate towns and regions to help you narrow down your choices and budget your time accordingly. Hotels and restaurants are rated on a scale of zero (recommended) to three stars (exceptional). Attractions, shopping, nightlife, towns, and regions are rated according to the following scale: zero stars (recommended), one star (highly recommended), two stars (very highly recommended), and three stars (must-see).

In addition to the star-rating system, we also use **eight feature icons** that point you to the great deals, in-the-know advice and unique experiences that separate travelers from tourists. Throughout the book, look for:

Finds	Special finds—those places only insiders know about
Fun Fact	Fun facts—details that make travelers more informed and their trips more fun
Kids	Best bets for kids, and advice for the whole family
Moments	Special moments–those experiences that memories are made of
Overrated	Places or experiences not worth your time or money
Tips	Insider tips—great ways to save time and money
Value	Great values—where to get the best deals
Warning	Warning—traveler's advisories are usually in effect

The following **abbreviations** are used for credit cards:

AE	American Express	DISC	Discover	V	Visa
DC	Diners Club	MC	MasterCard		

Frommers.com

Now that you have the guidebook to a great trip, visit our website at **www.frommers.com** for travel information on more than 3,000 destinations. With features updated regularly, we give you instant access to the most current trip-planning information available. At Frommers.com, you'll also find the best prices on airfares, accommodations, and car rentals—and you can even book travel online through our travel booking partners. At Frommers.com, you'll also find the following:

- Online updates to our most popular guidebooks
- Vacation sweepstakes and contest giveaways
- Newsletter highlighting the hottest travel trends
- Online travel message boards with featured travel discussions

What's New in Southeast Asia

Buddhism is all about accepting the inevitable changes in a constantly changing world and the countries of Southeast Asia, Buddhist or other, couldn't be better proving ground for that very philosophy. Much of what fascinates many travelers in the region is minutia: that friendly shopkeeper who invites you to try something new, a hole-in-the-wall antiques store, a local specialty served at street-side, seeming impromptu festivals, and the kindness of strangers. These very visceral experiences are what make travel in this part of the world so memorable and yet so maddening for the publisher of a guidebook to chronicle. Those quaint little corners of the region are as fickle as shooting stars and can often only be found by searching (and often disappear or change if sought after again). Our advice: search away! Ask around and go where the locals go. It's a great place to explore and to find new and interesting things whether a rural temple ruin, a night market, or small local festival.

Below we list just a few of the major changes in this updated edition. Travelers to anywhere in the region need to be hip to fluctuations in the international airline scene following the events of Sept. 11, 2001, and in today's cautious climate. While some Asian airlines have eliminated North American routes, many North American carriers have begun offering rock-bottom rates for premium flights. Time will tell the overall effect. Yet, while the travel industry in Southeast Asia will definitely suffer somewhat, peak season is still peak season, and all surcharges and advance booking requirements still apply.

THAILAND Starbucks and Mc-Donald's have invaded Ko Samui! Most will agree there is not a more poignant sign of the times—the mass market meets the alternative nooks of Southeast Asia's tourist gem. Oddly enough, while you can satisfy any "Big Mac Attack" in many parts of old Siam, you'll still have a bear of a time finding an ATM. Go figure.

Bangkok is a one of the more convenient (and affordable) international air hubs in the world, but domestic carriers are fickle at best so stay abreast of any changes. Check out the latest flights on **Bangkok Airways** (direct connection to Angkor Wat in Cambodia among them).

The most exciting news since our last guide is the completion of **Bangkok's Skytrain.** This means you no longer need suffer Bangkok traffic jams. The smooth, air-conditioned ride whisks you high above the smoggy tangle of city streets below. The two short routes are limited, but convenient to a few sites and many of the big hotels downtown (Be sure that your hotel is nearby to save cash and time).

The **Bangkok Tourist Bureau** (© 2225-7612), while not necessarily new, are promoting themselves more vigorously and are quite helpful about the city and connections throughout Thailand.

⌒Warning Regional Safety & Health Concerns

Just as the world was overcoming jitters following the terrorist attacks in the United States, a grisly bombing that targeted Western tourists on the Indonesian paradise island of Bali dealt another serious blow to international travel.

Indeed, Southeast Asia is no stranger to terrorism, with active groups in the Philippines (Abu Sayaff) and Indonesia (Jemaah Islamiah) being linked to Al Qaeda networks. These are grim days to be planning a holiday; however, the economic effects of these events have created a depressed travel industry that promises unbelievable bargains. While no country can guarantee your safety, some countries are handling travel security far better than others. While planning your trip, you'll be well advised to check the **U.S. Department of State** website at **travel.state.gov/travel_warnings.html** for the most up-to-the-minute travel advisories.

At the time of writing, travelers were being advised by the **World Health Organization (WHO)** to avoid China's capital city Beijing and southern Guangdong province, Hong Kong, Singapore, Hanoi, Taiwan, and Toronto as areas stricken by the **Severe Acute Respiratory Syndrome (SARS)**. This highly contagious atypical pneumonia is caused by organisms as yet unidentified that can travel through the coughing, sneezing, or other close contact with SARS infected persons. Symptoms include high fever, dry cough, and breathing difficulties, and in many cases infection has lead to death. Presently Singapore, Hanoi, and Toronto have taken excellent measures to contain the spread of the disease, according to the WHO, with the treatment of SARS patients in designated hospitals, home quarantine of those who have come in close contact with SARS sufferers, public education campaigns, closing of schools, and airport arrival checks for visitors who display symptoms. It comes as no surprise that tourism figures in SARS affected countries have plummeted as a result. However, with the global campaign to contain and treat the virus, it is widely believed that it is just a matter of time before it runs its course and global movement continues as before. For the latest health alerts, refer to the U.S. Center for Disease Control and Prevention website at www.cdc.gov.

A few developments that have created the loudest hullabaloo are ordinances that restrict Bangkok nightlife. Smoking is now prohibited in restaurants and it looks like the restriction, bolstered by hefty fines and police presence, is actually going to hold; places to puff-away in this heretofore smokers' paradise are getting fewer. On top of that, there's a new Bangkok city ordinance that closes bars and nightclubs at 2am, clipping the wings of any 'One Night in Bangkok' to more of a half-a-night. Crack-downs on juvenile delinquency and amphetamine abuse, zoning laws limiting the more lewd nighttime establishments, and a more vigorous education campaign about STD's all add-up to a slowly changing face on this once debaucherous destination.

New on the hotel scene, don't miss the **Hard Rock Hotel Pattaya** (✆ 3842-8755), a Vegas-style edifice with all the standard offerings of Hard Rock Cafes and hotels the world over.

If you follow brand loyalty, the **Marriott hotel chain** (North American reservation toll-free ✆ **800/344-1212**) has taken over four resort properties, in Bangkok, Pattaya, Hua Hin, and Phuket. Each has a fine spa and upholds Marriot's standard of quality. The Dusit hotel chain has brought a bit of luxury to the provinces by opening Royal Princess hotels, its sister brand, in such places as **Ranong** and **Narathiwat.**

VIETNAM The north-south (or vice-versa) coastal route through Vietnam is gaining in popularity and meeting the increased numbers with fine amenities. Convenient tour buses connect all major destinations, a steadily improving rail system traces the coast, and convenient international and domestic flights make connecting with this fascinating land easier than ever.

If you've got the time, and the funds, don't miss the new and interesting **Victoria Express Train,** a dolled-up old Pullman-type of rail car that carries you in style to the far north, near the China border, on an overnight ride from Hanoi. A short bus/car ride from the end of the line in Lao Cai brings you to **Sapa,** a picturesque hilltown and great place for trekking and visiting colorful minority villages. The **Victoria Sapa Hotel** (✆ 20/871-522) has got it all and is the finest hotel between Hanoi and Kunming (China). Sapa also boasts fine budget choices (in both accommodation and transport).

The beaches of Vietnam are booming, and construction is underway on a number of new resorts. The islands off the coast of **Nha Trang** will soon bear fruit with a new five-star resort (though anything new has a tough standard of comparison in the popular **Ana Mandara Resort** ✆ 058/829-829). Places like **Mui Ne Beach** near **Phan Thiet** are giving rise to some fine upscale resorts and seaside hotels. At Mui Ne, don't miss the **Coco Beach Resort** (✆ 62/847-111), a relaxing spot and one of the first to go up there.

Both Hanoi and Ho Chi Minh have more high-end hotels than you can shake a stick at and a host of affordable options. **Sheraton** is putting up a new tower in downtown Ho Chi Minh and the **Renaissance Riverside Hotel** (✆ 08/822-0033), a **Marriot** property, is one of the finest new upscale stops among the city's many (for my money, the **Caravelle Hotel** ✆ 08/823-4999 can't be beat).

Victoria Hotels, like the popular hotel in Sapa, are popping up in places like the Mekong Delta at **Can Tho** and **Chau Doc** (✆ 076/865-010), and there are great new boat connections from there to Phnom Penh, Cambodia.

LAOS Change comes slowly to sleepy Laos, but come it does. Outside of Luang Prabang, Laos' historic jewel of the north, don't miss the two new upscale resorts opened in recent years. The **Villa Santi** (✆ 071/212-267) is still the best choice in town, but they've just opened the sprawling **Villa Santi Resort** (✆ 071/253-470) a few kilometers outside of the busy town center. The new **Grand Luang Prabang (Xieng Kheo)** (✆ 071/253-8517) is built on a beautiful plot of land overlooking a wide bend in the Mekong, and the **Pansea Phuvao** (✆ 071/212-194) is the long-reigning resort of note and overlooks the town and Phousi Hill.

L'Elephant (✆ 071/252-482), an upscale French bistro in the heart of Luang Prabang, is the town's latest culinary coup, but don't pass up their sister property, the laid-back **Café Wat Sene** (✆ 071/212-517). The popular and atmospheric **Tum-Tum Cheng Restaurant** (© 071/253-224) is the star of the town's "restaurant row." Some might be disappointed to hear that the falls at **Kuang Si** have collapsed, but it's still one of the nicer day trips into the countryside.

In the sleepy capital of **Vientiane** there are all manner of good culinary delights, mostly to satisfy the appetites of the town's many expatriate aidworkers. Try **Sticky Fingers** (across from the Tai-Pan Hotel), a popular place with some nice foreign specialties. No visit to town would be complete without stopping in at **Khop-Chai-Deu** (© 021/212-106), a popular bar and restaurant and the defacto information center for backpackers, expatriates, and business visitors. The hotel scene hasn't changed much: The upscale and atmospheric **Settha Palace** (© 021/217-581) is still top dog and the **Lao Plaza Hotel** (© 021/218-800) is the main business stopover; but don't miss the mellow, affordable **Day Inn** (© 021/223-847), a tranquil spot near the town center.

Eco-tourism is taking Laos by storm, and small companies like **Wildside Eco Group** (© 023/511-440) are leading the way and creating environmentally and culturally sensitive tours to the hinterlands of this landlocked jungle paradise.

SINGAPORE Despite global terrorism alerts and troubles within the region, Singapore remains Southeast Asia's safest place thanks to the government's very serious efforts to take a proactive approach to detaining terrorist suspects and promoting racial and religious harmony. Development continues at Singapore's normal rocket speed—the much anticipated second phase of the Asian Civilisations Museum will open its doors at Empress Place any day now. Meanwhile the Singapore History Museum

has closed for a 2-year massive renovation. History buffs can catch a smaller exhibit at Robertson Quay, managed by the National Heritage Board, to be opened at some unspecified time in the future. Contact the Singapore Tourism Board (STB) at © **1800/ 238-2388** for opening information of both museums. Delays to the new northeast subway line have pushed its opening date to late June 2003. And finally, the Beaufort Sentosa has changed its name to **The Sentosa Resort & Spa** (© **65/6275-0331**).

MALAYSIA Malaysia continues to remain safe for travelers. The country's moderate politics means that even though Islam is the state religion, extremism or violence in the name of religion is dealt with strictly. Expect delays from overland travel into the country either from Singapore or Thailand, as security checks are stepped up. Holiday resorts such as Langkawi and Penang remain as peaceful and welcoming as ever. With tourism arrivals continuing to sag, travel bargains abound. If you're planning a trip to Malacca soon, make sure you call ahead for the latest museum closings—three of the city's main displays are closed for (much needed) restoration. The **Malacca Tourism Centre** can be reached at © **06/283-6538.**

BALI AND LOMBOK Even after the tragic bombing in Kuta on October 12, 2002, Bali is still the tourist paradise it always was. The Balinese are eager to again attract the many tourists who once flocked here and many steps are being taken to bolster tourist confidence in the famed isle. Security at air- and seaports is tightening and great deals can be had at some of the finest resorts in the region. In popular **Kuta** on Bali, don't miss **TJ's Restaurant** (© **361/751-093**), a place for a great Mexican feast in the most unlikely of places.

CAMBODIA   Listed as a "difficult destination" in the last edition of this guide, Cambodia is quickly opening to more and more Western visitors. Recent reforms and developments in Cambodia mean that travel in-country has opened to more than just the intrepid or foolhardy. All of the information in chapter 11 is new. Cambodia's rough, rural roads are still best left to the very adventurous, though, and it is important to stay abreast of the political situation (especially around the planned July 2003 election); but travel to the popular sites in and around Phnom Penh and Siem Reap is now convenient and comfortable. New flights connect Cambodia's premier attraction, the magnificent temples of **Angkor Wat,** with nearby air hubs in the region and accommodation in **Siem Reap.** The access town to the temples is rife with comfortable amenities. Don't miss Siem Reap's proud dame, the classic **Raffles Grand Hotel D'Angkor** (✆ 063/963-888), or **Sofitel Royal Angkor** (✆ 063/964-600) and the **Pansea Angkor** (✆ 063/963-390), two resplendent hideaways and great jumping-off points to the amazing temples of Angkor.

In busy **Phnom Penh** visitors will find all the comforts of home in another of Raffles' fine properties, the **Hotel Le Royal** (✆ 023/981-888), at **Sunway Hotel** (✆ 023/430-333) or a true international business standard at the **Intercontinental Hotel** (✆ 023/424-888). Dining in the main tour centers caters to the many business visitors and humanitarian aid-workers, and there's a great choice of good international fare. Don't miss the **Foreign Correspondent's Club (FCC)** in both towns for good familiar food and unique atmosphere. **Sihanoukville,** Cambodia's only beach destination, can't quite live up to nearby Thailand but does have it's charm.

Air connections to and from Phnom Penh and Siem Reap are frequent. Boats now connect Phnom Penh with **Chau Doc** on the border of Vietnam and convenient speedboats still ply the Tonle Sap between Phnom Penh and Siem Reap. Rural travel is four-wheel-drive only, but in-country tour operators can arrange exciting tours.

1

The Best of Southeast Asia

To the Western visitor, Southeast Asia is an assault on the senses, an immersion into a way of life utterly unlike that to which we're accustomed. From bustling cities like Hong Kong, Singapore, and Kuala Lumpur to tiny fishing villages in Vietnam, from the jungles of Malaysian Borneo to the deluxe resorts of Bali, from the temples of Luang Prabang in Laos to the bacchanal of Patpong in Thailand, Southeast Asia offers a glimpse of the extraordinary, an explosion of colors, sounds, smells, textures, and *life* that will send you home with a wider vision of the human experience. In this chapter, we share our picks of the region's unrivaled highlights.

1 The Most Unforgettable Travel Experiences

- **Riding the Star Ferry (Hong Kong).** To reacquaint myself with the city, one of the first things I do on each return trip is hop aboard the Star Ferry for one of the most dramatic—and cheapest—5-minute boat rides in the world. Hong Kong's harbor is one of the world's busiest, and beyond it rises one of Earth's most breathtaking skylines. See chapter 4.

- **Gazing upon Hong Kong from Victoria Peak (Hong Kong).** You don't know Hong Kong until you've seen it from here. Take the tram to Victoria Peak, famous for its views of Central, the harbor, and Kowloon beyond, followed by a 1-hour circular hike and a meal with a view. Don't miss the nighttime view, one of the most spectacular and romantic in the world. See chapter 4.

- **Making Merit (Thailand).** In Thailand, Buddhist monks do not earn income; they survive on gifts of food and necessary items given by devoted Buddhists in the community. The monk in his gold-colored robes who walks from house to house each morning is not begging for food, but is offering an opportunity for the giver to receive merit. In contributing to the monk's survival, the giver of food and gifts is supporting the *sangha,* the monkhood, and therefore gets closer to Buddhist ideals. If you are interested in making merit this way, talk to your hotel's concierge. You might be able to join kitchen staff as they head to a nearby monastery in the early morning or wait on the right byway to greet and feed a column of monks. See chapter 5.

- **Sailing the South China Sea (Vietnam).** With the sky above us a deep, red afterglow, we rounded a buoy marking the shipping lane off coastal Nha Trang and, with the wind now at our backs, settled the Hobie Cat into a perfect fantail, the mainsail and jib billowing on opposite sides as the rudders gave a low moan and the boat gained speed. Riding low swells, we sped toward a coast where twinkling lights might have belonged to a child's train set, and the sky continued its show, now in orange. Heavenly. Opportunities for water sports and sailing are many as you travel along Vietnam's coast. Most resorts have boats for rent, and Nha Trang is a good bet, as is the area off Mui Ne Beach near Phan Thiet, which is becoming a very popular windsurfing spot. See chapter 6.

- **Staying in a Hill-Tribe Village near the China Border (Laos).** They're still asking visitors, "Why do you come here, anyway?" in villages along the NamHa River in northern Laos. Thanks to the folks who run the NamHa Project, these vast tracts of pristine jungle won't be overrun by tourists anytime soon, and the many ethnic minority groups who've lived here in isolation won't be turned into human zoo exhibits. Tours here come with a price tag, but it's heartening to know that your money goes to support a model of sustainable eco-tour development in a fragile region. For visitors, this means that you're sure to be alone in your kayak as you float through lush jungle terrain, brave some good rapids, and see monkeys and exotic birds. You'll arrive in villages where kayaks are still an oddity, and you'll spend fun evenings around the fire communicating by charades or stick figures in a notebook. It's not about the villages being "pristine"; it's about the fact that your visit is part of a cultural exchange, not about disparate currency exchange rates. You can have a positive effect on people with your heart *and* your tourist dollars. See chapter 7.

- **Participating in a Baci Ceremony (Laos).** The Baci is a touching Lao ceremony used to say welcome or farewell and to honor achievements. Participants sit in a circle and receive group blessings, after which there is traditional dancing and *lao lao,* rice wine. It's a chance for the ultrafriendly Lao people to express their hospitality to you, their honored guest. See chapter 7.

- **Sipping a Singapore Sling in the Long Bar (Raffles Hotel, Singapore).** Ah, the Long Bar, home of the Singapore Sling. I like to come in the afternoons before the tourist rush. Sheltered by long timber shutters that close out the tropical sun, the air cooled by lazy punkahs (small fans that wave gently back and forth above), you can sit back in old rattan chairs and have your saronged waitress serve you sticky alcoholic creations while you toss back a few dainty crab cakes. Life can be so decadent. Okay, so the punkahs are electric and, come to think of it, the place is air-conditioned (not to mention that it costs a small fortune), but it's fun to image the days when Somerset Maugham, Rudyard Kipling, or Charlie Chaplin would be sitting at the bar sipping Slings and spinning exotic tales of their world travels. Drink up, my friend; it's a lovely high. See chapter 8.

- **Walking the Streets of Georgetown (Penang, Malaysia).** Evidence of former British colonization and early Chinese, Indian, and Arab immigration is apparent in many major cities in Malaysia, but Penang has a special charm. In some ways, the city still operates the way it did half a century ago. The shophouses are filled with small businesses—bicycle repair shops, hardware stores, Chinese medicine halls, and coffee shops. From upstairs windows, you can still see laundry hanging on bamboo poles. Life hums in these streets, and for anyone who has

Southeast Asia

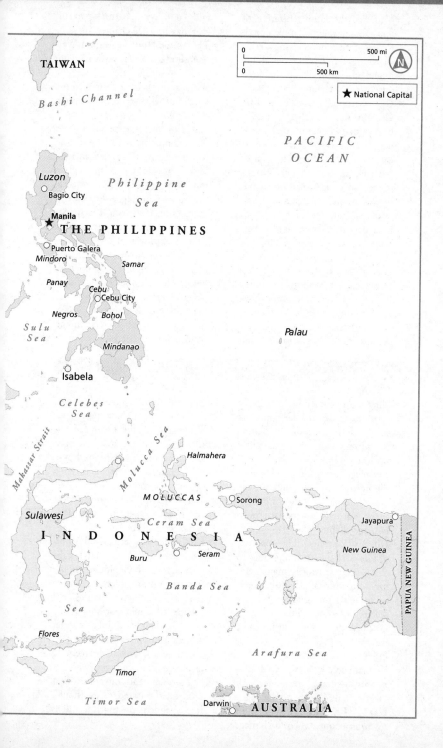

witnessed the homogenization of Singapore or the modernization of Kuala Lumpur, Penang is a charming reminder of what life might have been like in these old outposts. See chapter 9.

- **Observing Open-Air Public Cremations (Bali).** Hindus believe that cremation is the only way a soul can be freed of its earthly body and travel to its next incarnation (or to enlightenment), so cremations are joyous occasions, full of floats and fanfare that can resemble a Mardi Gras parade. Complicated towers hold the body, carried aloft by cheering men. At the burning ground, the body is placed in a receptacle resembling a winged lion, a bull, or some other fabulous creature, and is set on fire. It's beautiful and awesome, a marvelous show of pageantry and faith, and yet a natural part of everyday life. See chapter 10.

- **The Magic Hour at Angkor Wat (Cambodia).** You'll want to plan your day around it, and temple aficionados all have their favorite spots; but whether from a hillside overlooking a glowing temple facade or from the heights of the main temple itself with the horizon framed by the famed ancient towers, be sure to see an Angkor sunset. Sunrise is equally worth the early morning ride. At the more popular viewing spots, like Bakeng Hill, you'll ooh and aah in concert with lots of other travelers. Nobody likes crowds, but there is a certain cool oneness here, and the odd didgeridoo player or cross-legged character in meditation is all a nice throwback to the old hippy-trail days in the region. See chapter 11.

2 The Best Small Towns & Villages

- **Chiang Saen (Thailand).** Crumbling 11th-century temples and a splendid museum take you back to the birthplace of the Lanna Kingdom, one of Thailand's wealthiest and most influential. The neighboring Golden Triangle, the notorious trade point for the international opium industry, snaps you back to modern realities. See chapter 5.

- **Hoi An (Vietnam).** The small size of Hoi An belies its importance to Vietnam; it was once a major trading port, with canals leading right up to merchants' quarters for easy delivery of goods. The canals are now peaceful streets, but little else has changed. Almost every building in central Hoi An is a historic Vietnamese-, Japanese-, and Chinese-influenced residence or meeting hall. See chapter 6.

- **Luang Prabang (Laos).** This town, sanctioned a World Heritage site by UNESCO for its dozens of glorious Buddhist temples, also happens to be a charming retreat. Shady lanes are lined with French-style country homes that have been restored and converted to house cafes, galleries, shops, and some quaint guesthouses. The sunset over the lazy Mekong is the perfect end to a day spent in Luang Prabang. See chapter 7.

- **Kuala Terengganu (Malaysia).** The capital of Malaysian handicrafts has yet to be plotted on any standard tourist itinerary. Explore the city's cottage industries and experience a more orthodox side of Malaysian Islam in this quiet cultural gem. See chapter 9.

- **Ubud (Bali).** This is the teeming center of Bali, bursting with art and greenery and some of the best food on the island. Even though it's dependent on tourism and is far from a typical Bali village, you still get a sense of a real town, with real life going on around you. Ubud is the richest region in Bali for art production and, because it's centrally located, is the perfect base for exploring the rest of the island. See chapter 10.

- **Phnom Penh (Cambodia).** Few countries' capitals could be called quaint or fall under the category of a "town," and that's the very charm of this riverside burg. They say you either love it or hate it,

that it's a place for expats and not tourists, but in a short stroll through the town center, you'll come across a unique mix. First you'll see a row of crowded tourist cafes, streets buzzing with motorbikes and choked with dust, but you'll turn the corner and find a quiet alley, a row of colonials, a lone kid kicking a soccer ball, and a grim-looking grandmother breaking into a smile as you walk by. There's something special here. See chapter 11.

3 The Best Beaches

- **Chaweng Beach (Ko Samui, Thailand).** Chaweng is total fun in the sun. The beach itself is gorgeous, with bungalows nestled in the trees just beyond the sand. Behind the beach lies a small town full of life, from wonderful Thai and seafood eateries to shopping and wild nightlife options. See chapter 5.

- **Phan Thiet (Vietnam).** Just a few hours from Saigon, Phan Thiet is the latest getaway in Vietnam. Oceanside development is in full swing here, and there are some great boutique resorts along the stunning white sands of Mui Ne Beach. There's a golf course designed by Nick Faldo, and the town of Phan Thiet itself is an interesting little fishing port worth a wander. The seafood is good, and there are some great day trips to enormous remote dunes and smaller fishing villages. See chapter 6.

- **Tanjong Rhu (Langkawi, Malaysia).** This huge secluded cove has one of the longest

stretches of private beach I've ever seen. Wide with soft sand, the beach has cooling shady spots provided by palm trees overhead and beautiful deep blue waters for good swimming. Best of all, there's only one resort here (and the beach is kept picture perfect), so you won't have to elbow for space or suffer jet skis. See chapter 9.

- **Juara Bay (Tioman Island, Malaysia).** This beach is what they meant when they coined the word *isolated*. Be prepared to live like Robinson Crusoe—in tiny huts with cold-water showers and many with no electricity. But, oh, the beach! A wide crescent of palm-lined sand hugs the clearest blue water, with very few other people in sight. See chapter 9.

- **Lombok (Indonesia).** The pure white-sand beaches of Lombok, with clear aqua-blue water lapping against them, are sometimes so private that you can have one all to yourself. And Lombok is just a short hop from neighboring Bali. See chapter 10.

4 The Best Outdoor Adventures

- **Phang-nga Bay (Thailand).** From the island of Phuket, sea canoe operators guide visitors

through the caves hidden deep inside the craggy island-rocks of Phang-nga Bay. Outside, the islands thrust up to the sky, their jagged edges laced with scattered trees. Lie flat in your canoe to slip through the small cave openings, inside which you'll find magnificent chambers believed to have once hidden pirate operations. See chapter 5.

- **Sea Kayaking in Halong Bay (Vietnam).** The more than 3,000 arresting limestone karst formations rising out of Halong Bay's peaceful blue-green waters provide a natural obstacle course for paddling. Moving among them, you'll pass in and among intriguing grottos and caverns. Nights are spent camping out in natural parks or on the deck of a mother ship. See chapter 6.

- **Hill-Tribe Village Treks in Sapa (North Vietnam).** Dressed in elaborate costume of leggings, tunic, and headdress, Hmong and Yao people (among other groups) gather to sell their weavings, fine dyed clothing, or crude but intricate metalwork in the central market. In fact, the town of Sapa is famed for an ephemeral "Love Market," where people from surrounding villages converge to find that special someone. A trip to Sapa means that the hill-tribes come to you, but don't limit your trip to the town; be sure to get off into the countryside and trek in the shadow of Fansipan, the highest mountain in the region. Among lush terraced rice fields, you can visit many villages in even the shortest trek and experience different hill-tribe traditions and cultures. See chapter 6.

- **Caving and Kayaking in Vang Vieng (Laos).** Countless caves and caverns are hidden in the magnificent mountains surrounding Vang Vieng, a small village along the Nam Song River. Some of them are well known and some

are barely on the map. Kayak tours on the Nam Song include some fun caves that you'll swim into and can test your mettle on natural mud slides. Spend your days exploring and evenings talking about it over drinks in this laid-back little backpacker town. See chapter 7.

- **Tioman Island or Redang Marine Park (Malaysia).** If you scuba dive or want to learn how, the waters here are packed with exciting corals and creatures accessible through experienced dive operators. Snorkeling trips are also common and reveal the magic of the sea to those who want to stay closer to the surface. See chapter 9.

- **Jungle Trekking in Taman Negara (Malaysia).** With suitable options for all budgets, levels of comfort, and desired adventure, Malaysia's largest national park opens the wonders of primary rain forest and the creatures who dwell in it to everyone. From the canopy, walk high atop the forest to night watches for nocturnal life. This adventure is as stunning as it is informative. See chapter 9.

- **Hiking Gunung Agung (Bali).** Bali's highest mountain/volcano, Gunung Agung (3,014m/9,888 ft. high), is utterly sacred to the Balinese, who believe it to be the center of the world. Climbing it is a serious trek that absolutely calls for a guide and proper supplies. Most hotels can arrange for it, but you will have to start out in the middle of the night or very in the morning to make the top by sunrise. See chapter 10.

- **Born to Be Wild (Cambodia).** If you ride motorbikes, get your motor runnin' and head out on the dirt-track back roads. Rural Cambodia is just opening up for exploration, and the pioneers here are leading the way to the "back of beyond" on dirt bikes (find a bike with the best suspension). It's certainly a choice for the hearty, but it's a popular option for those who are looking for adventure. See chapter 11.

5 The Most Intriguing Temples, Shrines, Palaces & Archaeological Sites

- **The Giant Buddha (Hong Kong).** Laze on the open aft-deck during the hour-long ferry ride to Lantau island (and enjoy great views of the harbor and skyline along the way), followed by a ride over lush hills to see the world's largest seated outdoor bronze Buddha, located at the Po Lin Monastery. Complete your pilgrimage with a vegetarian meal at the monastery. See chapter 4.
- **The Grand Palace & Wat Phra Kaeo (Bangkok, Thailand).** These two places are no. 1 on every travel itinerary to Bangkok, and rightly so. The palace is indeed grand, with mixtures of traditional Thai and European Victorian architecture. Wat Phra Kaeo, the royal temple that houses Thailand's revered and mysterious Emerald Buddha, is a small city in itself, with a dozen or more picturesque outer buildings and monuments that devour rolls of film. See chapter 5.
- **Ayutthaya (Thailand).** Before Bangkok, there was Ayutthaya. This was the thriving capital of Siam that the first Europeans saw when they visited amazing Thailand. Ruling a rich and powerful kingdom of over a million inhabitants, the monarchy supported the arts, especially literature. As the city grew, international trade was encouraged. All that remains are brick remnants of a grand palace and many temples that were sacked during the Burmese invasion. It's best to hire a guide who can walk you through and point out the significance of each site. See chapter 5.
- **The Cao Dai Holy See (Tay Ninh) (North of Ho Chi Minh, Vietnam).** This is the spiritual home base of the Cao Dai religion, a faith characterized by philosophical inclusion and influence gathered from all beliefs, including the world's great scientists and humanitarians. Their headquarters is like a fantasyland of colored mosaic and elaborate painting. Followers are dressed in white turbans during the picturesque daily procession. It's quite unique. See chapter 6.
- **Tomb of Khai Dinh (Hue, Vietnam).** Khai Dinh was an egotistical, eccentric emperor, who was bad for the people of Vietnam but great for the tomb he left behind. A gaudy mix of Gothic, baroque, and classical Chinese architecture, the exterior is remarkable. The stunning interior is completely covered with intricate glass and ceramic mosaic work. See chapter 6.
- **Wat Xieng Thong (Luang Prabang, Laos).** The glittering Xieng Thong, built in 1560, sits grandly on a peninsula jutting out into the Mekong River. The facades of two of its buildings are covered by glittering glass mosaics; another building contains an ornate chariot with the heads of seven dragons and the remains of a king. About a dozen English-speaking monks roam the premises; all are excellent conversationalists. See chapter 7.
- **Plain of Jars (Xieng Khouang, Laos).** How did hundreds of huge stone urns, some measuring 10 feet tall, come to be placed on a few meadows in northern Laos?

No one really knows, and that's what's fun here. The most prevalent explanation is that the urns were made by prehistoric folk in the area about 2,000 years ago to be used as sarcophagi, but there's lots of room for conjecture. See chapter 7.

- **Thian Hock Keng (Singapore).** One of Singapore's oldest Chinese temples, it is a fascinating testimony to Chinese Buddhism combined with traditional Confucian beliefs and natural Taoist principles. Equally fascinating is the modern world that carries on just outside the old temple's doors. See chapter 8.
- **Jame Mosque (Kuala Lumpur, Malaysia).** Built at the central point of the city, this is one of the oldest mosques in Kuala Lumpur. It is the heart of Malay Islam, as evidenced by the Muslim shops, eateries, and daily activities carried on in the streets surrounding it. See chapter 9.
- **Jalan Tokong (Malacca, Malaysia).** This street, in the historical heart of the city, has a Malay mosque, a Chinese temple, and a

Hindu temple living peacefully side by side—the perfect example of how the many foreign religions that came to Southeast Asia shaped its communities and learned to coexist in harmony. See chapter 9.

- **Gunung Kawi (Bali).** Gunung Kawi is a shrine consisting of monolithic faux-tombs, the origin and purpose of which remain unknown—a fact that only adds to their power and mystery. It's an outstanding, awe-inducing sight. See chapter 10.
- **Angkor Wat (Cambodia).** One of the world's manmade wonders, Angkor Wat is the Disneyland of temples in Asia. This ancient city was known to the Western world only in myth until it was rediscovered and hacked free of jungle overgrowth in the late 1800s. The magnificent temples are arrayed over a 96.6-sq. km (60-sq.-mile) compound that dates from the rise and fall of the mighty Angkor Civilization (A.D. 802–1295). A visit here is unforgettable. See chapter 11.

6 The Best Museums

- **National Museum (Bangkok, Thailand).** From prehistory to recent events, this museum—the former palace of the brother of King Rama I—answers many questions about Thai history and culture through the ages. Inside buildings that are themselves works of fine Thai design, you'll find Buddha images, ancient arts, royal paraphernalia, and fine arts. Rama's sister also lived here, and her house is decorated in the same style as it was in the late 1700s. See chapter 5.
- **Vietnam Fine Arts Museum (Hanoi, Vietnam).** Proper art

museums are few and far between in the region, and this large colonial house is a nice collection of newer works and historical pieces. You'll find nothing too controversial or groundbreaking, but some good examples of lacquer and silk painting, wood-block, and folk and expressive work in oil. If you see anything you like, you're sure to find good copies in any of the city's many galleries. See chapter 6.

- **The Cham Museum (Danang, Vietnam).** This open-air colonial structure houses the largest collection of Cham sculpture in the world. Not only are relics of this ancient Hindu-inspired culture rare, but the religious artwork itself—more than 300 pieces of sandstone—is voluptuous, captivating, and intense. See chapter 6.

- **Images of Singapore (Sentosa Island, Singapore).** No one has done a better job than this museum in chronicling for the public the horrors of the Pacific Theatre and Japanese occupation in Southeast Asia. Video and audio displays take you on a chronological journey through Singapore's World War II experience. The grand finale is the Surrender Chambers, life-size wax dioramas of the fateful events. There's also dioramas depicting historical figures throughout Singapore's early development, as well as depictions of traditional cultural festivals. See chapter 8.
- **National Museum (Phnom Penh, Cambodia).** Don't miss this repository for the statues and relief sculpture that have been recovered from the Angkor temples and other ancient sites throughout Cambodia. Organized in a convenient chronology, it's a short course in Khmer art history. Later pieces are particularly quite expressive. See chapter 11.
- **Tuol Sleng S-21 Prison Museum (Phnom Penh, Cambodia).** Be warned that a visit here is quite intense—too much for some. The museum is simply the shell of Cambodia's largest prison from 1975 to 1979, when the entire country was turned into a concentration camp. Originally a high school, Tuol Sleng was the site of horrible atrocities and, though there are some exhibits of photos, the experience of the museum is in wandering the small cells and learning the tragic tale from experienced local guides. See chapter 11.

7 The Best Festivals & Celebrations

- **Chinese New Year (Hong Kong and Singapore).** If you're in Southeast Asia around the end of January or the beginning of February, hop up to Hong Kong or down to Singapore for the festivities. It's a 3-day party, with parades (complete with dragons and stilt-walkers) and fireworks. See chapters 4 and 8.
- **Songkran (Thailand).** Every year from April 13 to 15, Thais welcome the New Year (according to their calendar). Because Songkran falls in the middle of the hottest season in an already hot country, how do you think people celebrate? Every Thai heads out into the streets with water guns and buckets of ice water (sometimes laced with talcum powder, just to add to the mess), and spends the next 3 days soaking each other—and *you.* Foreigners are especially favorite targets. Don't get mad—arm thyself: Water bazookas are on sale everywhere. Have a ball! See chapter 5.
- **Mid-Autumn Festival (Vietnam).** This lunar celebration, which usually takes place in late September or early October, has the stuff of all great holidays: color, pageantry, and adorable children who dance and parade through towns carrying paper lanterns they've made themselves. See chapter 6.
- **That Luang Festival (Vientiane, Laos).** Thousands of Buddhist followers from all over the country, and even a few neighboring countries, converge on the spectacular That Luang temple in Vientiane. There are alms-giving ceremonies and flower processions, and then the whole affair dissolves into a carnival that

stretches over several days. See chapter 7.

- **Bun Song Hua/Dragon Boat Races (Laos).** Celebrating the end of Buddhist Lent, Dragon Boat races are held in every riverside town in Laos (and that's most towns, really). The races are exciting, the betting is frenzied, and there's always a small carnival with handmade rides and the standard rigged skill games. See chapter 7.
- **Thaipusam (Singapore and Malaysia).** Around the end of January and the beginning of February, Hindus celebrate Thaipusam. Men give thanks for prayers answered by carrying kavadis, huge steel racks attached to their bodies with skewers piercing the skin. Cheeks are pierced, and fruits are hung from the skin using sharp hooks. A parade of devotees carry these things in a deep trance—and the next day they wake up virtually unharmed. See chapters 8 and 9.

8 The Biggest Cultural No-Nos

- **Photographing a Villager Without Permission in Vietnam.** There's nothing a visitor wants more than to take away indelible images of the colorful, rustic lifestyles of the Vietnamese ethnic minorities. However, many rural people are superstitious about photographs or might resent the intrusion of privacy. Ask first. See chapter 6, plus "Etiquette Tips," in chapter 2.
- **Losing Your Temper in Laos or Thailand.** The Lao and Thai people enjoy a Buddhist sensibility in their daily life, approaching even unfortunate events with calm cheerfulness. They would be shocked and dismayed at anger or ill temper, and raising your voice won't achieve any purpose whatsoever. No matter how frustrated you become, keep it under wraps, or the people around you will see to it that you never get where you need to go. See chapters 7 and 5, plus "Etiquette Tips," in chapter 2.
- **Looking (or Being) Poor in Singapore.** You probably won't run into too many cultural faux pas in cosmopolitan Singapore, but poverty is the pits in this city. Bring your smartest clothes if you want to impress people here. See chapter 8, plus "Etiquette Tips," in chapter 2.
- **Using Offensive Body Language in Bali, Malaysia, Thailand, or Laos.** Muslims, Hindus, and Buddhists all reserve the left hand for "unclean" toilet duties, never for pointing at anyone or anything, handing objects to others, eating, or touching other people. Similarly, in Buddhist and Hindu cultures, the head is revered as the most sacred part of the body, while the feet are the lowest. Never touch another person's head or shoulders, not even a child's. Never point or gesture with your feet or use your feet to perform any tasks other than walking. See "Etiquette Tips," in chapter 2.
- **Hanging Clothes out to Dry in Bali.** Or otherwise out in public (off hotel balconies and chairs and the like). See chapter 10, plus "Etiquette Tips," in chapter 2.
- **Showing Too Much Skin (Regional).** Except perhaps in Hong Kong, Singapore and Bangkok or other heavily touristed areas, modest Southeast Asians accept beachwear at the beach, revealing vacation clothing

at resorts, and sexy attire at discos. Everywhere else, dress with respect for the locals and their traditions. See "Etiquette Tips," in chapter 2.

- **Wearing Shorts or Short Skirts to a Temple or Mosque (Regional).** It'll get you tossed out. See "Etiquette Tips," in chapter 2.

9 The Best Resorts & Luxury Hotels

- **The Peninsula Hotel (Hong Kong).** Hong Kong's most famous hotel exudes elegance, from its Rolls-Royce fleet to the white-gloved doormen who stand at attention outside the palatial, gilded lobby. Rooms in the 32-story tower sport unparalleled views of Victoria Harbour, and even jaded travelers are likely to be impressed with the sheer breadth of amenities offered here. See chapter 4.
- **Island Shangri-La Hong Kong (Hong Kong).** Viennese chandeliers, oriental carpets, and more than 500 paintings and artwork adorn this, the tallest hotel on Hong Kong Island. The 17-story atrium features a marvelous 16-story-high Chinese painting, believed to be the largest landscape painting in the world. Spacious, impeccable rooms face either the Peak or Victoria Harbour—both stunning views. See chapter 4.
- **The Oriental Hotel (Bangkok, Thailand).** The original address in Thailand, The Oriental has seen modernization detract from its charms of yesterday, but there's still ambience all around. See chapter 5.
- **The Amanpuri (Phuket, Thailand).** This seductive bungalow resort in exquisite Thai style will thrill even the most discerning guests. See chapter 5.
- **The Regent (Chiang Mai, Thailand).** Luxurious Thai-style suites, excellent restaurants, a multitude of activities, and the most amazing swimming pool you've ever seen await you. Don't forget to meet their resident water buffalo family—they work the resort's private rice paddies. See chapter 5.
- **Sofitel Metropole (Hanoi, Vietnam).** The history of the Metropole, one of Vietnam's premier grand dames, tells the history of the last tumultuous century in Vietnam. If the walls could only talk. Though everything is luxurious and comfortable, and you're in a prime downtown location, you'll certainly feel like you've walked into old Indochina. See chapter 6.
- **Ana Mandara (Nha Trang, Vietnam).** The details are perfect in this small-scale resort, from the incense burning in the open long-house-style lobby to the small signs identifying tropical fish in the lobby's pond. Each stylish room has the air of a secluded hut with its own verandah, many overlooking the palm-lined coast. Both the food and the staff's smiles are perfect. See chapter 6.
- **Settha Palace (Vientiane, Laos).** Once the address of note for visitors to the French colony, the Settha Palace only recently returned from obscurity and is now one of the finest hotels in the region. It's a nice marriage of colonial elegance and modern comfort. See chapter 7.
- **Pansea Phu Vao (Luang Prabang, Laos).** Lording it over the town in boutique luxury, the gardens and large suite rooms of the Pansea are comfort and atmosphere done to a T. This is typical of other Pansea properties in the region. See chapter 7.

- **Raffles Hotel (Singapore).** For old-world opulence, Raffles is second to none. This is a pure fantasy of the days when tigers still lurked around the perimeters. See chapter 8.
- **Four Seasons Hotel (Singapore).** Elegance and warmth combine to make this place a good bet. Consider a regular room here before you book a suite elsewhere. See chapter 8.
- **The Regent (Kuala Lumpur, Malaysia).** For my money, the Regent offers the smartest decor, best service, and best selection of facilities in the whole city. See chapter 9.
- **The Aryani Resort (Kuala Terengganu, Malaysia).** An exotic retreat, Aryani combines local Terengganu flavors with all the pampering you'd want from a getaway resort. See chapter 9.
- **Shangri-La's Rasa Sayang Resort (Penang, Malaysia).** The oldest resort on the beach has claimed the best stretch of sand and snuggled the most imaginatively modern yet traditionally designed resort in gardens just beyond. See chapter 9.
- **Four Seasons (Jimbaran, Bali).** With its individual bungalows and plunge pools overlooking the blue sea and its famous Four Seasons pampering, Four Seasons Jimbaran is one of the great hotels in the world. See chapter 10.
- **Amandari (Ubud, Bali).** Its individual bungalows overlook a deep green gorge, and the Amandari offers another sybaritic Bali experience. If you can afford it (or the Four Seasons Jimbaran), do. Even if you can't, do. See chapter 10.
- **Raffles Grand Hotel D'Angkor (Siem Reap, Cambodia).** Another grand colonial of Indochina, the Grand is indeed grand. With fine services to connect you to nearby Angkor Wat, a great central pool and spa/massage facility, and beautiful rooms, it doesn't get any better. See chapter 11.

10 The Best Hotel Bargains

- **Bossotel Inn (Bangkok, Thailand).** Located in a prime spot close to the Chao Phraya River, the Bossotel is the perfect budget answer to the Shangri-La and Orientals that dominate accommodations along the river. See chapter 5.
- **River Ping Palace (Chiang Mai, Thailand).** If you're going to travel on a budget, do it with style—and style is what River Ping Palace has wrapped up in its old Thai-style teak mansion buildings. See chapter 5.
- **Spring Hotel/Mua Xuan (Saigon, Vietnam).** Not especially luxurious, rooms in this privately owned downtown property (one of few nongovernment places in Saigon) has rooms starting at US$25. It's light on amenities but very comfortable, convenient, and friendly. See chapter 6.
- **Day Inn (Vientianne, Laos).** So it's just a few notches above your average guesthouse, but there's a comfortable, laid-back feel here and many long-stay visitors can't be wrong. You'll find rooms for US$25. See chapter 7.
- **RELC International Hotel (Singapore).** For a safe and simple place to call home in Singapore, RELC can't be beat. You might wonder how they keep costs so low when their location is so good. See chapter 8.
- **Traders Hotel (Singapore).** Value-for-money is the name of the game, with all sorts of promotional packages, self-service launderettes, vending machines, and a

checkout lounge—just a few of the offerings that make this the most convenient hotel in the city. See chapter 8.

- **Swiss-Inn (Kuala Lumpur, Malaysia).** Tucked behind the market tents in Chinatown, this bargain find has the look of a higher-quality hotel, but in mini-size. If you plan on spending your time out exploring the city, why pay more for empty space? See chapter 9.

- **Heeren House (Malacca, Malaysia).** Bargain or no bargain, this boutique hotel in the heart of the old city is *the* place to stay in Malacca if you want to really get a feel for the local atmosphere. See chapter 9.

- **Telang Usan Hotel (Kuching, Malaysia).** An informal place, Telang Usan is homey and quaint, and within walking distance of many major attractions in Kuching. See chapter 9.

- **The Home-Stay/Losmen of Bali.** These small-time accommodations will give you a large, comfortable (though no-frills) room or bungalow with a big, often fancy breakfast for about US$5 a night for two. See chapter 10.

- **Goldiana (Phnom Penh, Cambodia).** It's no-frills but friendly and cheap here in a quiet neighborhood south of the town center. It's popular with long-staying visitors and NGO workers. See chapter 11.

11 The Best Local Dining Experiences

- **Dining on Dim Sum (Hong Kong).** Nothing conveys a sense of Chinese life more vividly than a visit to a crowded, lively Cantonese restaurant where trolleys of dim sum in bamboo steamers are wheeled from customer to customer during breakfast and lunch. Simply peer into the passing bamboo baskets and choose what appears the most tempting. This is a great way to start the day. See chapter 4.

- **Taking High Tea at the Peninsula (Hong Kong).** The British rulers might be gone, but their legacy lives on in afternoon tea, complete with finger sandwiches and scones. Virtually all upper-class hotels offer afternoon tea, but none can compare with the experience offered in the lobby of Hong Kong's most venerable hotel, long a favored people-watching spot. Come for afternoon tea, listen to classical music, and gaze away. See chapter 4.

- **Street Food (Bangkok, Thailand).** On every street, down every alley, you'll find someone setting up a cart with an umbrella. Noodles, salads, and satay are favorites, and some hawkers set up tables and stools on the sidewalk for you to take a load off. This is Thai cafe life! See chapter 5.

- **Pho (Vietnam).** Don't leave the country without sampling one, if not many, bowls of this delicate noodle soup, made with vermicelli-thin rice noodles, chicken (*ga*) or beef (*bo*), and several fresh accompaniments, according to the chef's whim or local flavor: basil, mint, chile peppers, and bean sprouts. See chapter 6.

- **Restaurant Ngon (Ho Chi Minh, Vietnam).** It's a restaurant, but really like the classroom for "Vietnam Cuisine 101." It's loud and busy, but diners have their choice of food from the many authentic street stalls that line the central courtyard. Locals eat here; though they have an English menu, go with a Vietnamese friend or ask for a recommendation from the friendly (but always busy) staff. See chapter 6.

- **Kua Lao (Vientiane, Laos).** Kua Lao is traditional Lao cuisine in a similar setting, including music. Situated in a restored colonial, with a series of dining rooms, it is the premier Lao restaurant in the country. The extensive menu goes on for pages. There is an entire page of vegetarian entrees and another entire page of something you don't see often: traditional Lao desserts. See chapter 7.

- **Hawker Centers (Singapore).** Think of them as shopping malls for food—great food! For local cuisine, who needs a menu with pictures when you can walk around and select anything you want as it's prepared before your eyes? See chapter 8.

- **Gurney Drive (Penang, Malaysia).** Penang is king for offering a variety of Asian cuisine, from Chinese to Malay, Indian, and everything else in between. Visiting this large hawker center by the sea is like taking "Intro to Penang 101." See chapter 9.

- **Satri's Warung (Bali).** With 24 hours advance notice, Satri's will cook you a smoked duck or banana chicken feast, a whole bird, plus three plates of salad or fabulous vegetables, rice, and fruit for dessert, for about US$7 for two. See chapter 10.

12 The Best Markets

- **Stanley (Hong Kong).** Stall after stall of casual wear, silk clothing, bathing suits, tennis shoes, accessories, and souvenirs and crafts imported from China make this a shopper's paradise. After a day of bargaining, I like to recuperate in one of Stanley's trendy yet casual restaurants. See chapter 4.

- **Temple Street Night Market (Hong Kong).** Highlights include shopping for casual clothing, music, toys, and accessories; enjoying a meal at a *dai pai dong* (roadside food stall); watching amateur street musicians; and having your fortune told. See chapter 4.

- **Chatuchak Weekend Market (Bangkok, Thailand).** One word describes it: huge. You can easily get lost and certainly spend hours wandering this labyrinth. Don't buy anything until you spend at least a half day wandering down the endless aisles eyeballing the multitude of merchandise available. See chapter 5.

- **Night Bazaar (Chiang Mai, Thailand).** Most of those gorgeous handicrafts you find all over Thailand are made in the north, and at Chiang Mai's sprawling Night Bazaar, you'll find the widest selection, best quality, and best prices. See chapter 5.

- **Hoi An Central Market (Hoi An, Vietnam).** On the banks of the busy Perfume River lies this entire city block of narrow, roofed aisles. Produce of every description is for sale inside—handicrafts, household items, and services such as facials and massages. On the outskirts, an entire warehouse is devoted to silk and silk tailoring. See chapter 6.

- **Morning Market (Vientiane, Laos).** Laos's famous market is three huge buildings with traditional tiered roofs. Silver handicrafts, fabrics, jewelry, electronics, books, and much, much more occupy each building's several floors. The aisles are wide and made for wandering and poking through the wares, and the proprietors are friendly, gentle bargainers. See chapter 7.

- **Arab Street (Singapore).** Sure, Singapore is a shopper's paradise, but it needs more places like Arab Street, where small shops lining the street sell everything from textiles to handicrafts. Bargaining is welcome. See chapter 8.
- **Central Market (Kuala Lumpur, Malaysia).** This is one-stop shopping for all the rich arts and handicrafts Malaysia produces— and it's air-conditioned, too. See chapter 9.
- **Central Market (Phnom Penh, Cambodia).** This is where it all happens in Phnom Penh. The main building is a massive Art Deco rotunda with wings extending in all directions. It's an anthill of activity on any given day, and you can get some interesting bargains and unique finds. See chapter 11.

13 The Best Shopping Bargains

- **Custom-Tailored Clothes (Hong Kong).** Nothing beats the thrill of having something custom-made to fit you perfectly. If this is your dream, make a trek to a tailor one of your first priorities so that you'll have time for several fittings. See chapter 4.
- **Hill-Tribe Handicrafts (Night Bazaar, Chiang Mai, Thailand).** From unusual silver designs to colorful embroidery, you'll fill your birthday and holiday shopping list in about an hour, and it'll cost you a fraction of your budget. See chapter 5.
- **Antiques (Thailand).** Before you head out on vacation, visit some Asian galleries in your home country and take a look at the prices of the items you like. Once you're here, you'll be amazed at how little these things really cost. Most places will be glad to pack and ship purchases for you, and you'll still come out ahead. See chapter 5.
- **Tailored Silk Suits (Thailand and Hanoi, Hoi An, and Saigon, Vietnam).** For a fraction of what you'd pay at home, you can have a lined silk (or wool) suit tailored in a day or less, including a fitting or two. Bring pictures of your favorite designer outfits for a clever copy, and an empty suitcase or two for the trip home. See chapters 5 and 6.
- **Silver or Lacquer Handicrafts (Vietnam).** You'll find amazingly good workmanship and prices throughout the country, particularly for lacquerware. You can bargain like a demon, but be careful to ensure that the silver is genuine. See chapter 6.
- **Hand-Woven Textiles (Laos).** The Laos hand-weave textured fabrics piece by piece on primitive wooden looms. Such painstaking work costs more than a few dollars, but, ranging from sophisticated silk to gaily colored ethnic prints, the designs are pure art and uniquely Laotian. See chapter 7.
- **Silver Filigree Jewelry (Malaysia).** This fine silver is worked into detailed filigree jewelry designs to make brooches, necklaces, bracelets, and other fine jewelry. See chapter 9.
- **Pewter (Malaysia).** Malaysia is the home of Selangor Pewter, one of the largest pewter manufacturers in the world. Their many showrooms have all sorts of items to choose from. See chapter 9.
- **Fabric and Wood Carvings (Bali).** Even though as a tourist you might spend more than a

local, just about anything you buy in Bali is dirt cheap compared with the same stuff back home.

Commissioned fabric and wood carvings are a particularly good deal. See chapter 10.

14 The Hottest Nightlife Spots

- **Patpong (Bangkok, Thailand).** Yes, *that* Patpong. If go-go bars and sex shows aren't your style, you'll still find plenty to do. After you're finished shopping in the huge night market, plenty of restaurants, pubs, and discos cater to folks who prefer more traditional nightlife. See chapter 5.
- **Saigon (Vietnam).** From the tawdry Apocalypse Now bar to rooftop garden scenes like Saigon-Saigon and cool spots like Q-Bar, Saigon is famous for its rollicking nightlife. Most evenings begin with an elegant French or Vietnamese dinner at amazingly reasonable prices and then move on to incessant bar-hopping in the city's compact downtown, mingling with trendy locals and fun-loving expats. See chapter 6.
- **Disco Lives! (Laos).** Go to a disco . . . any disco. It's like a bad junior-high dance and just as innocent. In the basement of Vientiane's Lao Plaza Hotel is a reasonable big-city facsimile, but ask around in any small town for what's on. The music is Asian pop, but it's refreshing to watch young gentlemen ask the ladies to the floor with a bit of pomp and circumstance, and then it's cheek-to-cheek or stilted boogie until the big cheer when the music stops. It

hearkens to an America of the 1950s. See chapter 7.
- **Singapore (the Whole City).** Nightlife is becoming increasingly sophisticated in Singapore, where locals have more money for recreation and fun. Take the time to choose the place that suits your personality. Jazz club? Techno disco? Cocktail lounge? Wine bar? Good old pub? They have it all. See chapter 8.
- **Bangsar (near Kuala Lumpur, Malaysia).** Folks in Kuala Lumpur know to go to Bangsar for nighttime excitement. A couple blocks of concentrated restaurants, cafes, discos, pubs, and wine bars will tickle any fancy. There's good people-watching, too. See chapter 9.
- **The Heart of Darkness (Phnom Penh, Cambodia).** "Go Heart?" is how expats invite you, referring to Phnom Penh's notorious late-night rendezvous. You'll be glad you go through a metal detector here because there are some ornery-lookin' varmints about, but this place is the most interesting in this town where once, and even now, anything goes. One night in Bangkok wouldn't compare, I reckon. This is a good place to start or end the evening. See chapter 11.

2

Introducing Southeast Asia

While the rest of the world's continents fit into nice, tidy compartments—North America, South America, Europe, the Middle East, Africa—Southeast Asia seems more like a hodgepodge of islands than anything surely defined. Take a closer look at this region, and you'll see that the nations that make up Southeast Asia—Cambodia, Indonesia, Laos, Malaysia, Myanmar, Singapore, Thailand, and Vietnam—many times have more differences than similarities. Differences in geographical features, history, religious and cultural heritage, and political and economic viewpoints make this an incredibly diverse part of the world where even the shortest journey offers cross-cultural comparison and new perspective.

After the events of the September 11, 2001, terrorist attacks, the world is on high alert. Safety is, of course, our primary concern when making travel plans. The bombing of two nightclubs in Bali on October 12, 2002, serves as a cruel reminder of the continuing threat from terrorists and extremist groups to Westerners worldwide and in the region. Volatile groups such as Abu Sayef admit to vicious intent and are known to have significant bases in the island regions of the Philippines. That said, were we to stay in our homes, the terrorists win. Safety is always a concern when traveling, but if visitors stay abreast of any internal issues in any given country and steer clear of any hotspots, the exciting, adventurous tourist paths through this vibrant region are ripe for exploration and replete with mystery, beauty, and ancient culture and wisdom.

1 The Region Today

The region's many differences mean many choices for vacationers. Some travel as far as halfway around the world to visit—but with so much diversity, how can you decide which is the perfect beach or the most intriguing cultural adventure locale? In this chapter, we provide an overall view of the region and explain some of the special features and unique attractions of each destination to help you decide. And in the chapters that follow, we'll help you plan your trip from soup to nuts including trouble spots to stay clear of.

Geographically, Southeast Asia does not lack gorgeous scenery. The lush tropical rainforests of peninsular Malaysia and Borneo are some of the oldest in the world, and Singapore is one of only two cities that can boast a tropical rainforest within the city's limits. The islands and beaches of the region support famous resort areas in Phuket (Thailand) and Bali (Indonesia), plus countless other gorgeous islands and beaches that are relatively underexploited. Divers and snorkelers flock from around the world for stunning coral reefs bursting with colorful life in Thailand, Malaysia, Philippines, and Indonesia. Every country offers terrific natural diversity, opening up all kinds of choices for postcard-perfect experiences and exciting outdoor adventure, jungle trekking, sea and river kayaking, and trips to rural ethnic villages and sacred high peaks.

Southeast Asia's cultural diversity is also complex. Consider the Sri Lankans, who transplanted Theravada Buddhism, with its serene and orthodox ways, throughout Myanmar, Thailand, and Laos. Or the Indian traders, who brought ancient Hinduism to Cambodia, influencing the architecture of the magical city of Angkor; they contrast with the Hindus, who settled on Bali, mixing their dogma with local animism to create a completely unique sect. Meanwhile, seafaring Arab merchants imported Islam to coastal areas of Malaysia and Indonesia, adding a further element to the "oriental mystique" of these countries. Then there's Vietnam, the only Southeast Asian nation to fall directly under the control of past Chinese empires, whose cultural influences are still strong to this day. As if that weren't enough, Europeans from the late 1400s onward brought colonial elegance to cities such as Hong Kong, Singapore, Penang, and Malacca; the European colonial imprint can be found in the architecture and cuisine of most countries in the region. Basically, to cross an international border in Southeast Asia is to enter a completely different world from the one you just left.

Economic and political development have influenced tourism greatly. While cosmopolitan Hong Kong and Singapore guarantee the best luxury hotels, finest dining, and most refined cultural attractions, up-and-coming cities such as Kuala Lumpur, Bangkok, and Ho Chi Minh City promise cultural curiosities around every street corner as they struggle to justify traditional customs with modern development. And as Thailand's almost 3 decades of tourism development have created excellent facilities for travelers, those looking for a more down-and-dirty experience can head off to Cambodia, Myanmar, or Laos, almost completely new to the industry

and off the beaten path of most tourism agendas. Basically, for every luxurious Bali, there's a laid-back Tioman Island (Malaysia). For every crazy Hong Kong, there's a charming Luang Prabang (Laos).

It's important to talk about those Southeast Asian nations that present trouble spots for travelers in terms of politics and economics. The sections that follow discuss political turmoil in more detail, but basically you'll want to be aware in the Philippines, Indonesia, and Malaysia and in parts of Laos. Recent events in Bali and a general warning in the region have brought heightened awareness in the larger tourist areas, and it's important while traveling to stay abreast of current events in the region. Countries such as Cambodia and Myanmar are enjoying protracted periods of peace, but travelers should be aware of recent history in these countries and should remember that flairs of political upheaval are not uncommon in the region. Contact your country's overseas affairs bureau or check the U.S. Department of State's website posting current travel warnings (http://travel.state.gov).

HONG KONG

Okay, okay, you got us. Hong Kong is not *officially* part of Southeast Asia; however, we know that many of you will be stopping over in this happening hub and figure we'll save you some trouble by including the information you need in this guidebook. Even if it isn't a stop on the way, the incredible skyline alone is worth the trip. At night, the way the neon lights color Victoria Harbor, it has to be the world's most awesome cityscape next to New York.

The first reason people come to Hong Kong is for the **shopping**—the entire city is a Chinese emporium of cheap goods, exotic finds, and luxury bargains. The second is for the **dining**—everything from a 10-course

Chinese banquet fit for royalty to mouthwatering prawn wonton soup in a dingy shop front. Despite the city's **museums and exhibits,** many of which are excellent, and its well-maintained Chinese Taoist **temples,** the best sights to see are the streets themselves. Spend an afternoon getting lost in the back streets of **Yau Ma Tei** or **Mong Kok** and discover scenes of daily life and old traditions such as street markets and incense-saturated family altars. If you have the time, **Macau,** the charming Portugal-meets-China settlement, is only an hour away.

THAILAND

Thailand sees more international travelers each year than any of its neighbors, enticing everyone from luxury vacationers to young shoestring backpackers, Japanese junkets, and European group tours. You'll find professionals spinning their wheels for business ventures, tourists prowling for that "One Night in Bangkok," and soul-searchers hanging around for the Buddhist dharma and Asian hospitality. Most travelers to Southeast Asia either start here or end up here.

Most people fly into **Bangkok,** staying for a few days to take in the city's bizarre mix of old and new: royal palaces and skyscrapers, pious monks amid rush-hour commuters, sidewalk noodle vendors serving bankers in suits. That's not to mention the city's nightlife, with that seedy element that has made Bangkok infamous. Heading south, you'll find the legendary beaches and resorts of **Phuket** island, while **Ko Samui,** in the Gulf of Thailand, provides a lesser-developed "alternative" to Phuket. Another attraction to Thailand, the northern hills around **Chiang Mai,** presents a world of adventure trekking and tribal culture that has been well developed for visitors. Throughout the country are opportunities for **outdoor adventure** and **extreme sports,** organized by very professional firms that you can count on for safety and reliability.

And at the end of the day, there's that unbeatable taste of the **Thai cuisine**—tangy soups, hearty coconut curries, and the freshest seafood.

VIETNAM

If the thought of Vietnam stirs flashbacks of televised war coverage or scenes from dark movies, guess again. One of the fastest-growing destinations in the region also happens to be one of

---

Moments **Get Lost to Get Found**

Southeast Asia has drawn seekers from all over the world for many years and has long been an important stop on the hippy trails connecting Europe, India, and the Far East. Intrepid travelers began in the 1960s to explore the region and to plumb the depths and climb the heights for new and different ideologies, for spiritual paths that answer the call for introspection or the guidance of ancient wisdom; of course, many came just for the slow living, loose laws, and low rent. Whatever brings us, Southeast Asia still draws seekers, some to learn about Buddhism, meditation techniques, and traditional massage, and others to unhinge their perspective and explore unique cultures. Most come away from a trip with a different outlook. Whether you acquire just appreciation of the luxuries in your home country, new notions of culture, or a whole new set of loose-fitting duds and a relaxed demeanor, you're certain to come away from a visit here a changed person.

the most beautiful, most friendly, and most convenient places to travel.

Vietnam's major destinations fall in a line, and most travelers choose to travel from north to south, starting in Hanoi and ending in Ho Chi Minh City, or vice versa. Convenient tourist buses connect the main coastal stops, and there are increasing options for individual travelers and more unique stops along the way.

Ho Chi Minh City, or Saigon, is the gateway to the beautiful **Mekong Delta** region. Heading north, you'll pass through **Dalat,** a hill station in the cool mountains, and then down to **Nha Trang,** an emerging seaside town. Farther north, **Hoi An** is one of the region's most charming villages and a picturesque labyrinth of cobblestone streets, historic buildings, and lots of shopping. Still farther north, the former capital city at **Hue** is filled with many architectural gems of Chinese and European influence. But the merging of cultures is never more evident than in **Hanoi,** where the best elements of Vietnamese, French, and Chinese cultures collide. From here, head east to see the gorgeous **Halong Bay,** with hundreds of craggy rock formations plunging straight up from the sea, or travel north to **Sapa** and visit Vietnam's hill-tribe people in the mountains that divide northern Vietnam from China.

LAOS

Travelers who complain that Thailand has become too touristy can look to Laos. Here is a country where foreigners are still greeted as gracious guests rather than cash cows. Rarely will you find a tour bus or tacky souvenir stall—just quiet towns with laid-back markets, townsfolk carrying on their crafts in pretty street scenes, and farmers tending their chores in the beautiful countryside. That's the pace of life set by peaceful Buddhist values. You'll also meet some of the friendliest people in the world.

Some people fear that Laos will break into the "Tour Coach" market at any moment, that the ethnic villages in the north will be turned into safari parks and the country's beautiful temples turned into theme attractions. But the infrastructure of this developing nation won't yet support that, and Lao people are in no rush to cash in on the nation's tranquility.

For a capital city, Vientiane is startlingly parochial. With every other building dedicated to an international development agency, it's an eye-opening reminder that Laos is one of the top 10 poorest countries in the world. Next stop is **Luang Prabang,** UNESCO World Heritage site, a paradise of gorgeous Buddhist temples—dozens of them amid shady streets that lead to the Mekong River. If you have time, **Xieng Khouang,** in the east of Vientiane, is the home of Southeast Asia's Stonehenge, **The Plain of Jars,** huge mysterious stone monoliths that have somehow survived bombs and guerilla insurgents. **Eco-tourism** is growing rapidly, and some new and interesting avenues into the Lao jungle and rivers connect remote ethnic villages (especially in the north).

Note: Laos has experienced a return to the random acts of terror propagated by the Hmong, a northern hill tribe seeking autonomy. In two separate incidents in the winter and spring of 2003, buses on Rt. 13 north of Vang Vieng were attacked resulting in casualties. Visitors should stay abreast of the current situation and avoid that volatile stretch of road.

SINGAPORE

All of Southeast Asia's cultures seem to converge on Singapore, making it perhaps one of the best places to begin your exploration of the region. Excellent **museums** explore Asian civilizations, Southeast Asian art, and even World War II history. The city's hundreds of restaurants provide a wealth of choices in terms of **cuisine,** for a glimpse of regional specialties in one stop. And some of the best regional **fine arts, crafts, and antiques** end up in Singapore showrooms.

I'll be honest with you: Singapore gets trashed regularly by complaints that it is too Western, too modern, too sanitary—too Disneyland. Walk the streets of **Chinatown, Little India,** and the Malay Muslim area at **Kampong Glam,** and you can see where the buildings have been renovated and many former inhabitants have retired from traditional crafts. But some of these places have a few secrets left that are very rewarding if you are observant. For the past 200 years, Singapore has invented itself from many contributing cultures. If you consider the country today, it is still keeping up that tradition.

MALAYSIA

Possibly one of the most overlooked countries in Southeast Asia, Malaysia is one of my favorites for one very special reason: It's not Thailand! After so much time spent traveling around Thailand listening to every hawker yell "Hello! Special for you!" and every backpacker bragging about $5 roach-infested guesthouses, I look forward to Malaysia just to escape the tourism industry. Beaches on the islands of **Langkawi** and **Sabah** are just as beautiful as Thailand's, and resorts here are equally as fine. The quaint British colonial influences at **Penang, Malacca,** and **Kuching** (Sarawak) add to the beauty, as does the mysterious Arab-Islamic influences all over the country. That's not to mention an endless number of outdoor adventures, from mountain climbing to jungle trekking to scuba diving—in fact, the rainforest here is far superior.

Why is Malaysia so underestimated? To be honest, after experiencing the relative "freedom" and tolerance of Thai culture, many travelers find Malaysian culture too strict and prohibitive. Personally, I think it's a fair

trade—in Thailand, when I talk to Thai people, I'm often treated like a tourist with a fat wallet. In Malaysia, when I meet local people, I end up having interesting conversations and cherished personal experiences. And I don't have to suffer through blatant prostitution and drug abuse—the sad, sleazy side of the Thai tourism industry.

One word of caution regarding travel in Malaysia: On April 23, 2000, a group of tourists was kidnapped from the diving resort at Sipadan Island, off the east coast of Sabah (Malaysian Borneo). Abu Sayyaf, the Filipino Muslim separatists who were responsible for the incident, still remain at large in the southern islands of the Philippines close to Borneo. Exercise caution when traveling to this area.

BALI (INDONESIA)

Memories of the recent bombing of two nightclubs packed with Western tourists, mostly Australian, in the town of Kuta are written large on our collective consciousness, and no doubt the whole world is familiar with the trouble facing Indonesia. Since the economic crisis in 1997, the country has been plagued with civil unrest: ethnic and religious conflict, the struggle for independence in East Timor and now Aceh, and anti-American rioting in Jakarta. Meanwhile, despite injections of IMF funds and major changes in leadership, the economy continues to stall, spin, crash, and burn.

Until the bombings, Bali was the one safe haven, an enclave of upscale resorts that now, in the wake of bombing, struggles to regain its international allure. The beaches remain the stuff of legend, supporting dreamy resorts dripping with tropical ambience, world renowned among romantic honeymooners and well-heeled paradise seekers. Sports enthusiasts flock here for surfing, snorkeling, scuba diving, swimming, and windsurfing, as well as a number of on-land challenges. People who can pull themselves away from the seaside will venture into villages lively with friendly local smiles and markets packed with eye-boggling local handicrafts and treasures to bargain for. The artistic and intriguing community in Ubud is just as fascinating as the gorgeous scenery around the town, full of sacred Hindu temples, mysterious royal tombs, rice paddies, gorges, and rivers. Bali still has much to offer, and the friendly Balinese islanders are eager to see a return of the Western visitors who've brought so much to this magical isle.

CAMBODIA

It wasn't long ago that Cambodia was off the map, a land plagued by general lawlessness and banditry as the result of years of strife. In recent years, visitors have braved the remnants of the country's chaos and, by hook or crook, made their way to **Siem Reap** and Southeast Asia's premiere cultural attraction, **Angkor Wat,** the magnificent temple ruins of the mighty Angkor Civilization of A.D. 800–1200. The good news is that, though it will take years to catch up economically with its growing neighbors, Cambodia is on the mend. Most also agree that it will take a few generations to heal, though never forget, the tragic events of the mid-1970s, when the entire country was turned into a concentration camp under Pol Pot. But Cambodia is looking to the future. Bolstered by international humanitarian aid organizations, the country is disarming its citizens and enjoying a protracted period of peace not seen in many years. **Phnom Penh,** the capital, and **Siem Reap,** the access village for the Angkor Temples, are safe, and the countryside is open to more adventurous travelers ready to brave the rough roads and basic amenities and accommodation.

Despite a loosening of restrictions on travel, many still limit their trip in Cambodia to the temples of Angkor. Convenient direct flights from the larger cities throughout the region simplify the process.

It's important to remember that the country is still littered with UXO, unexploded ordnance, including dormant bombs and landmines. In the countryside, it's important to stay on well-worn trails and, farther afield, to go with a knowledgeable guide. Though the political situation is reputedly calm, general elections scheduled for summer 2003 mean that visitors should stay informed before going because the country has a history of flash political upheaval.

THE PHILIPPINES

With 7,107 islands in total, you can't throw a stone without hitting a beach in the Philippines. Though tourism isn't nearly as developed as in the mainland countries of Southeast Asia, there are some fine accommodations in Manila and some beautiful, high-end resorts that pepper the many miles of coastline. For the nature lover, adventure traveler, or outdoor enthusiast, the Philippine archipelago is a giant playground. Resorts of the highest caliber (and lowest price tag) dot the dynamic coast.

Unfortunately, recent events in the region put the Philippines under a general warning. Since April 2000, the Abu Sayef terrorist group has kidnapped many locals and tourists, including a group from the nearby Malaysian dive resort at Sipadan in eastern Sabah. Travelers should certainly avoid the southwestern islands, especially Mindanao, Cordillera, and the Bicol regions of Luzon, and should even stay alert in large urban areas.

MYANMAR

Endowed with magnificent scenic beauty and unique culture, Myanmar (or Burma) offers profound travel experiences to the more adventurous traveler—but it still begs caution. After being closed to tourism for years due to a series of wars and repressive regimes, the government of Myanmar has encouraged foreign tourists since the 1990s, but its policies still reflect disarray, repression, and an inability to deal constructively with internal and external problems.

For a decade now Ang San Suu Kyi, Myanmar's leading voice of democracy, has spoken out against any activity that might put money into the hands of the oppressive military regime that imprisons her. However, human rights groups are only beginning to debate the merits of tourism in Myanmar. Perhaps tourism will attract global exposure that could prove helpful in the long run. We present a few of the better international and local tour providers, along with limited travel specifics and a general caution.

2 A Southeast Asian Cultural Primer

A vast diversity of ethnic groups people Southeast Asia. Whether living in modern cities or remote hills, each group has its own special cultural practices, which are often influenced by religion. With so much mingling and mixing of peoples occurring throughout Southeast Asian history, it should come as no surprise that the region's cornucopia of cultures have intertwined and adopted various elements, beliefs, and practices from each other.

THE CULTURAL MAKEUP OF SOUTHEAST ASIA
HONG KONG
Although Western culture has had a strong impact on Hong Kong (5 of the world's 10 busiest McDonalds are located here), it still preserves its connection to many aspects of Chinese culture passed down from ancestors. Fortune-telling, astrology, superstition, and ancestor worship still play a role in the daily life of a people whose religions might include elements of Buddhist, Taoist, and Christian beliefs. In the morning, you might see men and women practicing the ancient art of tai chi in the shadow of a skyscraper; in the evening, outside a temple, you might encounter a fortune-teller interpreting someone's future.

Whether it's entertainment, cuisine, or the arts, the Chinese influence in Hong Kong is unmistakable. Among the most popular cultural pursuits are **puppet plays,** which tell the story of Chinese dynasties, and **Chinese Opera** (wayung), which is performed in the more modern Cantonese style as well as the classic Beijing style.

While the majority of Hong Kong's 30,000 restaurants serve Cantonese-style Chinese food, a good selection of establishments also serves Shanghai, Beijing, Hangzhou, Szechuan, and many other varieties of Chinese cooking.

English is spoken widely in Hong Kong; the island's two official languages are Chinese (Cantonese) and English.

THAILAND
Over centuries, migrating cultures have blended to create what is known as "Thai" today. Early waves of Southern Chinese migrants combine with Mon peoples from Burma, Khmers from Cambodia, Malays, and Lao people—it is said that Thailand's King Rama I could trace ancestry to all these, plus European, Indian, Han Chinese, and Arab families. Of the 75% of the population that calls itself Thai, a great number of people in northeastern Isaan are of Lao ancestry. In the past century, Thailand has also become home to many migrating hill tribes in the north—tribes who've come from Vietnam, Laos, Myanmar, and Southern China, many as refugees. As you travel south toward the Malaysian border, you find Thai people who share cultural and religious affinity with their southern Malay neighbors. Also in the past 50

Buddha and Buddhism in Southeast Asia

Born Siddhartha Gautama Buddha in the year 563 B.C., the historical Buddha was an Indian prince, a child who, legend has it, walked and spoke from his first breath and left lotus flowers for footsteps. His mother's dream while pregnant was confirmed by a passing sage who predicted the child's future as a great holy man. In an effort to spare him such tortures, Siddhartha was kept sheltered behind palace walls; knew nothing of sickness and death; married, had children, and lived a carefree, sheltered life, though one plagued by a certain soul sickness and discontent. His journey began when he first spied a sick man and a corpse. Renouncing his princely cloaks, he concluded that life is suffering; resolving to search for relief from that suffering, he went into the forest and lived there for many years as a solitary ascetic, ultimately following his moderate "middle way" and achieving enlightenment and Nirvana (escape from the cycle of reincarnation) while in meditation under the Boddhi Tree.

Buddha's peripatetic teaching is the basis of all Buddhism and, upon his death, two schools arose and spread throughout Asia. The oldest and probably closest to the original practice is **Theravada** (Doctrine of the Elders), sometimes referred to less correctly as **Hinayana** (the Small Vehicle). It prevails in Sri Lanka, Burma, Laos, Thailand, and Cambodia and believes in the enlightenment of individuals in this life, one at a time. The other school is **Mahayana** (the Large Vehicle), which is practiced in China, Korea, Vietnam, and Japan; it believes in collective enlightenment, that we all go up together.

Buddhism has one aim only: to abolish suffering. Most of us are pretty sure that we do, in fact, exist, and, if told otherwise, might object. But Buddhism tells us that our ideas of "self," our relentless egos, get in the way of understanding the world around us and finding peace. According to Buddhism, it is the attachment to self, to ownership in the material world, that brings us suffering.

The Buddhist assertion that "all life is suffering" conjures images of self-denial but should be understood in the context of Buddhist "impermanence." Because nothing remains as it is, even the most pleasant experiences (eating an ice-cream cone, falling in love, being healthy and

years, Thailand has seen a boom in Chinese immigrants. They're difficult to pinpoint because immigration laws have required that they change their name to a Thai equivalent.

The Thais are a warm and peaceable people, with a culture that looks heavily to Indian and Sri Lankan influences. Early Thais adopted many Brahman practices that today are evident in royal ceremony and social hierarchy—Thailand is a very class-oriented culture. Even their cherished national story, the *Ramakien*, the subject of almost all Thai classical dances and temple murals, finds its origin in the Indian Hindu epic the *Ramayana*. Thai Buddhism follows the Theravada sect, imported from Sri Lanka along with the classic bell-shape stupa seen in many temple grounds.

rich) will turn to suffering in the extreme and dissatisfaction in the main because they eventually will end or change. Buddhists tell us that our clinging to these states of impermanence causes us suffering and that seeing things as they are, without desire, malice, and delusion, means attaining enlightenment or nirvana. There is no god in Buddhism; the Buddha is but an example. Buddhist practices, particularly Theravada, center on meditation and require that individuals, according to Buddha himself, look within and come to understand the Four Noble Truths: The existence of suffering; its arising; and its ultimate passing by practice of the Eightfold Path, a road-map to right living and good conduct.

Buddhist philosophy pervades every aspect of life, morality, and thought in the countries of Thailand, Laos, Burma, and Cambodia. The monastic community, called the *Sangha,* is supported by local people; it serves as the cultural touchstone and often is an important avenue for education. Monks live in the "supramundane," free from the usual human concerns of finding food, clothing, and shelter. Instead, they focus on the rigorous practice of meditation, study, and austerities prescribed by the Theravada tradition. Mahayana traditions from China hold important sway over life in parts of the Malay Peninsula, Vietnam, and Hong Kong as well.

Lay practitioners adopt the law of **karma,** in which every action has effects and the energy of past action, good or evil, continues forever and is "reborn." Merit can be gained by entering the monkhood (and most males do so for a few days or months), helping in the construction of a monastery or a stupa, contributing to education, giving alms, or performing any act of kindness, no matter how small. When monks go daily with their bowls from house to house, they are not begging, but are offering people an opportunity to make merit by supporting them. Buddha images are honored and revered in the Eastern tradition and are said to radiate the essence of Buddha, ideals that we should revere and struggle to achieve; but the images themselves are not holy or spiritually charged, per se. That said, most laymen worship the Buddha by wearing talismans and amulets said to protect them from evil spirits, and they pray to the Buddha for good luck and prosperity.

Perhaps the two main influences in Thai life today are spirituality and the royal family. In every household throughout the country, you'll find a spirit house to appease the property's former inhabitants, a portrait of the king in a prominent spot and perhaps pictures of a few previous kings, a dais for Buddha images and religious objects, and portraits of each son as he enters the monkhood as almost all sons do.

VIETNAM, LAOS, CAMBODIA & MYANMAR (BURMA)

Together, the countries of Vietnam, Cambodia, Laos, and Myanmar (Burma) make up one of the most ethnically diverse regions of Southeast Asia. Outside the cities, little English is spoken in any of these countries except by tour guides and others who have frequent contact with Western visitors. Much of the architecture and art in Cambodia, Laos, and Burma is influenced by Buddhism and includes some of the world's most renowned temples, along with exquisitely sculpted Buddha images. The temple complexes of Angkor Wat in Cambodia and Bagan in Burma are among the architectural wonders of the ancient world, while the finest temples in Laos are found in the ancient capital of Luang Prabang.

One important note: The ethnic minorities, or hill tribes, of northern Vietnam, Laos, Thailand, and Myanmar (Burma) all share a common heritage with each other, originating from either Himalayan tribes or southern Chinese clans. You'll find startling similarities in the customs and languages of all these people.

VIETNAM In Vietnam, the ethnic Vietnamese are a fusion of Viet, Tai (a southern Chinese group), Indonesian, and Chinese who first settled here between 200 B.C. and A.D. 200. Although Vietnam has no official religion, several religions have significantly impacted Vietnamese culture, including **Buddhism, Confucianism, Taoism, and Animism.** Animism, which is the oldest religious practice in Vietnam and many other Southeast Asian countries, is centered on belief in a spirit world. Ancient cultural traditions lean toward borrowings from the mandarins of old Chinese dynasties that claimed sovereignty over Vietnam. In the 1900s, the French added a smattering of their own culture. Today the modern culture is defined by a pell-mell rush to capitalism.

LAOS In Laos, approximately half the population is ethnic Lao descended from centuries of migration, mostly from southern China. A landlocked country with little natural resources, Laos has had little luck entering the global trade scene and remains dependent on the international donor community. If you think the Thais are laid back, you'll have to check the Laos for a pulse. In fact, Lao culture is most often compared with the Thais because the two share common roots of language and culture although the Thais will never admit it because they often look down upon their northern neighbors. Large communities of ethnic minorities live in agrarian and subsistence communities, particularly in the north, and carry on rich traditional crafts and practices.

CAMBODIA The population of Cambodia is made up primarily of ethnic Khmers who have lived here since around the 2nd century A.D. and whose religion and culture have been influenced by interaction with Indians, Javanese, Thais, Vietnamese, and Chinese. The achievements of the ancient Angkor Empire were a long time ago, and modern Khmer culture still struggles in the aftermath of many years of war and terror. Relative political stability is new here and Cambodia has far to go to catch up economically and with the infrastructure of the other countries in the region. Basic medical necessities are still lacking and landmines still cover the countryside and kill an estimated four people each day. Time and effort by civil authorities and NGOs (nongovernment organizations) will only tell. Though our image of the country may be defined by "The Killing Fields," Khmer life is marked by devout Buddhist ritual, much like its neighbors, which fosters a pervasive gentleness among Khmer.

MYANMAR (BURMA) The majority of Myanmese people come from the Burmans. Today these are the people who hold positions of power in the government, occupying most of the territory of central and south Myanmar. A small group of Mons, descended from an ancient civilization that once ruled, still exists in the east and southeast of the country. The northern hills are occupied by scores of hill tribes, the most vocal of which is the **Shan.** Although the international community is aware that many tribes are fighting for "independence," it is interesting to note that, for many of these people, they already have their own state but feel that they are fighting Myanmese who are trying to occupy it.

SINGAPORE

Seventy-eight percent of Singaporeans trace their heritage to migrating waves from China's southern provinces, particularly from the Hokkien, Teowchew, Hakka, Cantonese, and Hainanese dialect groups. Back then, the Chinese community was driven by rags-to-riches stories—the poor worker hawking vegetables who opened a grocery store and then started a chain of stores and now drives a Mercedes Benz. This story still motivates them today.

But it's not just Chinese who have dominated the scene. The island started off with a handful of Malay inhabitants; then came the British colonials with Indian administrators, followed by Muslim Indian moneylenders, Chinese merchants, Chinese coolie laborers, and Indian convict labor, plus European settlers and immigrants from all over Southeast Asia. Over 2 centuries of modern history, each group made its contribution to "Singaporean culture."

Today, as your average Singaporean struggles to balance traditional values with modern demands of globalization, his country is raked over the coals for being sterile and overly Westernized. Older folks are becoming frustrated by younger generations who discard traditions in their pursuit of "The 5 C's"—career, condo, car, credit card, and cash. Temples and ethnic neighborhoods are finding more revenue from tourists than from the communities they once served. Although many lament the loss of the good old days, most are willing to sacrifice a little tradition to be Southeast Asia's most stable and wealthy country.

MALAYSIA

Malaysia's population consists primarily of ethnic **Malays,** labeled **Bumiputeras,** a political classification that also encompasses tribal people who live in peninsular Malaysia and Borneo. Almost all Malays are Muslim, with corresponding conservative values running throughout the land. The ruling government party supports an Islam that is open and tolerant to other cultures, but a growing minority favors strict Islamic law and government, further marginalizing the country's large Chinese and Indian population. These foreign cultures migrated to Malaysia during the British colonial period as trading merchants, laborers, and administrators. Today Malaysia recognizes ethnic **Chinese** and **Indian** citizens as equals under national law. However, government development and education policies always seem to favor Bumiputeras.

Among the favorite Malaysian recreational pastimes are **kite flying,** using ornately decorated paper kites, and top spinning. Some still practice **silat,** a Malaysian form of martial arts.

BALI

No country in Southeast Asia has a more ethnically diverse population than Indonesia, with more than 350 ethnic groups with their own languages and cultures scattered among the 6,000 inhabited islands of this vast archipelago of more than 14,000 islands.

Of all the islands, Bali stands out for its especially rich cultural life, which is inextricably linked with its Hindu beliefs. Life in Bali is marked by a unique flow of ritual; whether painting, carving, dancing, or playing music, it seems that all Balinese are involved in the arts or practice devout daily rituals of beauty. Flower offerings to the gods are a common sight, and the Balinese are forever paying homage to Hindu deities at more than 20,000 temples and during the 60 annual festivals on the island.

The majority of the island's population is native Balinese; there are quite a few people from other parts of Indonesia, and they are there for work opportunities. English is widely spoken in the tourist parts of Bali, which means that just about everywhere you go someone will speak enough English to help you out.

THE PHILIPPINES

In the Philippines, **English** is one of three official languages, along with Spanish and the Filipino dialect Tagalog. The country stands out from the rest of Southeast Asia as the only predominantly Christian country in the region. Islam is also practiced, with the Muslim population concentrated on the Philippines' second largest island, Mindanao.

Filipinos are primarily of **Malay** ancestry, with mixtures of **Spanish, Chinese,** and other groups. Altogether, several hundred languages and dialects are spoken in the islands.

ETIQUETTE TIPS

"Different countries, different customs," as Sean Connery said to Michael Caine in *The Man Who Would Be King.* And although each country covered in this book proves that rule by having their own twists on etiquette, some general pointers will allow you to go though your days of traveling without inadvertently offending your hosts. (For etiquette tips on individual countries, see the country chapters.)

GREETINGS, GESTURES & SOCIAL INTERACTION

In these modern times, the **common Western handshake** has become extremely prevalent throughout Southeast Asia, but it is by no means universal. There are a plethora of traditional greetings, so when greeting someone—especially an older man and even more especially a woman of any age—it's safest to wait for a gesture or observe those around you and then follow suit. In Muslim culture, for instance, it is not acceptable for men and women not related by blood or marriage to touch.

In interpersonal relations in strongly Buddhist areas (Laos, Vietnam, and Thailand), it helps to **take a gentle approach to human relationships.** A person showing anger or ill temper would be regarded with surprise and disapproval. A gentle approach will take you farther.

Here's a delicate matter that's best to get out of the way immediately: In countries with significant Muslim and Hindu cultures (Malaysia, Singapore, Indonesia, Bali) **use only your right hand in social interaction.** Traditionally, the left hand is used only for personal hygiene. Not only should you eat with your right hand and give and receive all gifts with your right hand, but you also should make sure that you make all gestures, especially **pointing** (and even more especially, pointing in temples and mosques), with your right hand. In all the countries discussed in this book, it's also considered more polite to point with your knuckle (with your hand facing palm down) than with your finger.

In all the countries covered in this guide, ladies seated on the floor should never sit with their legs crossed in front of them—instead, always tuck your legs to the side. Men may sit with legs crossed. Both men and women should also be careful **not to show the bottoms of their feet,** which are considered the lowliest, most unclean part of the body. If you cross your legs while on the floor or in a chair, don't point your soles toward other people. Also be careful not to use your foot to point or gesture. **Shoes should be removed** when entering a temple or

Understanding Feng Shui

Have you ever noticed how some homes seem to give off terrific vibes the moment you enter the front door, while others leave you feeling disturbed and wanting to get out fast? The Chinese believe that feng shui (pronounced "fung shway" and meaning "wind and water") has a lot to do with these positive and negative feelings.

The earliest record of feng shui dates from the Han Dynasty (202 B.C.–A.D. 220), and the practice is still widely and highly regarded in Asia today. In essence, the idea of feng shui revolves around the way physical surroundings relate to the invisible flow of chi (natural energy), which must move smoothly throughout the home or business in order for life to play itself out beneficially. Walls, doors, windows, or furnishings can throw off this flow through their color, balance, placement, or proportion—even by their points on the compass. Your bed, for example, placed on the wrong wall or facing the wrong way could encourage chi to rush into a room and out again, taking wealth and health with it. If your bed is situated directly under an exposed beam, you might as well make a standing appointment with the chiropractor, 'cause that's some bad feng shui.

In Singapore and Hong Kong, particularly (as both have large Chinese populations), company presidents regularly call upon feng shui masters to rearrange their office furniture, and the master is usually the first person called in on new construction jobs to assess the building plans for their adherence to good feng shui practices. It's not uncommon to hear stories about buildings being partially torn down late in the construction process, simply because a master hadn't examined the plans earlier and, when finally consulted, deemed that the structure did not promote good feng shui. The extra cost is considered a valid investment—after all, what's a few dollars saved now if bad feng shui will later cause the business to fail? For the average homeowner who doesn't want to consult a feng shui master (or can't afford to), a plethora of books is available to advise on creating successful living spaces.

For every life situation, there's a feng shui solution. And don't worry what people will think when they see those four purple candles in the corner of your living room or the pair of wooden flutes dangling from an exposed beam. Let 'em laugh—you'll be grinning all the way to the bank.

---

private home. And don't ever step over someone's body or legs.

On a similar note, in Buddhist and Hindu cultures, the head is considered the most sacred part of the body; therefore, do not casually touch another person's head—and this includes patting children on the head.

DRESSING FOR CULTURAL SUCCESS

The basic rule is, **dress modestly.** Except perhaps on the grounds of resorts and in heavily tourist areas such as Bali's Kuta and Thailand's beaches, foreigners displaying navels, chests, or shoulders, or wearing short

Tips Everything Has a Price: Haggling

In the smaller shops and at street vendors throughout Southeast Asia, you'll find that prices are never marked, and it is expected that you will bargain. The most important thing to remember when bargaining is to keep a friendly, good-natured banter between you and the seller. It's all in a day's work for him. Before you start out, it's always good to have at least some idea of how much your purchase is worth, to give you a base point for negotiation. Shop around and ask questions. A simple "How much?" is the place to start, to which the vendor will reply with the top price. Never accept the first price! Try a smile and ask, "Is that your best price?" Sometimes the vendor will ask what your paying price is. Knock the price down about 50%—they'll look shocked, but it's a starting point for bidding. Just remember to smile and be friendly, and you should be able to negotiate something you both can agree on. *Caveat:* If it's a larger, more expensive item, don't get into major bargaining unless you're serious about buying. If the shopkeeper agrees on what you say you're willing to pay, it's generally considered rude to not make the purchase. If no agreement is made, however, you can always say "Thank you" and walk away. See individual country chapters for more on shopping.

shorts or short skirts will attract stares. Although shorts and bathing suits are accepted on the beach, you should avoid parading around in them elsewhere, no matter how hot it is.

TEMPLE & MOSQUE ETIQUETTE

Many of Southeast Asia's greatest and most remarkable sights are its places of worship, usually Buddhist wats, Hindu temples, and Islamic mosques (masjids). When visiting these places, more so than at any other time, it's important to observe certain rules of decorum.

When visiting the **mosques,** be sure to dress appropriately. Neither men nor women will be admitted wearing shorts. Ladies should not wear short skirts or sleeveless, backless, or low-cut tops. Both men and women are required to leave their shoes outside. Also, never enter the mosque's main prayer hall; this area is reserved for Muslims only. No cameras or video cameras are allowed, and remember to turn off cellphones and pagers. Friday is the Sabbath day, and you should not plan to go to the mosques between 11am and 2pm on this day.

Visitors are welcome to walk around and explore most temples and wats. As in the mosques, remember to dress appropriately—some temples might refuse to admit you if you're showing too much skin—and to leave your shoes outside. Photography is permitted in most temples, although some, such as Wat Phra Kaeo in Thailand, prohibit it. Never climb on a Buddha image, and if you sit down, never point your feet in the direction of the Buddha. Do not cross in front of a person who is in prayer. Also, women should never touch a monk, try to shake his hand, or even give something to one directly (the monk will provide a cloth for you to lay the item upon, and he will collect it). Monks are not permitted to touch women or even to speak directly to them anywhere but inside a temple or wat.

3

Planning Your Trip to Southeast Asia

The country chapters in this guide provide specific information on traveling to and getting around in all of Southeast Asia's individual countries, but in this chapter, we give you some region-wide tips and information that will help you plan your trip.

1 Visitor Information

 Southeast Asia: Red Alert Checklist

- Are there any **special requirements** for your destination? Vaccinations? Special visas, passports, or IDs? Bug repellent? Appropriate attire?
- If you purchased traveler's checks, have you recorded the check numbers and stored the documentation separately from the checks?
- Did you stop the newspaper and mail delivery, and leave a set of keys with someone reliable?
- Did you pack your camera and an extra set of camera batteries, and purchase enough film? If you packed film in your checked baggage, did you invest in protective pouches to shield film from airport x-rays?
- Do you have a safe, accessible place to store money, like a money belt?
- Did you bring your ID cards that could entitle you to discounts, such as AAA and AARP cards, and student IDs?
- Did you bring emergency drug prescriptions and extra glasses or contact lenses?
- Did you find out your daily ATM withdrawal limit?
- Do you have your credit card pin numbers? Is there a daily withdrawal limit on credit card cash advances?
- If you have an E-ticket, do you have documentation?
- Did you leave a copy of your itinerary with someone at home?
- Do you have the measurements for people you plan to buy clothes for on your trip?
- Did you check to see if any travel advisories have been issued by the U.S. State Department (http://travel.state.gov/travel_warnings.html) regarding your destination?
- Do you have the address and phone number of your country's embassy with you?

2 Entry Requirements & Customs

ENTRY REQUIREMENTS

Most countries covered in this guide require that citizens of the U.S., U.K., Canada, Australia, and New Zealand have only a **passport** for entry, but Vietnam, Laos, Cambodia, and Myanmar (Burma) require citizens of these countries to have **visas.** Though most international airports offer visas upon arrival and there are more overland points where you can apply with a passport photos and money when you arrive, if you plan to enter Vietnam, Laos, or Cambodia from rural overland points, you often need to obtain a visa beforehand (often you even need to specify what entry point). See individual country chapters for more specific information.

BALI   Note: Word is out that Bali and Indonesia will soon require pre-arranged visas for most Western foreign nationals. Keep an eye out for news. As of this writing, visitors from the U.S., Australia, most of Europe, New Zealand, and Canada do not need visas. They will be given a stamp that allows them to stay for 60 days, provided that they are entering the country through an officially designated gateway: Ngurah Rai Airport or the seaports of Padang Bai and Benoa. If you want to stay longer than 60 days, you must get a tourist or business visa before coming to Indonesia. Tourist visas are valid only for 4 weeks and cannot be extended, while business visas can be extended for 6 months at Indonesian immigration offices.

CAMBODIA   All visitors are required to carry a passport and visa. A 1-month visa can be obtained upon entry at the Phnom Penh or Siem Reap international airports for US$20. Bring two passport photos for your application. Visa on arrival is now available at the land crossing from Poi Pet (Thailand) and the boat-crossing point from Chau Doc in Vietnam for just US$22.

HONG KONG   A valid passport is the only document that most tourists, including Americans, need to enter Hong Kong. Americans can stay up to 1 month without a visa. Australians, New Zealanders, Canadians, and other British Commonwealth citizens can stay 3 months without a visa, while citizens of the United Kingdom can stay for 6 months without a visa.

LAOS   Residents of every Western country need a passport and visa to visit Laos. Although the official time limit is 15 days, for US$35 (slightly more through an agent), most people get 30 days for just asking. If you haven't organized your visa in your home country, travel agents in Thailand and Vietnam can arrange them for you with little hassle. Visa-upon-arrival service is now available when crossing the Friendship Bridge from Nong Khai (Thailand) to Vientiane (bring 2 photos).

MALAYSIA   To enter Malaysia, you must have a valid passport. Citizens of the United States do not need visas for tourism and business visits. Citizens of Canada, Australia, New Zealand, and the United Kingdom do not require a visa for tourism or business visits not exceeding 1 month.

MYANMAR (BURMA)   Myanmar consulates issue visas for tourist visits of up to 4 weeks. *Be warned:* They might refuse your application if they suspect that you represent a media firm or a prodemocracy or human rights organization. Look like a tourist. No extensions are granted. There are special visas for the study of meditation; inquire at an embassy or consulate.

SINGAPORE   To enter Singapore, you'll need a valid passport. Visas are

Tips **Passport Savvy**

Allow plenty of time before your trip to apply for a passport; processing normally takes 3 weeks but can take longer during busy periods (especially spring). And keep in mind that if you need a passport in a hurry, you'll pay a higher processing fee. When traveling, safeguard your passport in an inconspicuous, inaccessible place like a money belt, and keep a copy of the critical pages with your passport number in a separate place. If you lose your passport, visit the nearest consulate of your native country as soon as possible for a replacement.

not necessary for citizens of the United States, Canada, the United Kingdom, Australia, and New Zealand. Upon entry, visitors from these countries will be issued a 30-day pass for a social visit only, except for Americans, who get a 90-day pass.

THAILAND All visitors to Thailand must carry a valid passport with proof of onward passage (either a return or through ticket). Visas are not required for stays of up to 30 days for citizens of the U.S., Australia, Canada, Ireland, New Zealand, or the U.K. but 3-month tourist visas can be arranged before arrival.

VIETNAM Residents of the U.S., Canada, Australia, New Zealand, and the United Kingdom need both a passport and a valid visa to enter Vietnam. A tourist visa usually lasts for 30 days and costs US$60. You need to specify your date of entry and exit. Though there's no official policy, tourist visas can commonly be extended with little hassle. Multiple-entry business visas are available that are valid for up to 3 months; however, you must have a sponsoring agency in Vietnam, and it can take much longer to process. For short business trips, it's less complicated simply to enter as a tourist.

For information on how to get a passport, go to the "Fast Facts" section of this chapter—the websites listed provide downloadable passport applications as well as the current fees for

processing passport applications. For an up-to-date country-by-country listing of passport requirements around the world, go the "Foreign Entry Requirement" website of the U.S. State Department at **http://travel. state.gov/foreignentryreqs.html**.

CUSTOMS
WHAT YOU CAN BRING INTO SOUTHEAST ASIA
Allowable amounts of tobacco, alcohol, and currency are comparable in all countries: usually 2 cartons of cigarettes, up to 2 bottles of liquor, and between US$3,000 and US$10,000. Check individual chapters for exact amounts. Plant material and animals fall under restrictions across the board.

WHAT YOU CAN TAKE HOME FROM SOUTHEAST ASIA
Restrictions on what you can take out of the various nations of SE Asia are loose, at best. Expect a red flag if you have any kind of plant materials or animals, but the most notable restriction has to do with antiques. To prevent the return to wholesale looting of the region's antiquities in the recent colonial past, you might be stopped if you are carrying any Buddhist statuary or authentic antiques or religious artifacts. This does not apply to tourist trinkets, however aged and interesting. In fact, despite any salesman's claim of authenticity, you'll be hard-pressed to

find authentic antiques, really. Returning **U.S. citizens** who have been away for at least 48 hours are allowed to bring back, once every 30 days, $400 worth of merchandise duty-free. You'll be charged a flat rate of 4% duty on the next $1,000 worth of purchases. Be sure to have your receipts handy. On mailed gifts, the duty-free limit is $100. With some exceptions, you cannot bring fresh fruits and vegetables into the United States. For specifics on what you can bring back, download the invaluable free pamphlet *Know Before You Go* online at **www.customs. gov.** (Click on "Traveler Information" and then "Know Before You Go.") Or, contact the **U.S. Customs Service,** 1300 Pennsylvania Ave. NW, Washington, DC 20229 (© **877/287-8867**) and request the pamphlet.

For a clear summary of **Canadian** rules, write for the booklet *I Declare,* issued by the **Canada Customs and Revenue Agency** (© **800/461-9999** in Canada, or 204/983-3500; www. ccra-adrc.gc.ca). Canada allows its citizens a C$750 exemption, and you're allowed to bring back duty-free 1 carton of cigarettes, 1 can of tobacco, 40 imperial ounces of liquor, and 50 cigars. In addition, you're allowed to mail gifts to Canada valued at less than C$60 a day, provided that they're unsolicited and don't contain alcohol or tobacco (write on the package "Unsolicited gift, under $60 value"). All valuables should be declared on the Y-38 form before departure from Canada, including serial numbers of valuables that you already own, such as expensive foreign cameras. *Note:* The $750 exemption can be used only once a year and only after an absence of 7 days.

U.K. citizens returning from **a non-EU country** have a Customs allowance of 200 cigarettes; 50 cigars; 250g of smoking tobacco; 2 liters of still table wine; 1 liter of spirits or strong liqueurs (over 22% volume); 2 liters of fortified wine, sparkling wine, or other liqueurs; 60cc (ml) of perfume; 250cc (ml) of toilet water; and £145 worth of all other goods, including gifts and souvenirs. People under 17 cannot have the tobacco or alcohol allowance. For more information, contact HM Customs & Excise at © **0845/010-9000** (from outside the U.K., 020/8929-0152), or consult the website www.hmce.gov.uk.

The duty-free allowance in **Australia** is A$400 or, for those under 18, A$200. Citizens can bring in 250 cigarettes or 250 grams of loose tobacco, and 1,125 milliliters of alcohol. If you're returning with valuables that you already own, such as foreign-made cameras, you should file form B263. A helpful brochure available from Australian consulates or Customs offices is *Know Before You Go.* For more information, call the **Australian Customs Service** at © **1300/363-263,** or log on to www.customs.gov.au.

The duty-free allowance for **New Zealand** is NZ$700. Citizens over 17 can bring in 200 cigarettes, 50 cigars, or 250 grams of tobacco (or a mixture of all 3, if their combined weight doesn't exceed 250g); plus 4.5 liters of wine and beer, or 1.125 liters of liquor. New Zealand currency does not carry import or export restrictions. Fill out a certificate of export listing the valuables that you are taking out of the country; that way, you can bring them back without paying duty. Most questions are answered in a free pamphlet available at New Zealand consulates and Customs offices: *New Zealand Customs Guide for Travelers, Notice no. 4.* For more information, contact **New Zealand Customs,** The Customhouse, 17–21 Whitmore St., Box 2218, Wellington (© **04/473-6099** or 0800/428-786; www.customs.govt.nz).

3 Money

The East Asian financial crisis is now a distant memory for most, and the countries of Southeast Asia are generally gaining economic clout in the world, but the rate of exchange, not to mention the price of most goods and services, means that travel in the region, apart from the few glitzy cities like Singapore or Hong Kong, is very budget friendly. In places like Laos or Cambodia, you'll find that you can live quite well on very little, and the region's resort destinations and luxury accommodations in general come at a fraction of what you might pay in your home country. ATM service is good in the larger cities but can be scant, at best, in some of the region's backwaters, with no service whatsoever in places like Laos, Cambodia, and Myanmar. Traveler's checks, an anachronism elsewhere in the world, are still not a bad idea, especially in the developing countries of the region; places like Malaysia Thailand and all urban centers, however, offer all the services of Western cities, although ATMs come with a fee (unless you can find a branch of your bank, such as Citibank). It's important to know that the U.S. dollar is the de facto currency for many of these countries. Hotels, in particular, prefer doing business in U.S. dollars to dealing in local currency, a practice that helps them stay afloat amid fluctuating currency values. In places like Vietnam and Laos, everybody down to the smallest shop vendor quotes prices in U.S. dollars, and particularly the big-ticket items are best handled with greenbacks instead of large stacks of local currency.

While dealing in U.S. dollars can make things less complicated, always keep in mind local currency values so that you know if you're being charged the correct amount. In this book, we've listed **hotel, restaurant, and attraction rates** in whatever form the establishments quoted them—in U.S. dollars (designated as US$) where those were quoted, and in local currencies (with U.S. dollar equivalents) where those were used.

Note that, with the exception of the Singapore dollar, Malaysian ringgit, and Hong Kong dollar (which have remained stable), all other Southeast Asian national currencies are still in a state of flux. Before you budget your trip based on rates we give in this book, be sure to check the currency's current status. CNN's website has a convenient **currency converter** at **www.xe.com/ucc/**.

CURRENCY

You will have to rely primarily on local currency when traveling in the countryside and visiting towns and villages situated off the main tourist routes, where neither traveler's checks nor credit cards are accepted. No matter where you travel, its always a good idea to have some U.S. dollars handy, preferably in small bills, which might help ease you through any unforeseen emergencies. The U.S. dollar has long been the most readily accepted foreign currency throughout Southeast Asia.

Below we've listed the currencies of all countries in this guide, with their denominations.

CAMBODIA   The monetary unit is the **riel,** which is available in 50, 100, 200, 500, 1,000, 5,000, 10,000, 20,000, and 50,000 riel notes. Cambodia's volatile exchange rate typically fluctuates but is currently at **3,900 riel to US$1.** It's a good idea to bring a supply of U.S. dollars, because the dollar is considered Cambodia's second currency and is accepted—even preferred—by many hotels, guesthouses, and restaurants. If paying in dollars, you'll get the small change in riel.

HONG KONG   The basic unit of currency is the **Hong Kong dollar,** which is divided into 100 cents. Three banks—the Hongkong and Shanghai Banking Corporation, the Bank of China, and, to a lesser degree, the Standard Chartered Bank—all issue their own colorful notes, in denominations of HK$10 (which is being phased out), HK$20, HK$50, HK$100, HK$500, and HK$1,000. Coins are minted in bronze for 10¢, 20¢, and 50¢ pieces; in silver for HK$1, HK$2, and HK$5; and in nickel and bronze for HK$10. The exchange rate is **HK$7.80 to US$1.**

Throughout Hong Kong you'll see the dollar sign ($), which, of course refers to Hong Kong dollars, not U.S. dollars. To avoid confusion, this guide identifies Hong Kong dollars with the symbol HK$ (followed in parentheses by the U.S. dollar conversion).

INDONESIA (BALI)   The **rupiah (Rp)** is the main currency, with bills of Rp100, Rp500, Rp1,000, Rp5,000, Rp10,000, Rp20,000, and Rp50,000, and coins in denominations of Rp25, Rp50, Rp100, and Rp500. Indonesia's currency was hit hard in 1998 and 1999, leading to exchange rates that fluctuated wildly. From a pre-crisis rate of approximately Rp2,300 to US$1, the rupiah plunged to Rp14,700 to US$1 in July 1998, but it has stabilized in recent years to **Rp10,800 to US$1.**

LAOS   The primary unit of currency is the **kip** (pronounced "keep"), which comes in denominations of 20,000, 10,000, 5,000, 2,000, 1,000, 500, 100, 50, 20, 10, and 5. The exchange rate is approximately **10,000 kip to US$1.** As in Cambodia, many tourist establishments prefer payment in U.S. dollars. In many areas of Laos, both U.S. dollars and Thai baht are preferred over the local currency.

MALAYSIA   The **ringgit,** which is also referred to as the Malaysian dollar, is the unit of currency, and prices are marked RM. One ringgit equals 100 sen, and notes come in RM1, RM2, RM5, RM10, RM20, RM50, RM100, RM500, and RM1,000. Coins come in denominations of 1, 2, 5, 10, and 50 sen, and 1 ringgit coins. Since the economic crisis, the value of the ringgit has been set at **RM3.80 to US$1.**

MYANMAR   (BURMA)   Upon arrival, you'll be asked to change US$200 into FEC (Foreign Exchange Certificates), with denominations and value equivalent to U.S. dollar amounts and for use in hotels. FEC can be converted to U.S. dollars or the Kyat (sounds like "chat"). The **Kyat** is made up of 100 pyas and come in notes with denominations of 1, 5, and 10. There are also 1-kyat coins and coins of 1, 5, 10, 25, and 50 pyas. The exchange rate is currently **6.70 kyat to US$1.** It is illegal to carry Myanmese currency out of the country, so be sure to exchange whatever you have remaining when you leave the country.

SINGAPORE   The **Singapore dollar** (commonly referred to as the Sing dollar) is the unit of currency, with notes issued in denominations of S$2, S$5, S$10, S$20, S$50, S$100, S$500, and S$1,000; coins come in denominations of 1, 5, 10, 20, and 50 cents and the gold-colored S$1. The exchange rate is approximately **S$1.73 to US$1.**

THAILAND   The Thai **baht,** (noted as B), which is made up of 100 satang, comes in colored notes of 10 baht (brown), 20B (green), 100B (red), and 500B (purple). Coins come in denominations of 1B, 5B, and 10B, as well as 25 and 50 satang. The exchange rate is approximately **42B to US$1.**

VIETNAM   The main unit of Vietnamese currency is the **dong,** (noted as VND), which comes in denominations of 200, 500, 1,000, 2,000,

> **Tips** **Small Change**
>
> When you change money, ask for some small bills or loose change. Petty cash will come in handy for tipping and public transportation. Consider keeping the change separate from your larger bills so that it's readily accessible and you'll be less of a target for theft.

5,000, 10,000, 20,000, and 50,000 notes. There are no coins. Most tourist venues accept dollars, and even in small towns you will at least be able to exchange greenbacks, if not use dollars directly. The exchange rate is approximately **15,000VND to US$1.**

It's a good idea to exchange at least some money—just enough to cover airport incidentals and transportation to your hotel—before you leave home. The currencies of the region's developing nations are only available in-country; however, Sing and Hong Kong dollars, as well as Thai baht and even Malaysian Ringgit, are available at your local American Express or Thomas Cook office or any major bank. If you're far away from a bank with currency-exchange services, American Express offers traveler's checks and foreign currency, though with a $15 order fee and additional shipping costs, at www.american express.com or ✆ **800/807-6233.**

ATMS

The easiest and best way to get cash away from home is from an ATM (automated teller machine). The **Cirrus** (✆ **800/424-7787;** www.master card.com) and **PLUS** (✆ **800/843-7587;** www.visa.com) networks span the globe; look at the back of your bank card to see which network you're on, and then call or check online for ATM locations at your destination. Be sure you know your personal identification number (PIN) before you leave home, and be sure to find out your daily withdrawal limit before you depart. Also keep in mind that many banks impose a fee every time a card is

used at a different bank's ATM, and that fee can be higher for international transactions (up to $5 or more) than for domestic ones (where they're rarely more than $1.50). On top of this, the bank from which you withdraw cash might charge its own fee. For international withdrawal fees, ask your bank.

You can also get cash advances on your credit card at an ATM. Keep in mind that credit card companies try to protect themselves from theft by limiting the funds someone can withdraw outside their home country, so call your credit card company before you leave home.

TRAVELER'S CHECKS

In most parts of the world, ATM service in major centers makes traveler's checks an anachronism from the days before the ATM made cash accessible at any time. But be forewarned that the developing countries in Southeast Asia (Laos, Cambodia, and Myanmar) have no ATM service. In fact, in most rural areas in the region service is scant at best. Traveler's checks are a sound alternative to traveling with dangerously large amounts of cash, and they can be replaced if lost or stolen.

You can get traveler's checks at almost any bank. **American Express** offers denominations of $20, $50, $100, $500, and (for cardholders only) $1,000. You'll pay a service charge ranging from 1% to 4%. You can also get American Express traveler's checks over the phone by calling ✆ **800/221-7282;** Amex gold and platinum cardholders who use this number are exempt from the 1% fee.

Tips **Dear Visa: I'm Off to Bangkok!**

Some credit card companies recommend that you notify them of any impending trip abroad so that they don't become suspicious when the card is used numerous times in a foreign destination and your charges get blocked. Even if you don't call your credit card company in advance, you can call always the card's toll-free emergency number (see "Fast Facts," later in this chapter) if a charge is refused—a good reason to carry the phone number with you. But perhaps the most important lesson is to carry more than one card on your trip; if one card doesn't work for any number of reasons, you'll have a backup card just in case.

AAA members can obtain checks without a fee at most AAA offices.

Visa offers traveler's checks at Citibank locations nationwide, as well as at several other banks. The service charge ranges between 1.5% and 2%; checks come in denominations of $20, $50, $100, $500, and $1,000. Call ✆ **800/732-1322** for information. **MasterCard** also offers traveler's checks. Call ✆ **800/223-9920** for a location near you.

If you choose to carry traveler's checks, be sure to keep a record of their serial numbers separate from your checks in case they are stolen or lost. You'll get a refund faster if you know the numbers.

CREDIT CARDS

Accepted widely at large hotels and the major restaurants in the region, credit cards are a safe way to carry money, they provide a convenient record of all your expenses, and they generally offer good exchange rates. Visa and MasterCard are the most widely accepted, but American Express is a close second (along with

JCB); Diner's Club is accepted only in some locations (mostly in major cities). You can also withdraw cash advances from your credit cards at banks or ATMs, provided that you know your PIN number. If you've forgotten yours, or didn't even know you had one, call the number on the back of your credit card and ask the bank to send it to you. It usually takes 5 to 7 business days, though some banks will provide the number over the phone if you tell them your mother's maiden name or some other personal information. Your credit card company will likely charge a commission (1% or 2%) on every foreign purchase you make, but don't sweat this small stuff; for most purchases, you'll still get the best deal with credit cards when you factor in things like ATM fees and higher traveler's check exchange rates.

For tips and telephone numbers to call if your wallet is stolen or lost, go to "Lost and Found" in the "Fast Facts" section of this chapter

4 When to Go

With a few exceptions, wherever and whenever you travel in Southeast Asia you are likely to encounter hot and humid weather. All of Southeast Asia lies within the tropics, and the countries closest to the equator—Singapore, Malaysia, Indonesia, and southern Thailand—have the hottest annual temperatures. Vietnam, Laos, Cambodia, Burma, and the rest of Thailand located 10 to 20 degrees above the equator also have high humidity but slightly "cooler" temperatures. The mountainous northern regions of Myanmar, Thailand, Laos, and Vietnam get pretty chilly during the winter

---

(**Tips Packing Sensibly**

Wherever you travel in Southeast Asia, you're sure to meet with tropical heat, and only in a few northern mountain towns will you need to bundle up at all. **Lightweight clothing** in natural fibers (or breathable travel gear) is essential in the tropical heat, as are a hat and a pair of sunglasses. The most practical clothing is lightweight long cotton trousers or a long skirt (below the knee) and a cotton shirt, especially if your sightseeing takes you to royal palaces or religious buildings where local customs favor conservative attire—no shorts or miniskirts, and please cover your shoulders (no tank tops).

For everyday wear, except at resorts and the beach, **avoid wearing shorts in Vietnam, Laos, and more conservative areas of Malaysia.** I highly recommend a light sweater or lined windbreaker for airports, bus trips, or theaters where the A/C always seems to be set at deep-freeze.

A pair of rugged open **sport sandals** is also a must, and a pair of **rubber flip-flops** comes in handy in hotel rooms with tile or wood floors, and for use in public showers. If you're going in and out of temples (as is always the case for sightseeing), you'll be happy to have shoes that slip off and on easily.

Most toiletries, even Western brands, are easily available at pharmacies and stores in the big cities.

Here's a list of items from home you might not want to be without:

- Antacid tablets
- Antidiarrhea medicine
- Antibacterial cream
- Anti-itch cream
- Bandages
- Acetaminophen, aspirin, or ibuprofen for fever or pain
- Batteries (it's also a good idea to bring an extra camera battery)
- Bug repellent
- Hydration powder packets
- Mild laxative tablets
- Moist towelette packets
- Full supply of any medications you need to take
- Nylon or fast-drying shorts
- Padlock and wire cable (good to lock your bag or rented bike)
- Sealable plastic bags for everything and anything
- Rain poncho/small umbrella
- Sunscreen
- Tampons (note that maxi pads are available everywhere)
- Tissues (good to carry with you at all times)
- Trash bags (to line your luggage on river trips)
- Water-purifying tablets
- Waterproof sandals

Tips **Quick ID**

Tie a colorful ribbon or piece of yarn around your luggage handle, or slap a distinctive sticker on the side of your bag. This makes it less likely that someone will mistakenly appropriate it. And if your luggage gets lost, it will be easier to find.

---

months between November and March, so bring a pullover.

Monsoon winds make weather patterns confusing to keep track of. The basic rule of thumb is this: Between the months of October and February, winds from the northeast create heavy rainfall and rough seas along the eastern coasts of Vietnam, Cambodia, Thailand (including Ko Samui), Malaysia, and Singapore; however, western coasts along Thailand (including Phuket) and Malaysia are peaceful and calm. In May, the winds shift, bringing rains and swelling seas from the northwest down upon the western coasts of Myanmar, Thailand, and Malaysia until October. Nearly everyplace feels a dry and hot spell in March and April—Bangkok swelters! The cooler months of October through March are also the most pleasant times to visit Hong Kong, while the most rain usually falls between July and September during typhoon season.

Singapore and Malaysia are hot and humid year-round, with annual average maximum and minimum daily temperatures of 90°F and 72°F (32°C and 24°C) and year-round humidity above 90%. Most major cities are located at or near sea level, where average daytime temperatures are in the range of 80°F to 90°F (28°C–32°C) range year-round. The best way to escape the heat and humidity is to head for the hills and mountains in the higher-altitude regions of Thailand, Malaysia, Vietnam, Myanmar, and Laos.

HOLIDAYS, CELEBRATIONS & FESTIVALS

Some of the holidays celebrated in Southeast Asia might affect your vacation plans, either positively or negatively. Wherever you are, you won't want to miss Chinese New Year or the many lunar festivals and myriad events like dragon boat races and small Buddhist fetes, but some holidays simply mean that businesses and attractions are closed. See the individual country chapters for listings of the major holidays celebrated in each country.

5 Travel Insurance

Check your existing insurance policies and credit card coverage before you buy travel insurance. You might already be covered for lost luggage, cancelled tickets, or medical expenses. The cost of travel insurance varies widely, depending on the cost and length of your trip, your age, your health, and the type of trip you're taking.

TRIP-CANCELLATION INSURANCE Trip-cancellation insurance helps you get your money back if you have to back out of a trip, if you have to go home early, or if your travel supplier goes bankrupt. Allowed reasons for cancellation can range from sickness to natural disasters, to the State Department declaring your destination unsafe for travel. (Insurers usually won't cover vague fears, though, as many travelers discovered who tried to cancel their trips in October 2001 because they were wary of flying.) In this unstable world, trip-cancellation insurance is a good buy if you're getting tickets well in advance—who knows what the state of the world, or of your airline, will be in 9 months? Insurance policy details vary, so read the fine print—and especially make sure that your airline is on the list of carriers covered in case of bankruptcy. For information, contact one of the following insurers: **Access America** (℃ 800/284-8300; www.access america.com), **Travel Guard International** (℃ 800/826-1300; www.travel guard.com), **Travel Insured International** (℃ 800/243-3174; www.travel insured.com), or **Travelex Insurance Services** (℃ 800/228-9792; www. travelex-insurance.com).

MEDICAL INSURANCE Most health insurance policies cover you if you get sick away from home—but check, particularly if you're insured by an HMO. With the exception of certain HMOs and Medicare/Medicaid, your medical insurance should cover medical treatment—even hospital care—overseas. However, most out-of-country hospitals make you pay your bills up front and then send you a refund after you've returned home and filed the necessary paperwork. And in a worst-case scenario, there's the high cost of emergency evacuation.

If you require additional medical insurance, try **MEDEX International** (℃ 800/527-0218 or 410/453-6300; www.medexassist.com) or **Travel Assistance International** (℃ 800/ 821-2828; www.travelassistance.com; for general information on services, call the company's Worldwide Assistance Services, Inc., at ℃ 800/777-8710).

LOST-LUGGAGE INSURANCE On international flights (including U.S. portions of international trips), baggage is limited to approximately $9.05 per pound, up to approximately $635 per checked bag. If you plan to check items more valuable than the standard liability, see if your valuables are covered by your homeowner's policy, get baggage insurance as part of your comprehensive travel-insurance package, or buy Travel Guard's Bag-Trak product. Don't buy insurance at the airport: It's usually overpriced. Be sure to take any valuables or irreplaceable items with you in your carry-on luggage; many valuables (including books, money, and electronics) aren't covered by airline policies.

If your luggage is lost, immediately file a lost-luggage claim at the airport, detailing the luggage contents. For most airlines, you must report delayed, damaged, or lost baggage within 4 hours of arrival. The airlines are required to deliver luggage, once found, directly to your house or destination free of charge.

6 Health & Safety

STAYING HEALTHY

Health concerns should comprise much of your preparation for a trip to Southeast Asia, and staying healthy on the road takes vigilance. Tropical heat and mosquitoes are the biggest dangers, and travelers should exercise caution over dietary change and cleanliness. Just a few pre-trip precautions and general prudence, though, is all

that is required for a safe and healthy trip.

GENERAL AVAILABILITY OF HEALTH CARE

The best hospitals and health-care facilities are located in the large cities and major tourist centers of countries that have the greatest number of Western tourists—Singapore, Hong

Kong, Malaysia (Kuala Lumpur), and Thailand (Bangkok). In rural areas of these countries and throughout the lesser developed countries of Vietnam, Cambodia, Laos, and Burma, there are limited health-care facilities: Hospitals are few and far between and generally are of poor quality. Even in heavily touristed Bali, you're better off evacuating to one of the more developed countries if faced with a serious medical situation. Over-the-counter medications are available anywhere, but it's a good idea to bring some antidiarrhea medication and rehydration salts, among others (see the "Packing Sensibly" box, above).

COMMON AILMENTS

Among Southeast Asia's tropical diseases carried by mosquitoes are **malaria, dengue fever,** and **Japanese encephalitis.** Reports about malaria prophylactics vary. While most local health agencies tell you not to waste your time with antimalaria drugs, the CDC still advises people to take tablets, most of which cause uncomfortable side effects. In truth, your only sure way to avoid mosquito-borne diseases is to avoid being bitten. Repellents that contain **DEET** are the most effective, but more gentle alternatives, like Johnson's Baby Clear Lotion Antimosquito (in the baby-care section of your pharmacy), provides terrific DEET-free mosquito protection without the chemicals. Also be aware that malaria mosquitoes bite between the hours 5 and 7 in the morning and the evening, so it's important to exercise caution at those hours (wearing long sleeves and long trousers and burning mosquito coils is a good idea). Dengue-fever mosquitoes bite during the day.

Hepatitis A can be contracted from water or food, and cholera epidemics sometimes occur in remote areas. Bilharzia, schistosomiasis, and giardia are parasitic diseases that can be contracted from swimming in or drinking from stagnant or untreated water in lakes or streams.

Anyone contemplating sexual activity should be aware that HIV is rampant in many Southeast Asian countries, along with other STDs such as gonorrhea, syphilis, herpes, and hepatitis B.

The **International Association for Medical Assistance to Travelers (IAMAT)** (℃ **716/754-4883** or 416/652-0137; www.sentex.net/~iamat) offers tips on travel and health concerns in the countries you'll be visiting, and lists local English-speaking doctors. The **United States Centers for Disease Control and Prevention** (℃ **404/332-4559;** www.cdc.gov) provides up-to-date information on necessary vaccines and health hazards by region or country (by mail, its booklet is US$20; on the Internet, it's free). The **U.S. State Department's 24-hour travel advisory** (℃ **202/647-5225;** http://travel.state.gov/travel_warnings.html) also lists the latest information on diseases affecting a particular country.

DIETARY PRECAUTIONS   Unless you intend to confine your travels to the big cities and dine only at restaurants that serve Western-style food, you will likely be sampling some new cuisine. This could lead initially to upset stomachs or diarrhea, which usually lasts just a few days as your body adapts to the change in your diet. Except for Singapore, where tap water is safe to drink, **always drink bottled water (never use tap water for drinking or even brushing teeth)**. It's also recommended to peel all fruits and vegetables and avoid raw shellfish and seafood. Also beware of ice unless it is made from purified water. (Any suspicious water can be purified by boiling for 10 minutes or treating with purifying tablets.) If you're a vegetarian, you will find that

Southeast Asia is a great place to travel; vegetarian dishes abound throughout the region. In terms of hygiene, restaurants are generally better options than street stalls, but don't forgo good local cuisine just because it's served from a cart. Be sure to carry diarrhea medication as well as any prescription medications you might need. It's acceptable to wipe down utensils in restaurants, and in some places locals even ask for a glass of hot water for just that purpose (some travelers even carry their own plastic chopsticks or cutlery). Carrying antiseptic hand-washing liquid is also not a bad idea for when you're out in the sticks.

So, how can you tell if something will upset your stomach before you eat it? Trust your instincts. Avoid buffet-style places, especially on the street, and be sure all food is cooked thoroughly and made to order. I've been plenty sick my share of times and have found that each time I get into trouble, I've usually felt dread from the start. If your gut tells you not to eat that gelatinous chicken foot, don't eat it. If your hosts insist but you are still afraid, explain about your "foreign stomach" with a regretful smile and accept a cup of tea instead. Be careful of raw ingredients, common in most Asian cuisines, but realize that questions like, "Are these vegetables washed in clean water?" are inappropriate anywhere. Use your best judgment or simply decline.

BUGS, BITES & OTHER WILDLIFE CONCERNS

There are all kinds of creepy critters to be aware of in any tropical climate. Mosquito nets in rural accommodations are often required and, if so, are always provided by hoteliers. Check your shoes in the morning (or wear sandals) just in case some little ugly thing is taking a nap in your Nikes. Keep an eye out for snakes and poisonous spiders when in jungle terrain or when doing any trekking. Having a guide doesn't preclude exercising caution. **Rabies** is rampant, especially in rural areas of the less developed nations, and extreme care should be taken when walking, particularly at night. In places like Thailand, dogs are simply fed and left to roam free, and you are likely to run into some ornery muts. A walking stick or umbrella is a suitable deterrent when out in the countryside. It's also important to know that all dogs have been hit with hurled stones sometime in their life, and, a nod to Pavlov here, the very act of reaching to the ground for a handful of stones is often enough to send an angry dog on the run, for fear of being pelted. If you are bitten, wash the wound immediately and, even if you suffer just the slightest puncture or scrape, seek medical attention and a series of rabies shots (now quite a simple affair of injections in the arm in a few installments over several weeks).

SUN/ELEMENTS/EXTREME WEATHER EXPOSURE

Sun and heatstroke are of great concern anywhere in Southeast Asia. Limit your exposure to the sun, especially during the first few days of your trip and, thereafter, from 11am to 2pm. Use a sunscreen with a high protection factor, and apply it liberally. Also, Asians are still big fans of parasols. Don't be shy about using an umbrella to shade yourself (all the Buddhist monks do). Remember that children need more protection than adults.

Always be sure to drink plenty of bottled water, which is the best defense against heat exhaustion and the more serious, life-threatening heatstroke. Also remember that coffee, tea, soft drinks, and alcoholic beverages should not be substituted for water because they are diuretics that dehydrate the body. In extremely hot and humid weather, try to stay out of the midday heat, and confine most of your daytime traveling to early morning and late afternoon. If you ever feel weak, fatigued, dizzy, or disoriented, get out of the sun immediately and go to a shady, cool place. To prevent sunburn, always wear a hat and apply sunscreen to all exposed areas of skin.

Be aware of major weather patterns; many island destinations are prone to typhoon or severe storm.

WHAT TO DO IF YOU GET SICK AWAY FROM HOME

In most cases, your existing health plan will provide the coverage you need. But double-check; you might want to buy **travel medical insurance** instead. (See the section on insurance, above.) Bring your insurance ID card with you when you travel. Make sure that any insurance covers **medical evacuation;** even in the more developed countries of the region, any chronic illness or injury could entail an expensive fixed-wing or helicopter charter to the closest international-standard urban hospital.

If you suffer from a chronic illness, consult your doctor before your departure. For conditions like epilepsy, diabetes, or heart problems, wear a **Medic Alert Identification Tag** (© 800/825-3785; www.medic alert.org), which will immediately alert doctors to your condition and give them access to your records through Medic Alert's 24-hour hotline.

Pack **prescription medications** in your carry-on luggage, in their original containers, with pharmacy labels—otherwise, they won't make it through airport security. Also bring along copies of your prescriptions, in case you lose your pills or run out. Don't forget an extra pair of contact lenses or prescription glasses.

Carry the generic name of prescription medicines, in case a local pharmacist is unfamiliar with the brand name.

Contact the **International Association for Medical Assistance to Travelers (IAMAT)** (© 716/754-4883 or 416/652-0137; www.iamat.org) for tips on travel and health concerns in the countries you're visiting and for lists of local, English-speaking doctors. The United States **Centers for Disease Control and Prevention** (© 800/311-3435; www.cdc.gov) provides up-to-date information on necessary vaccines and health hazards by region or country. Any foreign consulate can provide a list of area doctors who speak English. If you get sick, consider asking your hotel concierge to recommend a local doctor—even his or her own. You can also try the emergency room at a local hospital; many have walk-in clinics for emergency cases that are not life-threatening. You might not get immediate attention, but you won't pay the high price of an emergency room visit.

STAYING SAFE

Road conditions vary throughout the region, but most large cities, from Bangkok to Ho Chi Minh, are busy and chaotic. Even for intrepid travelers who climb all the mountains and get out into rural terrain, crossing big-city streets, even at prescribed crossings, can be the greatest risk on your trip; move slowly and exercise caution (Mom's advice to look both ways couldn't be more important). Rural roads in places like Laos, Cambodia and Burma are often no more than dirt track, but even where there's basic infrastructure, Western visitors are often shocked at the seeming lack of rules and the fact that, on most roads, might is right: The biggest, fastest, and most aggressive vehicle takes precedence in many areas. Visitors are often shocked (or annoyed) at how the horn is used more frequently than the turn signal, and on some bus rides you might want to just keep your eyes on the scenery and not the road ahead. It's better to rent a car with a hired driver instead of trying to drive yourself. Many come away from road travel rattled and shaky (or with the newfound ability to pray), but adventure-junkies will get their fix.

In places like the beach towns of Thailand, you're sure to meet one or two road-rashed victims of minor motorbike accidents. Exercise extreme caution on rented bikes, especially if you're inexperienced.

Anonymous, violent crime is less an issue in most countries in the region, but petty theft, pickpocketing, and purse-snatching is not uncommon.

Dicey political situations arise and pass with frequency and it's important to check travel warnings and double-check with the U.S. State Department (http://state.gov) or the most up-to-date sources on the region. Places like Laos, Myanmar, Cambodia, and Indonesia are known to flare with separatist movements and terrorism. Stay abreast of any and all news before flying.

Nancy Reagan's advice about drugs couldn't be more apt for a trip to Southeast Asia: "Just say no". Grown, produced, and shipped through the region, drugs like heroin, opium, and marijuana are readily available. There are island spots and mountain retreats where it might seem like the thing to do, but in all cases here, national laws are strict. Many visitors find themselves in an intensive language school of another variety (i.e. jail) in short order if they can't bribe their way out of it. It's certainly not worth it anywhere.

7 Specialized Travel Resources

TRAVELERS WITH DISABILITIES

Most disabilities shouldn't stop anyone from traveling. There are more options and resources out there than ever before. Most larger hotels in the major cities of the region have adequate facilities for visitors with disabilities, but in rural destinations, specialized amenities are scant, at best.

Many travel agencies offer customized tours and itineraries for travelers with disabilities. **Flying Wheels Travel** (✆ 507/451-5005; www.flying wheelstravel.com) offers escorted tours and cruises that emphasize sports and private tours in minivans with lifts. **Rumpleduck Travel** (✆ 877/401-7736 or 310-850-5340; www.rumpleduck.com) designs personal itineraries. **Accessible Journeys** (✆ 800/846-4537 or 610/521-0339; www.disabilitytravel.com) caters specifically to slow walkers and wheelchair travelers and their families and friends.

Organizations that offer assistance to travelers with disabilities include the **Moss Rehab Hospital** (www.moss resourcenet.org), which provides a library of accessible-travel resources online; the **Society for Accessible Travel and Hospitality** (✆ 212/447-7284; www.sath.org; annual membership fees: $45 adults, $30 seniors and students), which offers a wealth of travel resources for all types of disabilities and informed recommendations on destinations, access guides, travel agents, tour operators, vehicle rentals, and companion services; and the **American Foundation for the Blind** (✆ 800/232-5463; www.afb.org), which provides information on traveling with Seeing Eye dogs.

For more information specifically targeted to travelers with disabilities, the community website **iCan** (www. icanonline.net/channels/travel/index. cfm) has destination guides and several regular columns on accessible travel. Also check out the quarterly magazine *Emerging Horizons* ($14.95 per year, $19.95 outside the U.S.; www.emerginghorizons.com); **Twin Peaks Press** (✆ 360/694-2462;

http://disabilitybookshop.virtualave.net/blist84.htm), which offers travel-related books for travelers with special needs; and **Open World Magazine,** published by the Society for Accessible Travel and Hospitality (see above; subscription: $18 per year, $35 outside the U.S.).

GAY & LESBIAN TRAVELERS

Acceptance of alternative lifestyles in Southeast Asia, like anywhere, runs the gamut. One thing to remember is that many of the societies and cultures of the region are, by tradition, very modest, and public displays of affection of any kind are not acceptable. Gay nightlife choices are many and varied in larger cities like Bangkok, Singapore, and Hong Kong, but in rural areas, provincial attitudes vary and intolerance is not uncommon.

The International Gay & Lesbian Travel Association (IGLTA) (© **800/ 448-8550** or 954/776-2626; www.iglta.org), the trade association for the gay and lesbian travel industry, offers an online directory of gay- and lesbian-friendly travel businesses; go to its website and click on "Members."

Many agencies offer tours and travel itineraries specifically for gay and lesbian travelers. **Above and Beyond Tours** (© **800/397-2681;** www.abovebeyondtours.com) is the exclusive gay and lesbian tour operator for United Airlines. **Now, Voyager** (© **800/255-6951;** www.nowvoyager. com) is a well-known San Francisco–based gay-owned and operated travel service. **Olivia Cruises & Resorts** (© **800-631-6277** or 510/ 655-0364; www.olivia.com) charters entire resorts and ships for exclusive lesbian vacations and offers smaller group experiences for both gay and lesbian travelers.

The following travel guides are available at most travel bookstores and gay and lesbian bookstores, or you can order them from **Giovanni's Room** bookstore, 1145 Pine St., Philadelphia, PA 19107 (© **215/923-2960;** www.giovannisroom.com): **Out and About** (© **800/929-2268** or 415-644-8044; www.outandabout.com), which offers guidebooks and a newsletter 10 times a year packed with solid information on the global gay and lesbian scene; **Spartacus International Gay Guide** and **Odysseus,** both good annual English-language guidebooks focused on gay men; the **Damron** guides, with separate annual books for gay men and lesbians; and **Gay Travel A to Z: The World of Gay & Lesbian Travel Options at Your Fingertips,** by Marianne Ferrari (Ferrari Publications; Box 35575, Phoenix, AZ 85069), a very good gay and lesbian guidebook series.

SENIOR TRAVEL

Seniors traveling in the region can bask in the glow of filial piety and the region's notorious Confucian respect for elders, but they are less likely to enjoy the major discounts found in the West. Mention the fact that you're a senior citizen when you make your travel reservations, though. In some cases, people over the age of 60 qualify for reduced admission to theaters, museums, and other attractions, as well as discounted fares on public transportation.

Members of **AARP** (formerly known as the American Association of Retired Persons), 601 E St. NW, Washington, DC 20049 (© **800/ 424-3410** or 202/434-2277; www.aarp.org), get discounts on hotels, airfares, and car rentals. AARP offers members a wide range of benefits, including *Modern Maturity* magazine and a monthly newsletter. Anyone over 50 can join.

Many reliable agencies and organizations target the 50-plus market. **Elderhostel** (© **877/426-8056;** www.elderhostel.org) arranges study programs for those aged 55 and over (and a spouse or companion of any age) in the U.S. and in more than 80 countries around the world. Most courses last 5 to 7 days in the U.S. (2–4 weeks abroad), and many include airfare, accommodations in university dormitories or modest inns, meals, and tuition. **ElderTreks** (℡ 800/741-7956; www.eldertreks.com) offers small-group tours to off-the-beaten-path or adventure-travel locations, restricted to travelers 50 and older.

Recommended publications offering travel resources and discounts for seniors include the quarterly magazine *Travel 50 & Beyond* (www.travel50 andbeyond.com); *Travel Unlimited: Uncommon Adventures for the Mature Traveler* (Avalon); *101 Tips for Mature Travelers,* available from Grand Circle Travel (℡ 800/221-2610 or 617/350-7500; www.gct. com); *The 50+ Traveler's Guidebook* (St. Martin's Press); and *Unbelievably Good Deals and Great Adventures That You Absolutely Can't Get Unless You're over 50* (McGraw Hill).

FAMILY TRAVEL

If you have enough trouble getting your kids out of the house in the morning, dragging them thousands of miles away might seem like an insurmountable challenge. But family travel can be immensely rewarding, giving you new ways of seeing the world through smaller pairs of eyes. The rough roads of Southeast Asia can be a bit much for the little shaver, and concerns about communicable disease in rural areas should certainly be weighed. However, more accessible destinations and larger cities offer a glimpse into ancient civilization and varied culture that delights the kid in all of us. Most hotels can arrange extra beds at little additional cost, and connecting room capability is common.

Familyhostel (℡ 800/733-9753; www.learn.unh.edu/familyhostel) takes the whole family, including kids

ages 8 to 15, on moderately priced domestic and international learning vacations. Lectures, fields trips, and sightseeing are guided by a team of academics.

You can find good family-oriented vacation advice on the Internet from sites like the **Family Travel Network** (www.familytravelnetwork.com); **Traveling Internationally with Your Kids** (www.travelwithyourkids.com), a comprehensive site offering sound advice for long-distance and international travel with children; and **Family Travel Files** (www.thefamilytravel files.com), which offers an online magazine and a directory of off-the-beaten-path tours and tour operators for families.

How to Take Great Trips with Your Kids (The Harvard Common Press) is full of good general advice that applies to travel anywhere.

WOMEN TRAVELERS

Women traveling together or alone will find touring this region particularly pleasant and easy. The Buddhist and Islamic codes of conduct and ethics followed by many mean that you will be treated with respect and courtesy.

Wearing revealing clothing or sunbathing topless might appear to be tolerated, but that's only because your hosts wish to avoid confrontation. Deep inside, it is very embarrassing.

Although you will almost never find local women dining or touring alone, as a visitor, your behavior will be accepted. You will rarely, if ever, be approached or hassled by strangers. At the same time, you can feel free to start a conversation with a stranger without fear of misinterpretation. Note that if you are traveling with a man, public displays of affection are not welcome, and it's you, the female, who will be scorned. Also, you will have to take even more care than your male counterpart to dress modestly, meaning no cleavage- or midriff-baring tops, miniskirts, or short shorts. Otherwise, you risk offending people on the grounds of either religious or local moral standards.

All this said, it's still not advisable to take risks that you wouldn't normally take at home. Don't hitchhike, accept rides, or walk around late at night, particularly in dimly lit areas or in unfamiliar places. Be acutely aware of purse or jewelry snatchers in large cities. When meeting strangers in nightclubs, for example, buy your own drinks and keep an eye on them. **Women Welcome Women World Wide (5W) (**©️ **203/259-7832** in the U.S.; www.womenwelcomewomen. org.uk) works to foster international friendships by enabling women of different countries to visit one another (men can come along on the trips but just can't join the club). It's a big, active organization, with more than 3,500 members from all walks of life in some 70 countries.

Check out the website **Journeywoman** (www.journeywoman.com), a lively travel resource, with GirlTalk Guides to destinations like New York, Hong Kong, and Toronto, and a free e-mail newsletter; or the travel guide *Safety and Security for Women Who Travel,* by Sheila Swan Laufer and Peter Laufer (Travelers' Tales, Inc.), offering commonsense advice and tips on safe travel.

MULTICULTURAL TRAVELERS

Agencies and organizations that provide resources for black travelers include **Rodgers Travel (**©️ **215/473-1775;** www.rodgerstravel.com), a Philadelphia-based travel agency with an extensive menu of tours in destinations worldwide, including heritage and private group tours; the **African-American Association of Innkeepers International (**©️ **877/422-5777;** www.africanamericaninns.com), which provides information on member

B&Bs in the U.S., Canada, and the Caribbean; and **Henderson Travel and Tours (**800/327-2309 or 301/650-5700; www.hendersontravel.com), which has specialized in trips to Africa since 1957.

The Internet offers a number of helpful travel sites for the black traveler. **Black Travel Online** (www.black travelonline.com) posts news on upcoming events and includes links to articles and travel-booking sites. **Soul of America** (www.soulofamerica.com) is a more comprehensive website, with travel tips, event and family reunion postings, and sections on historically black beach resorts and active vacations.

For more information, check out the following collections and guides: *Go Girl: The Black Woman's Guide to Travel & Adventure* (Eighth Mountain Press), a compilation of travel essays by writers including Jill Nelson and Audre Lorde, with some practical information and trip-planning advice; *The African American Travel Guide,* by Wayne Robinson (Hunter Publishing; must be bought direct at www.hunterpublishing.com), with details on 19 North American cities; *Steppin' Out,* by Carla Labat (Avalon), with details on 20 cities; *Travel and Enjoy Magazine (*©️ **866/266-6211;** www.travelandenjoy.com; subscription: $24 per year), which focuses on discounts and destination reviews; and the more narrative *Pathfinders Magazine (*©️ **877/977-PATH;** www.pathfinderstravel.com; subscription: $15 per year), which includes articles on everything from Rio de Janeiro to Ghana.

STUDENT TRAVEL

Southeast Asia has become a very hot destination for budget-minded (I didn't say *poor*) students. Places like southern Thailand are becoming almost like spring break destinations; commonly, young backpackers hit the shores here and travel for extended periods of time. In fact, backpackers paved the way for tourism throughout the region. From bases like Bangkok's Khao San road, budget travelers roam the rugged highways and biways; often the more rural areas are relegated to only this hearty horde. Most find that the discounts to be had in Southeast Asia come from hard bargaining or tolerance for the most basic accommodation, but it's not a bad idea to have an **International Student Identity Card (ISIC),** which offers substantial savings on plane tickets and some museum entrance fees. The card does provide you with basic health and life insurance, and a 24-hour help line, for just $22. Contact **STA Travel** (© **800/781-4040;** and if you're not in North America there's probably a local number in your country; www.statravel.com), the biggest student travel agency in the world. If you're no longer a student but are still under 26, you can get an **International Youth Travel Card (IYTC)** for the same price from the same people, which entitles you to some discounts (but not on museum admissions). (*Note:* In 2002, STA Travel bought competitors **Council Travel** and **USIT Campus** after they went bankrupt. It's still operating some offices under the Council name, but it's owned by STA.)

Travel CUTS (© **800/667-2887** or 416/614-2887; www.travelcuts.com) offers similar services for residents of both Canada and the U.S. Irish students should turn to **USIT** (© **01/602-1600;** www.usitnow.ie).

SINGLE TRAVELERS

By and large, travelers in Southeast Asia are seekers of some kind, so many prefer to travel alone. For independent travelers, solo journeys offer many opportunities to make friends and meet locals. Unfortunately, some resorts and tours levy a "single supplement" to the base price. Single travelers can avoid

these supplements, of course, by agreeing to room with other single travelers on the trip. An even better idea is to find a compatible roommate before you go from one of the many roommate locator agencies.

Travel Companion Exchange (TCE) (© **631/454-0880;** www.travelcompanions.com) is one of the nation's oldest roommate finders for single travelers. Register here and find a travel mate who will split the cost of the room with you and be around as little, or as often, as you like during the day. **Travel Buddies Singles Travel Club** (© **800/998-9099;** www.travelbuddiesworldwide.com), based in Canada, runs small, intimate, single-friendly group trips and will match you with a roommate free of charge and save you the cost of single supplements. **TravelChums** (© **212/787-2621;** www.travelchums.com) is an Internet-only travel companion matching service with elements of an online personals-type site, hosted by the respected New York–based Shaw Guides travel service. **The Single Gourmet Club** (www.singlegourmet.com/chapters.html) is an international social, dining, and travel club for singles of all ages, with offices in 21 cities in the U.S. and Canada. Membership costs $75 for the first year and $50 to renew.

Many reputable tour companies offer singles-only trips. **Singles Travel International** (© **877/765-6874;** www.singlestravelintl.com) offers singles-only trips to places like London, Fiji, and the Greek Islands. **Backroads** (© **800/462-2848;** www.backroads.com) offers more than 160 active trips to 30 destinations worldwide, including Bali, Morocco, and Costa Rica.

For more information, check out Eleanor Berman's *Traveling Solo: Advice and Ideas for More Than 250 Great Vacations* (Globe Pequot), a guide with advice on traveling alone, whether on your own or on a group tour. (It's been updated for 2003.) Or turn to the **Travel Alone and Love It** website (www.travelaloneandloveit. com), designed by former flight attendant Sharon Wingler, the author of the book of the same name. Her site is full of tips for single travelers.

8 Planning Your Trip Online

SURFING FOR AIRFARES

The "big three" online travel agencies, **Expedia.com**, **Travelocity.com**, and **Orbitz.com**, sell most of the air tickets bought on the Internet. (Canadian travelers should try expedia.ca and Travelocity.ca; U.K. residents can go for expedia.co.uk and opodo.co.uk.) Each has different business deals with the airlines and might offer different fares on the same flights, so it's wise to shop around. Expedia and Travelocity will also send you **e-mail notification** when a cheap fare becomes available to your favorite destination. Of the smaller travel agency websites, **Side-Step** (www.sidestep.com) has gotten the best reviews from Frommer's authors. It's a browser add-on that purports to "search 140 sites at once," but in reality it beats competitors' fares only as often as other sites do.

Also remember to check **airline websites;** even with major airlines, you can often shave a few bucks from a fare by booking directly through the airline and avoiding a travel agency's transaction fee. But you'll get these discounts only by **booking online:** Most airlines now offer online-only fares that even their phone agents know nothing about. For the websites of airlines that fly to and from your destination, go to "Getting There," below.

Great **last-minute deals** are available through free weekly e-mail services provided directly by the airlines. Most of these are announced on Tuesday or Wednesday and must be purchased online. Most are valid for travel only that weekend, but some (such as Southwest's) can be booked weeks or months in advance. Sign up for weekly e-mail alerts at airline websites, or check megasites that compile comprehensive lists of last-minute specials, such as **Smarter Living** (smarterliving. com). For last-minute trips, **site59. com** in the U.S. and **lastminute.com** in Europe often have better deals than the major-label sites.

If you're willing to give up some control over your flight details, use an **opaque fare service** like **Priceline** (www.priceline.com; www.priceline. co.uk for Europeans) or **Hotwire** (www.hotwire.com). Both offer rock-bottom prices in exchange for travel on a "mystery airline" at a mysterious time of day, often with a mysterious change of planes en route. The mystery airlines are all major, well-known carriers and the airlines' routing computers have gotten a lot better than they used to be. But your chances of getting a 6am or 11pm flight are pretty high. Hotwire tells you flight prices before you buy; Priceline usually has better deals than Hotwire, but you have to play their "name our price" game. If you're new at this, the helpful folks at **BiddingForTravel** (www.biddingfortravel.com) do a good job of demystifying Priceline's prices. Priceline and Hotwire are great for flights within North America and between the U.S. and Europe. But for flights to other parts of the world, consolidators will almost always beat their fares.

For much more about airfares and savvy air-travel tips and advice, pick up a copy of *Frommer's Fly Safe, Fly Smart* (Wiley Publishing).

SURFING FOR HOTELS

Shopping online for hotels is not too practical in the region. You'll find any number of sites, but few list the

Frommers.com: The Complete Travel Resource

For an excellent travel-planning resource, we highly recommend Frommers.com (www.frommers.com). We're a little biased, of course, but we guarantee that you'll find the travel tips, reviews, monthly vacation giveaways, and online-booking capabilities indispensable. Among the special features are our popular **Message Boards,** where Frommer's readers post queries and share advice (sometimes we authors even show up to answer questions); **Frommers.com Newsletter,** for the latest travel bargains and insider travel secrets; and **Frommer's Destinations Section,** where you'll get expert travel tips, hotel and dining recommendations, and advice on the sights to see for more than 3,000 destinations around the globe. When your research is done, the **Online Reservations System** (www.frommers.com/book_a_trip/) takes you to Frommer's preferred online partners for booking your vacation at affordable prices.

smaller boutique properties and picturesque bungalow hideaways you'll find on your own, and even the most popular websites often list inflated prices. For all hotels in the major metropolitan areas, though, online booking is cheap and convenient. Of the "big three" sites, **Expedia** might be the best choice, thanks to its long list of special deals. **Travelocity** runs a close second. Hotel specialist sites **hotels.com** and **hoteldiscounts.com** are also reliable. An excellent free program, **TravelAxe** (www.travelaxe.net), can help you search multiple hotel sites at once, even ones you might never have heard of.

Priceline and Hotwire are even better for hotels than for airfares; with both, you're allowed to pick the neighborhood and quality level of your hotel before offering up your money.

Priceline's hotel product even covers Europe and Asia, although it's much better at getting five-star lodging for three-star prices than at finding anything at the bottom of the scale. *Note:* Hotwire overrates its hotels by one star—what Hotwire calls a four-star is a three-star anywhere else.

SURFING FOR RENTAL CARS

For booking rental cars online in the big cities, the best deals are usually found at rental-car company websites, although all the major online travel agencies also offer rental-car reservations services. Priceline and Hotwire work well for rental cars, too. The only "mystery" is which major rental company you get; for most travelers, the difference in Hertz, Avis, and Budget is negligible.

9 The 21st-Century Traveler

INTERNET ACCESS AWAY FROM HOME

Travelers have any number of ways to check their e-mail and access the Internet on the road. Of course, using your own laptop—or even a PDA (personal desk assistant) or electronic organizer with a modem—is a good option, but if you don't have a computer, you can still access your e-mail and even your office computer from cybercafes.

WITHOUT YOUR OWN COMPUTER

In some parts of Southeast Asia, it seems there's a cybercafe on every street corner and everywhere from the upscale business center of a glitzy high-rise hotel to a few terminals under a thatch roof in the most dingy guesthouse. Although there's no definitive directory for cybercafes—these are independent businesses, after all—three places to start looking are at **www.cybercaptive.com**, **www. netcafeguide.com**, and **www.cyber cafe.com**. **Hotels** that cater to business travelers often have **in-room dataports** and **business centers,** but the charges can be exorbitant. Most major airports now have **Internet kiosks** with per-minute access.

To retrieve your e-mail, ask your **Internet Service Provider (ISP)** if it has a Web-based interface tied to your existing e-mail account. If your ISP doesn't have such an interface, you can use the free **mail2web** service (www. mail2web.com) to view (but not reply to) your home e-mail. For more flexibility, you might want to open a free, Web-based e-mail account with **Yahoo! Mail** (mail.yahoo.com). (Microsoft's Hotmail is another popular option, but Hotmail has severe spam problems.) Your home ISP might be able to forward your e-mail to the Web-based account automatically.

If you need to access files on your office computer, look into a service called **GoToMyPC** (www.gotomypc. com). The service provides a Web-based interface for you to access and manipulate a distant PC from anywhere—even a cybercafe—provided that your "target" PC is on and has an always-on connection to the Internet (such as with Road Runner cable). The service offers top-quality security, but if you're worried about hackers, use your own laptop rather than a cybercafe to access the GoToMyPC system.

WITH YOUR OWN COMPUTER

Major Internet Service Providers (ISP) have **local access numbers** around the world, allowing you to go online by simply placing a local call. Check your ISP's website, or call its toll-free number and ask how you can use your current account away from home and how much it will cost.

If you're traveling outside the reach of your ISP, the **iPass** network has dial-up numbers in most countries. You'll have to sign up with an iPass provider, who will then tell you how to set up your computer for your destination(s). For a list of iPass providers, go to www. ipass.com and click on "Individuals." One solid provider is **i2roam** (www.i2 roam.com; ☏ **866/811-6209** or 920/ 235-0475).

Wherever you go, bring a **connection kit** of the right power and phone adapters, a spare phone cord, and a spare Ethernet network cable.

Most Southeast Asian countries run-on **220-volt electrical currents.** Plugs are two-pronged, with either round or flat prongs. If you're coming from the U.S. and you must bring electrical appliances, bring your own converter and adapter (a surge protector is a good idea for a laptop). Check the "Fast Facts" section of individual country chapters. Some hotels have 110-volt service.

Most business-class hotels offer dataports for laptop modems, but only a choice few in the big cities have high-speed Internet. You'll have to bring your own cables either way, so **call your hotel in advance** to find out what the options are.

USING A CELLPHONE

Like anywhere these days, hand phones are *de rigueur* for anyone from the businessman to the socialite in Southeast Asia. Local providers in the larger cities are many and varied, but the three letters that define much of

Online Traveler's Toolbox

Veteran travelers usually carry some essential items to make their trips easier. Following is a selection of online tools to bookmark and use.

- **Visa ATM Locator** (www.visa.com), for locations of PLUS ATMs worldwide, or **MasterCard ATM Locator** (www.mastercard.com), for locations of Cirrus ATMs worldwide.
- **Foreign Languages for Travelers** (www.travlang.com). Learn basic terms in more than 70 languages, and click on any underlined phrase to hear what it sounds like.
- **Intellicast** (www.intellicast.com) and **Weather.com** (www.weather.com). Get weather forecasts for all 50 states and for cities around the world.
- **Mapquest** (www.mapquest.com). This best of the mapping sites lets you choose a specific address or destination, and, in seconds, returns a map and detailed directions.
- **Universal Currency Converter** (www.xe.com/ucc). See what your dollar or pound is worth in more than 100 other countries.
- **Travel Warnings** (http://travel.state.gov/travel_warnings.html, www.fco.gov.uk/travel, www.voyage.gc.ca, www.dfat.gov.au/consular/advice). These sites report on places where health concerns or unrest might threaten American, British, Canadian, and Australian travelers. Generally, U.S. warnings are the most paranoid; Australian warnings are the most relaxed.

the world's **wireless capabilities** are GSM (Global System for Mobiles), a big, seamless network that makes for easy cross-border cellphone use throughout Europe and in dozens of other countries worldwide.

If your cellphone is on a GSM system and you have a world-capable phone such as many (but not all) Sony Ericsson, Motorola, or Samsung models, you can make and receive calls across civilized areas on much of the globe, from Andorra to Uganda. Just call your wireless operator and ask for international roaming to be activated on your account. Unfortunately, per-minute charges can be high—usually $1 to $1.50 in Western Europe and up to $5 in places like Russia and Indonesia.

World-phone owners can bring down their per-minute charges with a bit of trickery. Call up your cellular operator and say you'll be going abroad for several months and want to "unlock" your phone to use it with a local provider. Usually, they'll oblige. Then, in your destination country, pick up a cheap, prepaid phone chip at a mobile phone store and slip it into your phone. (Show your phone to the salesperson because not all phones work on all networks.) You'll get a local phone number in your destination country—and much, much lower calling rates.

Otherwise, **renting** a phone is a good idea. (Even world-phone owners will have to rent new phones if they're traveling to non-GSM regions.) Although you can rent a phone from any number of overseas sites, including kiosks at airports and at car-rental agencies, we suggest renting the phone before you leave home. That way, you can give loved ones your new number, make sure the phone works, and take the phone wherever you go—especially helpful when you rent overseas, where phone-rental agencies bill in local currency and might not let you take the phone to another country.

Phone rental isn't cheap. You'll usually pay $40 to $50 per week, plus airtime fees of at least a dollar a minute. If you're traveling to Europe, though, local rental companies often offer free incoming calls within their home country, which can save you big bucks. The bottom line: Shop around.

Two good wireless rental companies are **InTouch USA** (© **800/872-7626;** www.intouchglobal.com) and **Road-Post** (© **888-290-1606** or 905/272-5665; www.roadpost.com). Give them your itinerary, and they'll tell you what wireless products you need. For free, InTouch will also advise you on whether your existing phone will work overseas; simply call © **703/222-7161**

between 9am and 4pm EST, or go to http://intouchglobal.com/travel.htm.

For trips of more than a few weeks spent in one country, **buying a phone** becomes economically attractive; many nations have cheap, no-questions-asked prepaid phone systems. Stop by a local cellphone shop and get the cheapest package; you'll probably pay less than $100 for a phone and a starter calling card. Local calls can be as low as 10 cents per minute, and in many countries incoming calls are free.

True wilderness adventurers, or those heading to less-developed countries, should consider renting a satellite phone (see above). Per-minute call charges can be even cheaper than roaming charges with a regular cellphone, but the phone itself is more expensive (up to $150 a week), and depending on the service you choose, people calling you might incur high long-distance charges.

10 Getting There

BY PLANE

If you're flying to Southeast Asia, you will more than likely arrive via one of the region's three main hubs: Hong Kong, Bangkok, or Singapore, from where you can pick up flights to any other destination in Southeast Asia. Your home country's national carriers will almost certainly connect with all three of these airports. Check also with Southeast Asian–based airlines for fare deals: Cathay Pacific, Thai Airways International, Malaysian Airlines, and Singapore Airlines.

TO HONG KONG

The following carriers fly to Hong Kong's Chek Lap Kok Airport.

FROM THE UNITED STATES United Airlines, Northwest Airlines, Cathay Pacific Airways, China Airlines, Singapore Airlines, Thai Airways International, and Hong Kong's Dragonair.

FROM CANADA Cathay Pacific Airways, Canadian Airlines International, Air Canada, Singapore Airlines, and China Airlines.

FROM THE UNITED KINGDOM Cathay Pacific Airways, British Airways, Virgin Atlantic Airways, Singapore Airlines, China Airlines, and Dragonair.

FROM AUSTRALIA Cathay Pacific Airways, Qantas Airways, Ansett Australian Airlines, Singapore Airlines, and Dragonair.

FROM NEW ZEALAND Air New Zealand and Cathay Pacific Airways.

TO SINGAPORE

The following carriers fly to Singapore's Changi Airport.

FROM THE UNITED STATES Singapore Airlines has the most weekly flights from the U.S. to

Changi International Airport. United Airlines and Northwest Airlines are the only U.S. airlines offering flights to Singapore.

FROM CANADA Singapore Airlines provides service from Canada, along with Canadian Airlines International.

FROM THE UNITED KINGDOM
You can fly to Singapore via Singapore Airlines, British Airways, and Qantas Airways.

FROM AUSTRALIA Singapore Airlines, Qantas Airways, Ansett Australian Airlines, British Airways, and KLM Royal Dutch Airlines all provide service to Singapore.

FROM NEW ZEALAND Singapore Airlines and Air New Zealand offer New Zealand–Singapore flights.

TO BANGKOK

The following international airlines provide service to Bangkok's Don Muang International Airport.

FROM THE UNITED STATES
Service is provided by the national carrier, Thai Airways International, as well as United Airlines, Northwest Airlines, Cathay Pacific Airways, All Nippon Airways, Asiana Airlines, Japan Air Lines, China Airlines, Eva Airways, Korean Air, Malaysia Airlines, and Singapore Airlines.

FROM THE UNITED KINGDOM
Airlines with flights from the U.K. to Bangkok include Thai Airways International, British Airways, and Singapore Airlines.

FROM CANADA Canadian Airlines International flies to Bangkok from Vancouver via Hong Kong 4 days a week.

FROM AUSTRALIA Service is provided by Qantas Airways, Thai Airways International, Singapore Airlines, and British Airways.

GETTING THROUGH THE AIRPORT

With the federalization of airport security, security procedures at U.S. airports are more stable and consistent than ever. Generally, you'll be fine if you arrive at the airport **2 hours** before an international flight; if you show up late, tell an airline employee and you'll probably be whisked to the front of the line.

Bring a **current, government-issued photo ID,** such as a driver's license, and, of course, a passport for international flights. If you've got an E-ticket, print out the **official confirmation page;** you'll need to show your confirmation at the security checkpoint and your ID at the ticket counter or the gate. (Children under 18 do not need photo IDs for domestic flights, but the adults checking in with them need them.)

Security lines are getting shorter than they were during 2001 and 2002, but some doozies remain. If you have trouble standing for long periods of time, tell an airline employee; the airline will provide a wheelchair. Speed up security by **not wearing metal objects** such as big belt buckles or clanky earrings. If you've got metallic body parts, a note from your doctor can prevent a long chat with the security screeners. Keep in mind that only **ticketed passengers** are allowed past security, except for folks escorting passengers with disabilities or children.

Federalization has stabilized **what you can carry on** and **what you can't.** The general rule is that sharp things are out, nail clippers are okay, and food and beverages must be passed through the x-ray machine—but security screeners can't make you drink from your coffee cup. Bring food in your carry-on rather than checking it; explosive-detection machines used on checked luggage have been known to mistake food (especially chocolate, for some reason) for bombs. Travelers in the U.S. are allowed one carry-on bag, plus a "personal item" such as a purse, briefcase, or laptop bag. Carry-on hoarders can stuff all sorts of things into a laptop bag; as long as it has a laptop in it, it's still considered a personal item. The Transportation Security Administration (TSA) has issued a list of restricted items; check its website (www.tsa.gov/public/index.jsp) for details.

In 2003, the TSA will be phasing out **gate check-in** at all U.S. airports. Passengers with E-tickets and without checked bags can still beat the ticket-counter lines by using **electronic kiosks** or even **online check-in.** Ask your airline which alternatives are available and, if you're using a kiosk, bring the credit card you used to book the ticket. If you're checking bags, you will still be able to use most airlines' kiosks; again call your airline for up-to-date information. **Curbside check-in** is also a good way to avoid lines, although a few airlines still ban curbside check-in entirely; call before you go.

At press time, the TSA is also recommending that you **not lock your checked luggage** so that screeners can search it by hand, if necessary. The agency says to use plastic "zip ties" instead, which can be bought at hardware stores and can be easily cut off.

FLYING FOR LESS: TIPS FOR GETTING THE BEST AIRFARE

Passengers sharing the same airplane cabin rarely pay the same fare. Travelers who need to purchase tickets at the last minute, change their itinerary at a moment's notice, or fly one-way often get stuck paying the premium rate. Here are some ways to keep your airfare costs down.

- Passengers who can book their ticket **long in advance,** or who **fly midweek** or **at less-trafficked**

hours, will pay a fraction of the full fare. If your schedule is flexible, say so, and ask if you can secure a cheaper fare by changing your flight plans.

- You can also save on airfares by keeping an eye out in local newspapers for **promotional specials** or **fare wars,** when airlines lower prices on their most popular routes. You rarely see fare wars offered for peak travel times, but if you can travel in the off-months, you might snag a bargain.

- Search **the Internet** for cheap fares (see "Planning Your Trip Online," earlier in this chapter).

- Try to book a ticket **in its country of origin.** Try ticket consolidators in your country of origin and for domestic flights in the region. Know that Bangkok is perhaps one of the best budget travel hubs in the world, and cheap tickets can be purchased at small travel agents for next-day travel throughout the world.

- **Consolidators,** also known as bucket shops, are great sources for international tickets, although they usually can't beat the Internet on fares within North America. Start by looking in Sunday newspaper travel sections; U.S. travelers should focus on the *New York Times, Los Angeles Times,* and *Miami Herald.* For less-developed destinations, small travel agents who cater to immigrant communities in large cities often have the best deals. *Beware:* Bucket shop tickets are usually nonrefundable or rigged with stiff cancellation penalties, often as high as 50% to 75% of the ticket price, and some put you on charter airlines with questionable safety records.

- Several reliable consolidators are worldwide and available on the Net. **STA Travel** is now the world's leader in student travel, thanks to its purchase of Council Travel. It also offers good fares for travelers of all ages. **Flights.com** (© 800/TRAV-800; www.flights.com) started in Europe and has excellent fares worldwide, particularly to that continent. It also has local websites in 12 countries. **FlyCheap** (© 800/FLY-CHEAP; www.1800flycheap.com) is owned by package-holiday megalith MyTravel and has especially good access to fares for sunny destinations. **Air Tickets Direct** (© 800/778-3447; www.airticketsdirect.com) is based in Montreal and leverages the currently weak Canadian dollar for low fares; it'll also book trips to places that U.S. travel agents won't touch, such as Cuba.

- Join **frequent-flier clubs.** Accrue enough miles, and you'll be rewarded with free flights and elite status. It's free, and you'll get the best choice of seats, faster response to phone inquiries, and prompter service if your luggage is stolen, if your flight is canceled or delayed, or if you want to change your seat. You don't need to fly to build frequent-flier miles—**frequent-flier credit cards** can provide thousands of miles for doing your everyday shopping.
- For many more tips about air travel, including a rundown of the major frequent-flier credit cards, pick up a copy of *Frommer's Fly Safe, Fly Smart* (Wiley Publishing).

LONG-HAUL FLIGHTS: HOW TO STAY COMFORTABLE

Long flights can be trying; stuffy air and cramped seats can make you feel as if you're being sent parcel post in a small box. But with a little advance planning, you can make an otherwise unpleasant experience almost bearable.

- Your choice of airline and airplane will definitely affect your legroom. Among U.S. airlines, American Airlines has the best average seat pitch (the distance between a seat and the row in front of it). Find more details at www.seatguru.com, which has extensive details about almost every seat on six major U.S. airlines. For international airlines, research firm Skytrax has posted a list of average seat pitches at www.airlinequality.com.
- Emergency exit seats and bulkhead seats typically have the most legroom. Emergency exit seats are usually held back to be assigned the day of a flight (to ensure that the seat is filled by someone able-bodied); it's worth getting to the ticket counter early to snag one of these spots for a long flight. Keep in mind that bulkheads are where airlines often put baby bassinets, so you might be sitting next to an infant.

(*Tips*   **Travel in the Age of Bankruptcy**

At press time, two major U.S. airlines were struggling in bankruptcy court, and most of the rest weren't doing very well, either. To protect yourself, **buy your tickets with a credit card**: The Fair Credit Billing Act guarantees that you can get your money back from the credit card company if a travel supplier goes under (and if you request the refund within 60 days of the bankruptcy). **Travel insurance** can also help, but make sure it covers "carrier default" for your specific travel provider. And be aware that if a U.S. airline goes bust midtrip, a 2001 federal law requires other carriers to take you to your destination (albeit on a space-available basis) for a fee of no more than $25, provided that you rebook within 60 days of the cancellation.

Tips **Coping with Jet Lag**

After flying from Europe or the U.S. to Asia, you'll suffer some real jet lag, with symptoms caused by dehydration and the general stress of air travel as well as the very confusing time change. Everything from your digestion to your brain gets knocked for a loop. Traveling east, say, from Europe over the Middle East and Central Asia, is more difficult on your internal clock than traveling west, say, from Hawaii to Bangkok: Most peoples' bodies find it more acceptable to stay up late than to fall asleep early. Here are some tips for combating jet lag:

- **Reset your watch** to your destination time before you board the plane.
- **Drink lots of water** before, during, and after your flight. Avoid alcohol.
- **Exercise and sleep well** for a few days before your trip.
- **Daylight** is the key to resetting your body clock. At the website for **Outside In** (www.bodyclock.com), you can get a customized plan of when to seek and avoid light.
- If you need help getting to sleep earlier than you usually would, doctors recommend taking either the hormone **melatonin** or the sleeping pill **Ambien**—but not together. Take 2 to 5 milligrams of melatonin about 2 hours before your planned bedtime.

- To have two seats for yourself, try for an aisle seat in a center section toward the back of coach. If you're traveling with a companion, book an aisle and a window seat. Middle seats are usually booked last, so chances are good that you'll end up with three seats to yourselves. And if a third passenger is assigned the middle seat, he or she will probably be more than happy to trade for a window or an aisle.
- Ask about entertainment options. Many airlines offer seatback video systems with which you get to choose your movies or play video games—but only on some of their planes. (Boeing 777s are your best bet.)
- To sleep, avoid the last row of any section or a row in front of an emergency exit because these seats are the least likely to recline. Avoid seats near highly trafficked toilet areas. You also might want

to reserve a window seat so that you can rest your head and avoid being bumped in the aisle.
- Get up, walk around, and stretch every 60 to 90 minutes to keep your blood flowing. This helps avoid deep vein thrombosis, or "economy-class syndrome," a rare and deadly condition that can be caused by sitting in cramped conditions for too long.
- Drink water before, during, and after your flight to combat the lack of humidity in airplane cabins—which can be drier than the Sahara. Bring a bottle of water on board. Avoid alcohol, which will dehydrate you.
- If you're flying with kids, don't forget to carry on toys, books, pacifiers, and chewing gum to help them relieve ear pressure buildup during ascent and descent. Let each child pack his or her own backpack with favorite toys.

11 Packages for the Independent Traveler

Before you start your search for the lowest airfare, you might want to

consider booking your flight as part of a travel package. Package tours are not the same thing as escorted tours. Package tours are simply a way to buy the airfare, accommodations, and other elements of your trip (such as car rentals, airport transfers, and sometimes even activities) at the same time and often at discounted prices—kind of like one-stop shopping. Packages are sold in bulk to tour operators—who resell them to the public at a cost that usually undercuts standard rates.

One good source of package deals is the airlines themselves. Several big **online travel agencies**—Expedia, Travelocity, Orbitz, Site59, and Last-minute.com—also do a brisk business in packages. If you're unsure about the pedigree of a smaller packager, check with the Better Business Bureau in the city where the company is based, or go online at www.bbb.org. If a packager won't tell you where it's based, don't fly with it.

Travel packages are also listed in the travel section of your local Sunday newspaper. Or, check ads in the national travel magazines such as *Arthur Frommer's Budget Travel Magazine, Travel & Leisure, National Geographic Traveler,* and *Condé Nast Traveler.*

Package tours can vary by leaps and bounds. Some offer a better class of hotels than others. Some offer the same hotels for lower prices. Some offer flights on scheduled airlines, while others book charters. Some limit your choice of accommodations and travel days. You are often required to make a large payment up front. On the plus side, packages can save you money, offering group prices but allowing for independent travel. Some even allow you to add on a few guided excursions or escorted day trips (also at prices lower than if you booked them yourself) without booking an entirely escorted tour.

Before you invest in a package tour, get some answers. Ask about the **accommodation choices** and prices for each. Then look up the hotels' reviews in a Frommer's guide and check their rates for your specific dates of travel online. You'll also want to find out what **type of room** you get. If you need a certain type of room, ask for it; don't take whatever is thrown your way. Request a nonsmoking room, a quiet room, a room with a view, or whatever you fancy.

Finally, look for **hidden expenses.** Ask whether airport departure fees and taxes, for example, are included in the total cost.

12 Escorted General-Interest Tours

Escorted tours are structured group tours, with a group leader. The price usually includes everything from airfare to hotels, meals, tours, admission costs, and local transportation.

Whether you want to ride an elephant through the jungle, trek among indigenous people, shake hands with an orangutan, swim beneath a waterfall, snorkel in a clear blue lagoon, lounge on a white-sand beach, or wander through exotic markets, there's a Southeast Asia tour packager for you, offering a wide range of travel options using the finest and most reliable travel services available in the region.

Many people derive a certain ease and security from escorted trips. The logistics of travel in Southeast Asia can try the patience of the Buddha, so going by tour means you won't be hassled by touts or frustrated by confusing local transport schedules (or lack thereof). All the little details are taken care of, you know your costs up front, and there are few surprises. Escorted tours can take you to the maximum number of sights in the minimum amount of time, with the least amount of hassle—you don't have to sweat over the plotting and planning of a vacation schedule. Escorted tours are particularly convenient for people with limited mobility.

On the downside, an escorted tour often requires a big deposit up front, and lodging and dining choices are predetermined. As part of a cloud of tourists, you'll get little opportunity for serendipitous interactions with locals. The tours can be jam-packed with activities, leaving little room for individual sightseeing, whim, or adventure—plus, they often focus only on the heavily touristed sites, so you miss out on the lesser-known gems.

Before you invest in an escorted tour, ask about the **cancellation policy:** Is a deposit required? Can they cancel the trip if they don't get enough people? Do you get a refund if they cancel? If *you* cancel? How late can you cancel if you are unable to go? When do you pay in full? *Note:* If you choose an escorted tour, think strongly about purchasing trip-cancellation insurance, especially if the tour operator asks you to pay up front. See the section on "Travel Insurance," earlier in this chapter.

You'll also want to get a complete **schedule** of the trip to find out how much sightseeing is planned each day and whether enough time has been allotted for relaxing or wandering solo.

The **size** of the group is also important to know up front. Generally, the smaller the group is, the more flexible the itinerary is and the less time you'll spend waiting for people to get on and off the bus. Find out the **demographics** of the group as well. What is the age range? What is the gender breakdown? Is this mostly a trip for couples or singles?

Discuss what is included in the **price**. You might have to pay for transportation to and from the airport. A box lunch might be included in an excursion, but drinks might cost extra. Tips might not be included. Find out if you will be charged if you decide to opt out of certain activities or meals.

Before you invest in a package tour, get some answers. Ask about the **accommodation choices** and prices for each. Then look up the hotels' reviews in a Frommer's guide and check their rates for your specific dates of travel online. You'll also want to find out what **type of room** you get. If you need a certain type of room, ask for it; don't take whatever is thrown your way. Request a nonsmoking room, a quiet room, a room with a view, or whatever you fancy.

Finally, if you plan to travel alone, you'll need to know if a **single supplement** will be charged and if the company can match you up with a roommate.

Among the most experienced and knowledgeable tour operators specializing in Southeast Asia are **Absolute Asia** and **Asia Transpacific Journeys.** Outbound (or in-country) tour providers **Diethelm** and **Exotissimo** can do anything, from arranging deluxe tours to just helping out with any small details or bookings. Most companies allow clients to design their own trip or deviate from exact schedules (often at a small cost). See individual country chapters for other in-country tour operators. Companies like **Intrepid,** among others, offer unique itineraries for solo travelers.

Here are the top outfitters:

Abercrombie & Kent   Well-known luxury tour operator Abercrombie & Kent offers Southeast Asia programs with numerous comprehensive itineraries. Tours include Myanmar, Thailand (including spa tours in Thailand), Cambodia, Hong Kong, and other destinations, as well as connections with China. These tours also include stays at the finest hotels in Southeast Asia, such as the Oriental in Bangkok and the Mandarin Oriental in Hong Kong. 1520 Kensington Rd., Suite 212, Oakbrook, IL 60523-2141. © 800/323-7308. Fax 630/954-3324. www.aandktours.com.

Absolute Asia Founded in 1989, Absolute Asia offers an array of innovative itineraries, specializing in individual or small group tours customized to your interests, with experienced local guides and excellent accommodations. Talk to them about tours that feature art, cuisine, religion, antiques, photography, wildlife study, archaeology, and soft adventure—they can plan a specialized trip to see just about anything you can dream up for any length of time. They can also book you on excellent coach programs in Indochina. 180 Varick St., 16th Floor, New York, NY 10014. © **800/736-8187.** Fax 212/627-4090. www.absoluteasia.com.

Asia Transpacific Journeys Coordinating tours to every corner of South and Southeast Asia and the Pacific, Asia Transpacific Journeys deals with small groups and custom programs that include luxury hotel accommodations. The flagship package, the 23-day Passage to Indochina tour, takes you through Laos, Vietnam, and Cambodia's major attractions with a well-planned itinerary, and it is but one of many fun tours that promote cultural understanding. It's a model of sustainable tourism and a highly recommended choice. 2995 Center Green Court, Boulder, CO 80301. © **800/642-2742** or 303/443-6789. Fax 303/443-7078. www.asiatranspacific.com.

Backroads For those who want to explore Southeast Asia by bicycle, cycling and hiking specialist Backroads has a 12-day Vietnam tour and an 8-day Thailand Golden Triangle tour, among others. Check out their website; they're always coming up with innovative itineraries in the region. 801 Cedar St., Berkeley, CA 94710-1800. © **800/462-2848** or 510/527-1555. Fax 510/527-1444. www.backroads.com.

Diethelm The folks at this Swiss-based tour company, with offices throughout the region (and a popular choice for European tour groups), are friendly and helpful; they operate as de facto tourist information centers in places like Laos. Diethelm has full tour programs and, like Exotissimo (below), can help with any details for travelers in-country, can arrange car rental or vans for small groups, and offer discount options to all locations. Kian Gwan Building II, 140/1 Wireless Rd., Bangkok 10330, Thailand. © **662/255-9150.** Fax 662/256-0248. www.diethelm-travel.com.

Exotissimo A French outfit and outbound (in-country) agency with offices in every major city in the region, Exotissimo has excellent guides onsite. Agents not only can arrange all-inclusive tours, but they also are helpful with all travel details, from ticketing to visas. See the office locations in each chapter. **In France:** 40 bis, Rue du fg Poissonniére, 75010 Paris, France © **(33)149/490-360.** Fax (33)149/490-369. **In Saigon:** Saigon Trade Center, 37 Ton Duc Thang, District 1 Ho Chi Minh City, Vietnam. © **8/825-1723.** Fax 08/829-5800. www.exotissimo.com.

Intrepid This popular Australian operator is probably the best choice to get off the beaten track on a tour of Asia. Intrepid caters tours for the culturally discerning, those with humanitarian goals, those in search of comfort, adventurers, people on a budget, or those looking for a looser structure and lots of options. Their motto is their name, and with some of the best guides in Asia, these folks will take you to the back of beyond safely, in style, and with lots of laughs. Box 2781, Fitzroy, DC VIC 3065, 12 Spring St., Fitzroy, Victoria, Australia. © **613/9473-2626.** Fax 613/9419-4426. In the U.S.: **877/488-1616.** www.intrepidtravel.com.

Imaginative Traveler This U.K.–based firm gets rave reviews every time for organizing all sorts of cycling, trekking, and motorcycling adventures throughout Southeast Asia, particularly Indochina. 1 Betts Ave., Martlesham Heath, Suffolk IP5 3RH. © **0208/742-8612.** Fax 0280/742-3045. www.imaginative-traveler.com.

13 Getting Around Southeast Asia

Flying in Southeast Asia is the best way to go between and within countries, in terms of time conservation and convenience. It is also the most expensive, but if your time is short, it is definitely worth the cost. That said, sometimes half the fun of traveling is getting there—many walk away from land travel in this part of the world saying, "I'll never do it again, but what a trip!" When the massive Soviet 4X4 nearly lays on its side in the deep ruts of the road to Xieng Khouang in Laos, or that rattle-trap motorbike you rented in hill-tribe country in the north of Vietnam catches a flat and leaves you stranded, you might curse yourself or the very road you're on, but you'll have lots of stories to tell when you get back.

BY PLANE

Depending on your specific itinerary, you can fly on international carriers, including Silk Air (the regional arm of Singapore Airlines), Malaysia Airlines, Thai Airways International, Cathay Pacific Airways, Vietnam Airlines, Myanmar Airways International, or Garuda Indonesia, as well as various domestic carriers including Pelangi Air and Berjaya Air in Malaysia; Air Mandalay in Burma; Lao Aviation in Laos; or Bangkok Airways, P.B. Air, or Angel Airlines in Thailand and Cambodia. Competing airlines can often offer more interesting routes for you to select from.

Also bear in mind that international airports are not restricted to capital cities. In addition to Bangkok, Thailand has international access via Chiang Mai and Chiang Rai (to China, Burma, and Laos), U-Tapao and Phuket (to Cambodia), and Phuket and Ko Samui (to Singapore and Kuala Lumpur). You can fly into Malaysia to Penang, Langkawi, and Tioman Island, and to Borneo destinations direct from Singapore. Burma

has international access to Mandalay; Laos has international access at both Luang Prabang and Pakse, in addition to the capital, Vientiane. Vietnam has international flights to Ho Chi Minh City and Hanoi. And in Cambodia, you can fly directly to Siem Reap, the access city to Angkor Wat, from Bangkok, U-Tapao (near Pattaya), Phuket, Singapore, and other cities.

Check out the UNESCO World Heritage Tour, a new schedule of flights offered by Bangkok Airways (www.bangkokair.com). Originating in Bangkok, this tour connects Sukhotha (Thailand) with Luang Prabang (Laos), Hue (Vietnam), and Angkor Wat in Cambodia. Unique and convenient connections are offered between the regions' cultural centers. Ask any travel agent, and be sure to research all flight options for the most direct routes and best fares. Each chapter gives specific details for booking these flights.

BY TRAIN

With a few exceptions, trains that operate throughout Southeast Asia are poorly maintained, overcrowded, and slow. The most popular rail route—and the only one with interconnecting service among countries in all of Southeast Asia—runs from Singapore to Bangkok (and vice versa) through the heart of the Malaysian peninsula, with stops along the way at the cities of Johor Bahru, Malacca, Kuala Lumpur, and Butterworth (for Penang). It takes 6 hours from Singapore to Kuala Lumpur, and another 35 hours from Kuala Lumpur to Bangkok. You can board the train at the Singapore Rail Station in Tanjong Pagar, at the Kuala Lumpur Central Railway Station on Jalan Hishamuddin, and in Bangkok at the Hua Lamphong Railway Station on Rama IV Road.

Tips **Dial E for Easy**

For quick directions on how to call to or from the countries of Southeast Asia, see the "Telephone" entry in the "Fast Facts" section of each chapter.

Upscale travelers with unlimited budgets can book passage on one of the world's foremost luxury trains, the Eastern & Oriental Express, which covers the distance between Singapore and Bangkok in 42 hours. Find more details in either the Singapore or the Thailand chapters.

Reliable rail service also runs north to south along coastal Vietnam with interesting new luxury cars that connect Hanoi, the capital, with the northern hill country and make a further connection to the vast rail networks of China.

BY BUS

Although they're not the most comfortable option, buses save money and provide access to some places not available via commercial flights. Popular overland routes include Vietnam to Laos (between Hue/Danang and Savannakhet), Vietnam to Cambodia (between Ho Chi Minh City and Phnom Penh), Thailand to Cambodia (between Bangkok and Phnom Penh),

and extensive routes from southern Thailand, throughout Malaysia, and down to Singapore. Check each country's individual visa requirements because you often need to prearrange visas for land crossings (such as between Thailand, Laos, and Vietnam).

BY BOAT

More and more travelers are heading down the Mekong, starting at Chiang Khong in northern Thailand and ending in Luang Prabang in Laos. Get your visas from travel agents in Chiang Mai, and you'll have no problems. Thailand and Laos have a few border crossings over the Mekong, the most popular of which is the Friendship Bridge connecting Nong Khai (the last stop on Thailand's northeastern rail route) to Vientiane, Laos's capital. Don't miss the new boat connections along the Mekong tributaries between Vietnam's Mekong Delta and Phnom Penh, Cambodia's capital.

14 Suggested Itineraries

Routes through the region are as varied as the rag-tag bunch who travel them. With the many and frequent air connections, you can really just choose your destinations and connect them as you like really, but here are a few suggestions.

INDOCHINA TOUR

Clockwise or counterclockwise routes starting in Bangkok and including northern Thailand, Laos, Vietnam, and Cambodia are common. Connecting northern Thailand with Laos by boat is popular, and flying from Vientiane, the Lao capital, to Hanoi

or Ho Chi Minh is a better choice than the rough overland route (which also leaves you in the middle of the north-south route where a flight will get you to a terminus). Boats now connect Cambodia and Laos, and there is frequent service between Angkor Wat and Bangkok.

Length   This can take anything from a few weeks to 6 months, depending on your inclinations.

Highlights   These include the historic temple towns of Thailand, hill-tribe treks throughout the region, sleepy Luang Prabang, busy Hanoi and Ho Chi Minh, all of the stops along coastal Vietnam, and, of course, Angkor Wat. After a trip like this, you'll have earned your time on the beaches of Thailand, Malaysia, or Bali.

DOWN THE MALAY PENINSULA

Starting in Bangkok and heading south, you can connect the major resort destinations of southern Thailand with a tour down the length of Malaysia to Singapore and end in Bali.

Length This can take anywhere from a fly-by-night week to a few months.

Highlights These include pristine beaches (maybe even "The Beach")

in Thailand, great food, affordable cosmopolitan comforts, and unique cultural stops in Malaysia, "shop-til-you-drop" in Singapore, and the tranquil beaches of Bali.

START FROM A HUB

From Bangkok, Singapore, or other major urban centers, travelers can make short forays into the countryside or to the resort of their choice from a comfortable, familiar base in a big city with all the comforts of home. Many visitors aim for the cultural and historical sites recommended by UNESCO or connect with adventure outfits for short adventure trips before coming back to hot showers and room service.

 FAST FACTS: Southeast Asia

ATM Networks International ATMs abound in the major cities. See the "Money" section, earlier in this chapter, or in each specific country chapter.

Car Rentals See "Getting Around," in each country's chapter. In most places, it's best to hire a driver when renting a car because road conditions and traffic rules (or the seeming lack thereof) can make self-driving a bit harrowing; if this sounds like a luxury, hiring a driver for a day is affordable, for the most part, and drivers are often great sources of local information.

Currency See "Money," earlier in this chapter.

Driving Rules See "Getting Around," earlier in this chapter.

Drugstores You'll find over-the-counter medications readily available in each country. It's best to bring enough of any medication that you require regularly, and know the generic name of the medicines you carry, in case you lose one or run out.

Electricity Most countries run on 220 volts, with two-pronged (flat or round) plugs. Use a converter for U.S. appliances (some hotels actually run on 110 volts), and use a surge protector for a laptop.

Embassies and Consulates See the "Fast Facts" sections in each country's chapter.

Emergencies Check the "Fast Facts" sections in each country's chapter.

Etiquette & Customs Customs vary, but in the mostly Buddhist and Muslim countries of Southeast Asia, modesty in dress and conduct is the general rule. Check the culture sections in specific country chapters.

Appropriate Attire: Modesty is the rule throughout Southeast Asia. Though the cultures and religions of the many nations are more different than alike quite often, they all agree on respect for one another and staying covered in public. Ratty clothes are out of place here, as anywhere.

Gestures: See individual country chapters because there are some varied specifics here. Everywhere a scooping form of the wave that Westerners use to say "hello" means come here. Be aware of issues in most countries over eating with only the right hand (the left is considered dirty) or of how to offer things to people (commonly with both hands). Check individual country chapters under "Etiquette."

Business Etiquette: Be on time, shake hands when greeting, and look people in the eye: The basics are all the same here, but it gets tricky when different cultural modes of thought and communication come into play (volumes are written on the subject). You might have to change your definition of "Yes" and "No." Check individual country chapters.

Photography: Be aware that there are some superstitions about photography among hill tribes. In general, it's a good idea to ask before taking photos in houses of worship. Be careful not to photograph police or military installations or activity.

Film Film is easy to get in all of these countries and is usually much cheaper than in the West (the exceptions being Singapore and Hong Kong, where it costs about the same).

Holidays See "Holidays and Events," earlier in this chapter, or in the introductory material in each individual country chapter.

Information See "Visitor Information," earlier in this chapter.

Internet Access The Internet is accessible just about anywhere and everywhere you'll travel. The farther you are from urban centers, the slower the dial-up connections (at slightly inflated prices), but the region's boom in young backpacker travelers means that you'll find a cybercafe in any location (except Myanmar, where there are only a few, and those are censored).

Language The English language holds sway over the countries of Southeast Asia, and wherever you go you'll be sure to find helpful folks eager to practice a few phrases on you (certainly touts and people who want your tourist dollars will know a few words). Don't let this distract you from picking up some of the local lingo: The eclectic tapestry in the region, a melding of Indian, Chinese, and indigenous languages, is a rich source worth exploring, and a little goes a long way.

Liquor Laws Drinking ages vary (in most countries it's either 18 or 20), but you won't find too many constraints placed on the purchase or consumption of alcohol in the region. Bars in the major cities are open late and, in some rural areas or at beachside, are mandated only by the whims of the owner. Beer, wine, and liquor, both familiar imports and local rice-based varieties, are sold anywhere and everywhere.

Lost and Found Be sure to tell all of your credit card companies the minute you discover that your wallet has been lost or stolen, and file a report at the nearest police precinct. Your credit card company or insurer might require a police report number or record of the loss. Most credit card companies have an emergency toll-free number to call if your card is lost or stolen; they might be able to wire you a cash advance immediately or deliver an emergency credit card in a day or two. Visa's U.S. emergency number is (© 800/847-2911 or 410/581-9994. American Express cardholders and traveler's check holders should call (© 800/221-7282. MasterCard holders should call (© 800/307-7309 or 636/722-7111. For other credit cards, call the toll-free number directory at (© 800/555-1212.

If you need emergency cash over the weekend when all banks and American Express offices are closed, you can have money wired to you via **Western Union** ((© 800/325-6000; www.westernunion.com).

Identity theft and fraud are potential complications of losing your wallet, especially if you've lost your driver's license along with your cash and credit cards. Notify the major credit-reporting bureaus immediately; placing a fraud alert on your records could protect you against liability for criminal activity. The three major U.S. credit-reporting agencies are **Equifax** ((© 800/766-0008; www.equifax.com), **Experian** ((© 888/397-3742; www.experian.com), and **TransUnion** ((© 800/680-7289; www.transunion.com). Finally, if you've lost all forms of photo ID, call your airline and explain the situation; they might allow you to board the plane if you have a copy of your passport or birth certificate and a copy of the police report you've filed.

Mail Postage rates are comparable to those in Western countries, although service Is often less reliable and very slow, especially from the developing counties of Laos, Cambodia, or Burma. Express services such as DHL or Fed Ex are growing in number and abundant in large cities (many souvenir or antique dealers can arrange shipping on items large and small).

Newspapers and Magazines In the major urban centers, Hong Kong, Singapore, and Bangkok, foreign press material is available anywhere. There are good local English-language papers, like the *Bangkok Post* or Singapore's *StraitsTimes* and the *Asian Wall Street Journal,* that will keep you connected. Don't pass up small-press editions or *Time Out* guides to local happenings and attractions; expat newspapers are also a good glimpse into daily life in each country.

Passports Visitors to all the countries of Southeast Asia require a passport that is valid for the duration of their intended stay.

For Residents of the United States: Whether you're applying in person or by mail, you can download passport applications from the U.S. State Department website at **http://travel.state.gov.** For general information, call the **National Passport Agency** ((© 202/647-0518). To find your regional passport office, either check the U.S. State Department website or call the **National Passport Information Center** ((© 900/225-5674); the fee is 55¢ per minute for automated information and $1.50 per minute for operator-assisted calls.

For Residents of Canada: Passport applications are available at travel agencies throughout Canada or from the central **Passport Office,** Department of Foreign Affairs and International Trade, Ottawa, ON K1A 0G3 ((© 800/567-6868; www.dfait-maeci.gc.ca/passport).

For Residents of the United Kingdom: To pick up an application for a standard 10-year passport (5-yr. passport for children under 16), visit your nearest passport office, major post office, or travel agency, or contact the **United Kingdom Passport Service** at (© 0870/521-0410 or search its website at www.ukpa.gov.uk.

For Residents of Ireland: You can apply for a 10-year passport at the **Passport Office,** Setanta Centre, Molesworth Street, Dublin 2 (✆ **01/671-1633;** www.irlgov.ie/iveagh). Those under age 18 and over 65 must apply for a 3-year passport for 12€ You can also apply at 1A South Mall, Cork (✆ **021/272-525)** or at most main post offices.

For Residents of Australia: You can pick up an application from your local post office or any branch of Passports Australia, but you must schedule an interview at the passport office to present your application materials. Call the **Australian Passport Information Service** at ✆ **131-232,** or visit the government website at www.passports.gov.au.

For Residents of New Zealand: You can pick up a passport application at any New Zealand Passports Office or download it from the website. Contact the **Passports Office** at ✆ **0800/225-050** in New Zealand or 04/474-8100, or log on to www.passports.govt.nz.

Police See the "Fast Facts" sections in individual country chapters.

Restrooms Public restrooms are often a bit of a shocker for first-time visitors. Especially in rural areas, it's common that toilets flush manually, with a few scoops of water from a larger cistern, and paper is to be deposited not in the loo, but in a separate wastebasket. Standards of cleanliness vary, but many public toilets would make a run-down roadside gas station in the U.S. seem like a temple. Squat toilets are common, but most major hotels have amenities familiar to the Western visitor.

Safety See "Insurance, Health & Safety," earlier in this chapter.

Smoking The region is more or less a smoker's paradise, and there are few restraints on the habit in most destinations. In fact, in rural areas of the developing countries, smoking is even allowed on buses (a bit much, really). New laws in Bangkok ban smoking in restaurants, and similar rules are in place in the larger cities. If you're a smoker, be sure to read the rules before heading to Singapore.

Taxes Each country has its version of a VAT tax added to restaurant and hotel bills. It can go as high as 20%, so be sure to inquire beforehand.

Telephones See the "Fast Facts" and "Dialing at a Glance" sections in individual country chapters.

Time Zone The countries of Southeast Asia are between 7 and 8 hours ahead of Greenwich Mean Time (that means 12 or 13 hours ahead of New York, and 3 or 4 hours behind Sydney).

Tipping Though not as common as in the U.S., a small gratuity for taxi drivers, bellhops, and restaurant staff is appreciated.

Useful Phone Numbers

- U.S. Dept. of State Travel Advisory: ✆ **202-647-5225** (manned 24 hours)
- U.S. Passport Agency: ✆ **202-647-0518**
- U.S. Center for Disease Control International Traveler's Hotline: ✆ **404-332-4559**

Water Apart from in urban Singapore, **don't drink the water.** Buy inexpensive bottled drinking water, available everywhere. Some restaurants serve safe, treated ice and water.

4

Hong Kong

by Beth Reiber

Viewed from Victoria Peak, Hong Kong surely rates as one of the most stunning cities in Asia, if not the world. In the foreground rise the skyscrapers of Hong Kong Island, while beyond that is Victoria Harbour, with its incredibly busy traffic of everything from the historic Star Ferry to cruise liners, cargo ships, and wooden fishing vessels. On the other side is Kowloon Peninsula, growing larger seemingly by the minute with ambitious land-reclamation projects, housing estates, and ever-higher buildings, all against a dramatic backdrop of gently rounded mountains.

Though not part of Southeast Asia proper, many flights in the region pass through this busy hub and we include this chapter to aquaint visitors for the eventuality of a long lay-over or overnight. For more in-depth information, see the *Frommer's Hong Kong Guidebook.* If this is your first stop in Asia, Hong Kong will seem excitingly exotic, with its profusion of neon Chinese signs, roasted ducks hanging in restaurant windows, colorful street markets, herb medicinal shops, and crush of people, 98% of whom are Chinese.

If you're arriving from elsewhere in Asia, however, Hong Kong might seem welcomingly familiar, with its first-class hotels, restaurants serving everything from California-style pizzas to French haute cuisine, easy-to-navigate transportation system, English-language street signs, and gigantic shopping malls.

Hong Kong's unique blend of exotic and familiar, East and West, offers ancient curiosities as well as familiar comforts. To the first-time visitor to Asia, it's a cacophony of sights and smells, colorful markets and rushing crowds. Though rich in ancient history, Hong Kong's 156 years of British rule mean that English is an official language and Western standards abound. There are some great deals for the taking. Shopping is full-contact here and whether bargain hunting, browsing upscale boutiques, or in search of the best in new electronics, you'll find it here.

The city has some good attractions, including museums, parks, and temples, as well as good side-trips to outlying islands.

1 Getting to Know Hong Kong

The Hong Kong Special Administrative Region (SAR) is located at the southeastern tip of the People's Republic of China, some 2,000km (1,240 miles) south of Beijing and about the same latitude as Mexico City and Hawaii. Covering 1,100 sq. km (about 425 sq. miles), Hong Kong can be divided into four distinct parts: **Hong Kong Island,** with the Central District (Hong Kong's main financial and business district and usually referred to simply as Central), the Western District, Wan Chai, and Causeway Bay, along with such major attractions as

Hong Kong Park, Victoria Peak, Stanley Market, Ocean Park, and the Zoological and Botanical Gardens; **Kowloon Peninsula,** with Tsim Sha Tsui and its many hotels, restaurants, museums, and shops, as well Tsim Sha Tsui East and the Yau Ma Tei and Mong Kok districts; the vast **New Territories,** which stretch north from Kowloon all the way to the Chinese border and now house approximately half of the population in massive satellite towns; and 260 **outlying islands,** most of which are barren and uninhabited.

2 Planning Your Trip to Hong Kong

VISITOR INFORMATION

In addition to its tourist counter in the arrivals hall of the Hong Kong International Airport, the **Hong Kong Tourist Board (HKTB)** maintains two offices in town: In Tsim Sha Tsui at the Star Ferry concourse (daily 8am–6pm) and on Hong Kong Island at 99 Queen's Rd. Both offices are open 8am to 6pm daily or call the HKTB Visitor Hotline at *①* **852/2508 1234.** You can pick up any number of free local papers that list events and happenings; in addition, check the *Hong Kong Standard* newspaper or the *South China Morning Post* for specials on local events.

IN THE UNITED STATES

- **New York:** 115 E. 54th St., 2nd floor, New York, NY 10022-4512 (*①* **212/ 421-3382;** fax 212/421-4285; hktanyc@hkta.org). **Chicago:** 401 N. Michigan Ave., Suite 1640, Chicago, IL 60611 (*①* **312/329-1828;** fax 312/ 329-1858; hktachi@hkta.org). **Los Angeles:** 10940 Wilshire Blvd., Suite 2050, Los Angeles, CA 90024-3915 (*①* **310/208-4582;** fax 310/208-1869; hktalax@hkta.org).

IN CANADA

- **Toronto:** Hong Kong Trade Center, 3rd floor, 9 Temperance St., Toronto, ON M5H 1Y6 (*①* **416/366-2389;** fax 416/366-1098; hktayyz@hkta.org).

IN THE UNITED KINGDOM

- **London:** 6 Grafton St., London W1X 3LB, England (*①* **0171/533-7100;** fax 0171/533-7111; hktalon@hkta.org).

IN AUSTRALIA & NEW ZEALAND

- **Sydney:** Hong Kong House, Level 4, 80 Druitt St., Sydney, NSW 2000, Australia (*①* **02/9283 3083;** fax 02/9283-3383; hktasyd@hkta.org).
- **Auckland:** P.O. Box 2120, Auckland, New Zealand (*①* **09/307-2580;** fax 09/307-2581; hktaauk@hkta.org).

ENTRY REQUIREMENTS

A valid passport is the only document most tourists, including Americans, need to enter Hong Kong. Americans can stay up to 1 month without a visa. Australians, New Zealanders, Canadians, and other British Commonwealth citizens can stay 3 months without a visa, while citizens of the United Kingdom can stay for 6 months without a visa.

CUSTOMS REGULATIONS

Visitors are allowed to bring in, duty-free, 1 liter of alcohol and 200 cigarettes (or 50 cigars or 250g of tobacco). There are no restrictions on currencies brought into or taken out of Hong Kong.

Hong Kong Region

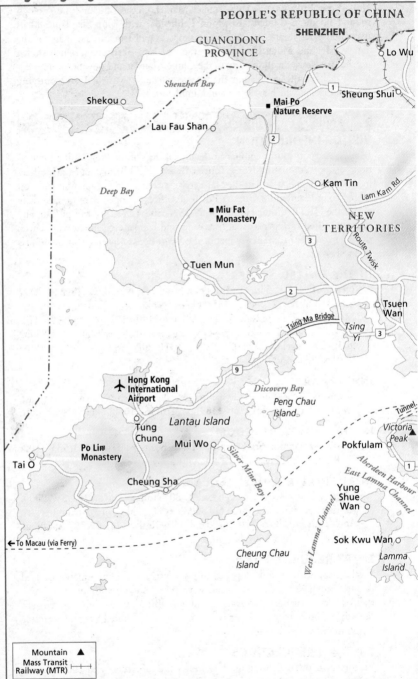

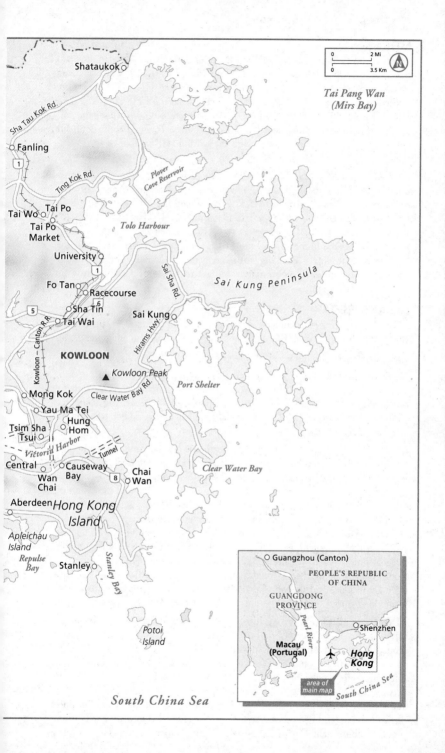

Shataukok

Tai Pang Wan
(Mirs Bay)

Sha Tau Kok Rd.

Fanling
1

Ting Kok Rd.

Plover
Cove Reservoir

Tai Po
Tai Wo
Tai Po
Market

Tolo Harbour

University
1

Sai Kung Peninsula

Fo Tan
Racecourse
6
Sha Tin
5
Tai Wai

Sai Sha Rd.

Sai Kung

Kowloon – Canton R.R.

Hirams Hwy.

KOWLOON

▲ Kowloon Peak

Port Shelter

Clear Water Bay Rd.

Mong Kok

Yau Ma Tei
Hung
Hom

Tsim Sha
Tsui

Victoria Harbor

Tunnel

Central

Clear Water Bay

Wan
Chai

Causeway
Bay
8
Chai
Wan

Aberdeen Hong Kong
Island

Apleichau
Island

Repulse
Bay

Stanley

Stanley Bay

Potoi
Island

South China Sea

Guangzhou (Canton)

PEOPLE'S REPUBLIC
OF CHINA

GUANGDONG
PROVINCE

Pearl River

Shenzhen

Macau
(Portugal)

✈ Hong
Kong

area of
main map

South China Sea

0   2 Mi
0   3.5 Km

77

MONEY

The basic unit of currency is the **Hong Kong dollar,** which is divided into 100 **cents.** Hong Kong dollars come in denominations of HK$10 (which is being phased out), HK$20, HK$50, HK$100, HK$500, and HK$1,000. Coins are minted in bronze for 10¢, 20¢, and 50¢ pieces; in silver for HK$1, HK$2, and HK$5; and in nickel and bronze for HK$10. In Hong Kong, you'll see the dollar sign ($) alone which denotes Hong Kong dollars. To avoid confusion, this guide identifies Hong Kong dollars with the symbol "HK$" (followed in parentheses by the U.S. dollar conversion).

CURRENCY EXCHANGE & RATES   The exchange rate is stable at approximately HK$7.80 to each US$1; however, at banks, hotels, and currency exchange offices, rates vary from HK$7.77 (at a bank) to HK$7.25 (at a hotel). For British readers, the exchange rate is approximately HK$12.25 to £1 (or HK$1 to 6 pence). You'll be charged a commission when exchanging **Traveler's Checks. ATMs** are found throughout Hong Kong (rates are favorable but the fees can be quite high). **Banking hours** are generally Monday through Friday from 9am to 4:30pm, and Saturday from 9am to 12:30pm. **Credit Cards** are accepted in most venues.

DEPARTURE TAX

Most plane tickets now include departure tax in their price, but if yours doesn't, you'll be required to pay HK$80 (US$10) for both adults and children.

WHEN TO GO

Hong Kong's peak tourist season used to be in the spring and fall, but now tourists are flocking to the territory year-round. No matter when you go, therefore, make hotel reservations in advance, particulary if you're arriving during the Chinese New Year or one of the festivals described below. Major conventions and trade fairs can also tie up the city's hotel rooms.

CLIMATE   Subtropical Hong Kong's weather is generally mild in winter and uncomfortably hot and humid in summer, with an average annual rainfall of 89 inches. The most pleasant time of year is late September to early December, when skies are clear and sunny, temperatures are in the 70s, and the humidity drops to 70%. January and February are the coldest months, with temperatures often in the 50s. In spring (Mar–May), the temperature can range between 60°F and 80°F (16°C and 27°C), and the humidity rises to about 84%, with fog and rain fairly common. Summer temperatures are often in the 90s, humidity can be 90% or more, and there's little or no relief even at night. This is when Hong Kong receives the most rain; it's also typhoon season but efficient warning systems are in place and the worst that tourists can expect is to be asked to stay inside for a time.

PUBLIC HOLIDAYS   Hong Kong has 17 public holidays a year, including some of the festivals described below. Because most shops, restaurants, and attractions remain open except during the Chinese New Year, the holidays should not cause any inconvenience to visitors. Banks, however, do close.

Public holidays are: New Year's Day (Jan 1), Chinese Lunar New Year (2 days between the end of Jan through mid-Feb), Easter (Good Fri, Sat, Easter Sun, and Easter Mon), Ching Ming Festival (early Apr), Labor Day (May 1), Buddha's Birthday (end of Apr or May), Tuen Ng Festival (Dragon Boat Festival, June), Establishment Day of the Special Administrative Region (Hong Kong's return to China; June), day following the Mid-Autumn Festival (Sept), National Day (Oct 1), Chung Yeung Festival (Oct), Christmas Day (Dec 25), and the first weekday after Christmas.

HEALTH CONCERNS

No shots or inoculations are required for entry to Hong Kong. Health facility standards are high.

Generally, you're safe eating anywhere in Hong Kong, even at roadside food stalls. Stay clear of local oysters and shellfish, however, and remember that many restaurants outside the major hotels and tourist areas include MSG in their dishes as a matter of course.

GETTING THERE
BY PLANE

Hong Kong is a major hub in the region with flights connecting to most destinations in Asia and the world.

Hong Kong International Airport (© 852/2181 0000) is located about 32.2km (20 miles) from Hong Kong's central business district. The arrivals hall is rife with information and ground transport access. The quickest way to get to downtown Hong Kong is via the sleek **Airport Express Line** (© 852/2881 8888). Trains run every 10 minutes between 6am and 1am, and connect with Kowloon and Hong Kong Island. The cost is between HK$90 and HK$113 (US$12–US$13). Shuttles connect the major train stops and downtown hotels.

The **Airport Shuttle Bus**(© 852/2735 7823) provides door-to-door service to major hotels for HK$120 (US$16), with buses departing every 30 minutes. **Cityflyer Airbuses** (© 852/2873 0818) offer similar but slower service with more stops for HK$33 to HK$45 (US$4.30–US$5.85).

A taxi from the airport to downtown will cost between HK$300 and HK$400 (US$39–US$52).

BY TRAIN

There is convenient rail connection from Hong Kong and all major stops in China. Remember that you'll need a Chinese visa (easily done in Hong Kong).

DEPARTING
BY BOAT

Hong Kong connects with mainland China and Macau by frequent ferry service. Tickets are sold at all ferry terminals and at the Shun Tak Centre 3/F, 200 Connaught Rd. Central, Hong Kong, the TurboJET Service Counter (Sheung Wan MTR Station Exit D), the Macau airport, and China Travel Service branches. Telephone reservations via credit card can be made up to 28 days in advance at © 852/2921 6688.

GETTING AROUND

Hong Kong is easy to navigate, with street, bus, and subway signs clearly marked in English. In addition, the city of Hong Kong is so compact and its public transportation system is so efficient and extensive that it's no problem at all to zip from Tsim Sha Tsui to Causeway Bay for a meal or some shopping.

Each mode of transportation—bus, ferry, tram, and train/subway—has its own fare system and requires you carry change for the exact fare; however, the **Octopus** is a reloadable electronic smart card that covers all for HK$150 (US$20) (that includes a HK$50/US$6.50 refundable deposit).

BY SUBWAY Hong Kong's **Mass Transit Railway (MTR)** is modern and easy to use and consists of four color-coded lines. Single-ticket, one-way fares range from HK$4 to HK$26 (US50¢–US$3.40), depending on the distance. Plastic, credit card–size tickets are inserted into slots at entry turnstiles.

BY TRAIN The **Kowloon-Canton Railway (KCR) East Rail** is useful for traveling north from Kowloon to the New Territories and China and links with the MTR subway.

BY BUS Hong Kong buses are a delight—especially the British-style double-deckers—and are good for traveling to places where subways don't go, such as to the southern part of Hong Kong Island and throughout the New Territories. Buses run from about 6am to midnight, with fares ranging from HK$1.20 to HK$45 (US15¢–US$5.85). Unless you have an Octopus card, good on most buses (see above), *you must have the exact fare,* which you deposit into a box as you get on. Drivers often don't speak English, so you might want to have someone at your hotel write down your destination in Chinese. In rural areas, you must flag down a bus to make it stop.

BY TRAM Tramlines, found only along the north end of Hong Kong Island, are a great nostalgic way to travel through the Western District, Central, Wan Chai, and Causeway Bay. Established in 1904, these old narrow, double-decker affairs clank their way from Kennedy Town in the west to Shau Kei Wan in the east, with one branch making a detour to Happy Valley. Enter the trams from the back and try to get a front-row seat on the top deck. Regardless of how far you go, you pay the exact fare of HK$2 (US25¢) into a little tin box next to the bus driver or with an Octopus card as you exit. Trams run daily from 6am to 1am.

BY FERRY A 5-minute trip across Victoria Harbour on one of the white-and-green ferries of the Star Ferry Company, in operation since 1898, is one of the most celebrated rides in the world and one of Hong Kong's top attractions. It costs only HK$1.70 (US22¢) for ordinary (2nd) class; if you really want to splurge, it's HK$2.20 (US28¢) for first class on the upper deck. Ferries ply the waters between Central and Tsim Sha Tsui daily from 6:30am to 11:30pm. Don't miss it. Other boats connect with Wan Chai and Hung Tom.

BY TAXI As a rule, taxi drivers in Hong Kong are strictly controlled and fairly honest. Taxis free to pick up passengers display a red "for hire" flag in the windshield during the day and a lighted taxi sign on the roof at night. Fares start at HK$15 (US$1.95) for the first 2km (1¼ miles) and then are HK$1.40 (US18¢) for each 200m (275 yards). Luggage costs an extra HK$5 (US65¢) per piece, and taxis ordered by phone add a HK$5 (US65¢) surcharge. Trips through tunnels cost extra: HK$20 (US$2.60) for the Cross-Harbour Tunnel, HK$30 (US$3.90) for the Eastern Harbour Crossing, HK$45 (US$5.85) for the Western Harbour Tunnel, and HK$5 (US65¢) for Aberdeen.

 FAST FACTS: Hong Kong

American Express American Express offices are located up on the first floor of the Henley Building, 5 Queen's Rd. Central, in the Central District (© **852/2110 2008**), and at 48 Cameron Rd. (© **852/2926 1606**) in Tsim Sha Tsui. Both offices are open Monday through Friday from 9am to 6pm, and Saturday from 9am to 12:30pm.

Business Hours Banks are generally open Monday through Friday from 9am to 4:30pm, and Saturday from 9am to 12:30pm.

Most business offices are open Monday through Friday from 9am to 5pm, with lunch hour from 1 to 2pm; Saturday business hours are generally 9am to 1pm.

Most shops are open 7 days a week and are open as late as 10pm. Most bars stay open until 2am; some stay open until dawn.

Doctors & Dentists Most first-class hotels have medical; otherwise, your concierge can refer you to a doctor or dentist. If it's an emergency, dial ℂ **999.**

Electricity Hong Kong uses 220 volts alternating current (AC) at 50 cycles with a three-prong system. Most hotels offer adapters.

Embassies/Consulates Because visa, passport, and other departments might have limited open hours, telephone for exact opening hours. **United States:** 26 Garden Rd., Central District (ℂ **852/2523 9011;** ℂ 852/2841 2211 for the American Citizens Service). **Canada:** 12th–14th Floor of Tower One, Exchange Square, 8 Connaught Place, Central District (ℂ **852/2810 4321). U.K.:** 1 Supreme Court Rd., Central District (ℂ **852/2901 3000;** ℂ 852/2901 3222 for passport inquiries). **Australia:** 23rd and 24th floors of Harbour Centre, 25 Harbour Rd., Wan Chai, on Hong Kong Island (ℂ **852/2827 8881). New Zealand:** 65th floor of Central Plaza, 18 Harbour Rd., Wan Chai (ℂ **852/2525 5044).**

Emergencies All emergency calls are free—just dial ℂ **999** for police, fire, or ambulance.

Hospitals The following hospitals can help you around the clock: **Queen Mary Hospital,** 102 Pokfulam Rd., Hong Kong Island (ℂ **852/2855 3111);** and **Queen Elizabeth Hospital,** 30 Gascoigne Rd., Kowloon (ℂ **852/2958 8888).**

Internet Access All upper range hotels in Hong Kong are equipped with in-room dataports and many have business centers with Internet. Outside hotels, **Itfans,** 12–13 Jubilee St., Central (near Central Market and HKTB), is open 24 hours with 100 computers, charging a HK$10 (US$1.30) membership fee and HK$18 ($2.35) per hour at peak times. **Pacific Coffee** is a chain of coffee shops with access; try their store above Hong Kong Station in Central (ℂ **852/2868 5100),** open Monday to Saturday 7am to 10pm, and Sunday 8:30am to 9pm.

Newspapers The *South China Morning Post* and the *Hong Kong iMail* (which carries mostly financial news) are the two local English-language daily newspapers. Most other international papers are available.

Pharmacies One of the best-known pharmacies in Hong Kong is Watson's, with more than 90 branches, most of them open 9am to 10pm.

Police You can reach the police for an emergency by dialing ℂ **999,** the same number as for a fire or an ambulance. There's a crime hotline (ℂ **852/2527 7177),** a 24-hour service that also handles complaints against taxis.

Post Offices Airmail letters up to 20g and postcards cost HK$3 (US40¢) to the United States or Europe. Most hotels have stamps and can mail your letters for you. Post offices are open Monday to Friday 9:30am to 5pm, and Saturday 9:30am to 1pm. The main post office is at 2 Connaught Place, Central District, Hong Kong Island, next to the Star Ferry concourse (② 852/2921 2222). On the Kowloon side, the main post office is at 10 Middle Rd., which is 1 block north of Salisbury Road (② 852/2366 4111).

Safety Hong Kong is a safe destination, but general rules of prudence apply. Pickpockets are a concern as anywhere, but violent crime is not common. If you need to carry your passport or large amounts of money, it's a good idea to conceal everything in a money belt. Don't leave your passport at your hotel unless it's in a room safe or safety-deposit box.

Taxes Hotels add a 10% service charge and a 3% government tax to your bill. Restaurants and bars automatically add a 10% service charge, but there is no tax. There's an airport departure tax of HK$80 (US$10) for adults and children older than 12, but this is usually—though not always—included in your ticket price.

Telephone The international country code for Hong Kong is 852.

For directory assistance, dial ② 1081 for local numbers and ② 10013 for international inquiries. Hotels offer direct dialing and public phones with international capability (using a prepaid phone card) are aplenty.

To make a direct-dial international call, dial ② 001 followed by the country code.

Alternatively, you can make a collect call from any public or private phone by dialing ② 10010. For matters pertaining to international calls, call ② 10013.

Time Zone Hong Kong is 8 hours ahead of Greenwich Mean Time, 13 hours ahead of New York, 14 hours ahead of Chicago, and 16 hours ahead of Los Angeles. Because Hong Kong does not have a daylight saving time, subtract 1 hour from the above times in the summer.

Tipping Even though restaurants and bars automatically add a 10% service charge to your bill, you're expected to leave small change for the waiter. A general rule of thumb is to leave 5%, but it's 10% for fine restaurants. It's also common practice to tip taxi drivers by rounding up the bill and bellhops between HK$5 and HK$10 (US$1.30–US$2.60).

3 Where to Stay

With the recent drop in international tourism, travelers can find great deals on hotels and Hong Kong is no exception. Rates listed below are only a point of departure for budget hunting. Contact hotels directly for the best rates. Hong Kong's many famous properties center around the Kowloon area (a short ferry-ride from downtown). Note that a 10% service charge and 3% tax is added to any bill.

KOWLOON
EXPENSIVE
Hotel Inter-Continental Hong Kong (formerly The Regent Hong Kong) ✸✸✸ It was no small shock when this famous property became the flagship Inter-Continental in 2001, but management has taken great pains to ensure continuity, maintaining the same staff and calling in the hotel's original

Kowloon

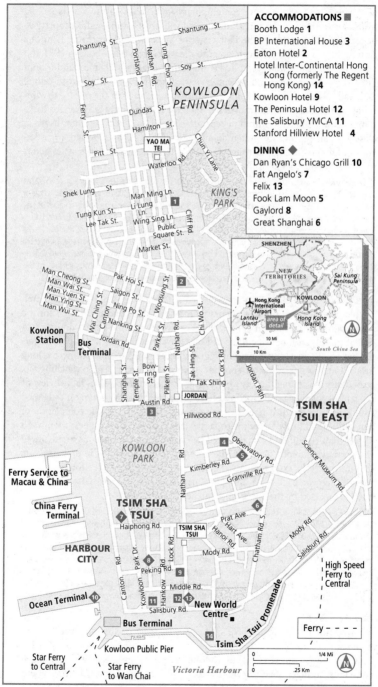

ACCOMMODATIONS ■
Booth Lodge **1**
BP International House **3**
Eaton Hotel **2**
Hotel Inter-Continental Hong Kong (formerly The Regent Hong Kong) **14**
Kowloon Hotel **9**
The Peninsula Hotel **12**
The Salisbury YMCA **11**
Stanford Hillview Hotel **4**

DINING ◆
Dan Ryan's Chicago Grill **10**
Fat Angelo's **7**
Felix **13**
Fook Lam Moon **5**
Gaylord **8**
Great Shanghai **6**

design team to create a more contemporary look. With half its guests hailing from North America, the Inter-Continental still has what made this property so beloved in the first place: the best views of Victoria Harbour from Tsim Sha Tsui. In fact, you can't get much closer to the water than this—built in 1981 and rising 17 stories, the hotel is located at the water's edge on reclaimed land. About 70% of its rooms command sweeping views of the harbor, with floor-to-ceiling and wall-to-wall windows, while less expensive rooms face the outdoor swimming pool and landscaped sun terrace. Notable hotel features are spacious bathrooms with a sunken bathtub, a separate shower unit, and adjoining walk-in closets; an air-purification system in all guest rooms; a spa renowned for its jetlag and Oriental healing treatments; and wireless broadband that enables guests to access the Internet even from poolside.

18 Salisbury Rd., Tsim Sha Tsui, Kowloon, Hong Kong. © 800/327-0200 in the U.S. and Canada, or 852/2721 1211. Fax 852/2739 4546. www.interconti.com. 514 units. HK$3,100–HK$4,500 (US$403–US$584) single or double; HK$700 (US$91) extra for Club Floors; from HK$5,500 (US$714) junior suite. Children under 18 stay free in parents' room. AE, DC, DISC, MC, V. MTR: Tsim Sha Tsui. **Amenities:** 4 restaurants (seafood, Cantonese, steaks, Continental); bar; lounge; outdoor pool and whirlpools overlooking Victoria Harbour; fitness room (open 24 hr.); spa; concierge; limousine service; business center; upscale shopping arcade; 24-hr. room service; massage; babysitting; same-day laundry/dry cleaning service; nonsmoking rooms; executive-level rooms; house doctor. *In room:* A/C, satellite TV w/pay movies, wireless broadband service, minibar, coffeemaker, hair dryer, safe, bathroom scale, and complimentary welcoming tea, fruit, and bottled water.

The Peninsula Hotel 🏰🏰🏰 *Finds*   This is Hong Kong's most famous hotel, *the* place to stay if you are an incurable romantic and have a penchant for the historical. Built in 1928, it exudes elegance, from its white-gloved doormen to one of the largest limousine fleets of Rolls-Royces in the world. Its lobby, reminiscent of a Parisian palace with high gilded ceilings, pillars, and palms, has long been Hong Kong's foremost spot for afternoon tea and people-watching. Its restaurants are among the city's best. After The Peninsula lost its fabled view of the harbor following construction of the unsightly Space Museum on reclaimed land across the street, it remedied the problem in 1993 with the completion of a magnificent 32-story tower, with fantastic harbor views from guest rooms and its top-floor restaurant Felix, designed by Philippe Starck. Spacious rooms are so wonderfully equipped that even jaded travelers are likely to be impressed. Note that it's worth the extra money for a stunning harbor view in the tower, because views facing the back are a disappointment and those in the older part of the hotel are marred by the Space Museum across the street.

Salisbury Rd., Tsim Sha Tsui, Kowloon, Hong Kong. © 800/462-7899 in the U.S. and Canada, or 852/2920 2888. Fax 852/2722 4170. www.peninsula.com. 300 units. HK$3,000–HK$4,900 (US$390–US$637) single or double; from HK$5,600 (US$727) suite. AE, DC, MC, V. MTR: Tsim Sha Tsui. **Amenities:** 6 restaurants (French, Pacific Rim crossover, Continental, Swiss, Cantonese, Japanese); 2 bars; lounge; gorgeous indoor pool w/sun terrace overlooking the harbor; health club; spa; concierge; limousine service; business center; designer-brand shopping arcade; salon; 24-hr. room service; massage; babysitting; same-day laundry/dry cleaning service; nonsmoking rooms; in-house nurse. *In room:* A/C, cable/satellite TV w/CD/DVD player (free CDs and movies available), fax, dataport, minibar, hair dryer, safe, bathroom scale, complimentary welcoming tea and fruit.

MODERATE

BP International House *Kids*   The word *House* in this accommodation's name is misleading, because it's actually a 25-story hotel, with a spacious but utilitarian lobby. It caters mainly to tour and school groups as well as budget-conscious business travelers, all of which give it a dormitorylike atmosphere. Built in 1993 at the north end of Kowloon Park, it's just a stone's throw from the park's indoor and outdoor public swimming pools and a short walk to a playground, making it good for families. The park's many paths also make it popular with joggers. Guest rooms, located on the 14th to 25th floors, are clean, pleasant, and modern. Although it's located inland, the best and priciest rooms on higher floors offer good views of the harbor (though future buildings will probably eclipse those views). Business travelers usually opt for one of the corporate rooms on the top five floors. There are also very simple family rooms equipped with bunk beds that sleep four for HK$1,340 (US$170).

8 Austin Rd., Tsim Sha Tsui, Kowloon, Hong Kong. © **800/223-5652** in the U.S. and Canada, or 852/2376 1111. Fax 852/2376 1333. www.bpih.com.hk. 535 units. HK$990–HK$1,450 (US$129–US$188) single; HK$1,100–HK$1,500 (US$143–US$195) double; HK$1,600–HK$1,800 (US$208–US$234) corporate double room; from HK$3,100 (US$403) suite. Children under 13 stay free in parents' room. Rates include buffet breakfast. AE, DC, MC, V. MTR: Jordan. **Amenities:** coffee shop; lounge; room service (6:30am–10pm); babysitting, coin-op laundry; laundry/dry cleaning service; nonsmoking rooms; executive-level rooms. In room: A/C, satellite TV w/pay movies.

Eaton Hotel ★★ *Finds* This accommodation has more class and facilities than most in its price range, making it one of my top picks. A handsome 21-story brick building, located above a shopping complex not far from the Temple Street Night Market, it features one of the longest hotel escalators I've ever seen—it takes guests straight up to the fourth-floor lobby, where a cheerful and efficient staff awaits your arrival. The lobby lounge is bright and cheerful, with a four-story glass-enclosed atrium that overlooks a garden terrace with a water cascade, where you can sit outside with drinks in nice weather. Another plus is the small but nicely done rooftop pool with sunning terrace. Guest rooms are small but welcoming, with all the basic creature comforts. I especially like the innovatively designed (and highest-priced) deluxe rooms, with curved, floor-to-ceiling windows giving views of a distant harbor.

380 Nathan Rd., Yau Ma Tei, Kowloon, Hong Kong. © **800/207-6900** in the U.S. and Canada, or 852/2782 1818. Fax 852/2782 5563. www.eaton-hotel.com. 460 units. HK$1,430–HK$2,130 (US$97–US$338) single or double; HK$2,430–HK$2,730 (US$316–US$355) executive room. AE, DC, MC, V. MTR: Jordan. **Amenities:** 3 restaurants (Cantonese, Asian/Western, coffee shop); bar, lounge; small outdoor pool; exercise room; concierge; business center; shopping arcade; room service (7am–1am); babysitting; same-day laundry/dry cleaning service; nonsmoking rooms. In room: A/C, satellite TV w/pay movies, minibar, coffeemaker, hair dryer, safe.

Kowloon Hotel ★ If you like high-tech hotels but don't want to pay a fortune, the Kowloon is the place for you. Its location is great, right behind The Peninsula and just a few minutes' walk from the Star Ferry. But the hotel's main selling point is that it has long offered the most technically advanced rooms in its price category, each equipped with an interactive telecenter, which allows free access to the Internet and such information as up-to-the-minute flight details and incoming messages, and contains video games. In addition, the telecenter, with word-processing capability, interfaces with in-room fax machines that double as printers. Guests can also retrieve voice mail messages electronically from outside the hotel. The downside: Rooms are minuscule and are plagued by traffic noise. Although they have V-shape bay windows, allowing unobstructed views up and down the street, The Peninsula's new tower has robbed harbor views from all but the most expensive rooms.

19–21 Nathan Rd., Tsim Sha Tsui, Kowloon, Hong Kong. © **800/262-9467** in the U.S., or 852/2929 2888. Fax 852/2739 9811. www.peninsula.com. 736 units. HK$1,300–HK$2,550 (US$169–US$331) single; HK$1,400–HK$2,650 (US$182–US$344) double; from HK$3,700 (US$480) suite. AE, DC, MC, V. MTR: Tsim Sha Tsui. **Amenities:** 3 restaurants (Italian, Cantonese, international buffet); bar; access to nearby YMCA pool and a nearby health club (fee charged); limousine service; business center; shopping arcade; room service (6:30am–2am); babysitting; same-day laundry/dry cleaning service; nonsmoking rooms. In room: A/C, satellite TV w/access to Internet, fax, minibar, coffeemaker, hair dryer, safe.

INEXPENSIVE

Booth Lodge ✪ *Finds*   About a 30-minute walk to the Star Ferry, but close to the Jade Market, Temple Street Night Market, Ladies' Market, and MTR Station, Booth Lodge is located just off Nathan Road on the seventh floor of the Salvation Army building. Recently renovated, it has a comfortable lobby and an adjacent coffee shop offering very reasonably priced dinner buffets. Rooms, all twins or doubles and either standard rooms or larger deluxe rooms, are spotlessly clean. Some that face Nathan Road have views of a harbor in the distance, though those facing the hillside are quieter. If you're looking for inexpensive yet reliable lodging in a convenient location, this is a good bet. *A bonus:* Local telephone calls are free.

11 Wing Sing Lane, Yau Ma Tei, Kowloon, Hong Kong. ✆ 852/2771 9266. Fax 852/2385 1140. www.booth lodge.netfirms.com. 53 units. HK$620–HK$1,500 (US$81–US$195) single or double. Rates include buffet breakfast. AE, MC, V. MTR: Yau Ma Tei. **Amenities:** coffee shop (international); tour desk; laundry/dry cleaning service. *In room:* A/C, TV, fridge, hair dryer.

The Salisbury YMCA ✪✪✪ *Kids*   For decades, the overwhelming no. 1 choice among low-cost accommodations has been the YMCA on Salisbury Road, right next to The Peninsula Hotel on the waterfront and just a 2-minute walk from both the Star Ferry and the subway station. It offers 19 single rooms (none with harbor view) and more than 280 twins (the most expensive twins provide great harbor views), as well as suites with and without harbor views that are perfect for families. Although simple in decor, these rooms are on par with those at more expensively priced hotels in terms of in-room amenities. For budget travelers, there are also 14 dormitory-style rooms, available only to visitors who have been in Hong Kong fewer than 10 days. Great for families is its sports facility boasting two indoor swimming pools (one a lap pool, the other a children's pool) and a fitness gym, two squash courts, and an indoor climbing wall, as well as a fourth-floor terrace with play equipment for children. Make reservations in advance, especially if booking for April or October.

Salisbury Rd., Tsim Sha Tsui, Kowloon, Hong Kong. ✆ 852/800 537-8483 in the U.S. and Canada, or 852/2268-7000 (852/2268 7888 for reservations). Fax 852/2739 9315. www.ymcahk.org.hk. 363 units. HK$710 (US$92) single; HK$790–HK$990 (US$103–US$129) double; from HK$1,300 (US$169) suite. Dormitory bed HK$210 (US$27). AE, DC, MC, V. MTR: Tsim Sha Tsui. **Amenities:** 2 restaurants (international buffet, international cafeteria); 2 indoor pools; squash courts; exercise room; Jacuzzi; sauna; tour desk; room service (7am–10pm); massage; babysitting; laundry/dry cleaning service; coin-op laundry; nonsmoking rooms; climbing wall. *In room:* A/C, satellite/cable TV w/complimentary in-house movies, dataport, minibar, coffeemaker, hair dryer, safe.

Stanford Hillview Hotel ✪ *Finds*   This small, intimate hotel, built in 1991, is near the heart of Tsim Sha Tsui, and yet it's a world away from it, located on top of a hill in the shade of some huge banyan trees, next to the Royal Observatory with its colonial building and greenery. Knutsford Terrace, an alley with trendy bars and restaurants, is just a minute's walk away. Its lobby is quiet and subdued (quite a contrast to most Hong Kong hotels), and its staff is friendly and accommodating. The most expensive rooms are on higher floors; ask for one that faces the observatory. All in all, it's a very civilized place, but it is a hike uphill to the hotel.

13–17 Observatory Rd., Tsim Sha Tsui, Kowloon, Hong Kong. ✆ 800/858-8471 in the U.S., or 852/2722 7822. Fax 852/2723 3718. www.stanfordhillview.com. 163 units. HK$880–HK$1,580 (US$114–US$205) single or double. AE, DC, MC, V. MTR: Tsim Sha Tsui. **Amenities:** Restaurant (international buffet); lounge; outdoor golf-driving nets; small exercise room; business center; 24-hr. room service; babysitting; same-day

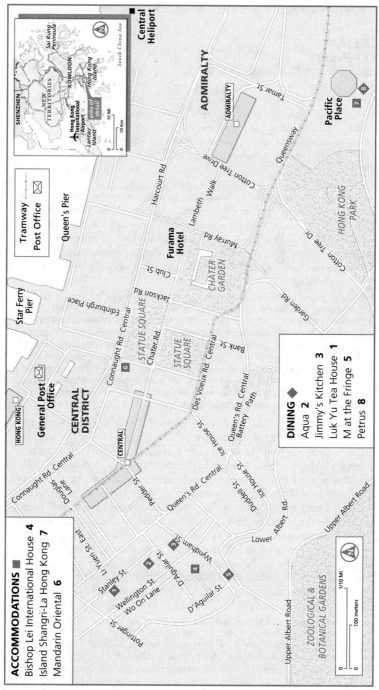

ACCOMMODATIONS ■
Bishop Lei International House **4**
Island Shangri-La Hong Kong **7**
Mandarin Oriental **6**

DINING ◆
Aqua **2**
Jimmy's Kitchen **3**
Luk Yu Tea House **1**
M at the Fringe **5**
Petrus **8**

Tramway
Post Office ⊠

laundry/dry cleaning service; nonsmoking rooms. *In room:* A/C, cable TV w/pay movies, minibar, coffeemaker, hair dryer.

CENTRAL
EXPENSIVE

Island Shangri-La Hong Kong ★★★ *(Finds)*   Hong Kong Island's tallest hotel offers the ultimate in extravagance and luxury, rivaling the grand hotels of Europe. More than 700 Viennese chandeliers, lush Tai Ping carpets, artistic flower arrangements, and paintings and artworks adorn the hotel. The 17-story atrium, which stretches from the 39th floor to the 56th floor, features a mar-velous 16-story-high Chinese painting, drawn by 40 artists from Beijing and believed to be the largest landscape painting in the world. Also in the atrium is a private lounge open only to hotel guests and a two-story old world–style library. The hotel itself is enhanced by the connecting Pacific Place shopping center; across the street is Hong Kong Park. Rooms, among the largest in Hong Kong, face either the Peak or the spectacular Victoria Harbour. Fresh flowers and teddy bears placed on pillows during nightly turndown are nice touches. Guests paying rack rates receive such additional services as free transportation from and to the airport, free laundry and dry cleaning throughout their stay, complimentary American or continental breakfast, free local telephone calls, and 6pm late checkout.

Pacific Place, Supreme Court Rd., Central, Hong Kong. © **800/942-5050** in the U.S. and Canada, or 852/2877 3838. Fax 852/2521 8742. www.shangri-la.com. 565 units. HK$2,500–$HK$3,650 (US$325–US$474) single; HK$2,700–HK$3,850 (US$351–US$500) double; from HK$5,800 (US$753) suite. Children under 18 stay free in parents' room. AE, DC, MC, V. MTR: Admiralty. **Amenities:** 5 restaurants (French, lobster/seafood, Can-tonese, Japanese, buffet); 2 lounges; outdoor heated pool big enough for swimming laps; health club (open 24 hr.); spa; Jacuzzi; sauna; steam bath; concierge; tour desk; limousine service; business center (open 24 hr.); adjoining shopping arcade; salon; 24-hr. room service; babysitting, same-day laundry/dry cleaning service; nonsmoking rooms; executive-level rooms; medical clinic; free shuttle to Queen's Pier in Central and Con-vention Centre. *In room:* A/C, satellite TV w/pay movies, fax, dataport; minibar, coffeemaker, hair dryer, safe, bathroom scale, complimentary welcoming tea and fruit.

Mandarin Oriental ★★   With so many newer hotels in Hong Kong, the Mandarin, a 25-story 1963 landmark, seems like a familiar old-timer. Truth be told, it's starting to look like an old-timer as well, with an increasingly shabby exterior, a lobby that seems dated, and a disappointingly small indoor pool. Still, the Mandarin is famed for its service and consistently rates as one of the top hotels in the world. Because of its great location in the heart of Central (not far from Star Ferry), it attracts a mostly business clientele, yet it's also a good choice for those wanting to escape the tourist crowds of Tsim Sha Tsui. In addition, the Mandarin's restaurants are among the best in Hong Kong. Elegant rooms, on the small side, come mostly with balconies (rare in Hong Kong and admittedly a bit noisy) and face either the harbor (complete with binoculars) or inland. Rooms feature all you could possibly want, including a keyboard that allows you to con-nect to the Internet through your TV, but if you are still in need of something, the staff will make every effort to fulfill your wishes.

5 Connaught Rd., Central, Hong Kong. © **800/526-6566** in the U.S. and Canada, or 852/2522 0111. Fax 852/2810 6190. www.mandarinoriental.com. 541 units. HK$2,950–HK$4,200 (US$383–US$545) single; HK$3,200–HK$4,450 (US$416–US$578) double; from HK$5,500 (US$714) suite. AE, DC, MC, V. MTR: Central. **Amenities:** 4 restaurants (Continental, Franco-Asian, Cantonese, coffee shop); 3 bars; lounge; indoor pool; health club (open 24 hr.); Jacuzzi; sauna; concierge; tour desk; limousine service; business center; shopping arcade; salon; 24-hr. room service; babysitting, same-day laundry/dry cleaning service; nonsmoking rooms; Cuban-style cigar divan. *In room:* A/C, satellite TV w/on-demand pay movies and Internet keyboard, dataport, minibar, hair dryer, safe, bathroom scale, and complimentary welcoming tea, fruit, and shoe shine.

MID-LEVELS
MODERATE

Bishop Lei International House 𝓕 *Finds*   If you want to pretend that you live in Hong Kong, this is the place for you. It's located in the Mid-Levels, popular with expats and Chinese working professionals, about halfway up Victoria Peak, but it is not as convenient as other hotels. However, the hotel makes up for its out-of-the-way location with free shuttle service to Central, and a half-dozen city buses stop outside its door. Opened in 1996, it offers tiny standard rooms (with even tinier bathrooms, most with showers instead of tubs) that have large windows letting in lots of sunshine but facing inland. If you can, spring for a more expensive room with fantastic harbor views and video players (video rental shops are located nearby), appealing to the hotel's many long-staying business travelers (long-term packages are available). In any case, in acknowledgment that rooms are small, there's a reading room for relaxation and, surprising for a hotel this size, also a small pool and exercise room. If the frenetic pace of Hong Kong sets you on edge, you'll find this a nice retreat.

4 Robinson Rd., Mid-Levels, Hong Kong. 𝓒 **852/2868 0828.** Fax 852/2862 1551. www.bishopleihtl.com.hk. 203 units. HK$1,080 (US$140) single; HK$1,280–1,680 (US$166–US$218) double; from HK$1,880 (US$244) suite. AE, DC, MC, V. Bus: Nos. 3B, 12, 12M, 23, 23A, and 40 to Robinson Rd. **Amenities:** Coffee shop; small outdoor pool; small exercise room; business center; 24-hr. room service; same-day laundry/dry cleaning service; nonsmoking rooms; free shuttle bus to Central. *In room:* A/C, cable TV, dataport, minibar, coffeemaker, hair dryer, safe.

CAUSEWAY BAY/WAN CHAI
EXPENSIVE

Grand Hyatt Hong Kong 𝓕𝓕𝓕 *Kids*   In a city with so many first-class hotels, sooner or later a hotel had to exceed all the others in opulence and grandeur. Walking into the lobby of the Hyatt International's Asian flagship hotel is like walking into the salon of a 1930s Art Deco luxury ocean liner, with huge black granite columns, massive flower arrangements, bubbling fountains, and furniture and statuettes reminiscent of that era. It's not the kind of place you want to be seen on a bad hair day. Located on the waterfront near the Convention Centre and only a 5-minute walk from the Wan Chai Star Ferry pier that delivers passengers to Tsim Sha Tsui, it offers smart-looking, contemporary rooms, equipped with cordless keyboards to access the Internet through an interactive TV, coffee-table books, and marble bathrooms with separate bathtub and shower areas. Some 70% of the rooms provide a harbor view, while the rest have views of Hong Kong's largest outdoor hotel pool and garden with partial glimpses of the harbor.

1 Harbour Rd., Wan Chai, Hong Kong. 𝓒 **800/233-1234** in the U.S. and Canada, or 852/2588 1234. Fax 852/ 2802 0677. www.hongkong.hyatt.com. 572 units. HK$3,600–HK$4,300 (US$467–US$558) single; HK$3,850– HK$4,550 (US$500–US$584) double; HK$4,350–HK$4,650 (US$565.50–US$604) Regency Club executive floor double; from HK$6,400 (US$831) suite. Children under 12 stay free in parents' room (maximum: 3 persons per room). AE, DC, MC, V. MTR: Wan Chai. **Amenities:** 4 restaurants (Italian, Cantonese, Continental, Japanese); lounge; nightclub; huge outdoor pool (shared w/adjacent Renaissance Harbour View Hotel and closed in winter); children's splash pool; golf driving range; 2 outdoor tennis courts; health club; concierge; tour desk; limousine service; business center; salon; 24-hr. room service; babysitting, same-day laundry/dry cleaning service; nonsmoking rooms; executive-level rooms; free shuttle to Central, Causeway Bay, and Admiralty. *In room:* A/C, satellite TV w/keyboard for Internet access and on-demand pay movies, fax, dataport; minibar, coffeemaker, hair dryer, safe, bathroom scale, complimentary bottled water.

MODERATE

Best Western Rosedale on the Park 𝓕𝓕 *Finds*   This hotel has lots going for it, including the fact that it opened in 2001, giving it a more contemporary, high-tech edge over older properties in the area. Targeting corporate accounts, it sweetens the deal with several innovative incentives, including complimentary broadband Internet service in each room, cordless phones, in-house mobile phones that allow you to receive calls throughout the hotel, free drinks in the fridge, and a lounge with computers and free Internet access. Only 13 rooms on each floor give it an atmosphere like a boutique hotel. Rooms are small but have everything you need, though note that the least expensive "superior" rooms are on lower floors and face another building. Some rooms on the 31st-floor executive level have side views of the harbor (you have to be standing at the window to see it), but the real benefits here are the microwaves and kitchen utensils, making this floor a good bet for long-staying guests.

8 Shelter St., Causeway Bay, Hong Kong. ℂ 800/528-1234 in the U.S. and Canada, or 852/2127 8888. Fax 852/2127 3333. www.rosedale.com.hk. 274 units. HK$1,180–HK$1,280 (US$153–US$166) single; HK$1,280–HK$1,380 (US$166–US$179) double; HK$1,580 (US$205) executive double; from HK$1,980 (US$257) suite. Children under 18 can stay free in parents' room. AE, DC, MC, V. MTR: Causeway Bay. **Amenities:** 2 restaurants (Cantonese, international/fusion); lounge; small fitness room; business center; room service (6:30am–midnight); babysitting; same-day laundry/dry cleaning service; nonsmoking rooms. *In room:* A/C, cable TV w/pay movies, dataport, fridge, coffeemaker, hair dryer, iron/ironing board, safe, and complimentary soda, beer, and bottled water.

Harbour View International House *(Value)*   Opened in 1986, this YMCA occupies a prime spot on the Wan Chai waterfront, right next to the Hong Kong Arts Centre and not far from the convention center. Rooms, all twin or double beds, are rather stylish for a YMCA, attracting guests mostly from mainland China and North America. Best of all, more than half the rooms face the harbor with V-shape windows, making this the cheapest place on Hong Kong Island with great views. Rooms that face inland are even cheaper.

4 Harbour Rd., Wan Chai, Hong Kong. ℂ 852/2802 0111. Fax 852/2802 9063. www.harbour.ymca.org.hk. 320 units. HK$1,200–HK$1,750 (US$156–US$227) single or double. Children under 12 stay free in parents' room. AE, DC, MC, V. MTR: Wan Chai. **Amenities:** Restaurant (Chinese/Western); lounge; tour desk; room service (10:30am–10pm); babysitting; laundry/dry cleaning service; nonsmoking rooms. *In room:* A/C, cable TV, minibar.

NEAR THE AIRPORT
MODERATE

Regal Airport Hotel *(★) (Kids)*   Opened in 1998 as Hong Kong's largest hotel and the only hotel at Hong Kong International Airport, this Regal chain hotel is only a 5-minute walk from the airport via covered walkway. Standout facilities include a 24-hour cafe offering Asian and Western fare (unique for its rotating art gallery, which moves through the restaurant on tracks) and a very good children's recreation room with games ranging from slides, toys, and books for youngsters to air hockey, pool, and electronic games for teenagers. Otherwise, though the hotel makes a conscious effort to brighten its interior with lots of mirrors and glass, including a glass dome over the lobby and gleaming black floors that reflect light, it can't seem to escape its airport connection; the futuristic decor (including a flying saucer–shape stage for live music in the lobby) also reminds me of a space ship. Captain Kirk would feel right at home. Guest rooms are large and soundproofed, with modern furniture in eye-popping colors of purple, red, or lime green; all but the cheapest also have TVs with keyboards for Internet access and electronic games.

9 Cheong Tat Rd., Chek Lap Kok, Hong Kong. ℂ 800/222-8888 in the U.S. and Canada, or 852/2286 8888. Fax 852/2286 8686. www.regalhotel.com. 1,100 units. HK$1,700–HK$2,400 (US$221–US$312) single; HK$1,850–HK$2,550 (US$240–US$331) double; HK$3,200 (US$416) Regal Club double; from HK$4,500 (US$584) suite. Children under 12 stay free in parents' room (maximum 2 children per room). AE, DC, MC, V.

Airport Express Liner: Hong Kong International Airport. **Amenities:** 5 restaurants (Cantonese, Shanghainese, Japanese, international, steaks); lounge; indoor and outdoor pools; health club and spa; children's recreation room; concierge; limousine service; business center (open 24 hr.); shopping arcade; salon; 24-hr. room service; babysitting, same-day laundry/dry cleaning service; nonsmoking rooms; executive-level rooms; house doctor. *In room:* A/C, satellite TV w/keyboard for Internet connection and games and pay movies, minibar, coffeemaker, hair dryer, safe.

4 Where to Dine

Dining is one of *the* things to do in Hong Kong. Not only is the food excellent, but the range of culinary possibilities is nothing short of staggering, with more than 10,000 restaurants from which to choose. In a few short days, you can take a culinary tour of China, dining on Cantonese, Szechuan, Shanghainese, Pekingese, Chiu Chow, and other Chinese specialties as well as choices of authentic international cuisine from every corner of the globe.

KOWLOON
EXPENSIVE

Felix ★★★ *Value* PACIFIC RIM FUSION/CROSSOVER Located on the top floor of The Peninsula, this strikingly avant-garde restaurant comes as something of a shock in this otherwise staid hotel, but what can you expect from a restaurant designed by Philippe Starck? Your first hint that Felix is not your ordinary dining experience begins with the elevator's wavy walls, which suggest a voyage to the world beyond, and continues inside the restaurant, with its huge aluminum wall and two glass facades that curve seductively to reveal stunning views of Kowloon and Hong Kong Island. Two eye-catching zinc cylinders vaguely resembling gigantic snails contain a cocoon-cozy bar and what might be one of the world's tiniest discos. The food, featuring Pacific Rim ingredients brought together in East-meets-West combinations, rarely disappoints. You might start with hot California rolls, followed by the Mongolian-style barbecued rack of lamb in a port wine and akala berry reduction served with a feta, cilantro, and mint salad. Bargain hunters can save bundles by dining early (before 7pm) and opting for the early-bird, three-course fixed-price dinner for HK$340 (US$44). You can also come just for a drink.

In The Peninsula Hotel, Salisbury Rd., Tsim Sha Tsui. ℭ 852/2920 2888, ext. 3188. Reservations required. Main courses HK$210–HK$280 (US$27–US$36). AE, DC, MC, V. Daily 6pm–2am (last order 10:30pm). MTR: Tsim Sha Tsui.

Fook Lam Moon ★★★ CANTONESE Upon entering this restaurant (look for the shrine to the kitchen god at the entrance), you immediately feel as if you've stepped back a couple of decades to a Hong Kong that has all but vanished. The decor is outdated, and unless you're a regular, the waiters are indifferent. Yet this remains *the* place to go for exotic dishes, including shark's fin, bird's nest, and abalone. Shark's fin is the obvious no. 1 choice, with 19 different renditions listed on the menu. If you feel like splurging, prices for half a bowl of shark's fin with crab meat or shredded chicken begin at HK$280 (US$36). If you are not careful, you could end up spending a small fortune (if you go for the exotic dishes, count on at least HK$1,000/US$130 per person), but whatever you order, it's apt to be memorable. Indeed, some Hong Kong old-timers swear this restaurant serves the best Cantonese food in the world, and it's a favorite of local movers and shakers.

There's another branch in Wan Chai at 35–45 Johnston Rd. (ℭ 852/2866 0663; MTR: Wan Chai), with the same hours.

53–59 Kimberley Rd., Tsim Sha Tsui. © 852/2366 0286. Main dishes HK$100–HK$190 (US$13–US$24). AE, DC, MC, V. Daily 11:30am–2:30pm and 6–11:30pm. MTR: Tsim Sha Tsui.

MODERATE

Dan Ryan's Chicago Grill 🌟 *Kids* AMERICAN   Located in the huge Ocean Terminal complex at it southernmost end where cruise ships dock, this casual restaurant serves real American food, with portions big enough to satisfy a hungry cowboy. The decor is Anywhere, U.S.A., but with a difference—it has views of the famous harbor. The lunch menu is substantial, including such classics as chicken wings, potato skins, nachos, New England clam chowder, barbecued ribs, spaghetti, lasagna, chili, great hamburgers (a hit with kids), and large deli sandwiches. There are also lunch specials, available Monday to Friday, priced at HK$65 and HK$75 (US$8.45–US$9.75). The dinner menu is more limited, confined mainly to barbecued steaks, chops, fish, and pasta. Admittedly, most dishes here are a bit pricey, but if you're hungering for the real thing, you might consider it a lifesaver. You can also come just for a drink at its bar, and there are English-language newspapers for customer perusal.

There's another Dan Ryan's at Pacific Place in Admiralty, 88 Queensway (© 852/2845 4600; MTR: Admiralty), open Monday to Thursday 11am to midnight, Friday 11am to 2am, Saturday 9am to 2am, and Sunday 9am to midnight.

200 Ocean Terminal, Harbour City, Tsim Sha Tsui. © 852/2735 6111. Main courses HK$75–HK$240 (US$9.75–US$32) before 6pm, HK$95–HK$298 (US$12–US$39) after 6pm. AE, DC, MC, V. Mon–Fri 11am–midnight; Sat–Sun 10am–midnight. MTR: Tsim Sha Tsui.

Gaylord 🌟 INDIAN   This long-established first-floor restaurant in the heart of Tsim Sha Tsui is classy and comfortable, with private booths and overstuffed sofas. It's popular for its authentic North Indian classics, including tandoori, lamb curry cooked in North Indian spices and herbs, chicken cooked in hot fiery vindaloo curry, prawns cooked with green pepper and spices, and fish with potatoes and tomatoes. There are a dozen vegetarian dishes, and the lunchtime buffet, served every day except Sunday and public holidays until 2:30pm, is a winner. There are also fixed-price dinners for two or more persons, beginning at HK$160 (US$21) per person.

23–25 Ashley Rd., Tsim Sha Tsui. © 852/2376 1001. Main dishes HK$78–HK$198 (US$10–US$26); lunch buffet HK$95 (US$12). AE, DC, MC, V. Daily noon–2:30pm and 6–11pm. MTR: Tsim Sha Tsui.

Great Shanghai 🌟 *Finds* SHANGHAINESE   Established in 1958, this well-known spot in Tsim Sha Tsui is a big old-fashioned dining hall with bright lights, white tablecloths, an army of waiters in green shirts, and a gigantic menu with more than 200 items, most priced under HK$140 (US$18) and about as close as you can get to food the way Mom used to cook in old Shanghai. Try the Shanghainese dumplings, prawns in chili sauce, vegetarian imitation goose, diced chicken with cashews, cold chicken in wine sauce, Szechuan soup, fried pork dumplings, or Peking duck. The house specialty is beggar's chicken for HK$260 (US$34), but it's available only at night; in addition, only a limited number are prepared daily, so call in your order by midafternoon if you want to be assured of getting a bird. My own particular favorite is braised shredded eel, which is cooked in an oily garlic sauce, but all eel dishes here are good. I've also left the ordering entirely up to the waiter and ended up with a well-rounded sampling of Shanghainese food.

26 Prat Ave., Tsim Sha Tsui. © 852/2366 8158. Main dishes HK$75–HK$195 (US$9.75–US$25). AE, DC, MC, V. Daily 11am–2:30pm and 6:30–11pm. MTR: Tsim Sha Tsui.

INEXPENSIVE

Fat Angelo's *Value* ITALIAN   With its checkered tablecloths, black-and-white family photographs (all hanging crooked on purpose?), wainscoting, ceiling fans, and other decor reminiscent of a New World, early-20th-century Italian restaurant, this chain offers good value with its hearty, American renditions of Italian food, including pastas ranging from traditional spaghetti marinara to fettuccini Alfredo and main courses that include rosemary roasted chicken, grilled salmon with pesto, and eggplant Parmesan, all of which come with salad and homemade bread. The emphasis is on quantity, not quality, though the food isn't bad. And they really pack 'em in; this place is like Grand Central Station, bustling, loud, and slightly chaotic. It's sometimes hard to flag down your waitress, but they're cheerful in a we're-all-in-this-together kind of way. It makes for a fun outing with a group.

There are two branches on the other side of the harbor, at 414 Jaffe Rd., Causeway Bay (℃ 852/2574 6263; MTR: Causeway Bay), and 49A-C Elgin St., Central (℃ 852/2973 6808), open the same hours.

33 Ashley Rd., Tsim Sha Tsui. ℃ **852/2730 4788**. Reservations recommended. Small pastas HK$88–HK$135 (US$11–US$18); small main courses HK$125–HK$170 (US$16–US$22); fixed-price lunch (Mon–Fri only) HK$28–$68 (US$3.65–US$8.85). AE, DC, MC, V. Daily noon–11:30pm. MTR: Tsim Sha Tsui.

CENTRAL
EXPENSIVE

M at the Fringe ★★★ *Finds* CONTINENTAL   For a memorable, unusual dining experience, head for this delightful restaurant, located on the upper floor of a former dairy farm building, also home of the Fringe Club. A meal here is a treat in more ways than one—the artsy furnishings are a feast for the eyes, while the food, influenced by cuisines along the Mediterranean, is to die for. The handwritten menu changes every 3 months but is always creative and always includes lamb and vegetarian selections. An example of the former is a salt-encased, slowly baked leg of lamb with celery root and potato gratin, French beans, and baby carrots. For dessert, don't pass up the Pavlova.

2 Lower Albert Rd., Central. ℃ **852/2877 4000**. Reservations strongly recommended. Main courses HK$188–HK$212 (US$24–US$28); fixed-price lunch HK$148–HK$168 (US$19–US$22). AE, MC, V. Mon–Fri noon–2:30pm; Mon–Sat 7–10:30pm; Sun 7–10pm. MTR: Central.

Petrus ★★★ *Finds* FRENCH   Simply put, the views from this 56th-floor restaurant are breathtaking, probably the best of any hotel restaurant on the Hong Kong side. If you can bear to take your eyes off the windows, you'll find the restaurant decorated like a French castle, with the obligatory crystal chandeliers, black marble and gilded columns, statues, thick draperies, Impressionist paintings, murals gracing dome-shape ceilings, and a pianist playing softly in the background. Tables are spaced far enough apart for intimacy. The cuisine emphasizes contemporary Mediterranean/French seasonal ingredients, spiced sparingly to complement the dishes' natural aroma and flavor. The menu changes often but has included such intriguing choices as black truffle soup with green asparagus and salsify, and roast Boston lobster served with fennel, morels, and tomato. As expected, the wine list—particularly Bordeaux—is among the best in Hong Kong, if not the world. With the impressive blend of great views, refined ambience, excellent cuisine, and professional staff, this restaurant is a top choice for a splurge, a romantic dinner, or a special celebration.

In the Island Shangri-La (56th floor), Pacific Place, Supreme Court Rd., Central. ℃ **852/2820 8590**. Reservations recommended. Jacket required. Main courses HK$320–HK$530 (US$42–US$69); fixed-price lunch

HK$290–HK$340 (US$38–US$44); fixed-price dinner HK$750–HK$900 (US$97–US$117). AE, DC, MC, V. Mon–Sat noon–3pm; daily 6:30–10:30pm. MTR: Admiralty.

MODERATE

Aqua ★★ *Finds* FUSION/CROSSOVER   Of the several dozen independent restaurants that have sprung up in the Central/SoHo area the past few years, this counts among the best. It sits on a busy corner with a glass facade, but inside it's cool and collected, with an open kitchen set unobtrusively in a corner and low lighting that sets the mood for romantic dining. Australian chef Gregory Bunt creates a constantly changing menu that capitalizes on his years working in Asia. For starters, try the tasting platter for two, followed by such entrees as yellowfin tuna grilled with olive crust, basil potatoes, confit tomato and anchovy sauce; or cumin-crusted lamb loin with smoky aubergine, tomato ginger, and spice jus. Fixed-price lunches include grazing at an ample salad bar, making it a very good bargain.

49 Hollywood Rd., Central. © 852/2545 9889. Reservations recommended. Main courses HK$135–HK$198 (US$18–US$26); fixed-price lunch HK$88–HK$108 (US$11–US$14); fixed-price dinner HK$388 (US$50). AE, MC, V. Mon–Thurs noon–midnight; Fri noon–2am; Sat 10:30am–2am; Sun 10:30am–midnight. MTR: Central.

Jimmy's Kitchen ★ CONTINENTAL   This restaurant opened in 1928, a replica of a similar American-owned restaurant in Shanghai. Now one of Hong Kong's oldest Western restaurants (some of its waiters are descendants from the original staff), it has an atmosphere reminiscent of an American steakhouse, with white tablecloths, dark-wood paneling, and elevator music, but it's a favorite with older foreigners living in Hong Kong and serves dependably good, unpretentious European food. The daily specials are written on a blackboard, and an extensive a la carte menu offers salads and soups, steaks, chicken, Indian curries, and a seafood selection that includes sole, scallops, and the local garoupa. It's a good place also for corned beef and cabbage, beef Stroganoff, and hearty German fare, including Wienerschnitzel (breaded veal), pig's knuckle, and Knockwurst sausage.

There's another branch at 29 Ashley Rd., Tsim Sha Tsui (© 852/2376 0327), open daily noon to 11pm.

1 Wyndham St., Central. © 852/2526 5293. Main courses HK$116–HK$205 (US$15–US$27). AE, DC, MC, V. Daily 11:30am–3pm and 6–11pm. MTR: Central.

Luk Yu Tea House ★★ CANTONESE   Luk Yu, first opened in 1933, is the most famous teahouse remaining in Hong Kong. In fact, unless you have a time machine, you can't get any closer to old Hong Kong than this wonderful Art Deco–era Cantonese restaurant with its ceiling fans, spittoons, individual wooden booths for couples, marble tabletops, and stained-glass windows. It's one of the best places to try Chinese teas like lung ching (a green tea) or sui sin (narcissus or daffodil), but Luk Yu is most famous for its dim sum, served 7am to 5:30pm. The problem for foreigners, however, is that the place is always packed with regulars who have their own special places to sit, and the staff is sometimes surly to newcomers. In addition, if you come after 11am, dim sum is no longer served by trolley, but from an English menu with pictures but no prices, which could end up being quite expensive unless you ask before ordering. Try to bring along a Chinese friend, or consider coming for dinner, when it's not nearly so hectic and there's an English menu listing more than 200 items, including all the Cantonese favorites.

24–26 Stanley St., Central. © 852/2523 5464. Main dishes HK$100–HK$220 (US$13–US$29); dim sum HK$25–HK$55 (US$3.25–US$7.15). MC, V. Daily 7am–10pm. MTR: Central.

CAUSEWAY BAY

EXPENSIVE

Tott's Asian Grill & Bar ★★★ INTERNATIONAL/FUSION   This flashy restaurant seems to suffer from an identity crisis: gigantic Chinese paintbrushes at the entrance and a blood-red interior with zebra-stripe chairs. I don't know whether I'm in Africa or China until I look at the fabulous view from the restaurant's 34th-floor perch. This is Hong Kong at its most eclectic, funky self, and though the setting seems contrived, the restaurant itself is relaxed, fun, and highly recommended for its innovative and varied East-meets-West fusion cuisine. Come early for a drink in the restaurant's bar, or retire there after dinner for live music and dancing. A glass-enclosed kitchen reveals food being prepared in woks, over charcoal grills, and in tandoori ovens. The menu is diverse in cuisine and price, allowing diners to eat moderately priced dishes like creamy risotto with pearl onions, broad beans, grilled mushrooms, and house-dried tomatoes, or go all out on tandoori-roasted salmon filet on basil whipped potatoes and crisp vegetable chips. This place is a good choice for those who want dining and entertainment in one spot, as well as for those entertaining first-time visitors to Hong Kong.

In the Excelsior Hotel, 281 Gloucester Rd., Causeway Bay. ℭ **852/2837 6786.** Reservations recommended for dinner (request a window seat). Main courses HK$168–HK$328 (US$22–US$43); fixed-price lunch buffet HK$198 (US$26); Sun brunch HK$298 (US$39). AE, DC, MC, V. Mon–Fri noon–3pm; Mon–Sat 6:30–11pm; Sun 11:30am–3pm and 6:30–10pm. MTR: Causeway Bay.

MODERATE

Red Pepper ★ SZECHUAN   Open since 1970, the Red Pepper has a large following among the city's expatriates, many of whom seem to come so often that they know everyone in the place. It's a very relaxing, small restaurant, with a rather quaint decor of carved dragons on the ceiling and Chinese lanterns. Specialties include fried prawns with chili sauce on a sizzling platter, sour-pepper soup, fried garoupa with sweet and sour sauce, smoked duck marinated with oranges, and shredded chicken with hot garlic sauce and dry-fried string beans. Most dishes are available in two sizes, with the small dishes suitable for two people. Lychee tea is a good accompaniment.

7 Lan Fong Rd., Causeway Bay. ℭ **852/2577 3811.** Reservations recommended, especially at dinner. Small dishes HK$85–HK$130 (US$11–US$17). AE, DC, MC, V. Daily 11:30am–11:15pm (last order). MTR: Causeway Bay.

INEXPENSIVE

Open Kitchen ★ *Finds* INTERNATIONAL   This self-serve cafeteria, near the convention center, gets my vote as the best place in Wan Chai for an inexpensive and quick meal. Bright with natural lighting, it boasts a view of the harbor and even has a tiny outdoor terrace. True to its name, chefs working in an open kitchen prepare everything from lamb chops, grilled steak, and tandoori chicken to grilled Cajun salmon and spring chicken. Diners can also choose from four or five kinds of pasta, along with a choice of sauce. Lighter fare includes a salad bar, soups, sandwiches, sushi, quiche, and desserts. You can also come just for a drink (I often see people writing postcards or reading a book here in the afternoon), but the minimum charge per person is HK$20 (US$2.60).

Hong Kong Arts Centre (6th floor), 2 Harbour Rd., Wan Chai. ℭ **852/2827 2923.** Main courses HK$70–HK$90 (US$9.10–US$12). AE, MC, V. Sat–Thurs 11am–9:30pm; Fri 11am–11pm. MTR: Wan Chai.

5 Exploring Hong Kong

Every visitor to Hong Kong should eat dim sum in a typical Cantonese restaurant, ride the Star Ferry across Victoria Harbour, and, if the weather is clear, take the Peak tram for the glorious views from Victoria Peak. If you have more time, I also recommend the Hong Kong Museum of History, Stanley Market for its inexpensive fashions and souvenirs, an excursion via ferry to one of the outlying islands, and a stroll through the Temple Street Night Market.

VICTORIA PEAK

At 399m (1,308 ft.), Victoria Peak is Hong Kong Island's tallest mountain and offers spectacular views; if possible, go on a clear day. Because the peak is typically cooler than the sweltering city below, it has always been one of Hong Kong's most exclusive places to live. More than a century ago, the rich reached the peak via a grueling 3-hour trip in sedan chairs, transported to the top by coolies. In 1888, the **peak tram** began operating, cutting the journey to a mere 8 minutes.

The easiest way to reach the Peak Tram Station, located in Central on Garden Road, is to take the no. 15C open-top shuttle bus that operates between the tram terminal and the Star Ferry in Central (turn left from the ferry pier). Otherwise, the tram terminal is about a 10-minute walk from the Star Ferry. Trams depart from Peak Tram Station every 10 to 15 minutes between 7am and midnight. Round-trip tickets cost HK$30 (US$3.90) for adults, HK$14 (US$1.80) for senior citizens, and HK$9(US$1.15) for children.

Upon reaching the Peak, you'll find yourself at the very modern **Peak Tower,** looking for all the world like a Chinese cooking wok. Head straight for the viewing terrace on Level 5, where you have one of the world's most breathtaking views, with the skyscrapers of Central, the boats plying Victoria Harbour, Kowloon, and the many hills of the New Territories undulating in the background.

Of the three attractions located in Peak Tower, most well known is probably **Madame Tussaud's,** Level 2 (© **852/3128 8288**), with more than 100 life-size wax figures of celebrities, politicians, and historical figures, including local heroes Jackie Chan and Bruce Lee. It's open daily 11am to 8pm and costs HK$75 (US$9.75) for adults and HK$50 (US$6.50) for senior citizens and children. Plan on about 30 minutes here. **Ripley's Believe It or Not! Odditorium,** Level 3 (© **852/2849 0698**), contains oddities (and replicas of oddities) collected by Robert L. Ripley on visits to 198 countries over 55 years, including a shrunken head from Ecuador, torture devices from around the world, a two-headed calf, and models of the world's tallest and fattest men. Be forewarned that some of the items are purely grotesque or, at best, out-of-date in a more socially correct world. It's open daily 9am to 10pm and costs HK$75 (US$9.75) for adults and HK$50 (US$6.50) for senior citizens and children. **Peak Explorer,** Level 4 (© **852/2849 0866**), is a 36-seat motion-simulator theater that features changing, 8-minute fast-paced films, and seats that move in accordance with the action on the screen. It's open Monday to Friday noon to 10pm, and Saturday and Sunday 9am to 10pm, with admission costing HK$45 (US$5.85) for adults and HK$32 (US$4.15) for children.

But the best thing to do atop Victoria Peak, in my opinion, is to take an hour-long circular hike on Lugard Road and Harlech Road, located just a stone's throw from the Peak Tower. Mainly a footpath overhung with banyan trees and passing lush vegetation alternating with secluded mansions, the road snakes along the side of the cliff, offering great views of Central District below, the harbor, Kowloon, and then Aberdeen and the outlying islands on the other side. This is one of the best walks in Hong Kong; at night, the lit path offers one of world's most romantic views. Don't miss it.

MUSEUMS

Keep in mind that municipal museums are closed December 25 and 26, January 1, and the first 3 days of Chinese New Year.

Hong Kong Heritage Museum ★★ *Kids*   Presenting both the history and culture of the New Territories, this museum is probably the best reason to take the KCR to Sha Tin in the New Territories. Come here to learn about the customs, religions, and lifestyles of the early fishermen and settlers, and how they have changed over the centuries. See a barge loaded for market, an ancestral hall, traditional clothing, models of Sha Tin showing its mind-numbing growth since the 1930s, musical instruments, elaborate costumes used in Chinese opera, porcelains, bronzes, furniture, jade, and other works of Chinese art dating from the Neolithic period to the 20th century. At the Children's Discovery Gallery, youngsters can practice being an archeologist, wear traditional costumes, and learn about marshes. Plan on 2 hours here.

1 Man Lam Road, Sha Tin. ✆ 852/2180 8188. www.heritagemuseum.gov.hk/. Admission HK$10 (US$1.30) adults, HK$5 (US65¢) children, students, and senior citizens. Free admission Wed. Mon and Wed–Sat 10am–6pm; Sun and holidays 10am–7pm. KCR: Tai Wai or Sha Tin, about a 10-min. walk from each.

Hong Kong Museum of Art ★★★   Because of its location on the Tsim Sha Tsui waterfront just a 2-minute walk from the Star Ferry terminus, this museum is the most convenient and worthwhile if your time is limited. I like popping in just to see the temporary exhibits, though it also boasts a vast collection of Chinese antiquities and fine art that makes this one of my top picks. Feast your eyes on ceramics, bronzes, jade, cloisonné, lacquerware, bamboo carvings, women's costumes, and textiles, as well as paintings, wall hangings, scrolls, and calligraphy dating from the 16th century to the present. The Historical Pictures Gallery is especially insightful, with oils, watercolors, pencil drawings, and prints that provide a visual account of life in Hong Kong, Macau, and Guangzhou in the late 18th and 19th centuries. Another gallery displays contemporary Hong Kong works by local artists. You'll want to spend at least an hour here, though art aficionados can devote more time by renting audio guides for HK$10 (US$1.30). A bonus is the beautiful backdrop of Victoria Harbour.

Hong Kong Cultural Centre Complex, 10 Salisbury Rd., Tsim Sha Tsui. ✆ 852/2721 0116. www.lcsd.gov.hk/ hkma/. Admission HK$10 (US$1.30) adults, HK$5 (US65¢) children, students, and senior citizens. Free admission Wed. Fri–Wed 10am–6pm. MTR: Tsim Sha Tsui.

Hong Kong Museum of History ★★★   If you visit only one museum in Hong Kong, this should be it. Opened in 2001, it's Hong Kong's ambitious attempt to chronicle 6,000 years of history, from its beginnings as a Neolithic settlement to its development as a fishing village and finally its transformation into a modern metropolis. Through displays that include life-size dioramas, replicas of fishing boats, reconstructed traditional housing, furniture, clothing, and items from daily life, the museum introduces Hong Kong's ethnic groups, traditional means of livelihood, customs, and beliefs. You can peer inside a fishing junk, see what Kowloon Walled City looked like before it became a park, view the backstage of a Chinese opera, read about the arrival of European traders and the Opium Wars, and study a map showing land reclamation since the

1840s. One of my favorite parts of the museum is a re-created street of old Hong Kong, complete with an original Chinese herbal medicine shop located in Central until 1980 and reconstructed here. There are also 19th- and early-20th-century photographs, poignantly showing how much Hong Kong has changed through the decades. You can easily spend 2 hours here.

100 Chatham Rd. S., Tsim Sha Tsui East. **852/2724 9042.** www.lcsd.gov.hk/hkmh/. Admission HK$10 adults (US$1.30), HK$5 (US65¢) children and senior citizens. Free admission Wed. Wed–Mon 10am–6pm. MTR: Tsim Sha Tsui (a 20-min. walk from exit B2). Bus: No. 5 from Star Ferry bus terminus.

Hong Kong Museum of Medical Sciences *(Finds)*　This museum, located in the Edwardian-style former Pathological Institute founded more than 100 years ago to combat the colony's most horrific outbreak of bubonic plague, charts the historical development of medical science in Hong Kong. Several rooms remain almost exactly as they were, including an autopsy room and a laboratory filled with equipment, while others serve as exhibition rooms devoted to such areas as the development of dentistry and radiology (note the x-ray of the bound foot), acupuncture, and traditional Chinese herbs. But what makes the museum particularly fascinating is its unique comparison of traditional Chinese and Western medicine. You can easily spend up to an hour here.

2 Caine Lane, Mid-Levels. © 852/2549 5123. www.hkmms.org.hk/. Admission HK$10 (US$1.30) adults, HK$5 (US65¢) children and senior citizens. Tues–Sat 10am–5pm; Sun and holidays 1–5pm. MTR: Central; then bus no. 26 from Des Voeux Rd. in front of Hongkong Bank headquarters to Man Mo Temple; walk up Ladder St. to Caine Lane.

Hong Kong Science Museum *(Kids)*　The mysteries of science and technology come to life with plenty of hands-on exhibits sure to appeal to children and adults alike. More than 500 exhibits are devoted to the life sciences; light, sound, and motion; meteorology and geography; electricity and magnetism; computers and robotics; construction; transportation and communication; occupational safety and health; energy efficiency; and food science and home technology. There is also an area specially designed for children 3 to 7. It's a great place to take kids on a rainy or humid day; you can easily spend 3 hours here.

2 Science Museum Rd., Tsim Sha Tsui East. © 852/2732 3232. www.lcsd.gov.hk/hkscm/. Admission HK$25 (US$3.25) adults, HK$12.50 (US$1.60) children, students, and senior citizens. Free admission Wed. Mon–Wed and Fri 1–9pm; Sat–Sun and holidays 10am–9pm. MTR: Tsim Sha Tsui (a 20-min. walk from exit B2). Bus: No. 5 from the Star Ferry bus terminus.

Hong Kong Space Museum *(Kids)*　Located opposite The Peninsula Hotel on the Tsim Sha Tsui waterfront, the Space Museum is easy to spot with its white-domed planetarium. The Hall of Space Science explores the human journey into space, with exhibits on ancient astronomical history, early rockets, manned space flights, and future space programs. There are also several interactive rides and exhibits (most with weight and height restrictions), including a ride on a virtual paraglider (a harness that holds occupants aloft with the same approximate gravity they'd experience walking on the moon) and a multiaxis chair developed for astronaut training to give the sensation of tumbling through space. The Hall of Astronomy presents information on the solar system and the universe. Personally, I find the museum, which opened in 1980, rather dated. Come only if you have kids and extra time on your hands, in which case you'll spend about an hour here.

The adjoining Space Theatre, with a 75-foot domed roof, presents mostly Omnimax screenings and sky shows with a Zeiss star projector that can project up to about 9,000 stars. Try to buy your ticket at least a day in advance, either at the museum or any URBTIX outlet. Call © 852/2734 2722 for show schedules.

Hong Kong Cultural Centre Complex, 10 Salisbury Rd., Tsim Sha Tsui. ℭ 852/2721 0226. www.lcsd.gov.hk/ hkspm/. Admission to Exhibition Halls HK$10 (US$1.30) adults, HK$5 (US65¢) children, students, and senior citizens. Free admission Wed. Space Theatre HK$24–HK$60 (US$3.10–US$7.80) adults, HK$12–HK$30 (US$1.55–US$3.90) children, students, and senior citizens. Mon and Wed–Fri 1–9pm; Sat–Sun and holidays 10am–9pm. MTR: Tsim Sha Tsui.

Sam Tung Uk Museum ★★ Located in the New Territories but easily accessible from either Central or Tsim Sha Tsui in about 25 minutes via MTR, this is actually a restored Hakka walled village, built in the 18th century by members of the farming Chan clan. It consists of tiny lanes lined with tiny tile-roof homes, four houses that have been restored to their original condition, an ancestral hall, two rows of side houses, an exhibition hall, and an adjacent landscaped garden. The four windowless restored houses are furnished much as they would have been when occupied, with traditional Chinese furniture (including elegant blackwood furniture). Although as many as 300 clan members once lived here, the village was abandoned in 1980. Today the museum is a tiny oasis in the midst of high-rise housing projects.

2 Kwu Uk Lane, Tsuen Wan. ℭ 852/2411 2001. Free admission. Wed–Mon 9am–5pm. MTR: Tsuen Wan (a few minutes' walk from exit E).

TEMPLES

Man Mo Temple ★ Hong Kong Island's oldest and most important temple was built in the 1840s and is named after its two principal deities: Man, the god of literature, and Mo, the god of war. Ironically, Mo finds patronage in both the police force (shrines in his honor can be found in all Hong Kong police stations today) and the infamous triad secret societies. Two ornately carved sedan chairs in the temple were once used during festivals to carry the statues of the gods around the neighborhood. But what makes the temple particularly memorable are the giant incense coils hanging from the ceiling, imparting a fragrant, smoky haze—these are purchased by patrons seeking fulfillment of their wishes, such as good health or a successful business deal, and might burn as long as 3 weeks.

Hollywood Rd. and Ladder St., Western District. ℭ 852/2803 2916. Free admission. Daily 8am–6pm. Bus: No. 26 from Des Voeux Rd. Central (in front of the Hongkong Bank headquarters) to the second stop on Hollywood Rd., across from the temple.

Wong Tai Sin ★★ Located six subway stops northeast of Yau Ma Tei in the far north end of Kowloon Peninsula, Wong Tai Sin is Hong Kong's most popular Taoist temple. Although the temple itself dates only from 1973, it adheres to traditional Chinese architectural principles with its red pillars, two-tiered golden roof, blue friezes, yellow latticework, and multicolored carvings. The temple is very popular among those seeking their fortunes—from advice about business or horse racing to determining which day is most auspicious for a wedding. Most worshippers make use of a bamboo container holding numbered sticks, which correspond to a certain fortune. On temple grounds are halls dedicated to the Buddhist Goddess of Mercy and to Confucius; the Nine Dragon Garden, a Chinese garden with a pond, waterfall, and a replica of the famous Nine Dragons mural (the original is in Beijing's Imperial Palace); the Good Wish Garden, a replica of the Yi He Garden in Beijing with circular, square, octagonal, and fan-shape pavilions as well as ponds, an artificial waterfall, and rocks and concrete fashioned to resemble animals; and a clinic with both Western medical services and traditional Chinese herbal treatments. A visit to this temple, surrounded by vast, government housing estates, provides insight into Chinese religious practices, and it is well worth a stop, despite its out-of-the-way location.

Wong Tai Sin Estate. Free admission to temple, though donations of about HK$1 (US13¢) are expected at the temple's entrance and for Nine Dragon Wall Garden; admission to Good Wish Garden HK$2 (US26¢) extra. Temple daily 7am–5:30pm; gardens Tues–Sun 9am–4pm. MTR: Wong Tai Sin (exit B2) and then a 3-min. walk (follow the signs).

6 Shopping

No doubt about it—shopping is one of the main reasons people come to Hong Kong, and at first glance the city does seem to be one huge department store. Good buys include products from mainland China (porcelain, jade, cloisonné, silk handicrafts and clothing, hand embroidery, jewelry, and artwork), Chinese antiques, clothing, shoes, jewelry, furniture, carpets, leather goods, luggage, handbags, briefcases, Chinese herbs, watches, toys, and eyeglasses. As for electronic goods and cameras, they are not the bargains they once were, though good deals can be found in recently discontinued models. Hong Kong is a duty-free port, so there is no sales tax.

Tsim Sha Tsui boasts the greatest concentration of shops in Hong Kong, particularly along Nathan Road, with its many electronics stores. Harbour City, one of the largest malls in the world, stretches along Canton Road, and Central is where to go for international designer labels and boutiques.

Stanley Market is probably the most popular and best-known market in Hong Kong and the ride out to this southern coastal area is a picturesque day trip. Located on the southern coast of Hong Kong Island, it's a great place to buy inexpensive clothing, especially sportswear, cashmere sweaters, casual clothing, silk blouses and dresses, linen blazers, and women's suits. Men's, women's, and children's clothing are available. Although prices are not the bargain they once were, I buy more of my clothes here than anywhere else in Hong Kong, especially when it comes to cheap, fun fashions. The inventory changes continuously: One year, it seems everyone is selling washable silk; the next year, it's Chinese traditional jackets or Gore-Tex coats. There are also souvenir shops selling Chinese paintings, embroidered linen, beaded purses, handicrafts, and other products from mainland China.

To get there, take bus nos. 6, 6A, 6X, or 260 from Central's Exchange Square bus terminal near the Star Ferry (a 30 min. trip).

7 Nightlife

DANCE CLUBS/DISCOS

C Club   With a seductive interior of velvet sofas and a curved bar, all bathed in red lighting, this basement club packs 'em in with underground house music, techno-beat, and noncommercial sounds created by international and resident DJs. If you come on a weekend, be prepared to wait in the queue of beautiful people lined up outside. It's open Monday to Thursday 6pm to 2am, Friday 6pm to 5am, and Saturday 9pm to 5am. California Tower, 30–32 D'Aguilar, Lan Kwai Fong, Central. ✆ 852/2526 1139. No cover Mon–Thurs; cover HK$100 (US$13) Fri–Sat. MTR: Central.

Joe Bananas   Appealing to Hong Kong's single yuppies, this is a bar and restaurant that transforms itself into a happening disco every evening after 11:30pm, but the action doesn't kick in until late. Ladies get in free until 1am and even get free drinks on Wednesday from 6pm to midnight. There's dancing Sunday to Thursday 11:30pm to 5am, and Friday and Saturday 11:30pm to 6am. 23 Luard Rd., Wan Chai. ✆ 852/2529 1811. No cover Sun–Thurs; cover Fri–Sat HK$100 (US$13), including 1 drink. Free for women until 1am. MTR: Wan Chai.

Propaganda   Hong Kong's longest-standing and most popular gay disco, Propaganda moved into upgraded quarters a few years back in the new SoHo nightlife district, with a discreet entrance in a back alley (off Pottinger St.). The crowd is 95% gay, but everyone is welcome. Come late on a weekend if you want to see this alternative hot spot at its most crowded. It's open Tuesday to Thursday 9pm to 3:30am, and Friday and Saturday 9pm to 5am. 1 Hollywood Rd., Central. ℂ 852/2868 1316. No cover Tues–Thurs; cover HK$80 (US$10) Fri; HK$80 (US$10) Sat before 10:30pm and after 3am; HK$120 (US$16) Sat 10:30pm–3am. MTR: Central.

THE BAR SCENE
KOWLOON

Chasers   One of several bars lining the narrow, alleylike Knutsford Terrace, which parallels Kimberley Road to the north, this is among the most popular, filled with a mixed clientele that includes both the young and the not-so-young, expats and Chinese. It features a house Filipino band nightly from 10:30pm playing rock, jazz, rhythm-and-blues, and everything in between, free of charge. Happy hour is noon to 9pm Sunday and, the rest of the week, 5 to 9pm. It's open daily noon to 6am. 2–3 Knutsford Terrace, Tsim Sha Tsui. ℂ 852/2367 9487. MTR: Tsim Sha Tsui.

Delaney's   This upmarket Irish pub is decorated in old-world style, with a convivial atmosphere that gets an extra boost from a DJ Thursday nights and a live Irish band Friday nights, both free of charge. Big soccer and rugby events are shown on a big screen. An a la carte menu lists Irish stew, beef and Guinness pie, corned beef and cabbage, and other national favorites. Happy hour is 5 to 9pm daily; open hours are daily 10:30am to 2:30am. There's another Delaney's in Wan Chai at 18 Luard Rd. (ℂ 852/2804 2880). 71–77 Peking Rd., Tsim Sha Tsui. ℂ 852/2301 3980. MTR: Tsim Sha Tsui.

Ned Kelly's Last Stand   This is a lively Aussie saloon, attracting a largely middle-age crowd with free live Dixieland jazz or swing Monday to Saturday from 9:30pm to 1am. It serves Australian chow and pub grub, and happy hour is 11:30am to 9pm. It's open daily 11:30am to 2am. 11A Ashley Rd., Tsim Sha Tsui. ℂ 852/2376 0562. MTR: Tsim Sha Tsui.

Sky Lounge   This plush and comfortable lounge on the top floor of the Sheraton affords one of the most romantic views of the harbor and glittering Hong Kong Island. There's soft live music every night except Sunday 9pm to midnight, with a minimum drink charge of HK$138 (US $18) per person (waived for hotel guests). It's open Sunday to Thursday 2pm to 1am, and Friday and Saturday 2pm to 2am. In the Sheraton Hotel and Towers, 20 Nathan Rd., Tsim Sha Tsui. ℂ 852/ 2369 1111. MTR: Tsim Sha Tsui.

CENTRAL DISTRICT

Alibi Bar and Brasserie   No alibi needed to visit this chic new bar above the madness of Lan Kwai Fong, though it's standing room only for the hip crowd that gathers here most nights. For a breath of fresh air, try to make your way to the outdoor terrace. Happy hour Monday to Saturday from 6 to 9pm includes complimentary canapes. It's open Monday to Thursday noon to 3am, and Friday and Saturday noon to 4am. 73 Wyndham St., Central. ℂ 852/2167 1676. MTR: Central.

California   Located in Central's nightlife district, this was once *the* place to see and be seen—the haunt of young nouveaux riches in search of a definition. Newer establishments have since encroached upon California's exalted position, but it remains a respected and sophisticated restaurant/bar. You might consider starting your night on the town here with dinner and drinks—the restaurant boasts a changing menu from an innovative American chef, though hamburgers (the house specialty) remain hugely popular. Happy hour is 5 to 9pm, and on Friday and Saturday nights from 11pm to 4am it becomes a happening disco. It's open Monday to Thursday noon to midnight, Friday and Saturday noon to 4am, and Sunday 6pm to midnight. 24–26 Lan Kwai Fong St., Central. ℂ 852/2521 1345. MTR: Central.

Club 97   Opened almost 20 years ago, this club underwent recent transformation that changed it from a disco to a sophisticated lounge, a reflection of an aging clientele more prone to drinking and conversation than dancing. It hasn't lost its edge, however, and remains a must for any decent pub crawl through Lan Kwai Fong. Weekly events to watch out for are the Friday gay happy hour complete with drag shows, and the Sunday reggae night, which draws a huge crowd wanting to chill out before the work week begins. It's open Monday to Thursday 6pm to 4am (happy hour 6–8:30pm), Friday 6 to 4am (happy hour 6–10pm), Saturday 7pm to 4am (happy hour 7–8:30pm), and Sunday 8pm to 3am (happy hour 8–10pm). 9 Lan Kwai Fong, Central. ℂ 852/2810 9333. MTR: Central.

Curve   This is one of Hong Kong's friendliest and most crowded gay bars, with a long bar upstairs and a mirrored dance floor downstairs. DJs get things rolling Wednesday through Saturday nights, but equally popular is the tea dance held the third Sunday of every month from 4pm to 2am (otherwise, open daily 5pm–4am). Everybody is welcome here—even single women. And it's fun! It's located on a hill above Lan Kwai Fong. 2 Arbuthnot Rd., Central. ℂ 852/2523 0998. No cover Sun–Thurs; cover (including 1 drink) Fri–Sat HK$60 (US$7.80); cover (including 2 drinks) night before a holiday HK$150 (US$19). MTR: Central.

Dublin Jack   With its bright red exterior, it's easy to spot this Irish pub next to the Central/Mid-Levels Escalator Link in Central's SoHo entertainment district. Top draws include more than 150 brands of Irish and Scottish whiskies, and the ubiquitous screens broadcasting rugby and other British sports. Happy hour is 11am to 9pm daily. It's open daily 11am to 2am. 37 Cochrane St., Central. ℂ 852/2543 0081. MTR: Central.

Insomnia   One of Lan Kwai Fong's most popular bars, it's aptly named, because live music by a Filipino band doesn't get underway until 10:30pm, and it's at its most packed in the wee hours of the morning when there's no room to spare on the crowded dance floor. Happy hour is 5 to 9pm. It's open daily 8am to 6am, leaving insomniacs 2 hours with nowhere to go. 38–44 D'Aguilar St., Central. ℂ 852/2525 0957. MTR: Central.

MadDogs   Catering to a mellow crowd of professional people during early evening hours and a wilder bunch at night, this is one of Hong Kong's longer-standing English pubs, with a traditional decor reminiscent of Britain during its imperial heyday. Happy hour is Monday to Saturday noon to midnight, and all day Sunday. There's a DJ every night; ladies get free drinks on Thursday nights from 9pm until "late." It's open Monday to Thursday 10am to 2am, Friday 10am to 3am, Saturday 10am to 3am, and Sunday 10am to 1am. 1 D'Aguilar St., Central. ℂ 852/2810 1000. MTR: Central.

CAUSEWAY BAY/WAN CHAI

Dusk til Dawn   This is one of my top picks for an evening out in Wan Chai. Classier than most of its competitors, it attracts a mostly expat and Southeast

Asian clientele, who take advantage of its 5 to 10pm daily happy hour, food and snack menu served until 5am, and nightly free live music starting at 10pm provided by rotating bands that include Filipino musicians and an all-girl band. It's open Monday through Saturday noon to 6am, and Sunday 3pm to 6am. 76–84 Jaffe Rd., Wan Chai. © 852/2528 4689. MTR: Wan Chai.

JJ's   This upscale, glitzy entertainment complex was the first in Hong Kong to offer several diversions under one roof. It's huge, with a main bar, pool table, food (pizza, tapas, and snacks) served in various places throughout, an upscale music room with live jazz and blues, and a supper club featuring contemporary Latin music, Brazilian flair (even the bartenders are flown in from Brazil), and an impressive list of rums. This is the place for those who like to move from one scene to the next, without actually having to go anywhere. Happy hour, including a free snack buffet, is Monday to Friday 6 to 8:30pm. JJ's is open Monday to Thursday 6pm to 2am, Friday 6pm to 3am, and Saturday 7pm to 4am. In the Grand Hyatt Hotel, 1 Harbour Rd., Wan Chai. © 852/2588 1234, ext. 7323. Cover (including 1 drink) HK$100 (US$13). No cover before 9:30pm. MTR: Wan Chai.

Thailand

by Jennifer Eveland

At the end of the last century, the Tourism Authority of Thailand kicked off a new tourism campaign called "Amazing Thailand." It could not have chosen a better adjective. Amazing are the clear blue waters that lap at sandy palm-lined shores on Thailand's coasts and islands. Amazing are the country's thousands of ornate and historic temples that house serene Buddha images amid the sweet smell of jasmine. Amazing are the Thai people, their warm smiles welcoming visitors to enjoy their world. Every experience is a thrill, from a sampling of the renowned spicy Thai cuisine to shopping adventures in sprawling bazaars, to the sexy shows that entice guests to experience "sanuk," fun Thai-style, for there is no better place in Southeast Asia to experience both the exotic and the pleasurable. Thailand invites the world to experience the allure of the Orient, while providing endless opportunities for the relaxation and good times that holiday travelers seek. Thailand is truly amazing.

The world has caught on to Thailand's magic. The country for years has enjoyed some of the highest tourism rates in the region, and even amid the economic crisis that had almost every Southeast Asian nation scurrying for tourism dollars, Thailand managed to increase its tourism traffic. Indeed, the collapse of the Thai baht in July 1997 accounts for much of this increase; the currency stretches a long way to make a fantastic vacation even more enjoyable. At the time of this writing, the baht still was a bargain, at about 43 baht per dollar, as opposed to the precrisis 25 baht per dollar.

One benefit of the developed tourism industry is the accessibility of the country to outsiders. While venturing into the unknown, you will rarely feel uneasy. Regional and local transportation, Western-style accommodations, and locals well versed in rudimentary English allow foreigners to roam with relative ease and comfort. And despite often incomprehensible cultural differences, widespread travel has increased the ease with which the Thai people greet outsiders and allow for foreign tastes and manners.

1 Getting to Know Thailand

THE LAY OF THE LAND

In the center of Southeast Asia, Thailand is located roughly equidistant from China and India, sharing cultural affinities with both. It borders Burma (Myanmar) to the north and west, Laos to the northeast, Cambodia (Kampuchea) to the east, and Malaysia to the south. Thailand's southwestern coast stretches along the Andaman Sea, and its southern and southeastern coastlines border the Gulf of Thailand (still often called the Gulf of Siam).

Thailand covers approximately 289,668 sq. km (180,000 sq. miles)—about the size of France. The country, which the Thais often compare in shape to the

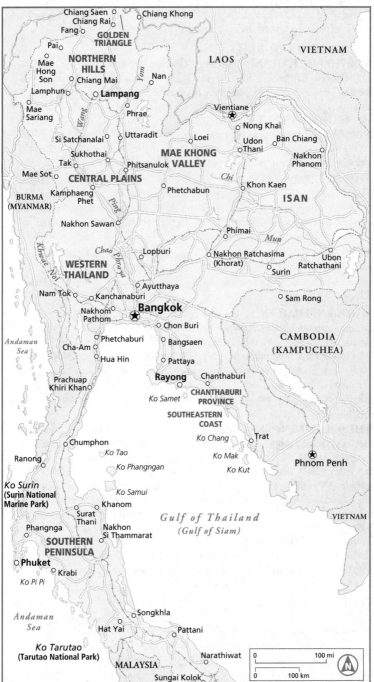

Thailand

profile of an elephant's head, facing right, is divided into six major geographic zones, within which there are 73 provinces.

THE REGIONS IN BRIEF

NORTHERN THAILAND Northern Thailand (the forehead of the elephant) is a relatively cool mountainous region at the foothills of the Himalayas. Like most of Thailand, the cool hills in the north are well suited for farming, particularly for strawberries, asparagus, peaches, litchis, and other fruits. At higher elevations many hill-tribe farmers cultivate opium poppies, a crop that is rarely profitable (and ruinous to farmers who become addicted), though the agricultural program advanced by the king is introducing more productive crops. The cities in the north covered in this chapter are Chiang Mai and Chiang Rai.

THE CENTRAL PLAIN The Central Plain is an extremely fertile region, providing the country and the world with much of its abundant rice crop. The main city of the area is Phitsanulok, northeast of which are the impressive remains of Sukhothai, Thailand's first capital. To the south is Lopburi, an ancient Mon-Khmer settlement.

THE SOUTHEAST COAST The southeast coast is lined with seaside resorts, such as Pattaya and the islands Ko Samet and Ko Chang. Farther east, in the mountains, is Thailand's greatest concentration of sapphire and ruby mines.

WESTERN THAILAND On the opposite side of the country, west of Bangkok, are mountains and valleys carved by the Kwai River, made infamous during World War II by the "Death Railway," built by Allied prisoners of war who worked and lived under horrifying conditions, and a bridge (made famous by the film *Bridge on the River Kwai*) over the river near Kanchanaburi. Just to the north of Bangkok (which is in every way the center of the country, along the Chao Phraya River banks) is Ayutthaya, Thailand's second capital after Sukhothai.

THE SOUTHERN PENINSULA The long, narrow Southern Peninsula (the elephant's trunk) extends south to the Malaysian border, with the Andaman Sea on the west and the Gulf of Thailand on the east. The eastern coastline along the gulf extends more than 1,802km (1,125 miles); the western shoreline runs 716km (445 miles) along the Andaman Sea. This region is the most tropical in the country, with heavy rainfall during monsoon seasons. The northeast monsoon, roughly from November to April, brings clear weather and calm seas to the west coast; the southwest monsoon, March to October, brings similar conditions to the east coast. There are glamorous beach resorts here (people visit them even during the rainy season; it doesn't rain all day), such as the western islands of Phuket and nearby Ko Phi Phi. Ko Samui, off the east coast, is a bit more relaxed and not yet as expensive as the former two.

ISAAN Finally, Isaan, the broad and relatively infertile northeast plateau (the ear of the elephant), is the least developed region in Thailand, bordered by the Mekong River (*Mae Nam Khong* in Thai). Isaan is dusty in the cool winter and muddy during the summer monsoon. Fewer tourists make their way to Isaan than any other part of the country, so we've opted not to cover it in this chapter.

THAILAND TODAY

Today, under a pyramid of king, nation, and religion, Thais enjoy greater freedom than any people in Asia and continue to tenaciously hold their nation together. The government is a constitutional monarchy (though the constitution is still biased toward military rule). The country's political structure remains relatively flexible, yet many Thais feel that despite constant changes in leadership as political parties form new alliances and old political figures are recycled, the government remains more or less the same mixture in a different cup. King Bhumibol Adulyadej holds a position outside of government but is recognized as the defender of all Thai people. On a few occasions, he has put his foot down when government monkey business is not beneficial to his people. His word is always heeded.

The nation's most pressing concern at the time of writing, and most likely for years to come, is recovery from the **economic crisis** and the politicians who stall the legislative process to protect their own business interests. Reform proposals for debt restructuring that are desperately needed to jump-start the economy have been stonewalled in parliament by politicians who are linked to many failed businesses. Media reporting of political activities is wide open, especially in comparison to most of Thailand's ASEAN neighbors, and the press here can't seem to resist any story involving accusations of corruption in politics. In international relations, at the time of this writing, Thailand's main concerns involved its immediate neighbors Cambodia and Myanmar. Refugees crossing over both borders have squeezed Thailand's resources, and pressure from the West to stop drug trafficking from Myanmar has put Thailand in the middle of some heated regional and global situations (though none of these should affect law-abiding visitors to the country in any way).

A LOOK AT THE PAST

Archaeologists believe that Thailand was a major thoroughfare for *Homo erectus* en route from Africa to China and other parts of Asia. Modern civilization did not arrive in Thailand until about a thousand years ago, when waves of people migrated from central and southern China, settling primarily in what is now Vietnam, Laos, Thailand, and Burma. These people, who are called *Tai,* became dispersed over a vast area of space, sharing a cultural and linguistic commonality. Their descendents are the core bloodline of the Thai people of today, plus some tribal peoples of Burma, Laos, southern China, Vietnam, and others in northeastern India. The **early Tais** lived in nuclear families with a dozen or two households forming an independently ruled *muang,* or village, eventually establishing loosely structured feudal states where both lord and villager benefited— the lord from manpower and the villager from stability.

From the 6th century, Southeast Asia underwent a gradual period of **Indianization.** Merchants and missionaries from India introduced Brahmanism and Buddhism to the region, as well as Indian political and social values and art and architectural preferences. Around the 6th century, the **Mon,** migrants from Burma, were responsible for establishing Sri Lankan Buddhism in central Thailand. The Mons supported extensive religious establishments, usually Buddhist, and their religious life was reinforced by regular contact with India, visiting monks, imported sacred scriptures, and works of art.

By the early 9th century, the **Khmer** Empire had risen to power in Cambodia, spreading into surrounding areas. Magnificent Khmer temples, originally built for the worship of Hindu deities, were constructed in outposts increasingly farther from the Cambodian center of the empire. Brahmanism, having been introduced by traders from southern India, influenced not only Khmer religion and temple design (with the distinct corncob-shape *prang,* or tower), but government administration and social order as well. Angkor Wat, Cambodia's great ancient temple city, was built during the reign of **Suryavarman II** (1113–5?). The last great Khmer ruler, **Jayavarman VII** (1181–1219), extended the empire to its farthest limits—north to Vientiane, west to Burma, and down the Malay peninsula. It was he who shifted Khmer ideology toward Buddhism, building temples in Khmer style, but with a Buddhist purpose. Many historians believe the decline of the Khmers was due to this overextension of territories.

In 1259, several powerful centers of Tai power in northern Thailand, southern China, and Laos were united by **King Mengrai**, who established the first capital of the **Lanna Kingdom** at Chiang Rai in 1263, and later at Chiang Mai in 1296. The Lanna Kingdom saw the rise of a scholarly Buddhism, with strict adherence to orthodox ways. Citizens enjoyed the benefits of infrastructure projects for transportation and irrigation, developed medicine and law, and created artistic expression through religious sculpture, sacred texts, and poetry. But the Mongols, under the fierce expansionist leadership of **Kublai Khan,** forced their way into the region. Mengrai, forming strategic alliances with neighboring kingdoms, succeeded in keeping the Mongols at bay.

In the vacuum left by the departing Khmers, a tiny kingdom based in **Sukhothai** rose to fame after its crown prince Rama single-handedly defeated an invasion from neighboring Mae Sot at the Burmese border. Upon his coronation in 1279, **Ramkhamhaeng,** or "Rama the Bold," set the scene for what is recognized as the first truly Siamese civilization, mixing all the people of the central plains—Tai, Mon, Khmer, and indigenous populations, with threads of India and China interwoven in their cultural tapestry. In response to the Khmer's hierarchical rule, Ramkhamhaeng established himself as an accessible king. He was a devout Buddhist, adopting the orthodox and scholarly Theravada Buddhism. A patron of the arts, the king commissioned many great Buddha images, initiated splendid architectural achievements, and developed the modern Thai written language. After his death in 1298, his successors failed to rule wisely and Sukhothai's brilliant spark faded almost as quickly at it had ignited.

Next came the kingdom of **Ayutthaya,** which swallowed what was left of Khmer outposts and the Sukhothai kingdom. Incorporating the strengths of its population—Tai military manpower and labor, Khmer bureaucratic sensibilities, and Chinese commercial talents, the empire grew wealthy and strong. Following Khmer models, the king rose above his subjects atop a huge pyramid-shape administration. A huge fortified city was built, with temples that glittered as any in Sukhothai. This was the Kingdom of Siam that the first Europeans, the Portuguese, encountered in 1511.

Burmese invasion forces took Chiang Mai's Lanna Kingdom in 1558 and finally Ayutthaya in 1569. However, during the occupation, **Prince Naresuan,** descended from Sukhothai kings, in a historic battle scene atop an elephant, challenged the Burmese crown prince and defeated him with a single blow. Ayutthaya continued through the following 2 centuries in grand style, and while its Southeast Asian neighbors were falling under colonial rule, the court of Siam retained its own sovereignty. *It has the distinction of being the only Southeast Asian nation never to have been colonized, a point of great pride for Thais today.* Unfortunately, the final demise of Ayutthaya was two more Burmese invasions in the 1760s.

The Siamese did not hesitate to build another kingdom. **Taksin,** a provincial governor, rose to power on military excellence, charisma, and a firm belief that he was divinely appointed to lead the land. Rebuilding the capital at Thonburi, on the western bank of the Chao Phraya River (opposite present-day Bangkok), within 3 years he reunited the lands under the previous kingdom. But Taksin suffered from paranoia—he had monks killed, along with eventually his own wife and children. Regional powers were quick to get rid of him—he was swiftly kidnapped, covered in a velvet sack, and beaten to death with a sandalwood club.

These same regional powers turned to **Chaophraya Chakri** in 1782 to lead the land. Crowned **King Ramathibodi,** he was the first king of Thailand's present dynasty, the **Chakri Dynasty.** He moved the capital across the river to Bangkok, where he built the **Grand Palace** and great temples. The city grew around a network of canals, with the river as the central channel for trade and commerce. Rama I reinstated Theravada Buddhist doctrine, re-established the state ceremonies of Ayutthaya, and revised all laws. He also wrote the *Ramakien,* based upon the Indian *Ramayana,* a legend that has become the subject for many Thai classical arts.

King Mongkut (1851–68) with his son, **King Chulalongkorn** (1868–1910), lead Siam into the 20th century as an independent nation, establishing an effective civil service, formalizing global relations, and introducing industrialization-based economics.

It was King Mongkut who hired Anna Leonowens (of *The King and I*) as an English tutor for his children. Thai people want everyone to know that Mongkut was not the overbearing, pushover fop described in her account. Historians side with the Thais, for she is barely mentioned in court accounts—the story had its origins more in her imagination than in realty.

During the reign of **King Prajadhipok,** Rama VII (1925–35), the growing urban middle class became increasingly discontent. Economic failings and bureaucratic bickering weakened the position of the monarchy, which was delivered its final blow by the Great Depression. In 1932, a group of midlevel officials staged a coup d'etat, and Prajadhipok abdicated in 1935.

Democracy had a shaky hold on Siam. Over the following decades, government leadership changed hands fast and frequently, many times the result of hostile takeover with the military at the helm. In 1939, the nation adopted the name Thailand—"Land of the Free."

During **World War II,** democracy was stalled in the face of the Japanese invasion in 1941. Thailand chose to side with the Japanese, but at the war's end, no punitive measures were taken against Thailand; the Thai ambassador in Washington had failed to deliver his country's declaration of war against the Allies.

Thailand managed to stay out of direct involvement in the **Vietnam War;** however, it continues to suffer repercussions from the burden of refugees. The U.S. pumped billions into the Thai economy, bringing riches to some and relative affluence to many, but further impoverishing the poor. Communism became an increasingly attractive political philosophy, and a full-scale insurrection seemed imminent. In June 1973, thousands of Thai students demonstrated in the streets, demanding a new constitution and the return to democratic principals. Tensions grew until October, when armed forces attacked a demonstration at Thammasat University in Bangkok, killing 69 students and wounding 800, paralyzing the capital with terror and revulsion.

The constitution was restored, a new government was elected, and democracy once again wobbled on. Many students, however, were not yet satisfied and continued to complain that the financial elite were still in control and still resisting change. In 1976, student protests again broke out, and there was a replay of the grisly scene of 3 years before at Thammasat University. The army seized control to impose and maintain order, conveniently spiriting away some bodies and prisoners, and another brief experiment with democracy was at an end. Thanin Kraivichien was installed as prime minister of a new right-wing government, which suspended freedom of speech and the press, further polarizing Thai society.

In 1980, Prem Tinsulanonda was named prime minister, and during the following 8 years, he managed to bring remarkable political and economic stability to Thailand. The Thai economy continued to grow steadily through the 1980s, fueled by Japanese investment and Chinese capital in flight from Hong Kong. Leadership since then has seen quite a few changes, including a military coup in 1991 and another student crackdown in 1992. It was under Gen. Chavalit Yongjaiyudh's administration that the economic crisis hit Thailand in July 1997. While his government sat on its hands in indecision over how to proceed, connections between public officials and bad financial institutions became more apparent and international investors lost confidence in Thailand. While in August 1997 Thailand accepted $17 billion in bailouts from the International Monetary Fund, political in-fighting stalled the government's action until November of the same year, when Chuan Leekpai, a previous prime minister, was elected into office again to try to straighten things out.

THAILAND'S PEOPLE & CULTURE

The Thais are a true melting pot of many people and cultures. They descended from immigrants from southern China who for centuries absorbed Mon, Khmer, Laotian, Persian, Indian, and Malay people and influences. Today the people of modern Thailand cannot credit their ethnic identity as anything other than Thai. The hill-tribe peoples of the north are descended from Tibeto-Burman people who migrated down the Himalayas to the hills of northern Indochina.

RELIGION

Thai culture cannot be fully appreciated without some understanding of **Buddhism,** which is followed by 90% of the population. Although Buddhism first came to Thailand in the 3rd century B.C., when missionaries were sent from India, it was not until the 14th century that the *sangha* (monastic order) was established. The king entered the order, thus beginning the close connection between the royal house and the *sangha* that continues to this day.

Other religions and philosophies are also followed in Thailand, including Islam, Christianity, Hinduism, and Sikhism. Sunni Islam is followed by more than 2 million Thais, mostly in the south. Even after centuries of evangelism, there are only a quarter of a million Christians living in the country.

ETIQUETTE

Disrespect for the royal family and religious figures, sites, and objects will cause great offense. While photography is permitted in temples (except for Wat Phra Kaeo), never climb on a Buddha image, and if you sit down, never point your feet in the direction of the Buddha image. Women should never touch a monk or give something to one directly. A monk will provide a cloth for you to lay the item upon, and he will collect it.

Thais consider the feet the lowest part of the body, so pointing your feet at someone is considered offensive. Shoes should be removed when entering a temple or private home. And don't ever step over someone's body or legs. Alternately, the head, as the highest part of the body, should never be touched, not even in jest.

Tips Wats 101

The wat, or Buddhist temple/monastery, is the defining architectural structure in Thailand. Bangkok alone has more than 400, with thousands more spread out across the land.

With their Chinese wooden building techniques, polychromatic schemes, and Japanese-influenced carved flowing lines, the **Sukhothai-era Thai wats** (13th and 14th centuries) represented the first "pure" Thai Buddhist style, and it was during this time that the mainstays of Thai wat architecture were created. They include (in order of artistic importance): the *phra chedi* (stupa), *bot, wihaan, phra prang, mondop,* and *prasat.*

The dome-shape **phra chedi**—usually called simply *chedi* and better known in the West as stupa—is the most venerated structure and an elaboration of the basic mound. Originally it enshrined relics of the Buddha; later it contained items of holy men and kings. A stupa consists of a dome (tumulus) constructed atop a round base (drum) and surmounted by a cubical chair representing the seated Buddha, over which is the *chatra* (umbrella) in one or several (usually 9) tiers.

The **bot** (*ubosoth* or *uposatha*) is where the *bhikku* (monks) meditate and all ceremonies are performed. It consists of either one large nave or one nave with lateral aisles built on a rectangular plan where the Buddha image is enshrined. At the end of each ridge of the roof are graceful finials, called *chofa* (meaning "sky tassel"), which are reminiscent of animal horns but are thought to represent celestial geese or the Garuda (a mythological monster ridden by the god Shiva). The triangular gables are adorned with gilded wooden ornamentation and glass mosaics.

The **wihaan** (*vihara* or *viharn*) is a replica of the bot that is used to keep Buddha images.

The **phra prang,** which originated with the corner tower of the Khmer temple, is a new form of Thai stupa, elliptical in shape and also housing images of the Buddha.

The **mondop** is made of wood or brick. On a square-pillared base, the pyramidal roof is formed by a series of receding stories, enriched with the same decoration tapering off in a pinnacle. It might serve to enshrine some holy object, or it might serve as a kind of library and storeroom for religious ceremonial objects, as it does at Wat Phra Kaeo in Bangkok.

The **prasat** ("castle") is a direct descendant of the Khmer temple, with its round-topped spire and Greek-cross layout. At the center is a square sanctuary with a domed *sikhara* and four porchlike antechambers that project from the main building, giving the whole a steplike contour. The *prasat* serves either as the royal throne hall or as a shrine for some venerated objects, such as the *prasat* of Wat Phra Kaeo in Bangkok, which enshrines the statues of the kings of the present dynasty.

Perhaps the most important advice I can give is this: In public, never show anger, temper, or frustration. The Thai people consider such public displays a sign of a less developed, primitive being. While banging your fist on the counter might get you better service back home, in Thailand you'll be promptly ignored. You'll catch more bees with honey.

A lovely Thai greeting is the *wai:* Place your palms together, raise the tips of your fingers to your chin, and make a subtle bow from the waist while bending your knees slightly. The person of lower social status initiates a wai. In general, you should not wai to children and to someone providing a service to you. Also, don't expect a monk to return a wai; they're exempt due to their unique social status.

Address a Thai person by his or her first name preceded by "Khun." For example, Methinee Pratoomsuvarn should be properly addressed as Khun Methinee. Don't be surprised if you are solely addressed by your first name—such as Mr. John or Ms. Mary. Closer Thai friends will use nicknames, which are usually much easier to remember.

Even though this is a tropical country and you've probably come in search of the ultimate beach experience, it is offensive to the Thais to see tourists bare themselves in public, wear bathing suits around town, or go topless on the beach. It is particularly inappropriate for men or women to wear shorts, halter tops, or miniskirts in temples. Cover thyself in the presence of the Buddha.

THAI CUISINE: TIGER PRAWNS TO PAD THAI

Enjoying exquisite food is one of the true joys of traveling in Thailand. If you aren't familiar with Thai cooking, imagine the best of Chinese food ingredients and preparation combined with the sophistication of Indian spicing and topped off with red and green chiles. The styles of cooking available in Bangkok run the gamut from mild northern khan toke to extremely spicy southern curries. Basic ingredients include a cornucopia of shellfish, fresh fruits, and vegetables—asparagus, tamarind, bean sprouts, carrots, mushrooms of all kinds, various kinds of spinach, and bamboo shoots, combined with pungent spices such as basil, lemongrass, mint, chile, garlic, and coriander. Thai cooking also uses coconut milk, curry paste, peanuts, and a large variety of noodles and rice.

Among the dishes you'll find throughout the country are: *tom yum goong,* a Thai hot-and-sour shrimp soup; satay, charcoal-broiled chicken, beef, or pork strips skewered on a bamboo stick and dipped in a peanut-coconut curry sauce; spring rolls, similar to egg rolls but with a thinner crust and usually containing only vegetables; *larb,* a spicy chicken or ground-beef concoction with mint and lime flavoring; salads, most with a dressing of onion, chile pepper, lime juice, and fish sauce; *pad thai* ("Thai noodles"), rice noodles usually served with large shrimp, eggs, peanuts, fresh bean sprouts, lime, and a delicious sauce; *khao soi,* a northern curried soup served at small food stalls; a wide range of curries, flavored with coriander, chile, garlic, and fish sauce or coconut milk; spicy *tod man pla,* one of many fish dishes; sticky rice, served in the north and made from glutinous rice, prepared with vegetables and wrapped in a banana leaf; and Thai fried rice, a simple rice dish made with whatever the kitchen has on hand. "American fried rice" usually means fried rice topped by an easy-over egg and sometimes accompanied by fried chicken.

A word of caution: Thai palates relish incredibly spicy food, normally much more fiery than is tolerated in even the most piquant Western cuisines. Protect your own palate by saying *"Mai phet, farang,"* meaning "Not spicy, foreigner."

Traditionally, Thai menus don't offer fancy desserts, but the local fruit is luscious enough. Familiar fruits are pineapple (served with salt to heighten its flavor), mangoes, bananas, guava, papaya, coconut, and watermelon, as well as the latest rage, apples grown in the royal orchards. Less familiar possibilities are durian, in season during June and July, which is a Thai favorite, but this is an acquired taste because it smells like rotten onions; mangosteen, a purplish, hard-skinned fruit with delicate, whitish-pink segments that melt in the mouth, available April to September; jackfruit, which is large and yellow-brown with a thick, thorned skin that envelops tangy-flavored flesh, available year-round; longan, a small, brown-skinned fruit with very sweet white flesh available July to October; tamarind, a spicy little fruit in a pod that you can eat fresh or candied; rambu-tan, which is small, red, and hairy, with transparent sweet flesh clustered round a woody seed, available May to July; and pomelo, similar to a grapefruit but less juicy, available October to December. Some of these fruits are served as salads—the raw green papaya, for example, can be quite good.

LANGUAGE

Thai is derived principally from Mon, Khmer, Chinese, Pali, Sanskrit, and, increasingly, English. It is a tonal language, with distinctions based on inflec-tion—low, mid, high, rising, or falling tone—rather than stress, and it can elude most speakers of Western languages. One interesting aspect of the language that can be confusing to first-time visitors is that the polite words roughly corre-sponding to our *sir* and *ma'am* are determined not by the gender of the person addressed, but by the gender of the speaker; females say *ka* and males say *krap.*

English is spoken in the major cities at most hotels, restaurants, and shops, and is the second language of the professional class, as well as the international business language.

Unfortunately, there is no universal transliteration system, so you will see the usual **Thai greeting** written in Roman letters as *sawatdee, sawaddi, sawasdee, sawusdi,* and so forth. Some consistency has been imposed in transliterating place names. For example, you will still see the Laotian capital written Wiang Chan as well as Vientienne or Viantiane, and the word *Ratcha* ("Royal"), as in Ratchadamnoen, can be rendered *Raja, Radja,* and *Raj.* Sometimes you'll see Ko Samet as Koh Samed, or the ancient city of Ayutthaya spelled Ayudhya, but for most destinations, the spelling has been more or less standardized as presented in this chapter.

Central Thai is the official written and spoken language of the country, and most Thais understand it, but there are three other major dialects: **Northeastern-Thai,** spoken in Isaan and closely related to Lao; **Northern Thai,** spoken in the northwest, from Tak Province to the Burmese border; and **Southern Thai,** spo-ken from Chumphon Province south to the Malaysian border. The hill tribes in the North have their own distinct languages, most related to Burmese or Tibetan.

USEFUL THAI PHRASES

Hello	**Sa-wa-dee-krup (males); sa-wa-dee-ka (females)**
How are you?	**Sa-bai-dee-rue**
I am fine.	**Sa-bai-dee**
Excuse me	**Kor-tod-krup (males); kor-tod-ka (females)**
I understand.	**Kao-jai.**
I don't understand.	**Mai-kao-jai.**
Do you speak English?	**Khun-pood-pa-sa-ang-rid-dai-mai?**
Not spicy, please	**Kor-mai-ped**
Thank you	**Kop-koon-krup (male); kop-koon-ka (female)**
How much?	**Tao-rai?**

That's expensive.	**Paeng**
Discount	**Lod-ra-ka**
Where is the toilet?	**Hong-nam-yoo-tee-nai?**
Stop here.	**Yood-tee-nee.**

2 Planning Your Trip to Thailand

VISITOR INFORMATION

The **Tourism Authority of Thailand (TAT)** publishes pamphlets and maps on many destinations throughout the country, even places that aren't on the usual travel agenda, and posts them upon request. Current schedules for festivals and holidays come in especially handy when planning your trip. Once in the country, you'll also find good, privately produced maps and tourist publications— many free—at most hotels and many businesses.

On the Internet, visit **www.tourismthailand.org** the **TAT's** virtual travel information center; or **Welcome to Thailand,** at **www.mahidol.ac.th/ Thailand/Thailand-main.html**, for cultural, geographic, historical, and economic information.

IN THE UNITED STATES & CANADA

- **Los Angeles:** 611 North Larchmont Blvd,, 1st Floor, , Los Angeles, CA 90004 (© **323/461-9894;** fax 323/461-9834).
- **New York:** (temporary address) c/o World Publications 304 Park Avenue South, 8 th Floor, New York, NY 10010 New York, NY 10048 (© **212/ 219-4655;** fax 212/219-4697).
- **Canada:** While there is no TAT office in Canada, the Chicago office represents this region.

IN AUSTRALIA & NEW ZEALAND

- **Sydney:** 2nd Floor, 75 Pitt St., Sydney 2000, N.S.W. (© **02/9247-7549;** fax 02/9251-2465).
- **New Zealand:** Like Canada, New Zealand has no TAT representative of its own, but the office in Sydney can forward information upon request.

IN THE UNITED KINGDOM

- **London:** 3rd Floor, Brook House, 98-99 Jermyn Street, London SW1Y6EE. (© 44 207/-925-2511; fax 44 207/ 925-2512).

ENTRY REQUIREMENTS

All visitors to Thailand must carry a valid **passport** with **proof of onward passage** (either a return or through ticket). Visa applications are not required if you are staying up to 30 days and are a national of 1 of 41 designated countries, including Australia, Canada, Ireland, New Zealand, the U.K., and the U.S. New Zealanders may stay up to 3 months. Visa extensions can be obtained at the nearest immigration office and cost 500 baht. Visitors who overstay their visa will be fined 200 baht (US$4.65) for each extra day, payable in cash upon exiting the country.

CUSTOMS REGULATIONS

Tourists are allowed to enter the country with 1 liter of alcohol and 200 cigarettes (or 250g of cigars or smoking tobacco) per adult, duty-free. There are no restrictions on the import of foreign currencies or traveler's checks, but you cannot export foreign currency in excess of 10,000 baht (US$233) unless declared to Customs upon arrival.

MONEY

The Thai unit of currency, the **baht,** is written on price tags and elsewhere as the letter B crossed with a vertical slash. In this chapter, I've written it as B, as in "100B." One baht is divided into 100 **satang,** though you'll rarely see a satang coin. Yellow coins represent 25 and 50 satang; silver coins are 1B, 5B, and 10B. Bank notes come in denominations of 10B (brown), 20B (green), 50B (blue), 100B (red), 500B (purple), and 1,000B (khaki). While the rate is still experiencing some flux following the 1997 Asian economic crisis, it's still relatively stable, hovering around 40B per U.S. dollar. For this book, I used an exchange rate of 43 baht per U.S. dollar. Obtain the latest money conversions before you plan your trip. For up-to-date conversions, visit the currency chart at www.xe.net/ict.

Most major banks in Bangkok now have **automated teller machines,** and ATMs are increasingly common in major tourist spots. The largest banks in Thailand all perform account debit and cash advance services through the Cirrus/MasterCard or PLUS/Visa networks (try **Bangkok Bank, Thai Farmers Bank,** and **Bank of Ayudhya**). Things to keep in mind: The fee for a withdrawal is US$1.25 per transaction, and time changes between here and home can affect your ability to withdraw cash on 2 consecutive business days.

Traveler's checks are negotiable in most banks, hotels, restaurants, and tourist-oriented shops, but you'll receive a better rate by cashing them at commercial banks.

Nearly all international hotels and larger businesses accept **major credit cards,** but few accept personal checks. Despite protests from credit card companies, many establishments add a 3% to 5% surcharge for payment. Use discretion in using your card—all major credit card companies list Thailand as a high-risk area for fraud. Don't let your card out of your sight, even for a moment, and be sure to keep all receipts. I generally don't like to use credit cards outside hotels anyway, as many retailers will give better discounts for cash payments.

In small towns and remote places, cash is the name of the game.

LOST/STOLEN CREDIT CARDS & TRAVELER'S CHECKS   To report a lost or stolen credit card, you can call these service lines: American Express ℂ 02/273-0022; Diners Club ℂ 02/238-3660; JCB (Japanese Credit Bank) ℂ 02/631-1938; MasterCard ℂ 02/232-2039; and Visa ℂ 02/256-7324.

WIRING EMERGENCY FUNDS   **Western Union** has branches throughout Bangkok and many provincial capitals—thanks to partnerships with Central Department Store and Bangkok Metropolitan Bank. The service allows you to either send or receive cash worldwide immediately at local branches connected with Western Union offices worldwide. *One word of warning:* Cash sent in foreign currencies will be exchanged to Thai baht using a seriously awful exchange rate. Use this service only in emergency and in the smallest necessary amounts. Call the Western Union Customer Service Center in Bangkok at 02/254-7000. The head office is at Central Department Store, Chidlom Branch (3rd floor, 1027 Ploenchit Rd.; ℂ **02/655-7777,** ext. 3357).

WHEN TO GO

CLIMATE   Thailand has two distinct climate zones: tropical in the south and tropical savanna in the north. The northern and central areas of the country (including Bangkok) experience three distinct seasons. The hot season lasts from March to May, with temperatures averaging in the upper 90s Fahrenheit (mid-30s Celsius); April is the hottest month. This period sees very little rain, if any at all. The rainy season begins in June and lasts until October; the average

Warning   The Thai Sex Industry & AIDS

Every day you're in Thailand, in any part of the country, you will see foreigners enjoying the company of Thai women and men. Although prostitution is illegal, it's as much a part of the tourism industry as superb hotels and stunning beaches.

With a legacy of royal patronage and social acceptance, the oldest profession has been part of Thailand's economy for centuries, although in the 19th century most brothels were operated by the Chinese and the majority of commercial sex workers (CSWs) were foreign until the 1930s. Today this burgeoning industry is still publicly ignored, and because the subject is controversial, the number fluctuates depending on whom you talk to. Some groups will say only 80,000, while others will put the number as high as 800,000.

Thailand has aggressively developed research and education programs on the subject of AIDS. The largest nongovernmental organization in Thailand, the PCDA, led by the courageous and innovative public health crusader Meechai Viravaidya, has enlarged the scope of its rural development programs from family planning and cottage-industry schemes, to distributing condoms and running seminars for CSWs. Even the royal family is in on it: Her Royal Highness Princess Chulaporn Walailuke, founder of the Chulaporn Research Institute and an internationally known activist, sponsored the 1990 International Global AIDS Conference in Bangkok and continues to be active.

If you patronize commercial sex workers, take proper precautions; use a latex condom.

---

temperature is 84°F (29°C), with 90% humidity. While the rainy season brings frequent showers, it's rare for them to last for a whole day or for days on end. Daily showers come in torrents, usually in the late afternoon or evening for maybe 3 or 4 hours—many times bringing floods. If you plan on trekking in the north, I don't recommend going during this time, when you'll be slogging through mucky trails. The cool season, from November through February, has temperatures from the high 70s to low 80s Fahrenheit (21°C–27°C), with moderate and infrequent rain showers. In the north during the cool season (which is also the peak season for tourism), day temperatures can be as low as 60°F (16°C) in Chiang Mai and 41°F (5°C) in the hills.

The southern Malay Peninsula has intermittent showers year-round and daily ones during the rainy season (temperatures average in the low 80s Fahrenheit/30s Celsius). If you're traveling to Phuket or Ko Samui, it will be helpful to note that the two islands alternate peak seasons somewhat. Optimal weather on Phuket occurs between November and April, when the island welcomes the highest numbers of travelers and the most expensive resort rates. Alternately, Ko Samui's great weather lasts from about February to October. Refer to each destination's section for more information about peak seasons and weather patterns.

PUBLIC HOLIDAYS   Many holidays are based on the Thai lunar calendar; check with TAT for the current year's schedule and for holidays and festivals specific to certain regions.

travel • news • classifieds • health • personals • maps • autos • spot

Plan your vacation

- flights, hotels, car rentals
- cruises & vacation packages
- destination guides
- fare alerts
- go to yahoo.com, click travel

© 2003 Yahoo! Inc.

powered by

The national holidays are: Makha Puja (Feb full moon), Chakri Day (Apr 6), Songkran (Thai New Year, Apr 12–14); Coronation Day (May 5), Visakha Puja (May full moon), Asalha Puja (July full moon), Her Majesty the Queen's Birthday (Aug 12), Chulalongkorn Day (Oct 23), His Majesty the King's Birthday (Dec 5), and Constitution Day (Dec 10), as well as New Year's Eve (Dec 31) and New Year's Day (Jan 1).

GETTING THERE
BY PLANE
Bangkok International Airport (aka Don Muang Airport) links all Southeast Asian nations with every other corner of the world. Because Bangkok is a regional hub, you might find yourself stopping through en route to other destinations, even if you don't plan to visit Thailand.

Thai Airways International (head office: 485 Silom Rd., Bangkok; © 02/ 280-0060; www.thaiair.com) covers virtually all Southeast Asian nations in its routing.

The best way to ensure the most economical airfare on direct flights to Thailand is to call a registered travel agent for your reservations and booking. Some of the best fares on direct flights can come from unexpected airlines. From Cambodia you can take Bangkok Airways, Kampuchea Airlines, or Royal Air Camboge. From Hong Kong, you can fly Cathay Pacific, China Airlines, Emirates, Gulf Air, Japan Airlines, or Sri Lankan Airlines. Indonesian routes are serviced by Garuda Indonesia, and from Laos there's Lao Aviation. From Myanmar, you can fly Biman Bangladesh Airlines or Myanmar Airways International; from Malaysia, you can fly Malaysian Airlines. From the Philippines, you can take Egypt Air, Lufthansa German Airlines, or Philippine Airlines. From Singapore, try Biman Bangladesh Airlines (one of the least expensive flights), Cathay Pacific, Finnair, Pakistan International Airlines, Royal Nepal Airlines (another good fare), Singapore Airlines, Swissair, or Turkish Airlines. Vietnam Airlines provides service from Vietnam.

Another important consideration is your desired point of entry. The above flights are to Bangkok, but there are additional direct flights into Chiang Mai from Kuala Lumpur, Singapore, and Vientiane and Luang Prabang in Laos; flights to Phuket from Hong Kong, Kuala Lumpur, Singapore, and Phnom Penh and Siem Reap in Cambodia; flights to Ko Samui from Singapore, and flights to U Tapao (Pattaya) from Phnom Penh.

Don't forget that if you leave Thailand by air, you're required to pay 500B (US$12) **international departure tax.**

BY TRAIN
Thailand is accessible via train from Singapore and peninsular Malaysia. Malaysia's Keretapi Tanah Melayu Berhad (KTM) begins in Singapore (© 65/ 222-5165), stopping in Kuala Lumpur (© 603/273-8000) and Butterworth (Penang; © 604/323-7962) before heading for Thailand, where it joins service with the **State Railway of Thailand.** Bangkok's Hua Lamphong Railway Station is centrally located on Krung Kassem Road (© 02/223-7010 or 02/223-7020). Taxis, tuk-tuks, and public buses are just outside the station.

The **Eastern & Oriental Express** (www.orient-expresstrains.com), sister to the Venice Simplon-Orient-Express, runs once a week between Singapore and Bangkok in exquisite luxury, with occasional departures between Bangkok and Chiang Mai. For international reservations, from the U.S. and Canada, call © 800/524-2420; from Australia, call © 3/9699-9766; from New Zealand, call

℄ **9/379-3708;** and from the U.K., call ℄ **020 7805 5100.** From Singapore, Malaysia, and Thailand, contact E&O in Singapore at (℄ **65/392-3500**).

BY BUS

From every major city in peninsular Malaysia (and even Singapore), you can pick up a bus to Thailand—at least to Hat Yai in southern Thailand, where you can transfer to another bus to your destination. Stop by the bus terminal in any city to find out about time schedules. VIP buses cost more but have fewer seats, which means more legroom. Traveling up the peninsula by bus is arduous, at best. If you can take the train, you'll be far more comfortable with a sleeping berth and a little walking space.

GETTING AROUND

Transportation within Thailand is accessible, efficient, and inexpensive. If your time is short, fly. But if you have the time to take in the countryside and you care to see a bit of provincial living, travel by bus, train, or private car.

BY PLANE

Domestic routes provided by Thai Airways, Bangkok Airways, and Angel Air make flying not only some of the most convenient traveling in the Kingdom, but some of the cheapest as well. Time was, Bangkok served as the hub for almost all connections between domestic flights, but these days you can find flights between provincial cities without stopping in Bangkok; for example, flights travel between Pattaya, Ko Samui, and Phuket.

Bangkok International Airport (Don Muang) can be reached at ℄ **02/535-2081** for domestic flights only. Most domestic flights are on **Thai Airways,** part of Thai Airways International, 6 Lam Luang Rd., Bangkok (℄ **02/535-2084**), with Bangkok as its hub. Flights connect Bangkok and 25 domestic cities, including Chiang Mai, Chiang Rai, and Phuket. There are also connecting flights between many cities.

Bangkok Airways (head office: 60 Queen Sirikit National Convention Center, New Ratchadaphisek Road; ℄ **02/229-3456**) covers routes between Bangkok, Ranong, Sukhothai, Chiang Mai, Ko Samui, Phuket, Krabi, and Pattaya (U-Tapao). The new **Angel Airlines** (3rd floor, Tower B, Benjajinda Bldg., 499 Vibhavadi Randsit Rd.; ℄ **02/953-2260**) serves Bangkok and Singapore, and domestically Bangkok, Chiang Mai, and Phuket.

BY TRAIN

From Bangkok, the **State Railway of Thailand** provides regular service to destinations north as far as Chiang Mai, northeast to Udon Thani, east to Pattaya, and south to Thailand's southern border, where it connects with Malaysia's Keretapi Tanah Melayu Berhad (KTM) with service to Penang (Butterworth), Kuala Lumpur, and Singapore. Complete schedules and fare information can be obtained at any railway station or by calling **Hua Lampong Railway Station** directly at ℄ **02/223-7010** or 02/223-7020. Advance bookings can be made by calling ℄ 02/223-3762 or 02/224-7788.

Fares are a bit tricky to figure out at first because they use a double charge system. The first charge depends on the distance you travel between stations; for example, a trip from Bangkok to Hua Hin (229km/142 miles) is 202B (US$4.70) for first-class travel, 102B (US$2.37) for second-class travel, and 44B (US$1.02) for third-class travel. From Bangkok to Chiang Mai (751km/465½ miles), the rates are something like 593B (US$14) for first class, 281B (US$6.53) for second class, and 121B (US$2.81) for third class.

The second, or "supplementary charge," is relative to the speed at which you travel and the comfort level you desire. There are more than a few different trains, each running at a different speed. The fastest is the Special Express, which is used primarily for long-distance hauls. These trains cut travel time by as much as 60% and have sleeper cars, which are a must for the really long trips. Supplementary charges range from 40B (US93¢) for the Rapid Train to 120B (US$2.79) for the Special Express with catering service. Sleeping berth supplementary charges are from 100B (US$2.33) for a second-class upper berth on a Rapid Train to 520B (US$12) per person for a double first-class cabin.

Warning: On trains, pay close attention to your possessions. Thievery is common on overnight trips.

BY BUS

Thailand has a very efficient and inexpensive bus system, highly recommended for budget travelers and short-haul trips. Options abound, but the major choices are public or private, air-conditioned or non-air-conditioned. Most travelers use the private, air-conditioned buses. Ideally, buses are best for short excursions; expect to pay a minimum of 50B (US$1.20) for a one-way ticket. Longer-haul buses are an excellent value, but their slowness and lack of comfort can be a real liability.

There are three main bus terminals in Bangkok, each servicing a different part of the country. Buses to and from the southern peninsula originate at the **Southern Bus Terminal** (© 02/435-1199), on Charan Sanitwong Road, across the river at the Bangkok Noi Station. Buses to the east coast arrive and depart from the **Eastern Bus Terminal** (© 02/390-1230), on Sukhumvit Road opposite Soi 63 (Ekamai Rd.). Buses to all the northern areas are at the **Northern Bus Terminal** (© 02/272-5761), on Phahonythin Road, near the Chatuchak Weekend Market.

Warning: When traveling by long-distance bus, pay close attention to your possessions. Thievery is common, particularly on overnight buses when valuables are left in overhead racks.

BY CAR

Renting a car is almost too easy in Thailand. I don't recommend driving yourself in Bangkok because the traffic patterns are very confusing and jams are entirely frustrating. Outside the city, it's a good option, though Thai drivers are quite reckless. *One caution:* In many places, if you have an accident you will most likely be held responsible, regardless of actual fault. Many times the person believed most able to pay is the person who ultimately foots the bill.

Among the many car-rental agencies, the company that offers the best cars and insurance policies at the most competitive rates is **Budget Car and Truck Rental.** They have offices in Bangkok (© 02/203-0250; fax 02/203-0249; www.budget.co.th) as well as Chiang Mai, Chiang Rai, Hua Hin, Krabi, Phuket, Pattaya, and Ko Samui. A Suzuki Caribian Mini 4WD soft top costs 1,375B (US$32) per day, while the top-end Honda Accord full-size sedan goes for 2,700B (US$63) per day. Discounts apply for weekly rentals. I've checked out Hertz and Avis, who also have offices around the country, and Budget seems to be the best deal.

Thailand drives on the left side of the road at a maximum speed limit of 60kmph (37mph) inside a city and 80kmph (50mph) outside.

TIPS ON ACCOMMODATIONS

Thailand has all kinds of accommodations, from world-renowned luxury hotels and resorts to great backpacker hotels and bungalows. Some pricier places have recently taken to quoting rates in U.S. dollars as opposed to Thai baht, as a buffer against fluctuating currency values. In places like Phuket and Ko Samui, you have a rainy season that brings with it special rates that can be between 30% and 50% off the rack rates. Other places, such as Hua Hin and Cha-Am, impose peak-season surcharges. The prices listed in this book are rack rates quoted at the time of publishing and are subject to change. However, be prepared to negotiate with reservations agents—these places almost always have special discounts, packages, or free service add-ons for extra value.

TIPS ON DINING

While Bangkok and the major tourist areas have a wide variety of quality international restaurants, you have a wide range of Thai food options as well, from fine dining to local coffee shop fare, to street food. As for street food, be cautious: Check out the stall to see that it's clean and the ingredients are fresh. If it passes your muster, the food's probably okay to eat. In smaller towns, your only options will be Thai food, with some Chinese and Western selections on the menu. Most places expect to use less spice for foreigners, but you can always remind the waiter. (Conversely, make sure you ask for spicy if you want the chiles, because some places will automatically turn down the heat when they see you coming.)

TIPS ON SHOPPING

In shopping malls and boutiques, where prices are almost always marked, you will be expected to pay full rate for any item. However, in markets and smaller shops, bargaining is the name of the game. Keep it nice and sporting, and you should be fine. If you spend a long time negotiating or suggest a price that is accepted, you might be considered rude if you walk away without finishing the sale. In rural areas such as the north, where some local people derive a large percentage of their income from handicrafts sales, I refrain from ferocious bargaining—the kind lady selling the silver bangle can probably do more with the extra 10 baht than I can. Keep in mind, however, that in high-traffic tourist areas, prices are always inflated. A major annoyance is the horrible 3% charge shops try to tack onto credit card purchases. There have been times when I've talked the shop owner into not charging me, but then there have been times when I've walked out of the store without making the purchase. They're not supposed to charge you extra, but, of course, nobody is really enforcing it.

ⓒ FAST FACTS: Thailand

American Express The American Express agent in Thailand is **Sea Tours Company,** with offices in Bangkok, Phuket, and Chiang Mai. In Bangkok, the Sea Tours office is at 88-92 Phayathai Plaza Building, 8th floor, 128 Phayathai Rd. (ⓒ **2216-5783**; fax 2216-5757).

ATM Networks Most major banks throughout the country have automated teller machines. In general, you can get cash with your debit card at any Bangkok Bank, Thai Farmers Bank, Siam Commercial Bank, or Bank of Ayudhya—provided that your card is hooked into the MasterCard/Cirrus or Visa/PLUS network. See the "Money" section, earlier in this chapter.

Banks Many international banks maintain offices in Bangkok, including **Bank of America**, next door to the Hilton at 2/2 Wireless Rd. (© 2251-6333); **Chase Manhattan Bank**, Bubhajit Bldg., Sathorn Nua Rd. (© 2234-5992); **Citibank**, 82 Sathorn Nua Rd. (© 2232-2000); **National Australia Bank**, 90 Sathorn Rd. (© 2236-6016); and **Standard Chartered Bank**, Abdulrahim Place, 990 Rama IV Rd. (© 2636-1000). However, even if your bank has a branch in Thailand, your home account is considered foreign here—conducting personal banking will require special arrangements before leaving home.

Business Hours Government offices (including branch post offices) are open Monday to Friday 8:30am to 4:30pm, with a lunch break between noon and 1pm. Businesses are generally open 8am to 5pm. Shops often stay open from 8am until 7pm or later, 7 days a week. Department stores are generally open 10am to 7pm.

Car Rentals See "Getting Around," above.

Climate See "When to Go," earlier in this chapter.

Currency See "Money," earlier in this chapter.

Customs See "Customs," earlier in this chapter. All items must be declared. Firearms and ammunition can be brought in only with a permit from the police department or local registration office.

Documents Required See "Visitor Information," earlier in this chapter.

Driving Rules See "Getting Around," above.

Electricity All outlets—except in some luxury hotels—are 220 volts AC (50 cycles). Outlets have two flat-pronged or round-pronged holes, so you might need an adapter. If you use a 110-volt hair dryer, electric shaver, or battery charger for a computer, bring a transformer and adapter.

Embassies & Consulates Your home embassy in Thailand can help you in emergencies—medical and legal (legal, to an extent), and is the place to contact if you've lost your travel documents and need them replaced. The following is a list of major foreign representatives in Bangkok: **Embassy of the United States of America**, 120-22 Wireless Rd. (© 2205-4000); **Canada Embassy**, 15th floor, Abdulrahim Place, 990 Rama IV Rd. (© 2636-0540); **Australian Embassy**, 37 South Sathorn Rd. (© 2287-2680); **New Zealand Embassy**, 93 Wireless Rd. (© 2254-2530); and **British Embassy**, 1031 Wireless Rd. (© 2253-0191).

Emergencies Throughout the country, the emergency number you should use is © 1699 for the Tourist Police. Don't expect many English speakers at normal police posts outside the major tourist areas. (Ambulances must be summoned from hospitals rather than through a central service.) You should also contact your embassy or consulate, the Tourist Police, or the local Tourist Authority of Thailand (TAT) office.

Etiquette See "Etiquette," later in this chapter.

Holidays See "When to Go," earlier in this chapter.

Information See "Visitor Information," earlier in this chapter.

Language Central (often called Bangkok) Thai is the official language. English is spoken in the major cities at most hotels, restaurants, and shops, and is the second language of the professional class, as well as the international business language.

Mail If shipping a parcel from Bangkok, take advantage of the Packing Service offered by the **GPO** (Post and Telegraph Office), Charoen Krung Rd. (© 2233-1050), open 24 hours. Small cardboard packing cartons cost 5B to 17B (US11¢–US38¢); they pack things for you for 5B (US11¢)! *Note:* Packing service is available only during normal office hours.

Shipping by air freight is expensive. Two major international delivery services have their main dispatching offices in Bangkok, though they deliver throughout the country; these are **DHL Thailand,** Grand Amarin Tower Building, Phetchaburi Road (© 2207-0600), and **Federal Express,** at Rama IV Road (© 2367-3222). **UPS Parcel Delivery Service,** with a main branch in Bangkok at 16/1 Soi 44/1 Sukhumvit Rd. (© 2712-3300), also has branches elsewhere in Thailand. Many businesses will also package and mail merchandise for a reasonable price.

Maps The **TAT** gives out excellent regional and city maps at its information offices, and there are a number of good privately produced maps, usually free, available at most hotels and many businesses. For specific map recommendations, see "Visitor Information" in each region.

Newspapers & Magazines The major domestic English-language dailies are the *Bangkok Post* and *The Nation,* distributed in the morning in the capital and later in the day around the country. They cover the domestic political scene, as well as international news from AP, UPI, and Reuters wire services, and cost 20B (US45¢). Both the *Asian Wall Street Journal* and the *International Herald Tribune* are available Monday to Friday on their day of publication in Bangkok (in the provinces a day or 2 later). *Time, Newsweek, The Economist, Asiaweek,* and the *Far Eastern Economic Review* are sold at newsstands in the international hotels, as well as in bookstores in all the major cities.

Pharmacies Bangkok has a great many pharmacies, though the drugs dispensed differ widely in quality. Thailand is notorious for producing generic knock-offs of name-brand drugs and selling them at a discount. Be warned that these drugs are not checked for quality. Bring with you any prescription medications you require. If something new arises that calls for a prescription, the treating hospital or clinic will be able to provide reliable drugs from its dispensary.

Police The **Tourist Police** (© 1699), with offices in every city, speak English (and other foreign languages) and are open 24 hours. You should call them in an emergency rather than the regular police because there is no guarantee that the regular police operator will speak English.

Tourist Police who patrol nightclub areas, especially where go-go bars are present, are incredibly efficient. If you run into any trouble in these areas, do not hesitate to contact them. They will take the most minor offence seriously and will work hard until the crime is solved.

Radio & TV In Bangkok, **95.5 FMX** plays the current charts, while **Smooth 105FM** and **Easy FM 105.5** play adult-oriented contemporary music. Every day at 6pm, every radio station plays the national anthem; at 8pm, they broadcast the daily news.

Television channels all broadcast either local Thai programs or English-language programs dubbed in Thai. **UBC** (United Broadcasting Company) provides satellite programming for the entire country. Most hotels, even those in rural areas, carry UBC channels such as CNN, CNBC, Star Movies, HBO, MTV and Star Sports, plus other channels.

Restrooms Many restaurants and all hotels above the budget level have Western toilets. Shops and budget hotels will have an Asian toilet, a.k.a. a "squatty potty," a hole in the ground with foot pads on either side. Near the toilet is a water bucket or sink with a small ladle. The water is for flushing and cleaning the toilet. Don't count on these places having toilet paper. Some shopping malls have dispensers outside the restroom—2B (US5¢) for some paper. Dispose of it in the wastebasket provided because it will clog up rudimentary sewage systems.

Safety Serious crime in Thailand is rare; petty crime such as purse snatching or pickpocketing is common. Particular care should be taken by those traveling over land (especially on overnight buses and trains) in remote parts of the country and near the Burmese and Lao borders; local bandits or rebel groups sometimes rob travelers.

Beware of credit-card scams; carry a minimum of cards, don't allow them out of your sight, and keep all receipts. Never leave your cards with others for safekeeping (such as during a trek). If you don't want to carry them, put them in a hotel safe. Don't carry unnecessary valuables, and keep those you do carry in your hotel's safe. Pay particular attention to your things, especially purses and wallets, on public transportation.

A special warning: Be wary of strangers who offer to guide you (particularly in Bangkok), take you to any shop (especially jewelry shops), or buy you food or drink. This is most likely to occur near a tourist sight. Be warned that this kind of forward behavior is simply not normal for the average Thai. There are rare exceptions, but most likely these new "friends" will try to swindle you in some way. This often takes the form of trying to persuade you to buy "high-quality" jewelry or gems (usually worthless) at "bargain" prices. Also, beware of anyone inviting you to his or her home and then offering to show you a famous Thai card game or engage you in any sort of gambling. You will lose. If you are approached about such schemes, call the Tourist Police immediately.

For those who contemplate bringing a prostitute to their hotel room, be advised of the danger of food or drink laced with sleeping potions. There are many incidents with victims waking up 2 days later to find their valuables gone. Women who work at go-go bars are more likely to be trustworthy—you know where they work.

Taxes & Service Charges Hotels charge a 7% government value added tax (VAT) and typically add a 10% service charge; hotel restaurants add 8.25% government tax. Smaller hotels quote the price inclusive of these charges.

Telephone, Telex & Fax Beware of hotel surcharges on international calls, usually 25% to 40% (check with the operator before dialing). A credit card or collect call placed from your room also carries a service charge.

The main government telephone office occupies a separate building on the grounds of the GPO (General Post Office) on Charoen Krung Road

(New Rd.) between the Oriental and Royal Orchid Sheraton Hotels and is open daily 24 hours. This office is for international calls.

All post offices and 7-Elevens sell prepaid phone cards for use with the **orange Lensko public phones**—if you can't find an orange Lensko phone, look outside the nearest 7-Eleven. These phones will also charge calls to credit cards and AT&T calling cards.

Blue or the newer silver long-distance telephones in strategic places throughout Bangkok (such as the airport) are used for domestic long-distance calls, at rates from 6B to 18B (US13¢–US40¢) per minute. You will need a pile of 5B coins, and you can observe your running total on the meter, putting in more coins as needed. For **information** within the Bangkok metropolitan area, dial ✆ **1133**, or find an English-language copy of the *Greater Bangkok Business Listing*.

Telegraph services, including fax service and telegram service, are offered in the telephone and telegraph office of the GPO, open daily 24 hours. The same services (except for telegram restante) are offered at the telephone and telegraph offices at Don Muang airport. A fax to the United States costs about 400B (US$9) and must be prepared on the official form. Every hotel offers normal fax service as well.

Time Zone Bangkok and all of Thailand are 7 hours ahead of Greenwich Mean Time. During winter months, this means that Bangkok is exactly 7 hours ahead of London, 12 hours ahead of New York, and 15 hours ahead of Los Angeles. Daylight saving time adds 1 hour to these figures.

Tipping If a service charge is not added to your restaurant check, a 10% to 15% tip is appropriate. In small noodle shops, a 10B (US20¢) tip can be given if the service is particularly good. Airport or hotel porters expect tips of 20B (US45¢) per bag (in expensive hotels, I'll double it to 40B/US90¢ or 50B/US$1.10 per bag). The gracious hostesses who show you to your room in the better hotels usually do not expect a tip, but you should feel free to reward good service wherever you find it. Tipping taxi drivers is not expected. Carry small bills because many cab drivers either don't have (or won't admit to having) small change.

Water Don't drink the tap water, even in the major hotels. Most hotels provide bottled water in or near the minibar or in the bathroom; use it for brushing your teeth as well as drinking. Most restaurants serve bottled or boiled water and ice made from boiled water, but always ask to be sure.

3 Bangkok

From the moment you arrive, Bangkok will grip your senses. Streets throb with traffic. The world's most opulent hotels cohabitate with squat buildings gray from smog. On every corner, street vendors fill the air with savory smells, and stalls packed with souvenirs, handicrafts, and cheap buys seem to clog every sidewalk. In the mornings, businesspeople rush to work with cellphones pressed to their ears while monks draped in saffron robes glide peacefully through the crowds. In the evenings, if the fiery and delicious Thai cuisine isn't racy enough, there's a nightlife unrivaled by any other city on the planet. Bangkok will suck you in with promises of a most exotic vacation and will never fail to deliver.

Vintage 19th-century photographs of Bangkok show vivid images of life on the Chao Phraya River, bustling with vessels ranging from the humblest rowboat to elaborate royal barges. Built along the banks of the broad, S-shape river, the city spread inland through a network of klongs (canals) that rivaled the intricacy—though never the elegance—of Venice.

As Bangkok became more densely populated and developed, more of the klongs were filled in to create broad thoroughfares. Cars, buses, motorcycles, and tuk-tuks (motorized 3-wheeler rickshaws) followed, and today the resultant rush-hour traffic jams are so horrendous (commuters spend, on average, 40 working days per year waiting in traffic!) that, once again, one of the best ways to travel around the city is via the river.

"Old Bangkok," or the **Historic District** nestled next to the Chao Phraya River, contains most of the city's historical sights such as the Grand Palace and most of the city's original wats (temples with resident monks). Following the river south, you'll run into the narrow lanes of Bangkok's **Chinatown.** Farther down, a few of Bangkok's best hotels, including the famous Oriental Hotel, have made their mark on the city. Inland from the river, Bangkok's **central business district** is situated on Sathorn, Silom, and Surawongse roads, beginning at Charoen Krung Road (sometimes still referred to by its old name, New Rd.) leading all the way to Rama IV Road. Connecting from here is **Wireless Road,** where many of the larger foreign embassies have built huge compounds. Bangkok's **main shopping thoroughfare,** on Rama I Road, between Payathai and Ratchadamri roads, sports huge modern shopping complexes like the World Trade Center and Siam Square. Follow Rama I east, and you'll run into Sukhumvit Road. While Sukhumvit isn't in the hub of the tourist area, it has a large concentration of expatriate residences, which makes for all sorts of good international restaurants, inexpensive shopping, and nightlife.

Get to know the Thai word *soi,* meaning "lane." Main thoroughfares in the city have individual names, with many of the smaller side streets numbered in sequence for identification purposes. For example, Sukhumvit Soi 5 is the home of the Amari Boulevard Hotel, while Sukhumvit Soi 8, a few minutes' walk east and across the street, is where you'll find Le Banyan restaurant. Once upon a time each little soi had an individual name—yikes! Some are still known today, such as Nana Tua, Sukhumvit Soi 4, and its sister, Nana Nua, Sukhumvit Soi 3.

VISITOR INFORMATION

The **TAT's** main office is at Le Concorde Office Building, 202 Ratchadaphisek Rd. (© **02/694-1222**), but the more convenient location is at 4 Ratchadam-noen Nok Ave., a short walk from the Khao San Road area (© **02/282-9773**). Call the **Tourist Service Line** at © **1155** for all sorts of general inquiries.

GETTING THERE

Because most people enter Thailand via Bangkok, specific information on travel to Bangkok is covered in the country's "Getting There" section earlier in this chapter.

BY AIR   Most travelers arrive at Bangkok International Airport (Don Muang), which has domestic (© **02/535-2081**) and international (© **02/535-1111**) terminals. The airport has conveniences such as currency exchange offices, restaurants, post offices, hotel reservations counters, duty-free shopping, and emergency medical service. **To get to central Bangkok,** limousines can be booked at the Arrival Hall starting from 650B (US$15). Just outside of the

Tips **Telephone Dialing Info at a Glance**

- **To place a call from your home country to Thailand,** dial the international access code (011 in the U.S., 0011 in Australia, 0170 in New Zealand, and 00 in the U.K.), plus the country code **(66)**, plus the Thailand area code (Bangkok: 2; Pattaya: 38; Hua Hin: 32; Surat Thani and Ko Samui: 77; Phuket: 76; Chiang Mai and Chiang Rai: 53), followed by the six- or seven-digit phone number (for example, from the U.S. to Bangkok, you'd dial 011-66-2-000-0000).

- **To place a call within Thailand,** you must use area codes if calling between states. Note that for calls within the country, area codes are all preceded by a 0 (for example, Bangkok: 02; Pattaya: 038; Hua Hin: 032; Surat Thani and Ko Samui: 077; Phuket: 076; Chiang Mai and Chiang Rai: 053).

- **To place a direct international call from Thailand,** dial the international access code (001), plus the country code of the place you are dialing, plus the area code, plus the residential number of the other party.

- To reach the international operator, dial ℂ **100.**

- **International country codes** are as follows: Australia: 61; Burma: 95; Cambodia: 855; Canada: 1; Hong Kong: 852; Indonesia: 62; Laos: 856; Malaysia: 60; New Zealand: 64; the Philippines: 63; Singapore: 65; U.K.: 44; U.S.: 1; Vietnam: 84.

Arrivals Hall you'll be able to catch a cab for less: the metered fare plus 50B (US$1.16) airport pickup surcharge—about 250B to 300B (US$5.81–US$6.98). For the best deal, check the Airport Shuttle Bus on the ground level of the Arrivals hall to see if your hotel is along one of the four routes. It'll set you back only 100B (US$2.33).

BY TRAIN Passengers arriving by train will alight at the Hua Lamphong Railway Station (ℂ **02/223-7010** or 02/223-7020) on Krung Kassem Road in central Bangkok. There never fails to be a line of taxis and tuk-tuks waiting outside.

BY BUS If you're arriving from the southern parts of Thailand, or from Malaysia, you'll come into the Southern Bus Terminal (ℂ **02/435-1199**) on Charan Sanitwong Road, across the river near the Bangkok Noi Station. From east coast destinations, you'll arrive at the Eastern Bus Terminal (ℂ **02/390-1230**) on Sukhumvit Road opposite Soi 63—Ekamai Road. From northern areas of the country, you'll be dropped at the **Northern Bus Terminal** (ℂ **02/272-5761**) on Phahonyothin Road near the Chatuchak Weekend Market. Metered taxis either are waiting at these terminals or are easy enough to flag down.

GETTING AROUND

Prepare yourself for traffic jams and pollution. Bangkok's notorious motor vehicle problem still remains a major issue, despite all sorts of ideas to lessen the load. The best one is the brand new BTS Skytrain, which rockets you over the bottlenecks below. While taxis are your next best bet, try to get around by boat to some of the sights, such as the Grand Palace, Wat Po, and the National Museum, for peace of mind as well as the fascinating river scenery.

BY SKYTRAIN   The **Bangkok Mass Transit System (BTS)**, known as the "Skytrain" is just about the hottest thing going in Bangkok. The elevated railways system brilliantly whisks you above the maddening traffic. While coverage isn't too extensive, there is access to Bangkok's central areas. The Silom Line takes runs from the Chao Phraya River at the King Taksin Bridge (next to the Shangri-La Hotel), along Sathorn and Silom roads, past Sala Daeng (at Patpong), and up Ratchadamri Road to the Siam Square shopping area. Here you can change to the Sukhumvit Line to head north to the Chatuchak Weekend Market near the airport, or go east down Ploenchit and Sukhumvit roads. Purchase single-journey tickets or stored-value tickets at each station for fares between 10B and 40B (US23¢ and US93¢).

BY TAXI   Unless you venture to the outer residential neighborhoods, you're never at a loss for a taxi in Bangkok. Metered taxis can be flagged down from sidewalks and will swing by hotels and shopping malls looking for fares. The meter starts at 35B (US81¢) for the first 2km (1¼ miles), and increases by about 5B (US12¢) per kilometer thereafter (increases will also depend on how fast traffic is moving). Basically, for most trips around town, you won't spend more than 100B (US$2.33). Tipping is not expected, but many will fumble for change in search of one. If you encounter a cabbie who tries to negotiate a fare up front, insist that he use the meter. *A useful tip:* Many drivers come from Isaan in the northeast of the country and have terrible English. It's always a good idea to have the concierge or desk clerk at your hotel write your destination for you in Thai before you venture out.

BY TUK-TUK These are some crazy little vehicles: three-wheeled scooters with an open cart, complete with flashing lights, metallic ornamentation, bright colors, and rumbling motors. Drivers will negotiate the fare before you set out; make sure you bargain. The fun part is that these guys are kamikazes, zipping through traffic as you grip the bars for support. The not-so-fun part is when you're stuck in traffic with exhaust fumes smoking all around you. Use them for short trips and never during rush hour.

Be wary of tuk-tuk drivers touting shopping trips. A lot of these drivers lurk in tourist areas, trying to chat folks up to come and see his friend's gem shop or his brother's tailor, but they're just trying to get commission, and you'll be ripped off. Make sure your driver takes you where you want to go and *only* where you want to go.

BY CAR & DRIVER A great option for sightseeing in comfort is to hire a car and driver for a full or half day. The larger hotels can arrange these for you, but a cheaper alternative is to contact a local travel agent or car-rental company. **World Travel Service Ltd.,** 1053 Charoen Krung Rd., 10500 Bangkok (© **02/ 233-5900**), can also provide an English-speaking tour guide and can help arrange a suitable itinerary.

BY BOAT Once upon a time Bangkok was a city of waterways, not unlike Venice. While today most *klongs,* or canals, have been paved over for motor vehicle traffic, some remain, and the mighty Chao Phraya River is still considered the lifeline of the city. Today the most common form of transportation around the city is by taxi, but if you can take a trip somewhere via the river or a klong, you'll experience a wonderful side to the city; a tranquil ride through neighborhoods, past temples and the Grand Palace. It is highly recommended.

The **Chao Phraya Express Company** (© **02/222-5330**) will shuttle you among the many piers on either side of the river (almost all maps indicate the location of the piers), the most common ones being the piers at the Oriental Hotel, the River City Complex (Wat Muang Khae Ferry Pier), and the Grand Palace (Tha Chang Ferry Pier).

The cost depends on how far you go. It is usually between 5B and 10B (US12¢ and US23¢). Look for the Chao Phraya Express logo on the side of the boat, and be prepared to jump quick as they briefly pull up to the pier.

At the ferry piers, you can also charter a private longtail boat to take you through the klongs in Bangkok and on the Thonburi side of the river. For only 300B (US$6.98) an hour, the trip is incredibly fun, passing riverside houses and shops and seeing how the locals live. Go to the pier at the River City Complex next to the Sheraton Hotel.

BY MOTORCYCLE TAXI If tuk-tuk drivers aren't kamikaze enough, you always have motorcycle taxis. Distinguished by their colored vests, these guys are great for getting you where you want to go in a jiffy, even if traffic is bumper to bumper. Just hop on the back. They'll weave you through, so be careful not to knock your knees on the sides of buses. At about 5B to 40B (US12¢–US93¢) for a short trip, they're a bargain.

BY BUS Bangkok has an extensive and dependable system of city buses. Maps are available at bookstores and magazine stands marked with the more popular routes. A trip on an air-conditioned bus will set you back only 6B (US14¢).

Beware of pickpockets and purse slashers, a serious problem on crowded rush-hour buses.

ON FOOT   Bangkok's heat, humidity, and air pollution prohibit walking long distances. Besides, half the sidewalks seem to be in a state of perpetual ruin. If you're walking around a limited area, you'll be fine. Walking around Old Bangkok, the area near the Grand Palace, and many of the city's wats is not too difficult, as long as you start in the morning while it's still cool.

FAST FACTS: Bangkok

Banks/Currency Exchange Banks with money changers and ATMs are easy to find in the areas around hotels and shopping malls. Bangkok Bank, Thai Farmers Bank, and Bank of Ayudhya are Thailand's three biggest banks, and they will accept debit and cash advance cards on the MasterCard/Cirrus and Visa/PLUS networks.

Internet/E-mail You've got a million options here. If you're staying near Khao San Road in Banglamphu, you can't throw a stone without hitting an Internet cafe. You can also look around the Patpong area, on Silom and Suriwongse roads—check in the shopping malls. You'll also find them around the Siam Square shopping area. Down Sukhumvit Road, a few of the sois are packed with them. Access rates vary between 2B (US5¢) per minute and 300B (US$6.98) per hour. There are so many to choose from that I recommend asking your hotel concierge for the nearest one. Don't be tempted to use the Internet in your hotel's business center; the expense is alarming.

Police The Tourist Police can be reached at ✆**1699**.

Post Office/Mail The General Post Office (✆ **02/233-1050**) is on Charoen Krung Road between the Oriental Hotel and the Sheraton Royal Orchid Hotel.

Telephone Bangkok's city code is 2.

WHERE TO STAY

Because of the currency fluctuation of recent years, many luxury hotels have chosen to quote room rates in U.S. dollars. All prices listed are the official published tariff. Be sure to ask for discount offers and any extra add-on incentives (free breakfast or airport transfer, etc.) when you book. Also, expect these prices to jump during the holiday peak season between December 20 and January 10. Except for those quoted for budget accommodations, prices do not include additional a 7% service charge and the 7% value-added tax (VAT).

The pricing categories for the following Bangkok hotels go like this: A Very Expensive room is above US$250 per night, while an Expensive room falls between US$150 and US$250 per night. Moderate rooms are between US$50 and US$150, but be warned that inexpensive rooms, those below US$50, can vary greatly. For example, a budget US$40 room will have air-conditioning, TV, private bathroom, and minibar, while a US$10 room will be a basic guesthouse room with minimal in-room amenities.

Bangkok Accommodations & Dining

ACCOMMODATIONS ■

Amari Boulevard Hotel **28**

Bangkok Marriott Resort & Spa **12**

Bangkok YWCA **20**

Bossotel Inn **10**

Chinatown Hotel **7**

City Lodge **29**

The Dusit Thani **18**

Grand Hyatt Erawan

Hilton International Bangkok at Nai Lert Park **27**

Holiday Inn Crowne Plaza **13**

Le Royal Meridien and Le Meridien President **26**

Montien Hotel **16**

New Merry V. Guesthouse **4**

Novotel Bangkok **24**

The Oriental **9**

The Regent **22**

Royal Princess **6**

Shangri-La Hotel **11**

Siam Inter-Continental Hotel **25**

The Sukhothai **19**

DINING ◆

Bangkok Bar and Restaurant **5**

Benjarong **21**

Cabbages & Condoms **30**

The Chinese Restaurant **23**

Commé **3**

Genji Restaurant **27**

Harmonique **8**

Kaloang Home Kitchen **1**

Le Banyan **31**

Le Dalat **32**

Le Normandie **9**

Lemongrass **34**

The Mango Tree **15**

Prik Kee Noo **17**

Salathip **11**

Seafood Market & Restaurant **33**

Somboon Seafood **14**

Spice Market **22**

Ton Pho Restaurant **2**

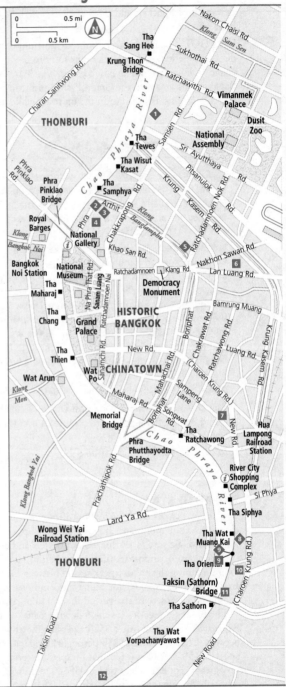

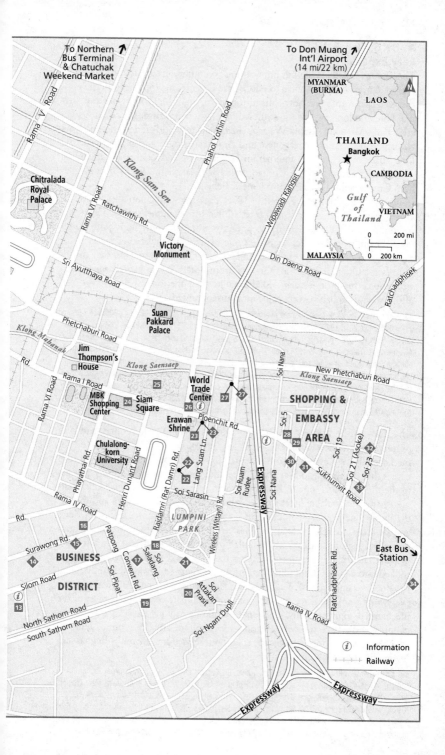

To Northern
Bus Terminal
& Chatuchak
Weekend Market

To Don Muang
Int'l Airport
(14 mi/22 km)

MYANMAR
(BURMA)

LAOS

THAILAND
Bangkok

CAMBODIA

Gulf
of
Thailand

VIETNAM

MALAYSIA

0   200 mi
0   200 km

Chitralada
Royal
Palace

Rama V Road

Klong Sam Sen

Phahol Yothin Road

Wipawadi Rangsit

Rama VI Road

Ratchawithi Rd.

Din Daeng Road

Ratchadphisek

Victory
Monument

Sri Ayutthaya Road

Klong Mahanak

Phetchaburi Road

Suan
Pakkard
Palace

Jim
Thompson's
House

Rd.

Rama I Road

Klong Saensaep

Soi Nana

New Phetchaburi Road

Klong Saensaep

Rama VI Road

MBK
Shopping
Center

Siam
Square

World
Trade
Center

SHOPPING &

EMBASSY

AREA

25

24

26

27   27

Erawan
Shrine

Ploenchit Rd.

23   23

28

29

Soi 5

Soi Nana

Soi 19

Soi 21 (Asoke)

Soi 23

32

Chulalong-
korn
University

Phayathai Rd.

Henri Dunant Road

Rajdamri (Rat Damri) Rd.

Lang Suan Ln.

22

22

Soi Sarasin

30

31

Sukhumvit Road

33

Rama IV Road

LUMPINI
PARK

Wireless (Wittayu) Rd.

Soi Ruam
Rudee

Expressway

Soi Nana

16

Rd.

Surawong Rd.

15

BUSINESS

Silom Road

14

DISTRICT

13

North Sathorn Road

South Sathorn Road

Patpong

Convent Rd.

Soi Pipat

Soi
Saladang

18

17

21

19

20

Soi
Attakan
Prasit

Soi Ngam Dupli

To
East Bus
Station

34

Ratchadphisek Rd.

Rama IV Road

Expressway

Expressway

Expressway

ⓘ   Information

├┼┼┼┤ Railway

131

ALONG THE RIVER
Very Expensive

The Oriental 🏰🏰   Cited in publications too numerous to list and favored by everyone from honeymooners to CEOs, the Oriental has long been in the pantheon of the world's best hotels. Its history dates from the 1860s, when the original hotel, no longer standing, was established by two Danish sea captains soon after King Mongkut (Rama IV) reopened Siam to world trade. The hotel has withstood occupation by Japanese and American troops and played host to a long roster of Thai and international dignitaries and celebrities, including adventurous authors Joseph Conrad, Somerset Maugham, Noël Coward, Graham Greene, John Le Carré, and James Michener.

Rooms in the older wing, built in 1876, pack the most colonial richness and charm, but are more or less minisuites stuffed into cramped spaces. The newer buildings (c. 1958 and 1976) are certainly more spacious, some with better views of the river, but they sacrifice some of that Oriental Hotel romance for modern convenience. It's the level and range of service, however, that distinguishes the Oriental from the other riverfront hotels. It's probably a more practical choice for businessmen and diplomats than for tourists, but if you can afford it, you probably won't come away disappointed.

48 Oriental Ave., Bangkok 10500 (on the riverfront off Charoen Krung Rd. [New Rd.]). ② **800/526-6566** or 2236-0400. Fax 2236-1937. www.mandarin-oriental.com. 396 units. 12,320B–13,640B (US$280–US$310) double; from 18,480B (US$420) suite. AE, DC, MC, V. 5-min. walk to Saphan Taksin BTS station. **Amenities:** 4 restaurants (French, Cantonese, seafood, Thai); lounge w/world-class live jazz performances; 2 outdoor pools; 2 lighted outdoor tennis courts; state-of-the-art fitness center; luxurious spa w/sauna, steam, massage, and traditional Thai beauty treatments; concierge; tour desk; car-rental desk; limousine service; helicopter transfer service; tour boats for river excursions; business center; up-market shopping arcade; salon; 24-hr. room service; babysitting; same-day laundry service/dry cleaning; nonsmoking rooms; executive-level rooms; cooking school. *In room:* A/C, TV w/satellite programming, minibar, hair dryer, safe.

The Peninsula Bangkok   Whether you land on the helicopter pad and promenade into the exclusive top-floor lounge, roll in from the airport in one of the hotel's Rolls-Royce limousines or step lightly off the wood-decked, custom barges that ply the Chao Praya, you'll feel like you've "arrived" however you get to the the Peninsula, one of Bangkok's most deluxe accomodations. Any possible amenity is available here, from elegant dining to great activites and top-of-the-line business services. Some of the largest in town, all rooms have river views and are done in a refined Thai and Western theme, a good marriage of Thai tradition and high-tech luxury with wooden paneling, silk wallpaper, and attractive carpets. The technical features of each room may make you may feel like you've walked into a James Bond film as each room is digitized in ways that only Agent Q could've conceived of: Each bedside features a panel control that operates everything from the three phones, voice-mail, climate control, TV, or even the mechanized room curtains. The large marble bathrooms have separate vanity counters and a large tub with a hands-free telephone and TV monitor built-in. "Ask and it will be done," seems the rule about service and the multi-lingual staff is friendly and very accommodating.

333 Charoennakorn Road, Klongsan, Bangkok 10600. (just across the Chao Praya River from Saphan Taksin Station) ② **800/262-9467** in the US; 207/730-0993 in the UK; 61/2)-9252-2888 in Australia, New Zealand; 02/861-2888. www.peninsula.com. 370 units. 10,660B–12,300B (US$260–US$300) deluxe; 16,400B–106,600 (US$400–US$2,600) suite. AE, DC, MC, V. Amenities: 3 restaurants (Thai, Chinese, international); 2 bars; 60m 3-tiered pool; tennis court; state-of-the-art fitness center; full spa service w/sauna, steam, massage and aromatherapy; concierge; tour desk; car-rental; fleet of Rolls Royce limousines; rooftop helicopter pad; tour boats

and complimentary ferry service; business center; fine shopping; extensive salon; 24-hr. room service; babysitting; laundry/dry cleaning; executive check-in. *In room:* A/C, TV w/satellite programming, minibar, hair dryer, safe, CD player.

Expensive

Shangri-La Hotel ⭐⭐   The opulent but thoroughly modern Shangri-La, on the banks of the Chao Phraya, boasts acres of polished marble, a jungle of tropical plants and flowers, and two towers with breathtaking views of the river. The higher-priced guest rooms have a view of the river, but all rooms are decorated with lush carpeting and teak furniture, and have marble bathrooms. The views are terrific from the higher-floor deluxe rooms, and most have either a balcony or a small sitting room, making them closer to junior suites and a particularly good value for on-the-river upscale accommodations. For such an enormous place, the level of service and facilities is surprisingly good.

The superluxurious Krung Thep Wing adds another 17-story, river-view tower to the grounds, as well as a riverside swimming pool and a restaurant and breakfast lounge. Guests register in their spacious rooms, surrounded by colorful Thai paintings and glistening Thai silk.

89 Soi Wat Suan Plu, Charoen Krung Rd. (New Rd.), Bangkok 10500 (adjacent to Sathorn Bridge, w/access off Chaoren Krung Rd. [New Rd.] at S end of Silom Rd.). © **800/942-5050** or 2236-7777. Fax 2236-8579. www. shangri-la.com. 850 units. 9,240B–14,080B (US$210–US$320) double; from 17,160B (US$390) suite. AE, DC, MC, V. Next to Saphan Taksin BTS station. **Amenities:** 6 restaurants (international, barbecue, Thai, Chinese, Italian, Japanese); dinner cruise; lounge and bar; 2 outdoor pools w/outdoor Jacuzzi; 2 outdoor lighted tennis courts; 2 squash courts; fitness center w/Jacuzzi, sauna, steam, massage, and aerobics classes; concierge; tour desk; car-rental desk; limousine service; helicopter transfer; city shuttle service; business center; small shopping arcade; salon; 24-hr. room service; same-day laundry service/dry cleaning; nonsmoking rooms; executive-level rooms. *In room:* A/C, TV w/satellite programming, dataport, minibar, coffee/tea-making facilities, hair dryer, safe.

Moderate

Bangkok Marriott Resort & Spa ⭐⭐ *(Kids)*   Formerly the Royal Garden Riverside Hotel, the name *resort* better describes this luxuriously sprawling complex. On the banks of the Chao Phraya across the river and a few miles downstream from the heart of Bangkok, the resort is best reached via longtail boat. It's a short trip downriver, as you feel the crazy city release you from its grip. Once at the resort, you'll think you're farther from the city than you actually are; the three wings of the hotel surround a large landscaped pool area with lily ponds and fountains, and there's a wonderful spa for a very uniquely calming Bangkok experience. As this book went to press, Marriott was just beginning a major renovation of all guest rooms to refurbish decor—look forward to hardwood floors replacing old wall-to-wall carpeting—so make sure you specify new rooms when you book. Boats go to and from River City shopping mall every half-hour, from early to late. Choose the Bangkok Marriott if you want to enjoy Bangkok but can't stand the insanity of big city life.

257/1–3 Charoen Nakhorn Rd., at the Krungthep Bridge, Bangkok 10600 (on the Thonburi [east] side of the Chao Phraya River, 15 min. by boat from River City). © **800/228-9290** or 2476-0022. Fax 2476-1120. www. marriotthotels.com. 420 units. 5,500B–6,380B (US$125–US$145) double; 7,700B–9,900B (US$175–US$225) suite. AE, DC, MC, V. **Amenities:** 6 restaurants (Thai, Trader Vic's Polynesian, Benihana teppanyaki, Japanese sushi bar, Cantonese, international cafe); bar and lounge; dinner cruise; large landscaped pool w/Jacuzzi; 2 outdoor lighted tennis courts; fitness center w/sauna; new spa w/massage and beauty treatments; children's recreation programs; concierge; tour desk; limousine service; business center; adjoining shopping arcade; salon; 24-hr. room service; babysitting; same-day laundry service/dry cleaning; nonsmoking rooms. *In room:* A/C, TV w/pay movies, minibar, safe.

Inexpensive

Bossotel Inn ★★ (Value)   It's not on the water and there isn't a view to speak of, but the spiffy, renovated new wing of the Bossotel, in particular, warrants consideration.

Many of the guests are either long-term visitors or repeat offenders because, quite frankly, Bossotel delivers large, clean rooms in a fantastic location without draining your wallet. Press them for a discount rate, and make sure you specify the newer Bossotel II. Rooms are very basic, and the furniture and decor are a monotone gray—at least it doesn't clash, which, believe me, is impressive for a budget hotel in these parts. My only big complaint is that the shower head clipped to the wall is a bit short. At least it unclips from its holder for manual use. The English spoken by the staff is limited, but that doesn't make for bad service. Check out the traditional Thai massage on the 2nd floor—hotel guests can get a pretty decent 2-hour massage for 300B (US$6.80).

55/12–13 Soi Charoen Krung 42/1, Bangrak, Bangkok 10500 (off Charoen Krung Rd., on Soi 42, near Shangri-La Hotel). ✆ **2630-6120.** Fax 2237-3225. www.bossotelinn.com. 46 units. 1,000B–1,800B (US$23–US$41) double. AE, MC, V. 5-min. walk to Saphan Taksin BTS station. **Amenities:** Coffee shop (Thai, Western); swimming pool; Jacuzzi; sauna; tour desk; small business center; limited room service; massage; same-day laundry service. *In room:* A/C, TV w/satellite programming, minibar.

HISTORIC BANGKOK—NEAR THE GRAND PALACE
Moderate

Royal Princess   This first-class hotel near the Grand Palace in the Ratanakosin Island area more than lives up to the high standards of the Thai-owned Dusit Thani Hotels and Resorts family. Completed in 1989, its proximity to government offices brings a steady flow of official visitors, but it's also great for travelers interested in the sights of old Bangkok.

Public spaces are wall-to-wall marble and bustle with activity, yet the scale is intimate. Guest rooms are very tastefully furnished and bright. While higher-priced deluxe rooms have balconies overlooking the tropically landscaped pool, the superior rooms of the same style look out over the neighborhood. It's a 10-minute taxi ride to either the Grand Palace or Vimanmek Palace, and though the area lacks a diversity of dining, the authentic flavor of this old neighborhood more than compensates.

269 Larn Luang Rd., Pomprab, Bangkok 10100 (E of Wat Saket). ✆ **2281-3088.** Fax 2280-1314. www.royal princess.com. 170 units. 3,600B–3,900B (US$82–US$89) double; from 7,500B (US$170) suite. AE, DC, MC, V. **Amenities:** 4 restaurants (international, Chinese, Italian, Japanese); lounge; small landscaped pool; fitness center w/massage; tour desk; shuttle bus service; business center; 24-hr. room service; babysitting; same-day laundry service/dry cleaning. *In room:* A/C, TV w/satellite programming, minibar, hair dryer, safe.

Inexpensive

Chinatown Hotel ★★   This smart boutique hotel is shiny and bright compared to other choices in this price category. More boutique than budget, the property is small, allowing for few facilities, but within a compact space they've included many comforts in the rooms. All rooms are basically decorated the same, the only difference being that as you travel up the price ladder, rooms get bigger. The showcase Empire Room has lovely mirror and light wood paneling. Personally, I really appreciated the helpful and very funny front desk staff. Chinatown is just outside the door.

562 Yaowaraj Rd., Samphuntawong, Bangkok 10100 (3 blocks from Grand China Princess Hotel). ✆ **2225-0203.** Fax 2226-1295. www.chinatownhotel.co.th. 60 units. 750B–2,300B (US$17–US$52) double; from 2,900B (US$66) suite. MC, V. **Amenities:** Coffee shop; tour desk; limited room service; massage; same-day laundry service/dry cleaning; *In room:* A/C, TV w/satellite programming, minibar, hair dryer, safe.

New Merry V. Guesthouse   This is a good traveler's center, where young and old come for simplicity and proximity to the river. Prices listed are for rooms with attached bathrooms (cheaper dorms with shared toilets are also available). The place is basically clean, air-conditioned rooms have better views, the beds are reasonably comfortable, and the water pressure in the shower's not bad. All in all, your basic necessities for an easy guesthouse stay. *Warnings:* It's a walk-up, so try to get a lower room if you can't hike it, and don't get one of the dreary rooms with inside-facing windows. Not to be confused with the older Merry V. Guesthouse around the corner, this newer facility is far superior.

18–20 Phra Athit Rd., Banglamphu, Bangkok 10200 (across from the Phra Athit boat pier). ℂ **2280-3315.** 70 units. 400B (US$9.10) double with A/C; 280B (US$6.35) double w/fan. No credit cards. **Amenities:** Coffee shop (Thai, international); tour desk; laundry service; Internet center; lockers and baggage storage. *In room:* No phone.

THE BUSINESS DISTRICT
Very Expensive
The Sukhothai ★★★   Inside The Sukhothai, visitors find a welcome, if studied, serenity. Avoiding the hype of a high-rise, the hotel's maze of low pavilions combines crisp, contemporary lines with earthy textures and tones. Broad, colonnaded public spaces surround peaceful lotus pools. Symmetry and simplicity form the backdrop for brick chedis, terra-cotta friezes, and celadon ceramics evoking the ancient kingdom of Sukhothai.

Large guest rooms carry the same signature style in fine Thai silk, mellow teak, and celadon tile. Gigantic luxurious bathrooms feature oversize bathtubs, separate shower and toilet stalls, plus two full-size wardrobes. Technologically up-to-date, these smart rooms also have personal fax machines and Internet connections. The Sukhothai is second to none in excellent service and an assured sense of privacy.

13/3 S Sathorn Rd., Bangkok 10120 (S of Lumphini Park, near intersection of Rama IV and Wireless rds. next to the YWCA). ℂ **800/223-6800** or 2287-0222. Fax 2287-4980. www.sukhothai.com. 224 units. 11,440B–13,640B (US$260–US$310) double; from 17,160B (US$390) suite. AE, DC, MC, V. **Amenities:** 2 restaurants (Thai, international); bar and lobby lounge; 25m outdoor pool; outdoor lighted tennis court; air-conditioned racquetball court; state-of-the-art fitness center w/Jacuzzi, sauna, steam, massage, and aerobics classes; concierge; limousine service; 24-hr. business center w/cutting-edge technology; salon; 24-hr. room service; babysitting; executive-level rooms. *In room:* A/C, TV w/satellite programming and in-house video, fax, dataport w/direct Internet access, hair dryer, safe.

Expensive
The Dusit Thani ★ *Overrated*   "The Dusit" continues to be a favorite meeting place for locals, the expatriate community, and visiting celebrities. After more than 3 decades of operation, it retains its legendary reputation as one of Bangkok's premier hotels. Too bad about the overhead pass that cuts so close to the front entrance—the government has been trying to squeak every last millimeter from the hotel to build a stop for its commuter rail service—testimony to the Dusit's fabulous location, but disastrous for the appearance of the grounds. The lobby, while grand, is not the same marble-and-mirror disaster as some of the newer hotels in Asia. Splashing lobby fountains, exotic flower displays, and a poolside waterfall cascading through dense foliage make it a welcome retreat at the end of a day's sightseeing. Unfortunately, the old gal could stand some renovations; some of the guest rooms look a little too well worn. Superior rooms in the Executive Wing are newer.

Rama IV Rd., Bangkok 10500 (corner of Silom and Rama IV rds. opposite Lumpini Park). ℂ **2236-0450.** Fax 2236-6400. www.dusit.com. 530 units. 8,360B (US$190) double; from 11,440B (US$260) suite. AE, DC, MC,

V. Sala Daeng BTS station. **Amenities:** 8 restaurants (2 Chinese, Thai, Vietnamese, steakhouse, California fusion, Japanese, international); lounge and bar; library w/high tea service; small landscaped pool; driving range and chipping green; fitness center and spa w/sauna, steam, massage, aerobics, and spa cafe; concierge; limousine service; business center; shopping arcade; salon; 24-hr. room service; babysitting; same-day laundry service/dry cleaning; executive-level rooms. *In room:* A/C, TV/VCR w/satellite programming, minibar, hair dryer, safe.

Holiday Inn Crowne Plaza 🏮 Crowne Plaza, Holiday Inn's upmarket chain of hotels, provides high-quality service and a level of luxury unexpected by those familiar with standard Holiday Inn accommodations in the United States. This is the top choice for families traveling to Bangkok; while there is a 500B (US$12) charge for an extra bed, there's no charge for children under 19 years of age accompanying parents. The very comfortable guest rooms are lovely, with masculine striped fabrics offsetting floral prints for a soft and homelike appeal. Rooms in the Plaza Tower are an especially good value, though smaller than those in the Crowne Tower, with high ceilings that give a spacious feel and over-size porthole windows, framed by heavy drapery, overlooking the city. The location is very convenient, near the expressway, a short walk from the river (and the Shangri-La and Oriental), in the middle of the gem-trade district. The huge lobby seating areas are always humming with travelers who are either resting from a day's adventure or waiting to begin a new one.

981 Silom Rd., Bangkok 10500 (1 block E of Charoen Krung Rd.). ✆ **800/465-4329** or 2238-4300. Fax 2238-5289. www.crowneplaza.com. 726 rooms. 7,876B–8,316B (US$179–US$189) double; from 10,516B (US$239) suite. AE, DC, MC, V. 10-min. walk to Surasak BTS station. **Amenities:** 3 restaurants (international, Thai, northern Indian); lounge; small outdoor pool; outdoor lighted tennis court; small fitness center; concierge; tour desk; limousine service; business center; salon; 24-hr. room service; babysitting; same-day laundry service/dry cleaning; executive-level rooms. *In room:* A/C, TV w/satellite programming and in-house video, dataport, minibar, hair dryer, iron.

Moderate

Montien Hotel 🏮 Like many of the first-class tourist hotels that are attempting to break into the business market in Bangkok, the Montien is really two facilities in one. The first is directed at its traditional market, mainly Australian groups, who occupy the lower floors of one of the Montien's two wings, with their dark teak hallways and bright, pleasant rooms. The other wing has been thoroughly upgraded and renamed the Executive Club. In this part of the hotel, dark teak has given way to bleached wood, granite, and matching gray carpet.

Here's a feature few other hotels can boast: The resident psychic at the Astrologer's Terrace, open daily from 10:30am to 7pm, will use a number of international techniques to peek into your future for just 500B (US$11).

54 Surawong Rd., Bangkok 10500 (near Patpong). ✆ **2233-7060.** Fax 2236-5218. www.montien.com. 475 units. 4,400B–6,000B (US$100–US$136) double; from 8,000B (US$182) suite. AE, DC, MC, V. 10-min. walk to Sala Daeng BTS station. **Amenities:** 3 restaurants (each serving a combination of international and Cantonese fare); bar, lounge, and karaoke; outdoor pool; fitness center w/sauna; tour desk; limousine service; business center; 24-hr. room service; babysitting; same-day laundry service/dry cleaning; executive-level rooms. *In room:* A/C, TV w/satellite programming and pay movies, minibar, hair dryer, safe.

Inexpensive

Bangkok YWCA For budget accommodations, the YWCA is a reasonable choice in Bangkok, with very clean, simple rooms for women, men, and couples. Many stay here while enrolled in the YWCA Cooking School or the Sri Pattana Thai Language School, the two main features that set YWCA apart from other guesthouses or budget accommodations. However, those are really the only great facilities to write home about.

13 Sathorn Tai Rd., Bangkok 10120 (a short walk S of intersection of Rama IV and Wireless rds.). ℂ **2286-3310.** 46 units (10 w/shared bathroom). 1,000B (US$23) double. No credit cards. **Amenities:** 2 restaurants (international); TV lounge; limited room service; babysitting; same-day laundry service. *In room:* A/C, TV.

THE SHOPPING/EMBASSY AREA
Very Expensive

Grand Hyatt Erawan ★★★ When the Thai government attempted to build this hotel 50 years ago, so many spooky occurrences happened on the site that a special spirit house, or shrine, was erected on the property to appease the spirits before the building could be completed. Honoring the four-faced Brahma god Than Tao Mahaprom, the Erawan Shrine gets its common name from the three-headed Erawan elephant, the Brahma god's steed. To this day the shrine is never neglected for the throngs of wish-seekers who come daily to offer joss, fruits, flowers, and teak elephant statues. As a result, the gods smile on this hotel.

Step from Bangkok's busy shopping district into this hotel's majestic lobby—with old columns and balustrades reminiscent of colonial architectural styles and indoor landscaping—a perfect setting for afternoon tea. The works of dozens of contemporary Thai artists grace hallways and spacious rooms, where earth-tone silks, celadon accessories, antique-finish furnishings, parquet floors, oriental rugs, large bathrooms, and city views abound. In addition to the facilities one expects from a five-star hotel, there is a delightful fifth-floor pool terrace, where a waterfall tumbles down a rocky wall into a full-size hot tub.

494 Ratchadamri Rd., Bangkok 10330 (corner of Rama I Rd.). ℂ **800/233-1234** or 2254-1234. Fax 2254-6308. www.hyatt.com. 400 units. 12,320B–13,420B (US$280–US$305) double; from 21,120B (US$480) suite. AE, DC, MC, V. 5-min. walk to Chit Lom BTS station. **Amenities:** 3 restaurants (international, Chinese, Italian); lounge, disco, and wine bar; rooftop pool and garden; outdoor grass tennis court; 2 squash courts; fitness center w/Jacuzzi, sauna, steam, and massage; spa; concierge; tour desk; limousine and helicopter service; 24-hr. business center; shopping arcade; salon; 24-hr. room service; babysitting; same-day laundry service/dry cleaning; nonsmoking rooms; executive-level rooms. *In room:* A/C, TV w/satellite programming, dataport, minibar, hair dryer, safe.

Le Royal Meridien and Le Meridien President ★★ The original hotel here, Le Meridien President, attracted many a tour group with attractive facilities, great location, and good rates. In 1998, alongside the original hotel, Le Royal Meridien opened a luxury property to surpass the original hotel. Now both stand side by side sharing facilities. The newer property has more expensive and deluxe accommodations—its tall tower block offers unobstructed views all around, and because it's a newer building, rooms sport dataports and Internet access. You'll pay a premium here. Le Meridien President is nevertheless maintained quite handsomely and will be the more attractive choice for leisure travelers. While rooms feel new, they have deep pile carpets and wood furnishings and decorative touches that set it apart from other city hotels that feel cold and impersonal.

971, 973 Ploenchit Rd., Lumphini, Pathumwan, Bangkok 10330 (near intersection of Rama I and Ratchadamri rds.). ℂ **800/225-5843** or 2656-0444. Fax 2656-0555. www.lemeridien-bangkok.com. 381 units. 11,660B (US$265) double; from 14,080B (US$320) suite. AE, DC, MC, V. Chit Lom BTS station. **Amenities:** 5 restaurants (grill, international, Thai, Japanese, Cantonese); tower lounge w/Latin bands and karaoke; 2 pools; 2 fitness centers; spa w/Jacuzzi, sauna, steam, massage, and beauty treatments; concierge; tour desk; car-rental desk; limousine service; business center; shopping arcade; salon; 24-hr. room service; babysitting; same-day laundry service/dry cleaning; nonsmoking rooms; executive-level rooms. *In room:* A/C, TV w/satellite programming, minibar, hair dryer, safe.

Expensive

Amari Boulevard Hotel ★ The Sukhumvit Road area doesn't provide the best street access to the sights in old Bangkok, but who needs street access when there's a perfectly good klong nearby? All you need do is hop a water taxi and take a fascinating trip through Bangkok's old "back alleys" to the old part of the city near the Grand Palace. And now, with the new Skytrain, you can whoosh to other parts of town in a snap. Many people choose to stay in the Sukhumvit Road area to be close to major shopping malls and plentiful food and entertainment options. If you pick this part of town, Amari Boulevard offers an excellent facility at good value. The newer Krung Thep Wing has spacious rooms with terrific city views, while the original wing has attractive balconied rooms that are a better value. When rooms are discounted 40% to 60% in the low season, this hotel is a very good bargain.

Amari Boulevard Hotel. 2 Soi 5, Sukhumvit Rd., Bangkok 10110 (N of Sukhumvit Rd., on Soi 5). 𝒞 2/255-2930. Fax 2255-2950. www.amari.com. 315 units. 8,800B (US$200) double; from 27,720B (US$630) suite. AE, DC, MC, V. 5-min. walk to Nana BTS station. **Amenities:** Restaurant (Thai and international); rooftop pool; fitness room; concierge; tour desk; car-rental desk, business center; 24-hr. room service; massage; babysitting; same-day laundry service/dry cleaning; In room: A/C, TV w/satellite programming, minibar, hair dryer, safe.

Hilton International Bangkok at Nai Lert Park 🏵🏵
Set in lushly landscaped Nai Lert Park, near the British and American embassies, this tropical paradise is something of a mixed blessing—you will sleep far from the madding crowd, but you might find the taxi ride to the river or tourist sights a minor nuisance (though the adventurous will ride the convenient klong boat to the Grand Palace Area). However, after a long day of business or sightseeing, returning to the peaceful tranquility of the Hilton has the very comfortable feeling of returning home. The airy atrium lobby, with its classic teak pavilion and open garden views, ranks as one of the great public spaces in Bangkok. And the gorgeous freeform pool in landscaped gardens is a total resort experience. The spacious guest rooms all have bougainvillea-draped balconies; the most preferred (and expensive) rooms overlook the pool. Other facilities include a fitness center with tennis and squash courts, and an exclusive shopping arcade.

Hilton offers many year-round packages to draw not only businesspeople, but leisure travelers as well. Special deals can be an excellent deal.

2 Wireless Rd., Bangkok 10330 (between Ploenchit and New Phetchaburi rds.). 𝒞 800/HILTONS or 02/253-0123. Fax 02/253-6509. www.bangkokhilton.com. 338 units. 8,800B–15,400B (US$200–US$350) double; from 16,192B (US$368) suite. AE, DC, MC, V. **Amenities:** 5 restaurants (French, Thai, international, Japanese, Cantonese); lobby lounge; lushly landscaped pool; outdoor lighted tennis courts; fitness center w/sauna; new spa center w/massage, body, and beauty treatments; concierge; tour desk; limousine service; business center; shopping arcade; salon; 24-hr. room service; babysitting; same-day laundry service/dry cleaning; nonsmoking rooms; executive-level rooms. In room: A/C, TV w/satellite programming and pay movies, dataport, minibar, coffee/tea-making facilities, hair dryer, safe.

The Regent 🏵🏵🏵
The Regent is a modern palace. From your first entrance through the massive lobby, you'll be captured by the grand staircase, huge gorgeous Thai murals, and gold sunbursts on the vaulted ceiling. The impeccable service begins at the front desk, where guests are greeted and then escorted to their room to complete check-in and enjoy the waiting fruit basket and box of chocolates. The air of luxury pervades each room: traditional-style Thai murals, handsome color schemes, and a plush carpeted dressing area off the tiled bathroom. The more expensive rooms have a view of the Royal Bangkok Sport Club and racetrack.

Cabana rooms and suites face the large pool and terrace area, which is filled with palms and lotus pools and all sorts of tropical greenery. Regent also has one of the finest hotel spas in Bangkok.

155 Ratchadamri Rd., Bangkok 10330 (S of Rama I Rd.). ℂ 800/545-4000 or 2251-6127. Fax 2253-9195. www.regenthotels.com 356 units. 10,120B–11,000B (US$230–US$250) double; US$380 cabana room; from 14,080 (US$320) suite. AE, DC, MC, V. Ratchadamri BTS station. **Amenities:** 4 restaurants (international, Italian, Thai, Japanese); excellent lobby lounge w/high tea and live jazz; landscaped outdoor pool; state-of-the-art fitness center w/sauna and steam; Clinique la Prairie spa; concierge; limousine service; 24-hr. business center; shopping arcade; salon; 24-hr. room service; babysitting; same-day laundry service/dry cleaning; non-smoking rooms; executive-level rooms. *In room:* A/C; TV w/satellite programming and Internet access; dataport; minibar; hair dryer; safe.

Moderate

Novotel Bangkok ★★

This elegant and opulent high-rise hotel in the Siam Square shopping area is one of this French chain's best inns. The grand marble, granite, and glass entrance leads into an expansive gray stone interior that is complemented by soft leather-upholstered sofas and chairs. Pastel tones carry over into guest quarters, where the rooms are spacious and fully equipped. Facilities include the 18th-floor nonsmoking suites, a fully-equipped business center that overlooks the hotel's kidney-shape pool, and a sleek chrome-and-mirror fitness center.

The location isn't too bad for visiting Bangkok's traditional tourist sites, but if you're in town on business or prefer one of Bangkok's better shopping areas, the Novotel is a fine choice. For the record, while "Siam" in the West is pronounced "*sigh*-yam" with a long *i*, in Thailand it's pronounced "*see*-yam." It'll help you explain where you're going to your taxi driver.

Siam Square Soi 6, Bangkok 10330 (in Siam Sq. off Rama I Rd.). ℂ 2255-6888. Fax 2254-1328. 465 units. 5,500B–6,300B (US$125–US$143) double; from 7,200B (US$164) suite. AE, DC, MC, V. Siam BTS station. **Amenities:** 4 restaurants (international, Chinese, Thai, seafood); huge popular disco; outdoor pool; fitness center w/massage; concierge; tour desk; limousine service; business center; shopping arcade; salon; 24-hr. room service; babysitting; same-day laundry service/dry cleaning; nonsmoking rooms; executive-level rooms. *In room:* A/C, TV w/satellite programming, minibar, safe.

Siam Inter-Continental Hotel ★★ (Value) (Kids)

Set in 26 acres of parkland—part of the Srapatum Royal Palace estate—the Siam Inter-Continental is an island of calm in frenetic Bangkok—which also allows it some of the best outdoor sports facilities in the city. It's hard to believe that just outside is the liveliest part of town: the main BTS station and Siam Square, with all its manic shopping and entertainment. But from the road, a graceful driveway leads to the sprawling ranch-style complex with its spacious lobby overlooking the well-landscaped grounds. Choose from rooms in a five-story tower or along two low-rise wings with views of the gardens. Pastel carpets and dark Chinese-style furniture provide a rich, pleasing ambience. The Club Inter-Continental Wing is the two-story equivalent of an "executive" floor, with slightly smarter furnishings and free breakfast and drinks in the private lounge.

967 Rama I Rd., Bangkok 10330 (opposite Siam Sq.). ℂ 2253-0355. Fax 2254-5474. www.interconti.com. 400 units. 4,752B (US$108) double; from 6,660B (US$150) suite. AE, DC, MC, V. Siam BTS station. **Amenities:** 4 restaurants (international, Thai); lounge w/live band; large resort-style pool; golf driving range and putting green; 3 outdoor tennis courts (1 grass); fitness center; children's playground; badminton court; volleyball and basketball courts; concierge; tour desk; limousine service; business center; shopping arcade; salon; 24-hr. room service; massage; babysitting; same-day laundry service/dry cleaning; nonsmoking rooms; executive-level rooms. *In room:* A/C, TV w/satellite programming, minibar, hair dryer, safe.

Inexpensive

City Lodge ★ (Value)

Budget watchers will appreciate the two small, spiffy City Lodges. Both the newer lodge on Soi 9 and its nearby cousin, the older, 35-room City Lodge on Soi 19 (ℂ 2254-4783; fax 2255-7340), provide clean, compact rooms with simple, modern decor. Each has a pleasant coffee shop (facing the bustle on Sukhumvit Rd. at Soi 9; serving Italian fare on Soi 19), a small but friendly staff, and facility-sharing privileges at the more deluxe Amari Boulevard Hotel on Soi 5—all three properties of the Amari Hotels and Resorts Group. Rooms are large, with some major furniture mismatching going on, but are clean and not musty. You'll find no frills here, there's but still a lot of comfort for your money.

137/1–3 Sukhumvit Soi 9, Bangkok 10110 (corner of Sukhumvit and Soi 9). © **2253-7705.** Fax 2255-4667. 28 units. 2,090B (US$47) double. MC, V. Nana or Asok BTS stations. **Amenities:** Coffee shop; access to Amari Boulevard's rooftop pool, fitness center, and business center; 24-hr. room service; babysitting; same-day laundry service/dry cleaning; In room: A/C, TV w/satellite programming, minibar.

Suk 11 Guesthouse ★★   For budget convenience in Bangkok, Suk 11 finds few rivals. With convenient access to the Skytrain and prices more befitting the budget spots on Khao San Road, this family-owned gem is often fully booked so call ahead (or book on their useful website). Rooms are basic: just plain linoleum floors and large beds in double rooms. Bathrooms are small, the shower-in-room variety, but clean. They have rooms with shared bathrooms for very little, but the single and double rooms with bathroom are the best bet. The hotel was recently refurbished and the common areas and hallways are done in a faux rustic style with wood-plank floors and are meant to look like old Thai streets. There are some quiet sitting areas and even a yoga room. It's a popular spot for folks studying Thai massage and a friendly comraderie pervades. A healthy Thai buffet breakfast is included and the staff couldn't be more friendly.

1/13 Soi Sukhumvit 11 (behind 7-Eleven) Sukhumvit Rd., Bangkok 10110. © **02/253-5927** www.suk11.com 500B (US$12) single; 600B (US$14) double. Cash only. **Amenities:** Restaurant; game-room; laundry; yoga room; Internet terminals; library. In room: A/C.

WHERE TO DINE

Chances are, your hotel will have at least one or two options for in-house dining; some hotels boast four or more different options. In fact, some of Bangkok's best dining is in its hotels, and I've included some of the better choices in this chapter. Usually the more authentic dining experience is out around town, from noodle hawkers on the sidewalks to traditional Thai dishes served in beautiful local settings. Bangkok also has some fine international dining establishments with guest chefs from Europe and America.

Thai food is among the finest cuisine in Southeast Asia and, some would argue, in the world. Bangkok offers a delightful variety of Thai restaurants, ranging from simple noodle stands to elegant dining rooms offering "royal" cuisine. It's so reasonably priced that even in the finest Thai restaurant, you'll have a hard time spending more than US$40 for two. The city also offers a spectacular array of excellent European, Chinese, and other Asian dining spots, generally more expensive than those catering to locals (up to $150 for 2 in the top hotels), but still a bargain compared to back home. Be prepared for ever-changing menus: Internationally renowned chefs are known for guest appearances in many top restaurants, adding their own masterful touches to the dishes offered. You'll find inexpensive Thai-style fast food, on the street or in the shopping malls. *Metro Magazine* contains reviews of recently opened restaurants plus short recaps of proven establishments.

ON THE RIVER
Very Expensive

Le Normandie ★★★ FRENCH   The ultraelegant Normandie, atop the renowned Oriental Hotel, with panoramic views of Thonburi and the Chao

Phraya River, is the apex in formal dining in Thailand, in both price and quality. The room glistens in gold and silver, from place settings to chandeliers, and the warm tones of golden silks impart a delicious glow. Some of the highest-rated master chefs from France have made guest appearances at Normandie, adding their own unique touches to the menu. The small menu features changing specialties, with classic selections such as pan-fried goose liver, followed by a pan-fried turbot with potato and leeks in a parsley sauce. The beef filet main course, in a red wine sauce, is a stroll through heaven. The set menu also includes cheese, coffee, and a sinful dessert. Order wines you only dreamed of from the masterful wine list, or faint from joy in the wine cellar.

The Oriental Bangkok, 48 Oriental Ave. (off Charoen Krung [New Rd.], overlooking the river). ℂ 2236-0400. Reservations required at least 1 day in advance. Jacket/tie required for men. Main courses 1,000B–1,600B (US$23–US$36); set menu w/wine selections 5,200B (US$118). AE, DC, MC, V. Daily noon–2:30pm and 7–10pm; closed Sun lunch. 10-min. walk from Saphan Taksin BTS station.

Expensive

Salathip ★★ THAI   Salathip, on the river terrace of the Shangri-La Hotel, is arguably Bangkok's most romantic Thai restaurant. Classical music and traditional cuisine are superbly presented under one of two aged, carved teak pavilions perched over a lotus pond or at outdoor tables overlooking the river. (For those who crave a less humid environment, grab a table in one of the air-conditioned dining rooms.) Although the food might not inspire aficionados, it is skillfully prepared and nicely served. Set menus help the uninitiated with ordering: Many courses include Thai spring rolls, pomelo salad with chicken, a spicy seafood soup, snapper with chili sauce, and your choice of Thai curries. Keep your eyes peeled for masked dancers performing between the tables at various intervals.

Shangri-La Hotel, 89 Soi Wat Suan Plu (overlooking Chao Phraya River, near Taksin Bridge). ℂ 2236-7777. Reservations recommended. Main courses 200B–450B (US$4.55–US$10). AE, DC, MC, V. Daily 6:30–10:30pm. Saphan Taksin BTS station.

Moderate

Harmonique ★★ THAI   A nice little find, Harmonique has special character that practically oozes from the courtyard walls of this century-old mansion. Small dining rooms set with cozy antiques and marble-top tables are inviting and friendly. While the cuisine here is Thai, it's not exactly authentic—much of it leans toward Western tastes, and there's a big Chinese influence here. But it's all still very good—the tom yam with fish was moderately spicy with enormous chunks of fish, and the sizzling grilled seafood platter is nice and garlicky (with chiles on the side). Also featured are good Thai salads. The service is far better during the week than on weekends.

22 Chaoren Krung (New Rd.) Soi 34. ℂ 2630-6270. Reservations recommended for dinner. Main courses 70B–200B. AE, MC, V. Mon–Sat 11am–10pm. 15-min. walk from Saphan Taksin BTS station.

HISTORIC BANGKOK—NEAR THE GRAND PALACE
Moderate

Bangkok Bar and Restaurant ★ THAI   A newer entry on the capital's dining scene, Bangkok is fresh and bold—a great alternative to places with more hype than taste. In a renovated 150-year-old mansion alongside Klong Banglamphu, all your senses are visited with local contemporary art on the walls (don't forget to walk upstairs for more exhibit space), deep jazz and funk rhythms wafting through the air, and sensational Thai food—but be warned, it's spicy. After scraping half the green chilis off my sea bass—steamed with lemon, garlic, and chili—it was no longer atomic, but delectable. But there are plenty of dishes that are not so spicy—the chicken wrapped in pandanus leaves is crispy and savory, and the coconut milk soup has a great creamy texture and sweet flavor. With a full bar and interesting cocktails, this place will be a success for years to come.

591 Phra Sumen Rd. (N of Democracy Monument). ✆ **2281-6237.** Reservations recommended for weekends. Main courses 70B–150B (US$1.60–US$3.40). No credit cards. Daily 6am–2am.

Kaloang Home Kitchen ★★ *Finds* THAI For ambience alone, the Kaloang Home Kitchen is a favorite. This riverside cafe, overlooking the Royal Yacht Pier and adjoining a lovely residential neighborhood, is as authentically Thai as any you'll find in the capital. The huge portions alone are well worth the trip. Make sure you ask about the daily specials, which don't appear on the menu, or try house specialties like yam paduk fu, a salad of roasted catfish whipped into a foam and crisply (and deliciously) fried, sam lee fish with mango, and marinated chicken.

There are two separate dining areas: a covered wooden pier set with simple outdoor furniture and a retired wooden boat that holds about 10 small tables. It might require patience to hunt this one down, but you'll be rewarded with a memorable off-the-beaten-tourist-track experience. The restaurant sometimes requires men to wear a sport coat.

2 Soi Wat Thevarajkunchorn, Si Ayutthaya Rd. (behind the National Library; go down Sri Ayutthaya Rd., cross Samsen Rd., and turn left and then right to the river). ✆ **2281-9228.** Reservations required for boat tables only. Main courses 70B–200B (US$1.60–US$4.55). AE, MC, V. Daily 11am–11pm.

Inexpensive

Commé ★ THAI Phra Athit Road has enjoyed a recent spark of trendy new restaurants and cafe openings in the past few years. Quite the place to hang out, it has the double joy of being hip and affordable at the same time. Of all the places here, I like Commé. Small and brightly lit, the staff is laid back and good-humored, the art will always give you something to talk about, and the menu (although somewhat limited) is quite good—and surprisingly inexpensive for the quality. Beer is served, but if you prefer wine or spirits, you'll have to bring your own.

Phra-Athit Rd. (opposite Ton Pho, 1 block N of Phra-Athit ferry pier). ✆ **2280-0647.** Reservations not accepted. Entrees 50B–120B (US$1.10–US$2.75). No credit cards. Tues–Sun 6pm–2am.

Ton Pho Restaurant THAI Another great choice for dining along the Chao Phraya River, Ton Pho is closer and easier to find, plus you still have a lovely riverside venue. I was lucky one day to have my lunch while watching the Royal Barges, the delicate gilt boats that parade the royal family through the city on special occasions, practice on the river. The extensive menu has a large selection of seafood specials, plus chicken and beef dishes (although the beef here was a bit too tough for my taste)—and the soups are lovely. Call the TAT to find out about Royal Barges practice, and then make your reservations for some great lunch entertainment.

43 Phra-Athit Rd., Banglamphu (1 block N of Phra-Athit ferry pier). ✆ **2280-0452.** Reservations recommended on weekends. Main courses 50B–260B (US$1.10–US$5.90). MC, V. Daily 11am–10pm.

THE BUSINESS DISTRICT

The touristy Silom Village Trade Center, 286 Silom Rd., at Soi 24, has a number of good dining venues. The Silom Village serves Thai and other Asian dishes, specializing in fresh seafood sold by weight. The Ruen Thep offers more elegant fare with classical Thai dance in the evenings.

Expensive

Benjarong ☆ THAI   You'll want to get dressed up for this elegant dining room, named for the exquisite five-color pottery once reserved exclusively for the use of royalty. Benjarong prides itself on offering the five basic flavors of Thai cuisine (salty, bitter, hot, sweet, and sour) in traditional "royal" dishes. While the a la carte menu is extensive, the most popular dishes are the sweet red curry crab claws and the exotic grilled fish with black beans in banana leaves. The illustrated menu will help you navigate your way through the choices and whet your appetite. For after-dinner treats, the kong wan is an ornate selection of typical Thai desserts—distinctive, light, and not too sweet.

The Dusit Thani, Rama IV Rd. (corner of Silom and Rama IV rds.). ✆ **2236-0450**. Reservations recommended. Main courses 180B–600B (US$4.10–US$14). AE, DC, MC, V. Daily 11:30am–2:30pm and 6:30–10:30pm. Closed for lunch Sat–Sun. Sala Daeng BTS station.

Moderate

The Mango Tree ☆ THAI   In a lovely 80-year-old Siamese restaurant house with its own tropical garden, Mango Tree offers a quiet retreat from the hectic business district. Live traditional music and classical Thai decorative touches fill the house with charm, and the attentive staff serves well-prepared dishes from all regions of the country. The mild green chicken curry and the crispy spring rolls are both excellent—but the menu is extensive, so feel free to experiment. The only trouble is, the food isn't exactly authentic. Yet although it has been toned down for foreign palates, it's still quite decent.

37 Soi Tantawan, Bangrak (off W end of Surawong Rd., across from Tawana Ramada Hotel). ✆ **2236-2820**. Reservations recommended. Main courses 90B–350B (US$2.05–US$7.95). AE, DC, MC, V. Daily 10am–2pm and 6–10pm. 10-min. walk from Sala Daeng BTS station.

Somboon Seafood SEAFOOD   This one's for those who would sacrifice atmosphere for excellent food. Though it's packed nightly, you'll still be able to find a table (the place is huge). The staff is extremely friendly—between them and the picture menu, you'll be able to order the best dishes and have the finest recommendations. Peruse the large aquariums outside to see all the live seafood options, like prawn, fishes, lobsters, and crabs (guaranteed freshness). The house specialty, chili crab, is especially excellent, as is the tom yang goong (they'll be glad to tone down the spice for any of the dishes here).

169/7–11 Surawongse Rd. (just across from the Peugeot building). ✆ **2233-3104**. Reservations not necessary. Seafood at market prices (about 800B/US$18 for 2). No credit cards. Daily 4–11pm.

Inexpensive

Prik Kee Noo ☆ THAI   Just so you know, Prik Kee Noo literally translates as "rat shit chili," which is the tiniest green chili pepper with the most lethal spice. Don't let it scare you away: The dishes here are spicy, but you can talk to your waiter about turning down the spice factor if you're worried. They have the full Thai menu, with great soups (a nice and hot tom yam), curries, salads, and fried foods—the appetizer menu is extensive, with great finger-food selections. I love this place for late-night stop-in snacks during a night on the town. If the chili doesn't wake you up, the bright coffee shop environment will.

1/2 Convent Rd., Silom (1 block S from Silom Rd.). ✆ **2631-2325**. Reservations not necessary. Main course 80B–180B (US$1.80–US$4.10). AE, DC, MC, V. Daily 11:30am–11pm. Sala Daeng BTS station.

THE SHOPPING/EMBASSY AREA
Expensive

The Chinese Restaurant ☆☆ CHINESE   Small dining nooks partitioned with crackled glass panels let in light but allow for privacy and intimacy. But the decor isn't the only thing contemporary here. The menu definitely goes for the nontraditional—while shark's fin and birds nest are available (what self-respecting Chinese restaurant can omit these?), the rest of it is a gastronomic storybook of live fish (the house specialty), baked lobster, and a highly recommended steamed crab with Chinese wine—aromatic and sumptuous. Nice, New Age music complements the modern edge here. It's a generic name, but definitely not a generic restaurant.

Grand Hyatt Erawan, 494 Ratchadamri Rd. ✆ **2254-1234**. Reservations recommended. Main courses 250B—1,500B (US$5.80—US$35). AE, DC, MC, V. Daily 11:30am–2:30pm and 6:30–10:30pm. 5-min. walk from Chit Lom BTS station.

Genji Restaurant ✿ JAPANESE

One of the best Japanese restaurants in Bangkok is located in a great hotel that caters to a large Japanese clientele. If you go to Genji for lunch, you'll likely discover a room full of Japanese businesspeople, a good sign for sushi eaters. Lunch served from the set menu is an excellent value. You can also save some money if you order local sashimi—a difference of about 1,500B (US$35) compared to the imported Japanese selections. The same goes for the U.S. beef over the Japanese imports, but it's a pity if you miss the Kobe beef sashimi with soy sauce and garlic, which is not only hard to find, but completely out of this world. The long menu also includes extensive teppanyaki and a host of seasonal specials.

Hilton International Bangkok at Nai Lert Park, 2 Wireless Rd. (in Nai Lert Park, N of Ploenchit Rd.). ✆ **2253-0123**. Reservations recommended; required for a tatami room. Main courses 100B–1,200B (US$2.30–US$27); set dinners 850B–2,000B (US$19–US$45). AE, DC, MC, V. Daily 11:30–2:30pm and 6:30–10:30pm.

Le Banyan ✿✿ FRENCH

In the same league as the top hotel French restaurants, this local favorite serves fine classic French cuisine with Thai touches. A spreading banyan tree on the edge of the gardenlike grounds, on a quiet Sukhumvit soi, inspires the name. Dining rooms are warmly furnished, with sisal matting and white clapboard walls adorned with Thai carvings, old photos, and prints of early Bangkok.

The most popular house special is pressed duck for two: Baked duck is carved and pressed to yield juices that are combined with goose liver, shallots, wine, and Armagnac or calvados to make the sauce. The sliced meat is lightly sautéed and, when bathed in the sauce, creates a sensational dish. Other fine choices include a rack of lamb a la Provençale and salmon with lemongrass. All are served with seasonal vegetables and can be enjoyed with one of the reasonably priced wines. A friendly and capable staff help make this a memorable dining experience.

59 Sukhumvit Soi 8 (1 block S of Sukhumvit Rd.). ✆ **2253-5556**. Reservations recommended. Main courses 350B–1,500B (US$7.95–US$34). AE, DC, MC, V. Mon–Sat 6–10pm. 10-min. walk from Nana BTS station.

Spice Market ✿✿ THAI

Many contend that the Spice Market is the city's finest pure Thai restaurant. The theatrical decor reflects the name: burlap spice sacks, ceramic pots, and glass jars set in dark-wood cabinets around the dining area playfully re-create the mercantile feel of a traditional Thai shop house. The food is artfully presented, authentically spiced, and extraordinarily delicious, with featured regional specialties for a great way to sample dishes from places you might or might not be traveling to in the kingdom. House specialties include nam prik ong, crispy rice cakes with minced pork dip; nua phad bai kraprow, fried beef with chili and fresh basil; and siew ngap, red curry with roasted duck in coconut milk. The menu's "chili rating" guarantees that spices are tempered to your palate.

In the Regent Bangkok, 155 Ratchadamri Rd. (S of Rama I Rd.). ✆ **2251-6127**. Reservations recommended. Main courses 150B–600B (US$3.40–US$14). AE, DC, MC, V. Daily 11:30am–2:30pm and 6–11pm. Ratchadamri BTS station.

Moderate

Lemongrass THAI   Nouvelle Thai cuisine, somewhat tailored to the Western tastes of its predominantly expatriate customers, is the specialty of this pleasant restaurant in an old Thai mansion handsomely converted and furnished with antiques. There are occasional complaints about small portions and slow service, but most of the waiters speak some English and will help guide you through the menu, which contains a full spectrum of Thai cuisine, including fiery southern dishes.

Try house favorites pomelo salad or chicken satay. Also excellent is the tom yang kung (a spicy sweet-and-sour prawn soup with ginger shoots), and the tender and juicy lemongrass chicken.

5/1 Sukhumvit Soi 24 (S of Sukhumvit Rd. on Soi 24). ✆ **2258-8637**. Reservations highly recommended. Main courses 120B–550B (US$2.70–US$12). AE, DC, MC, V. Daily 11am–2pm and 6–11pm. Phrom Pong BTS station.

Seafood Market & Restaurant ✪ SEAFOOD   *Warning:* This place is touristy, but I wouldn't recommend it if it weren't good food and fun. Chances are, you've never had a dining experience like this before, and if you're a seafood fan, you'll love it. After you've been seated, look over the list of preparation styles, and then walk to the back and take a shopping cart. Peruse the no fewer than 40 different creatures of the sea, either live or on ice, all priced by the kilo. Pay for it all at the cashier and then cart it back to the table. Waiters are skilled at making perfect suggestions for your catch, and what comes out of the kitchen is divine. I had the most tender squid broiled in butter and the meatiest grouper I've ever imagined, deep-fried with chilis. Cooking charges and corkage are paid separately at the end of the meal. The seafood is market price; the fish ranges from 195B to 625B (US$4.40–US$14) per kilo, with imported Alaskan king crab weighing in at a high 1,800B (US$41) per kilo and cuttlefish at only 245B (US$5.60) per kilo. Cooking charges range from 60B to 120B (US$1.35–US$2.70).

89 Sukhumvit Soi 24 (Soi Kasame). ✆ **2261-2071**. Reservations suggested for weekend dinner. Market prices, see above. AE, DC, MC, V. Daily 11:30am–midnight.

Inexpensive

Cabbages & Condoms ✪✪ THAI   Here's a theme restaurant with a purpose. Opened by local hero Mechai Viravaidya, founder of the Population & Community Development Association, the restaurant helps fund population control, AIDS awareness, and a host of rural development programs. Set in a large compound, the two-story restaurant has air-conditioned indoor dining—but if you sit on the garden terrace, you're in a fairy land of twinkling lights in romantic greenery. The house recommends the sam lee dad deao, which is a huge deep-fried cotton fish with chili and mango on the side. Another great dish is the kai hor bai teoy, fried boneless chicken wrapped in pandan leaves with a dark sweet soy sauce for dipping. There's also a large selection of vegetable and bean curd entrees.

Before you leave, be sure to check out the gift shop's whimsical condom-related merchandise. The restaurant apologizes for not providing after-dinner mints, but feel free to help yourself to a free condom instead.

10 Sukhumvit Soi 12. ✆ **2229-4610**. Reservations recommended. 70B–200B (US$1.60–US$4.55). AE, DC, MC, V. Daily 11am–10pm. 15-min. walk from Asok BTS station.

Le Dalat ★★ VIETNAMESE   Le Dalat's fine food and lovely garden setting make for a charming evening. The restaurant is casual and understatedly elegant, housed in an old Thai house done up in Vietnamese and Chinese antiques. The excellent food is prepared by Vietnamese-trained Thai chefs. Go for the bi guon (spring rolls with herbs and pork), chao tom (pounded shrimp laced on ground sugarcane in a basket of fresh noodles), and cha ra (fresh filet of grilled fish). In nice weather, you'll enjoy dining in the gracefully landscaped outdoor garden. This is a very highly recommended restaurant.

47/1 Sukhumvit Soi 23 (N of Sukhumvit Rd.). ⓒ **2258-4192.** Reservations recommended at dinner. Main courses 130B–180B (US$2.95–US$4.10). AE, DC, MC, V. Daily 11:30am–2:30pm and 6–10:30pm.

EXPLORING BANGKOK

When Rama I established Bangkok as the new capital city in the 1780s, he built a new palace and royal temple on the banks of the Chao Phraya River. The city sprang up around the palace and spread outward from this point as population and wealth grew. Today this area contains most of Bangkok's major historical sites, including a great number of **wats,** or Buddhist temples, that were built during the last 200 years. The city's attractions might seem like wat after wat, but they are each very unique in character, employing different architectural elements, cultural influences, and histories of their own. If you're short on time, the most interesting and easily accessible wats to catch are Wat Phra Kaeo, the royal wat that houses the Emerald Buddha at the Grand Palace, and Wat Po, home of the reclining Buddha.

BANGKOK'S WATERWAYS

The history of Bangkok was written on its waterways, which until recent years were the essential focus of the city's life. As Ayutthaya was before it, Bangkok came to be known as the "Venice of the East," but sadly, many of these klongs have been paved over for avenues. The magnificent Chao Phraya River ("the River of Kings"), however, continues to cut through the heart of the city, separating the early capital of Thonburi from today's Bangkok. On the Thonburi side, the klongs still branch off into a network of arteries that are relatively unchanged as the centers of neighborhood life. For an intimate glimpse of traditional Thai life, schedule a few hours to explore the waterways. You'll see people using the river to bathe, wash their clothes, and even brush their teeth at water's edge (a practice not recommended to tourists). Floating kitchens in sampans serve rice and noodles to customers in other boats.

There are several approaches to touring the klongs. Both **Sea Tours** (Suite nos. 88–92, 8th floor, Payathai Plaza Rajthavee; ⓒ **02/216-5783**) and **World Travel** (1053 Charoen Krung [New Road]; ⓒ **02/5900**) offer standard group tours: The basic canal tour is organized around a so-called "Floating Market" in Thonburi, but it has become very touristy and crowded (the morning trip, 8:30am–noon, is priced about 800B/US$19 per person). Better yet, charter a longtail *hang yao* for about 300B (US$6.98) an hour—expect to negotiate the price, and agree on the charge *before* you get in the boat. You'll find boats for hire at the Tha Chang ferry pier near Wat Phra Kaeo or the pier at River City Shopping Complex. Beware of independent boat operators that offer to take you to the nearby Thonburi Floating Market or to souvenir or gem shops. Take your time and explore Klong Bangkok Noi and Klong Bangkok Yai, with a stop at the Royal Barges Museum on the way back.

BANGKOK'S HISTORICAL TREASURES

The Grand Palace ⭐⭐⭐   The Grand Palace is almost always the first stop on any sightseeing agenda. Rama I built the oldest buildings in the square-mile complex when he moved the capital from Thonburi to Bangkok in the 1780s. It was the official residence and housed the offices of the kings until 1946, when the royal family moved to Chitralada Palace. These days, the palace is used only for royal ceremonies and as the royal guesthouse for visiting dignitaries. The focal point of the compound is the Chakri Maha Prasad, an intriguing mixture of Victorian architecture topped with a Thai temple-style roof that today houses the ashes of royal family members. To the left, the Amarinda Vinichai Hall is the venue for the highest royal ceremonies, including coronations. To the right of Chakri Maha Prasad stands the Dusit Hall, a perfect example of Thai architecture in the highest order. The Grand Palace compound also has a Royal Decorations and Coin Pavilion—its main draw is air-conditioning.

Near the river on Na Phra Lan Rd. near Sanam Luang. ℂ 2222-0094. Admission 125B (US$2.85). Price includes Wat Phra Kaeo and the Coin Pavilion inside the Grand Palace grounds, as well as admission to the Vimanmek Palace (near the National Assembly). Daily 8:30am–3:30pm; most individual buildings are closed to the public except on special days proclaimed by the king. Take the Chao Phraya Express Boat to the Tha Chang Pier, then walk E and S.

Jim Thompson's House ⭐   Jim Thompson was a New York architect who served in the OSS (Office of Strategic Services, now the CIA) in Thailand during World War II and afterward settled in Bangkok. Almost single-handedly he revived Thailand's silk industry, employing Thai Muslims as skilled silk weavers and building up a thriving industry. After expanding his sales to international markets, Mr. Thompson mysteriously disappeared in 1967 while vacationing in the Cameron Highlands in Malaysia. Despite extensive investigation, his disappearance has never been resolved.

His Thai house is composed of six linked teak and theng (harder than teak) wood houses from central Thailand that were rebuilt according to Thai architectural principles, but with Western additions (such as a staircase and window screens). In some rooms, the floor is made of Italian marble, but the wall panels are pegged teak. Volunteers guide you through rooms filled with Thompson's splendid collection of Khmer sculpture, Chinese porcelain, Burmese carving (especially a 17th-century teak Buddha), and antique Thai scroll paintings.

Soi Kasemsan 2 (on a small soi off Rama I Rd., opposite the National Stadium). ℂ 2216-7368. Admission 100B (US$2.30). Daily 9am–4:30pm.

The National Museum ⭐⭐   The National Museum, a short (15-min.) walk north of the Grand Palace and the Temple of the Emerald Buddha, is the country's central treasury of art and archaeology. It was originally the palace that the brother of Rama I built as part of the Grand Palace complex in 1782. Rama V converted the palace into a museum in 1884. Today it is the largest museum in Southeast Asia.

To see the entire collection, plan on at least 3 hours. If you're rushed, go straight to the Red House, a traditional 18th-century Thai building that was originally the living quarters of Princess Sri Sudarak, sister of King Rama I. It's furnished in period style, with many pieces originally owned by the princess.

Another essential stop is the Phuttaisawan (Buddhaisawan) Chapel, built in 1787 to house the Phra Phut Sihing, one of Thailand's most revered Buddha images, brought here from its original home in Chiang Mai. The main building of the royal palace contains gold jewelry, some from the royal collections, and

Exploring Bangkok

Grand Palace **10**

Jim Thompson's House **22**

Kamthieng House
(The Siam Society) **28**

Lak Muang (City Pillar Shrine) **9**

Lumpini Stadium **26**

National Museum **7**

Pak Klong Talaat
(Flower Market, also
called Talaat Taywait) **16**

Patpong Night Market **25**

Queen Sirikit National
Convention Center **27**

Ratchadamnoen Stadium **3**

Red Cross Snake Farm **24**

Royal Bangkok Sports Club **23**

The Royal Barges **6**

Royal Turf Club **20**

TAT Office (Tourist
Authority of Thailand) **4**

Vimanmek Mansion Museum **1**

Wang Suan Pakkard **21**

Wat Arun (Temple of Dawn) **12**

Wat Benchamabophit
(The Marble Wat) **2**

Wat Bovornivet **5**

Wat Kalaya Namit **17**

Wat Mahathat
(Temple of the Great Relic) **8**

Wat Phra Kaeo **11**

Wat Po **13**

Wat Prayunrawonsawat
(Wat Prayun) **18**

Wat Saket
(The Golden Mount) **15**

Wat Suthat and
the Giant Swing **14**

Wat Traimit
(The Golden Buddha) **19**

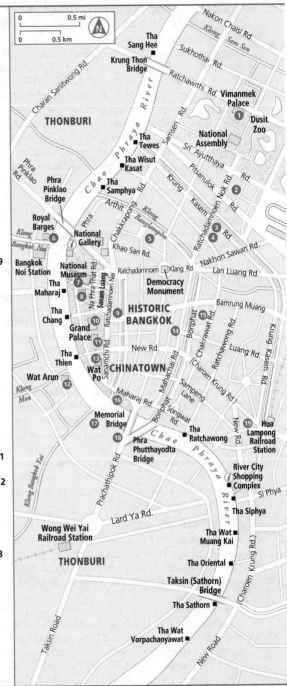

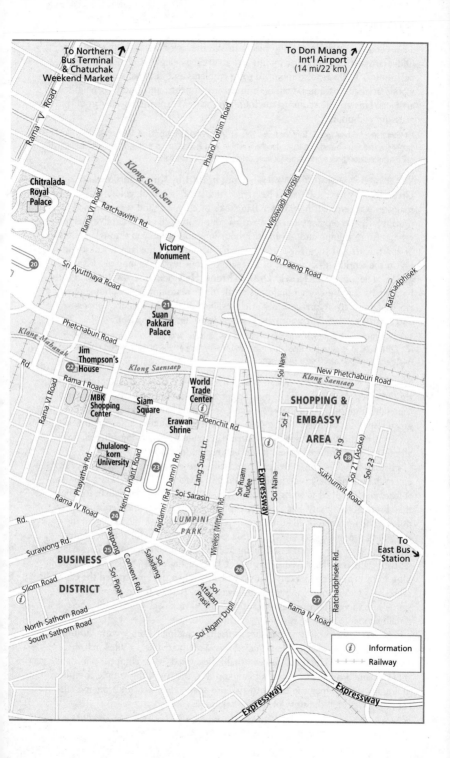

Thai ceramics, including many pieces in the five-color bencharong style. The Old Transportation Room contains ivory carvings, elephant chairs, and royal palanquins. There are also rooms of royal emblems and insignia, stone carvings, wood carvings, costumes, textiles, musical instruments, and Buddhist religious artifacts. Fine art and sculpture are found in the newer galleries at the rear of the museum compound.

Na Phra That Rd. (about ½ mile N of the Grand Palace). ✆ **2224-1333**. Admission 40B (US90¢). Wed–Sun 9am–4pm. Free English-language tours: Buddhism culture, Wed 9:30am; art, culture, religion, Thurs 9:30am; call the museum or check a newspaper for more details and current schedule.

Vimanmek Mansion Museum 🔆 Built in 1901 by King Chulalongkorn the Great (Rama V) as the Celestial Residence, this large, beautiful, golden teakwood mansion was restored in 1982 for Bangkok's bicentennial and was reopened by Queen Sirikit as a private museum with a collection of the royal family's memorabilia. An intriguing and informative hour-long tour takes you through a series of apartments and rooms (81 in all) in what is said to be the largest teak building in the world—the thought of all that gorgeous teakwood employed is staggering. The original **Abhisek Dusit Throne Hall** houses a display of Thai handicrafts, and nine other buildings north of the mansion display photographs, clocks, fabrics, royal carriages, and other regalia. Classical Thai dance, folk dance, and martial art demonstrations are given daily at 10:30am and 2pm.

193/2 Ratchavitee Rd., Dusit Palace grounds (opposite the Dusit Zoo, N of the National Assembly Building). ✆ **2281-8166**. Admission 50B (US$1.10); free if you already have a 125B (US$2.85) ticket to the Grand Palace and Wat Phra Kaeo. Daily 9:30am–4pm.

Wat Phra Kaeo 🔆🔆🔆 When Rama I built the Grand Palace, he included this temple, the royal temple most revered by the Thai people. The famed "emerald" Buddha, a 0.6m-tall (2-ft.-tall) northern Thai-style image made from green jasper, sits atop a towering gold altar. The statue dons a different costume for each of the three seasons in Thailand, changed by the king himself, who climbs up to the image because it can be lowered for no one.

Historians believe that artists created the statue in the 14th century. The emerald Buddha hid inside a plaster Buddha image until 1434, when movers accidentally dropped it, setting it free. The king at Chiang Mai demanded that it be brought to his city, but three attempts failed. Each time the elephant transporting the image stopped at the same spot in Lampang, so the king gave in to the will of the spirits and built a *chedi* (a sacred monument) for it there. Thirty-two years later, King Tiloka of Chiang Mai brought the image to Chiang Mai. The emerald Buddha stayed in the Wat Chedi Luang until 1552, when a later king from Luang Prabang carted it off to Laos. When the king moved the capital of Laos to Vientiane, the image followed him. Rama I finally recaptured the statue in a successful invasion of Laos and placed it in Wat Phra Kaeo, where it remains today.

The wat compound is a small city in itself, including a library with stunning Ayutthaya-style mother-of-pearl inlay doors; a reliquary like a golden bell-shape Sri Lankan style chedi; a *wihaan* (hall) bejeweled with chipped porcelain mosaics; and a miniature model of Angkor Wat, the sprawling temple complex at the ancient Khmer capital, with its corn-shape chedis. Murals on the surrounding walls tell the story of the *Ramayana*.

In the Grand Palace complex. ✆ **2222-0094**. Admission included in the Grand Palace fee, 125B (US$2.85). Daily 8:30–3:30pm. Take the Chao Phraya Express Boat to Tha Chang Pier, then walk E and S.

THE WATS

Wat Po ★★★   Wat Po (Wat Phra Chetuphon), the Temple of the Reclining Buddha, was built by Rama I in the 16th century and is the oldest and largest Buddhist temple in Bangkok. Considered Thailand's first public university, the temple's many monuments and artworks explain principles of religion, science, and literature.

Most people go straight to the enormous Reclining Buddha in the northern section. It's more than 46m (140 ft.) long and 16m (50 ft.) high, and was built during the mid-19th-century reign of Rama III. The statue is brick, covered with layers of plaster and always-flaking gold leaf; the feet are inlaid with mother-of-pearl illustrations of 108 auspicious *laksanas* ("characteristics") of the Buddha. Behind the Buddha, a line of 108 bronze bowls, each also representing one of the laksanas, awaits visitors to drop coins (acquired nearby for a 20B/US47¢ donation for luck).

Outside, the grounds contain 91 *chedis* (stupas or sacred mounds), four *wihaans* (halls), and a *bot* (the central shrine in a Buddhist temple). The Traditional Medical Practitioners Association Center teaches traditional Thai massage and medicine. Stop in for a massage (250B/US$5.80 per hr.), or ask about the 7- to 10-day massage courses.

Maharat Rd., near the river (about ½ mile S of the Grand Palace). ✆ 2222-0933. 20B (US45¢) admission. Daily 8am–5pm; massages offered until 6pm.

Wat Mahathat (Temple of the Great Relic) ★   Built to house a relic of the Buddha, Wat Mahathat is one of Bangkok's oldest shrines and the headquarters for Thailand's largest monastic order. Also the home of the Mahachulalongkorn Buddhist University, the most important center for the study of Buddhism and meditation, Wat Mahathat offers some programs in English.

Adjacent to it, between Maharat Road and the river, is the city's biggest amulet market, where a fantastic array of religious amulets, charms, talismans, and traditional medicine is sold. Each Sunday, hundreds of worshippers squat on the ground studying tiny images of the Buddha with magnifying glasses, hoping to find one that will bring good fortune or ward off evil.

Na Phra That Rd. (near Sanam Luang Park, between the Grand Palace and the National Museum). ✆ 2222-6011. 20B (US45¢) donation. Daily 9am–5pm.

Wat Arun (Temple of Dawn) ★★★   The 86m-high (260-ft.-high) Khmer-inspired tower rises majestically from the banks of the Chao Phraya, across from Wat Po. This religious complex served as the royal chapel during King Taksin's reign (1809–24), when Thonburi was the capital of Thailand.

The original tower was only 16m (50 ft.) high, but it was expanded during the rule of Rama III (1824–51) to its current height. The exterior is decorated with flower and decorative motifs made of colorful ceramic shards donated to the monastery by local people at the request of Rama III. Wat Arun is a sight to behold shimmering in the sunrise, but truly the best time to visit is in late afternoon for the sunset.

W bank of the Chao Phraya, opposite Tha Thien Pier. ✆ 2465-5640. 20B (US45¢) admission. Daily 8am–5:30pm. Take a water taxi from Tha Thien Pier (near Wat Po) or cross the Phra Pinklao Bridge and follow the river S on Arun Amarin Rd.

Wat Benchamabophit (the Marble Wat)   Wat Benchamabophit, simplified for tourists as the Marble Wat because of the white Carrara marble of which it's constructed, is an early-20th-century temple designed by Prince Narai, the half brother of Rama V. It's the most modern and one of the most beautiful of Bangkok's royal wats. Unlike the older complexes, there's no truly monumental wihaan or chedi dominating the grounds. Many smaller buildings reflect a melding of European materials and designs with traditional Thai religious architecture. Even the courtyards are paved with polished white marble. Walk inside the compound, beyond the main bot, to view the many Buddha images that represent various regional styles. In the early mornings, monks chant in the main chapel, sometimes so intensely that it seems as if the temple is going to lift off.

Si Ayutthaya Rd. (S of the Assembly Building near Chitralada Palace). © 2281-2501. 20B (US45¢) admission. Daily 8am–5pm.

Wat Saket (The Golden Mount) ★

Wat Saket is easily recognized by its golden chedi atop a fortresslike hill near the pier for Bangkok's east-west klong ferry. The wat was restored by King Rama I, and 30,000 bodies were brought here during a plague in the reign of Rama II. The hill, which is almost 80m high, is an artificial construction begun during the reign of Rama III. Rama IV brought in 1,000 teak logs to shore it up because it was sinking into the swampy ground. Rama V built the golden chedi to house a relic of Buddha, said to be from India or Nepal, given to him by the British. The concrete walls were added during World War II to keep the structure from collapsing.

The Golden Mount, a short but breathtaking climb that's best made in the morning, is most interesting for its vista of old Rattanakosin Island and the rooftops of Bangkok. Every late October to mid-November (for 9 days around the full moon), Wat Sakhet hosts Bangkok's most important temple fair, when the Golden Mount is wrapped with red cloth and a carnival erupts around it, with food and trinket stalls, theatrical performances, freak shows, animal circuses, and other monkey business.

Ratchadamnoen Klang and Boripihat rds. Entrance to wat is free; admission to the chedi 5B (US10¢) donation. Daily 9am–5pm.

Wat Suthat and the Giant Swing

The temple is among the oldest and largest in Bangkok, and Somerset Maugham declared its roofline the most beautiful. It was begun by Rama I and finished by Rama III; Rama II carved the panels for the wihaan's doors. It houses a beautiful 14th-century Phra Buddha Shakyamuni that was brought from Sukhothai, and the ashes of King Rama VIII, Ananda Mahidol, brother of the current king, are contained in its base. The wall paintings for which it is known were done during Rama III's reign.

The huge teak arch—also carved by Rama II—in front is all that remains of an original giant swing, which was used until 1932 to celebrate and thank Shiva for a bountiful rice harvest and to ask for the god's blessing on the next. The minister of rice, accompanied by hundreds of Brahman court astrologers, would lead a parade around the city walls to the temple precinct. Teams of men would ride the swing on arcs as high as 24.6m (82 ft.) in the air, trying to grab a bag of silver coins with their teeth. Due to injuries and deaths, the dangerous swing ceremony has been discontinued.

Sao Chingcha Sq. (near the intersection of Bamrung Muang Rd. and Ti Thong Rd.). © 2222-0280. 20B (US45¢) donation. Daily 9am–9pm.

Wat Traimit (The Golden Buddha)

Wat Traimit, which is thought to date from the 13th century, would hardly rate a second glance if not for its astonishing Buddha image, which is nearly 3m (10 ft.) high, weighs over 5 tons, and is believed to be cast of solid gold. It was discovered by accident in 1957 when an old stucco image was being moved from a storeroom by a crane, which dropped it and shattered the plaster shell, revealing the shining gold beneath. This powerful image has such a bright, reflective surface that its edges seem to disappear, and it is truly dazzling. The graceful seated statue is thought to have been cast during the Sukhothai period and later covered with plaster to hide it from the Burmese or other invaders. Pieces of the stucco are on display in a case to the left.

Traimit Rd. (W of Hua Lampong Station, just W of the intersection of Krung Kasem and Rama IV rds.). 20B (US45¢) donation. Daily 9am–5pm. Walk SW on Traimit Rd. and look for a school on the right w/a playground; the wat is up a flight of stairs overlooking the school.

CULTURAL PURSUITS

Anyone can tell you that cultural curiosities don't merely exist in the structures of buildings or cloistered in special collections. Daily activities, festivals and ceremonies, and cultural events expose elements of civilization, both modern and ancient, that are fascinating to the outside observer. Try to plan your time to include some of the following activities, which offer a peek into the lives of the Thai people.

Begin your travel plans by asking the Tourism Authority about upcoming **traditional festivals and ceremonies** (see "When to Go," earlier in this chapter). The **TAT** on Ratchadamnoen Nok Avenue (© **2282-9773**) has up-to-date information about celebration dates and locations, and encourages all visitors to attend even the smallest events. Some of my fondest experiences have been the times when I've come to these occasions out of curiosity only to find myself an active participant, welcomed and encouraged by friendly Thai hosts. By joining these events, even as a passive observer, you'll find yourself feeling less like a voyeur and more connected to the city and its people. Also inquire about events upcountry before you leave the capital to explore other cities and regions.

Muaythai, or **Thai Boxing** 𝄞𝄞𝄞, stretches beyond the boundaries of spectator sport in its presentation of Thai mores evident in prebout rituals, live musical performances, and the wild gambling antics of the audience (see "Phuket After Dark," later in this chapter). In Bangkok, catch up to 15 bouts nightly at either of two stadiums. The **Ratchadamnoen Stadium** (Ratchadamnoen Nok Ave.; © **2281-4205**) hosts bouts every Monday, Wednesday, Thursday, and Sunday, while the **Lumphini Staduim,** on Rama IV Road (© **2251-4303**), has bouts on Tuesday, Friday, and Saturday. Tickets are 1,000B (US$23) for ringside seats, 440B (US$10) for standing room only, and 220B (US$5) if you don't mind crowding in the cage at the back. Shows start at 6:30 or 7:30pm, depending on the stadium and the night.

Okay, so it's not exactly culture per se, but you'll have a hard time getting out of Thailand without encountering some kind of snake show. Bangkok's biggest venue is at the **Red Cross Snake Farm,** 1871 Rama IV Rd. (© **2252-0161**). Located in the heart of Bangkok opposite the Montien Hotel, this institute for the study of venomous snakes, established in 1923, was the second facility of its type in the world (the 1st was in Brazil). There are slide shows and snake-handling demonstrations weekdays at 10:30am and 2pm, and on weekends and holidays at 10:30am. You can also watch the handlers work with deadly cobras and equally poisonous banded kraits and green pit vipers, with demonstrations of venom milking. The venom is later gradually injected into horses, which produce antivenom for the treatment of snakebites. The Thai Red Cross sells medical guides and will also inoculate you against such maladies as typhoid, cholera, and smallpox in its clinic. The farm is open daily Monday to Friday 8:30am to

3pm, and Saturday and Sunday 8:30am to noon; admission is 70B (US$1.60). It's at the corner of Rama IV Road and Henri Dunant.

A good traditional **Thai massage** ★★ is one of life's true joys. A head-to-toe extravaganza, you don't just lie back and passively receive. Nay! Masseurs manipulate your limbs to stretch each muscle, and then apply acupressure techniques to loosen up tense muscles and get energy flowing. Basically, your body will be twisted, pulled, and sometimes pounded. But after you've spent the whole day on your dogs touring the sights, you'll be psyched to work out all those kinks. Talk to your hotel's concierge—all hotels can arrange massages for you. If your hotel doesn't have massage facilities, sometimes it has discount programs with neighboring businesses.

In the city there are countless massage places, and many of them are quite good. Be aware that many "massage parlors" cater to gentlemen, with services beyond standard service expectations. You can differentiate between the two different styles by looking for a sign specifically stating that the massage is TRADITIONAL. Some upstanding places have blatant signs indicating the place is free of hanky-panky. Try Po Thong Thai Massage, in the basement of the **Fortuna Hotel,** Sukhumvit Soi 5 (© **2255-1045;** 300B/US$6.80 per hr.), or **Arima Onsen,** 37/10–11 Soi Surawong Plaza, Surawong Road (© **2235-2142;** 200B/US$4.55 per hr.). The home of Thai massage, **Wat Po,** is a school to almost every masseuse in Bangkok and has cheap massages in an open-air pavilion within the temple complex—a very interesting but not necessarily relaxing, experience (Sanamchai Rd.; © **2221-2974;** 200B/US$4.55 per hr.). According to the experts, 2 hours is the minimum to experience the full benefits of Thai massage, but many will do it for 1 hour upon request. These places will also perform foot massages, which are equally divine.

Fancy a chance to learn cooking techniques from the pros? **Thai cooking classes** ★★ are extremely popular and fabulously presented, with hands-on practice in some of the most famous kitchens of Bangkok. Classes teach you all you need to know about Thai herbs, spices, and main ingredients—you'll never look at a produce market the same again. Lectures on Thai regional cuisine, cooking techniques, and menu planning complement classroom exercises to prepare all your favorite dishes. The best part is afterward, when you get to eat them! Classes are typically held in the mornings from 8 or 9am until noon, with lunch afterward. The Oriental Hotel's program offers 4-day programs, but you can join in for 1 or 2 days only, if you'd like. The cost is $120 per person. It's very expensive, but the chef is tops. Call © **2437-6211** for booking and information.

If you're traveling through Bangkok during February through April, you can't beat the fantastic sights of the **kite-fighting** competitions held at Lumphini Park in the center of the city and at Sanam Luang near The Grand Palace. Elaborate creations in vivid colors vie for prizes, and "fighting," a team spectator sport complete with sponsors, thrills onlookers. The TAT will have all the information you need about exact dates, or you can check the local papers or travel publications.

For Thais, **cockfighting** is a tradition as old as the hills. Country farmers raise cocks to be fighters, in the hope of bringing in a good one and making a small fortune. In markets, fighting cocks are kept under dome basket cages—in the animal section of Chatuchak Weekend Market (see "Shopping," below), you can see the birds up close. At the north end of the market you might catch a demonstration or an actual fight. The sport is legal in Thailand (so is the gambling involved). *Be forewarned:* Animal lovers will find this awful. Even though they've outlawed putting razors on the birds' wings, the fights get gory.

> **Tips**   **The Art of Bargaining**
>
> Nearly all shops will negotiate, so don't be shy. (If they don't want to hag-
> gle, they'll politely inform you that their prices are fixed—and even that
> ain't necessarily so.) Shop around a little first, to develop a sense of what
> things should cost. Let the seller make the first offer, and then counter
> with a reasonable offer somewhat less than you expect to pay. Always
> maintain a sense of humor; Thais resist unpleasant tactics. Take your time.
> (A companion might politely express disinterest or a desire to leave.) Once
> you've decided on an object, let your attention wander so that the seller
> doesn't know you're hooked. If there are several objects that interest you,
> work out a package deal. If you find something unusual that really
> appeals to you, don't pass it by hoping to find it cheaper later.

Wat Mahathat serves as one of Thailand's two Buddhist universities. As such, it has become a popular center for **meditation lessons and practice,** with Eng-lish-speaking monks overseeing the technique—Vipassana, also called insight meditation. If you haven't been around to **Wat Mahathat** (Temple of the Great Relic) during your trips out into the city, you'll find it at Na Phra That Road near Sanam Luang Park, between the Grand Palace and the National Museum, or you can call the Vipassana section at **Wat Mahathat** at ✆ **2623-6326.** Classes are held daily from 7 to 10am, 1 to 4pm, and again from 6 to 8pm. The length of time needed for practice and the results obtained vary from individual to individual.

SHOPPING

Don't even think about leaving Bangkok with money left over. With a huge assortment of **Thai silks,** tailors on every block, classical artwork and antiques, hill-tribe handicrafts, fine silver, beautiful gemstones, porcelain, and reptile skin products, shopping is your destiny in Thailand. I haven't even started describing all the **street bazaars** where you can find cheap batik clothing, knockoff watches, jeans and designer shirts, and all sorts of souvenirs. A friend of mine likes to pack a "goodie bag" when she comes to Thailand, an empty bag that she fills through-out her stay. Inevitably it's overflowing by day 3. Whatever your travel budget, set aside a large chunk of it for the many items you just won't resist.

Most major hotels have shopping arcades, in many cases with respectable, quality shops, though their prices are often much higher than those in less upscale neighborhoods. The finest arcades are those at the Oriental and Regent hotels, filled with antiques and haute couture. Similarly priced quality goods can be found at the high-end malls, particularly at **River City,** next to the Royal Orchid Sheraton. **The World Trade Center, Sogo, Siam Discovery Center,** and **Central** (a nationwide chain of department stores) are the city's leading malls; all of these are centrally located in Bangkok's shopping district.

Specific streets or areas are also known for excellent shopping. Among these are the **Chinatown streets,** off and on Sampeng Lane, where you'll find the so-called Thieves Market, the Pahurat cloth market, and a thousand and one notions stands; the compact and general **Bangrak Market,** behind the Shangri-La Hotel; **Pratunam Market,** at the intersection of Phetchaburi and Ratchaprarop roads, the wholesale and retail ready-to-wear center, with a vast array of inexpensive clothing; **Sukhumvit Road,** with its upscale antiques and handicrafts shops as well as bookstores; **Silom and Surawong** roads, with general merchandise, between the Oriental Hotel and Lumpini Park; **Thewet Market,** the wholesale flower outlet off Samsen Road; and the huge weekend market at **Chatuchak Park** (the Chatuchak Weekend Market).

In Bangkok, most shops are open from about 10am and sometimes stay open until 8 or 9pm. Most are closed on Sundays.

Charoen Krung (New Road) and the smaller outlet roads near the Oriental Hotel were once lined with antiques shops. There are still a few in this congested area, although some of the finest shops have moved to the notable **River City shopping mall,** creating Bangkok's greatest concentration of high-end antique galleries. In this great sampling of Thai antiques, you're certain to find something to your taste; however, the River City shops are among the most expensive in the city.

BANGKOK AFTER DARK

Bangkok is one of Asia's wildest nightlife scenes, with a huge range of cultural and hedonistic activities that should satisfy just about anyone. Artistic and cultural performances light up Bangkok evenings, after which countless discos and bars for all tastes keep you going until the wee hours. Most visitors won't leave without a stroll around Patpong, the famous sex strip, and the Night Market, with myriad vendors and blocks of bars and clubs.

For the hippest nightlife update, check out *Metro Magazine* (100B/US$2.27) available at bookstores. Featuring monthly listings of art events (by both foreign and local artists), theater performances (including local theater companies performing modern Thai plays), and the club scene (very up-to-date), it's the best single source of information about entertainment in the Big Mango and a must-buy for those serious about exploring Bangkok culture. Both the *Bangkok Post* and *The Nation* offer daily listings of cultural events and performance schedules. The **TAT** (in Bangkok; ✆ **1155**) will also provide schedule information. Your hotel concierge should also be able to guide you toward the evening of your choice.

THE PERFORMING ARTS

Although the large shopping malls and international hotels often sponsor a cultural show, most travelers experience the Thai classical performing arts at a commercially staged dance show accompanying a Thai banquet; several hotels and restaurants offer this program. Generally there's a fixed-menu dinner of Thai favorites accompanied by a small orchestra, followed by a dance performance.

For a different experience, visit the **Erawan Shrine,** at the corner of Ratchadamri and Ploenchit roads (near the Grand Hyatt Erawan Bangkok and Sogo Department Store). In front of the large, white marble altar to Brahma, the Hindu god of creation, and Erawan, his three-headed elephant—you'll often find musicians and beautifully costumed dancers commissioned to amuse Brahma by a grateful or hopeful worshiper.

There are two major theaters for Thai and international performances, the National Theater and the Thai Cultural Center. The **National Theater,** 1 Na Phra That Rd. (✆ **2224-1342**), presents demonstrations of Thai classical dancing and music by performers from the School of Music and Dance in Bangkok, which are generally superior to those at the tourist restaurants and hotels. There are also performances by visiting ballet and theatrical companies. Call the TAT or the box office for the current schedule.

The **Thailand Cultural Center,** Thiem Ruammit Road off Ratchadaphisek Road, Huai Khwang (✆ **2247-0028**), is the newest and largest performance center in town, offering a wide variety of programs. The Bangkok Symphony performs here during its short summer season. Other local and visiting companies also present theater and dance at the center. If you're to see the *Ramayana* performed in Bangkok, this is probably the place you'll see it. Call for the current schedule.

For a bit of tongue-in-cheek theater, a couple of Cabaret shows in Bangkok feature katoeys (aka "Lady-Boys") in 6-inch heels and feather boas performing to pop hits. Many times these shows are hilarious—the best to try is **Calypso Cabaret,** Asia Hotel, 296 Phayathai Rd. (② **2261-6355**). Calypso enjoys a certain amount of fame in Bangkok, with some performances that are creative than the standard drag parades at cabarets in Phuket or Pattaya. (Shows are nightly at 8:15pm and 9:45pm; tickets cost 700B/US$16.) A more typical show for Thailand, featuring much of the same routine as at the resorts, is **Mambo,** Washington Square, Sukhumvit Soi 22 (② **2259-5128**), with shows nightly 8:30 and 10pm; tickets cost 800B (US$18).

THE CLUB & BAR SCENE

Bangkok is huge, offering an endless selection of nighttime amusements. Most night places seem clustered around certain areas within the city, so I've broken down nightlife into the more popular areas—within each you can find all sorts of different entertainment. Drink prices range from about 80B (US$1.80) for a bottle of beer or a one-shot cocktail at a local bar, to double that at a hotel. If you'd just like to unwind with an evening cocktail, check out what's happening at your hotel's lobby bar; many set up jazzy live music to entertain folks. For the best lobby bar atmosphere, head for The **Bamboo Bar at the Oriental Hotel,** Oriental Lane off Charoen Krung Road (② **2236-0400**), with classy live jazz—some of the best in the city, or **The Colonnade** at the Sukhothai Hotel, 13/3 Sathorn Tai Rd. (② **2287-0222**), to enjoy the Sukhothai's sophisticated decor. For the infamous Bangkok sex show scene, check out "Patpong," below. Bars and discos are all over the city, with the bigger ones in the areas I've covered, plus an interesting local disco scene out on Ratchadaphisek Road. If you're looking for Bangkok's gay scene, start at Silom Soi 4 (see "Patpong," below).

A latest development, and major annoyance to Bangkok residents, is the current debate to close all bars and clubs at 2am. The city's growing concern for its youth has prompted this early closing time, and I've found more bars complying, often quite strictly. Also keep in mind that all bars close for major Buddhist holidays, including HRH Queen Sirikit's birthday on August 12 and HRH King Bhumibol's birthday on December 5.

Patpong

The Patpong scene is centered on Soi Patpong 1 and Soi Patpong 2 between Surawong and Silom roads. Most people know Patpong for its reputation as the home of Bangkok's sex shows, but even if you're not exactly interested in risqué entertainment, you'll probably find yourself there to explore this spot's large Night Market or array of other interesting bars and discos. The market packs in stalls full of cheap knock-off goods, pirate recordings, and all sorts of souvenirs—a great browse, but be prepared for some crowding.

Along the sides of the streets, men will try to lure you in to see a show. Take a peek at their menu boards to see what shows the girls will perform—it's definitely more circus spectacle than erotic dance. If you'd like to check out a show, be careful about the places you enter. Some add steep charges to your bill and threaten you if you can't pay the whole thing. If this (or anything else horrible) happens to you in one of these places, the best way to handle it is to pay the bill without argument, get a receipt (if you can), and report directly to the Tourist Police booth on Surawong Road. The Tourist Police here are a force to be reckoned with and have helped many a traveler out of just such a scam (see "The Sex Scene," below). For a place that will not cheat you, go to **Fire Cat**—you won't find any cover charge or hidden costs, drinks are reasonably priced, and the girls are less assertive than other places in terms of buying them drinks. If you're tipping, keep it limited to 20B notes, otherwise you'll be mobbed by a million girls. Another fun place is **King's Castle,** for basic go-go—but guess which women are really women?

Despite its rap as a go-go center, Patpong serves up some pretty great bars and discos. For a good watering hole, you can always count on **O'Reilly's Irish Pub,** 62 Silom Rd., on the corner of Soi Thaniya just east of Patpong (✆ **2632-7515**), a lively bar with regulars and travelers; or **The Barbican,** 9/4–5 Soi Thaniya off Silom Road (✆ **2234-3590**), for stylish hanging out (and great food), plus some nice live music. **Shenanigan's** (formerly Delaney's), across from Patpong on Convent Road (next to Silom Complex), 1/5–6 Sivadon Building (✆ **2266-7160**), caters to Bangkok yuppies and foreign expatriates with Irish pub style and live music after office working hours. For dancing, try the very techno **Lucifer's,** Radio City, 76/1–3 Patpong 1 (✆ **2234-6902**). There's also **Legends** in the Dusit Thani Hotel, at the corner of Silom Road and Rama IV Road (✆ **2236-0450**), for an upscale and fashionable place to see and be seen. I like heading to Silom Soi 4 (between Patpong 2 and Soi Thaniya off Silom Rd.), where you'll find small home-grown clubs spinning great music in a more intimate atmosphere. Silom Soi 4 is also where you'll find a lot of gay clubs, the most popular of which are **Telephone Bar,** 114/11–13 Silom Soi 4 (✆ **2234-3279**), and **The Balcony,** 86–8 Silom Soi 4 (✆ **2235-5891**).

Siam Square

Siam Square, on Rama I Road between Henri Dunant Road and Phayathai Road, houses quite a few popular joints. Here's where you'll find **Bangkok's Hard Rock Café,** 424/3–6 Siam Square Soi 11 (✆ **2254-0830**), featuring good live bands. At the Hartmannsdorfer Brauhaus, 2nd floor, **Siam Discovery Center,** Rama I Road (✆ **2658-0223**), you'll find home brews in a nice atmosphere—with special beer discounts on Sundays.

A great disco, **Concept CM²** has live bands (1 night there was a jazzy bebop band—great if you can remember how to jitterbug) with DJ dance music in between. Another very popular place is **Novotel Siam,** Siam Square Soi 6 (✆ **2255-6888**). **Spasso,** in the Grand Hyatt Erewan Hotel, 494 Ratchadamri Rd. (✆ **2254-1234**), a fabulous Italian restaurant, turns into an equally fabulous upscale club featuring live music, with superb decor and atmosphere.

If you must find the best karaoke in Bangkok, try **Sensations,** Novotel Siam, Siam Square Soi 6 (✆ **2255-6888**). It has a huge selection of songs and excellent equipment. Ask about group discounts.

A little bit north of this area (a short cab ride away), near the Victory Monument, check out live "jazz" (more blues than jazz, but still good) at **Saxophone Pub and Restaurant.** It's at Phayathai Road just across from the traffic circle (✆ **2246-5472**).

Khao San Road

Over on Rattanakosin Island in Old Bangkok, the backpackers on Khao San Road have created quite a scene, where many locals and expatriates come to join once in a while. Start at **Gulliver's** on the corner of Khao San and Chakrabongse roads to prime yourself, and then explore the back lanes off Khao San for small dance clubs (some the size of broom closets) and hangouts. You'll find plenty of other travelers here, mostly in their 20s, and the atmosphere is always laid back; anything goes.

Sukhumvit Road

Along the long stretch of Sukhumvit Road, expatriates and locals have created an assortment of great places to check out—but most are not within walking distance of each other. Most require a short hop by taxi or tuk-tuk in between.

The **Bull's Head,** Sukhumvit Soi 33/1 (© 2259-4444), a fun local pub, draws crowds with frequent theme parties and a clubhouse attitude. A few microbreweries draw crowds out to this area. **Bruahaus Bangkok,** President Park, Sukhumvit Soi 24, at the end of the soi (© 2661-1111), and **Taurus Brew House,** Sukhumvit Soi 26 (© 2661-2207), pack them in—especially on weekends—for home brews and live pop music. Taurus also boasts one of the better discos in the Sukhumvit area, just across from the Brew House; this hip and huge "complex" has live music, a giant disco, and good food. For the best live music, however, head for **Riva's,** Sheraton Grande Sukhumvit Hotel, 250 Sukhumvit Rd. (© 2653-0333), with international bands and lots of dancing.

Q Bar on 34 Sukhumvit Soi 11 (© 2252-3274) is *the* place for the slick urban hip of Bangkok. Wear black. Similar to the Patpong sex show scene, two other areas out on Sukhumvit have go-go bars but without the hype. Check out **Nana Plaza** just south of Sukhumvit Road on Sukhumvit Soi 4, or **Soi Cowboy** (the oldest go-go scene, dating from Vietnam War days) between Soi Asoke (Sukhumvit Soi 21) and Sukhumvit Soi 23.

Ratchadaphisek Road

Huge discos reign supreme at Ratchadaphisek—and it has a good local feel. The area attracts mostly young urban Thais; you'll find fewer foreigners here than you will at other places. **Dance Fever** (© 2247-4295) and **Hollywood** (© 2246-4311), opposite Oscar Palace, are big and cavernous, with DJs spinning thumping Western hits and popular Thai songs. I also like **Sparks,** in the Emerald Hotel (© 2276-4774), for a local disco experience—the people are friendly and welcoming, and in many ways more open to meeting you. Actually, some will be quite shocked to see a foreign face at their local joint. Chances are, you'll have a blast.

"MODERN" OR "PHYSICAL" MASSAGE PARLORS

This is not *exactly* traditional Thai massage. Bangkok has hundreds of "modern" or "physical" massage parlors, which are heavily advertised and offer something quite different from traditional Thai massage. Physical massage usually involves the masseuse using her entire body, thoroughly oiled to massage the customer, a "body-body" massage. If one wishes, a "sandwich," with two masseuses, can also be ordered.

Nearly all massage parlors are organized along the same lines. Guests enter the lobby where there's a coffee shop/bar and several waiting rooms where young Thai women wearing numbers pinned to their blouses sit on bleachers. Guests examine the women through a window and select their masseuse. Both guest and masseuse take a room in the building and typically spend between 1 and 2 hours on a massage. Rates for a physical massage start at about 600B (US$14).

THE SEX SCENE

Although the 1985 hit song "One Night in Bangkok" was actually about chess (from the musical *Chess*), the song celebrated the naughtiest aspect of life in Bangkok. Since the 1960s—and particularly since the Vietnam War—Bangkok has reigned supreme as the sin capital of Asia, with sex clubs, bars, massage parlors, and prostitutes concentrated in the Patpong, Nana Plaza, and Soi Cowboy districts. Recent acknowledgments by the Thai government of the startling increase in HIV-positive cases have toned down somewhat the sex-club scene, while some vendors have shifted their focus to younger and younger women. Prostitutes these days will insist their clients use a condom.

In the "Patpong" section above, I've included a few suggestions where anyone can see a "Bangkok Sex Show" without being hassled by extra charges and seedy goings on—the places I've recommended are basically on the up and up, and women are welcome, as are couples. To be honest, in all of these clubs, the girls look bored, with most of the acts being performed with studied routine. In addition to go-go bars and sex shows, you'll also find gay go-go bars in Patpong, small clubs with sex on the menu and rooms upstairs, and some bars where oral sex is performed en bar (in all 3 districts).

Let's be perfectly frank: The men and women in the clubs are all available to take out of the bar. You'll be required to pay a "bar fine" (about 350B–500B/US$7.95–US$12), and you can take the companion of your choice out to other clubs or to someplace more private. Some men buy girls out of bars just to go to the movies. If you're interested in having sex, you'll negotiate directly with him or her, and pay in cash. If this is your scene, stick with folks from the go-go bars and established clubs—these women and men are less likely to slip you drugs (which happens), rob your hotel room while you're sleeping (which happens), or get you mixed up with illegal activities (which happens). If you stick with club employees, you can always return to the club the next night to find them if something goes amiss. Also, know that many "gay" men working the scene are not really gay, but just in the business for the money.

If you're staying in a very expensive up-market hotel, many times you will not be allowed to bring prostitutes through the lobby. As an alternative, ask your new friend to recommend a cheap alternative hotel room nearby.

While prostitution is technically illegal in Thailand, this law is never enforced. International reports about poor farmers selling their children into prostitution are true—many children are held in brothels against their will. However, the majority of sex workers are adults who enter the industry of their own free will, for basic economic necessity. While most have an open-minded attitude toward the industry in general, there are some things going on in the scene that can be very upsetting for Western visitors. Child prostitution and pornography, slavery, and violence against sex workers all exist. In fact, Thai law can get serious about statutory rape—the legal age of consent is 15, and a few foreigners have served jail time for ignoring this law. If you encounter any of these activities, please report them to the **Tourist Police** (© **2694-1222,** ext. 1).

4 The Eastern Seaboard

Thailand's beaches along the Gulf of Thailand (aka the Gulf of Siam) are world-renowned for their clean white sand, palm groves, and warm water. Today most areas are served by a sophisticated tourism infrastructure and indulgent accommodations. Although no sandy crescent is protected from the hotel developer's hand, there are still areas that are relatively quiet.

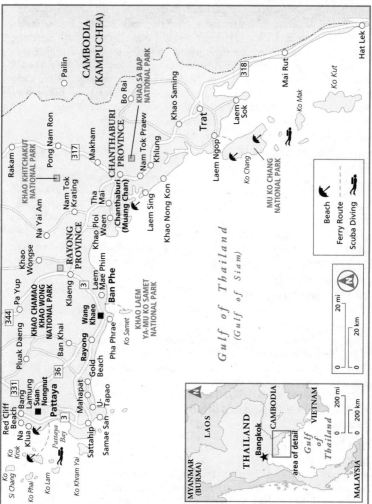

Pattaya, the oldest and most decadent of Thailand's resorts, lures people seeking a break from the big city because of its proximity to Bangkok (2½ hr. by bus). But don't come for the beach. Pattaya is better known as the sex playground of Southeast Asia, while its beaches rot from tourist pollution. The local government has been cleaning up Pattaya Bay and enacting strict new waste-management guidelines, but there's still far more work to be done. **Ko Samet** is the star of Rayong Province, a small island (somewhat protected as a national park) whose primitive bungalows create a very different feel from Pattaya's swinging hotels. Picture-postcard bays and soft white sands make this the tropical island many come to Thailand to experience. It's easily reached by a 45-minute ferry ride from the tiny port of Ban Phe (3½ hr. from Bangkok by bus); though isolated, it gets crowded on weekends due to its popularity with foreign low-budget tourists and Thais, especially during holidays.

5 Pattaya

You'll hear Pattaya, 147km (91 miles) east of Bangkok, called anything from "Asia's premier resort" to "one big open-air brothel"—its legacy as Thailand's R&R capital for Vietnam-weary American troops. It does indeed have several hundred beer bars, discos with scantily clad Thai teens, massage parlors, and transvestite clubs all jammed together along a beachfront strip. But it has another more elegant and sophisticated side in its big international resorts, retreats set in sprawling, manicured seaside gardens.

Okay, let me be honest here. If you want fun and relaxation on idyllic tropical beaches, don't come to Pattaya. The bay is a toilet—I wouldn't go near the water without a prescription for an antibiotic.

If you want to see crazy scenes from a wild nightlife—go-go bars, loose bar girls, cheap booze, and plenty of trouble to be had—then Pattaya's your kind of place. Come to think of it, I wouldn't go near the bars without a prescription for an antibiotic, either.

Pattaya has struggled to present a family resort atmosphere, and it surprises me just how many families come here to vacation. Really, if you're looking for something more wholesome, bypass Pattaya for tranquil Ko Samet or check out Hua Hin on the other side of the Gulf.

VISITOR INFORMATION

The TAT office, once in the center of Beach Road, has lost the battle with increasing rents and moved to a location south of Pattaya City, up the mountain on the road between Pattaya and neighboring resort Jomtien. You can hop any of the Jomtien-bound songtao, and they'll drop you off at the office for 20B (US45¢). The address is 609 Moo 10, Pratamnak Road (© **3842-8750**). Don't depend on them for critical details.

A couple of free publications, *What's On Pattaya* and *Explore Pattaya and the East Coast,* are widely distributed to hotels and guesthouses. They each contain good maps.

GETTING THERE

By Plane There's no airport in Pattaya; the nearest is in U Tapao, an hour east of the city (© **3824-5595**), served by **Bangkok Airways** with a daily flight from Ko Samui (trip time: 1 hr.). The airline also flies four times a week to and from Phnom Penh in Cambodia. Make reservations through its offices at Bangkok (© **2229-3456**) and Ko Samui (© **7742-5601**). There's also an office in Pattaya at Royal Garden Plaza, 218 Beach Rd., 2nd floor (© **3841-1965**). To get to and from the airport to Pattaya, you'll have to either arrange private transfer through your resort (a limo can be as steep as 1,000B/US$23), or take the Bangkok Airways minivan for 150B (US$3.40).

By Train Once-a-day train service leaves from **Bangkok's Hua Lampong station** at 6:55am and returns from Pattaya at 2:50pm. The 5-hour trip through the countryside is much more pleasant than that via the highway and costs only 31B (US75¢). Call Hua Lampong in Bangkok at © **2223-7010,** or the train station in Pattaya at © **3842-9285.** The train station is east of the resort strip off Sukhumvit Road near the intersection with North Pattaya Road. Outside you can catch a shared-ride songtao (minitruck) to the main beach (they'll drop you off anywhere along the main drag for about 20B/US45¢).

By Public Bus The most common and practical form of transportation to Pattaya is the bus. Buses depart from **Bangkok's Eastern Bus Terminal** on

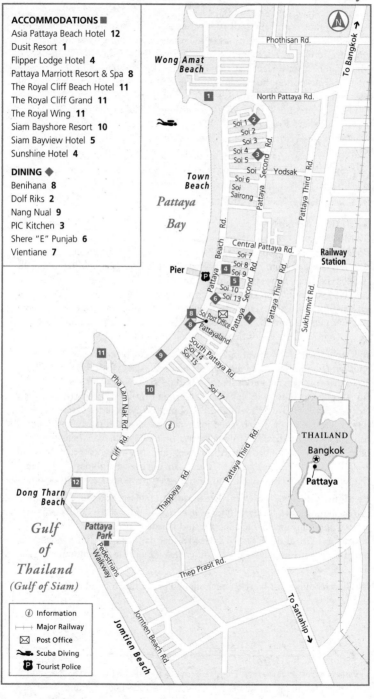

Pattaya

ACCOMMODATIONS ■
Asia Pattaya Beach Hotel **12**
Dusit Resort **1**
Flipper Lodge Hotel **4**
Pattaya Marriott Resort & Spa **8**
The Royal Cliff Beach Hotel **11**
The Royal Cliff Grand **11**
The Royal Wing **11**
Siam Bayshore Resort **10**
Siam Bayview Hotel **5**
Sunshine Hotel **4**

DINING ◆
Benihana **8**
Dolf Riks **2**
Nang Nual **9**
PIC Kitchen **3**
Shere "E" Punjab **6**
Vientiane **7**

Phothisan Rd.

Wong Amat Beach

North Pattaya Rd.

To Bangkok

Soi 1
Soi 2
Soi 3
Soi 4
Soi 5
Soi 6
Soi Sairong

Yodsak

Pattaya Second Rd.

Pattaya Third Rd.

Town Beach

Pattaya Bay

Central Pattaya Rd.

Soi 7
Soi 8
Soi 9
Soi 10
Soi 13

Railway Station

Pier

Pattaya Beach Rd.

Pattaya Second Rd.

Pattaya Third Rd.

Sukhumvit Rd.

Soi Post Office
Pattayaland

South Pattaya Rd.
Soi 14
Soi 15

Soi 17

Pha Lam Nak Rd.

Cliff Rd.

ⓘ

THAILAND

Bangkok

Pattaya

Dong Tharn Beach

Thappaya Rd.

Pattaya Third Rd.

Gulf
of
Thailand
(Gulf of Siam)

Pattaya Park

Pedestrians Walkway

Thep Prasit Rd.

To Sattahip

Jomtien Beach Rd.

Jomtien Beach

ⓘ Information
Major Railway
⊠ Post Office
Scuba Diving
🅟 Tourist Police

163

Sukhumvit Road opposite Soi 63, Ekamai Road (② **2391-2504**), every half-hour beginning from 5am until 10pm every day. For air-conditioned coach, the fare is 90B (US$2.05). There's also regular bus service from **Bangkok's Northern Bus Terminal,** on Kampaengphet 2 Road (Mor Chit) (② **2936-2841**), which can be a convenient way to avoid Bangkok rush-hour traffic if you're trying to get out during those hours (from central Bangkok, you can take advantage of the less-congested expressway).

The bus station in Pattaya for air-conditioned buses to and from Bangkok is on North Pattaya Road (② **3842-9877**). From there, catch a shared ride on a songtao to your resort or hotel for about (20B/US45¢).

By Taxi   You can arrange a taxi at the desk in either terminal of Don Muang Airport for 1,250B (US$28), or your hotel concierge can negotiate with a metered taxi driver to take you to a Pattaya resort, door to door, for about 1,500B (US$34).

By Car   Take Highway 3 east from Bangkok.

GETTING AROUND

By Minibus or Songtao   *Songtao* (also called baht buses), pickups with two wooden benches in their bed, cruise the major streets for passengers and are the best and cheapest form of transport. Fares within Pattaya should be from 10B (US20¢; however, I have yet to find a songtao from the bus terminal for less than 20B/US45¢); to far-flung beaches such as Jomtien, they're 30B (US70¢). Rates are fixed by the local governments, but most drivers will try to overcharge you, and you must negotiate firmly. Some hotels operate their own minibuses, but they charge much more for the same bumpy ride.

By Car   There are plenty of car-rental agencies, and you can negotiate the price with most, especially outside the high season. **Avis at the Dusit Resort** (② **3836-1628**) has self-drive rates from about 1,500B (US$34) per day for a Suzuki Caribian 4WD sport vehicle, to 2,000B (US$45) and up for a compact sedan. **VIA Rent-a-Car,** 215/15–18 Pattaya 2nd Rd. opposite Royal Garden Plaza (② **3842-6242**), has a good reputation, good insurance coverage, and rates a few hundred baht lower per day than Avis. Along Pattaya Beach Road, local car-rental agencies offer Caribians and huge souped-up Jeeps for anywhere between 900B and 1,500B (US$20–US$34) per day. These cars often have dubious maintenance records and even more suspicious insurance agreements—proceed with caution.

By Motorcycle   For those who dare brave the often drunk and reckless foreign drivers in downtown Pattaya, 150cc motorcycles rent for about 200B (US$4.55) a day without insurance. Big choppers and Japanese speed bikes (500cc) will go for about 500B to 800B (US$12–US$18) per day. Like the independent car-rental agencies, motorcycle rentals differ in bike quality and insurance agreements. Demand a helmet.

By Bicycle   Look for bicycle rentals along Pattaya Beach Road as low as 100B (US$2.30) per day.

ⓒ *FAST FACTS:* Pattaya

Banks/Currency Exchange There are many independent **money-changing booths;** many bank exchanges (with better rates) stay open 24 hours. They're all easily located on any of the Pattaya maps available, with ATMs as well.

Internet/E-mail There are little Internet centers everywhere, the average charge seems to be 2B (US5¢) per minute. I like the classy **Pattaya K@fe Net** at 219/59–60 Soi Yamato Beach Rd. (© **3842-1050**).

Hospital If you need an ambulance, call **Bangkok Pattaya Hospital** at © **3842-7751**. English-speaking staff can handle standard outpatient services as well.

Police In Pattaya, the number for the **Tourist Police** is © **1699** or © **3842-9371**.

Post Office/Mail The post office is suitably located on **Soi Post Office**, the street just before the Royal Garden Plaza (© **3842-9341**).

WHERE TO STAY
VERY EXPENSIVE
The Royal Cliff Grand ✦✦   If columned public spaces with fountains, staircases, chandeliers, and acres of granite mean grand, then this newer addition to the fine Royal Cliff Beach Club Resort complex lives up to the name. Everything about the place is larger than life.

Spacious rooms in the contemporary, scallop-shape tower have private VCRs and fax setups, as well as marble bathrooms with separate shower stalls and twin sinks. Speaking of showers, each room has a balcony with a shower. Rooms are elegantly appointed with classic furniture and coffered ceilings in tribute to the era of King Rama V, who inspired the Victoriana/Siam design. The Royal Club on the sixth floor boasts a private spa and sun deck, as well as seven Jacuzzis for its VIP and business guests.

353 Phra Tamnuk Rd., Pattaya, Chonburi 20150 (on cliff, S end of Pattaya Bay). © **3825-0421**. Fax 3825-0514. www.royalcliff.com. 290 units. 6,500B–8,000B (US$148–US$182) double; from 9,500B (US$216) suite. AE, DC, MC, V. **Amenities:** Full facilities sharing w/all Royal Cliff Beach Resort properties, including 9 restaurants (Thai, Chinese, Japanese, Continental grill, Italian, seafood, international coffee shops); 4 bars w/live music; 5 outdoor landscaped pools; golf course (or nearby); 3-hole putting green; 6 outdoor lighted tennis courts; large completely equipped fitness center w/spa, sauna, steam, and massage; Jacuzzi; watersports equipment rental, including private catamaran for chartered cruises; concierge; tour desk; limousine service; business center; salon; 24-hr. room service; babysitting; same-day laundry/dry cleaning; nonsmoking rooms. *In room:* A/C, TV w/satellite programming, minibar, hair dryer, safe.

The Royal Wing ✦✦   The dazzling Royal Wing is treated by both guests and its capable Swiss management as a separate entity within the impressive Royal Cliff resort. The level of service here is more personal (butlers on call 24 hr.), and the rooms are more regally furnished than anywhere else in town.

As opulent as Bangkok's Shangri-La, the Royal Wing is the pinnacle of Hong Kong–style glitz. The lobby is white marble, with lotus bud–capped columns combining Thai and Chinese influences. Each guest is catered to personally, with butlers unpacking your luggage on arrival and beach chaise lounges reserved with your brass nameplate. The large, bright, quietly tasteful rooms—decorated throughout with teak and fine pastel Thai cottons—are spaced around the cliff. For maximum privacy, each has two balconies, draped in fuchsia or orange bougainvillea, overlooking Pattaya Bay. In addition, there's an exclusive pool for Royal Wing guests that is not available to guests of other hotels within the resort, plus you'll have your own private pavilion reserved for you at the small but uncrowded and well-maintained beach.

353 Phra Tamnuk Rd., Pattaya 20150, Chonburi (on cliff, S of Pattaya Beach). © **3825-0421.** Fax 3825-0486. www.royalcliff.com.86 units. From 10,500B (US$239) suite. AE, DC, MC, V. **Amenities:** Full facilities sharing w/all Royal Cliff Beach Resort properties, including 9 restaurants (Thai, Chinese, Japanese, Continental grill, Italian, seafood, international coffee shops); 4 bars w/live music; 5 outdoor landscaped pools; golf course (or nearby); 3-hole putting green; 6 outdoor lighted tennis courts; large completely equipped fitness center w/spa, sauna, steam, and massage; Jacuzzi; watersports equipment rental, including private catamaran for chartered cruises; concierge; tour desk; limousine service; business center; salon; 24-hr. room service; babysitting; same-day laundry/dry cleaning; nonsmoking rooms. *In room:* A/C, TV w/satellite programming, minibar, hair dryer, safe.

EXPENSIVE

Dusit Resort ⭐ This beautifully landscaped resort offers watersports, a good health club, and some nightlife (far from the steamier side of Pattaya). Straddling a bluff on the north end of the main beach, the Dusit has two pools and sun decks, access to two small but well-kept sandy beach coves, several dining outlets, and a small shopping arcade.

Most of the balconied rooms overlook Pattaya Bay, but the best values are the garden view rooms in Wing B, which face manicured lawns, hibiscus beds, and a side view of the sea. Tastefully modern rooms trimmed with stained wood offer all-marble bathrooms, hair dryers, and bathrobes. Landmark deluxe rooms have large bathrooms with separate bathtubs and shower stalls, plus outdoor showers on their large balconies and comfortable and luxurious sitting areas.

240/2 Pattaya Beach Rd., Pattaya 20150, Chonburi (N end of Pattaya Beach). © **3842-5611.** Fax 3842-8239. www.dusit.com. 460 units. 3,600B–9,100B (US$82–US$207) double; from 10,500B (US$239) suite. AE, DC, MC, V. **Amenities:** 3 restaurants (Chinese, S European, international); lobby bar w/live music; 2 large free-form pools; golf course nearby; 2 outdoor tennis courts; small fitness center; unique spa w/traditional Thai massage; sauna w/TV; watersports equipment/rentals and private beach; games; concierge; tour desk; car-rental desk; limousine service; 24-hr. room service; babysitting; same-day laundry service/dry cleaning; non-smoking rooms. *In room:* A/C, TV w/satellite programming, minibar, hair dryer, safe.

Pattaya Marriott Resort & Spa ⭐⭐⭐ *(Kids)* Smack in the center of Pattaya Beach (you really can't get a better location), Royal Garden surprises guests with its large courtyard garden and landscaped pool area. You'd hardly know Pattaya City was just beyond the walls. With the helpful staff and handsome accommodations, this resort makes for a great retreat. Spacious balconied rooms have views of the gardens or the sea, and many creature comforts not found in other hotels, including an in-house video-on-demand service. The adjoining Royal Garden Plaza makes your dining and entertainment options even more attractive. The pool is the largest in Pattaya.

218 Beach Rd., Pattaya 20150, Chonburi. © **800/344-1212** or 3841-2120. Fax 3842-9926. 300 units. 5,016B–7,524B (US$114–US$171) double; from 10,076B (US$229) suite. AE, DC, MC, V. **Amenities:** 3 restaurants (Chinese, Japanese-American teppanyaki, international); lounge; pretty landscaped pool w/swim-up bar; golf course nearby; 2 lighted grass tennis courts; large, state-of-the-art fitness center w/sauna and steam; Thai herbal spa; watersports equipment/rentals; children's programs; game room; tour desk; limousine service; shopping mall w/more than 50 shops; salon; 24-hr. room service; babysitting; same-day laundry service/dry cleaning; nonsmoking rooms; executive-level rooms; Ripley's Believe It or Not Museum; Motion Master Theater. *In room:* A/C, TV w/pay movies, minibar, coffee/tea-making facilities, safe.

Royal Cliff Beach Hotel ⭐⭐ *(Value)* This is Pattaya's top family resort, on the same garden property as the more exclusive Royal Wing and Royal Cliff Grand. It was built and upgraded in phases: The Royal Cliff Terrace building houses four terraced stories of suites with patios; the nine-story sea-view hotel tower houses most of the guest rooms, including huge, perfect-for-families two-bedroom suites. Rooms are spacious, with bleached wood and pastel decor and large terraces, most with bay views. If you tire of the lushly planted grounds, there's an elevator from the precipice down to the sandy beach, which is relatively clean but disappointingly small. Go for the pools, the grounds, and the health club, not for the beach. The hotel has a staff of more than 1,500 waiting to serve. I found it friendly, luxurious, and relaxing.

353 Phra Tamnuk Rd., Pattaya 20150, Chonburi (on cliff, above S end of Pattaya Beach). ✆ 3825-0421. Fax 3825-0511. 550 units. 4,500B (US$102) double; from 5,500B (US$125) suite. AE, DC, MC, V. **Amenities:** Full facilities sharing w/all Royal Cliff Beach Resort properties, including 9 restaurants (Thai, Chinese, Japanese, Continental grill, Italian, seafood, international coffee shops); 4 bars w/live music; 5 outdoor landscaped pools; golf course nearby; 3-hole putting green; 6 outdoor lighted tennis courts; large, completely equipped fitness center w/spa, sauna, steam, and massage; Jacuzzi; watersports equipment rental, including private catamaran for chartered cruises; concierge; tour desk; limousine service; business center; salon; 24-hr. room service; babysitting; same-day laundry/dry cleaning; nonsmoking rooms. *In room:* A/C, TV w/satellite programming, minibar, hair dryer, safe.

MODERATE

Asia Pattaya Beach Hotel The Asia Pattaya offers immaculate grounds, all heavily planted, with a topiary A-S-I-A in the middle of a circular driveway. The rooms are aging but well kept and have numerous amenities. Many are decorated with kitschy 1960s paneling or with leather-look furniture. European tour groups abound. The well-priced rooms and two-bedroom family suites are a good value if you're looking for a nicely groomed private beach, tranquility, and relative seclusion.

Cliff Rd., Pattaya 20260, Chonburi (on cliff above S end of beach; 3km/1³⁄₄ miles S of town). ✆ 3825-0401. Fax 3825-0496. www.asiahotel.co.th. 314 units. 1,900B–2,300B (US$43–US$52) double; from 2,800B (US$64) suite. AE, DC, MC, V. **Amenities:** 3 restaurants (international, French, seafood); nightclub and lobby lounge; outdoor pool w/swim-up bar; private 9-hole golf course on premises; outdoor lighted tennis court; fitness center w/massage; children's playground; snooker room; tour desk; car-rental desk; limousine service; 24-hr. room service; babysitting; same-day laundry service/dry cleaning; executive-level rooms. *In room:* A/C, TV w/satellite programming, minibar, hair dryer.

Siam Bayview Hotel Managed by the same people as the nearby Siam Bayview Resort, what this hotel lacks in terms of spacious gardens and the recreational options of resort life it makes up for with rooms and services expected of a city hotel that is in the center of the beach action strip. Some might find this option preferable; some might find it disappointing. Rooms are bland, with few local touches, but are fine in terms of convenience and comfort. On higher floors, request the sea view. Some rooms have balconies, but cheaper rooms with city views are a waste—why stay in at a tall hotel when you don't take advantage of the view opportunity? There are two attractively landscaped pools, two lighted tennis courts, nearby watersports facilities, an exercise room, three good dining venues, and a pleasant pub, plus a friendly and attentive staff.

310/2 Beach Rd., Pattaya, Chonburi 20260 (center of beach, between sois 9 and 10). ✆ 3842-3871. Fax 3842-3879. www.siamhotels.com. 270 units. 2,500B (US$57) double. AE, MC, V. **Amenities:** Restaurant (international); lounge; 2 pools; 2 outdoor lighted tennis courts; fitness center; tour desk; business center; limited room service; babysitting; same-day laundry service/dry cleaning. *In room:* A/C, TV w/satellite programming, minibar.

Siam Bayshore Resort ⭐ For value-for-money in Pattaya, this resort is not a bad choice. With an intimate feel to it, you'd never realize this large resort was adjacent to the wild life at South Pattaya. You'd also never realize that this large resort is so large. Although it's on 20 acres, the 12 interconnecting low-rise buildings allow an intimate tropical garden setting in open areas without that feel of resort sprawl. I like the clean, airy feel to the rooms, especially the cabana rooms with tile floors that are cool under the feet; however, standard and deluxe doubles have light carpeting that is also fresh. Superior garden wing rooms are good value, with excellent discounts. All rooms have a balcony or patio.

Pattaya Beach Rd., Pattaya, Chonburi 20260 (S end of Pattaya Beach). ℭ **3842-8678.** Fax 3842-8730. www. siamhotels.com. 272 units. 2,500B–3,700B (US$57–US$84) double; 8,000B (US$182) suite. AE, DC, MC, V. **Amenities:** 4 restaurants (international, Swiss, Chinese); 2 lounges; 2 lagoon-style pools; golf course nearby; 4 outdoor lighted tennis courts; fitness center; Jacuzzi; watersports equipment rentals; snooker room; tour desk; limousine service; salon; 24-hr. room service; massage; babysitting; same-day laundry service/dry cleaning; nonsmoking rooms; football lawn; volleyball court. *In room:* A/C, TV w/pay movies and satellite programming, minibar, coffee/tea-making facilities.

INEXPENSIVE

Flipper Lodge Hotel ⭐ ⟨Value⟩ While new renovations have made the glass-enclosed lobby far more snappy to look at, they've taken away the life-size statue of Flipper the dolphin that was this place's mascot. Flipper or no Flipper, this small budget hotel is still a top choice for good value and location. The decor is basic and clean, without being a bit musty, and the bathrooms are new, with shiny tiles and white grout. That's a definite plus for an inexpensive place. The sea-view rooms (with that great view) can't be beat for the price. The pool is a bit on the short side, but the attractive coffee shop serves some pretty good Thai and Continental fare.

520/1 Soi 8, Pattaya Beach Rd., Pattaya 20260, Chonburi (midbeach strip, off Soi 8). ℭ **3842-6401.** Fax 3842-6403. 126 units. 800B–950B (US$18–US$22) double; 1,500B (US$34) suite. AE, MC, V. **Amenities:** Coffee shop; small outdoor pool; golf course nearby; tour desk; limited room service; massage; laundry service; Internet center. *In room:* A/C, TV w/satellite programming, minibar.

Sunshine Hotel This is about as budget as budget can go without losing respectability; Sunshine has a decent reputation for, well, being decent (which, in Pattaya, is saying something). The hotel is small and so are the rooms, with compact closet cabinets and limited space for luggage. But it's a clean facility with a small, personal staff that is very helpful for local information and activities planning.

217/1 Moo 10 Soi 8, Pattaya Beach Rd., Pattaya, 20260 Chonburi. ℭ **3842-9247.** Fax 3842-1302. 79 units. 550B (US$13) double. MC, V. **Amenities:** Coffee shop and Thai restaurant; 2 tiny outdoor pools; small game room. *In room:* A/C, TV w/satellite programming, minibar.

WHERE TO DINE
MODERATE

Benihana JAPANESE/AMERICAN Most American readers are thinking, "Benihana? In Thailand?" Well, for those of you who've sampled tom yam gung and pad thai till it's coming out your ears, you'll be happy to visit this place. It has all the fun of Benihana's original restaurants—fantastic teppanyaki grill displays performed by chefs who have as much humor as skill, and the food is just great. The beef is like butter. Come here for a good time and a lot of laughs. You won't be disappointed.

2nd Level, Royal Garden Plaza. ℭ **3842-5029.** Reservations not necessary. Set menus 150B–500B (US$3.40–US$12). AE, DC, MC, V. Daily noon–2pm and 5–10pm.

Dolf Riks INDONESIAN/EUROPEAN Dolf Riks is an Indonesian-born Dutch restaurateur who's also a bit of a character. His restaurant is Pattaya's oldest and remains something of a legend. Although Dolf's menu changes with his whims, he normally serves a delicious Indonesian Rijstaffel (good, but very different from Jakarta), as well as Continental favorites. His regulars prefer the seafood in a wine-drenched broth, the Spanish garlic soup, and his fragrant ramekin Madras, an oven-baked curry ragout.

463/77 Sri Nakorn Center, N Pattaya (1 block N of Soi 1). ✆ **3942-8269.** Reservations recommended during high season. Main courses 250B–550B (US$5.70–US$12). AE, DC, MC, V. Daily 11am–midnight.

PIC Kitchen ⭐ THAI   Named for the Pattaya International Clinic PIC Hospital next door (don't worry, they're unrelated), PIC Kitchen is highly recommended for its wonderful atmosphere. Small Thai teak pavilions, both air-conditioned and open-air, have seating areas on the floor, Thai style, or at romantic tables. Delicious and affordable Thai cuisine is served a la carte or in lunch and dinner sets. The spring rolls and deep-fried crab claws are mouthwatering. Other dishes come pan-fried, steamed, or charcoal grilled, with spice added to taste. At night, groove to a live jazz band from 7pm to 1am.

Soi 5 Pattaya 2nd Rd. ✆ **3842-8374.** Reservations not necessary. 75B–320B (US$1.70–US$7.30). AE, DC, MC, V. Daily 8am–midnight.

Shere "E" Punjab NORTHERN INDIAN   Glimpsing through the windows from the outside, you're immediately invited into this brand-new little restaurant by its candle-lit tables and pretty table settings. The menu serves a complete range of northern Indian cuisine, and the kitchen has a tandoor oven for cooking meats and breads. Fresh ingredients and while-you-wait preparation from scratch mean you'll get consistently excellent dishes. Do yourself a favor and bypass all the amateur English eateries for this good curry fix.

377/312 Moo 12, Beach Road. ✆ **3836-4218.** Main courses 120B–280B (US$2.75–US$6.35). AE, MC, V. Daily noon–1am.

INEXPENSIVE

Nang Nual ⭐ THAI/SEAFOOD   Nang Nual is an excellent breakfast, lunch, or dinner choice in Jomtien Beach. This Thai restaurant specializes in seafood, which you can select from the tanks out front. A cheery, fluorescent-lit, blue-and-white interior is the setting for steamed butterfish with Chinese lime sauce or the sumptuous seasonal grilled seafood combination. Our combination had grilled prawn, a whole local lobster, and fresh crab; it varies with the catch.

Pattaya Walking St. ✆ **3842-8708.** Reservations recommended for seaside tables. Main courses 60B–300B (US$1.40–US$6.80). AE, MC, V. Daily 10am–11pm.

Vientiane LAOTIAN/THAI   The large menu of this busy place includes Laotian, Vietnamese, Chinese, and Isan (northeastern Thai) specialties, plus the chef's suggested "not-too-hot dishes." I found the distinctively flavored roast chicken particularly delicious, and the seafood was fresh, not overcooked, and in generous portions. Excellent sea crab costs 60B (US$1.40) per 100g portions. The only drawback is its location on a noisy street, so head for the air-conditioned (smoking section) dining room or as far back as possible.

485/18 Pattaya Second Rd. (on E side of 2nd Rd., between Soi 14 and Soi Post Office). ✆ **3841-1298.** Main courses 60B–200B (US$1.40–US$4.55). AE, DC, MC, V. Daily 11am–midnight.

EXPLORING PATTAYA

Pattaya Beach, a 4km (2½-mile) strip of land, might seem harmless to the naked eye, but **be warned:** The rumors you've heard are true. It's very, very polluted. Rapid growth of the tourism sector was not accompanied by growth of public facilities works, and for years waste has been disposed of improperly, ironically destroying the very attraction that drew travelers here in the first place. As if raw sewage isn't enough, the waste attracts many varieties of poisonous sea snakes.

Water activities still reign in the area, but for swimming you should either stick to the very north of Pattaya Beach near the Dusit Resort, or head a little south to

Jomtien Beach (which isn't the most attractive beach, in my opinion). The best option is to take a day trip to one of the islands in the Gulf of Thailand.

On Pattaya Beach, there's windsurfing (150B/US$3.49 per hr.), parasailing (250B/US$5.81 for 5 min.), canoeing (100B/US$2.33 per hr.), and catamaran sailing (400B–600B/US$9.30–US$14 per hr.). You can wander the beach to find guys who arrange these activities.

On Jomtien, you can find even more activities than on Pattaya Beach. To get to Jomtien Beach, grab a songtao on Beach Road or Pattaya 2nd Road for around 30B (US70¢). Swimming is centered on the northern section of Jomtien Beach, while the southern parts are for other water sports such as catamarans, parasailing, water-skiing, and windsurfing.

Day trips to Ko Lan (Coral Island) or nearby Ko Pai are best if you want cleaner and less crowded beaches. Ko Lan, 7.7km (5 miles) west of Pattaya, has beaches with eateries, overnight accommodations, watersports, and other facilities. On weekends it gets very crowded, so you might want to try Ko Pai, which is beautiful but has no facilities at all. The local ferryboat to Ko Lan costs 20B (US47¢) per person and takes 45 minutes. The last ferry back is at 5pm. For a speedboat hire, expect to pay 800B to 2,000B (US$19–US$46) per day. Once at the island, you can take a motorcycle taxi to the various beaches for between 20B and 50B (US47¢–US$1.16). The easiest way to arrange the boat trip is through the **TAT office** (© 3842-9113). You will also need to see them for arrangements to Ko Pai.

Snorkeling and **scuba diving** are popular because of Pattaya Bay's clear waters (20m–25m average visibility), colorful coral reefs (including mushroom, lettuce, brain, and staghorn corals), and tropical fish (white- and black-tip sharks, stingrays, angelfish, and many others). Nearby Ko Larn, Ko Sak, and Ko Kroh can be reached within 45 minutes by boat. There are a number of good dive shops with PADI and NAUI certified instructors in the area. I liked the people at **Dolphin Diving Center** (183/31 Moo 10, Soi Post Office; © 0384-27185), who take small groups out for two daily dives. The total cost, including equipment, two tanks, transport, a hot meal, and a divemaster guide, is about 2,800B (US$65). Overnight dives can also be arranged.

For sports enthusiasts, **golf** is second only to water activities, and for reputation the area around the resort is known as the "Golf Paradise of the East," with international-class courses within a 40km (25-mile) radius of the city. If you're willing to travel a little, the finest course is at Bangphra International Golf Club (45 Moo 6, Tambon Bang Phra, Sri Racha; © 3834-1149; fax 2341-151). This par-72 championship course was designed in 1958 by a Japanese team and was redone in 1987. It's considered the prettiest course in the area. Also try The Laem Chabang International Country Club (106/8 Moo 4 Tambon Bung, Sri Ratcha; © 0383-38351; fax 3837-2273), a nine-hole course designed by Jack Nicklaus; or the Siam Country Club (50 Tambol Poeng, Banglamung; © 3824-9381; fax 3824-9387), believed to be one of the country's most challenging courses.

When your skin is charred, your head is waterlogged, and you want a change of pace from all that beach living, Pattaya has a few worthwhile activities that are both fun and cultural. On the culture side of life, there's **Wat Khao Phra Yai** on Big Buddha Hill (Pratumnak Rd. between South Pattaya and Jomtien). This 10.8m (32.5-ft.) gold-colored stucco Buddha, believed to be the protector of the city, peers out into the sea. The view of the bay is quite nice from the wat as well. Pattaya also has a **Mini Siam** theme park (387 Sukhumvit Rd. near N Pattaya

Road; ℂ 3842-1628), with replicas of major Thai attractions like the Temple of
the Emerald Buddha and the Bridge over the River Kwai, and, strangely, some
European monuments as well. It's open daily from 9am to 9pm, and charges
200B (US$4.65) for adults and 100B (US$2.33) for children.

There's a huge and highly entertaining elephant park only 18km (11 miles)
from the city. **Nong Nooch** stages performances three times daily, with elephants performing alongside some 100 dancers, musicians, and performers for
spectator crowds of up to 1,000. Cultural performances, music, Thai boxing,
audience participation, and dozens of funny photo ops make this really touristy
activity a load of laughs. Make your booking from Nong Nooch direct at
ℂ **3842-9321.** They arrange shuttles from Pattaya at either 8:30am or 1:15pm
with return. The half-day trip costs 350B (US$8.14) per person.

For something completely unusual, the **Ripley's Believe It or Not** showcase
(3rd Floor, Royal Garden Plaza, 218 Beach Rd.; ℂ **3871-0294;** open 10am–
midnight daily; admission 150B/US$3.49) is hilarious, with unusual exhibits
and odd facts from around the globe. Just next door is the Ripley's Motion Master simulator ride. Both are highly recommended if you're traveling with your
children.

The **Pattaya Elephant Village** (see the Elephant Desk at the Tropicana
Hotel, Beach Road; ℂ **3842-3031**) stages elephant shows daily at 2:30pm. You
can also arrange for a little jungle trekking on elephant back. If that's not quite
your speed, check out **Pattaya Go-Kart** (Sukhumvit Road next to Mini Siam;
ℂ **3842-2044**) with a 400m (1312-ft.) track that is also suitable for children.
Rates run between 100B and 200B (US$2.33–US$4.65) per 10 minutes,
depending on the power of your kart.

PATTAYA AFTER DARK

At first sight, Pattaya is an assault on the senses. Electricity bills must be staggering from all the neon displays, light-up signs, and flashing bulbs down every
soi. Take a stroll down the South Pattaya pedestrian area ("Pattayaland"), where
every alley is lined with open-air watering holes with bar girls hanging around
hoping for a lucky catch. Go-go bars are everywhere, with sex shows of the sort
you'd find in Bangkok's Patpong. Pattaya Land 1 and Pattaya Land 2, near South
Pattaya make up "Boyz Town," with rows of gay go-go clubs. This spectacle is
the nightlife most come to Pattaya to experience. (Pattayaland is actually pretty
cruel in the light of day, when lonely old guys blink bleary-eyed atop barstool
perches listening to "Hotel California" for the umpteenth time.)

Most of Pattaya's "physical" massage parlors are on Pattaya Second Road in
northern Pattaya. Typically, dozens of girls with numbered signs wait to be
selected by clients, who are then whisked away to private massage rooms.

All-night companionship is easy to come by, though payments to club owners, security guards, and so on, mount up. Beware of "companions" bearing
drinks laced with knockout drugs, and watch your wallet. AIDS continues to
spread at an alarming rate in Pattaya and all of Thailand. There's also a very
active katoey (transvestite) scene.

If it's not your scene, you'll be happy to know there are some swell spots that
don't have the sleaze. The biggest disco, **Palladium,** 78/33–35 Pattaya 2nd Rd.
(ℂ **3842-4922**), is cavernous, complete with an enormous dance floor, pulsing
music, karaoke, snooker, and even traditional Thai Massage. **Shenanigan's,** a
fun Irish bar hangout, has a branch at the Royal Garden Resort, with the front
entrance on Pattaya 2nd Road (ℂ **3841-2120**). My favorite place, though, is

Hopf Brewery, 219 Beach Rd. (© **3871-0650**), which brews its own beer served by the glass, goblet, or ampolla. The Hopf Band is the kick—playing everything from old Herb Alpert tunes to newer jazzy sounds.

The campy cabaret shows are touristy good fun. Pattaya's most beautiful katoeys (transsexuals) don sequined gowns and feather boas to strut their stuff for packed houses nightly. At **Alcazar,** 78/14 Pattaya 2nd Rd., opposite Soi 5 (© **3841-0505**), the shows are at times hilarious. If you've seen a cabaret show elsewhere in Thailand, you might be disappointed to see familiar acts, which are standard in almost every show.

6 Ko Samet

Beautiful **Ko Samet** first became popular with Thais from the poetry of Sunthon Phu, a venerated 19th-century author and Rayong native who set his best-known epic on this "tropical island paradise." In the 21st century, Samet remains a slice of heaven. From a lazy beach chair under a shady coconut palm, you can dig your toes into soft white powder sand while you contemplate whether you want to jump into the glittering green sea or order another fruit punch and have a massage. At night, the beach turns into a fairy land of glittering lights and barbecue pits—sumptuous seafood feasts under the stars.

Lucky for us, a shortage of potable water kept rampant commerce and tourism at bay for many years. In 1981, Samet became part of the six-island **Khao Laem Ya–Samet National Park,** a designation meant to preserve its relatively undeveloped status. However, since then, small-scale construction has boomed, and there are now more than 50 licensed bungalow hotels with nearly 2,500 rooms on the 6km-long (3¾-mile-long) island. In 1990, a TAT-sponsored effort to close the national park to overnight visitors met with such fierce resistance that 4 days later Samet was reopened for business as usual. Until inadequate water supplies, waste treatment, and garbage disposal are dealt with, the TAT encourages visitors to go to the still lovely Samet for day trips only, but that rarely happens.

These days Samui welcomes a diverse crowd, from Thai and expatriate weekenders unwinding from the stress of the big city to international travelers who seek an idyllic beach life that overexploited Pattaya can not provide. For this reason, weekends and public holidays get pretty crowded, rooms become scarce, and resorts tack on up to 20% rate surcharges. Book early or, better yet, come during the week. Monday through Friday, this place is quiet and lovely. Another planning consideration: Samet follows the same weather patterns as Bangkok. Basically, from December through April, you can expect less rain but more people. May through August is hit or miss as far as rain goes, but I've always had good luck. September through November, the weather gets iffy rainwise.

Tips   Ko Samet Survival Gear

Some tips: Arm yourself with **mosquito repellent,** and if you plan to stay in a smaller bungalow, hang a mosquito net over your bed. A **flashlight** is also a good idea for finding your way after dark and in the smaller bungalows that turn off electricity in the late evening. You might want to bring along a **towel.** The bigger resorts have towels, but the cheap bungalow places don't. **A good sarong** is the ultimate—beach blanket, towel, wrap, bed sheet, sun shield. I never leave home without at least two.

The small island's northern half is triangular, with a long tail leading to the south that looks somewhat like a kite. Most of the beaches are on the east coast of the tail; although Ko Samet is only about 1km (⁶⁄₁₀ of a mile) wide, it has a rocky spine and there are few paths that connect the two coasts. Passengers alight from the ferry at **Na Dan,** the island's main port. It's a 10-minute walk south past the **health center** and school to **Hat Sai Kaeo** (Diamond Beach, on the northeast cape), the island's most developed and crowded beach, which is linked by a dirt path to 10 other small beach developments. Most day-trippers take the regular ferry and then catch one of the songtaos that meet the boats and travel inland as far as Vong Deuan beach. You can also catch a ride with one of the individual resort ferries or hike the shoreline path between beaches.

The beaches at Hat Sai Kaeo, Ao Pai, and Vong Deuan have the best facilities but are also the most expensive, basically because everything, including water, must be imported from the mainland. Keep in mind that, on Samet, even the finest resorts are simple no-frills operations. Air-conditioning is extra; a hot-water shower is nonexistent.

VISITOR INFORMATION

There are no TAT offices in Ko Samet or Ban Phe, but the TAT offices in Bangkok and Pattaya can provide you with information before your departure. Ko Samet is pretty much a cash operation only. While there are no ATMs, there is a money-changing service at the post office at the Naga Bar along the main

> **Tips** **Water Taxis & Songtaos**
>
> One note about water taxis and songtaos: They don't like to make the trip if there's only one or two passengers: Premiums will be charged. A water taxi could soak you up to 300B (US$6.80), and a songtao could run you into the ground for 400B (US$9.10), especially if they know you have no other choice. So if you see a truck or boat full of people headed in your direction, don't hesitate to jump aboard. Otherwise, you could be waiting hours for the next group trip or paying out the nose for private hire. This is true everywhere around Thailand.

road in Ao Pai. (See how laid back this place is? The post office is at a bar.) This same bar also has an international phone and fax service. In Na Dan, also called Samet Village, as well as Vong Duean, there are some small provision shops by the main ferry landing.

GETTING THERE

By Bus Buses leave Bangkok every hour between 5am and 7pm for the 3½-hour journey, departing from Bangkok's Eastern Bus Terminal on Sukhumvit Road opposite Soi 63, Ekamai Road (© **2391-2504**). The one-way trip to Ban Phe costs 124B (US$2.80). From Pattaya, public bus transportation isn't the best way to go. You must wait for the Ban Phe bus along Sukhumvit Road (there are pavilions located across the street from the North Pattaya Rd. and Central Pattaya Rd. intersections) and flag it down. Buses from Bangkok are very popular on weekends and holidays, so you might not find a seat. Book your return to either Bangkok or Pattaya at the Ban Phe pier bus stop immediately on arrival, to make sure you have a seat for your return home.

By Private Bus Samet Island Tour, 109/22 Moo 10 Pratumnuk Rd., South Pattaya (© **3871-0676**), runs minivan service form Pattaya at 8am and again at noon (trip time: 1 hr.; 300B/US$6.80 round-trip).

By Taxi Malibu Travel Service in Pattaya will arrange a private car to take you to Ban Phe for 900B (US$20) one-way. Call © **3842-3180** for details and booking.

By Car Take Highway 3 east from Bangkok along the longer, more scenic coastal route (about 3½–4 hr.) or the quicker route: via Highway 3 east to Pattaya, then Highway 36 to Rayong, and then the coastal Highway 3 to Ban Phe (about 3 hr.).

Ferries to Ko Samet During the high season, from November to April, ferries leave Ban Phe pier for the main port, Na Dan, every half-hour (trip time: 40 min.; 40B/US90¢). The first boat departs at 9:30am, and the last leaves at 5pm. Several other agents in Ban Phe sell passage on their own boats to Vong Duean beach, which depart at least a few times daily. One-way fare is 50B (US$1.10).

From the ferry landing on Samet, you must catch a water taxi to the other beaches (20B–60B/US45¢–US$1.35) per person, depending on your destination). You can also take a songtao to other beaches for between 10B and 50B (US25¢–US$1.10). There is one road on Samet connecting the main town, Samet Village, halfway down the eastern shore of the island to Vong Duean. Beyond that, you won't find more than footpaths.

FAST FACTS: Ko Samet

Banks/Currency Exchange Ko Samet is pretty much a cash-only operation, except for Vong Deuan Resort and Malibu Garden Resort, where you can use Visa and MasterCard to settle your tab. While there are no ATMs on the island, many resorts will change money.

Post Office/Mail Talk to your resort front desk for postal services or directions to nearby services.

Provisions In Na Dan, Hat Sai Kaew, and Vong Deuan, you'll find small provision shops for basic goods.

Telephone International and domestic phone access is available through the major resorts on all beaches.

WHERE TO STAY

Vong Deaun Resort can be booked in Bangkok at the contact information listed below; it offers a wide range of accommodations. If you don't book one of the few bungalow complexes with a telephone before your arrival, never fear. Several travel agents, enterprising fishermen, teenage girls, and others hover at the Ban Phe pier with photo albums showing off their rooms to rent. Accommodations are similarly primitive around the island. Note that rates are higher than at other "undeveloped" island resorts because food and water must be imported from the mainland.

Ao Pai Hut Au Pai is a smaller beach but is less developed, with bungalows set in the jungle, just a hop from the beach. It's quiet, and you'll feel more privacy. The best of the bungalows (shacks) here are Ao Pai Huts along the main dirt road, about a 10-minute ride from the main jetty. These simple bungalows are tidy and well constructed, with clean concrete bathrooms and space to lay your baggage. Bring your own towels.

Pai Beach, Samet Island, Ban Phe, 121160. (C) 01-353-2644 in Rayong. 500B (US$12) bungalow with A/C; 300B (US$6.80) bungalow w/fan. **Amenities:** Restaurant (breakfast only). *In room:* No phone.

Malibu Garden Resort These clean, concrete motel-style rooms are clustered behind the tree line at the beach, surrounding a thatch dining pavilion where light meals are served and a small swimming pool. This is one of two cushy resorts on Ko Samet—it has hot water and air-conditioning. If you need some kind of comfort and organization, this place is recommended both for the quality of the facility and for the convenience of the Samet Island Tour in handling details of booking and transport.

77 Wong Duan Beach, Samet Island, Ban Phe, 121160 Rayong. (C) 3865-1057 in Ban Phe, or contact Samet Island Tour in Pattaya at 109/22 Moo 10 Pratumnuk Rd., South Pattaya (C) 3871-0676. 1,500B–2,200B (US$34–US$50) double with A/C; 800B–1,100B (US$18–US$25) double w/fan. **Amenities:** Restaurant (international); small pool; watersports rentals; convenience shop; laundry service. *In room:* No phone.

Vongduern Villas Simple, solid wood bungalows with air-conditioning and private hot-water showers vary in price according to the view and size of room. There are also elaborate VIP bungalows (perhaps the only ones on the island) with carpeting, a TV, a VCR with a private video collection, an intrabungalow phone, and a minibar—quite a change from what the average visitor to Ko Samet is seeking.

Wong Duan Beach, Samet Island, 22 Moo 4 Pae, 121160 Rayong. ✆ **3865-1292**, or 2392-4390 in Bangkok. 1,200B–2500B (US$27–US$57) bungalow with A/C; 650B–900B (US$15–US$20) bungalow w/fan. V. **Amenities:** Restaurant (international); watersports equipment/rentals; laundry service. *In room:* No phone.

WHERE TO DINE

All of the bungalows offer some sort of eating experience, mostly bland local food and beer, with some Western breakfast offerings. In the evenings on Vong Deuan beach, tables are set up under twinkling lights on the sandy beach, where seafood barbecues grill up the day's catch. It's very pretty. On other beaches, a few places entice dinner guests with video screenings of pirated movies, which are always popular. In Ao Pai, Naga Bar on the main road is quiet, with a fairly decent menu, a beer selection, and a bakery that has surprisingly wonderful fresh goods in the mornings. In Vong Deuan, places like Nice & Easy, Oasis, Baywatch, and Seahorse serve dinner, and get pretty lively later. You can expect most dishes in these places to cost you between 60B and 100B (US$1.35–US$2.30), with seafood barbecue a bit more.

EXPLORING KO SAMET

Windsurfing is particularly popular with weekenders from Bangkok. The island's best is said to be north of Hat Sai Kaeo (Diamond Beach), around the cape that bulges out of Samet's east side. The rocky north coast is even more challenging, with strong currents and sometimes erratic winds caused by the deep channel between the island and the mainland. Windsurfers are available at most guesthouses for 100B to 200B (US$2.30–US$4.55) per hour, without instruction. Hat Sai Kaeo also has jet skis for rent, so look out if you're swimming.

Up north on the west coast is **Ao Phrao** (Paradise Beach), the most isolated cove on the island. Aficionados prefer snorkeling off the rocky west coast, where coral reefs have escaped the damage caused by frequent ferries. The western coastline is mostly uninhabited; the easiest access is by sea, though there are two roads and several rough trails across the central spine of the island.

You can book any of the speedboats at the beaches for round-island tours (about 300B/US$6.80 per person) and for snorkeling on the rocky uninhabited western side of the island, which is said to be the best for underwater life. They'll be happy to do a morning drop-off and afternoon pickup. Samet's southern, narrow kite tail has calm waters, good for swimming and snorkeling.

7 The Southern Peninsula

From Bangkok, follow Thailand's narrow Malay Peninsula south through tropical terrain, past coconut plantations worked by clever monkeys and coastal villages that experience "rush hour" at dawn with the return of colorful fishing boats. To the Thai people, the south represents a robust side of life. The weather here gets a bit more hot and steamy, Thai dialects turn coarse and tough (and according to the rest of the country, so do the people), and the local food sets mouths on fire with fresh chiles. Visitors know this part of the country best for the gorgeous tropical islands off the peninsula's long coastlines.

In the Andaman Sea, world-famous Phuket draws countless visitors each year on its reputation for idyllic beaches and stellar resorts. To counter the glamour and hype of **Phuket, Ko Samui** in the Gulf of Thailand developed its own image of scaled-down, homegrown tropical paradise. While these two islands get the lion's share of visitors, seaside **Hua Hin and Cha-Am,** Thailand's oldest beach resort destination, entertain mostly locals and expatriates popping down from hectic Bangkok.

8 Southern Peninsula: Hua Hin & Cha-Am

Hua Hin and Cha-Am, neighboring villages on the Gulf of Thailand, form the country's oldest resort area. Developed in the 1920s as a relaxing getaway for Bangkok's elite, Thailand's "Riviera" was a mere 3- or 4-hours journey from the capital by train, thanks to the southern railway's completion in 1916. At the same time, Thailand opened its first golf course here, the Royal Hua Hin Golf Course, sealing this area's fate as a perfect golfing vacation destination.

When Pattaya, on Thailand's eastern coast, hit the scene in the 1960s, it lured vacationers away from Hua Hin and Cha-Am. If you ask me, it only makes this the perfect place to get away from the usual tourist din. The clean sea and wide beaches support excellent and unique resorts, plus there's the added thrill of nearby historic Phetchaburi, Khao Sam Roi Yod National Park, and islands for snorkeling trips.

Plan your trip for the months between November and May for the most sunshine and least rain, but note that from about mid-December to mid-January, Hua Hin and Cha-Am reach peak levels. Bookings must be made in advance, and hotels will slap a 500B to 1,500B (US$11–US$34) peak season surcharge onto your nightly room rate. The area is still pleasant during the other months. During the low season, while it's more likely to rain, it is highly improbable that it will rain all the time.

VISITOR INFORMATION

The **Hua Hin Tourist Information Center** (© 3251-1047 or 3253-2433) is in the center of town tucked behind the city shrine at the corner of Damnoenkasem and Petchkasem roads. Open hours are from 8:30am to 4:30pm daily. In Cha-Am, the TAT office (© 3247-1005 or 3247-1006) is inconveniently located on the corner of Phetchkasem Road and Narathip Road (the main Beach Road is about 1km/⅗₀ mile away).

An interesting source of information, *The Hua Hin Cha-Am Observer,* packs a lot of advertisers and local tidbits into a small, regularly updated magazine. Better still, it's free! Look for it at the tourism information offices and at travel agents.

GETTING THERE

By Plane   While there is a domestic airport in Hua Hin, no airlines have serviced it for years.

By Train   Both Hua Hin and Cha-Am are reached via the train station in Hua Hin. Ten trains make the daily trek from Bangkok's **Hua Lampong Railway Station** (© 2223-7010 or 2223-7020). For an idea of the fare, first class is 202B (US$4.50) on Special Express. The trip is just over 4 hours.

The **Hua Hin Railway Station** (© 3251-1073) is at the tip of Damnoenkasem Road, which slices through the center of town straight to the beach. Pickup-truck taxis (songtao) and tuk-tuks wait outside to take you to your hotel, starting at 50B (US$1.10).

By Bus   Most agree that the bus is the better choice for travel from Bangkok to Hua Hin because it takes less time. Buses depart from **Bangkok's Southern Bus Terminal** (© 2435-1199) every 20 minutes from 5am to 10pm (128B/US$2.90). There are also five daily buses to Cha-Am between 5am and 2pm (113B/US$2.50).

Buses from Bangkok arrive in **Hua Hin** at the air-conditioned bus station (© 3251-1230) on Srasong Road, 1 block north of Damnoenkasem Road. From here it's easy to find a songtao or tuk-tuk to take you to your destination. The **Cha-Am bus station** is on the main beach road (© 3242-5307).

By Car From Bangkok, take Route 35, the Thonburi-Paktho Highway, southwest; allow 2 to 4 hours, depending on traffic.

GETTING AROUND

By Songtao Pickup-truck taxis (songtao), make their way along the main streets of Hua Hin, passing the railway station and bus terminals at regular intervals. Flag one down that's going in your direction. Fares range from 10B to 20B (US20¢–US45¢) within town, while stops at outlying resorts will be up to 50B (US$1.10). Trips between Hua Hin and Cha-Am cost between 100B and 200B (US$2.30–US$4.50).

By Tuk-Tuk Tuk-tuks will take you door to door for between 20B and 50B (US45¢–US$1.10) within town.

By Motorcycle Taxi Within each town, motorcycle taxi fares begin at 20B (US45¢). The taxi drivers, identified by their colorful numbered vests, are also practically the only way to get to your resort if you're in Cha-Am after hours. The cost is usually 100B (US$2.30).

By Samlor Trishaws, or samlors, can be found around the center of town and can be hired for short distances as low as 20B (US45¢). You can also negotiate an hourly rate if you'd like to tour the town.

By Car or Motorcycle Avis has a desk at both the Hotel Sofitel Central in Hua Hin (℃ 3251-2021) and the Dusit Resort and Polo Club in Cha-Am (℃ 3252-0008). Avis has self-drive rates from 1,500B (US$34) per day for a Suzuki Caribian 4WD sport vehicle, to 2,000B (US$45) and up for a compact sedan. Luxury cars, including Volvo and Mercedes start at 7,000B (US$157).

Make sure you call ahead to reserve at least 1 day in advance. Cheaper alternatives can be rented from stands near the beach on Damnoenkasem Road. A Suzuki Caribian goes for around 800B (US$18) per day. These places will also rent 100cc motorcycles for 190B (US$4.25) per day.

On Foot This is the way I recommend seeing Hua Hin. The narrow back alleys reveal a treasure trove of funky guesthouses, bars full of local character, and a wide assortment of casual eating venues. Most everything in town is close enough to walk comfortably.

FAST FACTS: Hua Hin & Cha-Am

In Hua Hin Major banks are along Petchkasem Road to the north of Damnoenkasem, and money changers are peppered throughout the town. The **main post office** (℃ 3251-1350) is on Damnoenkasem Road near the Phetchkasem intersection. Both Hua Hin and Cha-Am have Internet cafes along the well-traveled roads. For the best price (1B/US2¢ per min.) and atmosphere, check out **Cups & Comp,** at 104/1 Naeb-Khehars Rd. (℃ 3251-1369). The **Hua Hin Hospital** (℃ 3252-0371) is located in the north of town along Petchkasem Road. Call the **Tourist Police** for either town at ℃ 3251-5995.

In Cha-Am Banks are centered on Phetchkasem Road, and the post office is on Beach Road just south of the Novotel. The **Thonburi Cha-Am Hospital** (℃ 3243-3903) is off Narathip Road close to the Phetchkasem intersection. Internet access can be found in a few places along the beach road.

Thung Wua Laem ○ ↑ **Hua Hin/Cha Am**
BURMA **Chumphon** ○
(MYANMAR)
41
○ Ranong ○ Lang Suan ○ Ko Tao
RANONG ← Ang Thong
National Park ← Ko Phangan
PROVINCE Ko Ta ○ ○
Luang ○ Ko Samui
Chaiya ○
No Dog Island
Surat Thani (Ko Taen)
401 ○ Sichon
○ Phanom 401
Phrasaeng ○ Tha Sala *Gulf of Thailand*
4009 *(Gulf of Siam)*
41
Thung Yai ○ **Nakhon Si**
Thammarat
401
403 41 ○ Hua Sai
○ Klong Thom 4
Huai Yot ○
Ko Phatthalung
Lanta Trang ○
Yai **TRANG** ○ Sathing Pra
PROVINCE
Ko Li Bong
○ ↑ Airport
○ Thung Wa ✈ Beach
Hat Yai - - - Ferry Route
☂ Scuba Diving
Ko **Songkhla**
Tarutao
4 ○ Pattani
Narathiwat
Andaman ○ Yala
Sea **YALA** ○ Tak Bai
PROVINCE
MALAYSIA **Sungai**
Kolok ○

THAILAND
Bangkok
★

The Southeast
Coast

0   30 mi
0   30 km

WHERE TO STAY

Hua Hin's resorts are relatively close to the town, with guesthouses clustered in the town itself. Cha-Am offers a host of inexpensive and casual guesthouses along the main beach road for as low as 300B to 500B (US$6.98–US$12) per night. Hop from house to house, and look at rooms till you find something you like (trust me, trying to make advance reservations by phone is just begging for frustration). For the best resorts in the area, the 8km (5-mile) strip of prime beach between the two villages hosts a variety of high-rise condo-hotels, luxury resorts, casual bungalow spots, and dingy budget motels. I've selected the best options below.

VERY EXPENSIVE

Chiva-Som International Health Resort ★★★   Chiva-Som will strip away any wear and tear the modern world can dish out, both mentally and physically. This ultrapeaceful resort is a sublime collection of handsome pavilions, bungalows, and central buildings dressed in fine teak and sea-colored tiles nestled in landscaped grounds just beyond a pristine beach. Choose a guest room in the main building for the fabulous morning sunrise over the water, or a bungalow with either ocean or garden view for extra privacy. Each are decorated in cooling natural tones and warm wood, with traditional Thai touches throughout.

The centerpiece is the spa. Carefully planned to ensure privacy and relaxation, the menu for treatments is phenomenal: health and beauty consultation, numerous facial and body treatments, medical treatments, diet programs, and fitness activities including personal training, swimming, yoga, tai chi, and Thai boxing. Check into one of the spa packages. A double-room package for 3 nights is $945, up to $3,660 for 14 nights. All packages include a fabulous list of treatments.

73/4 Petchkasem Rd., Hua Hin, 77110 Thailand (5-min. drive S of Hua Hin). ℂ **3253-6536.** Fax 3251-1615. www.chivasom.net. 57 units. All double rates are quoted per person. Ocean-view double 14,077B (US$315); Thai Pavilion 17,831B (US$399); ocean-view suite 24,133B–40,221B (US$540–US$900). Nightly rate includes 3 spa cuisine meals per day, health and beauty consultations, daily massage, and participation in fitness and leisure activities. AE, DC, MC, V. **Amenities:** 2 restaurants (international, organic); ozonated indoor swimming pool and outdoor swimming pool; golf course nearby; amazing fitness center w/personal trainer and exercise classes; his-and-hers spas w/steam and hydrotherapy treatments, massage, beauty treatments, flotation, and medical advisement; watersports equipment; bike rental; concierge; tour desk; limousine service; salon; 24-hr. room service; same-day laundry service/dry cleaning; nonsmoking rooms; library. *In room:* A/C, minibar.

EXPENSIVE

Anantara Resort & Spa ★★   A series of elegantly designed Thai-style pavilions makes up the structure of the lobby and the public facilities at this "village" away from the town center, off the main road. A lovely Kaliga tapestry hangs prominently in the open-air sala-style lobby, which is tastefully decorated with ornately carved teak wooden lanterns, warm wood floors, and furniture with rose-colored cushions. A series of teak pavilions houses 12 guest rooms each. Consistent with the lobby, rooms are furnished Thai style with teak-and-rattan furniture. Superior rooms have a garden view, and deluxe rooms overlook the sand and sea. For a few dollars more, the beach terrace rooms have large patios, perfect for requesting a fun (or romantic) barbecue set up by the staff.

43/1 Petchkasem Beach Rd., Hua Hin 77110. ℂ **3252-0250.** Fax 3252-0259. 162 units. 5,050B (US$115) double; 5,500B (US$125) terrace double; suite from 7,250B (US$165). AE, DC, MC, V. **Amenities:** 2 restaurants (Thai, international/seafood); lounge; outdoor pool w/children's pool; golf course nearby; outdoor lighted tennis courts; fitness center; spa w/sauna, steam, and massage; Jacuzzi; watersports equipment and instruction; bike and motorcycle rental; children's playground; concierge; tour desk; car-rental desk; limousine service; shopping arcade; salon; 24-hr. room service; babysitting; same-day laundry service/dry cleaning; nonsmoking rooms. *In room:* A/C, TV w/satellite programming, minibar, coffee/tea-making facilities, hair dryer, safe.

Dusit Resort and Polo Club ★   Intended for the country's wealthy elite and the well-heeled foreign tourist, the Dusit combines the amenities and facilities of the best international deluxe resorts with an English country and polo club theme. The grandly elegant marble lobby features bronze horses, plush carpets, and seating areas, with hunting-and-riding oil paintings hung throughout. Hall doors have polo mallet handles; each public area follows suit with "horsey" artwork and decor.

Guest rooms are spacious, with English country touches and oversize marble bathrooms. Room rates vary with the view, although every room's balcony faces out over the lushly landscaped pool, which could very well be the largest in Thailand. Patios for the ground-floor Lanai Rooms are landscaped for privacy, but you can still run straight out to the pool and beach. Landmark suites, with a very elegant living room, full pantry area, and dressing room off a huge bathroom, have the finest decor.

For all its air of formality, the resort is great for those who prefer swimsuits and T-shirts to riding jodhpurs. In fact, there's no polo field around at all, but if you'd like to go riding, the resort does care for its own stables. The beach is meticulous and calm, and all sorts of watersports with instruction are available.

1349 Petchkasem Rd., Cha-Am 76120. ℂ **3252-0009.** Fax 3252-0296. www.dusit.com. 305 units. 5,000B–5,500B (US$112–US$123) double; 11,000B (US$246) Landmark suite. AE, DC, MC, V. **Amenities:** 5 restaurants (international, grill, Italian, Thai, seafood); lounge; huge outdoor pool; minigolf; golf course nearby; outdoor lighted tennis courts; squash courts; fitness center; Jacuzzi; sauna; watersports equipment; bike and motorcycle rental; billiards and game room; concierge; tour desk; car-rental desk; limousine service; business center; shopping arcade; salon; 24-hr. room service; massage; babysitting; same-day laundry service/dry cleaning; nonsmoking rooms; executive-level rooms; horseback riding. In room: A/C, TV w/satellite programming, minibar, coffee/tea-making facilities, hair dryer, safe.

Hotel Sofitel Central ★★

The Hua Hin Railway Hotel opened in 1922 in response to the demand for luxury accommodations in what was then a newly emerging resort town. Adapted from European styles, the brick-and-wood design incorporated long, shady verandas with whitewashed wood detail under a sloped red-tile roof. Sofitel treasures the heritage of this old beauty, creating a hotel museum and preserving the hotel's original 14 bedrooms. Subsequent additions and renovations have expanded the hotel into a large and modern fullfacility hotel without sacrificing a bit of its former charm.

While the original rooms have their unique appeal, the newer rooms are larger, brighter, and more comfortable. With furnishings that reflect the hotel's old beach resort feel, they are still modern and cozy. Sofitel's three magnificent outdoor pools are landscaped for sun decks with shady spots. The new Spa Health Club, in its own beachside bungalow, provides full-service health and beauty treatments, and the new fitness center sports fine equipment with recent additions.

1 Damnoenkasem Rd., Hua Hin 77110 (in the center of town by the beach). ℂ **800/221-4542** in the U.S., or 3251-2021. Fax 3251-1014. www.sofitel.com. 214 units. 6,591B–7,533B (US$149–US$171) double; 10,358B–16,949B (US$235–US$385) suite. DC, MC, V. **Amenities:** 5 restaurants (seafood, Thai, international, high tea); lounge and bar; 3 outdoor pools; putting green and miniature golf; golf course nearby; outdoor lighted tennis courts; new fitness center; spa w/massage; watersports equipment; bike rental; billiards room; concierge; tour desk; car-rental desk; limousine service; business center; shopping arcade; salon; 24-hr. room service; babysitting; same-day laundry service/dry cleaning; nonsmoking rooms; executive-level rooms; daily craft and language lessons; nature tours. In room: A/C, TV w/satellite programming, minibar, hair dryer.

Hua Hin Marriott Resort & Spa ★

Formerly the Royal Garden Resort, this extremely well-outfitted and well-maintained property is best suited for those in search of beach and sports activities. Singles and families are here throughout the year, lured principally by the ponds, pools, boats, golf, tennis, and other racket sports, as well as by the pet elephant and the junglelike grounds leading out to the calm sea. Top it off with a children's playground and a fitness center, and you have the perfect equation for a family vacation. The hotel is relatively convenient, with complimentary shuttle service into town. Deluxe rooms are the best choice—large, filled with amenities, and facing the sea.

107/1 Petchkasem Beach Rd., Hua Hin 77110. ℂ **800/228-9290** in the U.S., or 3251-1881. Fax 3251-2422. 220 units. 4,270B (US$97) double; 5,320B (US$119) beach terrace; 8,600B–9,100B (US$193–US$204) suite.

AE, DC, MC, V. **Amenities:** 3 restaurants (seafood, Thai, Italian); lounge; outdoor pool; golf course nearby; outdoor lighted tennis courts; fitness center; spa; watersports equipment; bike rental; children's playground and zoo; concierge; tour desk; car-rental desk; limousine service; shopping arcade; salon; 24-hr. room service; massage; babysitting; same-day laundry service/dry cleaning; nonsmoking rooms. *In room:* A/C, TV w/satellite programming, minibar, coffee/tea-making facilities, hair dryer, safe.

MODERATE

Regent Chalet ★ I'm sure the Regent Chalet gets a lot of business because of name association, but the resort is not related to the famous Regent chain with hotels in Bangkok, Chiang Mai, and other Asian cities. Still, Regent Chalet is a popular choice in Cha-Am. The entire resort is a huge complex with 660 rooms and suites, 3 outdoor pools, a Jacuzzi, a fitness center, massage, 4 tennis courts, 2 squash courts, land and watersports, and a choice of restaurants. Sounds overwhelming? Well, in a quiet little section to the side of the resort grounds is the Regent Chalet, the resort's separate bungalow facility. The best part is, you enjoy a more relaxed and rustic experience, but you still have access to all the offerings of the larger resort—the best of both worlds. Bungalows are either on or close to the beach, with rattan and bamboo furniture in true beach home style. The last time I visited, they had a resident baby elephant make an appearance for an afternoon bath and snacks—very, very cute.

849/21 Petchkasem Rd., Cha-Am 76120. ✆ **3245-1240.** Fax: 3245-1277. www.regent-chaam.com. 660 units. 4,120B (US$93) double; 5,885 (US$134) family suite; 14,124B (US$321) bungalow suite. AE, MC, V. **Amenities:** 2 restaurants (Asian, international); lounge; 2 pools; golf course nearby; outdoor lighted tennis courts; squash courts; fitness center; Jacuzzi; watersports equipment; bike and motorcycle rental; game room; tour desk; limousine service; business center; salon; 24-hr. room service; massage; babysitting; same-day laundry service/dry cleaning. *In room:* A/C, TV w/satellite programming, minibar.

The Cha-Am Methavalai Hotel Compared to the other choices for accommodations in Cha-Am village, the Methavalai is certainly the better bet. This large hotel is modern and well suited for the demands of international travelers. Located on the main Beach Road in Cha-Am, it's convenient to the restaurants, shopping, and the small nightlife scene in town. Large guest rooms in soft palettes are peaceful, and all have balconies with a sun deck. The only downfall is that you have to share the beach here with residents of the many motels along the strip. Instead, you can always opt for the large outdoor lagoon-shape pool.

220 Ruamchit Rd., Cha-Am 76120. ✆ **3247-1028.** Fax 3247-1590. 118 units. 3,276B (US$74) double; 6,751B (US$153) suite. AE, DC, MC, V. **Amenities:** 2 restaurants (international, seafood); lounge and karaoke; pool; golf course nearby; tour desk; salon; limited room service; massage; babysitting; same-day laundry service. *In room:* A/C, TV w/satellite programming, minibar.

INEXPENSIVE

Jed Pee Nong Hotel This recently built hotel with Chinese flair is located less than 100m (328 ft.) from the Sofitel Central's elegant driveway. It's so clean and well kept that it's a good choice. A bevy of family or local workers maintain the tiny garden filled with songbirds and fountains, a small pool, and the simple balconied rooms. Many rooms are carpeted and have air-conditioning. The higher-priced rooms have better decor and hug the pool, cabana style. There's also a Thai seafood restaurant off the lobby and laundry service.

17 Damneonkasem Rd., Hua Hin 77110 (on the main st. near the town beach). ✆ **3251-2381.** Fax 3253-22036. 25 units. 700B (US$16) double with A/C; 500B (US$11) double w/fan. No credit cards. **Amenities:** Restaurant (international); pool; laundry service. *In room:* Minibar.

WHERE TO DINE

If you wake up at about 7am and walk to the piers in either Hua-Hin or Cha-Am, you can watch the fishing boats return with their loads. Workers sort all varieties of creatures, packing them on ice for distribution around the country. Still, much of the catch remains behind to be consumed locally. In Cha-Am, look for the docks at the very north end of the beach and stroll past to the open-air restaurants looking out over the water. Come here for lunch and enjoy enormous fish for 150B (US$3.40) and huge juicy tiger prawns for 500B (US$12) per kilo (compare that to 1,850B/US$42 per kilo in Bangkok's Seafood Market) ;there's scallops, squid, clams, cockles, mussels, a few varieties of prawn, snails, crabs, lobsters, all kinds of fish—all of it fresh like you've never seen before. Four of us gorged ourselves on a Mount Olympus–style seafood feast and spent under 600B (US$14). That's truly unbelievable.

Itsara THAI   Formerly called Ban Tuppee Kaow, Itsara resides in a two-story greenhouse built in the 1920s—not especially well maintained, though it is atmospheric. By the sea, the terrace seating is the best in the house, with views of the beach. During weekend lunches, it's quiet and peaceful. Specialties include a sizzling hot plate of glass noodles with prawn, squid, pork, and vegetables. A large variety of fresh seafood and meats are prepared steamed or deep fried, and can be served with either salt, chili, or red curry paste. Beer, Mekhong whiskey, and soft drinks are available.

7 Napkehard St., Hua Hin (seaside, a 40B–70B/US90¢–US$1.60 samlor ride N from the town center). ✆ 3253-0574. Reservations recommended Sat dinner. Main courses 60B–290B (US$1.30–US$6.50). MC, V. Mon–Fri 10am–midnight; Sat–Sun 2pm–midnight.

Meekaruna Seafood SEAFOOD   This small family-run restaurant serves fresh fish prepared in many Thai and Chinese styles on a wooden deck overlooking the main fishing pier in Hua Hin. The menu is in English (with photographs), and you'll find the lack of hype—compared to the other fish places, with their flashy entrances and hustling touts—refreshing. Naturally, a place like this has great tom yam goong—also try fried crab cakes, fish served in any number of styles, and, my favorite, baby clams fried in chili sauce. Wear bug repellent!

26/1 Naratdamri Rd., Hua Hin (near the fishing pier). ✆ 3251-1932. Reservations not necessary. Main courses 120B–500B (US$2.70–US$10). AE, DC, MC, V. Daily 10am–10pm.

Palm Seafood Pavilion ✿ CONTINENTAL   Hotel Sofitel Central's crystal pavilion close to the beach offers a very romantic dining experience. Attentive but discreet service, beautiful table settings and linen, soothing mood music, and excellent, elegantly prepared food all contribute in pleasing harmony. The menu changes quite often but always highlights fresh seafood, which is prepared in Continental style with Asian touches. For something different, I tried the simmered pomfret with Chinese plums, bacon, and mushrooms smothered in sautéed vegetables, which was light, healthful, and full of flavor. They also do a mean salmon poached with white wine in lobster sauce with sliced lobster and mushrooms. With a fine selection of wines and a dessert menu that is an eyeful of sweet goodies, this is the best choice for fine dining in Hua Hin. Be sure to call ahead because they frequently book private barbecues and parties.

Hotel Sofitel Central, 1 Damneonkasem Rd., Hua Hin (on the waterfront end of Main St.). ✆ 3251-2021. Reservations recommended. Main courses 540B–800B (US$12–US$18); seafood buffet 650B (US$15) per person. AE, DC, MC, V. Daily noon–2:30pm and 6–10:30pm.

EXPLORING HUA HIN & CHA-AM

While most of the larger resorts will plan **watersports** activities for you upon request, you can arrange your own from operators on the beach. Jet skis (which most of the resorts have given up due to accidents and pollution) can still be rented from these guys for 500B (US$11) per hour, in addition to windsurfing gear 300B (US$7) per hour and Hobie Cats at 600B (US$13) per hour. Call **Western Tours** at 11 Damnoenkasem Rd., Hua Hin (© **3251-2560**), for snorkeling trips to outer islands for about 1,500B (US$34) per person. For 750B (US$17) per person, **Lucky Sea Tours** (cellular © **1824-9419**) will take you fishing on a Thai fishing boat that heads out for nearby Ko Singtao (Lion Island) when they get enough takers. Scuba diving trips are coordinated by **Coral Divers,** 7 Naresdamri Rd., Hua Hin (cellular © **132-8180**), for 1,500B to 2,000B (US$34–US$45) per person, in addition to fishing, snorkeling, and island-hopping trips at Ko Singtao. Scuba trips are only as deep as 5m (16½ ft.) around the small island.

Meanwhile, back on terra firma, the other favorite activity in Hua Hin and Cha-Am is **golf,** and some really fine courses might lure you out despite the heat. The best places to try are the centrally located Royal Hua Hin Golf Course and the Springfield Royal Country Club, which is also home to the Springfield Golf Academy, staffed with PGA pros. Reservations are suggested and necessary most weekends. **Royal Hua Hin Golf Course** (Damnoenkasem Rd. near the Hua Hin Railway Station; © **3251-2475**), Thailand's first championship golf course, opened in 1924 and was recently upgraded. It features topiary figures along its fairways and is open daily 6am to 6pm. The course at **Springfield Royal Country Club,** 193 Huay-Sai Nua, Petchkasem Road, Cha-Am (© **3247-1303**), designed by Jack Nicklaus in 1993, is clever in design in a beautiful valley setting.

Outside the resort areas, there are a few wonderful natural and cultural attractions. Set aside a day for a trip to **Phetchaburi** (see "A Side Trip to Phetchaburi," below). Just outside Hua Hin, visit the Mareukatayawan Palace, also known as the Teakwood Mansion (it's open daily 8:30am–4pm, with free admission). Built and designed in 1924 by King Rama VI, it served for many years as the royal summer residence, and it is now open to the public.

For a little nature, **Khao Sam Roi Yot National Park** is a great day trip. The "Mountain of 300 Peaks" is comparatively small in relation to the nation's other parks, but has nice short hikes to see panoramic views of the sea and surrounds, plus a look at wildlife. Of the park's two caves, Kaew Cave is the most interesting, housing a sala pavilion that was built in 1890 for King Chulalongkorn. Call **Western Tours** (© **3251-2560**), which charges 700B (US$16) per person. A half-day trip to the Pala-U waterfall close to the Burmese border (63km/39 miles west of Hua Hin) is another nature-trekking option. Nature trails take you through hills and valleys until you end up at the falls. Western Tours does the trip for 700B (US$16) per person. The driver can stop at the **Dole Thailand pineapple factory** for a tour and tasting (© **3257-1177;** open daily 9am–4pm; 200B/US$4.50 admission), and the Kaew Cave.

Shopping action is had throughout the small streets in the center of Hua Hin, where you can find tailors and souvenir shops. The day market along Damnoenkasem Road, just at the beach, displays local crafts made from seashells, batik clothing, and many other handicraft finds. At night, the 2-block-long Night Market on Dechanuchit Road west of Phetchkasem Road packs in hawkers with sweet foods, cheap clothes, and all sorts of fun trinkets.

If you're looking for nightlife in the area, your best bet is Hua Hin. Cha-Am has a couple of notable spots: the Wild West saloon-style **Jeep Pub** (© **3247-2311**) and the tiki-style **Bamboo Bar** (© **3243-3292**), both on Soi Cattriya off Ruamchit (Beach) Road. But Hua Hin has a greater variety of life. A 15-minute stroll through the sois between Damnoenkasem, Poolsuk, and Deachanuchit roads near the beach reveals all sorts of small places to stop for a cool cocktail and some fun. For a little nighttime Thai culture, the small shack of a boxing stadium on Poolsuk Road has occasional Friday night bouts (9pm; admission 250B/US$5.60). Announcements are tacked up around the village.

A SIDE TRIP TO PHETCHABURI ★★

Phetchaburi, one of the country's oldest towns, possibly dates from the same period as Ayutthaya and Kanchanaburi, though it's believed to have been first settled during the Dvaravati period. After the rise of the Thai nation, it served as an important royal military city and was home to several princes who were groomed for ascendance to the throne. Phetchaburi's palace and historically significant temples highlight an excellent day trip.

Many tour operators coordinate day trips to Phetchaburi from Hua Hin; it's a mere 50-minute drive away. **Western Tours,** 11 Damnoenkasem Rd. (© 3251-2560), has day excursions for 700B (US$16) per person. While the Phra Nakorn Khiri and Khao Luang Cave are the two main stops on every tour itinerary, the city has a few other gems that are never included in the standard package. To see these, I recommend arranging your own ride from Hua Hin. A car can be hired through the **Hua Hin Tourist Information Center** (© 3251-1047 or 3253-2433) for the day for 1,200B (US$27). All the drivers know how to get to the palace and the cave, but few have ever been to any of the smaller temples in the city. Don't fret; everyone in the town knows where these places are, and the driver need only to stop and ask for directions.

The main attraction is **Phra Nakhorn Khiri** ★ (© 3242-8539), a summer palace atop the hills overlooking the city. Built in 1858 by King Mongkut (Rama IV), it was intended as a summer retreat not only for the royal family, but for foreign dignitaries as well. Combining Thai, European, and Chinese architectural styles, the palace buildings include guesthouses and a royal Khmer-style chedi, or temple. The Phra Thinang Phetphum Phairot Hall is open for viewing and contains period art and antiques from the household. Although it was once accessible only via a 4km (2½-mile) hike uphill, you'll be happy to hear that there's a funicular railway (called a "cable car," but not really) to take you to the top. The ride costs 40B (US90¢) for adults and 10B (US25¢) for children; it's open Monday through Friday 8:15am to 5pm, and Saturday and Sunday from 8:15am to 5:50pm. The museum charges 40B (US90¢) for admission and is open daily from 9am to 4pm.

Another fascinating sight at Phetchaburi, the **Khao Luang Cave,** houses more than 170 Buddha images underground. Outside the cave, hundreds of noisy monkeys descend upon the parking lot and food stalls looking for handouts. Sometimes you'll find guides outside who'll escort you through the caves for 40B (US90¢). If you're not with a group, it's a good idea—their English isn't too hot, but they do point out many cave features that might otherwise be missed. A 20B (US45¢) donation is optional once inside.

A small wonder is **Wat Yai Suwannaram** ★, a royal temple built during the Ayutthaya period. The teak ordination hall was moved from Ayutthaya after the second Burmese invasion on the city. The proof is in the axe chop battle scar on the building's carved wood doors. Inside, murals represent religious scenes filled with Brahmans, hermits, giants, and deities. The temple complex is usually locked, but if you wander to the back of the complex and talk to some of the young monk apprentices, they'll seek out a key and take you inside.

Southern Peninsula: West Coast

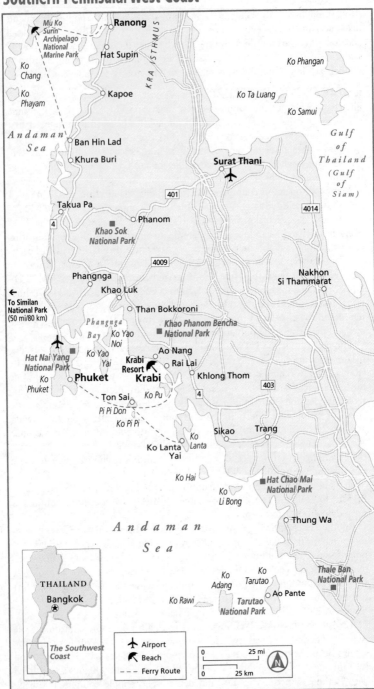

Mu Ko Surin Archipelago National Marine Park

Ranong

Ko Chang

Hat Supin

Ko Phayam

Kapoe

K R A   I S T H M U S

Ko Phangan

Ko Ta Luang

Ko Samui

Andaman Sea

Ban Hin Lad

Khura Buri

Surat Thani

Gulf of Thailand (Gulf of Siam)

401

4014

Takua Pa

4

Phanom

Khao Sok National Park

4009

Phangnga

Khao Luk

← To Similan National Park (50 mi/80 km)

Than Bokkoroni

Phangnga Bay

Ko Yao Noi

Ko Yao Yai

Khao Phanom Bencha National Park

Nakhon Si Thammarat

Ao Nang

Krabi Resort

Rai Lai

Krabi

Hat Nai Yang National Park

Phuket

Ko Phuket

Khlong Thom

403

Ton Sai

Ko Pu

4

Pi Pi Don

Ko Pi Pi

Sikao

Trang

Ko Lanta Yai

Ko Lanta

Ko Hai

Hat Chao Mai National Park

Ko Li Bong

Thung Wa

Andaman Sea

THAILAND

Bangkok

The Southwest Coast

Ko Adang

Ko Tarutao

Thale Ban National Park

Ko Rawi

Ao Pante

Tarutao National Park

✈ Airport

🏖 Beach

- - - Ferry Route

| 0 | 25 mi |
| 0 | 25 km |

N

The other wat with impressive paintings is **Wat Ko Keo Suttharam** ⍟, also built in the 17th century but with murals from the 1730s. These are far more representational. Of some interest to Westerners, there are several panels depicting the arrival in the Ayutthaya court of European courtesans and diplomats (including a Jesuit dressed in Buddhist garb). This one is more likely to be open, but if it's not, someone will be around to let you in if you ask.

Another fabulous wat, particularly for fans of Khmer architecture, is **Wat Kamphaeng Laeng,** originally constructed during the reign of Khmer ruler King Jayavaraman VII (1157–1207) as a Hindu shrine. Made of laterite, it was once covered in decorative stucco, some of which still remains. Each of the five prangs, or towers, was devoted to a deity—the center prang to Shiva. During the Ayutthaya period, it was converted to a Buddhist temple. The temple is amazing when you consider how far the Khmer empire extended through Thailand.

If you still have time, the **Phra Ram Raja Nivesana,** or **Ban Puen Palace** (© 3242-8506; open daily 8am–4pm, with free admission), is a nice stop. A royal palace built by Rama V, the German-designed grand summer home comes alive with colorful tile work, neoclassical marble columns, and floor motifs. Today it sits on military grounds and is a popular venue for ceremonies and large occasions.

As for spending the night in Phetchaburi, I don't really recommend it because there are no comfortable accommodations around. For a lunch break, **Num Tien,** 539 Moo 1, Phetchakasaemkao Rod (© 3242-5121), still reigns as the best lunch eatery in town. An open-air cafe cooled under a columned veranda, this well-established restaurant serves a combination of Thai and Chinese specialties at cheap prices. The menu is in English, and for extra help, Khun Natta, the oh-so-kind proprietor, will make good recommendations.

9 Ko Samui

The island of Ko Samui lies 84km (52 miles) off Thailand's east coast in the Gulf of Thailand, near the mainland commercial town of Surat Thani. Since the 1850s, Ko Samui has been visited by Chinese merchants sailing from Hainan Island in the South China Sea to trade coconuts and cotton, the island's two most profitable products.

Ko Samui's coconuts are among Southeast Asia's most coveted, principally for their flavor. More than 2 million coconuts a month are shipped to Bangkok. Much of the fruit is made into coconut oil, a process that involves scraping the meat out of the shell, drying it, and pressing it to produce a sweet oil. To assist farmers with Ko Samui's indigenous breed of tall palm trees, monkeys are trained to climb them, shake off the ripe coconuts, and gather them for the boss man.

You'll hear Ko Samui compared to Phuket all the time. While Phuket enjoys international fame (or notoriety, depending on your point of view) as a gorgeous beach resort heaven, Ko Samui attracts those who want to avoid the hype and settle for more down-to-earth relaxation. Once upon a time, Ko Samui's fine beaches were less crowded, and simple bungalow accommodations and eateries made for a more off-the-beaten-path island experience. As Ko Samui's reputation as the "alternative Thai island" grew, so did the number of visitors landing on its shores. Increasing demand inspired the opening of an international airport in 1988 that now has more than 20 packed daily flights. In recent years, big resorts have been getting in on the action, opening up huge accommodations a la Phuket. While they provide more comforts and facilities, in some ways they lack the carefree Ko Samui charm that drew travelers here in the first place.

The high season on Ko Samui is from mid-December to mid-January. January to April has the best weather, before its gets hot. October through mid-December are the wettest months, with November bringing extreme rains and fierce winds that make the east side of the island rough for swimming. Some years, the island's west side is buffeted by summer monsoons from the mainland.

VISITOR INFORMATION

The **TAT Information Center** opened a new office on Thawiratchaphakdi Road in the north of Nathon (© 7742-0504). A good place to stop before you head out to the beach, the center distributes, in addition to TAT pamphlets, the thin *Accommodations Samui* guidebook, a free booklet packed with information on hotel, dining, and activity options. Bangkok Airways produces the free **Samui Guide,** a color magazine with advertisements and practical information about the island. I like Bangkok Airways' free *Samui Guidemap,* an accurate map indicating locations for most major businesses and landmarks. All are distributed at TAT, the airport and many hotels and restaurants. At magazine stands, look for the *Greater Samui Guide* (80B/US$1.80), a glossy magazine with travel articles, photos, and advertisements for up-market establishments.

GETTING THERE

Getting to Ko Samui is more simple than it at first appears. Direct flights from Bangkok, Phuket, Pattaya (U-Tapao), and even Singapore and Phnom Penh make visiting the island a snap. In addition, there are several bus and train options to Surat Thani (the nearest mainland town), a ferry from a canal in south Surat Thani, and express ferries from Thathon, another port 5km (3 miles) south of Surat Thani.

BY PLANE   Up to 17 flights depart daily from Bangkok on **Bangkok Airways** (© 2229-3456 in Bangkok), pretty much one every 40 minutes between 6:20am and 7:20pm. Two daily flights from Phuket (Bangkok Airways Phuket office; © 7622-5033) and another daily from the U-Tapao airport near Pattaya (Bangkok Airways Pattaya office; © 3841-1965) connect these major beach destinations, with additional Bangkok Airways flights connecting the northern cities through Bangkok. From Singapore, Bangkok Airways flies direct each day. Its offices in Samui are at Chaweng Beach (© 7742-2512) and at the airport (© 7742-5601).

Ko Samui Airport is a little slice of heaven—open-air pavilions with thatch roofs surrounded by gardens and palms. For **airport information,** call © 7742-5012. If you're staying at a larger resort, airport minivan shuttles can be arranged when you book your room. There's also a minivan service that is very convenient. Book your ticket at the transportation counter upon arrival, and you'll get door-to-door service for 100B (US$2.30). To save a few baht, just out at the main road you'll find songtaos (pickup-truck taxis) that can take you to the beach you're staying at. If there are many of you, trips can be as low as 30B (US70¢), depending on how far you're going. For one or two people going a longer distance, they might try to up the price to more than 100B (US$2.30). If you depart Ko Samui via the airport, there's an additional 150B (US$3.40) airport tax that's usually added to your ticket charge.

Another flight option, while cumbersome, is also available. **Thai Airways** operates two daily flights to Surat Thani (© 2525-2084 for domestic reservations in Bangkok). While Thai Airways runs a shuttle from the airport to Surat Thani town, if you're moving on to Ko Samui, your best bet is to prearrange a

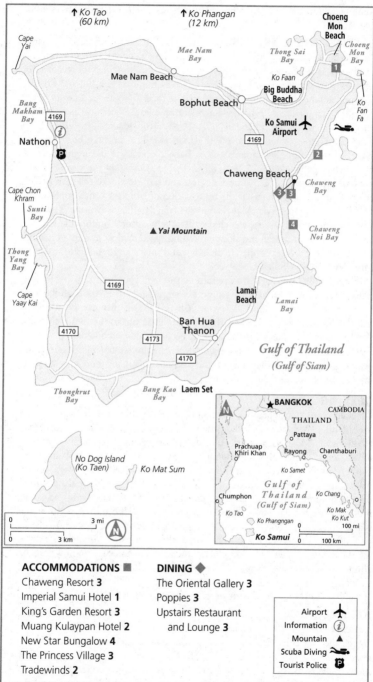

Ko Samui

↑ Ko Tao (60 km)

↑ Ko Phangan (12 km)

Choeng Mon Beach

Choeng Mon Bay

Cape Yai

Mae Nam Bay

Thong Sai Bay

Mae Nam Beach

Ko Faan

Bophut Beach

Big Buddha Beach

Ko Fan Fa

Bang Makham Bay

4169

Ko Samui Airport

Nathon

4169

Chaweng Beach

Chaweng Bay

Cape Chon Khram

Sunti Bay

▲ Yai Mountain

Chaweng Noi Bay

Thong Yang Bay

Cape Yaay Kai

4169

Lamai Beach

Lamai Bay

4170

Ban Hua Thanon

4173

4170

Gulf of Thailand (Gulf of Siam)

Thongkrut Bay

Bang Kao Bay Laem Set

No Dog Island (Ko Taen)

Ko Mat Sum

★ BANGKOK

CAMBODIA

THAILAND

Pattaya

Prachuap Khiri Khan

Rayong

Chanthaburi

Ko Samet

Gulf of Thailand (Gulf of Siam)

Chumphon

Ko Chang

Ko Tao

Ko Mak

Ko Kut

Ko Phangngan

0   100 mi

Ko Samui

0   100 km

0   3 mi

0   3 km

ACCOMMODATIONS ■

Chaweng Resort **3**
Imperial Samui Hotel **1**
King's Garden Resort **3**
Muang Kulaypan Hotel **2**
New Star Bungalow **4**
The Princess Village **3**
Tradewinds **2**

DINING ◆

The Oriental Gallery **3**
Poppies **3**
Upstairs Restaurant
   and Lounge **3**

Airport ✈
Information ⓘ
Mountain ▲
Scuba Diving
Tourist Police 🅿

combined airport shuttle and ferry trip through Songserm Travel (contact information below).

GETTING THERE FROM SURAT THANI If you're traveling overland, **Songserm** (📞 7720-5418 in Surat Thani) can link you out to Samui via **speedboat**—this is the fastest but not necessarily most comfortable way to go. They run a loop from Surat Thani with stops in Ko Samui, Ko Phangan, and Ko Tao, finishing at Chumphon (and back again). The total trip is about 4 hours, while the Surat–Samui leg is 2 hours. Rates are as follows: Surat to Samui 150B (US$3.40); Samui to Phangan 95B (US$2.16); Phangan to Tao 250B (US$5.70); Tao to Chumphon 400B (US$9.10). The morning boat leaves at 8am. Songserm can also connect you via Bangkok on a VIP overnight bus. Call the office in Bangkok at 📞 **2280-7897.**

Phanthip (📞 7727-2230) provides bus and ferry service to the island—you board a bus at Surat Thani (at the train station or from the office opposite the Thai Thani Hotel on Talat Mai Rd.) to the ferry landing at Donsak. The giant ferry (which also transports vehicles) is definitely a more comfortable journey, but between bus transfer and slower traveling speed, it does eat up a bit more time. At least eight ferries operate each day, and they take 2½ hours to make the trip (about 150B/US$3.40 each way).

If you haven't arranged transportation through your resort, you can find transportation once you reach Nathon, Ko Samui's ferry pier. Touts on the ferry offer very cheap rides, some as low as 20B (US45¢) if they can get a packed truckload from the boat (and be warned, they'll tie you to the roof if they can eke 20B/US45¢ out of it). If you have no accommodations booking, many will even make a few stops along the way so you can check a few places out before deciding. If you wait until you reach the pier, there are many more songtao waiting to take people to their destinations.

GETTING AROUND

BY SONGTAO Songtao are the easiest and most efficient way to get around the island. They advertise their destinations—to such beaches as Lamai, Chaweng, and Mai Nam—with colorfully painted signs. There are two primary routes, with songtao plying the circular Highway 4169, making stops between Nathon on the west coast over the north side of the island to Chaweng on the east coast, and another route between Chaweng and Nathon along the southern coast. For some trips, you have to change trucks between north and south routes. Some branch off to hit Choeng Mon in the northeastern tip of the island. You can hail one anywhere along the highway and along beach roads. To visit a site off the beaten track (or one other than that painted on a truck's sign), ask the driver to make a detour. Check when the songtao stop running, usually around sundown, after which some will hang around outside the discos in Chaweng to take night owls home to other beaches. The cost is 20B to 40B (US45¢–US90¢) one-way, with steep fares (up to 300B/US$6.80) after hours.

BY RENTAL CAR Ko Samui's roads are narrow, winding, poorly maintained, and dark at night. In the island's first decade of tourism, more than 350 foreigners died in vehicle accidents. Still, renting a car is safer than renting a motorcycle. Your defensive driving skills will be required to navigate around slow motorcycles at the side of the road and the occasional wandering dog.

From **Avis**'s office at Santiburi Dusit Resort (📞 7742-5031), you can have your vehicle delivered to your hotel, to the ferry pier, or to the airport. Avis provides excellent insurance but costs far more than local rental firms. Its brand-new fleet of **Suzuki Caribians** cost from 1,500B (US$34) per day; it costs 2,000B (US$45) and up for a compact sedan. Local rental companies and travel agents have great deals for car rentals, and while vehicles are sometimes a little beat up, they're generally mechanically sound. Look for bargains as low as 700B (US$16) per day, but don't expect solid insurance policy coverage. Read all the fine print, and make sure that if you don't have an international driver license, your local license is acceptable under the terms of the insurance agreement. In the event of an accident, you don't want to lose insurance eligibility for not being properly licensed according to the contract. A standard contract allows for liability coverage with a 5,000B (US$116) deductible. Do not leave your passport with any rental agency.

BY MOTORCYCLE   Upon first arrival, it's easy to see that motorcycles are the top choice for locals as well as visitors. Driving on the left, most motorcyclists stick to the side of the road, but where shoulders are narrow, they drift into car lanes. Keep to the side as much as you can, to make way for passing cars and trucks, and be mindful of other bikes. Helmet laws exist but aren't always enforced. Travel agencies and small operators rent motorcycles in popular beach areas. A 100cc Honda scooter goes for as little as 150B (US$3.40) per day, while a 250cc chopper is as expensive as 700B to 900B (US$16–US$20) a day. Insist on a helmet.

FAST FACTS: Ko Samui

Banks/Currency Exchange   All the major **banks** are in Nathon, along Thawiratchaphakdi Road, running parallel to the waterfront road where the pier is. In Chaweng, you'll find some money-changers and two (two!) ATMs. Krung Thai Bank's ATM, opposite Starbucks, always has a long queue, while farther north Siam Commercial Bank's ATM is out of the way for most. Hotels and guesthouses also accept traveler's checks—your safest bet here—but use conversion rates to their favor.

Emergencies   A good hospital with excellent emergency care, **Bandon International Hospital** has English-speaking physicians and good facilities. It's located in the north of Chaweng off Highway 4169, but doctors can also make house calls. Call ℰ 7742-5382.

Internet Service   On Chaweng, head for the **Go Internet Café**, opposite the Central Samui Beach Resort (ℰ 7723-0535). The best Internet (and business services) can be found at Sawadee Internet Service, 131 Moo 4, T. Maret Lamai, Lamai Beach (ℰ 7723-1176).

Police   For **Tourist Police** emergencies, dial ℰ 7742-1281.

Post Office/Mail   The main **post office** (ℰ 7742-1013) is on Chonwithee Road in Nathon, but you'll probably not hike all the way back to the main pier for posting. Any hotel or guesthouse will handle it for you, and stamps can be purchased in small provision shops in beach areas.

Telephone   There are pay telephones, both coin and card, and in the main villages at Chaweng and Lamai beaches you can find overseas calling offices to call home and send or receive faxes. The area code is 077.

CHAWENG & CHAWENG NOI BAYS

By far the largest assortment of accommodations is at Chaweng. Every inch of the beachfront is divvied up among all sorts of hotels and resorts—some are unique and lovely, but some I wouldn't let my dog stay in. The following are my favorites.

WHERE TO STAY
Very Expensive

Imperial Samui Hotel ⚑ This is one of the few luxury resorts on this long coastline; like its sister, the Boat House at Choeng Mon, it's a member of the Thai-owned Imperial Hotel chain. The hotel's two original wings are built up on a hill in a grove of coconut palms, overlooking Chaweng Noi; two newer wings, a second pool (with fewer people), and another indoor/outdoor restaurant have been added higher up the hillside.

Spacious rooms have sea views, lots of floral prints and rattan, large bathrooms with potted plants, and easy access (via steps) to the beach. Amenities include large balconies, tiled floors that seem impervious to sand, and an odd-shaped saltwater swimming pool that looks ready to spill into the bay. The staff was helpful, many with great senses of humor. Check to see if a local travel agent can get you a good rate here; it's a very pleasant resort.

86 Moo 3, Ban Chaweng Noi, Ko Samui 84320, Surat Thani (middle of Chaweng Noi Beach). ℂ **7742-2020.** Fax 7742-2396. www.imperialhotels.com. 155 units. 5,850B (US$133) double; from 7,000B (US$159) suite. AE, DC, MC, V. **Amenities:** 3 restaurants (Thai, international); lounge; 2 outdoor pools, 1 freshwater and 1 seawater; outdoor lighted tennis courts; Jacuzzi; watersports equipment and dive center; bike rental; snooker and badminton; concierge; tour desk; car-rental desk; limousine service; 24-hr. room service; massage; babysitting; same-day laundry service/dry cleaning. *In room:* A/C, TV w/free in-house movies, minibar.

Expensive

Chaweng Resort ⚑ Like a quaint Florida resort development, the Chaweng Resort consists of two columns of freestanding bungalows facing each other down to the sea. Cottages are comfortable and spacious, with one queen bed, one single bed, a spotless bathroom, and a personal safe in each. The suites are good value, in their own little houses sporting king beds, plenty of space, a small private pool, and funky wood-paneled bathrooms. The place has some neat local touches. Grounds are nicely landscaped, with a medium-size pool and Thai/Continental restaurant overlooking the fine beach. A good family choice, this place always bustles with activity.

Chaweng Beach, Ko Samui, 84320 Surat Thani (middle of Chaweng Beach). ℂ **7742-2230,** or 2651-0016 in Bangkok. Fax 7751-0018. www.chawengresort.com. 70 units. 2,200B–2,800B (US$50–US$64) double; 3,000B (US$68) suite. AE, DC, MC, V. **Amenities:** Restaurant (international); pool; tour desk; massage; laundry service. *In room:* A/C, TV w/satellite programming, minibar.

Muang Kulaypan Hotel ⚑⚑ I've never seen a resort like this in Thailand. Within this 3-year-old two-story building, some imaginative soul has combined warm natural woods and rich local textiles with clean contemporary lines and stylistic minimalism. While rooms are sparse, it's all part of the design concept—think of it as a sort of Shaker approach to resort decor. It's grace in simplicity, with some tasteful Thai touches. Of the platform beds, different in each room, the four-poster platform bed in the honeymoon room is the nicest. Almost all rooms have a sea view. Budsaba Restaurant serves all kinds of cuisine, including many vegetarian selections. The black-tile pool is just lovely.

100 Moo 2, Chaweng Beach Rd., Ko Samui 84320, Surat Thani (N tip of Chaweng Beach). ℂ **7723-0850.** Fax 7723-0031. www.kulaypan.com. 40 units. 3,200B–4,550B (US$73–US$103) double. AE, DC, MC, V. **Amenities:** Restaurant (international); lounge; outdoor pool; small fitness center; motorcycle rental; tour

desk; car rental limousine service; limited room service; massage; babysitting; same-day laundry service/dry cleaning. *In room:* A/C, minibar.

The Princess Village ★★
If you've wondered what sleeping in Jim Thompson's House or the Suan Pakkard Palace—both in Bangkok—might be like, try the regal Princess Village. Traditional teak houses from Ayutthaya have been restored and placed around a lushly planted garden. Several have sea views, and each is on stilts above its own lotus pond; use-worn stairs lead up to a large veranda with roll-down bamboo screens.

Inside, you'll find a grand teak bed covered in embroidered silk or cotton, and antique furniture and artwork worthy of the Ramas. Small, carved dressing tables and spacious bathrooms contain painted ceramics, silverware, a porcelain dish, a large khlong jar for water storage, or other Thai details amid the modern conveniences. Traditional shuttered windows on all sides have no screens, but lacy mosquito netting and a ceiling fan, combined with sea breezes, create Thai-style ventilation. There is air-conditioning for skeptics.

101/1 Moo 3, Chaweng Beach, Ko Samui 84320, Surat Thani (middle of Chaweng Beach). © 7742-2216. Fax 7742-2382. www.samuidreamholiday.com. 12 units. 3,000B (US$68) garden-view double; 3,600B–4,400B (US$82–US$100) sea-view double; from 4,600B (US$105) suite. AE, MC, V. **Amenities:** Restaurant (international); motorcycle rental; tour desk; Jeep rental; massage; laundry service; daily Chinese tea service on your veranda. *In room:* Minibar, coffee/tea-making facilities, safe.

Moderate

New Star Bungalow
This newer establishment offers a wide range of facilities clustered on Chaweng Noi. All are freestanding buildings with porches. Eight deluxe bungalows sit slightly up the hill, with full sea views, large rooms, air-conditioning, and charming stonework in the private bathrooms. Smaller, slightly cheaper superior rooms with air-conditioning sit on the beach, but five rows deep, so that only the first row is really desirable (the best value). However, prices include one full-size bed and an alcove single bed, ideal for small families. Most of the rooms are air-conditioned, but some are back from the beach and small, with fans and twin beds.

Chaweng Noi Beach, Ko Samui 84320, Surat Thani (N of Imperial Samui Hotel on Chaweng Noi). © 7742-2407. Fax 7742-2325. 50 units. 1,800B (US$41) double. MC, V. **Amenities:** Restaurant (international); water-sports equipment; bike rental; transfer service; same-day laundry service. *In room:* A/C.

Tradewinds ★
In the center of Chaweng, Tradewinds has one of the best locations. Step out of the front entrance, and you're in the center of it all: restaurants, clubs, and shopping. However, the other side of the resort opens out to Chaweng's long lovely beach. From the higher-priced bungalows, you can step right off your front porch into the sand. The other bungalows are placed in shady secluded gardens not far from the beach. The bungalows here are modern and fully furnished with large beds and rattan furnishings. Spotless and bright, they're perfect for travelers who want the intimate feeling of a bungalow village but don't want to sacrifice modern conveniences. If you don't want to go out for a meal, the superb Thai restaurant (with Western selections as well) is situated on the beach. Tradewinds is also the home of Samui's catamaran sailing center.

17/14 Moo 3, Chaweng Beach, Ko Samui 84320, Surat Thani. © 7723-0602. Fax 7723-1247. 32 units. 2,500B–3,000B (US$57–US$68) double. AE, V. **Amenities:** Restaurant (international); bar; catamaran sailing center; laundry service. *In room:* A/C, minibar.

Inexpensive

King's Garden Resort
These simple bungalows are fairly new, spacious, and comfortable, with fans and cold-water showers. The older, smaller cottages are

closer to the beach and cheaper, but they lack window screens. A larger, higher-priced cottage has air-conditioning and is a better value (2,500B/US$58), only about 30m (100 ft.) back from the beach.

12 Moo 2, Chaweng Beach, Ko Samui 84320, Surat Thani (middle of Chaweng Beach). ⊙ **7742-2304.** Fax 7742-0430. 32 units. 1,000B–2,500B (US$23–US$57) double with A/C; 350B–800B (US$7.95–US$18) double w/fan. No credit cards. **Amenities:** Restaurant (international); massage; laundry service. *In room:* no phone.

WHERE TO DINE

The Oriental Gallery 🌟 THAI   Opened in 1991, the Oriental Gallery combines a fine arts and antiques gallery with a swanky little cafe. Gorgeous treasures fill the dining area, both under cover and in the small outdoor patio garden. You'll almost be too busy admiring the pieces to look at the menu. Thai dishes are prepared and presented with similar good taste, and are not too spicy for tender foreign tongues. The friendly and knowledgeable gallery owners are around to chat about Thai antiques and art, and to explain any pieces that catch your eye.

39/1 Moo 3, Chaweng Beach. ⊙ **7742-2200.** Reservations recommended during peak season. Main courses 60B–200B (US$1.40–US$4.55). AE, MC, V. Daily 2–11:30pm.

Poppies THAI/INTERNATIONAL   Famous for its Bali-style feel, Poppies is equally famous for fresh seafood by the beach. The romantic atmosphere under the large thatch pavilion is enhanced by soft lighting and live international jazz music. Guest chefs from around the world mean the menu is ever changing, but you can be sure the seafood selections are some of the best catches around. This is a good place, especially if you're romancing someone special.

South Chaweng Beach. ⊙ **7742-2419.** Reservations recommended during peak season. Entrees 80B–240B (US$1.80–US$5.45). AE, MC, V. Daily 7am–10pm.

Upstairs Restaurant and Lounge 🌟🌟 INTERNATIONAL   The Oriental Gallery's sister restaurant, Upstairs, is exactly that—upstairs. But it's not just an extension of the original restaurant; it's a whole new venue with an entirely different groove. With a twist on contemporary, it mixes tropical style with bold colors and mod angles. The menu features seafood and meats in familiar Western recipes with delicate flavors and beautiful presentation. After 10pm, a DJ spins a sophisticated mix of soul music, so feel free to hang around enjoying cocktails until late.

39/1 Moo 3, Chaweng Beach. ⊙ **7742-2200.** Reservations recommended during peak season. Main courses 120B–350B (US$2.70–US$7.95). AE, MC, V. Daily noon–11:00pm (kitchen closes at 11pm, but the bar stays open until late).

LAMAI BAY

Despite the popularity of this beach, it's slim pickings in terms of decent accommodations. Most places are bargain hunters' dreams, at the expense of comfort. And sometimes this beach can be rowdier at night than its more infamous neighbor, Chaweng.

WHERE TO STAY
Expensive

The Pavilion Resort 🌟   One of Lamai's newer facilities, this resort has attached rooms in a hotel block and Polynesian-style octagonal bungalows, all scattered throughout the beachfront grounds (limited sea views). Hotel rooms are nicely appointed, each with its own safe, and have good-size patios for sunbathing. The larger bungalows have a campy primitive feel, as well as the comfort of a private bath and hot water. The pool and dining pavilion are right on the surf—combined with ground-floor hotel rooms, it makes a comfortable, easy access resort for travelers with disabilities. The proximity to Lamai's nightlife is a plus for most guests.

124/24 Moo 3, Lamai Beach, Ko Samui 84310, Surat Thani (N end of Lamai Beach). ✆ **7742-4030.** Fax 7742-4029. www.pavilionsamui.com. 64 units. 3,500B (US$80) double in hotel wing; 4,500B (US$102) double bungalow; 5,600B (US$127) suite. AE, DC, MC, V. **Amenities:** Restaurant (international); bar; outdoor pool; Jacuzzi; tour desk; car-rental desk; transfer service; limited room service; laundry service. *In room:* A/C, TV, minibar, safe.

Moderate

Samui Yacht Club   This tidy bungalow complex, a yacht club in name only, has an almost exclusive location in a small cove just north of Lamai Beach. It's very quiet and close to one of the best snorkeling areas off the island. Each bungalow has a little porch, glass wrap-around windows (with drapes), canopy beds with romantic mosquito netting, clean tiled floors, and rattan furnishings. I like the ample closet space. Best are the beachfront bungalows (which also have stereos), where you can just step off the porch into the sand. The restaurant is fine for breakfast, but I'd go out for dinner. This place is best for people who want to be left alone.

Ao Tongtakian, between Chaweng and Lamai Beaches, Koh Samui 84320, Surat Thani. ✆ **7742-2225.** Fax 7742-2400. www.samuiyachtclub.com. 43 units. 1,800B–2,800B (US$41–US$64) garden bungalow; 3,300B (US$75) beachfront bungalow. AE, MC, V. **Amenities:** Restaurant (international); outdoor pool; motorcycle rental; babysitting; laundry service. *In room:* A/C, TV w/satellite programming, minibar, safe.

Inexpensive

The Spa Resort ✦ *Value*   For long-term stays or just a daytime visit, The Spa Resort Health Center has an excellent reputation on the island. Register for one of its programs—the intensive cleansing and fasting program rejuvenates your system with prepared detox drinks and tablets plus twice daily colonic enema (US$260 per week). Other short-term programs are available. The trademark spa features local Thai herbs for steam baths, herbal massage, body wraps, and facial treatments. Classes and workshops on yoga, meditation, and massage techniques fill your days with relaxation. Day programs are available if you just want to stop in—Thai massage, herbal steam, cleansing facial, and body wrap for only 700B (US$16). Accommodations are the simplest of the simple—few have air-conditioning, and you won't find a TV or telephone. However, you will have mosquito nets, fans, and private bathrooms. Higher-priced bungalows are those situated closer to the beach. The vegetarian restaurant serves excellent dishes, with particular care to cleansing bodies. If you're trying to find the place, the road sign just says SPA.

171–2 Moo 4, Lamai Beach, Ko Samui 84320, Surat Thani (N of Lamai Beach). ✆ **7723-0855.** Fax 7742-4126. www.spasamui.com. 18 units. 250B–600B (US$5.70–US$14); 1,800B (US$41) suite. MC, V. **Amenities:** Restaurant (vegetarian Thai); spa; sauna; massage; laundry service. *In room:* No phone.

WHERE TO DINE

Mr. Pown Restaurant SEAFOOD   Of all the seafood places along the main drag in Lamai, Mr. Pown is the nicest. Fresh seafood is carefully laid on ice in front of the entrance, so you can choose your own toothy fish or local lobster. In this patio of a restaurant, tables near the front railing are great fun for people-watching. The menu is an extensive list of seafood of all kinds prepared in many Chinese, Thai, and Western styles. There's also an assortment of accompanying Chinese and Thai soups, vegetable, and meat dishes. ***Be warned:*** The lobster is delicious, but expensive.

124/137 Moo 3, Lamai Beach. ⓒ mobile **1970-7758**. Reservations not necessary. Seafood at market prices. MC, V. Daily 10am–10pm.

The Spa Restaurant VEGETARIAN I don't just recommend The Spa Restaurant to vegetarians (it serves a few seafood and chicken dishes as well), but I do recommend it to anyone who wants to relax with his feet in the sand, eating a healthful, tasty dish. Go for the delicious curries, or try the excellent local dishes. But leave plenty of time for an herbal steam and massage at the Health Center. For a vacation activity, this is tops for relaxation—an afternoon of pure indulgence, and it's good for you!

Rte. 4169, between Chaweng and Lamai Beaches. ⓒ **7723-0855**. Reservations recommended in peak season. Main courses 30B–150B (US70¢–US$3.40). MC, V. Daily 7am–10pm.

Vinmarnmek ✷✷ ASIAN FUSION/SEAFOOD You'll think you'd died and gone to heaven. Chef Khun Tangkuay, the genius behind the menu, knows his local cuisine like the back of his hand and has studied in prestigious kitchens abroad. He combines his knowledge of many cultural tastes to invent dishes with the best elements of the East and West, crafted from the freshest local ingredients. Presentation is perfect, service is true Dusit charm, and the atmosphere is royal elegance.

Santiburi Dusit Resort. 12/12 Moo 1, Tambol Mae Nam, Ko Samui, Surat Thani 84330. ⓒ **7742-5031**. Reservations recommended for peak season. Main courses 170B–350B (US$3.90–US$7.95). AE, DC, MC, V. Daily 10am–10pm.

EXPLORING KO SAMUI

Local aquanauts agree that the best **scuba diving** is off Ko Tao, a small island north of Ko Phangan and Ko Samui. Because conditions vary with the seasons, the cluster of tiny islands south of Samui, Mu Ko Angthong National Park, are often more reliable destinations. Follow the advice of a local dive shop on where to go. **Easy Divers,** in operation for 10 years, has locations in Chaweng (ⓒ **7741-3373**) and other beaches, indicated on just about every free map. They offer all sorts of PADI courses, daily dive tours to 13 different sites, international safety standard boats, good equipment, and complete insurance packages. Daily dives (2 dives per day) start at about 3,000B (US$68) per person, including land transportation, breakfast, equipment, lunch, and drinks.

Some of the finest **snorkeling** off Ko Samui is found along the rocky coast between Chaweng Noi and Lamai Bays. Several shops along Chaweng Beach rent snorkeling gear for about 100B (US$2.30) per day.

Blue Stars Sea Kayaking, at the Gallery Lafayette next to the Green Mango in Chaweng (ⓒ **7723-0497**), takes people kayaking and snorkeling to the Marine National Park. The rubber canoes are perfect for exploring the caverns underneath limestone cliffs. If you can't get to Phang Nga, for the most fantastic sea cave scenery, this trip is a fun alternative. The 4-hour trip costs 1,990B (US$45) per person.

For **catamaran sailing,** check out **Tradewinds Resort in Chaweng** (ⓒ **7723-0602**). It's run by John Stall, one of the pioneer bungalow operators here who is familiar with local sailing conditions and great routes. He'll also provide instruction for 2,500B (US$56 for a 3-hr. course), while straight rentals are 800B (US$18) per hour (with a guide, if you'd like).

Fishermen should talk to **Camel Fishing Game,** in Lamai across from Bauhaus Pub (ⓒ **7742-4523**), about daily trips with all equipment and lunch provided. Prices range from 230B to 270B (US$5.20–US$6.15) for a day trip.

Ko Samui's famed **Wonderful Rocks**—the most important of which are the shaped like sex organs, the **Hin Yaay & Hin Ta** (Grandmother and Grandfather Stones)—are located at the far southern end of Lamai Beach. To get to them, walk about an hour south of Chaweng Beach, or take any minitruck to Lamai Beach and get off at Paradise Bungalows.

The gold-tiled **Wat Phrayai** (Big Buddha), more than 24m (80 ft.) tall, sits atop Ko Faan (Barking Deer Island), a small islet connected to the shore by a dirt causeway almost 300m (1,000 ft.) long. Though it's of little historic value, it's an imposing presence on the northeast coast and is one of Samui's primary landmarks. It's open all day; a 20B (US45¢) contribution is recommended. It's easy to reach: Just hop on any songtao going to Big Buddha Beach. You can't miss it.

The main island road forks at Ban Hua Thanon in the southeast corner. Past the village of Ban Thurian, the road climbs north past **Na Muang Falls,** a pleasant waterfall once visited by many kings of the Chakri dynasty. After the rainy season ends in December, it reaches a height of almost 30m (100 ft.) and a width of about 19.8m (66 ft.). Na Muang is a steamy 5km (3-mile) walk from the coast road and makes for a nice bathing and picnic stop. Feel free to trek to the falls on the back of an elephant. **Na Muang Trekking** (cellular ✆ **1397-5430**) will take you for a half-hour trip (600B/US$14), or longer.

For something a little more tranquil, visit the **Butterfly Garden** (✆ **7742-4020**), off the 4170 Road near Laem Din on the southeast corner (open daily 9am–5pm; adults 50B/US$1.10, children 20B/US45¢).

OTHER THINGS TO SEE & DO IN KO SAMUI

There's a terrific cooking school on Ko Samui for daily Thai cooking lessons plus fruit carving. **Samui Institute of Thai Culinary Arts (SITCA)** ★ is highly recommended as a professional operation and a great way to have fun—especially if your beach plans get rained out. A 1-day course goes for 1,650B (US$37). Call ✆ **7741-3172** for more details, or stop in on Chaweng Beach across from the Central Samui Resort. The nicely packaged Thai spices and cooking pastes are sold at gift shops around the island and make excellent souvenirs for friends back home.

Along Samui's main roads, you'll find little hand-painted signs along the lines of **"Monkey Work Coconut."** These home-grown tourist spots show off monkey skills involved in the local coconut industry—they're trained to climb the trees, spin the coconuts to break them off their stems, and collect them from the bottom when they're finished. Trainers really use the beasts' natural smarts and talents—these monkeys might otherwise end up picking through resort garbage cans to eke out an existence. The proper **Samui Monkey Theater** (✆ **7724-5140**) is just south of Bophut village on 4169 Road. Shows are a little more vaudeville than the "working" demonstrations—with costumes and goofy tricks—and are a lot more fun for kids than for adults, who'll just feel sorry for the animals. Show times at 10:30am, 2pm, and 4pm daily cost 150B (US$3.35) for adults and 50B (US$1.10) for children.

I defy you to find a Thai tourist spot without the requisite **snake farm,** complete with young men who taunt audiences with scary serpents, catching them with their bare hands (and sometimes their teeth). If you're really scared of snakes, keep away—this stuff is fodder for months of nightmares. On the other hand, it's a lot of laughs to see the audience squirming all over each other in semiamused horror. Samui's snake farm is at the far southwest corner of the island on 4170 Road (✆ **7742-3247**), with daily shows at 11am and 2pm; tickets cost 250B (US$5.70).

The spa scene on Ko Samui has really skyrocketed in recent years. Resorts like **The Spa Resort** *✿*, between Chaweng and Lamai Beaches (© 7723-0855); **Health Oasis Resort,** at Bang Po Beach near Mae Nam (© 7742-0124); and **Axolotl Village,** at Bang Po Beach near Mae Nam (© 7742-0017), offer full-service health and beauty treatments, including yoga, meditation, chi kung, international styles of massage, herbal steam treatments, facials, and body wraps, plus lectures on health. All feature health cuisine in their restaurants and long- and short-term health programs for guests. I also recommend these places for people who just want to pop in for a day of relaxation. If it happens to be bad weather, can you think of a better way to get out of the rain and still enjoy Samui? I've recommended The Spa Resort in the "Where to Stay" section, above, mainly because its location is both secluded and near the conveniences of Chaweng and Lamai Beaches. Understand, however, that the health resorts on Ko Samui are not Chiva Som or Banyan Tree—they're more New Age than Guerlain (no doubt the effect of Ko Samui's development as an alternative vacation island). Health Oasis Resort, famous for its Healing Child Center, is pretty hard core, offering fasting and colonic programs, a holistic education program (for parents as well), and vortex destiny astrology (vortex destiny astrology?). Axolotl Village does all of that, plus tarot readings and lessons, past-life analysis, aura readings, and more.

Also recommended, the brand-new **Bodycare Spa at Poppies** *✿* in Chaweng Beach (© 7742-2419) features natural Thai skin-care products (which I highly recommend) from **The Hideaway Spa** in Phuket, and **Tamarind Springs** in Lamai (© 7742-4436) has a lovely hillside location, providing comforting surroundings for massage, even acupuncture.

Samui is not exactly a hotbed of **shopping.** There's very little in terms of local crafts production on the island—most everything is imported from the mainland. Do yourself a favor by saving your money for Bangkok or Chiang Mai, where you'll find a better selection of the same items for a better price. One thing I can suggest is to take a peek at local **pearls** from oysters that thrive in this area. For those seriously interested in learning about pearl cultivation and jewelry crafting, I recommend a trip offshore to the Naga Pearl Shop. The day trip includes a 20-minute boat ride to and from the island shop, the grand tour of the operation, lunch, and shopping at the showroom. That's all for only 1,300B (US$30) per person—one of the few places in the world that actually charges *you* to shop in its store! Call © 7742-3272 to make a booking.

KO SAMUI AFTER DARK

Some of the nights that you're on Samui, your dinner will be interrupted by a roaming pickup truck with a crackling PA system blaring incomprehensible Thai. They're advertising local Thai boxing bouts. Grab one of the flyers for times and locations, which vary. It's iffy whether the TAT office can tell you about upcoming bouts, but you can try.

Some resort restaurants stage **dinner theater** with Thai performances, but the schedules change regularly. Check with the **Santiburi Dusit Resort** (© 7742-5031), which does wonderful poolside theme nights, and the food is always excellent. Ask about the Floating Market parties, where people float various Thai foods around on wooden canoes in the pool right up to your table. Another venue known for throwing fine dinner performances is the **Imperial Samui Hotel** (© 7742-2020). With back-to-back shows featuring dances, Thai boxing, sword fighting, fruit and vegetable carving, and palm reading, they really put on a show.

Talk about shows, of course Ko Samui has a drag queen review. **Christy's Cabaret** (cellular ✆ **1676-2181**), on the north end of Chaweng, puts on a hilarious show that's free of charge. Come well before the show starts at 11pm to get a better seat, and be prepared to make up for that free admission with cocktail prices. This is also the island's preparty meeting place, so if you want to know where the action is, start off here.

For **bars and discos,** Chaweng is the place to be. A mainstream kind of fun seems to always be happening at **The Reggae Pub** (indicated on just about every island map—back from the main road around the central beach area). A huge thatch mansion, the stage thumps with some funky international acts, the dance floor jumps (even during low season, they do a booming business) and the upstairs pool tables are good for sporting around. Just outside is a collection of open-air bars, also found along Chaweng's beach road. During my last visit, flyers for various all-night raves were being passed around; these happen mostly on the beaches north of Chaweng. For something mellow and moody, walk to the beach. All along Chaweng's sandy strip, you'll find beach lounges with ambient music and lighting—lie on big straw mats and pillows and gaze at the stars while you enjoy your cocktails.

Over at Lamai Beach, the open-air bars get a little sleazier, with less originality but more bar girls. The big nightclub in Lamai is supposed to be Bauhaus (located in the center of the beach road), but when I was there it was empty save a few in to watch the satellite football match.

If it happens to be Sunday afternoon, truck on over to **The Secret Garden Pub** ★★, on Big Buddha Beach (✆ **7724-5253**), for live music and a barbecue on the beach. Many a famous performer has jumped up on the stage here (including a certain guitarist for a certain Grateful Dead). Call ahead of time, and they can book you on one of the free shuttles (one at 3pm and another at 4pm). There have been times where the pub has hosted thousands. That's not exactly "secret," but it's highly recommended.

10 Phuket

No other Thai destination has changed so rapidly as Phuket, yet it remains Thailand's finest resort destination. At its best, this island is almost idyllic. It has long sandy beaches and picturesque coves, warm tropical waters of the Andaman Sea, excellent snorkeling and scuba diving, ideal windsurfing conditions, inland rain forest and mountains, and the best seafood in all of Thailand. Over the past 20 years, Phuket's resort community has developed excellent properties—both exotic and luxurious—that can compete with the best of Bali. Today, as groups pour in from Singapore, Hong Kong, Germany, and Italy, low-key travelers head for nearby Ko Pi Pi, or Ko Samui on the Gulf.

The peak season on Phuket extends from November to April, with the late-December/early-January holiday season demanding the highest rates. The monsoon winds arrive in May and last through October. During the monsoon season, rains come often (with sunny patches in between storms) and the seas swell and become too rough for sea activities. Fewer people come to Phuket during this time, so resorts offer discounts of up to 50% of the peak period rate.

This section is largely dedicated to activities on the western coast of the island, mainly the Karon and Patong beaches where most people spend their time. However, many fine resorts are outside of these areas, so they're included as well.

VISITOR INFORMATION

The **Tourism Authority of Thailand** is on the ball in Phuket. Unfortunately, you have to travel all the way into Phuket Town to see it, at 73–75 Phuket Rd. (© **7621-2213**). It is well worth the trip, with all sorts of information, and the people behind the counter know everything there is to know about travel in the area.

Some great local publications to pick up include the free *Phuket Food-Shopping-Entertainment,* packed with dining suggestions and ads for many of the island's activities. Another free publication, *What's on South,* is not as comprehensive but has some information on Ko Phi Phi and Krabi. The bimonthly ultraglossy *Greater Phuket Magazine* provides articles and photo essays about the island and its people. Pick it up at bookstores in Phuket and Bangkok for 80B (US$1.80).

Maps are abundant, and most of them are free. For getting around Phuket Town, I like the detail, accuracy, and clarity of the free map given out by the TAT, but for driving around the island, the *Periplus Editions Map of Phuket* (at bookstores) is easier to use. The Periplus map also features good layouts of the major beaches.

GETTING THERE

BY PLANE   Thai Airways (© **2525-2084** for domestic reservations in Bangkok) flies more than 14 times daily from Bangkok from 7am to 9:30pm (trip time: 1 hr. 20 min.); and a daily flight from Hat Yai (trip time: 45 min.). In Hat Yai, its office is at 190/6 Niphat Uthit Rd. (© **7423-3433**). Thai Airways' office in Phuket is at 78 Ranong Rd. (© **7621-1195** domestic, 7621-2499 international). Also keep in mind that Thai Airways connects Phuket with international flights to and from Frankfurt, Hong Kong, Penang, Perth, Singapore, and Tokyo.

Bangkok Airways (© **2229-3434** in Bangkok, 7724-5601 on Ko Samui) connects Phuket with Ko Samui at least two times daily. The Bangkok Airways office in Phuket is at 158/2–3 Yaowarat Rd., Phuket Town (© **7622-5033,** or 7632-7114 at Phuket Airport).

Air Andaman (© **2251-4905** in Bangkok; 7635-1374 on Phuket), a relative newcomer on the scene, is targeting the tourism market with routes to various vacation destinations in the south, including Krabi, Surat Thani, Chumpon, and Nakhon Si Thammarat, with plans to expand routes. The small planes are usually booked up by travel agents and tour operators, so book early. They also accept charter bookings.

The attractive, modern **Phuket International Airport** (© **7732-7230** information) is located in the north of the island, about a 40-minutes drive from town or from Patong Beach. There are banks, money-changing facilities, car-rental agents (see "Getting Around," below), and a post office. The Phuket Tourist Business Association booth can help you make hotel arrangements if you haven't booked a room.

Many resorts will pick you up at the airport upon request for a fee, usually steep. The airport limousine counter, operated by **Tour Royale** (© **7634-1214**), offers many options for getting to your hotel from the airport. The cheapest way is the minibus, which operates every hour on the hour from 9am to 11pm daily. Stopping between Patong, Kata, Karon, and Phuket Town, prices run from 80B to 180B (US$1.80–US$4.10), depending on how far you're going. Taxi service from the airport, also arranged at the limousine counter, will cost from between 360B (US$8.20) to Phuket Town and 540B (US$12) to Kata beach. The VIP Volvo transfer will set you back between 480B and 750B (US$11–US$17).

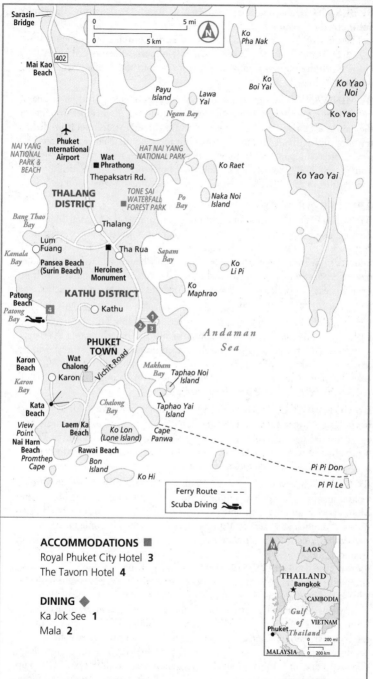

Sarasin Bridge

Mai Kao Beach

402

Ko Pha Nak

Ko Boi Yai

Ko Yao Noi

Ko Yao

Payu Island

Lawa Yai

Ngam Bay

Phuket International Airport

NAI YANG NATIONAL PARK & BEACH

Wat Phrathong

Thepaksatri Rd.

HAT NAI YANG NATIONAL PARK

Ko Raet

Ko Yao Yai

THALANG DISTRICT

TONE SAI WATERFALL FOREST PARK

Po Bay

Naka Noi Island

Bang Thao Bay

Thalang

Lum Fuang

Kamala Bay

Tha Rua

Sapam Bay

Pansea Beach (Surin Beach)

Heroines Monument

Ko Li Pi

Patong Beach

Patong Bay

KATHU DISTRICT

Kathu

Ko Maphrao

Andaman Sea

Karon Beach

Wat Chalong

PHUKET TOWN

Vichit Road

Makham Bay

Taphao Noi Island

Karon Bay

Karon

Kata Beach

Chalong Bay

Taphao Yai Island

View Point

Laem Ka Beach

Ko Lon (Lone Island)

Cape Panwa

Nai Harn Beach

Promthep Cape

Rawai Beach

Bon Island

Ko Hi

Pi Pi Don

Pi Pi Le

Ferry Route – – – –
Scuba Diving

ACCOMMODATIONS
Royal Phuket City Hotel **3**
The Tavorn Hotel **4**

DINING
Ka Jok See **1**
Mala **2**

LAOS

THAILAND
Bangkok

CAMBODIA

Gulf of Thailand

VIETNAM

Phuket

MALAYSIA

BY BUS   Three air-conditioned 24-seat VIP buses leave daily from **Bangkok's Southern Bus Terminal** (© **2435-1199**).

The intercity bus terminal is at the **City Park Complex** on Phangnga Road (© **7621-1480**), east of Phuket Town just opposite the Royal Phuket City Hotel. For information on how to get from here to the beaches, see "Getting Around," below.

BY MINIVAN   Minivans to and from Surat Thani, Krabi, Nakhon Si Thammarat, Ranong, and other southern cities leave on regular schedules throughout the day. In each city, it's best to book minivans through your hotel front desk, a travel agent, or the TAT office since minivan operators change locations and service often, plus the operators who man the phones never speak English. In Phuket, call © **7728-6131** for booking and hotel pickup—tickets will be from about 100B to 250B (US$2.30–US$5.70), depending on where you go.

GETTING AROUND

BY SONGTAO   The local bus terminal is in front of the Central Market on Ranong Road in Phuket Town. Fares to the most popular beaches range from 20B to 30B (US45¢–US70¢). Buses are typically scheduled to operate every 30 minutes from 7am to 6pm, but they usually run whenever there is a full load of passengers or produce. As mentioned above, you can take these buses only from town to beach or back again. They do not operate routes between beaches.

BY TUK-TUK   Within Phuket Town, tuk-tuks cost about 20B to 40B (US45¢–US90¢) for local trips, more or less, depending on your destination. They also wander up and down the beach areas for short trips along the strip.

Tuk-tuks are the only way to travel between beaches, and these guys will try to eke every baht out of you. Here's your rule of thumb: 300B (US$6.80) from town to the airport, 120B (US$2.75) from town to Patong Beach, and 120B (US$2.75) from Patong Beach to Karon Beach.

BY MOTORCYCLE TAXI   Drivers will try to talk you into a ride as you pass by, in both Phuket Town and Patong Beaches. As in other towns, drivers here are identified by their colored vests. For a quick trip within town or Patong beach, they're recommended, but don't let them talk you into a trip between beaches; I really doubt that it's safe enough.

BY CAR   When you self-drive on Phuket, you have to be especially careful. Coastal and inland roads have serious hills and curves that appear out of nowhere. Motorcycles swarm like bees, and Thai drivers will pass anything on a blind curve without so much as a care. Your defensive driving skills will come in handy.

Avis has a counter at **Phuket Airport** (© **7653-1243**). Plan on spending around 1,500B to 1,800B (US$34–US$41) per day for a Suzuki Caribian 4WD sport vehicle. **Budget** (© **7620-5398**) also has an airport location. They're a bit cheaper, at 1,375B (US$31) per day. Both companies offer sedans, and both also have sound insurance coverage available, which is highly recommended.

Inexpensive Suzuki Caribians can be rented from almost all travel agents and from hotels at the beach areas. Prices start at 1,000B (US$23) per day. Lining the beach at Patong, there are also oodles of Caribian cars for rent from independent agents who hang around under umbrellas. They'll charge 900B (US$20) a day for Caribians (which is negotiable), and 1,500B (US$34) and up for open-top Jeeps and souped-up four-wheel-drive off-road vehicles. While many resorts will rent you a car, I've found that the independent dealers have the same product for less money. Don't count on the insurance policy.

BY MOTORCYCLE Also along the Patong strip, the same car-rental people will provide you with a bike for cheap. A 100cc Honda scooter goes for 200B (US$4.55) per day, while a 400cc Honda CBR or a 600cc Honda Shadow chopper will set you back at least 500B (US$12) per day. If you plan to rent for longer, make sure to negotiate for a discount rate. Wear your helmet, keep to the left, and let cars pass. For God's sake, watch it out there—they're animals. I shudder to think of all the horror stories I've heard about vacation motorcycle accidents.

FAST FACTS: Phuket

American Express The American Express representative in Phuket is Sea Tours (© **7621-8417**), 95/4 Phuket Rd., Phuket Town, 1 block south of the TAT.

Banks Banks are located in Phuket Town, with many larger branches on Ranong and Rasada roads. There are bank offices at the airport as well as branches of major Thai banks at Kata, Karon, and Patong beaches. See each section for more complete information. **Money-changers** are also around in major shopping areas on each beach, and you can always change money at your resort; however, you'll get the best rates at banks.

Bookstores Near the TAT office in Phuket Town, look for **The Books** at 53–55 Phuket Rd. (© **7622-4362**). There's also an outlet at Patong at 198/2 Rat-U-Thit Rd. (© **7634-2980**).

Post Office The General Post Office in Phuket Town (© **7621-1020**) is at the corner of Thalang and Montri rds.

Hospitals The Bangkok Phuket Hospital, at 2/1 Hongyok-Uthit Rd. (off Yaowarat Rd. in Phuket Town; © **7625-4421**), has English-speaking staff and high-quality facilities, plus it claims to accept some international medical insurance. It also has clinics at Patong (Soi Patong Beach Hotel; © **7634-4699**), and Laguna Canal Village (Laguna Phuket; © **7632-5442**).

Internet Internet service is fairly easy to find on the island. In Phuket Town, head for Internet KSC at the ECC Building, 73/4 Rasada Rd., across from the Thavorn Hotel (© **7621-4496**).

Police The emergency number for the **Tourist Police** is fast-dial four digits, © **1699**. For **Marine Police**, call © **7621-4368**.

PHUKET TOWN

Phuket Town is not the first choice for vacationers who come to Phuket for beaches and sunshine. The island's capital city, the small town does have some good high-class facilities and more moderately priced ones as well. However, most will stay in town only if they're overnighting before the early boat to surrounding islands.

WHERE TO STAY
Expensive

Royal Phuket City Hotel ★ For a small town like Phuket, this hotel is surprisingly cosmopolitan. A true city hotel, Royal Phuket's facilities include possibly the largest and most modern fitness center facility on the island, an excellent spa and massage center, an outdoor swimming pool, and an executive business center good enough for even Bangkok itself. Above the cavernous marble lobby, guest rooms are smart—in contemporary hues and style, with amenities that simplify your stay. Don't expect too much from the views.

Pickles Restaurant serves international cuisine, with monthly regional features. At the time of this writing, it highlighted the foods of Malaysia. At the Chinatown Restaurant, you can dine in one of the poshest establishments in town.

154 Phang-Nga Rd., Amphur Muang, Phuket 83000 (located to the E of Phuket Town, across from the intercity bus terminal). © 7623-3333. Fax 7623-3335. www.royalphuketcity.com. 251 units. 3,500B–4,200B (US$80–US$95) double; from 6,000B (US$136) suite. AE, DC, MC, V. Amenities: 2 restaurants (international, Chinese); lobby lounge; outdoor pool; golf course nearby; fitness center w/sauna, steam, massage, and spa; tour desk; limousine service; business center; 24-hr. room service; babysitting; same-day laundry service/dry cleaning; nonsmoking rooms; executive-level rooms. In room: A/C, TV w/satellite programming, dataport, minibar, hair dryer, safe.

Moderate

The Tavorn Hotel   I'm ambivalent about this budget choice. The lobby of this unique and informal hotel doubles as a charming museum exhibit dedicated to the history of the island. Old photos and antiques create a fascinating period ambience to the dark wood-paneled entry hall and surrounding chambers. Too bad the look doesn't spill over into the rooms. Still, they're quite cheap, and in not too bad condition, although some renovations here and there would help. Besides, for in-town accommodations, you can't find a better location—close to the TAT office, banks, shopping, and dining.

74 Rasada Rd., Amphur Muang, Phuket 83000 (Rasada Rd. is in the center of Phuket Town). © 7621-1333. Fax 7621-5559. 200 units. 550B (US$12) double. MC, V. Amenities: Coffee shop; laundry service. In room: A/C, TV.

WHERE TO DINE

Ka Jok See ⭐⭐⭐ *Finds* THAI   This is one of my favorite restaurants in Thailand. I love the ambience—a small shop in town with a tiled floor and wood-beamed ceiling, antiques lit by candlelight, and classic jazz wafting throughout. Ka Jok See is smart and chic, cozy, and intimate. They prepare fabulous dishes like the house specialty, goong-saroong—vermicelli-wrapped shrimp fried quick and light and served with a velvety mustard dipping sauce. I also sampled smoky grilled eggplant and shrimp salad, and the stir-fried beef curry, which were both heavenly. This place is well worth a venture from the beach for an evening. Look for the shop hidden behind all the plants—they have no sign.

26 Takuapa Rd., Phuket Town (a short walk from Rasada Rd.). © 7621-7903. Reservations recommended for weekends. Main courses 150B–380B (US$3.40–US$8.65). No credit cards. Tues–Sun 6pm–midnight (kitchen closes around 11pm). Closed Mon.

Mala THAI/INTERNATIONAL   Mala serves inexpensive breakfast, lunch, and dinner in a small open-air coffee shop setting. Spacious and cooled by overhead fans, the charming wood and tile tables look out at the street scene past a potted terrace garden. With a full selection of Thai curries, Thai and Chinese dishes, plus some Western selections, you can't go wrong. Like many restaurants in town, Mala serves prawns wrapped with vermicelli and deep fried, only theirs is served with a more traditional sweet chili sauce. I also recommend the mee-sua, a noodle soup with pork that is a local specialty.

5/73 Mae Luan Rd. (located between Satun and Yaowarat rds.). © 7621-4201. Reservations not necessary. Main courses 30B–150B (US70¢–US$3.40). No credit cards. Daily 7am–9pm.

KATA & KARON

These are among the island's most attractive beaches, about 20km (12 miles) southwest of Phuket Town and several miles north of Nai Harn. By day, the beaches are beginning to resemble Saint-Tropez, with rows of rented beach chairs and umbrellas lining the fine white san, at times packed and even hectic in the high season. The two beaches are separated by a rocky promontory but are quite similar, in both ambience and development.

In Karon, there's a small post office on the north end of Karon Beach Road between My Friendship Hotel and South Sea Resort. At Karon, try the **Karon Beach Internet Center,** at 36/31 Patak Rd. (✆ **7628-6086**); at Kata, find the **Surfing Eagle,** 98/15 Patak Rd. (✆ **7633-3105**), opposite the Kata Post Office, which, for the record, is also on Patak Road.

WHERE TO STAY
Expensive

Kata Beach Resort ✪   As soon as you pull up to the soaring granite-and-marble lobby, you'll realize that you've arrived at the most formal facility on the Kata coast. This place works hard to attract conference groups, with full facilities for meetings and large groups. Individual leisure travelers will feel at home as well, especially with a staff this friendly. I prefer the beach-view rooms in the central building—it's the higher-priced choice, of course, but the view really is lovely. All rooms have balconies and are attractively decorated.

5/2 Patak Rd., Kata Beach, Phuket 83100 (in the Kata Beach strip). ✆ 7633-0530, or 2939-4062 in Bangkok. Fax 7633-0128. 200 units. 5,129B–5,650B (US$117–US$128) double; from 6,000B (US$136) suite. AE, DC, MC, V. **Amenities:** 3 restaurants (international, Asian, Italian); outdoor pool; golf course nearby; fitness center w/sauna and massage; watersports; children's center; concierge; tour desk; limousine service; business center; shopping arcade; salon; limited room service; babysitting; same-day laundry service/dry cleaning. In room: A/C, TV w/satellite programming, minibar, hair dryer, safe.

Kata Thani Hotel ✪   The Kata Thani is the dominant structure on lovely Kata Noi Beach and is a haven of quiet luxury. The top-end deluxe rooms are especially attractive, but even the standard ones are a good value, especially those with a sea view. A wide, well-groomed lawn surrounds sizable pools and leads to the graceful curve of the pristine cove. There is a nightly poolside buffet. Its best feature is that it's right up on the beach, meaning you don't have to cross the street to a messy beach shared with every other Joe. And while it's completely self-contained in terms of facilities and activities, you won't feel like you're in Phuket Siberia.

3/24 Patak Rd., Kata Noi Beach, Phuket 83100 (N end of Kata Noi Beach). ✆ 7633-0124. Fax 7633-0426. www.katathani.com. 530 units. 6,400B–7,200B (US$145–US$164) double; from 7,700B (US$175) suite. AE, DC, MC, V. **Amenities:** 5 restaurants (Italian, seafood/steak, Asian, international, theme buffet); lounge and library; 4 outdoor pools; golf course nearby; 2 outdoor lighted tennis courts; fitness center; aromatherapy spa; Jacuzzi; sauna; watersports equipment/scuba diving; game room; tour desk; car-rental desk; limousine service; salon; 24-hr. room service; massage; babysitting; same-day laundry service/dry cleaning. In room: A/C, TV w/satellite programming, minibar, coffee/tea-making facilities, hair dryer, safe.

Mom Tri's Boathouse & Villa Resort ✪✪   A.k.a. "The Boathouse," with its own beach at the quieter south end of Kata Beach, this small inn is a favorite pick. More inn than resort, there's a real home-style feeling here, with Thai touches on the side. All the comfortable, attractive rooms face the sea, each with a terrace overlooking the huge Jacuzzi pool in the courtyard. Nothing about the hotel calls attention to itself; it's the well-trained, friendly, attentive staff that makes it very special. The Boathouse high-style Thai and Continental restaurant serves some of the best food on the island and boasts without argument *the best* wine cellar in Thailand with 420 international labels. They also offer discount theme packages: Health Holidays, including massage and herbal steam treatments, and a Thai Cooking Class weekend getaway that is incredibly popular.

2/2 Patak Rd., Kata Beach, Phuket 83100. ℂ 7633-0557. Fax 7633-0561. 36 units. 8,200B (US$186) double; from 16,500B (US$375) suite. AE, DC, MC, V. **Amenities:** 3 restaurants (Thai, international, grill); lounge and library; outdoor pool; golf course nearby; fitness center; Jacuzzi; limousine service; 24-hr. room service; massage; babysitting; same-day laundry service/dry cleaning. *In room:* A/C, TV w/satellite programming, minibar, coffee/tea-making facilities, hair dryer, safe.

Phuket Arcadia Hotel   This modern, full-facility resort is a massive presence on Karon Beach and is quite pleasant, if a bit expensive for a not-so-great beach area. Rooms are attractive but rather bland, with standard bathroom facilities, all overlooking the beach and ocean. If you're traveling with children, the studio double, with more space, will fit a couple of extra beds with space left over. The landscaping is a little stark, but the elevated pool and sun deck offer wonderful views of the bay.

78/2 Patak Rd., Karon Beach, Phuket 83100 (Middle of Karon Beach Rd.) ℂ 7639-6433. Fax 7639-6136. www.phuketarcadia.com. 475 units. 5,530B (US$145) double; 6,290B (US$165) studio double. AE, DC, MC, V. **Amenities:** 5 restaurants (Thai, Chinese, Japanese, Italian, international); lounge and karaoke; large outdoor pool; golf course nearby; putting green on the premises; outdoor lighted tennis courts; fitness center w/Jacuzzi, sauna, steam, and massage; game room; tour desk; limousine service; salon; 24-hr. room service; babysitting; same-day laundry service/dry cleaning. *In room:* A/C, TV w/satellite programming, minibar, coffee/tea-making facilities, safe.

Phuket Club Mediterranee 🏀 *Kids*   Though it keeps up with renovations, the Club Med still lacks luxury. Quarters contain two tiny bedrooms, divided by a rattan wall, with a shared bathroom and foyer; in other words, unless you pay a 20% premium, you'll share a room.

Set in its own sealed compound, Club Med commands an enormous and enviable piece of beachfront real estate. In typical Club Med fashion, the Kata Beach facility is so completely equipped that contact with the outside world is hardly required. A full range of watersports is available, and if you do feel compelled to wander off, various excursions around the island are offered. Special kudos for the food, including much locally caught Phuket seafood.

Among the many positive aspects of staying at this Club Med is its provision for children. There is the Mini-Club (daily 9am–9:30pm), which involves play groups, special classes for craft making, supervised activities, and babysitting (for kids under 4), all performed by people who are well versed in child care. Many vacationing parents leave their kids in the Mini-Club in the morning, eat lunch with them in the afternoon, and pick them up at the end of the day, leaving them to enjoy their vacation relatively unburdened by family demands. For teenagers, there's an equivalent service. While many in-house sports activities are included in the price, be aware that things like massage, outside tours, alcohol, laundry service, and whatnot are all extra—make sure you know what all is included when you book.

7/3 Patak Rd., Kata Beach, Phuket 83000 (N end of Kata Beach). ℂ 7633-0455 or 2253-0108 in Bangkok. Fax 7633-0461 or 2253-9778 in Bangkok. www.clubmed.com. (The resort does not accept direct reservations.) 308 units. 4,300B (US$98) per adult; 2,550B (US$58) per child. AE, DC, MC, V. **Amenities:** 2 restaurants (international buffet); nightclub w/live music and karaoke; outdoor pool; golf course nearby (golf instruction); tennis courts w/instruction; squash courts; fitness center w/trainers; watersports equipment; children's programs; game room; tour desk; limousine service; salon; 24-hr. room service; massage; babysitting; same-day laundry service/dry cleaning; basketball; volleyball. *In room:* A/C, minibar, hair dryer, safe.

Thavorn Palm Beach Hotel 🏀   Located near the beach, this large resort covers a lot of territory, providing plenty of facilities. Most rooms have fine views overlooking the Karon dunes. The decor is minimal but pleasant, with tiled floors, rattan furnishings, and small balconies. Newly renovated and upgraded Bird of Paradise rooms, costing almost as much as a suite, are decorated in Thai style featuring teak woodcarvings and local textiles—these rooms also come with extra services. The beach is lovely, but it's across the busy beach road, and the roar of automobile traffic can sometimes drown out the sound of the surf.

128/10 Moo 3, Karon Beach, Phuket 83110 (in mid–Karon Beach area). © 7639-6091. Fax 7639-6555. www.thavornpalmbeach.com. 210 units. 10,560B (US$240) double; from 23,760B (US$540) suite. AE, DC, MC, V. **Amenities:** 5 restaurants (seafood, grill, Italian, Thai, international); lounge; 4 outdoor pools; golf course nearby; outdoor lighted tennis courts; fitness center; watersports equipment; game room; concierge; tour desk; car-rental desk; limousine service; 24-hr. room service; massage; babysitting; same-day laundry service/dry cleaning. In room: A/C, TV w/satellite programming, minibar, hair dryer.

Moderate

Marina Phuket ⭐ These simple cottages, tucked in the jungle above the cusp of Kata and Karon beaches, are slightly more comfortable than the older thatch bungalows nearby. Rates vary according to the view, but all have a jungle bungalow charm, connected by walkways past the lush greenery that creeps up the hillside. Guest rooms are decorated in lovely and exotic Thai style, some without air-conditioning. All are a hike down to the rocky shore; no, the beach here isn't the best, but the rocky shore makes for superb snorkeling. The Marina Phuket is home to **Marina Divers** (© **7638-1625**), a PADI International Diving School, which conducts classes, rents equipment, and leads expeditions around the island reefs; if you're a diver, Marina is a good pick for everything you need in-house. The pleasant restaurant cottage serves good, inexpensive Thai food.

120 Patak Rd., Kata Karon Beach, Phuket 83000 (on bluff at S end of Karon Beach Rd.). © 7633-0625. Fax 7633-0999. www.marinaphuket.com. 104 units. 4,400B–7,040B (US$100–US$160) double. MC, V. **Amenities:** Restaurant (international, seafood); pool; dive center; limited room service; same-day laundry service. In room: A/C, TV w/satellite programming, minibar, no phone.

Inexpensive

Golden Sand Inn Budget accommodations are disappearing on this part of the island. After looking hard and finding little, this is one of a couple of places that's fine to recommend. It's clean, reasonably quiet, and well maintained, and the management is friendly. Rooms are large and motel-like, but you can't see much of the nearby beach. There's a pleasant cafe-style coffee shop, a swimming pool, safes in the rooms, and VDO (movies on compact discs, *not* to be confused with the more sophisticated DVD). Rooms are 50% less in the low season.

Karon Beach, Phuket 83100 (across highway from N end of beach above traffic circle). © 7639-6493. Fax 7639-6117. 125 units. 2,200B (US$50) double. AE, DC, MC, V. **Amenities:** Restaurant (local, international); pool; laundry service. In room: A/C, TV, minibar, no phone.

Katanoi Bay Inn Here's a no-muss, no-fuss pick for Phuket. This budget accommodation provides you with a comfortable, clean, and spacious room without paying out the nose for resort facilities that you might or might not use. Fresh and bright rooms feature balconies and good firm beds. Yes, facilities are limited, but the beach, Phuket's main attraction, is only 20m (65½ ft.) away. Katanoi is an especially quiet beach, too—this small place is a bit remote, which for some is a plus.

4/16 Moo 2 Patak Rd., Kata Noi Beach, Phuket 83100 (Kata Noi is S of Kata Beach). © and fax **7633-3308**. katanoibayinn@phuket.com. 28 units. 1,200B (US$27). MC, V. **Amenities:** Restaurant (international, seafood); tour desk; car-rental desk; massage; same-day laundry service/dry cleaning; Internet center. In room: Fridge, no phone.

Sandy Inn   Those who don't require hot water or a view will find this a good-value choice. It's a 5-minute walk from the beach, near some inexpensive restaurants and a laundry. Rooms are simple, clean, and cool. Staff is very, very friendly, but this place is very, very budget.

102/12 Patak Rd., Karon Beach, Phuket 83100 (near S end of beach, inland on small road S of Thavorn Hotel). ℰ 7634-0275. Fax 7634-1519. 12 units (w/showers, no hot water). 1,000B (US$23) double. No credit cards. **Amenities:** Restaurant (coffee shop); laundry service. *In room:* A/C, minibar, no phone.

WHERE TO DINE

The Boathouse 𝄫𝄫𝄫 THAI/INTERNATIONAL   So legendary is the Thai and Western cuisine at the Boathouse that the inn where it resides offers popular holiday packages for visitors who want to come and take cooking lessons from its chef. Inside the restaurant, a large bar and separate dining area sport nautical touches, while outside huge picture windows, the sun sets on a deep blue sea. Cuisine is nouvelle, combining the best of East and West and the finest ingredients in satisfying portions. If you're in the mood for the works, the Phuket lobster is one of the most expensive dishes on the menu but is worth every baht. The Boathouse also has an excellent selection of international wines—420 labels. Bon appetit.

The Boathouse Inn, 114 Patak Rd., Kata Beach, Phuket 83110 ℰ 7633-0557. Reservations recommended during peak season. Main courses 200B (US$4.70) and up; seafood sold at market price. AE, DC, MC, V. Daily 7:30am–11pm.

The Cliff 𝄫 ASIAN/MEDITERRANEAN   They call it Mediter-Asian cuisine, but it seems really to be more Mediterranean than Asian, with recipes that include bouillabaisse, roast duck's breast, and rack of lamb Provençal. The Asian influences come into play with local ingredients such as rock lobster, tiger prawn, and mango used creatively in many dishes. It's located in the Central Karon Village Resort, between Karon and Patong beaches. Come early for cocktails with the setting sun.

Central Karon Village Resort, 8/21 Moo 1, Karon Beach. ℰ 7628-6300. Reservations recommended. Main courses 280B–590B (US$6.35–US$13). AE, DC, MC, V. Daily 5:30–midnight.

Sunset Restaurant SEAFOOD   While Patak Road, running perpendicular to the main beach road, doesn't really have a view of the sunset, this restaurant is notable for its fine seafood, prepared in both local and Western styles. The lobster thermidor and Western-style steamed fish are fresh and scrumptious, as are the mixed seafood platters. Thai dishes are either spicy or tempered upon request, depending on your preference. Simple tables have neat batik cloths, which is as stylish as the restaurant's decor gets. Nevertheless, it's a favorite spot for foreigners living in Phuket, and one of the best places in this part of the island.

102/6 Patak Rd., Karon Beach. ℰ 7639-6465. Reservations not necessary. Entrees 80B–180B (US$1.80–US$4.10); seafood at market price. AE, DC, MC, V. Daily 8am–11pm.

PATONG

In Patong, the post office is buried under all the touts and hawkers on Thaveewongse Road (the main beach road) in the center of the strip near the Banthai Hotel. My favorite place to frequent is **Pizzadelic,** a combination pizzeria, bar, and Internet cafe at 93/3 Taveewongse Rd. in Patong (ℰ 7634-1545). They have fairly reliable service, plus you can have a beer while you check your e-mail.

WHERE TO STAY
Expensive

Amari Coral Beach Resort ⭐⭐   The Coral Beach stands on the rocks high above Patong, at the southern tip well away from the din of Patong's congested strip, but close enough to enjoy the mayhem. While the beachfront is lacking—the rocks prevent swimming and watersports other than snorkeling—the two swimming pools overlook the huge bay, as do the terrace lobby, resort restaurants, and guest rooms. The rooms have seafoam tones, balconies, and full amenities, so you'll not miss any of the comforts of home.

104 Moo 4, Patong Beach, Phuket 83150 (far S end of Patong Beach). ℂ 7634-0106. Fax 7634-0115. www. amari.com. 200 units. 8,624B–10,120B (US$196–US$230) double; from 13,112B (US$298) suite. AE, DC, MC, V. **Amenities:** 3 restaurants (Italian, international, Thai); lounge; 2 outdoor pools; golf course nearby; 2 outdoor lighted tennis court; fitness room; brand-new spa; dive center; game room; tour desk; car-rental desk; limousine service; salon; 24-hr. room service; massage; babysitting; same-day laundry service/dry cleaning. *In room:* A/C, TV w/satellite programming, minibar, safe.

Diamond Cliff Resort ⭐   Located a 10-minute walk from the center of Patong Beach, the Diamond Cliff is a gleaming, well-maintained, full-facility resort, with rooms done in soothing sea greens and blues and light wood trim. All guest quarters command an ocean view, and the grounds are attractively landscaped (they even have a boardwalk to Patong that winds through the rocky coastline). Our one caveat (other than the high price) is that the Diamond Cliff is for those who enjoy a view but don't require a beach on the premises; they do operate a shuttle to a small private bit of sand across the bay, but for the money, you might want your own bit of sand. However, for facilities they sport quite a selection, with three outdoor pools, a spa, a game room, tennis, and beach club activities.

284 Prabaramee Rd., Patong, Phuket 83150 (far S end, on the road to Kamala Beach). ℂ 7634-0501. Fax 7634-0507. www.diamondcliff.com. 222 units. 7,436B (US$169) double; from 8,976B (US$204) suite. AE, DC, MC, V. **Amenities:** 8 restaurants; lounge; outdoor pool; minigolf plus golf course nearby; outdoor lighted tennis courts; fitness center; dive center; game room; concierge; tour desk; car-rental desk; limousine service; salon; 24-hr. room service; massage; babysitting; same-day laundry service/dry cleaning. *In room:* A/C, TV w/satellite programming, minibar, safe.

Holiday Inn Resort Phuket ⭐⭐ *Kids*   The buildings at this Holiday Inn are modern, concrete blocks; guest rooms are furnished with rattan furniture and have balconies—in terms of decor, this is not the most luxe place. What distinguishes the Holiday Inn is its excellent offerings for traveling families. Not only does it have a children's center with terrific programs, but it's open late 2 nights a week so parents can have an evening out. Even more unique are the special-value Kids Suites and Family Suites, with separate "kids rooms" that have jungle- or pirate-theme decor, TV with video and PlayStation, and stocked toy boxes; some have bunk beds. One of my favorite facilities for families, however, is the self-service launderette so you don't have to pay hotel laundry prices for the millions of play clothes your kids will rip through. It is the *only* hotel I've seen in Thailand that has such a facility.

The Holiday Inn has also added a new wing a couple of years ago, with more sophisticated accommodations, three new pools, and a spa. The Busakorn Wing features Thai-style resort decor, with modern furnishings dressed in elegant Thai touches like local woven tapestries, woodcarvings, and pottery. Suite rooms use a lot of golden teakwood flooring and paneling. It's definitely an upgrade from the old wing of the hotel.

52 Thaweewong Rd., Patong Beach, Phuket 83150 (Patong Beach strip). ℂ 800/HOLIDAY or 7634-0608. Fax 7634-0435. www.phuket.com/holidayinn. 272 units. 5,200B (US$118) double; from 6,800B (US$154) suite.

AE, DC, MC, V. **Amenities:** 3 restaurants (Thai, international, steaks); lounge; 4 outdoor pools; golf course nearby; fitness center w/sauna; spa; children's center and programs; tour desk; car-rental desk; limousine service; business center; 24-hr. room service; massage; babysitting; same-day laundry service/dry cleaning; self-service launderette. *In room:* A/C, TV w/satellite programming, fridge, coffee/tea-making facilities, hair dryer, safe.

Patong Merlin   The Merlin is well maintained and has a particularly attractive center courtyard. All rooms have balconies, some of which overlook the three pretty lagoon-style swimming pools (each with a pool bar) and a nicely manicured garden. The lobby is spacious and airy, with comfortable, clubby rattan furniture. Facilities also include a fitness club, watersports, a game room, a gym, a sauna, and snooker.

99/2 Moo 4, Patong Beach, Phuket 83150 (on Patong strip near S end of town). ✆ **7634-0037.** Fax 7634-0394. http://merlinphuket.com. 386 units. 4,500B (US$102) double; from 8,500B (US$193) suite. AE, DC, MC, V. **Amenities:** 3 restaurants (Thai, Asian, Western); lounge; 3 pools; golf course nearby; outdoor lighted tennis courts; fitness center; watersports equipment; game room; tour desk; limousine service; 24-hr. room service; massage; babysitting; same-day laundry service/dry cleaning. *In room:* A/C, TV w/satellite programming, minibar, safe.

Phuket Cabana Resort 🐾   These Thai island cabins are closely packed but are quiet and have some character: exposed wood beams, dark lacquered bamboo, rattan wall coverings, and stone floors. Though crowded, the beach is just through a nice jungle garden. There's no need to cross the street like all the other resorts on Patong—this is the only property on Patong beach that has direct beachfront access. While facilities are limited compared to other resorts in this category, the unique location makes it worthy of consideration. This is one of Patong's better-value lodgings.

41 Thaweewongse Rd., Patong Beach, Phuket 83150 (middle of beach road). ✆ **7634-0138.** Fax 7634-0178. www.phuket.com/cabana. 81 units. 6,318B (US$143) double; from 9,700B (US$220) suite. AE, DC, MC, V. **Amenities:** 2 restaurants (Thai, international); pool; golf course nearby; watersports equipment; concierge; tour desk; limousine service; limited room service; babysitting; same-day laundry service/dry cleaning; Internet center. *In room:* A/C, TV w/satellite programming, minibar, hair dryer, safe.

Moderate

Finding decent accommodations on Phuket that are truly "budget" is a task. In too many cases, what you get doesn't even closely resemble what you should probably pay. Just because this is Phuket, even the most pathetic place feels it can charge top rates. To be honest, the lower-priced accommodations near the beach are noisier and tawdrier than ever. You're better off looking at the lower-priced accommodations on Kata and Karon Beaches. However, if you must stay on Patong, here are a couple of suggestions.

Andaman Resortel   Of your budget choices, you're hard pressed to find a truly lovely little guesthouse that's quaint and cheap. It just doesn't exist, at least not anywhere near Patong. Budget accommodations here more closely resemble characterless modern blocks. Of these blocks, Andaman Resortel is perhaps your best bet. Located two streets from the beach, the surrounding area is quiet. Room decor is older—a face-lift is definitely in need, but they keep the place clean. The large lobby has a seating area where you can chat up the folks at the travel desk for reservations and tour ideas.

65/21–25 Soi Sansabai, Patong Beach, Phuket 83150 (off Soi Bangla). ✆ **7634-1516.** Fax 7634-1712. 45 units. 1,200B (US$32) double. MC, V. **Amenities:** Restaurant; lounge; pool; golf course nearby; outdoor lighted tennis courts; fitness center w/Jacuzzi, sauna, steam, and massage; spa w/Jacuzzi, sauna, steam, and massage; watersports equipment/rentals; bike scooter rental; children's center or programs; game room; concierge; tour desk; car-rental desk; limousine service; business center; shopping arcade; salon; 24-hr. room service; babysitting; same-day laundry service/dry cleaning; nonsmoking rooms; executive-level rooms. *In room:* A/C, TV w/pay movies and satellite programming, fax, dataport, minibar, fridge, coffee/tea-making facilities, hair dryer, iron, safe, no phone.

Royal Palm Resortel   If you want to be in the center of it all, Royal Palm is a better choice—in the middle of the crazy main thoroughfare, just across the street from the beach. Rooms are not bad, with king beds, closet space, and a bathroom that has a long bathtub. I was surprised to find such an inexpensive place at this location. But I wasn't surprised to hear so much noise outside the window.

66/2 Taweewong Rd., Patong Beach, Phuket 83150 (in the middle of the Patong Beach strip). © 7629-2510. Fax 7629-2512. 43 units. 1,800 (US$40) double. MC, V. **Amenities:** Restaurant (international); small rooftop pool; golf course nearby; limited room service; same-day laundry service/dry cleaning. *In room:* A/C, TV w/satellite programming, minibar.

WHERE TO DINE

Baan Rim Pa ⭐ THAI   In a beautiful Thai-style teak house, Baan Rim Pa has dining in the romantic indoor setting or with a gorgeous view of the bay from outdoor terraces. This is one of the most popular restaurants on the island, for locals who want to entertain as well as for visitors, so be sure to reserve your table early. Thai cuisine features seafood, with a variety of other meat and vegetable dishes, including a rich duck curry and a sweet honey chicken dish. The seafood basket is a fantastic assortment of prawns, mussels, squid, and crab.

Kalim Beach Rd., N end of Patong Beach. © 7634-0789. Reservations necessary. Entrees 250B–1,200B (US$5.70–US$27). AE, DC, MC, V. Daily noon–2:30pm and 6–10pm.

Patong Seafood Restaurant SEAFOOD   Take an evening stroll on the lively Patong Beach strip, and you'll find quite a few open-air seafood restaurants displaying their catches of the day on chipped ice at their entrances. The best choice of them all is the casual Patong Seafood, for the freshest and the best selection of seafood, including several types of local fish, lobster, squid (very tender), prawn, and crab. The menu has a fantastic assortment of preparation styles, with photos of popular Thai noodles and Chinese stir-fry dishes. Service is quick and efficient. The place fills up quickly, so it's best to arrive here early.

Patong Beach Rd., Patong Beach. © 7634-0247. Reservations not accepted. Main courses 80B–250B (US$1.80–US$5); seafood at market price. AE, DC, MC, V. Daily 7am–11pm.

Sala Bua THAI   Dining is breezy at Sala Bua, one of the few restaurants in Patong that enjoys a beachside location. The lunch menu features light Thai dishes, and Western sandwiches and burgers are inexpensive and well prepared. Dinners are expensive, but the southern-Thai-style seafood favorites—local Phuket lobster, huge juicy tiger prawns, and fresh fish steaks in a variety of local preparation styles—are good value. Sala Bua is a far more intimate option than the crowded seafood joints across the street. Under the pavilion, candlelight and local decor make for a nice touch, but to see the beach you must sit on the patio.

In the Phuket Cabana Hotel, 94 Thaweewong Rd., Patong Beach (at the N end of the beach at Phuket Cabana Hotel). © 7634-2100. Reservations recommended for weekends. Entrees 120B–260B (US$2.75–US$6). AE, DC, MC, V. Daily 6:30pm–midnight.

Sea Hag Restaurant ⭐⭐ THAI   The name is far from appealing, but everything else about the place is, making it one of Patong's favorite joints for local residents and travelers. The food is superb: The baked seafood in curry is rich and delicious, and the grilled fish with tamarind sauce is highly recommended. The casual dining atmosphere captures a local style of grace with an easy charm. The staff also is very nice.

78/5 Soi Permong III, Patong Beach. © 7634-1111. Reservations recommended for weekend dinner. Main courses 80B–200B (US$1.80–US$4.55). No credit cards. Daily 11am–2pm and 5pm–midnight.

EXPLORING PHUKET

You can spend a lot of time on Phuket and still not do everything. Thanks to years of resort growth, there are well-developed activities here and literally something for everyone. Upon arrival, you can't help but notice the hundreds of tour operators, each vying for your business. For each activity, I've provided the most reputable firms, those with the best quality of activities, and even some of the more unusual, to help steer you clear of any shoddy operators.

WATER ADVENTURES

Most of your watersports activities are almost exclusively on Patong Beach—centralized for convenience, but restricted to one beach so swimmers can enjoy other beaches without the buzz of a jet ski or power boat. There are no specific offices to organize such activities; just walk to the beach and chat up the guys under the umbrellas, who set up activities from impromptu operations. **Jet skis** are technically illegal but can still be rented out for 30 minutes at 700B (US$16), for better or worse. A 10-minute **parasailing rid**e is 600B (US$14). You'll also find **Hobie Cats** for around 600B (US$14) per hour, as well as **windsurf boards** for 200B (US$4.55) per hour.

For yachting, Phuket can't be rivaled in Southeast Asia. Facilities from recreational boating are better than anywhere else, while Phuket is a **sailing dream** come true, with the crystal blue waters of the Andaman Sea and gorgeous island scenery. A great guide, *Sail Thailand,* accurately documents all of them. It's distributed in the United States, the United Kingdom, and Australia.

Every December, Phuket hosts the increasingly popular **King's Cup Regatta,** in which almost 100 international racing yachts compete. For more information check out www.kingscup.com.

If you don't have your own yacht but still want a taste of the sea, you can charter a bareboat or crewed boat from **Thai Marine Leisure** (c/o Phuket Boat Lagoon, 20/2 Thepkasatri Rd., Tambon Koh Kaew, Phuket 83200; © **7623-9111;** www.thaimarine.com).

For game fishing, talk to **Blue Water Anglers,** deep-sea fishing experts with expertly equipped boats. They'll take you out for marlin, sailfish, swordfish, and tuna, and they also have special night-fishing programs. But be warned that if you're new to the sport, it ain't cheap—a trip will set you back thousands of baht. Stop by at 35/7 Sakadidet Rd., Phuket Town, or call © **7639-1287.** Or, you can check out www.bluewater-anglers.com.

For an interesting water adventure, try a **sea kayak** trip to **Phang-nga Bay National Park,** a 1½-hour drive north of Phuket (3 hr. by boat) off Thailand's mainland. Between 5 million and 10 million years ago, limestone thrust above the water's surface, creating more than 120 small islands. These craggy rock formations (the famous scenery for the James Bond classic *The Man with the Golden Gun*) look like they were taken straight from a Chinese scroll painting. Sea kayaks are perfect for inching your way into the many breathtaking caves and chambers that hide beneath the jagged cliffs. Most companies will drive you to Phang-Nga province, where you'll pick up the kayaks for the water adventure, and then bring you back to Phuket. The company to pioneer the cave trips, **Sea Canoe,** in Phuket Town, 367/4 Yaowarat Rd. (© **7621-2172**), is a very ecofriendly group and the most professional around. The full-day trip is 2,970B (US$67) per person. Be prepared for an entire day of grueling tourist sightseeing here.

For "the real-deal" sea-kayaking in and around Phuket (and throughout the region), contact Dave Williams at **PaddleAsia Co. Ltd.,** P.O. Box 1, Phuket or at their offices at 53/80 Moo 5 Thambon Srisoonthon, Thalang, Phuket 83110 © **76/311-222;** fax 76/313-689; www.paddleasia.com. Informed guides take you out in real sea kayaks (not inflatable) to explore places that the locals don't even know about and where you're likely to witness some rare and exotic wildlife. The folks at PaddleAsia can cater a trip to anyones needs; it's not just for the physically fit and families with young kids are certainly welcome.

For a different view of the gorgeous Phang-Nga Bay, book a trip aboard the *June Bahtra* ☆☆, a restored Chinese sailing junk, to cruise the islands. Full-day trips include lunch and hotel transfers. Adults pay 2,200B (US$50) per person (alcoholic beverages are separate), while children pay 1,500B (US$34) each. Contact East West Siam, 119 Rat-U-Thit 2000 Year Rd., Patong (© **7634-0912**).

In the smaller bays around the island, such as Nai Harn Beach or Relax Bay, you'll come across some lovely snorkeling just close to the shore. For the best coral just off the shoreline, trek up to **Had Nai Yang National Park** ☆☆ for the long reef in clear shallow waters. Most skin divers prefer day trips to outer islands such as the Similan Islands, Ko Phi Phi, or the newest favorite **Raya Island** (pronounced by the Thais as "Laya" Island). The best times to snorkel are from November to April before the monsoon comes and makes the water too choppy. Almost every tour operator arranges group day boating trips with hotel transfers, lunch, and gear—they all book people for groups on the same boats, so services are all the same. The prices are up to 1,000B (US$23) a day per person.

The island's more than 45 scuba operators are testimony to the beautiful attractions that lie deep within the Andaman Sea. Sites at nearby coral walls, caves, and wrecks can be explored in full-day, overnight, or long-term excursions. All operators advertise full PADI courses, Dive Master courses, and 1-day introductory lessons. Let me rave for a moment about **Dive Master's EcoDive 2000** ☆☆☆, which is timely and innovative. A program of special dives planned under the supervision of marine biologists and environmentalists, this unique program takes small groups beyond the standard dive routes to pristine areas, educating divers about sea creatures and ecodiving. Contact Dive Master in Phuket at 75/20 Moo 10, Patak Road, Chalong (© **7628-0330**); or plan your trip in advance through the Bangkok office (© **2259-3195;** fax 2259-3196). Trip prices vary according to program.

Fantasea Divers is the oldest and most reputable firm on Phuket. The main office is at Patong Beach, at 219 Rat-U-Thit Rd. (© **7634-0088;** fax 7634-0309; www.fantasea.net), but there are other branches along Thaveewongse Road (the main beach road) in Patong. Dive packages include live-aboards to the Burmese coast and 4-day PADI certification courses in addition to full-day dives around Phuket.

If you can spare only a day for diving, great day trips to nearby reefs and wrecks are put together by **Sea Bees Diving,** a highly respected firm on the island. Visit them at 1/3 Moo 9, Viset Road, Chalong Bay, or phone/fax © **7638-1765.** On the Web, visit www.sea-bees.com.

TREKKING & OTHER ACTIVITIES

To experience the wild side of Phuket's interior, try a **rainforest trekking journey** through the Khao Phra Thaew National Park. **Phuket Nature Tour** operates an ecofriendly small group trek through 3.5km (2¼ miles) of jungle paths past waterfalls and swimming holes. A typical half-day excursion includes hotel transfers, English-speaking jungle guides, and drinks. Booking is made by calling © 7625-5522.

Then there's **elephant trekking,** a perennial favorite for children, and a great time for adults, too. While it makes sense to think elephant tourism is harmful to these creatures, environmentalists claim the industry is a win/win situation. Elephants can no longer support themselves in the wild in Thailand, and many working elephants have found themselves out of jobs. Victims of starvation and ivory poachers, or working animals on city streets parading for tourists, these beasts are far better off under the expert care of quality tourism firms. **Siam Safari Nature Tours,** winner of numerous tourism awards, coordinates daily treks on elephants, Land Rovers, and river rafts. Their three-in-one Half-Day Eco-Adventure includes 4 hours of elephant treks through jungles to rubber estates, Jeep tours to see local wildlife, and a light river-rafting journey to Chalong Bay. A full-day tour is the three-in-one plus a trek on foot through Khao Pra Taew National Park and a Thai lunch. Siam Safari's office is at 70/1 Chaofa Rd. in Chalong (© **7628-0116;** www.phuket.com/safari).

Island Safari Adventure Company, 77 Moo 6 Chalong (© **7628-0858**), also does the elephant trekking thing, but it has activities for those who can't invest a whole 3 hours for the experience. A half-hour elephant trek is only 600B (US$14) for adults and 400B (US$9.30) for kids. Check out the free elephant shows daily at 8:45am, 9:45am, 10:45am, 2:45pm, 3:45pm, and 4:45pm. The babies are heartbreakingly cute.

Meanwhile, it wouldn't be an Asian resort without golf. The best course on Phuket is the **Banyan Tree Club & Laguna,** 34 Moo 4, Srisoonthorn Rd., at the Laguna Resort Complex on Bang Tao Bay (© **7627-0991;** fax 7632-4351; www.lagunaphuket.com/golf), a par-71 championship course with many water features (greens fees: 2,600B/US$59; guests of Laguna resorts pay 2,210B/US$50). The **Blue Canyon Country Club,** 165 Moo 1, Thepkasattri Road, near the airport (© **7632-7440;** fax 7632-7449. www.bluecanyonclub.com), is a par-72 championship course with natural hazards, trees, and guarded greens (greens fees: from 2,940/US$67, depending on the course you play). An older course, the **Phuket Country Club,** 80/1 Vichitsongkram Rd., west of Phuket Town (© **7632-1038;** fax 7632-1721; www.phuketcountryclub.com), has beautiful greens and fairways, plus a giant lake (greens fees: 2,350B/US$53).

CULTURAL PURSUITS

If you are on Phuket in October, ask the TAT about the **Vegetarian Festival** ✿✿✿. The name is misleading—this is not an animal rights health consciousness carnival, but a Thai Chinese tradition on Phuket that corresponds with the Buddhist lent. For 9 days, not only do devotees refrain from meat consumption, but many also submit to physical self-mutilation through bizarre body-piercing. It began as an act of penance to the spirits to help early inhabitants ward off malaria. It worked, so the festival became tradition. These days the rituals are more for teens to prove themselves than for malaria protection. Early morning processions follow through the streets of Phuket Town, with onlookers clad in white for the occasion. During this time, you can also feast on terrific vegetarian buffets at just about any restaurant.

When you're ready to take in a little culture, the first place to stop is the **Thalang National Museum,** toward the eastern side of the island on Sri Soonthorn in Thalang District, off Highway 402 just past the Heroine's Monument (© **7631-1426;** open daily 9am–4pm; admission 30B/US70¢). The museum has extensive displays on Phuket's indigenous cultures, the history of the Thais on Phuket, and crafts from the southern Thai regions. There's also a fascinating image of the Hindu god Vishnu that was uncovered from forest overgrowth in Phang-Nga in the early 1900s. The image dates from the 9th century, evidence of the presence of Indian merchants long ago and their influence on the Thai people.

Phuket might not be the center of traditional Thai culture like its northern cousins, Bangkok or Chiang Mai, but a few Buddhist temples on the island are quite notable. I highly recommend this little window on Thai culture, especially if Phuket is your only stop in Thailand. The most unique temple is **Wat Pra Tong,** located along Highway 402 in Thalang, just south of the airport. Years ago, a boy fell ill and dropped dead after tying his buffalo to a post sticking out of the ground. It was later discovered that the post was actually the top of a huge Buddha image that was buried under the earth. Numerous attempts to dig out the post failed—during one attempt in 1785, workers were chased off by hornets. Everyone took all this failure to mean that the Buddha image wanted to just stay put, so they covered the "post" with a plaster image of The Buddha's head and shoulders and built a temple around it.

Near **Wat Pra Tong, Wat Pra Nahng Sahng** (also on Hwy. 402, at the traffic light in Thalang) houses three very interesting Buddha images. Made from tin, a local natural resource once considered semiprecious, each image has a smaller Buddha in its belly.

The most famous temple among the Thais is **Wat Chalong.** Chalong was the first resort on Phuket, back when the Thais first started coming to the island for vacations. Nowadays, the discovery of better beaches on the west side of the island has driven most tourists away from this area, but the temple still remains the center of Buddhist worship. While the temple compound itself is pretty standard in terms of modern temples, the place comes to life during Buddhist holy days. See the section "When to Go," earlier in this chapter, for dates and descriptions of religious holidays. The temple is on the Bypass Road, about 8km (5 miles) south of Phuket Town.

Sea Gypsies, considered the indigenous people of Phuket, are fast disappearing from the island and surrounds. Commercial fishing interests and shoreline development continue to threaten their existence, which is primarily subsistence fishing. These people are related to both the **Orang Laut,** sea people of Malaysia, and the Sakai tribes on Thailand's southern peninsula. While many live primarily at sea, there remain two small settlements on Phuket island, one on Ko Sirey east of Phuket Town, and another at Rawai Beach just south of Chalong Bay. The small **fishing villages** are nothing more than simple shacks and longtail boats. It's an enlightening trip to see these people and their disappearing culture. Be prepared for panhandling children.

When just eating Thai cuisine isn't enough, you can learn how to make it yourself at **The Boathouse** ★★. Weekend cooking classes (10am–2pm) with Chef Tummanoon introduce students not only to preparation styles and ingredients, but to Thai culture as well. Two half-day sessions cost 2,200B (US$50) per person. Call The Boathouse at © **7633-0015** or fax 7633-0561.

SHOPPING

Patong Beach is the center of handicraft and souvenir shopping in Phuket. By day and night, a journey through the main streets and small sois is an assault on anyone's shopping senses. Tailors, leather shops, jewelers, and ready-to-wear clothing boutiques occupy storefronts, while vendors line the sidewalks selling

> **Moments The Best Sunset**
>
> There's a small point at the southern tip of the island that everybody will tell you has the best view of the sunset. And they're right. From the cliffs atop Promthep Cape, the view of the sky as it changes colors from deep reds to almost neon yellows can't compete with the best fireworks. The sun usually sets between 6:15 and 6:45pm. Get there early on weekends; the place isn't exactly a secret.

batik clothing, T-shirts, pirated CDs, local arts and handicrafts, northern hill-tribe handicrafts, silver, and souvenir trinkets. You'll also find people standing on corners holding out sarongs, fabrics, and even luggage, in the hopes someone will stop and buy. The shops and vendors stay open until around 10 or 11pm nightly, so it's a fun stroll after dinner. But *be warned:* Heavy tourist traffic has inflated prices in Patong to unbelievable levels (a batik sarong that costs 100B/US$2.30 in Bangkok was quoted as 380B/US$8.65 in Patong), so be prepared to bargain. It helps to know how much these items go for in other parts of the country. But here's my advice: If you are going to other parts of Thailand, do your shopping there. You can find any of these items in Bangkok. As for handicrafts, if something catches your eye, ask where it was made. Many northern hill-tribe crafts are sold here, and if you're headed up to Chiang Mai later in your trip, you'll find the selection there much wider, the quality of handicrafts better, and the prices far more realistic.

For other shopping around the island, it's best to have your own wheels. There are some cute shops in Phuket Town and others on Highway 402 (Thepkrasattri Rd.), the airport access highway. In town, you can find antiques at **Ban Boran Antiques,** 24 Takuapa Rd. (© 7621-2473), and **The Loft,** 36 Thalang Rd. (© 7625-8160). Along Highway 402, Chan's Antiques, 26/3 Thepkrasattri Rd. (© 7623-9344), is also a treat, as is **Thai Style Antique and Décor,** 25/7 Thepkrasattri Rd. (© 7621-5980). They are easily spotted as you drive on the highway.

I like to do my gift shopping at the Phuket Shell Museum. The huge gift shop has high-quality shell products for the home, novelty items and fun shell souvenirs. They also have all varieties of gorgeous perfect seashells for sale, some of them massive. You could only pray to find one of these on the beach. Friends and family love them.

PHUKET AFTER DARK

From the huge billboards and glossy brochures, **Phuket FantaSea** ★★, the newest theme attraction, seems like it could be touristy and tacky. Surprise—it is! But I must confess, I had a fabulous time. A giant theme park, Phuket FantaSea is as slick as Universal Studios. The festival village entrance, lined with more shopping than you can imagine, plus games, entertainment, and snacks, keeps you busy until dinner. The buffet is served in the palatial Golden Kinaree Restaurant, with decor fashioned after the kinaree mythical half-woman, half-bird creatures. Afterward, proceed to the Palace of the Elephants for the show. Frankly, the shopping is expensive and the dinner is nothing to rave about, but the show is incredibly entertaining, very professional and often amazing. Don't fear the hype. Phuket FantaSea is at Kamala Beach, north of Patong, on the coastal road. Call © 7627-1222 for reservations. The park opens at 5:30pm; the buffet begins at 6:30pm and the show starts at 9pm. Tickets for the show are 1,000B (US$22) for adults and 700B (US$15) for children, while dinner is 500B (US$12) for adults and 300B (US$6.80) for children. Hotel transfers are extra.

Phuket also has a resident cabaret troupe at **Simon Cabaret,** 100/6-8 Moo 4, Patong Karon Road (② **7634-2011**). There are shows at 7:30pm and 9pm nightly, costing 750B (US$17) between Patong and Karon beaches. It's a featured spot on every planned tour agenda, so be prepared for busloads. However, I still think the cabaret is a fun and interesting thing to see—many of the tourists who attend are Asians, and the show mainly caters to them, with lip-sync performances that, in turn, make all the Koreans laugh, the Japanese laugh, and the Chinese laugh. It can be a lot of fun. In between the comedy are dance numbers with pretty impressive sets, costumes, and, naturally, transsexuals.

Every night you can catch Thai boxing at **Vegas Thai Boxing** ☆☆ in Patong at the Patong Simon Shopping Arcade on Soi Bangla. Bouts start every night from 7pm and last until 3am. Best of all, admission is free.

Patong nightlife is a wild time. Lit up like Las Vegas, the beach town hops like Saturday every night of the week. Shops and restaurants stay open late, and there's a never-ending choice of bars (both straight and gay), nightclubs, karaoke lounges, snooker halls, massage parlors, go-go bars, and sex shows a la Patpong. Needless to say, Patong has a draw for those interested in sex tourism—most of the bars have hostesses who are not shy.

Patong has a couple of worthwhile discos. The centrally located **Banana Club,** 94 Thaweewong Rd. (② **7634-0301;** 100B/US$2.30 cover charge), has a fun mix of foreigners and locals, with a good DJ spinning dance music and chart hits, and it is almost always packed to the gills. **Mambo Beach Club** (68 Thweewong Rd., Patong Beach; ② **7629-2883;** no cover) is a friendly place with good live music and a clean reputation for singles, couples, and even families for a night out.

SIDE TRIPS FROM PHUKET

Ko Phi Phi, actually a pair of islands—Phi Phi Don and Phi Phi Le—were once the darlings of the backpacker set. Phi Phi Don, the larger of the two, was loved for its fabulous beaches, great snorkeling, and remote location. As dozens of bungalow complexes sprouted along the beaches, development went unchecked, pollution got out of hand, and corals started to fall to pieces. You'll be happy to know that Ko Phi Phi has started cleaning up its act as Thailand has become more aware of its environmental problems. The winter of 1998–1999 saw this small pair of islands making international headlines when Hollywood came to town to shoot *The Beach* based upon the Thailand-based novel by Alex Garland. The film's star, Leonardo DiCaprio, drew all kinds of rubbernecks to these parts, as well as environmental protection groups who, ironically, howled loudly about the negative effects the production might have on the environment here.

Boats to Phi Phi generally leave at 8:30am and take an hour and a half to complete the journey. Companies will arrange for your transfer to the jetty for an extra cost (50B–200B/US$1.16–US$4.65, depending on your hotel's location). During the high season, from November to April, these companies sometimes run an afternoon boat at 2:30pm if there's demand. **Songserm** (② **7622-2570**) has both ferries (250B–350B/US$5.81–US$8.14 per person) and a speedboat (350B/US$8.14). Round-trip, with returns in the afternoon, costs between 450B and 650B (US$10 and US$15). While the boats depart for Phi Phi year-round, you might want to be careful from May through October, when monsoon winds cause them to rock heavily—I've seen more than a few people lose their lunch over the side of the boat. It's not a pretty sight.

Pi Pi Le proves the most popular day trip from Pi Pi Don, and it's a fun excursion. Boats depart from Ton Sai town and take you on a tour that includes stops at the Viking Cave, known for its swallow nests (which fetch up to US$2,000 per kilo and are the key ingredient of bird's nest soup), cave paintings with vessels that look like Viking ships (hence the name of the cavern), inland bays with dramatic rock formations, and small beaches for swimming and snorkeling. Songserm (© 01-229-2480), along the main street in town, will take you on a day trip there, including lunch and snorkel gear, for 350B (US$8.14) per person. *Note:* Some of the Phuket-based day trips include stops at Pi Pi Le.

If you stay overnight on Phi Phi Don, the nicest place is **P.P. Princess Resort,** at 103 Moo 7, Tambon Ao Nang, Amphur Muang, Krabi 81000 (© 7561-2188; fax 7562-0615). There's an office on Phuket 2/39 Montri Rd., in Phuket Town (© 7621-0928; fax 7621-7106). During high season (Nov–Apr), rates are 2,000B to 3,000B (US$47–US$70) for a garden bungalow, 3,250B (US$76) for a beachfront bungalow, and 4,500B (US$105) for a suite bungalow. During low season (May–Oct), rates are 1,500B–2,000B (US$35–US$46) for a garden bungalow, 2,250B (US$52) for a beachfront bungalow, and 3,250B (US$76) for a suite bungalow. These beach bungalows are different from any others I've seen, especially within this moderate price category. While the bungalows and private decks are not huge, smooth stained woods and huge glass windows bring the outside indoors. You can't help but feel surrounded by nature. The garden and beachside bungalows are identical; only the location changes with the price. Just next door is Sea Fun, where you can arrange all your water activities.

The nine islands that form the Similan archipelago are so pristine that they have been cited by diving authorities as among the best in the world for undersea exploration. The beaches that encircle all nine islands are fine, white sand bordered by lush forests that lead to rocky interiors. Snorkeling is superb. The only development is on Ko Muang (also known as Ko 4), which has a park's office and a few very basic bungalows.

The Similan archipelago is 80km (50 miles) northwest of Phuket. Excursion boats take both day-trippers (it's a long way but is worth it) and campers to Similan daily for about 1,700B (US$39), including food and snorkel equipment. **Seatran Travel** (© 7621-1809) has a boat that departs every morning at 8am and can provide hotel transfers. Note that this trip is very much affected by weather conditions (for both travel and diving), so plan to visit from November to May (Feb and Mar are the best months), when the western monsoons are at their quietest. Under no circumstances should you fail to bring sunscreen with the highest possible rating; it's likely that the sun will be as hot and bright as you've ever encountered, and you can burn in as little as 10 minutes on the beach!

11 An Introduction to Northern Thailand

The southern regions of Thailand might be a vacation paradise of beaches and blue waters, but when many Thais nationals think of a holiday, they head for the northern hills, where the air is cooler and the atmosphere is more culturally stimulating. The historic cities of **Chiang Mai, Chiang Rai,** and the small but interesting **Golden Triangle** (Chiang Saen), a former cowboy town for the opium trade, are a welcome change for visitors who want to experience Thailand's beauty beyond the beaches.

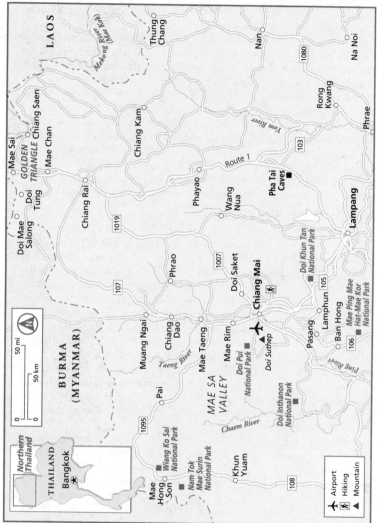

Northern Thailand is composed of 15 provinces, many of them sharing borders with Burma (Myanmar) to the north and west, and Laos to the northeast. This verdant, mountainous terrain, which includes Thailand's largest mountain, Doi Inthanon, at 2,563m (8,408 ft.), supports nomadic farming and teak logging at high altitudes and systematic agriculture in the valleys. Traditionally, opium poppies were the main cash crop for the people here, but government efforts have largely replaced their cultivation with rice, tobacco, soybeans, corn, and sugarcane.

A SHORT REGIONAL HISTORY

The tribal people living in the northern hills are actually recent immigrants in the grand scheme of the history of these parts, migrating only within the past

100 years or so from neighboring Burma, Tibet, Laos, and southern China to escape political strife and fighting.

The majority of northern Thais trace their heritage to the Tai people who migrated from Southern China in waves between the 1st and 8th centuries. King Mengrai, a brilliant leader who united the Tai tribes, established the first capital of the Lanna Kingdom at Chiang Rai in 1262. It was about this time that Kublai Khan invaded Burma. For added protection, King Mengrai forged ties with the Sukhothai Kingdom to the south, and in 1296 he moved his capital to Chiang Mai. For the next century, the Lanna Kingdom absorbed most of the northern provinces and, in alliance with the Sukhothai, held off invasion from the Mons and Khmers. After taking control of Sukhothai, Ayutthaya tried to conquer Chiang Mai and failed each time. The Lanna Kingdom enjoyed wealth and power until 1556, when the Burmese captured the capital. It remained in their hands until 1775, when King Taskin (of Ayutthaya) took it for Siam.

A LOOK AT THE HILL TRIBES

Since the 1970s, foreigners have caught on to the beauty of the north and to the cultures of the unique **hill-tribe people** who live here. Northern Thailand is home to the majority of Thailand's more than half a million tribal peoples, who live in villages that are a trek away from civilization and who often come to the larger cities to sell their excellent handicrafts and share their culture with visitors.

While many Thais in the central and southern regions of the country acknowledge the original Chinese Thais as their ancestral lineage, the people of the hill tribes retain a separate identity. They are divided into six primary tribes: the Karen, Akha (also known as the Kaw), Lahu (Mussur), Lisu (Lisaw), Hmong (Meo), and Mien (Yao), each with subgroups that are linked by history, lineage, language, costume, social organization, and religion. With close ethnic, cultural, and linguistic ties to the cultures of their Laotian, southwestern Chinese, Burmese, and Tibetan ancestors and neighbors, the hill tribes remain to this day different from the Thais of central and southern Thailand, retaining their own traditional costumes, religion, art, and way of life.

Numbering more than a quarter million—almost half of the entire tribal population—the **Karen** are the largest tribal group in Thailand and are among the most assimilated of the hill tribes, making it difficult to identify them by any outward appearance; however, the most traditional tribespeople wear silver armbands and don a beaded sash and headband, and the single women wear all white. In nearby Burma (Myanmar), it's estimated that there are more than 4 million people of Karen descent (and of Buddhist belief), many of whom have settled along the Thai-Burmese border. For years, Burma's military government has been battling Karen rebels seeking an autonomous homeland, and many Burmese Karen have sought refuge in Thailand.

The **Hmong** are a nomadic tribe scattered throughout Southeast Asia and China. About 65,000 Hmong live in Thailand, while there are approximately 4 million living in China. In Thailand, the Hmong generally dwell in the highlands, where they cultivate opium poppies more extensively than any other tribal group; corn, rice, and soybeans are also grown as subsistence crops. As with most of the other tribes, the Hmong are pantheistic and rely on shamans to perform spiritual rites, though their elite is staunchly Catholic. Like the Chinese, with whom they resided for so many centuries, Hmong are skilled entrepreneurs, and many are beginning to move down from the hills to pursue a less rigorous and more profitable life in other occupations.

The **Lahu** people, of whom about 40,000 abide in Thailand, are a fractured group with a great many subdivisions, and if any tribe reflects the difficulties of maintaining a singular cultural identity in the tumult of migration, it's the Lahu. Consider Lahu religion: Originally animist, they adopted the worship of a deity called G'ui sha (possibly Tibetan in origin), borrowed the practice of merit-making from Buddhism (Indian or Chinese), and ultimately incorporated Christian (British/Burmese) theology into their belief system. In addition, they practice a kind of Lahu voodoo and follow a messianic tradition. The Lahu are skilled musicians, their bamboo and gourd flutes being the most common instruments sold in the Night Market in Chiang Mai. They welcome strangers more than any other tribe in Thailand.

There are now estimated to be 33,000 **Mien** living in Thailand, concentrated in the Chiang Rai, Phayao, Lampang, and Nan provinces. Even more than the Hmong, the Mien are closely connected to their origins in southern China. They incorporated the Han (Chinese) spoken and written language into their own, and many Mien legends, history books, and religious tracts are recorded in Chinese. The Mien people also assimilated ancestor worship and a form of Taoism into their theology, in addition to celebrating their New Year on the same date (relying on the same calendar system) as the Chinese. Mien farmers practice slash-and-burn agriculture but do not rely on opium poppies; instead, they cultivate dry rice and corn. The women produce rather elaborate and elegant embroidery, which often adorns their clothing. Their silver work is intricate and highly prized even by other tribes, particularly the Hmong.

The **Lisu** are one of the smaller ethnic minorities in northern Thailand, representing less than 5% of all hill-tribe people. They arrived in the Chiang Rai province in the 1920s, migrating from nearby Burma, occupying high ground and growing opium poppies as well as other subsistence crops. Like their Chinese cousins (many have intermarried), the Lisu people are reputed to be extremely competitive and hardworking. Even their clothing is brash, with brightly colored tunics embellished with hundreds of silver beads and trinkets. The Lisu are achievers who live well-structured lives. Their rituals rely on complicated procedures that demand much from the participants. Everything from birth to courtship, to marriage, to death is ruled by an orthodox tradition, much borrowed from the Chinese.

Of all the tradition-bound tribes, the **Akha,** accounting for only 3% of all minorities living in Thailand, have probably maintained the most profound connection with their past. At great events in one's life, the full name (often more than 50 generations of titles) of an Akha is proclaimed, with each name symbolic of a lineage dating back more than a thousand years. All aspects of life are governed by the Akha Way, an all-encompassing system of myth, ritual, plant cultivation, courtship and marriage, birth, death, dress, and healing. They are widely spread throughout southern China, Laos, Vietnam, and Burma (Myanmar). The first Akha migrated from Burma to Thailand in the beginning of the 20th century. They are "shifting" cultivators, depending on subsistence crops planted in rotation, and raising domestic animals for their livelihood. The clothing of the Akha is among the most attractive of all the hill tribes: Simple black jackets with skillful embroidery are the everyday attire for both men and women.

WEATHER

There are three distinct seasons in the north. The **hot season** (Mar–May) is dry, with temperatures up to 86°F (30°C). The **rainy season** (June–Oct) is a bit cooler, with the heaviest daily rainfall in September. The **cool season** (Nov–Feb) is brisk, with daytime temperatures as low as 59°F (21°C) in Chiang Mai town and 41°F (5°C) in the hills. November to May is the best time for trekking, with February, March, and April (when southern Thailand gets extremely hot) usually being the least crowded months. Trekkers *beware:* During the rainy season, paths become mud-slides due to frequent showers.

12 Chiang Mai

The largest and most well known city in the north, Chiang Mai is the primary gateway to the hills and the people who live there. The city itself is a treasure trove of small but magnificent temples and, without argument, the epitome of shopping for Thai and hill-tribe arts and handicrafts. If you can be seduced away from the city limits, you'll find cottage industries, hill-tribe villages, and natural wonders.

Chiang Mai begins at the **"Old City,"** a square fortress surrounded by a moat, and some remains of its original massive walls. Several of the original gates have been restored and serve as useful reference points. Within the Old City are three of the area's most important wats (temples): Wat Chedi Luang, Wat Phra Singh, and Wat Chiang Man.

Most of the major streets radiate from the Old City and fan out in all directions. The **main business and shopping area** is the half-mile stretch between the east side of the Old City and the Ping River. Here you'll find **Chiang Mai's Night Market,** along with many shops, hotels, and restaurants.

VISITOR INFORMATION

The **TAT** office is at 105/1 Chiang Mai-Lamphun Rd., 400m (1,312 ft.) south of the Nawarat Bridge on the east side of the Ping River (© **5324-8604**). A couple of free magazines—*Guidelines Chiang Mai* and *Welcome to Chiang Mai and Chiangrai*—contain detailed maps, as well as useful and interesting information; they're available at hotels and businesses. I personally think the latter is better for maps and useful information.

GETTING THERE

BY PLANE　In planning your trip, keep in mind that Chiang Mai connects with many international cities. **Lao Aviation** (© **5340-4033**) links Chiang Mai to Vientiane and Luang Prabang twice weekly, while Air Mandalay (© **5327-6884**) offers twice-weekly flights to Yangon and weekly service to Mandalay, in Myanmar (Burma). **Silk Air** (© **5327-6459**), the regional arm of Singapore Airlines, connects Singapore with direct service three times a week. A new addition, **Mandarin Airlines** (© **5320-1268**), provides service from Taipei frequently throughout the week. Thai Airways International has service direct from Kunming in southern China. For international reservations in Chiang Mai, call © **5321-1044.**

Within Thailand, **Thai Airways,** 240 Propokklao Rd. (© **5321-0210**), flies from Bangkok to Chiang Mai 10 times daily (trip time: 1 hr., 10 min.). There's a direct flight from Phuket daily, plus a circular route connecting Phitsanulok, Nan, Phrae, and Chiang Mai four times a week. The 35-minute hop up to Chiang Rai departs twice daily, and another 35-minute hop is also the fastest way to get out to Mae Hong Son.

Bangkok Airways, with an office at the airport in Chiang Mai (© **5328-1519;** in Bangkok 2229-3434), has a daily flight from Bangkok with a stop in Sukhothai.

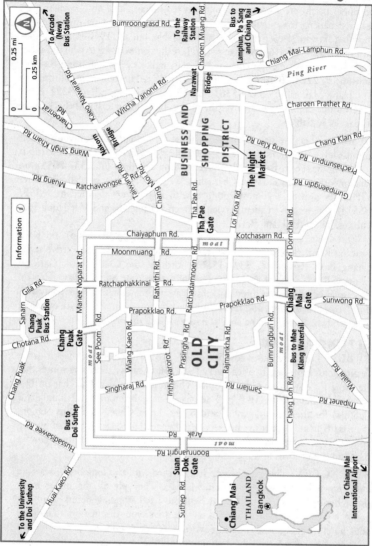

The **Chiang Mai International Airport** has several banks for changing money, a post and overseas call office, and an information booth.

Taxis from the airport are a flat 100B (US$2.30) to town, a bit more for places outside of Chiang Mai proper. Buy a ticket from the taxi booth in the arrival hall, and then proceed to the taxi queue with your ticket.

BY TRAIN Of the seven daily trains from Bangkok to Chiang Mai, the 8:25am Sprinter (trip time: 11 hr.; 481B/US$11 2nd-class air-conditioned seat) is the quickest, but you sacrifice a whole day to travel and spend the entire trip in a seat. The other trains take between 13 and 15 hours, but for overnight trips, second-class sleeper berths (611B/US$14 for a lower berth or 681B/US$15 for an upper berth) are a better option. They're only available on Special Express trains departing twice daily—at 4:25pm and 5:25pm, arriving early the next morning. Private sleeper cabins are also available, but at 1193B (US$27), they cost only 700B (US$16) less than flying. It really comes down to which you can spare—money or time. Purchase tickets at Bangkok's **Hua Lampong Railway Station** (© 2223-7010) up to 90 days in advance. For local train information in Chiang Mai, call © 5324-5363; for advance booking, call © 5324-2094. Reservations cannot be made over the phone, but you can call and check to see if space is available.

BY BUS There are several buses to choose from, depending on your budget and the level of comfort you desire—regardless of which you choose, the trip is still 10 hours. From **Bangkok's Northern Bus Terminal** (© 2537-8055), on Phahonyothin Road near the Chatuchak Weekend Market, six daily 24-seater VIP buses provide the most comfort, with larger seats that recline (625B/ US$14). There's also frequent service between Chiang Mai and Mae Hong Son, Phitsanulok, and Chiang Rai.

Most buses arrive at the **Arcade Bus Station** (© 5324-2664), on Kaeo Nawarat Road, 3km (2 miles) northeast of the Tha Pae Gate; a few arrive at the Chang Puak station (© 5321-1586), north of the Chang Puak Gate on Chotana Road. Some of the private bus companies drop off their passengers on the Superhighway, where guesthouse touts await them. Unless you're exhausted, don't accept their offers, and make the extra effort to get to your place of choice on your own. You should be able to find a tuk-tuk or songtao.

GETTING AROUND

BY BUS Local minibuses cost 5B to 40B (US10¢–US90¢) for most in-town destinations, but they are often packed and follow rather confusing routes that are more for out-of-town destinations. The minibus to Wat Pra That on Doi Suthep Mountain costs 35B (US80¢)to take you up the mountain, but only 25B (US60¢) for the easier downhill return trip. From Chang Puak Bus Station, there is frequent, inexpensive bus service to the nearby villages of Sankamphaeng and Bo Sang, Lamphun. These buses can also be flagged down on the highways that lead out of town to these destinations.

BY SONGTAO These red pickup trucks fitted with two long bench seats are also known locally as *seelor* ("four wheels"). They ply all the major roads throughout the city, day and night, with no fixed stopping points. Hail one going in your general direction, and tell the driver your destination. (*Tip:* have your hotel or guesthouse concierge write your destination in Thai before you head out.) If it fits in with the destinations of other passengers, you'll get a ride to your door for only 5B to 20B (US10¢–US45¢). If you can deal with a bit of uncertainty along the confusing twist of roads, it's a great way to explore the city—it's cheap and fast, and the drivers are honest.

BY TUK-TUK The ubiquitous tuk-tuk (motorized 3-wheeler) is the next-best option. The fare within Chiang Mai is always negotiable—and you will have to bargain hard to get a good rate—but expect to pay about 40B (US90¢) for an in-town ride. Actually, this most recent trip to Chiang Mai, none of the tuk-tuk drivers seemed interested in trying to rip me off. Then again, it was pretty hot and lazy weather.

Many tuk-tuk drivers will hustle you with a shopping tour of their "favorite" shops and factories, and then pocket hefty commissions on your purchases. And be careful of the drivers who lurk around major hotels, hounding guests as they exit. Their prices are always inflated. Still, many drivers have emigrated from Bangkok, speak good English, and are fun to ride with. Just make sure you go where *you* want to go: A favorite ploy is pretending they have never heard of your destination or telling you it's closed.

BY CAR **Avis** has an office conveniently located at the airport (© **5320-1574**). Avis self-drive rental rates for Chiang Mai are the same as they are elsewhere in Thailand, from 1,500B (US$34) per day for a Suzuki Caribian 4WD sport vehicle to 2,000B (US$45) and up for a compact sedan.

Dozens of local car-rental companies rent self-drive sedans for 1,000B to 1,400B (US$23–US$32) per day, and Suzuki Caribians for as low as 700B (US$16) per day. Most travel agents will arrange a car and driver for about 1,600B (US$36) per day. I've used **North Wheels,** 127/2 Moonmuang Rd. (© **5321-6189**), with great success. They'll greet you at the airport and drop you there when you leave, or make deliveries to your hotel, no problem. They even took me back to the lot to let me inspect and select the car I wanted myself.

BY BICYCLE Biking in the city is fun and practical if you avoid rush hour traffic, especially for getting around to the temples. Stop in one of the many guesthouses in or around the old city for a rental. You'll pay about 30B (US70¢) per day. Pay attention to one-way streets, as well as tuk-tuks, motorcycles, samlors, and other smaller vehicles that are known to weave through slower traffic.

BY MOTORCYCLE Many guesthouses along the Ping River and shops around Chaiyapoom Road (N of Tha Pae Rd. in the Old City) rent 100cc to 150cc motorcycles for about 200B (US$4.55) per day. The 250cc Hondas are commonly available and a good choice because of their added power and large fuel tanks; they rent for about 550B (US$12). Make sure you have the necessary insurance, wear a helmet, and expect to leave your passport as security (don't leave any credit cards). Traffic congestion makes driving within the city dangerous, so employ all your defensive driving techniques.

FAST FACTS: Chiang Mai

Airport See "Getting There," above.

American Express Sea Tours Co. Ltd., 2/3 Prachasampan Rd., off Chang Klan Road (© **5327-1441**), is the American Express representative.

ATMs For ATMs and money-changers, go to Chang Klan Road and Charoen Prathet Road, around the Night Market, for the most convenient major bank branches.

Bookstores There are a few with a good selection of English-language novels and travel books. The best is **Bookazine** (ground floor, Chiang Inn Plaza, 100/1 Chang Klan Rd.; © **5328-1370**)—it's the smallest in terms of floor space but has the largest selection of English-language titles. Also try **Suriwong Book Centre,** 54/1–5 Sri Dornchai (© **5328-1052**), and D. K. Books, 234 Tha Pae Rd. (© **5325-1555**).

Car Rentals See "Getting Around," above.

Climate See "When to Go," earlier in this chapter.

Consulates There are many representative offices in Chiang Mai. Contacts are as follows: **American Consulate General** © 5325-2629, **Canadian**

Honorary Consul ℂ **5385-0147**, Australian Honorary Consul ℂ **5322-1083**, and **British Consul** ℂ **5320-3405**.

Dentist/Doctor The American Consulate (see "Consulates," above) will supply you with a list of English-speaking dentists and doctors. There are also several medical clinics; check with your hotel about the best and nearest facility.

Emergencies Dial ℂ **1699** to reach the Tourist Police in case of emergency.

Holidays See "When to Go," earlier in this chapter.

Hospitals in Chiang Mai, hospitals offer excellent emergency and general care, with English-speaking nurses and physicians. The best private hospital is **McCormick,** on Kaeo Nawarat Road (ℂ **5324-1311**), out toward the Arcade Bus Terminal.

Internet If you're looking for Internet access, there are many cafes around, especially in or around guesthouses in the Old City. **Assign Internet** has two branches, the most convenient across from McDonald's in Chiang Mai Pavilion at the Night Market on 145/23 Chang Klan Rd. (ℂ **5381-8911**), with another branch outside the northwest corner of the Old City at 12 Huay Kaew Shopping Center, Huay Kaew Road, across from the Central Department Store (ℂ **5340-4550**).

Pharmacies There are dozens of pharmacies throughout the city; most are open daily 7am to midnight.

Police For police assistance, call the **Tourist Police** at ℂ **1699,** or see them at the TAT office.

Post Office The most convenient branch is at 186/1 on Chang Klan Road (ℂ **5327-3657**), with a 24-hour branch at the airport (ℂ **5327-7382**). The General Post Office is on Charoen Muang (ℂ **5324-1070**), near the train station. The Overseas Call Office, open 24 hours, is upstairs from the GPO and offers phone, fax, and telex services.

WHERE TO STAY

The largest number of hotels is concentrated in the business and shopping district to the east of the Old City, and staying in these hotels is very convenient for reaching most attractions, restaurants, and night spots. In addition, some smaller and very charming hotels sit on the banks of the Ping River. These tend to reflect more local character, and can be very relaxing.

EXPENSIVE

The Imperial Mae Ping Hotel ✪   This newer tower hotel is one of the city's most popular choices because of its attractive style and excellent location—a stroll away from the Night Market, yet far enough to get a good night's sleep—just make sure you book a room in the front of the hotel away from the busy beer garden out back. The unusual double height lobby interprets Thai architectural elements in bold white-and-gold decor, with shops, a tour desk, and other services discreetly included. Large, bright guest rooms have contemporary blond teak furnishings upholstered in peach, jade, or blue; modern conveniences; and mountain views. Sculpted lamp bases and reproductions of temple murals add a classic touch.

153 Sri Dornchai Rd., Chiang Mai 50100 (corner of Kampaengdin Rd., 2 blocks SW of Night Market). ✆ **5327-0160.** Fax 5327-0181. 371 units. 3,500B (US$80) double; from 4,700B (US$107) suite. AE, DC, MC, V. **Amenities:** 3 restaurants (coffee shop, Thai, Chinese); lounge and beer garden; outdoor pool; fitness center; tour desk; limousine service; business center; salon; 24-hr. room service; massage; babysitting; same-day laundry service/dry cleaning; nonsmoking rooms. *In room:* A/C, TV w/satellite programming, minibar.

Royal Princess Hotel ✿   The northern cousin of Bangkok's deluxe Dusit Thani is a first-rate city hotel. This time around, the hotel was just completing refurbishment, which included a much needed redecorating. And they've done a terrific job exploiting all those lovely locally produced rich crafts—textiles, ceramics, and traditional Thai ornaments all with a real eye for style. It makes you wonder why more properties here don't take advantage of such resources. The extremely busy staff is always helpful and courteous. Surprisingly quiet rooms overlook the glittering lights of the city. They're small yet much more comfortable, thanks to the new design scheme, which has brought in lighter, fresher colors. The sometimes frenetic lobby has a comfortable bar. The pleasant coffee shop serves an elaborate breakfast buffet with delicious pastries, and the Jasmine restaurant serves excellent dim sum at lunch. While the small swimming pool isn't the most atmospheric, the traditional Thai massage service in the basement is excellent, though expensive. ***Be warned:*** The Royal Princess is a favorite hangout for tuk-tuk drivers who try to charge visitors an arm and a leg and take them to places they don't want to visit.

112 Chang Klan Rd., Chiang Mai 50100 (located just at the Night Market, across from Chiang Mai Pavilion [shopping center]). ✆ **5328-1033.** Fax 5328-1044. www.royalprincess.com. 198 units. 3,200B–3,500B (US$73–US$80) double; from 10,500B (US$239) suite. AE, DC, MC, V. **Amenities:** 3 restaurants (international, Cantonese, Japanese); lobby lounge and pub; small outdoor pool; concierge; tour desk; limousine service; 24-hr. room service; massage; babysitting; same-day laundry service/dry cleaning. *In room:* A/C, TV w/satellite programming, minibar, hair dryer.

MODERATE

Chiang Inn Hotel ✿   The renovated Chiang Inn is just behind the Chiang Inn Plaza, an arcade of Western chain eateries and shops, but it's set back from the lively street and quieter at night than you'd expect. Location and convenience are its best features, adding special value for money to this modest hotel. The compact, teak-paneled lobby has a homey feel and is almost always crowded with Europeans. Spacious rooms are clean but are decorated in a bland fashion, and while hotel facilities are limited, with so many offerings around the hotel in terms of dining and entertainment, you won't be spending much time in your room. After touring the city and its sights, you'll appreciate relaxing around the pool and sun deck, though.

100 Chang Klan Rd., Chiang Mai 50100 (2 blocks S of Tha Pae Rd., 2 blocks W of river, just N of Night Market). ✆ **5327-0070.** Fax 5327-4299. chianginn@chiangmai.a-net.net.th. 190 units. 1,884B (US$43) double; from 7,060B (US$160) suite. AE, DC, MC, V. **Amenities:** 2 restaurants (international grill, coffee shop); lobby lounge; small pool; tour desk; business center; limited room service; babysitting; same-day laundry service/dry cleaning. *In room:* A/C, TV w/satellite programming, minibar.

The Empress Hotel ✿   This 17-story tower, opened in 1990, is a little bit south of the main business and tourist area, which makes it especially quiet. The impressive public spaces are filled with glass, granite, and chrome, along with well-integrated touches of Thai style. The large rooms with picture windows are done in a tasteful, modern interpretation of Asian decor, using primarily rose-and-peach tones. Bathrooms are small but include many toiletries. There's an outdoor pool that you can actually swim laps in.

199/42 Chang Klan Rd., Chiang Mai 50100 (a 15-min. walk S of Night Market, 2 blocks from river). © **5327-0240.** Fax 5327-2467. www.empresshotels.com. 375 units. 3,000B–4,000B (US$68–US$91) double; from 8,400B (US$191) suite. AE, DC, MC, V. **Amenities:** 3 restaurants (coffee shop, Cantonese, international grill); lobby lounge and disco; pool; fitness center w/sauna; concierge; tour desk; business center; shopping arcade; salon; 24-hr. room service; massage; babysitting; same-day laundry service/dry cleaning; executive-level rooms. *In room:* A/C, TV w/satellite programming, minibar, hair dryer.

River View Lodge ★★ Veteran shopper and mapmaker Nancy Chandler stays here when in Chiang Mai, and for good reason. First of all, River View's location makes for a peaceful retreat, yet it's only a short hop to the city's main business and shopping district. Second, the atmosphere is fabulous, from the antiques (all for sale) scattered throughout the hotel's public spaces to the quaint, shady garden that separates the small swimming pool from the open-sided cafe restaurant. Large guest rooms have fresh terra-cotta tile floors with simple but well-maintained wood furnishings and no-fuss decor. Bathrooms have shower stalls only, and some of the rooms have wall-to-wall carpeting, which doesn't feel as cooling as the tiled rooms. Rates vary depending on the view, and many rooms have balconies.

25 Charoen Prathet Rd., Soi 2, Chiang Mai 50100 (on river 2 blocks S of Thae Pae Rd.). © **5327-1109.** Fax 5327-9019. www.riverviewlodge.com 36 units. 1,450B–1,800B (US$33–US$41) double. MC, V. **Amenities:** Restaurant (international); tiny outdoor pool; laundry service. *In room:* A/C.

Suriwongse Hotel ★ The unique hardwood paneling that covers every inch of the lobby of this comfortable hotel gives it an appealing warmth—this much wood is hard to find in newer places these days. The spacious, teak-trimmed twin bedrooms are among Chiang Mai's better values. Unlike the woody decorative scheme downstairs, the colors in the upstairs guest areas are cheerier off-white and pastel. Higher-priced rooms offer a balcony and better views, but all are equipped with first-class amenities. For you caffeine junkies out there, Chiang Mai's first Starbucks just opened right outside the lobby—I know this information will be valuable to some!

110 Chang Klan Rd., Chiang Mai 50100 (corner of Loi Kroa Rd., just SW of Night Market, halfway between Old City and River). © **5327-0051.** Fax 5327-0063. www.geocities.com/suriwongsehotel. 168 units. 2,278B–2,516B (US$52–US$57) double; from 3,500B (US$79) suite. AE, DC, MC, V. **Amenities:** 2 restaurants (Thai, international); lounge; pool; tour desk; business center; limited room service; massage; babysitting; same-day laundry service/dry cleaning; nonsmoking rooms. *In room:* A/C, TV w/satellite programming, minibar.

INEXPENSIVE

River Ping Palace If you really want a taste of old Thailand, check into the River Ping Palace for a night. This old restored compound of teak houses that were once a private residence has been converted into a guesthouse, dressed in four-poster beds with romantic mosquito netting, antique cabinets, rattan armchairs, Victorian brass wall sconces, framed historical photos, and unique accessories. The upstairs lanai overlooking the river is especially scenic for enjoying lazy afternoon cocktails. That said, the facility is not exactly modern. The management needs to keep better tabs on maintenance because it's difficult fitting so many functioning bathrooms into the old dame; you must sacrifice a little convenience, especially during rainstorms when the roof gets leaky in spots. Yikes! Still, it's ambience and authenticity in one wild package. Its restaurant, Once Upon a Time, serves excellent northern cuisine and is reviewed below.

385/2 Charoen Prathet Rd., Chiang Mai 50100 (on the river, a 20-min. walk S of the Night Market, between Monfort College and the Mengrai Bridge). © **5327-4932.** Fax 5327-3675. 11 units. 600B–1,000B (US$14–US$23) double; 1,100B (US$25) suite. AE, MC, V. **Amenities:** Restaurant (Thai); laundry service. *In room:* A/C, no phone.

Top North Guest House ★★ _Value_ This is not your average guesthouse. Tucked away on one of the old city's narrow lanes, the quiet Top North is like a minihotel. It's quiet and comfortable, and guests are invited to relax by the pool, a large and popular hangout, or sit for a spell in the laid-back Thai/Western coffee shop. Rooms are big, with clean tiled floors, large bathrooms (some with bathtubs), and the most unique stencil painting on the walls. Prices vary depending on whether you prefer air-conditioning or fan-cooled rooms, TV (local Thai TV), or a phone, but all rooms have hot-water showers. Top North also has a good tour operation that organizes treks, an Internet cafe on premises, and video CD movies in the coffee shop in the evenings.

15 Moon Muang Rd., Soi 2, Chiang Mai 50100. © **5329-8900**. Fax 5327-8485. 90 units. 500B (US$12) double with A/C; 300B (US$6.80) double w/fan. MC, V. **Amenities:** Restaurant (international); outdoor pool; bike and motorcycle rental; tour desk; laundry service Internet cafe. _In room:_ A few rooms have A/C and TV, and a few have no phone.

WHERE TO DINE
EXPENSIVE

Jasmine ★ CHINESE Jasmine is an intimate, quiet, tastefully decorated, and expensive Cantonese restaurant that specializes in dim sum at lunch. The variety changes often, but there are normally 12 different mildly spiced, freshly steamed treats from which to choose. Dinner and lunch main courses are deliciously prepared by a Chinese chef. Specialties include bird's nest and shark's fin soups, barbecued pig, crystal prawns, and minced squab with lettuce.

In the Royal Princess Hotel, 112 Chang Klan Rd. © **5328-1033**. Reservations recommended. Main courses 250B–1,400B (US$5.70–US$32). AE, DC, MC, V. Daily 11am–2:30pm and 6:30–10pm.

La Grillade ★ FRENCH The Chiang Inn Hotel's formal Thai-style dining room serves some of the best Continental fare in the city, with an emphasis on French cuisine. Comfortable armchairs, crisp linens, gleaming crystal, and attentive service distinguish this from your average casual Thai dining experience. For starters, enjoy fresh asparagus with hollandaise, vegetable salads, and several soups. The red snapper, pan-fried with capers, is flown in daily from the south, and imported Australian tenderloin is marinated in red wine and cooked with artichoke hearts. French wines are served by the bottle or the glass.

In the Chiang Inn Hotel, 100 Chang Klan Rd. © **5427-0070**. Reservations recommended. Main courses 275B–600B (US$6.25–US$14). AE, MC, V. Daily 11:30am–2pm and 6:30–10pm.

Le Coq d'Or ★★ FRENCH In a romantic English country house setting, Le Coq d'Or is second to none in Chiang Mai for excellent atmosphere, food, presentation, and service. Well-trained waiters serve a small but mouthwatering assortment of imported beef, lamb, and fish in French and Continental styles on white linen and china. My chateaubriand came perfectly rare, with a delicate gravy and béarnaise on the side. For starters, the salmon tartar wrapped in smoked salmon is served with toast, a sour cream and horseradish sauce, and capers. They have a nice wine list to complement your meal. Don't wait for a special occasion.

68/1 Koh Klang Rd. (5-min. drive S of the Westin, following the river). © **5328-2024**. Reservations recommended for weekend dinner. 320B–850B (US$7.30–US$19). AE, DC, MC, V. Daily 11am–2pm and 6–11pm.

Piccola Roma Palace ★★ ITALIAN Locals have praised Piccola as the best of the city's many Italian restaurants for a long time. This year Piccola Roma became Piccola Roma Palace when it changed location to a larger more elegant venue. It's definitely an upgrade from its former tavern feel. Your host, executive chef Angelo Faro, prepares daily specialties that depend upon his latest fresh finds at the markets. If you're lucky enough to select a dish that is prepared at your table, there's no extra charge for the entertainment. A good regularly featured menu item is the black linguine in inky squid sauce. A small selection of wines is available to accompany your meal.

144 Charoen Prathet Rd. (corner of Charoen Prathet and Sri Dornchai rds.). © 5382-0297. Reservations recommended. AE. Daily 11am–2pm and 5–11pm. Main dishes 160B–400B (US$3.65–US$9.10).

MODERATE

Antique House ☆ THAI   As its name suggests, this restaurant is an antique house, a 100-year-old Thai-style teakwood mansion in a beautiful garden next to the river. As if that isn't charming enough, they've filled the place with gorgeous antiques, adding to the visual effect. What you end up with is one of the most romantic evenings in Chiang Mai. The menu is impressive, with page after page of Thai dishes, but I would have preferred something more simplified. If you order a khan toke set, a northern Thai traditional dinner with many small dishes presented on one large platter, you'll get a taste of many treats all in one. And the tom yam soup is served in a coconut shell, a cute presentation. Throughout the evening, you'll also hear live traditional music. This is a good pick for a memorable dinner.

71 Charoen Prathet Rd. (next to Diamond Riverside Hotel). © 5327-6810. Reservations recommended for weekend dinner. Main courses 80B–280B (US$1.80–US$1.35). MC, V. Daily 11am–midnight.

Once Upon a Time THAI   Here's some excellent Thai food in a beautiful compound of restored teak houses, along a quiet part of the river. The two-story teak dining pavilion shares a tranquil garden with the River Ping Palace guesthouse. Downstairs serves specialties such as *hohmok,* an array of seafood soufflés made with prawns, mussels, or fish and coconut milk; mildly spiced grilled duck in a coconut-milk curry; *pla chon,* fresh river fish served with dipping sauces; and delicious and distinctive *gai yang,* barbecue chicken. Upstairs, under the peaked roof, diners can sit on cushions in the khan toke style and sample the same specials or an array of northern Thai dishes, including pork curry and piquant chili pastes.

385/2 Charoen Prathet Rd. (W side of the river, just N on Mengrai Bridge). © 5327-4932. Reservations recommended. Main courses 80B–200B (US$1.80–US$4.55). AE, MC, V. Daily 4:30pm–midnight.

The Riverside ☆☆ THAI/INTERNATIONAL   Casual and cool is what The Riverside is all about. It's a tavern with riverside terrace views—make sure you get there before the dinner rush so you get your pick of tables. There's live music, from blues to soft rock; great Thai and Western food (including burgers); and a full bar. Even if you just stop by for a beer, it's a convivial place that always has a jolly crowd. Full of conversation and laughter, it's no wonder that it's such a favorite with travelers, locals, and expatriates. The Riverside also operates a night cruise at 8pm for 50B (US$1.10) per person.

9–11 Charoenrat Rd. (E side of river, N of Narawatt Bridge). © 5324-3239. Reservations recommended for weekend dinner. Main courses 65B–200B (US$1.50–US$4.55). AE, MC, V. Daily 10am–1:30am.

Whole Earth Restaurant ☆ VEGETARIAN/ASIAN   If you're looking for Asian food in the California/health food/Asian fusion vein, head for this New Age place in a traditional Lanna Thai pavilion. The extensive menu is prepared by a gifted Pakistani chef and is part vegetarian, Thai, and Indian. The old pavilion has an indoor air-conditioned, nonsmoking section, and a long open-air veranda set for dining with a view of the gardens (they'll bring a fan to your table upon request). In a good location, near the main shopping and business areas,

Whole Earth gets busy at lunch and dinner (but still retains a peaceful air), so try to call ahead if you can.

88 Sri Dornchai Rd. (2 blocks W of river, off Chang Klan Rd.). ✆ 5328-2463. Reservations recommended. Main courses 60B–250B (US$1.35–US$5.70). No credit cards. Daily 11am–10pm.

INEXPENSIVE

Aroon (Rai) Restaurant ★★ NORTHERN THAI For authentic northern food, adventurous eaters should try this nondescript garden restaurant. The khao soi, filled with egg noodles and crisp-fried chicken bits and sprinkled with dried fried noodles, is spicy and coconut-sweet at the same time. Chiang Mai sausages are served sliced over steamed rice; puffed-up fried pork rinds are the traditional (if not cholesterol-free) accompaniment. Dishes are all made to order in an open kitchen, so you can point to things that interest you, including the myriad fried insects, beetles, and frogs for which this place is famous. They've added a new attraction—prepackaged spices and recipes for make-it-yourself back at home.

45 Kotchasarn Rd. (2 blocks S of Tha Pae Gate, outside Old City). ✆ 5327-6947. Main courses 20B–60B (US45¢–US$1.35). No credit cards. Daily 9am–10pm.

Haus München GERMAN/CONTINENTAL This popular place is usually filled with shoppers in the evening. You can eat wurst, delicious Kasseler (smoked pork), fish and chips, spaghetti, or many German favorites, including homemade brown bread. You can also drink draft Amarit beer and check in with the international expatriate community. They say they're the first Western restaurant in Chiang Mai, which could be true.

115/3 Loi Kroa Rd. (at the corner of Chang Klan Rd. around the corner from the Night Market). ✆ 5327-4027. Main courses 90B–140B (US$2.05–US$3.20). No credit cards. Daily noon–midnight.

JJ Coffee Shop and Bakery ★★ INTERNATIONAL The closest thing I've seen to a diner in Thailand, JJ's has spotless booths and tables lining the long window front, pop music, and a wait staff with personality. The extensive menu includes excellent sandwiches and burgers, with good fries. They also have Thai dishes, but the Western food is particularly recommended. Breakfasts are tops and reasonably priced, with excellent bakery goods. The Moonmuang Road branch has a salad bar in the evenings, a rare find in Thailand. There's a second branch at the Chiang Inn Plaza off the Night Bazaar, and there's another location at Chiang Inn Plaza Basement, 100/1 Moo 3, Changklan Rd. (✆ 5328-1367).

Corner of Moonmuang and Ratchadamnoen rds. (in Old City across from Tha Pae Gate). ✆ 5341-8090. Main courses 40B–220B (US90¢–US$5). V. Daily 6:30am–11:30pm.

Khao Soi Suthasinee THAI This small Formica and fluorescent shop house isn't easy to find, but it's a sure bet for authentic khao soi, an aromatic concoction of coconut curry soup with noodles, *gai* (chicken), or *moo* (pork), including greens and seasonal vegetables, such as tangy green eggplant. The restaurant isn't touristy, so you might have to ask for help finding it.

164/10 Chang Klan Rd. (S of Sri Donchai Rd., just S of junction w/Prachasamphan Rd., across from Saengtawan Cinema). No phone. Main courses 20B–140B (US45¢–US$3.20). No credit cards. Daily 9am–8:30pm.

Shere Shiraz INDIAN/PAKISTANI/ARABIAN/THAI One step in the door, and the aroma of coriander, cardamom, and anise will convince you that the tastes are going to be authentic. It's also especially good for vegetarians—the *aloo paratha* (potato-stuffed bread) and the *bindi masala* (okra in tomato) melt in your mouth. Tandoori oven specialties are good value. This is an excellent meal for the money.

23–25 Charoen Prathet Soi 6 (across from Kalare Bazaar). ℂ 5327-6132. Main courses 50B–130B (US$1.10–US$2.95). AE, MC, V. Daily 10:30am–11pm.

Ta-Krite ⭑⭑ THAI   This small restaurant packs a lot of charm, with lots of green plants, lovely locally made blue-and-white pottery, and old finds here and there. Serving Thai cuisine more common to the central parts of the country, the house specialty is the duck curry in a coconut gravy hot with chilies and sweetened with fruits. It's also nice to know that the produce comes from the Royal Project. This is a great place to stop for a sightseeing lunch break; the Quick Lunch specials are numerous and cheap.

7 Samlarn Rd., Soi 1 (walk S from Wat Phra Sing and turn right on Soi 1). ℂ 5327-8298. Reservations not necessary. 50B–120B (US$1.10–US$2.75). No credit cards. Daily 10am–11pm.

EXPLORING CHIANG MAI

After Bangkok, Chiang Mai has the greatest concentration of exquisitely crafted **wats** (temples) in the country—more than 700 of them. Assuming that you aren't planning a wat-by-wat tour, you can see all the principal sights in 1 day if you start early in the morning, particularly if you travel by tuk-tuk.

Chiang Mai National Museum   This modern complex houses the province's fine collection of Lanna Thai art. Woodwork, stonework, and the many religious images garnered from local wats, all well labeled, help to chronicle the distinct achievements of the Lanna Kingdom from the 14th to 18th centuries. These works reveal how Burmese religious art grew more influential over the years of occupation. Knowledge of both cultures will serve you well while touring the north. Note the display of weapons that were used to combat the Burmese.

Superhighway, just N of the 7-spired Wat Chet Yot. ℂ 5322-1308. Admission 20B (US4¢5). Tues–Sun 8:30am–4pm. Closed holidays.

Tribal Museum ⭑   Formerly at Chiang Mai University's Tribal Research Institute, the museum moved to the peaceful Ratchamangkla Park just north of the city, not far from the Chiang Mai National Museum. It's a small but well-executed exhibit showing the cultures and daily lives of the hill-tribe people of Thailand's north. It is especially recommended as an introductory course for those who plan to visit the villages.

Ratchamangkla Park on Chotana Rd. ℂ 5322-1933. Free admission. Weekdays 9am–4pm.

Wat Chedi Luang ⭑⭑⭑   Because this temple is near the Tha Pae Gate, most visitors begin their sightseeing here, where there are two wats of interest. This complex, which briefly housed the Emerald Buddha now at Bangkok's Wat Phra Kaeo, dates from 1411, when the original chedi was built by King Saen Muang Ma. The already-massive edifice was expanded to 84m (280 ft.) in height in the mid-1400s, only to be ruined by a severe earthquake in 1545, just 11 years before Chiang Mai fell to the Burmese. (It was never rebuilt.) A Buddha still graces its exterior, and it's not unusual to spot a saffron-robed monk bowing to it as he circles the chedi.

Wat Phan Tao, also on the grounds, has a wooden wihaan and bot, a reclining Buddha, and fine carving on the eaves and door. After leaving the temple, walk around to the monks' quarters on the side, taking in the traditional teak northern architecture and delightful landscaping.

Prapokklao Rd. S of Ratchadamnoen Rd. Suggested donation 20B (US45¢). Daily 6am–5pm.

Wat Chet Yot ★★   Also called Wat Maha Photharam, Wat Chet Yot is one of the central city's most elegant sites. The chedi was built during the reign of King Tilokkarat in the late 15th century (his remains are in one of the smaller chedis), and in 1477, the World Sangkayana convened here to revise the doctrines of the Buddha.

The unusual design of the main rectangular chedi with seven peaks was copied from the Maha Bodhi Temple in Bodh Gaya, India, where the Buddha first achieved enlightenment. The temple also has architectural elements of Burmese, Chinese Yuan, and Ming influence. The extraordinary proportions; the angelic, levitating devata figures carved into the base of the chedi; and the juxtaposition of the other buildings make Wat Chet Yot (Seven Spires) a masterpiece.

The Lanna-style Buddha hidden in the center was sculpted in the mid–15th century; a door inside the niche containing the Buddha leads to the roof on which rests the **Phra Kaen Chan (Sandalwood Buddha).** There is a nice vista from up top, but only men are allowed to ascend the stairs.

Superhighway near the Chiang Mai National Museum (N of the intersection of Nimanhemin and Huai Kaeo rds., about ½ mile on the left). Suggested donation 20B (US45¢). Daily 6am–5pm.

Wat Chiang Man   Thought to be Chiang Mai's oldest wat, it was built during the 14th century by King Mengrai, the founder of Chiang Mai, on the spot where he first camped. Like many of the wats in Chiang Mai, this complex reflects many architectural styles. Some of the structures are pure Lanna. Others show influences from as far away as Sri Lanka; notice the typical row of elephant supports. Wat Chiang Man is most famous for its two Buddhas: Phra Sritang Khamani (a miniature crystal image also known as the **White Emerald Buddha**) and the marble **Phra Sri-la Buddha.** Unfortunately, the wihaan that safeguards these religious sculptures is almost always closed.

N of the intersection of Nimanhemin and Huai Kaeo rds., about ½ mile on the left.

Wat Phra Singh ★★★   This compound was built during the zenith of Chiang Mai's power and is one of the more venerated shrines in the city. It's still the site of many important religious ceremonies, particularly during the Songkran Festival. More than 700 monks study here, and you will probably find them especially friendly and curious.

King Phayu, of Mengrai lineage, built the chedi in 1345, principally to house the cremated remains of King Kamfu, his father. As you enter the grounds, head to the right toward the 14th-century library. Notice the graceful carving and the characteristic roofline with four separate elevations. The sculptural *devata* (Buddhist spirits) figures, in both dancing and meditative poses, are thought to have been made during King Muang Kaeo's reign in the early 16th century. They decorate a stone base designed to keep the fragile *sa* (mulberry bark) manuscripts elevated from flooding and vermin.

On the other side of the temple complex is the 200-year-old **Lai Kham (Gilded Hall) wihaan,** housing the venerated image of the Phra Singh or **Sighing Buddha,** brought to the site by King Muang Ma in 1400. The original Buddha's head was stolen in 1922, but the reproduction in its place doesn't diminish the homage paid to this figure during Songkran. Inside are frescoes illustrating the stories of Sang Thong (the Golden Prince of the Conchshell) and Suwannahong. These images convey a great deal about the religious, civil, and military life of 19th-century Chiang Mai during King Mahotraprathet's reign.

Samlarn and Ratchadamnoen rds. Suggested donation 20B (US45¢). Daily 6am–5pm.

Wat Suan Dok   This complex is special less for its architecture (the buildings, though monumental, are undistinguished) than for its contemplative spirit and pleasant surroundings. The temple was built amid the pleasure gardens of the 14th-century Lanna Thai monarch, King Ku Na. Unlike most of Chiang Mai's other wats (more tourist sights than working temples and schools), Wat Suan Dok houses quite a few monks who seem to have isolated themselves from the distractions of the outside world. Among the main attractions in the complex are the bot, with a very impressive **Chiang Saen Buddha** (one of the largest bronzes in the north) dating from 1504 and some garish murals; the chedi, built to hold a relic of the Buddha; and a royal cemetery with some splendid shrines.

Suthep Rd. (from the Old City, take the Suan Dok Gate and continue 1 mile W). Suggested donation 20B (US45¢). Open daily 6am–5pm

EXPLORING OUTSIDE THE CITY

Wat Phra That   The jewel of Chiang Mai, Wat Phra That glistens in the sun on the slopes of Doi Suthep mountain. One of four royal wats in the north, at 1,000m (3,250 ft.), it occupies an extraordinary site with a cool refreshing climate and expansive views over the city, the mountain's idyllic forests, waterfalls, and flowers. In the 14th century, during the installation of a relic of the Buddha in Wat Suan Dok (in the Old City), the holy object split in two, with one part equaling the original's size. A new wat was needed to honor the miracle. King Ku Na placed the new relic on a sacred white elephant and let it wander freely through the hills. The elephant climbed to the top of Doi Suthep, trumpeted three times, made three counterclockwise circles, and knelt down, choosing the site for Wat Phra That. The original chedi was built to a height of 26½ feet. Other structures were raised to bring greater honor to the Buddha and various patrons. The most remarkable is the steep 290-step naga staircase, added in 1557, leading up to the wat, one of the most dramatic approaches to a temple in all of Thailand. To shorten the 5-hour climb, the winding road was constructed in 1935 by thousands of volunteers under the direction of a local monk.

Suggested contribution 20B (US45¢). Daily 7am–5pm; come early or late to avoid the crowds.

Doi Inthanon National Park   Thailand's tallest mountain (at 2,563m/8,408 ft.), Doi Inthanon is 47km (29 miles) south of Chiang Mai. It crowns a 581-sq.-km (360-sq.-mile) national park filled with impressive waterfalls and wild orchids. Doi Inthanon Road climbs 48km (30 miles) to the summit. Along the way is the 30m (100-ft.-high) Mae Klang Falls, a popular picnic spot with food stands. Nearby Pakan Na Falls is less crowded because it requires a bit of climbing along a path to reach. At the top of the mountain, there's a fine view and two more falls, Wachirathan and Siriphum, both worth exploring.

Admission 200B (US$4.55). Daily sunrise to sunset. Camping is allowed in the park, but you must check w/the TAT or the national park office to obtain permits, schedule information, and regulations.

TREKKING FROM CHIANG MAI

Tourism in the north developed slowly during the 1970s but really took off in the early 1980s, when backpackers and other assorted intrepids made their way north to see this unique region and the colorful people who inhabit it. Today travelers are still drawn to the hill-tribe villages in search of a special experience—to come in contact with cultures that are unspoiled by modern development—to witness life here as it has been for past centuries. With this ideal in mind, all trekking companies advertise their offerings as "nontourist," "authentic," "alternative," or "remote," to set their tours and treks apart from tacky tourist operations or staged cultural experiences. The truth is, despite what these touts promise, not one village exists that has not experienced the modern world in some way.

The encroachment of civilization is inevitable, and tourists aren't the only ones to blame. The Thai government has made efforts to incorporate the tribes into the national political culture, environmentalists have worked to spare precious forests that are destroyed by their slash-and-burn agricultural techniques, and the royal family has taken huge strides to introduce crops to replace their staple opium production. Despite the overall positive effects of these efforts, the tribal peoples now must struggle to maintain their cultural identities, livelihoods, and centuries-old ways of life. But don't let this discourage you from joining a trek or tour. If you seek a truly *authentic* experience, come not to see primitive people, as the tour promoters suggest. Instead, come to learn how these cultures on the margin of society grapple with complex pressures from the national and international scene to maintain their unique identities. Within this frame of reference, you will find your authentic experience.

There are two kinds of hill-tribe operators in northern Thailand: those that offer **tribal village tours** and others that coordinate jungle treks. The former puts together large and small groups to visit villages that are close to major cities and towns. If you join one of these groups, you'll travel by van or coach to up to half a dozen villages, each inhabited by a different tribe, and you'll spend about an hour in each one. These villages have had decades of exposure to foreigners, and because they are connected by roads, have some modern conveniences. Day-trip village tours are carried out professionally by **Gem Travel,** 209/2 Sri Dornchai Rd., Soi 6 (© **5327-2855;** fax 5381-8755). They'll provide transportation, a guide, and lunch for a day trip to a few different hill-tribe villages. For two, the cost is 1,900B (US$43) per person, but this figure decreases if you can join a group.

For short-term jungle trekking, The Wild Planet is a highly reputable outfit. Combining treks and village stays with elephant treks, visits to caves, and relaxing bamboo raft river trips, they have quality guides and can even provide English-speaking guides upon request. Treks from Chiang Mai stop at Lisu, Lahu, and Karen villages. A 2-day/1-night trip is 1,300B (US$30) per person if you join the regular tour, or 3,900B (US$89) per person for a private group trip. A 3-day/2-night trip, which takes you to a greater variety of villages, is 4,300B (US$98) per person if you join the regular tour, or 5,900B (US$134) per person for a private group. For an additional 1,000B (US$23) per person, you can hire a porter to wrestle your bags along. The office in Chiang Mai is at 73/7 Charoen Prathet Rd. (© **5327-7178;** fax 5327-9505), and the head office in Bangkok is at No. 9 Thonglor Soi 25, Sukhumvit 55, Prakanong (© **2712-8407;** fax 2712-8748; www.wild-planet.co.th).

BIKING

Mountain biking is perhaps the best way to see this part of the country. Out in the fresh air, there's a more up-close and personal view of nature, sights, and people. The **Wild Planet** coordinates 2-, 3-, and 4-day trips from Chiang Mai, taking you to elephant camps, hill-tribe villages (with an overnight stay in the headman's house), temples, and some cave exploration. Some trips even end up in Chiang Rai—much more interesting than taking a Thai Airways flight. A day trip is 1,500B (US$34), while a longer 3-day/2-night trip is about 1,700B (US$39). Call them in Bangkok at © **2712-8407,** or in Chiang Mai, at Charoen Prathet Road between the Diamond Hotel and SK Money Changer, at © **5327-7178.** From atop Doi Inthanon, Thailand's highest peak, flows the

Mae Chaem River. Winding through ravines and past tall cliffs and small settlements, the river makes for a gorgeous and fun **river-rafting trip.** Maesot Conservation Tour puts together a 2-day/1-night trip that includes a drive to the summit of the mountain, followed by rafting (a rubber inflatable raft) with stops at villages and archaeological sites along the way. All equipment is provided. Contact them at 175/18 Ratchadamnern Rd. (© and fax **5381-4505**). The cost is 3,500B (US$80) per person, with everything included.

SHOPPING

While traveling through the many regions of Thailand, you're sure to find Thai arts and handicrafts in abundance in shops and at souvenir stalls. Most of the truly creative and unique items are made in the northern part of the country, and if Chiang Mai is on your itinerary, your best bet is to delay any purchases until you've arrived here. Not only will you find the best selection of jewelry, embroidery, silks, pottery, carved wood, and religious artifacts, but you'll probably buy them at a much more reasonable price as well.

The centerpiece of Chiang Mai shopping is the famous **Night Market.** In the late afternoon, merchants set up their tents on the sidewalks along Chang Klan Road, beginning at the intersection of Loi Kroa Road. Until about 11pm nightly, the street and the alleys beyond become a maze of good excuses to blow your vacation cash.

The **Anusarn Night Market,** located just southwest of the Night Bazaar, closes an hour earlier but has less tourist traffic and more bargains.

Dedicated shoppers will have to devote at least half a day to shopping along the Chiang Mai–Sankamphaeng Road (Rte. 1006). It runs due east out of Chiang Mai and after several kilometers becomes lined with shops, showrooms, and factories extending another 9km (5½ miles). Most are open daily from 8am to 6pm. If you plan on doing a lot of shopping, joining a "shopping tour" group is the best idea. These half-day or full-day excursions are planned by just about every tour operator. If you hire a private car, you can take your time, stopping at each place to peruse.

CHIANG MAI AFTER DARK

Most folks will spend at least 1 night at the Night Bazaar for an evening full of shopping adventure. If you get tired and hungry along the way, stop at the **Kalare Food & Shopping Center,** 89/2 Chang Klan Road, on the corner of Soi 6, behind the bazaar (© **5327-2067**). Free nightly traditional Thai folk dance and musical performances grace an informal beer garden where shoppers can stop for a drink or pick up inexpensive Chinese, Thai, and Indian food from stalls around. Just behind, local singer-guitarists play more modern selections. For an impromptu bar scene, duck into one of the back alleys behind the Night Bazaar mall that are lined with tiny bars.

For a more studied **cultural performance,** the **Old Chiang Mai Cultural Center,** 185/3 Wulai Rd. (© **5327-4093**), stages a good show at 7pm every night for 270B (US$6), which includes dinner. Live music accompanies female dancers in handsome costumes who perform traditional dances. In between sets, men dance with knives and swords. A khan toke dinner is served, and despite the crowds, the wait staff remains quite attentive. Yes, it's touristy—busloads find their way here—but I still had a great time. Call ahead, and they'll plan transportation from your hotel.

Most **discos and lounges,** located in major hotels, feature live music, whether it's a quiet piano bar or a rock pub featuring a Filipino band. If you want a nice lounge for a cocktail or two, **The Royal Princess Hotel's Casablanca Room,**

112 Chang Klan Rd. (© **5328-1033**), has live music nightly. The casual tavern atmosphere and live pop and rock at **The Riverside Restaurant & Bar,** 9–11 Charoenrat Rd. (© **5324-3239**), make up my pick for a great night out with friends. The Bubble Disco in Pornping Tower, 46 Charoen Prathit Rd. (© **5327-0099**), and the **Crystal Cave Disco at Empress Hotel,** Chang Klan Road (© **5327-0240**), are two of the most popular discos in the city. Pick up a copy of *Welcome to Chiang Mai & Chiang Rai* magazine at your hotel for listings of events that are happening while you're in town. If you're here during August and September, really try to stop by the annual Elvis festival at the **Imperial Mae Ping Hotel** (© **5327-0160**). Local artists join male and female impersonators from all over the world with names like Elvis Golden Hair, Elvis 3 in 1, and Elvis Roasted Chicken. Elvis Roasted Chicken? I laughed; I cried.

13 Chiang Rai

Chiang Rai (780km/485 miles NE of Bangkok; 180km/112 miles NE of Chiang Mai) is Thailand's northernmost province; the mighty Mae Kok River (known to most readers as the Mekong of Vietnam fame) shares borders with Laos to the east and Burma to the west. The scenic Mae Kok River, which supports many hill-tribe villages along its banks, flows right through the provincial capital of Chiang Rai.

Chiang Rai is 575m (1,885 ft.) above sea level in a fertile valley, and its cool, refreshing climate; tree-lined riverbank; small Night Market; and easy-to-get-around layout lure travelers weary of traffic congestion and pollution in Chiang Mai.

It's a small city, with most services grouped around the main north-south street, Phahonyothin Road, until it turns right (that is, E) at the **Clock Tower,** after which it's called Ratanaket. There are three noteworthy landmarks: the small clock tower in the city's center; the **statue of King Mengrai** (the city's founder) at the northeast corner of the city, on the superhighway to Mae Chan; and the **Mae Kok River,** at the north edge of town. Singhakai Road is the main artery on the north side of town, parallel to the river. The bus station is on Prasopsuk Road, 1 block east of Phahonyothin Road, near the Wiang Inn Hotel. The Night Market is on Phahonyothin Road near the bus station.

VISITOR INFORMATION

The **TAT** (© **5374-4674**) is located at 448/16 Singhakai Rd., near Wat Phra Singh on the north side of town, and the Tourist Police are next door. The monthly *Welcome to Chiang Mai & Chiang Rai* is distributed free by most hotels and has a good, reliable map of the town.

GETTING THERE

By Plane   **Thai Airways** has five flights daily from Bangkok to Chiang Rai (flying time: 85 min.), and two daily flights from Chiang Mai (flying time: 40 min.). Contact them in Bangkok at © **2535-2084,** or in Chiang Rai at 870 Phaholyothin Rd. (© **5371-1179**).

The **Chiang Rai International Airport** (© **5379-3048**) is about 10km (6¼ miles) north of town. There's a bank exchange open daily 9am to 5pm, and a gift shop. Taxis hover outside expectantly: It costs 150B (US$3.40) to town, and more to other towns in the province.

By Bus   Three air-conditioned VIP 24-seat buses leave daily from Bangkok's **Northern Bus Terminal** (© **5731-8055**) to Chiang Rai (trip time: 11 hr.; 700B/US$16). Buses leave hourly between 6am and 5:30pm from **Chiang**

Mai's Arcade Bus Terminal (© **5324-2664;** trip time: 3½ hr.; 66B/US$1.50 not air-conditioned; 119B/US$2.70 air-conditioned). Chiang Rai's **Khon Song Bus Terminal** (© **5371-1369**) couldn't be more conveniently located—it's on Phrasopsook Road, off Phaholyothin Road near the Night Market, just in the center of town. Tuk-tuks and samlors are easy to catch here for trips around town for 30B to 60B (US70¢–US$1.35).

By Car The fast, not particularly scenic route from Bangkok is Highway 1 North, direct to Chiang Rai. A slow, scenic approach on blacktop mountain roads is Route 107 north from Chiang Mai to Fang, and then Route 109 east to Highway 1.

By Boat Longtail boat taxis can be privately hired to ply the Mae Kok River between the village of Thaton and Chiang Rai (trip time: 5 hr.; 1,600B/US$36 per boat). You can take orange bus no. 1231 to Thaton town for 50B (US$1.10) early in the morning to arrange a whole day trip along the river with stops at interesting sites along the way. See "Exploring Chiang Rai," below, for more trip details. Songtao wait at the ferry in Chiang Rai to take you to town.

GETTING AROUND

By Trishaw or Tuk-Tuk You'll probably find walking the best method of transport. However, there are *samlors* (bicycle trishaws) parked outside the Night Market and on the banks of the Mae Kok River; they charge 10B to 30B (US20¢–US70¢) for in-town trips. During the day, there are tuk-tuks, which charge 30B to 60B (US70¢–US$1.35) for in-town trips.

By Bus Frequent local buses are the easiest and cheapest way to get to nearby cities. All leave from the bus station (© **5371-1369**) on Prasopsuk Road, near the Wiang Inn Hotel.

By Motorcycle Two local companies are recommended: **Soon Motorcycle,** 197/2 Trirath Rd. (© **5371-4068**), and **Lek House,** 95 Thanalai Rd. (© **5371-3337**). Daily rates run about 550B (US$12) for a 250cc motorcycle, 180B (US$4.10) for a 100cc moped, and 15B (US35¢) for a helmet.

By Car **Avis** has a branch at the airport (© **5379-3827**) and another at Dusit Island Resort Hotel (© **5371-5777**), where self-drive vehicles cost from 1,500B (US$34) for a Jeep to more than 2,000B (US$45) for a sedan.

C FAST FACTS: Chiang Rai

Banks/Currency Exchange Several bank exchanges are located on Paholyothin Road in the center of town. They are open daily 8:30am to 10pm.

Internet/E-mail There are plenty of **Internet cafes,** especially on the soi that leads off Paholyothin Road to Wiangcome Hotel, but the best one is **Chiang Rai Cyber Net** (© **5375-2513**) just opposite the hotel.

Hospital The **Overbrook Hospital** (© **5371-1366**) is on the north side of town at Singhakai and Trairat roads, west of the TAT.

Post Office/Mail The post office is on Utrakit Road 2 blocks north of the Clock Tower, also near the TAT.

Tourist Police The **Tourist Police** (© **5371-7796**) are next to the TAT on Singhakai Road.

WHERE TO STAY
VERY EXPENSIVE
Dusit Island Resort Hotel ★★ Chiang Rai's best resort hotel occupies a large delta island in the Mae Kok River. It's sure to please those looking for international luxury and resort comforts, though at the expense of local flavor and homeyness.

The dramatic lobby is a soaring space of teak, marble, and glass, as grand as any in Thailand, with panoramic views of the Mae Kok. Rooms are luxuriously appointed in pastel cottons and teak trim. The Dusit Island's manicured grounds, pool, and other facilities create a resort ambience, but that shouldn't dissuade you from exploring the town. The hotel's most formal dining room is the semicircular Peak on the 10th floor, with sweeping views and a grand terrace overlooking the Mae Kok. The fine Continental fare runs 1,100B to 2,200B (US$25–US$50) per person. Chinatown is a more casual Cantonese restaurant, with a large, tasty dim sum offering at lunch and excellent Chinese fare at dinner. The sunny coffee shop extends into an outdoor poolside terrace and makes for scenic dining. In the evening, there's the cozy Music Room bar and a new nightclub. An outdoor swimming pool, floodlit tennis courts, a health club, and Yogi traditional Thai massage round out the resort's recreational facilities.

1129 Kraisorasit Rd., Amphur Muang 57000, Chiang Rai (over bridge at NW corner of town). ☎ **5371-5777.** Fax 5371-5801. www.dusit.com. 271 units. 5,129B (US$117) double; from 11,000B (US$250) suite. AE, DC, MC, V. **Amenities:** 3 restaurants (Chinese, Western, international); lounge and pub; outdoor pool; lighted tennis courts; fitness center w/Jacuzzi, sauna, steam, and massage; spa w/Jacuzzi, sauna, steam, and massage; game room; concierge; tour desk; car-rental desk; limousine service; 24-hr. room service; babysitting; same-day laundry service/dry cleaning; nonsmoking rooms; executive-level rooms. *In room:* A/C, TV w/satellite programming, minibar, safe.

EXPENSIVE
Rimkok Resort Hotel ★ Though inconvenient, this riverside resort offers fine views. Well decorated and plush with first-class amenities, the rooms offer comforts rarely found in this town. The public spaces are also quite grand, thoroughly done over in Thai decor and arts and crafts, and lushly planted lawns open off large verandas. The Rimkok Resort has a free regular shuttle service to town, which is necessary because it's pretty far out. For meals, there's the attractive Saen Wee Coffee Shop and a poolside bar and terrace.

6 Moo 4, Tathorn Rd., Amphur Muang, 57100 Chiang Rai (on N shore of Kok River, about 6km/3¾ miles N of town center). ☎ **5371-6445.** Fax 5371-5859. 256 units. 1,700B (US$39) double; from 6,000B (US$136) suite. AE, DC, MC, V. **Amenities:** 3 restaurants (Thai, international grill); bar and lounge; large outdoor pool; Jacuzzi; tour desk; limousine service; limited room service; massage; babysitting; same-day laundry service. *In room:* A/C, TV w/satellite programming, minibar.

Wangcome Hotel ★ The Wangcome is the best city hotel in town, plus it has a fabulous central location. Rooms are small but comfortable, detailed with Lanna Thai style, such as carved teak headboards. In the center of the hotel complex, rooms look out to the outdoor swimming pool. There's a lively coffee shop and a moody cocktail lounge, a popular rendezvous spot after the Night Market (across the street) closes.

896/90 Penawibhata Rd., Chiang Rai Trade Center, Amphur Muang 57000, Chiang Rai (W off Paholyothin Rd.). ☎ **5371-1800.** Fax 5371-2973. 234 units. 1,600B (US$36) double; from 2,000B (US$45) suite. AE, DC, MC, V. **Amenities:** Restaurant (international); lounge; small pool; tour desk; limousine service; business center; massage; laundry service. *In room:* A/C, TV w/satellite programming, minibar.

MODERATE
The Golden Triangle Inn ★★★ A charming little hotel that offers comfort and lots of style and character, the Golden Triangle is set in lush gardens—once

inside you'd never believe bustling Chiang Rai is just beyond the front entrance. Large rooms have terra-cotta tiled floors, traditional-style furniture, and reproductions of Lanna artifacts and paintings. The owners and management are very down to earth and extremely helpful, and their operations are very well organized and professional. The restaurant is excellent and is reviewed separately in this chapter, as is the travel agency. It's my favorite pick for Chiang Rai.

590 Paholyothin Rd., Amphur Muang 57000, Chiang Rai (2 blocks N of bus station). ✆ **5371-1339.** Fax 5371-3963. 39 units. 650B–900B (US$15–US$20) double. MC, V. **Amenities:** Restaurant (international); tour desk; car-rental desk; laundry service. *In room:* A/C, no phone.

WHERE TO DINE

Cabbages & Condoms ✮ THAI   Sister restaurant to Cabbages & Condoms in Bangkok, this northern branch was opened by the Population & Community Development Association to help support population control, AIDS awareness, and a host of rural development programs in the north. An extensive Thai menu, with local catfish specialties, is excellent. It's popular for tour groups, which also come for the exhibit upstairs (see "Exploring Chiang Rai," below), but don't let that keep you away—it's good food for a good cause.

620/25 Thanalai Rd. ✆ **5371-9167.** Entrees 70B–200B (US$1.60–US$4.55). MC, V. Daily 10am–11pm.

Golden Triangle International Café ✮ THAI   The decor—antique artifacts and photos—is an ode to old Chiang Rai. The owner grew up in the town and loves it well. The best reason to eat here is for the menu, which is almost like a short book explaining Thai dinner menus, the various dishes that make up a meal, and the ingredients and preparation of each. The choose-your-own noodle dishes give you the chance to experiment with various tastes and are prepared in quick-and-tasty fashion. Go for the regional treats, especially the curry sweetened with local litchies.

Golden Triangle Inn, 590 Phaholyothin Rd. ✆ **5371-1339.** Entrees 80B–250B (US$1.80–US$5.70). MC, V. Daily 8am–10:30pm.

Islands Café INTERNATIONAL   Overlooking the Kok River, this casual restaurant has excellent quality food and great selection. The lunch buffet is extensive and fresh, and the atmosphere is cooling and relaxing. Like the rest of the resort's staff, waiters here provide excellent service.

In the Dusit Island Resort Hotel, 1129 Kraisorasit Rd. ✆ **5371-5777.** Entrees 60B–300B (US$1.35–US$6.80). AE, MC, V. Daily 6am–11pm.

The Night Market/Food Stalls MARKET   Every night after 7pm, the cavernous, tin-roofed Municipal Market, south of the Rama Hotel comes alive with dozens of chrome-plated food stalls that serve steamed, grilled, and fried Thai treats. This is a fun sight (about a 10-min. walk northwest from the souvenir Night Market), but not as hygienic as most people would like.

Trairat and Tanarai rds., NW of Clock Tower.

EXPLORING CHIANG RAI
THE WATS

Wat Doi Tong (Phra That Chomtong)   This Burmese-style wat offers an overview of the town and a panorama of the Mae Kok valley. It's said that King Mengrai himself chose the site for his new Lan Na capital from this very hill. The circle of columns at the top of the hill surrounds the new lak muang (city pillar), built to commemorate the 725th anniversary of the city and King Bhumibol's

60th birthday. It is often criticized for its failure to represent local style. (You can see the old wooden lak muang in the wihaan of the wat.)

Atop a hill above the NW side of town, up a steep staircase off Kaisornrasit Rd.

Wat Phra Kaeo   Phra Kaeo is the best known of the northern wats because it once housed the Emerald Buddha now at Bangkok's royal Wat Phra Kaeo. Near its Lanna-style chapel is the chedi, which (according to legend) was struck by lightning in 1436 to reveal the precious green jasper Buddha. There is now a green jade replica of the image on display.

On Trairat Rd. on the NW side of town, just N of Ruang Nakhon Rd.

Wat Phra Singh   The restored wat is thought to date from the 15th century. Inside is a replica of the Phra Singh Buddha, a highly revered Theravada Buddhist image; the original was removed to Chiang Mai's Wat Phra Singh.

2 blocks E of Wat Phra Kaeo.

VISITING THE HILL TRIBES

Most of the **hill-tribe villages** within close range of Chiang Rai have become somewhat assimilated by the routine visits of group tours. If your time is too limited for a trek, several in-town travel agencies offer day trips to the countryside. Prices are based on a two-person minimum and decline as more people sign up; rates include transportation and a guide.

The best operation in Chiang Rai is **Golden Triangle Tours** ✦, 590 Phaholyothin Rd. (© **5371-1339;** fax 5371-3963; gotour@loxinfo.co.th). With about 20 different day and overnight trips, their experience has created offerings that are well in tune with what travelers seek in this area. For hill-tribe treks, they have day trips and longer trips, from 2 days and 1 night to 6 days and 5 nights. **Day trips** to surrounding villages include light trekking (1,300B/US$29) per person for two or three people. If you include elephant trekking, it's 1,700B (US$39) per person for two or three people. Longer treks cost 3,200B (US$73) per person (for 2–3 people) for 2 days and 1 night, 4,200B (US$95) per person for 3 days and 2 nights, and 7,500B (US$170) per person for 6 days and 5 nights. You'll encounter numerous Akha, Hmong, Yao, Karen, or Lahu tribes, depending on the length of your trip.

LONGTAIL BOAT TRIPS ON THE MAE KOK RIVER

The Mae Kok River is a fascinating attraction here for its beautiful scenery along its banks. You can hire a longtail boat to zip you up and down the river, stopping at sites along the way. Charter boats begin at 7am and can be booked at any time until 11pm. A full-day trip to Thathon and back costs 2,100B (US$48) for boat hire. You'll have the option to stop at the Buddha cave, a temple within a cavern; an elephant camp, for trekking; a hot spring; and a riverside Lahu village. If you have limited time, you can hire a boat to view only one or two attractions from 300B to 700B (US$7–US$16), depending on the stops you make. The ferry pier is beyond the bridge across from the Dusit Island Resort. Call **C. R. Harbour** (© **5375-0009**) for information and taxi pickup.

Maesalong Tours, 882–4 Phaholyothin Rd. (© **5371-2515;** fax 5371-1011), conducts half-day river cruises north of Chiang Saen, with a stop on the Lao side at the small riverside town of Muang Mom (1,520B/US$35 per person). A full-day cruise includes additional stops at Stone Forest, with its picturesque natural rock formations, plus sand beaches and additional Lao villages (2,280B/US$52 per person).

SHOPPING

The recent influx of tourists has made Chiang Rai a magnet for hill-tribe cloth-ing and crafts. You'll find many boutiques in the Night Market near the bus ter-minal off Phaholyothin Road, as well as some fine shops scattered around the city. Most are open daily from 8:30am to 10pm and accept credit cards. There's much less available than in Chiang Mai, but prices are reasonable.

Chiang Rai Handicrafts Center, 273 Moo 5, Paholyothin Rd. (4km/2½ miles north of town on the superhighway; call ahead for a free pickup; ℰ **5371-3355**), is the largest of the hill-tribe shops, with a huge selection of well-finished merchandise, an adjoining factory, and a good reputation for air-mail shipping.

CHIANG RAI AFTER DARK

Most visitors stroll through the **Night Market** to shop for souvenirs. It's really a miniversion of the more famous market in Chiang Mai. Shops clustered along Paholyothin Road near the Wiang Inn, and around the two lanes leading off it to the Wangcome Hotel, stay open until 10pm.

There's a small and rather tawdry nightlife district west and south of the Clock Tower along Punyodyana Road, a private lane with clubs named **Lobo, La Cantina, My Way, Mars Bar,** and **Butterfly.** You can also hit the disco or karaoke bar at the **Inn Come,** across from Little Duck on the superhighway, or have a draft beer and toss a few darts at the **Cellar Pub,** at the Dusit Island Resort.

14 Chiang Saen ⟨★ & the Golden Triangle

The small village of Chiang Saen (935km/581 miles NE of Bangkok; 239km/148 miles NE of Chiang Mai) has the sleepy, rural charm of Burma's ancient capital of Pagan. The single-lane road from Chiang Rai (59km/37 miles) follows the small Mae Nam Chan River past coconut groves and rice paddies guarded by water buffalo. Little Chiang Saen, the birthplace of expansionary King Men-grai, was abandoned for the new Lanna Thai capitals of Chiang Rai, then Chi-ang Mai, in the 13th century. With the Mae Khong River and the Laos border hemming in its growth, modern developers went elsewhere. Today the slow rural pace, decaying regal wats, crumbling fort walls, and overgrown moat contribute greatly to its appeal. After visiting the excellent museum and local sites, most travelers head west along the Mae Khong to the Golden Triangle, the north's prime attraction.

VISITOR INFORMATION

There is no TAT, so make sure you talk to TAT in Chiang Rai before your trip. The staff at the few guesthouses speak some English and try to be helpful.

Route 1016 is the village's main street, also called Paholyothin Road, which intersects after 500m (1,640 ft.) with the Mae Khong River. Along the river road, there are a few guesthouses to the west and an active produce, souvenir, and clothing market to the east.

GETTING THERE

By Bus   Buses from **Chiang Rai's Kohn Song Bus Terminal** leave every 15 minutes from 6am to 6pm (trip time: 1½ hr.; 20B/US45¢). The bus drops you on Chiang Saen's main street. The museum and temples are walking distance, for convenient day trips, and songtao are across the street for trips to the Golden Triangle (about 10B/US20¢).

By Car   Take the superhighway Route 110 north from Chiang Rai to Mae Chan, and then take Route 1016 northeast to Chiang Saen.

GETTING AROUND

On Foot   There's so little traffic that it's a pleasure to walk; all of the in-town sights are within a 15-minutes walk of each other.

By Bicycle & Motorcycle   It's a great bike ride (45 min.) from Chiang Saen to the prime nearby attraction, the Golden Triangle. The roads are well paved and pretty flat. Chiang Saen House Rent Motor, on the river road just east of the main street intersection, has good one-speed bicycles for 30B (US70¢) per day, and 100cc motorcycles (no insurance, no helmets) for 180B (US$4.10) per day.

By Samlor   Motorized pedicabs hover by the bus stop in town to take you to the Golden Triangle for 60B (US$1.35) one-way. Round-trip fares with waiting time are negotiable to about 250B (US$5.70) for about 2 hours.

By Songao   Songtao (truck taxis) can be found on the main street across from the market; rides cost only 10B (US20¢) to the Golden Triangle or to nearby guesthouses.

By Longtail Boat   Longtail boat captains down by the river offer Golden Triangle tours for about 400B (US$9.10) per boat (seating 8) per half-hour. Many people enjoy the half-hour cruise, take a walk around the village of Sob Ruak after they've seen the Golden Triangle, and then continue on by bus.

FAST FACTS: CHIANG SAEN & THE GOLDEN TRIANGLE

There's a **Siam Commercial Bank** in the center of Phaholyothin Road, Route 1016, the main street, close to the **bus stop, post and telegram office** (no overseas service and few local telephones), and the police station. The Chiang Saen National Museum is on main street as well. There is a **currency exchange** booth at the Golden Triangle.

WHERE TO STAY & DINE

The Imperial Golden Triangle Resort ⍟   This five-story hotel block looms over the west corner of tiny, souvenir-soaked Ban Sob Ruak. Modern, spacious guest rooms with pastel and rattan decor have large balconies; the more expensive rooms overlook the Golden Triangle. It's a fine, totally comfortable choice if you're passing through, but not nearly the tribal experience that the Le Meridien Baan Boran provides. There's a three-story, Lanna Thai–style restaurant, with multipeaked roofs, that serves northern Thai specialties and some Continental cuisine, and has an evening cocktail lounge. There's also a small outdoor pool.

222 Golden Triangle, Chiang Saen, 57150 Chiang Rai (in Sob Ruak, 11km/7 miles NW of Chiang Saen). ℭ **5378-4001.** Fax 5378-4006. 73 units. 2,500B (US$57) double; from 7,000B (US$159) suite. AE, MC, V. **Amenities:** Restaurant (international); lounge; pool; tour desk; laundry service. *In room:* A/C, TV w/satellite programming, minibar.

Le Meridien Baan Boran Hotel ⍟⍟⍟   In stunning contrast to most new hotels, this one is a triumph of ethnic design. You'll never question whether you're in the scenic hill-tribe region because the Le Meridien Baan Boran's elegance and style depend on locally produced geometric and figurative weavings, carved teak panels, and pervasive views of the juncture of the Ruak and Mae Khong Rivers. On a hilltop just 2km (1¼ miles) west of the infamous Golden Triangle, the balconied rooms have splendid views. This oasis of comfort has attached rooms that are so spacious and private that you'll feel like you're in your own bungalow. Tiled foyers lead to large bathrooms and bedrooms furnished in teak and traditionally patterned fabrics.

Golden Triangle, Chiang Saen 57150, Chiang Rai (above river, 12km/7½ miles NW of Chiang Saen). ℂ 800/225-5843 in the U.S., or 5378-4084. Fax 5378-4090. 110 units. 4,840B–6,600B (US$110–US$150) double; 11,880B (US$270) suite. AE, DC, MC, V. **Amenities:** 2 restaurants (Thai, international); lounge and bar; outdoor pool; outdoor lighted tennis courts; fitness center w/Jacuzzi, sauna, and massage; Jacuzzi; bike rental; concierge; tour desk; car-rental desk; limousine service; business center; shopping arcade; salon; limited room service; babysitting; same-day laundry service. *In room:* A/C, TV w/pay movies and satellite programming, minibar, coffee/tea-making facilities, hair dryer, safe.

EXPLORING CHIANG SAEN

Allow at least half a day to see all of Chiang Saen's historical sights before exploring the Golden Triangle. To help with orientation, make the museum your first stop. There's a good map about local historical sites on its second floor.

The **Chiang Saen National Museum,** 702 Paholyothin Rd. (ℂ **5377-7102**), houses a small but very fine collection of this region's historic and ethnographic products. The ground floor's main room has a collection of large bronze and stone Buddha images dating from the 15th- to 17th-century Lanna Kingdom. Pottery from Sukhothai-era kiln sites is displayed downstairs and on the balcony.

The handicrafts and cultural items of local hill tribes are fascinating, particularly the display of Nam Bat, an ingenious fishing tool. Burmese-style lacquer ware, Buddha images, and wood carvings scattered through the museum reinforce the similarities seen between Chiang Saen and its spiritual counterpart, Pagan. Allow an hour to go through the museum carefully. It's open Wednesday to Sunday 9am to 4pm; it's closed holidays. Admission is 30B (US70¢).

Wat Pa Sak, the best preserved, is set in a landscaped historical park that contains a large, square-based stupa and six smaller chedis and temples. The park preserves what's left of the compound's 1,000 teak trees. The wat is said to have been constructed in 1295 by King Saen Phu to house relics of the Buddha, though some historians believe its ornate combination of Sukhothai and Pagan styles dates it later. The historical park is about 220m (656 ft.) west of the Chiang Saen Gate (at the entrance to the village). It's open daily 8am to 5pm; admission is 20B (US45¢).

The area's oldest wat is still an active Buddhist monastery. Rising from a cluster of wooden dorms, **Wat Phra Chedi Luang** (or Jadeeloung) has a huge brick chedi that dominates the main street. The wat complex was established in 1331 under the reign of King Saen Phu and was rebuilt in 1515 by King Muang Kaeo. The old brick foundations, now supporting a very large plaster seated Buddha flanked by smaller ones, are all that remain. Small bronze and stucco Buddhas excavated from the site are now in the museum. It's open daily from 8am to 5pm. Admission is free.

There are several other wats of note in and around the town. **Wat Mung Muang** is the 15th-century square-based stupa seen next to the post office. Above the bell-shape chedi are four small stupas. Across the street, you can see the bell-shape chedi from **Wat Phra Bouj.** It's rumored to have been built by the prince of Chiang Saen in 1346, though historians believe it's of the same period as Mung Muang. As you leave Chiang Saen on the river road, going northwest to the Golden Triangle, you'll pass **Wat Pha Kao Pan,** with some sculpted Buddha images tucked in niches and on its stupa, and then the unrestored vihara mound of **Wat Sangakaeo Don Tan.** Both are thought to date from the 16th century.

THE GOLDEN TRIANGLE

The infamous Golden Triangle (12km/7½ miles northwest of Chiang Saen) is the point where Thailand, Burma, and Laos meet at the confluence of the broad, slow, and silted Mekong and Mae Ruak Rivers. They create Thailand's north border, separating it from overgrown jungle patches of Burma to the east and forested, hilly Laos to the west. The area's appeal as a vantage point over forbidden territories is quickly diminishing because there is now a legal crossing into Laos from nearby Chiang Khong.

Nonetheless, a "look" at the home of ethnic hill tribes and their legendary opium trade is possibly interesting. Despite years of DEA-financed campaigns, the annual yield is still nearly 4,000 tons—about half of the heroin sold in the United States. The "surrender" of the notorious drug lord Khun Sa and his Muang Tai Army to the military dictators of Myanmar (Burma) effected little change—there were plenty of others waiting to take his place.

The appeal of this geopolitical phenomenon has created an entire village, Sob Ruak, of thatch souvenir stalls, cheap river-view soda and noodle shops, and very primitive guesthouses. The **House of Opium,** 212 Moo 1 (© **5378-4062**), is tiny and packed with visitors (if you see tour buses outside, go across the street and have a drink until they leave). Displays walk you through the opium process, from poppy cultivation, opium harvesting, drug production, and opium consumption. It makes a killing on camp appeal, but it is quite informative.

Golden Triangle doesn't take too long to see, so I recommend a relaxing afternoon beer at **Jang's Place,** a small local establishment just across from the sandbar. *Be warned:* You might get so comfortable you'll never leave. Don't worry, though; they'll send out for food.

6

Vietnam

by Charles Agar

Sadly, for so many, the very mention of Vietnam conjures images of jungle warfare and the strife that marks the country's late history. Though the events of that turbulent time just over a quarter century ago lie just below the surface for all combatants and those who lived through the war in Vietnam and abroad, Vietnam is long a vibrant tourist destination and a visit of any length will dispel many preconceptions. From lush jungle terrain to beautiful coastline, cosmopolitan cities to friendly hamlets, or among Vietnam's many hill tribes, travelers can experience the gamut in only a short trip here.

The country has more than 2,000 years of its own history to boast, and while occupation by the Chinese, French, and Americans has left its brutal imprints on the Vietnamese story, it has also left a rich cultural smorgasbord. Chinese and French food, language, and architecture have been assimilated smoothly into Vietnamese culture and exist as attractive embellishments to an already fascinating nation. An ancient Confucian university, a Zen monastery, a Buddhist temple built in the Hindu style, a Vietnamese puppet show, French country chalets, and gourmet restaurants—you'll find them all in Vietnam. The Kingdom of Cham, an Indian- and Khmer-influenced nation, also made what is present-day Vietnam its home from the 2nd through 18th centuries, leaving a stunning legacy of art in its temples and sculpture.

Ethnic Vietnam can be seen by visiting some of the country's more than 54 minority groups, usually living in rural, mountainous areas. Their distinct clothing, language, and customs present another side of the country entirely.

Then there is the land of natural beauty. From tall mountains and craggy limestone formations to dense jungles, river deltas, and pristine beaches, Vietnam's ecological treasures alone are worth a trip. Adventure and outdoor travel outfitters have discovered the country lately, and many travelers come to trek, bicycle, and paddle their way through scenic surroundings. On the other side of the spectrum, luxurious Vietnam is available in the form of five-star hotels and idyllic seaside resorts.

If you want to see the country's past in terms of its wars, you can easily do so. Many sites, like the tunnel city of Vinh Moc, near Hue; crumbling pillboxes of the DMZ; or old Viet Cong hideouts in the Mekong Delta are somber reminders of the past. American veterans and history buffs of all nationalities visit former bases and battle sites. The Vietnamese, though, would rather put their turbulent history behind them; the sentiment is almost a public policy, and you'll hear it like a mantra. You might have a chance to talk about the wars on a casual basis with people, and some might even share their stories, but expect no recrimination here.

Instead, the Vietnamese are going forward to establish their country as a unified whole, a unique entity in the world, a strong nation at peace at last. From the smallest northern village to frantic Saigon in the south, all seem to be rushing to develop infrastructure as quickly as possible, to make money and embrace foreign investment and tourism. Since the inception of *doi moi*, the Communist Party's policy of loosening stringent economic restrictions and opening trade, Vietnam has enjoyed exponential growth. Following the Asian Economic Crisis that hit Thailand in the 1990s and sent all neighboring economies for a spin, Vietnam is enjoying prosperity, with an influx of foreign investment and trade. In the larger cities, the central business districts rank with any in the world for quantity of glass and steel, and are peopled by busy Western business-people (they're the ones in suits unharried by touts). Expat residents bring along their pocketbooks and appetites, and local hotels and restaurants rise to the challenge, offering some great dining and luxe hotels.

If you've never been to Vietnam, you'll be amazed at how easy it is to navigate. Everybody seems to speak English and to be somehow connected with the tourism industry. Everybody wants to sell you something, too, and that means lots of touts, but that can work to your advantage: You'll have your pick of tour guides, ticket agents, and chauffeurs. That might not be necessary, though; Vietnam's relatively good roadways and newly efficient air system make much of this small country within very easy reach of the casual traveler.

So, whether to close a chapter on the past, to experience a lively ancient culture, to see beautiful countryside, to get your adventure fix, or to just get a bit of beachside or cosmopolitan comfort, Vietnam has it all. Be sure to bring your camera: The whole country is a photo op in motion.

1 Getting to Know Vietnam

THE LAY OF THE LAND

Vietnam is an S-shape peninsula that borders China to the north, Laos to the west, and Cambodia to the southwest. Covering about 331,520 sq. km (128,000 sq. miles), it is roughly the size of Italy. It has a varied and lush topography, with two deltas, tropical forests, craggy mountains and rock formations, and a coastline that stretches for 3,260km (2,025 miles), much of it white-sand beaches. Vietnam also claims thousands of islands off its coast.

THE REGIONS IN BRIEF

THE NORTH   The northern highlands, occupying the entire northwest tip of Vietnam, are known for their scenic beauty, with craggy mountains hovering over sweeping green valleys. The inhabitants of the region are ethnic minorities and hill tribes, scratching out a living from subsistence farming and still somewhat isolated from civilization. Popular tourism destinations are **Sapa, Lao Cai, Son La,** and **Dien Bien Phu,** the former French military garrison. Vietnam's tallest mountain, Fansipan (3,143m/10,312 ft.), hovers over Sapa near the border with China in the northwest, part of the mountain range the French dubbed "The Tonkinese Alps." The **Red River** Delta lies to the east of the highlands. It is a triangular shape off the **Gulf of Tonkin,** an extension of the South China Sea. In the gulf is spectacular **Halong Bay,** 3,000 limestone formations jutting up from still blue waters. South of the highlands but still in the northern region is **Hanoi,** Vietnam's capital city.

THE CENTRAL COAST   To the east is the central coastline, location of major cities **Hue, Hoi An,** and **Danang.** Hue is Vietnam's former capital and imperial city (1802–1945). Hoi An, a major trading port in the mid–16th century, still shows the architectural influences of the Chinese and Japanese traders who passed through and settled here, leaving buildings that are perfectly preserved. Danang, Vietnam's fourth-largest city, is a port town whose major attractions include the museum of Cham antiquities and nearby China Beach. Major flooding in the year 2000 caused immeasurable damage to the lowlands here, which will be apparent if you try to navigate Highway 1; at the printing of this book, the highway had yet to be repaired.

THE SOUTH CENTRAL COAST & HIGHLANDS   The central highlands area is a temperate, hilly region occupied by many of Vietnam's ethnic minorities. Travelers are most likely to visit historic **Dalat,** a resort town nestled in the Lang Bien Plateau, established by the French at the turn of the century as a recreation and convalescence center. On the coast is **Nha Trang,** Vietnam's preeminent sea resort.

THE MEKONG DELTA   Farthest south, the Mekong Delta is a flat land formed by soil deposits from the Mekong River. Its climate is tropical, characterized by heat, high rainfall, and humidity. The delta's sinuous waterways drift past fertile land used for cultivating rice, fruit trees, and sugar cane. The lower delta is untamed swampland. The region shows the influences of ancient Funan and Khmer cultures, as well as the scars from war misery, particularly in battles with neighboring Cambodia. **Saigon (Ho Chi Minh City),** Vietnam's largest cosmopolitan area, lies just past its northern peripheries.

VIETNAM TODAY

As a destination, Vietnam is impressive for the sheer variety of what it can offer. A history of more than 1,000 years has developed a rich and varied culture, heavily spiced with remnants of other occupants, like the Chinese, French, and Cham, a Hindu culture that has largely disappeared. Vietnam's 54 ethnic groups, many of them hill tribes living in remote villages, also make it ethnically one of the most diverse in Southeast Asia. The land's topography, with grandiose mountains, lush tropical forests, and beaches of plush sand, is perfect for trekking, paddling, biking, and enjoying every watersport you can name. Its major cities, Hanoi and Saigon, are exciting and cosmopolitan, and have countless cultural and historical attractions, as well as accommodations from budget to ultradeluxe. As a rapidly developing nation, Vietnam is inexpensive and yet comfortable enough to appeal to travelers of all tastes and budgets.

A LOOK AT THE PAST

Vietnam began in the Red River Valley, around the time of the 3rd century B.C., as a small kingdom of Viet tribes called Au Lac. The tiny kingdom was quickly absorbed into the Chinese Qin Dynasty in 221 B.C., but as that dynasty crumpled, it became part of a new land called Nam Viet, ruled by a Chinese commander. In 111 B.C., it was back to China again, this time as part of the Han empire. It remained part of greater China for the next thousand years or so. The Chinese form of writing was adopted (to be replaced by a Roman alphabet in the 17th century), Confucianism was installed as the leading ideology, and Chinese statesmen became the local rulers. Few effectively challenged Chinese rule, with the exception of a nobleman's two daughters, the Trung sisters, who led a successful but short-lived revolt in A.D. 39.

Vietnam

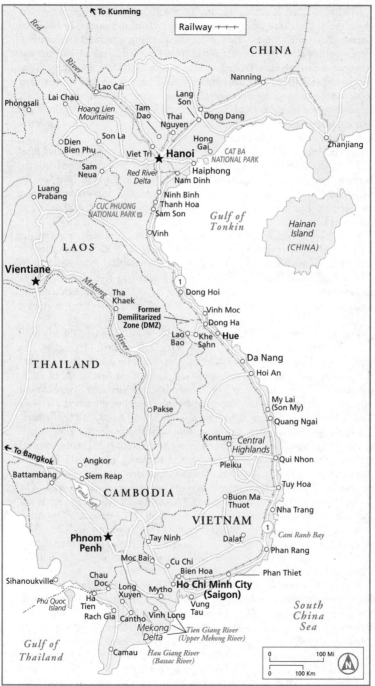

In A.D. 939, the Chinese were finally thrown off and the Vietnamese were left to determine their own destiny under a succession of dynasties. The kingdom flourished and strengthened, enough for the Vietnamese to repel the intrusion of Mongol invaders under Kublai Khan from the north, and armies from the kingdom of Champa from Danang and the east, in the mid–13th century. Gathering strength, Vietnam gradually absorbed the Cham empire and continued to move south, encroaching upon Khmer land, taking the Mekong Delta and almost extinguishing the Khmer as well. There followed a brief period of Chinese dominance in the early 1400s, but the biggest risk to the country's stability was to come from the inside.

Torn between rival factions in court, the country split along north-south lines in 1545; the north followed the Le Dynasty, and the south followed the Nguyen. The country was reunited under Emperor Gia Long in 1802, but by the 1850s, the French, already settled and on the prowl in Indochina, launched an offensive that resulted in the Vietnamese accepting protectorate status 3 decades later.

Although the French contributed greatly to Vietnamese infrastructure, the proud people of Vietnam bridled under colonial rule. In 1930, revolutionary Ho Chi Minh found fertile ground to establish a nationalist movement. As in China, World War II and occupation by the Japanese in 1940 helped fuel the movement by creating chaos and nationalist fervor. Upon the retreat of the Japanese, Ho Chi Minh declared Vietnam an independent nation in August 1945.

The French did not agree, however, and the two sides fought bitterly until 1954. The French, having lost a decisive battle at Dien Bien Phu, agreed to a cease-fire at the Geneva Convention that year. The two sides determined that the country would be split along north and south at the Seventeenth Parallel, with the Viet Minh (League for the Independence of Vietnam) having control of the north and the French supporters having control of the south. Elections were to be held in 2 years to determine who would lead a new, unified Vietnam.

Mainly because of resistance from an American-supported regime in the south, led by Ngo Dinh Diem, the elections were never held. The communists continued to gain power, and Diem was assassinated, putting the southern regime in peril. Finally, in 1965, American president Lyndon Johnson dispatched the first American combat troops to Danang to prop up the south. The Soviet Union and China weighed in with assistance to the north. The rest is history. After a decade of heavy fighting that took 58,000 American and as many as 4 million Vietnamese lives, the communists took Saigon on April 30, 1975. In 1976, north and south were officially reunited. Rather than enjoying the newfound peace, Vietnam invaded Cambodia after border skirmishes in 1978. China, friend of Cambodia, then invaded Vietnam in 1979.

In the mid-1980s, Vietnam began moving toward *doi moi,* a free-market policy, to save itself from bankruptcy. To further ingratiate itself with the international community, it withdrew its army from Cambodia in 1989, and as the 1990s began, the country began opening to the world. It further reorganized its economy toward a market-oriented model, sought diplomatic relations, and in 1991 signed a peace agreement with Cambodia. In 1994, America capitulated and lifted its long-standing trade embargo against Vietnam, and the two countries established diplomatic relations in 1995. Vietnam also joined ASEAN (Association of Southeast Asian Nations).

Today Vietnam is flourishing. It has become the world's third-largest rice exporter. Its per-capita income increases steadily each year, though pockets of extreme poverty still remain in rural areas. Foreign investment is booming following the setback of the Asian Economic Crisis in the late 1990s, and tourists are increasingly discovering its pleasures.

For historical background during the French occupation, read Graham Greene's *The Quiet American.* For history on the American War, Neil Sheehan's *A Bright Shining Lie* is considered the standard bearer. Michael Herr's *Dispatches* gives another view, and *In Retrospect,* by Robert McNamara, U.S. Secretary of Defense during the Vietnam War, is insightful. *The Things They Carried,* by Tim O'Brien, is an interesting fictional account of the war years in the U.S. and Vietnam and is a good read.

A few movies will whet your appetite: *Indochine,* a 1992 film with Catherine Deneuve set during the time of the communist revolution; *The Scent of Green Papaya,* a 1994 story of an elite Vietnamese family and their servant girl; *Cyclo,* a 1995 film about youth gangs in present-day Vietnam; and the film version of *The Quiet American,* with Michael Caine.

VIETNAMESE CULTURE

Vietnam has a cultural landscape as varied and colorful as its topography. The Viet ethnic group is well in the majority, comprising about 88% of the population, but there are 53 other minority ethnic groups, many of whom are hill tribes living in villages largely untouched by modern civilization.

Though Vietnam has rushed into modernization over the past several years, the economy has remained largely agrarian, with farmers, fishermen, and forestry workers accounting for 73% of the workforce and most of the population still residing in small villages. The Vietnamese have a strong sense of family and of community, and are accustomed to close human contact and far-reaching interrelationships. This might be one of the reasons why, despite centuries of occupation by foreigners, Vietnamese cultural traditions have survived. Moreover, outsiders are still welcomed. Americans, in fact, will get a wide smile and a thumbs-up, although the reception is notably better in the south than in the north.

One final note on the subject: Most westerners don't know that since the end of "The Vietnam War," this country has engaged in two other wars—one with Cambodia and another with China. To many Vietnamese, the war with the United States is considered ancient history.

CUISINE

Each region has its specialties, but the hallmarks of Vietnamese food are light, fresh ingredients, heavy on the rice, pork, and fish, with fresh garnishes such as mint, coriander, fish sauce, and chile pepper. Two of the local dishes you're most likely to encounter are *pho,* a noodle soup in a clear broth, and *bun cha,* fresh rice noodles with barbecued pork in sauce. Chinese-influenced dishes can be found, including hot pot, a cook-your-own group activity in which fresh vegetables and chunks of meat and fowl are dipped into boiling broth and then consumed. The French have left their mark as well. Along with excellent restaurants, you'll find espresso and crusty French bread on every street corner.

THE ARTS

Ancient, distinctive Vietnamese art forms remain today, like **water puppetry,** with wooden hand puppets actually dancing across water, and **cheo,** traditional **folk opera.** There is an emerging interest in fine arts, with countless galleries in almost every major Vietnamese city, and an emphasis on traditional techniques such as lacquer and silk painting and wood blocking. **Vietnamese music,** using string and woodwind instruments, bamboo xylophones, and metal gongs, is delicate, distinctive, and appealing. **Literature** has existed since the forming of the nation in folklore, proverbs, and idioms singular to each village and ethnic group, and passed down from century to century. Many of the old tales have been translated and printed in books that you can easily find in a foreign-language bookstore.

RELIGION
About 70% of all Vietnamese are **Buddhists,** mainly Mahayana practitioners of Chinese influence (see "Buddha and Buddhism in Southeast Asia" box in chapter 2), 10% are **Catholics,** and the rest are **Confucianists, animists** (believing in gods of nature), or followers of the unique Vietnamese religion **Cao Dai** (see the section on excursions from Ho Chi Minh), an interesting combination of the major world faiths. **Islam** and **Protestantism** also have small pockets of believers. While we're on the topic of -isms, it's hard for the casual observer to see any observance of communism at all, other than the prevalence of state-owned entities and the bureaucratic hoops you might have to jump through.

ETIQUETTE
Although the Vietnamese are generally tolerant of foreign ways, they dress very modestly. Foreigners displaying navels, chests, or shoulders, or wearing hot pants will attract stares. Swimsuit thongs and nude beach bathing are out of the question. Some temples flatly refuse to admit persons in shorts, and some smaller towns like Hoi An post signs asking tourists to dress "appropriately," which means you might have a run-in with the police if you don't.

Unfortunately, one by-product of the relative newness of tourism in Vietnam is an eagerness to separate you from your money. The child hawkers, "tour guides," and cyclo drivers can be extraordinarily persistent, following you for blocks, grabbing your arm, and hounding you at temples and open-air restaurants. Saying "no" is just an invitation to turn up the sales pitch; even if you don't want to be rude, avoiding eye contact and saying nothing is the best way to extricate yourself. It can be wearying, but things have calmed down a bit in recent years. In tour centers like Hoan-kiem Lake in Hanoi or the major sites in HCMC, you'll still be besieged, though; remember that you're not going to hurt anyone's feelings by ignoring them (but it's hard to do).

LANGUAGE
The ancient Vietnamese language, though not complex structurally, is tonal and, therefore, difficult for many Westerners to master. In its earliest written form, it was based on the Chinese pictographic writing forms, and you'll see remnants of that tradition on temple walls, but in the 17th century, a French scholar developed the Roman alphabet that is used today. Unlike other Asian countries, it looks like you can read this stuff, but the system of accent marks is quite involved (you'll still do double-takes at some signs that look like you might read them). Today most city dwellers seem to speak at least a little English, the older generation speaks some French, and, with increased influence from China (the Chinese comprise well more than 50% of all visitors here), younger people are increasingly studying Mandarin. Students especially will be eager to practice English with you. Solo travelers, being less intimidating, are at an advantage; you'll have many opportunities (and invitation) to have a squat on a street corner, drink a "Bia Hoi" (beer Hoi), and meet people.

USEFUL VIETNAMESE PHRASES

Hello	**Xin chao**
Goodbye	**Tam biet**
Yes	**Vang**
No	**Khong**
Thank you	**Cam on**
You are welcome.	**Khong co gi.**
Excuse me	**Xin loi**
Where is . . .	**O dau . . .**
Turn right.	**Re phai.**
Turn left.	**Re trai.**
Toilet	**Nha ve sinh**
Hotel	**Khach san**
Restaurant	**Nha hang**
Potable water	**Nuoc khoang**
I don't understand.	**Toi khong hieu.**
How much?	**Bao nhieu?**
When?	**Luc nao?**
I need a doctor.	**Toi can bac si.**
Hospital	**Benh vien**
Antibiotic	**Thuoc khang sinh**

2 Planning Your Trip to Vietnam

VISITOR INFORMATION

Vietnam's national tourism administration is a government agency rather than a fount of information, although it does have a fairly good website at www. vietnamtourism.com. It operates mainly through its state-run tourism agencies, **Saigontourist** (www.saigon-tourist.com) and **Vietnamtourism** (www. vietnamtourism.com), with offices all over Vietnam. They provide comprehensive services, including tours and bookings. The website www.vietnamembassy-usa.org (the Vietnam Embassy in the U.S.) is also very helpful, or click on "Vietnam" at the Mekong subregion's cross-referenced site, www.visit-mekong.com.

ENTRY REQUIREMENTS

Residents of the U.S., Canada, Australia, New Zealand, and the United Kingdom need both passports and a valid visa to enter Vietnam. A tourist visa usually lasts for 30 days and costs US$65. You'll pay a bit more through an agent but will save yourself some paper shuffling (can be done for a nominal fee at any travel agent in Bangkok). Getting a visa takes 5–7 days to process. Applicants must submit an application, a passport, and two passport photos. Though there's no official policy, once inside Vietnam, most tourists can extend their visa twice, each time for 30 days, but they go case by case and it's possible only through a travel agent (government-owned Saigontourist is a good bet, but try any of the agents listed in each section). If someone gives you trouble about extending your visa, stick to your guns and ask around. Multiple-entry business visas are available that are valid for up to 3 months, but you must have a sponsoring agency in Vietnam and it can take much longer to process. For short business trips, it's less complicated simply to enter as a tourist.

Tours for Vietnam Veterans

Travelers in Vietnam these days are from all walks of life, but a good percent of them are, surprisingly, American Vietnam veterans. It's not unusual to run across groups or individuals as you make your way across the country, some simply seeing how the story ended or others on more somber missions, such as staging memorial services.

But why would a veteran want to return to Vietnam, the scene of such tragic events? Most say they seek closure and that only by finally crossing the 17th Parallel can they find that; many also say that a trip to Vietnam gives them a chance to truly experience Vietnamese culture this second time around and visit peaceful villages devoid of barbed wire.

Tours of Peace (TOP), a nonprofit organization started by Jess DeVaney, a retired U.S. Marine, arranges tours of Vietnam for Veterans not only to come to terms with their past, but also to participate in the future. DeVaney's tours bring friends and family to points of historical or personal significance, but what is unique here is their humanitarian focus: The folks at TOP believe that through helping others, we heal ourselves, so humanitarian aid projects are part of every tour. TOP visits orphanages, homes for the elderly and the homeless, poor rural villages, and schools, providing food, medicines, and supplies that save lives and give hope. Participants have a chance to return again as jolly-green-giants of yore, only this time able to help and spread kindness. Trip participants say that the tour is a great step in their recovery and toward acceptance of the past.

According to a spokesperson, "TOP participants come home from Vietnam this time feeling whole and understood. Vietnam is no longer a secret and a source of nightmares for them. A Tour of Peace helps participants exorcise the demons of war and find peace of mind."

TOP offers financial assistance for those who find it difficult to foot the bill (see the application on its website) and organizes tours year-round.

Applications for a Tour of Peace can be printed from TOP's website, www.topvietnamveterans.org, or by writing to TOP Vietnam Veterans, 7400 N. Oracle Rd., Suite 100-W, Tucson, AZ 85704.

A few tour operators cater to Veterans and can tailor individual tours to follow a division's history or customized travel for an individual returning veteran's wishes. Most groups visit general operating areas. An itinerary might include starting out in Saigon with an excursion to the Cu Chi tunnels, going down to the Mekong Delta, then heading up to Qui Nhon and to the Central Highlands and Pleiku, and then moving on to Danang, China Beach, Hue, and of course, the demilitarized zone (DMZ).

Contact the following: **The Global Spectrum,** 5683 Columbia Pike, Suite no. 101, Falls Church, VA 22041 (✆ **800/419-4446** or 703/671-9619; fax 703/671-5747; www.vietnamadventuretours.com), or **Nine Dragons Tours,** P.O. Box 24105, Indianapolis, IN 46224-0105 (✆ **800/909-9050** or 317/329-0350; fax 317/329-0117; www.nine-dragons.com).

You no longer need to specify an entry point; Vietnam visas are good for any legal port of entry—land, sea, or air—but remember that your visa begins on the date that you specify on your application.

VIETNAMESE EMBASSY LOCATIONS
IN THE UNITED STATES
- **Vietnam Embassy:** 1233 20th St. NW, Suite 400, Washington, DC 20036 (© **202/861-0737;** fax 202/861-0917)
- **Consulate General of Vietnam:** 1700 California St., Suite 430, San Francisco, CA 94109 (© **415/922-1577;** fax 415/922-1848)
- **Permanent Mission of Vietnam to the United Nations:** 866 UN Plaza, Suite 435, New York, NY 10017 (© **212/644-0594;** fax 212/644-5732)

IN CANADA
- **Vietnam Embassy:** 470 Wilbrod St., Ottawa, Ontario, Canada K1N 6M8 (© **613/236-0772;** fax 613/236-2704)

IN THE UNITED KINGDOM
- **Vietnam Embassy:** 12–14 Victoria Rd., London W8-5RD, U.K. (© **0171/ 937-1912;** fax 0171/937-6108)

IN AUSTRALIA
- **Vietnam Embassy:** 6 Timbarra Crescent, Malley, Canberra, ACT 2606 (© **2/6286-6059;** fax 2/6286-4534)
- **Consulate General of Vietnam:** 489 New South Head Rd., Double Bay, Sydney, NSW 2028 (© **02/9327-2539;** fax 02/9328-1653)

IN THAILAND
- **Vietnam Embassy:** 82/1 Wireless Rd., Bangkok 10500 (© **251-7202,** 251-5835; fax 251-7201, 251-7203)

CUSTOMS REGULATIONS
The first and most important thing to remember is **not to lose your entry/ exit slip,** the colored piece of paper that will be clipped to your passport upon arrival. If you do, you might be fined. If you are entering the country as a tourist, you do not need to declare electronic goods and jewelry if these things are for personal consumption. Declaration forms are only to make sure you're not importing goods without paying a tariff. You must declare cash in excess of US$3,000 or the equivalent. You can also import 200 cigarettes, 2L of alcohol, and perfume and jewelry for personal use. Antiques cannot be exported, although the laws are vague and irregularly enforced. If you're buying a reproduction, have the shop state as much on your receipt, just in case.

MONEY
The official currency of Vietnam is the **dong (VND),** which comes in notes of 100,000, 50,000, 10,000, 5,000, 1,000, 500, and 200 VND.

CURRENCY EXCHANGE & RATES At the time I did my research, the exchange rate was 15,000 Vietnamese VND to 1 U.S. dollar. The U.S. dollar is used as an informal second currency, and most items that cost more than a few dollars are priced in the greenback. I've listed prices in this guide as they are quoted, and conversions were calculated at a rate of 15,000 VND per US$1. Every hotel, no matter how small, will gladly change money for you with some commission or at a slightly lower rate (for US$100, it works out to about 1% in most places). You might squeeze an extra 100 VND or so to the dollar from the black market. Changers usually loiter outside banks or post offices. Count the money you're given carefully, and be alert to counterfeits. The bigger the bill you change, the better your rate will be. Don't accept torn or very grubby bills because you might have a problem reusing them. It might make more sense to pay in U.S. dollars whenever possible, unless you get a very good exchange rate on the black market.

Banks in any city I've mentioned can cash traveler's checks for you in U.S., Canadian, and Australian dollars or pounds sterling, although U.S. dollars get the best rate. A service charge of anywhere between US$1 and US$4 will be levied. Vendors and retailers usually don't like to accept traveler's checks, however. Hanoi and Saigon each have a few automated teller machines (ATMs) that dispense cash in dong and dollars.

As a general rule, credit cards are accepted only at major hotels, restaurants, tour guide operators, and some shops in Hanoi and Saigon, though they're increasingly accepted outside these two major cities. Any Vietcombank branch, as well as big foreign banks, will handle credit card cash withdrawals.

LOST/STOLEN CREDIT CARDS & TRAVELER'S CHECKS   To report lost or stolen cards or traveler's checks, call the nearest branch of Vietcombank. Otherwise, you can go to a post office to place a collect call to the card's international toll-free collect number for cash and a card replacement. The international numbers are operational 24 hours and are as follows: **Visa** Global Customer Assistance Service ✆ **410/581-3836,** and **MasterCard** Global Services ✆ **314/542-7111.** Note that foreigners aren't permitted to make collect calls, so you'll have to get a Vietnamese to assist you. Or, you can use AT&T, whose access number in Vietnam is ✆ **1/201-0288.** For American Express, visit or call the nearest representative office, listed below in "Fast Facts."

WHEN TO GO
PEAK SEASON   For some reason, most people end up coming to Vietnam from September through April, the official "peak season" which doesn't necessarily present them with the best weather. See "Climate," below.

CLIMATE   Vietnam's climate varies greatly from north to south. The north has four distinct seasons, with a chilly but not freezing winter from November to April. Summers are warm and wet. Dalat, in the central highlands, has a temperate climate year-round. The south (which means Nha Trang on down) has hot, humid weather throughout the year, with temperatures peaking March through May into the 90s (30s Celsius). In addition, the south has a monsoon season from April to mid-November, followed by a "dry" season.

If, like many people, you're planning to do a south-north or north-south sweep, you might want to avoid both the monsoons and heat in the south by going sometime between November and February. If you're planning a beach vacation, however, keep in mind that the surf on the south central coast (China Beach, Nha Trang) is too rough for watersports from October through March (but is bringing out the wind-surfers in droves).

⌒Tips Travel Tip
Film is cheap in Vietnam, at about US$2.50 per roll, and the quality of developing services is good. If your camera breaks down, though, have it fixed at home. Disposables are available.

PUBLIC HOLIDAYS   Public holidays are New Year's Day (Jan 1), Tet/Lunar New Year (early to mid-Feb; state holiday that lasts 4 days), Saigon Liberation Day (Apr 30), International Labour Day (May 1), and National Day of the Socialist Republic of Vietnam (Sept 2). Government offices and tourist attractions are closed at these times.

While **Tet** (the lunar new year, in late Jan/early Feb) is Vietnam's biggest holiday, it's very much a family-oriented time and is food-focused, like American Thanksgiving. Folks travel far to get home for some of Mom's cooking. Beginning on the evening exactly 3 days from the Lunar New Year and lasting for 4 days, much of the country closes down, including stores, restaurants, and museums, and accommodations might be difficult to find.

HEALTH CONCERNS

In chapter 3, we outline general information about vaccinations and general issues that affect the region. Health considerations should comprise a good part of your Vietnam trip planning, even if you're going for only a few weeks. You'll need to cover all the bases to protect yourself from tropical weather and illnesses, and you will need to get special vaccinations if rural areas are on your itinerary. You should begin your vaccinations as necessary at least weeks before your trip, to give them time to take effect. If you follow the guidelines here and those of your doctor, however, there's no reason you can't have a safe and healthy trip.

DIETARY PRECAUTIONS

First, you'll want to avoid contaminated food and water, which can bring on a host of ills: bacillary and amoebic dysentery, giardia (another nasty intestinal disease), typhoid, and cholera, to name a few. *Take note:* **There is no public potable water in Vietnam. Drink only bottled or boiled water, without ice,** except in very upscale places that assure you that they make their own ice from clean water. **Wash your hands often** with soap, particularly before eating, and eat fruit only if you have peeled it yourself. **Try to avoid uncooked food,** and with fruit and vegetables follow the old adage: **Boil it, cook it, peel it, or forget it.** This is difficult with Vietnamese cuisine, which uses fresh condiments, and, of course, you'll want to try the fresh fruit milk shakes, ice cream, and so forth. So use your best judgment. Find the cleanest small restaurants (**tip:** look at the floors), and carry your own pair of plastic or disposable chopsticks or eating utensils for the inevitable moment a restaurant gives you a pair of used wooden ones.

If despite all your precautions you still fall ill with diarrhea or stomach problems, stick to easily digested foods until they clear up. Any Vietnamese will tell you to eat rice porridge and bananas and to drink lots of weak green tea, which is sound advice. Yogurt (packaged only—avoid the fresh on-the-street stuff) can also help replenish necessary bacteria that you might lose. You should also dose yourself with a rehydration solution to replace lost salt in the body. Bring some with you. In a pinch, you can purchase it at pharmacies in Vietnam. Once you feel like branching out, try a bowl of *pho ga*, noodle soup with shredded chicken. If your symptoms persist for more than a few weeks, seek medical attention, and if you become ill after returning home, tell your doctor about your travels.

VACCINATIONS

It's always good to check the most recent information at the Center for Disease Control: Search its website (www.cdc.gov) by region under the heading "Traveler's Health," or call **877/394-8747.**

> **Tips   Dress Codes**
>
> Dress codes in Vietnam are casual except for some big-city restaurants, so pack with this in mind. As in most Asian countries, most men don't wear shorts (considered childish), so long pants are preferable, but "Bermuda shorts" or longer athletic shorts are okay. Be sure to keep it light, too, because you end up carrying your own goods more than once or twice along the way. A good pair of light cotton trousers will suffice in almost all situations and is the best defense against mosquitoes.

The following vaccinations are important for Vietnam: Hepatitis A or immune globulin (IG), Hepatitis B, typhoid, and Japanese encephalitis, if you plan to visit rural areas during the rainy season or stay longer than 4 weeks, and rabies if you're planning to go to rural areas where you might be exposed to wild animals. You should also consider booster doses for tetanus-diphtheria, measles, and polio.

Malaria is not a problem in the cities, but if you're going rural, you should take an oral prophylaxis. Most Vietnamese mosquitoes are chloroquine-resistant, so mefloquine, also known as Larium, is commonly prescribed. It can have side effects, including dizziness and nausea. Before taking Larium, tell your doctor if you are pregnant or plan to become pregnant. The best prevention is to wear clothing that fully covers your limbs and to use an insect repellant that contains DEET (diethylmethyltoluamide). Some people have allergic reactions to DEET, so test it at home before you leave.

GETTING THERE
BY PLANE
There is a myriad of air routes into Vietnam. You can fly almost any carrier that goes into Bangkok, Hong Kong, Taipei, or Tokyo and get a regional carrier from there. See the section "Getting There," in chapter 3 for more international flight tips.

Pretty much every country in Southeast Asia is connected to both Hanoi and Ho Chi Minh City. Malaysia Airlines, Singapore Airlines, Thai Airways International, and Bangkok Airways fly regular routes from the big hubs, but prices might be expensive compared with those for flights on Vietnam Airlines. Vietnam Airlines has the benefit of being price-regulated by the government. It connects Vietnam (Ho Chi Minh City) with Vientiane, Phnom Penh, Siem Reap, Bangkok, Kuala Lumpur, Singapore, and Manila. Just about the only Southeast Asian country without a direct connection is Myanmar.

Reconfirmation of your ticket out of Vietnam is a must. Call your airline's in-country office at least 72 hours before your departure. Be prepared for a 20,000 VND (US$1.35) airport departure tax for each domestic flight, and a 180,000 VND (US$12) departure tax for your international flight out.

BY BUS
From Laos, it is possible to enter Vietnam overland via a bus ride from Savannakhet in the south. It's 520km (323 miles) to Danang (US$27) or 405km (252 miles) to Hue (US$22). Buses leave at midnight. For more information, contact the Lao National Tourism Authority in Savannakhet at © **041/212-755.** It's a long, bumpy overnight, and travelers in the rainy season have reported wading chest deep, backpacks held aloft, to ford streams and cross rivers and connect with ongoing buses. Ask around to be sure the road is okay before leaving.

BY BOAT

A new and interesting option, boats now connect Vietnam with neighboring Cambodia by one of the larger tributaries of the Mekong, connecting Phnom Penh, Cambodia's capital, with the Mekong Delta border town Chau Doc. The trip takes all day and costs US$15. Contact the **Capital Guesthouse** (© 023/724-104), Cambodia's budget travel cafe, or make more luxury arrangements on a private outboard speedboat with the **Victoria Chau Doc** (© 076/865-010). Be sure to have a prearranged Vietnam visa. The trip takes from morning until late afternoon, depending on water level and weather, and is an interesting adventure with great perspective on Indochine river life.

GETTING AROUND

It is almost ridiculously easy to get around Vietnam. First, it seems like everybody is in the tourist business. A passerby on the street could probably book you a tour, if you asked. Along with established government-run and private tour agencies, hotels and cafes provide booking services. They all feed into a few big contractors, like tributaries into a river, so prices for the same services can vary. There hasn't been much of a problem with fraud yet, but do stick with the well-established agencies, tourist cafes, or hotels and remember that, despite any elaborate descriptions and promises (especially at the cafes), you get what you pay. Get all the details before booking.

BY PLANE   Vietnam Airlines is the only domestic airline carrier in the country, but prices are reasonable and the service is good. Seats are usually easy to come by. Purchasing tickets is also very easy; all travel agents book for a nominal fee, and many major hotels have V.A. agents in the lobby.

BY TRAIN   Vietnam's major rail network runs from Hanoi to Saigon and back, with stops along the way including coastal towns like Hue, Danang, and Nha Trang. Ironically, the Reunification Express is the nonexpress train; there is an express route as well. To give you an idea of timing, from Hanoi all the way to Saigon is 34 hours on the express train; from Hanoi to Hue is about 14 hours on an overnight express. It's an interesting way to get around, although not much cheaper than flying. Make sure you get "soft-sleeper" berths; "hard-sleeper" berths are a good value, but you're stacked three high and cannot sit when the bunks are down, while in "soft-sleep" there is plenty of room. Air-conditioning will cost you an additional price per ticket but might be most welcome, depending on when you're there. If you don't have time to buy tickets at the station (it's not too difficult, but it takes time away from the finer things), most hotels and tour agencies will gladly simplify the process and arrange tickets for you for only a nominal fee (check each section for contacts). Soft-sleeper berths and special tourist cars are available on most routes. Contact **Ratraco,** Vietnam's rail tour provider (just across from the station: 2nd floor, 95-97 Le Duan Str., Hanoi; © 04/942-2889; ratraco@hn.vnn.vn), or book through any travel agent.

From Hanoi to Lao Cai (Sapa) near the China border, be sure to check out the new luxury cars on either the **Royal Express** or the **Victoria Express** (run by the **Victoria Sapa;** © 20/871-522; fax: 84 20 871-539; victoriasapa@hn.vnn.vn). For a price, you'll ride in the high style of a bygone era for a unique experience (see "Sapa," later in this chapter).

BY BUS/MINIVAN   Public buses are not an option. Even if you're a traveler of the most intrepid variety or are fluent in Vietnamese, you'll be shooed off if you even try (though some travelers report squeezing on unnoticed). You're not missing out in terms of convenience, though; local buses are slow and incredibly crowded, and they break down often, but, even so, it's always a shame to lose an option, especially one that brings travelers close to the locals (they might just think it's a bit "too close").

Begun as small storefronts making arrangements for early backpackers in the 1990s, the **tourist cafes** are now franchised, with offices dotting the country; these convenient outfits run **open-tour bus tickets** that connect all the major points: Saigon, Dalat, Phan Thiet, Nha Trang, Hoi An, Danang (optional), Hue, and Hanoi. You can travel either direction, north to south or vice versa, for about US$25 to US$27. The buses leave at set times (most in the morning, though a few overnights are possible), and you just decide the day before if you want to be on one. This gives you tremendous freedom to plan your own itinerary. These operations are intensely competitive and will solicit you wherever you go. In recent years, **Sinh Café,** which now has computerized reservation services and can do just about anything, has really beat out the pack. **AtoZ Queen Café, Kim Café,** and **TM Brothers** (in the south) all have comparable service; don't be surprised if the companies trade you over to another if their buses are full. Check "Information & Tours," later in this chapter.

BY CAR   For all practical purposes, it is possible to rent a car in Vietnam only if it comes with a driver. However, it is a good way to see things outside of a city, or to take a 1-day city tour of major sights. Any major hotel or tour agency can assist you. For distances of longer than a few hours' drive, stick to minivans for safety unless you have a very trustworthy driver and a heavy-duty vehicle.

TIPS ON ACCOMMODATIONS

Vietnam is gaining popularity as a very safe and affordable tourist destination, so book early, especially during the high season of November/December; accommodations ranging from the glitziest five-stars to the grungiest guesthouses are often booked up or able to demand the unheard of: tourists paying the published

---

Ⓒ Have You Hugged Your Taxi Driver Today?

"Motorbike? Motorbike? Where you go?" You'll hear it on every street corner in most cities, the relentless ploys of the motorbike taxi drivers. These guys drive like maniacs, but, especially for the individual traveler, there is no better way to get around any town in Vietnam. They're called Xe Om or Honda Om in Vietnamese, with Om meaning "hug"—thus, it's really a "hugging taxi." In crowded HCMC and Hanoi, this is the cheapest and best way to get around and makes for good bargaining practice. They'll start at around 10 times the price here, and you'll need to walk away a few times to get anything near the 5,000 VND (US35¢) or so that the locals pay to get around or across one quadrant of the city. A price of 10,000 VND (US70¢) is not a bad compromise for most rides. You can also hire these guys at about US$1 to US$2 per hour to take you around to the sites. It's a good way to learn Vietnamese and gives a unique perspective on any town. Ask for a helmet, and don't be afraid to tap the guy's shoulder and give a "slow-down" hand signal.

Tips **Nonsmokers Beware**

There is no such thing as "nonsmoking" in Vietnam. Only top-end restaurants serving Western cuisine are likely to have a **nonsmoking section.** Some hotels offer nonsmoking rooms or floors. Inquire when booking, especially at hotels popular with business travelers, because the rooms can get pretty musty.

(or "rack") rate. Now making a splendid recovery from the regional currency crisis of a few years back, accommodations are enjoying a real boom, and that has brought hotel prices crashing down here. Always ask for seasonal reductions or promotional rates; discounts can be as high as 50%.

While this means that deluxe hotels now have midrange prices, the level of cleanliness and amenities is so high that you can stay in lower-range hotels, pay very little, and still come away smiling. A 20% value-added tax (VAT) was instituted in January 1999, but expect differences in how hotels follow the policy (often it's just 10%). Inquire carefully.

TIPS ON DINING

Many of the world's finest culinary traditions are represented in Vietnam, including French, Chinese, Japanese, and, of course, Vietnamese. Explore all of your options, particularly in the French arena, because you won't find lower prices anywhere. There are some interesting new upscale Vietnamese food venues, but ask locals and expats where to eat, and you'll get a blanket recommendation for the local market and many street stalls: They offer fantastic local delicacies like *bun bo* (cold rice noodles with fried beef), *banh khoi* (crispy thin rice-based crepes filled with chopped meat and shrimp), and *chao* (rice porridge with garnishes of meat, egg, or chiles). Note that many upscale places levy a 10% government tax plus a 5% service charge, or might add the new 10% to 20% VAT.

TIPS ON SHOPPING

Bring an empty suitcase. Vietnam offers fabulous bargains on silk, as both fabric and made-to-order clothing, as well as lacquer ware, silver, and fine art. Hanoi is probably best for most buys, particularly paintings; save the lacquer ware and home furnishings for Saigon. Furthermore, all prices are negotiable except for those in the most upscale shops, and the more relentless bargainers can walk away with incredible deals on some unique finds.

FAST FACTS: **Vietnam**

American Express Amex is represented by agencies in both Hanoi and Ho Chi Minh City. *Be warned:* They do not provide complete travel services, but can direct you if you lose your card. In Hanoi, contact Exotissimo Travel, 24–26 Tran Nhat Duat, Hanoi (© **04/828-2150**); in Ho Chi Minh City, contact Exotissimo Travel, Saigon Trade Center, 37 Ton Duc Thang St., HCMC (© **08/825-1723**). Hours are Monday to Friday 8am to 5pm.

Business Hours Vendors and restaurants tend to be all-day operations, opening at about 8am and closing at 9 or 10pm. Government offices, including banks, travel agencies, and museums, are usually open from 8 to 11:30am and 2 to 4pm.

Crime Violent crime isn't common in Vietnam, but petty thievery, especially against tourists, is a risk. Pickpocketing is rampant, and Ho Chi Minh City (HCMC), in particular, has a special brand of drive-by purse-snatching via motorbike. Don't wear flashy jewelry or leave valuables in your hotel room, especially in smaller hotels. There are small-time rackets perpetrated against tourists by taxi and cyclo drivers, usually in the form of a dispute on the agreed-upon price after you arrive at your destination. Or, the driver doesn't seem to have change. Simply agree on a price by writing it down first, and always smile and demand change; it will eventually appear.

Doctors & Dentists Vietnamese health care is not yet up to Western standards. However, there are competent medical clinics in Hanoi and Saigon (see "Fast Facts," in individual sections) with international, English-speaking doctors. The same clinics have dentists. If your problem is serious, it is best to get to either one of these cities as quickly as possible. The clinics can arrange emergency evacuation. If the problem is minor, ask your hotel to help you contact a Vietnamese doctor. He or she will probably speak some English, and pharmacies throughout the country are surprisingly well stocked. Check the products carefully for authenticity and expiration dates. The Vietnamese are big believers in prescription drugs (without prescriptions), although there are still some folk remedies around.

Drug Laws Possessing drugs can mean a jail sentence, and selling them or possessing quantities in excess of 300g means a death sentence. Don't take chances.

Electricity Vietnam's electricity carries 220 volts, so if you're coming from the U.S., bring a converter and adapter for electronics. Plugs have either two round prongs or two flat prongs. If you're toting a laptop, bring a surge protector. Big hotels will have all these implements.

Embassies Embassies are located in Hanoi at the following addresses: **United States,** 7 Lang Ha St., Ba Dinh District (✆ **04/843-1500**); **Canada,** 31 Hung Vuong St., Ba Dinh District (✆ **04/823-5500**); **Australia,** 8 Dao Tan, Van Phuc Compound, Ba Dinh District (✆ **04/831-7755**); **New Zealand,** 32 Hang Bai St., Hoan Kiem District (✆ **04/824-1481**); **United Kingdom,** 31 Hai Ba Trung St., 4th Floor, Hoan Kiem District (✆ **04/825-2510**).

Emergencies Nationwide emergency numbers are as follows: For police, dial ✆ **113;** for fire, dial ✆ **114;** and for ambulance, dial ... **115.** Operators speak only Vietnamese.

Hospitals In Hanoi, **International SOS** medical services can be found at 31 Hai Ba Trung St.; call the 24-hour service center for emergencies at ✆ **04/934-0056.** They have both Vietnamese and foreign doctors. In Ho Chi Minh City, International SOS is at 65 Nguyen Du St., District 1 (24-hr. hotline ✆ **8/829-8424**). **The French Hospital,** at 1 Phuong Mai St. (✆ **574-0740**), provides some of the finest medical attention at a fraction of the cost of SOS. They were building a new facility in HCMC at the time of this writing.

Internet/E-mail There are heaps of Internet cafes in cities throughout Vietnam, many of them in popular guesthouse and hotel areas. At cafes, rates are dirt cheap—usually around 4,000 VND per hour (a little less than US25¢). In rural areas, it can be as much as 500 VND per minute (US$2 per hr.), and hotel business centers usually charge at least double that. Take a short walk in most towns, and you can find affordable service.

Language Vietnamese is the official language of Vietnam. Older residents speak and understand French, and young folks are busily learning Chinese these days. While English is widely spoken among those in the service industry in Hanoi and Saigon, it is harder to find in other tourist destinations. Off the beaten track, arm yourself with as many Vietnamese words you can muster (see "Useful Vietnamese Phrases," earlier in this chapter) and a dictionary.

Liquor Laws There are virtually no liquor laws in Vietnam as far as age limits and when or where you can buy the stuff. It's not uncommon to find that your motorbike or taxi driver has had a few, so be cautious, especially at night.

Police You won't find a helpful cop on every street corner—just the opposite. Count on them only in cases of dire emergency, and learn a few words of Vietnamese to help you along. Moreover, police here can sometimes be part of the problem. Especially in the south, you and your car/motorbike driver might, for instance, be stopped for a minor traffic infraction and "fined." If the amount isn't too large, cooperate. Corruption is the rule, and palm-greasing and graft pose as police process. Be aware.

Post Offices/Mail A regular airmail letter will take about 10 days to reach North America, 7 to reach Europe, and 4 to reach Australia or New Zealand. Mailing things from Vietnam is expensive. A letter up to 10g costs 13,000 VND (US86¢) to North America, 11,000 VND (US73¢) to Europe, and 9,000 VND (US60¢) to Australia/New Zealand; postcards, respectively, cost 8,000 VND (US53¢), 7,000 VND (US46¢), and 6,000 VND (US40¢). Express mail services such as FedEx and DHL are easily available and are usually located in or around every city's main post office.

Safety Vietnam is considered a safe place to visit, but take heed of the following: First, the chaotic bike, motorbike, and car traffic can literally be deadly, so be cautious when crossing the street; maintaining a steady pace helps. In a taxi, belt up, if possible, and lock your door. Second, women should play it safe and avoid going out alone late at night. Third, and most important, beware of unexploded mines when hiking or exploring, especially through old war zones such as the DMZ or My Son. Don't stray off an established path, and don't touch anything.

Taxes A 20% VAT was instituted for hotels and restaurants in January 1999, but expect variation in how it's followed. Upscale establishments might add the full 20%, and some might even tack on an additional 5% service charge. Others might absorb the tax in their prices, and still others will ignore it entirely. Inquire before booking or eating.

Telephone & Fax Most hotels offer international direct dialing, but with exorbitant surcharges of 10% to 25%. It is far cheaper to place a call from a post office. There are plenty of phone booths that accept phone cards (local and international) that can be purchased at any post office or phone company branch. A local call costs 1,000 VND (US6¢) per minute. See the "Telephone Dialing Information at a Glance" box, below, for more specific information.

Time Zone Vietnam is 7 hours ahead of Greenwich Mean Time, in the same zone as Bangkok. It is 12 hours ahead of the U.S. and 3 hours behind Sydney.

Tipping Tipping is common in Hanoi and in Saigon. In a top-end hotel, feel free to tip bellhops anywhere from 10,000 VND to 15,000 VND (about US$1). Most upscale restaurants throughout the country now add a service surcharge of 5 to 10%. If they don't, or if the service is good, you might want to leave another 5%. Taxi drivers will be pleased if you round up the bill (again, mainly in the big cities). Use your discretion for tour guides and others who have been particularly helpful. Contrary to rumor, boxes of cigarettes as tips don't go over well. The recipient will say regretfully, "I don't smoke," when what he really means is "Show me the money." Exceptions to this are chauffeurs or minibus drivers.

Toilets Public toilets (*cau tieu*) are nonexistent in Vietnam outside of tourist attractions, but you'll be welcome in hotels and restaurants. Except for newer hotels and restaurants, squat-style toilets prevail. You'll often see a tub of water with a bowl next to the toilet. Throw two or three scoops of water in the bowl to flush. Finally, bring your own paper and antiseptic hand wipes—just in case.

Water Water is not potable in Vietnam. Outside of top-end hotels and restaurants, drink only beverages without ice, unless the establishment promises that it manufactures its own ice from clean water. Bottled mineral water, particularly the reputable La Vie and "A&B" brands, is everywhere. Counterfeits are a problem, so make sure you're buying the real thing, with an unbroken seal. A sure sign is typos. "La Vile" water speaks for itself.

3 Hanoi

Vietnam's capital, Hanoi, ranks among the world's most attractive and interesting cities. It was first the capital of Vietnam in 1010, and though the nation's capital moved to Hue under the Nguyen Dynasty in 1802, the city continued to flourish after the French took control in 1888. In 1954, after the French departed, Hanoi was declared Vietnam's capital once again. The remnants of over 1,000 years of history are still visible here, with that of the past few hundred years marvelously preserved.

Hanoi has a reputation, doubtless accrued from the American war years, as a dour northern political outpost. While the city is certainly smaller, slower, and far less developed than chaotic Saigon, and there are some vestiges of Soviet-influenced concrete monolith architecture, there are some beautiful, quiet streets and neighborhoods in Hanoi, and such placid air gives it a gracious, almost regal flavor. It is set amid dozens of lakes of various sizes, around which you can usually find a cafe, a pagoda or two, and absorbing vignettes of street life.

Among Hanoi's sightseeing highlights are the **Ho Chi Minh mausoleum and museum,** the **National Art Museum,** the grisly **Hoa Lo prison** (also known to Americans as the infamous Hanoi Hilton), and the **Old Quarter,** whose ancient winding streets are named after the individual trades practiced there. Hanoi is also Vietnam's cultural center. The galleries, puppetry, music, and dance performances are worth staying at least a few days to take in. You might also want to use the city as a base for excursions to Halong Bay and Cat Ba island, to Cuc Phuong nature reserve, or north to Sapa.

GETTING THERE

BY PLANE Hanoi is one of Vietnam's major international gateways, the other being Saigon. For details, see the country's "Getting There" section, earlier in this chapter.

The airport is located about a 45-minutes drive outside the city. If you haven't booked a hotel transfer through your hotel, an airport taxi costs US$10. To save a few dollars, you can take the Vietnam Airlines minivan into town. It costs US$2 for a drop-off at the Vietnam Airlines office, but sometimes for an extra buck you can get the driver to drop you at your hotel.

BY TRAIN Hanoi Railway Station, on the western edge of Hoan Kiem district (120 Le Duan; ℂ **04/942-3949**), is a major connection on the Reunification Railroad. US$35 will get you a comfortable, air-conditioned soft-berth to Hue, and the same is US$87 to Ho Chi Minh. Buying tickets at the stations is easy (but takes time), and any travel agent can handle it for a small fee.

BY BUS Traveler Café open-tour options are numerous in the Old Quarter on Hang Bac or Hang Be. Service and price are similar: about US$27 for an open-tour ticket from Hanoi to Saigon with all stops in-between. See "Tourist Cafes," below. Tour buses connect to all major destinations from Hanoi.

 Telephone Dialing Information at a Glance

- **To place a call from your home country to Vietnam:** Dial the international code (011 in the U.S., 0011 in Australia, 0170 in New Zealand, or 00 in the U.K.), plus the country code (84), the city code (4 for Hanoi, 8 for Ho Chi Minh City, 54 for Hue, 511 for Danang, 510 for Hoi An, 63 for Dalat, 58 for Nha Trang), and the phone number (for example, 011 84 4 000-0000).

- **To place a call within Vietnam:** First dial 0 before the city code. Note that not all phone numbers have seven digits, and establishments might have several different numbers, one for each line.

- **To place a direct international call from Vietnam:** Most hotels offer international direct dialing, but with exorbitant surcharges of 10% to 25%. Faxes often have high minimum charges. To place a call, dial the international access code (00) plus the country code, the area or city code, and the number (for example, to call the U.S., you'd dial 00 01 000/000-0000).

- **International country codes are as follows:** Australia: 61; Myanmar: 95; Cambodia: 855; Canada: 1; Hong Kong: 852; Indonesia: 62; Laos: 856; Malaysia: 60; New Zealand: 64; the Philippines: 63; Singapore: 65; Thailand: 66; U.K.: 44; U.S.: 1.

- Post offices in Vietnam also provide international calling services. If you must call home, this is your best cost-saving option.

Hanoi Accommodations & Dining

ACCOMMODATIONS ■
Army Hotel **20**
Dan Chu Hotel **23**
De Syloia **22**
Eden Hotel **28**
Galaxy Hotel **8**
Guoman Hotel **32**
Ha Long Hotel **9**
Hanoi Daewoo Hotel **1**
Hilton Hanoi Opera **18**
Melia Hotel **29**
Hoa Binh Hotel **24**
Hoang Cuong Hotel **35**
Hong Ngoc Hotel **11**
Phuc Loi **34**
Sofitel Metropole Hanoi **15**

DINING ◆
Al Fresco's **25**
Brother's Café **38**
Cha Ca La Vong **10**
Emperor **21**
Il Grillo **27**
Indochine **33**
Le Café des Arts de Hanoi **12**
Luna d' Autuno **36**
The Press Club **16**
Restaurant Bobby Chinn **26**
Revival **14**
Seasons of Hanoi **7**
Tamarind Café **13**

ATTRACTIONS ●
Army Museum **37**
Hanoi Opera House **17**
Ho Chi Minh's Mausoleum **6**
Ho Chi Minh's Residence **3**
Hoa Lo Prison
  (Hanoi Hilton) **30**
Hun Tiep Lake and the
  Downed B-52 **2**
National Museum of
  Vietnamese History **19**
One-Pillar Pagoda **4**
Quan Su Pagoda **31**
Temple of Literature and
  National University (Van
  Mieu–Quoc Tu Giam) **40**
Vietnam Fine Arts Museum **39**

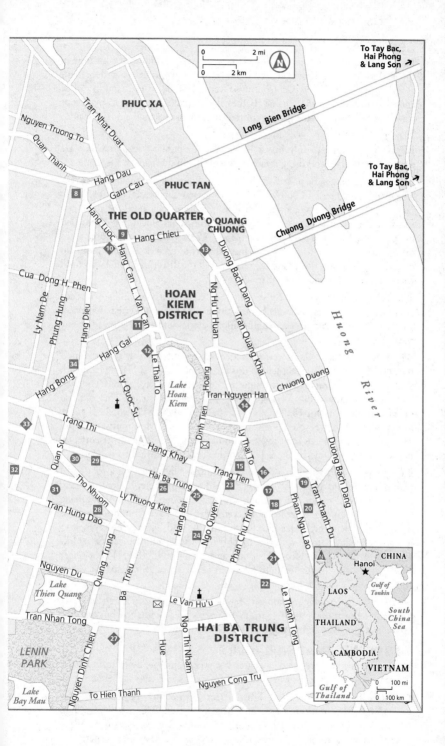

GETTING AROUND

Hanoi is divided into districts. You will most likely spend most of your time in the Hoan Kiem (downtown) and Ba Dinh (west of town) districts, with perhaps a few forays into Dong Da (southwest) and Hai Ba Trung (south). Most addresses include a district name. If they don't, ask. You'll want to plan your travels accordingly because getting from district to district can be time-consuming and expensive.

BY BUS   Hanoi has only **buses** in the way of public transport. They are extremely crowded, and using them is difficult if you don't speak Vietnamese.

BY TAXI   Taxis can be hailed off the street, at hotels, and at major attractions. The meter should read 14,000 VND (US94¢) to start, and 4,000 to 5,000 VND (about US30¢) for every kilometer thereafter. You can call ahead (or ask at any front desk or concierge) to contact a few companies, including **Vina Taxi** (✆ **04/811-1111**) and **52 Taxi** (✆ **04/852-5252**). Make sure the cabbie turns on the meter. Be sure to get your change; drivers often seek a surreptitious tip by claiming that they don't have the change. Tell the driver that you'll wait until it's obtained, and it will materialize.

BY CAR   Renting a car is convenient. You can book one with a driver for about US$33 a day (or US$5 per hr., minimum 3 hr.). If an upscale hotel quotes you more, call a **tourist cafe** (combination eateries and travel agents) or any travel agent.

BY MOTORBIKE   Motorcycle taxis are a cheap and easy way to get around the city, but they go like madmen, so this is only for the brave. Haggle hard with these guys because, no matter the distance, they'll start with a few dollars but will come down as far as 5,000 VND (US30¢) with some persistence. They can also be hired by the hour for 15,000 VND to 30,000 VND (US$1–US$2). If you're feeling especially brave, you can rent your own motorbike. Most tourist cafes and mid- to low-range hotels offer them, as do the numerous street-corner entrepreneurs. The price should be about US$6 or US$7 per day. Ask for a helmet.

BY CYCLO   Cyclos are two-seated carts powered by a man on a foot-pedal bike riding behind you. You can flag them down anywhere, particularly near hotels and tourist attractions, where they're certain to find (or follow) you. Being trundled along among whizzing motorcycles isn't always very comfortable and is definitely unsafe at night. It's nice for touring the Old Quarter, however, with its narrow streets. Bargain with the driver before setting out. You can pay as low as 10,000 VND (US66¢) for a short ride, and 15,000 VND (US$1) for a longer haul. You can also hire by the hour for about US$2. If you're inclined, they'll let you try and ride just for fun.

BY BICYCLE   Another option is to rent a bicycle for the day for about US$1 from a hotel or tourist cafe. Again, it's an easily available method but one best used during the day. Bring your own helmet from home.

VISITOR INFORMATION & TOURS

Most tour companies are based in Saigon; however, many have branches in Hanoi. Operators can usually assist with local tours as well as country-wide services.

- **Ann's Tours.** 26 Yet Kieu, Hoan Kiem District (✆ **04/822-0018;** fax 04/832-3866; www.anntours.com). Ask for the manager, Mr. Hoan. This company offers private deluxe tours to Halong Bay and elsewhere. We've had feedback from Frommer's readers who tell us what great experiences they've had with this operation.

- **Buffalo Tours.** 11 Hang Muoi (© **04/828-0702;** www.buffalotours.com). This reputable outfit offers a range of standard tours and some good eco-adventures, like cycling, trekking, and kayaking.
- **Exotissimo.** 26 Tran Nhat Duat (© **04/828-2150;** fax04/828-2146; www.exotissimo.com). You'll get comprehensive service both in-bound and out-bound throughout the region.
- **Handspan.** The main address is 80 Ma May St. (© **04/962-0446;** fax 04/926-0445; www.handspan.com). This is an excellent option for organized trips around Hanoi, in the northern hills and Halong Bay, plus some adventure options.
- **Hanoi Tourism.** 18 Ly Thuong Kiet St. (© **04/825-7886;** fax 04/825-4209; www.hanoitourism.com.vn). A government affiliated company, it covers all bases and offer good city tours.

TOURIST CAFES

A good option for tours and transport or for 1- or 2-day excursions to sites like Halong Bay is to visit one of Hanoi's tourist cafes, which are small eateries/Internet cafes and travel agents all rolled into one. Minitrip prices to Halong Bay and Cat Ba Island range from US$16 to US$28, but the lodging provided is quite basic. You'll see them everywhere. Here are a few:

- **Sinh Café.** 25 Hang Be St., Hoan Kiem District (© **04/926-1288;** fax 04/756-7862; www.sinhcafe.com).
- **A-Z Queen Café.** 65 Hang Bac, Hoan Kiem District (© **04/826-0860;** fax 04/826-0300; www.azqueentravel.com).
- **Kim Tours.** 82 Ma May St., Hoan Kiem District (© **04/926-0804**).

 **FAST FACTS: Hanoi**

Banks/Currency Exchange Major banks in Hanoi include: Australia New Zealand Bank (ANZ), 14 Le Thai To St. (© **04/825-8190**); Citibank, 17 Ngo Quyen St. (© **04/825-1950**); and Vietcombank, 198 Tran Quan Khai (© **04/826-8045**). ATMs are located at ANZ Bank and Citibank.

Internet/E-mail The **Emotion CyberNet Café,** at 60 Tho Nhuom and 52 Ly Thuong Kiet (© **04/934-1066;** emotioncafe@hn.fpt.vn), across from the Hanoi Hilton, sells snacks and Internet access. Small Internet storefronts are numerous in the Old Quarter on Hang Bac or Hang Be, and in all traveler cafes.

Post Office/Mail The General Post Office is located at 6 Dinh Le St., Hoan Kiem District (© **04/825-7036**). It's open daily 6:30am to 10pm. You can also send faxes or telexes and make international phone calls. FedEx (© **04/826-4925**) is located in the same building as the post office but has its own storefront.

Telephone The city code for Hanoi is 04. Most hotels provide international direct dialing, although none allows you to access an international operator or AT&T (whose Vietnam access code is 12010288). To do that, you will have to go to the General Post Office (above). There are public phone booths throughout the city for local calls that accept phone cards purchased from the post office.

WHERE TO STAY

From historic charm to ultra-efficient business hotel to budget hole-in-the-wall, you'll find what you want in Hanoi. There has been a boom in high-end accommodation in town (we list 3 of 6 five-stars), and though some are a bit officious businesslike properties, they all offer every facility a holiday-maker could wish for. Amenities and cleanliness levels are high across the board; virtually every hotel over US$10 a night will have a phone, air-conditioning, in-room safes, and hair dryers. Children under 12 usually stay free.

Ask for discounts! Lingering effects of the Asian Economic Crisis and recent construction have every reservations desk offering cut rates, many of up to 50%. Shown here are listed high-season (Oct–Feb) rates, so use them as guidelines only. Prices do not include a government VAT of up to 20%, except where noted.

VERY EXPENSIVE

Hanoi Daewoo Hotel ★★   Just 7 years in business, the Daewoo is the most popular choice in recent years for heads of state and dignitaries (with a long list including President Clinton and Jiang Zemin) and, fittingly, everything is done large—the hotel lobby, the bars, the rooms with king beds, and the 80m-long (262-ft.-long) curving pool. All interior space is tessellated in marble, deep-toned wood, or in sumptuous fabrics. It's almost a bit too much. The plush rooms are decorated with local accents, and the halls are graced with over 1,000 interesting modern paintings by Vietnamese artists. Bathrooms are surprisingly small in the lower-end rooms but quite well appointed, with hair dryers and thick, soft linens and towels. There's an attractive lobby lounge and a pool bar. Overlooking the large park surrounding Thu Le Lake, the Daewoo is like a city unto itself. There's a nightclub (Club Q) with five karaoke rooms. For dining, Edo (Japanese) and La Paix (Italian) are among the best restaurants in Hanoi—both are formal, expensive, excellent power lunch spots with private rooms. Café Promenade features Asian and European buffets, and Silk Road offers fine Chinese (Cantonese and Szechuan) food. There are three nonsmoking floors and a very efficient business center—perhaps the best in Hanoi—with Internet access. You're a good distance from town here at the Daewoo, but the amenities make it self-contained. You might not want to, or have to, leave.

360 Kim Ma St., Ba Dinh District. ✆ 04/831-5000. Fax 04/831-5010. www.hanoi-daewoohotel.com. 411 units. US$199 double; US$269–US$359 executive-floor room; US$319–US$1,500 suite. AE, DC, MC, V. **Amenities:** 4 restaurants; 2 bars; outdoor tennis court; elegant health club; spa; Jacuzzi; sauna; family play program; concierge; tour desk; car rental; limo service; business center; shopping arcade; salon; barber shop; 24-hour room service; massage; laundry service; babysitting; dry cleaning; Internet. *In room:* A/C, satellite TV, dataport, minibar, fridge, coffeemaker, hair dryer, safe, phone w/IDD.

Hilton Hanoi Opera ★★   This hotel opened before the millennium in grand style—the reproduction colonial exterior is quite stunning and describes an elegant arc around the perimeter of the splendid Opera building. The inside matches the fine facade, with a lobby done in grand scale. Rooms are carpeted in rich, contrasting colors with a unique cushioned wallpaper, subdued lighting, and faux Chinese lacquer cabinetry that fits well. Rooms on the fifth floor have balconies. Suites offer similar services as standard rooms but are much larger and nicely appointed. Television with satellite service, daily newspaper delivery, voice-mail telephone system, and in-room Internet access keep business travelers up to speed. The hotel also has plenty of features for vacation travelers, like in-house tour services and a concierge. There is fine dining at Turtle's Poem (try the dim sum for lunch), and Café Opera has gourmet sandwiches and baked goods, or you can have a pint at JJ's Sports Bar and catch up on scores or play a game of pool. On the executive floor, business travelers can enjoy the luxury of private check-in, as well as an executive lounge with a bar and snacks. The courtyard pool area is quite lovely.

1 Le Thanh Tong St., Hoan Kiem, Hanoi. ⓒ **800/774-1500** or 04/933-0500. Fax 04/933-0530. www.hilton. com. 269 units. US$210–US$230 double; US$250 executive room. AE, MC, V. **Amenities:** 3 restaurants; bar; club lounge; pool; fitness center; business center; meeting and executive services; handicapped rooms; ballroom. *In room:* A/C, TV, dataport, safe, hair dryer.

Melia Hotel ★★   This downtown behemoth, popular with tour groups and conventions, might just warrant its own postal code, but you'll find all the comforts of home in this oversized but friendly setup. The lobby is grand and full of wide-eyed conventioneers quite often, but the service is good and the room standard is top-notch. Done in an understated Art Deco theme that toes a comfortable line between bland and sleek, rooms are large, with firm beds, large bathrooms done in nice marble tile with granite counters, and fresh flowers in every available nook and cranny. It's all about elegance and acreage here, whether in the rooms or among the hotel's many facilities. The executive floor is refined, rivaling the services and standards of any high-end hotel in the world. Because this building sticks out like such a sore thumb in the Hanoi skyline, you have great views of the whole town, from the Red River to Hoan Kiem and West Lake. The staff is friendly and efficient and can cater to any need. It might pay to ask about the convention schedule before checking in because, with capacity for 1,200 in the meeting facilities, you might feel a bit overrun if it's the International Mooselodge Week. Overall, this is a high standard that's close to town and friendly.

44B Ly Thuong Kiet St., Hanoi. ⓒ **04/934-3343.** Fax 04/934344. www.solmeliea.com. 308 units. US$200 deluxe; US$290 executive suite; US$240 deluxe royal; US$330–US$1,500 suite. AE, MC, V. **Amenities:** 2 restaurants; bar; outdoor pool; health club; Jacuzzi; concierge; tour desk (Saigon Tourism); car rental; business center; shopping; 24-hour room service; babysitting on request; laundry service. *In room:* A/C, satellite TV, dataport w/in-house personal Internet accounts, minibar, fridge, coffeemaker, safe, IDD phone.

Sofitel Metropole Hanoi ★★★   Built in 1901, the Metropole is one of the world's treasures. This is where invading, liberating or civil armies have found billet and raised their flags, where the first film was shown in Indochina, where Charlie Chaplin spent his honeymoon, where Jane Fonda and Joan Baez took cover in a bomb shelter, and where heads of state and embassy officials resided for many years. In fact, the history of the Metropole is the history of the last hundred years in Hanoi, and the folks here have even published a short volume telling the tale. The hotel had a major renovation in 1992 and added a second building in 1994; rooms in the new wing are more spacious, but push for the old wing and walk into a bit of history (keep an eye out for ghosts) in these medium-size rooms with wood floors, cane furniture, classic fixtures, and high ceilings. The very modern bathrooms are large and have little touches like woodframe mirrors, fresh flowers, and toiletries in hand-painted ceramics jars. The staff couldn't be nicer or more efficient. The pool is small, but the adjoining Bamboo lounge is an oasis of calm in the city center. The health club with sauna and massage is superb and has a good street view. Le Beaulieu is popular in Hanoi for classic French fare, and the Spices Garden is a great place to sample local delights (the lunch buffet is a safe and tasty place to try Hanoi street fare like Pho and Bun Cha). The Metropole also offers cooking classes. Among the three bars, the Met Pub is a casual spot to have a beer and listen to live music.

The downtown location can't be beat, and there's a nice mix of tourists and businesspeople here.

15 Ngo Quyen St., Hanoi. © **800/221-4542** or 04/826-6919. Fax 04/826-6920. Sofmet@netnam.org.vn. 232 units. US$230–US$280 double; from US$290 suite. AE, DC, MC, V. **Amenities:** 4 restaurants; 3 bars; top-notch health club; nice courtyard pool; spa; Jacuzzi; sauna; concierge; tour desk; car rental; limo; business center; shopping; salon; massage; laundry; Internet. *In room:* TV, dataport, minibar, fridge, hair dryer, safe, phone w/IDD.

EXPENSIVE

De Syloia ★   Not trying to be more than it is, the De Syloia is an upscale little gem just south of the city center. Rooms are large and clean, not especially luxe but comfortable with tidy carpet, dark-wood appointments and furniture, and large bathrooms with tubs (deluxe rooms and suites have Jacuzzis). The lobby is compact and clean but not particularly atmospheric, and the whole setup seems like a feisty minihotel, but it's a nice standard throughout. The staff is friendly on a good day, and the amenities are limited, but this is a popular choice away from the downtown traffic. Ask to see a room before checking in, and be sure to inquire about Internet and promotional rates.

17a Tran Hung Dao St., Hoan Kem District. © **08/245-346.** Fax 08/241-083. www.desyloia.com. 33 units. US$90–US$105 double; US$115 deluxe; US$145 suite (discount available). AE, MC, V. **Amenities:** Restaurant; bar; minigym; tour desk; car rental; business center; laundry; dry cleaning; small meeting room; Internet. *In room:* A/C, satellite TV, minibar, fridge, hair dryer, safe, IDD phone.

Guoman Hotel ★★   For a high standard of service and comfort in Hanoi, the Guoman is a real find. Only a year and a half old, the uppity downtown four-star caters to the business crowd and is popular for semi-permanent residents; with a good location and nice amenities, it's a great choice for all. From the large central chandelier and toothed filigree of the stylish lobby to the subdued Helmsman lounge's live music and low-slung couches, there is a laid-back boutique feel here that's much finer than the low price tag. Rooms are big, carpeted, and very nicely furnished (albeit bland), and they still have that brand-new feeling. They are very well equipped, with coffeemakers, safes, and even a power outlet and phone jack for laptops. Other highlights include comfy, just-right firm beds; fat pillows; and big spic-and-span marble-and-tile bathrooms. The fitness center is quite nice, too, and the second-floor restaurant serves a great breakfast and good Western and Asian fare. There are two nonsmoking floors, a rarity in Vietnam. Service is excellent, and the staff can help you with any business or travel need.

83A Ly Thuong Kiet St., Hanoi. © **04/822-2800.** Fax 04/822-2822. www.guomanhanoi.com.vn. 149 units. US$70–US$75 double; US$120–US$180 suite. AE, MC, V. **Amenities:** 2 restaurants; 2 bars (live music); health club; dry sauna; concierge; tour desk; car rental; limo; business center; small gift shop; massage; babysitting; nonsmoking floors; meeting rooms. *In room:* A/C, satellite TV, dataport, minibar, fridge, coffeemaker, safe.

MODERATE

Army Hotel ★★ *Value*   Though in a sprawling complex owned by the Vietnamese military, there's no need to salute here and the friendly staff won't ask you to drop for 20 push-ups. For basic comforts and good value close to downtown (and a nice pool), the Army Hotel is a good bet. Here you'll find the kind of services, and prices, of a basic midrange hotel, but with a location on a quiet street just a short walk east of downtown (behind the opera house). It's popular with long-term visitors like businessmen or couples who come to adopt in Vietnam. Rooms vary greatly, so ask to see one before you check in; most are large and clean, with tile floors and nice-size bathrooms with a shower/bathtub combo.

Each room has a balcony, and be sure to ask for one with a view of the pool (the 1st floor has direct access to the pool area). The staff is friendly, the lobby business center is convenient, and though the courtyard health club has seen better days, the pool is inviting and there's a nice open sitting area. This is great value and a welcome oasis just a short walk or ride from the town center. Try for one of the large suites; some are quite eclectic, with a raised floor, Japanese-style rooms, and a larger private balcony for not much more money.

33 C Pham Ngu Lao St., Hanoi (just behind the opera house). (C) 04/825-2896. Fax 04/825-9276. army hotel@fpt.vn. 82 units. US$50–US$60 standard single–double;. US$70 deluxe; US$72–US$198 suite. AE, MC, V. **Amenities:** Restaurant; outdoor pool in large central courtyard; basic fitness equipment; sauna; small business center (Internet is US$3 per hr.); room service 6am–10pm; babysitting. *In room:* A/C, TV, fridge, hot water for coffee, hair dryer, IDD phone.

Dan Chu Hotel ★★ Pronounced like "Zahn Shoe," the Dan Chu was originally a French government building nearly 100 years ago, and the long history and columned facade lends to the funky but pleasant feeling here. It's just a short walk from Hoan Kiem Lake, in the heart of the downtown district; you can choose from a selection of spotless, atmospheric, high-ceiling rooms with handsome carved wood furniture and large, clean, but rather spare bathrooms with hair dryers. There is a useful travel counter, car rental, popular massage and sauna, a restaurant, and a nice gift shop on the premises; you'll also find satellite TV and in-room safes. The deluxe rooms are the best value, with high ceilings bordered in filigree crowning a room large enough for a game of racquetball. A long, common balcony overlooks the courtyard and active street scene below. Rooms could do without the polyester bedspreads, and the downtown location means a bit of street noise, but for history, character, and convenience, this place is a great value. Buffet breakfast and US$2 buffet lunch make it a great deal.

29 Trang Tien St., Hanoi. (C) 04/825-4344. Fax 04/826-6786. 42 units. US$40 standard; US$55 superior; US$65 deluxe; US$75–US$90 suite. AE, DC, MC, V. **Amenities:** Restaurant; bar; tour desk (Hanoi Tourism); car rental; small business center; massage. *In room:* Satellite TV, minibar, fridge, coffeemaker, safe, IDD phone.

Eden Hotel Rooms at this 8-year-old hotel all face a small faux-brick courtyard atrium on a quiet street south of the city center. Popular with large groups on a budget and often booked, it's down to basics here, with few amenities and overworked front-desk indifference as a rule. Still, it's a good middle-of-the-road standard for comfort and affordability. Nicely carpeted rooms have high ceilings and feature traditional Asian carved-wood furniture, but standard and deluxe rooms are quite small and all are a bit dark. Mattresses are foam, but they are extremely sturdy and comfortable. Bathrooms are basic and spotless, without bathtubs except in the suites. It's laid back and affordable, but you won't find any frills.

78 Tho Nhuom St., Hanoi. (C) 04/942-3273. Fax 04/824-5619. eden@hn.vnn.vn 35 units. US$25 single; US$30 double; US$35–US$40 single/double deluxe; US$50–US$60 suite (not including tax). Children under 12 free. Discounts available for long-term guests. AE, DC, MC, V. **Amenities:** Restaurant; bar; laundry. *In room:* A/C, TV.

Galaxy Hotel ★★ Popular with tour groups (but don't let that stop you), the Galaxy is on a busy corner just north of the Old Quarter and is a comfortable spot to begin exploring this colorful part of the city. If you elect to stay here, it will quickly become a home away from home. Converted from a 1929 factory, the recently renovated building is colorless but comfortable. Good-size rooms are spotless, with familiar amenities, and recent reductions in price make this a very affordable option. Rooms are nondescript but tidy, some quite spacious, with nice touches like a bit of filigree on the ceiling and immaculate tile bathrooms (although they're a bit small). There is an Asian restaurant on the premises and a nice little bar with current Western magazines. The breakfast (included in the price) is good and even has pancakes and sausage. The staff members will remember your name and are friendly and helpful with advice and suggestions. The corner suites on each floor are a great option, with windows facing two directions over the Old Quarter.

1 Phan Dinh Phung St., Hanoi. ℂ **04/828-2888.** Fax 04/828-2466. galaxyhtl@netnam.org.vn. 60 units. US$50 double; US$60 suite. Breakfast included. AE, DC, MC, V. **Amenities:** Restaurant; bar; tour desk; car rental; 24-hour room service; babysitting; laundry; dry cleaning. *In room:* A/C, satellite TV, minibar, fridge, coffeemaker, hair dryer, safe, IDD phone.

Hoa Binh Hotel ☆ Built in 1926 and recently renovated, the Hoa Binh is a good, atmospheric choice. Comfort and history meet at just the right level, and whether you're walking up the big, creaky grand stair or opening French doors onto a balcony overlooking the busy street, you know that you're in Hanoi here. Sizable rooms have original light fixtures, molded ceilings, and gloss-wood furniture. The shiny, polyester bedspreads; velveteen drapes; and spongy mattresses detract from the effect only slightly. Deluxe rooms and suites are a great bargain, at US$50, but are just larger versions of the standard with the same amenities. Bathrooms are very plain and small but spotless. The hotel is in a prime downtown location, and the bar has a view of the city. Le Splendide, a restaurant on the ground floor, carries on the tradition of a departed French chef and serves a good set lunch. Ask to see a room before checking in because they vary in size, shape, and degree of smoke or must; in general, though, this is a good bet. It's popular with tour groups.

27 Ly Thuong Kiet St., Hoan Kiem District, Hanoi. ℂ **04/825-3315** or 04/825-3692. Fax 04/826-9818. www.hoabinhhotel.com. 103 units. US$40–US$60 double; US$80 suite. Breakfast included. AE, MC, V. **Amenities:** 2 restaurants; 2 bars; sauna; concierge; tour desk; car rental; small business center; shopping; limited room service; massage; laundry; dry cleaning (next day); nonsmoking rooms available. *In room:* A/C, TV, minibar, fridge, hair dryer, safe.

INEXPENSIVE

Ha Long Hotel ☆ On one of the quieter streets in the north end of the Old Quarter, the Ha Long is a great base for exploration. You might feel like you've come to stay at the YMCA when you board the rattle-trap elevator, but it's just no frills, clean, and affordable in this older minihotel. All rooms have hard mattresses (foam) and nice dark furniture, but everything's a bit drab. The suites are a bit too big for their britches, with inlaid woodwork tables and overly ornate purple curtains befitting another ouvre (I didn't say brothel). You'll find good value here, though, and rooms on the upper floors have especially nice views of either the Red River or the town center. It's a good place to get your bearings in town, and it's far enough away from the lake that the hassling touts seem to leave this part of the Old Quarter alone (a big relief).

77 Hang Luoc St., Old Quarter, Hanoi. ℂ **04/828-3525.** Fax 04/828-3526. halong.hotel.fpt.vn. 18 units. US$20 double; US$30 superior; US$40 deluxe. AE, MC, V. **Amenities:** Restaurant. *In room:* A/C, TV.

Hoang Cuong Hotel ☆ This attractive little gem is one of the best among Hanoi's budget choices and is located on the same street as many of them, near the Old Quarter. Family-run, it has large carpeted rooms, with attractive inlaid Asian furniture and very firm foam mattress beds. There are some nice details, like hair dryers, hot-water thermoses, and fans in the room. The tile bathrooms are functional and spotless. There is no elevator, and room prices are based on how far you'll have to hike up the six or so flights of stairs. But you'll soon become firm friends with the very nice staff.

15 Nguyen Thai Hoc St., Hoan Kiem District, Hanoi. ☎ **04/822-0060.** Fax 04/822-0195. 10 units. US$15–US$30 double. AE, DC, MC, V. *In room:* A/C, TV, minibar, hair dryer.

Hong Ngoc Hotel ✿   With three locations all right in the heart of the Old Quarter, this is a good no-frills option close to Hoan Kiem. Friendly to a fault, the staff has a can-do attitude and can help you with any detail, like renting a car, motorcycle, or bicycle. Rooms are sparse, but all have quality amenities of a proper hotel, with dark wooden trim and small but clean bathrooms. If this location is full, they can arrange something at one of their other comparable spots. For my money, this is top-notch downtown affordability, a minihotel with attitude (like a terrier who thinks himself a Great Dane). You'll make fast friends with the helpful staff.

14 Luong Van Can St., Hoan Kiem District, Hanoi. ☎ **04/826-7566.** Fax 04/8245362. hongngochotel@hn. vnn.vn. 10 units. US$20–US$30. MC, V. **Amenities:** Restaurant; tour desk; limited room service; Internet. *In room:* A/C, satellite TV, minibar, fridge, IDD phone.

Phuc Loi ✿   Here's an affordable little gem in the heart of the Old Quarter. This is your standard minihotel, but everything is super-tidy and ornate. Rooms are small but spotless, with faux-wood floors and high ceilings. This place is just 1 year old, and everything is in good shape. The bathrooms are nice-size, with shower/tub combo, granite counters, and patterned wall tiles. Try for one of the three large split-level VIP rooms; they're very comfortable and a steal at US$35. Rooms on higher floors have great views of the Old Quarter, and the top-floor terrace promises to be a cafe some day, but now it affords access to the city's panorama. The staff is very friendly.

128 HangBong St., Old Quarter. ☎ **04/928-5235.** Fax 04/828-9897. phucloihotel@fpt.vn. 18 units. US$22–US$50. **Amenities:** Bar; small gym room on top floor; bike rental. *In room:* A/C, satellite TV, minibar, fridge, hair dryer, IDD phone.

WHERE TO DINE

It's hard to have a bad meal in Hanoi. The French influence is here in both classical and Vietnam-influenced versions, neither to be missed, especially at these prices. Almost every ethnic food variation is well represented in the city; in fact, and you'll be hard pressed to choose among them.

Hanoi has savory specialties that must be sampled. For that, hit the streets and dine in small local eateries. *Pho,* by far the most popular local dish, is noodles with slices of beef (*bo*) or chicken (*ga*), fresh bean sprouts, and condiments. *Bun cha,* a snack of rice noodles and spring rolls with fresh condiments, has made Dac Kim restaurant (at No. 1 Hang Manh, in the Old Quarter) city-renowned. And don't miss *Cha Ca,* Hanoi's famed spicy fish fry-up (see below under "Inexpensive").

EXPENSIVE

Emperor ✿✿✿ VIETNAMESE   For atmosphere and decor alone, the Emperor is Hanoi's address of note. A beautiful restored colonial stands sentinel at the busy street-side entrance and is the fine-dining area, posh and elegant. But this hushed elegance, perhaps a bit stiff for some, gives way to a lovely interior courtyard and a classic open-air building. With elegant torches and candles well placed, the hush mumble of conversation, and the gliding forms of staff in traditional ao-dai dresses, you might think you've gone into a time warp. The entry ticket is none too dear by Western standards; basic dishes fit any budget, but specialty items like the ubiquitous bird's nest or shark's fin soup will run up the bill. This is Vietnamese fine dining at its best, a tourist and expat favorite. I enjoyed the steamed garuppa in a subtle "slightly dark" sauce after an appetizer of crabmeat and asparagus soup. Everything was excellent. Try the soft-shell crab, spicy grilled squid, or any seafood specials of the day. Whether sampling light fare over a game of billiards in the back or putting on a spread in the main dining room, this is affordable elegance and the benchmark for comparison.

18b Le Thanh Tong Str., Hoan Kiem District. ℂ **04826-8801.** Fax 04/824-0027. Reservations highly recommended. Main courses US$4.75–US$22.50. MC, V. Daily 11:30am–2pm and 5:30pm–10:30pm (pub open until midnight).

The Press Club 🏵🏵 CONTINENTAL   Subdued and elegant, this place states firmly, in hushed tones, "power lunch" and offers cuisine and prices to match. The indoor restaurant is sizable yet private, done in dark tones of maroon and forest green with solid-looking wood furniture and detailing. There is outdoor seating on the terrace, next to a pseudo-jazz band, which imparts a more casual atmosphere. The service is impeccable. The menu is full of safe Continental standards: antipasto starters, goat cheese salad, tuna steak, smoked trout and Novia Scotia lobster (1¾ lb.), and various wood-grilled steaks, including, of course, "The Ultimate Steak" (22oz U.S. rib chop). The deserts are outstanding. Try the banana créme brûlée or New York cherry cheesecake. The second and third floors house event facilities and meeting rooms, and on the ground floor there's a casual coffee corner and a downscaled Deli. A good place to grab a local or international paper (and also browse a good book corner), the **Deli** is an expat standby and famous for its sandwiches and gourmet pizzas, not to mention the Aussie pie with chips or "Mom's Meatloaf." This is a good place to get a casual dose of home.

59A Ly Thai To St., Hoan Kiem District. ℂ **04/934-0888.** Reservations recommended. Main courses US$17–US$40. AE, MC, V. Daily 11am–3pm and 5–10:30pm. Weekend brunch 11am–3pm.

MODERATE

Al Fresco's 🏵🏵 TEX-MEX   Run by Australian expats, which practically guarantees a good time, Al Fresco's is two floors of friendly, casual dining. With checkered tablecloths, good oldies music, and a great view from the second floor to the street below, this is the place to bring the kids (or yourself) when they're griping or in need of a slice of home. The place serves very good Tex-Mex, pizza, chicken wings, and the like. The ribs are the house specialty. There are excellent imported and local Aussie steaks, and the burgers are the real deal, with all the fixins. The fajitas are simply out of this world, too. Desserts are good old standbys like brownies a la mode. There is a healthy wine list featuring name-brand Australian wines and some inexpensive Bulgarian and Chilean reds. If you've had enough of fried rice or noodle soup, come here for something to stick to your ribs and have a chat with the friendly owner.

23L Hai Ba Trung St., Hoan Kiem District. ℂ **04/826-7782.** Main courses US$5–US$11.50. MC, V. Daily 9:30am–10:30pm.

Brother's Café 🏵 VIETNAMESE   Buffet only, Brother's is an inexpensive starting point to explore gourmet Vietnamese cuisine. Lunch includes dishes such as salted chicken, sweet and sour bean sprouts, shrimp, noodles, and spring rolls; a full dessert table of sweet tofu, sweet baby rice, dragon fruit, and other exotic offerings; and fresh lemon or melon juice. Dinner features grilled items— shrimp, fish, lamb, and pork—and a glass of wine. There are faux street stalls encircling the garden with Vietnamese favorites like pho (noodle soup) and bun cha (cold rice noodles, spring rolls, and lettuce eaten by dipping into a slightly sweet sauce with meat). Don't expect anyone to explain anything, though; the staff here does little more than schlep drinks and smilingly point to the buffet, but it's about the food, really, and a meal here is not without nice details like pressed linen napkins and tiny fresh flowers. There's nice seating in both the courtyard (under canvas umbrellas) and the casual corners of this lushly restored colonial. The word is out, though so, especially at lunch, it's not uncommon to see tour buses pulled up in front. Get there early or get ready for an old-time smorgasboard push and shove.

26 Nguyen Thai Hoc. ℭ **04/733-3866.** Buffets 80,000 VND (US$5.25) lunch; 150,000 VND (US$10) dinner. AE, DC, MC, V. Daily 11:30am–2pm and 6:30–10pm.

Il Grillo ⭐ CLASSIC ITALIAN Il Grillo is your standard Italian restaurant, with a very casual, intimate atmosphere along with print tablecloths, hand-painted pottery, and chalkboard specials. You won't find any Vietnamese here, but it's a favorite with the expat crowd and, by virtue of its size, seems to ward off big tour groups. Portions are huge and good, and the service is friendly and attentive, including personal attention from the Italian owner. With a list of starters including bruschetta, prosciutto, and salad with anchovies, Il Grillo offers an impressive roster of grilled items, but the specialty here is pasta. Whether dry, homemade, or filled with goodies, pasta dishes here are simple and simply delicious. There's also a nice Italian wine list.

116 Ba Trieu (in the N of Hai Ba Trung District). ℭ **04/822-7720.** Reservations recommended on weekends. Main courses US$5–US$10.50. AE, MC, V. Daily 11am–11pm.

Indochine ⭐ VIETNAMESE Set in a beautifully restored colonial, this place has long been a favorite with the expat and tourist crowd. Although the food is beautifully presented and very good, the staff is indifferent, as if they're too aware that this is, in fact, "the place" (or they're angry over having to wear their funny old-style getups). There certainly are some fine things on the menu though, such as the spring rolls, banana flower salad, and crispy fried prawn-cakes with ginger. Ask about any specials. With indoor and patio seating, it is well worth a visit just for the beautiful colonial setting alone or the traditional Vietnamese music performances (call ahead for time). Take a cab; it's hard to find.

16 Nam Ngu St., Hoan Kiem District. ℭ **04/942-4097.** Main courses US$2–US$6.50. MC, V. Daily 11:30am–10pm.

Luna d' Autuno ⭐⭐ ITALIAN It's all about pizza here and it's hands-down the best in town. In a laid-back little courtyard and connected to a popular wine bar out front, this longtime expat standby is just the ticket for a casual meal and beers after work, a treat for the kids, or even a romantic night out. The portions are big, and all ingredients are good and fresh. The wood-fired, thin-crust pizza (you can specify how crunchy) lets the ingredients do the talking. You'll find no pretensions here, and the staff makes you feel welcome; any language barriers are overcome by the international language of pizza. Enjoy.

11b Din Bien Phu, Hanoi. ℭ **08/237-338.** Main courses US$4.60–US$10.50. Daily 10am–11pm.

Restaurant Bobby Chinn ⭐⭐ CALIFORNIA/VIET/FRENCH With a decor and panache that would hold its own on a side street of Soho or a lofty perch in the Bay Area, Restaurant Bobby Chinn makes for an interesting evening. On the southwest corner of Hoan Kiem Lake, longtime expat and raconteur Mr. Chinn holds court and runs the show from behind the proscenium of his large, open bar at the entrance. It's where to see and be seen these days in Hanoi, and it's a popular late-night spot where local jazz artists like to drop by. There's a good revolving collection of local artists' works on the walls and always good music playing. The front dining area is simple tables and a few booths at bar-side with picture-window views of the lake and the street. Seating in the back is choice overstuffed couches and low tables in a maze of discreet nooks with hanging cloths blown by ceiling fans that offer fickle privacy. It's all quite cinematic, really. Oh, right, and there's food. However you feel about the atmosphere, Mr. Chinn serves up a delightfully eclectic menu of fine French and Vietnamese dishes with slight variations and cross-cultural flair. With an excellent affordable tapas menu billed as "Zenlike" for simple elegance, try the rib sampler or "symphony of flavors" (a selection of all). Main courses like pan-roasted salmon with wasabi mashed potatoes, and green tea smoked duck have a certain Franco-Japanese appeal all their own. The menu is a work in progress, so try to get a recommendation from the charismatic owner; that means jockeying for "face-time."

> **Tips   Restaurant Tip**
>
> Note that many upscale restaurants in Hanoi levy a 5% service charge on top of the 10% government tax.

1 Ba Trieu St., Hoan Keim District, Hanoi. ✆ **04/934-8577.** Reservations recommended. AE, MC, V. Main courses US$7–US$12; tapas menu from US$2. Daily 12am–2pm and 5pm to last customer.

Revival ★★ NORTHERN INDIAN   Expats agree that Revival is tops in town for authentic and tasty Indian food. It's tidy Indian-themed Western decor here with excellent service and presentation (curries served in small metal crocks with brass ladles). It's a favorite of the business lunch crowd, and the US$5 set menus are popular. Manager Ajay Sandhir explains the ingredients of each dish with much pinache and with good reason: My *Achari Goshi* (mutton in pickled masala) was delicious. Try one of the many unique starters, like a chicken-cheese kebab. The menu is exhaustive and everything's good.

41B Ly Thai To St., Hoan Kiem District. ✆ **04/824-1166.** Main courses 45,000–75,000 VND (US$3–US$5). MC, V. Mon–Sat 11:30am–2pm and 6:30–10pm.

Seasons of Hanoi ★ VIETNAMESE   The atmosphere is picture-perfect at Seasons: intimate, candlelit, romantic, earth-colored surroundings in a casual yet beautifully restored colonial with authentic native furniture. There are two floors. Try to sit on the first to avoid tourists traveling in packs. The spring rolls are heaven, as are the tempura soft-shell crabs. Fish is everywhere on the menu—fried, boiled, on kabobs, and in hot pots. If you fancy it, try the sautéed eel with chile and lemongrass—that is, unless you don't decide on the fried chicken in panda leaves first. Everything comes beautifully presented, and there is a nice wine list.

95B Quan Thanh. ✆ **04/843-5444.** Reservations recommended, especially for groups. Main courses 40,000–80,000 VND (US$2.65–US$5.35). MC, V. Daily 11:30am–2pm and 6–11pm.

INEXPENSIVE

Cha Ca La Vong ★★ *Finds* HANOI/VIETNAMESE   On a street called Cha, Ca there's a restaurant (one of many) called Cha Ca, and it serves one dish: You guessed it, Cha Ca. So what in blazes is Cha Ca? Very simple. It's monkfish, a fine white fish, fried at high heat in peanut oil with dill, tumeric, rice noodles, and peanuts—and it's delicious. The place is pretty grungy, and to call the service "indifferent" would be to sing its praises, but that's the beauty here: It's all about the food. You order by saying how many you are, (for a flat rate per pax) and how many bottles of beer or soda you'd like. Then it's do-it-yourself (with some friendly guidance) as you stir in the ingredients on a frying pan over a charcoal hibatchi right at the table. It's a rich dish and great with some hot sauce (go easy on it at first), and it makes for a fun and interesting evening. Just say "Cha Ca," and any cab driver can take you there, but ignore entreaties to go to copycats (cabbies will certainly have commission-giving friends). Cha Ca La Vong is the top dog.

14 Cha Ca St. ✆ 04/826-8801. Main courses US$4. No credit cards. Daily 10am–2pm and 4pm–10pm.

Le Café des Arts de Hanoi ✿ BISTRO/CONTINENTAL   After strolling around Hoan Kiem Lake, stop off its northwest end for a drink or a bite at this friendly bistro-style eatery, run by French expats and open all day. Spacious, with tiled floors and shuttered windows looking into the narrow Old Quarter street below, the cafe has casual rattan furniture and a long, inviting bar, and it doubles as an art gallery, which explains the interesting paintings hanging throughout. The Vietnamese art crowd also provides some attractive local color. Most inviting, however, is the excellent food. Ask for the special of the day, and stick to bistro standbys like the omelets or a *croque madame*—toasted bread and cheese sautéed in egg—and house specialty *salade bressare* (very fresh chicken and vegetables in a light mayonnaise sauce). There is also good house wine by the glass and excellent lunch set specials.

11b Ngo Bao Khanh, Hoan Kiem District (in the Old Quarter). ✆ 04/828-7207. Main courses US$6–US$12. No credit cards. Daily 9am–11pm (bar open until midnight).

Tamarind Café ✿✿ VEGETARIAN   Tamarind is a laid-back, friendly spot, and, even if you're not a vegetarian, this welcoming cafe's inventive menu will tickle your fancy. Soups such as vegetarian wonton and two-color soup (spinach and sweet potato) take the chill off Hanoi winter nights and go great with the selection of sandwiches. Other inventive options here include "Ratatofu," ratatouille over tofu, and an all-day breakfast served with delicious homemade fruit condiments. Fruit shakes and excellent teas round out the meal, and with a bottomless cup of coffee for just US$1, it's a great place to take a break from the hectic traffic of the Old Quarter. They have street-side tables out front and funky, raised floor seating in the back for reading, relaxing (a good place to meet other travelers and pick up advice.

80 Ma May St. ✆ 04/926-0580. Main courses US$1.72–US$2.76. MC, V. Daily 9am–11pm.

SNACKS & CAFES

For great coffee and desserts, try **Moca Café,** at 14–16 Nha Tho (✆ **04/825-6334**). This area has become the popular spot for a growing little Bohemian community in Hanoi, and businesses are sprouting up all along Nha Tho, the street that extends from St. Christopher's Church. Check out one of the main attractions around Hoan Kiem Lake, **Fanny's Ice Cream,** 16 Hang Bong, which serves exquisite French-style ice cream and sorbets from 8am to 11pm.

   Pepperonis, at 29 Ly Quoc Su (✆ **04/928-5246**), serves up the pizza that backpackers have been longing for along the tough travel trails throughout Asia. It's cheap and best on the popular bar street (across from Café des Arts).

   Little Hanoi, 21 Hang Gai St. (✆ **04/828-8333**), just north of the lake, is little local-styled fast-food joint, with basic but tidy bamboo and wood decor.

Finds Have You Tried the Snake?

Six kilometers to the east of Hanoi, across the Red River, lies the town of Le Mat, known as the "snake village" by most. In among shanty houses and the winding alleyways of this town, you'll find some very flash restaurants with Chinese-style roofs sheltering elegant dining areas, all strangely tucked away or down small alleys. What's the big secret? For years, the town has been the de facto hub of the very taboo snake-restaurant industry. The Vietnamese taboo is not much different than that in the West (something like "Eat snake? Ooooh, Yuck!"), but it also has to do with what snakes represent (again this parallels western cultural paradigms). It's also considered a male aphrodisiac, a kind of fried Viagra, so at night it's not uncommon to see groups of businessmen drunk as skunks piling into these places for a bit of medicine.

So, here's the drill. Finding it is half the battle (or adventure). Any taxi driver will be happy to take you to his friend's place, and you will commonly be able to negotiate a low fare in anticipation of a hefty commission from the restaurant of his choice. Feel free to ask to see another restaurant (some of them are pretty grotty), but expect to pay about US$5 to get there (cheaper by moto-taxi).

You'll be greeted by a friendly owner who'll usher you back to the cages and put on quite a show of stirring up the snakes before using his forked stick to select one he thinks will feed your party. He'll then quote you a ridiculous price, but expect to pay somewhere between US$5 and US$10 per person, depending on your bargaining ability (he will likely start with something like quadruple that).

Then the show begins. You'll be seated and, before your eyes, the owner will adeptly kill the snake, drain the blood into a jar of rice whiskey, and systematically disembowel the animal, extracting the liver and showing you the still-beating heart before adding it to the whiskey/blood concoction. The guest of honor is meant to eat the heart and take the first sip of whiskey before the bottle circulates to all. Thus begins a lengthy seven-course meal, starting with fried snake skin, grilled snake filet (okay, it tastes like chicken), snake spring rolls, snake soup with rice cake, minced snake dumpling, copious amounts of rice whiskey, and orange wedges for dessert. It's a decent meal, really, and certainly something to write home about.

One might make ethical claims against places like this, and, in fact, many of these places are part of the underground market in endangered species such as rare, nocturnal jungle animals and the disappearing Asiatic Bear. That said, the snakes are common cobras found everywhere in Vietnam, and a trip here makes for an interesting night. Be clear with the driver about where you want to go (i.e., not to a brothel afterward), and don't pay until you arrive at the destination (always a good rule).

There are lots of restaurants in LeMat; after driving around and doing some comparative price shopping, I chose **O Sin** (© **04/827-2984),** kind of a midrange place. Some are quite upscale. Bargain hard.

Open 7:30am to 11pm, it serves up a limited menu of local favorites like banana flower salad and noodle soup (without the resultant bellyache), and makes a good central meeting point. It delivers, too.

ATTRACTIONS

While sightseeing, remember that state-owned attractions will usually close for lunch from 11:30am to 1:30pm (or thereabouts). Also, foreigners will be charged approximately twice what the Vietnamese are charged, so you'll pay 10,000 VND (US66¢) for most public attractions. Don't bother arguing. Be sure not to accept any extraneous pamphlets or unwanted guides for a hidden fee.

BA DINH DISTRICT

Army Museum ★★   This building opened in 1959, presents the Vietnamese side of the country's struggle against colonial powers. There are three buildings of odds and ends from both the French and American wars here, including evocative photos. Most interesting, though, is the actual war equipment on display, including aircraft, tanks, bombs, and big guns, some with signs indicating just how many of which enemy the piece took out. There is a tank belonging to the troops that crashed through the Presidential Palace gates on April 30, 1975, Vietnamese Liberation Day. Outside there is also a spectacular, room-size bouquet of downed French and U.S. aircraft wreckage. Also on the grounds is Hanoi's ancient flag tower (Cot Co), constructed from 1805 to 1812. The exhibits have English translations, which makes this an easy and worthwhile visit.

28A Dien Bien Phu St. ✆ **04/823-4264.** Admission 10,000 VND (US69¢). Tues–Sun 8–11:30am and 1:30–4:30pm.

Ho Chi Minh's Mausoleum ★★   In an imposing, somber granite-and-concrete structure modeled on Lenin's tomb, Ho lies in state, embalmed and dressed in his favored khaki suit. He asked to be cremated, but his wish was not heeded. A respectful demeanor is required, and the dress code mandates no shorts or sleeveless shirts allowed. Note that the mausoleum is usually closed through October and November, when Ho goes to Russia for body maintenance of an undisclosed nature. The museum might be closed during this period as well.

On Ba Dinh Square, Ba Dinh District. Tues–Thurs and Sat 8am–11am.

Ho Chi Minh's Museum ★★   English-language explanations help to piece together the fragments of Ho's life and cause here, and there are personal items, photos, and documents detailing the rise of the nation's communist revolution. The rhetoric is laid on a bit thick, but all in all it's an interesting and informative display. Completely unique to Vietnam are the conceptual displays symbolizing freedom, reunification, and social progress through flowers, fruit, and mirrors. Have a look.

3 Ngo Ha. Left of 1 Pillar Pagoda, near Ba Dinh Square. Ba Dinh District. ✆ **04/845-5455.** Admission 10,000 VND (US69¢). Tues–Sun 8–11:30am and 1:30–4pm.

Ho Chi Minh's Residence ★★   Ho's residence, the well-known house on stilts, is behind the Presidential Palace, a gorgeous French colonial building built in 1901 for the resident French governor. Shunning the glorious structure nearby, Ho instead chose to live here from 1958 to 1969. Facing an exquisite landscaped lake, the structure does have its charm, and the spartan room is an interesting glimpse into the life of this enigmatic national hero. The basement was a meeting place for the politburo; upstairs are the bedroom and a study, and little details like his phone and walking cane are kept behind glass. Behind the house is a garden of fruit trees, many of them exotics imported from other lands, including miniature rose bushes and areca trees from the Caribbean.

Behind the Presidential Palace. Admission 10,000 VND (US69¢). Tues–Sun 8–11am and 1:30–4:30pm.

Hun Tiep Lake and the Downed B-52

This is not a site that will knock you off your feet for its size or beauty; in fact, what brings many here is that it's an ordinary neighborhood, a maze of quiet lanes broken only by a small pond and, in the pond, the wreckage of an American B-52 shot down during the Christmas air-raids of 1972. Many folks, veterans among them, find that a visit here puts a perspective on the war and that the rusting wreckage brings our abstract historical impressions back to the concrete present; others see landing gear, struts, and metal sheeting in a grungy pond. There's a partly submerged memorial plaque, and the area is cordoned off; entrance fees are soon to follow, no doubt. Most taxi drivers know it, or some creative charades will get the point across. Drivers will drop you off at the head of the alley (Lane 55) leading to the site (a handwritten sign says B-52).

Located just S of W Lake along Hoang Hoa Tham Rd., and a short walk down Lane 55 heading S. No admission price.

One-Pillar Pagoda ★

To the right of the Ho Chi Minh Museum is the unique One Pillar Pagoda, a wooden structure built in 1049 that sits on stilts over a lake. A king of the Ly Dynasty, Ly Thai Thong King, had it built after having a dream in which Bodhisattva Avalokitesvara, the goddess of mercy, presented him with a lotus flower. The existing pagoda is a miniature reproduction of the original, which was said to represent a lotus emerging from the water. It is certainly interesting, and a visit to pray for fertility or good health reportedly has miraculous results. However, you will not be admitted if you're wearing shorts.

Right of Ho Chi Minh Museum, near Ba Dinh Square. Ba Dinh District.

Vietnam Fine Arts Museum ★★

The very worthwhile arts museum features Vietnamese art of the 20th century, up to the 1970s or so. While the presentations are a bit crowded and rustic, there are explanations in English. Much of the art is outstanding, although you won't really see any works of an innovative or controversial nature. Entire rooms are devoted to the Vietnamese style of lacquer and silk painting, woodblock, and folk art. Techniques are explained—a nice touch. Interesting also are the modern works of wood statuary interspersed among the exhibits. Some are patriotic in nature, depicting daily life or events during the war or done in Soviet-influenced caricature with heavy-limbed peasants striking triumphant poses or depictions of the brotherhood of the army and the working class. The top floors are devoted to prehistoric artifacts and Buddhist sculptures, some of which are huge and impressive. Don't miss the famous 11th-century goddess of mercy (Kouan Yin), with her thousand arms and eyes in the far-left room on the second floor. Best of all, the museum itself is in an old colonial, and, unless there's a tour group milling around, you can stroll around in relative serenity and rest on one of the many benches provided (no napping). The gift shop has some nice modern works from known artists for sale.

66 Nguyen Thai Hoc. ✆ 04/846-5801. Admission 10,000 VND (US69¢). Tues–Sun 9:15–11am and 1–5pm.

West Lake ★★

In Hanoi, West Lake is second only to Hoan Kiem as a nerve center for the city, steeped in legend and sporting several significant pagodas. Vietnam's oldest pagoda, **Tran Quoc,** was built in the 6th century and is located on Cayang Island in the middle of the lake, a beautiful setting. An actual fragment of

the Boddhi tree under which Buddha achieved Enlightenment was given as a gift from the Prime Minister of India in 1959 and now grows proudly in the main courtyard. Constructed by an early Zen sect and a famous center for Dharma study, and later as an imperial feasting grounds, the temple has a visitors' hall, two corridors, and a bell tower; it still houses a group of diligent monks. They recommend not wearing shorts here, but it is not enforced. Farther along the lake, **Quan Thanh Temple,** by the northern gate, was built during the reign of Le Thai To King (1010–28). It is dedicated to Huyen Thien Tran Vo, the god who reigned over Vietnam's northern regions. Renovated in the 19th century, the impressive temple has a triple gate and courtyard, and features a 3.6m (12-ft.) bronze statue of the god. West Lake is also a hub of local activity, particularly on weekends when families go paddle-boating on it.

Bordered by Thuy Khue and Thanh Nien sts.

DONG DA DISTRICT

Temple of Literature and National University (Van Mieu–Quoc Tu Giam) ★★ If Vietnam has a seat of learning, this is it. There are two entities here: Van Mieu, a temple built to worship Chinese philosopher Confucius in 1070; and Quoc tu Giam, literally "Temple of the King Who Distinguished Literature," an elite institute established in 1076 to teach the doctrines of Confucius and his disciples. It existed for more than 700 years as a center for Confucian learning. Moreover, it is a powerful symbol for the Vietnamese, having been established after the country emerged from a period of Chinese colonialism that lasted from 179 B.C. to A.D. 938. It is a testament to the strong cultural heritage of the Mandarins. As such, it stands for independence and a solidifying of national culture and values.

What exists today is a series of four courtyards that served as an entrance to the university. Architecturally, it is a fine example of classic Chinese with Vietnamese influences. Still present are 82 stone stelae—stone diplomas, really— erected between 1484 and 1780, bearing the names and birthplaces of 1,306 doctor laureates who managed to pass the university's rigorous examinations. Beyond the final building, known as the sanctuary, the real university began. Damaged in the French war, it is currently being restored.

Quoc Tu Giam St. ✆ 04/845-2917. Admission 10,000 VND (US66¢). Daily 8am–5pm.

HOAN KIEM DISTRICT

Hanoi Opera House This gorgeous, historic Art Nouveau building was built near the turn of the century. Unfortunately, to get inside, you'll have to attend a performance, but that should be enjoyable as well (see "Hanoi After Dark," below).

1 Trang Tien St. ✆ 04/933-0113. Intersection of Le Thanh Tong and Trang Tien sts., District 1.

Hoa Lo Prison (Hanoi Hilton) ★★ For sheer gruesome atmosphere alone, this ranks near the top of the must-see list. It was constructed by the French in 1896 mainly to house political prisoners, and the Vietnamese took it over in 1954. It was subsequently used to house prisoners of war. From 1964 to 1973, it was a major POW detention facility. U.S. senator John McCain was a particularly famous inmate, as was Pete Peterson, the ambassador to Vietnam, and Lieut. Everett Alvarez, officially the first American pilot to be shot down over Vietnam. Their stories are told from the Vietnamese perspective in photographs and writings grouped in one small room. To the west is the guillotine room, still with its original equipment, and the female and Vietnamese political prisoners' quarters. The courtyard linking the two has parts of original tunnels once used by a hundred intrepid Vietnamese revolutionaries to escape in 1945. Only part of the original complex is left; the rest of the original site was razed and is ironically occupied by a tall, gleaming office complex popular with foreign investors. There are basic English explanations, but this is a good spot to have a guide who is certain to be armed with a tale or two.

1 Hoa Lo St., off Quan Su St. ✆ 04/824-6358. Admission 10,000 VND (US66¢). Tues–Sun 8am–4:30pm.

National Museum of Vietnamese History This is an exhaustive repository of Vietnamese ancient and historical relics nicely displayed with some barebones explanations in English. Housed in a building that was the French consulate until 1910 and a museum in various incarnations since, this collection walks you from prehistoric artifacts and carvings to funerary jars and some very fine examples of Dong Son drums from the north, excavations of Han tombs, Buddhist statuary, and everyday items of early history. It's the kind of place where schoolchildren are forced to go (and be careful if you see buses out front), and for anyone but history buffs, you might feel just as bored as the kids. For those on any kind of historical mission in Vietnam, I recommend contacting a tour agency and booking a knowledgeable guide for an excellent overview and a good beginning to any trip.

1 Trang Tien St. (just E of the opera). ✆ 04/825-3518. Entrance 15,000 VND (US$1). Daily 8am–11:30am and 1:30pm–4:30pm.

Old Quarter & Hoan Kiem Lake ★★★ The Old Quarter evolved from workshop villages clustered by trades, or guilds, in the early 13th century. It's now an area of narrow, ancient, winding streets, each named for the trade it formerly featured. Even today, streets tend to be for either silk, silver, or antiques. It's a fascinating slice of centuries-old life in Hanoi, including markets that are so pleasantly crowded that the street itself narrows to a few feet. Hoan Kiem is considered the center of the city. It is also known as the Lake of the Recovered Sword. In the mid–15th century, the gods gave emperor Le Thai To a magical sword to defeat Chinese invaders. While the emperor was boating on the lake one day, a giant tortoise reared up and snatched the sword, returning it to its rightful owners and ushering peace into the kingdom. Stroll around the lake in the early morning or evening to savor local life among the willow trees and see elders playing chess or doing tai chi. In the center of the lake is the Tortoise Pagoda; on the northern part is Ngoc Son pagoda, reachable only by the Bridge of the Rising Sun and open daily from 8am to 5pm.

Bordered by Tran Nhat Duat and Phung Hung sts. Daily 8am–5pm.

Quan Su Pagoda ★ Quan Su is one of the most important temples in the country. Constructed in the 15th century along with a small house for visiting Buddhist ambassadors, in 1934 it became the headquarters of the Tonkin Buddhist Association and today it is headquarters for the Vietnam Central Buddhist Congregation. It's an active pagoda and usually thronged with worshippers; the interior is dim and smoky with incense. To the rear is a school of Buddhist doctrine. For good luck (or for fun), visitors of any stripe are welcome to buy sticks of incense and make offerings at the various altars and sand urns. It's easy to just follow suit, and folks will be glad to show you what to do.

73 Quan Su St., as it intersects Tran Hung Da, Hoan Kiem District. Daily 8–11am and 1–4pm.

SIGHTS OUTSIDE THE CITY CENTER
Vietnam Ethnology Museum ★★ If you're interested in learning more about the 53 ethnic minorities populating Vietnam's hinterlands, stop in at this new museum. The different groups, with their history and customs, are explained via photos, videos, and displays of clothing and household and work implements. You'll need to take a taxi to get here, though.

Nguyen Van Huyen, 6km (3¾ miles) W of town. ℂ 04/756-2193. Admission 10,000 VND (US66¢). Tues–Sun 8:30–11:30am and 1:30–4:30pm.

ACTIVITIES
Bicycles are easily rented from almost every hotel for about US$1 a day. Wake up early and join the hordes of people doing tai chi, stretching, walking, and running in the parks of Hanoi: This is a great place for people-watching and a little morning wake-up, best near the Botanical Gardens, Lenin Park, and Hoan Kiem Lake. Get your run in before about 6:30am, though, before traffic starts to snarl. The **Clark Hatch Fitness Center,** at the Metropole Hotel (ℂ **04/826-6919**), has top-end equipment, a sauna, and a Jacuzzi, with day rates for nonguests.

SHOPPING
Hanoi is a fine place to shop and features Vietnamese specialties such as silk, silver, lacquer ware, embroidered goods, and ethnic minority crafts. Silk is good quality and an easy buy. Shops will tailor a suit in as little 24 hours, but allow yourself extra time for alterations. Many of the shops are clustered along Hang

Gai St., aka "Silk Street," on the northeast side of the Old Quarter. **Daily hours are generally from 8am to 9pm.** A silk suit will run from about US$25 to US$65, depending on the silk, and a blouse or shirt will cost US$15 to US$20. Virtually every shop takes credit cards (MC, V). Bargain hard for all but the silk; offer 50% of the asking price and end up paying 70% or so.

Khai Silk, with branches in various hotel lobbies and at 96 Hang Gai St. (© 04/825-4237) and 121 Nguyen Thai Hoc St. (© 04/823-3508), is justly famous for its selection, silk quality, and relatively pleasant store layout. Also try **Thanh Ha Silk,** 114 Hang Gai St. (© 04/928-5348), and **Oriental House,** 28 Nha Chung (© 04/828-5542). **Tan My,** at 109 Hang Gai St. (© 04/826-7081), has exquisite embroidery work, especially for children's clothing and bedding.

For silver, antique oddities, and traditional crafts, try **Hong Hoa,** on 18 Ngo Quyen St., near the Metropole Hotel (© 04/826-8341), which has a good selection. **Giai Dieu,** on 82 Hang Gai St. (© 04/826-0222), has interesting lacquer paintings and decorative items, so stop in; you'll probably be in the neighborhood at some point. There is also a branch at 93 Ba Trieu St. Silver jewelry, handbags, and other ornaments are sold at 80 Hang Gai St. For fine ceramics, look to **Quang's Ceramics,** at 22 Hang Luoc St. (© 04/828-3440), in the Old Quarter. Unique lacquer ware, including business card holders and tissue boxes, can be had at **DeltaDeco,** 12 Nha Tho St. (© 04/828-9616). Wood, stone, and brass lacquer reproduction sculptures of religious icons are at **KAF Traditional Sculptures and Art Accessories,** 31B Ba Trieu St. (© 04/822-0022).

ART GALLERIES

Vietnam has a flourishing art scene, and Hanoi has many galleries of oil, silk, water, and lacquer paintings. Don't forget to bargain here, too. One of the best is **Nam Son,** at 41 Trang Tien (© 04/826-2993). Others include **Thanh Mai,** 64 Hang Gai St. (© 04/825-1618); **Apricot Gallery,** 40B Hang Bong St. (© 04/828-8965); and **Thang Long,** 15 Hang Gai St. (© 04/825-0740), in the Old Quarter. Paintings are originals, meaning that they're painted by one artist and commonly not the factory-style knock-offs so popular in the rest of Asia, like Taiwan Art. But you're just buying copies here of well-known Vietnamese artists. The original that you buy today is being reproduced at the local art school and will be replaced by something identical when you walk out the door. Still, it's some nice stuff, and it's cheap for originals.

BOOKS

For foreign books in Hanoi, check out one of the many shops lining Trang Tien Street, a popular backpacker repository and some good deals on photocopied bootlegs of regional sources and interesting cast-offs from other travelers. Also try **Le Comptoirs,** on the first floor of the **Press Club** (see the "Expensive" category in the "Where to Dine" section, earlier in this chapter); here they have all international papers and a good selection of new books.

CONVENIENCE

To pick up good snacks for a long train or bus ride, check out **Intimex** (© 04/825-6148), down a small alley at 22–23 Le Thai To St., on the west side of Hoan Kiem Lake. With groceries on the first floor and a small department store on the second level, you can find what you need. For Western wines and canned products from home, try the aptly named **Western Canned Foods,** at 66 Ba Trieu (© 04/822-9217), just south of Hoan Keim.

HANOI AFTER DARK

When it comes to nightlife, Hanoi is no Saigon, but there are a variety of pleasant watering holes about town and a few rowdy dance spots. Hanoi is also the best city in which to see **traditional Vietnamese arts** such as opera, theater, and water puppet shows. Invented during the **Ly Dynasty** (1009–1225), the art of water puppetry is unique to Vietnam. The puppets are made of wood and really do dance on water. The shows feature traditional Vietnamese music and depict folklore and myth. Book for the popular puppets at least 5 hours ahead.

THEATER & PERFORMANCE

The **Hanoi Opera House** (Hanoi Municipal Theatre), 1 Trang Tien St., Hoan Kiem District (© 04/933-0113), hosts performances by local and international artists. The **Hanoi Traditional Opera,** 15 Nguyen Dinh Chieu, Ba Dinh District (© 04/826-7361), has shows on Monday, Wednesday, and Friday at 8pm.

   Central Circus, in Lenin Park, Hai Ba Trung District (© 04/822-0277), has shows at 7:45pm every day except Monday. It's a real circus done on a small scale, so see it only if you're desperate to entertain the kids.

Thang Long Water Puppet Theater ★★★ *Finds*   Shows are nightly at 8pm. This might sound like one for the kids, but there is something enchanting about the lighthearted comedy and intricately skilled puppetry of this troupe. They perform numerous vignettes of daily life in the countryside and ancient tales, including the legend of Hoan Kiem Lake and the peaceful founding of the city of Hanoi. Puppeteers use bamboo poles to extend their puppets from behind the proscenium and up through the surface of a small pond that forms the stage. You will be amazed at their ingenuity, and it doesn't take much to "suspend disbelief" here as you find yourself getting caught up in this magical hour of otherworldly escape in Hanoi. The kids will like it, too. Buy tickets early in the high season.

57B Dinh Tien Hoang St., Hoan Kiem District. (© 04/825-5450. Fax: 04/824-9494. Thanglong.wpt@fpt.vn. Admission 20,000–40,000 VND (US$1.33–US$2.66).

BARS, PUBS & DISCOS

The old standard in town is **Apocalypse Now,** 5C Hoa Ma (© 04/971-2783), a down and dirty joint with black walls, a thatched-roof bar, and lights with "blood" streaks on them. Everybody comes—backpackers, locals, expats—and it's all somehow great fun. Plus, it's open later than practically any bar in Hanoi, until 4am or so—this is definitely an "end of the night" place. While they don't serve food, they do serve up great music and beer for US$1. There's a pool table and a small dance floor as well.

   Bao Khanh Street, just down a short lane in the northwest corner of Hoan Kiem Lake (near Café des Arts), is now home to lots of popular bars and late-night spots. Some are a bit seedy, but there are a few nice, laid-back spots that seem to ward off the international "lager-lout" set. Check out **Polite Pub** (© 04/825-0959), at 5 Bao Khanh, with a snooker table from Hong Kong and a pool table (open 5pm–2 or 3am). **Gecko Bar,** at 14b across from Café des Arts (© 04/928-6125), is three floors of fun, open late; be sure to check out French proprietor Michel's new French menu. Just around the corner, at 15b Hang Hanh, the **Funky Monkey** (© 04/928-6113) has music, pool tables, pizzas, and a cool black-light menu. All of these spots are open late, and the street's always hoppin'.

   The Spotted Cow, at 23C Hai Ba Trung, just next to Al Fresco (© 04/824-1028; see dining), is a good choice for a night out with the boys: There's just drinkin' and darts here.

For a more upscale experience, try a cocktail at the famous **Press Club,** 59A Ly Thai To (℧ **04/934-0888**), or just up the street at the **Diva Café,** 57 Ly Thai To ℧**04/934-4088**), where they put on a flamboyant and entertaining fire show when preparing their special Irish coffee.

Cau Lac Bo Nhac Jazz Club, in the heart of the Old Quarter at 31 Luong Van Can St. (℧ **04/828-7890**), has no cover charge and offers some of the best local acts here nightly. Call ahead to see what's going on of an evening. **The New Century,** at 10 Trang Thi (℧ **04/928-5285**), another popular jazz venue, has acts nightly; the cover charge varies with the performers, so be sure to call ahead.

The folks at **Bobby Chin's** (1 Ba Trieu St. on the S end of Hoan Kiem Lake ℧ **04/934-8577**) can serve up just about any cocktail. It's kind of a hip, late-night hangout, depending on the crowd.

EXCURSIONS FROM HANOI
HALONG BAY

Halong Bay, a natural wonder, is 3,000 islands of varying sizes in the Gulf of Tonkin, many housing spectacular limestone grottos. It has been declared a UNESCO World Heritage Site. The bay itself is a 4-hour drive from Hanoi among often almost unbearably bad roads, and usually includes at least one overnight stay. Given the logistics, the trip is best done via an agent or with a group. When you book a tour with an overnight stay, you'll probably cruise on a junk for 4 to 6 hours along the bay, stopping to explore two grottos. You might pause for a swim as well. If you're really pressed for time, the tourist cafes do a daily trip for US$24 per person, departing Hanoi at 7am and getting you back by midnight. But that's really pushing it. Overnight trips can cost anywhere from US$16 to upward of US$150 for one overnight. It depends on whether you hire a bus or a private driver, where you stay, and what you eat. Sinh Café does a fine job on the low end, and Ann's Tourist is a good choice for the higher end (see "Visitor Information & Tours," earlier in this chapter).

Ecotourism is taking off here, and the steep karst outcrops of the bay are not only beautiful, but ideal for **rock climbing.** You might also want to consider one of the 2- or 3-day **sea-kayaking** adventures that are becoming popular here. Contact Buffalo Tours or Handspan Adventure Travel (see "Visitor Information & Tours," earlier in this chapter,) for memorable, exciting packages starting from US$180 for multiday trips.

CUC PHUONG NATIONAL PARK

Cuc Phuong, established in 1962 as Vietnam's first national park, is a lush mountain rainforest with more than 250 bird and 60 mammal species, including tigers, leopards, and the unique red-bellied squirrel. The park's many visitors—and poachers—might keep you from the kind of wildlife experience you might hope for in the brush, however. It's still the perfect setting for a good hike, and it features goodies like a 1,000-year-old tree, a waterfall, and Con Moong Cave, where prehistoric human remains have been discovered. Cuc Phuong is a good day trip from Hanoi, and some tourist cafes offer programs for as little as US$20 (if you have 4 people in your group). It is also possible to overnight there in the park headquarters.

HOA LU

From A.D. 968 to 1010, Hoa Lu was the capital of Vietnam under the Dinh Dynasty and the first part of the Le Dynasty. It is located in a valley surrounded by awesome limestone formations, and is known as the inland Halong Bay. It is a similarly picturesque sight and much easier to reach. Most of what remains of the kingdom are ruins, but there are still temples in the valley, renovated in the 17th century. The first honors Dinh Tien Hoang and has statues of the king. The second is dedicated to Le Dai Hanh, one of Dinh's generals and the first king of the Le Dynasty, who grabbed power in 980 after Dinh was mysteriously assassinated. Hoa Lu can easily be seen on a day trip from Hanoi. Seat-in-coach tours from a tourist cafe run about US$12 per person.

4 The Far North

The north and northwest highland regions are becoming increasingly popular destinations for hardy travelers. In addition to breathtaking landscapes amidst the **Tonkinese Alps** and off-the-map destinations like **Dien Bien Phu,** one of the main attractions of going farther afield is the **villages of the ethnic minority hill tribes,** among them the Muong, Hmong, Tai, Tay, and Dao. The villagers truly haven't seen many outsiders, and visits from foreigners usually involve a lot of staring and some friendly touching on both sides. If you can make it this far, it will be a rewarding experience; a few new upscale options are quite exciting.

Another relatively easy destination is **Mai Chau,** a gorgeous valley about 4 hours from Hanoi. It is the homeland of the ethnic Tai people. The road is somewhat better than the one to Sapa, and the destination is not yet as developed. **Dien Bien Phu,** to the far northwest, is a former French commercial and military outpost, and the site of one of Vietnam's biggest military victories over the French. You can fly directly to Dien Bien Phu from Hanoi.

Apart from Sapa (see below), this region is definitely one in which independent travel could prove to be extremely challenging, if not well nigh impossible. The best way to take in the splendor of the natural surroundings is to do perhaps a 4- or 5-day tour, with a jeep and a driver. You could tackle only one or two of the destinations in a 2-day trip.

INFORMATION AND TOURS

Any tourist cafe or travel agent in Hanoi can arrange trips by private jeep or a combo jeep and train tour. Apart from Sapa, the vast tracts of the north are untouristed and best visited on a tour. Here are some good options:

Ann's Tours, 26 Yet Kieu, Hoan Kiem District (© **04/822-0018;** anntours@ yahoo.com), offers custom-tailored, reasonable packages.

Buffalo Tours, 11 Hang Muoi, Hoan Kiem District (© **04/828-0702;** www. buffalotours.com), also has an excellent reputation, offering similar tours. Some do involve arduous climbing and overnights in hill-tribe villages without electricity and running water. Other groups offer adventure travel in the region, including camping and hiking.

Handspan Adventure Travel, 80 Ma May St. (© **04/962-0446;** fax 04/926-0445; www.handspan.com), organizes light, intermediary, and tough treks with home stays for between US$75 and US$102 per person (minimum 2 people); it also offers jeep tours at US$160 to US$180.

Every **tourist cafe** offers a **Sapa package** and wide circuits through the north, but keep in mind that low-end travel to this area will be particularly rugged (packages run between US$25 and US$30 per person for 4 days and 3 nights).

5 Sapa

This small market town has been a gathering spot for many local hill tribes for nearly 200 years, and Hmong and Yao, among others, still come here to conduct trade, socialize, and attend an ephemeral **"love market"** where young men and women choose one another for marriage (it's not likely you'll see anything but a staged re-creation of it here). Seeing this, French missionaries as early as 1860 said "Mon Dieu!" and set up camp to save souls; their stone church still stands sentinel and is well attended at the center of town. With the mercifully cooler climate and colorful gatherings of hill-dwellers (not to mention the advantages gained by trade and control of this region), Sapa became an instant tourist site for French colonists, complete with rail connection, upscale hotels, and a tourist bureau as early as 1917. The French alternately deserted and rebuilt the town over the years, depending on the state of the colony, and the outpost was retaken by the Vietnamese in 1950 and attacked and destroyed later by the French. Chinese troops found billet here but aren't responsible for any destruction. The town began rebuilding for tourism in the early 1990s. It's a bit like an old trading post in the American West perhaps, and just as kitschy and picturesque.

Now connected by luxury train with Hanoi, Sapa boasts some great upscale and budget accommodation and is a great jumping-off point for trekking and ecotours. Even a 1- or 2-day trip, bracketed by overnight train journeys from Hanoi, will give you a unique glimpse of local hill-tribe culture. You can trek out to nearby villages with or without a guide, or simply wait for members of the various hill tribes to come to sell their wares. Their costumes alone are an eyeful: colorful embroidered tunics embellished with heavy silver ornaments that, to those in the know, signify marital status or place in their group's hierarchy.

And Sapa is a feast for the eyes; hills striated by terraced rice-farms in vast, green valleys are like a stairway up to Mt. Fansipan, Southeast Asia's tallest mountain, which, at 3,143m (10,312 ft.), seems to be smiling down on all the proceedings. *Note:* Bring a few layers here because, especially in the winter months, it's can get chilly.

GETTING THERE

BY TRAIN Guests of the Victoria Hotel won't want to miss the **Victoria's Orient Express** train from Hanoi to Sapa. With wood-paneled luxury sleeping cars and a restaurant rightly billed as the finest dining between Hanoi and Sapa, this is an exciting new option. Trains depart four times per week with a similar return schedule, making possible convenient 2- or 3-day trips with overnight transport. Prices range from US$85 for a midweek round-trip in superior class to US$220 in a deluxe compartment on the weekend. Children under 12 ride for 50% regular price. Contact the Victoria Sapa (© **20/871-522;** fax 20/871-539; victoriasapa@hn.vnn.vn) for details and reservation.

Any number of standard and tourist trains make the overnight run from Hanoi. You can make arrangements with any travel agent for a small fee, or do it yourself at the Hanoi Railway Station (where the western edge of Hoan Kiem district meets Dong Da district at 120 Le Duan; © **04/942-3949**). Prices range from US$16 to US$30 one-way. Trains passing through Lao Cai also continue north and make connections in China. (*Note:* This requires a Chinese visa.)

To get to Sapa, you'll need to transfer by bus for the 2-hour ride from Lao Cai station. This can mean anything from a 25,000 VND (US$1.66) fare in a rattle-trap Russian cast-off, or a price of US$40 for a ride in a Japanese Pajero Mini (SUV). The road is cut into the hillside and is bumpy and windy, but the views of the terraced rice farms of the valley are beautiful as you ascend.

BY BUS Hanoi's tourist cafes all run frequent buses to Sapa for US$12 one-way. Some include Sapa in larger tours of the north. You get what you pay for, and for my money, the train is the best option.

BY CAR   Any Hanoi travel agent can arrange a car and driver from Hanoi (for a small fortune) and from Lao Cai to Sapa.

VISITOR INFORMATION

For tours and trekking in the region, the Danish outfit **Topas Travel** (20 Cau May, Sapa; ℂ **020/871-331;** fax 020/871-596; www.topas.dk/vietnam), with offices worldwide and experienced guides, is a great option. Whether it's a day trek to nearby villages, an extended tour with home stays in villages, or the 5-day push to the top of Fansipan, these guys can cover it.

BANKS AND COMMUNICATION   The post office is on Cau May Street (the main drag; ℂ **020/821-206**), but most hotels can send postcards and letters and have stamps for sale. There are a few store-front Internet cafes but service is slow and unreliable. All hotels provide exchange service for traveler's checks and even credit-card cash advances.

WHERE TO STAY
EXPENSIVE

Victoria Sapa 🏵🏵🏵   This is Sapa's crème de la crème and one of the nicest rural resorts in Indochina. Set on a small hill with panoramic views of the town, the standard here, from the comfortable rooms and fine dining to the hilltop health club and pool, is without rival. Situated around a cozy courtyard, all rooms have balconies with wood-spindled railings and, inside, deep-toned wood floors offset by saturated wall colors, cane and fine wooden finish work, and local weavings and art. The decor in guest rooms and common areas work together in a nice unity to remind guests of the local hill-tribe culture. Beds are big and comfy, and the bathrooms are large, with fine granite counters, wood fixtures, and even a small heater to warm up the tiles. If you're here with the kids, family rooms are huge, with up to six beds and some with bunks (they can rearrange them) and are a great option; suites are similarly sized with elegant canopy beds and sitting area. The heated pool and hilltop spa facilities are incredible, and with a billiard table and comfortable reading nooks and scenic viewing points here and there, this hotel is so inviting and comfortable that many prolong their stay. Don't miss having at least one meal in the Tapas Restaurant (see "Where to Dine," below).

At the top of the hill overlooking town. Sapa district, Lao Cai Province. ℂ **020/871-522.** Fax 020/871-539. www.victoriahotels-asia.com. 77 units. US$85–US$103 double; US$178 suite (promotional rates available). AE, MC, V. **Amenities:** Restaurant; bar; indoor/outdoor pool (heated); tennis court; health club; sauna; kids' playroom; tour desk (can arrange treks w/Topas); car rental; salon; massage; laundry; nonsmoking rooms. *In room:* Satellite TV w/in-house movies, minibar, fridge, coffeemaker, hair dryer, safe, IDD phone.

MODERATE

Bamboo Green   This good budget standby is a quaint labyrinth of basic but comfortable rooms connected by catwalks on Sapa's steep hillside. Rooms are tile and a basic guesthouse standard (shower-in-room style of bathroom, plain tile floor, spongy mattresses), but the views are great and the staff couldn't be friendlier. There's a nice bar in what appears a small French grotto, and, like most places in town, you can arrange any tour under the sun from the front desk.

Cau May St. ℂ **020/871-411.** nhanhoa@hn.vnn.vn. 28 units. US$10–US$25. Cash only. **Amenities:** Bar; tour desk; laundry. *In room:* Hot water.

Cat Cat Guesthouse   The view—that's what it's all about here. At this basic guesthouse, buildings are stacked like an unlikely pile of children's blocks against a steeply sloping hill, and there are some of the best views back to town, of Fansipan and the valley below. Rooms are concrete and plain, but all have big windows and hot water, and many have nice balconies. Owner Mrs. Loan will make you feel at home, and you're sure to meet other travelers who'll be saying, "Did you check out the view?" Stop by for a coffee even if you don't stay.

Cat Cat Rd. (at the base of the town on the way to the Cat Cat village). ℂ **020/871-946** or 871-387. Fax ℂ 020/871-133. catcatht@hn.vnn.vn. US$5–US$25 double. Cash only. **Amenities:** Restaurant; bar (w/best view in town). *In room:* Hot water.

Chau Long Sapa Hotel ⭐ A tour group favorite, the Chau Long has the look of an old hilltop castle in Europe and is similarly dismal, but it's in a nice location down a quaint lane from the main street of town and has good views. The super-friendly staff will bend over backward to make your stay here fun and interesting (they can arrange treks and tours). Rooms are none too special but are clean and comfortable, with small, clean bathrooms, most with balconies, and dark, aged-wood appointments throughout. The roof-top restaurant is a unique stop to have a spot of grog and take in the valley below. This is a good midstandard that's often booked with tour groups.

33 Cau May St. ℂ 020/871-245. Fax 020/871-844. www.chaulonghotel.com. 35 units. US$28–US$51 double. MC, V. **Amenities:** Restaurant; bar; bike and motorbike rental; car rental; limited room service; laundry; Internet. *In room:* Satellite TV, hair dryer, IDD phone.

Royal Hotel ⭐ It's backpacker central at this picturesque five-story tower in the heart of Cau May Street. With just the right blend of comfort and affordability, this hotel is a real budget traveler favorite, but if you aren't a real budget traveler, you might be a bit turned off by the sparse tile and concrete decor, busy hallways (this place is always packed), and indifferent service: "Next!" It's a good bargain and a popular choice with the tourist café's tours. The Friendly Café is aptly named; waitstaff here seem to be chosen for their desire (read: not ability) to speak English, and the food is good, basic, affordable traveler fare (fried rice, fried noodles, and beer). Don't miss a chance to talk with the friendly young owner. Every room has a balcony, and some even come with a fireplace. The Royal also has its own train service, kind of a scaled-down version of Victoria's trains; ask at any travel agent to arrange it.

Cau May St. ℂ 020/871-313. royalhotel_sapa@yahoo.com. 30 units. US$10–US$15. AE, MC, V. **Amenities:** Restaurant; laundry. *In room:* TV, IDD phone.

WHERE TO DINE

The Gecko ⭐⭐ FRENCH/VIETNAMESE There is a pervasive feeling of warmth here in the candle-lit comfort of the dark timbers and earth tones of this bar, salon, and comfy dining room. On chilly nights, Sapa can feel like a pretty lonely little outcropping in the shadow of Fansipan, and there is nowhere better to warm up with fine cuisine, good wine, and friendship. Alain, the French proprietor, gives a hearty greeting and can explain the day's specials. Try Magret D' Oie Grille, a fine grilled goose breast served with a rum and pepper-cream sauce, or chicken with sapa mushrooms in a cream and wine sauce. Everything is good. They also have pizza and burgers, as well as beef bourgignon, good Vietnamese specials, and some nice appetizers, like carpaccio, tomato with real mozzarella, and Swiss Rosti or cheese fondue. The prices are high for this part of the world, which means you won't find many backpackers, which is shame because there aren't many places in the world where a gourmet meal costs about the same as buying a hot chocolate at the local ski hill. Enjoy!

Just below the Victoria Sapa. Post Office Place, Ham Rong St. © 020/871-504. Fax 020/871-898. www.gecko hotel.com. Main courses US$4–US$6.15. MC, V. Open daily 8am to last-customer.

Tavanh ★★ FRENCH/VIETNAMESE   This is elegant dining in the Tonkinese Alps. The menu is rich with imports; everything from lamb to filet and salmon steaks is shipped in. They serve all the right dishes to keep you warm on a chilly eve; be sure to try the cheese fondue. The dining room is candle-lit and romantic, done up with burgundy walls and rich wood floors and local hangings all around. You might end up taking all your meals in Sapa in this affordable, elegant spot; if so, don't feel bad about it because it's arguably the best in town. You'll find some nice Vietnamese specials on the evolving menu, and the pastas are homemade and delicious. Bon appetit!

At the Victoria Sapa Hotel. © 020/871-522. Main courses US$5–US$15. AE, MC, V. Daily 7am–10pm.

ATTRACTIONS

The town itself is the attraction here, and **Cau May Street,** the main drag, and the **central market area** (all very close together) are, on any given day, teeming with hill-tribe folks in their spangled finest, putting on and practicing the hard sell with some great weaving, fine silver work, and interesting trinkets like mouth harps and flutes. Especially on the weekend, it can be quite a scene. The small alleys and streets of the town are imminently wanderable, and a short walk in any direction offers great views.

Bac Ha Market ★   Some 100km (62 miles) from Sapa, this is probably the most famous market in the region and more along the lines of what Sapa was once like. Here, various hill tribes converge every Sunday morning to conduct commerce. As a visitor, you're certainly part of the trade here because folks are keen to sell you their wares, but this market isn't as much about the tourist buck (yet) as it is about small-time commerce and fellowship. Bring a camera. Sunday mornings from dawn to late morning is prime-time, but the market continues until about noon. Most visitors make the 3-hour drive from Sapa in the early morning.

By jeep from Sapa for US$60 (contact hotels for a guide). Also can be arranged from nearby Lao Cai (contact Hanoi travel agents).

Cat-Cat Village ★   At the base of the hill below the town of Sapa, this Hmong village is accessible by road most of the way, and cement path for the rest. The small waterfall is a good spot to kick back and rest. The whole trip can be made in just a few hours and offers a nice glimpse of rural life.

Entrance fee (paid at the top of the hill) 20,000 VND (US33¢) You can walk all the way down or hire a motorbike/car taxi to pick up and drop off.

Lao Cai to Tavanh ★★   This is the premier day trip from Sapa and is convenient to the town center. It's a good chance to traipse around the rice terraces and experience a bit of rural village life. Hire a car or motorbike for the 9km (5½-mile) road down the valley from Sapa to the Hmong village of Lao Cai (some folks even walk it); it's a nice ride in itself, with great views of the lush terraces. From there, you'll just follow the valley for a few miles to the next town of Tavanh. Along the way, you'll walk through terraced rice fields and among some picturesque villages, and experience a bit of rural life (I had a chance to help with some rice threshing). The short trek walks you through a few different hill-tribe villages (Hmong, Zay, and Dao people), and it's good to have a guide to explain any customs or practices and perhaps translate. You're sure to see other tourists on the trail (and this puts many people off), but this is a good example of the many great treks in the area; ask at your hotel front desk, or contact Topas Travel (under "Visitor Information," above) for longer, less touristic treks. You'll still be greeted with hearty "Bonjour, madam! Bonjour, monsieur!" wherever you go.

Entrance fee is 5,000 VND (US33¢). Drop-off at Lao Cai and later pick-up at Tavan is about US$4 w/a motorbike taxi and US$25 for a jeep (contact hotels for a guide).

The Mission Church 𝄢 An aging stone edifice, the church of the early French missionaries still stands on the high end of Cau May and is a popular meeting point for locals. There are masses held on Saturday night and throughout the day on Sunday.

6 An Introduction to the Central Coast

Many of Vietnam's most significant historical sites and some of its best beaches are clustered along its central coast. Here you'll find Hue, the former Vietnamese capital, with its Imperial City and emperors' tombs. Here also is Hoi An, a historic tiny trading town that had its heyday in the 17th century, with more than 800 perfectly preserved classic Chinese and Vietnamese houses and temples. Formerly the seat of the Cham kingdom from the 2nd through 14th centuries, the central coast also has the greatest concentration of Cham relics and art, the highlight of which is the Cham Museum at Danang. And you can sample the Vietnamese beach scene in its youthful stages at China Beach and Cua Dai. The proximity and convenient transportation between towns means you'll be able to cover ground efficiently. Danang and Hoi An are so close (about ½ hr. by car) that you can easily stay in one and make day trips to the other.

GETTING THERE
BY PLANE   You can fly into both Hue and Danang from Saigon or Hanoi.

BY TRAIN   Both Hue and Danang are stops on the north-south rail line.

BY CAR/BUS/MINIVAN   Tourist cafe buses connect all major towns in this region. Driving with a rented vehicle and driver is possible but will probably cost several hundred dollars and leave your teeth chattering from the bumpy roads.

GETTING AROUND
BY CAR/BUS/MINIVAN   The three main coastal towns in the central part of the country are linked by roads that are prone to flooding. Potholes are an understatement, and the dust that gets kicked up dries out your throat pretty quickly. You can easily rent a car or get a seat on a bus or minivan in any of the towns or in a hotel or booking agency—if you take a bus, be prepared for the trip to take a bit longer than they advertise, due to the poor condition of the roads. From Hue to Danang is about 3½ hours; from Danang to Hoi An is about 90 minutes. See individual city listings for suggested prices.

7 Hue

Hue (pronounced "hway") was once Vietnam's imperial city, the capital of the country from 1802 to 1945 under the Nguyen Dynasty. Culturally and historically, it might be the most important city in the entire country. While much of it (tragically including most of Vietnam's walled citadel and imperial city) was decimated during the French and American wars, there is still much to see. One of the most interesting sights is simply daily life on the **Perfume River,** a

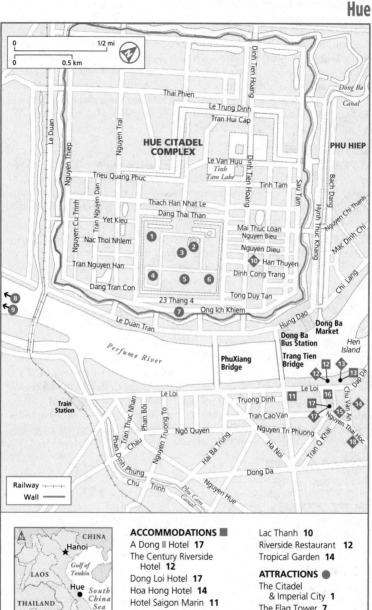

0   1/2 mi
0   0.5 km

Dinh Tien Hoang

Thai Phien

Le Trung Dinh

Tran Hui Cap

Le Duan

Nguyen Thiep

Nguyen Trai

HUE CITADEL COMPLEX

PHU HIEP

Dong Ba Canal

Le Van Huu

Tinh Tam Lake

Tinh Tam

Sau Tam

Bach Dang

Huynh Thuc Khang

Nguyen Chi Thanh

Mac Dinh Chi

Trieu Quang Phuc

Nguyen Cu Trinh

Tran Nguyen Dan

Thach Han Nhat Le

Dang Thai Than

Yet Kieu

Nac Thoi Nhlem

Mai Thuc Loan

Nguyen Bieu

Nguyen Dieu

10 Han Thuyen

Dinh Tien Hoang

Chi Lang

Tran Nguyen Han

1

3 **2**

4 **5** **6**

Dang Tran Con

Dinh Cong Trang

23 Thang 4

Tong Duy Tan

8
9

7

Ong Ich Khiem

Le Duan Tran

Hung Dao

Dong Ba Market

Perfume River

Dong Ba Bus Station

Hen Island

PhuXiang Bridge

Trang Tien Bridge

12 **13**

12 **13** Dap Da

Train Station

Le Loi

Truong Dinh

11

Le Loi

16

17

17 Nguyen Thai Hoc

Chu Van An

14

15

Tran Thuc Nhan

Phan Boi

Chau

Nguyen Truong To

Ngo Quyen

Tran Cao Van

Nguyen Tri Phuong

Ha Noi

Tran Q. Khai

18

Hai Ba Trung

Phan Dinh Phung

Chu

Trinh

Dong Da

Nguyen Hue

Phu Cam Canal

Railway ┼┼┼
Wall ━━━

CHINA

Hanoi ★

Gulf of Tonkin

LAOS

Hue ● *South China Sea*

THAILAND

CAMBODIA

VIETNAM

Gulf of Thailand

0   100 mi
0   100 km

ACCOMMODATIONS ■
A Dong II Hotel **17**
The Century Riverside
  Hotel **12**
Dong Loi Hotel **17**
Hoa Hong Hotel **14**
Hotel Saigon Marin **11**
Huong Giang Hotel **13**

DINING ◆
An Phu Restaurant **18**
Club Garden **15**
Hoa Mai Restaurant **13**
La Carambole **15**

Lac Thanh **10**
Riverside Restaurant **12**
Tropical Garden **14**

ATTRACTIONS ●
The Citadel
  & Imperial City **1**
The Flag Tower **7**
Forbidden Purple City **2**
The Imperial Tombs **9**
the Mieu Temple **4**
Trieu Mieu Temple **6**
Thai Hoa Palace **5**
Thien Mu Pagoda **8**

mélange of dragon and houseboats and longtail vessels dredging for sand. You'll visit many of the attractions, including the tombs of **Nguyen Dynasty emperors,** by boat. The enjoyable town has a seaside-resort sort of air, with a laid-back attitude; low-slung, colorful colonial-style buildings; and strings of lights at outdoor cafes at night. There are many local cuisine specialties to sample as well.

You might want to plan for a full-day **American war memorial excursion** to the nearby demilitarized zone (DMZ), the beginning of the Ho Chi Minh trail, and underground tunnels at **Vinh Moc.**

GETTING THERE

BY PLANE   Hue connects from both Hanoi and Saigon with Vietnam Airlines. A taxi from the airport costs 100,000 VND (USD\$6.30). There's also an airport bus that picks you up at your hotel and covers the half-hour trip to the airport for 25,000 VND (US\$1.60). You can book it through your hotel's front desk or any tour operator in town.

BY TRAIN   Trains depart daily from both Hanoi and Saigon to Hue. A trip from Hanoi to Hue takes 14 hours on an express train; with two nightly departures, 7 and 11pm, these trains have both soft-berth compartments with air-conditioning for about US\$35. From Saigon, in a soft-berth, it's about US\$50, which is a good way to go.

BY CAR   If you're coming from the south, Vietnamtourism Danang can arrange a car for the 3½-hour ride from Danang to Hue for US\$40. Contact travel agents in any section to rent a car with driver.

BY BUS   Many travelers choose to take an overnight private bus or minivan from Hanoi to Hue. Tickets are USD\$9 through one of Hanoi's tourist cafes (see "Visitor Information & Tours," earlier in this chapter), and the trip takes an excruciating 17 hours, with several rest stops. Hue is a major stop on any open-tour ticket, and, from the south, open-tour cafe buses connect with Danang and Hoi An for just US\$2.50, or Nha Trang for US\$6 (these are long, bumpy trails but are cheap and convenient).

GETTING AROUND

Taxis are much cheaper here than in Hanoi: 5,000 VND (US33¢) starting out and 5,000 VND for each kilometer after. Flag 'em down or call **Gili** at ⓒ **054/ 828-282** or **ThanhDo** at ⓒ **054/835-835.** Because Hue is relatively small, renting a cyclo by the hour for 15,000 VND to 20,000 VND (US\$1–US\$1.33) works well. Even the tiniest hotel provides motorbike rentals at US\$3 to US\$5 per day and bicycles for US\$1.

VISITOR INFORMATION

There are a number of tour companies in Hue through which you can book boat trips and visits to the DMZ. Every hotel will also be able to assist you, although the tour companies will be cheaper, especially for car services.

The **Huong Giang Company,** at 17 Le Loi St. (ⓒ **054/832-220** or 054/ 832-221; fax 054/821-426; hgtravel@dng.vnn.vn), organizes the usual tours to the tombs and the DMZ, although it is more flexible than most in terms of hours and transport. This is Hue's most upscale and efficient group, and also the most expensive. An all-day tour by car and boat, with guide, to the Citadel and tombs, with lunch, is US\$25. If you want a private boat to take you up the Perfume River, they can organize one for you for US\$20. And to the DMZ, they'll take you for US\$13.

On the other hand, **Sinh Café V,** 7 Nguyen Tri Phuong (℃ **054/848-262**) does a DMZ seat-in-coach tour for US$10 per person and can book a group boat up the river for 25,000 VND (US$1.70) per person.

Both can handle any onward travel needs.

✐ FAST FACTS: Hue

Banks/Currency Exchange Most hotels change currency in Hue. Vietcombank is at 46 Hung Vuong St. (℃ **054/846-058**). Vietinde, the foreign exchange bank, has an office at 41 Hung Vuong St. (on the roundabout at the terminus of the main tourist drag); it can do cash advances and is a Western Union representative.

Internet/E-mail Sinh Café, at 07 Nguyen Tri Phuong, has good service for 10,000 VND (US70¢) per hour, and there are many good spots on Hung Vuong (the main tourist street S of the river). If you're by the Century Hotel, walk down Pham Ngu Lao (just across from the Century), and you'll find good service for 4,000 VND to 5,000 VND per hour (about US33¢).

Post Office/Mail There are mini–post offices in the Century and Huong Giang hotels. The main post office is at 8 Hoang Hoa Tham St., and is open from 7am to 9pm. You can also place international calls there.

Telephone The city code for Hue is 54. You can place IDD calls at the post office (above) and from most hotels.

WHERE TO STAY

For the volume of tourists coming through this town, there isn't much in the way of quality accommodation, and even the nicest options are bland, with lots of "It's nice, but . . . ." Budget accommodation abounds, but there are some real duds. Always ask to see the rooms first if it's not a hotel I recommend. Don't expect the service you might get in Saigon, except that all provide tour services and almost all include breakfast in their prices. As always in Vietnam, the prices are eminently flexible, so press for a discount.

EXPENSIVE

The Century Riverside Hotel ✿ This is one of Hue's three best (see below). For comfort, friendliness, and location, it's quite nice. Rooms are bland chain-hotel style, smallish, clean, and comfortable, with new tile and marble bathrooms (be sure to ask for a room with recent renovations). The cheaper US$65 rooms have older carved-wood furniture. The river-view rooms are more than worth the extra US$10, and if you're lucky enough, you'll find yourself composing haikus or singing Old Man River if you are on one of the upper floors as you watch longtail boats putter by or men in small dugouts eek out a living from the river. The pool is in a prime lounge spot by the river, and there are some nice restaurant choices here, including The Riverside Restaurant, one of Hue's best (with many rivals), serving Vietnamese and Western dishes (see "Where to Dine," below). The hotel also has a very nice English-speaking staff.

49 Le Loi St., Hue. ℃ **800/536-7361,** 054/823-390, or 823-391. Fax 054/823-394. 147 units. US$65–US$100 double; US$170 suite. AE, MC, V. **Amenities:** 3 restaurants; 2 bars; outdoor pool overlooking river; 2 tennis courts; small gym; bicycles/motorbikes for rent; concierge; tour desk arranging popular boat trip to tombs; car

rental; small business center; shopping in lobby; salon; 24-hr. room service; massage; laundry; postal service. *In room:* A/C, satellite TV, minibar, fridge, hair dryer, IDD phone.

Hotel Saigon Morin ★★
The Morin is a nice government-run, recently refurbished colonial. They're trying to be something they're not here, a ritzy riverside palace, but the effort is genuine and the overall effect, something like a hollowed-out wedding cake lit with neon, is kind of fun. The staff is friendly and can make all the arrangements you might need. The hotel forms a large court-yard around a nice central garden and pool area with dining; rooms face this comfortable spot or overlook the river and are large and attractive, with repro-duction French colonial furniture, nice carpet, and floral drapes. Suites are just larger versions of deluxe rooms with the same furniture; you'll get only more real estate, and some have board rooms. It's rough around the edges, but everything's a bit frilly, with filigree and statuary anywhere and everywhere: The whole place is certainly clean, comfortable, and deluxe, by Hue standards. Nice-size new marble bathrooms are just that and have hair dryers. With more than 100 years of history, the Morin was originally the foreign visitor's address of prestige. It's interesting to note that the street in front of the Morin was where a young Ho Chi Minh carried his first placard in protest of foreign occupation. If he could only see the place now.

30 Le Loi St., Hue. © **054/823-526.** Fax 054/825-155. www.morinhotel.com.vn. 127 units. US$80–US$100 double; US$100–US$120 deluxe double; US$200–US$400 suite. AE, MC, V **Amenities:** Outdoor buffet area, (breakfast included); lobby restaurant; 2 bars/cafe (1 on the roof w/good views); small outdoor pool (in court-yard); small gym; sauna; bicycle/motorbike rental; concierge; helpful in-house tour desk; car rental; shopping in lobby; salon; 24-hr. room service; massage; laundry; Internet; postal service; Jacuzzi in executive suites. *In room:* A/C, satellite TV, minibar, fridge, coffeemaker, hair dryer, safe, IDD phone.

Huong Giang Hotel ★★
This hotel is a veritable Asian wonderland, so enamored is it of heavy carved wood and bamboo furnishings. Some might call it tacky, but it's great fun and well worth being your choice in Hue because "imperial" is what the city's all about. The rooms are clean and comfortable, in basic bamboo, but the bathrooms are a disappointing dormitory style, with plas-tic shower curtains and no counter space. Try to get a good deal on one of the Royal Suites, with carved-wood walls, grandiose furniture with inlaid mother-of-pearl, and a massive wood room divider—sort of a minipagoda right in your room. The words *emperor* and *bordello* both leap to mind. The Royal Restaurant, worth a photo just for its gaudy gold-and-red-everything design alone, is for pre-arranged group dinners, where the costumed staff serves a fancy traditional din-ner at a hefty price (popular in town). The River Front Terrace Bar is the best place in Hue to have a drink and watch life on the river. Be sure to splurge for a river-view room and enjoy a fine meal at the Hoa Mai restaurant.

51 Le Loi St., Hue. © **054/822-122** or 054/823-958. Fax 054/823-102. 150 units. US$55–US$75 garden-view double; US$65–US$85 river view; US$160–US$230 suite. AE, MC, V. **Amenities:** 3 restaurants; 2 bars; pool; tennis court; basic health club; sauna; concierge; tour desk; car rental; small business center; cool, kitsch shopping area; salon; massage; laundry. *In room:* A/C, cable TV, minibar, fridge, hair dryer, IDD phone.

MODERATE
Hoa Hong Hotel ★
This is a nice hotel bargain in Hue. Built in 1996, it has very nondescript rooms—think navy and beige, with ugly polyester spreads (a shame)—but is comfortable, with good, firm beds. The bathrooms are nice-size and tidy, with hair dryers; all have bathtubs, and some are enormous. Ask for a city view rather than a noisy street-view room. The suites are worth it and have authentic Asian furniture. There are two restaurants, one of which specializes in the popular "royal dinner" theme evenings, when both staff and guests dress like

emperors and empresses. The lobby has a fun little bar on one end with very expensive drinks. Tour and car rental services are available, as is round-the-clock room service. Hoa Hong II is hugely popular with tour groups (many from France), so book early. **Hoa Hong II,** around the corner, is same-same but different.

46 Le Loi St., Hue. ✆ **054/824-377** or 054/826-943. Fax 054/826-949. hoahonghotel@dng.vnn.vn. 50 units. US$30–US$60 double; US$80 suite. AE, MC, V. **Amenities:** Large restaurant (breakfast included); bar; tour desk; car rental; souvenir shop; Internet in reception. *In room:* A/C, satellite TV, minibar, fridge, IDD phone.

INEXPENSIVE

Dong Loi Hotel ⭐   There are plenty of inexpensive hotels in Hue, but the Dong Loi is a particularly good bargain. Family-run, it has spotless rooms with tile floors and firm beds. The attractive bathrooms are small but clean, and the most expensive rooms have bathtubs. Rooms here are snowflakes, none the same, so ask to see one before checking in. Even the less expensive rooms are comfy, though, and all are economical. The folks here are friendly and have lots of good services above and beyond standard guesthouses: tour planning, Internet service, and genuine smiles that you won't get elsewhere. Next door, the La Carambole restaurant, reviewed below, provides much better cuisine than your average budget hotel coffee shop.

11A Pham Ngu Lao St. ✆ **054/822-296** or ✆/fax 054/826-234. interser@dng.vnn.vn. US$15–US$35. No credit cards. **Amenities:** Restaurant next door; bicycle/motorbike rental; tour desk; car rental; laundry. *In room:* A/C, cable TV, IDD phone.

WHERE TO DINE

There are some good local dishes to sample in Hue, but relatively few spots with English menus and high-quality food. Still, the ones I found were good enough to visit more than once. Do try *bun bo Hue,* a noodle soup with pork, beef, and shredded green onions; and *banh khoi,* a thin, crispy pancake filled with ground meat and crispy vegetables.

MODERATE

An Phu VIETNAMESE   Another big group restaurant, this one serves good, inexpensive Vietnamese without much ado. The service is friendly, and everything is good. I had a fine meal of corn and crab-meat soup, a European salad, and stir-fried beef with vegetables for just US$6—can't beat that. You also get a chance to observe tour groups from many countries in action; it's funny when they discover en mass that it's fun to "pop" the moist towelette packs that the waiters hand out and the restaurant fills with loud popping sounds, laughs, and guttural guffaws of "Très bien!" and "Ganz Gut!" and "Omoshiroi desu ne!"

48 Chu Van An St. ✆ **054/826-090** or 054/828-856. Main courses US$2–US$5; set menu US$5–US$7. Cash only. Daily 7am–10pm.

Club Garden ⭐ VIETNAMESE   One of the best meals in Vietnam can be had at this unpretentious little restaurant. Newly decorated, there is nice seating both outdoors and in. The menu's emphasis is on fish and crab, all prepared in the local style (grilled, in lemon leaves) and absolutely delicious. And note the prices! The *banh khoi,* a crispy pancake stuffed with ground meat and shrimp, is the best in town. Other musts include the fried shrimp with garlic, crispy fried noodles with vegetables, and chicken cooked in lemon leaf. Dessert is fried bananas. Breakfast is served here as well.

08 Vo Thi Sau St. ✆ **054/826-327.** Fax 054/849-836. Main courses US$3–US$7; set menus US$8–US$12. No credit cards. Daily 7am–11pm.

Hoa Mai Restaurant ☆☆ VIETNAMESE   This most attractive restaurant is large, open, and airy, with bamboo furnishing and detail and a great view of the Perfume River. It serves excellent local cuisine. Try *banh rom Hue,* little triangular fried rolls stuffed with ground meat, shrimp, and vegetables. Daily special set menus are tops; mine featured a unique fried cuttlefish with grapefruit, crab soup, and shrimp with fig and rice cake. There is even wine by the glass. The muzak gets a bit much, and be sure to choose a table near the riverside window and away from any banquet-size setups that say RESERVED. The breakfast buffet is incredible, including every kind of egg and pancake, as well as Vietnamese sweets and a table full of exotic fruit.

51 Le Loi St., third floor, Huong Giang Hotel. ✆ **054/822-122.** Main courses US$2–US$6; set menus US$7–US$15. AE, MC, V. Daily 6am–10pm.

Riverside Restaurant ☆ VIETNAMESE/CONTINENTAL   This very nice upscale restaurant has scenic views over the Perfume River and fine food. The extensive menu includes dozens of varieties of noodles and fried rice, from spaghetti with cheese to Vietnamese rice noodles with seafood. Main dishes include sautéed shrimp with mushroom sauce over rice, and grilled duck wrapped in lemon leaf.

40 Le Loi, at the Century Riverside Hotel. ✆ **054/823-390.** Main courses US$3–US$6. AE, MC, V. Daily 7am–10pm.

Tropical Garden ☆☆ VIETNAMESE   Though it's a popular tour bus stop, this cousin of the Club Garden (above) has a good laid-back feel; serves fine, affordable Vietnamese grub from a good English menu; and features a nice live music show nightly. Even when it's packed here, there are enough intimate corners that you'll feel comfortable; the atmosphere also is laid back, and the service is quite friendly and casual. The place seems to specialize in "embarrassing entrees" here, the kind of flaming dishes and multitiered platters that would impress that eccentric uncle of yours; I got spring rolls served on toothpick skewers around the rind of a hollowed pineapple with a candle in the middle a la a Halloween Jack-o'-lantern. Hmmm. It's fun here, so just go with it, and the food is excellent. Set menus are quite reasonable and walk you through some house specialties, like the banana flower soup, the grilled chicken with lemon leaf, and the steamed crab with beer. As an appetizer, don't miss the grilled minced shrimp with sugar cane wrapped in rice paper and served with peanut sauce; it's unique and delicious.

05 Chu Van An St. ✆ **054/847-143.** Fax 054/828-074. adongcoltd@dng.vnn.vn. Main courses US$2–US$4; set menus US$7–US$25. 8:30am–11pm. MC, V.

INEXPENSIVE

La Carambole ☆☆ VIETNAMESE/CONTINENTAL   Good music is the first thing you might notice here; I heard an unlikely mix from CCR to Beck in my relaxing evening here. The cheerful decor features nice indirect lighting, red tablecloths, and playful mobiles hanging from ceiling, and is as welcoming as the kind waitstaff. The gregarious French proprietor and his Vietnamese wife will certainly make you feel at home here, and the good "comfort items" on the menu, like spaghetti, burgers, pizzas, and various French-style meat-and-potatoes specials, will stick to your ribs. The set menus are a good deal (salad and pizza at US$5, for example), and portions are ample. There's a game table, and you're sure to meet lots of other travelers here.

19 Pham Ngu Lao St. ✆ **054/810-491.** Fax 054/826-234. Main courses US$1.38–US$5.52; set menu US$4–US$9. Cash only. Daily 7am–12pm.

Lac Thanh Restaurant ⭐ VIETNAMESE   You'll find very good eats and a lively good time here. Everybody knows it, so there's a good chance you'll run into some fellow wayfarers at this popular crossroad (if not, there's a good chance you'll find their signature or business card on the wall, as is the custom here). It's basically a grubby street-side place, but one that serves very nice grilled pork wrapped in rice paper, sautéed bean sprouts, grilled crab, and spareribs, among dozens of choices. There's balcony seating, too. For dessert, try the local specialty, *ché nong*, a warm congee with coconut, bananas, and nuts; the glutinous texture takes some getting used to but is worth trying at least once. As you approach the restaurant, you'll be mobbed by hucksters trying to take you to the knock-off next door, which is reportedly not bad, either. You'll find lots of folks selling trinkets here, so don't be afraid to say a firm "no" if you want to have a quiet meal.

6A Dien Tien Hoang St. ✆ 054/824674. Main courses US50¢–US$3.25. No credit cards. Daily 7am–12pm.

CAFES, BARS & NIGHTLIFE

Hue is a tourist town really, so the nightlife isn't much. Across from the major riverside hotels is the **DMZ Café,** which stays up late a la a beer-swilling frat party, and along Hung Vuong you'll find a few backpacker bars open till midnight, but this is a pretty sleepy town. There is a branch of the club **Apocalypse Now** in town, but it opens and closes with the changing local ordinance.

SHOPPING

All along Le Loi Street, you'll find souvenir stalls that vary from the cute to the kitschy. You can find good deals on commemorative spoons and Velvet Ho Chi Minh's here, but nothing too traditional or authentic. However, you will find a few good silversmiths.

ATTRACTIONS

Except for the remains of its fabulous Imperial City, Hue in itself has sadly seen the worst of the French and American/Vietnam wars. Most of the star attractions other than the Citadel, therefore, involve half-day or day trips outside the city.

The Citadel & Imperial City ⭐⭐⭐   The **Citadel** is often used as a catchall term for Hue's Imperial City, built by Emperor Gia Long beginning in 1804 for the exclusive use of the emperor and his household, much like Beijing's Forbidden City. The city actually encompasses three walled enclosures: the Exterior Exclosure or Citadel; the Yellow Enclosure, or Imperial City, within that; and, in the very center, the Forbidden Purple City, where the emperor actually lived.

The Citadel is a square 2km (1½-mile) wall, 7m (23 ft.) high and 20m (66 ft.) thick, with 10 gates. Ironically, it was constructed by a French military architect, though it failed to prevent the French from destroying the complex many years later. The main entrance to the Imperial City is the Ngo Mon, the southwest gate or "Noon" Gate, and is where you can get a ticket and enter.

Admission 55,000 VND (US$3.66). Daily 7am–5:30pm.

SITES WITHIN THE IMPERIAL CITY

The Flag Tower ⭐⭐   The focal point of the Imperial City, a large rampart to the south of the Noon Gate, this tower was built in 1807 during Gia Long's reign. The yellow flag of royalty was the first to fly here and was exchanged and replaced by many others in Vietnam's turbulent history. It's a national symbol.

The Noon Gate (Cua Ngo Mon) ⭐⭐   One of 10 entrances to the city, this southern entrance is the most dynamic. It was the royal entrance, in fact, and was built by Emperor Gia Long in 1823. It was used for important proclamations, such as announcements of the names of successful doctoral candidates (a list still hangs on the wall on the upper floor) and, most memorably, the announcement of the abdication of the last emperor, Bao Dai, on August 13, 1945, to Ho Chi Minh. The structure, like most here, was damaged by war but is now nicely restored, with classic Chinese roofs covering the ritual space, complete with large drums and an altar. Be sure to climb to the top and have a look at the view.

Thai Hoa Palace   Otherwise known as the Palace of Supreme Harmony, it was built in 1833 and is the first structure you'll approach at the entrance. It was used as the throne room, a ceremonial hall where the emperor celebrated festivals and received courtiers; the original throne still stands. The Mandarins sat outside. In front are two mythical *ky lin* animals, which walk without their claws ever touching ground and which have piercing eyesight for watching the emperor, tracking all good and evil he does. Note the statues of the heron and turtle inside the palace's ornate lacquered interior: The heron represents nobility and the turtle represents the working person. Folklore has it that the two took turns saving each other's lives during a fire, symbolizing that the power of the emperor rests with his people, and vice versa.

The Forbidden Purple City ⍟   Once the actual home of the emperor and his concubines, this second sanctum within the Citadel is a large open area dotted with what's left of the king's court. Almost completely razed in a fire in 1947, a few buildings are left among the rubble. The new **Royal Theater** behind the square, a look-alike of the razed original, is under construction. The partially restored **Thai Binh Reading Pavilion,** to the left of it as you head north, is notable mostly for its beautifully landscaped surroundings, including a small lake with a Zen-like stone sculpture, and the ceramic and glass mosaic detailing on the roof and pillars, favored by flamboyant emperor Khai Dinh.

The Mieu Temple ⍟⍟   Constructed in 1921–22 by Emperor Minh Mang, this temple has funeral altars paying tribute to 10 of the last Nguyen Dynasty emperors, omitting two who reigned for only days, with photos of each emperor and his empress(es) and various small offerings and knickknacks. The two empty glass containers to the side of each photo should contain bars of gold, probably an impractical idea today.

Across from The Mieu you'll see Hien Lam, or the Glorious Pavilion, to the far right, with the **Nine Dynastic Urns** in front. Cast from 1835 to 1837, each urn represents a Nguyen emperor and is richly embellished with all the flora, fauna, and material goods that Vietnam has to offer, mythical or otherwise.

Thien Mu Pagoda ⍟⍟   Often called the symbol of Hue, Thien Mu is one of the oldest and loveliest religious structures in Vietnam. It was constructed beginning in 1601. The Phuoc Dien Tower in front was added in 1864 by Emperor Thieu Tri. Each of its seven tiers is dedicated to either one of the human forms taken by Buddha or the seven steps to enlightenment, depending upon whom you ask. There are also two buildings housing a bell reportedly weighing 2 tons, and a stele inscribed with a biography of Lord Nguyen Hoang, founder of the temple.

Once past the front gate, observe the 12 huge wooden sculptures of fearsome temple "guardians"—note the real facial hair. A complex of monastic buildings lies in the center, offering glimpses of the monks' daily routines: cooking, stacking wood, and whacking weeds. Stroll all the way to the rear of the complex to look at the large graveyard at the base of the Truong Son mountains, and wander through the well-kept garden of pine trees. Try not to go between the hours of 11:30am and 2pm, when the monks are at lunch, because the rear half of the complex will be closed.

On the bank of the Perfume River. Daily 8am–5pm.

The Imperial Tombs   As befits its history as an Imperial City, Hue's environs are studded with tombs of past emperors. They are spread out over a distance, so the best way to see them is to hire a car for a half day or take one of the many organized boat tours up the Perfume River. Altogether, there were 13 kings of the Nguyen Dynasty, although only 7 reigned until their death. As befits an emperor, each had tombs of stature, some as large as a small town. Most tomb complexes usually consist of a courtyard, a stele (a large stone tablet with a biography of the emperor), a temple for worship, and a pond.

Tomb of Tu Duc ⚜⚜   With the longest reign of any Nguyen Dynasty emperor, from 1848 to 1883, Tun Duc was a philosopher and scholar of history and literature. His reign was unfortunate: His kingdom unsuccessfully struggled against French colonialism, he fought a coup d'état by members of his own family, and although he had 104 wives, he left no heir. The "tomb" was constructed from 1864 to 1867 and also served as recreation grounds for the king, having been completed 16 years before his death. He actually engraved his own stele, in fact. The largest in Vietnam, at 20 tons, it has its own pavilion in the tomb. The highlight of the grounds is the lotus-filled lake ringed by frangipani trees, with a large pavilion in the center. The main cluster of buildings includes Hoa Khiem (Harmony Modesty) Pavilion, where the king worked, which still contains items of furniture and ornaments. Minh Khiem Duong, constructed in 1866, is said to be the country's oldest surviving theater. It's great fun to poke around in the wings. There are also pieces of original furniture lying here and there, as well as a cabinet with household objects: the queen's slippers, ornate chests, and bronze and silver books. The raised box on the wall is for the actors who played emperors; the real emperor was at the platform to the left.

Admission 55,000 VND (US$3.66). Summer daily 6:30am–5:30pm; winter daily 7am–5pm.

Khai Dinh's Tomb ⚜⚜   Completed in 1931, the tomb is one of the world's wonders. The emperor himself wasn't particularly revered, being overly extravagant and flamboyant (reportedly he wore a belt studded with lights that he flicked on at opportune public moments). His tomb, a gaudy mix of Gothic, baroque, Hindu, and Chinese Qing Dynasty architecture at the top of 127 steep steps, is a reflection of the man. Inside, the two main rooms are completely covered with fabulous, intricate glass and ceramic mosaics in designs reminiscent of Tiffany and Art Deco. The workmanship is astounding. The outer room's ceiling was done by a fellow who used both his feet and his hands to paint, in what some say was a sly mark of disrespect for the emperor. While in most tombs the location of the emperor's actual remains are a secret, Khai Minh boldly placed his under his de facto tomb itself.

Admission 55,000 VND (US$3.66). Summer daily 6:30am–5:30pm; winter daily 7am–5pm.

Tomb of Minh Mang ⚜   One of the most popular Nguyen emperors and the father of last emperor Bao Dai built a restrained, serene, classical temple, much like Hue's Imperial City, located at the confluence of two Perfume River tributaries. Stone sculptures surround a long walkway, lined with flowers, leading up to the main buildings.

Admission 55,000 VND (US$3.66). Summer daily 6:30am–5:30pm; winter daily 7am–5pm.

> **Tips   Taking a Boat to the Tombs**
>
> If you take the boat trip to see the tombs, note that you'll pay US$2 to US$4 for the boat ride (depending on which agent you use), *plus* 55,000 VND (US$3.66) for *each* tomb. Be prepared for when the boat pulls to shore at the first two tombs; you'll have to hire one of the motorcycle taxis at the bank to shuttle you to and from the site. You will not have enough time to walk there and back, so you're basically at their mercy.
>
> Haggle as best you can—I got one guy down to 10,000 VND (US69¢), but they'll try to quote you something like 40,000 VND (US$2.76). Anywhere in between is acceptable and don't be too stubborn. Admission is 55,000 VND (US$3.66). Summer hours are daily 6:30am–5:30pm; winter hours are daily 7am–5pm.

8 Danang & China Beach

Danang, the fourth-largest city in Vietnam, is one of the most important seaports in the central region. It played a prominent historical role in the American war, being the landing site for the first American troops officially sent to Vietnam. Even with the bustle of ships coming and going, poor Danang has to be one of the world's ugliest cities, and there isn't a major attraction except for the **Cham Museum** (a must-see). Unfortunately, it has been given the shaft by all the tour buses that used to make a stop here en route between Hoi An and Hue. Nowadays, if you can get them to stop for the museum, they'll give you only about 20 minutes to look. **Furama Resort,** a short ride from the city center, is one of the finest high-end resorts in Indochina.

There are a few excellent-value hotels in Danang, so an option is to actually stay in the city and take day trips to nearby Hoi An.

China Beach, or My Khe, as it's known locally, is worth a stop. This former U.S. recreation base has a light-sand coast with excellent views of the nearby Marble Mountains, and is just beginning to draw international tourists.

GETTING THERE
BY PLANE   You can fly to Danang from both Hanoi and HCMC. A taxi from the airport costs about US$3.

BY BUS   If you're traveling on the open-tour ticket, Danang is not a specified stop, but they'll drop you off at the Cham Museum. You'll have to call the office in either Hue or Hoi An for pick-up when you're ready to leave. Travelers to Laos should contact **Vietnamtourism** for buses to **Savanakhet** for US$25.

BY CAR   Danang is about 3½ hours by car from Hue, and the route covers the very scenic **Hai Van Pass.** You'll pay US$40 for the trip. From Hoi An, it's about an hour and costs US$25. This ride makes a good day trip along with the Marble Mountains (see "Attractions," below). Contact **Vietnamtourism** for good rentals.

VISITOR INFORMATION & TOURS
Vietnamtourism Danang is located at 83 Nguyen Thi Minh Khai (© **0511/ 823-660** or 822-142; fax 0511/821-560). They can arrange trips to the Marble Mountains and My Son, as can nearly every hotel; Vietnamtourism is just a lot more helpful and professional.

Exotissimo Danang, 73 Ham Nghi, Thanh Khe District (© **0511/690-364;** fax 0511/891-553; www.exotissimo.com) is very professional, as in any location, and can arrange any necessity.

An Phu Tourism, 147 Le Loi St, Danang (© 0511/818-366; anphucndn@ yahoo.com), is the local tourist cafe contact and can arrange any low-budget arrangements (there also are offices in Hoi An).

FAST FACTS: DANANG
Banks/Currency Exchange   Vietcombank is at 104 Le Loi St. (© **0511/821-955**). In a pinch, you can get traveler's checks cashed at An Phu Tourist Travel, 147 Le Loi St. (© **0511/818-366**). Hours of operation are better than the bank's, but the exchange rate is awful. Still, in a pinch . . .

Telephone   The city code for Danang is 511.

WHERE TO STAY
EXPENSIVE
Furama Resort Danang ★★★   The Furama is a full-service resort and one of the finest in the region. Just a short ride southwest of Danang and situated in elegant relation to a beautiful sandy beach, this popular up-scale gem greets you in style with a grand lobby that is more or less the gilded frame to the beautiful scenery you'll be enjoying here: sand, sun, and sky (and some good garden nooks). Whether you're a yacht racer, a beach bum, or a comfort junky, you'll find what you want here. There are two gorgeous swimming pools: one a minimalist still-life with tiers leading to the open beach, and the other a faux lagoon, complete with small waterfall and bridge, a romantic hideaway. Many guests enjoy just lounging around the Viet-style low-rise buildings, taking in the beautiful beach surroundings and elegant decor, but there's always something to do here: The hotel offers local tours, yoga, tai chi, a full aesthetic salon, and excellent massage, to top it off. Rooms are simple yet luxe: big with solid wood floors, Vietnamese-style furniture, and sliding doors to balconies that overlook the ocean or pool. The huge modern marble bathrooms have all the amenities. Prices are determined by the view, and oceanfront units are only steps from the beach. Note that most of the watersports are available only from February through September—the surf is far too rough in other months, often even for swimming. There is an hourly shuttle bus to the city.

68 Ho Xuan Huong St. (oceanside 11km/7 miles S and W of Danang). © **0511/847-333.** Fax 0511/847-220. www.furamavietnam.com. 200 units. US$140–US$160 garden view; US$190–US$200 ocean view; US$400 suite. AE, MC, V. **Amenities:** 3 restaurants; 3 bars; 2 outdoor pools (1 in courtyard, 1 multilevel w/ocean view); 4 lighted tennis courts; luxe health club; spa; sauna; diving; sail-boat (Laser) and kayak rental; concierge; tour desk; business center w/Internet; nice lobby shopping (gallery); salon; 24-hr. room service; massage; laundry; conference and banquet rooms. *In room:* A/C, satellite TV, dataport, minibar, fridge, coffee/ tea, hair dryer, safe, IDD phone.

MODERATE
Bamboo Green Hotel ★★   Operated by Vietnamtourism and the nicest of its three properties in town (Bamboo Green II and III are comparable but less luxe), this hotel opened in 1997 and is the nicest in the city of Danang. Rooms are large and immaculate, with clean beige carpets, and are well furnished in light wood (just try to overlook the hideous poly bedspreads). The nice-size marble bathrooms with hair dryers look brand new, and everything resembles your average midrange chain hotel. Ask for a room on the top floor for a good city view. There is a big restaurant with decent Asian/Vietnamese fare and good tour services. The staff is friendly and snaps to.

158 Phan Chau Trinh St. © **0511/822-996** or 0511/822-997. Fax 0511/822-998. www.vietnamtourism-vi
tours.com. 46 units. US$99–US$119 superior; US$119–US$139 deluxe; US$149–US$169 suite. AE, MC, V.
Amenities: 2 restaurants; bar; sauna; tour desk; motorbike/car rental; souvenir shopping; limited room service; massage; laundry; dry cleaning. *In room:* A/C, satellite TV, dataport, minibar, fridge, coffeemaker, hair
dryer, IDD phone.

Saigon Tourane Hotel ★   Popular with European tour groups, it's comfort
at low cost here in this nondescript, friendly hotel on the north end of town.
Carpeted rooms are clean, with tidy, good-size bathrooms; some have good city
views from upper floors. Nonetheless, it's all a bit low-luxe, with a general
atmosphere marked by failing neon signs and worn carpets that speak of the volumes that pass through. The hotel is owned by Saigontourist, and guests of this
three-star standard are well-connected and can make any necessary arrangements
with little hassle. The staff couldn't be any more kind. Be sure to ask for a room
away from the karaoke—far away.

5 Dong Da St., Danang. © **0511/821-021.** Fax 0511/895-285. 82 units. US$50–US$70 double; US$80–
US$90 suite. **Amenities:** 2 restaurants; bar; basic gym; sauna; Saigontourist tour desk; car rental; business
center; massage; laundry; dry cleaning; nonsmoking rooms; karaoke; basic souvenirs for sale. *In room:* A/C,
satellite TV, minibar, fridge, hair dryer, IDD phone, complimentary water.

WHERE TO DINE

Indochine ★★ VIETNAMESE   A bank for many years until its recent conversion, this building still maintains some colonial charm and when well-lit at
night is almost ostentatious. The interior is an open, airy space with large French
doors and windows and mercifully mellow indirect lighting. The menu reads like
a catalog of Vietnamese cuisine from every region, and the fare here compares
with the other new Vietnamese places in larger cities. I had a nice chicken with
ginger and fried rice *au co* style. They feature some nice clay pot baked dishes,
and brave diners, or linguists, will leap at the "stewed pork's brain with Chinese
drug in pot." Everything's tasty, the waitstaff is at ease but efficient, and the
atmosphere is old-style Indochine. You might find yourself lounging in languid
conversation or mesmerized by the ceiling fans and geckos on the wall. Enjoy.

18 Tran Phu St. © **0511-887-009.** Fax 0511/887-010. Main courses US$2–US$6. Daily 7am–2pm and
4–10pm.

Kim Do Restaurant ★★ CHINESE   Here it's good, if somewhat standard,
Canton fare served in that faux-gilded elegance popular with Chinese restaurants
the world over (and here they pull it off well). Some of the woodwork is quite
impressive. They've got some nice, light dim sum for lunch specials, and I had an
excellent dish of eggplant, garlic, and chilis that would put hair on your chest.
The menu here is exhaustive, and if you don't see what you want, the friendly and
accommodating owner will be glad to spin up something to your fancy. The staff
is still amazed that foreigners are apt to walk in the door in the afternoon, so go
gently with them; you'll find no shortage of smiles here, though.

180 Tran Phu St. © **0511/821-846.** Main courses US$1.66–US$7. Daily 7am–10pm.

ATTRACTIONS

The Cham Museum ★★   The Cham Museum was established in 1936 as the
École Française d'Extreme Orient. It has the largest collection of Cham sculpture
in the world, in works ranging from the 4th to 14th centuries, presented in a
rough outdoor setting that suits the evocative, sensual sculptures well. The more
than 300 pieces of sandstone artwork and temple decorations were largely influenced by Hindu and, later, Mahayana Buddhism. Among the cast of characters,

you'll see symbols of Uroja, or "goddess mother," usually breasts or nipples; the linga, the phallic structure representing the god Shiva; the holy bird Garuda; the dancing girl Kinnari; the snake god Naga; and Ganesha, child of the god Shiva, with the head of an elephant. The sculptures are arranged by period, which are, in turn, named after the geographic regions where the sculptures were found. Note the masterpiece Tra Kieu altar of the late 7th century, with carved scenes telling the story of the Asian epic *Ramayana.* The story is of the wedding of Princess Sita. Side one tells of Prince Rama, who broke a holy vow to obtain Sita's hand. Side two tells of ambassadors sent to King Dasaratha, Prince Rama's father, to bring him the glad tidings. Side three is the actual ceremony, and side four depicts the celebrations after the ceremony.

Explanations are written in English and French. There is a permanent photo exhibition of Cham relics in situ at various locations throughout Vietnam that helps put everything in context.

At Tran Phu and Le Dinh Duong sts. No phone. Admission 20,000 VND (US$1.38). Daily 7am–6pm.

The Marble Mountains ☆   The "mountains" are actually a series of five marble and limestone formations, which the locals liken to the shape of a dragon at rest. The hills contain numerous caves, some of which have become Buddhist sanctuaries. They also served as sanctuaries for the Viet Cong during the American war. The highest mountain, Thuy Son, is climbable via a series of metal ladders beginning inside the cave and extending. Its highlight is the Ling Ong Pagoda, a shrine within a cave. The quarries in Non Nuoc village, at the bottom of the mountains, are as interesting as the caves are. Fantastic animals, including a roaring lion said to watch over the village from the peaks, are carved from the rock. Try to get a good look before you are set upon by flocks of hawkers. What's more, even if you're interested in the items they hawk—incredibly cheap mortise and pestle sets, some very nice chess sets—who wants to drag *marble* all the way back home? You can easily see the mountains as part of your trip en route either to or from Hoi An.

11km (7 miles) S of Danang and 9.5km (6 miles) N of Hoi An along Hwy. 1. All tours stop here. Admission 30,000 (US$2).

AN EXCURSION TO MY SON ☆☆

My Son, 71km (44 miles) outside of Danang, is one of the most important Cham temple sites, established in the late 4th century. The temples were constructed as a religious center for citizens of the Cham capital, Danang, from the 7th through 12th centuries. My Son might also have been used as a burial site for Cham kings after cremation. Originally, there were over 70 towers and monuments here, but bombing during the American war (the Viet Cong used My Son as a munitions warehouse) has sadly reduced many to rubble. Additionally, many of the smaller structures have been removed to the Cham Museum in Danang. The complex has a very serene and spiritual setting, however, and what does remain is powerful and evocative. It's not hard to imagine what a wonder My Son must once have been.

Much of what remains today are structures built or renovated during the 10th century, when the cult of Shiva, founder and protector of the kingdom, was predominant in the Cham court. Each group had at least the following structures: a **kalan,** or main tower; a gate tower in front of that, with two entrances; a **mandapa,** or meditation hall; and a repository building for offerings. Some have towers sheltering stelae with kingly epitaphs. A brick wall encircles the compound.

Architecturally, a temple complex shows Indian influences. Each is a microcosm of the world. The foundations are Earth, the square bases are the temple itself, and the pointed roofs symbolize the heavens. The entrance of the main tower faces east, and surrounding smaller towers represent each continent. A trench, representing the oceans, surrounds each group. Vietnamese architecture is represented in decorative patterns and boat-shape roofs.

Group A originally had 13 towers. A-1, the main tower, was a 20.7m-tall (69-ft.-tall) masterpiece before it was destroyed in 1969. Group B shows influences from Indian and Indonesian art. Note that B-6 holds a water repository for statue-washing ceremonies. Its roof is carved with an image of the god Vishnu sitting beneath a 13-headed snake god, or **naga.** Group C generally followed an earlier architectural style called Hoa Lai, which predominated from the 8th century to the beginning of the 9th. Groups G and H were the last to be built, at around the end of the 13th century.

You can make arrangements for a half-day trip to see My Son through any tourist agent in Danang, or from Hoi An. Entrance to the site is 50,000 VND (US$3.33), and a private half-day tour with a guide is US$35 for a car and US$43 for a van. From Hoi An, the half-day seat-in-coach tour by Sinh Café costs US$2 per person and is nothing more than a ride there, with no explanations.

9 Hoi An

If you go, Hoi An will be one of the highlights of your Vietnam visit. From the 16th to the 18th centuries, Hoi An was Vietnam's most important port and trading post, particularly in ceramics. Today it is a quaint old town (844 structures have been designated historical landmarks) still showing the influences of the Chinese and Japanese traders who passed through and settled here. Moreover, it's small enough to cover easily on foot; you can wander through the historic homes and temples on a quiet Saturday afternoon, perhaps stop to lounge in an open-air cafe, gaze at the endless oddities and exotic foods in the market, or take a **sampan ride** down the lazy river. In the afternoons when school is out, the streets are thronged with skipping children in spotless white shirts. While the city is eagerly courting tourism and your tourist dollars—meaning there're plenty of pesky vendors and hawkers—it's still relatively low-key and genuinely friendly.

On the full moon of every month, local shop owners turn off the electricity and hang lanterns bearing their shop's name, and a candlelight lantern procession, complete with a few small floats, makes its way through the Old Town and along the riverfront. It's well worth timing a visit to enjoy the spectacle and the post-processional festivities.

GETTING THERE
BY PLANE OR TRAIN   Major public transport connections go through Danang. From there, you can take a car to Hoi An for US$25 through the **Vietnamtourism** office in Danang (✆ **0511/823-660**).

BY BUS   This is a major stop on all open-tour cafe buses. Connection with Danang is just US$3.

GETTING AROUND
Hoi An is so small that you'll memorize the map in an hour or two. Most hotels and guesthouses rent out bicycles for 5,000 VND to 7,000 VND (US34¢–US48¢) a day, as does Hoi An Tourism (see below), to explore the outer regions of the city or Cao Dai beach. **Motorbikes** are US$3 to US$5 per day and are

Hoi An

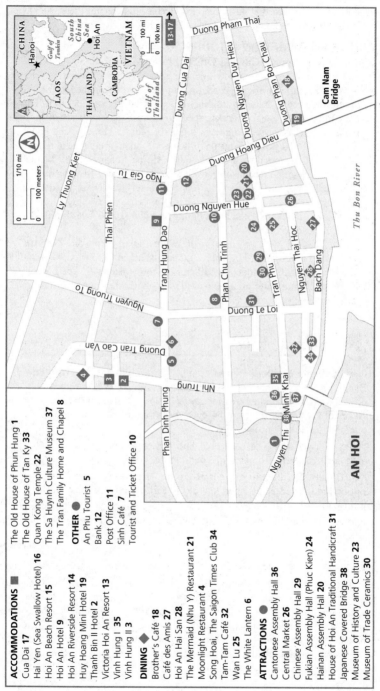

ACCOMMODATIONS ■
Cua Dai **17**
Hai Yen (Sea Swallow Hotel) **16**
Hoi An Beach Resort **15**
Hoi An Hotel **9**
Hoi An Riverside Resort **14**
Huy Hoang Mini Hotel **19**
Thanh Bin II Hotel **2**
Victoria Hoi An Resort **13**
Vinh Hung I **35**
Vinh Hung II **3**

DINING ◆
Brother's Café **18**
Café des Amis **27**
Hoi An Hai San **28**
The Mermaid (Nhu Y) Restaurant **21**
Moonlight Restaurant **4**
Song Hoai, The Saigon Times Club **34**
Tam-Tam Café **32**
Wan Lu **25**
The White Lantern **6**

ATTRACTIONS ●
Cantonese Assembly Hall **36**
Central Market **26**
Chinese Assembly Hall **29**
Fukian Assembly Hall (Phuc Kien) **24**
Hainan Assembly Hall **20**
House of Hoi An Traditional Handicraft **31**
Japanese Covered Bridge **38**
Museum of History and Culture **23**
Museum of Trade Ceramics **30**

The Old House of Phun Hung **1**
The Old House of Tan Ky **33**
Quan Kong Temple **22**
The Sa Huynh Culture Museum **37**
The Tran Family Home and Chapel **8**

OTHER ●
An Phu Tourist **5**
Bank **12**
Post Office **11**
Sinh Café **7**
Tourist and Ticket Office **10**

not difficult to drive in this tiny, calm city. **Cyclos** are here and there; 10,000 VND (US69¢) or so should get you anywhere within the city.

VISITOR INFORMATION & TOURS

- **The Hoi An Tourist Guiding Office,** 12 Phan Chu Trinh St. (© **0510/ 862-715**), offers tours of the old town and sells the entrance ticket to the Hoi An World Cultural Heritage. A one-ticket purchase offers limited admission to all of the town's museums, old houses, and Chinese assembly halls. For more information about the ticket, see "Attractions," later in this chapter.
- **Hoi An Tourist Service Company,** inside the Hoi An Hotel, 6 Tran Hung Dao St. (© **0510/861-373;** fax 0510/861-636), books every type of tour of the city and surrounding areas, including China Beach and the Marble Mountains, and is a reliable operation. Many tourist cafes, booking offices, and small hotels can do the same job, but these specialize in backpacker minibus tours.
- **The Sinh Café IV,** 37 Phan Dinh Phung St. (© **0510/863-948**), provides bus tours and tickets onward.
- **An Phu Tourist,** with a main office at 29 Phan Dinh Phung St. (© **0510/ 862-643;** anphutourist@hotmail.com) and two others in town, does everything that Sinh Café does. The difference? Your preference. The benefit? Competition and lower prices. No need to ask both; they match each other on everything.

⟨C⟩ *FAST FACTS:* Hoi An

Banks/Currency Exchange The Vietcombank branch at 4 Huong Dieu St. changes money of most major currencies and does credit card cash withdrawal transactions. Hours are Monday to Saturday 7:30am to 7pm. At no. 78 Le Loi St., 1 block up from the river, there's a money-changing booth operated by Hoi An Income Bank.

Internet/E-mail Along Le Loi, you'll find service at prices between 300 VND and 400 VND (a couple cents) per minute. Access is good.

Post Office/Mail The post office is at the corner of Trang Hong Dao and Huong Dieu streets and is open Monday to Saturday 6am to 9:30pm.

Telephone The city code for Hoi An is 510. You can place international phone calls from the post office listed above and from most hotels.

WHERE TO STAY

Hoi An has seen a recent boom in upscale resorts on the outskirts of town and there are some interesting new in town. Large-scale new construction in Hoi An proper is prohibited by UNESCO, so in the town center, apart from the Hoi An Hotel below, there are just a few older budget hotels and basic atmospheric choices; ask to see rooms before checking in because two rooms in the same hotel can have completely different amenities. The new resorts outside of town come with a price tag but are worth it.

EXPENSIVE

Victoria Hoi An Resort ⟨★★⟩ It's peace and palm trees here just a short ride (4.8km/3 miles) from ancient Hoi An. The Victoria is impressive yet comfortable, with all the amenities, and begs at least a few days' stay. The staff is very professional, the place has any activity you could imagine, and the guest rooms have it right in every detail, from the in-room sandals and beach robes to the finest decor. This is luxurious oceanside Vietnam at its best. Rooms are either the bungalow variety in low-slung buildings at beachside or are set in parallel two-story rows to mimic Hoi An's ancient streets, not displeasing, but a bit like a theme park. Prices reflect beachside proximity, but even the least expensive rooms are laid back and classy. Some bungalows are decorated in themes of French country style, with canopy beds and wicker furniture; others are unique Japanese rooms, with open-timber construction, bamboo floors, and large bathtubs. All rooms are finished with fine dark-wood appointments, many with high, exposed tile ceilings and comfortable, nonslip tile leading into large bathrooms. There is a certain flow to this property that invites guests to wander the high-ceilinged common areas of the lobby, with billiards, gaming tables, and reading nooks connected by catwalk. Or, you can take a tranquil stroll through the gardens. Amenities like the large oceanside pool, great indoor gym, Jacuzzi, aesthetic salon, and massage are top-notch. The hotel's resident elephant, Darling, offers rides to kids of all ages (priced per hr.) and gives demonstrations on elephant hygiene early each morning (he takes his bath). Convenient shuttles, one an old Renault bus, connect to town frequently.

Cua Dai Beach, 5km (3 miles) from Hoi An. ⓒ **0510/927-041.** Fax 0510/927-041. www.victoriahotels-asia. com. 100 units. US$120–US$130 superior (river/sea view); US$150–US$170 deluxe (river/sea view); US$220 suite. **Amenities:** 2 restaurants; 2 bars; outdoor pool (beachside); 2 tennis courts; nice health club; spa; Jacuzzi; kayak/windsurfer/Hobie cat rental; children's play area; snooker/billiards room; tour desk; car rental; shopping; extensive salon; 24-hr. room service; foot massage; babysitting; laundry; dry cleaning; small library; elephant rides; Internet. *In room:* A/C, satellite TV, minibar, fridge, coffeemaker, safe, IDD phone.

Hoi An Riverside Resort ★★
For upscale, tranquil, and intimate surroundings, you'll find no better than this lush little resort between road and river just outside of Hoi An (just 3km/1¾ miles). The address of choice for some of Vietnam's more recent celebrity guests (you'll have to ask at reception to find out), it almost feels like the guest rooms and other building kind of grew around the winding path of the garden and the tranquil courtyard pool. Rooms are neat and clean, not especially big, but with nice views of the meandering bend in the river here or the quiet garden. Vietnamese- or Japanese-theme rooms are a similar standard of amenities and comfort, with smallish but immaculate bathrooms and nice wood appointments throughout. The staff is invisible, meaning that this place carries on like an immaculately trimmed golf course that gets a once-over each night. The Song Do restaurant serves fine Vietnamese and Continental fare. Just a short visit to the Faifo bar, with its open terraces and finely crafted balconies, might have you fancying yourself a visiting Graham Greene or Somerset Maugham. They give cooking lessons here and lead daily boat rides and fishing trips on the river.

Cua Dai Rd. 3km (1¾ miles) from Hoi An. ⓒ **0510/864-800.** Fax 0510/864-900. www.hoianriverresort.com. 60 units. US$109 Vietnamese standard; US$119 Japanese standard; US$129 superior (river view). Promotional rates available in off season. AE, DC, MC, V. **Amenities:** Restaurant; bar; outdoor pool; health club; snooker/billiards room; business center w/Internet; nice souvenir shop; salon; 24-hr. room service; foot massage; babysitting; laundry; dry cleaning; small library; conference room. *In room:* A/C, satellite TV, dataport, minibar, fridge, coffeemaker, safe, IDD phone.

Hoi An Beach Resort ★
Opened in August 2000, this is the flagship of Hoi An Tourist, a government-owned company, and it's their answer to recent upscale development in town. Across the road from Cua Dai beach and close to

the small restaurant row and popular tourist sun-bathing area, this resort has a more riverside orientation. Everything from the casual open-air restaurant to the more expensive rooms and suites faces the De Vong River as it approaches the sea, offering a unique glimpse of everyday riverside life (all within walking distance of the beach, though). All rooms here are nice, but the villas are certainly worth the extra few bucks: They're quite large, with high ceilings and large private balconies (deluxe rooms are okay but are stacked in a courtyard a la an American motel). Villas and suites have vaulted ceilings like a Vietnamese house, and some have separate entrances directly to the bathroom for cleaning up after the beach. Service and general standards here are "just okay," not quite up to their high-end competition in town, but they're trying. Removing the neon signs scattered about would do well to tone down the wanna-be vibe. This seems a popular stop for large European tours and can get a bit wild in the busy season, but if you can't beat 'em, join 'em. They have shuttles to town or can arrange private cars for US$3 one-way.

Cua Dai Beach. ⓒ **0510/927-011** or 0510/927-015. Fax 0510/927-019. www.hoiantourist.com. 85 units. US$80–US$100 single/double garden deluxe; US$100–US$120 oceanview and river-view villas; US$180–US$200 suite. AE, MC, V. **Amenities:** Restaurant; 3 bars; 2 outdoor pools; tennis court; small health club; spa; Jacuzzi; sauna; steam bath; in-house tour desk that can do all; car rental; souvenir shops; salon; limited room service; foot massage; laundry; Internet. *In room:* A/C, satellite TV, minibar, fridge, coffeemaker, hair dryer, safe, IDD phone.

MODERATE

Hoi An Hotel ⚹⚹   The Hoi An Hotel was the first high-end hotel serving the town and is still the only international standard in the downtown area. As a result, it's pretty busy here with lots of tour groups; the friendly staff does a great job, though, and seems to handle large numbers with a modicum of grace. Don't expect anything fancy, but rooms are unusually large and impeccably clean, with tile floors and comfortable beds. Basic bathrooms are all tile and in good condition. There are three buildings, one very new with upscale rooms featuring new furniture and nice carpeted floors (also a new area under construction). The older wing with the US$35 rooms is nearly as nice as the newer, though, so my advice is to save your money. They've got good basic amenities like a nice, albeit small, pool, casual open-air dining facilities, and a good tour desk. It's the best for convenience and comfort to tour Hoi An's main sites.

6 Tran Hung Dao St. ⓒ **0510/861-373.** Fax 0510/861-636. www.hoiantourist.com. 160 units. US$26–US$60 double; US$100 suite. AE, MC, V. **Amenities:** Restaurant; garden bar; nice courtyard pool; tennis court; Jacuzzi; concierge; In-house tour desk can do all; car rental; business center; lobby souvenir shops; 24-hr. room service' babysitting' laundry; dry cleaning. *In room:* A/C, satellite TV, minibar, fridge, hair dryer, IDD phone.

Hai Yen (Sea Swallow Hotel) ⚹   This is a good, basic standard on the edge of the old town (a short walk or ride toward the beach). It's a popular choice for big tour groups that come here for the low price and consistency. Slick diagonal black-and-white (or blue-and-white) tile throughout gives everything a tidy edge, and rooms are good-size, with funky Chinese relief carvings, overly fancy curtains, and shiny polyester spreads. It gets an "A" for effort, but the general effect is kind of unsettling. The pool is a surprise luxury in this price range and is quite nice (if small), but it's a bit rough around the edges here, kind of a faded 1970s pallor over the whole place (and it's not so old). The staff is friendly, though, and can help with any detail.

22A Cua Dai St., Hoi An. ⓒ **0501/862-445** or 0501/862-446. 41 units. US$25–US$30 double (seasonal). AE, MC, V. **Amenities:** Restaurant; bar; small outdoor pool; all rentals; tour desk; laundry. *In room:* A/C, satellite TV, minibar, fridge, IDD phone.

Cua Dai ★★   For my money, this is one of Hoi An's true gems. A long walk or short ride toward the beach (on a road of the same name), the Cua Dai is a good marriage of affordability and comfort. With nice open sitting areas of comfy wicker furniture on black-and-white tile and a faux colonial edifice that is quite elegant, it's easy to settle in here, and the kind staff will make you feel right at home. The only drawback is the busy road out front, but all rooms have double glass and are quiet. Rooms in the new wing in back have fine wooden appointments and creative, local decoration; older rooms in the main building are quite large, basic, and comfortable. This is a great base from which to explore downtown and is a good spot to meet expats and long-stay travelers here on cultural or humanitarian missions. Take any opportunity to chat with the Cua Dai's knowledgeable owner, Ms. Vy, and don't miss the little Zen garden in the entry. Buffet breakfast is included.

18A Cua Dai St. ✆ **0510/862-231** or 864-604. Fax 0510/862-232. 27 units. US$18–US$25. MC, V. **Amenities:** Restaurant; bicycle/motorbike available; help w/any travel need; laundry. *In room:* A/C, TV, minibar, fridge, IDD phone.

INEXPENSIVE

Vinh Hung I and II ★   Whether in the downtown property, a classic old Chinese house with both basic and gawdy deluxe rooms, or the new hotel just outside the historic town center, you'll find affordable comfort and atmosphere here. Rooms are large, with nice wooden appointments and cool retro features like mosquito nets and Chinese latticework on wood balconies. The two deluxe rooms at the old Vinh Hung are almost museum pieces and are alone worth a visit here, but they're not especially luxe or comfortable. The new property has a pool and is popular with tour groups.

143 Tran Phu St.: ✆ **0510/861-621.** Fax 0510/861-893. Nhi Trung St. ✆ **0510/863-717.** Fax 0510/864-094. US$15–US$30 double. AE, MC, V. **Amenities:** Restaurant; small outdoor pool; rentals; tour desk; laundry. *In room:* A/C, TV, IDD phone.

Thanh Bin II Hotel ★   The Thanh Bin II hotel is newer and nicer than its sister property, the Thanh Bin I over on Le Loi Street. The three-story building has a very Chinese-inspired lobby, with carved dark-wood furnishings and cafe tables. Upstairs, the very clean and basic rooms are spacious, and just a bit loud (decor-wise, that is). The decor is a mish-mosh—somehow they've color-coordinated it all. There's not a musty smell to be found, bathrooms are tidy, and the staff is really friendly. For fun, ask about one of the suite: It's a huge room that sports wood paneling, carved Chinese-style furnishings (and a mosquito net over the bed), a nice balcony with beaded curtains, and, in the center of the room, a large wooden carving of a fat, happy Buddha.

Nhi Trung St. ✆ **0510/863-715.** 31 units. US$12–US$30 double. AE, MC, V. **Amenities:** Restaurant; rentals; laundry. *In room:* A/C, TV, minibar, fridge, IDD phone.

Huy Hoang Mini Hotel ★   This is a very good bargain hotel, in a new yellow-and-white faux colonial close to the Central Market. Rooms are spotless, big, and bright, with tile floors and some older carved furniture. There are no phones or other amenities, and only the few US$25 rooms have bathtubs. Breakfast is served in a patio in the back with views of the river. The staff is exceedingly friendly.

73 Phan Boi Chau St. ✆ **0510/862-211.** Fax 0510/863-722. kshuyhoang@dgn.vnn.vn. 19 units. US$10–US$25 double. No credit cards. **Amenities:** Restaurant; laundry. *In room:* Some w/A/C, TV.

WHERE TO DINE

Hoi An is a feast for the stomach as well as the eyes. Local specialties include *cao lau* (rice noodles with fresh greens, rice crackers, and croutons), white rose dumplings, shrimp in clear rice dough, and fried wontons. Seafood, particularly steamed fish, is excellent and available everywhere, and some new high-end options have popped up in town alongside some popular standbys. Each of the resorts has its own fine dining (see above), but be sure to get to town and check out some of the more atmospheric choices. The riverfront road, Bach Dang, has become the de facto "restaurant row," and I've suggested a few good spots, but if you take a stroll down here any time in the day, you're sure to be besieged by some friendly but persistent touts who'll drag you bodily into their restaurants. All of these places are comparable in price and serve similar local specialties and budget standbys (fried rice and noodles), and it's sometimes fun to let the restaurant choose you. *Note:* Hassles don't end, though, even when you're seated. Here you're a prime target for young salesmen with their Tiger Balm and trinkets. For a peaceful meal, choose a table a bit off the street and say a consistent and calm "No."

EXPENSIVE

Brother's Café ★★★ VIETNAMESE   Serving similar fine Vietnamese fare as its sister restaurant in Hanoi (but here it's a la carte, not buffet), Brother's Café is the town's top choice for cuisine and atmosphere. A bland street-side facade gives way to the lush, garden sanctuary formed by this grand U-shape colonial by the river. Indoor seating is upscale Indochina of a by-gone era, and the courtyard is dotted with canvas umbrellas to while away a balmy afternoon or enjoy a candlelight evening riverside. The fare is gourmet Vietnamese at its finest, with changing daily set menus and great specials; be sure to ask for a recommendation. It's a good place to try local items like the white rose, a light Vietnamese ravioli, or *cao lao* noodles. Set menus are great here and change daily. With a group, it's a great spot to order up family style and sample it all. They also feature a cooking school (just ask the staff). Everything's good, the atmosphere is great, and the staff couldn't be friendlier. This is a strong recommendation.

27 Pham Boi Chau St. ✆ **0510/914-150**. Main courses US$1.50–US$12. AE, MC, V. Daily 10am–11pm.

Song Hoai, The Saigon Times Club ★★ VIETNAMESE   Newly opened and set in a picturesque corner colonial at riverside, this Saigon-managed restaurant is as much about atmosphere as it is about dining. Rivaled only by Brother's, above, the two open floors here are true rustic, colonial elegance. The second floor has great views of the river and is dramatic, with a high, exposed tile ceiling and languid ceiling fans. They're just getting up and running and the menu is still in the works, but I had the Vietnamese-style ravioli, the local white rose specialty, and enjoyed fresh pan-fried shrimp. They serve regional dishes like Hanoi *cha ca* and *mi quang* wide noodles. Presentation is arguably the classiest in town, with fine China, stemware, and lacquered dishes on linen, and the service is refreshingly attentive but not hovering. It's a fine spot.

(Riverside) 119-121 Nguyen Thai Hoc. ✆ **0510/910-369**. Fax 0510/910-436. Main courses US$1–US$11.33. AE, MC, V. Daily 10am–11pm.

Tam-Tam Café ★★ ITALIAN/CONTINENTAL   Tam-Tam is the place to be in Hoi An. The brainchild of three French expats, it's historic and laid back, serving good, familiar food. The decor is very local and extremely well done, with hanging bamboo lamps, a high wooden ceiling, and fantastic wooden figurines. The dinner menu, served in a separate restaurant room with checkered tablecloths, is simple—featuring generous portions of homemade pastas, steaks, and salads—but the food is delicious. The dessert menu includes flambéed crepes, sorbet, and hot chocolate. There are two bar rooms: The bigger one to the left or the entry has a pool table, a book swap shelf, comfortable lounge chairs, and sofas, and is the place to hang out in Hoi An. The extensive drink menu features all kinds of bang-for-the buck rum specials, and there's even a small counter on the balcony where you can sip a cocktail and watch life go by on the street below. Even for just a coffee, don't miss this place.

110 Nguyen Thai Hoc St. (on the 2nd floor). ✆ 0510/862-212. Main courses US$2–US$10. AE, MC, V. Daily 24 hrs.

MODERATE

The White Lantern ⭐⭐ VIETNAMESE   This is a very popular tour group stop, so try to get there early (or late); if you see buses parked out front, head for the hills. Everyone's here for good reason, though: delicious, affordable Vietnamese cuisine and mellow atmosphere. Strumming guitarists roam the tables playing old Beatles melodies and some nice local numbers, and the large open area on the first floor, with long tables for groups, and the second-floor balcony space are dimly lit and romantic. Owned by the same folks that run Nhu Y, below, this is a slightly upscale version. Set menus are a great bet; I had a fine meal of a delicate won-ton soup, spring rolls, and chicken in a light curry. It's a good find just north of the town center.

11 Nhi Trung St. ✆ 0510/863-023. Main courses 30,000–45,000 VND (US$2–US$3); set menu 75,000–120,000 VND (US$5–US$8). MC, V. Daily 9am–10pm.

Café des Amis ⭐⭐ VIETNAMESE   This unique place serves some of the best food in Vietnam in a nothing-special setting—just an average storefront on Bach Dang. There is no menu, but you'll be greeted by the effusive owner, Mr. Kim, who'll walk you through your choice of either the seafood or the vegetarian course: a series of delicious dishes such as clear soup, fried wontons with shrimp, broiled fish, stuffed calamari, or scallops on the half shell. Mr. Kim is a practiced raconteur with rich material from his years as a taster for the army and a chef for heads of state. He is careful to explain the intricacies of each dish and even demonstrates how to eat some of the more unique entrees. The food is great, and a meal here makes for a memorable evening. Be sure to sign and peruse the guest book.

52 Bach Dang. ✆ 0510/861-616. Set menu 50,000 VND (US$3.45). No credit cards. Daily 6–10pm.

The Mermaid (Nhu Y) Restaurant ⭐⭐ VIETNAMESE   This quiet spot in the heart of downtown is an ivy-draped, unassuming storefront that serves some of the best authentic Vietnamese food in town (for next to nothing). If you like what you eat, stick around and take a **cooking class** in the large adjoining kitchen that's open to the street: Here's a unique chance to bring some of Vietnam home to your kitchen. I had a scrumptious tuna filet cooked in a banana leaf with tumeric. The spring rolls are light and fresh, with a whole jumbo shrimp in each, and they serve the most unique dish, called white eggplant: It's eggplant covered in spring onion, garlic, and chili, and then pressed, sliced, and served in a light oil. Everything is good. The staff members also teach the class and are very friendly and can explain it all.

02 Tran Phu St. ✆ 0510/861-527. Main courses 12,000–40,000 VND (US80¢–US$2.33). Cash only. Daily 7am–10pm.

Hoi An Hai San ✹✹ VIETNAMESE/CONTINENTAL   Hai-san means "seafood" in Vietnamese and "hello" in Swedish: The owners, longtime Swedish expat Calle and Hoa, his Vietnamese wife, offer just that: "Hello, seafood!" This is one of the few spots on Hang Bac that won't drag you in (much) because it's the food that brings folks here. I had delicious grilled, marinated tuna filet with ginger, garlic, and lemongrass and served in a light coconut milk. Try the pasta marinara, a rich mix of all kinds of seafood in a fine homemade sauce. Everything's good here, and it's a good place to linger after a meal, enjoy the Swedish lingenberry (a kind of cranberry) ice cream, and watch the goings-on on busy Bach Dang.

64 Bach Dang St. ✆ 0510/861-652. Main courses 20,000–75,000 VND (US$1.33–US$5). Daily 9am–10pm.

INEXPENSIVE

Moonlight Restaurant ✹ VIETNAMESE   In a quiet little courtyard just off the main street in the center of town, and complete with a little pond and stream trickling beneath hanging ivy, this unassuming little gem serves up standard backpacker fare and is a great place to catch breakfast or to just get out of the noontime heat. They've got *cao lao,* the local favorite of white noodles, as well as the lightly fried wontons, called white rose, that are popular in town. They offer things like hamburgers and pizza, but stick to the fried rice and noodles or try one of the good curries.

23 Phan Dinh Phung. ✆ 0510-861-203. Main courses 10,000–30,000 VND (US66¢–US$2). Cash only. Daily 7am–10pm.

Wan Lu ✹   Pull up a chair and try the special, *cao lao,* a thick but tender white noodle in light soy with fresh vegetables, garnish, and croutons. This is where the locals eat it, and if it's not your cup of tea, then you're out only 6,000 VND (about US40¢). It's an open-air place, and the atmosphere is a little rough, but they serve a nice selection of local favorites, too, all for next to nothing. The portions are big and everything's authentic, right down to the kindness in this little Mom and Pop. There are no touts here; it's the food that brings 'em in.

27 Tran Phu. ✆ 0510/861-212. Main courses 5,000–30,000 VND (US33¢–US$2). No credit cards. Daily 7am–11pm.

ATTRACTIONS

The whole town is an attraction, its narrow streets filling your eyes with the beauty of historical buildings mixed with the everyday lives of the Vietnamese who live and work here today. The oldest streets, Tran Phu and Nguyen Thai Hoc, supported Chinese immigrant merchants and their families who built traditional Chinese wooden houses, stone shop houses, and clan association houses. Many of these buildings have been restored with a tenderness that has salvaged the structure yet retained much of each building's true charm. While many today house cafes, art galleries, and silk and souvenir shops, building facades still retain their historical dignity. If you're an artist, bring your sketchpad and watercolors; photographers, bring plenty of film.

The Hoi An World Cultural Heritage Organization (www.hoianworld heritage.org) has the dilemma of financing the restorations and maintaining the old portions of the town. They sell a 50,000 VND (US$3.33) ticket that allows limited admission to the sights within the old town, each of which is listed below. I say "limited" because it's sort of a "One from column A, one from column B" sort of thing. One ticket gets you one of the three museums, one of the three assembly halls, one of the four old houses, plus a choice of either the

Japanese Bridge, the Quan Cong's Temple, or the local handicraft workshop; finally, a "wild card" lets you see one additional place in any category that you didn't see. So, to see everything, you'll have to purchase three tickets. The three-star choices in each category are your best bet if you don't have time to see it all.

Don't forget to admire the small details on the inside of each building, especially the old wooden houses that employ traditional Chinese construction methods. And don't be distracted by the tourist cafes and shops—stop and notice the trades that are worked behind some of the doors, and the locals living their everyday lives in this unique setting.

THE MUSEUMS

Museum of Trade Ceramics ★★★ Located in a traditional house, this museum describes the origins of Hoi An as a trade port and displays its most prominent trade item. Objects are from the 13th through 17th centuries and include Chinese and Thai works as well. While many of the exhibits are in fragments, the real beauty of the place is that the very thorough descriptions are in English, giving you a real sense of the town's origins and history. Furthermore, the architecture and renovations of the old house are thoroughly explained, and you're free to wander through its two floors, courtyard, and anteroom. After all the scattered explanations at the other historic houses, you'll finally get a sense of what Hoi An architecture is all about.

80 Tran Phu St. Daily 8am–5pm.

Museum of History and Culture ★ This tottering building erected in 1653 houses works that cross 2,000 years of Hoi An history from Cham relics to ancient ceramics and photos of local architecture.   There are English explanations, but they are scanty. If you're seeing only one museum, make it the Museum of Trade Ceramics (below). One interesting tidbit: The name Hoi An literally means "water convergence" and "peace."

7 Nguyen Hue St. Daily 8am–5pm.

The Sa Huynh Culture Museum ★ After local farmers around Hoi An dug up some strange-looking pottery, archaeologists identified 53 sites where a pre-Cham people, called the Sa Huynh, buried their dead in ceramic jars. The two-room display here includes some of the burial jars, beaded ornaments, pottery vessels, and iron tools and weapons that have been uncovered. English descriptions are sketchy. Upstairs, the little-visited Museum of the Revolution includes such intriguing items as the umbrella "which Mr. Truong Munh Luong used for acting a fortune-teller to act revolution from 1965 to 1967." Huh? This is for connoisseurs only.

149 Tran Phu St. Daily 8am–6pm.

THE OLD HOUSES

The Tran Family Home and Chapel ★★★ In 1802, a civil service mandarin named Tran Tu Nhuc built a family home and chapel to worship his ancestors. A favorite of Viet Emperor Gia Long, he was sent to China as an ambassador, and his home reflects his high status. Elegantly designed with original Chinese antiques and royal gifts such as swords, two parts of the home are open to the public: a drawing room and an ancestral chapel. The house does a splendid job of conveying all that is exotic and interesting about these people and their period. It has even been featured as a stylish layout in a fashion magazine. The drawing room has three sections of sliding doors: the left for men, the right for women, and the center, open only at Tet and other festivals, for dead ancestors to return home. The ancestral altar in the inner room has small boxes behind it containing relics and a biography of the deceased; their pictures hang, a little spookily, to the right of the altar. A 250-year-old book with the family history resides on a table to the right of the altar. In back of the house are a row of plants, each buried with the placenta and umbilical cord of a family child, so that the child will never forget its home. As if it could.

21 Le Loi (on the corner of Le Loi and Phan Chu Trinh sts.). Daily 8am–5pm.

The Old House of Phun Hung ⋆

This private house, constructed in 1780, is two floors of combined architectural influences. The first floor's central roof is four-sided, showing Japanese influence, and the upstairs balcony has a Chinese rounded "turtle shell" roof with carved beam supports. The house has weathered many floods. In 1964, during a particularly bad bout, its third floor served as a refuge for other town families. The upstairs is outfitted with a trap door for moving furniture rapidly to safety. You might be shown around by Ms. Anh, who claims to be an eighth-generation member of the family. Tour guides at every house make such claims; however, like Quan Thang's house, the family really does seem to live here.

4 Nguyen Thi Minh Khai St. Daily 8am–5pm.

The Old House of Tan Ky ⋆

There have been either five or seven generations of Tans living here, depending on whom you speak with. Built over 200 years ago, the four small rooms are crammed with dark-wood antiques. The room closest to the street is for greeting visiting merchants. Farther in is the living room, then the courtyard, and, to the back, the bedroom. The first three are open to the public. A guide who will greet you at the door will hasten to explain how the house is a perfect melding of three architectural styles: ornate Chinese detailing on some curved roof beams, a Japanese peaked roof, and a simple Vietnamese cross-hatch roof support. The mosaic decorations on the wall and furniture are aged, intricate, and amazing. Take your time to look around.

101 Nguyen Thai Hoc St. Daily 8am–5pm.

THE ASSEMBLY HALLS

Cantonese Assembly Hall (Quang Trieu/Guangzhou Assembly Hall)

Built in 1885, this hall is quite ornate and colorful. All of the building materials were completed in China, brought here, and then reassembled. The center garden sports a fountain with a dragon made of chipped pottery, the centerpiece. Inside, look for the statues depicting scenes from famous Cantonese operas and, in the rooms to each side, the ancestral tablets of generations past.

176 Tran Phu St. Daily 8am–6pm.

Fukian Assembly Hall (Phuc Kien)

This is the grandest of the assembly halls, built in 1697 by Chinese merchants from Fukian Province. It is a showpiece of classical Chinese architecture, at least after you pass the first gate, which was added in 1975. It's loaded with animal themes: The fish in the mosaic fountain symbolizes scholarly achievement, the unicorn flanking the ascending stairs symbolizes wisdom, the dragon symbolizes power, the turtle symbolizes longevity, and the phoenix symbolizes nobility. The main temple is dedicated to Thien Hau, goddess of the sea, on the main altar. To the left of her is Thuan Phong Nhi, a goddess who can hear ships in a range of thousands of miles, and on the right is Thien Ly Nhan, who can see them. Go around the altar for a view of a fantastic detailed miniature boat. There are two altars to the rear of the temple, the one on the left honoring a god of prosperity and the one on the right honoring a goddess of fertility. The goddess of fertility is often visited by local couples hoping for children. She is flanked by 12 fairies or midwives, 1 responsible for each of a baby's functions: smiling, sleeping, eating, and so forth.

46 Tran Phu St. Daily 7am–6pm.

OTHER SITES

Japanese Covered Bridge ★★★   The name of this bridge in Vietnamese, Lai Vien Kieu, means "Pagoda in Japan." No one is exactly sure who first built it in the early 1600s (it has since been renovated several times), but it is usually attributed to Hoi An's Japanese community. The dog flanking one end and the monkey at the other are considered to be sacred animals to the ancient Japanese, and my guide claimed the reasoning is that most Japanese emperors were born in the year of either the monkey or the dog by the Asian zodiac. Later I read something else that claimed maybe it meant construction began in the year of the dog and was completed in the year of the monkey. I'm sure there are many other interesting dog and monkey stories going around. Pick your favorite. The small temple inside is dedicated to Tran Vo Bac De, god of the north, beloved (or cursed) by sailors because he controls the weather.

At the W end of Tran Phu St.

Quan Kong Temple ★   This temple was built in the early 1600s to honor a famous Chin Dynasty general. Highlights inside are two gargantuan 3m-high (10-ft.-high) wooden statues flanking the main altar, one of Quan Kong's protector and one of his adopted son. They are fearsome and impressive. Reportedly the temple was a stop for merchants who came in from the nearby river to pay their respects and pray for the general's attributes of loyalty, bravery, and virtue.

168 Tran Phu St. (on the corner of Nguyen Hue). Daily 8am–5pm.

Attractions Not on the World Cultural Heritage Ticket

Chinese Assembly Hall ★   This hall was built in 1740 as a meeting place for all of the resident Chinese, regardless of their native province.

64 Tran Phu St. Daily 8am–5pm.

Hainan Assembly Hall   The Chinese merchants from Hainan Island, in the South China Sea east of Danang, built this hall. Although it is newer than most and is mostly made of concrete, it is nice.

178 Nguyen Duy Hieu St. Free admission. Daily 8am–5pm.

House of Hoi An Traditional Handicraft ★★   This is basically a silk shop with an interesting gimmick: On the first floor you can see both a 17th-century silk loom and a working, machine-powered cotton one. On the second, you can see where silk comes from: There are trays of silkworms feeding, then a rack of worms incubating, and then a tub of hot water where the pupae's downy covering is rinsed off and then pulled, strand by strand, onto a large skein. It's cool. They have the best selection of silks, both fine and raw, in many colors and weights good for clothing and for home interiors.

41 Le Loi St. Daily 8am–5pm.

Central Market ★★   If you see one Vietnamese market, make it this one, by the river on the southeast side of the city. There are endless stalls of exotic foodstuffs and services, and a special big shed for silk tailoring at the east end (these

tailors charge much less than the ones along Le Loi). Check out the ladies selling spices—curries, chile powders, cinnamon, peppercorns, and especially saffron—at prices that are a steal in the West. But don't buy from the first woman you see; the stuff gets cheaper and cheaper the deeper you go into the market. Walk out to the docks to see activity there (best early in the morning), but be careful of fish flying through the air, and stand back from the furious bargaining (best before 7am).

At Nguyen Hue and Tran Phu sts. along the Thu Bon River.

HITTING THE BEACHES

Cua Dai beach★★ is an easy 20-minute bicycle ride from Hoi An through vistas of lagoons, rice paddies, and stilt houses. Simply follow Tran Hung Dao Street out of town for about 3km (2 miles). It will turn into Cau Dai Street halfway to the beach. The small beach seems crowded, with its orderly lines of deck chairs and endless child hawkers, but the surf and sand are good, and the setting, gazing at the nearby **Cham Islands,** is spectacular. The tour companies offer boat excursions in season (Mar–Sept) to the Cham Islands, a group of seven islands about 12.9km (8 miles) east of Hoi An; prices vary, but expect to pay about 30,000 VND (US$2). Contact the traveler cafes in town. There are also boat trips on the Thu Bon River.

SHOPPING

Southeast Asia is packed with would-be Buddhists, travelers on a real spiritual mission espousing lives of detachment from material desires. These folks usually walk away with just the "one suit, two shirts, trousers, and a tie package" when they leave Hoi An. Shopaholics wander the streets in a daze.

Hoi An is a silk mecca. The quality and selection are the best in the country, and you'll have more peace and quiet while fitting than in Hanoi. **Silk suits** are made to order within 24 hours for about US$35; **cashmere wool** is US$45. There are countless shops, and the tailoring is all about the same quality and fast. Overnight service is commonplace, and suits can be made in a matter of hours. A good way to choose a shop is by what you see out front—if you see a style you like, it'll help with ordering. Make sure you take the time to specify your style, down to the stitch (it can come back looking pretty cheap without specifics). Many people buy their desired silk in bulk to take to a tailor back home. For the best silk selection, go to no. 41 Le Loi, upstairs. You'll find great colors and styles.

Tran Phu Street is lined with **art galleries,** and the **pottery** and **carved wood** items near the market and on Tran Phu are unique and of good quality. Along the river, lots of places sell blue and white **ceramics.** However cumbersome your finds are, like those lovely **Chinese lanterns,** shopkeepers are masters at packing for travel and to fit in your luggage, and will do so before you've even agreed on a price or decided to buy. Haggle hard.

HOI AN AFTER DARK

For the most part, Hoi An is a town that sleeps early, but **Hai's Scout Café,** at 98 Nguyen Thai Hoc St. (✆ **0510/863-210**), is a popular late-night hangout for travelers, expats, and locals alike; it's a good crossroads with your standard bar drinks as well as cappuccino and espresso and some great baked treats. **Treat's Same Same Café,** at 158 Tran Phu St. (at the intersection with Le Loi; ✆ **0501/861-125**), is also usually hopping as late as it can and has a pool table and a guillotine (for show, of course). You can try the new **Same Same Not Different Café** on Phan Dinh Phung next to An Phu Tourist Co. (both locations are, in short, similar). **The Yellow Star Café,** at 73 Nguyen Thai Ho. (© **090/ 512-4422;** www.yellowstarcafe.com), serves up drinks, while the next-door **ChamPa,** 75 Nguyen Thai Hoc (© **0510/862-974;** anguyen1269@hotmail. com), serves good Italian but might be best enjoyed for comfy chairs, good wine, and a cozy, late-night atmosphere.

10 An Introduction to South Central Vietnam

South central Vietnam comprises the highlands, a land of rugged mountainous terrain mainly inhabited by members of Vietnam's ethnic minorities, and a stunning coastline bordered by small islands. Outside of two established resort destinations, **Nha Trang** and **Dalat,** the rest of the region is relatively unexplored by tourists. The area saw its share of fighting during the American war, though. Names like Buon Me Thot and Pleiku will undoubtedly ring a bell. Dalat, the top destination in the region, is popular with both Vietnamese and foreigners. It's a former French colonial outpost nestled among the hills, and it still retains a serene, formal air due to the overwhelming presence of historic buildings. Nha Trang, not far from Dalat but on the coast, is an easygoing seaside town that offers little but merrymaking, which is just as welcome in its own way.

GETTING THERE

BY PLANE   Both Nha Trang and Dalat are easily accessible by plane from Hanoi and Saigon, plus there's a nonstop flight between the two.

BY TRAIN   Nha Trang is a stop on the north-south railway line.

BY BUS/MINIVAN   Travel between the two major cities is a 6-hour ride by bus or minivan, easily organized through a local travel agency. Both towns are included on tourist cafe open-tours, except some tickets connect Ho Chi Minh City direct to Nha Trang, skipping Dalat. For details, see "Getting There," in individual town listings.

11 Nha Trang

Welcome to Vietnam's Ocean City. The capital of Khanh Hoa Province, Nha Trang has a full-time population that stands at about 200,000 people, but it far exceeds that with the heavy local and international tourist influx, especially in the summer months. While it's not a particularly charming town, its surf isn't bad and the beach is a breathtaking setting, with views of the more than 20 surrounding islands. There are a few very nice places to stay, and dining is about good fresh seafood.

Unfortunately, far from becoming a gracious hideaway, Nha Trang is becoming raucous. With the development of water slide parks and more young folk out "cruisin' the strip" of oceanside, palm-lined **Tran Phu Street** (on scooters, of course), it's starting to look like a spring-break town and might as well just go ahead. If you accept it as such, it's a fine place to spend 2 or 3 days frolicking in the surf, snorkeling and diving, or taking a cruise to the nearby islands.

Culturally, there are a few things to keep you occupied: The **Pasteur Institute** is here, offering glimpses into the life and work of one of Vietnam's most famous expats; there also are the interesting **Long Son Pagoda** and the well-preserved **Po Nagar Cham Temple.**

Off season (Oct–Mar), the surf is far too rough for swimming and sports, and you might want to rethink stopping at Nha Trang at all.

GETTING THERE

BY PLANE   Nha Trang is 1,350km (839 miles) from Hanoi and 450km (280 miles) from Saigon. Vietnam Airlines, with a local office at 91 Nguyen Thien Thuat St. (© **058/826-768**), operates daily flights from Saigon, Hanoi, and Dalat.

BY TRAIN   Nha Trang is a stop on the Reunification Express and is 12 hours from Ho Chi Minh on a soft sleeper for **US$18,** and 20 hours to Hanoi for US$67. Buy your ticket at least 1 day in advance at the Nha Trang train station, 26 Thai Nguyen St. (© **058/822-113**), or from any travel agent. There is a convenient overnight connection with Ho Chi Minh.

BY CAR/BUS   If you choose to drive from Hoi An to Nha Trang, it's a 10-hour trip and will cost you about US$120 by car. An arduous 12-hour bus or minibus ride with a cafe tour bus will cost only US$8. There are overnight schedules to Ho Chi Minh City and Hoi An; that's tiring, but it's a good option if you're short on time and don't want to waste your precious daylight hours looking out the window of a tour coach.

GETTING AROUND

The main street in Nha Trang, **Tran Phu,** runs along the coast for about 4km (2½ miles), and the hotels and beach attractions form the city center along its path. Attractions like the **Po Ngar Cham** towers are yet another mile out. **Biet Thu** Street runs perpendicular to Tran Phu and is where you'll find lots of smaller restaurants and tour operators (tourist cafes, etc.). Taxis are scarce and tend to congregate around the major hotels. **Renting a bike** from your hotel for US$1 to US$2 a day is a very good option, as are cyclos, which you can rent for US$3 per hour from your hotel. A **cyclo** across town will cost abt 10,000 VND (US66¢). In addition, **motorcycle taxis** can be had for 20,000 VND (US$1.33) per hour and an average 5,000 VND (US33¢) per trip in town (bargain hard).

VISITOR INFORMATION & TOURS

You'll more than likely end up booking tickets and boat tours through your hotel in Nha Trang, or from one of the many ticketing agencies around the town and along the beach. They all sell tickets to the same buses and boats, and prices are consistent (though it's good to compare).

One-day city tours visit Long Son Pagoda, Bao Dai's Villa, the Oceonographic Institute, and Cham Tower. Country tours take you to Ba Ho Waterfall and secluded Doc Let Beach, as well as Monkey Island. *Important:* No matter what anyone tells you, Monkey Island is not worth the trip, especially if you like animals and don't like wasting your time (you can just buy a "monkeys on bikes" postcard and be done with it).

Warning   Crime in Nha Trang

With droves of tourists wandering about, Nha Trang is notorious for petty crime, particularly the motorbike "snatch and run." With one guy on the back, perps cruise the beach and grab bags from the unsuspecting, so be careful on the road, whether walking or in a cyclo. Go by taxi at night, if possible. Be aware on the beach also because, unless you're at a private resort, you'll be hassled by sellers all the live-long day; say no, keep an eye on valuables, and leave what you can in a hotel safe.

Nha Trang

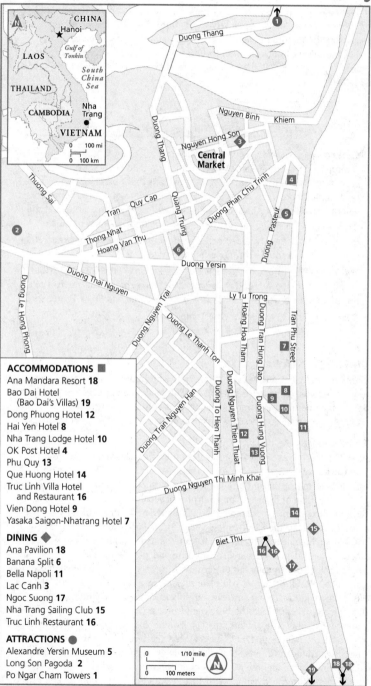

Inset map:

CHINA
★ Hanoi
Gulf of Tonkin
LAOS
South China Sea
THAILAND
CAMBODIA
Nha Trang
VIETNAM

0   100 mi
0   100 km

Main map labels:

Duong Thang
Nguyen Binh   Khiem
Nguyen Hong Son
Central Market
Duong Phan Chu Trinh
Pasteur
Duong
Duong Thang
Tran Quy Cap
Quang Trung
Thuong Sai
Thong Nhat
Hoang Van Thu
Duong Yersin
Duong Thai Nguyen
Duong Le Hong Phong
Duong Nguyen Trai
Ly Tu Trong
Hoang Hoa Tham
Duong Tran Hung Dao
Tran Phu Street
Duong Le Thanh Ton
Duong To Hien Thanh
Duong Nguyen Thien Thuat
Duong Hung Vuong
Duong Tran Nguyen Han
Duong Nguyen Thi Minh Khai
Biet Thu

ACCOMMODATIONS ■
Ana Mandara Resort **18**
Bao Dai Hotel
  (Bao Dai's Villas) **19**
Dong Phuong Hotel **12**
Hai Yen Hotel **8**
Nha Trang Lodge Hotel **10**
OK Post Hotel **4**
Phu Quy **13**
Que Huong Hotel **14**
Truc Linh Villa Hotel
  and Restaurant **16**
Vien Dong Hotel **9**
Yasaka Saigon-Nhatrang Hotel **7**

DINING ◆
Ana Pavilion **18**
Banana Split **6**
Bella Napoli **11**
Lac Canh **3**
Ngoc Suong **17**
Nha Trang Sailing Club **15**
Truc Linh Restaurant **16**

ATTRACTIONS ●
Alexandre Yersin Museum **5**
Long Son Pagoda **2**
Po Ngar Cham Towers **1**

0   1/10 mile
0   100 meters

Diving is quite popular in Nha Trang, and you can contact **Rainbow Diver** (ℂ **058/829-946**) or **Octopus Divers** (ℂ **058/810-629**) just about anywhere; 1-day **tour boats** to outlying islands can be booked in any hotel or agency.

For bus tickets and connection to Dalat, contact **TM Brother's Café,** at 22B Tran Hung Dao St. (ℂ **058/814-556**), or **Sinh Café III,** 10 Biet Thu St. (ℂ **058/ 811-981**).

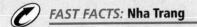

FAST FACTS: Nha Trang

Currency Exchange/Banks Vietcombank's local branch is located at 17 Quang Trung St. (ℂ **058/821-483**). Hours are 7:30 to 11am and 1:30 to 4pm. It offers the usual currency and traveler's check exchange and credit card cash withdrawal services. Along Biet Thu, some of the tour operators will cash traveler's checks and change money—rates are the same as at the bank (except for a small service fee), and they're open longer hours.

Internet/E-mail Biet Thu has a cluster of Internet cafes for between 200 and 300 VND (a couple cents) per minute usage.

Post Office/Mail The main branch is at 4 Le Loi St. (ℂ **058/823-866**). Hours are 6:30am to 10pm Monday to Saturday. DHL express mail services and Internet access are available. There is another branch at 50 Le Thanh Ton.

Telephone The city code for Nha Trang is 58.

WHERE TO STAY

There are many options in Nha Trang, but, with minor exception, the scene in town is dominated by faceless midend and substandard budget choices. Ana Mandara is the finest address, but there's lots of construction on nearby islands and more remote stretches of beach, so keep an eye peeled for new resort openings.

EXPENSIVE

Ana Mandara Resort ★★★   It's the little things that make this resort special: the native art and handiwork in the halls and rooms, the bowl with floating flowers in the bathroom, homemade bathroom cosmetics in cork-stop bottles, the basin of rainwater on your private veranda for rinsing sandy feet, the burning incense in the open-air lobby. This attention to detail, as well as the secluded layout of the "Vietnamese village" units, gives the whole resort a personable, small-scale feel. Each room has a rattan rising ceiling with wood beams. Rooms are good-size, with stylish furniture and tile floors; the staff makes the beds in the most exquisite fan pattern, with flowers artfully scattered and mosquito nets. Buddhist statues complete the amazing effect here. Each bathroom has a large window facing a private outdoor enclosure, like your own Zen garden. Thirty-six units face the beach, and others face a courtyard with exotic-plant landscaping (the plants are labeled, of course). The restaurant, Ana Pavilion (see "Where to Dine," below), has the best food and atmosphere in town. Ana Mandara means "beautiful home" in the Cham language; though it comes with a price tag, the hospitality and kindness extended here is quite sincere. Whether in the warm glow of floating candles in the pool at one of the informal cocktail parties, on one of the informative "market tours" with staff and guests, or out on the open water on a sailboat, you're sure to make friends and feel at home; you might never want to leave this seaside dreamscape.

Beachside, Tran Phu Blvd. ✆ **058/829-829.** Fax 058/829-629. www.sixsenses.com/ana-mandara. 68 units. Low season: US$175–US$225 double/villa; US$330 suite villa. High season: US$199–US$260 double/villa; US$362 suite villa. AE, DC, MC, V. **Amenities:** Restaurant; 2 bars; beautiful outdoor pool w/hot tub; tennis court; fine health club; Jacuzzi; sauna; cyclo rental (US$3 per hr.); sailboat, runabout, wave runner, and wind-surfer rental; beach rental; small air-conditioned library w/games; concierge; tour desk and in-house tour pro-grams (can arrange diving [w/Octopus Divers]); nice business center; boutique shopping; 24-hr. room service; massage; laundry; dry cleaning; nonsmoking rooms. *In room:* A/C, satellite TV, dataport, minibar, fridge, coffeemaker, hair dryer, safe IDD phone, nice touches like slippers and umbrella.

Yasaka Saigon-Nhatrang Hotel ★★

On the main strip and looking out over the ocean blue, this 3-year-old Japan/Vietnam joint venture bridges the gap in upper-end accommodation in NhaTrang. Short of the finer rooms at the Ana Mandara, the suites are undoubtedly the best in town, with good amenities and incredible corner views of this lovely beach town. All rooms have good views, some with balconies. The lowest standard, the superior, is quite comfortable and large, if bland; the deluxe room, an upgraded version of the superior and on higher floors, is the best bet for atmosphere, comfort, and price. Everything is done in cream or tan carpet, and rooms have flower-print spreads (no slippery polyester); the large, clean tile bathrooms are homey. Service is friendly, there are lots of good dining options on-site (the Red Onion is a local favorite), the rooftop pool is inviting, and it's just a short hop across busy Tran Phu Street to the beach. A nice breakfast buffet is included.

18 Tran Phu St., Nha Trang. ✆ **058/820-090** or 058/825-227. Fax 058/820-000. www.yasanhatrang.com. 201 units. US$98 superior; US$118 deluxe; US$158 senior deluxe; US$178 executive; US$198–US$350 suite. AE, MC, V. **Amenities:** 4 restaurants; bar; night club; karaoke; liver-shape rooftop pool w/ocean view; roof-top tennis court; small health club; Jacuzzi by pool; sauna; all rentals available; Saigontourist tour desk; car rental; business center; 24-hr. room service; massage; laundry. *In room:* A/C, satellite TV w/in-house movies, minibar, fridge, upper standards w/coffeemakers, safe, IDD phone.

MODERATE

Bao Dai Hotel (Bao Dai's Villas) ★★

Next to the Ana Mandara, the Villas are the most atmospheric place to stay in Nha Trang. Built in 1923 as a seaside resort for then-Emperor Bao Dai, the hotel is a cluster of plain colonial-style buildings set high on an oceanside hill south of town, so far south that you're in the next town, really. There's an interesting Gothic quality to the place, though, and one could certainly imagine a king wandering the promontory at night, watching the hotel's lighthouse scan the sea and sky, and worrying about the loss of his kingdom. In fact, Bao Dai's very room is the master suite and makes for a memorable stay. The less expensive rooms are musty monk's cells, but the Stan-dard 1 rooms, in their own villa, have high ceilings and large, shuttered windows overlooking the coast: They're a good bet. The more top-end rooms vary; some are quite spectacular and others are dingy, but all are palatial in size, even if they're wanting in amenities (the furniture can't keep up with the space). The bathrooms are nothing special but are sizable and clean, with bathtubs. The two deluxe suites in the villa closest to the promontory's tip are not particularly luxe but are eerily charming (ever wanted to sleep in a former king's lighthouse room overlooking the South China Sea?). Some of the buildings have big, funky, winding wooden staircases and rooftop access. The restaurant, in its own build-ing, has a nice buffet breakfast and delicious evening meals with a set menu or a la carte dishes. The staff is extremely affable and can help with any arrange-ments, including discount car and motorbike rental. They arrange private boat trips; prices start at US$10 and go up according to destination and number of people (also seat-in-boat tours).

Cau Da, Vinh Nguyen/Nha Trang. ⓒ **058/590-147** or 058/590-148. Fax 058/590-146. www.vngold.com/nt/baodai/. 45 units. US$25–US$50 standards 3 and 2; US$50 standard 1; US$70 superior; US$80 suite. MC, V. **Amenities:** Restaurant; bicycle/motorbike rental; in-house tour desk for island/snorkeling trips; car rental; souvenir shop; limited room service; laundry; Internet terminal (500 VND/US3¢ per min.). *In room:* A/C, satellite TV, minibar, fridge, hair dryer, IDD phone.

Nha Trang Lodge Hotel ⓡ

The 3-year-old lodge calls itself a "business hotel," and indeed it is a well-run and accommodating 12-story high-rise. Average-size rooms are chain-hotel style, with clean, new carpet; floral bedspreads; and modern furniture that matches. It's all quite pleasing, solid, and comfortable, particularly the beds. The bathrooms are a nice size, with marble finishes. There are in-room safes and big TVs, too. Spring for the US$95 ocean-view rooms with balcony (on an upper floor away from street noise, if possible). The staff is professional, and this comfortable seaside address covers all the bases with amenities and services. It's a nice, uninspired, affordable standard here and a bit like the Yasaka's (above) younger, less-accomplished brother. Don't miss a meal in the popular outdoor seafood barbecue area: You'll find great food and atmosphere.

42 Tran Phu St. ⓒ **058/810-500** or 058/810-900. Fax 058/828-800. www.nt-lodge.com. 121 units. US$50–US$95 double; US$145 suite. AE, MC, V. **Amenities:** 2 restaurants; bar; swimming pool; tennis court; small fitness center; sauna; tour desk; car rental; business center; souvenir shops in lobby; salon; 24-hr. room service; massage; laundry; dry cleaning; banquet/meeting rooms. *In room:* A/C, satellite TV, minibar, fridge, IDD phone.

Hai Yen Hotel ⓡ

The Hai Yen is owned by the Khanh Hoa tourism company, the same folks who own Vien Dong (below), and the two are virtually indistinguishable. It's next door, and they share recreational facilities, most notably the large pool in the central courtyard where you can swim laps, learn the basics of scuba, or frolic the night away at the poolside bar. The Hai Yen has outdoor hallways and an open, airy feeling, but the unfortunate blue indoor/outdoor carpeting lends a strange aura of an aging public high school. The super-basic rooms here are clean and, well, that's about it. Plastic furniture and plastic flowers round out features like old carpeting and cracked walls; suites are even more of the same but have bathtubs. The price is right, though, and it's a popular spot for large tour groups. Avoid a room directly facing noisy Tran Phu Street.

40 Tran Phu St. ⓒ **058/822-828** or 058/822-974. Fax 058/821-902. www.nhatrangtourist.com.vn 110 units. US$22–US$30 single; US$26–US$35 double; US$45 suite (tax incl.). AE, MC, V. **Amenities:** Shared w/Vien Dong (below). Large restaurant and bar (open-air at poolside and open late); big outdoor pool w/fun slide; tennis; sauna; all rentals available; tour desk; business center (Internet is 500 VND per min.); limited room service; massage; laundry; dry cleaning. *In room:* A/C, satellite TV, minibar, fridge, safe, IDD phone.

Vien Dong Hotel

If you're on a tour, you're probably booked here. It's big and blah and impersonal, but it's a comfortable three-star with all the amenities, and having lots of people around somehow helps. Rooms have basic blue carpet, nice yellow bedspreads, and simple wood furniture, but they aren't especially large. Mattresses are sturdy foam. Bathrooms are clean and tidy tile but have no counters. A college dorm room comes to mind. Suites have almost unbearably ugly plastic furniture and flowers, although they also have bathtubs. There is an inviting outdoor restaurant featuring nightly music and a cultural dance show; the pool, shared with Hai Yen (above), is big. You're sure to meet other travelers here, and the general atmosphere is friendly. The staff is kind and, though taxed by the large groups coming in and out, will do its best to help, whether that means sending a fax, changing money, or arranging onward travel.

1 Tran Hung Dao St. ℭ **058/821-606** or 058/821-608. Fax 058/821-912. www.nhatrangtourist.com. 103 units. US$19–US$26 single; US$22–US$30 double; US$52 suite. AE, MC, V. **Amenities:** Shared w/Hai Yen (above). Large restaurant; bar (open-air at poolside and open late); big outdoor pool w/fun slide; tennis; sauna; all rentals available; tour desk; business center (Internet is 500 VND per min.); limited room service; massage; laundry; dry cleaning. *In room:* A/C, satellite TV, minibar, fridge, hair dryer, IDD phone.

Que Huong Hotel   Another Khanh Hoa Tourism property, this 3-year-old hotel is a bright, bland, four-story block just across the street from the beach. Set back far enough from the road to be quiet and close enough to be convenient, it has rooms around the large, central courtyard and pool. All are average-size, with clean but worn carpets, warm pastel tones, nice padded wooden furniture, and balconies: It makes an overall good impression. There are signs of wear here and there, like crumbly tile bathrooms, but suites are huge and are a nice option for families (some even have two bathrooms). This is the land of the tour group, though, and the staff is not versed in individual graces; in the high season, the front desk is run like a busy Manhattan Deli: "Next!" That said, it's affordable, clean, and close to the beach, and the pool is quite lovely. There are capable travel agents in the lobby and nice amenities, like the nice Asian/Continental restaurant, small pool hall, and fun little disco.

60 Tran Phu Blvd. ℭ **058/825-047** or 058/827-365. Fax 058/825-344. www.nhatrangtourist.com.vn. 56 units. US$50–US$60 single/double deluxe; US$100 suite. MC, V. **Amenities:** Restaurant; bar/club and karaoke lounge; nice outdoor pool (courtyard); tennis; sauna; billiards; tour desk; car rental; small business center; salon; massage; laundry. *In room:* A/C, satellite TV, minibar, fridge, hair dryer, IDD phone, complimentary water.

INEXPENSIVE

OK Post Hotel ⊛   This is a decent, unassuming budget hotel, nothing more, but it's one of the best options in this category. The large rooms have old tile floors, wooden wainscoting, and carved wood furniture. Bathrooms are large and in good condition, with shower-in-room guesthouse fixtures; only the ground-floor rooms have bathtubs. Beds are adorned with old red blankets, the kind your grandma would drag out of the linen closet when you visited. Some rooms have funky floor-to-ceiling alpine murals, and there are glassed-in sitting areas at the end of each hall; it's a bit surreal, really, and basic but clean. The neat facade of this white colonial mock-up faces the ocean on a quiet stretch of Tran Phu Street, just a short walk away from the town center (out of the fray, but still convenient). Try for a room facing the beach. Other than Internet access, there are no services and the staff speaks little English. Rate includes breakfast.

2 Le Loi St. ℭ **058/821-252** or 058/821-250. Fax 058/824-205. posthotel@dng.vnn.vn. 20 units. US$18–US$22 double (promotional and seasonal rates available). MC, V. **Amenities:** Restaurant; will gladly arrange any rentals or travel; laundry; Internet; international phone-card pay phone in lobby. *In room:* A/C, satellite TV, minibar, fridge, IDD phone.

Dong Phuong Hotel ⊛   It's function, not form, as a rule in this motel-style block that typifies the budget accommodation in town (this is one of three properties of the same name and standard in Nha Trang). Rooms are bright but spartan, with spotless tile and not much more than a bed and a good-size, shower-in-room style of bathroom. Some rooms have a good city view, and if you're lucky, you'll be blessed with a classy nude done in painted tile mosaic in the bathroom (the only decoration I could find throughout). The family rooms are large and a good value, and the staff is indifferent, at best—but, again, it's function, not form.

103 Nguyen Thien Thuat St., Nha Trang. © 058/825-986 or 058/828-247. Fax 058/825-986. dongphuongnt@ dng.vnn.vn. 30 units. US$15–US$20 double; US$30–US$40 deluxe (family). MC, V. **Amenities:** Restaurant; will arrange tours; laundry. *In room:* A/C, satellite TV, fridge, hair dryer, IDD phone.

Truc Linh Villa Hotel and Restaurant   If you like the Ana Mandara (see above) but don't like the price tag, check out the "Villa," where a savvy, young former employee of the resort applies what he learned. The rooms are in a court-yard just off the busy backpacker street (Biet Thu), and everything from the gar-den to the basic setup of terra-cotta floor, high ceiling, and comfortable balconies is the Ana Mandara done in a nearly exacting miniature, low-end replica. The folks at the Ana Mandara take it as a compliment. Just like the pop-ular resort, you'll find details like a small rock-garden enclosure behind glass just outside of the shower, large ceramic pottery in the rooms, and even small details like cork-stopped bottles for shampoo. It's kind of a fun, affordable break from the usual minihotel, but be sure you know that the similarity to the Ana Man-dara stops at vague copies of decor. This is just a dolled-up budget choice, but it's friendly and fun.

21 Biet Thu St., Nha Trang. © 058/820-089 or 058/820-1259. 9 units. US$10–US$30 double. No credit cards. **Amenities:** Restaurant; bar. *In room:* A/C, TV.

Phu Quy ★★   This is the granddaddy of NhaTrang's many minihotels, and if you're looking for your basic "cheap and best" accommodations, you can't go wrong here. The Phu Quy is an interesting conglomeration of three properties, and some of the passages between buildings require you to duck through the most unlikely doors. It's Chinese-style business growth in action (start small, go big), so rooms vary; smile and ask for something nice, and be sure to bargain a bit. All of the buildings sport small, bright, and very clean rooms with brand-new plastic furniture. The beds are comfortable and bathrooms are small, with shower-in-room facilities. There are no views to speak of, but go for the top floors to escape street noise. Of course, that means climbing lots of stairs. This place has no amenities whatsoever, but breakfasts are good and cheap, and, of course, the hotel will book tickets. This is backpacker central and an ant hill of activity, and that, along with the price, makes it worth a stay. The large, shaded penthouse area has hammocks and lawn chairs, and is a good place to relax (they'll deliver food to you there, too). It is family-run, and owner Mr. Quy is as nice as they come.

54 Hung Vuong St. © 058/810-609 or 058/816-444. Fax 058/812-954. phuquyhotel@dng.vnn.vn. 47 units. US$6–US$16 double w/fan; US$8–US$25 w/A/C. Visa accepted (4% commission). **Amenities:** Restaurant/ bar; can arrange tours and any rentals; laundry. *In room:* Some A/C, some w/fan, some w/TV and phone.

WHERE TO DINE
EXPENSIVE
Ana Pavilion ★★★ ASIAN/CONTINENTAL   Without question the finest dining on this beautiful stretch of coast, the Ana Pavilion is the jewel in the crown of the Ana Mandara resort and serves exquisite food in elegant, natural surroundings. Whether you're on the oceanfront veranda, under a canvas umbrella in the courtyard, or eating by candlelight over the open ocean on the seaside jetty, the location alone is breathtaking. The food is creatively prepared and beautifully presented, and portions are healthy. With an evolving list of local and seasonal specials, the menu is a nice East-West fusion, with anything from sandwiches made from ingredients like bread baked on-site and imported cheese or imported Aussie steaks, to local favorites like banana flower salads and even sushi done to a T for the many Japanese guests. Don't miss the seafood hot-pot

served in a large, coal-fired crock and brimming with the catch of the day delicately stewed with vegetables. There is an excellent daily lunch buffet, and evening set menus are a great value. This is the best choice for romantic ambience and fine dining.

Tran Phu Blvd. (at the Ana Mandara Resort). © 058/829-829. Main courses US$6–US$16; prix-fixed menus US$15–US$22. AE, MC, V. Daily 6am–11pm.

MODERATE

Ngoc Suong ★★ SEAFOOD   Nha Trang has dozens of good seafood restaurants, but this one leads the pack. Whether in the very pleasant thatched outdoor pavilion or the vaguely nautical, softly lit interior, it's "seafood as you like it" served by a helpful, friendly staff. Whole fish and crustaceans can be chosen by pointing in the large tank and smiling greedily; the day's catch, including shrimp and crab, is ordered by the pound, grilled, fried, or boiled with basic spices like tamarind or pepper and lemon. The oysters, if they have them, are small but succulent. The name of the restaurant refers to a delicate marinated whitefish salad, one of the specialties and a great appetizer. This is a popular local and expat favorite.

(Might be moving soon, so call ahead.) 16 Tran Quang Khai St. © 058/827-030. Main courses 20,000–240,000 VND (US$1.33–US$18). No credit cards. Daily 10am–midnight.

Nha Trang Sailing Club ★ VIETNAMESE/CONTINENTAL   Stop by this oceanside open-air bar/restaurant for a real Western breakfast, if nothing else. A good bet is the pancakes, not greasy (as usual) and served with real butter. There are other Western standbys, such as macaroni and cheese and hamburgers (tasty, if not authentic), as well as the usual Nha Trang seafood selections. The setting, in a large hut just off the beach, can't be beat, and there are now different "stations" for dining here, including good Japanese eats, an Italian menu, and even an Indian menu. You can lounge on the beach and buy or swap a book from the well-stocked rack, and book a boat tour or a day of scuba with Rainbow Divers. The bar swings at night.

72–74 Tran Phu St. © 058/826-528. Main courses 30,000–125,000 VND (US$2–US$8.33). No credit cards. Daily 7am–11pm. Bar open until 2am.

Bella Napoli ★★ ITALIAN   It's all about the cheese here, and I'm talking homemade mozzarella served atop a fine thin-crust pizza done in a wood-fire oven with any topping you can imagine. Plus, you'll get great views of the beach. What else is there to say? Bring some friends, choose a nice wine, and enjoy. It's not just pizza, either, but a roster of specials from northern Italy. The effusive Italian proprietor always has some good daily specials and will keep you laughing with her good stories. Pizza by the South China Sea, anyone? Why not?

(Beachside, across from the Nha Trang Lodge.) Tran Phu St. © 058/829-621. Main courses US$4.33–US$8 No credit cards. Daily 8:30am–10pm.

INEXPENSIVE

Lac Canh ★★ CHINESE/VIETNAMESE   Two words: grilled shrimp. The Chinese-influenced Vietnamese cuisine here is all about ingredients, so go for the basics: fresh seafood in a light marinade that you grill yourself on a rustic, cast-iron brazier. The place is packed with locals and tourists. The new location is a little more airy, but try to sit outdoors because the atmosphere is smoky. This is definitely the local "greasy spoon," and it makes for a fun evening.

11 Hang Ca St. © 058/821-391. Main courses US$1.24–US$7.93. No credit cards. Daily 7am–11pm.

Truc Linh Restaurant ⍟ VIETNAMESE   An eclectic menu here has anything from the backpacker standbys of fried rice and noodles to sirloin steak and T-bone: It kind of runs the gamut. There's a seafood smorgasboard out front from which you can choose your own jumbo shrimp, crab, squid or fresh fish of the day and then have it weighed and cooked to your taste. They've got fondue and clay-pot specials, barbecued beef on clay tile, and rice-paper spring rolls with shrimp that are delicious.

21 Biet Thu St., Nha Trang. ℂ **058/820-089** or 058/820-1259. Main courses US80¢–US$10. Daily 6am–11pm.

Banana Split ⍟ VIETNAMESE/WESTERN   Banana Split is traveler central, the place to come for a snack and to meet fellow wanderers. With good burgers, soup, and sandwiches, this popular little storefront serves up good treats from home for next to nothing. The owners and staff are very friendly, the list of fruit shakes is as long as a sunny beachside day, and the ice cream is aces. Go for the gargantuan banana split. You're sure to meet other travelers and get the scoop on what's new in town or out on the road.

58 Quang Trung St. ℂ **058/829-115.** Main courses US66¢–US$4. No credit cards. Daily 7am–11pm.

ATTRACTIONS

Po Ngar Cham Towers ⍟   This standing temple complex was built from the 8th to 13th centuries to honor goddess Yang Ino Po Ngar, mother of the kingdom. It was built over a wooden temple burned by the Javanese in A.D. 774. There were originally 10 structures; 4 remain. The main tower, or Po Ngar Kalan, is one of the tallest Cham structures ever built. Its square tower and three-story cone roof are exemplary of Cham style. It has more remaining structural integrity than many sites, giving you a good idea of how it might have looked in all its glory. In the vestibule can be seen two pillars of carved epitaphs of Cham kings, and in the sanctuary there are two original carved doors. The statue inside is of the goddess Bharagati, a.k.a. Po Ngar, on her lotus throne. It was carved in 1050. The Po Ngar temples are still in use by local Buddhists, and the altars and smoking incense add to the intrigue of the architecture. Detracting from the whole experience are kitsch stands and endless hawkers.

Some advice: Go by taxi. A bike, cyclo, or motorbike ride along the truck-heavy road out of town is dangerous and unpleasant.

2km (1¼ miles) out of the city center at 2 Thang 4, at the end of Xom Bong Bridge. Admission 10,000 VND (US66¢). Daily 7:30am–5pm.

Long Son Pagoda ⍟   The main attraction at this circa-1930s pagoda is the huge white Buddha on the hillside behind, the symbol of Nha Trang. Around the base of the Buddha are portraits of monks who immolated themselves to protest against the corrupt Diem regime. After climbing the numerous flights of stairs, you'll also be rewarded with a bird's-eye view of Nha Trang.

Thai Nguyen St. Daily 8am–5pm.

Alexandre Yersin Museum ⍟⍟   Here you can get an inkling of the work of one of Vietnam's greatest heroes. Swiss doctor Yersin founded Dalat, isolated a plague-causing bacteria, and researched agricultural methods and meteorological forecasting, all to the great benefit of the Vietnamese. He founded the institute in 1895. On display are his desk, overflowing library, and scientific instruments.

In the Pasteur Institute, 10 Tran Phu St. ℂ **058/822-355.** Admission 15,000 VND (US$1). Mon–Sat 8–11am and 2–4:30pm.

Hon Mieu Island The largest of the surrounding islands, Hon Mieu has a fishing village, Bai Soi, that isn't very active any longer but that features many seafood restaurants. There is also an aquarium of sorts, consisting of a lake divided into three sections: one for ornamental fish, one for edible fish, and one for carnivorous varieties. There's also a wharf to stand on. A trip here is good in combination with other outlying islands.

The folks at the Bao Dai Villa (© 058/881-049) operate good trips to all the islands. Also contact the Nha Trang Sailing Club (© 058/826-528).

SPORTS & OUTDOOR ACTIVITIES

Diving is big in Nha Trang, in season (Mar–Sept). There are a number of professionally run operations; whether you're a beginner or an expert, make your choice based on safety more than anything. **Rainbow Divers** has taken advertising to the level of pollution in Nha Trang, with seemingly every storefront claiming a connection, but whatever your belief is in truth in advertising, these guys are some of the best in town and you can book anywhere: Try the **Nha Trang Sailing Club** (© 058/826-528; see "Where to Dine," above), or call © 058/829-946 (or visit www.divevietnam.com). For a guaranteed safe and fun time, try the folks at **Octopus Diving,** 62 Tran Phu St. (© 058/810-629; octopusdivingclub@yahoo.com), where the expert, mostly expat staff can devise dives for any and all (you can also contact them through the **Ana Mandara**).

You can also take a **boat cruise** to some of the 20 surrounding islands. For many years, Nha Trang was famed for the rowdy day trips of "Mama Hahn," but she's temporarily out of service and her antics are sorely missed. However, there has been a shift in Nha Trang from the kind of "daytime raves" popular in the past. There are any number of operators running; **Mama Linh** (© 058/ 826-693) is just one of many, including **Sinh Café** and **TM Brothers** (see the listing of travel agents above). The going rate is US$6 per day and includes 9am hotel pick-up and afternoon drop-off. It's a mellow day of motoring through some lovely bays to three different islands, and you're guaranteed some snorkeling, a big feast for lunch; beer and drinks are available all day (at one point, you can swim out to a floating bar for complimentary grape wine) and there's a great spread of fruit in the afternoon. The tour terminates at a fish farm and a small harbor where you can rent a traditional bamboo-basket boat to paddle about. It's all as friendly and laid back as it sounds, and the party boat scene has been toned down in recent years. Just about everyone in town will want to book you on one of these tours, so ask at any hotel front desk and be sure to nail down all specifics (meals, transport included, etc.).

Bao Dai Villa's (058/590-147) is a good bet for **private boat charters** to nearby islands, where you can witness and learn about local trades like boat building, pottery making, and weaving, or go for specialized fishing or snorkeling tours.

For **sailing,** contact the **Nha Trang Sailing Club** (© 058/826-528) or the **Ana Mandara** (© 058/829-829). Go for a Hobie Cat if it's available and hire a captain if you are not experienced; the strong ocean breezes and choppy waters make for a memorable sail. Runabouts and jet-skis are also available.

NHA TRANG AFTER DARK

Nha Trang has a few lively beachfront bars where tourists congregate to swap stories. The **Nha Trang Sailing Club,** at 72–74 Tran Phu St. across from the Hai Yen Hotel, has open-air bamboo huts and a dance scene on some nights until late. **Crazy Kim Bar,** at 19 Biet Thu St. in the backpacker area (© 058/816-072), is open late and asks customers to "Be hot. Be cool. Be crazy. Just be." There are many versions of that walking around this place, and it's popular with the diving crowd and the few expats in town.

12 Dalat

Known as "Le Petit Paris" by the early builders and residents of this hillside resort town, Dalat is still considered a kind of luxury retreat for city dwellers and tourists tired out from the steamy coastline in Vietnam. Here you can have a game of golf on one of the finer courses in Indochina, visit some beautiful temples, and enjoy the town's honeymoon atmosphere and delightfully hokey tourist sites.

At 1,500m (4,900 ft.), Dalat is mercifully cool year-round—there's no air-conditioning here—and is a unique blend of pastoral hillside Vietnam and European alpine resort. Alexander Yersin, the Swiss geologist who first traipsed across this pass, established the town in 1897 as a resort for French commanders weary of the Vietnamese tropics. In and around town are still scattered the relics of colonial mansions, as well as some serene pagodas in a lovely natural setting; you've escaped from big-city Vietnam for real. A few ethnic minorities, including the Lat and the Koho, live in and around the picturesque hills surrounding Dalat, and you can visit their small villages.

Dalat is the no. 1 resort destination for Vietnamese couples getting married or honeymooning. If the lunar astrological signs are particularly good, it's not unusual to see 10 or so wedding parties in a single day. Many of the local scenic spots, like the Valley of Love and Lake of Sighs, pander to the giddy couples. The waterfalls are swarming with vendors, costumed "bears," and "cowboys" complete with sad-looking horses and fake pistols. A carnival air prevails. It's tacky, but it's one of those "so bad that it's good" kind of tacky that's kind of fun. You'll also get a chance to travel, lodge, and dine with Vietnamese on holiday, a rare opportunity.

GETTING THERE

BY PLANE   The only direct flights to Dalat are from Ho Chi Minh City (flight time: 50 min). In Dalat, call to confirm your ticket, or direct inquiries to Vietnam Airlines at © **063/822-895.** Departing, you'll pay an airport tax of 20,000 VND (US$1.66). A taxi from the airport to the city is US$3 and takes about 30 minutes.

BY BUS/CAR   Dalat is the first stop on the "open tour" bus from Ho Chi Minh City; the next connection is Nha Trang to the north. From Ho Chi Minh City, it's a 7-hour trip for US$5. From Nha Trang, it's the same: US$5 for the 7-hour ride.

From Saigon, you can hire a private car for the trip and save about an hour. In Ho Chi Minh City, call **Dalattourist,** 80 Truong Dinh St., District 1 (© **08/823-7176**), to rent a car. The charge is about US$100 for the 4-hour trip. If you're coming from Nha Trang, the trip time is about the same, but the cost is US$80 per car. Make your booking from the Dalattourist head office in Dalat by calling © **063/822-520.**

VISITOR INFORMATION & TOURS

- **Dalattourist** 02 Nguyen Thai Hoc St., on the lake at the Thanh Thuy restaurant (© **063/822-520;** fax 063/834-144; www.dalattourist.com), is the local favorite for higher-end tours and is a good place to go to hire a car and driver for the day (a nice way to see Dalat).

- **Phat Tire Ventures,** 73 Truong Cong Dinh (𝄐 **063/829-422;** fax 063/829-422; www.phattireventures.com), offers a unique ecotourist option in Dalat. Contact Brian and Kim (young U.S. expats), who can arrange anything from day treks to jungle expeditions, mountain biking (they have a stable of top-quality bikes and hold daily clinics), rock climbing, repelling, or canyoning. Daily rates for most activities start at US$19 and include lunch, transport, and a knowledgeable guide. Safety and environmental stewardship are their trademark. They also book classic tours through their affiliate, **Dalat Tours.**
- **Sinh Café,** 4A Bui Thi Xuan St. (𝄐 **063/822-663**), has an information and tour office adjacent to Trung Cang, the company's budget accommodation (see the section on accommodations below). Standard services here are arrangements for the open tour and the budget countryside and city tours.
- **TM Brothers,** 02 Nguyen Chi Thanh St (𝄐 **063/828-282**), can book standard budget tours for you from its office on "cafe street" (overlooking the market). These guys will pick you up at your hotel and are very accommodating and professional for their prices.

GETTING AROUND

There are no cyclos in Dalat, but walking is very pleasant in the cool air. You can catch most of the city sites, like the market and the lake, **on foot.**

Dalat is a good place to rent a **motorbike,** cheapest with the street-side places on Nguyen Thi Minh Khai (between the market and the lake), for about US$3 per day (US$4–US$5 from hotels and cafes). Be sure to check the brakes, and be sure the horn is working because you should beep-beep all the way, especially when passing or on curves. The hillside, windy roads will have you feeling like you're "born to be wild," if you can forget that you're riding the motorcycle equivalent of a hair dryer. This is the best way to get to all the funky sites outside the city.

Another option is to get a **motorbike with a driver** for the day (about US$1–US$2 per hr., or fix a rate for the day and the destinations), or you can **rent a car** with a driver (about US$25 a day with Dalattourist). Because most sites are outside city limits, it makes sense to take a **half- or full-day tour** with **Dalattourist** or through your hotel or **tourist cafe.**

𝄐 FAST FACTS: Dalat

Banks/Currency Exchange Industrial & Commercial Bank at 46 Hoa Binh St. (𝄐 **063/822-495**), offers the best rate, but most hotels offer comparable exchange services for a small fee. There is no ATM service in Dalat.

Internet/E-mail The most accessible Internet cafe in town is on the hill that overlooks the main market street—**Viet Hung Internet Café,** 7 Nguyen Chi Thanh (𝄐 **063/835-737;** dhoaithu@hcm.vnn.vn). It charges VND 5,000 (US33¢) per hour, but there are many scattered about.

Post Office/Mail The main office is located at 14 Tran Phu St., across from the Novotel, and is open Monday to Saturday from 6:30am to 9:30pm.

Telephone The area code for Dalat is 63.

WHERE TO STAY

With a long history as a popular resort area for both foreigners and Vietnamese, Dalat offers some nice lodging choices. There are plenty of minihotels, but they're not of the quality you might find in Hanoi, for example. You'll note that no Dalat hotel has air-conditioning; with the year-round temperate weather, none is needed.

VERY EXPENSIVE

Sofitel Dalat Palace ✿✿✿   Built in 1922 and once the Langbian Palace of Bau Dai, this recently renovated beauty, with its understated old-world opulence, is one of the finest five-star choices in all of Indochina. From the huge fireplace and mosaic floor in the lobby to the hanging tapestries, 500 oil reproductions of classic European art, and thick swag curtains, it's a French country chateau with a Southeast Asian colonial flair. The large rooms, with glossy original wood floors, are finished with fine fabrics and throw rugs, and all beds are crowned with an ornate wooden housing for a mosquito net (purely for decoration). The bathrooms feature hand-painted tiles and large, claw-foot bathtubs with antique-style fixtures. Genuine antique French clocks and working reproduction telephones complete the picture, yet nothing feels overdone. Every room has a foyer and a fireplace. Lake-view rooms open to a huge shared veranda with deck chairs. The high, high ceilings and huge corridors with hanging lamps contribute to the palatial feeling. Service is superb. All in all, this is an exquisite place that should not be missed. Le Rabelais Restaurant serves mediocre French food in an exquisite setting, but Café de La Poste is good for lunch and snacks. The whole place is the brainchild of the late Larry Hillblom, the enigmatic American entrepreneur and co-owner of DHL who invested heavily in the property out of love and generosity as much as anything. He is still remembered and revered by the many who knew him; Larry's Bar, a great little grotto establishment with a pool table, darts, and good pub grub, does his memory proud.

12 Tran Phu St. ✆ **800/221-4542** or 063/825-444. Fax 063/825-666. www.accorhotels-asia.com. 43 units. US$169–US$214 double; US$319–US$414 suite. Extra bed US$40. Ask about discounts and specials. AE, DC, MC, V. **Amenities:** 2 restaurants; 3 bars; tennis; golf (can arrange); all rentals available; kids' playroom and outdoor playground; concierge; tour desk; business center; shopping boutique; limited room service; laundry; dry cleaning; horseback riding and carriage rental; hotel history corner. *In room:* Satellite TV, minibar, fridge, hair dryer, safe, IDD phone.

EXPENSIVE

Novotel Dalat Hotel ✿✿   This is the scaled-down companion hotel to the Sofitel Palace. It was renovated in 1997 from a 1932 building that was originally the Du Parc hotel, and a lovely job was done of it. The lobby has a very interesting open-face wrought-iron lift. The smallish rooms have attractive historic touches: glossy wood floors, tastefully understated wood furniture, and molded high ceilings. A superior room (the lowest standard) is a bit cramped and not the greatest value (US$119), but deluxe rooms are clean, compact, and classy and worth the upgrade (US$139). Everything is tidy and convenient, with nice local artwork throughout and a homey warmth in tone and atmosphere. The bathrooms are nice-size, efficient, and spotless, with sleek granite and dark wooden trim. The staff is businesslike and friendly, and the Novotel shares fine amenities with neighboring Dalat Palace (above).

7 Tran Phu St. ✆ **800/221-4542** or 063/825-777. Fax 063/825-888. www.accorhotels-asia.com. 144 units US$119–US$139 double; US$189 suite. Discounts and specials are common. AE, MC, V. **Amenities:** 2 restaurants; 3 bars; tennis; golf (can arrange); all rentals available; concierge; tour desk; business center; shopping. *In room:* Satellite TV, minibar, fridge, coffeemaker, safe, IDD phone.

MODERATE

Golf III Hotel ⭐

The Golf is a three-star chain hotel and a good choice in Dalat (local Golf I and II are low-end versions). Large rooms here have tacky purplish upholstery and some gawdy carved wood detailing, and are frayed just a tiny bit around the edges, but they're perfectly clean and comfortable. It's worth springing for a deluxe room (US$50) with parquet floors rather than carpet and larger bathrooms with big sunken tubs; this is a honeymoon hotel, after all. In fact, the constant stream of Vietnamese wedding parties in and out lends a welcome festive air to the proceedings, and this hotel is at its best when trying to be a little more than it is; blooming bonsais, overstuffed chairs, and a glitzy sheen over the lobby area stand testament. If that's not your thing, consider staying elsewhere. Although the hotel is near the market and not far from the golf course, it is set back from the road and the rooms are relatively quiet. Suites and VIP rooms come in all shapes, but all are large and there are some interesting options. Amenities are just basic, like a rooftop steam, sauna, and massage area, and the lobby restaurant serves a fine breakfast. As the name betrays, the Golf properties all have an arrangement with the local course; this hotel's just seems to be the most economical. The staff seems happy you're here.

4 Nguyen Thi Minh Khai St. (near the market). ✆ 063/826-042 or 063/826-049. Fax 063/830-396. 78 units. US$45–US$60 double; US$70–US$100 suite. AE, MC, V. **Amenities:** Restaurant; bar; golf; sauna; steam; tour desk (work w/Dalat Tourist); small business center; limited room service; massage; laundry. *In room:* Satellite TV, minibar, fridge, hot water for coffee/tea, safe in higher standard rooms, IDD phone.

Empress Hotel ⭐⭐

This Hong Kong/Vietnamese joint venture is a good, up-scale but affordable oasis just a stone's throw from the lake and close to all the action. Tucked into the side of a hill, the hotel has rooms that form a courtyard, with the steep gable of a European lodge-style reception and restaurant on one side and two floors of rooms all facing the courtyard on the other. With dark wood walls, terra-cotta tile floors, rattan furniture, and nice details all around, rooms are comfortable. All have mellow, indirect lighting along with nice local artwork and elegant cotton and silk bedspreads. Bathrooms are large, with granite counters and nice fixtures, some with bathtubs and others with an open arrangement with a combined shower/toilet area (like a guesthouse, but spotless). The suites are large and luxe, with a sunken tub and large sitting area, but for my money, I'll take a deluxe room (US$110), which is a larger version of a standard and has views of the stone courtyard and lake below. There's a nice restaurant serving good local and Continental fare; if the staff is slightly cool, it's almost refreshingly real of them. They also have a great old Mercedes for rental or airport transfers. (overlooking the north end of the lake).

5 Nguyen Thai Hoc St. ✆ 063/833-888. Fax 063/829-399. empress@hcm.vnn.vn. US$60–US$110; US$198 suite. AE, MC, V. **Amenities:** Restaurant; tour desk; car rental (classic Mercedes to airport for US$16); laundry; dry cleaning. *In room:* Satellite TV w/in-house movies, minibar, fridge, hair dryer, safe, IDD phone.

INEXPENSIVE

Hang Nga Guest House ⭐

In addition to being an interesting architectural experiment, Hang Nga (see "Attractions," below) is also a guesthouse. Or, it's a "guest-tree," you might call it—the nine small rooms are hollowed out of huge fantasy tree trunks, and each has a theme: the bear room, ant room, bamboo room, and so forth. Statues of said animals dominate the rooms, some of which have stalactites (perfect for head-bumping) and small fireplaces. It's like living in a small high-brow installation, really. Furniture consists of tree trunk chairs and tables and the like, and mirrors are at odd angles on the wall and ceilings (I know what you're thinking). The eagle room, which Ms. Hang says represents the U.S., is the most majestic and has a huge mosaic concrete tub, but I found the ant room the best of all. The honeymoon suite has two floors, the upper consisting solely of a bed in a nook. You can stay here for kicks, and it will be quite memorable, but don't expect it to be very comfortable. Thin foam mattresses, small rooms, cold cement floors, and a slight must are the wee price you'll pay for staying in fantasyland.

3 Huynh Thuc Khang St. ℂ 063/822-070. 9 units. US$29–US$60 double. AE, MC, V. **Amenities:** Restaurant.

Hotel Dai Loi (Fortune Hotel) ★★   If you want value for money, look no further. It's affordable, and even the lowest-priced rooms are terrific, with high ceilings, fresh paint, comfortable and firm mattresses, marble floors, new furnishings, and nicely tiled bathrooms. Most other places in this category have musty smells and dingy decor, but not the Fortune. The place is spotless, the location is far enough from the center of town for quiet yet close enough for access, and the price is right—most doubles are US$14 to US$15; the US$25 rooms have two double beds and nice, large bathtubs, and most have balconies. The second-floor restaurant is open and inviting. The small lobby bar has white walls and white plastic chairs, and could be airlifted to a museum as a "minimalist installation," but there is nice black-and-white tile throughout to give it a nice, crisp look. The staff members speak little English but are quite helpful.

3A Bui Thi Xuan. ℂ 063/837-333. 39 units. US$14–US$25 double. AE, MC, V. **Amenities:** Restaurant; bar; all rentals available; laundry. *In room:* TV, minibar, fridge, IDD phone.

Ngoc Lan Hotel ★   This 12-year-old two-star alternative is centrally located and has good views of the lake, but it has seen better days. Rooms are huge; tiled, if you're lucky (you'll get grotty old carpet, if not); and airy, with comfy beds; unfortunately, they have hideously mismatched plastic/wood furniture and red velveteen bedspreads, and they are showing lots of wear and tear. Bathrooms are roomy as well and are similarly shoddy, with aged tile, but all have a tub and a hair dryer. City noise permeates all the rooms, which is inevitable for such a central location. Ask for a room with a "garden view"—these are as quiet as you can get. Otherwise, go for one of the corner rooms overlooking the lake. The restaurant is like an old moose lodge fraternity: large, dark, and musty; it doubles as a dance hall on special occasions. There's a good pool table in the bar, and breakfast isn't bad. Folks on staff here either speak very basic English or are geniuses at charades.

42 Nguyen Chi Thanh St., Dalat. ℂ 063/822-136 or 063/823-522. Fax 063/824-032. 33 units. ctcpdlngoc lan@hcm.vnn.vn. US$10–US$30 double. MC, V. **Amenities:** Restaurant; bar; sauna; steam; tour desk; laundry; conference rooms. *In room:* TV, minibar, fridge, IDD phone.

Trung Cang Hotel ★★   The Sinh Café expands its monopoly on budget traveler amenities here with this new, centrally located little gem. Rooms have clean tile floors and basic amenities; and any lack of decoration is compensated for by clean, airy rooms for next to nothing, though some even have nice filigreed ceilings and cool, subdued lighting. Time will tell with this place, but get there while it's new, ask to see a room, and do a bit of haggling. This is a good option for those on a budget, and the folks at Sinh Café are always accommodating when arranging tours or getting you around town. All room rates include breakfast.

4A Bui Thi Xuan St. ℂ 063/822-663. US$10–US$20. MC, V. **Amenities:** Restaurant; rentals available; tour desk; laundry service. *In room:* Satellite TV, minibar, fridge, IDD phone.

WHERE TO DINE

Dalat dining is pretty basic. Meals are simply prepared and heavily influenced by Chinese cuisine. The huge variety of local ingredients, particularly fruit and vegetables, makes for freshly tasting food. Many small restaurants are located at Phan Dinh Phung Street, and some of the best dining, according to locals, is at the many stalls in the central market. Do try the artichoke tea and strawberry jam, two local specialties (and good souvenirs to take home from the market).

Café de la Poste ★★ CONTINENTAL   This cozy, colonial gem, part of the Dalat Palace Hotel, is located in an open, airy corner building across from the post office (go figure). It's more a restaurant than cafe, really, and has a great selection of light choices, sandwiches and desserts on top of hearty entrees like spare ribs, T-bone steak and fresh pasta. The salads are big and fresh, and they have a great French onion soup. Don't miss the cheesecake for dessert. It's pricey for Dalat, but it's worth it in a way that the Dalat palace's fine dining venue, Les Rabelais, is not.

12 Tran Phu St. ✆ 063/825-444. Main courses US$4–US$10.50. MC, V. Daily 6am–10pm.

Long Hoa ★★ VIETNAMESE/CONTINENTAL   On a busy street just opposite the hilltop cinema, this small bistro has checkered tablecloths and a cozy atmosphere that attract passersby. The owner, a vivacious, self-taught linguist, is very welcoming and will walk you through any menu choices, travel recommendations, or local lore in the language of your choice. You'll feel like a regular, or will become one, even if you're here for only a few days. The menu is grouped by ingredients (chicken, beef, fish, etc.), and they have any kind of sauté or steamed dish you can imagine, as well as a variety of hot-pots and soups for those cold Dalat nights. It's inexpensive, excellent local fare with a French flare here; I had a delicious meal of barbecued deer with french fries. Don't miss the homemade yogurt, a real treat.

6 Duong 3 Thang 2 (Duy Tan) Dalat. ✆ 063/822-934. Longhoa@hcm.vnn.vn. Main courses US$1–US$4. No credit cards. Daily 10:30am–9:30pm.

Ngoc Hai Restaurant ★ VIETNAMESE/CHINESE   Just down the street from the market and a popular stop for tours, this local spot is two floors of bright, clean, indoor/outdoor dining. It's none too spectacular, but with the Ngoc Hai has a friendly staff and an ambitious menu; ask for anything, and you'll hear hearty replies of, "Have. Have." Selections from the Western end of the spectrum include roasted chicken with potatoes and a mock-up of British fish and chips, but go for the nice Chinese-influenced Vietnamese stir-fries, one-dish meals, and soups. Reasonable set menus vary daily and are a good bet. Test your mettle with menu items like anteater or porcupine. You'll also find some good veggie selections.

6 Nguyen Thi Minh Khai St. ✆ 063/825-252. Main courses US$2–US$5.33; set menus US$3.33–US$8. Daily 9am–10pm.

Nam Do ★ CHINESE   For an unassuming, inexpensive Chinese meal of a hot-pot and rice for one or a cover-the-table feast for many, this little market-side gem is friendly and a comfy on a chilly night. The food is nongreasy and good. There are some exotics on the menu, like bear claw marinated in Chinese medicine, and grilled porcupine, but the restaurant was strangely all out of those.

6 Nguyen Thi Minh Khai St., next to Ngoc Hai Restaurant. ✆ 063/824-550. Main courses 10,000–60,000 VND (US66¢–US$4). No credit cards. Daily 8:30am–10:00pm

Café V ★★ *Finds* CONTINENTAL   It's good for the budget and good for the tummy here at homey Café V. Tell me where you can sit at a table with linen and candlelight and enjoy a great burger for a buck? Also, you'll find the only burritos in town here. The owner, V, and her husband Michael, a long-time expat, serve up hospitality smothered in gravy and will welcome you as their own. With only a short time in business, the place is full of travelers and expats, but there's room for one more. Pull up a chair!

1/1 Bui Thi Xuan St. (across from Sinh Café), Dalat. ℂ **063/837-576.** Main courses 10,000–40,000 VND (US66¢–US$1.66). No credit cards. Daily 8:30am–10:00pm.

CAFES

Ngyen Chi Thanh Street is lined with cafes, one indistinguishable from another in many ways. Each building hangs over the main market street and all serve ice cream, tea, and beer to oogling couples. Try **Coffee Artista** (ℂ **063/821-749**), at 9 Nguyen Chi Thanh St., for some good ice cream, classic rock, and friendly folks. Just next door the **Viethung Internet Café** (ℂ **063/835-737**) has laid-back porch seating.

ATTRACTIONS

Much of what there is to see in Dalat hinges on the outdoors: lakes, waterfalls, and dams dominate the tourist trail. Things are spread over quite some distance, so consider booking a tour or renting your own car or motorbike.

Remember to avoid visiting pagodas between 11:30am and 2pm, when nuns and monks will be having their lunch. You might disturb them and also miss a valuable opportunity for a chat. It is also correct to leave a thousand VND or two in the donation box near the altar.

Dalat Market (Cho Da Lat) ★★★   Huge, crowded, and stuffed with produce of all varieties, this is the top stroll-through destination in Dalat. Here's where you can see all the local specialties—and even have a try! Some of the vendors will be happy to give you a sample of some local wine or a few candied strawberries. Dalat in general is low on the hassling tourist touts that plague the big towns and tourist sites in Vietnam, and entreaties from the merchants are friendly; you can walk around without too much hassle here because the locals are doing all the shopping.

Central Dalat.

Xuan Huong Lake ★★   Once a trickle originating in the Lat village, Dalat's centerpiece, Huan Huong, was created from a dam project that was finished in 1923, demolished by a storm in 1932, and reconstructed and rebuilt (with heavier stone) in 1935. You can rent windsurfing boards and swan-shape paddleboats, although in two visits here I have yet to see anyone actually using them—I cannot vouch for the cleanliness of the water.

Central Dalat.

Bao Dai's Palace ★   Completed in 1938, this monument to bad taste provided Bao Dai, Vietnam's last emperor, with a place of rest and respite with his family. It has never been restored and, indeed, looks veritably untouched since the emperor's ousting and hasty exile; on a busy weekend in high season, you might get a rush by imagining you're there to liberate the place and are part of the looting masses—that's not hard to imagine, with the crowds ignoring any velvet ropes and posing for pictures in the aging velvet furniture. You'll be asked to go in stocking feet or wear loose shoe covers, which make it fun for sliding around the home's 26 rooms, including Bao Dai's office and the bedrooms of the royal family. You can still see the grease stains on Bao Dai's hammock pillow and the ancient steam bath in which he soaked. The explanations are in English, and most concern Bao Dai's family. There is pathos in reading them and piecing together the mundane fate of the former royals: This prince has a "technical" job, while that one is a manager for an insurance company. There are three other Bao Dai palaces in town, the Sofitel Dalat Palace Hotel among them, but this is the most choice.

S of Xuan Huong Lake and up the hill behind "Crazy House." Admission 5,000 VND (US33¢). Daily 7am–8pm.

Hang Nga Guest House and Art Gallery ★★   Otherwise known as the "Crazy House," this Gaudi-meets-Sesame Street theme park is one not to miss. It's a wild mass of wood and wire fashioned into the shape of a giant tree house and smoothed over in concrete. It sounds simple, but there's a vision to this chaos; just ask the eccentric owner/proprietor and chief architect, Ms. Dang Viet Nga. Daughter of aristocracy, Ms. Nga is well heeled after early schooling in China and has a degree in architecture from university in Moscow. In Dalat she has been inspired to undertake this shrine to the curved line, what she calls an essential mingling of nature and people. The locals deem her eccentric for some reason, but she's just misunderstood; don't pass up any opportunity to have a chat with the architect herself. On a visit here, you'll follow a helpful guide and are sure to have fun clambering around the concrete ladders, tunnels, and hollowed-out nooks, and in the unique "theme" rooms of this huge fantasy tree trunk. It's an actual guesthouse, too (see "Where to Stay," above). There's a small family shrine in a large common area at the back. It all spoke to me about Vietnam's refreshingly lax zoning laws, but to many it's an interesting, evolving piece of pop art. This is a fun visit.

3 Huynh Thuc Khang St. © 063/822-070. Admission 5,000 VND (US33¢). Daily 7am–7pm.

Lam Ty Ni Pagoda: Home of Thay Vien Thuc, "The Crazy Monk"   A visit with the man is a highlight for some and is just plain creepy for others. The temple itself is nothing special, though the immaculate garden in the back is nice; the attraction here is the large studio of Mr. Thuc, a Vietnamese Zen practitioner who seems to be painting, drawing, and scribbling his way to Nirvana. It's a unique glimpse into the inner sanctum of a true eccentric, and though locals say that he's not a real monk, just a painter and salesman, it's an interesting visit. A polyglot afflicted with graphophilia perhaps (a language genius who can't stop drawing), Mr. Thuc has a message of "peace and connectedness" characteristic of the Zen sect, and he conveys that message in Vietnamese, Chinese, French, English, Japanese, German, and Swedish as he continually cranks out poems with small stylized drawings when you talk with him. Your part in the plan is that for US1$ (bargain if you will), he'll scribble an original before your eyes and pose for a photo; he has tentative plans to visit everyone who buys one of his paintings and bring us all together. Hmm. You're free to ask him questions, browse his stacks of finished works in the studio, and sign the guest book. This is a standard stop on city/country tours.

2 Thien My, Dalat. © 063/822-775. Admission free, but most feel obliged (or compelled) to buy one of his paintings.

The French Quarter ★★   The whole town has the look and feel of a French replica, but on the ridge-running road, Tran Hung Dao, don't miss the derelict shells of the many French colonial summer homes once populated and popular;

it's where the connected and successful came to escape the Saigon heat in summer. Most are owned by the folks at Sofitel, and who's to say what will become of them in years to come, but they are a beautiful and eerie reminder of the recent colonial past. The road itself, one you'll take to many of the sites outside of town, offers panoramic views.

Best visited by motorbike or in a car w/driver. Follow Tran Hung Dao Rd. a few kilometers SE from town. Some of the houses are on private rds. at the end of promontories.

Truc Lam (Bamboo Forest) Zen Monastery ⭐⭐   What's refreshing is that you can walk around Truc Lam with no harassment, unlike many other temples and most pagodas in Vietnam. This is a working temple, and though it's packed with tourists at certain times of the day, you'll be wandering amid meditation halls and classrooms that are utilitarian, not museum pieces. You'll get to see monks at work and have an informative glimpse into the daily rhythms of temple life. The complex was completed in 1994 with the aim of giving new life to the Truc Lam Yen Tu Zen sect, a uniquely Vietnamese form of Zen founded during the Tran Dynasty (1225–1400). Adherents practice self-reliance and realization through meditation. The shrine, the main building, is notable mainly for its simple structure and peaceful air, and there is a large relief sculpture of Boddhidarma, Zen's wild-eyed Indian heir, at the rear of the main temple. The scenery around the monastery, with views of the nearby man-made lake, Tuyen Lam Lake, and surrounding mountains is breathtaking.

Near Tuyen Lam Lake, 6km (3¾ miles) from Dalat. A popular spot on any countryside tour. Daily 7am–5pm.

Thien Vuong Pagoda ⭐   Otherwise known as the "Chinese Pagoda," built as it was by the local Chinese population, this circa 1958 structure is unremarkable except for its serene setting among the hills of Dalat and the very friendly nuns who inhabit it. It does have three awe-inspiring sandalwood Buddhist statues that have been dated to the 16th century. Each is 4m (13 ft.) high and weighs 1½ tons. Left to right, they are Dai The Chi Bo Tat, god of power; Amithaba or Sakyamuni, Buddha; and Am Bo Tat, god of mercy.

3km (2 miles) SE of town at the end of Khe Sanh St. Daily 9am–5pm.

Dalat Railway Station (Cremaillaire Railway)   Built in 1943, the Dalat station offers an atmospheric slice of Dalat's colonial history. You can see an authentic old wood-burning steamer train on the tracks to the rear, and stroll around inside looking at the iron-grilled ticket windows, empty now. Although the steamer train no longer makes tourist runs, a newer Japanese train makes a trip to Trai Mat Street and the Linh Phuoc pagoda (below). A ride costs US$5 and leaves when full.

Near Xuan Huong Lake, off Nguyen Trai St. Daily 8am–5pm.

Linh Phuoc Pagoda ⭐   Here is another example of one of Vietnam's fantasyland glass and ceramic mosaic structures. Refurbished in 1996, this modern temple features a huge golden Buddha in the main hall, and three floors of walls and ceilings painted with fanciful murals. Go to the top floor for the eye-boggling Bodhisattva room and views of the surrounding countryside. In the garden to the right, there is a 3m-high (10-ft.-high) dragon climbing in and out of a small lake. You'll find very cool little nooks and crannies to explore.

At the end of Trai Mat St. (20 min. by car/bike). Daily 8am–5pm.

Valley of Love ⭐⭐   The Valley is scenic headquarters in Dalat and a popular stopover for honeymooners. It's a good place to find some real bizarre kitsch, the kind whose precedent can only be roadside America; here I mean guys in bear suits and huge-headed cowboys with guns that spout "bang" flags. There are a few nice walking paths among the rolling hills and quaint little lakes, and everyone enjoys the antics of Vietnamese honeymooners zipping around on motorboats and posing for pictures with guys in fuzzy jumpsuits. Don't miss it.

Phu Dong Thien Vuong St., about 3.2km (2 miles) N of town center. Admission 5,000 VND (US33¢). Daily 6am–5pm.

Lake of Sighs (Ho Than Tho) ⚐   This lake has such romantic connotations for the Vietnamese that you would think it was created by a fairy godmother rather than French dam work. Legend has it that a 15-year-old girl named Thuy drowned herself after her boyfriend of the same age, Tam, fell in love with another. Her gravestone still exists on the side of the lake, marked with the incense and flowers left by other similarly heart-broken souls, even though the name on the headstone reads "Thao," not "Thuy." The place is crammed with honeymooners in paddleboats and motorboats.

NE of town, along Ho Xuan Huong Rd. Admission 5,000 VND (US33¢). Daily 7am–5pm.

Prenn Falls ⚐   The falls are actually quite impressive, especially after a good rain. You can ride a rattle-trap little cable car over them if you're brave or follow a stone path behind the falling water (prepare to get your feet wet). That is a little thrill, of course, but the true Prenn experience is all about staged photos for Vietnamese tourists: couples preening, boys looking macho, and girls looking wan and forlorn. Professional photographers run the show and pose their willing actors on a small wooden bridge, on the back of a costumed horse, with an arm around a guy in a bear suit, on a small inflatable raft in front of the falls, or perched in one of the cool tree houses high above (be careful of the loose rungs when climbing up). Come here to have a laugh and observe until you find out that, as a foreign tourist, it's you that's being observed; in that case, say "Xin Chao" or return a few "hellos" and go from there (you'll be getting your photo snapped for sure). You might walk away with some new chums, not to mention some good tourist chachki, if that is your wont (plastic samurai sword anyone?).

At the foot of Prenn Mountain pass, 10km (6¼ miles) from Dalat. Admission 6,000 VND (US41¢). Daily 7am–5pm.

SPORTS & OUTDOOR ACTIVITIES

Dalat is the perfect setting for **hiking and mountain biking.** Check with the folks at **Phat Tire Ventures,** 73 Truong Cong Dinh (© **063/829-422;** see "Visitor Information and Tours," earlier in this chapter), for some remote jungle treks in among hill-tribe towns, good mountain biking, or any kind of day trip (these folks are extremely amenable and can customize to your needs).

Golfers can try the **Dalat Palace Golf Club**'s impressive 18-hole course. One round costs Sofitel Palace or Novotel guests US$65; guests of Golf 1, 2, or 3 pay US$75, and all others pay US$85, plus a mandatory caddie fee (US$6 for 9 holes, and US$12 for 18 holes). For reservations, call © **063/821-201.** Rental clubs and shoes are available; private lessons, by appointment, begin at US$30 for a half-hour. There is a nice driving range.

13 Phan Thiet Town & Mui Ne Beach

This is one of the best laid-back getaways in Vietnam. The town of Phan Thiet itself is a bustling little fishing port. Though it's picturesque and good for a day's visit, you'll want to get out to the long stretch of beach to the east: the sprawling sandy shore at Mui Ne. This is a popular weekend getaway from nearby Saigon, and anybody with wood and a hammer is putting up a roof and welcoming visitors. Still, there are some very nice upscale resorts and comfy little boutique bungalow properties.

Nick Faldo's golf course at the Novotel in Phan Thiet is a big draw here, and the consistent winds of Mui Ne bay bring windsurfers from all over the world. Farther east and north along the coast, some 19.3km (12 miles), there are vast sand dunes, like a beachside Sahara, and inland there is the famous and strangely verdant Silver Lake amid the towering, shifting sands: It's worth a visit. These spots, as well as other small fishing villages, make for great day trips. There are also some local Cham ruins, and the town of Phan Thiet, famous for a brand of fish sauce (nuoc mam) made here, is worth exploring (especially the market).

Don't expect the world, but this is a good getaway from Saigon or to take a break as you make your way down the coast.

GETTING THERE

By Bus/Car: Phan Thiet is just 3 hours from Saigon. The tourist cafe buses connect here from Nha Trang and Dalat as well as Saigon. **TM Brothers** (in HCMC: ☏ **08/836-1791**) and **Sinh Café** (in HCMC: ☏ **08/369-420**) are the top choices. Any hotel front desk can make the necessary arrangements for car rental or return bus tickets.

WHERE TO STAY

The Novotel is the only international standard in the town of Phan Thiet. Along the beach at Mui Ne, about 9km (5½ miles) to the east, accommodations run the gamut from bamboo bungalows with no running water to five-star luxury (and these are often incongruously right next door to one another—so much for zoning). All accommodations offer promotional and long-stay rates. Many find that they plan to stay only a short time and end up in a hammock for a few extra days. *Note:* Addresses are listed by their distance from Phan Thiet.

EXPENSIVE

Novotel Coralia Ocean Dunes Phan Thiet ★★ "Fore!" Sandwiched between Nick Faldo's golf course on one side and an open lawn and sandy beach on the other, the Novotel is the most international standard in Phan Thiet. It's got all the amenities of a resort, and rooms and facilities are in a "traditional" hotel style, with clean carpet and floral prints; it's a clean but drab "chain hotel" style. Rooms aren't particularly big but are comfy, and bathrooms have nice bathtubs, the only ones in town. Every room has a balcony, and prices are according to the view of either the beach or the golf course. The only drawback is that it's an old Soviet-era building that's been dolled up; though they've made lemonade out of lemons, its still a bit dull. Novotel is close to the town of Phan Thiet but is insulated by the surrounding golf course and far from any road. This means tranquility and not even distant sounds of honking, unique in Vietnam. It's about 9km (5½ miles) to the beaches of Mui Ne. It's a popular getaway for Saigon expats and their families, and there is a comfortable, airy feel to the pool area and surrounding yard: It's great for kids (there's even a jungle gym). The hotel has resort-style activities and children's programs, rents jet-skis and sailboats, and offers limo service to town or to Saigon. Like the Sofitel in Dalat, this resort is the brainchild of the well-loved and eccentric Larry Hillblom, a founder of DHL, who was lost to a plane crash in 1995. His portrait is in the lobby.

1 Ton Duc Than St., Phan Thiet. © 62/822-393. Fax 062/828-045. www.accorhotels-asia.com. 123 units. US$110–US$125 golf/sea view; US$156 suite. AE, MC, V. **Amenities:** Restaurant (indoor and outdoor seating); 2 bars (poolside and inside); golf; 2 tennis courts; health club; kids' room; concierge; tour desk; car rental; business center; lobby shopping; salon; massage; babysitting; laundry; nonsmoking rooms; Internet. *In room:* A/C, TV, minibar, fridge, coffeemaker, hair dryer, safe, phone w/IDD.

Victoria Phan Thiet Resort 🌴🌴   Just as the road descends to meet with the sandy beaches of Mui Ne, the Victoria stands on a quiet little knoll overlooking the sea. It's a grass-and-garden campus traced by small brick pathways that connect their tidy, upscale bungalows; the overall feel and impression is as comfortable, laid back, and luxe as the other famed Victoria properties in the region. You enter the lobby over a small catwalk. The layout is done in interesting, interlacing levels, with many of the buildings made of fine natural stone. The pool area is luxe and lovely, and the new massage facility, in a small seaside grove, is in quiet harmony with nature. Each private massage room is done in wood and bamboo and is open to the sound of the nearby surf. Guest rooms are large, private bungalows, some with two tiers and all done in terra-cotta, bamboo catay, and dark wood; it's refined comfort with nice touches like stylish indirect lighting disguised as pottery, large ceiling fans, and local artwork. Family bungalows have multiple sleeping areas and a pull-out couch. Shower and toilet are in separate rooms in most, and are compact but luxe. The beach here is a bit rocky, but the resort overlooks its own quiet cove and there are nice beach-side thatch awnings. Service is top-notch, and the staff members here, from the bar and fine dining area to the front desk and beach, all make you feel at home. This resort has all the amenities of a much larger property, only here done in intimate and friendly miniature. Come for the weekend, and you'll stay for the week.

Km. 9, Phu Hai, Phan Thiet. © 62/813-000. Fax 062/813-007. www.victoriahotels-asia.com. 50 units. US$113–US$134 bungalow; US$154 villa. AE, MC, V. **Amenities:** Restaurant (indoor and outdoor dining); large thatch-roofed poolside bar area; outdoor pool w/Jacuzzi; tennis court; small health club; all rentals available; billiards; private tours available; shopping arcade below reception; massage; laundry; Internet. *In room:* A/C, satellite TV, minibar, fridge, coffeemaker, safe, phone w/IDD.

MODERATE

Bien Xanh Blue Ocean Resort 🌴   This is a basic but comfy three-star resort. It's open and airy here around the large, central pool, and the bar and restaurant overlook the beach, but it's all a bit plain. Rooms have terra-cotta floors and are sparse but neat, with either a low false ceiling or an exposed catay vaulted roofs. All have balconies, and some have nice views. Baths are the shower-in-room, guesthouse variety and are done in basic yellow tile. This is an affordable option popular for young expats more for the price tag than anything. There's a good Irish pub, and the staff is friendly.

Km 12. 200 Ham Tien, Phan Thiet. © 62/847-322. Fax 62/847-351. www.blueoceanresort.com. 58 units. Bungalow US$55, which includes breakfast. AE, MC, V. **Amenities:** (Shares amenities w/Saigon Mui Ne.) Restaurant; pub; outdoor pool; all rentals; Binthanh tour desk; business center; limited room service; babysitting; laundry. *In room:* A/C, TV (satellite), minibar, fridge, phone w/IDD.

Coco Beach 🌴🌴   This is the little slice of heaven you've been looking for in your hard travels along the coast. On the main strip in Mui Ne, Coco Beach doesn't look like much from the road—just a wall to keep out the noise—but it is a real seaside, garden oasis. Rooms are wooden bungalows on stilts, each with a comfy balcony area with a couch and a table. It's a basic but nice standard, intimate and tidy, though not particularly luxe. There are nice rustic touches like fine dark beams, exposed thatch roofs, bamboo catay lanterns, and mosquito nets. All bungalows have subdued, indirect lighting. Bathrooms are small and basic but are tidy, done in small tile with glass stall showers. Rooms are priced by their proximity to the beautiful sandy beach, where you'll find comfy lounge chairs and umbrellas. Service is attentive and genuine here; the two restaurants, the picturesque seaside Paradise Beach Club and the more upscale Champa, are arguably the best in town. There are no TVs \(though there's a library and video area), so there are no distractions. This is a good place to have a go at that novel you've been wanting to start (whether reading or writing) or just relax in the quiet garden after a day of swimming or boating.

km 12.5 Ham Tien, Phan Thiet. ℂ 62/847-111. Fax 62/847-115. 31 units. US$70–US$85 bungalow; US$140–US$170 2-room villa (prices are net; long-stay rates are available). **Amenities:** 2 restaurants; pool/beach bar and shop, central pool; Jacuzzi at poolside; motorboat and sailboat rental; family programs; in-house tour programs; car rental business center; limited room service; massage; laundry *In room:* A/C, mini-bar, fridge, IDD phone.

Saigon Mui Ne Resort ⭐

The Saigon Mui Ne is the most popular spot in town for larger group tours. Run by Saigontourist, the resort has all the amenities. Rooms are comparable to any in this category in town, but there's that hazy indifference of a government-run, tour-group hotel. The good news is the price tag and the many amenities. It's a sprawling campus of manicured lawns and tidy bungalows with terra-cotta tile floors, unique wrought-iron furniture, and bathrooms with granite counters and bamboo lattice-work. Especially in the more expensive rooms, the decor is an unsettling mish-mash of styles and tries to be more than it is though. Bungalows have balconies, and some open onto the central pool area. The poolside bar is popular and open late.

Km. 12.3 Ham Tien, Phan Thiet, Binh Thuan. ℂ **62/847-302.** Fax 62/847-307. www.saigonmuineresort.com. 69 units. US$60–US$115. AE, MC, V. **Amenities:** Restaurant (Sea Breeze); beachside bar; nice courtyard pool w/Jacuzzi; tennis; sauna; all rentals; Saigon tour desk; salon; 24-hr. room service; massage; laundry; Internet. *In room:* A/C, TV, minibar, fridge, IDD phone.

Mui Ne Sailing Club ⭐⭐

This new seaside spot is owned by the same Aussie folks who run the popular Sailing Club in Nha Trang. Rooms run the gamut from budget rooms with a fan, comfortable but like an American motel, to top-notch bungalows at seaside. All rooms have terra-cotta tile with bamboo matting, cloth hangings, and bamboo floor lamps. There's almost an American Southwest feel in the artful beveled edges of the plaster walls and in the similarly rounded built-in night stands. Bathrooms are separated from the bedroom by only a hanging cloth and are large and nicely appointed in tile and dark wooden trim. The high-end sea-view bungalows are a great choice. The pool is small, but in a picturesque seaside courtyard with the open-air colonial-style restaurant. This is a popular stop for windsurfers and sailors, and boat rentals are available. Rooms are priced by their relation to the beach, and you can choose air-conditioning or not and pay accordingly.

24 Nguyen Dinh Chieu St., Han Tien Ward, Phan Thiet. ℂ **62/847-440.** Fax 62/847-441. www.sailingclub vietnam.com. 32 units. US$35–US$55 bungalow; US$75 deluxe bungalow. AE, MC, V. **Amenities:** Restaurant; bar; outdoor pool; all rentals; tour desk; business center; room service 7am–10pm; babysitting; laundry; Internet. *In room:* A/C, IDD phone.

Budget accommodations line the main drag in Mui Ne. The scene is constantly changing, but expect to pay between US$8 and US$15 for basic guesthouse accommodation. If you come by cafe bus, they will take you around to shop for the spot you'd like. It gets cheaper and more rustic the farther east you go on the main road. One good bet in the budget department is **Full Moon Beach,** a popular spot for windsurfers. Rooms vary from unique little second-floor wood perches overlooking the beach to midrange comfort in the newest building.

Contact Phuong or Pascal at ✆ **062/847-008.** (14km/8¾ miles from Phan Thiet, Thon 3–Xa Ham Tien, Muin Ne; fax 062/847-160; www.windsurf-vietnam.com).

WHERE TO DINE

Your best bet along the beach is to eat in any of the resorts. Foremost among these is the **Paradise Beach Club,** at the Coco Beach Resort (km 12.5 Ham Tien, Phan Thiet; ✆ **62/847-111**), where you can dine on fine fresh seafood and barbecue in an informal, seaside setting. The more upscale restaurant **Champa** is also a great choice.

The **Mui Ne Sailing Club** (24 Nguyen Dinh Chieu St., Han Tien Ward, Phan Thiet; ✆ **62/847-440**) serves good, basic Western in a nice open-air building at poolside overlooking the ocean. Farther east, **Full Moon Beach** (14km/8¾ miles from Phan Thiet, Thon 3–Xa Ham Tien, Muin Ne; ✆ **062/ 847-008**) is a good stop for coffee or breakfast on your way to Silver Lake or the big dunes outside of town.

Thatched-roof eateries line the main beach-side road in Mui Ne, and there is also a **Good Morning Vietnam** restaurant (km 11.8 Ham Tien Mui Ne; ✆ **091/802-2760**), Vietnam's pizza and pasta franchise that serves good, affordable, familiar meals for little.

ATTRACTIONS

Cape Mui Ne 𝄢𝄢, some 20km (12½ miles) from town to the northeast, is a dynamic area where you'll find Mui Ne's phenomenal sand dunes or where you can visit any of a number of lovely seaside villages that are well worth a wander. Coming from the beach, you'll first reach a small fishing town and can explore its fine little rural market, with photo ops aplenty. Heading inland away from the beach, you'll first come to **The Red Dunes** 𝄢𝄢 towering over town. A walk to the top offers great views of the town and surrounding countryside, and you're sure to be followed by a gaggle of friendly kids trying to sell you on the idea of renting one of their little plastic sleds for the ride down the steep dune slopes. From the Red Dunes, if you have time, the unique **Silver Lake** 𝄢𝄢 is reached only after a long bumpy ride, but the views of the coast are dynamic and this unique little verdant lake in the large, parched silver dune makes the trip worth it. It's a long day, though. Ask at any hotel or resort for tours. Expect to pay US$10 per person for two or more to go to the tip of the cape and the Red Dunes, and more to go inland.

At the highest point on the road between Phan Thiet Town and Mui Ne beach, you won't miss **Cham Tower,** an impressive spire of crumbling brick. The tower dates from the end of the 13th century and is worth a stop if you weren't able to catch any of the Cham sites near Hoi An and Danang. Any taxi will be happy to make a brief stop on the way. There are also Cham sites some 2 hours drive inland near Phan Rang, and all hotels and resorts can arrange tours.

Phan Thiet Market 𝄢 is a large but pretty standard central market in town. It's certainly worth a wander. This is where you can pick up a bottle of locally made Nuoc Mam (fish sauce). Go early for the bringing-in of the day's catch, and don't forget your camera.

OUTDOOR ACTIVITIES

The wind conditions in Mui Ne are steady and strong in the dry season (Oct–May), and the beach is becoming a real windsurfing mecca (it's over 12 knot winds for ⅔ of the year). **Jibe's,** a popular rental shop, windsurfer club, and bar, is a good place to check in or rent a board. It's next to the **Full Moon Beach** restaurant and guesthouse (14km/8¾ miles from Phan Thiet, Thon 3–Xa Ham Tien, Muin Ne; www.windsurf-vietnam.com); contact Pascal at © **062/847-008.** One-hour rental is US$10, and all-day rental is US$40. Sailors and wind-surfers will want to contact the folks at the **Mui Ne Sailing Club** (24 Nguyen Dinh Chieu St., Han Tien Ward, Phan Thiet; © **062/847-440**) or at any hotel or resort about renting Hobie Cat and Laser sailboats, jet-skis, and runabouts.

The outstanding Nick Faldo–designed **Ocean Dunes Golf Course** (1 Ton Duc Than St., Phan Thiet; © **062/821-511**) is a big draw here in town.

14 Ho Chi Minh City (Saigon)

Ho Chi Minh City, or, Saigon as it is once again commonly known, is a rela-tively young for Asia, founded just in the 18th century. Settled mainly by civil-war refugees from north Vietnam and Chinese merchants, it quickly became a major commercial center. When the French took over a land they called Cochin China, Saigon became the capital. After the French left in 1954, Saigon remained the capital of south Vietnam until national reunification in 1975.

Saigon is still Vietnam's commercial headquarters, brash and busy, with a keen sense of its own importance. Located on the Saigon River, it's Vietnam's major port and largest city, with a population of almost 5 million people. True to its reputation, it is noisy, crowded, and dirty, but the central business district is rap-idly developing in steel and glass precision to match any city on the globe. The old Saigon still survives in wide downtown avenues flanked by pristine colonials. Hectic and eclectic, Ho Chi Minh City has an attitude all its own.

Some of Saigon's tourism highlights include the **Vietnam History Museum;** the grisly **War Remnants Museum;** and **Cholon, the Chinese district,** with its pagodas and exotic stores. Dong Khoi Street—formerly fashionable Rue Catinat during the French era and Tu Do, or Freedom Street, during the American war—is still a strip of grand colonial hotels, chic shops, and cafes. The food in Saigon is some of the best Vietnam has to offer, the nightlife sparkles, and the shopping is good. The city is also a logical jumping-off point for excursions to other southerly destinations: the **Mekong Delta,** the **Cu Chi tunnels,** and **Phan Thiet beach.**

GETTING THERE

BY PLANE   Of the regional airlines, pretty much all of them fly to Vietnam, including Malaysian Airlines, Thai Airways International, Bangkok Airways, Silk Air/Singapore Airlines, Lao Aviation, Garuda Indonesia, Philippine Air-lines, and Cathay Pacific (from Hong Kong). My suggestion is to always check the price of the Vietnam Airlines flight first. That's usually the best fare, thanks to government controls. If you're flying to Vietnam directly from North Amer-ica, look into Cathay Pacific for good fares and itineraries. Domestically, Saigon is linked by Vietnam Airline flights from Hanoi, Hue, Danang, Hoi An, Nha Trang, and Dalat.

At the airport in Saigon, you'll be able to change foreign currency for VND, but taxi drivers to town don't mind payment in U.S. dollars, either. Arranging a hotel limousine to greet you will certainly make life a bit easier, but taxis are aplenty outside the arrivals hall. The trip to town is US$5, even though the cab-bie will always quote you US$5. Stick firmly to your offer of US$5, and they give in without too much hassle.

In town, the Vietnam Airlines office is at 116 Nguyen Hue, District 1 (© **08/ 829-2118;** fax 08/823-8454). Call to book a flight or confirm your reservation.

> ⌐ *Warning* **Scam Alert**
>
> If you go with a taxi driver, even a metered one, from the airport in Saigon, watch out for the hotel bait-and-switch scam. Drivers get commissions for leading tourists to one hotel or another, and it's common for them to insist that the hotel you're going to is full, or closed, or has some other problem. The driver will pull a dour face and even sound pretty convincing as he tries to take you to his friend's hotel. Sit tight until you're at your intended destination. It might help for you to agree in writing where you're going before setting out.

To get to the airport, if you can't find a taxi, you can call Airport Taxi at © **08/844-6666.** There is an international departure tax of US$12. The departure tax for domestic flights is 20,000 VND (US$1.33).

BY BUS/MINIVAN   By bus, Saigon is about 5½ hours from Dalat, the nearest major city. All of the cafes connect here, of course, and line the streets around the Pham Ngu Lao area. See the tour information below.

BY CAR   For safety reasons alone, if you're taking wheels, it is better to book a minivan with a tour or group.

GETTING AROUND

BY BICYCLE & MOTORBIKE   Saigon is blessed with the country's most chaotic traffic, so you might want to think twice before renting a motorbike or bicycle, which aren't as easily available as in other towns. You can, however, hop a motorcycle taxi—a quick trip is 5,000 VND (US33¢), while hourly booking can be in the ballpark of US$1 per hour with some haggling. It's a bit hair-raising sometimes but is a good way to get around.

BY CYCLO   Cyclos are available for an hourly rental of about 20,000 VND (US$1.33). But they simply are not a good option in Saigon, especially outside District 1. First, drivers have an odd habit of not speaking English (or indeed, any other language) halfway through your trip and taking you to places you never asked to see, or simply driving around in circles pretending to be confused. Second, riding in a slow, open conveyance amid thousands of motorbikes and cars is unpleasant and dangerous, and cyclo passengers are low to the ground and in the front, something like a bumper. Third, drive-by thefts from riders is common even during daylight hours! Don't even think about it at night.

BY TAXI   Taxis are clustered around the bigger hotels and restaurants. They cost 12,000 VND (US80¢) at flag fall and 6,000 VND or so for every kilometer after. You can call Airport Taxi (© **08/844-6666**) or Saigon Taxi (© **08/822-6688**), among others.

BY CAR   You can simplify your sightseeing efforts if you hire a car and driver for the day from Ann Tours or Saigontourist (see "Visitor Information & Tours," below).

VISITOR INFORMATION & TOURS

Every major tourist agency has its headquarters or a branch in Saigon. They will be able to book tours and travel throughout the city and the southern region, and usually the countrywide as well.

Ho Chi Minh City (Saigon)

ACCOMMODATIONS ■
Bong Sen Hotel Annex **22**
Caravelle Hotel **21**
Grand Hotel **24**
Hong Hoa Hotel **46**
Hotel Continental **20**
Hotel Majestic **28**
Huong Sen Hotel **23**
Kim Do Royal City Hotel **37**
Mondial Hotel **29**
New World Hotel Saigon **44**
Norfolk Hotel **36**
Omni Saigon Hotel **1**
Palace Hotel **30**
Renaissance Riverside Hotel Saigon **27**
Rex Hotel **34**
Saigon Prince Hotel, a Duxton Hotel **39**
Sofitel Plaza Saigon **8**
Spring Hotel (Mua Xuan) **16**
Windsor Hotel **48**

DINING ◆
Allez Boo **47**
Amigo **40**
Augustin **31**
Bi Bi **14**
Blue Ginger **42**
Café Mogambo **17**
Camargue **18**
Chao Thai **15**
Gartenstadt **26**
Hoi An **13**
Lemongrass **32**
Mandarin **12**
Ngon Restaurant **5**
Restaurant **19**
Sushi Bar **11**
Temple Club **38**
ZEN **45**

ATTRACTIONS ●
Ben Thanh Market **43**
City Hall **33**
Emperor Jade Pagoda (Phuoc Hai) **2**
General Post Office (Buu Dien) **7**
Ho Chi Minh Museum **41**
Notre Dame Cathedral **6**
Reunification Palace **4**
Revolutionary Museum **35**
Saigon Opera House
   (Ho Chi Minh Municipal Theater) **19**
Vietnam History Museum **9**
War Remnants Museum **3**
Zoo and Botanical Gardens **10**

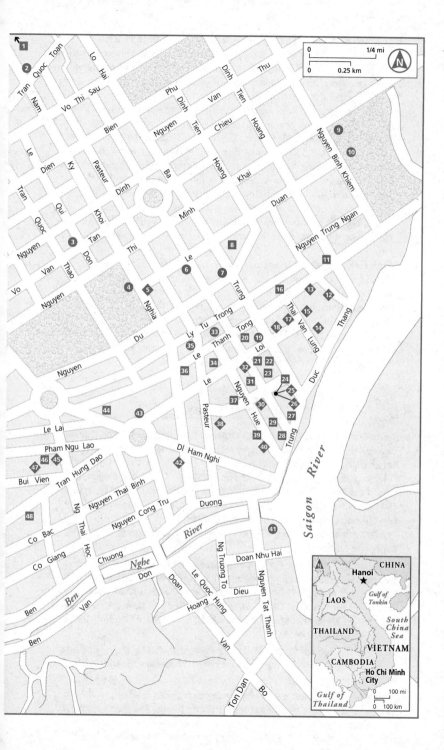

349

- **Ann Tours,** 58 Ton That Tung St., District 1 (© **08/833-2564** or 833-4356; fax 08/832-3866; www.anntours.com), has a great reputation that is well deserved. It's hard to imagine a friendlier, better-run travel organization. Ann's specializes in custom tours for individuals or small groups. They can be relatively expensive, but that's in comparison to the seat-in-coach cattle-drive tours. These guys will help you do virtually anything you want to in Vietnam. Ask for director Tony Nong, and tell him Frommer's sent you.
- **Exotissimo,** Saigon Trade Center, 37 Ton Duc Than, District 1 (© **08/825 1723;** fax 08/829 5800; vietnam@exotissimo.com) has a chic downtown office and can arrange just about any tour or international itinerary. It's popular for expats and has convenient offices throughout the region.
- **Saigontourist,** 49 Le Thanh Ton St., District 1 (© **08/829-8914;** fax 08/822-4987; sgtvn@hcmc.netnam.vn), is a faceless, pricey, government-run group, but it'll get you where you want to go. Plus, you'll never have trouble finding it because there are outlets in practically every hotel lobby in the city.
- **Sinh Café,** 246–248 De Tham, District 1 (© **08/369-420** or 08/8369322; sinhcafevietnam@hcm.vnn.vn), is a backpacker choice for inexpensive trips and tours. On paper, the tours seem exactly the same as others offered at private tour agents, but with a cheaper price tag—actually, they're pretty standard tours. This is a good option for shoestring travelers.
- **TM Brothers,** 269 De Tham St. or 139 Bui Vien St., District 1 (© **08/836-1791**), is pure "same-same but different here" on the cafe tip. This is a good place to check in comparison with Sinh.

✐ FAST FACTS: Ho Chi Minh City

Banks/Currency Exchange As with elsewhere in Vietnam, you can change money in banks, hotels, and jewelry stores. The exchange rate in Saigon is better than in many smaller cities.

Major banks in Saigon include these: ANZ Bank, 11 Me Linh Square, District 1 (© **08/829-9319**); Citibank, 115 Nguyen Hue St. (© **824-2118**); HSBC, 75 Pham Hong Thai St., District 1 (© **08/829-2288**); and Vietcombank, 29 Ben Chuong Duong, District 1 (© **08/829-7245**).

ATMs dispensing dollars and dong around the clock are at HSBC, ANZ Bank, and Citibank.

Embassies & Consulates For embassies, see "Fast Facts: Hanoi," earlier in this chapter. Consulates are all in District 1, as follows: United States, 4 Le Duan St. (© **08/822-9433**); Canada, 235 Dong Khoi St. (© **08/824-5025**); Australia, 5B Ton Duc Thang St. (© **08/829-6035**); New Zealand, 41 Nguyen Thi Minh Khai St. (© **08/822-6908**); and United Kingdom, 25 Le Duan St. (© **08/829-8433**).

Emergencies For police, dial © **113**; for fire, dial © **114**; and for ambulance, dial © **115**. Have a translator on hand, if necessary; operators don't speak English.

Internet/E-mail Almost every upscale hotel provides Internet services in Saigon, and you can bet they charge a pretty penny. You won't find any service on Dong Khoi, but a short walk in any direction brings you to service for an average of 200 VND (US1¢) per minute. My personal favorite:

Thumbs up to **Café Cyber Business Center** for serving drinks as well as providing full business center services in a laid-back, plush atmosphere with very private terminals. It's at 48 Dong Du St., just off Dong Khoi in District 1 (© **08/823-3668**; info@cgcybercfe.com; 300 VND/US2¢ per min.). Also try **Welcome Internet**, at 15B Le Thanh Ton (© **08/822-0981**). Service in the Pham Ngu Lao backpacker area is fast, and cheap; Internet cafes line De Tham and charge 5,000 VND per hour (that's less than US1¢ per min.).

Post Office/Mail   The main post office is located at 2 Coq Xu Paris, District 1 (© **08/823-2541** or 08/823-2542), just across from Notre Dame cathedral. It's open daily from 6:30am to 10pm. All services are available here, including long-distance calling and callback, and the building itself is a historic landmark (see "Attractions," later in this chapter). Postal service is available in most hotels and at various locations throughout the city.

Safety   The biggest threat to your health in Saigon is likely to be the street traffic. Cross the wildly busy streets at a slow, steady pace. If you're having a really hard time getting across, find a local who is crossing and stick to his heels!

Pickpocketing is a big problem in Saigon, especially motorbike drive-bys with someone slashing the shoulder strap, grabbing the bag, and driving off. Keep your bag close and away from traffic. Hang on to your wallet, and don't wear flashy jewelry. Be especially wary in crowded places like markets. Women should avoid wandering around in the evenings alone past 11pm or so. Contact your consulate or your hotel if you have a serious problem. If you insist on going to the local police, bring a translator. Also, the Saigon police tend to throw up their hands at "minor" infractions such as purse snatching or thievery.

Telephone   The city code for Saigon is 8. When dialing within Vietnam, the city code should be preceded by 0.

Toilets   There are no public toilets, per se. Seek out hotels, restaurants, and tourist attractions.

SAIGON'S DISTRICTS

Saigon is divided into districts, as is Hanoi, and is very easy to navigate. Be sure to know the district along with any addresses, and try to group your travels accordingly (try not to criss-cross districts in a day). Most of the hotels, bars, shops, and restaurants are in District 1, easily covered on foot, while sightseeing attractions are spread among Districts 1, 3, and 5 (Cholon).

WHERE TO STAY

Saigon presents the best variety of hotels in Vietnam, from deluxe business and family hotels to spotless smaller options. Most of the upper-end hotels are clustered around Nguyen Hue Street in District 1, as are the restaurants, shops, and bars.

Remember that prices listed here are guidelines only. Depending on occupancy, the season (low season in Saigon is Mar–Oct), and how long you're staying, you might get up to 50% off the rack rate. Cleanliness and amenities are very easy to come by. If your room doesn't have a hair dryer or hot water, for example, you need only ask.

If you're traveling on a budget, head for De Tham, a backpacker haven loaded with guesthouses. You can get a fan-cooled room with a cold-water shower for as little as US$5 per night, or an air-conditioned room with hot water for around US$15. Most of these places are very basic (and a bit noisy from street traffic) but are tidy, well run, and friendly.

Sheraton, among other international investors, is hard at work on a large high-rise here, so keep an eye out for grand-opening deals and price shifts resulting from the competition.

Remember that all hotels are listed by rack rate, an almost hypothetical price that few actually pay. Internet, group, and standard promotional rates are the rule, and especially in the off season (Mar–Sept), expect discounts up to 50%. Remember that many hotels levy a VAT of up to 20%.

VERY EXPENSIVE

Caravelle Hotel ★★★   Named for a type of light, fast ship, this hotel gives you that very impression here in its self-contained, sleek downtown location. The original was built by a French company in 1956 and, after honeymoon years as the town's address of note, the hotel became a shabby hangout for wartime journalists and fell into obscurity as the Doc Lap (Independence) Hotel in postwar years. The Caravelle was renovated and expanded beyond recognition in 1998 and is now an extremely attractive, efficient, and well-appointed hotel, the most prestigious in town. With five-star amenities and finely appointed rooms, luxury accommodations here attract a good number of business travelers as well as tourists. The big, new rooms are large and plush, with neutral furnishings and firm beds; higher floors have the best views in town. Bathrooms are sizable, in marble. The executive signature floors have fax machines, computer hookups, VCRs, and CD players in each room. The suites are luxe beyond belief. Everything is nice here, perhaps a little too nice, but the charismatic old Caravelles lives on in the popular Saigon-Saigon bar, an open-air colonial throwback in its original rooftop location; it has a laid-back Indochina flair completed by rattan shades, low-slung chairs, and twirling ceiling fans. If you squint, you might just see Graham Greene or a war-time correspondent sidling up to the bar. The popular restaurant, Port Orient, requires reservations 1 week in advance and serves fine international and Vietnamese fare. The lobby bar is a great meeting point. Here you'll find the best service, the best location, and a fine, friendly standard.

19 Lam Son Square, District 1. ℂ **08/823-4999.** Fax 08/824-3999. www.caravellehotel.com. 335 units. US$190–US$270 double; US$310–US$980 suite. AE, DC, MC, V. **Amenities:** 2 restaurants; 3 bars; lovely rooftop pool; top-notch health club; spa; Jacuzzi; sauna; all rentals available; tour desk; expensive but extensive business center; salon, facials, manicures; 24-hr. room service; massage; laundry; dry cleaning; executive-level rooms; banquet facility for 250; rooms for travelers w/disabilities. In room: A/C, satellite TV, fax; dataport, minibar, fridge, coffeemaker, hair dryer, safe, IDD phone.

Hotel Majestic ★   This 1925 landmark on the picturesque, riverside corner of Dong Khoi St. (formerly Catinat) still has some historical charm despite many renovations. Owned by Saigontourist and the jewel in the crown of its local empire, the Majestic is a picture-postcard colonial. Although botched details abound on the interior (tacky decor where something plain would stand, and vice versa), rooms and facilities here are classy and comfortable for the cost. High ceilings, original wood floors, and retro fixtures are a nice touch in all rooms, but clunky furniture and the red velveteen cabinets housing the TV sets kind of miss the mark. The hallways look as old as they are and don't befit a hotel of this price range and stature. Bathrooms are large, though, all with tubs and old-style taps. Majestic suites have large Jacuzzis. The small courtyard pool is surrounded by palms and the hotel's picturesque shuttered windows and walkways; in fact, the best choice are the fine deluxe rooms facing this quiet spot. Suites are just larger versions of deluxe rooms, and standards are small and bland, some without windows. The lobby lounge offers buffet meals at the fine restaurant, Cyclo, with either pianist or traditional music as live accompaniment. The staff couldn't be nicer and has a genuine desire to make your stay memorable, whether that means explaining the eccentricities of Vietnamese cuisine or hailing you a taxi. Don't miss the great views from the rooftop Sky-Bar, a good spot to have a chat and popular for weddings and parties.

1 Dong Khoi St., District 1. © 08/829-5514. Fax 08/829-5510. www.majestic-saigon.com. 122 units. US$130 single; US$150 standard double; US$165–US$180 superior; US$195–US$215 deluxe; US$295–US$575 suite. AE, DC, MC, V. **Amenities:** 2 restaurants; 2 bars; small courtyard pool; basic health club; sauna; Saigontourist tour desk; car rental; business center; shopping; massage; babysitting; laundry; dry cleaning. In room: A/C, satellite TV w/HBO, minibar, fridge, hair dryer, safe, IDD phone.

New World Hotel Saigon ⭐⭐   This first-rate hotel is where President Clinton called home during his brief stay in Saigon and is a fine choice indeed, whether you're a business traveler, a tourist, or a world leader. Everything's big, flashy, and deluxe. The location is in the very center of town and a short walk from Ben Than Market (see "Attractions," later in this chapter). It has a popular park out front, and there's a nice bustle and feeling of connectedness to the place uncommon to similar self-contained luxury hotels. The impeccable, plush rooms are done in a soothing array of neutrals, and the bathrooms are a sharp contrast in black and gray marble. The fat pillows are a little mushy and the beds are a bit too firm, but you can't have everything. The place is loaded with amenities. The four executive floors, with an executive lounge, have an impressive list of benefits: late check-out, all-day refreshments, free pressing, computer hookups, and free access to financial newswire information. If convenience is your game, it is well worth the US$30 more you'll pay over a standard double room. The staff snaps to; service is ultraefficient. It's also one of the few places to ask straight away if you'd like a nonsmoking room.

76 Le Lai St., District 1. © 08/822-8888. Fax 08/823-0710. www.newworldvietnam.com. 570 units. US$140 double; US$170 executive floor; from US$300 suite. AE, DC, MC, V. **Amenities:** 2 restaurants; bar; outdoor pool; lighted tennis court; health club; spa; sauna; rentals available; concierge; tour desk; business center; shopping arcade; 24-hr. room service; massage; babysitting; laundry; dry cleaning; executive/club rooms; banquet facilities. In room: A/C, satellite TV, minibar, fridge, coffeemaker, safe, IDD phone.

Omni Saigon Hotel ⭐⭐   Once quarters for the U.S. Army (some say a base for the CIA), the edifice recalls a Soviet-era post office. Inside is another story. The lobby, with a colonial period flavor and Art Deco details, is gorgeous and welcoming. The rooms are quite comfortable, and the amenities, like the company's many fine-dining outlets, popular Irish pub, Mulligan's, or extensive fitness center, rival any in town. Here's the drawback: Though it's just 10 minutes from the airport, you're in District 3 and some 15 minutes from town. Shuttles and taxis are consistent, but traffic can be hellish and you might feel distanced from the action (though this is what some seek). There are many perks here: Rooms are lush and well equipped, with coffeemakers, safes, comfy beds with fine linen, and a somewhat formal but immaculate decor. The one executive floor has a small business center of its own, in-room faxes and broadband hookup (the only in town), and a particularly elegant lounge; the service is flawless. The Omni is renowned around town for its Sunday brunch at the Café Saigon, featuring Asian and international cuisine, and Lotus Court for Cantonese and Nishimura, unbeatable for upscale Japanese dining. This is a very popular stop for Asian travelers and businessmen.

251 Nguyen Van Troi St., Phu Nhuan District (District 3). © 08/844-9222. Fax 08/844-9198. www.omnisaigon hotel.com. 240 units. US$110–US$120 double; US$150–US$160 club floor; US$200–US$500 suite. (long-stay rates available). AE, DC, MC, V. **Amenities:** 5 restaurants; bar; outdoor patio pool; health club; nice spa; Jacuzzi; sauna; steam; tour desk; fleet of cars for rent; business center; shopping, salon; 24-hr. room service; massage; babysitting; laundry; book borrowing corner. In room: A/C, TV, dataport (special in-room broadband for executive floor), minibar, fridge, hair dryer, safe, IDD phone.

Renaissance Riverside Hotel Saigon ☆☆
Owned and managed by Marriot, you'll find high standards and still that "new car smell" in this convenient downtown 22-floor tower. The lobby is done in a crisp, boutique colonial theme with a small central domed ceiling and a grand spiral stair connecting to the mezzanine. Rooms have black-and-white tile entries giving way to acres of carpet and comfort, with light furniture in small windowside sitting areas, interesting primitive artwork, and cool electric control-panels near the headboard (like a 1970s bachelor pad). Bathrooms are spacious and comfortable, with black marble countertops and an antique black-and-white tile pattern throughout. The drawback is that you could be anywhere really, and everything's nice in the same way an upscale hotel might be nice in Bangkok, Paris, or Pittsburgh; nevertheless, the staff is kind and the amenities, like the rooftop pool, fine health club, and executive floors, can't be beat (or, at least, match the others in town). Don't miss the dim sum lunch at the fine Cantonese restaurant, Kabin.

8-15 Ton Duc Thang St., District 1. **08/822-0033.** Fax 08/823-5666. www.renaissancehotels.com/sgnbr. 349 units. US$95 single/double; US$220–US$550 suite. AE, MC, V. **Amenities:** 2 restaurants; bar; rooftop pool w/great city view; health club; nice massage and spa facility; can arrange all rentals; business center; shopping; 24-hr. room service; babysitting; nonsmoking floor; executive/club floor. In room: A/C, satellite TV, dataport, minibar, fridge, coffeemaker, iron, safe, IDD phone.

Sofitel Plaza Saigon ☆☆
The Sofitel hotel chain is famous in Southeast Asia for finding grand old colonial dames and converting them into the most charming hotel properties. This is not one of them. Opened in 1999, it's one of the newest and shiniest facades on the Saigon skyline. However, what it lacks in colonial charm it more than compensates for in modern luxury, convenience, and comfort. Guest rooms are handsome and cooling, with fine Art Deco touches like the curving, clean-lined desks in most rooms. You'll never be wanting for any amenity here, and the staff is helpful and professional. In a convenient spot just across from the former U.S. and French embassies, this is a popular choice for the international business crowd, who can enjoy the sleek executive floor with a small lounge, a daily buffet, drinks, and some basic business services. With similar high-luxe suites and comparable standards throughout, the Sofitel is the top-notch Caravelle's closest competitor in town.

17 Le Duan Blvd., District 1. In the U.S., © **800/221-4542** or 08/824-1555. Fax 08/824-1666. www.accor hotels.com/asia. 290 units. US$150 superior; US$200–US$210 club single/double; US$350–US$1,450 suite. AE, MC, V. **Amenities:** 2 restaurants; bar; luxury rooftop pool; health club; spa; sauna; steam; concierge; car rental; business center; 24-hr. room service; massage; babysitting; laundry; dry cleaning; 1 nonsmoking floor; club rooms; meeting rooms for 500. In room: A/C, satellite TV, dataport, minibar, fridge, coffeemaker, safe, IDD phone.

EXPENSIVE

Grand Hotel ☆☆
This is it—the Real McCoy: a 1930s colonial building, done just right (okay, close, at least). It's owned by Saigontourist—fancy that! The recently renovated Grand has a serene, tasteful atmosphere, and there are

some choice features, like the lovingly restored iron elevator with views through some stunning original stained glass. The lobby is bright, the staff is friendly, and the location on Dong Khoi is, in a word, grand. Rooms are big, with simple dark-wood furniture and large wardrobes, and without the musty smell that plagues many Saigon hotels. The bathrooms are small but have big counters and hair dryers. Deluxe rooms clustered in the old building near the elevator have classic high ceilings, rich wood floors, and a comfortable, colonial charm for the price tag (US$125). Standard rooms are no less charming—just smaller. The quiet atmosphere here suggests tourists rather than business, though and they've got all the right amenities: Most notable are the quiet sitting areas and bar, and the central courtyard's small but peaceful pool area, a unique escape from busy Ho Chi Minh City.

8–24 Dong Khoi St., District 1. ℂ **08/823-0163.** Fax 063/823-5781. www.grandsaion.com. 107 units. US$85–US$125 double; US$160 deluxe suite; US$260–US$490 grand/presidential suite. AE, MC, V. **Amenities:** Restaurant; 2 bars; outdoor pool (nice courtyard); small health club; Jacuzzi; sauna; steam; Saigontourist tour desk; car rental; business center; shop; massage; laundry; dry cleaning. *In room:* A/C, satellite TV, minibar, fridge, safe, IDD phone, complimentary water.

Hotel Continental ✿   Owned by Saigontoursm, this place is a big shame. It's not that it's so horrible, but it could be gorgeous, and it's a shambles. Built in 1890, it is the pre-eminent historic hotel in Saigon, of Graham Greene's *The Quiet American* fame. Its last renovation was in 1980. The very heart of downtown, it has a lovely colonial facade, but the lobby is overly ornate, with oversize chandeliers, Chinese vases, and that fake, semigloss shine of a lower standard trying to be something more. Rooms are absolutely huge, with high ceilings, but it's the red velveteen curtains, tatty red carpets, and general run-down feel that spoil the fantasy. It looks more like an aging cathouse, really, and the furniture can't seem to fill the big, empty space. The beds are comfortable and plush, though, as are the towels; all bathrooms are done plain, like a guesthouse, and lack counters, but are big and clean and have bathtubs. "First-class rooms," for US$120, are big and comfy, with roll-top desks, ornate columns, and a wood archway separating a small sitting area—they're a good bet. The restaurant is a lovely period piece, and the hotel staff is friendly but more or less dazed and confused. With a renovation, this historic gem could be a contender.

132–134 Dong Khoi St., District 1. ℂ **08/829-9201.** Fax 08/824-1772. 83 units. US$100–US$130 double; US$160 suite. Includes breakfast, tax, and service charge. AE, MC, V. **Amenities:** 2 restaurants; 2 bars; small fitness center; tour desk; car rental; small business center in lobby; shopping; limited room service; massage; laundry; dry cleaning. *In room:* A/C, satellite TV w/video rental, minibar, fridge, safe (in higher standard only), phone w/IDD.

Norfolk Hotel ✿✿   This snappy 10-year-old Australian/Vietnamese joint venture has one of the highest occupancy rates in town, for good reason: It's affordable and convenient, and it covers all the bases. Rooms are bright and good-size, furnished in slightly mismatched chain-hotel style, but everything is like new and there are even in-room safes. The beds are soft and deluxe, and the TVs are large. Bathrooms are small but finished with marble. Extremely efficient and friendly, the Norfolk's staff could conduct its own world school of languages; and all speak great English and are helpful. The restaurant is bright and upscale, featuring extensive breakfast and lunch buffets, as well as monthly themes and special menus. It's perfect for the business traveler or tourist seeking amenities and affordability; there's a business center with Internet, a basic health club, a sauna, room service, and a travel desk to cater to any need—all at reasonable prices. Book early.

117 Le Thanh Ton St., District 1. © 08/829-5368. Fax 08/829-3415. www.norfolkgroup.com. 104 units. US$100–US$140 double; from US$220 suite. Promotional and Internet rates available. AE, MC, V. **Amenities:** Restaurant; bar/club; small health club; sauna; steam; concierge; tour desk; business center; 24-hr. room service; massage; laundry; nonsmoking rooms; meeting facilities. *In room:* A/C, satellite TV, minibar, fridge, coffeemaker, safe, IDD phone.

Saigon Prince Hotel, a Duxton Hotel ★★   The Saigon Prince is in a good location, at the quieter end of hotel row and near several excellent restaurants. Run by Duxton, an Australian standard, it's got all the bases covered at very affordable rates. The beige rooms are nice-size, tasteful, and comfortable, with plush beds, carpets, and coffeemakers. The bathrooms are smart black-and-white marble. The lobby, entered by swooping stairs from a circular drive and, inside, circled by a mezzanine, is classy but not overly grand: It's a good downtown meeting point. This place is popular with business travelers, especially those on an extended stay, who come here for all the comforts of home at cost. The staff is efficient and personable. The second-floor spa offers excellent Hong Kong massage service, along with steam and Jacuzzi (ask about special mid-week spa rates). Also try the authentic Japanese restaurant on the mezzanine floor. Club Lido is a happening nightspot.

63 Nguyen Hue Blvd., District 1. © 08/822-2999. Fax 08/824-1888. 203 units. US$70 deluxe; US$90 deluxe w/break; from US$156 suites (add tax). Promotional rates available. AE, DC, MC, V. **Amenities:** 2 restaurants; bar, nightclub; small health club; Jacuzzi; sauna; steam; concierge; tour desk; fleet of cars for rent; business center; shopping; 24-hr. room service; massage; laundry; dry cleaning; nonsmoking rooms; meeting rooms for 310. *In room:* A/C, satellite TV w/in-house movies, dataport, minibar, fridge, coffeemaker, safe, IDD phone.

MODERATE

Huong Sen Hotel   This is an outstanding hotel for the price and has a great location on Dong Khoi, but this is another of the many government-owned places whose service is marked only by varying levels of indifference. It's a popular choice for big tour groups, and great group rates (and Internet prices) are available. Rooms are big and newly renovated, with simple, colorfully painted wood furniture and floral drapes and headboards. Nice touches include molded ceilings and marble-topped counters in the spotless bathrooms. Some rooms have balconies. Beds are ultracomfortable. This hotel is comparable to any other in this category, but it's bland.

66–70 Dong Khoi St., District 1. © 08/829-9400. Fax 08/829-0916. huongsen@hcm.vnn.vn. 50 units. US$52–US$95 double. AE, DC, MC, V. **Amenities:** Restaurant; bar; sauna; car rental; business center; limited room service; massage; laundry; dry cleaning; Internet. *In room:* A/C, TV, minibar, fridge, IDD phone.

Kim Do Royal City Hotel ★★   This is a good bargain right downtown. The Kim Do is the kind of place with a wooden tree trunk clock in the lobby, pink plastic hangers, polyurethane slippers in the closet, and bedspreads of some indeterminate man-made-material. It is still immensely likeable, however, thanks to its very friendly staff, good restaurant, perfect downtown location, and absolute cleanliness. It was built nearly 100 years ago and underwent a renovation in 1994. All rooms have interesting Asian carved furniture, carpets, and rock-hard beds (you can request a soft one). Aged bathrooms are clean but have no counter space. There are coffeemakers, though, and everything is spotless. Rooms are big; the junior suites simply huge. On-premises dining options include the Saigon Restaurant (which serves excellent Vietnamese cuisine), two bars, and a lobby lounge. Don't miss a dip in the top-floor hot tub, if just to look at the funky sea nymphs on the wall and fake stars on the ceiling.

133 Nguyen Hue Ave., District 1. © 08/822-5914 or 08/822-5915. Fax 08/822-5913. www.kimdohotel.com. US$44–US$57 double; US$79 junior suite; US$97 executive suite. These are Internet rates. AE, DC, MC, V.

Amenities: Rooftop restaurant; bar; steam bath; all rentals; concierge; tour desk; car rental; business center; 24-hr. room service; massage; nonsmoking floor; Internet. *In room:* A/C, TV, minibar, fridge, coffeemaker, hair dryer, safe, IDD phone.

Palace Hotel   This downtown tower has been around for a while. In fact, it was popular for U.S. soldiers on R&R. There have been some recent updates, but the history shows. What holds this place above its fellow downtown Saigon-tourist properties is the rooftop pool; though small, like a big bathtub, it's unique in this category. Standard rooms are nondescript, really, and a bit run down, with older carpet; they're also in need of a bit of paint. The high-end suites have large beds, desks, and sitting areas that are raised on parquet and with decent views; they're a good bet. This is a popular group option (because of good group and Internet rates), and though the staff members are often swamped, they're yet to be jaded and couldn't be friendlier. Whatever amenities they lack, these folks will point you in the right direction. There's also a useful Saigon-tourist desk in the lobby.

56-66 Nguyen Hue Blvd., Dist 1. (*C*) **08/824-4231.** Fax 08/824-4229. www.palacesaigon.com. US$55–US$80 double; US$110–US$165 suite (plus tax). AE, MC, V. **Amenities:** 2 restaurants; 2 bars (1 up, 1 down); rooftop pool; sauna; rentals available; Saigontourist desk in lobby; business center; 24-hr. room service; massage; laundry. *In room:* A/C, TV, minibar, fridge, phone w/IDD.

Rex Hotel ⭐⭐   The Rex has an unorthodox history; it used to be a French garage, was expanded by the Vietnamese, and then was used by the United States Information Agency (and some say the CIA) from 1962 to 1970. The hotel was transformed in a massive renovation and opened in 1990 as the hugely atmospheric government-run place it is today. There are a variety of rooms, but all are large and clean, with fluffy carpets and bamboo detailing on the ceilings, the mirrors—everywhere, in fact. The lampshades are big royal crowns, which are a hoot. There is good indirect lighting throughout. Some of the suites have beaded curtains and Christmas lights over the bathroom mirrors. The beds and pillows are incredible, firm but fat, and there are good views from some balconies. Each suite has a fax machine. The Rex is in a fabulous location downtown, across from a square that has a lively carnival atmosphere at night. It is also known for its rooftop bar, with its panoramic Saigon view. The pool is small, just a toe-dipper, but is in a quiet courtyard. Amenities here cover all the bases, if you can find them in this labyrinth. Call ahead because this place is often booked.

141 Nguyen Hue Blvd., District 1. (*C*) **08/829-2185** or 08/829-3115. Fax 08/829-6536. 207 units. US$70–US$120 double; US$155–US$495 suite. AE, MC, V. **Amenities:** 2 restaurants; 2 bars; outdoor pool; tennis; small health club; Jacuzzi; sauna; tour desk; car rental; business center; shopping; salon; 24-hr. room service; massage; babysitting; laundry; dry cleaning; nonsmoking rooms; Internet. *In room:* A/C, satellite TV w/in-house movies, safe, IDD phone.

Windsor Hotel ⭐   This handy business gem, around the corner from the backpacker area, is a converted block of service apartments, so the rooms are very spacious. Ask for onerecently renovated with a tile floor instead of the aging, drab carpets of other rooms. The one-bedroom suites are a bit plain, but it's like your own apartment and just as cozy and quiet (double-pane windows keep out the street noise). Bathrooms are not especially large but are clean, with good, high-pressure showers. There's a popular Chinese restaurant and newly opened French boulangerie in the lobby. The multilingual staff is "all business" but is helpful. Though you're a good distance from the central business district, it's easy to catch a cab on this busy thoroughfare. This is a good middle-of-the-road choice.

193 Tran Hung Dao St., District 1. ✆ **08/836-7848.** Fax 08/836-7889. www.windsorsaigonhotel.com. 65 units. US$60–US$75 double; US$130–US$145 suite. Discount rates available. AE, MC, V. **Amenities:** 2 restaurants; bar; all rentals available; tour desk; business center; laundry; dry cleaning. *In room:* A/C, TV, minibar, fridge, IDD phone.

INEXPENSIVE

Bong Sen Hotel Annex   This small annex to the large Saigontourist-owned Bong Sen provides many of the same amenities at a much lower price. The rooms are bright and attractive, with light-wood furniture, new carpet, and blue tile bathrooms. It's very chain-hotel floral. Everything is kind of on the small side, though, and the economy rooms have only one small window. The junior suite isn't much bigger. Make sure you're getting the Annex and not the main Bong Sen, which isn't as attractive or as much of a value. Service is indifferent, but this is a good place to just lay your head for cheap; you can arrange any travel necessities elsewhere.

61–63 Hai Ba Trung St., District 1. ✆ **08/823-5818.** Fax 08/823-5816. bongsen2@hcm.vnn.vn. 57 units. US$30–US$35 double; US$45 junior suite. AE, MC, V. **Amenities:** Restaurant; rentals available; tour desk; laundry. *In room:* A/C, TV, minibar, fridge, hair dryer, IDD phone.

Spring Hotel (Mua Xuan) ★★   If you don't care about fancy amenities and want to be downtown, look no further than this amazing place, with nicer rooms than many hotels twice the price. Accommodations here are neat and clean, with comfy double and super-king beds, big TVs, well-finished bathrooms done in decorated tiles, and nice, solid dark-wood or light rattan furniture. The floral motif isn't bad, and the carpeted floors are impeccably clean. Go as high up as you can to escape street noise, which is the hotel's one failing (and the elevator's kind of slow, too). Lowest-priced "economy" rooms have no windows. Suites are large, with couches in large, separate sitting rooms. The Spring has an improbable Greco-Roman motif, with statues and filigreed molding here and there; if the lobby's hanging ivy, colonnades, and grand staircase are a bit over the top, rooms are a bit more toned down, utilitarian, and pleasant. It's all quite forgivable, though. A short walk from Dong Khoi and the central business district, this is a popular choice for long-term business travelers. The staff couldn't be nicer or more helpful.

44–46 Le Thanh Ton St., District 1. ✆ **08/829-7362.** Fax 08/822-1383. 45 units. US$25–US$40 double; US$59 suite. Includes breakfast. AE, MC, V. **Amenities:** Restaurant/bar; can arrange rentals and tours; room service 7am–10pm; laundry; free Internet in lobby (but slow). *In room:* A/C, TV w/HBO, minibar, fridge, wooden safe, phone w/IDD.

Hong Hoa Hotel ★★   You found it! This minihotel is the top dog of the lower-end category in the Pham Ngu Lao backpacker area. Rooms are sizable and nicely furnished, with real light-wood furniture and tile floors. Only three of the rooms have bathtubs, but the rest have separate shower areas (all rooms

---

⌐ *Tips* **Things You Forgot from Home**

A large store on the corner of Nguyen Hue and Le Loi streets, across from the Rex Hotel, advertises itself as "duty-free." You'll find a good selection of brand-name toothpastes, face creams, sunscreens, and the like, or try the **Diamond Department Store** (in the Diamond Plaza just N of the Notre Dame Cathedral, at 34 Le Duan St.; ✆ **08/822-5500**) for everything but the kitchen sink (and maybe that, too).

have hot water), and all are clean, inviting, and well designed. The mattresses are those foam pads, but they're very comfortable and the pillows carry weight. The satellite TV and phones are a real luxury in this category. Downstairs is a popular Internet center, and the room rate includes 2 hours of free access daily. If it looks like two addresses here, it is, with one entrance through a small grocery storefront on busy De Tham street and the other off Pham Ngu Lao. Connect with folks back home with the cheap international Internet phone in the lobby. It's comfortable, safe, and friendly, and if you stay here long enough, you'll be adopted (and certainly learn some Vietnamese). If the place is full, which is more often than not the case, with just seven rooms, ask for a recommendation and they'll point you to a good neighbor.

185/28 Pham Ngu Lao St., 250 De Tham St., District 1. ℂ 08/836-1915. honhoarr@hcm.vnn.vn. 7 units. US$10–US$15 double. Includes tax and service charge. MC, V. **Amenities:** Rentals available; tour information; laundry; good Internet service; small grocery connected. *In room:* A/C, satellite TV, phone.

WHERE TO DINE

Saigon has the largest array of restaurants in Vietnam, and virtually every world cuisine is represented. The area around Dong Khoi is filled with some fine dining choices, and there are a few exciting new upscale spots for Vietnamese; ask locals where to eat, though, and they'll point you to the Ben Thanh Market or a local vendor on wheels. Ho Chi Minh's famous street stalls serve up local specials like *mien ga,* vermicelli, chicken, and mushrooms in a delicate soup; *lau hai san,* a tangy seafood soup with mustard greens; and, of course, *pho,* Vietnam's staple noodle soup. If the stalls scare you off, try a little gem of a restaurant called Ngon, where they bring the street stalls to you in a restaurant setting.

EXPENSIVE

Amigo ★★ ARGENTINE/STEAKHOUSE   One of the best steaks I've ever had was here, and I don't mean just in Saigon. This is one of those little expat gems you'll want to seek out. In a roomy two-floor downtown setting, it's a cozy and atmospheric Argentinean steakhouse theme (maybe the only in Asia), laid back but classy. You'll be greeted at the door by a kindly maître d' who will make you feel at home, as will the friendly staff and chummy atmosphere around the imposing wooden bar. But it's the food that sells this place, and here I mean imported steak done just how you like it, chargrilled to perfection, not panfried, as is common in this part of the world. I had a filet mignon with red shallots that would hold its own in the heart of Chicago. The restaurant also features seafood specials and has a nice salad bar. Entrees come with big baked potatoes and corn; for a real slice of home, follow it up with apple strudel or ice-cream roulade. There's also a great wine list featuring good Argentine and Chilean reds, among others, and a full-service bar.

55 Nguyen Hue St., District 1. ℂ 08/836-9890. Main courses US$5–US$20. AE, MC, V. Daily 11am–2pm and 5–11pm.

Bi Bi FRENCH/MEDITERRANEAN   The food is the star at this small restaurant and art cafe, although the atmosphere has its charms as well. Bi Bi's cozy interior is fashioned with bright Mediterranean-style furnishings and Impressionist paintings; the artwork collection changes periodically. Popular with expats, the place has chairs that are all embossed with names of notorious or beloved patrons past and present. A table near the front is devoted to drinking and card playing, and upstairs there are a few sofas for drinking and lounging. The menu is an interesting mix: cannelloni, ratatouille, pastas, and veal escalope, with fine hot and cold starters like salad with goat cheese and grill items. The beef tenderloin is trés bien. For dessert, there are perfectly done staples like crème brulée, mousse, or homemade ice cream. The starters are almost as expensive as the main courses, and the short wine list comprises pricey selections, making this one of Saigon's more expensive choices. The food is well worth it, though, and service is seamless.

8A/8D Thai Van Lung, District 1. ⓒ **08/829-5783**. Main courses US$5–US$13. MC, V. Daily 11:30am–2pm and 5:30–10:30pm.

Camargue ⓐ FRENCH/CONTINENTAL Camargue is two floors of enchanting surroundings in a renovated colonial. You can choose from softly lit interior or spacious outdoor terrace seating surrounded by palm fronds. The menu changes regularly. A sampling from our visit included warm goat cheese salad, roast pork rondalet, and venison. Camargue also seems to have given tourists the nod by adding ubiquitous, lower-priced pasta dishes. The food, alas, isn't as perfect as the surroundings and the service is substandard, but it's a quaint, laid-back spot downtown. The bar on the first floor is as fashionable as any in the country.

16 Cao Ba Quat St., District 1. ⓒ **08/824-3148**. Reservations recommended on weekend nights. Main courses US$5–US$12. AE, DC, MC, V. Daily 5:30–11pm.

Gartenstadt ⓐ GERMAN   It's everything but the oompah band here at this authentic German restaurant in the heart of downtown. A longtime favorite with expats, this place is a meat lover's dream, serving fine homemade sausage, rich dishes like sauerbraten, imported steaks, and a beef roulade that will have you saying "Gott im Himmel!" And what's German food without German beer? They've got fine German brands on tap and a good selection of schnapps and cognac. Seating is cozy in the popular downstairs bar area or in a classy second-floor dining room, but ask about the small balcony, with good views of busy Dong Khoi below.

34 Dong Khoi St., District 1. ⓒ **08/822-3623**. Main courses US$4.66–US$13.33. AE, MC, V. Daily 10:30am–12am.

Hoi An ⓐⓐ VIETNAMESE   Run by the same folks who bring you Mandarin just around the corner (see below), Hoi An serves a similar compliment of fine, authentic Vietnamese; here the focus is on central Vietnam's light fare. On busy Le Thanh Ton Street just north of the town center, the building is a nice re-creation of a traditional Vietnamese home, and the upstairs dining room is an interesting faux-rustic blend of wood and bamboo. Presentation here is unique, like the hollowed coconut that was used to serve a fine crab and asparagus, and everything is good. Try the drunken shrimp, large prawns soaked in rice whiskey and pan-fried at tableside. Order a cover-the-table meal for a group, and you're sure to go away smiling. Call ahead to ask about the authentic Vietnamese classical music (most nights).

11 Le Thanh Ton St., District 1. ⓒ **08/823-7694**. Main courses US$5–US$20. AE, MC, V. Daily 5:30–11:00pm.

Mandarin ⓐⓐ VIETNAMESE/CHINESE   On a quiet side-street between busy Le Than Thon and the river, cross the threshold at Mandarin and you enter a quaint, elegant oasis that will have you forgetting the seething city outside. Decor is an upscale Chinese motif with timber beams, fine Chinese screen paintings, and artwork on two open-plan floors. It's plush but not stuffy, and you'll feel comfortable in casual clothes or a suit. The staff is professional and attentive but doesn't hover, and it is helpful with suggestions and explanations. Ask about daily specials and set menus. I had an excellent spicy sautéed beef served in bamboo with rice. For a memorable meal, don't miss the famed duck done in a sweet "Mandarin style." The restaurant features a live classical trio (call ahead for schedule)

11A Ngo Van Nam, District 1. ✆ **08/822-9783**. Fax 08/825-6185. Main courses US$2–US$22; set menu US$16 per person (minimum 2). AE, MC, V. Daily 11am–2pm and 5:30–10pm.

Sushi Bar ★★ JAPANESE   The food speaks for itself (in Japanese, no less) at this friendly little corner sushi bar. At the end of Le Thanh Ton, an as-yet dubbed "Little Tokyo," this is one of many Japanese eateries popping up and is popular among longtime residents. It's a typical busy, big-city sushi bar, complete with a friendly, wise-cracking sushi master from Japan. Upstairs there are tatami mat rooms, and the place always seems full, which is a good sign. Everything's fresh, and the lunch specials are a good bargain, but it's good sushi and sashimi, worth the price.

2 Le Thanh Ton, District 1. ✆ **08/823-8042**. A la carte dishes US$1–US$5.33; set menu US$2.33–US$12. MC, V. Daily 11:30am–2pm and 5:30–11:30pm. Delivery until 10pm.

MODERATE

Augustin ★ FRENCH   On the quaint, up-and-coming "restaurant row" off Nguyen Hue Street, this is a bright, lively little French restaurant, a great favorite with French expats and tourists. The food is simple yet innovative French fare, including beef pot au feu and sea bass tartare with olives. Try the seafood stew, lightly seasoned with saffron and packed with fish, clams, and shrimp. The seating is quite cozy, especially because the restaurant is always full, and the Vietnamese wait staff is exceptionally friendly, speaking both French and English. The menu is bilingual, too. A large French wine list and classic dessert menu finish off a delightful meal.

10 Nguyen Thiep. ✆ **08/829-2941**. Main courses US$2–US$6. No credit cards. Daily noon–2pm and 6–11pm.

Blue Ginger   Also called the Saigon Times Club, this Vietnamese bistro is an atmospheric choice with fine local specialties; as a result, it's a tour group favorite, but that doesn't spoil the atmosphere. It features a nightly performance of folk music, and the dulcit tones mingle nicely with clinking glasses and the low hum of conversation in the candlelit dining room; it makes for a nice, casual evening. The specialty here are large seafood steamboats, a veritable cornucopia of seafood done like Japanese *nabe* in a large pot in front of you (for 2 or more). I had the caramelized pork served in a clay pot, and it was excellent. There are great set menus of up to 10 courses, and the desserts are all there: ice cream, crème caramel, and fried bananas.

37 Nam Ky Khoi Nghia, District 1. ✆ **08/829-8676**. Main courses US$2–US$6; set menu US$10–US$20. MC, V. Daily 7am–10:30pm.

Café Mogambo AMERICAN   Run by American expat Mike and his Vietnamese wife, Lani, Mogambo is the laid-back Yank hangout in Saigon. It's a small, dimly lit place with cane ceilings and walls, animal head trophies, and memorabilia. There is a long bar with television and a row of regulars bellied up to it. Before long, you'll be joining in the conversation and hanging out longer than you planned. Long, diner-style banquettes that stick to your legs are one contribution to an American experience. The other is the beef; the hamburgers and steaks are the real thing, as are the sausages and meat pies. Entrees are all quite affordable; it's just the steaks that jack up the high end of the price range. Dessert is apple pie, of course, and a plain, hearty cup of coffee.

20 Bis Thi Sach St., District 1. ✆ **08/825-1311**. Main courses US$4–US$13. MC, V. Daily 7am–11pm.

Chao Thai THAI   The food and setting are both flawless here. The restaurant is over two floors of an elegant, roomy Thai longhouse, with wide plank wood floors, black-and-white photos of Thai temples, and some small statuary. Chao Thai is famous for its fiery papaya salad, fried catfish with basil leaves, and prawn cakes with plum sauce. The flavors are subtle and not overdone; you won't leave feeling drugged on spices or too much chile. It's a popular power lunch spot, but the atmosphere is just as warm and welcoming to walk-in tourists. The service is gracious and efficient.

16 Thai Van Lung, District 1. ✆ **08/824-1457**. Reservations recommended only for groups of 5 or more. Main courses US$3.66–US$5; set lunch menu US$5.52. AE, MC, V. Daily 11:00am–2pm and 6:00–10:30pm.

Lemongrass VIETNAMESE   The atmosphere is candlelit and intimate, very Vietnamese, with cane furniture and tile floors, yet it's not overly formal. On a small romantic side street that's becoming it's own "restaurant row" in the downtown area, this restaurant is three floors of subdued cool and fine dining; a great place to duck out of the midday sun. Set lunches are an affordable and light option: soup, spring rolls, and a light curry for US$2. The long menu emphasizes seafood and seasonal specials. Particularly outstanding are the deep-fried prawn in coconut batter and the crab sautéed in salt and pepper sauce. The portions are very healthful, Asian family-style, so go with a group, if at all possible, and sample as many delicacies as possible.

4 Nguyen Thiep St., District 1. ✆ **08/822-0496**. Main courses US$2–US$8; lunch set menus from US$2. AE, MC, V. Daily 11am–2pm and 5–10pm.

Temple Club ★★ VIETNAMESE   For atmosphere alone, the Temple Club is a must-see in Ho Chi Minh. As the name suggests, this is an old Chinese temple, circa 1900, with original wood and masonry. Though it has gone upscale with recent renovations, that special air about the place remains. The ceiling is high, and the walls are exposed brick. The floor is terra-cotta draped in antique throw rugs, and there are some great Buddhist tapestries and statuary about. There's a classic old wooden bar and a formal but comfortable dining room, as well as a lounge area in the back for coffee and dessert. The cuisine is standard Vietnamese from all parts of the country. This place does a good Hanoi-style *cha ca*, fried monkfish, and the *tom me*, a dish of prawns in tamarind sauce, is a good choice. They have a "Western Corner" and serve sandwiches and salad. For dessert, the banana coconut cream pudding, served with sesame seeds, is decadent, and the coffee is the real thing, even cappuccino. This is one of the most atmospheric and romantic spots in town.

29 Ton That Thiep St., District 1. ✆ **08/829-9244**. Main courses US$3–US$8. Daily 10am–2pm and 5–11pm.

INEXPENSIVE

Allez Boo ★ VIETNAMESE/WESTERN   This little corner eatery is on De Tham Street in the very heart of the Pham Ngu Lao backpacker area. It serves affordable one-plate meals and a good selection of Vietnamese and faux-Western in an open-air corner bar. Come for dinner and stay for drinks or a game of pool table in this busy but cozy spot, all done up in a beachside bamboo-and-thatch theme. You're sure to meet some fellow travelers, the food is good (stick to Vietnamese and curry), and it's always hoppin' till late. It's pickpocket central, though, so keep an eye out at the window tables.

187 Pham Ngu Lao ☎ 08/837-2505. Main courses US$1–US$3. V, MC. Daily 8am–late.

Ngon Restaurant ★★ *Finds* VIETNAMESE   In Vietnamese, *Ngon* means "delicious"; for authentic Vietnamese, this unpretentious find gets my vote for the best in Vietnam. It's always packed (mostly with locals), and the atmosphere is like a busy marketplace. Fans blow mist to quell the smoky cooking fires of the many stalls in the courtyard around this stately colonial. There's another building at the rear and balcony overlooking the whole scene, and seating is just about everywhere: bar-side, at large banquet tables, at small romantic perches on the balcony, or on squat stools in the busy courtyard. Individual stalls on the courtyard perimeter each serve their own specialty, like someone went around the country head-hunting all of the best street-side chefs; the waitstaff simply act as liaisons among the many cooks. The menu is a survey course in Vietnamese cooking, and the tuition is low. Go with a Vietnamese friend, if you can, or someone who can explain some of the regional specialties. If you're alone, just point and shoot. Everything is good, from the Hue-style *bun bo,* cold noodles with beef; a catalog of *pho,* noodle soup; and all kinds of seafood prepared the way you like. Meals here are best dragged-out, many-course affairs, but go just for a snack if you're visiting the Reunification Palace or any sites downtown. Don't miss it!

138 Nam Ky Khoi Nghia, District 1 ☎ 08/829-9449. Main courses US50¢–US$3. AE, MC, V. Daily 6:30am–11pm.

Restaurant 19 ★ VIETNAMESE   With all the upscale eateries popping up in the downtown area, you might miss out on an old-school standby like this little storefront. Tucked between high-rises and just off Dong Khoi, this is one of many restaurants whose name is its street number (if this one is busy, try no. 13). The atmosphere might be somewhat institutional in this eatery, but it serves excellent traditional Vietnamese food without any fine wooden trim, upscale decoration, or sticker shock. The place is jolly and filled with locals, tourists, and expats. Ask what's good, and try the seafood, anything done in coconut broth, or the delectable lemongrass chicken.

19 Ngo Duc Ke, District 1. ☎ 08/298-882. Main courses US$2–US$6. No credit cards. Daily 6:30am–10pm.

ZEN ★ VEGETARIAN   Just a little storefront tucked away amid many on tiny Pham Ngu Lao, this little vegetarian hideaway serves some great light fare: It's a good break from heavy sauces and fried food. It's got nothing in atmosphere, but it's always busy and is a good people-watching spot in the alley. The staff couldn't be friendlier, and they seem downright happy you're there (though you can express that to one another only in smiles). The menu's a bit too ambitious, with Japanese, Indian, and even Mexican selections (some decent facsimiles, though). Ask what's good, and you can enjoy some good, wholesome veggie fare and pull a book from the shelf or strike up a conversation.

185/30 Pham Ngu Lao, District 1 ☎ 08/837-3713. Main courses US35¢–US$1.33. Cash only. Daily 7am–10pm.

SNACKS & CAFES

While shopping on Dong Khoi, stop to savor a few moments at the **Paris Deli,** 31 Dong Khoi (☎ **08/829-7533**), a retro spot with fantastic pastries and sandwiches. There's another storefront at 65 Le Loi St. (☎ **08/821-6127**), which serves the same good sandwiches and treats.

O'Brien's Pub, at 74 Hai Ba Trung (© **08/829-3198**), serves great pizza in its comfortable wooden bar room, as does the **Underground** (basement of Lucky Plaza, 69 Dong Khoi St.; © **08/829-9079**), a popular hangout in a little basement storefront right on Dong Khoi.

Pho 2000, riverside, next to the Renaissance Riverside Hotel, serves the popular Vietnamese noodle-soup staple. It's simplicity taken to a new height here. Though you can eat pho on any street corner and in any market, this is a good place to find English explanations and more comforting standards of cleanliness.

Café Central, in the Sun Wah Tower, 115 Nguyen Hue, District 1 (© **08/821-9303**), is a great little international deli. Stop in for breakfast or a sandwich any time; the kind staff makes you feel like you've stepped into an old greasy spoon (with all the same standbys on the menu).

Ciao Café, at 02 Hang Bai St. downtown (© **08/822-9796**), is a good spot for snacks and ice cream. **Fanny,** just below the Temple Club at 48 Le That Thiep (© **08/821-1630**), and serves the real-deal French glacées (ice cream, that is).

ATTRACTIONS
ATTRACTIONS IN DISTRICT 1

Ben Thanh Market 👁👁👁   The clock tower over the main entrance to what was formerly known as Les Halles Centrale is the symbol of Saigon, and the market might as well be, too. Opened first in 1914, it's crowded, a boon for pickpockets with its narrow, one-way aisles, and loaded with people clamoring to sell you cheap goods (T-shirts, aluminum wares, silk, bamboo, and lacquer) and postcards. There are so many people calling out to you that you'll feel like the bell of the ball or a wallet with legs. Watch for pickpockets. The wet market, with its selection of meat, fish, produce, and flowers, is interesting and hassle-free; no one will foist a fish on you. In open-air stalls surrounding the market are some nice little eateries. The adventurous can try all kinds of local specialties for next to nothing.

At the intersection of Le Loi, Ham Nghi, Tran Hung Dao, and Le Lai sts., District 1.

General Post Office (Buu Dien) 👁   In a grand old colonial building, you can check out the huge maps of Vietnam on either side of the main entrance and the huge portrait of Uncle Ho in the rear. The specialty stamps counter has some great collector sets for sale.

2 Coq Xu Paris, District 1. Daily 6:30am–10pm.

Saigon Opera House (Ho Chi Minh Municipal Theater)   This magnificent building was built at the turn of the century and renovated in the 1940s. Three stories and 1,800 seats are inside. Today it does very little in terms of performances, but it is a stalwart atmospheric holdout amid steel and glass downtown.

At the intersection of Le Loi and Dong Khoi sts.

Notre Dame Cathedral 👁   The neo-Romanesque cathedral was constructed between 1877 and 1883 using bricks from Marseilles and stained glass windows from Chartres. The cathedral is closed to visitors except during Sunday services, which are in Vietnamese and English. Whatever your faith is, don't miss it.

Near the intersection of Dong Khoi and Nguyen Du sts., District 1.

City Hall   Saigon's city hall was constructed between 1902 and 1908, a fantastic ornate example of colonial architecture. Unfortunately, it's not open to the public.

Facing Nguyen Hue Blvd.

Vietnam History Museum ★★ If there is one must-see in Saigon (or maybe "should-see"), this is it. The museum, in a rambling new concrete pagodalike structure, does a good job of presenting important aspects of Vietnam's southern area, in particular. There is an excellent selection of Cham sculpture and the best collection of ceramics in Vietnam. Weaponry from the 14th century onward is on display, including a yard with nothing but cannons. One wing is dedicated to ethnic minorities of the south, including photographs, costumes, and household implements. Nguyen Dynasty (1700–1945) clothing and housewares are also on display. There are archaeological artifacts from prehistoric Saigon. Its 19th and early 20th century histories are shown using photos and, curiously, a female corpse unearthed as construction teams broke ground for a recent housing project. There are even some general background explanations in English, something missing from most Vietnamese museums.

2 Nguyen Binh Khiem. ✆ **08/829-8146.** Admission 10,000 VND (US69¢). Daily 8–11:30am and 1:30–4:30pm.

Revolutionary Museum ★ This museum, situated in a grand historical structure built in the 1880s, is one of many in Vietnam exploring a familiar theme: the struggle of the nation against the French and Americans. It is probably the best of its breed, with various photos, documents, models, and military artifacts detailing local activism as well as long military struggles. The signs are in Vietnamese only at the moment, which actually doesn't present much of a problem. There is a model of the Cu Chi tunnels, the underground network built by the North Vietnamese for weapons transport and living quarters during the American war. Outside are the typical but always interesting captured U.S. fighter planes, tanks, and artillery. Underneath the building is a series of tunnels leading to the Reunification Palace, once used by former president Ngo Dinh Diem as a hideout before his eventual capture and execution in 1962.

65 Ly Tu Trong St. ✆ **08/829-8250.** Admission 10,000 VND (US66¢). Daily 8:30am–4:30pm.

Reunification Palace ★ Designed to be the home of former President Ngo Dinh Diem, this building is most notable for its symbolic role in the fall of Saigon in April 1975, when its gates were breached by North Vietnamese tanks and the victor's flag occupied the balcony. In the former century, the French governor general lived on the site in a building called Norodom Palace, destroyed in 1962 in an assassination attempt on Diem. The current "modern" nightmare was completed in 1966, after Diem's death. Like the Bao Dai Palace in Dalat, this is a series of rather empty rooms that are nevertheless interesting because they specialize in period kitsch and haven't been gussied up a single bit. You will tour private quarters, dining rooms, entertainment lounges, and the president's office. Most interesting is the war command room, with its huge maps and old communications equipment.

106 Nguyen Du St. Admission 15,000 VND (US$1). Daily 7:30–11am and 1–4pm.

OTHER DISTRICTS

Emperor Jade Pagoda (Phuoc Hai) ★★ One of the most interesting pagodas in Vietnam, the Emperor Jade is filled with smoky incense and fantastic carved figurines. It was built by the Cantonese community around the turn of the century and is still buzzing with worshippers, many lounging in the front gardens. Take a moment to look at the elaborate statuary on the pagoda's roof. The dominant figure in the main hall is the Jade Emperor himself; referred to as the "god of the heavens," the emperor decides who will enter and who will be refused. He looks an awful lot like Confucius, only meaner. In an anteroom to the left you'll find Kim Hua, a goddess of fertility, and the King of Hell in another corner with his minions, who undoubtedly gets those the Jade Emperor rejects. It's spooky.

73 Mai Thi Luu St., District 3. Daily 8am–5pm.

War Remnants Museum 👁️👁️   This museum houses a collection of machinery, weapons of all sorts, and photos documenting both the French and American wars, although the emphasis is heavily on the latter. The museum's former name was the War Crimes Museum, which should give you some tip whose side of the story is being told here. Some of the facts, including some gory photos and relics of the effects of bombing, are undeniably gripping. It is interesting to see how the Vietnamese propaganda machine works; short of being outright recrimination, this museum calls for peace, asking visitors to sign a petition against aerial bombing. Exhibits are more a testimony to the hellishness of war. A room at the entrance lists facts like troop numbers, bomb tonnage, and statistics on international involvement in the conflict. Displays change frequently and just recently there was a room dedicated to the journalists who were lost in wartime. One entire room is devoted to biological warfare, another to weaponry, and another to worldwide demonstrations for peace (and denunciations of the U.S.). The explanations, which include English translations, are amazingly thorough for a Vietnamese museum. There's a good collection of well-labeled bombs, planes, and tanks in the courtyard outside. Kids will love it, but you might want to think twice before taking them inside to see things like wall-size photos of the My Lai massacre and the bottled deformed fetus supposedly damaged by Agent Orange.

28 Vo Van Tan St., District 3. ✆ **08/829-0325.** Admission 10,000 VND (US69¢). Daily 7:30–11:30am and 1:30–5:15pm.

Giac Lam Pagoda 👁️   Giac Lam Pagoda, built in 1744, is the oldest pagoda in Saigon. The garden in the front features the ornate tombs of venerated monks, as well as a rare bodhi tree. Next to the tree is a regular feature of Vietnamese Buddhist temples, a gleaming white statue of Quan The Am Bo Tat (Avalokitesvara, the goddess of mercy) standing on a lotus blossom, a symbol of purity. Inside the temple is a spooky funerary chamber, with photos of monks gone by, and a central chamber chock full of statues. Take a look at the outside courtyard as well.

118 Lac Long Quan St., District 5. Daily 8am–5pm.

Cholon District 5 👁️👁️   Cholon is a sizable district bordered by Hung Vuong to the north, Nguyen Van Cu to the east, the Ben Nghe Chanel to the south, and Nguyen Thi Nho to the west. Cholon is the Chinese district of Saigon and probably the largest Chinatown in the world. It exists in many ways as a city quite apart from Saigon. The Chinese began to settle the area in the early 1900s and never quite assimilated with the rest of Saigon, which causes a bit of resentment among the greater Vietnamese community. You'll sense the different environment immediately, and not only because of the Chinese-language signs.

A bustling commercial center, Cholon is a fascinating maze of temples, restaurants, jade ornaments, and medicine shops. Gone, however, are the brothels and opium dens of earlier days. You can lose yourself in the narrow streets or hit the highlights. Here is one district, by the way, in which taking a cyclo by the hour makes sense to see the sites.

Start at the **Binh Tay Market** 👁️👁️, on Phan Van Khoe Street, which is even more crowded than Ben Thanh and has much the same goods, but with a Chinese flavor. There's much more produce, along with medicines, spices, and cooking utensils, and you'll find plenty of hapless ducks and chickens tied in heaps. From Binh Tay, head up to Nguyen Trai, the district's main artery, to see some of the major temples on or around it. Be sure to see Quan Am, on Lao Tu Street off Luong Nhu Hoc, for its ornate exterior. Back on Nguyen Trai, Thien Hau pagoda is dedicated to the goddess of the sea and was popular with seafarers making thanks for their safe trip from China to Vietnam. Finally, as you follow Nguyen Trai Street past Ly Thuong Kiet, you'll see the Cholon Mosque, the one indication of Cholon's small Muslim community.

SPORTS & OUTDOOR ACTIVITIES

There are two excellent 18-hole golf courses at the **Vietnam Golf and Country Club.** Fees are US$50 to US$80 during the week for nonmembers, depending on which course you want to play, and US$100 on Saturday and Sunday. The Clubhouse is at Long Thanh My Ward, District 9, © **08/733-0126;** fax 08/733-0102).

Tennis enthusiasts can find courts at **Lan Anh International Tennis Court,** 291 Cach Mang Than Tam, District 10 (© **04/862-7144**).

The pool and well-equipped gym and spa at the **Caravelle Hotel** (see the accommodations section) are available for nonguests at a day rate of US$12.

SHOPPING

Saigon has a good selection of silk, fashion, lacquer, embroidery, and housewares. Prices are higher than elsewhere, but the selection is more sophisticated, and Saigon's cosmopolitan atmosphere makes it somewhat easier to shop (meaning, shop owners aren't immediately pushing you to buy). Stores are open 7 days a week from 8am until about 7pm. Credit cards are widely accepted, except for the markets.

Dong Khoi is Saigon's premier shopping street. Formerly Rue Catinat, it was a veritable Rue de la Paix in colonial times. The best blocks are the last two heading toward the river. Notable shops include **Heritage,** 53 Dong Khoi (© **08/823-5438**), for wood carvings and other ethnic arts. **Les Epices,** at 25 Dong Khoi St.(© **08/823-6795**), also has a nice collection of lacquer ware and other gift items, and **Authentique Interiors,** 38 Dong Khoi (© **08/822-133**), specializes in gorgeous pottery and table settings. **Viet Silk,** at 21 Dong Khoi (© **08/823-4860**), has a quality selection of ready-made clothing and can, of course, whip something up for you in a day.

Nearby Le Thanh Ton Street is another shopping avenue. Look for **Kenly Silk,** at 132 Le Thanh Ton (© **08/829-3847**), a brand-name supplier with the best ready-to-wear silk garments in the business. Unique, tasteful, hand-embroidered pillows, table linens, and hand-woven fabrics can be found at **MC Decoration,** 92C5 Le Thanh Ton, across from the Norfolk Hotel (© **08/822-6003**).

Stop in at the **Saigon Duty Free Shop,** at 102 Nguyen Hue (© **08/823-4548**), catty-corner from the Rex Hotel, a full-size department store of bargains. You must have an international plane ticket, and you can pick up your goods at the airport upon departure.

ART GALLERIES

The **Ho Chi Minh Fine Arts Museum,** at 97A Pho Duc Chinh St., District 1 (© **08/829-4441;** Tues–Sun 9am–4:45pm; admission 10,000 VND/US66¢), is the place to start if you're truly keen. Here there are three floors of an evolving modern collection, featuring new and established Vietnamese artists' works in sculpture, oil, and lacquer, as well as a nice collection of ancient Buddhist artwork and some Cham statuary: It offers a good glimpse into the local scene. From there, have a look at **Lac Hong Art Gallery,** located on the ground floor of the museum (© **08/821-3771**), which features the works of many famous Vietnamese artists. There are galleries throughout the city, many clustered around Dong Khoi and near all the major hotels. Here you can get some great deals on reproductions of popular works (reproduction being a big industry in town), and those who're extremely keen or with deep pockets will find easy introductions to the artists or their representatives themselves. For a price, you can turn any photo into an enormous oil painting. Here are a few popular galleries in town: **Ancient Gallery,** 50 Mac Thi Buoi St., District 1, near Saigon Sakura Restaurant (© **08/822-7962**); **Hien Minh,** 32 Dong Khoi St., District 1 (© **08/829-5520**); **Particular Art Gallery,** 123 Le Loi St., District 1 (© **08/ 821-3019**); and **101 Catinat,** 101 Dong Khoi (© **08/822-7643**). If these pique your curiosity, pick up a copy of *Vietnam Discovery* or *The Guide*, two local "happenings guides," for further listings.

BOOKSTORES

HCMC's official foreign-language bookstore, Xuan Thu, is at 85 Dong Khoi St. across from the Continental Hotel (© **08/822-4670**). It has a good selection of classics in English and French, as well as some foreign-language newspapers. It's open daily from 7:30am to 9pm. There are also several small bookshops on De Tham Street, carrying many pirate titles and used books; some of these places do swaps, but you're certain to come away frustrated.

SAIGON AFTER DARK

When Vietnam made a fresh entry onto the world scene in the mid-1990s, Ho Chi Minh City quickly became one of the hippest party towns in the east. The mood has sobered somewhat, but it's still a fun place. Everything is clustered in District 1; ask expats in places like **Saigon Saigon** or **Maya** (below) about any club happenings.

As for cultural events, Saigon is sadly devoid of anything really terrific, except for a few cultural dinner and dance shows. If you try to find other types of performances, you'll be met with blank stares.

There is lots of sex for sale, as you might have heard. Gentlemen traveling alone are likely prey. Accepting a scooter ride from a lady, by the way, is tantamount to saying "yes" to lots more.

THE BAR SCENE

The most popular place, hands down, is **Saigon Saigon,** at the top of the Caravelle Hotel at 19 Lam Son (© **08/823-4999**). Here you have live music and a terrific view. It's Indochina meets the Hard Rock Cafe on any given evening. **Maya's,** a posh martini bar also serving Latin cuisine, is always good for a chic evening of cocktails. **Vasco's Bar,** on the first floor of Camarque (see the dining section), 16 Cao Ba Quat, (© **08/824-3148**) is a chic, atmospheric choice.

Don't miss the brick-walled Irish pub **O'Briens,** at 74A Hai Ba Trung (© **08/ 829-3198**), for pints and pizza. **Sheridan's,** at 17/13 Le Thanh Ton St. (© **08/ 823-0793**), is another good, friendly watering hole with character.

The Pham Ngu Lao area stays up late, and **Allez Boo,** 187 Pham Ngu Lao (© **08/837-2505**), is always up late, as are the many little street-side beer stalls selling Bia Hoi for pennies a glass.

CLUBS

Apocalypse Now, at 2C Thi Sach, District 1 (② **08/824-1463**), is a still-popular HCMC landmark and is good for a short stop on your night crawl. Try to make it toward the end of the night (or early morning), when the obvious decorations, drunk tourists, and platform-shod hookers will seem more fun than sad. Watch your belongings! **Q Bar,** in the basement of the central opera house at 7 Cong Truong Lam Son (② **090/810-9043**), is a fun and funky little catacomb with good music, cozy cocktail nooks, and an eclectic mix of homo sapiens.

MUSIC & THEATER

A few hotels stage traditional music and dance shows a la dinner theaters. The **"Au Co" Traditional Troupe** has performed abroad but calls home the Skyview Restaurant at the **Mondial Hotel,** 109 Dong Khoi St., District 1 (② **08/849-6291**). The **Rex Hotel,** 141 Nguyen Hue Blvd. (② **08/829-2185**), has regular performances as well. Call each place ahead of time to double-check the performance schedule.

15 The Mekong Delta

I can't emphasize this enough: Don't leave without seeing the Mekong Delta, at least for a day. The delta is a region of waterways formed by the Mekong, covering an area of about 60,000km (37,200 miles). Most of it is cultivated with bright green rice paddies, fruit orchards, sugarcane fields, vegetable gardens, and traditional fish farms. There are a few cities, too, but rather than seeing any cosmopolitan area, you get out to see the outlying canals by boat for a fascinating glimpse into a way of life that has survived intact for hundreds of years. As you cruise slowly along the meandering canals, you'll see locals living right beside the water, above it in stilt houses, and, in some cases, in it on houseboats. Trading is conducted from boat to boat, often in canal bends teeming with boats and their wares (hung from a tall pole as a form of advertising). The people are friendly and unaffected, and the cuisine of the upper delta is delicious and leans heavily toward seafood.

Coming south from Saigon, the town you'll probably reach first is **My Tho,** but you should try to make it down at least as far as **Can Tho,** the delta's largest city. It has a bustling riverfront and waterway. About 32km (20 miles) from Can Tho is **Phung Hiep,** the biggest water market in the region. The water is literally covered by the bobbing merchants. **Chau Doc** is another picturesque town and a popular gateway to Cambodia.

To cope with the necessary logistics, going with a tour agent is your best bet to the delta. All travel agents offer everything from day trips to "3 days, 4 nights" tours. Our pick is **Ann Tours,** at 58 Ton That Tung St., District 1 (② **08/833-2564** or 08/833-4356; fax 08/832-3866; www.anntours.com), for custom-made tours with six or fewer people at reasonable prices. The main reason to go with Ann's is the company's dedication to bringing you to places that are off the beaten path; you'll see the Mekong up close and personal. For the day trip, you'll be charged about US$45 per person; for 2 days, it's about US$85 to US$115 per person; and for 3 days, it's about US$165 per person (prices according to a 2-person minimum).

The **tourist cafes** all run standard, affordable tours here. Contact **Sinh Café,** 246-8 De Tham St., District 1 (② **08/376-833**), or **TM Brothers,** 269 De Tham St. or 139 Bui Vien St., District 1 (② **08/836-1791**), for 2- and 3-day tours starting at US$10 per day (with optional connection to Cambodia). As always, you get what you pay for.

Think twice about going to the delta at all during the rainy season, however. Many of the roads might be washed out, or the tides might be too high for canal travel.

16 Chau Doc

This little riverside border town is the main stopover for travelers going to and from Cambodia, but it is itself worthy of a brief visit. The town is a real throwback: You'll still see old-style Ho Chi Minh surries, a two-wheel cart on the back of a regular bicycle, instead of the standard cyclo. There's a floating market, a unique floating village, ethnic Cham villages, and a small pilgrimage peak outside of town, and all can be visited through most tours.

GETTING THERE

Chau Doc is part of most tours of the Mekong Delta. Contact any traveler cafe or travel agent in Ho Chi Minh, and you can arrange a visit here as part of a tour either returning to Ho Chi Minh or with connections to Cambodia. Chau Doc is 285km (177 miles) southwest of Saigon, and the bus ride combines with visits to other hamlets in the delta, boat trips, and lunch stops, and makes for a fun, full day.

VISITOR INFORMATION & TOURS

Saigontourist, in Ho Chi Minh City at 49 Le Thanh Ton St., District 1 (© **08/ 829-8914;** fax 08/822-4987; www.saigon-tourist.com), has regular bus schedules and tours, and can arrange onward boat travel to Cambodia. **Ann Tours,** 58 Ton That Tung St., District 1, Saigon (© **08/832-3866**), runs similar packages for smaller groups.

WHERE TO STAY AND DINE

There are a few minihotels around town. If you come with a cafe tour, you'll stay at **77 Thanh Tra Hotel,** 77 Thu Khoa Nghia St. (© **076/866-788**), or something similar: cell-block basic, but cheap, with air-conditioning. Dine at the Victoria, in the market, or in one of the basic storefront eateries in the town center that serve some good local fish, among other Vietnamese specialties.

Victoria Chau Doc ★★   This is the only option for quality accommodations in town, and it's a good one, at that. Of the same high standard of Victoria properties in the region, the riverside Victoria Chau Doc stands proud on the banks of the Bassac, a busy but captivating stretch of the Mekong. Rooms are good-size and simple, with wood floors and detail throughout. Bathrooms are nice black-and-white tile affairs and are large, with stylish granite countertops. Halls are done in a comfortable antique tile, and the general atmosphere of this old riverside dandy is quite pleasant. There's a nice, albeit small, pool and decks with great views. The restaurant, **Bassac,** serves fine Vietnamese and Western cuisine in an air-conditioned dining room or on a picturesque deck. They can arrange all necessities here: They have a private boat for tours or connection to Cambodia, and the helpful front-desk staff can arrange any local tours.

32 Le Loi St., Chau Doc Town, An Giang. © 076/865-010. Fax 076/865-020. www.victoriahotels-asia.com. US$83–US$98 double; US$154 suite. **Amenities:** Restaurant; bar; riverside pool; health club; spa; bicycle and all other rentals; concierge; tour desk; business center; shopping; room service 7am–11pm; massage; laundry; Internet. *In room:* A/C, satellite TV, minibar, fridge, safe, IDD phone.

ATTRACTIONS

The riverside and sprawling central market, a crossroads for goods to and from nearby Cambodia, are the real attractions. A stroll in the central market area any given morning is a real feast for the eyes (and the nose), and there are some small temples in the small downtown area. Even the most budget tour will take you to the **floating villages** ★★ in wooden sampans rowed in the unique "forward stroke" Vietnamese style (give it a try). You'll get to see a unique way of life and visit one of the many catfish farms that, collectively, are taking the world market by storm.

About 7km (4¼ miles) out of town to the north, and not a bad day trip by bicycle, is the **Sam Mountain** ★, a popular local pilgrimage peak. There's a colorful temple at the base of the mountain, and the path up is dotted with smaller spots for worship and shade-giving awnings where you can buy a Coke, stretch out in a hammock, and enjoy the view. It a tough little hike and might have you saying, "What in the Sam Hill?" but this is the only high spot for miles and the view is like looking at a map of the overflowing tributaries of the Mekong.

Laos

by Charles Agar

When you leave, don't worry that you find it difficult to summarize your experiences in "The Jewel of Southeast Asia"; many travelers come away from Laos with only a vague sense that they'd like to return and do so quickly before that special "something" is gone. Fear not, though, for change comes slowly here, and the genuine smiles of Laos' kind people endure.

So, what is Laos about? Sixty percent of Lao people are practicing Buddhists, and that fact colors every facet of life and is the overriding impression you'll carry away. Temples and stupas seem to dominate the architecture of even the most rural village, and flocks of monks in colorful robes on the streets are hard to miss. Try to catch the daily *pintabot,* or begging rounds, of monks, especially in Luang Prabang. Following centuries-old tradition, the *Sangha,* or monastic community, provides a moral fabric and plays a major role in society and education. Monks are highly respected in the social hierarchy, and Buddhist notions of personal morality and compassion still prevail, though generations change and modernize. The Buddhist philosophy of acceptance and compassion plays in everyday Lao life; arguments are the exception (and arguing by foreign visitors only achieves the opposite of desired aims). Even the shortest visit to Laos offers unique insight into Buddhist culture.

A developing country, one of the poorest in the world, Laos has been a long-time favorite for hearty backpackers willing to brave rough roads and basic accommodations for a bit of adventure. Laos defines the adage that it's all about the journey, and not the destination, and there's something special about the traveler camaraderie and connection to locals on an all-day bumpy bus ride or meandering boat journey. Pastoral villages and dusty, one-horse towns are the sparse destinations outside of the two major cities, and there are exciting options for getting off-the-track in pristine jungle and among the ethnic minorities of the north. Only in the capital of Vientiane and in Luang Prabang will you find quality accommodation. The infrastructure is still in its infancy, and rural travel begs caution, but many travelers find Laos a great place to arm themselves with a bit of insider information and jump off the track, to forgo comfort for a night in a minority village or rural town.

From citified Vientiane to the placid, tropical south and jungle north, Laos has a diverse geography and population. The north is a unique tapestry of ethnic minorities, and Lao people themselves have unique cultural and ethnic enclaves that differ from north to south, hill to plain. The country boasts vast tracts of deep jungle, open farmland, and even tropical river islands in the south. Remnants of ancient civilizations are here as well, including the odd **Plain of Jars** and **Wat Phu,** a Hindu site that might predate Angkor Wat. With current development in tourism and industry, many fear for the natural and cultural

(Warning) **Travel Advisory**

Travelers to Laos should refer to the U.S. State Department Travel Advisory regarding the present situation in the area (go to www.travel.state.gov and click "Travel Warnings"). Laos is not a dangerous destination, by any means, but it's important to remember that the current climate of calm and openness to visitors is quite short historically. Visitors should just keep in mind some late events and keep an ear to the ground when in-country.

In the winter and spring of 2003 there have been a number of attacks on buses traveling on Rte. 13, the major north-south highway, just north of Vang Vieng. As a result, visitors are advised to avoid the journey between Vang Vieng and Luang Prabang and stay abreast of the situation through the CDC or press. The attacks are attributed to Hmong rebels who have been fighting the Lao government for a number of years. Neither news nor government sources support the notion of anything like large-scale insurgency, but the group has been active, targeting tourist destinations in Vientiane in 2000 and forcing periodic road closures.

Travelers in the countryside should also remember that bus and boat breakdowns are frequent, and road conditions and poor infrastructure make rural travel unpredictable. Hospital facilities, even in the capital, are rudimentary, at best, and any serious medical condition requires evacuation (see "Fast Facts," later in this chapter, for hospital information). UXO, unexploded ordnance left from years of conflict, is still a major concern, especially in Xieng Khouang near the Plain of Jars.

It should also be mentioned that Lao Aviation has yet to pass any international standards for safety.

resources of this peaceful land-locked land. If Laos follows neighboring Thailand's model, as it does in many areas, Laos might further exploit its forests and waterways and, by packaging tourism for mass consumption, turn ethnic villages into human zoos. Working with United Nations agencies, the Laos government is taking steps to see that rural development proceeds slowly in order to protect these vital resources, but cultural change is coming in urban areas and modes of dress are changing as fast as attitudes. The sum of this is the loss of a unique and gentle way of life; one woman explained it to me, saying, "When the girls trade the traditional skirt for the miniskirt, then it's all over." So Laos is a place to tread lightly, but foreign travelers are made quite welcome and encouraged to do their part to preserve and participate in cultural practices. Laos' unique Buddhist heritage and gentle traditions are as open to us as we are to receiving them.

In Laos, travelers can enjoy some of Southeast Asia's most untamed natural beauty, kayak or trek in the back of beyond, experience ancient architectural wonders, enjoy the kindness and lightheartedness of Laos's unique hospitality, and experience Buddhist ritual and culture in a way that might add tranquility to your travels. It's an enchanting land that demands that you slow your pace to match its own.

The beauty of Laos exists not only along the Mekong at sunset, but in smiles at the market or impromptu Laotian lessons on the street corner, things that are easily missed if you're in a hurry.

1 Getting to Know Laos

THE LAY OF THE LAND

Comprising 147,201 sq. km (91,429 sq. miles), roughly the size of Great Britain or the state of Utah, Laos shares borders with China and Myanmar in the north and the northwest, Cambodia in the south, Thailand in the west, and Vietnam to the east. It is divided into 16 provinces. Seventy percent of its land is mountain ranges and plateaus, and with an estimated population of nearly 5.7 million, Laos is one of the most sparsely populated countries in Asia. Natural landmarks include the Annamite Mountains along the border with Vietnam, and the Mekong River, which flows from China and along Laos's border with Thailand. About 55% of the landscape is pristine tropical forest, sheltering such rare and wild animals as elephants, leopards, the Java mongoose, panthers, gibbons, and black bears.

THE LAO PEOPLE & CULTURE

A group of Russian ethnologists on a recent survey estimated that there are more than 100 distinct ethnic groups in Laos, but it is commonly believed that Laotians fall into 68 different groups. Only 47 groups are fully researched and identified; sadly, many are disappearing by attrition or intermarriage. Whatever the number, all Lao ethnicities fit into one of three categories. The lowlanders are **Lao Loum,** the majority group, who live along the lower Mekong and in Vientiane. The **Lao Theung,** low mountain dwellers, live on mountain slopes, and the **Lao Soung** are the hill tribes, or *montagnards.* Eighty percent of the population lives in villages or small hamlets, practicing subsistence farming.

The earliest **Lao religions** were animist, and most hill tribes still practice this belief, often in combination with Buddhism. In minority villages, you'll see elaborate spirit gates, small structures of bamboo and wood often depicting weapons to protect the village (tread lightly if you come across one of these markers because they are of great significance, and touching or even photographing is a major faux pas). Buddhism predominates, though, and 60% to 80% of all Laotians are practicing Theravada Buddhists. In the morning, monks walk the streets collecting food or alms, eagerly given by the Laotians, who believe it will aid them in the next life. Laos worship regularly and can often be seen making temple visits. Most young males spend at least 3 months in a *wat,* or monastery, usually around the time of puberty or before they marry. Impressive **religious art** and **architecture** is expressed in a singular Lao style, particularly the "standing" or "praying for rain" Buddha, upright with hands pointing straight down at the earth.

Music and dance are integral to the Lao character, and you'll get a taste of it during your stay. Folk or *khaen* music is played with a reed mouth organ, often accompanied by a boxed string instrument. The *lamvong* is the national folk dance, in which participants dance in concentric circles.

Laos are friendly and easygoing, but you might find it hard to make a close friend. Language will usually be a barrier. There is also a sense that the Lao people are just learning how to approach their foreign visitors. Solo travelers probably have the best chance of making entry into society, and any effort with the Lao language goes a long way to that effect. While Laos suffered brutally throughout

Laos

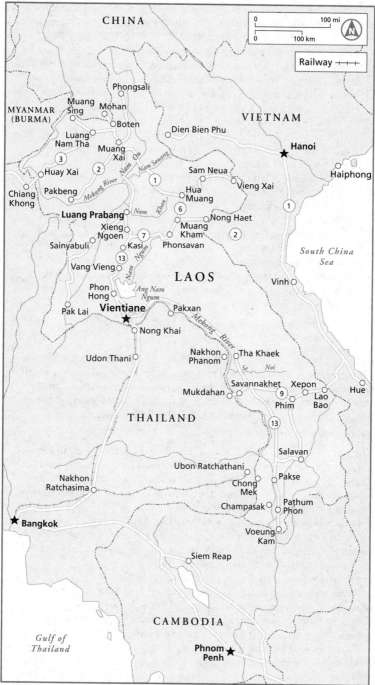

Baci Ceremony

At first it might look a bit like your average drinking contest, but a Baci ceremony is an ancient rite used as a blessing, to perform a marriage, to say welcome or farewell, or to honor achievement. Ceremonies vary in formality, but most are inclusive by nature (i.e., the more the merrier). As a foreign visitor, you might be invited or find yourself dragged in, offered a seat in the circle on the floor (often in a place of esteem), and offered plates of food passed your way. Lao-Lao, or local rice wine, flows freely and has a nasty habit of creeping up on you, so go easy. Many hotels have a special area for Baci, and you're likely to come across one even on the shortest trip to Laos.

The ceremony itself is slow, taking many hours. Folks come and go and casually chit-chat over the sound of chants and singing. Participants sit in a circle around a bouquet of flowers or offerings of food and join hands, saying prayers and blessings in both chanting and song. White string is tied around all celebrants' wrists and are to be worn for 3 days thereafter for good luck (a common sight). If you don't catch one in your travels, you can witness a Baci ceremony at the Royal Theater in Luang Prabang (see the Royal Palace Museum under "Attractions," in the Luang Prabang section).

its colonial history and most horrifically during the Vietnam War, the Lao people want to move on to peace and prosperity rather than dwell on the past. It's very unlikely that an American will be approached with recrimination, but memories are still fresh. Lao people still deal with war fallout literally and figuratively, a result of the unexploded bombs (or UXO) that litter 50% of the country.

ETIQUETTE

The Lao are generally tolerant people, but there are a few things to keep in mind. First, upon entering a temple or wat, you must always remove your shoes. There will usually be a sign, but a good rule of thumb is to take them off before mounting the last flight of stairs. You should also take off your shoes before entering a private home, unless told otherwise.

Dress modestly. It's unusual to see bare Lao skin above the elbow or even above the midcalf. Longer shorts and even sleeveless tops are permissible for foreigners of both sexes, but short shorts or skirts and bare bosoms and navels will cause stares and possibly offense, especially in a wat.

Men and women should avoid public displays of affection.

Women should never try to shake hands with or even hand something directly to a monk; monks are not permitted to touch women or even to speak directly to them anywhere but inside a wat. On buses, you'll find that Lao people will change seats so that monks sit only near men.

The **traditional greeting** is called the *nop* or *wai*. To perform this, place your hands together at chest level as if you are praying, but do not touch your body. Bow your head to your hands, and your upper body slightly. The nop is also used to say thank you and goodbye. Its use is fading in the big cities, but return the greeting if you're given it. In a business setting, a handshake is also appropriate.

The head is considered the most sacred part of the body, and the feet are the lowliest. Therefore, do not casually touch another person's head or even nonchalantly tussle the hair of a child, and don't sit with your legs crossed or otherwise point your feet at something or someone. As in most cultures, pointing with the finger is also considered rude; Laos often use a palms-up hand gesture when signifying direction or indicating a person or thing. If you are seated on the floor, men may sit with the legs crossed, but women should tuck them to one side.

As in many Asian countries, it is important not to step over people on a bus or in a crowded place, and it is common to make room (even when you think there is none) for others to pass rather than inviting them to go over.

In interpersonal relations with the Lao, it helps to remember that many are strong Buddhists and take (or try to take) a gentle approach to human relationships. A person showing violence or ill temper is regarded with surprise and disapproval. A gentle approach will take you farther, and patient persistence and a smile go further, especially when haggling, than an argument. It is important to haggle, of course, but just one or two go-rounds are usually enough, and "no" means no. If you have a disagreement of any kind, keep your cool.

A common greeting in Laos is to ask, "Have you eaten yet?" telling of the importance, not unlike many cultures, of offering and accepting hospitality whenever possible. Western visitors are often asked to join impromptu feasts. Hospitality is one thing, but don't feel pressed into drinking rice wine (I've had offers at breakfast); if something looks just unsavory or really turns you off, it is okay to politely decline an offer (but just a taste will make your host happy).

LANGUAGE

The **Lao language** resembles Thai, with familiar tones and sounds found in each. Yet while some vocabulary words might cross over, the two tongues—spoken and written—are quite distinct. However, many Lao understand Thai (learned from school texts and TV), so if you've picked up some words and phrases in Thailand, they'll still be useful here and people will understand and correct you with the appropriate Lao phrase. Thankfully, many people in Vientiane and Luang Prabang speak **English,** and older citizens will usually be able to speak **French. Russian** is not uncommon, and **Chinese** is growing in accord with the rising Chinese population (mostly in the north).

Like Thai, Lao has no officially recognized method of Roman alphabet transliteration. As a result, even town and street names have copious spelling irregularities, so for the vocabulary below we have chosen to list only phonetic pronunciations. Most Lao will understand you, even without tones, and will very much appreciate your efforts to speak their language.

When trying to figure out the correct pronunciation of certain names, it's helpful to remember that the original transliteration of Lao was done by francophones, so consider the French pronunciation when faced with a new word. For example, in Vientiane (pronounced wee-en-*chan*), the wide central avenue spelled Lane Xang is pronounced *Lahn Sahng*. Also in Vientiane, Mixay sounds like *Mee-sigh*. Phonexay is *pawn-sigh*. It takes a while, but it's easy to catch.

USEFUL LAO PHRASES

Hello	**Sa bai dee**
Good bye	**Laa kawn**
Yes	**Chow/ur**

No	**Baw/baw men** (Baw is also a tag to form questions.)
Thank you	**Khawp chai**
Thank you very much	**Khawp chai lai lai/khawp chai deu**
You're welcome/it's nothing	**Baw pen nyahng**
No problem	**Baw mi banhaa**
How are you?	**Sa bai dee baw?**
I'm fine./ I'm not fine.	**Sabai dee!/ baw sabai.**
Where are you going?	**Pai sai?**
I'm going traveling/to the market/to eat.	**Pai tiao/Pai talaat/Pai kin kao.**
Excuse me	**Khaw thoot** (rhymes with "put")
Where is the toilet?	**Hawng suam/Hawng nam yoo sai?**
May I wear shoes here?	**Sai Goop baw pen nyang baw?**
Do you have . . . ?	**Mii . . . Baw?**
drinking water	**nam-deum**
a room	**hawng**
a husband/wife	**mia**(common question)
Have/ don't have	**Mii/ baw mii**
I would like . . .	**Kaaw . . .**
coffee (black)/with cream	**Café daam/café sai noom**
tea	**Nam saa**
I want to go to . . .	**Koi yak pai . . .**
I don't understand.	**Baw kau jai.**
Do you speak English/French?	**Passah Angit/Falang dai baw?**
How do you say that in Lao?	**Ani Passah Lao nyang?**
How much kip/bot/dollar?	**Tao dai kip**(sounds like "keep")/**bot/dollah?**
Expensive/tToo expensive	**peng/peng pout**
Can you make it cheaper?	**Lut dai baw?**
Help!	**Sue-wee dah!**
Call the police!	**Sue-wee un tam luat dah!**
I need a/an . . .	**khaw-ee tawng kahn . . .**

2 Planning Your Trip to Laos

VISITOR INFORMATION

The Lao Tourism Authority serves as more of an administrative arm of the government than that of an information service for visitors. It provides some basic brochures if contacted at **National Tourism Authority of Lao P.D.R.,** 08/02 Lane Xang Ave., P.O. Box 2511, Vientiane, Lao P.D.R. (© **021/212-248** or 212-251; fax 021/212-769). The information office has a few good English speakers and is not a bad place to start.

The **Lao Tourism Company** (© **021/216-671**), the government's official travel services operation, provides limited visitor services. In addition to organizing tours in and around Vientiane city and province, it can help obtain visa extensions and offer advice on travel around the country. Write to the same address as the National Tourism Authority (above).

The official Visit Laos website, **www.visit-laos.com**, is sponsored by both the Lao government and private organizations, and is now cross-referenced with other countries in Southeast Asia at **www.mekongcenter.com**. These sites are detailed and accurate, and are very useful supplements with links to other sources of information in the region. For current domestic and international news and government affairs, log on to **http://laoembassy.com**, sponsored and maintained by the Lao Embassy in Washington, D.C.

ORGANIZED TOURS AND TRAVEL AGENTS

In chapter 3, "Planning a Trip to Southeast Asia," we've outlined major tour operators that organize trips to Laos in addition to other Southeast Asian destinations. Most arrange tours throughout the region, though they can plan a trip to Laos only.

Getting around underdeveloped Laos can be difficult (see "Getting Around," later in this chapter), so group travel is, of course, the simplest option and any of the companies that we recommend offer a range of options.

Independent travel is quite feasible, though, and the same companies that organize group tours can help with hotel and travel arrangements and even create quite affordable independent tour itineraries, almost a necessity outside of Vientienne and Luang Prabang. There are also some new and exciting options in eco-tourism, and some agencies specialize in getting you into the jungly back of beyond or into remote villages for a bit of cultural immersion.

The most established and widely represented tour operators provide basic, mainstream tours to most provinces within the country for either short trips or extended visits, including in and around Vientiane, Luang Prabang, Xieng Khouang (Plain of Jars), and Champasak, plus trips to visit Laos's hill tribes or for adventure trips and ecotourism. You can make arrangements with these companies from home before your trip or after you've arrived in the country. Like most tour services, these companies take the hassle out of your trip but cost more than a do-it-yourself itinerary. Prices among companies seem comparable. The following are the most established, but in each town there are small agencies able to take care of any details. As always, buyer beware: When arranging tours or travel with even the larger agents, be absolutely clear about the specifics (meals included of what variety, driver's expenses, taxes, etc.). Many local tour companies offer the world and come up short, so find out the details to avoid miscommunication on your tour.

In the high season (Nov–Feb) rooms are at high demand, so to play it safe, it's not a bad idea to use an agency to book ahead, even if just to avoid language troubles and save some time.

- **Diethelm Travel,** Namphu Square, Setthathirath Road, P.O. Box 2657, Vientiane, Laos P.D.R. (© **021/213-833;** fax 021/217-151; www.diethelm travel.com), is open Monday to Friday 8am to noon and 1:30 to 5pm, and Saturday 8am to noon. Operating almost like a de facto tourist information and help center, the folks at Diethelm are the most professional in the country and can arrange deluxe, personalized trips and cover all necessities. Offices are in all major towns (see the information sections in the coverage of each town).
- **Exotissimo Travel,** Pangkham Road (© **021/241-861;** fax 021/252-382; www.exotissimo.com) is a slick and helpful French-owned company. Exotissimo offers fine upscale group and individual, classic, and eco tours. It's popular among expats for outbound travel throughout the region.
- **Sodetour,** Fa Ngum Road, Vientiane, Lao P.D.R. (© **021/216-314;** fax 021/216-313; sodetour@laotel.com) is an experienced company offering a range of classic and eco-tours.

- **Inter-Lao Tourism,** 07/073 Luang Prabang Road, P.O. Box 2912, Vientiane, Lao P.D.R. (✆ **021/214-832;** fax 021/216-306; www.interlao.laopdr. com) is helpful and has convenient offices in Luang Prabang and Xieng Khouang.
- **Wildside Eco Group,** 54 Sethathirat Rd., Nam Phu Fountain Circle, Vientiane (✆ **021/251-563;** www.wildside-laos.com), offers some exciting rafting, kayaking, climbing, and trekking trips on anything from one-day trips to one-month expeditions. The helpful international staff caters to budget travelers and custom adventurers.

Small tour operators abound in Vientiane, Luang Prabang, and other tourist centers. In most places, even the smallest guesthouse is able to arrange many necessities. Be sure to compare prices and ask for specifics before booking; for example, ask about meals included, what kind of vehicles are used for tours and land travel, and exact details about any accommodation. Assume nothing.

AIR BOOKING

Making your own air arrangements from Vientiane and Luang Prabang is simple, and most travel offices can help for a small fee. Below are some air-booking offices in Vientiane.

- **Lao Aviation.** 2 Pangkham Road, P.O. Box 4169 (✆ **021/212-057;** www. lao-aviation.com). This office books Lao Air flights only.
- **Lao Air Service Ltd.** 77 Fa Ngum Rd. (next to Sodetour; ✆ **021/213-372;** fax 021/215-694; laoairsvc@laonet.net).
- **Lao Air Booking Co.** 44/3 Setthathirath Rd. (just S of Namphu in Vientiane; ✆ **021/ 216-761**).
- **Blue Bird.** 2 Pangkham Rd. (across from Laos Aviation; ✆ **021/168-9;** fax 021/251-169; bluebird@laotel.com).
- **Khamchalean Air Booking.** 110/5 Samsenthai Rd. (✆ **021/216-943**).

ENTRY REQUIREMENTS

Citizens of every Western country need a valid passport and visa to visit Laos. For convenience's sake, it's best to obtain a visa before your trip at one of the Lao Embassy locations listed below. At an embassy, the going rate for a 15-day visa is US$35, and you'll have to wait up to 5 days for processing (less in Bangkok). Some embassies will grant a 30-day visa if you ask. In addition, travel agents all over Southeast Asia offer visa services—the bigger agencies are very reputable. For a fee, they'll process your application and help it jump over any bureaucratic hurdles. Many Bangkok agents can deliver in as quickly as 1 day.

Laos offers three official entry sites where visas are granted upon arrival. If you're flying to Vientiane or Luang Prabang or are traveling over the Friendship Bridge from Nong Khai, citizens from most Western countries can apply for a visa at the arrival checkpoint for US$30. Call your nearest Lao embassy to find out if you qualify.

Once in Laos, you can extend your visa up to 30 days. To apply, head for the immigration office in Vientiane on Khoun Boulum Road off Lane Xang Avenue opposite the Morning Market, but they often tell you that you require a sponsor (and that means a travel agent). Many hotels and guesthouses offer the service as well as tour operators (Diethelm has a counter devoted solely to visa affairs), but I recommend letting **Lao Tourism,** 08/02 Lane Xang Ave., adjacent to the National Tourism Authority (✆ **021/216-671**), handle it. They charge the same fee, US$2 for each additional day, are quick (that day or overnight), and are an official government agency.

Check for the most current information; there are murmurs that other land crossings (Huay Sai from Thailand, Lao Bao from Vietnam, and Boten from China) might soon open visa-on-arrival services (check **http://laoembassy.com** for more information).

Overstaying your visa will cost you a fine of US$5 a day upon exiting the country.

LAOS EMBASSY LOCATIONS OVERSEAS

In the U.S.: Embassy of the Lao People's Democratic Republic, 2222 S St. NW, Washington, DC, 20008 (© **202/332-6416;** fax 202/332-4923; www.lao embassy.com); or the Lao P.D.R. Permanent Mission to the United Nations, 317 E. 51st St., New York, NY 10022 (© **212/832-2734;** fax 212/750-0039; www. laoembassy.com/laomission/index.html).

In Australia: 1 Dalmain Crescent, O'Malley, Canberra, ACT 2606 (© **02/ 6286-4595;** fax 02/6290-1910).

OTHER LAOS EMBASSIES:

In Thailand: 520/502/1–3 Soi Sahakarnpramoon, Wangthonglang, Bangkok 10310, Pracha Uthit Road (end of Soi Ramkhamhaeng 39; © **539 6667-8** or 539 7341; fax 539 3827 or 539 6678; sabaidee@bkklaoembassy.com).

CUSTOMS REGULATIONS

You may bring 500 cigarettes, 100 cigars, or 500g of tobacco; 1L of alcohol; two bottles of wine; and unlimited amounts of money, all for personal use, into Laos without taxation or penalty. Not that the Customs officials do much, if any, searching. However, if you purchase silver or copper items during your stay, you might be required to pay duty upon exiting Laos, according to their weight. Antiques, especially Buddha images or parts thereof, are not permitted to leave the country.

MONEY

The **kip** (pronounced *keep*), the official Lao unit of currency, comes in denominations of 5, 10, 20, 100, 500, 1,000, 2,000, 5,000, and, only recently issued by the Lao government (and a cause of inflation), 10,000 and 20,000 notes. The new notes are an improvement, but with the current exchange rate (10,000 kip to the dollar), that still means that the largest unit of currency is just $2. You'll want to use U.S. dollars, accepted widely, or Thai bot, commonly accepted but more popular near the border, for your larger purchases; be prepared to handle bricks of Lao cash when you exchange foreign currency. You might enjoy the comical scene at local banks where businesses cash in and out by toting their large bundles of cash in brimming shopping bags.

CURRENCY EXCHANGE & RATES   At press time, the exchange rate was US$1 to 10,000 kip. I've used this rate as the standard for all currency conversions in this chapter.

Laos is very much a cash country, especially outside Vientiane. Virtually all hotel and guesthouse rates, up-market restaurant menus, transportation charges, and expensive purchases are quoted in U.S. dollars, and payment is always accepted in either U.S. dollars, Thai baht, or Lao kip, so it doesn't always pay to convert all your currency into cumbersome wads of local scraps. For smaller purchases, local transportation, and pocket money, you can exchange currency at Wattay International Airport, in hotels, in banks, and on the black market, with the rate of exchange worst at hotels and best on the black market (but the difference is only negligible).

Traveler's checks in U.S. dollars and other major currencies are accepted in all banks in Vientiane and Luang Prabang, and some in Xieng Khouang and Pakse, but very rarely by vendors; even the American Express travel representative won't take them. In other provinces, it's best to carry cash in U.S. dollars, Thai baht, or Lao kip. It's not a bad idea to change traveler's checks into U.S. dollars at a major bank before going for any extended time out of the larger towns this (can be done in most banks with a 2% charge). **Credit cards** are accepted only at major hotels or tour operators (Visa is the most widely accepted). Lao Aviation accepts American Express, MasterCard, and Visa. You can get cash advances from your Visa card at **La Banque pour le Commerce Extérieur Lao (BCEL)** and at **Lane Xang Bank** branches in larger towns throughout the country. Both banks have local ATM service but have yet to make the international link.

LOST/STOLEN CREDIT CARDS & TRAVELER'S CHECKS   To report a lost or stolen American Express card, contact the Amex representative in Vientiane, **Diethelm Travel,** Setthathirat Road, Namphou Square, Vientiane (© 021/ 213-833 or 215-920). If you're upcountry, you can get help from one of Diethelm's regional offices. Addresses and telephone numbers are provided in each city's corresponding section. Your card can be replaced within 3 working days.

To report a lost or stolen Visa or MasterCard, you'll have to contact their customer service hot lines in Bangkok, the closest hot lines available from Laos. To report a lost or stolen credit card, you can call these service lines: **American Express** (© 66-2/273-0022); **Diners Club** (© 66-2/238-3660); **JCB** (Japanese Credit Bank; © 66-2/631-1938); **MasterCard** (© 66-2/232-2039); and **Visa** (© 66-2/256-7324).

WHEN TO GO

PEAK SEASON   High season for tourism is November through March and the month of August, when weather conditions are favorable (but accommodations run at full capacity and transportation can be overbooked).

CLIMATE   Laos's topical climate ushers in a wet monsoon season lasting from early May through October, followed by a dry season from November to April. In Vientiane, average temperatures range from 71°F (22°C) in January to 84°F (29°C) in April. The northern regions, which include Xieng Khouang, get chilly from November to February and can approach freezing temperatures at night in mountainous areas. Beginning in mid-February, temperatures gradually climb, and April can see temperatures over 100°F (39°C).

In order to avoid the rain and heat, the best time to visit the south is probably November through February. In the mountains of the north, May to July means still-comfortable temperatures. The monsoon season begins a bit later there as well.

PUBLIC HOLIDAYS   Businesses and government offices close for these holidays, but restaurants remain open. Ask about local festivals; on the full moon of each month, called a *Boun,* there's a festival somewhere, which is lots of fun.

- **International New Year's Day:** January 1, nationwide. Your standard countdown and party sans Dick Clark.
- **Lunar New Year (Pimai Lao):** Full moon in mid-April, nationwide. The Luang Prabang festivities include a procession, a fair, a sand-castle competition on the Mekong, a Miss New Year pageant, folk performances, and cultural shows. Make sure you're booked and confirmed in hotels before you go.

- **Buddhist Lent:** At local temples, worshippers in brightly colored silks greet the dawn on **Buddhist Lent (Boun Khao Phansaa)** by offering gifts to the monks and pouring water into the ground as a gesture of offering to their ancestors. Lent begins in July and lasts 3 months. Monks are meant to stay at their temple throughout this time, for more rigorous practice. Lent ends in the joyous **Boun Ok Phansa** holiday in September, usually commemorated with boat races (below), carnivals, and the release of hundreds of candle-bearing paper and bamboo floats on the country's rivers.
- **Dragon Boat Races (Bun Song Heua):** Held at different times in late summer and early fall in every riverside town. These races celebrates the end of Buddhist Lent. Teams of 50 paddle long boats in a long sprint, and winners parade through town. The **Vientiane Boat Race Festival** (Vientiane and Savannakhet) is held the second weekend in October to mark the end of Buddhist Lent. The **Luang Prabang Boat Races** are held in early September along the Nam Kan, with a major market day preceding the races and festivities throughout the night on race day.
- **That Luang Festival:** Full moon in early November, Vientiane. This major Buddhist fete draws the faithful countrywide and from nearby Thailand. Before dawn, thousands join in a ceremonial offering and group prayer, followed by a procession. For days afterward, a combined trade fair and carnival offers handicrafts and flowers, games, concerts, and dance shows.
- **Hmong New Year:** End of November/beginning of December, in the north. Although this is not a national holiday, it's celebrated among this northern hill tribe.
- **National Day:** December 2, nationwide. The entire country celebrates a public holiday, while in Vientiane, you'll find parades and dancing at That Luang temple.

HEALTH CONCERNS
VACCINATIONS
Laos does not require any special vaccinations to enter; however, you're recommended to have the vaccinations discussed in chapter 3 before you visit Laos or any other Southeast Asian nation.

HEALTH PRECAUTIONS
In chapter 3, we discuss the major health issues that affect travelers to Southeast Asia and recommend precautions for avoiding the most common diseases.

No water in Laos is considered potable, so stick with bottled water readily available from vendors all over the country (1,500 kip/US15¢ is a standard price). Also, Lao cuisine uses many fresh ingredients and garnishes, and condiments made from dried fish that might have been stored under unsanitary conditions. Exercise caution when eating from roadside and market stalls and smaller local restaurants, but remember that if Lao folks are eating it, it's okay. Questions like "Do you wash your vegetables in purified water?" are embarrassing for all involved.

In Laos, medical facilities are scarce and rudimentary. Emergency medical facilities exist in Vientiane, but outside the capital you'll require medical evacuation. Contact information is provided under "Fast Facts: Laos," below.

GETTING THERE
When planning travel to Laos, it's important to remember that you're not permitted to cross Laos's borders with Myanmar. Also, some intrepid travelers have

---

⌒Warning **Watch Out for Unexploded Bombs**

Per square inch, Laos is the most heavily bombed country in the world to date, thanks to the Vietnam War. Certain parts of the country, in the north around the Plain of Jars and in the south around the Ho Chi Minh Trail, are laden with unexploded bombs (or unexploded ordnance—UXO), some of which are as small as a fist. There is not much of a risk to tourists, provided that you avoid wandering through the unexplored jungle in risky areas and don't pick up anything. If you're traveling with children, warn them and keep an eye on them in those areas.

---

reported success crossing from Southern Laos to Cambodia, and vice versa, but it's not recommended because you might be forced to bribe your way out of no-man's-land (this could change soon). Official land borders are with China, Vietnam, and Thailand *only,* and not all border points are open to foreign nationals. For example, to China, the crossing point is at Boten, and though it looks encouraging on a map, you cannot cross north of Muang Sing. Similarly, the Laos/Vietnam borders in the north at Dien Bien Phu or Sam Neua are not open to most overseas passport-holders; only in the south at Lao Bao can you cross to and from Vietnam.

BY PLANE Bangkok provides Laos's main link with global air routes; however, with regular flights from neighboring Vietnam, Cambodia, and Myanmar, it's easy to hop a direct flight from anywhere in Indochina. See each individual country chapter for carriers to the countries mentioned above.

Lao Aviation, the national carrier, coordinates international flights from its head office in Vientiane, at 2 Pangkham Rd., P.O. Box 4169 (© **021/212-057** international; www.lao-aviation.com). Lao Aviation connects Vientiane with Bangkok, Hanoi, Ho Chi Minh City, Phnom Penh, and Siem Reap. It's also possible to fly from Bangkok or Chiang Mai direct to Luang Prabang. Other convenient routes link Cambodia (Phnom Penh and Siem Reap) and Pakse in the south.

Thai Airways International, Angel Air (from Thailand), Bangkok Air, Vietnam Airlines, and Myanmar Airways all provide service to Laos.

Check www.bangkokair.com for information about Bangkok Airways and new routes between the UNESCO World Heritage Sites of Bangkok, Sukhothai, Luang Prabang, and Hue. It's quite unique.

If you leave Laos by air, keep 100,000 kip (US$10) tucked away safely for the **international departure tax,** paid at the airport as you pass through the immigration checkpoint.

BY TRAIN The State Railway of Thailand's northeastern line originates at Bangkok's Hua Lampong Railway Station (© **02/223-7010** or 02/223-7020). Running north, it connects many major provincial capitals in Isan, Thailand's northeastern region, before terminating at Nong Khai across the Mekong from Vientiane. Buying tickets at Hua Lampong is a cinch, but for second-class sleeper cars (the most popular, and a great value at B400–B500/US$8.50–$11), it's best to book a few days in advance. Once you arrive in Nong Khai, you'll need to hire a tuk-tuk from the train station to the immigration checkpoint at the Thai-Lao Friendship Bridge (about 30B/US70¢ for the trip). The checkpoint is open daily from 8:30am to 5pm. Once across to Laos, you'll need to grab a taxi to Vientiane (which is actually not *exactly* across from Nong Khai). By tuk-tuk and with a bit of hard bargaining, you could pay as little as B150 (US$3). Just across the Thai-Lao border and on the other side of the taxi parking area (though the taxi drivers will tell you otherwise), there is infrequent bus service to the Morning Market in Vientiane for just 1,000 kip (US10¢).

BY BUS   Tourist buses, the VIP, reclining-seat, air-conditioned variety, connect Bangkok and Vientiane via the Friendship Bridge. The overnight trip can be booked from most tour services for about B700 (US$16) and will leave you at the Thai side of the border. From Vietnam, a lot of people choose to take the bus overnight from Danang or Hué to Savannakhet. In Danang, the bus leaves at 7pm every Monday, Wednesday, Thursday, and Sunday. Talk to **Vietnamtourism,** 83 Nguyen Thi Minh Khai (© **0511/823-660**); the cost is 37,000 VND (US$25). From Hue, the bus leaves at 7pm on Tuesday and Saturday. Contact Huong Giang Tourist Company, 17 Le Loi St. (© **054/832-220**) for more information.

BY BOAT   Thailand and Laos maintain three official border checkpoints (not including the Friendship Bridge) along the Mekong between the two countries. The Mekong border crossing between Thailand's Chiang Khong (near Chiang Mai) and Laos's Houeixay has proven wildly popular in the past few years with folks who want to float downriver from northern Thailand to Luang Prabang while taking in all the Mekong sights.

Visas can be secured in Chiang Mai, Chiang Rai, and Chiang Khong from travel agents and guesthouses. Once you reach Houeixay, book the passenger boat that departs every morning (arrive early). The trip costs 110,000 kip (US$11) and takes about 1½ days to complete. You'll stay overnight in Pak Beng, a village with basic accommodation, before arriving in Luang Prabang in the afternoon of the next day, pending no engine trouble or delay. Be prepared for all kinds of discomfort, but you'll have many tales to tell sitting in the cafes or getting a massage in Luang Prabang.

Diethelm Travel and **LuangSay Cruises** run the same trip with comfy tour boats and will put you up for the night in Pak Beng with their own respective, upscale accommodation priced to match (see "Getting Around," below, for details).

Additional crossing points along the Mekong are between Mukhdahan (Thailand) and Tha Khaek (Laos), and between Ubon Ratchathani (Thailand) and Chong Mek (Laos).

GETTING AROUND

Laos's underdeveloped infrastructure begs for endless cautions. The U.S. Department of State warns travelers that Lao Aviation has not passed international safety standards. Laos has no railroads, and of the country's highway system, only 40% is paved (and "paved" might be defined as 1 crumbly lane shared by opposing traffic). Bandit and insurgent activity along Highway 13 means that road travel between Vang Vieng and Luang Prabang can be prohibited; and elsewhere, poor road conditions, especially during the rainy season and in the north, and often overcrowded public transport relegate road travel to the hearty.

River travel is subject to the whims of Mother Nature, and boats leave irregularly. Even with the right number of tourists to charter a boat on smaller rivers in the north, arranging a departure would try the patience of Buddha.

That said, these very obstacles are what attract many to traveling in Laos; there's nothing like the feel of pulling into a northern town covered in dust or hopping from a boat to a muddy riverbank in a rural village to be greeted by a friendly delegation of kids. For many, though, the difficulties outweigh (or overshadow) any reward. Laos is a great place to get off the track, but you might even feel so when trying to stay on the track; arm yourself with current information if traveling far out of Vientianne and Luang Prabang, and consider carefully the travel options below.

BY AIR   Though Lao Aviation, the country's major domestic carrier, has yet to pass international safety standards, frequent flights connect the country's main destinations. Contact Lao Aviation at its head office in Vientiane, 2 Pangkham Rd. (© **021/212-058;** www.lao-aviation.com), about domestic routes linking Vientiane, Luang Prabang, Xieng Khouang, Pakse, and other places around the country. Ticket prices range from about 370,000 kip (US$37) from Luang Prabang to Xieng Khouang, to 950,000 kip (US$95) from Vientiane to Pakse. Lao Aviation accepts payment in U.S. dollars, traveler's checks, Lao kip, American Express, MasterCard, and Visa. Keep in mind that for each domestic flight you take, there's a **domestic departure tax** of 1,000 kip (US10¢) payable at the airport before you board your plane.

If you have the cash to spare and don't want to waste time with Lao Aviation domestic flights, **Lao Westcoast Helicopter** (© **021/512-023**) will be more than happy to charter a helicopter to take you where you need to go at your convenience. You'll have to negotiate the fare for your itinerary because prices vary based on many factors.

Lao Flying Service (© **021/222-687;** laofly@laotel.com) offers chartered fixed-wing options (strictly small planes) and sells blocks of time and package deals for charter, air taxi, and aerial survey in destinations throughout the country.

BY BUS   Mostly bought secondhand from Korea, **public buses and minibuses** connect most major destinations in Laos; however, many towns (especially in the north) are still serviced by only songthaew, a four-valve pickup truck fitted with an open-sided cover and bench seats definitive of Lao-style "hard travelin.'" Routes from Vientiane north to Luang Prabang and south to Savannakhet are handled by private companies with relatively comfortable buses, but road travel is still rough in Laos. Buses are often overcrowded (you might find yourself sitting on a plastic chair in the center aisle, with no air-conditioning and a wriggling bag of chickens or pigs under your seat), they stop frequently for new passengers, and the roads are rough by any standard. Again, that said, it's a good way to meet locals and is certain to be good grist for any travel journal; it can be a bit harrowing for some.

BY CAR   One alternative is to hire a **private vehicle,** a car with a driver (self-drive vehicles are virtually impossible to find). The most popular routes for car hire are the 8-hour trip up to Luang Prabang from Vientiane, or shorter trips throughout Vientiane Province. Also handy, car rentals provide the most convenient way around the southern parts around Pakse. You can find contacts for private vehicle hires in each corresponding section to follow.

BY BOAT   **Tour boats** operated by **LuangSay Cruises,** Ban Vat Sene, Sakarine Road, Luang Prabang, near Diethelm Travel (© **071/252-553,** or **021/ 215-958** in Vientiane; www.mekongcruises.com), are a luxury option along the Mehkong both in the north from Thailand to Luang Prabang and in the south from Pakse. With onboard accommodation on their flagship, the **Vat Phou,** LuangSay offers 4 nights and 3 days beginning and ending in Pakse and stopping at the famed **Wat Phou** and various villages and natural sites along the way.

As a more luxury option to the popular but uncomfortable barge rides down the Mehkong, take the 2-day trip from the Thai border town Houaixay to Luang Prabang (or vice versa), with 1 night at the up-market riverside bungalows near Pak Beng.

For those with a yen for a bit of adventure, **riverboats** ply the length of the Mehkong in Laos, and smaller boats of the longtail variety navigate smaller waterways throughout the country (particularly in the north). There's nothing like floating on the mighty Mekong, but sadly, Laos has little quality river transport with any sort of comfort, and departures are so infrequent that travelers need to charter boats for themselves, a true exercise in patience. From Nong Kiao just north and east of Luang Prabang, for example, it is common for travelers in groups of 10 or more to take the time to negotiate a charter to Luang Prabang on the Nam Ou. Options like this abound for those with the time and temperament (or who can speak Lao) to sort it out. Many tours in Laos include boat trips, often just 1-day excursions, and this is a good way to get on the river for good perspective on some pristine jungle or riverside village life (check the "Visitor Information and Tours" section or see the recommended tour operators in any city section).

A much more reliable option that is popular with backpackers is the **river barges** that ply between Chiang Khong in Thailand and Luang Prabang. If you're floating downriver, the trip is an interesting day and a half, full of great scenery and crazy travel companions. However, the chug upriver against the current takes about 3½ days and is not recommended. The alternative is a **speed-boat** hire between the two stops, which gets you there much faster but in a bone-jarring, ride that, though brief, is more uncomfortable than riding the barge (I recommend ear plugs, and many opt for the helmets offered). It is possible to hop cargo boats between Vientiane and Luang Prabang, but they're just that: cargo boats.

Local boats from Pakse to Champasak and farther south are a possibility but are similarly uncomfortable and loosely scheduled.

Navigating on foot through Laos's small cities is easy. You can use **taxis** and **tuk-tuks** (covered carts behind motorbikes) in Vientiane, Luang Prabang, and Pakse, or you can rent **bicycles** and **motorbikes** in Vientiane, Luang Prabang, and Vang Vieng.

TIPS ON ACCOMMODATIONS, DINING & SHOPPING

Book your hotel early during the peak season (Nov–Feb), using travel agents and tour operators as necessary. Language difficulties can make booking outside of Vientiane almost impossible to do yourself. Don't expect discounts, either, because facilities aren't plentiful and occupancy is usually high. That said, you'll be generally happy with the standards and prices you'll encounter.

Lao Cuisine is varied and interesting, with sticky rice (or glutinous rice) a delightful staple that, over a longer visit, often loses its appeal in simple redundancy. Lao cuisine is an interesting mixture of Thai and Chinese, with a bit of French thrown in for good measure, but it features some unique dishes and regional favorites. Try it at real restaurants whenever possible because the street stands aren't up to those in neighboring countries. French colonial influence is clear in the many excellent Continental options in Vientienne and Luang Prabang, and in the bigger towns there's some excellent Chinese, Thai, and Italian restaurants.

You'll undoubtedly leave with a few pieces of hand-woven Lao textiles, hand-crafted silver, and other lovely objects. Many things are one-of-a-kind, so if you see something you like, get it. Remember that the Lao do, of course, haggle, and for foreigners the starting price might be high, but bargaining here is not as relentless as with Lao's neighboring countries. Suggest prices carefully, beginning with something like half of the shop's suggested price (a smile helps); you'll likely agree somewhere in the middle.

FAST FACTS: Laos

American Express The country's one Amex representative is **Diethelm Travel,** Namphou Square, Setthathirat Road, Vientiane (① **021/215-920** or 213-833). *Good to know:* Diethelm will not cash American Express traveler's checks (available at all banks), and for lost or stolen traveler's checks, they'll have to make all arrangements through the representative in Bangkok. On the other hand, they can handle the American Express letter-holding service and will perform emergency check-cashing services.

Business Hours With a few exceptions, hours are 8:30am to noon and 1:30 to 5pm on weekdays and 8am to noon on Saturday. Restaurants are open from about 11am to 2pm and 6 to 10pm daily, although many are closed for lunch on Sunday.

Doctors & Dentists Medical care in Laos is primitive by Western standards. For major problems, most foreigners choose to hop the border to Thailand for the Nong Khai Wattana General Hospital just over the Friendship Bridge. In an emergency, call ① **66-42/465-201.** Vientiane has one International Medical Clinic, Mahosot Hospital, on Fa Ngum Road at the Mekong riverbank (① **021/214-022**). It's open 24 hours. Facilities are very basic. The doctors speak French but little English. For emergency evacuation, call **Lao Westcoast Helicopter Company** in Vientiane at ① **021/512-023.**

Drug Laws Opium is openly grown in northeast Laos and is easily available, as is marijuana. Neither are legal, and although you might see many travelers indulging, it is highly recommended that you don't. You could face high fines or jail if you're caught.

Electricity Laos runs on 220-volt electrical currents. Plugs are two-pronged, with either round or flat prongs. If you're coming from the U.S. and you must bring electrical appliances, bring your own converter and adapter. Outside of Vientiane and Luang Prabang, electricity is sketchy, sometimes available for a few hours a day. A surge protector is a must for laptops.

Embassies **U.S.:** Thatdam Bathrolonie Road (① **021/212-582;** fax 021/212-584). **Australia:** Nehru Road, Bane Phonsay (① **021/413-600**). The Australian embassy also assists Canada, New Zealand, and U.K. nationals.

Emergencies In Vientiane, for police dial ① **991;** for fire, dial ① **190;** and for ambulance, dial ① **195.** For medical evacuation, call **Lao Westcoast Helicopter Company** at ① **021/512-023.**

Internet/E-mail You can find Internet access in Vientiane, Luang Prabang, Pakse, Phonsavan, and Vam Vieng. I've listed Internet cafes in each city. Prices vary with proximity to Vientienne because most service is patched throughout the capital; it's often overpriced and too slow to be worth it. In Vientienne and Luang Prabang, the connections are generally not too slow and prices are reasonable.

Language   Lao is the major language, and many people in Vientiane and Luang Prabang speak **English.** If you've picked up a bit of Thai, feel free to use it here because many understand at least basic Thai. A rare few also speak some Russian and French, and Mandarin Chinese is growing concurrently with the Chinese population (mostly in the north). See "Language," above, for more information.

Liquor Laws   There are no real liquor laws in Laos, but most bars refuse to admit patrons under the age of 18. Bars usually close around midnight.

Post Offices/Mail   A letter or postcard should take about 10 days to reach the U.S. Overseas postage runs about 800 kip (US11¢) for 100g, and up to 2,300 kip (US30¢) for 500g. Postcards are 900 kip (US12¢). The mail service is reportedly unreliable, however, so if you're sending something important, use an express-mail service. FedEx and DHL have offices in the major cities.

Safety   Buddhist Laos is an extremely safe country by any standard. Violent or even petty crime is not a big risk for tourists. Quiet Vientiane isn't much of a threat, except for the traffic—there are few lights, and because traffic isn't all that heavy, it moves very, very quickly. There have been rare instances of robbery or rape in remote areas. Solo travelers should take care when going too far off the beaten track, even on a day hike. Some of the country's highways, like Route 13 near Kasi and Route 7 in the northeast, have seen rebel and bandit attacks in the past. Check with your consulate before doing any overland travel. Of course, petty crime does exist. Watch your belongings, and don't leave valuables in your hotel rooms, particularly in smaller guesthouses.

When trekking in the north or in the south around the Ho Chi Minh Trail, even in well-visited areas such as the Plain of Jars, **beware of unexploded bombs.** Don't stray into remote areas, and don't touch anything on the ground.

Telephone & Fax   The international country code for Laos is 856. Phone rates during my most recent visit were as follows: 1 minute to the U.S., the U.K., or Canada: 23,000 kip (US$2.30); to Australia: 11,500 kip (US$1.50); and to New Zealand, 22,000 kip (US$2.20). Buy a stored-value phone card at any post office or telecom center to use at international phone booths located just outside (there are just 300 phone booths in the whole country, and only a small percent are international). Most newer hotels have international direct dialing at surcharges of about 10%. Collect calls are impossible anywhere, and the long-distance companies haven't made it to Laos yet. Internet cafes often have Internet phone service at 5,000 kip (US50¢) per minute and charge 2,000 kip (US20¢) for callback service. See the "Telephone Dialing Info at a Glance" box for more information. Local calls are 100 kip (US1¢) per minute. Like the international phone booths, local phone booths accept only prepaid phone cards. Laos has no coins.

Time Zone   Laos is 7 hours ahead of Greenwich Mean Time, in the same zone as Bangkok. That makes it 12 hours ahead of the U.S. and 3 hours behind Sydney.

Tipping   Tipping has arrived in Laos, particularly in Vientiane. Feel free to tip bellhops, chauffeurs, and tour guides, and to leave 5% to 10% or round up your bill in upscale restaurants. Foreign currency, especially U.S. dollars, is appreciated.

Toilets You'll find toilets or *hawng nam* in hotels, restaurants, tourist attractions, and even wats. Only in the very newest hotels will you find Western-style sit-down toilets, but squat-style toilets (if they have clean floors) are actually more hygienic. Bring your own paper and sanitary hand wipes. You'll notice a bowl and a pail of water nearby for flushing. Throw two to three buckets of water into the toilet. In the sticks, expect buses to just pull to the side for bathroom breaks; in some villages, one is just expected to go au natural. Carry tissues.

Water There is no potable water in Laos. Drink only boiled or bottled water, which is available on virtually every street corner for 1,000 kip (10¢; or more in tourist areas). Don't take ice with your drinks, especially outside of Vientiane. You might even want to consider brushing your teeth with boiled or bottled water.

3 Vientiane

Vientiane (wee-en-*chan*) has to be one of the world's most unique capitals. Like many cities in developing countries, on arrival it's a bit of a shock; the main roads in town were only recently paved, and it's a place where the 3-month overdue repairs on a traffic light on one of the main intersections are the stuff of news in the local English-language paper. A short ride in any direction from Lane Xang, the main north-south avenue, will quickly carry you into the beginnings of rural Laos. Vientiane's population of 280,000 in a country of just under 6 million reflects the nation's rural makeup, and despite the infusion of foreign aid and steady local growth, the infrastructure even here in the capital is basic.

Vientiane's small scale means you'll be constantly confronted by startling incongruities. The town is peopled with monks in vermilion or mustard-color robes attending to their business at temples, but you might wonder at seeing those very pious figures hard at work on their website or playing games online at the local Internet cafe. The recent cellphone boom in Vientiane has urbanites well connected, but you'll be hard-pressed to find a public phone even in the city center. Crumbling French colonial mansions house the likes of the World Bank, International Monetary Fund, and every UN agency known to man. The airport still uses the grab-your-bag-off-the-cart method of dispensing luggage, and you can ride to town in a motorized cart. At the same time, the city has advertising agencies, embassies, and investment advisors. There are luxury business hotels with swimming pools and gourmet restaurants with fine wines, and the streets are crowded with big, gleaming sport utility vehicles.

As far as tourism goes, the city was ransacked by the Vietnamese in 1828, so it lacks some of the ancient history you find in the former capital of Luang Prabang. But its temples have been beautifully reconstructed, and some good examples of colonial buildings are still standing: **That Luang** is the pre-eminent temple in the country and the scene of a huge festival every November, the **Patuxay victory monument** is a peculiarly Lao version of the Arc de Triomphe, the **Morning Market** has a full city block of goods to explore, and the **Mekong** glows pink at sunset. It is worth a stay of several days to take it all in and enjoy Vientiane's laid-back atmosphere while it lasts.

Telephone Dialing Info at a Glance

- **To place a call from your home country to Laos,** dial the international access code (011 in the U.S., 0011 in Australia, 0170 in New Zealand, 00 in the U.K.), plus the country code (856), plus the city or area code (21 for Vientiane, 71 for Luang Prabang) and the 6-digit phone number (for example, 011 + 856 + 21/000-000).
- **To place a call within Laos,** dial the city or area code preceded by a 0, and then the six-digit number (for example, 021/000-000). A local call costs 45 kip (US1¢) a minute from a phone booth. You must use a phone card, which you can buy at the post office, the telephone office, and minimarts.
- **To place a direct international call from Laos,** dial the international access code (**00**) plus the country code, the area or city code, and the number (for example, 00 + 1 + 212/000-0000).
- **International country codes** are as follows: Australia: 61; Burma: 95; Cambodia: 855; Canada: 1; Hong Kong: 852; Indonesia: 62; Malaysia: 60; New Zealand: 64; the Philippines: 63; Singapore: 65; U.K.: 44; U.S.: 1; Vietnam 84.

VISITOR INFORMATION

It might seem that anyone with a shingle, or anything to write on it with, calls himself a travel agent or "tourist information" in Vientiane (not to mention the tuk-tuk drivers, who will offer to adopt you for the length of your stay), but there are some high-quality services in town. See the "Travel Agent" section in the introduction to this chapter for tour providers in Laos, but below are the most established in the capital:

- **Diethelm Travel Laos.** Namphou Square, Setthathirat Road, P.O. Box 2657, Vientiane, Lao P.D.R. (© **021/215-920;** fax 021/216-294. www.diethelm travel.com; ditralao@laotel.com).
- **Sodetour.** 114 Quai Fa Ngum, P.O. Box 70, Vientiane, Lao P.D.R. (© **021/ 216-314;** fax 021/216-313; sodetour@laotel.com).
- **Inter-Lao Tourisme.** Setthathirat Road, P.O. Box 2912, Vientiane, Lao P.D.R. (© **021/214-232;** fax 021/216-306; www.interlao.laopdr.com).
- **Lao Tourism.** 08/02 Lane Xang Ave., P.O. Box 2511, Vientiane, Lao P.D.R. (© **021/216-671;** fax 021/212-013).
- **Exotissimo Travel.** Pangkham Road (© **021/241-861;** fax 021/252-382; www.exotissimo.com).
- **Wildside Eco Group.** 54 Sethathirat Rd., Nam Phu Fountain Circle, Vientiane (© **021/251-563;** www.wildside-laos.com).
- **Lane Xang Travel.** Pangkham Road, P.O. Box 4452, Vientiane, Lao P.D.R. (© **021/212-469;** fax 021/215-804).
- **Tavanh Tour.** Luang Prabang Rd. 10, across from Fujiwara (see "Dining," below), Box 9847, Vientiane (© **021/214-907;** ttslao@yahoo.com). New on the scene, this growing company has good budget tours for rural itineraries and classic tours and can help with any travel detail.

Vientiane

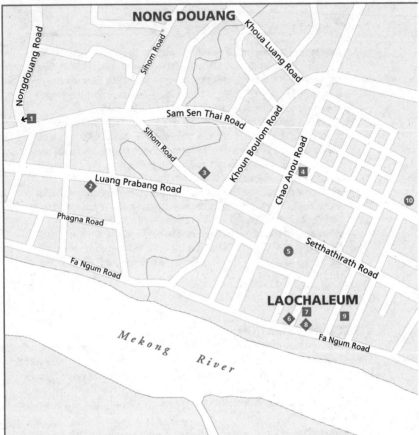

NONG DOUANG

Nongdouang Road

Sihom Road

Khoua Luang Road

Sam Sen Thai Road

Sihom Road

Khoun Boulom Road

Chao Anou Road

Luang Prabang Road

Phagna Road

Fa Ngum Road

Setthathirath Road

LAOCHALEUM

Fa Ngum Road

Mekong River

ACCOMMODATIONS ■
Anou Hotel **4**
Asian Pavillion Hotel **22**
Day Inn **12**
Douang Denane Hotel **9**
Lane-Xang Hotel **21**
Lao Plaza Hotel **13**
Novotel Vientiane **1**
Royal Dokmaideng Hotel **28**
Settha Palace Hotel **11**
Tai-Pan Hotel **7**

DINING ◆
Arawan **30**
Fujiwara **2**
The Hong Kong Restaurant **14**
Just For Fun Restaurant **17**
Khop Chai Deu **16**
Kua Lao **23**
Le Provençal **15**
L'Opera **18**
La Belle Epoque **11**
Le Silapa **3**
Nazim Restaurant **8**
Restaurant Namphou **17**
Sticky Fingers **6**

ATTRACTIONS ●
Buddha Park **32**
Ho Phra Keo **25**
Morning Market **29**
Lao National Museum **10**
Phra That Luang **28**
Patuxay (Victory Monument) **27**
That Dam (Black Stupa) **22**
Wat Ong Teu **5**
Wat Si Muang **31**
Wat Si Saket **24**

OTHER ●
Diethelm Travel **19**
Lao Aviation **20**

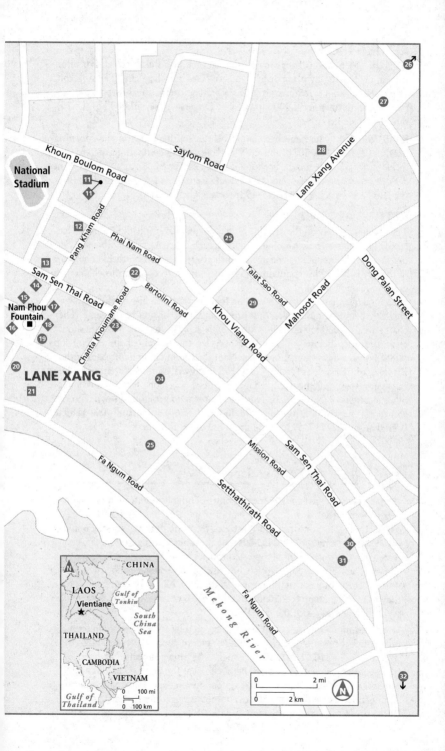

National
Stadium

Khoun Boulom Road

Saylom Road

Lane Xang Avenue

11
11

28

Pang Kham Road

12

Phai Nam Road

25

Dong Palan Street

13

Talat Sao Road

Mahosot Road

Sam Sen Thai Road

14

22

Bartolini Road

29

Khou Viang Road

Nam Phou
Fountain

15

17

16

18

23

19

Chanta Khoumane Road

20

LANE XANG

24

21

25

Mission Road

Sam Sen Thai Road

Fa Ngum Road

Setthathirath Road

30

31

CHINA

LAOS

Vientiane ★

Gulf of
Tonkin

South
China
Sea

THAILAND

CAMBODIA

VIETNAM

Gulf of
Thailand

0   100 mi

0   100 km

Mekong River

Fa Ngum Road

0   2 mi

0   2 km

32

N

GETTING THERE

BY AIR   Vientiane is Laos's major international hub for air travel. For information on arriving by plane or by train, see "Getting There" in "Planning Your Trip to Laos," above. If you're arriving via Wattay International Airport in Vientiane, a taxi to town is 30,000 kip (US$3). Drivers will say 50,000 kip (US$5), but be persistent.

BY BUS/CAR   The large bus station on the southern end of the **Morning Market** (✆ 021/216-507) connects Vientiane with all destinations in Laos (and to Nong Khai in Thailand). For long-distance car rental, ask at any hotel front desk or travel agent, or contact **Asia Vehicle Rental,** 354-356 Samsenthai (near the Lao Paris Hotel; ✆ 021/217-493; www.avr.laopdr.com).

GETTING AROUND

The city lies entirely on the east side of the Mekong River (the other side is Thailand). The main streets, running parallel to each other, are Samsenthai and Setthathirat, with Lane Xang, the north-south artery, intersecting them. The heart of the city is Nam Phu Fountain, and many of the directions in this chapter are given in relation to it.

Central Vientiane is easily covered on foot. You can also hire a **tuk-tuk,** a covered cart behind a motorbike, or a **jumbo,** a bigger version of the same. They charge about 5,000 kip to 10,000 kip (US50¢–US$1) around town. You should settle the price before you ride. **Motorcycles** can be rented for 80,000 kip (US$8) or so a day—look around the Nam Phu Fountain or along Samsenthai. **Bicycles** are available at Orchid Guest House (as well as other storefronts) along Fa Ngum Road near the river, at Sabaidy Guesthouse along Setthathirat, and at other locations on Samsenthai: This is a great way to get around town. You can also rent a car with a driver for 600,000 kip (US$60) a day. Call **Asia Vehicle Rental** at ✆ 021/217-493, or inquire at any hotel front desk.

✆ FAST FACTS: Vientiane

Banks/Currency Exchange   Banque Pour Le Commerce Extérieur Lao is on Pangkham Street down by the river, just west of the Lane Xang hotel (✆ 021/213-200), or just a short distance from the river at Lao May Bank, at 39 Pankham St. (✆ 021/330-001). At these and most other banks, you can exchange money in all major currencies, change traveler's checks to U.S. dollars, and withdraw cash on Visa cards. You can also exchange money at Banque Setthathirat, near Wat Mixay. All banks are open Monday to Friday 8:30am to 3:30pm. Other banks line Lane Xang Avenue, and exchange counters dot the city.

Internet/E-mail   Internet cafes seem to be on nearly every corner in town, and connections are generally good. Phet-Phim, along Fa Ngum Road (by the river; ✆ 021/252-757) and Contact Café, along Setthathirat (west of the fountain—look for the giant Pepsi can over the door; ✆ 020/527-007) are just two of many. Most are 100 kip per minute, and 150 kip for a faster connection (under $1 per hr.). Most hotel business centers charge at least three times this rate for the same service.

Emergencies For police, dial ✆ **991**; for fire, dial ✆ **190**; and for ambulance, dial ✆ **195**. For medical evacuation, call Lao Westcoast Helicopter Company at ✆ **021/512-023**.

Post Office/Mail The General Post Office is on the corner of Khou Vieng Road and Lane Xang Avenue, opposite the Morning Market. Hours are Monday to Friday 8am to noon and 1 to 5pm, and Saturday and Sunday 8am to noon only. EMS and FedEx services are just next door.

Telephone/Fax The central telephone office, where you can place local and international direct dialing (IDD) calls, is located on Setthathirat Road just east of Nam Phu Circle (Nam Phu Fountain), and is open from 8am to 10pm daily. You can also send faxes.

WHERE TO STAY

Vientiane has some good options that range from luxury rooms to backpacker dives. Book ahead, especially in late November and early December, and ask for a discount if you come during the rainy season (some places post their low-season rates). More expensive hotels list their prices in dollars (but accept other currencies), and be warned that the prices listed in this chapter do not always include a government tax of 10% or any additional service charges (sometimes applicable in high season). All hotels provide airport transfers (for free in the Expensive and Moderate categories).

EXPENSIVE

The Lao Plaza Hotel 🐵🐵   This is the best choice in town for the high-end business traveler or those seeking all of the comforts and amenities of an international hotel (rare elsewhere in developing Laos). With a convenient, central location, accommodation at the Lao Plaza is bland but plush and comfortable. Sizable rooms are either beige or blue, with solid wood furniture in perfect condition, thick rugs, firm beds, and small marble-tiled bathrooms with hair dryers and terry-cloth robes. You can get a computer and Internet hookup in your room. Nonsmoking rooms are available on two floors. The pool is big and inviting. Lao Plaza's staff is professional enough, but not especially friendly or helpful. The May Yuan restaurant has admirable Chinese food, and Dok Champa is a cheery cafe, with buffet meals and a deli/bakery. The Plaza is sufficiently self-contained and convenient to any destination in town, and one of only a few accommodations in Laos where you cross the threshold and enter such an international standard of accommodation and service that you might forget that you're in Laos.

63 Samsenthai Rd., P.O. Box 6708, Vientiane. ✆ **021/218-800.** Fax 021/218-808. www.laoplazahotel.com. 142 units. US$100–US$120 superior single/twin; US$130–US$140 executive single/twin; US$200–US$400 suite. AE, MC, V. **Amenities:** 2 restaurants; bar; popular nightclub; beergarden; nice pool; gym (guests are charged $8 to use it); Jacuzzi; sauna; business center w/Internet; bookstore and gift shop; massage; laundry; conference rooms; banquet facilities. *In room:* A/C, satellite TV, minibar, IDD phone.

Novotel Hotel Vientiane 🐵🐵   Just a short ride west of the town center, the Novotel Vientiane is a pleasant oasis from the dusty streets and downtown tuk-tuk clamor. The lobby, with stylish rounded woodwork and domed ceiling painted in a muted, pastel yellow, is decorated in a classic Art Deco theme and is an attractive invitation to Novotel's fine rooms and services. The renovated executive-floor rooms have attractive carpets, fine wood furniture, and marble

Tips   **Living Without Street Addresses**

You'll notice that many of the businesses in Vientiane don't seem to have street addresses. The city is so small that they hardly need them. Note also that transliterations of Laos street names differ from map to map, some favoring French pronunciation, others English, and often used inter-changably (see Nam Phu and Nam Phou for example). Also note that *thanon* simply means "street."

bathrooms with nice big counters. The older "standard" rooms are less luxe, with cane furniture, pastel colors, and tile bathrooms. Deluxe rooms include free laundry, local calls, and complimentary drinks. All rooms are spotless and have small details like local hangings and artwork that keep your mind in Indochina. Adjoining the lobby is a well-appointed Continental restaurant with indoor and outdoor by-the-pool seating. A popular daily breakfast buffet and brunch are featured on weekends. The staff is friendly and helpful, and the hotel offers a wealth of facilities and services, including its smart business center and chic executive lounge, and even a well-stocked book corner in the lobby. It's a bit far from town but has very convenient amenities and good transportation.

Unit 9, Samsenthai Rd., P.O. Box 585, Vientiane. ⓒ **800/221-4542** or 021/213-570. Fax 021/213-572. novot lao@loxinfo.co.th. 168 units. US$60–US$70 double; US$128 suite. AE, MC, V. **Amenities:** Restaurant; bar; nice outdoor pool; health club; sauna; free and frequent transport to the town center; gift shop; 24-hr. room service; massage. *In room:* A/C, satellite TV, minibar, coffeemaker, hair dryer, IDD phone.

Settha Palace Hotel 🐦🐦🐦   For elegance in Vientiane, there is no finer choice than this masterfully restored, early-20th-century French colonial mansion. Once the distinguished address of visitors from the adjacent colonies of Indochina, the building traced a long history of decline before its recent multi-million-dollar face-lift and 1999 reopening. A small circular drive ushers you into the high, columned marble entry, and light coming through the large windows lends a softness to the lobby that is not unlike stepping into a sepia photograph of a distant time. The rooms are small for the price but cozy, with antique detail and dark-wood reproduction furnishings that include four-poster beds. Bathrooms are small but elegant, and the black-and-white tile floors and marble counters stand in attractive contrast to the wood tones of the room. If a stay at the Palace is a trip to the past, modern amenities like in-room Internet access and satellite TV will keep you connected in the present (a good standard for the upscale business traveler). The hotel's elegant restaurant, La Belle Epoque (see "Where to Dine," below), serves excellent French and Continental cuisine in a setting that can't be beat. With service unmatched in town, the Palace offers quality far exceeding its price tag. You have arrived.

6 Pangkham (P.O. Box 161). ⓒ **021/217-581.** Fax 021/217-583. www.setthapalace.com. 48 units. US$88–US$98 double; US $120–US$220 deluxe; US$320 suite. AE, MC, V. **Amenities:** Restaurant (see dining section); bar; outdoor pool (nonguests welcome for $4); Jacuzzi; laundry. *In room:* A/C, satellite TV, minibar, safe, IDD phone, Internet connection.

MODERATE

Royal Dokmaideng Hotel 🐦   A good value can be found in this clean, friendly 7-year-old hotel. Owned and managed by a Taiwanese group, the hotel has large rooms, though devoid of much character, with attractive carpet and-wood furnishings, comfortable beds, and plump pillows. There are nice-size marble bathrooms with hair dryers, and you can get hot-water thermoses for tea and coffee upon request. The suites are huge and excellent for families, and the Chinese restaurant is bright and inviting (so is the small courtyard pool). With a central location on Lane Xang Avenue, just north of the Morning Market, the Royal Dokmaideng is a favorite for businessmen, and the multilingual staff offers efficient and friendly service. Nonsmokers, be sure to ask for a nonsmoking rooms because otherwise they're a bit musty. There's a popular karaoke area on the second floor.

Lane Xang Ave., P.O. Box 3925, Vientiane. © **021/214-455.** Fax 021/214-454. 40 units. US$28–US$40 double; US$60 suite. AE, MC, V. **Amenities:** Restaurant; bar; small courtyard swimming pool; basic gym; sauna; conference room; laundry. *In room:* A/C, TV, minibar, IDD phone.

Tai-Pan Hotel ★★ *Value* This very attractive 9-year-old midsize hotel is convenient to downtown, on a quiet street just off the Mekong, and offers the amenities and service of its larger, high-end competition. The large rooms, all spotless, bright, and cheerful, have dark parquet floors with painted wood furniture and floral bedspreads for contrast. The sizable bathrooms are done in white, with clean tile and bathtubs. Ask for a third-floor room with a balcony and river view. With a sister property in Bangkok, the Tai-Pan is popular for business travelers and is a popular spot for long-stay businesspeople and the humanitarian NGO set. The lobby restaurant is tops, and the location can't be beat.

22/3 François Nginn Rd., Ban Mixay, Muong Chanthabury, Vientiane. © **021/216-907.** Fax 021/216-223. taipan@lox2.loxinfo.co.th. 44 units. US$49 double; US$54 deluxe; US$71 junior suite; US$81 suite. AE, MC, V. **Amenities:** Restaurant; bar; health club w/sauna; airport transfer; conference rooms. *In room:* A/C, satellite TV, minibar, IDD phone.

INEXPENSIVE

Anou Hotel *Value* Here's a bargain for you. The Anou has clean, bright, good-size rooms, some with tidy beige carpet and others with hardwood floors. The beds are comfortable and the bathrooms are liveable, with tile floors and spiffy marble counters. Some are the shower-in-room variety, without bathtubs, so let the hotel know if that matters to you. The suites are simply huge, and all have wood floors, but they're just larger versions of the standard rooms (with a larger fridge). The downstairs restaurant is inviting, and the hotel has a good location in downtown Chinatown, surrounded by shops and restaurants; the area is abuzz with activity into the evening.

01–03 Heng Boun St., Vientiane. © **021/213-630.** Fax 021/213-632. anouhotel@laonet.net. 50 units. US$20 double; US$40 suite. AE, MC, V. **Amenities:** Restaurant; bar; laundry. *In room:* A/C, TV, minibar, IDD phone.

Day Inn Hotel ★★ *Finds* This charming little inn in the shadow of the Lao Plaza was once the Indian Embassy, and it retains some of that urban, colonial dignity in its large, airy rooms, with high ceilings and tall French doors. Though it's all a bit stark and simple, you're in an ideal downtown location; rooms are furnished in basic but tidy wicker, with hard beds and clean but basic bathrooms (some with a tub). The Day Inn is like an upscale guesthouse, really, but it has the basic in-room amenities of a proper hotel (satellite TV and IDD phone). Ask for a spot in the front, where doors and windows open to small private balconies. With a young and friendly staff, a fine Lao restaurant, and a laid-back feel, the Day Inn is popular with tourists who are in need of some amenities but who are here to relax and learn about "Lao Time."

059/3 Pangkham Rd., P.O. Box 4083, Vientian. © **021/223-847.** Fax 021/222984. dayinn@laotel.com 25 units. 250,000 kip (US$25) single; 300,000 kip (US$30) double; 450,000 kip (US$45) suite. Cash only. **Amenities:** Restaurant; laundry; Internet service in lobby. *In room:* A/C, satellite TV, minibar, IDD phone.

Douang Deuane Hotel (Value) Popular with tour groups, this is a clean and basic budget option just off the Mekong and close to the center of town. Rooms have tacky fluorescent paintings and discolored wallpaper, but they are spacious, with wood floors and large, tiled bathrooms (the shower-in-room variety). Call ahead; the word is out on the value of this little spot and the place is often booked. Bike and scooter rentals are available out front. A basic breakfast buffet is included.

Nokeo Koummane Rd., Ban Mixay, P.O. Box 6881, Vientiane. ℂ 021/222-301. Fax 021/222-300. DD_Hotel@ hotmail.com. 30 units. US$18 single; US$23 double. MC, V. **Amenities:** Restaurant; motorbike rental; laundry. *In room:* A/C, TV, minibar.

Lane-Xang Hotel 🏛 This 40-year-old hotel, once the prize of Vientiane, has seen better days, but there's a certain fallen-angel quality here, like an old Vegas casino or your favorite greasy spoon, that makes for an interesting stay. Considering the great riverfront location with good views of the Mekong (be sure to ask for a higher floor facing the river) and the many hotel facilities, you can't beat the price. Recent minor renovations, part of a larger effort to eventually bring the Lane Xang back to its former glory, have at least improved cosmetic detail (peeling wallpaper and water stains), but be sure to ask to see the room before you check in. There are lots of facilities on the hotel compound (including a pool and tennis), but none are well maintained, like everyone left in the 1970s and just dropped everything. The rooms are nice-size and comfortable, with clean beds and wood floors, but despite recent efforts, they're a bit rundown, with chipped furniture and old polyester bedspreads. The suites aren't much to write home about—just larger and seemingly grungier versions of the standard rooms. If the cigarette holes and stained carpet could talk, it might be a good story, but it makes for less than an ideal stay. Check out the snooker area and nightclub just outside for a bit of a bizarre late-night local scene.

Fa Ngum Rd., P.O. Box 280, Vientiane. ℂ **021/214-102.** Fax 021/214-108. 109 units. US$22 single; US$25 double; US$45–US$55 suite. AE, V. **Amenities:** 2 restaurants; bar; outdoor pool; tennis; a basic gym w/sauna and massage; snooker/billiard parlor; car rental; business center; salon; shopping; meeting rooms. *In room:* A/C, TV, minibar, IDD phone, room service.

BUDGET OPTIONS

The **Lao-Paris Hotel** (ℂ 021/222-229), just across the street at 100 Samsenthai, offers good value for basic rooms that are a bit dingy.

For a good budget value at the high end of the backpacker category, try the **Orchid Guesthouse,** on 33 Fa Ngum Rd. near the Mekong (ℂ **021/252-825**); it has very friendly staff and a laid-back feel, and it's right in the thick of things along the river. There are 22 rooms with air-conditioning, priced from US$12. Bicycle rental is available.

Vientiane, like the rest of Laos, has experienced a boom in backpacker accommodation over the years, and accommodations for US$2 to US$8 are abundant in and around Nam Phu Fountain; you get what you pay for here, but it's a good value compared with, for example, Vietnam.

WHERE TO DINE

French is very big in the Lao capital, and good restaurants of this ilk (along with a few serving Italian) actually outnumber those serving native Lao fare. It might sound like a pity, but the food is generally so good and so reasonably priced that you probably won't complain. There's usually a decent French wine list, or you can try *lao lao* (rice wine served warm, with or without herbs). A few other local specialties to watch out for are *khao poun,* rice vermicelli with vegetables, meat, or chiles in coconut milk; *laap,* minced meat, chicken, or fish tossed with fresh mint leaves; or a tasty Lao-style paté. Try sticky rice, eaten with the hands, as an accompaniment to most Lao dishes (it's a thrice-a-day staple for Laotians), and face your fears when local menus offer snake blood, tree bark, or elephant innards.

EXPENSIVE

Fujiwara ★★ JAPANESE   A culinary refuge for the many Japanese NGO workers here in Vientiane, Fujiwara serves up a good mix of sushi, sashimi, and grilled items in an understated Japanese atmosphere. You'll be greeted with a hearty "Irashaimase" (Japanese for "welcome!") at the sushi bar in the front, and you can have privacy behind a shogi-screen in one of the back rooms (don't step in the little rock garden and fake river on the way). Eating raw seafood in a land-locked, developing nation might sound a bit ill fated, but the fish is trucked in from Thailand and served directly (the menu is ambitious, and not all items are always available) and though the prices reflect the transport costs for some items, Fujiwara is an affordable and novel treat if you've had your fill of sticky rice. The set lunches are cheap and good light fare on a hot day.

002/2 Luang Prabang Rd., just W of the town center. ✆ 021/222-210. Main courses US$2–US$12. V. Daily 10am-11pm.

The Hong Kong Restaurant ★ CHINESE   Run by a family from Beijing, the Hong Kong is a long-time favorite in town. The decor is standard "Chinese restaurant"—bright and colorful in whites and reds. Whole fish of all types cooked to order and various shrimp and seafood stir-fries top the menu. Try the garlic shrimp. Specialty items like duck and suckling pig can be ordered in advance (and cost a bit more). At the Hong Kong, they firmly follow the Chinese axiom that dining out is about the food, not the atmosphere. If you're look-ing for a candlelit corner, you've come to the wrong place, but for a great meal and clamorous dish-clanging and conversation, the Hong Kong makes for a good evening.

80/4 Samsenthai Rd., across from the Lao Hotel Plaza. ✆ 021/213-241. Main courses US$5–US$15. No credit cards. Daily 11:30am–2pm and 6–10pm.

L'Opera ★★ ITALIAN   For nearly 10 years, L'Opera has been serving-up "real Italian" and garnering nothing but praise. Even if you've got good Italian at home, come here for the homemade egg noodle pasta, good Italian wine list, excellent grill and broiled specialties, and fantastic authentic desserts and espresso. There is also a large selection of pizzas—pizza Lao is a surprisingly good combination of tomatoes, cheese, chiles, Lao sausage, and pineapple. The ambience is good—a rather formal Italy-meets-Lao—with linen tablecloths, brick walls, and wood-beam ceilings in a large, open setting. Lao staff in fine restaurants often act as if their foreign patrons are armed and dangerous (please read: fear you), but here the service is confident and professional. There's a menu of daily specials, and groups of four or more can try the Opera Menu, featuring nine different special appetiz-ers, pastas, and main courses for $20 per person. It's very popular with expats.

On the Fountain Circle. ✆ 021/215-099. Main courses US$5–US$13. AE, V. Daily 11:30am–2pm and 6–10pm.

La Belle Epoque ★★ FRENCH/CONTINENTAL   This restaurant is at the top of dining experiences in Vientiane—the place for a power lunch or to enter-tain friends. In the atmospheric Settha Palace Hotel (see the section on accom-modations), you can't beat the atmosphere—colonial elegance mixed with Vientiane's laid-back appeal. The service is efficient, but with a friendliness that's sincere. The menu covers a wide range of French and Continental specialties, with meat, game, and seafood prepared to order. Imported Australian steaks and salmon top off a fine list of specialties, like grilled lamb with ratatouille or terrine of duck liver marinated in wine. Try one of the creative appetizers, like the goat cheese pasty; also sample the exhaustive wine list and, whatever you do, don't pass up the crème brulée. For such atmosphere, presentation, and service you would pay an arm and a leg anywhere but here.

Settha Palace Hotel, 6 Pangkham St., P.O. Box 1618. ✆ 021/217-581. Reservations recommended. Main courses US$6–US$13. AE, MC, V. Open daily 6am–10:30pm.

MODERATE

KhopChaiDeu ✾ LAO/INTERNATIONAL   The name means "Thank you very much" (with the last syllable, "do," elongated), and even if your time in Vientiane is brief, you can't miss this place if you want to. Just south and west of the Nam Phu Fountain and set in a large colonial building, KhopChaiDeu is the crossroads for expats, backpackers and tourists, and folks who come to get connected with the local scene as much as anything. The menu is extensive, with some tasty barbecue and good Lao selections; consider the "Lao Discovery" set, which walks you through various short courses of typical Lao dishes. The old standbys of fried rice, noodles, and spring rolls are featured on the menu's "backpackers page," while the "expats page" offers pizza, spaghetti, and all the things Mom used to heat up in the microwave so many miles away. Sit on one of the many balconies of this multitiered building, or pull up a chair in the courtyard or at the bar and enjoy overhearing some good NGO shop-talk or English teachers and backpackers sharing notes. KhopChaiDeu is abuzz late into the evening, and the 3,000 kip (US30¢) draft beer flows freely. It's a good spot to find out about any good happenings in town, club events, festivals, and even road conditions from long-time locals.

54 Sethathirat, SW of Nam Phu Fountain. ✆ 021/212-106. Main courses US$2–US$5. Set menu US$5.70. MC, V. Dining daily 7am–10:30pm. Bar open late.

Kua Lao ✾✾ LAO   Kua Lao offers excellent Lao fare in a traditional atmosphere that makes for a unique dining experience. Set in a restored colonial mansion, there is music and Lao dancing each evening. Though at times the whole scene pushes the bounds of kitsch, the staff is very kind; their hope to infuse your dining experience with Lao culture is quite genuine. Nowhere else will you find such an extensive menu of Lao food with English descriptions (and pictures), and many will appreciate the numerous options for vegetarians, not to mention a whole page of tempting Lao desserts. Try the Laap (or larp), a mince of fish, chicken, or beef mixed with spices and mint; it's excellent when accompanied by a basket of sticky rice and eaten by hand. The set menus, at US$10, are a bargain, especially for smaller groups hoping to sample a larger selection. Staff can answer questions or will find someone who can. If you're going up-country or heading out to the back of beyond, this is a good place for a primer in Lao cuisine.

111 Samsenthai Rd., Box 1873 (at the intersection w/Chanta Khoumane). ✆ 021/214-813. Fax 021/215-777. Main courses US$2–US$6; set menu US$10. Daily 11am–2pm and 5–11:30pm.

Le Provençal ✾ FRENCH/CONTINENTAL   If it's a good pizza you want, you've come to the right place. It's affordable, beginning at just $3, and hearty, with excellent cheeses and toppings. I ordered the supreme and was greeted with a proper pizza topped off with a fried egg smack in the middle—odd, but not a bad addition to an old favorite. Le Provençal also features standard French fare; the specialty is the terrine maison (potted beef). Head right next door to the Scandinavian Bakery for coffee and sweets for dessert.

On the N edge of Nam Phu Fountain, 78/2 Pangkham Rd. (C) 021/219685. Main courses US$3–US$5. MC, V. Mon–Sat 11:30m–2pm and 6–10pm.

Le Silapa *FRENCH/CONTINENTAL* For cozy atmosphere and authentic French cuisine, this is a find in Vientiane (if you can find it). It's small and a bit rustic, but the wine list holds up to any standard and everything on the menu is excellent. I had a steamed whitefish subtly garnished with capers, lemon, and parsley. The effusive French proprietor will make you feel welcome. I found myself one evening just leaning back in my chair, listening to the muffled street sounds diminishing at the day's end, and watching the candlelight overtake the waning sun's glow, and thinking about how I could extend my visa.

17/1 Sihom Rd., Ban Haysok. (C) 021/219-689. Main courses US$4.75–US$12.75; set lunch US$5.50. MC, V. Mon–Sat 11:30am–2pm and 6–10pm.

Restaurant Namphou *ASIAN/CONTINENTAL* Whether you opt for a bit of people-watching from one of the outdoor semi-reclined chairs or choose the intimate, bamboo-walled dining room, dinner or drinks at Restaurant Namphou is a laid-back, atmospheric affair. It's semi-casual native Lao, yet formal enough for a business lunch. The menu is an eclectic mix of Thai, Lao, French, and Continental that somehow works. Specialties of the house are filet mignon, a hamburger with bleu cheese, and, for a price, imported seafood and specialty steaks from Australia. Ask for the daily special and take your time.

On the Fountain Circle. (C) 021/216-248. Main courses US$4.50–US$13. AE, V. Daily 11am–3pm and 6:30–11:30pm.

Sticky Fingers *INTERNATIONAL* Started by two Australians who came to Laos with the UN and are involved in NGO work, Sticky Fingers serves up soups, salads, sandwiches, and snacks in a relaxed atmosphere. Here they've got the corner on the casual business lunch and the after-work crowd. Try a burger, sandwich, or steak, and be sure to choose from the impressive list of homemade dips and sauces (available for carry-out). This is the place to get your hummus fix or grab a falafel and a bit of respite from the afternoon heat. Bon appetit.

10/3 François Nginn St., P.O. Box 7034, just across the road from the Tai-Pan Hotel. (C) 021/215-972. Main courses US$2.50–US$7.50 Daily 10am–11pm.

INEXPENSIVE

Arawan *RUSTIC FRENCH* For inexpensive grilled or one-pot meals, try Arawan. The menu features all manner of meats: chicken, pork, and steak (imported from New Zealand). The food is fresh, simply prepared, and very good. Most entrees are served with salad and french fries. There are other French specialties to be had as well, including coq au vin and ragoût de mouton. Arawan has no ambience to speak of, but the place is clean and inviting and has an amiable French proprietor who will be eager to chat with you—that is, if you speak some French. The menu has English translations. Most main courses go up to only about 15,000 kip (US$1.50); it's the steaks that cost the big bucks.

478 Samsenthai Rd., about 2 blocks past Wat Simuang. (C) 021/215-373. Main courses US$1.18–US$3.95. No credit cards. Daily 11am–2pm and 5–10pm.

Nazim Restaurant *INDIAN* For great Indian cuisine at affordable prices, Nazim has cornered the market in Laos and now has branch locations in Vang

Vieng and Luang Prabang. Serving up anything from Biryani to tandori and any kind of curry you can imagine, Nazim offers a survey of Indian cuisine (and the beer to wash it down) in a no-frills storefront along the Mekong. Everything is good, and the prices are reasonable (one avoids the word *cheap*), making this a popular backpacker spot and an expat standby. In the evenings in high season, it's packed and you might find yourself seated family style with other travelers, crackin' beers, swappin' tales, and making friends. Enjoy.

Fa Ngum Rd. © 021/223-480. www.nazim.laopdr.com. Main courses US$1.05–US$2.50. No credit cards. Daily 11am–11pm.

SNACKS & CAFES

Stop at the **Healthy & Fresh Bakery,** at 44/4 Ban Xieng Yeun, Setthathirat Road. It's everything it says it is, and great-tasting as well. You'll find quiche and salads along with breads, sweets, and fantastic coffee.

The Scandinavian Bakery, off Nam Phu Fountain Circle, has specialties from that region (and daily bread specials) and is always packed with travelers. This is a good place to pick up a foreign newspaper and people-watch on the terrace.

Just for Fun Restaurant, 57/2 Phangkhoum Rd. (© 021/213-642), just opposite Lao Aviation, is a good spot to kick back and relax; pick up a paper or the latest bit of local, international, or NGO news; and have a good, inexpensive one-plate meal (fried rice, noodles, etc.) or just a coffee.

Xayoh Café, just across from the Lao National Culture Hall (© 020/612-051), serves pub grub of all sorts and is a good place to relax and have a beer or a coffee anytime.

PVO, an open-air storefront on Samsenthai near the Lao-Paris Hotel, serves great Vietnames Bo Bun (cold noodles and spring roll) and is a longtime traveler's favorite.

For ice cream, crepes, and desserts, don't miss **La Terrasse** in Ban Mixay, just down Kokeokoumane Street (© 021/218-550).

ATTRACTIONS

While Vientiane doesn't have the sheer number of wats enjoyed by Luang Prabang, they still dominate the list of must-sees. Most sights are still within the city limits, which means you'll be able to cover them by bicycle or even on foot, getting to know the city intimately as you go (and getting to know the city might be the real attraction in this little burg).

Finds **Vientiane's Street Fare**

The busy area of **Ban Haysok** on the western edge of the town center is Vientiane's small **Chinatown** and a great place for an evening stroll and some great snacks. One-dish meals of rice or noodles, Lao/Chinese desserts, and super-sweet banana pancakes are sold by street vendors. It's an area that stays up late for sleepy Vientiane, and its charm is in the clamorous chaos. Don't miss it.

The many storefronts along riverside **Fa Ngum Road** are popular gathering spots for travelers, and across the street, on the riverside, are a row of **thatched-roof eateries** serving all the basics. This is a great spot for viewing the Mekong and neighboring Thailand at sunset.

Buddha Park ★★ *Finds*   It's said that if a fool persists in his folly, he will become wise. Buddha Park is more like a fanciful sculpture garden, full of Hindu and Buddhist statues, and it is concrete testament to the obsession of Luang Pu, a shamanist priest who conceived and started building the park in the 1950s. The statues are captivating, whether they are snarling, reposing, or saving maidens in distress (or carrying them to their doom—it's hard to tell). The huge reclining Buddha is outstanding; you can climb on its arm for a photo. There is also a big concrete dome to climb, itself filled with sculptures. The half-hour jumbo ride to get here, if you choose that route, is very dusty but fulfilling: You get a clear view of Thailand across the Mekong.

About 24km (15 miles) SE of town. Admission 500 kip (US7¢), plus an additional 500 kip (US7¢) for jumbo parking and 500 kip (US7¢) to use a camera. Daily 7:30am–5:30pm.

Ho Phra Keo ★★   Also built by King Setthathirat in 1565, Phra Keo was constructed to house an emerald Buddha that the king took from Thailand (which the Thais took back in 1779). Today there are no monks in residence, and the wat is actually a museum of religious art, including a Khmer stone Buddha and a wooden copy of the famous Luang Prabang Buddha. In the garden, there's a transplanted jar from the Plain of Jars (see section 7, later in this chapter).

On Setthathirat Rd., opposite Wat Sisaket. Admission 1,000 kip (US13¢). Daily 8am–noon and 1–4pm.

Lao National Museum   Housed in an interesting old colonial that was once used for government offices, the Museum of the Revolution has photos, artifacts, and re-creations of the Lao struggle for independence against the French and Americans. The exhibits (firearms, chairs used by national heroes, and the like) are rather scanty, barely scratching the surface of such a complicated subject, but most are in English at least. Archaeological finds and maps presented on the first floor (probably because there is no other museum to house them at present) help make a visit here worthwhile. Actually, one of the most interesting exhibits is in the last room before you exit, sort of a Laos trade and commodities exhibit of produce, handiwork, and manufactured goods. Though dated, it will give you some idea of Laos's geography and commerce.

Samsenthai Rd., near the Lao Plaza Hotel. Admission 3,000 kip (US30¢). Daily 8am–noon and 1–4pm.

Morning Market (Talaat Sao) ★★   Full of surprises around every corner, the Morning Market is the hub of local commerce and really where the action is. Here you can find anything from the Thai version of that Britney Spears CD you've been chasing after or a Buddhist keepsake from one of the tourist shops or small-time trinket salesmen. Bargain hard. This is the Laos version of "mall culture," and sometimes the everyday tool department or stationery area gives a special glimpse into everyday life (and with a few well-placed "sabaidees," you'll be making friends, without doubt). Enjoy a good wander and the unique experience of hassle-free shopping; there are few touts, but, as always in crowded places, mind your valuables.

On Talat Sao Rd., off Lane Xang Ave. Daily 7am–5pm.

Patuxay (Victory Monument) ★   This monument was completed in 1968 and dedicated to those who fought in the war of independence against the French. Ironically, the monument is an arch modeled on the Parisian Arc de Triomphe. Its detailing is typically Lao, however, with many *kinnari* figures—half woman, half bird. It's an imposing sight, and you can climb up for a good city view. This is the town's pre-eminent teenage strutting ground and is busy and crowded on weekends.

At the end of Lane Xang Ave. Admission 1,000 kip (US10¢). Daily 8am–4pm.

Phra That Luang ⚑   This is the pre-eminent temple in Lao, actually a 44.4m (148-foot) stupa. It is not the original; the first, built in 1566 by King Set-thathirat over the ruins of a 12th-century Khmer temple, was destroyed when the Siamese sacked Vientiane in 1828. It was rebuilt by the French in 1900, but the Lao people criticized it as not being true to the original. It was torn down in 1930 and remodeled to become the temple you see today. As you approach, the statue in front depicts Setthathirat. After you enter the first courtyard, look to the left to see a sacred bodhi tree, the same variety as that under which Buddha sat to achieve enlightenment. It has a tall, slim trunk, and the shape of its foliage is almost perfectly round. According to the Laotians, bodhi trees appear only in sacred places. You'll never see one, for example, in someone's backyard. The stupa is built in stages. On the second level, there are 30 small stupas, representing the 30 Buddhist perfections, or stages to enlightenment. That Luang is the site of one of Lao's most important temple festivals, which takes place in early November.

At the end of That Luang Rd. Admission 2,000 kip (US20¢). Daily 8am–noon and 1–4pm.

That Dam (the Black Stupa)   This ancient stupa was probably constructed in the 15th century or even earlier, though it has never been dated. It is rumored to be the resting place of a mighty *naga*, or seven-headed dragon, that protected the local residents during the Thai invasion in the early 1800s.

In the center of the traffic circle at the intersection of Chanta Khumman and Bartholomie Rd.

Wat Ong Teu ⚑   Wat Ong Teu is in a particularly auspicious location, surrounded by four temples: Wat Inpeng to the north, Wat Mixay to the south, Wat Haysok to the east, and Wat Chan to the west. Its name comes from its most famous inhabitant, a huge (*ongteu*) bronze Buddha. The temple, famous for its beautifully carved wooden facade, was built in the early 16th century and rebuilt in the 19th and 20th centuries. Home to the Patriarch of Lao Buddhism, the temple also serves as a national center for Buddhist studies.

Intersection of Setthathirat and Chau Anou rds. Daily 8am–5pm

Wat Si Muang   Wat Si Muang, another 1566 Setthathirat creation, houses the foundation pillar of the city. According to legend, a pregnant woman named Nang Si, inspired by the gods to sacrifice herself, jumped into the pit right before the stone was lowered. She has now become a sort of patron saint for the city. The temple is very popular as a result and is the site of a colorful procession 2 days before the That Luang festival every November.

East on Samsenthai, near where it joins Setthathirat. Daily 8am–5pm.

Wat Si Saket ⚑⚑   Wat Si Saket, completed in 1818, is the only temple in Vientiane to survive the pillaging of the city by the Siamese in 1828, perhaps because the temple is built in traditional Thai style. It is renowned for the more than 10,000 Buddha images in the outer courtyard, of all shapes and sizes, in every possible nook and cranny. Look for Buddha characteristics that are unique to Laos: the standing or "praying for rain" Buddha; or the pose with arms up and palms facing forward, the "stop fighting" or calling for peace Buddha. The pose in which Buddha points the right hand downward signifies a rejection of evil and a calling to mother earth for wisdom and assistance. Lao Buddhas also have exaggerated nipples and square noses, to emphasize that Buddha is no longer human. The sim features a Khmer-style Buddha seated on a coiled cobra for protection.

At the corner of Setthathirat and Lane Xang aves. Admission 2,000 kip (US20¢). Daily 8am–noon and 1–4pm.

SHOPPING

Laos is famous for its hand-woven silk textiles. You can buy them in fabric or in ready-made wall hangings, accessories, and clothing. Silver is everywhere, in jewelry and ornamental objects. The main shopping streets are **Samsenthai** and **Setthathirat,** around the Nam Phu Fountain area and the **Morning Market** (see "Attractions," above).

Perhaps best known not just in town but worldwide is **Carol Cassidy: Lao Textiles,** off Setthathirat on Nokeo Koummane Road (② 021/212-123; www. laotextiles.com). Since 1990, Carol has employed local weavers and, using traditional Lao motifs as a base, has a great reputation for fine contemporary pieces.

Be sure to visit **Satri Lao Silk,** at 79/4 Setthathirat, for fabrics, clothing, and housewares; and **Ikho 2,** Phangkhoum Road, next to Just for Fun Restaurant, also a good gift shop. The unusual furniture and artworks displayed at **T'shop Lai Gallery,** Vat Inpeng Road (② 021/223-178), is worth a visit as well. For anything from small carvings and authentic Buddhist do-dads all the way up to priceless statues, furniture, and antiques, try **Oot-Ni,** just west of the Lao Cultural Hall on Samsenthai (② 021/215-911). Check out the cut-work household linens, bedspreads, kitchen textiles, place settings, plus baby items in great colors and quality at **Camacrafts,** on Nokeo Koummane Road (② 021/416-597).

For a unique shopping experience in Vientiane, contact Sandra Yuck at her private studio, **Caruso,** housed in a charming colonial property west of the hospital on Fa Ngum Road (P.O. Box 7866, Vientiane; ② 021/223-644; fax 021/223-645; sandrina@loxinfo.co.th). Sandra carries a unique line of ebony wood boxes, trays, and accessories, as well as unique Lao bedspreads.

BOOKS AND NECESSITIES

Just across from Lao Aviation and next to Just for Fun Restaurant is the **Vientiane Book Center,** 54/1 Pangkham Rd. (② 021/212-031), a great spot to exchange that novel you've finished or to pick up maps and information. Or, try nearby **Kosila Bookshop,** across from La Terrasse (② 021/241-352), in Ban Mixay (the parallel street just east of Pangkham Rd.).

For foreign-made staples, from Spam to fine French wine, check out **Phimphone Minimart,** 110/1 Samsenthai Rd. (② 021/216-963).

VIENTIANE AFTER DARK

There are a few places around town to meet and greet other English-speakers. The **KhopCaiDeu** (see "Where to Dine," above), on the southwest corner of the Nam Phu Fountain, is the hot spot for expats and travelers, and a good place to find out what's going on in town; often you'll find some good local cover bands. There is also a wine bar, **Le Cave de Châteaux,** on Fountain Circle; the bar also serves some fine French fare. The **Lao Plaza Hotel** has a nightclub/disco and a popular beer garden, and on Samsenthai Road just before Novotel, you'll find **Wind West** on the right and **Bamboo Bar** on the left side: Called discos, they're a bit grungy but can be fun with the right folks. For live music, try the **Chess Café** on Sakkaline Road, just off Fa Ngum Road to the east of the hospital when heading toward the Friendship Bridge (away from the airport). Be careful if you're strolling about after dark, though, because Vientiane has a good number of open sewers.

4 Vang Vieng

Just 3 hours north of Vientiane, Vang Vieng is a picturesque little town surrounded by beautiful limestone spires, called karst, and is a great base for some good trekking and kayaking. The town itself is more or less an old backpacker ghetto, with rows of budget guesthouses, small sit-on-the-floor (or raised bamboo platforms) eateries, and bars blaring techno or showing films (a rural Khao San Road). But there's a certain laid-back allure that makes up for any lack of fine accommodation. It's a majestic setting and great for day-time adventures and twilight tall tale telling and camaraderie. You might want to stay a night or two and enjoy a single-day or multiday kayak tour in combination with trekking and cave exploration.

GETTING THERE

Bus   Just 3 hours north from Vientiane on Highway 13, it's a smooth ride most of the way; there are numerous daily departures from the Morning Market (© 021/216-507), and tickets are just 8,000 kip (US80¢). Bus connection to Luang Prabang was once a popular option, a rugged but scenic all-day ride for just 40,000 kip (US$4), but recent attacks just north of town mean that road travel is prohibited. Ask around as the situation will surely change.

INFORMATION AND TOURS

Diethelm Travel (see "Planning Your Trip to Laos," earlier in this chapter) includes Vang Vieng in many of its tours and can make any custom arrangements. The town itself is brimming with small operators, but for good ecotours, contact local **Wildside Eco Group** (© 023/511-440; www.wildside-laos.com).

WHERE TO STAY

Budget accommodations are choc-a-bloc in town; most is concrete basic with no hot water. You'll find some real grungy options, but what can you expect for US$2 per night? The two below are the best in town.

Bungalow Thavansouk and Sunset Restaurant ⭐   Adjacent to the Hotel Nam Sang and also in a prime riverside spot, at the Thavansouk you'll find a range of neatly fitted, affordable bungalows starting with a basic guesthouse standard up to a unique riverside suite with, get this, a picture window next to the bathtub with views of the river. Rooms vary in age, quality, and mildew smell in this casual work in progress, so ask to have a peek before checking in. In general, though, these bungalows are a good value. Lounge chairs on the lawn face the breathtaking wall of karst peaks across the river. The attached Sunset restaurant and bar serves good local fare and is the most happening spot each day at, go figure, dusk.

Along the Nam Song just S and W of the town center. © 023/511-096. Fax 023/511-096. www.geocities. com/thavonsouk/index.html. 29 units. US$16–US$35 for a range of bungalows; US$50 for suite. **Amenities:** Restaurant; can arrange tours and all rentals; laundry. In room: A/C, hot water.

Hotel Nam Song   Named for the river that rolls by out front, and just a stone's throw from the major takeout point for most kayaking or tubing trips on the Nam Song, this is a basic, tidy, and comfortable option in Vang Vieng. With clean tile floors, the air-conditioned rooms are small but cozy, and the spacious, shaded common area viewing the river is a fine spot to while away some lazy days. It's about a 10-minute walk from town.

Along the river just SW of the town center, in Vang Vieng. © 023/511-016. 16 units. Double rooms US$30–US$35 (seasonal discount available). **Amenities:** Restaurant; can arrange tours and all rentals; laundry. In room: A/C, hot water.

WHERE TO DINE

There are lots of small eateries of the storefront variety all over town, and you can get good, basic traveler's fare (fried noodles and rice and "faux-Western") for next to nothing. Also, **Nazim Restaurant,** on the main drag (© **023/511-214**), serves the same good, affordable Indian cuisine as in its other locations in Laos. **Xayoh Café,** at the main intersection in town (© **023/511-440**), serves good burgers and basics.

OUTDOOR ACTIVITIES

Eco-tour operators offering kayak tours now line the main road, but the folks at **Wildside Eco Group,** at the main intersection in town (© **023/511-440**), are probably your best bet for a fun day in inflatable two-man kayaks on the small rapids of the Nam Song; the trip will take you to some of the local caves, one where you'll actually swim in wearing headlamps before a return by river to the town itself. Another option is a day on the **Nam Lik River,** a more exciting whitewater journey (done by raft, depending on the season) just a few hours by pickup from town. Check in with these guys and ask about other trips, like their trekking and kayaking connection back to Vientiane. Day trips start at US$8 (most competing companies offer similar options and prices).

5 Luang Prabang

It's a town that wakes early each day when, beginning ever so faintly, the bells, gongs, and drums of local temples crescendo around 4:30am to send Luang Prabang's estimated 1,000 resident monks and novices on their morning begging rounds. Making a circuit around the small peninsula formed by the Nam Khan and Mehkong, the crisp column of barefoot, orange-robed figures collect rice for their one daily meal. Visitors can even take part and do their good karmic deed for the day by handing handfuls of rice to each monk as they pass—a unique way to connect in a city that is alive with Buddhist culture and history. The colonial legacy still thrives and the torch of French culture and custom is borne by Luang Prabang's architecture and cuisine. Even the most brief visit to this magically tranquil town is memorable.

Designated a UNESCO World Heritage Site in 1995, Luang Prabang is named after the golden statue that's kept here, the Prabang (the town's name means "great holy image"). With a long history as a center for the study of Buddhism, Luang Prabang was the first capital of Laos and has mercifully remained relatively untouched by war or even by the ravages of time; this means that many of the 33 temples are original, and the town's charm arises from the ancient and authentic.

This small town has magic—so many come and get lost in its charm. It's a place to wander, to watch streetside craftsmen, get lost in lazy back alleys amid stately colonials, and stop for a chat down by the river or in one of the many cozy streetside cafes. Allow yourself at least 3 days to sink into the city's languid rhythms, but *beware:* You might end up staying longer than you planned.

VISITOR INFORMATION & TOURS

- **Diethelm Travel,** Sakarinh Road, near the Villa Santi (© **071/212-277;** fax 071/212-032; www.diethelm-travel.com). Open Monday to Saturday 8am to noon and 2 to 5pm. Diethelm arranges city tours and excursions to out-of-town sights and is the top agent.
- **Exotissimo,** with offices in The Grand Luang Prabang Hotel, Ban Xieng Keo (© **071/253-851;** fax 071/253-027; www.exotissimo.com). It's not the

most convenient office locale, but it has the same high standard of service as throughout the region.

- **Sodetour,** 105/6 Souvannabalang Rd., Ban Xiengmouan, near the boat docks on the river (© **071/212-092**). Open Monday to Friday 8am to noon and 1:30 to 4pm, and Saturday 8am to noon. This is a very professional outfit.
- **Inter-Lao Tourism,** in the Hotel Souvannaphoum on Phothisarath and on Kingkisarath Road near the Talat Dala (Dala Market; © **071/212-200;** www.interlao.laopdr.com).
- **Savanh Banhao Tourism,** 023 Luang Prabang Rd., Ban Akat (© **021/218-291;** fax 021/251-246). Here you'll find good eco and classic tours.
- **All Lao Services,** 5/7 Sisavangvong Rd., Luang Prabang (© **071/252-785;** fax 071/253-522; kamvanh-k@yahoo.com). One of many storefront travel agents on the main drag, this operation can do just about anything and has very helpful staff, especially with bus and boat travel on the lower end of the scale. It's also an Internet cafe.

GETTING THERE

BY PLANE Lao Aviation has three daily flights from Vientiane to Luang Prabang for US$55 one-way; it connects with other major towns in the north (to Xieng Khouang daily for US$35; to Luang Namtha for US$37). The Luang Prabang airport also handles international flights from Chiang Mai and Bangkok in Thailand. This airport allows you to get a visa on arrival. Outside the airport, if you haven't arranged pickup via your hotel, try to hop a jumbo with other travelers—the more passengers, the better the rate. For flight information, call the Lao Aviation office in Luang Prabang at © **071/212-172.**

BY BUS/MINIVAN The overland route to Luang Prabang from Vientiane takes about 11 hours by public bus, depending on how many times it breaks down. However, the jaw-dropping scenery, past the mountains and limestone formations at Vang Vieng and several Hmong hill villages along the way, is well worth making the trip by land at least once. The bus costs 50,000 kip (US$5) and departs from Vientiane's Morning Market several times a day (© **021/216-507**).

BY JEEP OR TRUCK Taking the mountain route by jeep or truck (it's not very safe to go by car) takes 7 hours and costs about 2,300,000 kip (US$230), plus 600,000 kip (US$60) per day *plus* extra for the driver's meals and accommodations. If it seems steep, blame all the nongovernmental organizations operating in Laos for driving up the prices—they all get reimbursed from expense accounts (in case you were wondering where your charity money ends up).

BY BOAT Options for boat travel to and from Luang Prabang are many and varied; all are, in a word, "adventurous." The only regular departure is between Luang Prabang and the Thai border at Houayxay (see "Getting There," in the introduction to Laos section, earlier in this chapter). Daily departures leave in the morning and cost 120,000 kip (US$12). **Luang Say cruises** also operates tour boats on the same route (contact them at Ban Vat Sene, Sakarine Rd., Luang Prabang, near Diethelm Travel; © **071/252-553;** www.mekongcruises). On all other routes, like the Nam Tha and the Nam Ou, you'll essentially be chartering the boat with other tourists; departures, rates, and duration of trips vary in a way almost unique to Laos. Contact any travel agent or tour provider listed to make arrangements or get more details (availability varies with season). Speedboats connect Vientiane with Luang Prabang if they get enough passengers to make the trip worthwhile (contact the main port at © **021/215-924**).

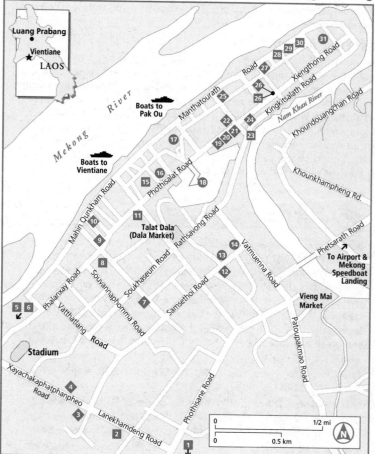

Luang Prabang

Luang Prabang
Vientiane
LAOS

Boats to Pak Ou

Boats to Vientiane

Talat Dala (Dala Market)

Stadium

Vieng Mai Market

To Airport & Mekong Speedboat Landing

Mekong River
Nam Khan River

Manthatourath Road
Xiengthong Road
Kingkitsalath Road
Khoundouangchan Road
Khounkhampheng Rd
Phetsarath Road
Phothisalat Road
Mahin Ounkham Road
Phalanxay Road
Souvannaphomma Road
Soukhaseum Road
Rathsavong Road
Samsethoi Road
Vatmuenna Road
Patoupakmao Road
Vatthatlang Road
Xayachakaphatphanpheo Road
Lanekhamdeng Road
Phothisane Road

| 0 | | 1/2 mi |
| 0 | 0.5 km | |

ACCOMMODATIONS ■
The Grand Luang Prabang
  (Xieng Keo) **5**
L'hotel Souvannaphoum **8**
Le Calao **29**
Manoluk Hotel **2**
Mouang Luang Hotel **7**
New Luang Prabang
  Hotel **15**
Pan Sea Hotel **1**
Phousi Hotel **11**
Rama Hotel **14**
Say Nam Khan Guest
  House **23**
Sayo Guesthouse **28**
Tum-Tum Cheng **30**
Villa Santi Hotel **26**
Villa Santi Resort **6**

DINING ◆
Café des Arts **21**
Café Vat Sene **24**
Couleur Café
  and Restaurant **22**
Indochina Spirit **9**
L'Elephant **27**
Malee Lao Food **3**
Nisha **19**
Ole Ole **20**
Sinxay Restaurant at the
  Villa Sinxay **4**
Somchan Restaurant **10**
Tum-Tum Cheng **22**
Villa Santi **26**
Visoun Restaurant **12**

ATTRACTIONS ●
Mount Phu Si
  (Phousi) **18**
Royal Palace Museum **17**
Wat Mai **16**
Wat Wisunalat/
  Visounarath **13**
Wat Xieng Thong **31**

The 10-hour trip is uncomfortable and noisy, and costs 180,000 kip (US$18) if you have enough people to fill a boat.

GETTING AROUND

Luang Prabang is easy to cover on foot or bicycle, and if you get tired, tuk-tuks and jumbos cost about 5,000kip (US50¢) per trip (less with more people and some haggling). For sights outside the city, jumbos usually gather along Xieng Thong Road across from the popular cafes and restaurants; prices are negotiable. **Vatthanaluck Vehicle Rental,** just around the corner form the Villa Santi, rents bicycles for US$1 to US$2 and motorbikes for US$10. Motorbikes and bicycles are also available for rent in many spots along Xieng Thong, the main road in town. **Longtail boats** are for hire at Luang Prabang's main pier and can take you to adjacent villages and the **Pak Ou Caves.**

FAST FACTS: Luang Prabang

Banks/Currency Exchange The Lane Xang Bank is at Phothisarat Road, next to the New Luang Prabang Hotel. Hours are Monday to Saturday 8:30am to 3:30pm; it's closed Sunday and holidays. You can exchange cash and traveler's checks in most major currencies to kip and can withdraw cash using a Visa card. There's another Lane Xang money-changing office on Xieng Thong Road next to the Luang Prabang Bakery. Lao May Bank (open 8am–3:30pm), in the middle of restaurant row, is convenient, and you can also change money at hotels. Dollars and Thai bot are accepted widely.

Emergencies For police, dial © 071/212-453; for a medical emergency, call © 071/252-049.

Post Office/Mail The post office is on the corner of Phothisarat and Kitsalat roads, across from Luang Prabang Travel and Tourism. Hours are Monday to Friday 8am to noon and 1 to 5pm, and Saturday 8am to noon.

Internet Look for PlaNet Online on Phothisarat Road (the main restaurant drag), on the corner of Ban Wat Sene (© 071/252-291). There's another branch at the other end of Phothisarat, 3 blocks past the Palace Museum. Small Internet cafes line this busy block, but service is patched through Vientiane and is quite slow. It's 300 kip per minute (US3¢) and 18,000 kip per hour (US$1.80).

Telephone The city code for Luang Prabang is 71. Dial a 0 first inside Laos. The telephone center in town consists of two booths around the corner from the post office on Kitsalat Road. You can buy local and international phone cards in an office across the street.

WHERE TO STAY

There has been a real boom in accommodation in recent years in LPB. The city's UNESCO status mercifully prevents large-scale construction in the historic center; as a result, developers have renovated existing hotels and converted old guesthouses to low-luster boutiques, and a few resorts have sprung up on the outskirts of town to keep up with demand. Though there are more options these days, it's still a good idea to book ahead from November through March.

Tips **Where the Streets Have No Names**

In Luang Prabang, though there are some named streets, the same road can change names as it progresses through the city, making it a bit confusing at first. For example, the main street (I refer to it as "restaurant row" at the town center) is either Chao Fa Ngum, Sisavongvong, or Sakkarine Road, depending where you are. Locals use village names, not streets, to navigate, and villages are commonly named for the local Wat (or temple); when checking into your hotel, it's good to find out the village or nearby wat's name, important for taxis and tuk-tuks. Also note that the Western spelling of many streets and wat names is very inconsistent (hard to represent a tonal language), so just "sound it out" as best as possible.

Working televisions with satellite service and amenities like hair dryers and coffeemakers are still in short supply, though, and service in general, even at the finest properties, is a bit lax. It's hot and cold character in a town that is all about atmosphere. Promotional and low-season rates are available at most hotels, but be aware that a surcharge is often levied in the busy months.

EXPENSIVE

The Grand Luang Prabang (Xieng Keo) ★★
Despite new road signs and advertising, you won't get far in a taxi if you ask to go to "The Grand." The site will forever be known to locals by its former name, Xieng Keo, in reverence to its previous owner, Lao nationalist and peace-broker Prince Petsarath. Suffering years of exile, Petsarath followed his country, in and out of power, from colony to communism. The site of Petsarath's former palatial home is on a high, sloping hill at the apex of a wide bend in the Mekong. Words can't describe the view from this open campus to river and surrounding mountains; the hotel's aptly named Sunset Bar overlooks such a vista at the "magic hour" that you might want to make a visit here just to see the afterglow. That said, the Grand is just getting up and running and seems to be going through some growing pains. Without a swimming pool and only just developing amenities, any billing as a "resort" comes up a bit short, but it's popular spot for conventions and is attracting more individual travelers. The rooms are average in size but are quite lovely, with teak floors and high ceilings. The tile bathrooms are a bit small but spotless, and the one wall left in rough brick is a unique touch. All rooms have a balcony and a view of either the colonnaded walkways and the courtyard or the majestic Mekong. Prince Petsarath's home stands at the middle of the compound and promises to be a museum honoring his legacy. Like the other resorts in Luang Prabang, the biggest drawback is the distance from town and fickle transport.

Baan Xiengkeo, Khet Sangkalok, Luang Prabang. (About 6km/3¾ miles S of the town center). © 071/253-851-7. Fax 071/253-027-8. www.grandluangprabang.com. 78 units. US$150 deluxe; US$250–US$300 suite. AE, MC, V **Amenities:** 2 restaurants; bar; tour desk operated by Exotissimo Travel; airport and city shuttle available; handicapped-access rooms. *In room:* A/C, satellite TV, minibar.

Pan Sea Hotel ★★
Hands down the finest hotel in Luang Prabang, the Pan Sea (or Phou Vao, as many call it, after the hill on which it stands) was just finishing major restorations at the time of this writing. It offers only superior suites; rooms are priced accordingly but are worth it. Shallow ponds trace the courtyards connecting each block of rooms, and bushes of bougainvillea, palm, and

frangipani frame views of Phoussi hill in the distance, especially lovely from the pool area and the balconies of the more choice rooms. Each suite has a large marble bathroom with oversize tub, dark teak sink stands, and wooden slat blinds that open to reveal a private balcony with two low, Lao-style divans. Rooms are large and tastefully decorated with a bamboo-and-wood inlaid headboard, fine rosewood furniture, and even some retro fixtures like a classic fan and mosquito netting. At the Pan Sea you'll find all the amenities of a hotel in a larger city (safe, IDD, satellite TV) with a boutique, up-scale rustic charm, and service that's only shortcoming is youthful vigor. There's a good indoor French/Lao restaurant and bar overlooking the main courtyard. The only drawback is the long ride to town.

Phou Vao St., P.O. Box 50, Luang Prabang. (℃ **071/212-194**. Fax 071/212-534. www.pansea.com. 34 units. US$95 low season/superior suite; US$150 high season/superior suite. AE, MC, V. In room: A/C.

Villa Santi Hotel ★★★   Considering luxury, convenience, and charm, the Villa Santi is without a doubt the most choice residence in town. Formerly the home of Lao princess Manilay, this low-key villa reopened in 1992. With consistent upgrades in decor and amenities in recent years, the Villa Santi has achieved a standard unmet anywhere in the downtown area. Whether in the original building, in the nearby annex, or at the latest venture some 6km (3¾ miles) from town (see below), you'll find peaceful elegance and a connection with culture and nature. Rooms have parquet floors and rosewood furniture, and the decor is deluxe colonial but laid back and comfortable, with overstuffed pillows, fine linen, mosquito nets and local weaving. The tile bathrooms are neat but not especially large. Everything is spotless and plush, down to details like old-fashioned sun umbrellas provided for walks to town, fresh flowers, and a welcome drink. A new wing, built 4 years ago, has common balcony sitting areas and a charm all its own. Only four rooms have king beds, so be sure to specify when you book if that's what you want. The staff is friendly and professional. The overall charm and the convenient downtown location make this the top choice in Luang Prabang.

P.O. Box 681, Sakkarine St., Luang Prabang. (℃ **071/212-267**. Fax 071/252-158. www.villasantihotel.com. 25 units. US$80–US$120 deluxe room high–low season; US$200–US$250 suite low–high season (Internet rates available). AE, MC, V. **Amenities:** Restaurant; bar; all rentals available; tour desk; limited room service; laundry/dry cleaning. In room: A/C, minibar, fridge, safe, IDD phone.

Villa Santi Resort ★★   This resort is a roomier rural companion to the popular downtown Villa Santi and similarly sophisticated without being stuffy. Tucked among lush rice paddies and picturesque hills, this little Eden has a tranquil stream that tip-toes through the grounds, a placid pond, and an open garden area; the buildings seem at ease with the surroundings, and from the open-air, high-ceilinged lobby to the two story villas scattered about, there's a certain harmony to the place. Rooms are very like those at the downtown Villa Santi and have similar tile floors, dark rosewood trim, and local decoration but are slightly larger with TV sets and bigger bathrooms. The resort is also just getting up and running, which might mean there are some kinks to work out. Still, the staff is kind and courteous and will make sure of efficient transport to and from town (like the other resorts, the biggest drawback).

6km (3¾ miles) from town (a 10-min. drive). Santi Resort Road, Ban Nadeuay, P.O. Box 681, Luang Prabang, Laos. (℃ **071/253-470**. US$170 deluxe double; US$300–US$500 suite. **Amenities:** Restaurant; bar; tours and rentals can be arranged; limited room service; laundry. In room: A/C, satellite TV w/in-house movies, minibar, fridge, hair dryer, IDD phone.

MODERATE

L'hotel Souvannaphoum ★★ Formerly the villa of Prince Souvanna-phouma, there's a comfortable, colonial malaise among the quiet open-air build-ings and courtyards of this hotel. It's the kind of place where one feels at home hanging up the old pith helmet and reclining on a wicker guest chair in the shade with a cool drink. The rooms are basic but clean, each with a balcony and immaculate marble-tiled bathrooms. And if the wicker furniture seems a bit aged or the wood floors are a bit nicked, it's in keeping with the Southeast Asian country-house decor throughout (some nice antique touches include an old gramophone, swords, photos, and hangings). The two suites (the former royal bedrooms) are exceptionally large, with a balcony and a unique sunken tub: They're well worth the price, if available. Just a short walk from the center of town, yet far enough from the tourist hoards, the location is ideal. Inter-Lao Tourism mans a desk in the main building and can handle any arrangements.

Phothisarath Rd., Namphou Square, P.O. Box 741, Luang Prabang. ✆ **071/212-200.** Fax 071/212-577. 0sunaphum@Laotel.com. 25 units. US$54 double; US$40 double/low season; US$80 suite; US$60 suite/low season. AE, DC, MC, V. **Amenities:** Restaurant; bar; all rentals available; tour desk; laundry. *In room:* A/C, hair dryer, safe, some w/complimentary tea and coffee, IDD phone.

Le Calao ★★ This restored 1904 villa stands near the tip of Luang Prabang's peninsula on the banks of the Mekong. Unique and picturesque, it has a loca-tion, size, and style all its own. The second-floor rooms are a nice size, with high, sloping ceilings of exposed under-tile, wood furniture, neat tile floors, and beds that are firm and comfortable. Bathrooms have wood cabinetry but are other-wise rather spartan, with no bathtubs. The staff is, well, "Hey, where did the staff go?" What sells these rooms and commands the seemingly high price tag is that each room has a large private balcony facing the majestic Mekong. The casual ambience at the Calao comes at a premium but is quite popular (be sure to book ahead). The newly renovated downstairs suite (formerly a kitchen and staff room) has two double beds and a private balcony; perfect for a family with kids.

Khaem Khong Rd. (on the Mekong River, close to Wat Xieng Thuong), Luang Prabang. ✆ **071/212-100.** Fax 071/212-085. www.calaoinn.laopdr.com. 6 units. US$60 double. V. **Amenities:** Cafe/bar; laundry. *In room:* A/C.

Manoluk Hotel It's an interesting choice, the Manoluk; it's eccentric but comfy and affordable. You're a bit away from town, though, which is a draw-back. Rooms are large and have polished wood floors; high ceilings; big, clunky tables and chairs; and amazingly comfortable beds. The bathrooms are similarly large, finished with tile and clean. The huge restaurant and second-floor lounge, complete with wooden deer heads, give the place the feel of a lodge, and if your taste runs to good quality kitsch, the Manoluk is the "Velvet Elvis" of Luang Pra-bang: You'll appreciate the many large carved elephants, fluorescent village-scene paintings, and shiny bedspreads with fringe. The one suite is similarly fancy in a way that your eccentric uncle might like. Two buildings are separated by a large covered courtyard. The staff seems to be nonexistent, save for a person or two at the front desk watching the lobby television. Somehow, that seems to suit the laid-back, private feel of the place. There are motorcycles and bicycles for rent.

121/3 Phou Vao St., Luang Prabang. ✆ **071/212-250** or 071/212-509. Fax 071/212-508. 30 units US$40–US$45 double; US$70–US$80 suite. MC, V. **Amenities:** Restaurant; bar; motorcycle rental; laundry. *In room:* A/C, TV, IDD phone.

Mouang Luang Hotel ★ A 10-minute walk from town on a quiet street north of the Souvanophoum, this place has many tiers of traditional Lao tem-ple-style roofs adorning it. Comparable to the Manoluk in amenities and value, the rooms at the Mouang Luang are clean, with parquet floors and marble-tiled bathrooms (all with smallish tubs). Streetside rooms have balconies. There's an open-air Lao restaurant in the back, and just above it is an enormous balcony reserved for Baci ceremonies. Mouang Luang has the distinction of being the only hotel in town, besides the Phou Vao, with a pool (there's a charge of US$4 for nonguests). The staff is very friendly, and the place is popular with groups.

Bounkhong Rd., P.O. Box 779, Luang Prabang. ℭ **071/212-791**. Fax 071/212-790. mgluang@laotel.com. 35 units. US$35/$40 single/double low season. US$40/$45 single/double high season. AE, DC, MC, V. **Amenities:** Restaurant; outdoor swimming pool; conference room; laundry/dry cleaning. *In room:* A/C, TV, minibar, IDD phone.

Phousi Hotel ✪   For overall comfort, price, and convenience, this is a good middle-of-the-road bet in Luang Prabang. The rooms are neat and clean, with teak furniture, floral fabrics, and little touches like Lao carvings and prints. Bathrooms are large and spotless, and the more expensive doubles have wood floors and are a bit larger; they're certainly worth the upgrade. The hotel is situated in a prime downtown spot, across from the market. At night it glitters with strings of lights (a somehow soothing rather than tacky effect in magical Luang Prabang), and traditional musicians serenade. The staff is accommodating and efficient. Try to book early because it's a tour group favorite.

Setthathirat Rd., Luang Prabang. ℭ **071/212192**. Fax 071/212719. www.phousihotel.laopdr.com. 43 units. US$35 standard; US$40 superior; US$56 family rooms (seasonal rates available). MC, V. **Amenities:** Restaurant; bar; car rental and tours can be arranged; laundry. *In room:* A/C, TV, IDD phone.

INEXPENSIVE

New Luang Prabang Hotel   The New Luang Prabang has the dubious distinction of being the only hotel in town that doesn't comply with UNESCO's maximum standards for height. What that means is this dull facade is the tallest building downtown, and the small rooftop restaurants, serving only breakfast, have some of the best views of Phousi hill. There is little else of distinction. Rooms are nicer than the faded-carpet hallways, but the overall impression is aged. Beds come in sets of two twins but are comfortable, and the parquet floors are tidy. Bathrooms have no separate showers or tubs; it's the all-in-one variety. The staff is very kind, but don't expect the service or facilities of a real hotel. There are no elevators.

Sisavangvong Rd., Luang Prabang. ℭ **071/212-264**. Fax 071/212-804. 15 units. US$20–US$30 high/low season double. No credit cards. **Amenities:** Restaurant; laundry service available. *In room:* A/C, minibar.

Rama Hotel *Value*   With renovations just a year old, this hotel is a good standby in the busy season. Just north of the center of town, the Rama has 26 air-conditioned rooms, basic and clean, with parquet floors and clean bathrooms. You'll find no frills here, but the walls and furniture are without the usual nicks and scrapes of age so common in hotels of this category. It's a good value.

Visounnarath Rd. (across from the Red Cross and Visoun Rest.). ℭ **071/212-247**. Fax 071/253-266. 30 units. US$8 w/fan; from US$16 with A/C. **Amenities:** Restaurant; bar; laundry. *In room:* A/C, TV, IDD phone.

Say Nam Khan Guest House ✪   This little renovated colonial on the banks of the Nam Kham River is basic but centrally located and has its own quiet, riverside charm. The smallish rooms have comfortable beds and wood furniture, but nothing too plush. The bathrooms are clean, tile with shower-in-room. Some of the rooms have ugly red carpet; others have a teak floor. Located within walking distance of the main restaurant row and with a downstairs balcony viewing the river, Say Nam Khan is an unassuming gem for convenience and cost.

Ban Wat Sene (off Kingkitsalath Rd. near the Nam Khan River), Luang Prabang. © **071/212-976.** Fax 071/ 213-009. 14 units. US$30–US$35 for front rooms w/view; US$25 for back side. No credit cards. **Amenities:** Bar; can arrange rentals and tours; laundry. In room: A/C.

Sayo Guesthouse ⭐ This 3-year-old guesthouse is basic on amenities and the frills of a fancy lobby (it looks like a grungy guesthouse from the front), but the rooms on the second floor are enormous, with ceilings the height of a barn and tasteful Lao decorations. Bathrooms are clean, large, and of the all-in-one variety (shower and toilet together). The rooms in the back are varied, similarly large, with exposed brick and decorations. It's an eccentric place, high on character but basic and convenient to the main street.

In front of Vat Xieng Mouane (between the main road and the Mekong), P.O. Box 1060 Luang Prabang. © **071/252-614.** 10 units. US$12–US$28. No credit cards. **Amenities:** Laundry. In room: Fan, hot water.

Tum-Tum Cheng ⭐⭐ It's atmosphere on a budget at the tidy, laid-back Tum-Tum Cheng guesthouse. Rooms are basic but immaculate, with good, solid mattresses; tile floor; and small bathrooms, the shower-in-room variety. The staff is friendly and helpful, and the large, common balcony on the second floor has low tables and cushions and is a great place to relax, meet people, or play a game of cards by candlelight. There are bicycles for rent, and the friendly owners at nearby Tum-Tum Cheng restaurant and cooking school (see "Where to Dine," below), are a wealth of information about the area. This place is very "Sabai, sabai" (relaxed), and you might stay longer than you'd planned.

50/1 Baan Xieng Thong, Luang Prabang (just E of the town center on the main road behind Wat Xieng Thong). © **071/253-224.** Fax 071/253-262. tumtumcheng@yahoo.com. 10 units. US$20–US$25 standard; US$35 suite. **Amenities:** Restaurant (around the corner); bicycle rental; laundry. In room: A/C.

WHERE TO DINE

Not only is the hotel market of Luang Prabang reflecting up-market tourist demands, but many newly arrived foreign restaurateurs are adding some spice to the local standards. There is still a great variety of inexpensive and very good restaurants in Luang Prabang, along with some new, gourmet options and hidden bistros. This is a wonderful place to explore local cuisine or savor some excellent French and Western meals. It's local practice to linger after a long repast, and whether viewing the Mekong, meeting other travelers along "restaurant row," or enjoying a romantic corner of a quiet neighborhood, you'll find what you're after.

EXPENSIVE

L'Elephant ⭐⭐ FRENCH This chic bistro is where it's at for fine dining in Luang Prabang. Run by French expats, it has a laid-back retro-chic atmosphere in a high-ceilinged colonial; the fine cuisine is unrivalled in town. There are daily and weekly specials, and everything is good. Don't pass up the imported steaks. In fact, L'Elephant imports many of the staples like the cheeses and, of course, wine, but local stock is used whenever possible; local boar and venison specials are popular, for example. The wine list could hold its own in a much larger city, and it's unlikely that you can stump the barman. A meal at L'Elephant is memorable, but be sure to make your reservation because it's quite often fully booked. The restaurant is expensive and worth it.

Ban Vat Nong, P.O. Box 812, Luang Prabang © **071/252-482.** Main courses US$6–US$12.80. MC, V. Daily 11am–2pm and 5:30–10pm.

MODERATE

Café Vat Sene Owned and run by the same folks who have brought true gourmet to town, Café Vat Sene is an atmospheric little espresso stop serving some great lunch specials and desserts. The pizzas are scrumptious, and the Greek and chicken salads are ample and a treat in this part of the world. There are lots of daily dessert specials and bread baked on-site, but don't pass up the warm apple tart. They also serve full breakfasts and have a good specials, like two croissants and one cappuccino for $1 (this ain't Starbucks). There are some local crafts for sale in the open-air first floor, and there's a small upstairs gallery.

Ban Vat Sene (across from the Villa Santi). ℭ **071/212-517.** Main courses US$2.50–US$6. Daily 7am–10pm.

Couleur Café and Restaurant ⭑ LAO/FRENCH   A fine meal can be had here in this unassuming but atmospheric little down-alley bistro. The decor is elegantly sparse, with one bare wall an empty plane broken only by a unique Buddha relief. Though run by a young French expat, the bistro has Lao specialties like steamed fish in banana leaf with coconut or fried prawns in oyster sauce; served with sticky rice, of course, these are your best bet. Also on the menu are good sandwiches, French omelets and a unique Casserole Luang Prabang, a baked mix of eggplant, mushrooms, and crispy green beans. Order up some Mekong seaweed for an interesting appetizer, and ask about the fine Lao whiskey and imported wines. It's a quiet little getaway for next to nothing.

48/5 Ban Vat Nong, Luangprabang. ℭ **020/621-064.** Main courses US$1–US$2. Daily 8am–10pm.

Indochina Spirit ⭑ LAO/THAI/WESTERN   Housed in a restored 70-year-old wooden home, Indochina Spirit, as its name denotes, dishes up as much atmosphere as it does good grub. This gorgeous traditional Lao home has been put to lovely use and now features traditional Lao music most evenings from 7:30 to 8:00pm (check the chalkboard in front to make sure). Indochina Spirit has done a great job with the simple local decor inside and charming garden dining outside. The menu is an ambitious list of Lao, Thai, and Western. It's a good place to have a drink, enjoy an affordable appetizer plate, and hear some good music before strolling the city at night.

Ban Vat That 52, opposite the fountain across from L'hotel Souvannaphoum. ℭ **071/252-372.** Main courses US70¢–US$3. Daily 8am–11pm.

Malee Lao Food ⭑ LAO   Malee Lao dishes up inexpensive and delicious local cuisine in a large, casual, open-air setting. It's an old-time favorite for Laos's wayfarers, the kind of place to have a full-table banquet when returning from rough roads or long boat rides in the north. Curries predominate; try the chicken curry soup, which is actually big pieces of chicken and potato in sauce. Don't be daunted by menu items like "chicken cut up into small pieces eaten with green vegetables" because where they're short on linguistic pizzazz, they're bang-on with some local specialties like *aulam,* a curry soup flavored with a unique bitter root. It's the obligatory "cheap and best" here, so order some sticky rice to sop it all up and enjoy. It's always crowded at dinner.

Near the intersection of Phu Vao and Samsenthai. Main courses US35¢–US$2. Daily 10am–10pm.

Sinxay Restaurant at the Villa Sinxay LAO/FRENCH   Sinxay serves local specialties in a charming, wooden, open-air villa with courtyard seating. Now featuring a culture show and music along with an extensive buffet 4 nights each week (Mon, Wed, Fri, and Sat 7:30–9:30pm), it has become a popular spot for tourists. The cuisine is quite good, especially for the price, and the buffet allows you to sample some local favorites. Lots of people just come for the show and one of the excellent Laos desserts, like sticky rice and coconut.

Phu Vao Rd. ℭ **071/212-587.** Main courses US80¢–US$1.80; show/buffet/dessert $4; show/dessert $1.50. No credit cards. Daily 7am–10pm.

Somchan Restaurant ★★ LAO   In a corner building at the edge of Ban Wat That, the old silver smith's neighborhood now backpacker's ghetto, the Somchan serves up Lao specialties rivaled only by Malee Lao (above) for authenticity and price. Ignore the Backstreet Boys CD playing on a loop in the background; there are lovely views of the river in the open-air dining room (more like a patio), but what sells this place is the grub, not the hubbub. Spicy coconut curries, flavored with the unique bitter-root aulum; fried dishes of all sorts; and various soups round out a menu that is refreshingly limited. Here they don't make the mistake of offering the world, but they list what's good and follow through (as opposed to many local restaurants that have a menu more like an atlas of world cuisine, and what you get are watered-down versions of everything). The prices are a steal, everything is good, and they follow it up with complimentary fruit in season.

Soulingsvonsa Rd., near the Mekong in Ban Vatthat, Luang Prabang. ✆ 071/252-021. Main courses US80¢–US$1.80. Daily 10am–10pm.

Tum-Tum Cheng ★★ *Finds* LAO   With a new location on restaurant row, this is an excellent spot for a relaxed or romantic meal. Owners Chandra, a Laos chef of note, and Elizabeth, a long-time expat from Hungary, will certainly make you feel welcome. It's one of those special, atmospheric places to just stick around and learn about life in this colorful corner of the world. The atmosphere in the first-floor open-air dining room is chic and comfortable, and decor is Laos original. The food is fantastic. Portions are hearty, but the fare is light, with fresh, local ingredients left to speak for themselves and not overly sauced or cooked away. The spring rolls are without rival, and specials like a unique fried-rice salad, fine local curries, and lots of vegetarian specials are all good. You can't go wrong. And if you like what you eat, be sure to sign up for a **cooking course** and find out how to make it back home. Students meet at 9am at the restaurant, take a short ride to the market and shop for the necessary ingredients, and spend a fun and informative day learning not only about Laos food, but also about Laos culture and history. Chef Chandra is a wealth of information. Classes are US$20 for 1 day and US$45 for 3 days; it comes with the bonus of being able to eat your creations.

On Sisavangvong ("restaurant row") across from the Scandinavian Bakery. ✆ 071/253-224. Main courses US$2–US$4.50. Daily 8am–10pm.

Villa Santi ★★ LAO/CONTINENTAL   You've heard the adage "Location, location, location." On the upper floor of the popular hotel's main building (see "Accommodations," above), this atmospheric open-air perch has just the right angle on the busy street below. With linen and silver, a candlelight table on the balcony is hands down the town's most romantic spot. The food is local and traditional Lao, along with some creative Asian-influenced Continental (on the whole, though, it's a bit uninspired—stick to Lao and Thai specials, and sample one of the fine curries). The daily set menus are always a good choice and walk you through a few courses of local cuisine. The desserts are scrumptious: bananas flambéed in Cointreau, and fruit salad in rum. There are more casual offerings for lunch, including hamburgers. Most evenings, there is traditional music and dancing in the courtyard below, and the restaurant is casual enough to allow you to stroll to the window for a look. Dining will be a memorable experience.

Sakkarine St., Luang Prabang (in the Villa Santi Hotel). ✆ 071/212-267. Main courses US$2–US$6. V. Daily 7am–10pm.

Visoun Restaurant ⭐ CHINESE   This low-scale open-air restaurant is perhaps a bit too casual, but it serves tasty Chinese food. The menu is a bit hard to decipher, getting no more specific than "fried chicken" or "pork with long beans," but the food is fresh and good. Visoun has a very large vegetarian selection as well.

Visounnalat (also spelled Wisunalat) Rd., next to the immigration office and Laos Red Cross. © **071/212-268.** Main courses US$1–US$2.50. No credit cards. Daily 7am–9pm.

INEXPENSIVE

For good, cheap eats and the company of many fellow travelers, don't miss what we've called **"restaurant row"** (it's hard to miss on any trip to Luang Prabang). Easily found along the end of Phothisarat Road as it turns into Xieng Thong, it's also about the only place in town alive past 9pm, before it quickly dies at 11pm. The restaurants are too many to list, and most are pretty blah, but here are a select few.

Café des Arts ⭐ FRENCH/CONTINENTAL   Pasta, hamburgers, crepes, filet de boeuf, and tartines round out the very appetizing menu. Breakfast is omelets galore. Open-air like all the others on restaurant row, Café des Arts has a better atmosphere than most, with real tables and chairs (not plastic), linen tablecloths, and a gallery of local artwork for sale.

Xieng Thong Rd. (on "restaurant row"). No phone. Main courses US50¢–US$1.64. No credit cards. Daily 7am–11pm.

Ole Ole LAO/CONTINENTAL   Pull up a chair and play a game of cards, or have a chat here. Granted, you'll be hard pressed to find anywhere that's too uptight in mellow Luang Prabang, but you won't find any power lunches in this little storefront—just young travelers staying up late. They serve some good sandwiches here and have excellent Thai specials, like the Tom Yam Kai (spicy chicken soup) and a unique coconut curry rice that's worth trying. This place is usually hopping in the late evening.

Xieng Thong Rd. (on "restaurant row"). No phone. Main courses US50¢–US$1.50. Open daily 7am–11:30pm (or so).

Nisha INDIAN   Just across the road from the popular Indian franchise in Laos, Nazim's, it's "same-same but different" (interpret as you will), but expats favor this place over the competition. Bright neon lights conspire with plastic chairs and a general indifference to decor to drive you away, but the food is what brings 'em in droves. Try the chicken tika masala or any of the excellent curries and tandoori.

Xieng Thong Rd. (on "restaurant row"). No phone. Main courses US50¢–US$3. Daily 7am–10pm.

SNACKS AND CAFES

A popular restaurant on "restaurant row," the **Luang Prabang Bakery,** 11/7 Sisavangvong Rd. (© **071/212-617**), serves some good pizza as well as a host of baked goods, and has an extensivecollection of books (also try their small storefront restaurant just across the street). But there's some healthy competition in town: the **Scandinavian Bakery,** farther east at 52/6 Sisavangvong (© **071/252-223**), and **Healthy and Fresh,** farther along on the main drag (© **071/253-363**), both serve similar fine coffee and baked goods and ensure that you won't go wanting for the delights of home.

A number of riverside restaurants overlook the Mekong, and all are good spots to watch the sunrise over a beer and a snack. For desserts, try any of the small creperies on restaurant row. Whether doused in Courvoisier or topped with a dollop of vanilla, it's sweet done as you like it.

ATTRACTIONS

Mount Phu Si (Phousi) ★★   Rising from the center of town, Phu Si has temples scattered on all sides of its slopes and a panoramic view of the entire town from its top. **That Chomsi Stupa,** built in 1804, is its crowning glory. Taking the path to the northeast, you will pass **Wat Tham Phousi,** which has a large-bellied Buddha, Kaccayana. **Wat Phra Bat Nua,** farther down, has a yard-long footprint of the Buddha. Be prepared for the 355 steps to get there. Try to make the hike, which will take about 2 hours with sightseeing, in the early morning or late afternoon, to escape the sun's burning rays.

Admission 10,000 kip (US$1). Open daily dawn–dusk.

Royal Palace Museum ★★   The palace, built for King Sisavang Vong from 1904 to 1909, was the royal residence until the Pathet Lao seized control of the country in 1975. The last Lao king, Sisavang Vattana, and his family were exiled to a remote region in the northern part of the country and never heard from again. Rumor has it that they perished in a prison camp, though the government has never said so. The palace remains now as a repository of treasures, rather scanty but still interesting. You can begin your tour by walking the length of the long porch; the gated, open room to your right has one of the museum's top attractions, an 83cm-high golden standing Buddha that was a gift to King Fa Ngum from a Khmer king. It's the namesake of Luang Prabang: the "holy image." This is only a copy, however; the real thing is in a vault of the State Bank, and a temple is under construction to enshrine the famed statue. To your right as you enter, note the fantastic murals, dating from about 1930, on the wall of the receiving room. Each panel is shown to best effect as the sun hits it at different times of the day. The main throne room features lavish colored glass murals and, in a cabinet near the door, the coronation robes of the last prince. Throughout the palace are numerous *dong san* drums, huge priceless bronze floor ornaments, some of them 1,000 years old.

Outside the palace, a large Soviet-made statue of Sisavang Vong, the first king under the Lao constitution, gives a stylized, ham-fisted wave like a caricature of Lenin. Don't miss it. The temple on the right as you face the palace, **Phra Bang,** has doors created by Thid Tud, considered Laos's greatest sculptor. The temple renovations are nearly complete and will soon house the golden standing Pra Bang Buddha.

The palace grounds now continue the tradition of the Royal Theater. On Monday, Wednesday, and Friday, tourists can take part in a baci ceremony and view the historical reenactment of the Ramayana (tickets start at US$3 for the 2-hr. performance).

Phothisarat Rd. Admission 10,000 kip (US$1). Mon–Sat 8–11am and 1:30–4pm. (**Warning:** at 11am, they will kick you out, and you'll have to pay *again* if you come back after lunch.)

Wat Mai ★★   Wat Mai is considered one of the jewels of Luang Prabang. Its golden bas-relief facade tells the story of Phravet, one of the last avatars, or reincarnations, of the Buddha. It held the Pra Bang Buddha from 1894 until 1947. Stop by at 5:30pm for the evening prayers, when the monks chant in harmony.

Phothisarat Rd., near the Lane Xang Bank. Open daily dawn–dusk.

Wat Wisunalat/Visounarath ★   Wisunalat is known for its absolutely huge golden Buddha in the sim, the largest in town at easily 6.1m (20 ft.) tall. The wat was constructed in 1512 and held the famous Pra Bang Buddha from 1513

Moments   **Going to Refuge: Making Friends at the Temple**

There is little that's spectacular on the sleepy peninsula of Luang Prabang. Time spent here is about soaking in the atmosphere and taking liesurely walks along the dusty lanes lined with French colonial buildings. It's hot, though, and you can walk only so far, so how can you spend the day if not with your feet on a chair in a corner cafe (that's not a bad option, though)? Stop in at a temple—any temple, really—and you're sure to meet up with some of the many monks or young novices wandering about. Most notable during the early fall months of Buddhist Lent, when monks cannot leave their temples, these guys are bored out of their trees and are great sources of information and insight into Laos culture, Buddhism, or the vagaries of human existence; they're also linguists, a big part of their training, and study Pali and Sanskrit as well as English and French (and even Chinese and Japanese). Wats are not much more than schools, really, and novices will be keen to practice their English on you or even get help with their homework. A short chat in a temple often ends in visitors giving impromptu English instruction to a group of monks. It's a good way to strip away any preconceptions or Western stereotypes about Buddhism or monks (they are all quite approachable and personable) and a unique opportunity to share ideas or get a free lesson in Lao language and culture. Women should be careful not to touch or sit too close to monks and novices, but all are welcome in the temple and it's a good way to beat the heat and connect with local culture.

to 1894. On the grounds facing the sim is the famous **That Makmo,** or watermelon stupa, a survivor since 1504. Wat Aham is a few steps away from the Wisunalat sim.

At the end of Wisunalat Rd. Daily 8am–5pm.

Wat Xieng Thong ⟨⟨   Xieng Thong is the premier wat of Luang Prabang. Built in 1560 by King Say Setthathirat, it is situated at the tip of a peninsula jutting out into the Mekong. Xieng Thong survived numerous invading armies intact, making its facade one of the oldest in the city. One of the outstanding characteristics of the complex is the several glass mosaics. Note the "tree of life" on the side of the sim. Facing the courtyard from the sim's steps, the building on the right contains the funeral chariot of King Sisavang Vong with its seven-headed *naga* (snake) decor. The chariot was carved by venerated Lao sculptor Thid Tun. There are also some artifacts inside, including ancient marionettes. Facing the sim, the building on the left, dubbed the "red chapel," has a rare statue of a reclining Buddha that dates back to the temple's construction. Its exterior is adorned with fun mosaics depicting a popular folk tale.

At the end of Xieng Thong Rd. Admission 2,000 kip (US20¢). Daily 8am–6pm.

SHOPPING

Luang Prabang features a fantastic array of the hand-woven textiles for which Laos is well known, so stock up here. In the parking lot on the corner of Phothisarat and Kitsalat (near the post office and Lane Xang Bank), a group of Hmong women sell embroidered items, also good buys. You can buy 100% gold jewelry at good prices in and around the Morning Market, although the workmanship is crude. There are a few shops with excellent handicrafts on Phothisarat Road across from Wat Hosian, and there are some funky new boutiques and gift shops scattered about town.

Check out the **Blue House** (© 071/252-383), just cater-corner to the Villa Santi, where there's a revolving display of local handicrafts. **OckPopTok**, in a two-story colonial between L'Elephant restaurant and the Mekong (© 020/ 570-148), carries a fine line of contemporary Lao textiles in its gallery and workshop. It features Lao skirts, home furnishings, and an array of interesting fabrics. It's open 9am to 8pm.

Natural paper-making has taken the town by storm, and **Baan Khily Gallery,** at 43/2 Baan Khily (on the eastern end of Sisavong Rd. near Diethelm; © 071/ 212-611; baankhily@hotmail.com), is where long-time German expat Oliver Bandmann produces and exhibits in the same roadside space.

NIGHTLIFE

Luang Prabang is a morning town, really, but there are a few good spots for drinks and some music. Backpackers fill the quiet lanes of Ban Wat That, the old silversmith quarter near the Mekong on the east end of town, and you'll sometimes find folks up late. Take a walk down any alley and you'll find fellow travelers in among the budget guesthouses and bamboo bars.

For atmosphere, there is nowhere better than **Letranger: Books & Tea** (booksinlaos@yahoo.com), in Ban Vat Aphay on the back side of Phousy Hill (the opposite side from the main street and royal palace) near the Nam Khan River. The friendly Canadian owners are full of good advice and lend books from their downstairs collection (loans at 5,000 kip/US50¢ per day). Have a pot of tea or a cocktail (don't miss the lao-lao marguerita) in their atmospheric upstairs teahouse; its also a good place in the steamy afternoons to choose from one of the old National Geographic magazines lining the walls and relax on the floor against a cozy Lao cushion.

Mayleck Pub is an atmospheric little martini bar on the busy corner of Visounnalath and Samsenthai (past the market going southeast from town) and is a popular late-night spot.

MASSAGE

Perhaps one of the most pleasant ways to do your deed for charity, the **Red Cross of Luang Prabang,** near Wat Visoun to the southeast of the city, offers traditional massage and herbal sauna to raise money for its education programs. There are a number of good spots for traditional massage and herbal sauna in town, but the Red Cross is the cheapest and funds a good cause. The herbal sauna is open daily from 4:30 to 8:30pm; a 1-hour massage is available from 9am to 8:30pm and costs just US$3 per hour.

6 Luang Namtha & the Far North

North of Luang Prabang, things get a little rough. It's where Laos travel separates the men from the boys (or the "travelers" from the "tourists"). Roads are, in the main, just dirt track, and most towns leave an impression of "outpost" or the Asian equivalent of a dusty main street in the old American West. It's a part of the country best visited with a tour company (try **Diethelm** out of Luang Prabang), but the north has long been a favorite destination for intrepid individual travelers who brave the long, bumpy rides to see some beautiful mountain scenery, jungle, and rivers. The north is a patchwork of ethic minorities, and there are some exciting trekking and ecotourism options.

Luang Namtha itself is not much to see, really—just a row of low concrete and wood storefronts on a dusty avenue and a few miles of bucolic road that takes you to a picturesque little **Old Town** (6km/3¾ miles down the main road); nonetheless, it's connected by air with Luang Prabang and is a great base to explore the surrounding countryside. Trekking, kayaking, and visiting remote villages in the phenomenal **Nam Ha Biodiversity Conservation Area** bring so many up to this outpost. Again, come with the knowledge that travel here is off the track and can be very frustrating (even if you could ask, no one really knows when the bus will get there). It's important to remember that you're far from all but the most basic medical assistance, and even electricity flows only a few hours each day, but many are drawn here for that very reason: a bit of adventure, beautiful scenery, and the chance to visit rural villages.

VISITOR INFORMATION & TOURS

Wildside Eco Group, with a storefront office on the main street, puts together great kayak and raft trips in the pristine Nam Ha NBCA. You'll visit villages where they'll ask, through a translator, "Why are you here?" because foreign wayfarers are still an anomaly. The Nam Ha River is an exciting whitewater ride through cavernous jungle overgrowth or steep-walled gullies teeming with life (they have a list of what you might spot, including monkeys and bears). The folks at **Wildside** do a good job of making these trips fun and also ensure that their clients set a good example and tread lightly, especially in the villages (it's all up to us). They're highly recommended.

NamHa Trekking, in a neighboring office, offers similar whitewater trips and trekking to many of the same villages. Contact them at their office in the town center (Nam Ha Biodiversity Project: P.O. Box 7, Luang Nam Tha, Laos).

GETTING THERE

BY AIR   From Vientiane, there are a few flights each week, depending on the season, and they cost US$80. There are connections with Luang Prabang for US$37. The airport is 6km (3¾ miles) from town; a songthaew (covered pickup) will run about US$3 with some friendly bargaining.

BY BUS   Luang Nam Tha is a major hub in the north, connecting by bus with **Jinhong, China** via Boten (you'll need to have a prearranged visa), **Muang Sing,** and **Houaysay** (Thai border). From Luang Prabang, you'll be bounced and jounced for 5 hours (25,000 kip/US$2.50) until the dusty bus stop in **Oudomxay.** If your teeth are still in your head and buses are leaving (most buses have morning departures), you can connect with Luang Namtha for 20,000 kip (US$2); sometimes there is no same-day connection, and travelers hole up for a US$2 night in Oudomxay before the early-morning connection with Luang Namtha. There are more Korean-style minibuses plying these routes, but chances are good that you'll end up on the back of a pickup truck with no suspension for at least one leg of the journey. Bus travel here offers beautiful views and a chance to meet locals (and sit among often live cargo of chickens and pigs) but this is pretty grueling in the best of circumstances. Veterans of these bus rides have plenty to brag about at the traveler cafe back in the luxury of Luang Prabang.

BY CAR   Contact Diethelm in Luang Prabang (© **071/212-277; fax 071/ 212-032**) for jeep or minivan rental. It's an expensive option but a good way to see the rugged north.

FAST FACTS: LUANG NAMTHA

Bank and Post   There are a few foreign exchange counters on the main road (Rte. 3), and Lane Xang bank has a branch on the south end of town. You can change U.S. and Thai currency to kip in the central market.

Internet   Service is limited in this little burg. On the north end of town is a popular computer school with an occasional connection at an inflated price.

Telephone   Service in town is also limited, but most guesthouses can do call-back service, and there are phone booths on the main road that are IDD-capable and require a local card (buy at any store or the post office).

WHERE TO STAY & DINE

The Boat Landing is a rustic little gem on the banks of the Namtha River (P.O. Box 28; © **086/312-398;** www.theboatlanding.laopdr.com). Some 6km (3¾ miles) from the town center (just past the old town in Luang Namtha), basic bamboo bungalows at riverside start at US$8, with tile bathrooms (shower-in-room variety) and private balconies. It's laid back and picturesque, but the room's rustic charms might be more like musty boy-scout camp to some; nonetheless, this is the best standard in town. As an "ecolodge," they practice "reduce, reuse, and recycle" and have solar-powered lights and solar hot water; they also provide lots of important information on local history, flora and fauna, and low-impact ecotour options. The Landing is family-run and very friendly; the restaurant serves the best food around in a roomy, Lao-style thatch-peeked common area. Mountain bikes also are available for rent.

In **Luang Namtha** proper, there is an array of budget accommodations starting at US$2, and all are pretty grungy and basic. Try **Manichan Guesthouse** in Ban Phonsay (© **086/312-398**), an old budget standby with 10 basic rooms (US$2–US$4) and a good Lao restaurant that's a popular meeting place for trekkers. Other budget guesthouses and eateries line the main drag.

7 Xieng Khouang Province: Phonsavan

Xieng Khouang, whose top attraction is the mysterious Plain of Jars, is relatively well developed for tourism compared to other provinces in the north—*relatively* being the operative word here. Its capital city, Phonsavan, still has an eerie "edge of the Earth" feeling even though it's slowly growing. Electricity is available only between 6pm and 11pm, so bring a flashlight and some candles. It's the jumping-off point to visit the Plain of Jars, a little-understood group of archaeological sites comprised of enormous stone jars, or drums, half buried in the earth. This is also the land of "the secret war" waged by the CIA and American military against Vietnam from bases in the area; as a result, halved bombshells serve as pig troughs, metal tracks airlifted for make-shift runways are converted to convenient driveways, and there is even a village dedicated to and decorated by found shrapnel and military ordnance. If all this sounds a bit intense, and it is, these sites are as much an excuse to get out into the countryside where the landscape will likely steal the show. The jars are a fun and interesting mystery, and a visit to this region is certainly educational; you'll learn about the Hmong rebels, the mysterious recent history, and the many demining projects going on here

---

> **Warning Beware of Unexploded Ordnance**
>
> Xieng Khouang Province is one of the most heavily bombed areas on the Earth. UXO, or unexploded ordnance, is numerous, particularly in the form of small cluster bombs, blue or gray metal balls about the size of a fist. Don't stray into uninhabited unexplored areas without a good guide, and don't touch anything on the ground.
>
> Jar sites 1, 2, and 3 were all demined and fenced in a yearlong effort, completed in 1990, that removed 3 tons of UXO. That is only the tip of the iceberg for what still remains in the area. International and grassroots efforts at demining are ongoing, but be mindful and stay on the path.

---

and in other parts of the county. You might also want to see one of the nearby hill tribe villages. You'll certainly want to spring for a good guide to take you around to the many sites. *Note:* Higher altitude and weather patterns mean that it can get chilly here, especially in the rainy season, so bring a few layers.

VISITOR INFORMATION AND TOURS

At **Sousath Travel,** at the Maly Guesthouse, P.O. Box 649, Xieng Khouang (② **061/312-031;** fax 061/312-395) the effusive Mr. Sousath is the definitive source on local history and a true steward of the jar sites. The man is like a local institution really, and a tour with Mr. Sousath himself, if you are so fortunate, is one of the town's most interesting activities. A car and driver can be arranged.

Diethelm, on the main in Ban Phonsavan, PekDistrict (② **061/211-118**) meets its usual high standard and can cater guided tours to any sites, local and remote.

Two other options are **Inter-Lao Tourism,** Ban Phonsavan, Pek District (② **061/312-169**) and **Sodetour,** Ban Phonsavan, Pek District (② **061/312-403**).

GETTING THERE

BY AIR   Lao Aviation flies from Vientiane to Phonsavan every day except Saturday for US$45 one-way, or from Luang Prabang four times a week for US$37. Make sure you reconfirm your flight out of there *every day until you leave* to guarantee a seat back (flights overbook in the high season and get cancelled in the low season). Either your hotel or your tour agent will greet you and can help with any detail during your stay (return flight etc.).

BY BUS   Route 7 begins at a junction some 150km (93 miles) north of Vientiane on the main north-south artery, Route 13, and daily buses connect Phonsavon with Vientiane and Luang Prabang (60,000 kip/US$6 from Vientiane, and 68,000 kip/US$6.80 from Luang Prabang). But *be forewarned:* The road has been paved but follows a dynamic, precipitous route and is prone to landslides. That means that the 2 hours from Route 13 to Phonsavon might take 6 hours and require a transfer to large, Soviet 4-wheel-drive trucks for many miles of what I can only call "mud-bogging" rivaled only at a tractor pull. You'll make it, but not without a tiring adventure. Ask travel agents and fellow travelers about current road conditions, but fly if you're not keen on some drama.

GETTING AROUND

Once you get to Phonsavan, your best bet is to hook up with a local tour company to get to the Plain of Jars and surrounding villages. Renting a car or jeep with a driver for the day will cost between US$35 and US$55 (see "Visitor Information & Tours," above).

FAST FACTS: PHONSAVON

Bank and Post   There are a few foreign exchange counters on the main road (Rte. 7), and Lane Xang Bank has a branch near the post office, all centrally located around the town's central market.

Internet   Next to the large Konica sign at the center of town, you'll find very slow service for the hefty price of 500 kip per minute (US$3 per hr.). That's not really worth it unless you're in a pinch.

WHERE TO STAY & DINE

Budget accommodations line the main street in town (Rte. 7), and if you don't care to dine at your hotel, take a short stroll and you'll find a few good noodle and snack shops near the town center.

Auberge de la Plaine des Jarres ★   Throw another log on the fire and gaze across the deep green fields and rolling mountain scenery below from the comfort of your own rustic bungalow nestled into a peaceful grove of pine on a mountain overlooking town. The word *rustic* should be stressed here, but the Auberge is a great place to rest up after a day exploring the countryside. Rooms are tidy, with interesting local decorations and photos, and all have small balconies and fireplaces. They can get musty, though. Beds are spongy and the bathrooms are small, but the gas-powered showers are the best in town. There are a few suites with multiple bedrooms and a sitting room that are great for families. A popular stop for French tour groups, the restaurant serves good French and Lao, but the place is light on amenities; come with your own car and driver from town. This is certainly the atmospheric choice in the area though, and the friendly staff will make you feel at home.

Atop Mount Pupadeng overlooking the town from the SE. © 061/312-044. plainjar@samart.co.th. US$45–US$60 double. Cash only. **Amenities:** Restaurant; laundry. *In room:* Fireplace.

Maly Hotel   Owned and operated by local historian and racontour Mr. Sousath, this is a good low-luxe but comfortable base for exploring the jars. Built pell mell in a series of additions, rooms vary and the decoration runs the gamut from comfortable wooden lodge to musty cell. Ask to see the room before checking in. A few luxe setups have floor-to-ceiling windows and fine views. Baths are guesthouse basic with fickle solar showers. They serve good Lao and Western food in their popular lobby restaurant, the staff is friendly and helpful, and the convenient offices of **Sousath Travel** are the best place in town to arrange a guide and travel to the site. There's some useful literature about the jars, and don't miss any chance to chat with Mr. Sousath.

A short ride S from the town center. P.O. Box 649, Xieng Khouang. © 061/312-031. 24 units. US$8–US$55 double. MC, V (the only credit-card outlet in town). **Amenities:** Restaurant; tour service; car/jeep rental. *In room:* TV.

ATTRACTIONS

Thought to date back some 2,000 years, the archaeological finds at the **Plain of Jars** are stunning and mysterious. Hundreds of jars of varying sizes, the largest a bit over 2.7m (9 ft.) high, cover a plateau stretching across 24km (15 miles). Jars have been found in 15 different sites in the area so far. Visit these sites with a guide, if only to buoy up any fears over landmines (all areas within the sites are safe, though) and to get some perspective on local history and to hear what is known about the jars. There are some great photo ops, and be sure to get the obligatory "This is me in a jar!" shot before they make restrictions on touching or climbing on them. You can cover the main sites in 1 day, but you might want to take a few days and explore the surrounding Hmong villages or follow a guide to little-known war fallout like the rusting shell of an old Soviet tank in a small wood, or some interesting local villages done up with military ordnance. There's much to explore. **The Central Market** in Phonsavon is standard for Laos, but it's enormous; because of trade with nearby Vietnam, you might find some unique items. It's definitely worth a stoll.

Site 1 ★★ If you're short on time, this is the one to see. Set on a high hill is one of the largest of the jars, called the Doloman jar, amid a cock-eyed collection of 300 jars. This is the largest and most dynamic. It's all quite surreal and a unique photo op; a visit here gives you a great perspective on the surrounding countryside, and it's a nice walk to the jars scattered at the foot of the hill. Burn scars where no grass grows still dot the area, and legend has it that a few enterprising American military once tried to lift one of the jars with a helicopter and failed. This is the easiest site to access and the most picturesque.

11km (7 miles) from town, near Ban Hang Village. Entrance 5,000 kip (US50¢).

Sites 2 and 3 ★ These sites are both a little off the beaten track and require some fancy driving and a bit of picturesque rice-paddy and pasture walking to get there, but they are certainly worth it. Site 2 is situated near a small waterfall and is some 60 jars in a grove atop a small hill. Site 3 will have you crossing a bamboo bridge and picking your way through fields to get to open pasture on a high hill with some 100 jars.

Site 2 is 22km (13 miles) from town, and Site 3 is just a short drive from there. Both have entrance fees of 5,000 kip (US50¢).

8

Singapore

by Jennifer Eveland

Singapore thrives on a history that has absorbed a multitude of foreign elements over almost 2 centuries, melding them into a unique modern national identity. Beginning with the landing of Sir Stamford Raffles in 1819, add to the mix the original Malay inhabitants, immigrating waves of Chinese traders and workers, Indian businessmen and laborers, Arab merchants, British colonials, European adventure-seekers, and an assortment of Southeast Asian settlers—this tiny island rose from the ingenuity of those who worked and lived together here. Today, all recognize each group's importance to the heritage of the land, each adding unique contributions to a culture and identity that we know as Singaporean.

With all its shopping malls, fast-food outlets, imported fashion, and steel skyscrapers, Singapore could look like any other contemporary city you've ever visited—but to peel through the layers is to understand that life here is far more complex. While the outer layers are startlingly Western, just underneath lies a curious area where East blends with West in language, cuisine, attitude, and style. At the core, you'll find a sensibility rooted in the cultural heritage of values, religion, superstition, and memory. In Singapore, nothing is ever as it appears to be.

For me, this is where the fascination begins. I detect so many things familiar in this city, only to discover how these imported ideas have been altered to fit the local identity. Like the Singaporean shop house—a jumble of colonial architectural mandates, European tastes, Chinese superstitions, and Malay finery. Or Singlish, the unofficial local tongue, combining the English language with Chinese grammar, common Malay phrases, and Hokkien slang to form a *patois* unique to this part of the world. This transformation of cultures has been going on for almost 2 centuries. So, in a sense, Singapore is no different today than it was 100 years ago. And in this I find my "authentic" travel experience.

1 Getting to Know Singapore

THE LAY OF THE LAND

The country is made up of one main island, Singapore, and around 60 smaller ones, some of which—like Sentosa and Pulau Ubin—are popular retreats. The main island is shaped like a flat, horizontal diamond, measuring in at just over 42km (25 miles) from east to west and almost 23km (14 miles) north to south. With a total land area of only 584.8 sq. km (351 sq. miles), Singapore is almost shockingly tiny.

Singapore's geographical position, sitting approximately 137km (82 miles) north of the equator, means that its climate offers uniform temperatures, plentiful rainfall, and high, high humidity.

As a city-state, Singapore is basically a city that *is* the country. That doesn't necessarily mean that the entire country is urban, but that the whole of the country and the city is "Singapore," without provincial divisions.

Singapore does, however, have an urban center and smaller suburban neighborhoods: The urban area centers on the Singapore River at the southern point of the island, and within it are neighborhood divisions: the **Historic District** (also referred to as the city center or cultural district), **Chinatown, Tanjong Pagar** (which is often lumped together with Chinatown due to its proximity), the **Orchard Road area, Little India,** and **Kampong Glam** (also referred to as the Arab District).

Just beyond the urban area lie suburban neighborhoods. Some older suburbs, like **Katong** and **Geylang,** date from the turn of the 20th century. Others are new and are therefore referred to as "HDB New Towns." (HDB stands for Housing Development Board, the government agency responsible for public housing.) HDB New Towns such as **Ang Mo Kio** and **Toa Payoh** are clusters of public housing units, each with their own network of supporting businesses: provision shops, restaurants, health-care facilities, and sometimes shopping malls.

THE CITY   The urban center of Singapore spans quite far from edge to edge, so walking from one end to the other—say, from Tanjong Pagar to Kampong Glam—might be a bit much. However, once you become handy with local maps, you'll be constantly surprised at how close the individual districts are to one another.

The main focal point of the city is the **Singapore River,** which on a map is located at the southern point of the island, flowing west to east into the Marina. It's here that Sir Stamford Raffles, a British administrator, landed and built his settlement for the East India Trading Company. As trade prospered, the banks of the river were expanded to handle commerce, behind which neighborhoods and administrative offices took root. In 1822, Raffles developed a Town Plan, which allocated neighborhoods to each of the races who came in droves to find work and begin new lives. The lines drawn then still remain today, shaping the major ethnic enclaves within the city limits.

On the south bank of the river, go-downs (warehouses) were built along the waterside, behind which offices and residences sprang up for the Chinese community of merchants and "coolie" laborers who worked the river and sea trade. Raffles named this section **Chinatown,** a name that stands today.

Neighboring Chinatown to the southwest is **Tanjong Pagar,** a small district where wealthy Chinese and Eurasians built plantations and manors. With the development of the steamship, Keppel Harbour, a deep natural harbor just off the shore of Tanjong Pagar, was built up to receive the larger vessels. Tanjong Pagar quickly developed into a commercial and residential area filled with workers who flocked there to support the industry.

In these early days, both Chinatown and Tanjong Pagar were amazing sites of city activity. Row houses lined the streets, with shops on the bottom floors and homes on the second and third floors. Chinese coolie laborers commonly lived 16 to a room, and the area flourished with gambling casinos, clubs, and opium dens for them to spend their spare time and money. Indians also thronged to the area to work on the docks, a small reminder that although races had their own areas, they were never exclusive communities.

As recently as the 1970s, a walk down the streets in this area was an adventure: The shops housed Chinese craftsmen and artists; on the streets, hawkers peddled food and other merchandise. Calligrapher scribes set up shop on

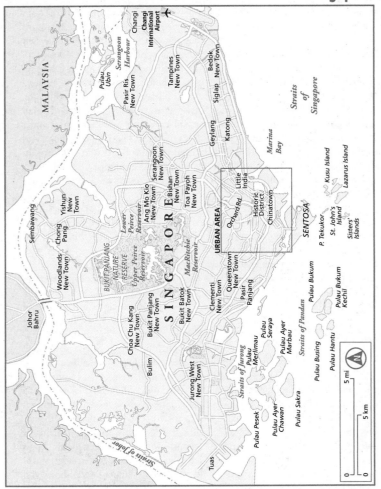

sidewalks to write letters for a fee. Housewives would bustle, running their daily errands; children would dash out of every corner; and bamboo poles hung laundry from upper stories. Today, however, both of these districts are sleepy by comparison. Modern HDB apartment buildings have siphoned residents off to the suburbs, and though the Urban Redevelopment Authority has renovated many of the old shop houses in an attempt to preserve history, they're now tenanted by law offices and architectural, public relations, and advertising firms. About the only time you'll see this place hustle anymore is during weekday lunchtime, when all the professionals dash out for a bite.

The **north bank** was originally reserved for colonial administrative buildings and is today commonly referred to as the **Historic District.** The center point was The Padang, the field on which the Europeans would play sports and hold outdoor ceremonies. Around the field, the Parliament Building, Supreme Court, City Hall, and other municipal buildings sprang up in grand style, and behind these buildings, Government Hill—the present-day **Fort Canning Park**—was the home of the governors. The Esplanade along the waterfront was a center for European social activities and music gatherings, when colonists would don their finest Western styles and walk the park under parasols or cruise in horse-drawn carriages. These days, the Historic District is still the center of most of the government's operations, and close by, high-rise hotels and shopping malls have been built. The area on the bank of the river is celebrated as Raffles's landing site.

To the northwest of the Historic District, in the areas along **Orchard Road and Tanglin,** a residential area was created for Europeans and Eurasians. Homes and plantations were eventually replaced by apartment buildings and shops, and in the early 1970s, luxury hotels ushered tourism into the area in full force. In the 1980s, huge shopping malls sprang up along the sides of Orchard Road, turning the landscape into the shopping hub it continues to be. The Tanglin area is home to most of the foreign embassies in Singapore.

The original landscape of **Little India** made it a natural location for an Indian settlement because the Indians were the original cattle hands and traders in Singapore; the area's natural grasses and springs provided their cattle with food and water, while bamboo groves supplied necessary lumber for their pens. Later, with the establishment of a jail nearby, Indian convict laborers and the Indian workers who supplied services to them came to the area for work and ended up staying. Today, although fewer Indians actually reside in this district, Little India is still the heartbeat of Indian culture in Singapore; shops here sell the clothing, cultural and religious items, and imported goods from "back home" that keep the Indian community linked to its cultural heritage. Although the Indian community in Singapore is a minority in its numbers, you wouldn't think so on Sundays, when all the workers have their day off and come to the streets here to socialize and relax.

Like Little India, the area around **Bugis Street** is adjacent to the Historic District. This neighborhood was originally allocated for the Bugis settlers who came from the island of Celebes, part of Indonesia. The Bugis were welcomed in Singapore, and because they originated from a society based on seafaring and trading, they became master shipbuilders. Today, regrettably, nothing remains of Bugis culture outside of the national museums. In fact, for most locals, Bugis Street is better remembered as a 1970s den of iniquity where transvestites, transsexuals, and other sex performers would stage seedy Bangkok-style shows and beauty contests. The government "cleaned up" Bugis Street in the 1980s so that all that remains is a huge shopping mall and a sanitized night market.

Kampong Glam, the neighborhood beyond Bugis Street, was given to Sultan Hussein and his family as part of his agreement to turn control of Singapore over to Raffles. Here he built his *istana* (palace) and the Sultan Mosque, and the area subsequently filled with Malay and Arab Muslims who imparted a distinct Islamic flavor to the neighborhood. The presence of the Sultan Mosque ensures that area remains a focal point of Singapore Muslim society, but the istana has fallen into disrepair and serves as a sad reminder of the economic condition into which Singapore's Malay community has fallen. **Arab Street** is perhaps the most popular area attraction for tourists and locals, who come to find deals on textiles and regional crafts.

Two areas of the city center are relatively new, having been built atop huge parcels of reclaimed land. Where the eastern edges of Chinatown and Tanjong Pagar once touched the water's edge, land reclamation created the present-day downtown business district, which is named after its central thoroughfare, **Shenton Way.** This Wall Street–like district is home to the magnificent skyscrapers that grace Singapore's skyline and to the banks and businesses that have made the place an international financial capital. During weekday business hours (9am–5pm), Shenton Way is packed with scurrying businesspeople. After hours and on weekends, it's nothing more than a quiet forest of concrete, metal, and glass.

The other reclaimed area is **Marina Bay,** on the other side of the river, just east of the Historic District. **Suntec City,** Southeast Asia's largest convention and exhibition center, is located here and has become the linchpin of a thriving hotel, shopping mall, and amusement zone.

OUTSIDE THE URBAN AREA

The heart of the city centers around the Singapore River but outside the city proper are suburban neighborhoods and rural areas. In the immediate outskirts of the main urban area are the older suburban neighborhoods, such as **Katong, Geyland,** and **Holland Village.** Beyond these are the newer suburbs, called **HDB New Towns.** The HDB, or Housing Development Board, is responsible for creating large towns, such as **Ang Mo Kio** and **Toa Payoh;** each have their own network of supporting businesses: restaurants, schools, shops, health-care facilities, and sometimes department stores.

2 Planning Your Trip to Singapore

VISITOR INFORMATION

The long arm of the **Singapore Tourism Board (STB)** reaches many overseas audiences through its branch offices, which will gladly provide brochures and booklets to help you plan your trip, and through its website, at www.newasia-singapore.com. The STB also has websites with special tips directed specifically to American and Canadian travelers; see **www.tourismsingapore.com**.

IN THE UNITED STATES
- **New York:** 590 Fifth Ave., 12th Floor, New York, NY 10036 (© **212/302-4861;** fax 212/302-4801)
- **Chicago:** Two Prudential Plaza, 180 North Stetson Ave., Suite 2615, Chicago, IL 60601 (© **312/938-1888;** fax 312/938-0086)
- **Los Angeles:** 8484 Wilshire Blvd., Suite 510, Beverly Hills, CA 90211 (© **323/852-1901;** fax 323/852-0129)

IN CANADA
- **Toronto:** The Standard Life Centre, 121 King St. West, Suite 1000, Toronto, Ontario, Canada M5H 3T9 (© **416/363-8898;** fax 416/363-5752)

IN THE UNITED KINGDOM
- **London:** 1st Floor, Carrington House, 126–130 Regent St., London W1R 5FE, United Kingdom (© **207/4370033;** fax 207/7342191)

IN AUSTRALIA & NEW ZEALAND
- **Sydney:** Level 11, AWA Building, 47 York St., Sydney NSW 2000, Australia (© **2/9290-2888;** fax 2/9290-2555)

IN SINGAPORE
- **Tourism Court:** 1 Orchard Spring Lane, across the street from Traders Hotel (© **65/736-6622;** fax 65/736-9423; the toll-free Touristline in Singapore is © **800/736-2000**)

Urban Singapore Neighborhoods

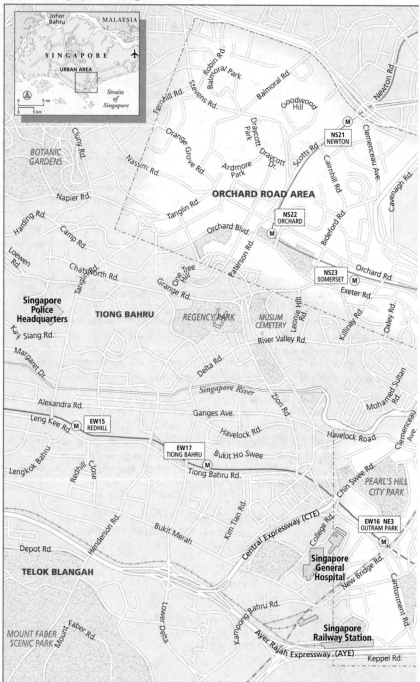

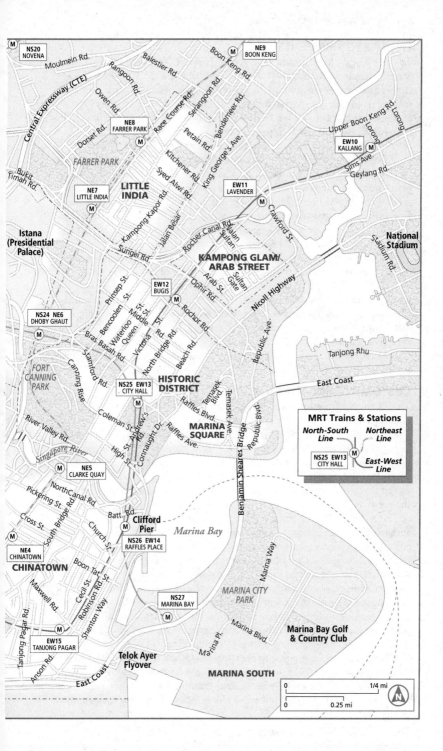

ENTRY REQUIREMENTS

To enter Singapore, you must have a valid passport. Visitors from the United States, Canada, Australia, New Zealand, and the United Kingdom are not required to obtain a visa prior to their arrival. A Social Visit Pass (with combined social and business status) good for up to 30 days is awarded upon entry for travelers arriving by plane, or for 14 days if your trip is by ship or overland from Malaysia. Good news for U.S. passport holders: In the fall of 1999, the United States allowed Singaporeans to travel socially in the United States without a visa, so Singapore has reciprocated by allowing Americans a 90-day social/business-class Social Visit Pass upon entry. Be advised that this and all other types of passes are at the discretion of the immigration officer, who might not award you the full amount of time. Singapore is trying to cut down on foreigners living here without proper documentation—many make illegal "Visa Runs" to Malaysia to allow them to stay longer in Singapore. However, if this is your first trip to Singapore, you should have no problems.

The **Singapore Immigration & Registration (SIR) Department** operates a 24-hour automated inquiry system for questions about visa requirements at © **65/391-6100,** but if you need to speak to a representative, call between the hours of 8am and 5pm Monday through Friday, or 8am and 1pm on Saturday. The Singapore Immigration & Registration office is located at 10 Kallang Rd., SIR Building (above the Lavender MRT station). Business hours are Monday through Friday 8am to 5pm, and Saturday 8am to 1pm. For immigration information on the Net, visit the Ministry of Home Affairs website at www.mha. gov.sg.

CUSTOMS REGULATIONS

There's no restriction on the amount of currency you can bring into Singapore. For those over 18 years of age who have arrived from countries other than Malaysia and have spent more than 48 hours outside Singapore, allowable duty-free concessions are 1 liter of spirits; 1 liter of wine; and 1 liter of either port, sherry, or beer, all of which must be intended for personal consumption only. There are no duty-free concessions on cigarettes or other tobacco items. If you exceed the duty-free limitations, you can bring in your excess items after paying the goods and services tax (GST) and Customs duty.

The following items are not allowed through Customs unless you have authorization or an import permit: animals; birds and their by-products; plants; endangered species or items made from these species; arms and explosives; bulletproof clothing; toy guns of any type; weapons, including decorative swords and knives; cigarette lighters in the shape of pistols; toy coins; pornographic prerecorded videotapes and cassettes, books, or magazines; controlled substances; poisons; and materials that might be considered treasonable (plutonium, military maps—that kind of thing). For all pharmaceutical drugs, especially sleeping pills, depressants, or stimulants, you must provide a prescription from your physician authorizing personal use for your well-being.

All inquiries can be directed to the **Customs Office** at Changi International Airport (© **65/6542-7058**) or to the automated **Customs hotline** at © **65/ 6355-2000** (Mon–Fri 8am–5pm, Sat 8am–noon). A detailed rundown can be found on the Net at the Ministry of Home Affairs home page, **www.mha. gov.sg**.

DEPARTURE TAX   Upon departure, you'll be required to pay a **departure tax of S$15.** Nowadays, this tax is usually added onto your airfare. Ask your airline if this is the case. If not, coupons for the amount can be purchased at most hotels, travel agencies, and airline offices.

THE TOURIST REFUND SCHEME　Singapore has a great incentive for travelers to drop big bucks: the Tourist Refund Scheme. If you purchase goods at a value of S$300 (US$171) or more at a shop that displays the Tax Free Shopping sign, Customs will reimburse the 3% GST (goods and services tax) you paid for the purchase. You are allowed to pool receipts from different retailers for purchases of S$100 (US$57) or more. Here's how it works: When you purchase the item(s), apply with the retailer for a Tax Free Shopping Check. When you're leaving Singapore, present your Shopping Checks and the items purchased at the Tax Refund Counters located in the Departure Hall at Changi Airport's terminals 1 or 2. Within 12 weeks, you'll receive a check for the GST refund—or, if you used a credit card for the purchase, your bill can be credited (a surcharge might be levied). For more information, contact the **Singapore Tourism Board** at © 800/736-2000.

MONEY

The local currency unit is the **Singapore dollar.** It's commonly referred to as the "Sing dollar," and retail prices are often marked as S$ (a designation I've used throughout this book). Notes are issued in denominations of S$1, S$2, S$5, S$10, S$50, S$100, S$500, and S$1,000. Notes vary in size and color from denomination to denomination. Coins are issued in denominations of S1¢, S5¢, S10¢, S20¢, S50¢, and the fat, gold-colored S$1. Singapore has an interchangeability agreement with Brunei, so the Brunei dollar is accepted as equal to the Singapore dollar.

Singapore's currency weathered the Southeast Asian economic crisis in 1997 rather successfully, so if you were hoping for a more favorable exchange rate, you're looking in the wrong place; the Sing dollar has decreased in value only slightly from precrisis rates. At the time of this writing, exchange rates on the Singapore dollar were as follows: US$1 = S$1.76, C$1 = S$1.12, £1 = S$2.80, A$1 = S$.99, NZ$1 = S87¢. The exchange rate used throughout this book is US$1 = S$1.75, to use an average figure, but before you begin budgeting your trip, I suggest that you obtain the latest conversions so that you don't suffer any shocks at the last minute. A neat and easy customizable currency conversion program can be found on the Internet through **www.xe.com**.

CURRENCY EXCHANGE　Although hotels and banks will perform currency exchanges, you'll get a better rate at any one of the many money-changers that can be found in all the shopping malls and major shopping districts (look for the certificate of government authorization). Many shops are also authorized to change money and display signs to that effect. Money-changers usually give you the official going rate for the day, and sometimes the difference in rate between hotels and money-changers can be as much as US8¢ to the dollar. Finally, although some hotels and shops might accept your foreign currency as payment, they will always calculate the exchange rate in their favor.

ATMS　Singapore has thousands of conveniently located 24-hour ATMs. Whether you're in your hotel, a shopping mall, or a suburban neighborhood, I'd be surprised if you're more than 1 or 2 blocks from an ATM—ask your concierge or any passerby for directions. With debit cards on the MasterCard/ Cirrus or Visa/PLUS systems, you can withdraw Singapore currency from any of these machines, and your bank will deduct the amount from your account at that day's official exchange rate. This is a very good way to access cash for the most favorable currency rate, but make sure you check with your bank before you leave home to find out what your daily withdrawal limits are. It's also a good idea to keep track of ATM charges—your home financial institution can levy a fee of up to US$1.50 per transaction for this convenience, and rumor has it that Singapore banks will be charging a fee as well.

TRAVELER'S CHECKS   These days, traveler's checks seem less necessary because most cities have 24-hour ATMs that allow you to withdraw small amounts of cash as needed. However, keep in mind that you will likely be charged an ATM withdrawal fee if the bank is not your own, so if you're withdrawing money every day, you might be better off with traveler's checks—provided that you don't mind showing identification every time you want to cash one.

You can get traveler's checks at almost any bank. **American Express** offers denominations of $20, $50, $100, $500, and (for cardholders only) $1,000. You'll pay a service charge ranging from 1% to 4%. You can also get American Express traveler's checks over the phone by calling © **800/221-7282;** Amex gold and platinum cardholders who use this number are exempt from the 1% fee. AAA members can obtain checks without a fee at most AAA offices.

Visa offers traveler's checks at Citibank locations nationwide, as well as at several other banks. The service charge ranges between 1.5% and 2%; checks come in denominations of $20, $50, $100, $500, and $1,000. Call © **800/732-1322** for information. **MasterCard** also offers traveler's checks. Call © **800/223-9920** for a location near you.

CREDIT CARDS   American Express (AE) is accepted widely, as are Diner's Club (DC), MasterCard (MC), Japan Credit Bank (JCB), and Visa (V), although you'll find that some budget hotels, smaller shops, and restaurants will accept no credit cards at all. Purchases made with credit cards will appear on your bill at the exchange rate on the day your charge is posted, not what the rate was on the day the purchase was made. It's also worth noting that if your signature is slightly different on the slip than it is on your card, shop owners will make you redo the slip. They're real sticklers for signature details, so don't leave out a middle initial or forget to cross a T.

WHEN TO GO

The busy season is from January to June. In the late summer months, business travel dies down, and in fall, even tourism drops off somewhat, making the season ripe for budget-minded visitors. These might be the best times to get a deal. Probably the worst time to negotiate is between Christmas and the Chinese New Year.

CLIMATE   At approximately 137km (82 miles) north of the equator, with exposure to the sea on three sides, it's a sure bet that Singapore will be hot and humid year-round. Temperatures remain uniform, with a daily average of 81°F (27°C); afternoon temperatures reach as high as 87°F (31°C), and an average sunrise temperature is as low as 75°F (24°C). Relative humidity often exceeds 90% at night and in the early morning. Even on a "dry" afternoon, don't expect it to drop much below 60%. (The daily average is 84% relative humidity.) Rain falls year-round, much of it coming down in sudden downpours that end abruptly and are followed immediately by the sun.

The Northeast Monsoon occurs between December and March, when temperatures are slightly cooler, relatively speaking, than other times of the year. The heaviest rainfall occurs between November and January, with daily showers that sometimes last for long periods of time; at other times, it comes down in short, heavy gusts and goes quickly away. Wind speeds are rarely anything more than light. The Southwest Monsoon falls between June and September. Temperatures are higher, and, interestingly, it's during this time of year that Singapore gets the *least* rain (with the very least reported in July).

Between monsoons, thunderstorms are frequent. Also interesting, the number of daylight hours and number of nighttime hours remain almost constant year-round. February is the sunniest month, while December is generally more overcast.

PUBLIC HOLIDAYS & EVENTS   There are 11 official public holidays: New Year's Day, Chinese New Year or Lunar New Year (2 days), Hari Raya Puasa, Good Friday, Hari Raya Haji, Labour Day, Vesak Day, National Day, Deepavali, and Christmas Day. On these days, expect government offices, banks, and some shops to be closed.

Holidays and festivals are well publicized by the **Singapore Tourism Board (STB),** which loves to introduce the world to the joys of all Singapore's cultures. As with any schedule of upcoming events, the following information is subject to change; always confirm the details before you plan your trip around an event. A call or visit to an STB office either before your trip or once you arrive will let you know the what, where, and when of all that's happening during your stay. See the listing of STB offices in the United States, Canada, the United Kingdom, and Australia under "Visitor Information," earlier in this chapter. Its website at www.newasia-singapore.com also has information about upcoming holidays and festivals.

HEALTH CONCERNS

Generally, you'll have no problem with the food in Singapore, other than the possible digestive problems you might experience simply because you're not used to the ingredients. All fruits and vegetables should be thoroughly washed to rinse away any bacteria. Chinese restaurants in Singapore still use monosodium glutamate (MSG), the flavor enhancer that was blamed for everything from fluid retention to migraine headaches, and has been squeezed out of most Chinese restaurant cuisine in the West. The MSG connection has just started to catch on here, but not in full force. Many restaurants can now prepare dishes without MSG upon request, but smaller places will probably think you're insane for asking.

Singapore doesn't require that you have any **vaccinations** to enter the country, but it strongly recommends immunization against diphtheria, tetanus, hepatitis A and B, and typhoid. If you're particularly worried, follow that advice; if you're the intrepid type, ignore it. Although there's no risk of contracting malaria (the country has been declared malaria-free for decades by the World Health Organization), there is a similar deadly virus, **dengue fever** (also just called dengue), that's carried by mosquitoes and has no immunization. Symptoms of dengue fever include sudden fever and tiny red, spotty rashes on the body. If you suspect that you've contracted dengue, seek medical attention immediately (see the listing of hospitals under "Fast Facts," later in this chapter). If left untreated, this disease can cause internal hemorrhaging and even death. Your best protection is to wear insect repellent, especially if you're heading out to the zoo, a bird park, or any of the gardens or nature preserves.

For further health and insurance information, see chapter 3.

GETTING THERE
BY PLANE

If you're hunting for the best airfare, there are a few things you can do. First, plan your trip for the low-volume season, which runs from September 1 to November 30. Between January 1 and May 31, you'll pay the highest fares. Plan your travel on weekdays only, and, if you can, plan to stay for at least a full week. Book your reservations in advance—waiting until the last minute can mean you'll pay sky-high rates. Also, if you have access to the Internet, there are a number of great sites that'll search out super fares for you. See chapter 3 for more information.

FROM THE UNITED STATES Singapore Airlines (✆ 800/742-3333 in the U.S., or 65/6223-6030 in Singapore; www.singaporeair.com) has a daily flight from New York, two daily flights from Los Angeles, two daily flights from San Francisco (only 1 on Sun), and a flight four times weekly from Newark, New Jersey. Flights originating from the East Coast travel over Europe, stopping in either Frankfurt or Amsterdam. Flights from the West Coast stop over in either Tokyo or Hong Kong. **United Airlines** (✆ 800/241-6522 in the U.S., or 65/6873-3533 in Singapore; www.ual.com) has daily flights connecting pretty much every major city in the United States with Singapore via the Pacific route. Expect a stopover in Tokyo en route. **Northwest Airlines** (✆ 800/447-4747 in the U.S., or 65/6336-3371 in Singapore; www.nwa.com) links all major U.S. airports with daily direct flights to Singapore from the following ports of exit: New York, Detroit, Minneapolis, Los Angeles, Seattle, and San Francisco, with direct flights from Las Vegas on Monday and Thursday only. All flights have one short stopover in Tokyo.

FROM CANADA Singapore Airlines (✆ 604/681-7488 in the U.S., or 65/6223-6030 in Singapore; www.singaporeair.com) has flights from Vancouver three times a week, with a stopover in Seoul.

FROM THE UNITED KINGDOM Singapore Airlines (✆ 181/747-0007 in London, 161/832-3346 in Manchester, or 65/6223-6030 in Singapore; www.singaporeair.com) has three daily flights departing from London's Heathrow Airport with a daily connection from Manchester. Depending on the day of departure, these flights stopover in either Amsterdam, Zurich, or Bombay. **British Airways** (✆ 0345/222111 local call from anywhere within the U.K., or 65/6839-7788 in Singapore; www.british-airways.com) has daily nonstop flights from London. **Quantas Airways Ltd.** (✆ 0345/747767 in Australia, or 65/6839-7788 in Singapore; www.quantas.com) has daily nonstop flights on weekdays and flights twice daily on weekends from London.

FROM AUSTRALIA Singapore Airlines (✆ 65/223-6030 in Singapore; www.singaporeair.com) has twice-daily flights from Melbourne (✆ 3/9254-0300) and Sydney (✆ 2/9350-0100); three dailies from Perth (✆ 8/9265-0500); a daily from Brisbane (✆ 7/3259-0717); flights from Adelaide (✆ 8/8203-0800) four times a week; and from Cairns (✆ 70/317-538) three times a week. **Quantas Airways Ltd.** (✆ 2/131313 toll free, or 65/6839-7788 in Singapore; www.quantas.com) links all major airports in Australia with daily direct flights to Singapore from Sydney and Melbourne. **British Airways** (✆ 8/9425-7711 in Perth, 7/3223-3133 in Brisbane, or 65/6839-7788 in Singapore; www.british-airways.com) has daily flights from Perth and Brisbane. British Airways and Quantas work in partnership to provide routing from Australia, so be sure to consult Quantas for connecting flights from your city.

FROM NEW ZEALAND   **Singapore Airlines** (℡ 303-2129 in Auckland, or 366-8003 in Christchurch; www.singaporeair.com) has daily flights from Auckland and Christchurch. **Air New Zealand** (℡ **0800/737000;** www.airnew zealand.co.nz) has daily flights from Christchurch and a daily flight from Auckland, in partnership with Singapore Airlines (so you can still use or accumulate frequent-flier miles for this trip).

GETTING INTO TOWN FROM THE AIRPORT

Most visitors to Singapore will land at **Changi International Airport,** which is located toward the far eastern corner of the island. Compared to so many other international airports, Changi is a dream come true, providing clean and very efficient space and facilities. Expect to find in-transit accommodations, restaurants, duty-free shops, money-changers, ATMs, car-rental desks, accommodation assistance, and tourist information all marked with clear signs. When you arrive, keep your eyes peeled for the many Singapore Tourism Board brochures that are so handily displayed throughout the terminal.

The city is easily accessible by public transportation. A taxi trip to the city center will cost around S$22 to S$25 (US$13–US$14) and takes around 20 minutes. You'll traverse the wide Airport Boulevard to the Pan-Island Expressway (PIE) or the East Coast Parkway (ECP), past public housing estates and other residential neighborhoods in the eastern part of the island, over causeways, and into the city center.

CityCab offers an airport shuttle, a six-seater maxicab that traverses between the airport and the major hotel areas. It covers most hotels and is very flexible about drop-offs and pickups within the central areas, including MRT (subway) stations. Bookings are made at the airport shuttle counter in the arrival terminal or by calling ℡ **65/6542-8297.** Pay S$7 (US$4) for adults and S$5 (US$2.85) for children directly to the driver.

The **MRT** now operates to the airport, linking you with the city and areas beyond. Follow signs in the terminal buildings. Trains operate roughly from 6am to midnight daily, and the trip takes about a half-hour. You'll pay S$1.40 (US80¢) to travel to City Hall Station.

A couple of **buses** run from the airport into the city as well. SBS bus no. 16 will take you on a route to Orchard Road and Raffles City (in the Historic District). SBS bus no. 36 runs a direct route to and from the airport and Orchard Road. Both bus stops are located in the basement of the arrival terminal. A trip to town costs about S$1.40 (US80¢).

For arrival and departure information, you can call **Changi International Airport** toll-free at ℡ **65/6542-4422.**

GETTING AROUND

The many inexpensive mass transit options make getting around Singapore pretty easy. Of course, taxis always simplify the ground transportation dilemma. They're also very affordable, and, by and large, drivers are helpful and honest, if not downright personable. The **Mass Rapid Transit (MRT) subway service** has lines that cover the main areas of the city and out to the farther parts of the island. Buses present more of a challenge because there are so many routes snaking all over the island, but they're a great way to see the country while getting where you want to go. In the bus section, below, I've thrown in some tips that will hopefully demystify the bus experience for you.

Of course, if you're just strolling around the urban limits, many of the sights within the various neighborhoods are within walking distance, and indeed, some of the neighborhoods are only short walks from each other—getting from Chinatown to the Historic District requires only crossing over the Singapore River, and from Little India to Kampong Glam is not far at all. However, I advise against trying to get from, say, Chinatown (in the west) to Kampong Glam (in the east). The distance can be somewhat prohibitive, especially in the heat.

Stored-fare EZ-Link fare cards can be used on both the subway and the buses, and can be purchased at TransitLink offices in the MRT stations. These save you the bother of trying to dig up exact change for bus meters. The card does carry a S$5 (US$2.85) deposit—for a S$15 (US$8.55) initial investment, you'll get S$10 (US$5.70) worth of travel credit.

BY MASS RAPID TRANSIT (MRT)

The MRT is Singapore's subway system. It's cool, clean, safe, and reliable, providing service from the far west reaches of the island to the far east parts on the east-west line and running in a loop around the north part of the island on the north-south line. The lines are color-coded to make it easy to find the train you're looking for (see the MRT map in this chapter for specifics). The two lines intersect at the Raffles Place Interchange in Chinatown/Shenton Way, at City Hall in the Historic District, and in the western part of the island at the Jurong East Interchange. (By the way, don't let the "East" fool you—Jurong East is actually in the western part of the island.) MRT operating hours vary between lines and stops, with the earliest train beginning service daily at 5:15am and the last train ending at 12:47am.

Fares range from S80¢ to S$1.80 (US45¢–US$1.05), depending on which stations you travel between. System charts are prominently displayed in all MRT stations to help you find your appropriate fare, which you pay with an EZ-Link fare card. Single-fare cards can be purchased at vending machines at MRT stations. See above for information on stored-fare cards. (**One caution:** A fare card cannot be used by 2 people for the same trip; each must have his own.)

For more information, call **TransitLink TeleInfo** at ℂ **1800/767-4333** (daily 24 hr.).

BY BUS

Singapore's bus system comprises an extensive web of routes that reach virtually everywhere on the island. It can be intimidating for newcomers, but once you get your feet wet, you'll feel right at home. There are two main bus services, SBS (Singapore Bus Service) and TIBS (Trans-Island Bus Service). Most buses are clean, but not all are air-conditioned.

Start off first by purchasing the latest edition of the *TransitLink Guide* for about S$1.50 (US85¢) at the TransitLink office in any MRT station, at a bus interchange, or at selected bookstores around the city. This tiny book is a very handy guide that details each route and stop, indicating connections with MRT stations and fares for each trip. Next to the guide, the best thing to do is simply ask people for help. At any crowded bus stop, there will always be somebody who speaks English and is willing to help out a lost stranger. You can also ask the bus driver where you need to go, and he'll tell you the fare, how to get there, and even when to get off.

All buses have a gray machine with a sensor pad close to the driver. Tap your EZ-Link care when you board and alight, and the fare will be automatically

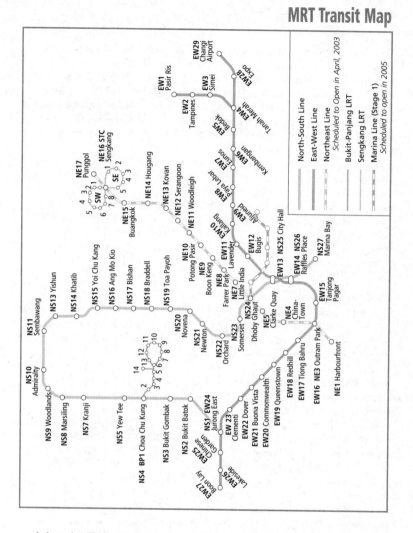

deducted. It'll be anywhere between S80¢ and S$1.60. If you're paying cash, be sure to have exact change; place the coins in the red box by the driver and announce your fare to him. He'll issue a ticket, which will pop out of a slot on one of the TransitLink machines behind him.

The **Tourist Day Ticket** is a great deal for travelers. The 1-day pass costs S$10 (US$5.70) and is good for 12 rides on either SBS or TIBS buses or the MRT. Using one of these will save you having to worry about calculating the correct fare or coming up with exact change. You can pick one up at any TransitLink office and at hotels, money-changers, provisioner shops, or travel agents. Unfortunately, there's no handy sign identifying which shops sell them, so you'll have to ask around.

For more information, contact either of the two operating bus lines during standard business hours: **Singapore Bus Service (SBS)** (✆ **1800/287-2727**) or **the Trans-Island Bus Service (TIBS)** (✆ **1800/482-5433**).

BY TROLLEY

You have a couple of trolley options; both services are offered for the convenience of travelers, making stops at most major tourist destinations. The Singapore Explorer shuttles down Orchard Road, through the Historic District and over the Singapore River, and down to Marina Square. For S$15 (US$8.50) for adults and S$9.90 (US$5.65) for children, you can enjoy unlimited rides for 1 day (this price also includes a free riverboat tour). Buy your tickets either from your hotel's front desk or directly from the driver. Call Singapore Explorer at © 65/6339-6833.

Singapore Airlines hosts the **SIA Hop-on bus.** Plying between Bugis Junction, Suntec City, the Historic District, the Singapore River, Chinatown, Orchard Road and the Singapore Botanic Gardens, the Hop-on comes every 30 minutes between the hours of 8:30am and 7pm. Unlimited rides for 1 day cost S$6 (US$3.45) for adults and S$4 (US$2.30) for children. Buy your tickets from your hotel's front desk, from a Singapore Airlines office, or from the bus drivers. If you've traveled to Singapore via Singapore Airlines, you're entitled to free passage aboard the Hop-on. Just show your boarding pass to the driver. For more information, call **SH Tours** © 65/6374-9923.

BY TAXI

Taxis are a very convenient and affordable way to get around Singapore, and there's every chance that you'll get a good conversation with the driver into the bargain. Despite this, I advise against relying completely on taxi cabs, since Singapore's excellent public transportation system will take you practically anywhere you need to go for a fraction of the price. Even in the middle of nowhere, there's always a bus route to take you to familiar territory—just remember to keep your *TransitLink Guide* (see above) handy so you'll know where the bus you're about to hop is headed.

In town, all of the shopping malls, hotels, and major buildings have taxi queues, which you're expected to use. During lunch hours and the evening rush, the queues can be very long; though taxis are generally convenient, don't count on finding one fast during the evening rush hours between 5pm and 7pm. Especially if it's raining, you'll be waiting for an hour, easy. Everybody wants a cab at this time, and for some strange reason, this is the time the cabbies choose to change shifts. Brilliant. During this time, I recommend that you call to book a taxi pickup, but even that could mean up to a half-hour wait. You pay a little extra, but, believe me, some days it can really be worth it.

Most destinations in the main parts of the island can be reached fairly inexpensively, while trips to the outlying attractions can cost from S$10 to S$15 (US$5.70–US$8.55) one-way. If you're at an attraction or restaurant outside of the central part of the city, where it is more difficult to hail a cab on the street, you can ask the cashier or service counter attendant to call a taxi for you. The extra charge for pickup is between S$3 and S$3.20 (US$1.70 and US$1.85), depending on the cab company. (CityCab is the cheapest.) Call these main cab companies for bookings: **CityCab** (© 65/6552-2222), **Comfort** (© 65/6552-1111), and **TIBS** (© 65/6552-8888).

CityCab and Comfort charge the metered fare, which is S$2.40 (US$1.35) for the first kilometer and S10¢ (US6¢) for each additional 225m to 240m or 30 seconds of waiting. TIBS's meter starts at S$2.10 (US$1.20). Extra fares are levied on top of the metered fare, depending on where you're going and when you go. At times, figuring your fare seems more like a riddle. Here's a summary.

Trips during peak hours: Between the hours of 7:30 and 9:30am Monday to Friday, 4:30 and 7pm Monday to Friday, and 11:30am and 2pm on Saturday, trips carry an additional S$1 (US55¢) peak-period surcharge. But if you're traveling outside the Central Business District (CBD), you won't need to pay this surcharge during the morning rush. (To accurately outline the boundaries of the CBD, I'd need to fill a couple of encyclopedic volumes, so for this purpose, let's just say it's basically Orchard Rd., the Historic District, Chinatown, and Shenton Way.)

Additional charges rack up each time you travel through an Electronic Road Pricing (ERP) scheme underpass. On the Central Expressway (CTE), Pan-Island Expressway (PIE), and selected thoroughfares in the CBD, charges from S30¢ to S$1.70 (US15¢–US95¢) are calculated by an electronic box on the driver's dashboard. The driver will add this amount to your fare.

And for special torture, here are some more charges: From midnight to 6am, add 50% to your fare. From 6pm on the eve of a public holiday to midnight the following day, you pay an additional S$1 (US.55¢). From Changi Airport, add S$5 (US$2.85) if you're traveling Friday, Saturday, or Sunday between 5pm and midnight. Other times, it's S$3 (US$1.70). And for credit card payments (yes, you can pay with plastic!), add 10%.

BY CAR

Singapore's public transportation systems are so extensive, efficient, and inexpensive that you shouldn't need a car to enjoy your stay. In fact, I don't advise it. Although most hotels and restaurants and many attractions do have parking facilities, parking in lots can be expensive, and on-street parking is by prepurchased, color-coded parking tickets that are a pain to purchase. In addition, if you're not accustomed to driving on the left side of the road, you'll need to take the time to pick up a new skill.

Because of heavy government taxes aimed at reducing traffic congestion and air pollution, everything to do with cars in Singapore is outlandishly expensive—the going price for a Toyota Camry, for instance, can be as high as S$125,000 (US$71,429). This attempt to reduce automobile traffic is also extended to you, the traveler, through rental charges up to S$1,000 (US$571) plus taxes for 1 week's rental of the smallest car on the lot.

One of the few good reasons to rent a car is if you plan to drive into Malaysia. Back in the 1970s, driving in Malaysia was risky because of highway bandits. These days, though, it's relatively safe traveling, and thanks to the new toll road—the North-South Highway from Singapore all the way up to the Thai border—it's pretty convenient (see chapter 9 for more on this subject and on renting a car in Malaysia rather than Singapore, which can save you some cash).

Two good places to seek out a rental car are these:

- **Avis:** Changi Airport Terminal 2 (℃ **65/6542-8855**), no. 01–01 Concorde Shopping Centre (℃ **65/6737-1668**). You must be at least 23 years old to rent, and the minimum rental period is 24 hours. Rates in Singapore run daily from S$100 (US$57) for a Mitsubishi Lancer to S$160 (US$91) for a Mitsubishi Gallant. For travel to Malaysia, the daily rates are somewhat higher. One-way rentals are available, with varying drop-off fees for Malacca, Kuala Lumpur, Kuantan, Alor Setar, Ipoh, and Penang. All major credit cards are accepted.

- **Hertz:** Changi Airport Terminal 2, Arrival Meeting Hall South (℃ **65/542-5300**), or 125 Tanglin Rd., Tudor Court Shopping Gallery (℃ **1800/734-4646**). You must be at least 21 years of age to rent, and the minimum rental period is 24 hours. Daily rates for rental within Singapore run from S$199 (US$119) for a Mitsubishi Lancer to S$559 (US$335) for a BMW or Mercedes Benz, and S$1,194 (US$715) to S$3,354 (US$2,008) per week, respectively. Hertz does not rent luxury cars for driving to Malaysia. For Malaysia driving, Hertz charges an extra S$25 (US$15) per day. For one-way trips to Malaysia, there are varying drop-off charges for Johor Bahru, Kuala Lumpur, Kuantan, and Penang. Hertz accepts all major credit cards.

An additional solution to getting around is to hire a car and driver. A **City-Cab Mercedes** can be hired for S$39 per hour, which is about the best rate available. For bookings, call ✆ **65/6454-2222.**

✆ FAST FACTS: Singapore

American Express The American Express office is located at 300 Beach Rd., no. 18-01 The Concourse, ✆ **65/6880-1333.** It's open Monday to Friday 9am to 5pm, and Saturday 9am to 1pm. There's a more convenient kiosk that handles traveler's checks and simple card transactions (including emergency check guarantee) on Orchard Road just outside the Marriott Hotel at Tang Plaza ✆ **65/6735-2069.** It's open daily from 9am to 9pm. An additional foreign exchange office is open at Changi Airport Terminal 2 (✆ **65/6543-0671**). It's open from noon to midnight daily. See the "Money" section earlier in this chapter for more details on member privileges.

Business Hours Shopping centers are open Monday through Saturday from 10am to 8pm, and they stay open until 10pm on some public holidays. Banks are open from 9:30am to 3pm Monday through Friday, and from 9am to 11am on Saturday. Restaurants open at lunchtime from around 11am to 2:30pm, and for dinner they reopen at around 6pm and take the last order sometime around 10pm. Nightclubs stay open until 2am on weekdays and until 3am on Friday and Saturday. Government offices are open from 9am to 5pm Monday through Friday, and from 9am to 3pm on Saturday. Post offices conduct business from 8:30am to 5pm on weekdays, and from 8:30am to 1pm on Saturday.

Car Rentals See "Getting Around," earlier in this chapter.

Climate See "When to Go," earlier in this chapter.

Currency See "Money," earlier in this chapter.

Documents See "Visitor Information & Entry Requirements," earlier in this chapter.

Driving Rules See "Getting Around," earlier in this chapter.

Drugstores **Guardian Pharmacies** fills prescriptions with name-brand drugs (from a licensed physician within Singapore) and carries a large selection of toiletry items. Convenient locations include no. B1-05 Centrepoint Shopping Centre (✆ 65/737-4835), Changi International Airport Terminal 2 (✆ 65/545-4233), no. 02-139 Marina Square (✆ 65/333-9565), and no. B1-04 Raffles Place MRT Station (✆ 65/535-2762).

Electricity Standard electrical current is 220 volts AC (50 cycles). Consult your concierge to see if your hotel has converters and plug adapters in-house for you to use. If you are using sensitive equipment, do not trust the

cheap voltage transformers. Nowadays, a lot of electrical equipment—
including portable radios and laptop computers—comes with built-in
converters, so you can follow the manufacturer's directions for changing
them over. FYI, videocassettes taped on different voltage currents are
recorded on machines with different record and playback cycles. Prerecorded videotapes are not interchangeable between currents unless you
have special equipment that can play either kind.

Embassies & Consulates See "Visitor Information & Entry Requirements,"
earlier in this chapter.

Emergencies For **police,** dial © **999.** For **medical** or **fire** emergencies, call
© **995.**

Etiquette & Customs See "Etiquette & Customs," above.

Holidays See the "Public Holidays & Events," earlier in this chapter.

Information See "Visitor Information," earlier in this chapter.

Internet Access Internet cafes are becoming common throughout the
city, with usage costs between S$4 and S$5 (US$2.30 and US$2.85) per
hour (keep in mind that if you use the Internet in your hotel's business
center, you'll pay a much higher price). Almost every shopping mall has
one, especially along Orchard Road, and there are cybercafes in both terminals at Changi Airport. In the Historic District, there are a few in Stamford House, just across from City Hall MRT Station. Check out **Chills Café,**
no. 01-01 Stamford House, 39 Stamford Rd. (© **65/883-1016;** open
9:30am–midnight daily).

Language The official languages are Malay, Chinese (Mandarin), Tamil,
and English. Malay is the national language, while English is the language
for government operations, law, and major financial transactions. Most
Singaporeans are at least bilingual, with many speaking one or more
dialects of Chinese, English, and some Malay

Liquor Laws The legal age for alcohol purchase and consumption is
18 years. Some of the smaller clubs rarely check identification, but the
larger ones will and sometimes require patrons to be 21 years old to enter,
just to weed out younger crowds. Public drunk-and-disorderly behavior is
against the law and could snag you for up to S$1,000 in fines for the first
offense, or even imprisonment—which is unlikely but still a great way to
ruin a vacation. There are strict drinking and driving laws, and roadblocks
are set up on weekends to catch party people on their way home to the
housing developments.

Mail Most hotels have mail services at the front counter. Singapore Post
has centrally located offices at no. 04-15 Ngee Ann City/Takashimaya
Shopping Centre (© 65/6738-6899); Tang's department store at 320 Orchard
Rd. no. 03-00 (© 65/6738-5899); Chinatown Point, 133 New Bridge Rd. no.
02-42/43/44 (© 65/6538-7899); Change Alley, 16 Collyer Quay no. 02-02
Hitachi Tower (© 65/6538-6899); and 231 Bain St. no. 01-03 Bras Basah
Complex (© 65/6339-8899). Plus, there are five branches at Changi Inter-
national Airport.

The going rate for international air-mail letters to North America and
Europe is S$1 (US55¢) for 20g, plus S35¢ (US20¢) for each additional 10g.

For international airmail service to Australia and New Zealand, the rate is S70¢ (US40¢) for 20g, plus S30¢ (US15¢) for each additional 10g. Postcards and aerograms to all destinations are S50¢ (US30¢).

Your hotel will accept mail sent for you at its address. American Express has a special mail delivery and holding deal for card members.

Maps The Singapore Street Directory, a book detailing every section of the island, is carried by most taxi drivers and can be very helpful if you're trying to get someplace and the driver either doesn't know where it is or can't understand you. The street listing in the front will direct you to the corresponding map. A good cabbie can take it from there. Other good maps of the major city areas can be found in free STB publications, and there are also a few commercially produced maps sold in all major bookstores here.

Newspapers & Magazines Local English newspapers available are the *International Herald Tribune, The Business Times, The Straits Times, Today,* and *USA Today International.* Following an article criticizing the Singapore government, the *Asian Wall Street Journal* was banned from wide distribution in Singapore. Most of the major hotels are allowed to carry it, though, so ask around and you can find one. The *New Paper* is an "alternative publication" that might be a useful source for finding out what's happening around town. Major hotels, bookstores, and magazine shops sell a wide variety of international magazines.

Pets Singapore has strict quarantine regulations, so don't even think about bringing a pet.

Police Given the strict law enforcement reputation in Singapore, you can bet that the officers here don't have the greatest senses of humor. If you find yourself being questioned about anything, big or small, be dead serious and most respectful. For emergencies, call ✆ **999.** If you need to call the police headquarters, dial ✆ **65/6224-0000.**

If you are arrested, you have the right to legal council, but only when the police decide that you can exercise that right. You get no call unless they give you permission. Bottom line: Don't get arrested.

Smoking It's against the law to smoke in public buses, elevators, theaters, cinemas, air-conditioned restaurants, shopping centers, government offices, and taxi queues.

Taxes Many hotels and restaurants advertise rates followed by "+++." The first + is the goods and services tax (GST), which is levied at 3% of the purchase. The second + is 1% cess (a 1% tax levied by the STB on all tourism-related activities). The third is a 10% gratuity. See the "Customs Regulations" section earlier in this chapter for information on the GST Tourist Refund Scheme, which lets you recover the GST for purchases of goods over S$300 (US$171) in value.

Telephones **To call Singapore:** If you're calling Singapore from the United States:

1. Dial the international access code: 011.

2. Dial the country code: 65.

3. Dial the 8-digit phone number. So, the whole number you'd dial would be 011-65-0000-0000.

To make international calls: To place a direct international call from Singapore, dial the international access code (001), the country code (U.S. and Canada: 1; Australia: 61; Republic of Ireland: 353; New Zealand: 64; U.K.: 44), the area or city code, and the number.

For operator assistance: If you need operator assistance in making a call, dial ℂ **104.**

For telephone directory assistance, dial ℂ **100.**

Time Zone Singapore Standard Time is 8 hours ahead of Greenwich mean time (GMT). International time differences will change during daylight saving or summer time. Basic time differences are: New York -13, Los Angeles -16, Montreal -13, Vancouver -16, London -8, Brisbane +3, Darwin +1, Melbourne +2, Sydney +3, and Auckland +4. For the current time within Singapore, call ℂ **1711.**

Tipping Tipping is discouraged at hotels and bars and in taxis. Basically, the deal here is not to tip. A gratuity is automatically added into guest checks, and there's no need to slip anyone an extra buck for carrying bags or such. It's not expected.

Water Tap water in Singapore passes World Health Organization standards and is potable.

⌜*Tips* Telephone Dialing Info at a Glance

- **To place a call from your home country to Singapore:** Dial the international access code (011 in the U.S., 0011 in Australia, or 00 in the U.K., Ireland, and New Zealand), plus the country code (**65**), plus the seven-digit phone number (for example, 011-65/000-0000). Note that many hotels have toll-free numbers for calling from all these countries; where this is the case, I've listed them in the individual hotel reviews.

- **To call Malaysia from Singapore:** Via an operator, dial 109. To call direct, dial the access code for the trunk line that links the two countries (007), plus Malaysia's country code (60), plus the city code and the number (for example, 005-60/000-0000).

- **To place a direct international call from Singapore:** Dial the international access code (001), the country code (U.S. and Canada: 1; Australia: 61; Republic of Ireland: 353; New Zealand: 64; U.K.: 44), the area or city code, and the number.

- **To reach the international operator:** Dial 104.

- **To place a call within Singapore:** Dial the seven-digit number. The "65" prefix need not be used. Toll-free numbers in Singapore use the standard "1-800" prefix.

3 Where to Stay

Budget accommodations are not a high priority in Singapore. Between the business community's demand for luxury on the one hand and the inflated Singaporean real estate market on the other, room prices tend to be high. What this means for leisure travelers is that you might end up paying for a business center you'll never use or a 24-hour stress-reliever masseuse you'll never call—and all this without the benefit of a corporate discount rate. Don't fret, though: there's a range of accommodations out there—you just have to know where to find 'em.

In considering where you'll stay, think about what you'll be doing in Singapore—that way, you can choose a hotel that's close to the particular action that suits you. (On the other hand, because Singapore is a small place and public transportation is excellent, nothing's really ever too far away.)

Orchard Road has the largest cluster of hotels in the city and is right in the heart of Singaporean shopping mania—the malls and wide sidewalks where locals and tourists stroll to see and be seen. The **Historic District** has hotels that are near museums and sights, while those in **Marina Bay** center more on the business professionals who come to Singapore for Suntec City, the giant convention and exhibition center located there. **Chinatown** and **Tanjong Pagar** have some lovely boutique hotels in quaint back streets, and **Shenton Way** has a couple of high-rise places for the convenience of people doing business in the downtown business district. Many hotels have free morning and evening shuttle buses to Orchard Road, Suntec City, and Shenton Way. I've also listed two hotels on **Sentosa,** an island to the south that's a popular day or weekend trip for many Singaporeans. (It's connected to Singapore by a causeway.)

Rates for double rooms range from as low as S$95 (US$54) at the Strand on Bencoolen (a famous backpacker's strip) to as high as S$650 (US$371) a night at the exclusive Raffles Hotel. Average rooms are usually in the S$300 (US$330) range, but keep in mind that although all prices listed in this book are the going rates, they rarely represent what you'll actually pay. In fact, you should never have to pay the advertised rate in a Singapore hotel because many offer promotional rates. When you call for your reservation, always ask what special deals they are running and how you can get the lowest price for your room. Many times hotels that have just completed renovations offer discounts, and most have special weekend or long-term stay programs. Also be sure to inquire about free add-ons. Complimentary breakfast and other services can have added value that makes a difference in the end.

For the purposes of this guide, I've divided hotels into the categories very expensive, S$450 (US$257) and up; expensive, S$350 to S$450 (US$200–US$257); moderate, S$200 to S$350 (US$114–US$200); and inexpensive, under S$200 (US$114).

TAXES & SERVICE CHARGES   All rates listed are in Singapore dollars, with U.S. dollar equivalents provided as well (remember to check the exchange rate when you're planning, though, because it might fluctuate). Most rates do not include the so-called "+++" taxes and charges: the 10% service charge, 5% goods and services tax (GST), and 1% cess (a 1% tax levied by the STB on all tourism-related activities). Keep these in mind when figuring your budget. Some budget hotels quote discount rates inclusive of all taxes.

THE BUSY SEASON   The busy season is from January to around June. In the late summer months, business travel dies down and hotels try to make up for drooping occupancy rates by going after the leisure market. In fall, even tourism drops off somewhat, making the season ripe for budget-minded visitors. These might be the best times to get a deal. Probably the worst time to negotiate is between Christmas and the Chinese New Year, when folks travel on vacation and to see their families.

MAKING RESERVATIONS ON THE GROUND   If you are not able to make a reservation before your trip, there is a reservation service available at Changi International Airport. The Singapore Hotel Association operates desks in both Terminals 1 and 2, with reservation services based upon room availability for many hotels. Discounts for these arrangements are sometimes as high as 30%. The desks are open daily from 7:30am to 11:30pm.

THE HISTORIC DISTRICT
VERY EXPENSIVE

The Fullerton Singapore ★★   The newest darling of Singapore's luxury hotel market, The Fullerton is giving competitors like the Ritz-Carlton and the Four Seasons a run for their money. Originally built in 1928, this squat administrative building at the mouth of the Singapore River once housed the General Post Office. Today it is flanked by the urban skyline, and its classical facade, with its Doric columns and tall porticos, looks more mundane than opulent. But designers have done a superb job, restoring Italian marble floors, coffered ceilings, and cornices inside. The courtyard lobby is grand, with skylights above and Courtyard guest-room windows lining the inner face of the building. Rooms have been cleverly arranged to fit the original structure, featuring vaulted ceilings and tall windows. While the architectural style is antique, the rooms are anything but. In fresh shades of champagne, they feature large writing desks, deluxe stationery kits, flat-screen TVs, Sony PlayStations, and electronic safes big enough to hold your laptop. Big bathrooms have separate bathtub and shower stalls, mini-Stairmasters, and stylish Philippe Starck fixtures. The attentive service here is second to none.

1 Fullerton Sq., Singapore 049178. © 800/44-UTELL in the U.S. and Canada, 800/221-176 in Australia, 800/933-123 in New Zealand, or 65/6733-8388. Fax 65/6735-8388. www.fullertonhotel.com. 400 units. S$450–S$650 (US$257–US$371) double; from S$800 (US$457) suite. AE, DC, MC, V. 5-min. walk to Raffles Place MRT. **Amenities:** 3 restaurants; bar and lobby lounge; outdoor infinity pool w/view of the Singapore River; fitness center w/Jacuzzi, sauna, and steam; spa w/massage and beauty treatments; concierge; limousine service; business center; shopping arcade; salon; 24-hr. room service; babysitting; same-day laundry service; dry cleaning; nonsmoking rooms; executive-level rooms. *In room:* A/C, TV w/satellite programming and in-house movies, dataport w/direct Internet access, minibar, coffee/tea-making facilities, hair dryer, iron, safe.

Raffles Hotel ★★   Legendary since its establishment in 1887, and named after Singapore's first British colonial administrator, Sir Stamford Raffles, this posh hotel is one of the most recognizable names in Southeast Asian hospitality. Originally it was a bungalow, but by the 1920s and 1930s it had expanded to become a mecca for celebrities like Charlie Chaplin and Douglas Fairbanks, writers like Somerset Maugham and Noël Coward, and various and sundry kings, sultans, and politicians (the famous Long Bar, where the Singapore Sling was invented, is located here). Always at the center of Singapore's colonial high life, it has hosted balls, tea dances, and jazz functions, and during World War II it was the last rallying point for the British in the face of Japanese occupation and the first place for refugee prisoners of war released from concentration camps. In 1987, the Raffles Hotel was declared a landmark and was restored to its early-20th-century splendor, with grand arches, 4.2m (14-ft.) molded ceilings with spinning fans, tiled teak and marble floors, oriental carpets, and period

Urban Singapore Accommodations

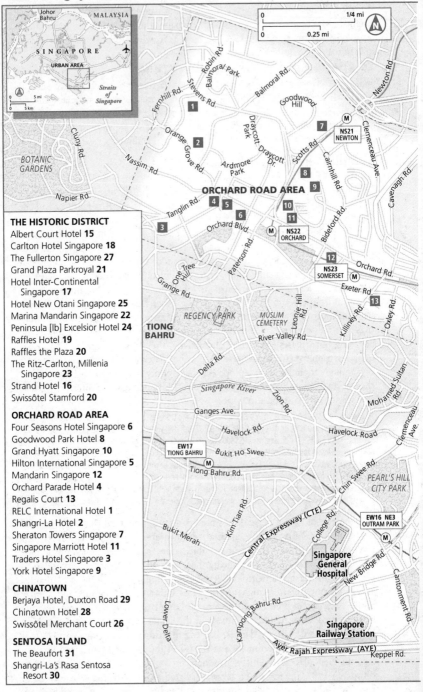

THE HISTORIC DISTRICT
Albert Court Hotel **15**
Carlton Hotel Singapore **18**
The Fullerton Singapore **27**
Grand Plaza Parkroyal **21**
Hotel Inter-Continental
  Singapore **17**
Hotel New Otani Singapore **25**
Marina Mandarin Singapore **22**
Peninsula [lb] Excelsior Hotel **24**
Raffles Hotel **19**
Raffles the Plaza **20**
The Ritz-Carlton, Millenia
  Singapore **23**
Strand Hotel **16**
Swissôtel Stamford **20**

ORCHARD ROAD AREA
Four Seasons Hotel Singapore **6**
Goodwood Park Hotel **8**
Grand Hyatt Singapore **10**
Hilton International Singapore **5**
Mandarin Singapore **12**
Orchard Parade Hotel **4**
Regalis Court **13**
RELC International Hotel **1**
Shangri-La Hotel **2**
Sheraton Towers Singapore **7**
Singapore Marriott Hotel **11**
Traders Hotel Singapore **3**
York Hotel Singapore **9**

CHINATOWN
Berjaya Hotel, Duxton Road **29**
Chinatown Hotel **28**
Swissôtel Merchant Court **26**

SENTOSA ISLAND
The Beaufort **31**
Shangri-La's Rasa Sentosa
  Resort **30**

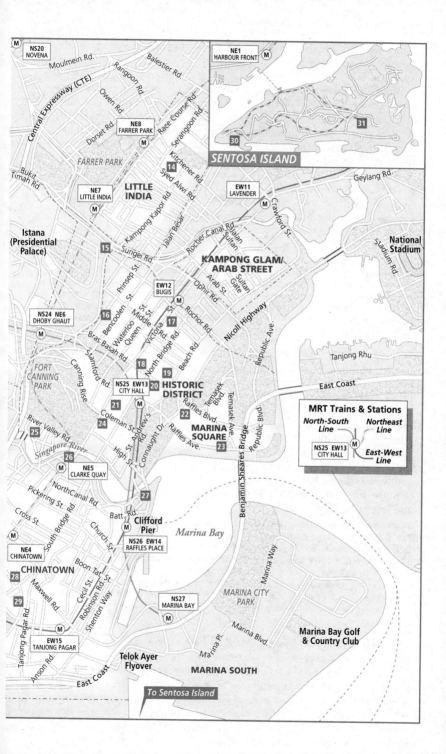

furnishings. Outside, the facade of the main building was similarly restored, complete with the elegant cast-iron portico and the verandas that encircle the upper stories.

Because it is a national landmark, thousands of people pass through the open lobby each day, so in addition there's a private inner lobby marked off for "residents" only. Nothing feels better than walking along the dark teak floors of the verandas, past little rattan-furnished relaxation areas overlooking the green tropical courtyards. Each suite entrance is like a private apartment door: Enter past the small living and dining area dressed in oriental carpets and reproduction furniture; then pass through louvered doors into the bedroom with its four-poster bed and beautiful armoire, ceiling fan twirling high above. Now imagine that you're a colonial traveler, fresh in town from a long ocean voyage. Raffles is the only hotel in Singapore where you can still fully play out this fantasy, and it can be a lot of fun. Other unique features include a hotel museum, a popular theater playhouse, and an excellent culinary academy.

1 Beach Rd., Singapore 189673. ℂ 800/232-1886 in the U.S. and Canada, or 65/6337-1886. Fax 65/6339-7650. www.raffleshotel.com. 103 suites. S$650–S$6,000 (US$371–US$3,429) suite. AE, DC, MC, V. Next to City Hall MRT. **Amenities:** 8 restaurants; 2 bars and a billiard room; small outdoor pool; fitness center w/Jacuzzi, sauna, steam, and spa; concierge; limousine service; business center; shopping arcade; salon; 24-hr. room service; babysitting; same-day laundry service/dry cleaning; personal butler service. *In room:* A/C, TV w/satellite programming and in-room VCR, fax, dataport w/direct Internet access, minibar, coffee/tea-making facilities, hair dryer, safe.

The Ritz-Carlton, Millenia Singapore ★★★ The ultimate in luxury hotels, The Ritz-Carlton blazes trails with sophisticated ultramodern design, sumptuous comfort, and stimulating art. Grand public spaces, lighted by futuristic window designs and splashed with artworks from the likes of Frank Stella, Dale Chihuly, David Hockney, and Andy Warhol, are a welcome change from international chain hotel design cliché. In comparison, guest rooms display a great deal of warmth and hominess. All rooms have spectacular views of either Kallang Bay or the more majestic Marina Bay. Even the bathrooms have views; the huge tubs are placed under octagonal picture windows so you can gaze as you bathe. Oh, the decadence! Guest rooms here are about 25% larger than most five-star rooms elsewhere, providing ample space for big two-poster beds, and have full walk-in closets.

7 Raffles Ave., Singapore 039799. ℂ 800/241-3333 in the U.S. and Canada, 800/241-33333 in Australia, 800/241-33333 in New Zealand, 800/234-000 in the U.K., or 65/6337-8888. Fax 65/6338-0001. www.ritz carlton.com. 610 units. S$515–S$595 (US$294–US$340) double; from S$698 (US$399) suite. AE, DC, MC, V. 10-min. walk to City Hall MRT. **Amenities:** 3 restaurants; lobby lounge; outdoor pool and Jacuzzi; outdoor lighted tennis court; fitness center w/sauna, steam, and massage; concierge; limousine service; business center; shopping mall adjacent; 24-hr. room service; babysitting; same-day laundry service/dry cleaning; non-smoking rooms; executive-level rooms. *In room:* A/C, TV w/satellite programming and in-house movies, dataport w/direct Internet access, minibar, coffee/tea-making facilities, hair dryer, iron, safe.

EXPENSIVE

Carlton Hotel Singapore ★★★ In April 2002, Carlton opened its new Premier Wing, a 19-story building, just next door to its 26-story Main Wing. Leisure travelers will be most interested in the newly refurbished and lower-priced superior and deluxe rooms in the Main Wing. While rooms in both categories are the same size and have all been smartly redone in contemporary neutral tones, deluxe rooms have broadband Internet access in-room, a flat-screen TV, plus marble bathroom decor (superiors are humble ceramic tile). The new building houses premier deluxe rooms, which, for a premium, feature larger bathrooms with separate bathtub and shower stall, an in-room safe to fit your laptop, and access to a coin-operated launderette. All public spaces have been upgraded as well, including the lobby entrance, an alfresco coffee shop, and a tiny wine and cigar room. The location, in the center of the historic district, is terrific. Ask for a room with a view of the city.

76 Bras Basah Rd., Singapore 189558. (C) **65/6338-8333**. Fax 65/6339-6866. www.carlton.com.sg. 627 units. S$350–S$400 (US$200–US$229) double; from S$480 (US$274) suite. AE, DC, MC, V. 5-min. walk to City Hall MRT. **Amenities:** 2 restaurants; lobby lounge; outdoor pool; fitness center w/sauna, steam, and massage; concierge; tour desk; car-rental desk; limousine service; shuttle service; business center; 24-hr. room service; babysitting; same-day laundry service/dry cleaning; nonsmoking rooms; executive-level rooms. *In room:* A/C, TV w/satellite programming and in-house movies, minibar, coffee/tea-making facilities.

Hotel Inter-Continental Singapore ★

The government let Inter-Continental build a hotel in this spot with one ironclad stipulation: The hotel chain had to retain the original shophouses on the block and incorporate them into the hotel design. No preservation, no hotel. Reinforcing the foundation, Hotel Inter-Continental built up from there, giving touches of old architectural style to the lobby, lounge, and other public areas on the bottom floors while imbuing it with the feel of a modern hotel. Features like beamed ceilings and wooden staircases are warmly accentuated with Chinese and European antique reproductions, oriental carpets, and local artwork. The second and third floors have "Shophouse Rooms" styled with such Peranakan trappings as carved hardwood furnishings and floral linens, and with homey touches like potted plants and carpets over wooden floors. These rooms are very unique, presenting a surprising element of local flair that you don't often find in large chain hotels. Guest rooms on higher levels are large, with formal European styling and large luxurious bathrooms.

80 Middle Rd., Singapore 188966 (near Bugis Junction). (C) **800/327-0200** in the U.S. and Canada, 800/221-335 in Australia, 800/442-215 in New Zealand, 800/0289-387 in the U.K., or 65/6338-7600. Fax 65/6338-7366. www.interconti.com. 406 units. S$440–S$480 (US$251–US$275) double; from S$630 (US$360) suite. AE, DC, MC, V. Bugis MRT. **Amenities:** 3 restaurants; bar and lobby lounge; outdoor pool; fitness center w/Jacuzzi, sauna, and massage; concierge; limousine service; business center; shopping mall adjacent; 24-hr. room service; babysitting; same-day laundry service/dry cleaning; executive-level rooms. *In room:* A/C, TV w/satellite programming and in-house movies, minibar, coffee/tea-making facilities, hair dryer, safe.

Marina Mandarin Singapore ★★

There are a few hotels in the Marina Bay area built around the atrium concept, and, of them, this one is the loveliest. The atrium lobby opens up to ceiling skylights 21 stories above, guest corridor balconies fringed with vines line the sides, and in the center hangs a glistening metal mobile sculpture in red and gold. One of the most surprising details is the melodic chirping of caged songbirds, which fills the open space every morning. In the evening, live classical music from the lobby bar drifts upward.

The guest rooms are equally impressive: large and cool, with two desk spaces and balconies standard for each room. Try to get the Marina view for that famous Shenton Way skyline towering above the bay. All bathrooms have double sinks, a separate shower and tub, and a bidet. Unique Venus Rooms, for women travelers, include potpourri, bath oils, custom pillows, and hair curler. **One plus:** The Marina Square Shopping Center attached to the lobby adds dozens of shops and services.

6 Raffles Blvd., Marina Square, Singapore 039594. (C) **65/6338-3388**. Fax 65/6845-1001. www.marina-mandarin.com.sg. 575 units. S$380–S$450 (US$217–US$257) double; S$480 (US$274) executive club; from S$600 (US$343) suite. AE, DC, MC, V. 10-min. walk to City Hall MRT. **Amenities:** 3 restaurants; English pub and lobby lounge; outdoor pool; outdoor lighted tennis courts; squash courts; fitness center w/Jacuzzi, sauna, steam, and massage; concierge; limousine service; business center; shopping mall adjacent; salon; 24-hr. room

service; babysitting; same-day laundry service/dry cleaning; nonsmoking rooms; executive-level rooms. *In room:* A/C, TV w/satellite programming and in-house movies, minibar, coffee/tea-making facilities, hair dryer, safe.

Raffles the Plaza ★★★   This has to be the best location in the city. Above an MRT hub and next to one of the largest shopping centers in Singapore, you won't find any inconveniences here. The lobby is studied serenity with soft lighting and music, a lovely escape from the crazy mall and hot streets. Perhaps the best reason to stay is the Amrita spa and fitness center, the largest of its type. It includes a huge state-of-the-art gym with exercise and relaxation classes, a pool, hot and cold plunge pools, steam and sauna, and endless treatment rooms with Asian and European treatments from beauty and rejuvenation. Standard rooms are large and comfortable, having been recently updated with new soft goods. Premier deluxe rooms, however, are stunningly contemporary, with cushy bedding, big desk spaces, Bose Wave systems, and incredible bathrooms—crisp white tiles, glistening glass countertops, polished chrome fixtures, and a shower that simulates rainfall.

2 Stamford Road, Singapore 178882. © **65/6339-7777.** Fax 65/6337-1554. www.raffles-theplazahotel.com. 769 units. S$210–S$420 (US$120–US$241) double; from S$1,000–S$3,150 (US$576–US$1,815) suite. AE, DC, MC, V. **Amenities:** 10 restaurants; martini bar; lobby lounge; a live jazz venue; outdoor pool; spa w/gym, Jacuzzi, sauna, steam, and massage; concierge; limousine service; business center; shopping arcade adjacent; 24-hr. room service; babysitting; same-day laundry service/dry cleaning; nonsmoking rooms; executive-level rooms. *In room:* A/C, TV w/satellite programming and in-house movies, minibar, coffee/tea-making facilities, hair dryer, safe.

MODERATE

Grand Plaza Parkroyal ★★   The Grand Plaza was built on top of (and incorporating) 2 blocks of prewar shophouses, and you can see hints of shophouse detail throughout the lobby, which is otherwise like any other hotel's. The old alleyway that ran between the shophouse blocks has been transformed into a courtyard where dinner is served alfresco. The hotel is located at the corner of Coleman and Hill streets, just across from the Armenian Church, the Asian Civilisations Museum, the Singapore Arts Museum, and Fort Canning Park— and if that's not convenient enough, a shuttle will take you to Orchard Road. Guest rooms are of smaller size, have decent closet space, and sport sharp Italian contemporary furniture in natural tones, with homey touches like snugly comforters on all the beds. This property does not stand out from the crowd, except for the St. Gregory Marine Spa, a popular and discrete full-service facility.

10 Coleman St., Singapore 179809. © **65/6336-3456.** Fax 65/6339-9311. www.plazapacifichotels.com. 326 units. S$320–S$340 (US$183–US$194) double; from S$500 (US$286) suite. AE, DC, MC, V. 5-min. walk to City Hall MRT. **Amenities:** 3 restaurants; lobby lounge; outdoor pool w/view of Armenian Church across the street; fitness center; spa w/Jacuzzi, sauna, steam, and massage; concierge; shuttle service; business center; 24-hr. room service; babysitting; same-day laundry service/dry cleaning; executive-level rooms. *In room:* A/C, TV w/satellite programming, minibar, coffee/tea-making facilities, safe.

Hotel New Otani Singapore   The Hotel New Otani sits along the Singapore River just next to Clarke Quay (a popular spot for nightlife, dining, and shopping) and a stroll away from the Historic District. At night, you have access to nearby Boat Quay bars and restaurants to one side, and to the unique clubs of Mohamed Sultan Road on the other. The hotel was renovated in 1993, and unique additions (to all rooms) include multimedia PCs with Microsoft Office and tourist information. Internet access and computer games are also available for an extra charge. All rooms have small balconies with good views of the river, the financial district, Fort Canning Park, or Chinatown, and the standard rooms have large luxurious bathrooms like those you typically see in more deluxe accommodations. Facilities include a large outdoor pool and a fitness center with aerobics, a Jacuzzi, sauna, facials, and massage (you can even get a massage poolside). The hotel runs daily shuttle service to Orchard Road, Shenton Way, and Marina Square, plus a complimentary evening river cruise for all room categories.

177A River Valley Rd., Singapore 179031. ℂ 800/421-8795 in the U.S. and Canada, or 65/6338-3333. Fax 65/6339-2854. www.newotanisingapore.com. 408 units. S$320–S$360 (US$183–US$206) double; from S$600 (US$343) suite. AE, DC, MC, V. Far from MRT stations. **Amenities:** 3 restaurants; lobby lounge; outdoor pool; fitness center; concierge; tour desk; limousine service; shuttle service; business center; shopping mall adjacent; 24-hr. room service; babysitting; same-day laundry service/dry cleaning; executive-level rooms. *In room:* A/C, TV w/satellite programming, minibar, coffee/tea-making facilities, safe, in-room PC w/direct Internet access.

Peninsula • Excelsior Hotel ★★ *Value*   In 2000, two of Singapore's busiest tourist-class hotels merged, combining their lobby and facilities into one giant value-for-money property. The location is excellent, in the Historic District within walking distance to Chinatown and Boat Quay. It's a popular pick for groups, but don't let the busloads of tourists steer you away. There are some great deals to be had here, especially if you request the guest rooms in the Peninsula tower. These are large and colorful, with big picture windows, some of which have stunning views of the city, the Singapore River, and the marina. Surprisingly, these rooms are priced about S$10 (US$5.70) lower than rooms in the Excelsior tower, which are smaller and, frankly, look like they haven't seen a decor update since the far-out 1970s. At the time of writing, they were in the process of wiring the place for in-room Internet access.

5 Coleman St., Singapore 179805. ℂ 65/6337-2200. Fax 65/6336-3847. www.ytchotels.com.sg. 600 units. S$240–S$260 (US$144–US$156) double; S$360–S$440 (US$216–US$263) suite. AE, DC, MC, V. 5-min. walk to City Hall MRT. **Amenities:** Restaurant; bar and lobby lounge; 2 outdoor pools; fitness center w/Jacuzzi; concierge; tour desk; business center; shopping mall adjacent; 24-hr. room service; babysitting; same-day laundry service/dry cleaning. *In room:* A/C, TV, minibar, coffee/tea-making facilities, hair dryer, safe.

Swissôtel Stamford ★★★ *Value*   You'd think a room in the tallest hotel in the world would cost a bundle, but this gem is reasonably priced. Besides, with an amazing location, right on top of a subway hub and a huge shopping complex, walking distance from many sights and attractions, this hotel is great value for money. On a clear day, you can see Indonesia, so make sure you request a room with a view. Done in fresh white linens, cool neutral fabrics, and new furnishings in golden wood tones, these large rooms also feature private balconies and full toiletries in marble bathrooms. Executive rooms in The Stamford Crest also have Bose hi-fi systems; ergonomically designed writing tables and chairs; a multifunction printer, fax, and copier; plus bathrooms with a view. It's managed by Raffles International, so you can be sure of friendly and professional service.

2 Stamford Rd., Singapore 178882. ℂ 800/637-9477 in the U.S. and Canada, and 800/121-043 in Australia, or 65/6338-8585. Fax 65/6338-2862. www.swissotel-thestamford.com. 1,200 units. S$195–S$420 (US$110–US$236) double; S$600–S$3300 (US$337–US$1,854) suite. AE, DC, MC, V. City Centre MRT. **Amenities:** 10 restaurants; martini bar; lobby lounge; a live jazz venue; outdoor pool; spa w/gym, Jacuzzi, sauna, steam, and massage; concierge; limousine service; business center; shopping arcade adjacent; 24-hr. room service; babysitting; same-day laundry service/dry cleaning; nonsmoking rooms; executive-level rooms. *In room:* A/C, TV w/satellite programming and in-house movies, minibar, coffee/tea-making facilities, hair dryer, safe.

INEXPENSIVE

Albert Court Hotel ★★ *Value*   This hotel was first conceived as part of the Urban Renewal Authority's master plan to revitalize this block, which involved the restoration of two rows of prewar shophouses. The eight-story boutique hotel that emerged has all the Western comforts but has retained the charm of its shophouse roots. Decorators placed local Peranakan touches everywhere from the carved teak furnishings in traditional floral design to the antique china cups used for tea service in the rooms. (**Guaranteed:** The sight of these cups brings misty-eyed nostalgia to the hearts of Singaporeans.) Guest room details like the teak molding, bathroom tiles in bright Peranakan colors, and old-time brass electrical switches give this place true local charm and distinction. A recent refurbishment, completed in 2001, gives an added freshness to the rooms. Albert Court will offer new courtyard rooms, in the renovated houses that front the hotel's courtyard, from spring 2003. They are guaranteed to contain all the local touches that make this hotel stand out from the rest.

180 Albert St., Singapore 189971. ⓒ 65/6339-3939. Fax 65/6339-3252. www.albertcourt.com.sg. 136 units. S$185–S$200 (US$106–US$114) double. AE, DC, MC, V. 5-min. walk to Bugis MRT. **Amenities:** 3 restaurants; small lobby lounge; tour desk; limited room service; babysitting; same-day laundry service/dry cleaning. *In room:* A/C, TV w/satellite programming, minibar, coffee/tea-making facilities, hair dryer, safe.

Strand Hotel ⓡ (Value) The Strand is by far the best of the backpacker places in Singapore. The lobby is far nicer than you'd expect, and for a promotional price of S$69 (US$39.35), you get a clean and neat room. Although there are some hints that you really are staying in a budget hotel—older decor and uncoordinated furniture sets, for instance—the place provides some little niceties, like hotel stationery. The no-frills bathrooms are clean and adequate. There are no coffee/tea-making facilities, but there is 24-hour room service and a cafe on the premises. Free parking is available.

25 Bencoolen St., Singapore 189619. ⓒ 65/6338-1866. Fax 65/6338-1330. 130 units. S$95 (US$54) double; S$110 (US$63) triple; S$140 (US$80) 4-person sharing. AE, DC, MC, V. 10-min. walk to City Hall MRT. **Amenities:** Restaurant; 24-hr. room service; same-day laundry service. *In room:* A/C, TV.

CHINATOWN
EXPENSIVE

Swissôtel Merchant Court ⓡ Merchant Court's convenient location and facilities make it very popular with leisure travelers. Situated on the Singapore River, the hotel has easy access not only to Chinatown and the Historic District, but also to Clarke Quay and Boat Quay, with their multitude of dining and nightlife options. It will become even more convenient when the new MRT stop opens just outside its doors in early 2003. Although this hotel's guest rooms aren't the biggest or most plush in the city, I never felt claustrophobic due to the large windows, uncluttered decor, and cooling atmosphere. Try to get a room with a view of the river or landscaped pool area. Convenience is provided by a self-service launderette, drink and snack vending machines on each floor, and unstocked minibar fridge, so you can buy your own provisions. The hotel touts itself as a city hotel with a resort feel, with a landscaped pool area (with a view of the river).

20 Merchant Rd., Singapore 058281. ⓒ 800/637-9477 in the U.S. and Canada, 800/121-043 in Australia, 800/637-94771 in the U.K., or 65/6337-2288. Fax 65/6334-0606. www.swissotel.com. 476 units. S$315–S$375 (US$180–US$214) double; from S$810 (US$463) suite. AE, DC, MC, V. 10-min. walk to Raffles Place MRT. **Amenities:** Restaurant; bar; outdoor pool; fitness center and spa w/Jacuzzi, sauna, steam, massage, and beauty treatments; 24-hr. room service; babysitting; same-day laundry service/dry cleaning; nonsmoking rooms; executive-level rooms. *In room:* A/C, TV w/satellite programming and in-house movies, dataport w/direct Internet access, minibar, coffee/tea-making facilities, hair dryer, safe.

MODERATE

Berjaya Hotel, Duxton Road ⭐   Formerly The Duxton, this was one of the first accommodations in Singapore to experiment with the boutique hotel concept, transforming its shophouse structure into a small hotel, and doing it with an elegance that earned it great international acclaim. From the outside, the place has old-world charm equal to any lamplit European cobblestone street, but step inside and there are very few details to remind you that you are in a quaint old shophouse—or in the historic Chinese district, for that matter. It's done entirely in turn-of-the-20th-century styling that includes reproduction Chippendale furniture, hand-painted wallpapers, and pen-and-ink Audubon-style drawings. Unfortunately, in recent years the hotel has dropped in service quality and the place has grown frayed around the edges. The recent takeover by Malaysian four-star hotel chain Berjaya is the first clue that this former luxury accommodation has gone downhill. Berjaya has no plans for refurbishment, which this place really needs. Each room is different (to fit the structure of the building), and some can be quite small, with limited views. Garden suites feature a lovely little courtyard. Building regulations do not allow for a pool, and space does not allow for fitness centers (they will arrange access to a nearby fitness center for you).

83 Duxton Rd., Singapore 089540. © 65/6227-7678. Fax 65/6227-1232. www.berjayaresorts.com. 50 units. S$210–S$250 (US$120–US$143) double; S$290 (US$166) suite. AE, DC, MC, V. 5-min. walk to Tanjong Pagar MRT. **Amenities:** Restaurant; lobby bar; shuttle service; limited room service; babysitting; same-day laundry service/dry cleaning. *In room:* A/C, TV w/satellite programming and in-house movies, minibar, coffee/tea-making facilities, hair dryer, safe.

INEXPENSIVE

Chinatown Hotel ⭐   Chinatown Hotel definitely has its pros and cons, but for clean rooms, friendly service, and a good rate, it's one of my favorites. *Be prepared:* Because this is a boutique hotel with limited space, the rooms, though modern and well maintained, are tiny, and the bathrooms are the shower—just a shower head coming out of the wall as you stand in front of the sink. Some rooms have no windows, so specify when you make reservations if you're fond of natural light. Guest room TVs have one movie channel, and some rooms have been recently supplied with coffee/tea-making facilities, hair dryers (unique for this price category), and unstocked refrigerators. Or, you can enjoy free coffee, tea, and toast in the lobby. Larger hotels will charge higher rates so you can enjoy the luxury of a pool, fitness center, and multiple food and beverage outlets, but if you're in town to get out and see Singapore, it's nice to know you won't pay for things you'll never use. Besides, the folks at the front counter will always remember your name and are very professional without being impersonal.

12–16 Teck Lim Rd., Singapore 088388. © 65/6225-5166. Fax 65/6225-3912. www.chinatownhotel.com. 42 units. S$80–S$90 (US$48–US$54) double. AE, DC, MC, V. 5-min. walk to Outram MRT. **Amenities:** Same-day laundry service/dry cleaning; complimentary toast, coffee, and instant noodles in the lobby. *In room:* A/C, TV.

ORCHARD ROAD AREA
VERY EXPENSIVE

Four Seasons Hotel Singapore ⭐⭐⭐   Many upmarket hotels strive to convince you that staying with them is like visiting a wealthy friend. The Four Seasons delivers this promise. The guest rooms are very spacious and inviting, and even the standard rooms have creature comforts that you'd expect from a suite, such as complimentary fruit, terry bathrobes and slippers, CD and video disk players, and an extensive complimentary video disk and CD library that the concierge is just waiting to deliver selections from to your room. Each room has two-line speakerphones with voice mail and an additional dataport. The Italian marble bathrooms have double vanities, deep tubs, bidets, Neutrogena amenities, and surround speakers for the TV and stereo. Did I mention remote-control drapes? Everything here is comfort and elegance done to perfection (in fact, the beds here are so comfortable that they've sold almost 100 in the gift shop.) In the waiting area off the lobby, you can sink into soft sofas and appreciate the antiques and artwork selected from the owner's private collection. The fitness center has a state-of-the-art gymnasium with TV monitors, videos, tape players and CD and video disk players, a virtual-reality bike, aerobics, sauna, steam rooms, massage, facials, body wraps and aromatherapy treatments, and a staff of fitness professionals. Want more? How about a flotation tank and a Mind Gear Syncro-Energiser (a brain relaxer that uses pulsing lights), a billiards room, and an OptiGolf Indoor Pro-Golf System. Two indoor, air-conditioned tennis courts and two outdoor courts are staffed with a resident professional tennis coach to provide instruction or play a game. There are two pools: a 20m lap pool and a rooftop sun deck pool, both with adjacent Jacuzzis. Consider a standard room here before a suite in a less expensive hotel. You won't regret it.

190 Orchard Blvd., Singapore 248646. (C) 800/332-3442 in the U.S., 800/268-6282 in Canada, or 65/6734-1110. Fax 65/6733-0682. www.fourseasons.com 254 units. S$475–S$530 (US$271–US$303) double; S$620–S$4,500 (US$354–US$2,571) suite. AE, DC, MC, V. 5-min. walk to Orchard MRT. **Amenities:** 2 restaurants; bar; 2 outdoor pools w/adjacent Jacuzzis; 2 outdoor, lighted tennis courts and 2 indoor air-conditioned tennis courts; Singapore's best-equipped fitness center; spa w/sauna, steam, massage, and full menu of beauty and relaxation treatments; billiards room; concierge; limousine service; business center; 24-hr. room service; babysitting; same-day laundry service/dry cleaning; nonsmoking rooms; executive-level rooms. *In room:* A/C, TV w/satellite programming and in-room laserdisc player w/complimentary disks available, minibar, coffee/tea-making facilities, hair dryer, safe.

Goodwood Park Hotel ⚐

This national landmark, built in 1900, resembles a castle along the Rhine—having served originally as the Teutonia Club, a social club for the early German community. During World War II, high-ranking Japanese military used it as a residence, and later it served as a British war crimes court before being converted into a hotel. Since then, the hotel has expanded from 60 rooms to 235 and has hosted a long list of international celebrities and dignitaries.

For the money, there are more luxurious facilities, but while most hotels have bigger and better business and fitness centers (Goodwood has the smallest fitness center), only the Raffles Hotel can rival Goodwood Park's historic significance. The poolside suites off the Mayfair Pool are fabulous in slate tiles and polished wood, offering direct access to the small Mayfair Pool with its lush Balinese-style landscaping. There are also suites off the main pool, which is much larger but offers little privacy from the lobby and surrounding restaurants. The original building has large and airy guest rooms in a classic European decor, but beware of the showers, which have hand-held shower heads that clip to the wall, making it difficult to aim and impossible to keep the water from splashing out all over the bathroom floor. Newer rooms in the main wing are renovated in stark contemporary style. The extremely attentive staff always serves with a smile.

22 Scotts Rd., Singapore 228221. (C) 800/772-3890 in the U.S., 800/665-5919 in Canada, 800/89-95-20 in the U.K., or 65/6737-7411. Fax 65/6732-8558. www.goodwoodparkhotel.com.sg. 235 units. S$425–S$465 (US$243–US$266) double; S$615–S$650 (US$351–US$371) poolside suite; S$888–S$3,000 (US$507–US$1,714) suite. AE, DC, MC, V. 5-min. walk to Orchard MRT. **Amenities:** 6 restaurants; bar and

lobby lounge; 2 outdoor pools; tiny fitness center; spa; concierge; limousine service; business center; 24-hr. room service; babysitting; same-day laundry service/dry cleaning. *In room:* A/C, TV w/satellite programming and in-house movies, minibar, coffee/tea-making facilities, hair dryer, safe.

Grand Hyatt Singapore ⟨⟨

Rumor has it that, despite its fantastic location, this hotel was doing pretty poorly until it had a feng shui master come in and evaluate it for redecorating. According to the Chinese monk, because the lobby entrance was a wall of flat glass doors that ran parallel to the long reception desk in front, all the hotel's money was flowing from the desk right out the doors and into the street. To correct the problem, the doors are now set at right angles to each other, a fountain was built in the rear, and the reception was moved around a corner to the right of the lobby. Since then, the hotel has enjoyed some of the highest occupancy rates in town. Feng shui or not, the new decor is modern, sleek, and sophisticated, an elegant combination of polished black marble and deep wood. Terrace Wing guest rooms invite with plush duvet and golden colors, plus unique glass-enclosed alcoves looking over the hotel gardens. Bathrooms are large, with lots of marble counter space. The Grand Wing rooms are really suites, with separate living areas, small walk-in closets, and a separate work area. It's a very deluxe choice, especially after it complete its refurbishment plans to freshen the decor in mid-2003. The pool and fitness center are amazing. Located in the center of this city hotel, a four-story waterfall provides the perfect soundscape to match a lush jungle garden hugging the free-form pool and state-of-the-art gym.

10–12 Scotts Rd., Singapore 228211. © **800/223-1234** in the U.S. and Canada, or 65/6738-1234. Fax 65/ 6732-1696. www.hyatt.com. 685 units. S$450–S$490 double (US$257–US$280). AE, DC, MC, V. Near Orchard MRT. **Amenities:** 3 restaurants; lobby lounge; live music bar; landscaped outdoor pool; 2 outdoor lighted tennis courts; squash court and badminton court; excellent fitness center w/Jacuzzi, sauna, steam, massage, and spa treatments; concierge; limousine service; business center; 24-hr. room service; babysitting; same-day laundry service/dry cleaning; executive-level rooms. *In room:* A/C, TV w/satellite programming and in-house movies, dataport w/direct Internet access, minibar, coffee/tea-making facilities, hair dryer, iron, safe.

Shangri-La Hotel ⟨⟨⟨

The Shangri-La is a lovely place, with strolling gardens and an outdoor pool paradise that are great diversions from the hustle and bustle all around. Maybe that's why visiting VIPs like George Bush, Benazir Bhutto, and Nelson Mandela have all stayed here.

The hotel has three wings: The Tower Wing is the oldest, housing the lobby and most of the guest rooms, which were completely redone. Instead of the usual square, block hotel rooms of typical city hotels, Shang's added unusual angles and curves, sophisticated contemporary furnishings, and a refreshing wall of glass blocks that welcomes natural light into the giant bathroom and dressing area. Balconies were melded into the rooms to become reading nooks. The Garden Wing surrounds an open-air atrium with cascading waterfall and exotic plants. Rooms here are more resortlike, with natural textured wall coverings, tweedy carpeting, and woven bedspreads. These larger-size rooms also have bougainvillea-laden balconies overlooking the tropical landscaped pool area. The exclusive Valley Wing has a private entrance and very spacious rooms, linked to the main tower by a sky bridge that looks out over the hotel's 6 hectares (15 acres) of landscaped lawns, fruit trees, and flowers. These enormous rooms, with large bathrooms and dressing areas, will be refurbished during 2003, to brighten their classical European styling.

Orange Grove Rd., Singapore 258350. © **800/942-5050** in the U.S. and Canada, 800/222-448 in Australia, 800/442-179 in New Zealand, or 65/6737-3644. Fax 65/6733-3257. www.shangri-la.com. 760 units. S$480 (US$274) Tower double; S$560 (US$320) Garden double; S$520 (US$297) Horizon Club; S$590 (US$337)

Valley double; S$1,000–S$3,200 (US$571–US$1,829) suite. AE, DC, MC, V. 10-min. walk to Orchard MRT. **Amenities:** 4 restaurants; lobby lounge; resort-style outdoor landscaped pool; 3-hole pitch and putt course; 4 outdoor lighted tennis courts; fitness center w/glass walls looking out into gardens, w/Jacuzzi, sauna, steam, and massage; concierge; limousine service; business center; shopping arcade; salon; 24-hr. room service; babysitting; same-day laundry service/dry cleaning; nonsmoking rooms; executive-level rooms. *In room:* A/C, TV w/satellite programming and in-house movies, minibar, coffee/tea-making facilities, hair dryer, iron, safe.

EXPENSIVE

Hilton International Singapore ⟡   If you count the luxury cars that drive up to the valet at the Hilton, you'd think this is a good address to have while staying in Singapore. Well, to be honest, this Hilton doesn't measure up with some of the other properties worldwide and definitely can't compete with other hotels in this price category in Singapore. Probably the most famous feature of the Hilton is its shopping arcade, where you can find your Donna Karan, Louis Vuitton, Gucci—all the greats. Ask the concierge for a pager, and he'll page you for important calls while you window-shop or try some of the 45 fragrant vodkas at the lobby bar. With all this, the guest rooms should be pretty sumptuous, no? Well, no. The rooms are simpler than you'd expect, with nothing flashy or overdone. There are floor-to-ceiling windows in each, and while views in the front of the hotel are of Orchard Road and the Thai Embassy property, views in the back are not so hot. In this day and age, when business-class hotels are wrestling to outdo each other, the Hilton has a lot of catching up to do.

581 Orchard Rd., Singapore 238883. ℂ 800/445-8667 in the U.S., or 65/6737-2233. Fax 65/6732-2917. www.singapore.hilton.com. 423 units. S$380–S$400 (US$217–US$229) double; S$470 (US$269) club; from S$620 (US$354) suite. AE, DC, MC, V. Near Orchard MRT. **Amenities:** 2 restaurants; lobby lounge; outdoor pool; fitness center w/sauna and steam; concierge; limousine service; business center; shopping arcade; salon; 24-hr. room service; babysitting; same-day laundry service/dry cleaning; nonsmoking rooms; executive-level rooms. *In room:* A/C, TV w/satellite programming and in-house movies, minibar, coffee/tea-making facilities, hair dryer, safe.

Mandarin Singapore ⟡   Smack in the center of Orchard Road is the Mandarin Hotel, a two-tower complex with Singapore's most famous revolving restaurant topping it off like a little hat. The 39-story Main Tower opened in 1973, and with the opening of the South Wing 10 years later, the number of rooms expanded to 1,200. True to its name, the hotel reflects a Chinese aesthetic, beginning in the lobby with the huge marble mural of the *87 Taoist Immortals* and the carved wood chairs lining the walls. The South Wing is predominantly for leisure travelers, who have access to the tower via a side entrance. These guest rooms are slightly smaller than average and are furnished with Chinese-style dark wood modular units. Mandarin is planning to upgrade wall, floor, bed, and furniture coverings in 2003—thank God, because the old colors were dull and uninviting. New tones are promised to be warmer and more cozy. Larger Tower Wing rooms are for corporate travelers—they're larger, with posh Chinois decor, including carved rosewood furnishings, silk walls, and a translucent Chinese watercolored panel separating the bathroom from the sleeping area.

333 Orchard Rd., Singapore 238867. ℂ 65/6737-4411. Fax 65/6732-2361. www.mandarin-singapore.com. 1,200 units. S$365–S$427 (US$211–US$247) double; S$457 (US$264) club; from S$590 (US$341) suite. AE, DC, MC, V. Near Orchard MRT. **Amenities:** 4 restaurants; revolving observation lounge and lobby lounge; outdoor pool; fitness center w/Jacuzzi, sauna, steam, and massage; concierge; tour desk; limousine service; business center; shopping arcade; salon; 24-hr. room service; babysitting; same-day laundry service/dry cleaning; nonsmoking rooms; executive-level rooms. *In room:* A/C, TV w/satellite programming and in-house movies, minibar, coffee/tea-making facilities, safe.

Sheraton Towers Singapore ★★ One of the first things you see when you walk into the lobby of the Sheraton Towers is the service awards the place has won; check in, and you'll begin to see why they won 'em. With the deluxe (standard) room, they'll give you a suit pressing on arrival, daily newspaper delivery, shoeshine service, and complimentary movies. These newly refurbished rooms are handsome, with textured walls, plush carpeting, and a bed luxuriously fitted with down pillows and dreamy 100% Egyptian cotton bedding. Upgrade to a Tower room, and you get a personal butler, complimentary nightly cocktails and morning breakfast, free laundry, free local calls, your own pants press, and free use of the personal trainer in the fitness center. The cabana rooms, off the pool area, have all the services of the Tower Wing in a very private resort room. The 23 one-of-a-kind suite rooms each feature a different theme, Chinese regency, French, Italian, jungle, you name it—all are very unique, with hand-picked furnishings. Although the Sheraton is a luxe choice, you can find better deals.

39 Scotts Rd., Singapore 228230. © **800/325-3535** in the U.S. and Canada, 800/073535 in Australia, 800/ 325-35353 in New Zealand, 800/353535 in the U.K., or 65/6737-6888. Fax 65/6737-1072. www.sheraton.com. 413 units. S$400 (US$229) double; S$560 (US$320) cabana room; S$1,000–S$3,000 (US$571–US$1,714) suite. AE, DC, MC, V. 5-min. walk to Newton MRT. **Amenities:** 3 restaurants; lobby lounge; outdoor landscaped pool; fitness center w/sauna and massage; concierge; limousine service; 24-hr. business center; 24-hr. room service; babysitting; same-day laundry service/dry cleaning; nonsmoking rooms; executive-level rooms. *In room:* A/C, TV w/satellite programming and in-house movies, dataport w/direct Internet access, minibar, coffee/tea-making facilities, hair dryer, safe.

Singapore Marriott Hotel ★★ You can't get a better location than at the corner of Orchard and Scotts roads. Marriott's green-roofed pagoda tower is a well-recognized landmark on Orchard Road, but guest rooms inside tend to be smaller than average to fit in the octagonal structure. Luckily, the recent refurbishing scheme added lively colors to brighten the spaces with natural greens and floral fabrics. The palatial lobby has been overtaken by the Marriott Cafe, with weekend buffets that are so popular with the locals that there's a long queue. Outside, the Crossroads Café, spilling out onto the sidewalk, is a favorite place for international and Singaporean celebrities who like to be seen.

Marriott, which took over management of this property in 1995, caters to the business traveler, so the rooms on the club floors get most of the hotel's attention. The club lounge, for instance, has a great view, and there's not a tacky detail in the comfortable seating and dining areas.

320 Orchard Rd., Singapore 238865. © **800/228-9290** in the U.S. and Canada, 800/251-259 in Australia, 800/22-12-22 in the U.K., or 65/6735-5800. Fax 65/6735-9800. www.marriott.com. 373 units. S$380 (US$217) double; S$420 (US$240) executive club; S$650–S$1,880 (US$371–US$1,074) suite. AE, DC, MC, V. Orchard MRT. **Amenities:** 4 restaurants; lobby lounge; bar w/live jazz; dance club w/live pop bands; outdoor pool w/Jacuzzi; fitness center w/Jacuzzi, sauna, steam, and massage; concierge; limousine service; 24-hr. business center; shopping arcade; 24-hr. room service; babysitting; same-day laundry service/dry cleaning; nonsmoking rooms; executive-level rooms; outdoor basketball court. *In room:* A/C, TV w/satellite programming and in-house movies, dataport w/direct Internet access, minibar, coffee/tea-making facilities, hair dryer, iron, safe.

MODERATE

Orchard Parade Hotel ★★ *(Value* *(Kids* This fine hotel, after a S$40 million (US$22.8 million), 2-year renovation, sports a new swimming pool, guest rooms, lobby, driveway, front entrance, and food and beverage outlets, decorated in a Mediterranean theme integrating marble mosaics, plaster walls, beamed ceilings, and wrought-iron railings. The midsize pool on the sixth-floor roof features colorful tiles and draping arbors, a motif carried over through the new fitness center. Rooms also feature Mediterranean style in terra-cotta wall sconces, wrought-iron table legs, and shades of teal and aqua. If it's important to you, you need to specify a room with a view here. For good value, the Family Studio fits a king-size bed and two twins with a separate family room and dining area and plenty of space for just S$100 (US$58) extra. Just outside, a long terrace along Orchard Road hosts many restaurant choices, the most popular of which, Modestos, serves good pasta and pizzas at an affordable price.

1 Tanglin Rd., Singapore 247905. ✆ 65/6737-1133. Fax 65/6733-0242. www.orchardparade.com.sg. 387 units. S$260–S$290 (US$149–US$166) double; S$360–S$420 (US$206–US$240) family studio; S$400 (US$229) junior suite; from S$500 (US$286) suite. AE, DC, MC, V. Orchard MRT. **Amenities:** 5 restaurants; lobby lounge; outdoor pool; fitness center; concierge; tour desk; business center; salon; 24-hr. room service; babysitting; same-day laundry service/dry cleaning; executive-level rooms. *In room:* A/C, TV w/satellite programming, minibar, coffee/tea-making facilities, hair dryer.

Traders Hotel Singapore 🏨🏨　A fantastic bargain for leisure travelers in Singapore, Traders advertises itself as a "value-for-money" hotel. A spin-off of the Shangri-La (see above), this hotel anticipates the special needs of travelers and tries on all levels to accommodate them. Rooms have an empty fridge that can be stocked from the supermarket next door (show your room card key at nearby Tanglin Mall for discounts from many of the shops); there are spanking-clean self-service launderette facilities with ironing boards on six floors; and there are vending machines and ice machines. They even provide a hospitality lounge for guests to use after checkout, with seating areas, work spaces with dataports, card phones, safe-deposit boxes, vending machines, and a shower.

Guest rooms are smaller than average but feature child-size sofa beds and large drawers for storage. The large landscaped pool area has a great poolside alfresco cafe, Ah Hoi's Kitchen, serving up tasty Chinese dishes at reasonable prices. Be sure to ask about promotion rates when you book your room. If you're planning to stay longer than 2 weeks, they have a long-stay program that offers discount meals, laundry and business center services, and half-price launderette tokens.

1A Cuscaden Rd., Singapore 249716. ✆ 800/942-5050 in the U.S. and Canada, 800/222448 in Australia, 0800/442179 in New Zealand, or 65/6738-2222. Fax 65/6831-4314. www.shangri-la.com. 547 units. S$305–S$350 (US$174–US$200) double; S$385 (US$220) club; S$520–S$1,200 (US$297–US$686) studio apt. and suite. AE, DC, MC, V. 10-min. walk to Orchard MRT. **Amenities:** 2 restaurants; bar and lobby lounge; outdoor pool; fitness center w/Jacuzzi, sauna, steam, and massage; spa; concierge; limousine service; shuttle service; business center; salon; 24-hr. room service; babysitting; same-day laundry service/dry cleaning; self-service launderette; executive-level rooms. *In room:* A/C, TV w/satellite programming, dataport w/direct Internet access, minibar, coffee/tea-making facilities, hair dryer, iron, safe.

York Hotel Singapore 🏨🏨　This small tourist-class hotel can boast some of the most consistently professional and courteous staff I've encountered. A short walk from Orchard, York is convenient though far enough removed to provide a relaxing atmosphere. A recent renovation has redressed previously flavorless rooms in a sharp contemporary style in light woods, natural tones, and simple lines. Combined with an already spacious room, the result is an airy, cooling effect. Bathrooms throughout are downright huge. Cabana rooms look out to a pool and sun deck decorated with giant palms. Despite surrounding buildings, it doesn't feel claustrophobic, as do some of the more centrally situated hotels. There's a Jacuzzi, but the business center is tiny, as is the fitness center. This year, rates have been raised a bit, so make sure you ask for promotional discounts.

21 Mount Elizabeth, Singapore 228516. ✆ 800/223-5652 in the U.S. and Canada, 800/553-549 in Australia, 800/447-555 in New Zealand, 800/89-88-52 in the U.K., or 65/6737-0511. Fax 65/6732-1217. www.york hotel.com.sg. 406 units. S$290–S$310 (US$166–US$177) double; S$310 (US$177) cabana; S$440 (US$251)

split-level cabana; S$460–S$910 (US$263–US$520) suite. AE, DC, MC, V. 10-min. walk to Orchard MRT. **Amenities:** Restaurant; lobby lounge; outdoor pool; fitness center; Jacuzzi; tour desk; business center; 24-hr. room service; babysitting; same-day laundry service/dry cleaning. *In room:* A/C, TV w/satellite programming, minibar, coffee/tea-making facilities.

INEXPENSIVE

Regalis Court ★★ For a bit of local charm at an affordable price, Regalis Court is a favorite. Centrally located just a 10-minute walk from Orchard Road, this old charming bungalow has been restored beautifully and outfitted with Peranakan-inspired touches. Everything here will make you feel as if you're staying in a quaint guesthouse rather than a hotel, from the open-air lobby (under the porte-cochere) and corridors to the guest rooms, which have comforting touches like teakwood furnishings, textile wall hangings, oriental throws over wooden floors, and bamboo blinds to keep out the sun. Although guest rooms are slightly smaller than conventional rooms, they are still quite comfortable. Facilities are few. Laundry services and car hire are also offered.

64 Lloyd Rd., Singapore 239113. © **65/6734-7117.** Fax 65/6736-1651. www.regalis.com.sg. 43 units. S$115–S$165 (US$66–US$94) double. AE, DC, MC, V. 10-min. walk from Somerset MRT. **Amenities:** Restaurant; car-rental desk; babysitting; same-day laundry service; nonsmoking rooms. *In room:* A/C, TV, dataport w/direct Internet access, coffee/tea-making facilities, safe.

RELC International Hotel ★★ (Value For real value, my money is on RELC. Sure the location is terrific (only a 10-min. walk to Orchard Rd.), but the added value is in the quality of the facility. I found the service and convenience here superior to that of some hotels in the higher-priced categories. RELC has four types of rooms—superior twin, executive twin, Hollywood queen, and alcove suite—but no matter what the size, none of the rooms ever feels cluttered, close, or cramped. All rooms have balconies, TVs with two movie channels, and a fridge with free juice boxes and snacks. Bathrooms are large, with full-length tubs and hair dryers standard. If you're interested in the higher-priced rooms, I'd choose the Hollywood queen over the alcove suite—its decor is better and it can sleep a family very comfortably. The "superior" rooms don't have coffee/tea-making facilities. A self-service launderette is available.

30 Orange Grove Rd., Singapore 258352. © **65/6885-7888.** Fax 65/6733-9976. www.hotel-web.com. 128 units. S$110 (US$66) double; S$165 (US$99) suite. AE, DC, MC, V. 10-min. walk to Orchard MRT. **Amenities:** Restaurant; tour desk; same-day laundry service; self-service launderette; nonsmoking rooms. *In room:* A/C, TV w/in-house movies, dataport w/direct Internet access, minibar.

4 Where to Dine

Dining out in Singapore is the central focus of family quality time, the best excuse for getting together with friends, and the proper way to close that business deal. That's why you find such a huge selection of local, regional, and international cuisine here, served in settings that range from bustling hawker centers to grand and glamorous palaces of gastronomy. But to simply say "If you like food, you'll love Singapore!" doesn't do justice to the modern concept of eating in this place. The various ethnic restaurants, with their traditional decor and serving styles, hold their own special sense of theater for foreigners, but Singaporeans don't stop there: They dream up new concepts in cuisine and ambience to add fresh dimensions to the fine art of dining. For a twist, new variations on traditions pop up, like the French-service Chinese cuisine at Chang Jiang or the East-meets-West New Asia cuisine dished up at Doc Cheng's. Theme restaurants turn regular meals into attractions. Take, for example, Imperial Herbal's intriguing predinner medical examination or House of Mao's Cultural Revolution menu.

Urban Singapore Dining

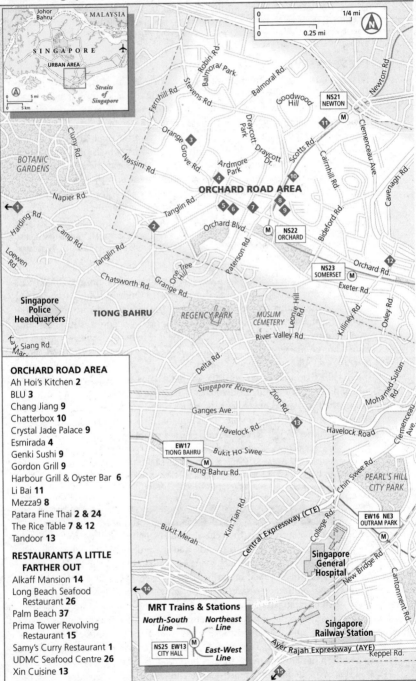

ORCHARD ROAD AREA
Ah Hoi's Kitchen **2**
BLU **3**
Chang Jiang **9**
Chatterbox **10**
Crystal Jade Palace **9**
Esmirada **4**
Genki Sushi **9**
Gordon Grill **9**
Harbour Grill & Oyster Bar **6**
Li Bai **11**
Mezza9 **8**
Patara Fine Thai **2 & 24**
The Rice Table **7 & 12**
Tandoor **13**

**RESTAURANTS A LITTLE
FARTHER OUT**
Alkaff Mansion **14**
Long Beach Seafood
  Restaurant **26**
Palm Beach **37**
Prima Tower Revolving
  Restaurant **15**
Samy's Curry Restaurant **1**
UDMC Seafood Centre **26**
Xin Cuisine **13**

MRT Trains & Stations
*North-South
Line*   *Northeast
                Line*
NS25 EW13   *East-West
CITY HALL   Line*

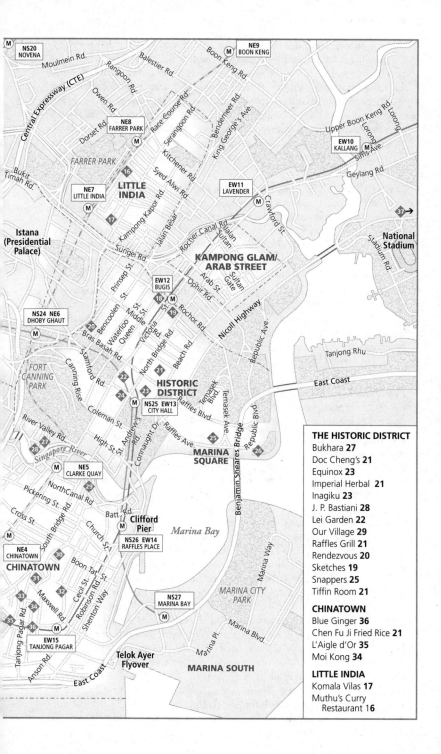

THE HISTORIC DISTRICT
Bukhara **27**
Doc Cheng's **21**
Equinox **23**
Imperial Herbal **21**
Inagiku **23**
J. P. Bastiani **28**
Lei Garden **22**
Our Village **29**
Raffles Grill **21**
Rendezvous **20**
Sketches **19**
Snappers **25**
Tiffin Room **21**

CHINATOWN
Blue Ginger **36**
Chen Fu Ji Fried Rice **21**
L'Aigle d'Or **35**
Moi Kong **34**

LITTLE INDIA
Komala Vilas **17**
Muthu's Curry
  Restaurant **16**

Many of Singapore's best restaurants are in its hotels, whether they're run by the hotel itself or operated by outfits just renting the space. Hotels generally offer a wide variety of cuisine, and coffee shops almost always have Western selections. Shopping malls have everything from food courts with local fast food to midpriced and upmarket establishments. Western fast-food outlets are always easy to find—McDonald's burgers, Dunkin' Donuts, or Starbucks coffee—but if you want something a little more local, you'll find coffee shops (called *kopitiam*) and small home-cookin' mom-and-pop joints down every back street. Then there are hawker centers, where, under one roof, the meal choices go on and on.

CHINESE CUISINE   The large Chinese population in Singapore makes this obviously the most common type of food you'll find, and by right, any good description of Singaporean food should begin with the most prevalent Chinese regional styles. Many Chinese restaurants in the West are lumped into one category—Chinese—with only mild acknowledgment of Cantonese, Szechuan and dim sum. But China's a big place, and its size is reflected in its many different tastes, ingredients, and preparation styles.

MALAY CUISINE   Malay cuisine combines Indonesian and Thai flavors, blending ginger, turmeric, chiles, lemongrass, and dried shrimp paste to make unique curries. Heavy on coconut milk and peanuts, Malay food can at times be on the sweet side. The most popular Malay curries are **rendang,** a dry, dark, and heavy coconut-based curry served over meat; **sambal,** a red and spicy chile sauce; and **sambal belacan,** a condiment of fresh chiles, dried shrimp paste, and lime juice.

PERANAKAN CUISINE   Peranakan cuisine came out of the Straits-born Chinese community and combines such mainland Chinese ingredients as noodles and oyster sauces with local Malay flavors of coconut milk and peanuts.

INDIAN CUISINE   **Southern Indian food** is a superhot blend of spices in a coconut milk base. Rice is the staple, along with thin breads such as *prata* and *dosai,* which are good for curling into shovels to scoop up drippy curries. Vegetarian dishes are abundant, a result of Hindu-mandated vegetarianism, and use lots of chickpeas and lentils in curry and chile gravies. **Vindaloo,** meat or poultry in a tangy and spicy sauce, is also well known.

Banana leaf restaurants, surely the most interesting way to experience southern Indian food in Singapore, serve up meals on banana leaves cut like place mats. It's very informal. Spoons and forks are provided, but if you want to act local and use your hands, remember to use your right hand only, and don't forget to wash up before and after at the tap. **Northern Indian food** combines yogurts and creams with a milder, more delicate blend of herbs and chiles than is found in its southern neighbor. It's served most often with breads like fluffy *nans* and flat *chapatis.* Marinated meats like chicken or fish, cooked in the tandoor clay oven, are always the highlight of a northern Indian meal. Northern Indian restaurants are more upmarket and expensive than the southern ones, but while they offer more of the comforts associated with dining out, the southern banana leaf experience is more of an adventure.

One tip for eating very spicy foods is to mix a larger proportion of rice to gravy. Don't drink in between bites, but eat through the burn. Your brow may sweat, but your mouth will build a tolerance as you eat, and the flavors will come through more fully.

SEAFOOD   One cannot describe Singaporean food without mentioning the abundance of fresh seafood. But most important is the uniquely Singaporean chile crab, chopped and smothered in a thick tangy chile sauce. Restaurants hold competitions to judge who has the best. Pepper crabs and black pepper crayfish are also a thrill. Instead of chile sauce, these shellfish are served in a thick black-pepper-and-soy sauce.

FRUITS   A walk through a wet market at any time of year will show you just what wonders the tropics can produce. Varieties of banana, fresh coconut, papaya, mango, and pineapple are just a few of the fresh and juicy fruits available year-round; in addition, Southeast Asia has an amazing selection of exotic and almost unimaginable fruits. From the light and juicy **star fruit** to the red and hairy **rambutan,** they are all worthy of a try, either whole or juiced.

Dare it if you will, the fruit to sample—the veritable king of fruits—is the **durian,** a large, green, spiky fruit that, when cut open, smells worse than old tennis shoes. The "best" ones are in season every June, when Singaporeans go wild over them. In case you're curious, the fruit has a creamy texture and tastes lightly sweet and deeply musky.

TIPS ON DINING

Of course, in any foreign land, the exotic cuisine isn't the only thing that keeps you guessing. Lucky for you, the following tips will make dining no problem.

- Most restaurants are open for lunch as early as 11am but close around 2:30 or 3pm to give them a chance to set up for dinner, which begins around 6pm. Where closing times are listed, that is the time when the last order is taken.
- **Don't tip.** Restaurants always add a gratuity to the bill, and to give extra cash can be embarrassing for the wait staff.
- Some restaurants, especially the more fashionable or upscale ones, might require that **reservations** be made up to a couple days in advance. Reservations are always recommended for Saturday and Sunday lunch and dinner; eating is a favorite national pastime, and a lot of families take meals out for weekend quality time.
- Because Singapore is so hot, "dress casual" (meaning a shirt and slacks for men and a dress or skirt/slacks and top for women) is always a safe bet in moderate to expensive restaurants. For the very expensive restaurants, formal is required. For the cheap places, come as you are, as long as you're decent.

ORDERING WINE WITH DINNER   Singaporeans have become more wine savvy in recent years, and have begun importing estate-bottled wines from California, Australia, New Zealand, Peru, South Africa, France, and Germany. However, these bottles are heavily taxed. A bottle of wine with dinner starts at around S\$50 (US\$29), and a single glass runs between S\$10 and S\$25 (US\$5.70 and US\$14), depending on the wine and the restaurant. Chinese restaurants usually don't charge corkage fees for bringing your own.

LUNCH COSTS   Lunch at a hawker center can be as cheap as S\$3.50 (US\$2), truly a bargain. Many places have set-price buffet lunches, but these can be as high as S\$45 (US\$26). Indian restaurants are great deals for inexpensive buffet lunches, which can be found as reasonably as S\$10 (US\$5.70) per person for all you can eat.

DINNER COSTS   In this chapter, prices for Western restaurants list the range for standard entrees, and prices for Asian restaurants list the range for small dishes intended for two. As a guideline, here are the relative costs for dinner in each category of restaurant, without wine, beer, cocktails, or coffee, and ordered either a la carte or from a set-price menu:

Note: See map "Urban Singapore Dining," above.

THE HISTORIC DISTRICT
VERY EXPENSIVE

Inagiku ★★ JAPANESE   At Inagiku, you'll have excellent Japanese food that gets top marks for ingredients, preparation, and presentation. In delicately lighted and subtle decor, you can enjoy house favorites like sashimi, tempura, and teppanyaki—with separate dining areas for tempura and a sushi bar. The tokusen sashimi morikimi is masterful in its presentation: An assortment of raw fish—including salmon, prawns, and clams—is laid out in an ice-filled shell inside of which nestles the skeleton of a whole fish. It's odd and delightful at the same time. I recommend the tempura moriawase, a combination of seafood and vegetables that's very lightly deep fried. Also highly recommended are the teppanyaki prawns. In addition to sake, there is also a good selection of wines.

The Westin Plaza Level 3, 2 Stamford Rd. ℂ 65/6431-6156. Reservations recommended. Set lunch S$30–S$50 (US$17–US$29); set dinner S$60–S$180 (US$34–US$103). AE, DC, MC, V. Daily noon–2:30pm and 6:30–10:30pm.

Raffles Grill ★★★ FRENCH   Dining in the grande dame of Singapore achieves a level of sophistication unmatched by any other five-star restaurant. The architectural charm and historic significance of the old hotel will transform dinner into a cultural event, but don't just come here for the ambience; the food is outstanding as well. Three set dinners allow you to select from the a la carte menu dishes like roasted veal tenderloin or roasted rack of suckling pig, the latter a highly recommended choice for its juicy meat under crispy, mouthwatering skin. The 400-label wine list (going back to 1890 vintages) could be a history lesson, and if you'd like, you can request that the cellar master select a wine to match each course. The fabulously attentive service from the wait staff will make you feel like you own the place. Formal dress is required.

Raffles Hotel, 1 Beach Rd. ℂ 65/6412-1240. Reservations recommended. Entrees S$42–S$52 (US$24–US$30); set dinner S$120 and S$130 (US$69 and US$74) per person. AE, DC, MC, V. Mon–Fri noon–2pm and 7–10pm; Sat–Sun 7–10pm.

EXPENSIVE

Equinox ★ CONTINENTAL/NEW ASIA   What a view! From the top of the tallest hotel in Southeast Asia, you can see out past the marina to Malaysia and Indonesia—and the restaurant's three-tier design and floor-to-ceiling windows means every table has a view. It's decorated in contemporary style with nice Chinese accents. Lunch is an extensive display of seafood served in a host of international recipes, with chefs searing scallops to order. Dinner is a la carte, with dishes that combine Eastern and Western ingredients and cooking styles such as *yuzu*-marinated cod with braised *enoki* and *tasoi* and grilled beef tenderloin with foie gras. For dessert, order the Equinox Temptation—a sample plate of desserts.

Swissôtel Stamford, 2 Stamford Rd., Level 70. ℂ 65/6431-6156. Reservations required. Buffet lunch Mon–Sat S$36 (US$22), Sun and public holidays S$42 (US$25); dinner entrees S$41–S$45 (US$24–US$27). AE, DC, MC, V. Daily noon–2:30pm and 7–10:30pm.

J. P. Bastiani ★ MEDITERRANEAN   The real-life J. P. Bastiani owned a pineapple cannery at Clarke Quay; today, he lends his name to this cozy Mediterranean place, with its walled courtyard patio in the back for cocktails, a wine cellar with a huge international collection on the first floor (buy your wine here for dinner), and a gorgeous dining room upstairs that's just dripping with romance. The seafood dishes are the best, with a choice of a delicious coriander-crusted salmon with ginger and onion confit, or the pan-roasted sea bass, which is stuffed with leeks and potato. You can also try one of the excellent meat entrees, such as rack of lamb or filet mignon. The dishes are rich, and servings are quite large, so make a mental note in advance to save room for the fantastic tiramisu.

3A River Valley Rd., Clarke Quay Merchant's Court no. 01-12. ⓒ **65/6433-0156.** Reservations recommended. Entrees S$29–S$42 (US$17–US$24). AE, DC, MC, V. Daily 11:30am–2:30pm and 6:30–10:30pm.

Lei Garden ⭐⭐ CANTONESE   Lei Garden, with three locations in Singapore, six in Hong Kong and Kowloon, and two in Guangzhou, lives up to a great reputation for the highest-quality Cantonese cuisine in one of the most elegant settings. Actually, of the three local branches, this one is special for the unique ambience of CHIJMES just outside its towering picture windows. Highly recommended dishes are the "Buddha jumps over the wall," a very popular Chinese soup made from abalone, fish maw (stomach), shark's fin, and Chinese ham. It's generally served only on special occasions. To make the beggar's chicken, they wrap up and bake a whole stuffed chicken in a lotus leaf covered in yam, which makes the chicken moist, with a delicate flavor you'll never forget. For either of these dishes, you must place your order at least 24 hours in advance when you make your dinner reservation. Also try the barbecued Beijing duck, which is exquisite. Dim sum here is excellent. A small selection of French and Chinese wines is available.

30 Victoria St., CHIJMES no. 01-24. ⓒ **65/6339-3822.** Reservations required. Small dishes S$18–S$58 (US$10–US$33). AE, DC, MC, V. Daily 11:30am–2:30pm and 6–10:30pm.

Snappers ⭐⭐ SEAFOOD   With a view of The Ritz-Carlton's lovely pool and gardens, this restaurant is hardly your typical poolside snack bar. Snappers invents mouthwatering recipes for new ways to enjoy fresh seafood. The crispy sea bass with eggplant and walnut coriander dressing melts in your mouth. The seafood platter is awesome. But if the a la carte menu doesn't have what you're looking for, you can have your choice of live seafood prepared to your specs. This is one of the city's top choices for delicious dining, with a terrific wine list and impeccable service. You will never be disappointed.

The Ritz-Carlton Millenia Singapore, Level 1, 7 Raffles Ave. ⓒ **65/6836-3333.** Reservations required for dinner. Entrees S$31–S$38 (US$17–US$22). AE, DC, MC, V. Daily noon–2:30pm and 6:30–10:30pm.

Tiffin Room ⭐ SOUTHERN INDIAN   Tiffin curry came from India and is named after the three-tiered containers that Indian workers would use to carry their lunch. The tiffin box idea was stolen by the British colonists, who changed the recipes a bit so they weren't as spicy. The cuisine that evolved is pretty much what you'll find served at Raffles's Tiffin Room, where a buffet spread lets you select from a variety of curries, chutneys, rice, and Indian breads. The restaurant is just inside the lobby entrance of Raffles Hotel and carries the trademark Raffles elegance throughout its decor.

Raffles Hotel, 1 Beach Rd. ⓒ **65/6337-1886.** Reservations recommended. All meals served buffet style. Breakfast S$30 (US$17); lunch S$35 (US$20); high tea S$27 (US$15); dinner S$45 (US$26). AE, DC, MC, V. Daily noon–2pm, 3:30–5pm (high tea), and 7–10pm.

MODERATE

Doc Cheng's CHINESE NEW ASIA/FUSION   Doc Cheng's calls itself "The Restaurant for Restorative Foods," but you won't find any ancient Chinese secrets here. Doc Cheng, the hero of the joint, was part man and part mythological colonial figure. Educated in Western medicine in England, he was a sought-after physician who became a local celebrity and notorious drunk. His concept of restorative foods is therefore rather skewed, but the restaurant banks on the decadence of the attraction and serves up "transethnic" dishes smothered in tongue-in-cheek humor. Guest chefs make the menu ever changing—the latest and greatest, an unbelievably scrumptious tamarind charcoal beef short ribs dish on portobello mushrooms. Equally well prepared (though lighter) is the charcoal-fried shutome swordfish on risotto. The house wine is a Riesling (sweet wines are more popular with Singaporeans) from Raffles's own vineyard. Three separate dining areas allow you to dine under the veranda, on the patio, or in cozy booths inside.

Raffles Hotel Arcade no. 02-20, Level 2. (C) **65/6331-1612.** Reservations recommended. Entrees S$22–S$32 (US$12–US$18). AE, DC, MC, V. Daily noon–2pm and 7–10pm.

Imperial Herbal ★★ CHINESE HERBAL   People come again and again for the healing powers of the food served here, enriched with herbs and other secret ingredients prescribed by a resident Chinese herbalist. Upon entering, go to the right, where you'll find the herb counter. The herbalist, who is also trained in Western medicine, will ask for the symptoms of what ails you and take your pulse. While you sit and order, he'll prepare a packet of ingredients and ship them off to the kitchen, where they'll be added to the food in preparation. Surprisingly, dishes turn out tasty, without the anticipated medicinal aftertaste. If all this isn't wild enough for you, order the scorpion.

The herbalist is in-house every day but Sunday. It's always good to call ahead, though, because he's the main attraction. When you leave, present him with a small ang pau—a gift of cash in a red envelope—maybe S$5 or S$7 (US$2.85 or US$4). Red envelopes are available in any card or gift shop.

Metropole Hotel, 3rd Floor, 41 Seah St. (near Raffles Hotel). (C) **65/6337-0491.** Reservations recommended for lunch, necessary for dinner. Small dishes S$14–S$24 (US$8–US$14). AE, DC, MC, V. Daily 11:30am–2:30pm and 6:30–10:30pm.

INEXPENSIVE

Bukhara NORTHERN INDIAN   I like to recommend Bukhara for the buffet, which is a great way to savor many treats without going over the top with the expense. Tandoori lamb kabobs, fish, prawns, chicken, and more will make meat lovers' eyes pop—the food just keeps coming. Plu, tandoori veggies like cauliflower and stuffed potatoes and peppers are quite good. The decor is a little bit India-kitsch, with carved stonelike accents and beat-up wooden chairs. The buffet includes breads and dal. You can also order from an a la carte menu of standard northern Indian fare. If you're in Clarke Quay, this is the best choice in this price range.

3C River Valley Rd., no. 01-44 Clarke Quay. (C) **65/6338-1411.** Reservations recommended. Buffet lunch S$14 (US$7.75); buffet dinner S$20 (US$11). AE, DC, MC, V. Daily noon–2:30pm and 6:30–10:30pm.

Magic Wok (Value THAI/CHINESE MIXED   Here's an excellent value-for-money restaurant in town. The decor doesn't do much, it's usually crowded, and staff don't pamper, but food is reliably good and cheap. Thai favorites include a spicy tom yam seafood soup that doesn't skimp on the seafood, a mild green curry with chicken, and sweet pineapple rice. If you come too late, the yummy fried chicken chunks wrapped in pandan leaf will be sold out. If you're adventurous, the fried baby squid look like cute, tiny octopi and are crunchy and sweet. During busy times, you'll have to queue, but it moves fast. Other outlets are located at no. 04-22/24 Far East Plaza on Scotts Road (℃ 65/6738-3708) and no. 02-05 Marina Liesureplex (℃ 65/6837-0826).

No. 01-20 Capitol Building, Stamford Rd. ℃ **65/6338-1882.** Reservations not accepted. S$4–S$18 (US$2.30–US$10) small dishes. MC, V. Daily 11am–10pm.

Our Village ✦ NORTHERN INDIAN With its antique white walls stuccoed in delicate and exotic patterns and glistening with tiny silver mirrors, you'll feel like you're in an Indian fairyland here. Even the ceiling twinkles with silver stars, and hanging lanterns provide a subtle glow for the heavenly atmosphere— it's a perfect setting for a delicate dinner. Everything here is handmade from hand-selected imported ingredients, some of them coming from secret sources. In fact, the staff is so protective of its recipes, you'd almost think the secret ingredient was opium—and you'll be floating so high after tasting the food that it might as well be. There are vegetarian selections as well as meats (no beef or pork) prepared in luscious gravies or in the tandoor oven. The dishes are light and healthy, with all natural ingredients and not too much salt.

46 Boat Quay (take elevator to 5th floor). ℃ **65/6538-3058.** Reservations recommended on weekends. Entrees S$9–S$20 (US$5.15–US$11). AE, MC, V. Mon–Fri 11:30am–1:30pm and 6–10:30pm; Sat–Sun 6–10:30pm.

Rendezvous MALAY/INDONESIAN I was sad when, after a few months away from Singapore, I couldn't find Rendezvous at its previous location in Raffles City Shopping Center, only to learn it had shifted to a nicer space at the new (coincidentally named?) Rendezvous Hotel. Line up to select from a large number of Malay dishes, cafeteria style, like sambal squid in a spicy sauce of chile and shrimp paste, and beef rendang, in a dark spicy curry gravy. The waitstaff will bring your order to your table. The coffee shop setting is as far from glamorous as the last Rendezvous, but on the wall black-and-white photos trace the restaurant's history back to its opening in the early '50s. It's a great place to experiment with a new cuisine.

No. 02-02 Hotel Rendezvous, 9 Bras Basah Rd. ℃ **65/339-7508.** Reservations not necessary. Meat dishes sold per piece S$3–S$5 (US$1.70–US$2.85). AE, DC, MC, V. Daily 11am–9pm. Closed on public holidays.

Sketches (Value ITALIAN Pasta is always an easy and agreeable choice, and sometimes when you're traveling, familiar tastes can be welcome from time to time. Not only is this place fast, inexpensive, and good, but it's also pretty unique. The concept is "Design-a-Pasta," where they give you a menu on which is a series of boxes you check off: one set for pasta type; one set for sauce type; another for add-ins, like meats, mushrooms, and garlic; and boxes for chile, Parmesan, and pine nuts. The kitchen is in the center of the restaurant, with bar seating all around. This is the best place to be if you want to watch those cooks hustle through menu card after menu card—it's a great show. You can also sit at one of the tables in the restaurant or out on the patio inside the shopping mall, but then you'd miss the fun of eating here.

200 Victoria St., no. 01-85/86/87 Parco Bugis Junction. ℃ **65/6339-8386.** S$11 (US$6) hungry; S$14.50 (US$8.30) starving. AE, DC, MC, V. Daily 11am–10pm.

CHINATOWN
VERY EXPENSIVE
L'Aigle d'Or ✦✦✦ FRENCH L'Aigle d'Or's reputation in Singapore is second to none, and after you dine here, you'll understand why. The French menu

is perfection, the setting is classic, and the staff is extremely attentive and charming. Like many of the other European restaurants in Singapore, the menu changes regularly with the seasons, so you might find different dishes than on your last visit. This time around, the menu featured a gorgeous veal rib, pan-fried and tender. For something different, try the pan-fried foie gras and rhubarb ravioli, a current house specialty and unbelievably tasty in a tangy raspberry sauce. As you would expect, the wine list is top of the line, the cheese selection is excellent, and the desserts are unmentionable. If you're looking for someplace truly special, you can't do better.

83 Duxton Rd., Berjaya Hotel Singapore. ℂ 65/6227-7678. Reservations recommended. Entrees S$75–S$96 (US$43–US$55); set lunch from S$36 (US$21). AE, DC, MC, V. Daily noon–2pm and 7–10pm.

INEXPENSIVE

Blue Ginger ✯ PERANAKAN   The standard belief is that Malay and Peranakan cooking is reserved for home-cooked meals, and therefore restaurants are not as plentiful—and where they do exist, are very informal. Not so at Blue Ginger, where traditional and modern mix beautifully in a style so fitting for Singapore. Snuggled in a shophouse, the decor combines clean and neat lines of contemporary styling with paintings by local artists and touches of Peranakan flair like carved wooden screens. The cuisine is Peranakan from traditional recipes, making for some very authentic food—definitely something you can't get back home. A good appetizer is the *ngo heong:* fried rolls of pork and prawn that are deliciously flavored with spices but not at all hot. A wonderful entree is the *ayam panggang* "Blue Ginger," really tender grilled boneless thigh and drumstick with a mild coconut-milk sauce. One of the most popular dishes is the *ayam buah keluak* (my favorite), a traditional chicken dish made with a hard black Indonesian nut with sweet meat inside. The favorite dessert here is *durian chendol,* red beans and pandan jelly in coconut milk with durian purée. Served with shaved ice on top, it smells strong.

97 Tanjong Pagar Rd. ℂ 65/6222-3928. Reservations recommended. Entrees S$6.50–S$23 (US$3.70–US$13). AE, DC, MC, V. Daily 11:30am–2:30pm and 6–10pm.

Chen Fu Ji Fried Rice SINGAPOREAN   With bright green walls glaring under fluorescent lighting, the fast-food ambience is nothing to write home about, but once you try the fried rice here, you'll never be able to eat it anywhere else again, ever. These people take loving care of each fluffy grain, frying the egg evenly throughout. The other ingredients are added abundantly, and there's no hint of oil. On the top is a crown of shredded crabmeat. If you've never been an aficionado, you'll be one now. Other dishes are served here to accompany the fried rice, and the soups are also very good.

7 Erskine Rd. ℂ 65/6323-0260. Reservations not accepted. S$10–S$20 (US$5.70–US$11). No credit cards. Daily noon–2:30pm and 6–9:45pm.

Moi Kong HAKKA   Located down a back alley called Murray Food Court, Moi Kong is a restaurant that looks more like somebody's kitchen, from the plastic tablecloths and dishes to tea served in simple glasses. The staff is very helpful about offering suggestions from the Hakka menu, dishes that are heavier on tofu and flavored more with homemade Chinese wine. Try house specialties like red wine prawn or salted chicken baked and served plain. The deep-fried bean curd stuffed with minced pork and fish is a traditional standard and can be served either dry or braised with black bean sauce. If you don't believe the food here is top rate, just ask Jackie Chan, whose happy photos are on the wall by the cash register!

22 Murray St. (between Maxwell House and Fairfield Methodist Church). ℂ **65/221-7758**. Reservations recommended on weekends. Small dishes S$4–S$30 (US$2.30–US$17). AE, MC, V. Daily 11:30am–2:30pm and 5:30–10pm.

LITTLE INDIA

Komala Vilas ⚘ SOUTHERN INDIAN   Komala Vilas is famous with Singaporeans of every race. Don't expect the height of ambience—it's pure fast food—but to sit here during a packed and noisy lunch hour is to see all walks of life come through the doors. Vegetarian dishes are southern-Indian style, so there's nothing fancy about the food; it's just plain good. Order the dosai, a huge, thin pancake used to scoop up luscious and hearty gravies and curries. Even for carnivores, it's very satisfying. What's more, it's cheap: two samosas, a dosai, and an assortment of stew-style gravies (dal) for two are only S$8 (US$4.55) with tea. For a quick fast-food meal, this place is second to none.

76/78 Serangoon Rd. ℂ **65/293-6980**. Reservations not accepted. Dosai S$2 (US$1.15); lunch for 2 S$8 (US$4.55). No credit cards. Daily 11:30am–3pm and 6:30–10:30pm.

Muthu's Curry Restaurant SOUTHERN INDIAN   We're not talking the height of dining elegance here. It's more like somebody's kitchen where the chairs don't match, but you know there's got to be a reason why this place is packed at mealtimes with a crowd of folks from construction workers to businesspeople. The list of specialties is long and includes crab masala, chicken biryani, and mutton curry, and fish cutlet and fried chicken sold by the piece. Of course, you can get the local favorite, fish head curry (this is a great place to try it). The fish head floats in a huge portion of curry soup, its eye staring and teeth grinning. The cheek meat is the best part of the fish, but to be real polite, let your friend eat the eye. Go toward the end of mealtime so you don't get lost in the rush and can find staff with more time to help you out.

76/78 Race Course Rd. ℂ **65/6293-2389**. Reservations not accepted. Entrees S$3.50–S$6.50 (US$2–US$3.70); fish head curry from S$16 (US$9.15). AE, DC, MC, V. Daily 10am–10pm.

ORCHARD ROAD AREA
EXPENSIVE

BLU ⚘⚘⚘ CALIFORNIA   The top floor of the Shangri-La commands a lovely view of Orchard Road and the gardens of the most fashionable residential district in the city. BLU is Singapore's cutting edge in stylish dining, decorated with modern glass sculpture by Danny Lane, table lamps by Philippe Starck, and Wedgewood table settings. The Maine lobster paella with saffron, black mussel, and lobster chorizo jus is mind blowing. Even your plain old chicken is sumptuously flavored, with apricots, foie gras, and Swiss chard. The wine list here is excellent. After hours, BLU turns into an atmospheric lounge with live jazz Monday to Thursday till 12:45am, and Friday and Saturday till 1:45am. BLU is my pick for the hottest date venue.

24th floor Shangri-La Hotel, 22 Orange Grove Rd. ℂ **65/6730-2598**. Reservations required. Entrees S$48–S$59 (US$27–US$34). AE, DC, MC, V. Mon–Sat 7–10:30pm.

Chang Jiang ⚘ CHINESE SHANGHAINESE   The small and elegant Chang Jiang is a unique blend of Chinese food and European style. A fine setting, which mixes refined Continental ambience with Chinese accents, has a view of the courtyard and pool of the historic Goodwood Park Hotel through its large draped picture windows. The food is Chinese, but the service is French Gueridon style, in which dishes are presented to diners and taken to a side table to be portioned into individual servings. Some dishes are prepared while you watch, especially coffee, which is a veritable chemistry showcase. A couple of the more sumptuous dishes are the tangy and crunchy crisp eel wuxi and the sweet batter-dipped prawns with sesame seed and salad sauce. If you order the Beijing duck, after the traditional pancake dish they serve the shredded meat in a delicious sauce with green bean noodles.

Goodwood Park Hotel, 22 Scotts Rd. © 65/6730-1752. Reservations recommended. Small dishes S$15–S$58 (US$8.55–US$33). AE, DC, MC, V. Daily noon–2:30pm and 6:30–10:30pm.

Esmirada ★ MEDITERRANEAN Ask any expatriate about restaurants, and you'll hear about Esmirada. This place revels in the joys of good food and drink, bringing laughter and fun to the traditional act of breaking bread with friends and family. The menu is easy: There's one dish each from Italy, Spain, Greece, France, Portugal, and Morocco, and they never change. Huge portions are served family style, from big bowls of salad to shish kebab skewers hanging from a rack, all placed in the center of the table so everyone can dig in. Don't even bother with paella anywhere else—this is the best. The place is small, so make your reservations early. Stucco walls, wrought-iron details, and terra-cotta floors are mixed with wooden Indonesian tables and chairs with kilim cushions in an East-meets-West style that works very nicely.

Orchard Hotel, 442 Orchard Rd., no. 01-29. © 65/735-3476. Reservations recommended for dinner. Entrees S$24–S$42 (US$14–US$24). AE, DC, MC, V. Daily 11am–11pm.

Gordon Grill ★★ CONTINENTAL Bringing meat and potatoes to the high life, Gordon Grill wheels out a carving cart full of the most tender prime rib and sirloin you could imagine, cut to your desired thickness. The menu of traditional English and Scottish fare includes house specialties like the pan-fried goose liver with apple and port wine sauce appetizer and the house recipe for (perfect) lobster bisque. Featured entrees are the mixed seafood grill of lobster, garoupa (grouper), scallops, and prawns in a lemon butter sauce and roast duck breast glazed with honey and black pepper. The traditional English sherry trifle is the dessert to order here, but if you want a little taste of everything, the dessert variation lets you have small portions of each dessert, with fresh fruit. The dining room, which is small and warmly set with dark tartan carpeting and portraits of stately Scotsmen, feels more comfortable than claustrophobic, and light piano music drifts in from the lounge next door. Dress formal.

Goodwood Park Hotel, 22 Scotts Rd. © 65/6730-1744. Reservations recommended. Entrees S$32–S$50 and up (US$18–US$29). AE, DC, MC, V. Daily noon–2:30pm and 7–10:30pm.

Harbour Grill & Oyster Bar ★★★ CONTINENTAL Grilled seafood and U.S. prime rib are perfectly prepared and served with attentive style in this award-winning restaurant. The Continental cuisine is lighter than most, with recipes that focus on the natural freshness of their ingredients rather than on creams and fat. Caesar salad is made at your table so you can request your preferred blend of ingredients, and the oyster bar serves fresh oysters from around the world. For the main course, the prime rib is the best and most requested entree, but the rack of lamb is another option worth considering—it melts in your mouth. Guest chefs from international culinary capitals are flown in for monthly specials. The place is small and cozy, with exposed brick and a finishing kitchen in the dining room. Windows have been replaced with murals of the Singapore harbor in the 1850s, but in the evenings it is still airy and fresh feeling.

Hilton International Singapore, Level 3, 581 Orchard Rd. ✆ **65/6730-3393**. Reservations recommended. Entrees S$34–S$36 (US$19–US$21). 2 courses S$55 (US$31), 3 courses S$75 (US$43), or 4 courses S$90 (US$51) per person. AE, DC, MC, V. Daily noon–2:30pm and 7–10:30pm.

Li Bai ⊀⊀⊀ CHINESE CANTONESE   Chinese restaurants are typically unimaginative in the decor department—slapping up a landscape brush painting or two here and there is sometimes about as far as they go. Not at Li Bai, though, which is very sleekly decorated in contemporary black and red lacquer, with huge vases of soft pussy willows dotted about. Creative chefs and guest chefs turn out a constantly evolving menu, refining specialties, and jade and silver chopsticks and white bone china add opulent touches to their flawless meals. Make sure you ask for their most recent creations—they're guaranteed to please. Or, try the farm chicken smoked with jasmine tea, a succulent dish. The crab fried rice is fabulous, with generous chunks of fresh meat, and the beef in mushroom and garlic brown sauce is some of the most tender meat you'll ever feast upon. The wine list is international, with many vintages to choose from.

Sheraton Towers, 39 Scotts Rd. ✆ **65/6839-5623**. Reservations required. Entrees S$18–S$48 and up (US$10–US$27). AE, DC, MC, V. Daily 11am–2:30pm and 6:30–10:30pm.

Mezza9 ⊀⊀ FUSION   This is your best bet if your party can't agree on what to eat. Mezza9 offers an extensive menu that includes Chinese steamed treats, Japanese, Thai, deli selections, Italian, fresh seafood, and Continental grilled specialties. Start with big and juicy raw oysters in the half-shell. If you want to consider more raw seafood, the combination sashimi platter is also very fresh. Grilled meats include various cuts of beef, rack of lamb, and chicken dishes with a host of delicious sides to choose from. The enormous 450-seat restaurant has a warm atmosphere, with glowing wood and contemporary Zen accents. Before you head in for dinner, grab a martini in the très chic martini bar.

Grand Hyatt, 10 Scotts Rd. ✆ **65/6416-7189**. Reservations required. Entrees S$18–S$40 (US$14–US$23). AE, DC, MC, V. Daily noon–3pm and 6–11:30pm.

MODERATE

Ah Hoi's Kitchen SINGAPOREAN   I like Ah Hoi's for its casual charm and its selection of authentic local cuisine. The menu is extensive, specializing in local favorites like fried black pepper kuay teow (noodles), sambal kang kong (vegetable), and fabulous grilled seafood. The alfresco poolside pavilion location gives it a real "vacation in the tropics" sort of relaxed feel—think of a hawker center without the dingy florescent bulbs, greasy tables, and sludgy floor. Also good here is the chile crab—if you can't make it out to the seafood places on the east coast of the island, it's the best alternative for tasting this local treat. Make sure you order the fresh lime juice; it's very cooling.

Traders Hotel, 1A Cuscaden Rd., 4th level. ✆ **65/6831-4373**. Reservations recommended. Entrees S$8–S$27 (US$4.55–US$15). AE, DC, MC, V. Daily 11:30am–2:30pm and 6:30–10:30pm.

Crystal Jade Palace ⊀ CHINESE CANTONESE   Although Crystal Jade Palace is an upmarket choice, it's a fantastic way to try Chinese food as it was intended. From the aquariums of soon-to-be-seafood-delights at the entrance, you can survey the rows of big round tables (and some small ones, too) packed with happy diners feasting away. The food here is authentic Cantonese, prepared by Hong Kong master chefs. Dim sum, fresh seafood, and barbecue dishes accompany exotic shark's fin and baby abalone. Scallop dishes are very popular and can be prepared either sautéed with cashews, chile, and soy; pan-fried with chiles, white pepper, and salt; or sautéed with green vegetables. The tender pan-fried cod in light honey sauce proves worthy of its reputation as a time-honored favorite. For a unique soup, try the double-boiled winter melon with mixed meats, mushrooms, crab, and dried scallops served in the halved melon shell. You can order Chinese or French wines to accompany your meal.

391 Orchard Rd., no. 04-19 Ngee Ann City. ℂ 65/735-2388. Reservations required. Small dishes S$12–S$38 (US$6.85–US$22); set lunch for 2 from S$50 (US$29). AE, DC, MC, V. Daily 11:30am–2:30pm and 6:30–10:30pm.

Patara Fine Thai THAI   Patara might say "fine dining" in its name, but the food here is home cooking: not too haute, not too traditional. Seafood and vegetables are big here. Deep-fried garoupa (grouper) is served in a sweet sauce with chile that can be added sparingly upon request. Curries are popular, too. The roast duck curry in red curry paste with tomatoes, rambutans, and pineapple is juicy and hot. For something really different, Patara's own invention, the Thai taco, isn't exactly traditional, but it's good, filled with chicken, shrimp, and sprouts. The green curry, one of my favorites, is perhaps the best in town. The Thai-style iced tea (which isn't on the menu, so you'll have to ask for it) is fragrant and flowery. A small selection of wines is also available. Patara has another outlet at Swissôtel Stamford Level 3, Stamford Road (ℂ 65/6339-1488).

No. 03-14 Tanglin Mall, 163 Tanglin Rd. ℂ 65/6737-0818. Reservations recommended for lunch, required for dinner. Entrees S$17–S$30 (US$9.70–US$17). AE, DC, MC, V. Daily noon–2:30pm and 6–10:30pm.

Tandoor 𝒢𝒢 NORTHERN INDIAN   Live music takes center stage in this small restaurant, adorned with carpets, artwork, and wood floors and furnishings. Entrees prepared in the tandoor oven come out flavorful and not as salty as most tandoori dishes. The tandoori lobster is rich, but the chef's specialty is crab lababdar: crabmeat, onions, and tomato sautéed in a coconut gravy. Fresh cottage cheese is made in-house for fresh and light saag panir, a favorite here. Chefs keep a close eye on the spices to ensure that the spice enhances the flavor rather than drowning it out—more times than not, customers ask them to add more spices. A final course of creamy masala tea perks you up and aids digestion. If you're curious, the tandoor oven is behind a glass wall in the back, so you can watch them prepare your food.

Holiday Inn Parkview, 11 Cavenagh Rd. ℂ 65/730-0153. Reservations recommended. Entrees S$11–S$40 (US$6.30–US$23). AE, DC, MC, V. Daily noon–2:30pm and 7–10:30pm.

INEXPENSIVE

Chatterbox SINGAPOREAN   If you'd like to try the local favorites but you don't want to deal with street food, then Chatterbox is the place for you. The Hainanese chicken rice is highly acclaimed, and other dishes—like nasi lemak, laksa, and carrot cake—are as close to the street as you can get. For a quick and tasty snack, order tahu goreng, deep-fried tofu in peanut chile sauce. This is also a good place to experiment with some of those really weird local drinks. Chin chow is the dark brown grass jelly drink; cendol is green jelly, red beans, palm sugar, and coconut milk; and bandung is the pink rose syrup milk with jelly. For dessert, order the ever-favorite sago pudding, made from the hearts of the sago palm. This informal and lively coffee shop dishes out room service for the Mandarin Hotel and is open 24 hours a day.

Mandarin Hotel, 333 Orchard Rd. ℂ 65/6737-4411. Reservations recommended for lunch and dinner. Entrees S$15–S$39 (US$8.55–US$22). AE, DC, MC, V. Daily 24 hr.

Genki Sushi *Value* JAPANESE   I ducked into Genki Sushi for lunch. I sat at the counter, where a tiny conveyor belt snaked along in front of me carrying colored plates full of glistening sushi, rolls, sashimi, and other treats. Just pick and eat—and pay per plate. So the goofy Japanese guy next to me got chatty. We discussed the conveyor-belt sushi bar concept and how much we both loved it, and then he poked some buttons on his electronic translator and showed me the screen. "This name in Japan." The translator spelled *revolution*. Makes sense, a "revolving" sushi bar, but now I'll never shake the image of Che Guevara sitting there plucking sushi off the belt.

No. 01-16 Forum The Shopping Mall, Orchard Rd. © 65/6734-2513. Reservations not accepted. Revolving plates S$1.90–S$6.50 (US$1.10–US$3.70). AE, DC, MC, V. Sun–Thurs 11:30am–9pm; Fri–Sat 11:30am–10pm.

The Rice Table MALAY/INDONESIAN   Indonesian Dutch rijsttafel, meaning "rice table," is a service of many small dishes (up to almost 20) with rice. Traditionally, each dish would be brought to diners by beautiful ladies in pompous style. Here, a busy waitstaff brings all the dishes out and places them in front of you—feast on favorite Indo-Malay wonders like beef rendang, chicken satay, otak otak, and sotong assam (squid) for a very reasonable price. It's an enormous amount of food, and everything is terrific. You pay extra for your drinks and desserts. There's an additional outlet at Cuppage Terrace at 43-45 Cuppage Rd. H$_2$O Zone (© 65/6735-9117).

International Bldg., 360 Orchard Rd., no. 02-09/10. © 65/6835-3783. Reservations not necessary. Lunch set S$13 (US$7.30); dinner set S$18.50 (US$11). AE, DC, MC, V. Tues–Sun noon–2:30pm and 6–9:30pm.

RESTAURANTS A LITTLE FARTHER OUT

There are some other really fantastic dining finds if you're willing to hop in a cab for 10 or 15 minutes. These places are worth the trip—for a chance to dine along the water at UDMC or amid lush terrace gardens at Alkaff Mansion, or to just go for superior seafood at Long Beach Seafood Restaurant. And don't worry about finding your way back: Most places always have cabs milling about. If not, restaurant staff will always help you call a taxi.

EXPENSIVE

Alkaff Mansion ☆ MALAY/INDONESIAN   Alkaff Mansion was built by the wealthy Arab Alkaff family not as a home, but as a place to throw elaborate parties; true to its mission, Alkaff Mansion is tops for elegant ambience. The mansion allows for indoor and outdoor patio dining at small tables glistening with starched white linens and small candles. The forest outside is a stunning backdrop. The dinner cuisine here is rijsttafel—home-style Indonesian fare that was influenced by Dutch tastes and is served in set menus that rotate weekly. A typical set dinner might include gado gado (a cold salad with sweet peanut sauce) and a soup. To announce the main course, a gong is sounded and ladies dressed in traditional kebaya sarongs carry out the dishes on platters. Main courses include the siakap masak asam turnis (fish in a tangy sauce); the udang kara kuning, which is a great choice for lobster; and the crayfish in chile sauce. In rijstaffel tradition, the dinner is served with rice, which is accompanied by an array of condiments like varieties of sambal and achar. Downstairs, Alkaff serves a huge buffet with nightly changing themes. I strongly recommend this place for a truly unique and memorable dining experience.

10 Telok Blangah Green (off Henderson Rd.), Telok Blangah Hill Park. © 65/6415-4888. Reservations recommended. Set rijstaffel menu S$60 (US$34) per person; buffet S$35 (US$20) per person. AE, DC, MC, V. Daily 11:30am–2:30pm and 6–10:30pm.

MODERATE

Long Beach Seafood Restaurant SEAFOOD   They really pack 'em in at this place. Tables are crammed together in what resembles a big indoor pavilion, complete with festive lights and the sounds of mighty feasting. This is one of the best places for fresh seafood of all kinds: fish like garoupa (grouper), sea bass, marble goby, and kingfish, and other creatures of the sea from prawns to cray-fish. The chile crab here is good, but the house specialty is really the pepper crab, chopped and deliciously smothered in a thick concoction of black pepper and soy. Huge chunks of crayfish are also tasty in the black pepper sauce and can be served in variations like barbecue, sambal, steamed with garlic, or in a bean sauce. Don't forget to order buns so you can sop up the sauce. You can also get veg-etable, chicken, beef, or venison dishes to complement, or choose from the menu selection of local favorites.

1018 East Coast Pkwy. ✆ 65/445-8833. Reservations recommended. Seafood is sold by weight according to seasonal prices. Most dishes S$9–S$16 (US$5.15–US$9.15). AE, DC, MC, V. Daily 5pm–1:15am.

Palm Beach ⚝ SEAFOOD   Palm Beach has two levels. Downstairs you have a dining hall that is extremely underdressed and informal, while upstairs is a lovely upscale setting. The food is great in either setting (the menu is the same) and very reasonably priced. Australian lobster graces the finest dish here—cooked in a clay pot with coconut milk and chile sauce. The chile crab is also great, but to me it seems a bit "local" if you're dining upstairs. Besides, it's very messy. A gift shop outside lets you bring home jars of hot pot sauce, achar (sweet sauce), chile sauce, and sambal. On weekends, if you don't have a reservation, you'll have to queue up.

5 Stadium Walk, no. 01-16 Leisure Park. ✆ 65/6344-3088. Reservations for dinner required. Seafood is sold by the gram according to seasonal prices. Most small dishes S$12–S$28 (US$6.85–US$16). AE, MC, V. Daily noon–2:30pm and 6–11:30pm.

Prima Tower Revolving Restaurant CHINESE BEIJING   One of the main attractions here is the fact that the restaurant revolves, giving you an ever-chang-ing view of the city from your table. The other main attraction is the food, which is Beijing-style Chinese. Naturally, the best dish is the Beijing duck, which has been a house specialty since this restaurant opened 20 years ago. All of the noodles for the noodle dishes are prepared in-house using traditional recipes and techniques, so the word of the day is *fresh*. Try them with minced pork and chopped cucumber in a sweet sauce. The restaurant manager comes to each table to present the daily specials. It's a good time to chat him up for the best dishes and ask questions about the menu.

201 Keppel Rd. ✆ 65/6272-8822. Reservations required. Small dishes S$14–S$50 (US$8–US$29) and up. AE, DC, MC, V. Mon–Sat 11am–2:30pm and 6:30–10:30pm; Sun 10:30am–2:30pm and 6:30–10:30pm. Closed Chinese New Year.

UDMC Seafood Centre ⚝⚝ SEAFOOD   Eight seafood restaurants are lined side by side in 2 blocks, their fronts open to the view of the sea outside. UDMC is a fantastic way to eat seafood Singapore style, in the open air, in restaurants that are more like grand stalls than anything else. Eat the famous local chile crab and pepper crab here, along with all sorts of squid, fish, and scallop dishes. Noo-dle dishes are also available, as are vegetable dishes and other meats. But the seafood is the thing to come for. Of the eight restaurants, there's no saying which is the best, as everyone seems to have their own opinions about this one or that one. (I like Jumbo at the far eastern end of the row; call ✆ **65/6442-3435** for reservations, which are recommended for weekends.) Have a nice stroll along the walkway and gaze out to the water while you decide which one to go for.

Block 1202 East Coast Pkwy. No phone. Seafood dishes are charged by weight, w/dishes from around S$12 (US$6.85). AE, DC, MC, V. Daily 5pm–midnight.

Xin Cuisine CHINESE CANTONESE/CHINESE HERBAL   A recent trend is to bring back the Chinese tradition of preparing foods that have special qualities for beauty, health, and vitality, balancing the body's yin and yang and restoring energy. Xin (new) cuisine transforms these concepts into light and flavorful creations, listed in a menu that's literally a book. The chef is famous for East-meets-West creations, but be assured that the cuisine is mostly Chinese. The concentrated seafood soup with chicken and spinach is a light and delicious broth that's neither too thick nor too thin and that has chunks of meat and shredded spinach. Stewed Mongolian rack of lamb is obviously not Cantonese but is as tender as butter and served in a sweet brown sauce with buns to soak up the gravy. The steamed eggplant with toasted sesame seed is fantastic, with warm, tender slices served in soy sauce. For the more adventurous, they serve up a mean dish of hasma scrambled egg whites. Hasma is frog glands, which are believed to improve the complexion. The dish is a little alarming to some, but served with a hint of ginger and scooped onto walnut melba toast, it's actually quite nice.

Concorde Hotel, 317 Outram Rd., Level 4. ✆ 65/6732-3337. Reservations recommended. Small dishes S$10–S$30 (US$5.70–US$17). AE, DC, MC, V. Daily noon– 2.30pm and 6:30–10:30pm.

INEXPENSIVE

Samy's Curry Restaurant ✦ SOUTHERN INDIAN   There are many places in Singapore to get good southern Indian banana leaf, but none quite so unique as Samy's out at Dempsey Road. Because it's part of the Singapore Civil Service Clubhouse, at lunchtime nonmembers must pay S50¢ (US30¢) to get in the door. Not that there's much of a door, because Samy's is situated in a huge, high-ceilinged, open-air hall, with shutters thrown back and fans whirring above. Wash your hands at the back and have a seat, and soon someone will slap a banana-leaf place mat in front of you. A blob of white rice will be placed in the center, and then buckets of vegetables, chicken, mutton, fish, prawn, and you name it will be brought out, swimming in the richest and spiciest curries to ever pass your lips. Take a peek in each bucket, shake your head yes when you see one you like, and a scoop will be dumped on your banana leaf. Eat with your right hand or with a fork and spoon. When you're done, wipe the sweat from your brow, fold the banana leaf away from you, and place your tableware on top. Samy's serves no alcohol, but the fresh lime juice is nice and cooling.

Block 25 Dempsey Rd. ✆ 65/6472-2080. Reservations not accepted. Sold by the scoop or piece, S80¢–S$3 (US46¢–US$1.70). V. Daily 11am–3pm and 6–10pm. No alcohol served.

HAWKER CENTERS

Hawker centers—large groupings of informal open-air food stalls—were Singapore's answer to fast and cheap food in the days before McDonald's came along, and are still the best way to sample every kind of Singaporean cuisine. They can be intimidating for newcomers, especially during the busy lunch or dinner rush, when they turn into fast-paced carnivals, so if it's your first time, try this: First, walk around to every stall to see what they have to offer. The stalls will have large signs displaying principal menu items, and you should feel free to ask questions before placing your order. Special stalls have drinks only. The fresh lime goes with any dish, but to be truly local, grab a giant bottle of Tiger beer.

Next, find a table. Some stalls have their own tables for you to use; otherwise, sit anywhere you can and when you order, let the hawker know where you are (tables usually have numbers to simplify). If it's crowded and you find a couple of free seats at an already occupied table, politely ask if they are taken, and if the answer is no, have a seat—it's perfectly customary. Your food will be brought to you, and you are expected to pay upon delivery. When you're finished, don't clear your own plates, and don't stack them. Some stalls observe strict religious customs that require different plates for different foods, and getting other scraps on their plates might be offensive.

For the record, all hawkers are licensed by the government, which inspects them and enforces health standards.

The most notorious hawker center in Singapore is **Newton.** Located at Newton Circus, the intersection of Scotts Road, Newton Road, and Bukit Timah/Dunearn Road, this place is notorious, as opposed to famous, for being an over-commercialized tourist spectacle where busloads of foreigners come and gawk at the Singaporean fast-food experience. All in all, if you want to check it out, it is a good initiation before moving on to the real places. **Lau Pa Set Festival Village** (Telok Ayer Market) is located in Chinatown at the corner of Raffles Way and Boon Tat Street, and sometimes gets touristy, too, but for the record, both Newton and Lau Pa Set are open 24 hours.

In the Historic District, there are a few. Try the one on Hill Street next to the Central Fire Station or the one on Stamford Road between the National Museum and Armenian Street intersection. You'll also find a couple on Victoria Street on either side of Allson Hotel, and another at Bugis night market.

In Little India, Zhujiao Centre is a nice-size hawker center. **On Orchard Road,** try Cuppage Terrace, just beyond the Centrepoint Shopping Centre.

One place that's been near and dear to Singaporeans for years (though now they've mostly been chased away by overcommercialization) is the **Satay Club** (★). It used to be down at the Esplanade, but constant building and land-reclamation efforts moved it around a bunch of times, so they eventually moved it to Clarke Quay off River Valley Road. Yes, it is very touristy now, but it's still worth a visit. Satay, by the way, is perhaps the most popular Malay dish of all time. The small kabobs of meat are skewered onto the stiff veins of palm leaves and barbecued over a hibachi. Order them by the stick. They come with cucumbers and onion on the side, and a bowl of peanut chile sauce to dunk it all in. Find yourself a table, get some beer, order yourself up a whole plate, and you'll be happy as a clam, whether you look like a tourist or not.

5 Attractions

A note: Many of the sights to see in Singapore are not of the "pay your fee and see the show" variety, but rather historic buildings, monuments, and places of religious worship. The city's historic buildings, such as City Hall or Parliament House, must be appreciated from the outside, their significance lying in their unique architecture and historical context combined with the sensual effect of the surrounding city. Monuments and statues tell the stories of events and heroes important to Singapore in both the past and the present. The places of worship listed in this section are open to the public and free of entrance charge. Expect temples to be open from sunup to sundown. Visiting hours are not specific to the hour, but unless it's a holiday (when hours might be extended), you can expect these places to be open during daylight hours.

THE HISTORIC DISTRICT

Armenian Church ✦ The first permanent Christian church in Singapore, it was funded primarily by the Armenian community, which was at one time quite powerful. Today few Singaporeans can trace their heritage back to this influential group of immigrants. The church was consecrated in 1836, and the last appointed priest serving the parish retired in 1936. Although regular Armenian services are no longer held, other religious organizations make use of the church from time to time. The cemetery in the back of the church is the burial site of many prominent Armenians, including Ashgen Agnes Joachim, discoverer of the Vanda Miss Joachim, Singapore's national flower.

60 Hill St., across from the Grand Plaza Hotel. ✆ 65/6334-0141.

Asian Civilisations Museum ✦✦✦ The old Tao Nan School, which dates from 1910, was completely renovated and reopened in 1997 to house the Asian Civilisations Museum. Beautiful and clear exhibits display fine collections of jade, calligraphy, ceramics, furniture, and artworks, all offering visitors the chance to trace the archipelago's rich Chinese heritage. Changing exhibits in the temporary galleries represent the other Asian civilizations.

39 Armenian St. ✆ 65/6332-3015. Adults S$3 (US$1.70), children and seniors S$1.50 (US86¢). Tues–Sun 9am–6pm (extended hr. Fri until 9pm). Free guided tours in English Tues–Fri 11am and 2pm, w/an extra tour on weekends at 3:30. City Hall MRT, and follow Stamford Rd. to Armenian St.

Bugis Street/Bugis Junction If you happened to visit Singapore in the 1970s and remember Bugis as a haven for transvestites and sex shows, you're in for a big surprise: Bugis Street ain't what it used to be. In place of the decadence is a giant shopping mall, Parco Bugis Junction. There's also a night market with a few bargains on cheap chic, curio items, accessories, and video disks.

The area around Bugis Street has a more benign history. The Bugis, fierce and respected warriors, were some of the first people to settle on Singapore in its early years. Raffles took note of their boat-building skills and, as part of his master town plan, included Bugis Town to attract more of them to the island.

Bugis MRT stop, across from Parco Bugis Junction shopping mall.

Cathedral of the Good Shepherd This cathedral was Singapore's first permanent Catholic church. Built in the 1840s, it brought together many elements of a fractured parish—Portuguese, French, and Spanish—to worship under one roof. Designed in a Latin cross pattern, much of its architecture is reminiscent of St. Martin-in-the-Fields and St. Paul's in Covent Garden.

4 Queen St., at the corner of Queen St. and Bras Basah Rd. ✆ 65/6337-2036. Open to the public during the day.

CHIJMES (Convent of the Holy Infant Jesus) CHIJMES (pronounced "Chimes") is a bustling enclave of retail shops, restaurants, and nightspots. It's difficult to imagine that this was once a convent that, at its founding in 1854, consisted of a lone, simply constructed bungalow. After decades of buildings and add-ons, this collection of unique yet perfectly blended structures was enclosed within walls, forming peaceful courtyards and open spaces encompassing an entire city block. In late 1983, the convent relocated to the suburbs, and some of the block was leveled to make way for the MRT headquarters. Thankfully, most of the block survived and the Singapore government, in planning the renovation of this desirable piece of real estate, wisely kept the integrity of the architecture. For an evening out, the atmosphere at CHIJMES is exquisitely romantic.

Urban Singapore Attractions

HISTORIC DISTRICT
Armenian Church **22**
Asian Civilisations Museum **19**
Boat Quay **32**
Bugis Street/Bugis Junction **12**
Cathedral of the Good Shepherd **16**
Chettiar's Hindu Temple **4**
CHIJMES **17**
City Hall (Municipal Building) **26**
Clarke Quay **23**
Empress Place Building **31**
Esplanade Park **27**
Fort Canning Park **20**
Hill Street Building **24**
Kuan Yin Thong Hood Cho
    Temple **13**
Merlion Park **28**
Parliament House **29**
Raffles Hotel **18**
Raffles Landing Site **30**
St. Andrew's Cathedral **25**
Singapore Art Museum **14**
Singapore History Museum **15**
Singapore Philatelic Museum **21**
Statue of Raffles **31**
Supreme Court **26**
Victoria Theatre and
    Concert Hall **31**

LITTLE INDIA
Abdul Gafoor Mosque **8**
Sri Perumal Temple **6**
Sri Veerama Kaliamman Temple **7**
Temple of a Thousand Lights **5**

**ARAB STREET &
    KAMPONG GLAM**
Alsagoff Arab School **9**
Hajjah Fatimah Mosque **10**
Istana Kampong Glam **11**
Sultan Mosque **11**

CHINATOWN
Al-Abrar Mosque **38**
Chinatown Heritage Centre **34**
Jamae Mosque **35**
Lau Pa Sat Festival Pavilion **40**
Nagore Durgha **39**
Sri Mariamman Hindu Temple **36**
Thian Hock Keng Temple **39**
Urban Development Association
    (URA) Gallery **37**
Wak Hai Cheng Bio Temple **33**

ORCHARD ROAD AREA
The Istana **2**
Peranakan Place **3**
Goodwood Park Hotel **1**

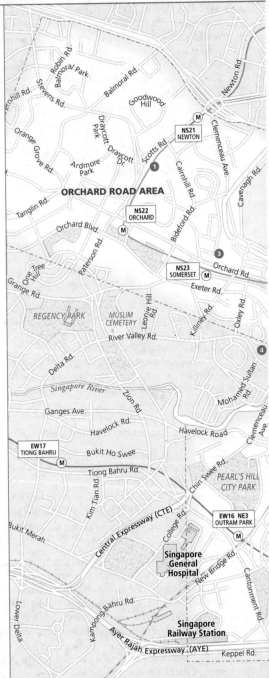

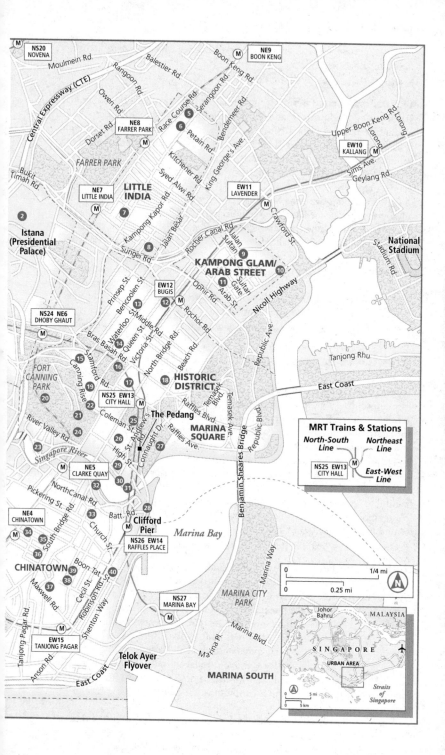

At the same time, you can enjoy a special decadence when you party in one of the popular bars here.

30 Victoria St. Free admission. ✆ 65/6337-7810.

City Hall (Municipal Building)   During the Japanese occupation, City Hall was a major headquarters, and it was here in 1945 that Adm. Lord Louis Mountbatten accepted the Japanese surrender. In 1951, the Royal Proclamation from King George VI was read here declaring that Singapore would henceforth be known as a city. Fourteen years later, Prime Minister Lee Kuan Yew announced to its citizens that Singapore would henceforth be called an independent republic.

City Hall, along with the Supreme Court, was judiciously sited to take full advantage of the prime location. Magnificent Corinthian columns march across the front of the symmetrically designed building, while inside, two courtyards lend an ambience of informality to otherwise officious surroundings. For all its magnificence and historical fame, however, its architect, F. D. Meadows, relied too heavily on European influence. The many windows afford no protection from the sun, and the entrance leaves pedestrians unsheltered from the elements. In defining the very nobility of the Singapore government, it appears the Singaporean climate wasn't taken into consideration.

St. Andrew's Rd., across from the Padang. Entrance to the visitor's gallery is permitted, but all other areas are off-limits.

Empress Place Building   Standing as a symbol of British colonial authority as travelers entered the Singapore River, Empress Place Building housed almost the entire government bureaucracy around the year 1905 and was a government office until the 1980s, housing the Registry of Births and Deaths and the Citizenship Registry. Every Singaporean at some point passed through its doors. In the late 1980s, the government offices moved out and the building was restored as an historical cultural exhibition venue.

· The oldest portion is the part nearest Parliament House; it was designed by colonial engineer J. F. A. McNair and built by convict labor between June 1864 and December 1867. Four major additions and other renovations have been faithful to his original design. Inside, there are many surviving details, including plaster moldings, cornices, and architraves. It is currently being renovated as the second phase of the Asian Civilisations Museum.

1 Empress Place, at the S end of the Padang next to the Parliament Bldg.

Fort Canning Park   When Stamford Raffles first navigated the Singapore River, he was already envisioning a port settlement and had designs to build his own home atop the hill that is today this park. His home, a simple wooden structure (at the site of the present-day lookout point), later became a residence for Singapore's Residents and Governors. In 1860, the house was torn down to make way for **Fort Canning,** which was built to quell British fears of invasion but instead quickly became the laughingstock of the island. In 1907, the fort was demolished to make way for a reservoir. Today the only reminders of the old fort are some of the walls and the Fort Gate, a deep stone structure. Behind its huge wooden door, you'll find a narrow staircase that leads to the roof of the structure.

Fort Canning was also the site of a **European cemetery.** To make improvements in the park, the graves were exhumed and the stones were placed within the walls surrounding the outdoor performance field that slopes from the Music and Drama Society building. A large Gothic monument was erected in memory of James Napier Brooke, infant son of William Napier, Singapore's first Law Agent, and his wife, Maria Frances, the widow of prolific architect George Coleman. Although no records exist, Coleman probably designed the cupolas as well as two small monuments over unknown graves. The Music and Drama Society building itself was built in 1938. Close by, in the wall, are the tombstones of Coleman and of Jose D'Almeida, a wealthy Portuguese merchant.

© 65/3663-3307. Major entrances are from behind the MITA building, Percival Rd. (Drama Centre), Fort Canning Aquarium, National Library Carpark, and Canning Walk (behind Park Mall). Free admission. Dhoby Gaut or City Hall MRT.

Kuan Yin Thong Hood Cho Temple

It's said that whatever you wish for within the walls of Kuan Yin Temple comes true, so get in line and have your wishes ready. It must work because there's a steady stream of people on auspicious days of the Chinese calendar. The procedure is simple: Wear shoes easily slipped off before entering the temple. Light several joss sticks. Pray to the local god, pray to the sky god, and then turn to the side and pray some more. Now pick up the container filled with inscriptions and shake it until one stick falls out. After that, head for the interpretation box office to get a piece of paper with verses in Mandarin and English to look up what your particular inscription means. (For a small fee, there are interpreters outside.) Now for the payback: If your wish comes true, be prepared to return to the temple and offer fruits and flowers to say thanks (oranges, pears, and apples are a thoughtful choice and jasmine petals are especially nice). Be careful what you wish for. Once you're back home and that job promotion comes through, your new manager might nix another vacation so soon. To be on the safe side, bring the goods with you when you make your wish.

Waterloo St., about 1½ blocks from Bras Basah Rd. Open to the public during the day.

The Padang

This large field—officially called Padang Besar but known as the Padang—has witnessed its share of historical events. It is bordered on one end by the Singapore Recreation Club and on the other end by the Singapore Cricket Club, and flanked by City Hall. The Padang is mainly used for public and sporting events—pleasant activities—but in the 1940s it felt more forlorn footsteps when the invading Japanese forced the entire European community onto the field. There they waited while the occupation officers dickered over a suitable location for the "conquered." Presently, they ordered all British, Australian, and Allied troops as well as European prisoners on the 22km (13½-mile) march to Changi.

An interesting side note: Frank Ward, designer of the Supreme Court, had big plans for the Padang and surrounding buildings. He would have demolished the Cricket Club, Parliament House, and the Victoria Hall & Theatre to erect an enormous government block if World War II hadn't arrived, ruining his chances.

St. Andrew's Rd. and Connaught Dr.

Parliament House

Parliament House, built in 1826, is probably Singapore's oldest surviving structure, even though it has been renovated so many times that it no longer looks the way it was originally constructed. The original house was designed by architect George D. Coleman, who had helped Raffles with his Town Plan of 1822. Coleman's design was in the English neo-Palladian style. Simple and well suited to the tropics, this style was popular at the time with Calcutta merchants. Major alterations have left very little behind of Coleman's design, however, replacing it with an eclectic French classical style, but some of his work survives. Today the building has been transformed once again, into part of a larger S$80 million (US$45.6 million) Parliament Complex.

The bronze elephant in front of Parliament House was a gift to Singapore in 1872 from His Majesty Somdeth Phra Paraminda Maha Chulalongkorn (Rama V), Supreme King of Siam, as a token of gratitude following his stay in the previous year.

1 High St., at the S end of the Padang, next to the Supreme Court. Closed to the general public, but worth seeing from the outside.

Raffles Hotel ⭐⭐   Built in 1887 to accommodate the increasing upper-class trade, Raffles Hotel was originally only a couple of bungalows with 10 rooms, but, oh, the view of the sea was perfection. The owners, Armenian brothers named Sarkies, already had a couple of prosperous hotels in Southeast Asia (the Eastern & Oriental in Penang and The Strand in Rangoon) and were well versed in the business. It wasn't long before they added a pair of wings and completed the main building—and reading rooms, verandas, dining rooms, a grand lobby, the Bar and Billiards Room, a ballroom, and a string of shops. By 1899, electricity was turning the cooling fans and providing the pleasing glow of comfort.

As it made its madcap dash through the 1920s, the hotel was the place to see and be seen. Vacancies were unheard of. Hungry Singaporeans and guests from other hotels, eager for a glimpse of the fabulous dining room, were turned away for lack of reservations. The crowded ballroom was jumping every night of the week. During this time, Raffles's guest book included famous authors like Somerset Maugham, Rudyard Kipling, Joseph Conrad, and Noël Coward. These were indeed the glory years, but the lovely glimmer from the chandeliers soon faded with the stark arrival of the Great Depression. Raffles managed to limp through that dark time—and, darker still, through the Japanese occupation—and later pull back from the brink of bankruptcy to undergo modernization in the fifties. But fresher, brighter, more opulent hotels were taking root on Orchard Road, pushing the "grand old lady" to the back seat.

The hotel was in limbo for a period of time due to legal matters, and in 1961 it passed through several financial institutions to land on the doorstep of the Development Bank of Singapore (DBS). It was probably this journey that saved the Raffles from a haphazard renovation nightmare. Instead, history-minded renovators selected 1915 as a benchmark and, with a few changes here and there, faithfully restored the hotel to that era's magnificence and splendor. Today the hotel's restaurants and nightlife draw thousands of visitors daily to its open lobby, its theater playhouse, the Raffles Hotel Museum, and 65 exclusive boutiques. Its 15 restaurants and bars—especially the Tiffin Room, Raffles Grill, and Doc Cheng's, all reviewed in chapter 4—are a wonder, as is its famous Bar and Billiards Room and Long Bar.

1 Beach Rd. © 65/337-1886.

Raffles Landing Site   The polymarble statue at this site was unveiled in 1972. It was made from plaster casts of the original 1887 figure located in front of the Victoria Theatre and Concert Hall (see below), and it stands on what is believed to be the site where Sir Stamford Raffles landed on January 29, 1819.

North Boat Quay.

St. Andrew's Cathedral   Designed by George Coleman and erected on a site selected by Sir Stamford Raffles himself, St. Andrew's was the colonial's Anglican

Church. Completed toward the end of the 1830s, its tower and spire were added several years later to accord the edifice more stature. By 1852, because of massive damage sustained from lightning strikes, the cathedral was deemed unsafe and was torn down. The cathedral that now stands on the site was completed in 1860. Of English Gothic Revival design, the cathedral is one of the few standing churches of this style in the region.

Coleman St., between North Bridge Rd. and St. Andrew's Rd., across from the Padang. ℂ 65/6337-6104. Open during daylight hours.

Singapore Art Museum ⋆

The Singapore Art Museum (SAM) officially opened in 1996 to house an impressive collection of more than 3,000 pieces of art and sculpture, most of it by Singaporean and Malay artists. A large collection of Southeast Asian pieces rotates regularly, along with visiting international exhibits. Once a Catholic boys' school established in 1852, SAM has retained some visible reminders of its former occupants: Above the front door of the main building, you can still see inscribed ST. JOSEPH'S INSTITUTION, and a bronze-toned cast-iron statue of St. John Baptist de la Salle with two children stands in its original place.

71 Bras Basah Rd. ℂ 65/6332-3222. www.museum.org.sg. Adults S$3 (US$1.70), children and seniors S$1.50 (US86¢). Tues–Sun 9am–6pm (extended hr. Fri until 9pm). Free guided tours in English Tues–Fri 11am and 2pm, w/additional weekend tour at 3:30pm. City Hall MRT, across Bras Basah Park from the Singapore History Museum.

Singapore History Museum ⋆⋆

Originally called Raffles Museum, the museum was opened in 1887, in a handsome example of neo-Palladian architecture designed by colonial architect Henry McCallum. It was the first of its kind in Southeast Asia, housing a superb collection of regional natural history specimens and ethnographic displays. In both 1907 and 1916, the museum outgrew its space and was enlarged. Renamed the National Museum in 1969, its collections went through a transformation, focusing on Singapore's history rather than that of the archipelago. Several years later, it became known as the Singapore History Museum.

93 Stamford Rd., across the street from Bras Basah Park. ℂ 65/6332-3659. National Heritage Board www. museum.org.sg/nhb.html. Adults S$3 (US$1.70), children and seniors S$1.50 (US86¢). Tues–Sun 9am–6pm (extended hr. Fri until 9am). Free guided tours in English Tues–Fri 11am and 2pm, w/an extra tour on weekends at 3:30pm.

Singapore Philatelic Museum

This building, constructed in 1895 to house the Methodist Book Room, recently underwent a S$7 million (nearly US$4 million) restoration and reopened as the Philatelic Museum in 1995. Exhibits include a fine collection of old stamps issued to commemorate historically important events, first-day covers, antique printing plates, postal service memorabilia, and private collections. Visitors can trace the development of a stamp from idea to the finished sheet, and can even design their own. Free guided tours are available upon request.

23B Coleman St. ℂ 65/6337-3888. Adults S$2 (US$1.15), children and seniors S$1 (US55¢). Tues–Sun 9am–6pm. Take the MRT to City Hall and walk toward Coleman St.

Statue of Raffles

This sculpture of Sir Stamford Raffles was erected on the Padang in 1887 and moved to its present position after getting in the way of one too many cricket matches. During the Japanese occupation, the statue was placed in the Singapore History Museum (then the Raffles Museum) and was replaced here in 1945. The local joke is that Raffles's arm is outstretched to the

Bank of China building, and his pockets are empty. (*Translation:* In terms of wealth in Singapore, it's Chinese one, Brits nil.)

Victoria Theatre and Concert Hall.

Supreme Court The Supreme Court stands on the site of the old Hotel de L'Europe, a rival of the Raffles Hotel until it went bankrupt in the 1930s. The court's structure, a classical style favored for official buildings the world over, was completed in 1939. With its spare adornment and architectural simplicity, the edifice has a no-nonsense, utilitarian attitude, and the sculptures across the front, executed by the Italian sculptor Cavaliere Rodolpho Nolli, echo what transpires within. Justice is the most breathtaking, standing 2.7m (9 ft.) high and weighing almost 4 tons. Kneeling on either side of her are representations of Supplication and Thankfulness. To the far left are Deceit and Violence. To the far right, a bull represents Prosperity and two children hold wheat, to depict Abundance.

Two and a half million bricks were used in building this structure, but take a moment to note the stonework: It's fake! Really a gypsum type of plaster, it was applied by Chinese plasterers who fled from Shanghai during the Sino-Japanese conflict, and molded to give the appearance of granite.

While taking in the exterior, look up at the dome, which is a copy of the dome of St. Paul's Cathedral in London. The dome covers the courtyard, which is surrounded by the four major portions of the Supreme Court building.

St. Andrew's Rd., across from the Padang. Closed to visitors, but worth seeing from the outside.

Victoria Theatre and Concert Hall Designed by colonial engineer John Bennett in a Victorian Revival style that was fashionable in Britain at the time, the theater portion was built in 1862 as the Town Hall. Victoria Memorial Hall was built in 1905 as a memorial to Queen Victoria, retaining the same style of the old building. The clock tower was added a year later. In 1909, with its name changed to Victoria Theatre, the hall opened with an amateur production of the *Pirates of Penzance*. Another notable performance occurred when Noël Coward passed through Singapore and stepped in at the last moment to help out a traveling English theatrical company that had lost a leading man. The building looks much the same as it did then, though, of course, the interiors have been modernized. It was completely renovated in 1979, conserving all the original details, and was renamed Victoria Concert Hall. It housed the Singapore Symphony Orchestra until the opening of The Esplanade—Theatres on the Bay, when it shifted to the larger digs.

9 Empress Place, at the S end of the Padang. © 65/339-6120.

ALONG THE RIVER

The Singapore River had always been the heart of life in Singapore even before Raffles landed, but for many years during the 20th century, life here was dead—quite literally. Rapid urban development that began in the 1950s turned the river into a giant sewer, killing all plant and animal life in it. In the mid-1980s, though, the government began a large and surprisingly successful cleanup project. Shortly thereafter, the buildings at Boat Quay and Clarke Quay were restored. Now the areas on both banks of the river offer entertainment, food, and pubs day and night.

Boat Quay ⭑ Known as "the belly of the carp" by the local Chinese because of its shape, this area was once notorious for its opium dens and coolie shops.

Nowadays, thriving restaurants boast every cuisine imaginable, and the rocking nightlife offers up a variety of sounds—jazz, rock, blues, Indian, and Caribe—that are lively enough to get any couch potato tapping his feet. Remember to pronounce *quay* as "key" if you don't want people to look at you funny.

Located on the S bank of the Singapore River between Cavenagh Bridge and Elgin Bridge.

Chettiar's Hindu Temple (aka the Tank Road Temple)   One of the richest and grandest of its kind in Southeast Asia, the Tank Road Temple is most famous for a **thoonganai maadam,** a statue of an elephant's backside in a seated position. It's said that there are only four others of the kind, located in four temples in India. The original temple was completed in 1860, restored in 1962, and practically rebuilt in 1984. Used daily for worship, the temple is also the culmination point of Thaipusam, a celebration of thanks, and the Festival of Navarathiri.

15 Tank Rd., close to the intersection of Clemenceau Ave. and River Valley Rd.

Clarke Quay   The largest of the waterfront developments, Clarke Quay was named for the second governor of Singapore, Sir Andrew Clarke. In the 1880s, a pineapple cannery, iron foundry, and numerous warehouses made this area bustle. Today, with 60 restored warehouses hosting restaurants and a shopping section known as Clarke Quay Factory Stores, the Quay still hops. **River House,** formerly the home of a *towkay* (company president), occupies the oldest building. The **Bar Gelateria Bellavista** ice cream parlor (River Valley Rd. at Coleman Bridge) was once the icehouse. On Thursday and Friday from 6:30 to 8:15pm, enthusiasts can catch a **Chinese opera performance** and makeup demonstration—it's a treat to watch. Get up early on Sunday, forgo the comics section, and take in the **flea market,** which opens at 9am and lasts all day. You'll find lots of bargains on unusual finds.

River Valley Rd. west of Coleman Bridge. ✆ 65/6337-3292.

Esplanade Park   Esplanade Park and Queen Elizabeth Walk, two of the most famous parks in Singapore, were established in 1943 on land reclaimed from the sea. Several memorials are located here. The first is a fountain built in 1857 to honor **Tan Kim Seng,** who gave a great sum of money toward the building of a waterworks. Another monument, **the Cenotaph,** commemorates the 124 Singaporeans who died in World War I; it was dedicated by the Prince of Wales. On the reverse side, the names of those who died in World War II have been inscribed. The third prominent memorial is dedicated to **Major General Lim Bo Seng,** a member of the Singaporean underground resistance in World War II who was captured and killed by the Japanese. His memorial was unveiled in 1954 on the 10th anniversary of his death. At the far end of the park, the Esplanade—Theatres on the Bay opened in October 2002. Fashioned after the Sydney Opera House, the unique double-domed structure is known locally as The Durians, because their spiky domes resemble halves of durian shells (the building itself is actually smooth—the "spikes" are sun shields).

Connaught Dr., on the marina, running from the mouth of the Singapore River along the Padang to The Esplanade–Theatres on the Bay. Daily until midnight.

Merlion Park   The Merlion is Singapore's half-lion, half-fish national symbol, the with lion representing Singapore's roots as the "Lion City" and the fish representing the nation's close ties to the sea. Bet you think a magical and awe-inspiring beast like this has been around in tales for hundreds of years, right? No such luck. He was the creation of some scheming mind at the Singapore Tourism Board in the early 1970s. Talk about the collision of ancient culture and the modern world. Despite the Merlion's commercial beginnings, he has been adopted as the national symbol and spouts continuously every day at the mouth of the Singapore River.

S bank, at the mouth of the Singapore River, adjacent to One Fullerton. Free admission. Daily 7am–10pm.

CHINATOWN/TANJONG PAGAR

Al-Abrar Mosque   This mosque was originally erected as a thatched building in 1827 and was also called Masjid Chulia and Kuchu Palli, which in Tamil means "hut mosque." The building that stands today was built in the 1850s, and even though it faces Mecca, the complex conforms with the grid of the neighborhood's city streets. In the late 1980s, the mosque underwent major renovations that enlarged the mihrab and stripped away some of the ornamental qualities of the columns in the building. The one-story prayer hall was extended upward into a two-story gallery. Little touches like the timber window panels and fanlight windows have been carried over into the new renovations.

192 Telok Ayer St., near the corner of Telok Ayer St. and Amoy St., near Thian Hock Keng Temple.

Jamae Mosque   Jamae Mosque was built by the Chulias, Tamil Muslims who were some of the earlier immigrants to Singapore, and who had a very influential hold over Indian Muslim life centered in the Chinatown area. It was the Chulias who built not only this mosque, but Masjid Al-Abrar and the Nagore Durgha Shrine as well. Jamae Mosque dates from 1827 but wasn't completed until the early 1830s. The mosque stands today almost exactly as it did then.

18 South Bridge Rd., at the corner of South Bridge Rd. and Mosque St.

Lau Pa Sat Festival Pavilion   Though it used to be well beloved, the locals think this place has become an atrocity. Once the happy little hawker center known as Telok Ayer Market, it began life as a wet market, selling fruits, vegetables, and other foodstuffs. Now it's part hawker center, part Western fast-food outlets, and all tourist. Lau Pa Sat is one of the few hawker centers that's open 24 hours, in case you need a coffee or snack before retiring.

18 Raffles Quay, located in the entire block flanked by Robinson Rd., Cross St., Shenton Way, and Boon Tat St.

Nagore Durgha Shrine   Although this is a Muslim place of worship, it is not a mosque, but a shrine, built to commemorate a visit to the island by a Muslim holy man of the Chulia people (Muslim merchants and money-lenders from India's Coromandel Coast), who was traveling around Southeast Asia spreading the word of Indian Islam. The most interesting visual feature is its facade: Two arched windows flank an arched doorway, with columns in between. Above these is a "miniature palace"—a massive replica of the facade of a palace, with tiny cutout windows and a small arched doorway in the middle. The cutouts in white plaster make it look like lace. From the corners of the facade, two 14-level minarets rise, with three little domed cutouts on each level and onion domes on top. Inside, the prayer halls and two shrines are painted and decorated in shockingly tacky colors.

140 Telok Ayer St., at the corner of Telok Ayer St. and Boon Tat St. ✆ 65/6324-0021.

Sri Mariamman Hindu Temple   As the oldest Hindu temple in Singapore, Sri Mariamman has been the central point of Hindu tradition and culture. In its early years, the temple housed new immigrants while they established themselves and also served as social center for the community. Today the main celebration here is the Thimithi Festival in October or November. The shrine is dedicated to the goddess Sri Mariamman, who is known for curing disease, but as is the case at all other Hindu temples, the entire pantheon of Hindu gods is present to be worshipped as well.

244 South Bridge Rd., at the corner of South Bridge Rd. and Pagoda St.

Thian Hock Keng Temple ★★★   Thian Hock Keng, the "Temple of Heavenly Bliss," is one of the oldest Chinese temples in Singapore. Before land reclamation, when the shoreline came right up to Telok Ayer Road, the first Chinese sailors landed here and immediately built a shrine, a small wood-and-thatch structure, to pray to the goddess Ma Po Cho for allowing their voyage to be safely completed. For each subsequent boatload of Chinese sailors, the shrine was always the first stop upon landing. Ma Po Cho, the Mother of the Heavenly Sages, was the patron goddess of sailors, and every Chinese junk of the day had an altar dedicated to her. The temple that stands today was built in 1841 over the shrine with funds from the Hokkien community. All of the building materials were imported from China, except for the gates, which came from Glasgow, Scotland, and the tiles on the facade, which are from Holland.

158 Telok Ayer St., ½ block beyond Nagore Durgha Shrine. ℂ 65/6423-4626.

Wak Hai Cheng Bio Temple ★★   Like most of Singapore's Chinese temples, Wak Hai Cheng Bio had its start as a simple wood-and-thatch shrine where sailors, when they got off their ships, would go to express their gratitude for sailing safely to their destination. Before the major land-reclamation projects shifted the shoreline outward, the temple was close to the water's edge, so it was named "Temple of the Calm Sea Built by the Guangzhou People." It's a Teochew temple, located in a part of Chinatown populated mostly by the Teochews. The temple itself is quite a visual treat, with ceramic figurines and pagodas adorning the roof, and every nook and cranny of the structure adorned with tiny three-dimensional reliefs that depict scenes from Chinese operas. The spiral joss hanging in the courtyard adds an additional picturesque effect.

30-B Phillip St., at the corner of Phillip St. and Church St.

LITTLE INDIA

Abdul Gafoor Mosque   Abdul Gafoor Mosque is actually a mosque complex consisting of the original mosque, a row of shop houses facing Dunlop Street, a prayer hall, and another row of houses ornamented with crescent moons and stars, facing the mosque. The original mosque was called Masjid Al-Abrar and is commemorated on a granite plaque above what could have been either the entrance gate or the mosque itself. It still stands and, even though it is badly dilapidated, retains some of its original beauty. One beautiful detail is the sunburst above the main entrance, its rays decorated with Arabic calligraphy.

Restoration of the shophouses is underway, including transformation of the facing shophouses into a religious school.

41 Dunlop St., between Perak Rd. and Jalan Besar.

Sakya Muni Buddha Gaya (Temple of a Thousand Lights)   Thai elements influence this temple, from the chedi (stupa) roofline to the huge Thai-style Buddha image inside. Often this temple is brushed off as strange and tacky, but there are all sorts of surprises inside, making the place a veritable Buddha theme park. On the right side of the altar, statues of baby boddhisattvas receive toys and sweets from worshippers. Around the base of the altar, murals depict scenes from the life of Prince Siddhartha (Buddha) as he searches for enlightenment. Follow them around to the back of the hall, and you'll find a small doorway to a chamber under the altar. Another Buddha image reclines inside, this one shown at the end of his life, beneath the Yellow Seraka tree. On the left side of the main part of the hall is a replica of a footprint left by the Buddha in Ceylon. Next to that is a wheel of fortune. For 50¢, you get one spin.

336 On Race Course Rd., 1 block past Perumal Rd. ℂ 65/6294-0714. Daily 7:30am–4:45pm

Sri Perumal Temple   Sri Perumal Temple is devoted to the worship of Vishnu. As part of the Hindu trinity, Vishnu is the sustainer, balancing out Brahma the creator and Shiva the destroyer. When the world is out of whack, he rushes to its aid, reincarnating himself to show mankind that there are always new directions for development.

The temple was built in 1855 and was most recently renovated in 1992. During Thaipusam, the main festival celebrated here, male devotees who have made vows over the year carry *kavadi*—huge steel racks decorated with flowers and fruits and held onto their bodies by skewers and hooks—to show their thanks and devotion, while women carry milk pots in a parade from Sri Perumal Temple to Chettiar's Temple on Tank Road.

397 Serangoon Rd., ½ block past Perumal Rd. Best times to visit are daily 7–11am or 5–7:30pm.

Sri Veerama Kaliamman Temple 🌂🌂   This Hindu temple is used primarily for the worship of Shiva's wife Kali, who destroys ignorance, maintains world order, and blesses those who strive for knowledge of God. The box on the walkway to the front entrance is for smashing coconuts, a symbolic smashing of the ego, asking God to show "the humble way." The coconuts have two small "eyes" at one end so they can "see" the personal obstacles to humility they are being asked to smash. Inside the temple in the main hall are three altars, the center one for Kali (depicted with 16 arms and wearing a necklace of human skulls) and two altars on either side for her two sons—Ganesh, the elephant god, and Murugan, the four-headed child god. To the right is an altar with nine statues representing the nine planets. Circle the altar and pray to your planet for help with a specific trouble.

On Serangoon Rd. at Veerasamy Rd. Daily 8am–noon and 5:30–8:30pm.

ARAB STREET & KAMPONG GLAM

Hajjah Fatimah Mosque 🌂🌂   Hajjah Fatimah was a wealthy businesswoman from Malacca and something of a local socialite. She had originally built a home on this site, but after it was robbed a couple of times and later set fire to, she decided to build a mosque here and moved to another home. Inside the high walls of the compound are the prayer hall, an ablution area, gardens and mausoleums, and a few other buildings. You can walk around the main prayer halls to the garden cemeteries, where flat square headstones mark the graves of women and round ones mark the graves of men. Hajjah Fatimah is buried in a private room to the side of the main prayer hall, along with her daughter and son-in-law.

4001 Beach Rd., past Jalan Sultan.

Istana Kampong Glam   The Istana Kampong Glam hardly seems a fitting palace for Singapore's former royal family, but there's a fascinating and controversial story behind its current state of sad disrepair. In 1819, Sultan Hussein signed the original treaty that permitted the British East India Trading Company to set up operations in Singapore. Then, in 1824, he signed a new treaty in which he gave up his sovereign rights to the country in return for Kampong Glam (which became his personal residence) and an annual stipend for himself and his descendants. Shortly after his death some 11 years later, his son, Sultan Ali, built the palace. The family fortunes began to dwindle over the years that followed, and a decades-long dispute arose between Ali's descendants over ownership rights to the estate. In the late 1890s, they went to court, where it was decided that no one had the rights as the successor to the sultanate, and the land reverted to the state, though the family was allowed to remain in the house. Trouble is, because the place had become state owned, the family lost the authority to improve the buildings of the compound, which is why they've fallen into the dilapidated condition you see today.

Located at the end of Sultan Gate, 1 block past the intersection of Sultan Gate, Bagdad St., and Pahang St. This is a construction site, so no entry is permitted.

Sultan Mosque 🎯   Though there are more than 80 mosques on the island of Singapore, Sultan Mosque is the real center of the Muslim community. The mosque that stands today is the second Sultan Mosque to be built on this site. The first was built in 1826, partially funded by the East India Company as part of its agreement to leave Kampong Glam to Sultan Hussein and his family in return for sovereign rights to Singapore. The present mosque was built in 1928 and was funded by donations from the Muslim community. The Saracenic flavor of the onion domes, topped with crescent moons and stars, are complemented by Mogul cupolas. Funny thing, though: The mosque was designed by an Irish guy named Denis Santry, who was working for the architectural firm Swan and McLaren.

Sultan Mosque, like all the others, does not permit shorts, miniskirts, low necklines, or other revealing clothing to be worn inside. However, they do realize that non-Muslim travelers like to be comfortable as they tour around, and they provide cloaks free of charge. They hang just to the right as you walk up the stairs.

3 Muscat St. Daily 9am–1pm and 2–4pm. No visiting is allowed during mass congregation Fri 11:30am–2:30pm.

ORCHARD ROAD AREA

The Istana and Sri Temasek   This building serves as the official residence of the President of the Republic of Singapore. Used mainly for state and ceremonial occasions, the grounds are open to every citizen on selected public holidays, though they're not generally open for visits. The house's domain includes several other houses of senior colonial civil servants

Orchard Rd., between Claymore Rd. and Scotts Rd.

Peranakan Place 🎯   The houses along Emerald Hill have all been renovated, and the street has been closed to vehicular traffic. As you pass Emerald Hill, though, don't just blow it off as a tourist trap. Walk through the cafe area and out the back. All of the terrace houses have been redone magnificently. The facades have been freshly painted and the tiles have been polished, and the dark wood details add a contrast that is truly elegant. When these places were renovated, they could be purchased for a song, but as Singaporeans began grasping at their heritage in recent years, their value shot up, and now these homes fetch huge sums.

Located at the intersection of Emerald Hill and Orchard Rd.

WESTERN SINGAPORE ATTRACTIONS

The attractions grouped in this section are on the west side of Singapore, beginning from the Singapore Botanic Gardens at the edge of the urban area all the way out to the Singapore Discovery Centre past Jurong. Remember if you're traveling around this area that transportation can be problematic; the MRT system rarely goes direct to any of these places, taxis can be hard to find, and bus routes get more complex. Keep the telephone number for taxi booking handy. Sometimes ticket salespeople at each attraction can help and make the call for you.

Bukit Timah Nature Reserve ★★   Bukit Timah Nature Reserve is pure primary rainforest. Believed to be as old as 1 million years, it's the only place on the island with vegetation that exists exactly as it was before the British settled here. The park is more than 81 hectares (202 acres) of soaring canopy teeming with mammals and birds and a lush undergrowth with more bugs, butterflies, and reptiles than you can shake a vine at. Here you can see more than 700 plant species, many of which are exotic ferns, plus mammals like long-tailed macaques, squirrels, and lemurs. There's a visitor center and four well-marked paths, one of which leads to Singapore's highest point. At 163m (535 ft.) above sea level, don't expect a nosebleed, but some of the scenic views of the island are really nice. Along another walkway is Singapore's oldest tree, estimated to be 400 years old. Also at Bukit Timah is Hindhede Quarry, which filled up with water at some point, so you can take a dip and cool off during your hike.

177 Hindhede Dr. ✆ 1800/468-5736. Free admission. Daily 24-hr. MRT to Newton, then TIBS bus no. 171 or SBS bus no. 182 to park entrance.

Chinese and Japanese Gardens   Situated on two islands in Jurong lake, the gardens are reached by an overpass and joined by the Bridge of Double Beauty. The **Chinese Garden** dedicates most of its area to "northern-style" landscape architecture. The style of Imperial gardens, the northern style integrates brightly colored buildings with the surroundings to compensate for northern China's absence of rich plant growth and natural scenery. The Stoneboat is a replica of the stone boat at the Summer Palace in Beijing. Inside the Pure Air of the Universe building are courtyards and a pond, and there is a seven-story pagoda, with the odd number of floors symbolizing continuity. Around the gardens, special attention has been paid to the placement of rock formations to resemble true nature, and also to the qualities of the rocks themselves, which can represent the forces of yin and yang, male and female, passivity or activity, and so on.

I like the Garden of Beauty, in Suzhou style, representing the southern style of landscape architecture. Southern gardens were built predominantly by scholars, poets, and men of wealth. Sometimes called Black-and-White gardens, these smaller gardens had more fine detail, featuring subdued colors as the plants and elements of the rich natural landscape gave them plenty to work with. Inside the Suzhou garden are 2,000 pots of *penjiang* (bonsai) and displays of small rocks.

While the Chinese garden is more visually stimulating, the **Japanese garden** is intended to evoke feeling. Marble-chip paths lead the way so that as you walk you can hear your own footsteps and meditate on the sound. They also serve to slow the journey for better gazing upon the scenery. The Keisein, or "Dry Garden," uses white pebbles to create images of streams. Ten stone lanterns, a small traditional house, and a rest house are nestled between two ponds with smaller islands joined by bridges.

Toilets are situated at stops along the way, as are benches, to have a rest or to just take in the sights. Paddle boats can be rented for S$5 (US$2.85) per hour just outside the main entrance.

1 Chinese Garden Rd. ℂ 65/6261-3632. Admission free; admission to bonsai garden adults S$5 (US$2.85), children S$3 (US$1.70). Daily 9am–7pm. MRT to Chinese Garden or bus nos. 335, 180, and 154.

Haw Par Villa (Tiger Balm Gardens) ☆   In 1935, brothers Haw Boon Haw and Haw Boon Par—creators of Tiger Balm, the camphor and menthol rub that comes in those cool little pots—took their fortune and opened Tiger Balm Gardens as a venue for teaching traditional Chinese values. They made more than 1,000 statues and life-size dioramas depicting Chinese legends and historic tales, and illustrating morality and Confucian beliefs. Many of these were gruesome and bloody, and some of them were really entertaining.

But Tiger Balm Gardens suffered a horrible fate. In 1985, it was converted into an amusement park and reopened as Haw Par Villa. Most of the statues and scenes were taken away and replaced with rides. Well, business did not exactly boom. In fact, the park has been losing money fast. But recently, in an attempt to regain some of the original Tiger Balm Garden edge, they replaced many of the old statues, some of which are a great backdrop for really kitschy vacation photos. Last year they also lowered the admission price from S$16 (US$9) for adults to the more affordable S$5 (US$3) they charge today. Catch the two theme rides: the Tales of China Boat Ride and the Wrath of the Water Gods Flume.

262 Pasir Panjang Rd. ℂ 65/6872-2780. Admission free. Daily 9am–5pm. MRT to Buona Vista and transfer to bus no. 200.

Jurong BirdPark ☆ *Kids*   Jurong BirdPark, with a collection of 8,000 birds from more than 600 species, showcases Southeast Asian breeds plus other color-ful tropical beauties, some of which are endangered. The more than 20 hectares (50 acres) can be easily walked, or, for a couple dollars extra, you can ride the panorail for a bird's-eye view (so to speak) of the grounds. I enjoy the Waterfall Aviary, the world's largest walk-in aviary. It's an up-close-and-personal experi-ence with African and South American birds, plus a pretty walk over pathways and babbling brooks through landscaped tropical forest. This is where you'll also see the world's tallest man-made waterfall, but the true feat of engineering here is the panorail station, built inside the aviary. Another smaller walk-in aviary is for Southeast Asian endangered bird species; at noon every day this aviary expe-riences a man-made thunderstorm. The daily guided tours and regularly sched-uled feeding times are enlightening. Other bird exhibits are the flamingo pools, the World of Darkness (featuring nocturnal birds), and the penguin parade, a favorite for Singaporeans, who adore all things Arctic.

Two shows feature birds of prey either acting out their natural instincts or per-forming falconry tricks. The **Fuji World of Hawks** is at 10am and the **King of the Skies** is at 4pm. The **All-Star Birdshow** takes place at 11am and 3pm, with trained parrots that race bikes and birds that perform all sorts of silliness, includ-ing staged birdie misbehaviors. Try to come between 8am and 10:30am for breakfast among hanging cages of chirping birds at the **Songbird Terrace.**

2 Jurong Hill. ℂ 65/6265-0022. Adults S$12 (US$6.85), children under 12 S$5 (US$2.85). Daily 8am-6pm. MRT to Boon Lay Station, transfer to SBS nos. 194 or 251.

Jurong Reptile Park   The newly renovated Jurong Reptile Park (fixed up just in time because the older facility was smelling up the entire neighborhood) houses more than 50 species of reptiles from the region and around the world.

Feedings are fun, as are the reptile shows (at 11:45am and 2pm daily). Snakes are happy to wrap themselves around your neck for a souvenir photo (10:30am and 5pm daily). In itself, it's no reason to trek out to Jurong, but it makes a convenient add-on to a visit to the Jurong BirdPark.

241 Jalan Ahmad Ibrahim. © 65/6261-8866. Adults S$7 (US$4), children under 12 and seniors S$3.50 (US$2.10). Daily 9am–6pm. MRT to Boon Lay Station, transfer to SBS nos. 194 or 251.

Ming Village   Tour a pottery factory that employs traditional pottery-making techniques from the Ming and Qing dynasties, and watch the process from mold making, hand throwing, and hand painting to glazing each piece. After the tour, shop from the large selection of beautiful antique reproduction dishes, vases, urns, and more. Certificates of authenticity are provided, which describe the history of each piece. They are happy to arrange overseas shipping for your treasures, or if you want to carry your purchase home, they'll wrap it very securely.

32 Pandan Rd. © 65/6265-7711. Admission and guided tour free. Daily 9am–5:30pm. MRT to Clementi, then SBS no. 78.

Singapore Botanic Gardens ★★   In 1822, Singapore's first botanic garden was started at Fort Canning by Sir Stamford Raffles. After it lost funding, the present Botanic Garden came into being in 1859, thanks to the efforts of a horticulture society; it was later turned over to the government for upkeep. More than just a garden, this space occupied an important place in the region's economic development when "Mad" Henry Ridley, one of the garden's directors, imported Brazilian rubber tree seedlings from Great Britain. He devised improved latex-trapping methods and led the campaign to convince reluctant coffee growers to switch plantation crops. The garden also pioneered orchid hybridization, breeding a number of internationally acclaimed varieties.

Carved out within the tropical setting lies a rose garden, a sundial garden with pruned hedges, a banana plantation, a spice garden, and sculptures by international artists dotted around the area. As you wander, look for the cannonball tree (named for its cannonball-shape fruit), para rubber trees, teak trees, bamboos, and a huge array of palms, including the sealing wax palm—distinguished by its bright scarlet stalks—and the rumbia palm, which bears the pearl sago. The fruit of the silk-cotton tree is a pod filled with silky stuffing that was once used for stuffing pillows. Flowers like bougainvilleas and heliconias add beautiful color.

The **National Orchid Garden** is 3 hectares (7½ acres) of gorgeous orchids growing along landscaped walks. The English Garden features hybrids developed here and named after famous visitors to the garden—there's the Margaret Thatcher, the Benazir Bhutto, the Vaclav Havel, and more. The gift shops sell live hydroponic orchids in test tubes for unique souvenirs.

The gardens have three lakes. Symphony Lake surrounds an island band shell for "Concert in the Park" performances by the local symphony and international entertainers like Chris de Burg. Call visitor services at the number below for performance schedules.

Main entrance at corner of Cluny Rd. and Holland Rd. © 65/6471-7361. Free admission. Daily 4am–11:30pm (closing at midnight on weekends). The National Orchid Garden adults S$2 (US$1.15), children under 12 and seniors S$1 (US55¢). Daily 8:30am–7pm. MRT to Orchard. Take SBS no. 7, 105, 106, or 174 from Orchard Blvd.

Singapore Discovery Centre (Kids   The original plan was to build a military history museum here, but then planners began to wonder if maybe the concept wouldn't bring people running. What they came up with instead is a fascinating display of the latest military technology with hands-on exhibits that cannot be resisted—one of 19 interactive information kiosks, for instance, lets you design tanks and ships. Airborne Rangers, a virtual reality experience, lets you parachute from a plane and manipulate your landing to safety. In the motion simulator, feel your seat move in tandem with the fighter pilot on the screen. The Shooting Gallery is a computer-simulated combat firing range using real but decommissioned M16 rifles. Other attractions are an exhibit of 14 significant events in Singapore history, including the fall of Singapore, self-government, racial riots, and housing block development. And then there's Tintoy Theatre, where the robot Tintoy conducts an entertaining lecture on warfare! Tintoy fights a war, seeking the help of Sun Tzu and other ancient military tacticians. IMAX features roll at the five-story iWERKS Theatre regularly. When you get hungry, there's a fast-food court.

You also get a 30-minute bus tour of the neighboring Singapore Air Force Training Institute free with SDC admission. Inquire about tour times at the front counter.

510 Upper Jurong Rd. ℂ 65/6792-6188. Adults S$9 (US$5.15), children under 12 S$5 (US$2.85). Tues–Sun 9am–7pm. MRT to Boon Lay; transfer to SBS nos. 192 or 193.

CENTRAL & NORTHERN SINGAPORE ATTRACTIONS

The northern part of Singapore contains most of the island's nature reserves and parks. Here's where you'll find the Singapore Zoological Gardens, in addition to some sights with historical and religious significance. Despite the presence of the **MRT** in the area, there is not any simple way to get from attraction to attraction with ease. Bus transfers to and from MRT stops is the way to go—or you could stick to taxi cabs.

Kong Meng San Phor Kark See Temple   The largest and most modern religious complex on the island, this place, called Phor Kark See for short, is comprised of prayer and meditation halls, a hospice, gardens, and a vegetarian restaurant. The largest building is the Chinese-style Hall of Great Compassion. There is also the octagonal Hall of Great Virtue and a towering pagoda. For S50¢ (US30¢), you can buy flower petals to place in a dish at the Buddha's feet. Compared to other temples on the island, Phor Kark See seems shiny—having been built only in 1981. As a result, the religious images inside carry a strange, almost artificial, cartoon air about them.

If you're curious, find the crematorium in the back of the complex. Arrive on Sunday after 1pm and wait for the funeral processions to arrive. Chairs line the side and back of the hall, and attendees do not mind if you sit quietly and observe, as long as you are respectful. The scene is not for the faint of heart, but it makes for a touching moment of cultural difference and human similarity.

88 Bright Hill Dr. Located in the center of the island to the east of Bukit Panjang Nature Preserve. Bright Hill Dr. is off Ang Mo Kio Ave. ℂ 65/6453-4046. Take MRT to Bishan, then take bus no. 410.

Kranji War Memorial   Kranji Cemetery commemorates the men and women who fought and died in World War II. Prisoners of war in a camp nearby began a burial ground here, and after the war it was enlarged to provide space for all the casualties. The Kranji War Cemetery is the site of 4,000 graves of servicemen, while the Singapore State Cemetery memorializes the names of more than 20,000 who died and have no known graves. Stones are laid geometrically on a slope with a view of the Strait of Johor. The memorial itself is designed to represent the three arms of the services.

Woodlands Rd., located in the very N part of the island. ℂ 65/6269-6158. Daily 24 hr. MRT to Kranji.

MacRitchie Nature Trail   Of all the nature reserves in Singapore, the Central Catchment Nature Reserve is the largest, at 2,000 hectares (5,000 acres). Located in the center of the island, it's home to four of Singapore's reservoirs: MacRitchie, Seletar, Pierce, and Upper Pierce. The rainforest here is the secondary forest, but the animals don't care; they're just as happy with the place. There's one path for walking and jogging (no bicycles allowed) that stretches 3km (1¾ miles) from its start in the southeast corner of the reserve, turning to the edge of MacRitchie Reservoir and then letting you out at the Singapore Island Country Club.

Central Catchment Nature Reserve. No phone. Free admission. From Orchard Rd. take bus no. 132 from the Orchard Parade Hotel. From Raffles City take bus no. 130. Get off at the bus stop near Little Sisters of the Poor. Next to Little Sisters of the Poor, follow the paved walkway, which turns into the trail.

Mandai Orchid Gardens   Owned and operated by Singapore Orchids Pte Ltd. to breed and cultivate hybrids for international export, the gardens double as an STB tourist attraction. Arranged in English garden style, orchid varieties are separated in beds that are surrounded by grassy lawn. Tree-growing varieties prefer the shade of the covered canopy. On display is Singapore's national flower, the Vanda Miss Joaquim, a natural hybrid in shades of light purple. Behind the gift shop is the Water Garden, where a stroll will reveal many houseplants common to the West, as you would find them in the wild.

Mandai Lake Rd., on the route to the Singapore Zoological Gardens. ℂ 65/6269-1036. Adults S$2 (US$1.15), children under 12 S50¢ (US30¢). Daily 8:30am–5:30pm. MRT to Ang Mo Kio and SBS no. 138.

Night Safari ★★★ *Kids*   Singapore takes advantage of its unchanging tropical climate and static ratio of daylight to night to bring you the world's first open-concept zoo for nocturnal animals. Here, as in the zoological gardens, animals live in landscaped areas, their barriers virtually unseen by visitors. These areas are dimly lit to create a moonlit effect, and a guided tram leads you through "regions" designed to resemble the Himalayan foothills, the jungles of Africa, and, naturally, Southeast Asia. Some of the free-range prairie animals come very close to the tram. The 45-minute ride covers almost 3.5km (2 miles) and has regular stops to get off and have a rest or stroll along trails for closer views of smaller creatures.

Staff, placed at regular intervals along the trails, help you find your way, though it's almost impossible to get lost along the trails; however, it is nighttime, you are in the forest, and it can be spooky. The guides are there more or less to add peace of mind (and all speak English). Flash photography is strictly prohibited, and be sure to bring plenty of insect repellent. *A weirder tip:* Check out the bathrooms. They're all open-air, Bali style.

Singapore Zoological Gardens, 80 Mandai Lake Rd., at the W edge of the Bukit Panjang Nature Reserve, on the Seletar Reservoir. ℂ 65/6269-3411. Adults S$15.45 (US$8.85), children under 12 S$10.30 (US$5.90). Daily 7:30pm–midnight. Ticket sales close at 11pm. Entrance Plaza, restaurant, and fast-food outlet open from 6:30pm. MRT to Ang Mo Kio and take SBS no. 138.

Sasanaransi Buddhist Temple   Known simply as the Burmese Buddhist Temple, it was founded by a Burmese expatriate to serve the overseas Burmese Buddhist community. His partner, an herbal doctor also from Burma, traveled home to buy a 10-ton block of marble from which was carved the 3.3m (11 ft.) Buddha image that sits in the main hall, surrounded by an aura of brightly colored lights. The original temple was off Serangoon Road in Little India and was moved here in 1991 at the request of the Housing Development Board. On the third story is a standing Buddha image in gold, and murals of events in the Buddha's life.

14 Tai Gin Rd., located next to the Sun Yat-sen Villa near Toa Payoh New Town. Daily 6:30am–9pm. Chanting Sun 9:30am, Wed 8pm, and Sat 7:30pm. Take MRT to Toa Payoh, then take a taxi.

Singapore Zoological Gardens ★★ Kids
This is called the Open Zoo because, rather than coop the animals in jailed enclosures, they're allowed to roam freely in landscaped areas. Beasts of the world are kept where they are supposed to be using psychological restraints and physical barriers that are disguised behind waterfalls, vegetation, and moats. Some animals are grouped with other species to show them coexisting as they would in nature. For instance, the white rhinoceros is neighborly with the wildebeest and ostrich—not that wildebeests and ostriches make the best company, but certainly contempt is better than boredom. Guinea and pea fowl, Emperor tamarinds, and other creatures are free roaming and not shy; however, if you spot a water monitor or long-tailed macaque, know that they're not zoo residents—just locals looking for a free meal.

Major zoo features are the Primate Kingdom, Wild Africa, the Reptile Garden, the children's petting zoo, and underwater views of polar bears, sea lions, and penguins. Daily shows include primate and reptile shows at 10:30am and 2:30pm, and elephant and sea lion shows at 11:30am and 3:30pm. You can take your photograph with an orangutan, chimpanzee, or snake, and there are elephant and camel rides, too.

The literature provided includes half-day and full-day agendas to help you see the most while you're there. The best time to arrive, however, is at 9am, to have breakfast with an orangutan, which feasts on fruits, putting on a hilarious and very memorable show. If you miss that, you can also have tea with it at 4pm. Another good time to go is just after a rain, when the animals cool off and get frisky.

Also see listing for "Night Safari," above.

80 Mandai Lake Rd., at the western edge of the Bukit Panjang Nature Reserve, on the Seletar Reservoir. ℭ **65/6269-3411.** Adults S$12 (US$6.85), children under 12 S$5 (US$2.85). Discounts for seniors. Daily 8:30am–6pm. MRT to Ang Mo Kio and take SBS no. 138.

Siong Lim Temple
This temple, in English "the Twin Groves of the Lotus Mountain Temple," has a great story behind its founding. One night in 1898, Hokkien businessman Low Kim Pong and his son had the same dream(of a golden light shining from the West. The following day, the two went to the western shore and waited until, moments before sundown, a ship appeared carrying a group of Hokkien Buddhist monks and nuns on their way to China after a pilgrimage to India. Low Kim Pong vowed to build a monastery if they would stay in Singapore. They did.

Laid out according to feng shui principles, the buildings include the Dharma Hall, a main prayer hall, and drum and bell towers. They are arranged in cong lin style, a rare type of monastery design with a universal layout so that no matter how vast the grounds are, any monk can find his way around. The entrance hall has granite wall panels carved with scenes from Chinese history. The main prayer hall has fantastic details in the ceiling, wood panels, and other wood carvings. In the back is a shrine to Kuan Yin, goddess of mercy.

Originally built amid farmland, the temple became surrounded by suburban high-rise apartments in the 1950s and 1960s, with the Toa Payoh Housing Development Board New Town project and the Pan-Island Expressway creeping close by.

184-E Jalan Toa Payoh. ℭ **65/6259-6924.** Located in Toa Payoh New Town. Take MRT to Toa Payoh, then take SBS nos. 232, 237, or 238.

Sun Yat-sen Nanyang Memorial Hall ⟨⋆⟩ Dr. Sun Yat-sen visited Singapore eight times to raise funds for his revolution in China, and he made Singapore his headquarters for gaining the support of overseas Chinese in Southeast Asia. A wealthy Chinese merchant built the villa around 1880 for his mistress, and a later owner permitted Dr. Sun Yat-sen to use it. The house reflects the classic bungalow style, which is becoming endangered in modern Singapore. Its typical bungalow features include a projecting carport with a sitting room overhead, verandas with striped blinds, second-story cast-iron railings, and first-story masonry balustrades. A covered walkway leads to the kitchen and servants' quarters in the back.

Inside, the life of Dr. Yat-sen is traced in photos and watercolors, from his birth in southern China through his creation of a revolutionary organization.

12 Tai Gin Rd., near Toa Payoh New Town. ⟨⋆⟩ 65/6256-7377. Admission S$2 (US$1.15). Tue–Sun 9am–5pm. Take the MRT to Toa Payoh, then take bus no. 45.

Sungei Buloh Wetland Reserve ⟨⋆⟩ Located to the very north of the island and devoted to the wetland habitat and mangrove forests that are so common to the region, 87-hectare (218-acre) Sungei Buloh is out of the way and not the easiest place to get to, but it's a beautiful park, with constructed paths and boardwalks taking you through tangles of mangroves, soupy marshes, grassy spots, and coconut groves. Of the flora and fauna, the most spectacular sights here are the birds, of which there are somewhere between 140 and 170 species in residence or just passing through for the winter. Of the migratory birds, some have traveled from as far as Siberia to escape the cold months from September to March. Bird observatories are set up at different spots along the paths. Also, even though you're in the middle of nowhere, Sungei Buloh has a visitor center, a cafeteria, and souvenirs.

301 Neo Tiew Crescent. ⟨⋆⟩ 65/6794-1401. Adults S$1 (US55¢), children and seniors S50¢ (US30¢). Mon–Fri 7:30am–7pm; Sat–Sun and public holidays 7am–7pm. Audiovisual show Mon–Sat 9am, 11am, 1pm, 3pm, and 5pm; hourly Sun and public holidays. MRT to Kranji, bus no. 925 to Kranji Reservoir Dam. Cross causeway to park entrance.

EASTERN SINGAPORE ATTRACTIONS

The east coast leads from the edge of Singapore's urban area to the tip of the eastern part, at Changi Point. Eastern Singapore is home to the Changi International Airport, nearby Changi Prison, and the long stretch of East Coast Park along the shoreline. The **MRT** heads east in this region but swerves northward at the end of the line. A popular **bus line** for east coast attractions not reached by MRT is the SBS no. 2, which takes you to Changi Prison, Changi Point, Malay Village, and East Coast Park (a short walk from Joo Chiat Centre).

Changi Chapel and Museum ⟨⋆⟩ Upon successful occupation of Singapore, the Japanese marched all British, Australian, and allied European prisoners to Changi by foot, where they lived in a prison camp for 3 years, suffering overcrowding, disease, and malnutrition. Prisoners were cut off from the outside world except to leave the camp for labor duties. The hospital conditions were terrible; some prisoners suffered public beatings, and many died. In an effort to keep hope alive, they built a small chapel from wood and attap. Years later, at the request of former POWs and their families and friends, the government built this replica.

The museum displays sketches by W. R. M. Haxworth and secret photos taken by George Aspinall—both men POWs who were imprisoned here. Displayed with descriptions, the pictures, along with writings and other objects from the camp, bring this period to life, depicting the day-to-day horror with a touch of high morale.

169 Sims Ave., off Upper Changi Rd., in the same general area as the airport. © 65/6543-0893. Free admission. Daily 9:30am–4:30pm. Changi Chapel Sun Service (all are welcome) 5:30–6:30pm. MRT to Tanah Merah station, then transfer to SBS no. 2.

East Coast Park   East Coast Park is a narrow strip of reclaimed land, only 8.5km (5¼ miles) long, tucked in between the shoreline and East Coast Parkway. It serves as a hangout for Singaporean families on the weekends. Moms and dads barbecue under the trees while the kids swim at the beach, which is nothing more than a narrow lump of grainy sand sloping into yellow-green water that has more seaweed than a sushi bar. Paths for bicycling, in-line skating, walking, or jogging run the length of the park and are crowded on weekends and public and school holidays. On Sunday, you'll find kite flyers in the open grassy parts. The lagoon is the best place to go for bicycle and in-line skate rentals, canoeing, and windsurfing.

Because East Coast Park is so long, getting to the place you'd like to hang out can be a bit confusing. Many of the locators I've included sound funny (for example, McDonald's Carpark C) but are recognizable landmarks for taxi drivers. Sailing, windsurfing, and other sea sports happen at the far end of the park, at the lagoon, which is closer to Changi Airport than it is to the city. Taxi drivers are all familiar with the lagoon as a landmark. Unfortunately, public transportation to the park is tough—you should bring a good map and expect to do a little walking from any major thoroughfare.

East Coast Park is also home to **UDMC Seafood Centre** (see "Where to Dine," above), located not far from the lagoon.

East Coast Pkwy. No phone. Free admission. Bus no. 16 to Marine Parade and use the underpass to cross the highway.

Malay Village   In 1985, Malay Village opened in Geylang as a theme village to showcase Malay culture. The Cultural Museum is a collection of artifacts from Malay culture, including household items, musical instruments, and a replica of a wedding dais and traditional beaded ceremonial bed. Kampung Days lets you walk through a kampung house (or Malay village house) as it would have looked in the 1950s and 1960s. The 25-minute **Lagenda Fantasy show** is more for kids, using multi-image projection, Surround Sound, and lights to tell tales from the Arabian Nights and the legend of Sang Nila Utama, the founder of Temasek (Singapore). The village has souvenir shops mixed with places that sell everything from antique knives to caged birds.

Two in-house groups perform **traditional Malaysian and Indonesian dances** in the late afternoons and evenings. Call during the day on Saturday to find out if they'll be performing the **Kuda Kepang** in the evening. If you're lucky enough to catch it, it's a long performance but worth the wait because at the end the dancers are put in a trance and walk on glass, eat glass, and rip coconuts to shreds with their teeth. Arrive early because the place gets packed with locals.

39 Geylang Serai, in the suburb of Geylang, an easy walk from the MRT station. © 65/6748-4700 or 65/6740-8860. Free admission to village. Kampong Days and Cultural Museum adults S$5 (US$2.85), children S$3 (US$1.70). Daily 10am–10pm. MRT to Paya Lebar.

The Singapore Crocodilarium   Head to the Crocodilarium if you're interested in seeing alligators from India and four types of crocodiles—from Singapore, Africa, Louisiana, and Caiman (South Africa). Of the total 1,800 crocodiles that reside here, 500 are on display. The Singapore crocodile, one of the largest, reaches a maximum size of 5.5 meters (6 yd.) and can weigh up to 500 kilograms (1,100 lb.). They're pretty fierce because they have bigger heads, which means bigger mouths. However, midsize ones are the most dangerous to people because they have better mobility on land. Every so often, the place picks up when a couple of them have a brutish fight. On a sweeter note, the Crocodilarium has approximately 400 births per year. Some young ones are on display—and they're very cute—but the Crocodilarium won't let you see the newborn babies because they're delicate and spook easily. While many are intended for the booming pelt industry, some are just for show. A huge gift shop peddles crocodile products, which are both made in-house and imported from outside designers. Here you can also find ostrich hide, stingray skin, and antelope pelt goods.

The best way to get back to town is to ask the front counter to call you a cab.

730 East Coast Pkwy., running along East Coast Park. ℂ **65/447-3722.** Adults S$2 (US$1.20), children under 12 S$1 (US60¢). Daily 9am–5pm. MRT to Paya Lebar or Eunos and take a taxi.

SENTOSA ISLAND

In the 1880s, Sentosa, then known as Pulau Blakang Mati, was a hub of British military activity, with hilltop forts built to protect the harbor from sea invasion from all sides. Today it has become a weekend getaway spot and Singapore's answer to Disneyland, both rolled into one. You'll find a lot of people recommending Sentosa as a must-see on your vacation, but although some travelers do visit the island for some part of their trip, it might not be the best way to spend your time if you're in town for only a few days. Basically, for those who like to do hard-core cultural and historical-immersion vacations, Sentosa will seem too contrived and cartoonish.

If you're spending the day, there are numerous restaurants and a couple of food courts. For overnights, the Shangri-La's Rasa Sentosa Resort and the Beaufort Sentosa, Singapore (see chapter 3), are popular hotel options. For general **Sentosa inquiries,** call ℂ **1800/736-8672.**

GETTING THERE

Private cars are not allowed entry to the island except between the hours of 6:30pm and 3am, but there are more than a few other ways to get to Sentosa. The cable car and ferry fares are exclusive of Sentosa admission charges, which you are required to pay upon arrival; bus fares include your admission charge. **Island admission** is S$6 (US$3.45) for adults and S$4 (US$2.30) for children. Tickets can be purchased at the following booths: Mount Faber Cable Car Station, World Trade Centre Ferry Departure Hall, Cable Car Towers (next to the World Trade Centre), Cable Car Plaza (on Sentosa), Sentosa Information Booth 4 (at the start of the causeway, opposite Kentucky Fried Chicken), and Sentosa Information Booth 3 (at the end of the causeway bridge, upon entering Sentosa). Many attractions require purchase of additional tickets, which you can get at the entrance of each.

BY CABLE CAR Cable cars depart from the top of Mount Faber and from the World Trade Centre daily from 8:30am to 9pm at a cost of S$8.50 (US$4.85) for adults and S$7.50 (US$4.30) for children, not including island admission. You can also take a glass-bottomed car for S$15 (US$8.55) for adults and S$8 (US$4.55) for children. The ticket is good for the round-trip, and you can decide where you choose to depart and arrive (at either Mt. Faber or World Trade Centre every 5 or 10 min. on the Singapore side) for one price. Plan at

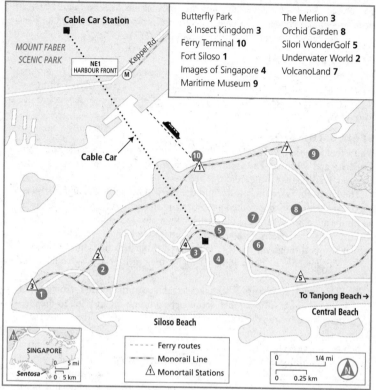

Butterfly Park
& Insect Kingdom **3**
Ferry Terminal **10**
Fort Siloso **1**
Images of Singapore **4**
Maritime Museum **9**

The Merlion **3**
Orchid Garden **8**
Silori WonderGolf **5**
Underwater World **2**
VolcanoLand **7**

least one trip on the cable car because the view of Singapore, Sentosa, and especially the container port is really fantastic from up there. The round-trip cable car ticket is also good for a return on the ferry, in case you've had enough view. **Be warned:** If you return to Singapore at the Mt. Faber stop, you'll have to walk down the mountain to find a cab or bus. For more information, call ☎ **65/ 6270-8855.**

BY FERRY The ferry departs from the World Trade Centre on weekdays from 9:30am to 10pm at 30-minute intervals, and on weekends and public holidays from 8:30am to 10pm at 20-minute intervals. The round-trip fare for adults is S$8.30 (US$4.75) and for children is S$6.30 (US$3.60), which includes admission.

BY BUS Sentosa Bus Service Leisure Pte Ltd operates bus service to and from Sentosa. Service A operates between 7am and 10:30pm daily from the World Trade Centre (WTC) Bus Terminal. Service C runs from the Tiong Bahru MRT Station. Service E stops along Orchard Road at Lucky Plaza, the Mandarin Hotel, Peranakan Place, Le Meridien Hotel, Plaza Singapura, and then Bencoolen Street, POSB Headquarters, Raffles City, and Pan Pacific Hotel; it operates from 7am to 10:35pm daily. Fares are S$7 (US$4) for adults and S$5 (US$2.85) for children. Fares are paid to the driver as you board, and the Sentosa admission fee is included in your fare. The last bus out of Sentosa is at 10:30pm.

BY TAXI   Taxis are allowed to drop off and pick up passengers only at the Beaufort Sentosa, Singapore; Shangri-La's Rasa Sentosa Resort; and NTUC Sentosa Beach Resort. The taxi surcharge is S$3 (US$1.70).

GETTING AROUND

Once on Sentosa, a free monorail operates from 9am to 10pm daily at 10-minute intervals to shuttle you around to the various areas. If you're staying at one of the island's major hotels, you can take advantage of free shuttle services to get into Singapore's urban area.

SEEING THE SIGHTS

The attractions that you get free with your Sentosa admission are the **Fountain Gardens** and **Musical Fountain,** the **Enchanted Garden of Tembusu,** the **Dragon Trail Nature Walk,** and the **beaches.**

The **Fountain Gardens,** just behind the Ferry Terminal, are geometric European-style gardens with groomed pathways and shady arbors. In the center is an amphitheater of sorts, the focus of which is a fountain—actually three fountains—that creates water effects with patterns of sprays and varying heights. During regular shows throughout the day, the fountains burst to the sounds of everything from marches to Elton John. At night, they turn on the lights for color effects.

The **Dragon Trail Nature Walk** takes advantage of the island's natural forest for a 1.5km (1-mile) stroll through secondary rainforest. In addition to the variety of dragon sculptures, there are also local squirrels, monkeys, lizards, and wild white cockatoos to try to spot.

Sentosa has three beaches. **Siloso Beach** is on the western end, and **J Central Beach** and **Tanjong Beach** are on the eastern end, each dressed in tall coconut palms and flowering trees. At Central Beach, deck chairs, beach umbrellas, and a variety of **watersports equipment,** like pedal boats, aqua bikes, fun bugs, canoes, surfboards, and banana boats, are available for hire at nominal charges. Bicycles are also available for hire at the bicycle kiosk at Siloso Beach. Shower and changing facilities, food kiosks, and snack bars are at rest stations. Siloso Beach is open at night for barbecue picnics and has a really nice view of the tiny lights of ships anchored in the port. About once a month, rumors spread throughout the island about a full-moon party on Siloso that lasts until the sun comes up. The parties are never publicized but are anticipated by the many folks looking for an alternative to the bar scene at night. Ask around at the bars, and they'll let you know if there's something going on.

Unless noted, all of the following Sentosa attractions have admission charges separate from the Sentosa charge, and operating hours that differ from place to place.

Butterfly Park and Insect Kingdom Museum of Singapore   This walk-in enclosure provides an up-close view of some 60 live species of native butterflies, from cocoon to adult. At the Insect Kingdom, the exhibits are mostly dead but extensive, with its collection carrying more than 2,500 bugs.

ⓒ 65/6275-0013. Adults S$6 (US$3.45), children S$3 (US$1.70). Daily 9am–6:30pm. Monorail stop 4.

Fort Siloso   Fort Siloso guarded Keppel Harbour from invasion in the 1880s. It's one of three forts built on Sentosa, and it later became a military camp in World War II. The buildings have been decorated to resemble a barracks, a kitchen, a laundry, and military offices as they looked back in the day. In places, you can explore the underground tunnels and ammunition holds, but they're not as extensive as you would hope they'd be.

Ⓒ **1800/736-8672.** Adults S$3 (US$1.70), children S$2 (US$1.15). Daily 9am–7pm. Monorail stop 3.

Images of Singapore ★★ Images of Singapore is without a doubt one of the main reasons to come to Sentosa. There are three parts to this museum/exhibit: the Pioneers of Singapore, the Surrender Chambers—which date back as far as I can remember—and Festivals of Singapore, a recent addition.

Pioneers of Singapore is an exhibit of beautifully constructed life-size dioramas that place figures like Sultan Hussein, Sir Stamford Raffles, Tan Tock Seng, and Naraina Pillai, to name just a few pioneers, in the context of Singapore's timeline and note their contributions to its development. Also interesting are the dioramas depicting scenes from the daily routines of the different cultures as they lived during colonial times. It's a great stroll that brings history to life.

The powers that be have tried to change the name of the **Surrender Chambers** to the Sentosa Wax Museum, but it still hasn't caught on because the Surrender Chambers are oh so much more than just a wax museum. The gallery leads you through authentic footage, photos, maps, and recordings of survivors to chronologically tell the story of the Pacific theater activity of World War II and how the Japanese conquered Singapore. The grand finale is a wax museum depicting, first, a scene of the British surrender and, last, another of the Japanese surrender.

Recently, Images of Singapore added the **Festivals of Singapore,** another life-size diorama exhibit depicting a few of the major festivals and traditions of the Chinese, Malay, Indian, and Peranakan cultures in Singapore. For each group, wedding traditions are shown in complete regalia, with brief explanations of the customs. Although this exhibit is not quite like being there and would be dull as a standalone, it's not bad tacked on to the other two. Try to catch the video presentation at the end—a tribute to Singapore's strides in "cultural integration" told in true "It's a small world after all" style.

Ⓒ **65/275-0388.** Adults S$5 (US$2.85), children S$3 (US$1.70). Daily 9am–9pm. Monorail stop 4.

The Maritime Museum The Maritime Museum is a showcase devoted to Singapore's ever-important connection to the sea. From ship models to artifacts, sea charts, and photos, the museum tells the story of 14 centuries of maritime life.

Ⓒ **65/6270-8855.** Free admission. Daily 10am–7pm. Closest to monorail stop 7, then walk along Gateway Ave.

The Merlion Imagine, if you will, 12 towering stories of that half-lion, half-fish creature, the Merlion. That's a lot of mythical beast. Admission buys you an elevator ride to the ninth floor, where you can peer out the mouth, and to the top of its head for a 360-degree view of Singapore, Sentosa, and even Indonesia. Be at the Fountain Gardens at 7:30, 8:30, and 9:30pm nightly for the "Rise of the Merlion" show, where they light up the thing with 16,000 fiber-optic lights and shoot red lasers out its eyes. Poor Merlion. Hope this never happens to the national symbol of *your* home country.

Ⓒ **65/6275-0388.** Adults S$3 (US$1.70), children S$2 (US$1.15). Daily 9am–10pm. Monorail stops 1 and 4.

Silori WonderGolf Sentosa This place is definitely miniature golf, but without the windmill. Instead, holes are made tricky using greens landscaped with rock designs and water features set on tiny terraces up the side of a steep slope.

65/6275-2011. Adults S$8 (US$4.55), children S$4 (US$2.30). Daily 9am–9pm. Monorail stop 4.

Underwater World ★ *Kids*   Underwater World is without a doubt one of the most visited attractions on Sentosa. Everybody comes for the tunnel: 83m (272 ft.) of transparent acrylic tube through which you glide on a conveyor belt, gaping at sharks, stingrays, eels, and other creatures of the sea drifting by, above and on both sides. At 11:30am, 2:30pm, and 4:30pm daily, a scuba diver hops in and feeds them by hand. In smaller tanks, you can view other unusual sea life like the puffer fish and the mysteriously weedy and leafy sea dragons. Then there's the latest display of bamboo shark embryos, developing within egg cases—what's keeping you?

ⓒ 65/6275-0030. Adults S$13 (US$7.45), children S$7 (US$4). Daily 9am–9pm. Monorail stop 2.

VolcanoLand   It's hard to say whether VolcanoLand is amusing or whether it's touristy and weird. A walk-through exhibit takes you on a journey to the center of the Earth with a mythological explorer and his Jules Verne–style robot buddy. Inside the "volcano" there's a multimedia show about the mysteries of life and the universe and a simulated volcano eruption.

VolcanoLand. ⓒ 65/6275-1828. Adults S$12 (US$6.85), children S$6 (US$3.45). Daily 10am–7pm. Monorail stop 1 or 4.

6 Sports & Recreation

BEACHES

Besides the beach at East Coast Park (see "Eastern Singapore Attractions," earlier in this chapter) and those on Sentosa Island (see above), you can try the smaller beach at Changi Village, called Changi Point. From the shore, you have a panoramic view of Malaysia, Indonesia, and several smaller islands that belong to Singapore. The beach is calm and frequented mostly by locals who set up camps and barbecues to hang out all day. There's kayak rentals along the beach, and in Changi Village you'll find, in addition to a huge hawker center, quite a few international restaurants and pubs to hang out in and have a fresh seafood lunch when you get hungry. To get there take SBS bus no. 2 from either the Tanah Merah or the Bedok MRT stations.

BICYCLE RENTAL

Bicycles are not for rent within the city limits, and traffic does not really allow for cycling on city streets, so sightseeing by bicycle is not recommended for city touring. If you plan a trip out to **Sentosa,** cycling provides a great alternative to that island's tram system and gets you closer to the parks and nature there. For a little light cycling, most people head out to **East Coast Park,** where rentals are inexpensive, the scenery is nice on cooler days, and there are plenty of great stops for eating along the way. One favorite place where the locals go for mountain-biking sorts of adventures (and to cycle amid the old kampung villages) is **Pulau Ubin,** off the northeast coast of Singapore.

AT EAST COAST PARK   Bicycles can be rented at East Coast Park from **Ling Choo Hong** (ⓒ 65/449-7305), near the hawker center at Carpark E; **SDK Recreation** (ⓒ 65/445-2969), near McDonald's at Carpark C; or **Wimbledon Cafeteria & Bicycle Rental** (ⓒ 65/444-3928), near the windsurfing rental places at the lagoon. All of these are open 7 days from about 9am to 8 or 9pm. Rentals are all in the neighborhood of S$4 to S$8 (US$2.40–US$4.80) per hour, depending on the type and quality of bike you're looking for. Identification might be requested.

ON SENTOSA ISLAND Try **SDK Recreation** (© 65/272-8738), located at Siloso Beach off Siloso Road, a short walk from Underwater World (see "Sentosa Island," above). It's open 7 days from around 10am to 6:30 or 7pm. Rental for a standard bicycle is S$4 (US$2.40) per hour. A mountain bike goes for S$8 (US$4.80) per hour. Identification is required.

IN PULAU UBIN When you get off the ferry, there are a number of places to rent bikes. The shops are generally open between 8am and 6pm and charge between S$5 (US$3) and S$8 (US$4.80) per hour, depending on which bike you choose. Most rental agents have a map of the island for you—take it. Even though it doesn't look too impressive, it'll be a great help.

GOLF

Golf is a very popular sport in Singapore. There are quite a few clubs, and though some of them are exclusively for members only, many places are open for limited play by nonmembers. All require you bring a par certificate. Most hotel concierges will be glad to make arrangements for you, and this might be the best way to go.

Best bets are the **Changi Golf Club,** 20 Netheravon Rd. (© **65/545-5133**); **Jurong Country Club,** 9 Science Centre Rd. (© **65/560-5655**); **Seletar Base Golf Course,** 244 Oxford St., 3 Park Lane (© **65/481-4745**); and **Sentosa Golf Club,** 27 Bukit Manis Rd., Sentosa Island (© **65/275-0022**).

SCUBA DIVING

If you're heading for one of the beach areas on Sentosa, or out at East Coast Park or Changi Point, you can rent canoes with paddles and life jackets for about S$6 to S$10 per hour (US$3.60–$6) for a one-person model, or S$8 to S$12 per hour (US$4.80–US$7.20) for a two-person canoe, depending on the make and quality of the canoe and gear. These outfits are small operators on the beach; look for their stacks of canoes on display. Basically, they have phone contact only if the guy on duty that day brought his own personal hand phone. For the best experience, I recommend canoeing out at Changi Point, where your rental person must point out to you the international boundaries between Singaporean, Malaysian, and Indonesian waters, and which islands you're permitted to land on.

TENNIS

Quite a few hotels in the city provide tennis courts for guests, many floodlit for night play (which allows you to avoid the midday heat), and even a few that can arrange lessons, so be sure to check out listings for hotel facilities in chapter 3. You'll have to travel about 15 minutes by taxi form the city center to reach the Singapore Tennis Centre on East Coast Parkway near the **East Coast Park** (© **65/442-5966**). Its courts are open to the public for day and evening play. Weekdays offer discount rates of S$8.50 (US$5.10) per hour, while weekday evening peak hours (6–9pm) jump to S$13 (US$7.50). Weekends and public holidays, expect to pay S$13 (US$7.50) per hour also. If you need to stay closer to town, you can play at the **Tanglin Sports Centre** on Minden Road (© **65/473-7236**). Court costs are S$3.50 (US$2.10) per hour on weekdays, with charges upped to S$9.50 (US$5.70) on weekday nights from 6 to 10pm, on weekends, and on all public holidays.

WATER-SKIING

The Kallang River, located to the east of the city, has hosted quite a few international water-skiing tournaments. If this is your sport, contact the Cowabunga

Ski Centre, the authority in Singapore. Located at **Kallang Riverside Park,** 10 Stadium Lane (© **65/344-8813**), they'll arrange lessons for adults and children and water-skiing by the hour. Beginner courses will set you back S$140 (US$84) for five half-hour lessons, while more experienced skiers can hire a boat plus equipment for S$80 (US$48) on weekdays and S$100 (US$60) on weekends. It's open on weekdays from noon to 7pm and weekends from 9am to 7pm. Call in advance for a reservation.

WINDSURFING & SAILING

You'll find both windsurfing boards and sailboats for rent at the lagoon in East Coast Park, which is where these activities primarily take place. The largest and most reputable firm to approach has to be the **Europa Sailing Club,** 1212 East Coast Pkwy. (© **65/449-5118**). For S$20 an hour (US$12), you can rent a small sailboat, while windsurf boards go for about the same. Expect to leave around S$30 (US$18) for a deposit. Although Europa does offer courses, instruction is really not recommended for short-term visitors because classes usually occur over extended periods of time on a set schedule.

7 Shopping

In Singapore, shopping is a sport—from the practiced glide through haute couture boutiques to skillful back-alley bargaining to win the best prices on Asian treasures. The shopping here is always exciting, with something to satiate every pro shopper's appetite. See the "Customs Regulations" section earlier in this chapter for information on the GST Tourist Refund Scheme, which lets you recover the GST for purchases of goods over S$300 (US$180) in value.

HOURS   Shopping malls are generally open from 10am to 8pm Monday through Saturday, with some stores keeping shorter Sunday hours. The malls sometimes remain open until 10pm on holidays. Smaller shops are open from around 10am to 5pm Monday through Saturday, but are almost always closed on Sunday. Hours vary from shop to shop. Arab Street is closed on Sunday.

PRICES   Almost all of the stores in shopping malls have fixed prices. Sometimes these stores have seasonal sales, especially in July, when they have the month-long **Great Singapore Sale,** during which prices are marked down, sometimes up to 50% or 75%. In the smaller shops and at street vendors, prices are never marked, and vendors will quote you higher prices than the going rate, in anticipation of the bargaining ritual. These are the places to find good prices, if you negotiate well.

DUTY-FREE ITEMS   Changi International Airport has a large duty-free shop that carries cigarettes, liquor, wine, perfumes, cosmetics, watches, jewelry, and other designer accessories. There's also a chain of duty-free stores in Singapore called **DFS.** The main branch is at no. 01-58 Millenia Walk, 9 Raffles Blvd., next to the Pan Pacific Hotel (© **65/6332-2188**). The store is huge and impressive, but unfortunately, the only truly duty-free items are liquor, which you can arrange to pick up at the airport before you depart—everything else carries the standard 5% GST. Feel free to apply for the Tourist Refund Scheme here, though.

ORCHARD ROAD AREA   The malls on Orchard Road are a tourist attraction in their own right, with smaller boutiques and specialty shops intermingled with huge department stores. **Takashimaya** and **Isetan** have been imported from Japan. **Lane Crawford** comes out of the West, as does **Kmart. John Little Pte. Ltd.** is one of the oldest department stores in Singapore, followed by **Robinson's. Tang's** is historic, having grown from a cart full of merchandise nurtured by the business savvy of local entrepreneur C. K. Tang. Boutiques range from the younger styles of **Stussy** and **Guess?** to the sophisticated fashions of **Chanel** and **Salvatore Ferragamo.** You'll also find antiques, oriental carpets, art galleries and curio shops, Tower Records and HMV music stores, Kinokuniya and Borders bookstores, video arcades, and scores of restaurants, local food courts, fast-food joints, and coffeehouses—even a few discos, which open in the evenings. It's hard to say when Orchard Road is not crowded, but it's definitely a mob scene on weekends, when folks have the free time to come and hang around, looking for fun.

Some of the larger and more exciting malls to check out are **Centrepoint,** 176 Orchard Rd.; **Ngee Ann City/Takashimaya Shopping Centre,** 391 Orchard Rd.; **Specialists' Shopping Center,** 277 Orchard Rd; and **Wisma Atria,** 435 Orchard Rd. The **Hilton Shopping Gallery,** 581 Orchard Rd., deals only in exclusive top-designer boutiques.

At **Far East Plaza,** 14 Scotts Rd., and **Lucky Plaza,** 304 Orchard Rd., there are some bargains to be had on electronics, camera equipment, and luggage, among other things, but be wary of rip-off deals. **Eyeglasses** are a surprising bargain in Singapore. A reputable outlet is Capitol Optical at no. 03–132, Far East Plaza (✆ **65/736-0365**). If you're in the mood for **jewels,** the most trusted dealer in Singapore is **Larry Jewelry (S) Pte. Ltd.,** Orchard Towers, Level 1, 400 Orchard (✆ **65/732-3222**), but be prepared to drop a dime. **Royal Selangor,** the famous Malaysian pewter manufacturer since 1885, has eight outlets in Singapore. The Orchard branch is at no. 02–40 Paragon by Sogo, 290 Orchard Rd. The **Tanglin Shopping Centre** (Tanglin Rd., at the northern end of Orchard) is a treasure trove of antiques dealers and carpet shops. For the best selection of carpets, visit **Hassan's Carpets,** no. 03–01/06 Tanglin Shopping Center (✆ **65/737-5626**).

THE HISTORIC DISTRICT   Although the Historic District doesn't have as many malls as the Orchard Road area, it still has some good shopping. **Raffles City Shopping Centre** can be overwhelming in its size, but convenient because it sits right atop the City Hall MRT stop. Men's and women's fashions, books, cosmetics, and accessories are sold in shops here, along with gifts. One of my favorite places to go, however, is the very upmarket **Raffles Hotel Shopping Arcade,** 328 North Bridge Rd. These shops are mostly haute couture; however, there is the Raffles Hotel gift shop for interesting souvenirs. For golfers, there's a Jack Nicklaus signature store.

CHINATOWN   In Chinatown, I've stumbled on some of my most precious treasures. My all-time favorite gift idea? Spend an afternoon learning the traditional Chinese tea ceremony at either **The Tea Village,** 45A–51A Pagoda St. (✆ **65/221-7825**), or **The Tea Chapter,** 9A Neil Rd. (✆ **65/226-1175**), and then head down to **D'Art Station,** 65 Pagoda St. (✆ **65/225-8307**), to pick up a good-quality tea set and accessories. After a stop at **Kwong Chen Beverage Trading,** 16 Smith St. (✆ **65/223-6927**), for some Chinese teas in handsome tins, you'll be ready to give a fabulous gift—not just a tea set, but your own cultural performance as well, as you teach your friends a new art. Although the teas are really inexpensive, they're packed in lovely tins—great to buy lots to bring back as smaller gifts.

Another neat place, **Gary Lee,** 20 Smith St. (𝄐 **65/221-8129**), carries a fantastic selection of linens imported from China. These hand-embroidered gems include bedding, dining linens, tea towels and handkerchiefs, and other decorative items for the home. They're priced right and won't break on the trip back home. For something a little more unusual, check out **Chinatown Joss Stick & Ceremonial Trading,** 54 Smith St. (𝄐 **65/227-6821**), or **Siong Moh Paper Products,** 39 Mosque St. (𝄐 **65/224-3125**), both of which carry a full line of ceremonial items. Pick up some joss sticks (temple incense) or joss paper (books of thin sheets of paper, stamped in reds and yellows with bits of gold and silver leaf). It's definitely a conversation piece, as is the Hell Money, stacks of "money" that believers burn at the temple for their ancestors to use in the afterlife. Perfect for that friend who has everything? Also, if you duck over to **Sago Lane** while you're in the neighborhood, there are a few souvenir shops that sell Chinese kites and Cantonese Opera masks—cool for kids.

For one-stop souvenir shopping, you can tick off half your shopping list at Chinatown Point, a.k.a the **Singapore Handicraft Center,** 133 New Bridge Rd. The best gifts there include hand-carved chops, or Chinese seals. **Chinatown Seal Carving Souvenir,** no. 03–72 (𝄐 **65/534-0761**), has an absolutely enormous selection of carved stone, wood, bone, glass, and ivory chops ready to be carved to your specifications. Simple designs are really quite affordable, while some of the more elaborate chops and carvings fetch a handsome sum. At **Inherited Arts & Crafts,** no. 03–69 (𝄐 **65/534-1197**), you can commission a personalized Chinese scroll painting or calligraphy piece. The handiwork is quite beautiful. Amid the many jade and gold shops at Chinatown Point, **La Belle Collection,** no. 04–53 (𝄐 **534-0231**), stands out for its jewelry crafted from orchids. The coating lets the flowers' natural colors show, while delicate gold touches add a little extra sparkle.

For Chinese goods, however, nothing beats **Yue Hwa,** 70 Eu Tong Sen St. (𝄐 **65/538-4222**). This five-story Chinese Emporium is an attraction in its own right. The superb inventory includes all manner of silk wear (robes, underwear, blouses), embroidery and house linens, bolt silks, tailoring services (for perfect mandarin dresses), cloisonne jewelry and gifts, lacquerware, pottery, musical instruments, traditional Chinese clothing for men and women (from scholars' robes to coolie duds), jade and gold, cashmere, traditional items, art supplies, herbs, home furnishings—I could go on and on. Plan to spend some time here.

ARAB STREET   Shop for handicrafts from Malaysia and Indonesia. I go for sarongs at **Hadjee Textiles,** 75 Arab St. (𝄐 **65/298-1943**), for their stacks of folded sarongs in beautiful colors and traditional patterns. They're perfect for traveling because they're lightweight, but they can serve you well as a dressy skirt, bed sheet, beach blanket, window shade, bath towel, or whatever you need—when I'm on the road, I can't live without mine. Buy a few here, and the prices really drop. If you're in the market for a more masculine sarong, **Goodwill Trading,** 56 Arab St. (𝄐 **298-3205**), specializes in pulicat, or the plaid sarongs worn by Malay men. For modern styles of batik, check out **Basharahil Brothers,** 99–101 Arab St. (𝄐 **65/296-0432**), for its very interesting designs, but don't forget to see the collection of fine silk batiks in the back. For batik household linens, you can't beat **Maruti Textiles,** 93 Arab St. (𝄐 **65/392-0253**), where you'll find high-quality place mats and napkins, tablecloths, pillow covers, and quilts. The buyer for this shop has a good eye for style.

I've also found a few shops on Arab Street that carry handicrafts from other countries in Southeast Asia. **Memoirs,** 18 Baghdad St. (✆ **65/294-5900**), sells mostly Indonesian crafts, from carved and hand-painted decorative items to scored leather shadow puppets and unusual teak gifts. **Ahn Yeu Em De Paris,** 15 Baghdad St. (✆ **65/292-1523**), carries boxes of velvet hand-beaded evening shoes made in Vietnam. So inexpensive! For antiques and curios, try **Gim Joo Trading,** 16 Baghdad St. (✆ **65/293-5638**), a jumble of the unusual, some of it old. A departure from the more packed and dusty places here, **Suraya Betawj,** 67 Arab St. (✆ **65/398-1607**), carries gorgeous Indonesian and Malaysian crafted housewares in contemporary design—the type you normally find for huge prices in shopping catalogues back home.

Other unique treasures include the large assortment of fragrance oils at **Aljunied Brothers,** 91 Arab St. (✆ **65/291-8368**). Muslims are forbidden from consuming alcohol in any form (a proscription that includes the wearing of alcohol-based perfumes as well), so these oil-based perfumes re-create designer scents plus other floral and wood creations. Check out their delicate cut-glass bottles and atomizers as well. Finally, for the crafter in your life, **Kin Lee & Co.,** 109 Arab St. (✆ **65/291-1411**), carries a complete line of patterns and accessories to make local Peranakan beaded slippers. In vivid colors and floral designs, these traditional slippers were always made by hand, to be attached later to a wooden sole. The finished versions are exquisite, plus they're fun to make.

LITTLE INDIA   The best shopping is on Serangoon Road, where Singapore's Indian community shops for Indian imports and cultural items. Little India offers all sorts of small finds, especially throughout Little India Arcade (48 Serangoon Rd.) and just across the street on Campbell Lane at **Kuna's,** no. 3 Campbell Lane (✆ **65/294-2700**). Here you can buy inexpensive Indian costume jewelry like bangles, earrings, and necklaces in exotic designs, and a wide assortment of decorative dots (called *pottu* in Tamil) to grace your forehead. Indian handicrafts include brass work, wood carvings, dyed tapestries, woven cotton household linens, small curio items, very inexpensive incense, colorful pictures of Hindu gods, and other ceremonial items. Look here also for Indian cooking pots and household items. If after you pick up these items you care to try your hand at making your own curry, head for **Mannan Impex,** 118 Serangoon (✆ **65/299-8424**), to peruse all the necessary spices.

OUTDOOR MARKETS   A few outdoor markets still exist in Singapore, though it ain't like the old days. At the Bugis MRT station, across from Parco Bugis Junction, a well-established **night market** (which is also open during the day) delivers overpriced cheap chic, some curio items, accessories, and video compact discs (VCDs) to tourists. In **Chinatown,** on the corner of South Bridge Road and Cross Street, look for the old guys who come out with blankets full of odd merchandise—old watches, coins, jewelry, Mao paraphernalia, Peranakan pottery, and local artifacts from decades past. There's not many of these guys there, but for impromptu markets, I thought their merchandise was far more imaginative than at Bugis. If you're really desperate for a **flea market,** you can always head for the field between Little India and Arab Street (just behind the Johor bus terminal), where you'll find about five times more vendors than at Chinatown, but *be warned:* The goods are weird. Old nasty shoes, Barry Gibb records, broken radios—the same stuff you'd see at garage sales back home, only local style. It could be interesting culturally, if you're in the mood.

8 Singapore After Dark

What do you want to do tonight? Do you want to go out for a cultural experience and find a traditional dance or music performance or a Chinese opera, or
do you want to put on your finery and rub elbows with society at the symphony?
If it's live performance you're looking for, you have your choice not only of the
local dance and theater troupes, but of the many West End and Broadway shows
that come through on international tours. Or you might want to try a local
performance—smaller theater groups have lately been hitting nerves and funny
bones through stage portrayals of life in the Garden City. Singapore has been
transforming itself into a center for the arts in this part of the world and is beginning to achieve the level of sophistication you'd come to expect from a Western
city. If partying it up is more your speed, there's all kinds of nighttime revelry
going on. Society might seem puritanical during the daylight hours, but once
the night comes, the clubs get crazy.

INFORMATION   Major cultural festivals are highly publicized by the **Singapore Tourism Board (STB),** so one stop by the office will probably provide
enough information to fill your evening agenda for your whole trip. Another
source is the *Straits Times,* which lists events around town, as well as the *New
Paper,* which also lists musical events like local bands and international rock and
pop tours. Both of these papers also provide cinema listings and theater reviews.

Theartsmagazine, a bimonthly publication with articles about the local
scene plus coming events, is on sale at bookstores and magazine stands for
S$5.80 (US$3.30).

TICKETS   Two ticket agents, **TicketCharge** and **Sistic,** handle bookings for
almost all theater performances, concert dates, and special events. You can find
out about schedules before your visit through their websites: www.ticket
charge.net and www.sistic.com.sg. When in Singapore, stop by one of their centrally located outlets to pick up a schedule, or call them for more information.
Call TicketCharge at © **65/6296-2929,** or head for Centrepoint, Forum—The
Shopping Mall, Funan—The IT Mall, Marina Square Shopping Centre, or
Tanglin Mall. For **Sistic** bookings, call © **65/6348-5555,** or see them at the
Victoria Concert Hall Box Office, Parco Bugis Junction, Raffles Shopping Centre, Scotts, Specialists' Shopping Center, Suntec Mall, or Wisma Atria. The STB
also carries information about current and coming events.

HOURS   Theater and dance performances can begin anywhere between 7:30
and 9pm. Be sure to call for the exact time. Many bars open in the late afternoon, a few as early as lunchtime. Disco and entertainment clubs usually open
around 6pm but generally don't get lively until 10 or 11pm. Closing time for
bars and clubs is at 1 or 2am on weekdays and 3am on weekends.

DRINK PRICES   Because of the government's added tariff, alcoholic beverage
prices are high everywhere, whether in a hotel bar or a neighborhood pub. "House
pour" drinks (generics) are between S$8 and S$14 (US$4.55–US$8). A glass of
house wine costs between S$10 and S$15 (US$5.70–US$8.55), depending on
whether it's a red or a white. Local draft beer (Tiger), brewed in Singapore, is,
on average, S$10 (US$5.70). Hotel establishments usually are the most expensive venues, while standalone pubs and cafes are better values. Almost every bar
and club has a happy hour in the early evenings, and discounts can be up to 50%
off for house pours and drafts. Most of the disco and entertainment clubs charge

covers, but they usually include one drink. Hooray for ladies' nights—at least 1 night during the week—when those of the feminine persuasion get in for free.

DRESS CODE   Many clubs require smart casual attire. Feel free to be trendy, but stay away from shorts, T-shirts, sneakers, and torn jeans. Be forewarned that you might be turned away if not properly dressed. Many locals dress up for their night on the town, either in elegant garb or in fashionista threads.

SAFETY   You'll be fairly safe out during the wee hours in most parts of the city, and even a single woman alone has little to worry about. Occasionally, groups of young men catcall, but by and large those groups are not hanging out in the more cosmopolitan areas. On the weekends, police set up barricades around the city to pick up drunk drivers, so if you rent a car, be careful about your alcohol intake or appoint a designated driver. Otherwise, you can get home safely in a taxi, which, fortunately, isn't too hard to find even late at night, with one exception: When Boat Quay clubs close, there's usually a mob of revelers scrambling for cabs. (Note that after midnight, a 50% surcharge is added to the fare, so make sure you don't drink away your ride home!)

THEATER, DANCE & MUSICAL PERFORMANCE

Singapore is not a cultural backwater. Professional and amateur theater companies, dance troupes, opera companies, and musical groups offer a wide variety of not only Asian performances, but Western as well. Broadway road shows don't stop in San Francisco, where the road ends; they continue on to include Singapore in their itineraries. Major musical performers from opera to rock stars have been equally as successful. The Merce Cunningham Dance Company and the Bolshoi Ballet have both graced the boards, and the New York Philharmonic, under the baton of maestro Zubin Mehta, thrilled Singaporeans and visitors alike.

The **Singapore Symphony Orchestra** performs regularly in its new home at Esplanade—Theatres on the Bay, with regular special guest appearances by international celebrities. For information about the orchestra, check out www.sso.org.sg; for performance dates, see www.esplanade.som.

The **Singapore Lyric Opera,** Stamford Arts Centre, 155 Waterloo St. no. 03–06 (© 65/336-1929), also appears regularly. For the millennium, it staged the ever-popular **Die Fledermaus** with local talents. Call for upcoming schedules, or call Sistic.

The **Singapore Chinese Orchestra,** the only professional Chinese orchestra in Singapore, has won several awards for its classic Chinese interpretations. The orchestra performs every 2 weeks at a variety of venues (including outdoor concerts at the Botanic Gardens). Contact it c/o People's Association, Block B, Room 5, No. 9 Stadium Link (© 65/440-3839; www.sco-music.org.sg). Ticket sales are handled by Sistic.

BARS & CLUBS

Singaporeans love to go out at night, whether it's to lounge around in a cozy wine bar or to jump around on a dance floor until 3am. And this city has become pretty eclectic in its entertainment choices, so you'll find everything from live jazz to Elvis, from garage rock to techno, world beat, or just plain rock. The truth is, the nightlife is happening. Local celebrities and the young, wealthy, and beautiful are the heroes of the scene, and their quest for the "coolest" spot keeps the club scene on its toes. The listings here are keyed in to help you find the latest or most interesting place. *A tip:* At press time, the most happening bars and clubs were anything on Mohamed Sultan Road and the new Chinese-chic Lan Kwai Fong. Start from there.

BARS

Anywhere Music Pub   This perennial favorite has weathered fashion trends and the economic crisis to become one of the oldest and most established bars in the city. Resident band Tania plays pop and rock covers to packed crowds Monday through Saturday. It's a casual joint, come as you are, with a mixed crowd of mostly 30s and up, locals and foreign expatriates. Hours are Sunday to Thursday 6pm to 2am, and Friday and Saturday 6pm to 3am. Happy hours are held on weekdays 6 to 9pm. 19 Tanglin Rd. no. 04-08/08, Tanglin Shopping Centre. ℂ 65/6734-8233.

Brix   In the basement of the Grand Hyatt Regency, Brix has inherited the spot once reserved for Brannigan's, a rowdy upmarket watering hole and pickup joint. Grand Hyatt decided to clean up its act and had Brix move in instead. Decidedly more sophisticated than its predecessor, Brix has a new air of class but somehow lacks a certain seedy spontaneity. Still, it's a nice new place on the scene for those who prefer a more discriminating kind of fun. The Music Bar features live jazz and R&B, while the Wine & Whiskey Bar serves up a fine selection of wines, Scotch, and cognacs. Hours are Sunday to Thursday 7pm to 2am, and Friday and Saturday 7pm to 3am; there is a nightly happy hour from 7 to 9pm. Basement, Grand Hyatt Singapore, 10–12 Scotts Rd. ℂ 65/6416-7108. Cover charge Thurs, Fri, and Sat S$20 (US$11.45) that includes 1 standard drink.

Carnegie's   Carnegie's rocks. Here's the place where you'll hear rowdy old favorites to make the room shake from dancing and roar with singing, everything from the latest hot pop songs to cheesy old Grease medleys, disco, and drinking favorites. Time was, the rowdier girls would jump up on the bar to dance (including yours truly), but a recent converisal law banning bartop dancing in the city has put a damper on that (at least for now). It's a great time, but it's also a notorious *ang moh* place (that's Hokkien for Westerners, so don't count on rubbing elbows with too many locals here). On busy nights sometimes the doorman will charge 10 bucks to let you jump the queue. Hours are Sunday to Thursday 11am to 2am, and Friday and Saturday 11am to 3am. There is a happy hour daily 11am to 9pm and a crazy hour 6 to 7pm except Saturday and Sunday. 44-45 Pekin St., no. 01-01 Far East Sq. ℂ 65/6534-0850.

The Crazy Elephant   The Crazy Elephant is the city's address for blues. Hang out in cooling breezes blowing off the river while listening to classic rock and blues by resident bands. This place has hosted, in addition to the best local and regional guitarists, international greats such as Rick Derringer, Eric Burdon, and Walter Trout. It's an unpretentious place to chill out and have a cold one. Beer is reasonably priced as well. Hours are Sunday to Thursday 5pm to 1am, and Friday and Saturday 5pm to 2am, with a daily happy hour 5 to 9pm. 3E River Valley Road, no. 01-06/07 Traders Market, Clarke Quay. ℂ 65/6337-1990.

The Fat Frog Café   More a cafe than a bar, the Fat Frog draws folks who prefer conversation without intrusive music. The patio at the back of this place stays quiet in the afternoons, and at night fills up, but it rarely becomes overcrowded. The main attraction is its location—behind the Substation, a hub for Singapore's visual and performing-arts scene, making this place a good stop after a show. Sometimes you can even run into performers and other majors from the local scene. Inside you'll find a bulletin board promoting current shows, performances, and openings. Around the patio courtyard walls, local painters contribute mural work to the decor. There is a limited menu available. Hours are Sunday to Thursday 11:30am to midnight, and Friday and Saturday 11:30am to 1am. 45 Armenian St. (behind the Substation). ℂ **65/6338-6201.**

Hard Rock Cafe   The Hard Rock Cafe in Singapore is like the Hard Rock Cafe in your hometown. You probably don't go to that one, so don't bother spending your vacation time in this one, either. Not that it's all bad—the Filipino bands are usually pretty good, and, of course, so are the burgers. Other than that, it's not much more than a tourist pickup joint. Bring mace. Hours are Sunday to Thursday 11am to 2am, and Friday and Saturday 11am to 3am. Happy hour is Monday to Saturday 4 to 6pm, and Sunday 4 to 6pm and 10:30pm to 2am. No. 02-01 HPL House, 50 Cusacaden Rd. ℂ **65/6235-5232.** There is a cover charge of S$23 (US$13) Fri–Sat only, which includes your first drink. Sun–Mon 1-drink minimum charge.

JJ Mahoney   If you're looking for a real bar-type bar, JJ Mahoney comes pretty close. You have the tile floor, the dark wood bar and paneling, stools lining the sides, and everyday people sidling up for another round. The first floor is a nice place to hang out and meet people (until about 10:30pm, when the band kicks in with contemporary but rather loud music), and it broadcasts soccer games from time to time. The second floor, up a wide hardwood staircase, has small tables where you can order drinks and play games like Scrabble, Yahtzee, chess, and checkers. The third floor is reserved for KTV, a karaoke lounge where you can sing without worrying about con-women hitting you up for overpriced and watered-down drinks. Hours are Sunday to Thursday 5pm to 1am, and Friday and Saturday and the eve of public holidays 5pm to 2am. Happy hour is held nightly 5 to 8pm. 58 Duxton Rd. ℂ **65/6225-6225.**

The Long Bar   Here's a nice little gem of a bar, even if it is touristy and expensive. With tiled mosaic floors, large shuttered windows, electric fans, and punkah fans moving in waves above, Raffles Hotel has tried to retain much of the charm of yesteryear, so you can enjoy a Singapore Sling in its birthplace and take yourself back to when history was made. And truly, the thrill at the Long Bar is tossing back one of these sweet, juicy drinks while pondering the Singapore adventures of all the famous actors, writers, and artists who came through here in the first decades of the 20th century. If you're not inspired by the poetry of the moment, stick around and get juiced for the pop/reggae band at 9pm, which is quite good. Hours are Sunday to Thursday 11am to 1am, and Friday and Saturday 11am to 2am. Happy hour is nightly 6 to 9pm, with special deals on pitchers of beer and some mixed drinks. A Singapore Sling is S$18.30 (US$10), and a Sling with a souvenir glass costs S$28 (US$16). Raffles Hotel Arcade, Raffles Hotel, 1 Beach Rd. ℂ **65/6337-1886.**

Muddy Murphys   This is one of a few Irish bars in Singapore. Located on two levels in the shopping mall, on the upper level you have the more conservative business set having drinks after their 9-to-5 gigs, while downstairs the party lasts a little longer and gets a little more lively. Irish music rounds out the ambience created by the mostly Irish imported trappings around the place. Occasionally, they'll even have an Irish band. There is a limited menu for lunch, dinner, and snacks. Hours are Sunday to Thursday 11am to 1am, and Friday and Saturday 11am to 3am. Happy hour is daily 11am to 7:30pm (happy hour begins earlier, but the discount is not as great as at other places). No. B1-01/01-06 Orchard Hotel Shopping Arcade, 442 Orchard Rd. ℂ **65/6735-0400.**

The Next Page Few bars stand out for ambience like The Next Page, which is a freaky Chinese dream in an old Singaporean shophouse. Creep through the pintu pagar front door into the main room, its old walls of crumbling stucco washed in sexy Chinese red, and lanterns glowing crimson in the air shaft rising above the island bar. The crowd is mainly young professionals who by late night have been known to dance on the bar (and not only on weekends). The back has a bit more space for seating, darts, and a pool table. There is a small snack menu available. It's open daily 3pm to 3am. Happy hour is daily 3 to 9pm. 17 Mohamed Sultan Rd. © 65/6235-6967.

No. 5 Down Peranakan Place there are a few bars, one of which is No. 5, a cool, dark place just dripping with Southeast Asian ambience, from its old shophouse exterior to its partially crumbling interior walls hung with rich wood carvings. The hardwood floors and beamed ceilings are complemented by seating areas cozied with oriental carpets and kilim throw pillows. Upstairs is more conventional table-and-chair seating. The glow of the skylighted air shaft and the whirring fans above make this an ideal place to stop for a cool drink on a hot afternoon. In the evenings, be prepared for a lively mix of people. It's open Monday to Thursday noon to 2am, Friday and Saturday noon to 3am, and Sunday 5pm to 2am. Happy hour is daily noon to 9pm. 5 Emerald Hill. © 65/6732-0818.

MICROBREWERIES

Brewerkz Brewerkz, with outside seating along the river and an airy contemporary style inside—like a giant IKEA room built around brewing kettles and copper pipes—brews the best house beer in Singapore. The bar menu features five tasty brew selections from recipes created by the English brew master: Nut Brown Ale, Red Ale, Wiesen, Bitter, and Indian Pale Ale (which, by the way, has the highest alcohol content). The American cuisine lunch, dinner, and snack menu is also very good—I recommend planning a meal here as well. It's open Sunday to Thursday 5pm to 1am, and Friday and Saturday 5pm to 3am. Happy hour is held daily 3 to 9pm with two-for-one beers. No. 01-05 Riverside Point, 30 Merchant Rd. © 65/438-7438.

JAZZ BARS

Harry's Quayside Bar & Upstairs at Harry's Wine Bar The official afterwork drink stop for finance professionals from nearby Shenton Way, Harry's biggest claim to fame is that it was bank-buster Nick Leeson's favorite bar. But don't let the power ties put you off. Harry's is a cool place, from airy riverside seating to cozy tables next to the stage. Harry's is known for its live jazz and R&B music, which is always good. Of all the choices along Boat Quay, Harry's remains the most classy; and even though it's also the most popular, you can usually get a seat. Dig their Sunday jazz brunches. Upstairs, the wine bar is very laid back, with plush sofas and dimly lit seating areas. Look for Harry's latest installment, scheduled to open in early 2003 at The Esplanade. It's being touted as the hottest hub for musicians and other artiste-types. It's open Sunday to Thursday 11am to 1am, and Friday and Saturday 11am to 2am. Happy hour daily is 11am to 9pm. 28 Boat Quay. © 65/6538-3029.

Raffles Bar & Billiards Talk about a place rich with the kind of elegance only history can provide. Raffles Bar & Billiards began as a bar in 1896 and over the decades has been transformed to perform various functions as the hotel's needs dictated. In its early days, legend has it that a patron shot the last tiger in Singapore under a pool table here. Whether or not the tiger part is true, one of its two billiards tables is an original piece, still in use after 100 years. In fact, many of the fixtures and furniture here are original Raffles antiques, including the lights above the billiards tables and the scoreboards, and are marked with small brass placards. In the evenings, a jazzy little trio shakes the ghosts out of the rafters, while from 6pm to 1am nightly, people lounge around enjoying single malts, cognacs, coffee, port, Champagne, chocolates, and imported cigars. Expect to drop a small fortune. It's open daily 11:30am to 12:30am. Raffles Hotel, 1 Beach Rd. ✆ 65/6331-1746.

Somerset's Bar   This huge hotel lounge can accommodate large crowds very comfortably. Good thing, because the place serves quite a lot of patrons, mostly jazz lovers who come for the best live jazz in the city. At least two sets of live music are featured every night: country, pop, and rock from 6:15 to 8:15pm except Saturday, and a jazz set from 9pm to around 1am every night. From time to time, the lounge has hosted internationally renowned performers like bassist Eldee Young, pianist Judy Roberts, and vocalist Nancy Kelly. Call ahead to find out the schedule of performances, and plan some time here for a nice evening in the relaxing environment. It's open daily 5pm to 2am. Happy hour is 5 to 8:30pm daily. The Westin Stamford and Westin Plaza hotels, 2 Stamford Rd. ✆ 65/6431-5332.

CLUBS

Bar None   In Singapore's trendy club scene, nightclubs have been known to come and go. Bar None is one place that has enjoyed steady success, probably because it does a great job keeping up with patrons' needs, with regularly scheduled theme parties and comedy nights. Resident band Energy is the best club band in town, playing a high-voltage mix of R&B, Top-40 and rock. Be prepared to queue up on weekends. Hours are Tuesday to Sunday 7pm to 3am, and Monday 7pm to 2am. Happy hour is 7 to 9pm. Basement Marriott Hotel, 320 Orchard Road. ✆ 65/6831-4656. Cover Fri–Sat S$26 (US$15), which includes 1 drink.

China Jump Bar & Grill   China Jump combines a disco, bar, and restaurant—sounds tame, but this place has been known to hop. It's especially famous for its Wednesday "Babe Central Night" that draws hordes of women after office hours. On any night, however, you can count on a fun crowd, dancing to pop and dance music. Restaurant cuisine is a passable American and Mexican grill offering, with huge portions. It's open daily 5pm to 3am and features no happy hour. 30 Victoria St., No. B1-07/08 CHIJMES Fountain Court. ✆ 65/6338-9388. Cover Wed Ladies' Night, men pay S$18 (US$10). Cover Fri–Sat S$18 (US$10) for everybody.

Liquid Room   Liquid Room was one of the first dance clubs in Singapore to spin techno, trance, and house music nightly. Local and guest DJs are very selective about the music they play, highlighting the best of each genre. The upstairs dance floor is open only Wednesday through Saturday. Downstairs, a moody lounge provides some downtime. The crowd here is young and energetic. It's open daily 7pm to 3am. Happy hour is daily 7 to 9pm. 76 Robertson Quay, Evason Hotel. ✆ 65/6333-8117.

Top Ten   This is one of the sleazier joints in Singapore and does a booming business. The huge space is like an auditorium, with a stage and dance floor at one end, seating areas on levels grading up to the top of the other end, and a lighted cityscape scene surrounding the whole thing. A cover band plays three sets of pop 7 days a week, but people don't come here for the decor or even the music: Top Ten is a notorious pickup joint for Asian women. Gentlemen, you'll be buying drinks all night. It's open daily 5pm to 3am, with a happy hour daily

9 to 11pm. No. 04-35/36 Orchard Towers, 400 Orchard Rd. ℭ **65/6732-3077.** Cover Fri–Sat S$18 (US$10), which includes 1 drink.

Zouk/Phuture/Velvet Underground Singapore's first innovative danceteria, Zouk introduced the city to house music, which throbs nightly in its cavernous disco, comprised of three warehouses joined together. This place plays the best in modern music, so even if you're not much of a groover, you can still have fun watching the party from the many levels that tower above the dance floor. If you need a bit more intimacy in your nightlife, Velvet Underground, within the Zouk complex, drips in red velvet and soft lighting—a good complement to the more soulful sounds spinning here. The newer addition to Zouk, Phuture, draws a younger, more hip-hop-loving crowd than VU. Including the wine bar outside, Zouk is basically your one-stop shopping for a party; and in Singapore, this place is legendary. At Zouk, cover is S$20 (US$12) Wednesday, and S$20 (US$12) for women and S$25 (US$15) for men Friday and Saturday. At Phuture, cover is S$23 (US$14) Wednesday, S$10 (US$6) Thursday, and S$20 (US$12) for women and S$25 (US$15) for men Friday and Saturday. At Velvet Underground, cover is S$20 (US$12) Tuesday and Thursday, S$25 (US$15) Wednesday, and S$20 (US$12) for women and S$25 (US$15) for men Friday and Saturday. All clubs are open 6pm to 3am. Jiak Kim St. ℭ **65/738-2988.** Payment of highest cover charge among the 3 clubs in the complex allows admission to the other clubs as well; otherwise, additional charges will incur when moving between clubs.

CABARET
Boom Boom Room Singapore's fun night out with female impersonators and somewhat bawdy vaudeville-style acts. Local TV stars Kumar and Leena perform regularly, in elaborate costumes, to Japanese and Bollywood hits in between bawdy jokes and audience participation. Drinks are moderately priced. Hours are Sunday to Thursday 8:30pm to 2am, and Friday and Saturday 8:30pm to 3am. 130-132 Amoy St., Far East Square, ℭ **65/6435-0030.** Cover S$20 (US$11) weekdays; S$25 (US$14) weekends.

GAY NIGHTSPOTS
It seems a few of Singapore's better known gay and lesbian spots have closed down in the past couple of years, but new places are popping up regularly. The Web has listings at www.utopia-asia.com/tipsing.htm. For the latest information, I recommend one of the chat rooms suggested at the address above, where you can talk to the experts. Velvet Underground, part of the Zouk complex (see above), welcomes a mixed clientele of gays, lesbians, and straight folks. There are a couple of gay bars that have asked to remain unlisted in this book, so ask around for a better sense of the scene in Singapore.

WINE BARS
Beaujolais This little gem of a place, in a shophouse built on a hill, is smaller than small, but its charm makes it a favorite for loyal regulars. Two tables outside (on the Five-Foot-Way, which serves more as a patio than a sidewalk) and two tables inside doesn't seem like much room, but there's more seating upstairs. They believe that wine should be affordable, so their many labels tend to be more moderately priced per glass and bottle. Hours are Monday to Thursday 11am to midnight, Friday 11am to 2am, and Saturday 6pm to 2am. Happy hour is held from opening until 9pm. 1 Ann Siang Hill. ℭ **65/6224-2227.**

Que Pasa   One of the more mellow stops along Peranakan Place, this little wine bar serves up a collection of some 70 to 100 labels with plenty of atmosphere and a nice central location. It's another bar in a shophouse, but this one has as its centerpiece a very unusual winding stairway up the air shaft to the level above. Wine bottles and artwork line the walls. In the front, you can order Spanish-style finger food—tapas, anyone?—and cigars. The VIP club on the upper floor has the look and feel of a formal living room, complete with wing chairs and board games. Hours are Sunday to Thursday 6pm to 2am, and Friday to Saturday 6pm to 3am. 7 Emerald Hill. © 65/235-6626.

9

Malaysia

by Jennifer Eveland

Compared with spicy Thailand to the north and cosmopolitan Singapore to the south, Malaysia is a relative secret to many from the West, and most travelers to Southeast Asia skip over it, opting for more heavily traversed routes.

Boy, are they missing out. Those who venture here wander through streets awash with international influences from colonial times and trek through mysterious rain forests and caves, often without another tourist in sight. They relax peacefully under palms on lazy white beaches that fade into blue, blue waters. They spy the bright colors of batik sarongs hanging to dry in the breeze. They hear the melodic drone of the Muslim call to prayer seeping from exotic mosques. They taste culinary masterpieces served in modest local shops—from Malay, with its deep mellow spices to succulent seafood punctuated by brilliant chile sauces. In Malaysia, I'm always thrilled to witness life without the distracting glare of the tourism industry, and I leave impressed by how accessible Malaysia is to outsiders while remaining true to its heritage.

Malaysia just doesn't get the tourism press it deserves, but it's not because foreign travelers aren't welcome. True, the Malaysian Tourism Board has almost no international advertising campaign—and you'll be hard-pressed to get any useful information out of them—but everyone from government officials in Kuala Lumpur to boat hands in Penang seems delighted to see the smiling face of a traveler who has discovered just how beautiful their country is.

This chapter covers the major destinations of peninsular Malaysia. We begin with the country's capital, **Kuala Lumpur,** and then tour the peninsula's west coast—the cities of **Johor Bahru** and **Malacca** (Melaka), the hill resorts at **Cameron** and **Genting Highlands,** plus islands like the popular **Penang** and the luxurious **Langkawi.** Next we take you up the east coast of the peninsula, through resort areas such as **Desaru, Kuantan,** and **Cherating,** all the way north to the culturally stimulating cities of **Kuala Terengganu** and **Kota Bharu.** My coverage will also include **Taman Negara,** peninsular Malaysia's largest national forest. Finally, we cross the South China Sea to the island of Borneo, where the Malaysian states of **Sarawak** and **Sabah** feature Malaysia's most impressive forests as well as unique and diverse cultures.

Malaysia is easily accessible to the rest of the world through its international airport in Kuala Lumpur. Or, if you want to hop from another country in the region, daily flights to Malaysia's many smaller airports give you access to all parts of the country, and you can also travel by car, bus, or train from Singapore or Thailand.

1 Getting to Know Malaysia

THE LAY OF THE LAND

Malaysia's territory covers peninsular Malaysia—bordering Thailand in the north just across from Singapore in the south—and two states on the island of Borneo, Sabah and Sarawak, approximately 240km (150 miles) east across the South China Sea. All 13 of its states total 336,700 sq. km (202,020 sq. miles) of land. Of this area, **Peninsular Malaysia** makes up about 465,000 sq. km (134,680 sq. miles) and contains 11 of Malaysia's 13 states: Kedah, Perlis, Penang, and Perak are in the northwest; Kelantan and Terengganu are in the northeast; Selangor, Negeri Sembilan, and Melaka are about midway down the peninsula on the western side; Pahang, along the east coast, sprawls inward to cover most of the central area (which is mostly forest preserve); and Johor covers the entire southern tip from east to west, with two vehicular causeways linking it to Singapore, just over the Strait of Johor. Kuala Lumpur, the nation's capital, appears on a map to be located in the center of the state of Selangor, but it is actually a federal district similar to Washington, D.C., in the United States.

Tropical evergreen forests, estimated to be some of the oldest in the world, cover more than 70% of Malaysia. The country's diverse terrain allows for a range of forest types, such as montane forests, sparsely wooded tangles at higher elevations; lowland forests, the dense tropical jungle type; mangrove forests along the waters' edge; and peat swamp forest along the waterways. On the peninsula, three national forests—Taman Negara (or "National Forest") and Kenong Rimba Park, both inland, and Endau Rompin National Park, located toward the southern end of the peninsula—welcome visitors regularly, for quiet nature walks to observe wildlife or hearty adventures like white-water rafting, mountain climbing, caving, and jungle trekking. Similarly, the many national forests of Sabah and Sarawak provide a multitude of memorable experiences, which can include brushes with the indigenous peoples of the forests.

Surrounded by the South China Sea on the east coast and the Strait of Malacca on the west, the waters off the peninsula vary in terms of sea life (and beach life). The waters off the east coast house a living coral reef, good waters, and gorgeous tropical beaches, while more southerly parts host beach resort areas. By way of contrast, the surf in southern portions of the Strait of Malacca is choppy and cloudy from shipping traffic—hardly ideal for diving or for the perfect Bali Hai vacation. But once you get as far north as Penang, the waters become beautiful again. Meanwhile, the sea coast of Sabah and Sarawak counts numerous resort areas that are ideal for beach vacationing and scuba diving. In fact, one of the world's top 10 dive sites is located at Sipadan in Sabah.

MALAYSIA'S PEOPLE, ETIQUETTE & CUSTOMS

The mix of cultural influences in Malaysia is the result of centuries of immigration and trade with the outside world, particularly with Arab nations, China, and India. Early groups of incoming foreigners brought wealth from around the world, plus their own unique cultural heritages and religions. Furthermore, once imported, each culture remained largely intact; that is, none has truly been homogenized. Traditional temples and churches exist side by side with mosques.

Likewise, **traditional art forms** of various cultures are still practiced in Malaysia, most notably in the areas of dance and performance art. Chinese opera, Indian dance, and Malay martial arts are all very popular cultural activities. Silat, originating from a martial arts form (and still practiced as such by

---

> **Tips   Abbreviating Malaysia**
>
> The first tip here is that people are always abbreviating Kuala Lumpur to KL. Okay, that's pretty obvious. But these people will abbreviate everything else they can get away with. So, Johor Bahru becomes JB, Kota Bharu KB, Kota Kinabalu, KK—you get the picture. Malaysia itself is often shortened to M'sia. To make it easier for you, the only shortened version I've used in this book is KL.

---

many), is a dance performed by men and women. Religious and cultural festivals are open for everyone to appreciate and enjoy. Unique arts and traditions of indigenous people distinguish Sabah and Sarawak from the rest of the country.

Traditional **Malaysian music** is very similar to Indonesian music. Heavy on rhythms, its constant drum beats underneath the light repetitive melodies of the stringed gamelan (no relation at all to the Indonesian metallophone gamelan, with its gongs and xylophones), will entrance you with its simple beauty.

Questions of etiquette in Malaysia are very similar to those in Singapore, so please see chapter 8 for more information.

2 Planning Your Trip to Malaysia

VISITOR INFORMATION
The **Malaysia Tourism Board (MTB)** can provide some information by way of pamphlets and advice before your trip, but keep in mind they are not yet as sophisticated as the Singapore Tourism Board. Much of the information they provide is vague, broad-stroke descriptions with few concrete details that are useful for the traveler. Overseas offices are located as follows.

The nationwide tourist hot line is ✆ **1300/88-5776.** The official website of the Malaysia Tourism Board is www.tourismmalaysia.gov.my.

IN THE UNITED STATES
- **New York:** 595 Madison Ave., Suite 1800, New York, NY 10022 (✆ **212/ 754-1113;** fax 212/754-1116)
- **Los Angeles:** 818 W. 7th St., Suite 804, Los Angeles, CA 90017 (✆ **213/ 689-9702;** fax 213/689-1530)

IN CANADA
- **Vancouver:** 830 Burrard St., Vancouver, B.C., Canada V6Z 2K4 (✆ **604/ 689-8899;** fax 604/689-8804)

IN AUSTRALIA
- **Sydney:** 65 York St., Sydney, NSW 2000, Australia (✆ **02/9299-4441;** fax 02/9262-2026)
- **Perth:** 56 William St., Perth, WA 6000, Australia (✆ **08/9481-0400;** fax 08/9321-1421).

IN THE UNITED KINGDOM
- **London:** 57 Trafalgar Square, London, WC2N 5DU, UK (✆ **071/930- 7932;** fax 071/930-9015)
- **In Malaysia:** 17th Floor, Menara Dato' Onn, Putra World Trade Centre, 45 Jalan Tun Ismail, 50480 Kuala Lumpur (✆ **03/293-5188;** fax 03/293- 5884).

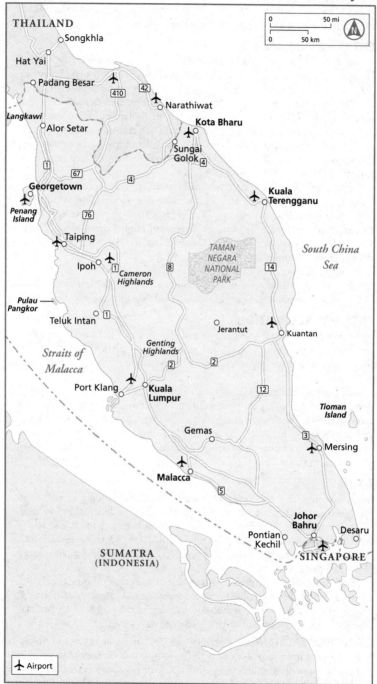

Peninsular Malaysia

THAILAND

Songkhla

Hat Yai

Padang Besar

Langkawi

Alor Setar

Narathiwat

Kota Bharu

Sungai Golok

Georgetown

Penang Island

Taiping

Ipoh

Cameron Highlands

Kuala Terengganu

South China Sea

TAMAN NEGARA NATIONAL PARK

Pulau Pangkor

Teluk Intan

Straits of Malacca

Jerantut

Genting Highlands

Kuantan

Port Klang

Kuala Lumpur

Gemas

Tioman Island

Mersing

Malacca

Johor Bahru

Pontian Kechil

Desaru

SINGAPORE

SUMATRA (INDONESIA)

0   50 mi
0   50 km

✈ Airport

For MTB offices in other cities, refer to individual city listings. The official website of the Malaysia Tourism Board is http://tourism.gov.my.

ENTRY REQUIREMENTS

To enter the country, you must have a valid passport. Citizens of the United States do not need visas for tourism and business visits, and upon entry are granted a Social/Business Visit Pass good for up to 3 months. Citizens of Canada, Australia, New Zealand, and the United Kingdom can also enter the country without a visa, and will be granted up to 30 days pass upon entry. For other countries, please consult the nearest Malaysian consulate before your trip for visa regulations. *Also note:* Travelers holding Israeli passports are not permitted to travel within Malaysia (likewise, Malaysians are forbidden from traveling to Israel).

While in Malaysia, if you need to contact an official representative from your home country, the following contact information in Kuala Lumpur can help you: the **United States Embassy** (© 03/2168-5000), the **Canadian High Commission** (© 03/2718-8333), the **Australian High Commission** (© 03/2146-5555), the **New Zealand High Commission** (© 03/2078-2533); and the **British High Commission** (© 03/2148-2122).

If you are arriving from an area in which yellow fever has been reported, you will be required to show proof of yellow fever vaccination. Contact your nearest MTB office to research the specific areas that fall into this category.

CUSTOMS REGULATIONS

With regard to currency, you can bring into the country as many foreign currency notes or traveler's checks as you please, but you are not allowed to leave the country with more foreign currency or traveler's checks than you had when you arrived.

Social visitors can enter Malaysia with 1 liter of hard alcohol and 1 carton of cigarettes without paying duty—anything over that amount is subject to local taxes. Prohibited items include firearms and ammunition, daggers and knives, and pornographic materials. Be advised that, similar to Singapore, Malaysia enforces a very strict drug abuse policy that includes the death sentence for convicted drug traffickers.

MONEY

Malaysia's currency is the **Malaysian ringgit.** It's also commonly referred to as the Malaysian dollar, but prices are marked as RM (a designation I've used throughout this book). Notes are issued in denominations of RM2, RM5, RM10, RM20, RM50, RM100, RM500, and RM1000. One ringgit is equal to 100 sen. Coins come in denominations of 1, 5, 10, 20, and 50 sen, and there's also a 1-ringgit coin.

Following the dramatic decline in the value of its currency during the Southeast Asian economic crisis, the Malaysian government has sought to stabilize the ringgit to ward off currency speculation by pegging the ringgit at an artificial exchange rate. At the time of writing, exchange rates were RM3.80 to US$1.

CURRENCY EXCHANGE   Currency can be changed at banks and hotels, but you'll get a more favorable rate if you go to one of the money-changers that seem to be everywhere: in shopping centers, in little lanes, and in small stores—just look for signs. They are often men in tiny booths with a lighted display on the wall behind them showing the exchange rate. All major currencies are generally accepted, and there is never a problem with the U.S. dollar.

AUTOMATED-TELLER MACHINES   Kuala Lumpur, Penang, and Johor Bahru have quite a few automated teller machines (ATMs) scattered around, but they are few and far between in the smaller towns. In addition, some ATMs do not accept credit cards or debit cards from your home bank. I have found that debit cards on the MasterCard/Cirrus or Visa/PLUS networks are almost always accepted at **Maybank,** with at least one location in every major town. Cash is dispensed in ringgit deducted from your account at the day's rate.

TRAVELER'S CHECKS   Generally, travelers to Malaysia will never go wrong with American Express and Thomas Cook traveler's checks, which can be cashed at banks, hotels, and licensed money-changers. Unfortunately, they are often not accepted at smaller shops. Even in some big restaurants and department stores, many cashiers don't know how to process these checks, which might lead to a long and frustrating wait.

CREDIT CARDS   Credit cards are widely accepted at hotels and restaurants, and at many shops as well. Most popular are American Express, MasterCard, and Visa. Some banks might also be willing to advance cash against your credit card, but you have to ask around because this service is not available everywhere.

In Malaysia, to report a lost or stolen card, call American Express via the nearest **American Express** representative office (see individual city listings) or the head office in Kuala Lumpur (© 603/2026-1770); for **MasterCard Emergency**

Assistance for International Visitors, call ✆ 800/88-4594; and for **Visa Emergency Assistance,** call ✆ 800/80-1066. Both numbers are toll-free from anywhere in the country. For more on credit cards and what to do if your wallet gets stolen, see chapter 3.

WHEN TO GO

There are two **peak seasons** in Malaysia, one in winter and another in summer. The peak winter tourist season falls roughly from the beginning of December to the end of January, covering the major winter holidays—Christmas, New Year's Day, Chinese New Year, and Hari Raya. These dates can change according to the full moon, which dictates the exact dates of the Chinese New Year and Hari Raya holidays. Note that due to the monsoon at this time (Nov–Mar), the east coast of peninsular Malaysia is rainy and the waters are rough. Resort areas are deserted and often closed. Tourist traffic slows down from February through the end of May, and then picks up again in June. The peak summer season falls in the months of June, July, and August, and can last into mid-September. After September it's quiet again until December. Both seasons experience approximately equal tourist traffic, but in summer months that traffic might ebb and flow.

CLIMATE   Climate considerations will play a role in your plans. If you plan to visit any of the east coast resort areas, the low season is between November and March, when the monsoon tides make the water too choppy for water sports and beach activities. On the west coast, the rainy season is from April through May, and again from October through November.

The temperature is basically static year-round. Daily averages are between 67°F and 90°F (21°C–32°C). Temperatures in the hill resorts get a little cooler, averaging 67°F (21°C) during the day and 50°F (10°C) at night.

CLOTHING CONSIDERATIONS   You will want to pack light, loose-fitting clothes, sticking mostly to natural fibers. Women have additional clothing requirements because it can sometimes be uncomfortable walking through Muslim streets wearing short shorts or a sleeveless top—in many areas people *will* stare. The traditional dress for Good Muslim Women in Malaysia is that which covers the body, including the legs, arms, and head. And while many Malay women choose to continue this tradition (and with color and pizzazz, I might add), those who do not are still perfectly acceptable within Malaysia's contemporary society. As a female traveler, I pack slacks and jeans, long skirts and dresses (below the knee is fine), and loose-fitting, short-sleeve cotton tops. In modern cities such as Kuala Lumpur, Johor Bahru, Malacca, Penang, and Kuching, I don't feel conspicuous in modest walking shorts, and at beach resorts I'm the first to throw on my bikini and head for the water. I always bring one lightweight long-sleeve blouse and a scarf large enough to cover my head—visits to mosques require it. If you get worried about what's appropriate, the best thing to do is to look around you and follow suit.

A tip for both male and female travelers is to wear shoes that are easily removed. Local custom asks that you remove your shoes before entering any home or place of worship

PUBLIC HOLIDAYS & EVENTS   During Malaysia's official public holidays, expect government offices to be closed, as well as some shops and restaurants, depending on the ethnicity of the shop owner or restaurant owner. **Hari Raya Puasa** and **Chinese New Year** fall close to the same dates, during which time you can expect many shop and restaurant closings. However, during these holidays, look out for special sales and celebrations. Also count on public parks, shopping malls, and beaches to be more crowded during public holidays, as locals will be taking advantage of their time off.

Official public holidays fall as follows: Hari Raya Aidil Fitri (Dec or Jan), New Year's Day (Jan 1), Chinese New Year (Jan or Feb), Hari-Raya Aidil-Adha (Mar or Apr), Wesak Day (May), Prophet Mohammed's Birthday (June 26), National Day (Aug 31), and Christmas (Dec 25). Where general dates are given above, expect these holidays to shift from year to year, depending on the lunar calendar. The MTB can help you with exact dates as you plan your trip. In addition, each state has a public holiday to celebrate the birthday of the state Sultan.

HEALTH & INSURANCE

The **tap water** in Kuala Lumpur is supposedly potable, but I don't recommend drinking it—in fact, I don't recommend drinking tap water anywhere in Malaysia. Bottled water is inexpensive enough and readily available at convenience stores and food stalls. **Food** prepared in hawker centers is generally safe—I have yet to experience trouble, and I'll eat almost anywhere. If you buy fresh fruit, wash it well with bottled water and carefully peel off the skin before eating it.

Malaria has not been a major threat in most parts of Malaysia, even Malaysian Borneo. **Dengue fever,** on the other hand, which is also carried by mosquitoes, remains a constant threat in most areas, especially rural parts. If left untreated, dengue can cause fatal internal hemorrhaging, so if you come down with a sudden fever or skin rash, consult a physician immediately. There are no prophylactic treatments for dengue; the best protection is to wear plenty of insect repellent. Choose a product that contains DEET or is specifically formulated to be effective in the tropics.

For further health and insurance information, see chapter 3.

SAFETY/CRIME

While you'll find occasional news reports about robberies in the countryside, there's not a whole lot of crime going on, especially crime that would impact your trip. There's very little crime against tourists, like pickpocketing and purse slashing. Still, hotels without in-room safes will keep valuables in the hotel safe for you. Be careful when traveling on overnight trains and buses where there are great opportunities for theft (many times by fellow tourists, believe it or not). Keep your valuables close to you as you sleep.

GETTING THERE
BY PLANE

Malaysia has five international airports—at Kuala Lumpur, Penang, Langkawi, Kota Kinabalu, and Kuching—and 14 domestic airports at locations that include Johor Bahru, Kota Bharu, Kuantan, and Kuala Terengganu. Specific airport information is listed with coverage of each city.

A passenger service charge, or **airport departure tax,** is levied on all flights. A tax of RM6 (US$1.58) for domestic flights and RM45 (US$12) for international flights is usually included when you pay for your ticket.

Few Western carriers fly directly to Malaysia. If Malaysian Airlines does not have suitable routes directly from your home country, you'll have to contact another airline to work out a route that connects to one of Malaysia Airline's routes. I have found Malaysia Airlines service to be of a very good standard, and they have possibly the lowest rates to Southeast Asia from North American destinations.

FROM THE UNITED STATES Malaysia Airlines (℡ 800/552-9264) flies at least once daily from Los Angeles to Kuala Lumpur, and three times a week from New York.

FROM CANADA North American carriers will have to connect with a Malaysian Airlines flight, either in East Asia or in Europe.

FROM THE UNITED KINGDOM Malaysia Airlines (℡ 0171/341-2020) has two daily nonstop flights from London Heathrow airport, operating domestic connections from Glasgow, Edinburgh, Teesside, Leeds Bradford, and Manchester. British Airways (℡ 0345/222111, a local call from anywhere within the U.K.) departs London to KL daily, except on Monday and Friday.

FROM AUSTRALIA Malaysia Airlines (℡ 02/132627) flies directly to Kuala Lumpur from Perth, Adelaide, Brisbane, Darwin, Sydney and Melbourne, and Cairns. Quantas Airlines (℡ 02/131211) provides service from Sydney to KL on Tuesday, Friday, and Saturday.

FROM NEW ZEALAND Malaysia Airlines (℡ 09/373-2741 or 0800/657-472) flies a direct route from Auckland.

BY TRAIN
FROM SINGAPORE The Keretapi Tanah Melayu Berhad (KTM), Malaysia's rail system, runs express and local trains that connect the cities along the west coast of Malaysia with Singapore to the south and Thailand to the north. Trains depart three times daily from the **Singapore Railway Station** (℡ 65/6222-5165), on Keppel Road in Tanjong Pagar, not far from the city center. About five daily trains to Johor Bahru cost S$4.20 (US$2.50) for first-class passage, S$1.90 (US$1.15) for second class, and S$1.10 (US65¢) for third class for the half-hour journey. **Johor Bahru's train station** is very centrally located at Jalan Campbell (℡ 07/223-4727), and taxis are easy to find. Trains to Kuala Lumpur depart five times daily for fares from S$60 (US$36) for first class, S$26 (US$16) for second class, and S$15 (US$8.90) for third. The trip takes around 6 hours. Kuala Lumpur's KL Sentral railway station is a 10-minute taxi ride from the center of town and is connected to the Putra LRT, KL Mono-rail city public transportation trains, and the Express Rail Link (ERL) to Kuala Lumpur International Airport (KLIA).

FROM THAILAND KTM's international service departs from the **Hua Lamphong Railway Station** (℡ 662/223-7010 or 662/223-7020) in Bangkok, with operations to Hua Hin, Surat Thani, Nakhon Si Thammarat, and Hat Yai in Thailand's southern peninsula. The final stop in Malaysia is at Butterworth (Penang), so passage to KL requires you to catch a connecting train onward. The daily service departs at 3:15pm and takes approximately 22 hours from Bangkok to Butterworth. There is no first- or third-class service on this train, only air-conditioned second class; an upper berth goes for about RM76 (US$20), and a lower is RM87 (US$23).

For a fascinating journey from Thailand, you can catch the **Eastern & Orient Express (E&O),** which operates a route between Bangkok, Kuala Lumpur, and Singapore. Traveling in the luxurious style for which the Orient Express is renowned, you'll finish the entire journey in about 42 hours. Compartments are classed as Sleeper (approximately US$1,490 per person double occupancy), State (US$2,200 per person double occupancy), and Presidential (US$3,000 per person double occupancy). All fares include meals on the train. Overseas reservations for the E&O Express can be made through a travel agent, or, from the United States and Canada, call ✆ **800/524-2420;** from Australia, call ✆ 3/ 9699-9766, and from the United Kingdom, call ✆ 0207/805-5100. From Singapore, Malaysia, and Thailand, contact the E&O office in Singapore at ✆ 65/ 6392-3500.

BY BUS

From Singapore, there are many bus routes to Malaysia. The easiest depart from the Johor-Singapore bus terminal at the corner of Queen and Arab streets. Buses to Kuala Lumpur leave three times daily and cost S$25. Contact **The Singapore-KL bus service** at ✆ **65/6292-8254.** Buses to Johor Bahru and Malacca can also be picked up at this terminal, leaving at regular intervals throughout the day. Call ✆ 65/6292-8149 for buses to Johor Bahru (S$2.10/US$1.20)) and ✆ 65/6293-5915 for buses to Malacca (S$11/US$6.30). If you wish to travel by bus to a smaller destination, the best way is to hop a bus to Johor Bahru and then transfer to a bus to your final stop.

By the way, it is possible to take local SBS bus no. 170 between Singapore and Johor Bahru, which is the cheapest way to go, but really I don't recommend it. During peak travel hours, I've seen the bus queues snaking for miles at the immigration checkpoints and thought, "Thank God I'm not those guys."

From Thailand, you can grab a bus in either Bangkok or Hat Yai (in the southern part of the country) heading for Malaysia. I don't recommend the bus trip from Bangkok. It's just far too long a journey to be confined to a bus. You're better off taking the train. From Hat Yai, many buses leave regularly to northern Malaysian destinations, particularly Butterworth (Penang).

BY TAXI (FROM SINGAPORE)

From the Johor-Singapore bus terminal at Queen and Arab streets, the **Singapore Johor Taxi Operators Association** (✆ **65/6296-7054**) can drive you to Johor Bahru for S$28 (US$16) if you get to the terminal yourself, or S$40 (US$23) if you ask to be picked up at your hotel.

BY CAR

For convenience, driving to Malaysia from Singapore can't be beat. You can go where you want to go when you want to go, and without the hassle of public transportation—but it is quite expensive. Cars can be rented in Singapore (see chapter 3 for details), and then driven to and even dropped off in Malaysia. A slightly cheaper option is taking the ferry from Singapore to Johor and renting there.

GETTING AROUND

The modernization of Malaysia has made travel here—whether it's by plane, train, bus, taxi, or self-driven car—easier and more convenient than ever. Malaysia Airlines has service to every major destination within the peninsula and East Malaysia. Buses have a massive web of routes between every city and town. Train service up the western coast and out to the east provides even more options. And a unique travel offering—the outstation taxi—is available to and from every city on the peninsula. All the options make it convenient enough for you to plan to hop from city to city and not waste too much precious vacation time.

By and large, all the modes of transportation between cities are reasonably comfortable. Air travel can be the most costly of the alternatives, followed by outstation taxis and then buses and trains.

BY PLANE

Malaysia Airlines links from its hub in Kuala Lumpur to the cities of Johor Bahru, Kota Bharu, Kota Kinabalu, Kuala Terengganu, Kuantan, Kuching, Langkawi, Penang, and other smaller cities not covered in this volume. Malaysian Airline's national hot line ℂ **1300/88-3000** can be dialed from anywhere in the country. Individual airport information is provided in sections for each city that follows. One-way domestic fares can average RM100 to RM372 (US$26–US$98).

A new domestic airline competes with incredibly affordable rates. AirAsia links all the country's major cities with fares that average run from RM35 to RM180 (US$9.20–US$47). Call the KL office at ℂ **03/7651-2222,** or visit the website www.airasia.com.

BY TRAIN

The **Keretapi Tanah Melayu Berhad (KTM)** provides train service throughout peninsular Malaysia. Trains run from north to south between the Thai border and Singapore, with stops between including Butterworth (Penang), Kuala Lumpur, and Johor Bahru. There is a second line that branches off this line at Gemas, midway between Johor Bahru and KL, and heads northeast to Tempas near Kota Bharu. Fares range from RM64 (US$17) for first-class travel between Johor Bahru and KL, to RM158 (US$42) for first-class passage between Johor Bahru and Butterworth. Train station information is provided for each city in individual city headings in the following chapters.

BY BUS

Malaysia's intercity coach system is extensive, reliable, and inexpensive. Buses depart several times daily for many destinations on the peninsula, and fares are charged according to the distance you travel. Air-conditioned express bus service (called Executive Coach service or Business Class) will cost you more, but because the fares are so inexpensive, it's well worth your while to spend the couple of extra dollars for the comfort. For an idea of price, it costs about RM50 (US$13) for business class service from KL to Johor Bahru, and RM27 (US$7.10) from KL to Penang. While there are more than a few independent bus companies around, for this book I've stuck to only the two major route providers, **Transnasional** and **Park May** (which operate the NiCE and Plusliner buses). I've found these companies to be more reliable and comfortable than the others. For each city covered, I've listed bus terminal locations, but scheduling information must be obtained from the bus company itself.

BY TAXI

You can take special hired cars, called **outstation taxis,** between every city and state on the peninsula. Rates depend on the distance you plan to travel. They are fixed and stated at the beginning of the trip, but many times they can be bargained down. In Kuala Lumpur, go to the second level of the Puduraya Bus Terminal to find cabs that will take you outside the city, or call the **Kuala Lumpur Outstation Taxi Service Station,** 123 Jalan Sultan, Kuala Lumpur (ℂ **03/2078-0213**). A taxi from KL to Malacca will cost you approximately RM120 (US$32), KL to Cameron Highlands costs RM180 (US$47), and KL to Butterworth or Johor Bahru costs RM220 (US$58). Outstation taxi stand locations are included under each individual city heading.

Also, within each of the smaller cities, feel free to negotiate with unmetered taxis for hourly, half-day, or daily rates. It's an excellent way to get around for sightseeing and shopping without transportation hassles. Hourly rates are anywhere from RM15 to RM25 (US$3.95–US$6.60).

BY CAR

As recently as the 1970s, there was trouble with roadside crime—bandits stopping cars and holding up the travelers inside. Fortunately for drivers in Malaysia, this is a thing of the past. In the mid-1990s, Malaysia opened the North-South Highway, running from Bukit Kayu Hitam in the north on the Thai border to Johor Bahru at the southern tip of the peninsula. The highway (and the lack of bandits) has made travel along the west coast of Malaysia easy. There are rest areas with toilets, food outlets, and emergency telephones at intervals along the way. There is also a toll that varies depending on the distance you're traveling.

Driving along the east coast of Malaysia is actually much more pleasant than driving along the west coast. The highway is narrower and older, but it takes you through oil palm and rubber plantations, and the essence of kampung Malaysia permeates throughout. As you near villages, you'll often have to slow down and swerve past cows and goats, which are really quite oblivious to oncoming traffic. You have to get very close to honk at them before they move.

The speed limit on highways is 110kmph. On the minor highways the limit ranges from 70 to 90kmph. Do not speed: There are traffic police strategically situated around certain bends.

Distances between major towns are: from KL to Johor Bahru, 368km (221 miles); from KL to Malacca, 144km (86 miles); from KL to Kuantan, 259km (155 miles); from KL to Butterworth, 369km (221 miles); from Johor Bahru to Malacca, 224km (134 miles); from Johor Bahru to Kuantan, 325km (195 miles); from Johor Bahru to Mersing, 134km (80 miles); and from Johor Bahru to Butterworth, 737km (442 miles).

To rent a car in Malaysia, you must produce a driver's license from your home country that shows you have been driving at least 2 years. There are desks for major car-rental services at the international airports in Kuala Lumpur and Penang, and additional outlets throughout the country (see individual city sections for this information).

Hitchhiking is not common among locals, and I don't really think it's advisable for you, either. The buses between cities are very affordable, so it's a much better idea to opt for those instead.

TIPS ON ACCOMMODATIONS

Peak months of the year for hotels in western peninsular Malaysia are December through February and July through September. For the east coast, the busy times are July through September. You will need to make reservations well in advance to secure your room during these months.

TAXES & SERVICE CHARGES   All the nonbudget hotels charge a 10% service charge and 5% government tax. As such, there is no need to tip. But bellhops still tend to be tipped at least RM2 per bag, and car jockeys or valets should be tipped at least RM4 or more.

TIPS ON DINING

Malaysian food seems to get its origins from India's rich curries, influenced by Thailand's herbs and spices. You'll find delicious blends of coconut milk and curry, shrimp paste and chiles, accented by exotic flavors of galangal (similar to turmeric), lime, and lemongrass. Sometimes pungent, a few of the dishes have a deep flavor from fermented shrimp paste that is an acquired taste for Western palates. By and large, Malaysian food is delicious, but in multicultural Malaysia, so is the Chinese food, the Peranakan food, the Indian food—the list goes on. The Chinese brought their own flavors from their points of origin in the regions of southern China. Teochew, Cantonese, and Szechuan are all styles of Chinese cuisine that you'll find throughout the country. Peranakan food is unique to Malacca, Penang, and Singapore. The Peranakans, or "Straits Chinese," combined local ingredients with some traditional Chinese dishes to create an entirely new culinary form. And Indian food, both northern and southern, can be found in almost every city, particularly in the western part of the peninsula. And, of course, you'll find gorgeous fresh seafood almost everywhere.

I strongly recommend eating in a hawker stall when you can, especially in Penang, which is famous for its local cuisine.

Also, many Malaysians eat with their hands off banana leaves when they are having *nasi padang* or *nasi kandar* (rice with mixed dishes). This is absolutely acceptable. If you choose to follow suit, wash your hands first and try to use your right hand because the left is considered unclean (traditionally, it's the hand used to wash after a visit to the toilet). While almost all of the food you encounter in a hawker center will be safe for eating, it is advisable to go for freshly cooked hot or soupy dishes. Don't risk the precooked items.

Also, avoid having ice in your drink in the smaller towns because it might come from a dubious water supply. If you ask for water, either make sure it's boiled or buy mineral water.

TAXES & SERVICE CHARGES   A 10% service charge and 5% government tax are levied in proper restaurants, but hawkers charge a flat price.

TIPS ON SHOPPING

Shopping is a huge attraction for tourists in Malaysia. In addition to modern fashions and electronics, there are great local handicrafts. In each city section, I've listed some great places to go for local shopping.

For **handicrafts,** prices can vary. There are many handicraft centers, such as Karyaneka, with outlets in cities all over the country, where goods can be priced a bit higher but where you are assured of good quality. Alternatively, you could hunt out bargains in markets and at roadside stores in little towns, which can be much more fun.

Batik is one of the most popular arts in Malaysia, and the fabric can be purchased just about anywhere in the country. Batik can be fashioned into outfits and scarves or purchased as sarongs. Another beautiful Malaysian textile craft is songket weaving. These beautiful cloths are woven with metallic threads. Sometimes songket cloth is patterned into modern clothing, but usually it is sold as sarongs.

Traditional wood carvings have become popular collectors' items. Carvings by *orang asli* groups in peninsular Malaysia and by the indigenous tribes of Sabah and Sarawak have traditional uses in households or are employed for ceremonial purposes to cast off evil spirits and cure illness. They have become much sought after by tourists.

Malaysia's **pewter products** are famous. Selangor Pewter is the brand that seems to have the most outlets and representation. You can get anything from a picture frame to dinner sets.

Silver designs are very refined, and jewelry and fine home items are still made by local artisans, especially in the northern parts of the peninsula. In addition, craft items such as *wayang kulit* (shadow puppets) and *wau* (colorful Malay kites) make great gifts and souvenirs.

SUGGESTED ITINERARIES

Planning a trip to Malaysia requires a few considerations. It's important to consider the time required for traveling around the country. The trip overland from Singapore to Penang, for instance, takes up a whole day. Similarly, flying from, say, Langkawi Island to Kota Kinabalu can take up a whole day. If your time is limited, your best bet is to narrow your destinations within Malaysia depending on the activities that are important to you.

While Kuala Lumpur presents the most obvious choice of destinations, if you have only 3 days, I recommend **Malacca** for its cultural charm, **Penang** for its British colonial history and good food, and **Langkawi** for its luxurious beach resorts. Each is easily accessible by air, bus, or ferry from Singapore, and your travel time will be minimal. If you have a week, you can add **Kuala Lumpur** to your itinerary, or maybe a 3-day trip to **Taman Negara,** peninsular Malaysia's most exciting national park.

FAST FACTS: Malaysia

American Express See individual city sections for offices.

Business Hours Banks are open from 10am to 3pm Monday through Friday, and 9:30 to 11:30am Saturday. Government offices are open from 8am to 12:45pm and 2 to 4:15pm Monday through Friday, and from 8am to 12:45pm Saturday. Smaller shops like provision stores might open as early as 6 or 6:30am and close as late as 9pm, especially those near the wet markets. Many such stores are closed on Saturday evenings and Sunday afternoons and are busiest before lunch. Other shops are open 9:30am to 7pm. Department stores and shops in malls tend to open later, about 10:30am or 11am till 8:30pm or 9pm throughout the week. Bars, except for those in Penang and the seedier bars in Johor Bahru, must close at 1am. Note that in Kuala Terengganu and Kota Bharu, the weekday runs from Saturday to Wednesday. The above hours generally apply to that part of the country, too.

Dentists & Doctors Consultation and treatment fees vary greatly depending on whether the practitioner you have visited operates from a private or public clinic. Your best bet is at a private medical center if your ailment appears serious. These are often expensive, but, being virtual minihospitals, they have the latest equipment. If you just have a flu, it's quite safe to go to a normal M.D.—most doctors have been trained overseas and display diplomas on their walls. The fee at a private center ranges from RM20 to RM45 (US$5.25–US$12). Call ✆ **999** for emergencies.

Drug Laws As in Singapore, the death sentence is mandatory for drug trafficking (defined as being in possession of more than 15g of heroin or morphine, 200g of marijuana or hashish, or 40g of cocaine). For lesser quantities, you'll be thrown in jail for a very long time and flogged with a cane.

Electricity The voltage used in Malaysia is 220–240 volts AC (50 cycles). The three-point square plugs are used, so buy an adapter if you plan to bring any appliances. Also, many larger hotels can provide adapters upon request.

Internet Service is available to all of the nation, and I have found Internet cafes in the most surprisingly remote places. While the major international hotels will have access for their guests in the business center, charges can be very steep. Still, most locally operated hotels do not offer this service for their guests. For each city, I have listed at least one alternative, usually for a very inexpensive hourly cost of RM5 to RM10 (US$1.30–US$2.65).

Language The national language is Bahasa Malaysia, although English is widely spoken. Chinese dialects and Tamil are also spoken.

Liquor Laws Liquor is sold in pubs and supermarkets in all big cities, or in provision stores. In Terengganu and Kelantan, liquor is strictly limited to a handful of Chinese restaurants. Hotels are having an increasingly difficult time keeping their bars open. A recent ruling requires pubs and other nightspots to officially close by 1am nationwide.

Newspapers & Magazines English-language papers the *New Straits Times, The Star, The Sun,* and *The Edge* can be bought in hotel lobbies and magazine stands. Of the local KL magazines, *Day & Night* has great listings and local "what's happening" information for travelers.

Postal Services Post office locations in each city covered are provided in each section. Overseas airmail postage rates are RM.50 (US15¢) for postcards and RM1.50 (US40¢) for a 100g letter.

Taxes Hotels add a 5% government tax to all hotel rates, plus an additional 10% service charge. Larger restaurants also figure the same 5% tax into your bill, plus a 10% service charge, whereas small coffee shops and hawker stalls don't charge anything above the cost of the meal. Although most tourist goods (such as crafts, camera equipment, sports equipment, cosmetics, and select small electronic items) are tax-free, a small, scaled tax is issued on various other goods such as clothing, shoes, and accessories that you'd buy in the larger shopping malls and department stores.

Telephone **To place a call from your home country to Malaysia:** Dial the international access code (011 in the U.S., 0011 in Australia, or 00 in the U.K., Ireland, and New Zealand), plus the country code (60), plus the Malaysia area code (Cameron Highlands: 5; Desaru: 7; Genting Highlands: 9; Johor Bahru: 7; Kuala Lumpur: 3; Kuala Terengganu: 9; Kota Bharu: 9; Kota Kinabalu: 88; Kuantan: 9; Kuching: 82; Langkawi: 4; Malacca: 6; Mersing: 7; Penang: 4), followed by the six-, seven-, or eight-digit phone number (for example, from the U.S. to Kuala Lumpur, you'd dial 011-60-3/ 0000-0000).

To place a direct international call from Malaysia: Dial the international access code (00), plus the country code of the place you are dialing (U.S. and Canada: 1; Australia: 61; Republic of Ireland: 353; New Zealand: 64; U.K.: 44), plus the area/city code and the residential number.

To reach the international operator: Dial © 108.

To place a call within Malaysia: You must use area codes if calling between states. Note that for calls within the country, area codes are preceded by a 0 (Cameron Highlands: 05; Desaru: 07; Genting Highlands: 09; Johor Bahru: 07; Kuala Lumpur: 03; Kuala Terengganu: 09; Kota Bharu: 09; Kota Kinabalu: 088; Kuantan: 09; Kuching: 082; Langkawi: 04; Malacca: 06; Mersing: 07; Penang: 04).

Television Guests in larger hotels will sometimes get satellite channels such as HBO, Star TV, or CNN. Another in-house movie alternative, Vision Four, preprograms videos throughout the day. Local TV stations TV2, TV5, and TV7 show English-language comedies, movies, and documentaries.

Time Malaysia is 8 hours ahead of Greenwich Mean Time, 16 hours ahead of U.S. Pacific Standard Time, 13 ahead of Eastern Standard Time, and 2 hours behind Sydney. It is in the same zone as Singapore. There is no daylight saving time.

Tipping People don't tip, except to bellhops and car jockeys. For these, an amount not less than RM4 is okay.

Toilets To find a public toilet, ask for the tandas. In Malay, lelaki is male and perempuan is female. Be prepared for pay for toilets. Coin collectors sit outside almost every public facility, taking RM20 (US$5.25) per person, or RM30 (US$7.90) if you want paper. Once inside, you'll find it obvious that the money doesn't go for cleaning crews.

Water Water in Kuala Lumpur is supposed to be potable, but most locals boil the water before drinking it—and if that's not a tip-off, I don't know what is. I advise against drinking the tap water anywhere in Malaysia. Hotels will supply bottled water in your room. If they charge you for it, expect inflated prices. A 1.5L bottle goes for RM7 (US$1.85) in a hotel minibar, but RM2 (US55¢) at 7-Eleven.

3 Kuala Lumpur

The most popular destinations in Malaysia dot the west coast of the peninsula where the main rail line passes through, connecting Singapore with Kuala Lumpur and on to Bangkok.

The convenience of train travel isn't the only draw of this part of the country; it also holds some of Malaysia's most significant historical towns. As you travel north from Singapore, **Johor Bahru** makes for a great day trip for those with only a short time to experience Malaysia. Three hours north of Johor Bahru, the sleepy town of **Malacca** reveals the evidence of hundreds of years of Western conquest and rule. Three hours north of Malacca, you're in **Kuala Lumpur,** the cosmopolitan capital of the country, full of shopping, culture, history, and nightlife. Close by, **Genting Highlands** draws tourists from all over the region for the casino excitement, while the more relaxed **Cameron Highlands** offers a cool and charming respite from Southeast Asia's blaring heat. Still farther north, **Penang,** possibly Malaysia's most popular destination, retains all the charm of an old-time Southeast Asian waterfront town, full of romance (and great food), with the added advantage of beach resorts nearby. Still farther north, just before you reach the Thai border, **Langkawi** proves that there are still a few tropical paradise islands left on the planet that are not swarming with tourists.

Kuala Lumpur (or KL, as it is commonly known) is more often than not a traveler's point of entry to Malaysia. As the capital, it is the most modern and developed city in the country, with contemporary high-rises and world-class hotels, glitzy shopping malls, and international cuisine.

Today the original city center at **Merdeka Square** is the core of KL's history. Buildings like the Sultan Abdul Samad Building, the Royal Selangor Club, and the Kuala Lumpur Railway Station are gorgeous examples of British style peppered with Moorish flavor. South of this area is KL's **Chinatown.** Along Jalan Petaling and surrounding areas are markets, shops, food stalls, and the bustling life of the Chinese community. There's also a **Little India** in KL, around the area occupied by Masjid Jame, where you'll find flower stalls, Indian Muslim and Malay costumes, and traditional items. Across the river you'll find **Lake Gardens,** a large sanctuary that houses Kuala Lumpur's bird park, butterfly park, and other attractions and gardens. Modern Kuala Lumpur is rooted in the city's **"Golden Triangle,"** bounded by Jalan Ampang, Jalan Tun Razak, and Jalan Imbi. This section is home to most of KL's hotels, office complexes, shopping malls, and sights like the KL Tower and the Petronas Twin Towers, the tallest buildings in the world.

VISITOR INFORMATION

In Kuala Lumpur, the Malaysia Tourism Board has several offices. The largest is at the **MATIC,** the **Malaysia Tourist Information Complex** (see "Attractions," later in this chapter), located on 109 Jalan Ampang (© **03/2164-3929**). In addition to a tourist information desk, MATIC has a money-exchanger, tourist police post, travel agent booking for Taman Negara trips, souvenir shops, an amphitheater, and Transnasional bus ticket bookings.

Vision KL Magazine is offered for free in many hotel rooms and has listings for events in KL and around the country, plus ads for restaurants and shops.

GETTING THERE

BY PLANE   The **Kuala Lumpur International Airport (KLIA)** (© **03/8776-2000**) opened in June 1998. Located in Sepang, 53km (32 miles) outside the city, KLIA is a huge complex with business centers, dining facilities, a fitness center, medical services, shopping, post offices, and an airport hotel operated by **Pan Pacific** (© **03/8787-3333**). Although there are money-changers, they are few and far between, so hop on the first line you see, and don't assume there's another one just around the corner.

From KLIA, domestic flights can be taken to almost every major city in the country.

GETTING INTO TOWN FROM THE AIRPORT

By Taxi   City taxis are not permitted to pick up fares from the airport, but **special airport taxis** (© **03/8787-3030**) operate round the clock, charging RM88 (US$23) for a premier car (Mercedes) and RM63 (US$17) for a standard vehicle (locally built Proton). Coupons must be purchased at the arrival concourse.

An **express coach** connects KLIA to most of the city's major hotels. Operating every 30 minutes from 5:30am to 10:15pm daily, the trip takes 1 hour and costs RM25 (US$6.60) for adults and RM13 (US$3.40) for children.

The **Express Rail Link** runs between KLIA and KL Sentral train station from 5am to 1am daily. Trains depart every 15 minutes and take 28 minutes to complete the journey. Tickets cost RM35 (US$9.20) for adults and RM15 (US$3.95) for children. From KL Sentral, you can catch one of the city's commuter trains to a station near your hotel.

The outstation taxi stand in Kuala Lumpur is located at **Puduraya Bus Terminal** on Jalan Pudu. Call © **03/2078-0213** for booking to any city on the peninsula. Fares will run you about RM180 (US$47) to Cameron Highlands, RM120 (US$32) to Malacca, RM220 (US$58) to Johor Bahru, and RM220 (US$58) to Penang and to Kuantan. These taxis can pick you up at your hotel for an additional RM10 (US$2.65) upon request.

Kuala Lumpur

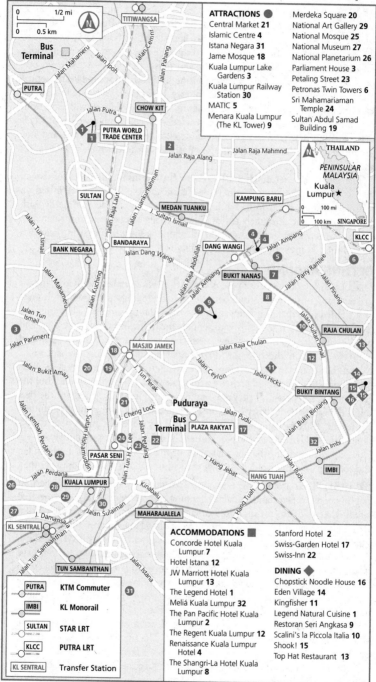

0 | 1/2 mi
0 | 0.5 km

Bus Terminal

TITIWANGSA

PUTRA

CHOW KIT

PUTRA WORLD TRADE CENTER

SULTAN

MEDAN TUANKU

KAMPUNG BARU

KLCC

BANK NEGARA

BANDARAYA

DANG WANGI

BUKIT NANAS

MASJID JAMEK

RAJA CHULAN

BUKIT BINTANG

Puduraya
Bus Terminal | PLAZA RAKYAT

PASAR SENI

KUALA LUMPUR

IMBI

HANG TUAH

MAHARAJALELA

KL SENTRAL

TUN SAMBANTHAN

Jalan Mahameru · Jalan Ipoh · Jalan Pahang · Jalan Cermet · Jalan Putra · Jalan Raja Alang · Jalan Raja Mahmnd · Jalan Raja Laut · Jalan Tuanku Abdul Rahman · J. Sultan Ismail · Jalan Ampang · Jalan Tun Ismail · Jalan Kuching · Jalan Dang Wangi · Jalan Raja Abdullah · Jalan Parry Ramlee · Jalan Pinang · Jalan Mahameru · Jalan Ampang · Jalan Sultan Ismail · Jalan Tun Ismail · Jalan Parliment · Jalan Raja Chulan · Jalan Bukit Aman · Jalan Ceylon · Jalan Hicks · J. Tun Perak · Jalan Bukit Bintang · Jalan Lembah Perdana · J. Sultan Hishamuddin · J. Cheng Lock · Jalan Pudu · Jalan Imbi · Jalan Petaling · Jalan Pudu · Jalan Perdana · Jalan Tun H.S. Lee · J. Hang Jebat · J. Kinabalu · J. Hang Tuah · J. Damansara · Jalan Sulaiman · Jalan Istana · J. Tun Sambanthan

THAILAND

PENINSULAR MALAYSIA

Kuala Lumpur ★

0 | 100 mi
0 | 100 km

SINGAPORE

ATTRACTIONS ●

Central Market **21**
Islamic Centre **4**
Istana Negara **31**
Jame Mosque **18**
Kuala Lumpur Lake Gardens **3**
Kuala Lumpur Railway Station **30**
MATIC **5**
Menara Kuala Lumpur (The KL Tower) **9**
Merdeka Square **20**
National Art Gallery **29**
National Mosque **25**
National Museum **27**
National Planetarium **26**
Parliament House **3**
Petaling Street **23**
Petronas Twin Towers **6**
Sri Mahamariaman Temple **24**
Sultan Abdul Samad Building **19**

ACCOMMODATIONS ■

Concorde Hotel Kuala Lumpur **7**
Hotel Istana **12**
JW Marriott Hotel Kuala Lumpur **13**
The Legend Hotel **1**
Meliá Kuala Lumpur **32**
The Pan Pacific Hotel Kuala Lumpur **2**
The Regent Kuala Lumpur **12**
Renaissance Kuala Lumpur Hotel **4**
The Shangri-La Hotel Kuala Lumpur **8**
Stanford Hotel **2**
Swiss-Garden Hotel **17**
Swiss-Inn **22**

DINING ◆

Chopstick Noodle House **16**
Eden Village **14**
Kingfisher **11**
Legend Natural Cuisine **1**
Restoran Seri Angkasa **9**
Scalini's la Piccola Italia **10**
Shook! **15**
Top Hat Restaurant **13**

PUTRA — KTM Commuter
IMBI — KL Monorail
SULTAN — STAR LRT
KLCC — PUTRA LRT
KL SENTRAL — Transfer Station

BY BUS   There's more than one bus terminal in Kuala Lumpur, and it can be somewhat confusing. The main bus terminal, **Puduraya Bus Terminal,** is on Jalan Pudu right in the center of town—literally. Buses heading in and out of the station block traffic along already congested city streets, spewing noxious gasses. The terminal itself is hot, filthy, and noisy; the heavy-metal boom box wars between the provision shops is amusing for about 30 seconds. This terminal handles bus routes to all over the country, but more specifically to areas on the west coast from north to south. Buses to Penang or Malacca will leave from here. I think Puduraya is a mess to be avoided at all costs. It is a well-kept secret that many business-class and executive coaches to Penang, Johor Bahru, and Singapore depart peacefully from the **KL Railway Station,** which is a far saner alternative.

The other main terminals are the **Putra Bus Terminal** on Jalan Tun Ismail just across from the Putra World Trade Centre and the **Pekililing terminal** on Jalan Ipoh, also not far from Putra WTC. Both terminals deal primarily with buses to east-coast cities such as Kota Bharu, Kuala Terengganu, and Kuantan.

The bus terminals have no general telephone inquiry numbers in their own right. Inquiries must be made directly to individual bus companies.

GETTING AROUND

Kuala Lumpur is a prime example of a city that was not planned, per se, from a master graph of streets. Instead, because of its beginnings as an outpost, it grew as it needed to, expanding outward and swallowing up suburbs. The result is a tangled web of streets too narrow to support the traffic of a capital city. Cars and buses weave through one-way lanes, with countless motorbikes sneaking in and out, sometimes in the opposite direction of traffic or up on the sidewalks. Expect traffic jams in the morning rush between 6 and 9am, and again between 4 and 7pm. At other times, taxis are a convenient way of getting around, but the commuter train system, if they're going where you need to, is perhaps the best value and easiest route. City buses are hot and crowded with some very confusing routes. Walking can also be frustrating. Many sidewalks are in poor condition, with buckled tiles and gaping gutters. The heat can be prohibitive as well. However, areas within the colonial heart of the city, Chinatown, Little India, and some areas in the Golden Triangle are within walking distance of each other.

BY TAXI   Taxis around town can be waved down by the side of the road, or can be caught at taxi stands outside shopping complexes or hotels. The metered fare is RM2 (US55¢) for the first 2km and an additional 10 sen for each 200m after that. Between midnight and 6am you'll be charged an extra 50% of the total fare. If you call ahead for a cab, there's an extra charge of RM1 (US25¢). Truth be told, many cabbies in KL are really lousy. Government regulations have made it compulsory for cabbies to charge the metered fare, but many still try to fix a price, which is invariably higher than what the metered fare would be. The worst is during peak hours or if it's raining, when they'll jack up the price depending on how badly they think you need their services. There are times when empty cabs will just pass you right by, or when cabbies will refuse to take you to your destination if it's "out of their way." The city has been trying to crack down on the poor quality of service; as a matter of fact, a government minister got into some hot water when in late 2002 he suggested that errant cabbies be shot! But I haven't noticed any change for the better.

To request a cab pickup, call **KL Teksi** at © **03/9221-8999** or **Comfort** at © **03/8024-2727.** Maybe they'll show up. Maybe they won't.

BY BUS   There are regular city buses and minibuses to take you around the city. The fare is 20 sen for the first kilometer and 5 sen for each additional kilometer. Know, however, that the buses in Kuala Lumpur are not dependable. You can wait at a stop for a long time only to find when the bus arrives that it's hot and packed so full that passengers seem to be hanging out every window. It's not the most relaxing way to get around.

BY RAIL   KL has a network of mass transit trains that snake through the city and out to the suburbs, and it'll be worth your time to become familiar with them, because taxis are sometimes unreliable and traffic jams can be unbearable. Trouble is, there are five train routes and each one is operated by a different company. How confusing! The lines don't seem to connect in any logical way.

The four lines that are most useful to visitors are the **Putra LRT,** the **Star LRT,** the **KL Monorail,** and the **ERL Express Rail Link** to the airport. The latter route is explained earlier under "Getting into Town from the Airport," earlier in this chapter.

Putra LRT has stops at Bangsar (featured in the nightlife section), KL Sentral (train station), Pasar Seni (Chinatown), Masjid Jamek, Dang Wangi, and KLCC shopping center. An average fare would be about RM1.40 (US35¢).

The **Star LRT** is convenient only if you need to get to the Putra World Trade Centre. It also stops at Masjid Jamek and Plaza Rayat. An average trip will cost well under RM2 (US55¢).

The newly opened **KL Monorail** provides good access through the main hotel and shopping areas of the city, including stops at KL Sentral, Imbi, Bukit Bintang (the main shopping strip), and Raja Chulan (along Jalan Sultan Ismail, where many hotels are). Fares run between RM1.20 (US30¢) and RM 2.50 (US65¢).

As a rough guide, all lines operate between 5 or 6am till around midnight, with trains coming every 10 minutes or so. Tickets can be purchased at any station either from the station master or from single-fare electronic ticket booths.

ON FOOT   The heat and humidity can make walking between attractions pretty uncomfortable. However, sometimes the traffic is so unbearable that you'll get where you're going much faster by strapping on your tennis shoes and hiking it.

FAST FACTS: KUALA LUMPUR

The main office for **American Express** is located in KL at The Weld, 18th floor, Jalan Raja Chulan (© **03/2050-0888**). You'll also find headquarters for all Malaysian and many international banks, most of which have outlets along Jalan Sultan Ismail, plus ATMs at countless locations thought the city. Look for money exchangers in just about every shopping mall; they're a better bargain than banks or hotel cashiers.

KL's **General Post Office,** on Jalan Sultan Hishamuddin (© **03/2274-1122**), can be pretty overwhelming. If you can, try to use your hotel's mail service for a much easier time. Internet service in KL will run about RM6 (US$1.60) per hour for usage. I like **Master-World SurfNet Café,** 23 Jalan Petaling, M floor (technically it's on Jalan Cheng Lock around the corner; © **03/2031-0133**), which charges RM6 (US$1.60) per hour. If you're near the KL City Centre, try **Café Caravali,** Lot 346, third floor next to the cinema (© **03/382-9033**). It's a bit more expensive (RM10/US$2.65 per hr.) but is a nice setting.

If you have a medical **emergency,** the number to dial is © **999.** This is the same number for **police and fire emergencies** as well.

For facts about Malaysia, see "Planning Your Trip to Malaysia," earlier in this chapter.

WHERE TO STAY

There are dozens of hotels in Kuala Lumpur, most of them within city limits; an especially large number of them are in the Golden Triangle area. Other hotels listed in this chapter are located in the Chinatown area, within walking distance of plenty of shopping attractions and nightlife.

VERY EXPENSIVE

The Regent Kuala Lumpur ★★★ *Value*   Of the best five-star properties in Kuala Lumpur, nobody delivers first-class accommodations with the finesse of The Regent. The lobby and guest rooms are contemporary and elegant, without a single sacrifice to comfort. Touches like soft armchairs and cozy comforters in each room will make you want to check in and never leave, and the large marble bathrooms will make you feel like a million bucks even on a bad-hair day. The outdoor pool is a palm-lined free-form escape, and the fitness center is state-of-the-art, with sauna, steam, spa, and Jacuzzi.

160 Jalan Bukit Bintang, 55100 Kuala Lumpur. ℂ **800/545-4000** in the U.S. and Canada, 800/022-800 in Australia, 800/440-800 in New Zealand, 800/917-8795 in the U.K., or 03/2141-8000. Fax 03/2142-1441. 468 units. RM550 (US$145) double; from RM880 (US$232) suite. AE, DC, MC, V. **Amenities:** 3 restaurants (international, Italian, Cantonese); bar and lobby lounge; outdoor pool; 2 squash courts; 24-hr. fitness center w/Jacuzzi, sauna, steam, and massage; concierge; limousine service; business center; 24-hr. room service; babysitting; same-day laundry service/dry cleaning; nonsmoking rooms; executive-level rooms. *In room:* A/C, TV w/satellite programming and in-house movies, minibar, coffee/tea-making facilities, hair dryer, safe.

Renaissance Kuala Lumpur Hotel ★★   The Renaissance has become a very elegant address in KL; its most recent claim to fame was hosting the U.S. secretary of state during his last visit to the city. It's actually two hotels in one, since the Renaissance absorbed its neighbor, The New World. Renaissance's lobby is a huge oval colonnade with a domed ceiling and massive marble columns rising from the sides of a geometric star burst on the floor. Guest rooms in the Renaissance Wing have an equally "official" feel to them—very bold and impressive, and completely European in style. In fact, you'll never know you're in Malaysia. The New World Wing is less opulent, with plain furnishings and bathrooms devoid of luxurious touches. Renaissance is essentially two hotels in one, with facilities sharing, so expect restaurants and leisure facilities to be more crowded than at other places, and service to be less personalized.

Corner of Jalan Sultan Ismail and Jalan Ampang, 50450 Kuala Lumpur. ℂ **800/HOTELS-1** in the U.S. and Canada, 800/251-259 in Australia, 800/441-035 in New Zealand, or 03/2162-2233. Fax 03/2163-1122. 910 units. RM460–RM535 (US$121–US$141) double; RM755 (US$199) executive double; from RM955 (US$251) suite. AE, DC, MC, V. **Amenities:** 3 restaurants (Pan-Asian, Japanese, Mediterranean); lounge; large, landscaped outdoor pool; outdoor lighted tennis court; fitness center w/sauna and massage; concierge; limousine service; business center; shopping arcade; salon; 24-hr. room service; babysitting; same-day laundry service/dry cleaning; nonsmoking rooms; executive-level rooms. *In room:* A/C, TV w/satellite programming and in-house movies, minibar, coffee/tea-making facilities, hair dryer, safe.

EXPENSIVE

Hotel Istana ★   Fashioned after a Malay palace, Hotel Istana is rich with Moorish architectural elements, and songket weaving patterns are featured in decor elements throughout. The guest rooms have Malaysian touches like hand-woven carpets and upholstery in local fabric designs, capturing the exotic flavor of the culture without sacrificing modern comfort and convenience. Located on Jalan Raja Chulan, Istana is in a favorable Golden Triangle location, within walking distance to shopping and some of the sights in that area. Ask about big-rate discounts in the summer months.

73 Jalan Raja Chulan, 50200 Kuala Lumpur. © **03/2141-9988.** Fax 03/2144-0111. 516 units. RM550–RM575 (US$145–US$151) double; RM690 (US$182) executive club; RM1,095 (US$288) suite. AE, DC, MC, V. **Amenities:** 4 restaurants (international, Japanese, Cantonese, and Italian); lobby lounge; outdoor pool; 2 outdoor lighted tennis courts; 2 squash courts; fitness center w/Jacuzzi, sauna, steam, and massage; concierge; limousine service; business center; 24-hr. room service; babysitting; same-day laundry service/dry cleaning; executive-level rooms. *In room:* A/C, TV w/satellite programming and in-house movies, minibar, coffee/tea-making facilities, hair dryer, safe.

JW Marriott Hotel Kuala Lumpur ☞

Opened in July 1997, the Marriott is one of the newer hotels in town. The smallish lobby area still allows for a very dramatic entrance, complete with wrought-iron filigree and marble. The modern guest rooms have a European flavor, decorated in deep greens and reds with plush carpeting, large desks, and a leather executive chair that are all beginning to show some wear. If you've stayed at Marriotts in other locations, this one might disappoint you. It's not their hottest property; however, the staff is very motivated and enthusiastic. Another great plus: The hotel is next door to some of the most upmarket and trendy shopping complexes in the city.

183 Jalan Bukit Bintang, 55100 Kuala Lumpur. © **800/228-9290** in the U.S. and Canada, 800/251-259 in Australia, 800/221-222 in the U.K., or 03/2715-9000. Fax 03/2715-7000. 518 units. RM300 (US$79) double, from RM500 (US$132) suite. AE, DC, MC, V. **Amenities:** 4 restaurants (Malay, international, Shanghainese, delicatessen); lounge and cigar bar; outdoor pool; outdoor lighted tennis court; fitness center w/Jacuzzi, sauna, and steam; new spa w/massage and beauty treatments; concierge; limousine service; business center; shopping mall w/designer boutiques adjacent; salon; 24-hr. room service; babysitting; same-day laundry service/dry cleaning; executive-level rooms. *In room:* A/C, TV w/satellite programming, dataport, minibar, coffee/tea-making facilities, hair dryer, safe.

The Pan Pacific Hotel Kuala Lumpur ☞

One thing you'll love about staying at the Pan Pacific is the view from the glass elevator as you drift up to your floor. The atrium lobby inside the main entrance is bright and airy and filled with the scent of jasmine. The hotel staff handles the demands of its international clientele with courtesy and professionalism, but when Pan Pac's running a full house, help can be a little weary and hard to find. The rooms are spacious and stately, in pale pastels. Sunken windows with lattice work frame each view. The large shopping mall across the street makes this hotel more convenient; otherwise, it's a bit out of the city center—the inconvenience is felt during rush hour, when it can take 30 minutes to make an otherwise 10-minute taxi hop. A recent dramatic drop in rates makes this an especially good choice for value.

Jalan Putra, P.O. Box 11468, 50746 Kuala Lumpur. © **800/327-8585** in the U.S. and Canada, 800/252-900 in Australia, 800/969-496 in the U.K., or 03/4042-5555. Fax 03/4041-7236. 565 units. RM199–RM259 (US$52–US$68) double. AE, DC, MC, V. **Amenities:** 3 restaurants (international, Chinese, Japanese); lobby lounge; outdoor pool; outdoor lighted tennis court; squash court; fitness center w/Jacuzzi, sauna, and massage; concierge; limousine service; business center; 24-hr. room service; babysitting; same-day laundry service/dry cleaning; nonsmoking rooms; executive-level rooms. *In room:* A/C, TV w/satellite programming and in-house movie, minibar, coffee/tea-making facilities, iron, safe.

The Shangri-La Hotel Kuala Lumpur

I don't know how they do it, but Shangri-La can always take what could easily be a dull building in a busy city and turn it into a resort-style garden oasis. Their property in KL is no different. With attention paid to landscaping and greenery, the hotel is one of the more attractive places to stay in town. The guest rooms are large, with cooling colors and nice views of the city. Shangri-La hotels always have great choices for dining. This one offers Restaurant Lafite for classic French cuisine, Nadaman

Japanese restaurant, Shang Palace Cantonese restaurant, and a coffee garden and pool cafe. Also check out the pub, cigar bar, and wine shop.

11 Jalan Sultan Ismail, 50250 Kuala Lumpur. ℭ **800/942-5050** in the U.S. and Canada, 800/222-448 in Australia, 0800/442-179 in New Zealand, or 03/232-2388. Fax 03/202-1245. 681 units. RM420–RM505 (US$111–US$133) double; RM575 (US$151) executive club room; RM1,300 (US$342) suite. AE, DC, MC, V. **Amenities:** 5 restaurants (international, Continental, delicatessen, Chinese, Japanese); outdoor pool; outdoor lighted tennis courts; fitness center w/Jacuzzi, steam; sauna; and massage; concierge; limousine service; salon; 24-hr. room service; babysitting; same-day laundry service/dry cleaning; nonsmoking rooms; executive-level rooms. *In room:* A/C, TV w/satellite programming and in-house movies, minibar, coffee/tea making facilities, hair dryer, in-room safe, Internet access.

MODERATE

Concorde Hotel Kuala Lumpur ⭐⭐ Ⓥ*alue*   Jalan Sultan Ismail is the address for the big names in hotels, like Shangri-La and Hilton, but tucked alongside the giants is the Concorde, a very reasonably priced choice. What's best about staying here is that you don't sacrifice amenities and services for the lower cost. Although rooms are not as large as those in the major hotels, they're well outfitted in an up-to-date style that can compete with the best of them. Choose Concorde if you'd like location and comfort for less. It also has a small outdoor pool facing a fitness center. A well-equipped business center lends additional value. Better yet, the Hard Rock Cafe, located on the premises, is one of the more fun clubs in town.

2 Jalan Sultan Ismail, 50250 Kuala Lumpur. ℭ **03/2144-2200.** Fax 03/2144-1628. 570 units. RM200–RM350 (US$53–US$92) double; from RM800 (US$211) suite. AE, DC, MC, V. **Amenities:** 3 restaurants; lobby lounge and Hard Rock Cafe; small outdoor pool; fitness center w/sauna, steam, and massage; concierge; limousine service; business center; shopping arcade; salon; 24-hr. room service; babysitting; same-day laundry service/dry cleaning; executive-level rooms. *In room:* A/C, TV w/satellite programming and in-house movies, minibar, coffee/tea-making facilities, safe.

The Legend Hotel   Sitting on top of a very large shopping complex, this hotel doesn't actually start until you reach the ninth story. From an unimpressive entrance, you're whisked on an express elevator to the vast lobby, which features earthy-toned marble Chinese touches such as carved wood furniture and terra-cotta warrior statues. Guest rooms are spacious, and all overlook the city, but ask to face the Twin Towers for the best view. Also, the less expensive rooms seem to have the nicest decor, with softer tones and modern touches. The executive rooms are rather strange—mine had a bright pink frilly bedcover, and amenities included a packet of generic pantyhose made in China. Facilities are highlighted by an outdoor pool with a great view and the convenience of the shopping mall beneath. Another good features to consider here is free in-room Internet via your flat-screen interactive TV. However, the hotel is located a little outside the main shopping and dining action of the city.

Putra Place, 100 Jalan Putra, 50350 Kuala Lumpur. ℭ **800/573-8483** in the U.S., 800/126-533 in Australia, 800/894351 in the U.K., or 03/4042-9888. Fax 03/4043-0700. 400 units. RM435–RM525 (US$114–US$138) double; from RM785 (US$207) suite. AE, DC, MC, V. **Amenities:** 4 restaurants (international, Chinese, Japanese, haute cuisine vegetarian); bar and lobby lounge; outdoor pool and Jacuzzi w/good views; squash courts; concierge; limousine service; business center; large shopping mall; salon; 24-hr. room service; babysitting; same-day laundry service/dry cleaning; executive-level rooms; Internet cafe. *In room:* A/C, TV w/satellite programming and in-house movies, minibar, coffee/tea-making facilities, hair dryer, safe, Internet access.

Meliá Kuala Lumpur ⭐ Ⓥ*alue*   This tourist-class hotel had nothing special to boast until recently. The opening of a KL Monorail station just outside, combined with a giant shopping and entertainment complex across the street, has certainly added great value. The small lobby is functional, with space for tour groups and a very active and efficient tour desk. Newly renovated guest rooms have light wood furnishings, contemporary decorator fixtures, wall desks with a swivel arm for extra space, and large-screen TVs. Bathrooms, while small, are well maintained, with good counter space. Mealtimes in the hotel's coffee shop can be a little crowded.

16 Jalan Imbi, 55100 Kuala Lumpur. (*C*) **03/2142-8333**. Fax 03/2142-6623. www.solmelia.com. 301 units. RM280–RM380 (US$74–US$100) double; from RM500 (US$132) suite. AE, DC, MC, V. **Amenities:** 2 restaurants (international, Chinese); bar and karaoke lounge; small outdoor pool; health center w/massage; tour desk; small business center; shopping arcade; salon; 24-hr. room service; babysitting; same-day laundry service/dry cleaning; nonsmoking rooms. *In room:* A/C, TV w/satellite programming and in-house movies, minibar, coffee/tea-making facilities, iron.

Swiss-Garden Hotel   For midrange prices, Swiss-Garden offers reliable comfort, good location, and affordability that attracts many leisure travelers to its doors. It also knows how to make you feel right at home, with a friendly staff (the concierge is on the ball) and a hotel lobby bar that actually gets patronized (by travelers having cool cocktails at the end of a busy day of sightseeing). The guest rooms are simply furnished but are neat and comfortable. Swiss-Garden is just walking distance from KL's lively Chinatown district, and close to the Puduraya bus station. Facilities include an outdoor pool, a brand-new spa, and a fitness center.

117 Jalan Pudu, 55100 Kuala Lumpur. (*C*) **03/2141-3333**. Fax 03/2141-5555. www.swissgarden.com. 310 units. RM350–RM425 (US$92–US$112) double; from RM580 (US$153) suite. AE, DC, MC, V. **Amenities:** 2 restaurants (international, Cantonese); lobby lounge; small outdoor pool; small fitness center; spa w/massage; concierge; limousine service; business center; 24-hr. room service; babysitting; same-day laundry service/dry cleaning; nonsmoking rooms. *In room:* A/C, TV w/satellite programming and in-house movies, minibar, coffee/tea-making facilities, hair dryer, safe.

INEXPENSIVE

Stanford Hotel (*Value*)   The Stanford Hotel is a good alternative for the budget-conscious traveler. The lobby feels like a miniversion of a more upmarket hotel, a tiny marble room with glass front facing the street. A small stairway leads to the tiny business center, coffee shop, and lifts to guest floors. Guest rooms have new carpeting, fresh paint, and refurbished furnishings and bathrooms; the place provides accommodations that are good value for your money. And some of the rooms even have lovely views of the Petronas Twin Towers. Discounted rates as low as RM100 (US$26) can be had if you ask about promotions. Facilities are thin, but if you plan to spend most of your time out and about, you won't notice.

449 Jalan Tuanku Abdul Rahman, 50100 Kuala Lumpur. (*C*) **03/2691-9833**. Fax 03/2691-3103. 168 units. RM150 (US$39) double. AE, MC, V. **Amenities:** Restaurant (international); tour desk; limousine service; business center; limited room service; same-day laundry service; nonsmoking rooms. *In room:* A/C, TV, fridge, coffee/tea-making facilities.

Swiss-Inn   This minisize hotel is one of KL's better bargains. Tucked away in the heart of Chinatown, Swiss-Inn's best asset is its location, amid the jumble of vibrant night market hawkers. The place is small and offers almost no facilities. Higher-priced rooms have a small window and a bit more space (but are still compact), and are somewhat better maintained. Budget rooms, on lower floors, are very small, the cheapest having no windows at all. Beige carpeting can use a deep cleaning, the walls can use a fresh coat of paint, and the bathrooms some new grout work. On my last visit, housekeeping wasn't up to snuff, which added to the problem. Still, these rooms can be had for as little as RM80 (US$20) per night. Make sure you reserve your room early because this place runs at high occupancy year-round.

62 Jalan Sultan, 50000 Kuala Lumpur. ℂ **03/2072-3333**. Fax 03/2031-6699. www.swissgarden.com. 110 units. RM150–RM184 (US$39–US$48) double. AE, DC, MC, V. **Amenities:** Restaurant (international); bar; tour desk; limited room service; babysitting; same-day laundry service/dry cleaning; nonsmoking rooms; Internet terminals for guest use (extra charge). *In room:* A/C, TV w/in-house movies, coffee/tea-making facilities.

WHERE TO DINE

Kuala Lumpur, like Singapore, is very cosmopolitan. Here you'll not only find delicious and exotic cuisine, but you'll find it served in some pretty trendy settings.

Chopstick Noodle House ☆ *Value* CANTONESE   I was in the mood for something cheap and good in the center of town, and was thrilled to find this place. The menu is vast, with no fewer than 20 kinds of noodles, served either in soup or dry (with soup on the side). The fresh prawn won ton noodle is light and flavorful, and you can also get them fried. They have barbecue dishes—duck, pork, honey spare ribs, and seafood dishes are reasonably priced. Also good are the clay-pot dishes, with rice and meats baked in a clay pot with dark soy, mushrooms, and crunchy onions. It's a good alternative to formal dining.

Lot F 003, 1st Floor, KL Plaza, 179 Jalan Bukit Bintang. ℂ **03/2148-2221**. Main courses RM9–RM22 (US$2.35–US$5.80). AE, MC, V. Daily 11:30am–midnight.

Eden Village SEAFOOD   Uniquely designed inside and out to resemble a Malay house, Eden Village has great local atmosphere. Waitresses are clad in traditional sarong kebaya and serve up popular dishes like braised shark's fin in a clay pot with crabmeat and roe, and the Kingdom of the Sea (a half lobster baked with prawns, crab, and cuttlefish). The terrace seating is the best in the house.

260 Jalan Raja Chulan. ℂ **03/2141-4027**. Reservations recommended. Main courses RM18–RM100 and up (US$4.75–US$26). AE, MC, V. Daily noon–3pm and 7pm–midnight; closed for lunch Sun.

Kingfisher ☆☆ SEAFOOD   This street, lined with simple low-rise houses and commercial buildings in the center of KL's fashionable shopping and hotel district, has in recent years become a hot address for trendy restaurants and bars, the best of which is Kingfisher. The very freshest fishes are crafted into lovely haute cuisine dishes with delicate Asian accents for flavor. With the help of the friendly waitstaff, you select your fish of choice and then decide the best preparation style in a "one from column A, one from column B" approach. Everything is fresh and delicious—a good pick.

20 Changkat Bukit Bintang. ℂ **03/2141-9266**. Reservations recommended. Main courses RM58–RM128 (US$15–US$33). MC, V. Mon–Sat noon–2:30pm and 6:30–10:30pm.

Legend Natural Cuisine INTERNATIONAL   Legend Natural Cuisine's menu is selected by dieticians, with its dishes incorporating organically grown produce and calorie-conscious recipes with a mind toward health awareness. Off the Legend Hotel's lobby, the restaurant is spacious and cozy, and the food is so good you'll never know it's healthful. It's easy to forget about dieting when you're traveling, but Legend Natural Cuisine makes it incredibly easy to stick to one. Try the rack of lamb, and the forest mushroom soup is an unbelievably good appetizer.

The Legend Hotel and Apartments, 100 Jalan Putra. ℂ **03/4042-9888**. Reservations recommended for lunch and dinner; required for high tea. Main courses RM38–RM55 (US$10–US$14). AE, DC, MC, V. Daily 6:30am–1am.

Restoran Seri Angkasa MALAYSIAN At the top of the Menara KL (KL Tower) is Restoran Seri Angkasa, a revolving restaurant with the best view in the city. Better still, it's a great way to try all the Malay-, Chinese-, and Indian-inspired local dishes at a convenient buffet, with a chance to taste just about everything you have room for—like nasi goreng, clay-pot noodles, or beef rendang

Jalan Punchak, off Jalan P. Ramlee. ⓒ 03/2020-5055. Reservations recommended. Lunch buffet RM55 (US$14); dinner buffet RM75 (US$20). AE, DC, MC, V. Daily noon–2:30pm lunch; 3:30–5:30pm high tea; 6:30–11pm dinner.

Scalini's la Piccola Italia ★★★ ITALIAN Four chefs from Italy create the dishes that make Scalini's a favorite among KL locals and expatriates. From a very extensive menu, you can select pasta, fish, and meat, as well as a large selection of pizzas. The specials are superb and change all the time. Some of the best dishes are salmon with creamed asparagus sauce and ravioli with goat cheese and zucchini. Scalini's has a large wine selection (that is actually part of the romantic decor), with labels from California, Australia, New Zealand, France, and, of course, Italy.

19 Jalan Sultan Ismail. ⓒ 03/2145-3211. Reservations recommended. Main courses RM26–RM58 (US$6.85–US$15). AE, DC, MC, V. Sun–Thurs noon–2:30pm and 6–10:30pm; Fri noon–2:30pm and 6–11pm; Sat 6–11pm.

Shook! JAPANESE/CHINESE/ITALIAN/WESTERN GRILL This place is unique for a number of reasons. First, Shook! is located on the ground floor of a shopping center, in a cavernous space decorated in a sort of Zen minimalism with splashes of color. Above, escalators glide shoppers to floors over the glass stage where the pop and jazz band plays nightly. Second, the menu features four different types of cuisine that are prepared in four separate show kitchens. It will take a few minutes to read the menu, which offers a mind-boggling selection of Japanese, Chinese, Italian, and Western grill specialties—very inventive. This is a good spot if your party can't agree on where to eat—there's something for everyone. One caveat: The waitstaff sometimes seem lost in Shook!'s enormity.

Starhill Centre, Lower Ground Floor, 181 Jalan Bukit Bintang. ⓒ 03/2716-8535. Main courses RM20–RM200 (US$5.25–US$53). AE, DC, MC, V. Daily noon–2:30pm and 6:30–10:30pm.

Top Hat Restaurant ★★★ *Finds* ASIAN MIX Let me tell you about my favorite restaurant in Kuala Lumpur. First, Top Hat has a unique atmosphere. In a 1930s bungalow that was once a school, the place winds through room after room, its walls painted in bright hues and furnished with an assortment of mix-and-match teak tables, chairs, and antiques. Second, the menu is fabulous. While a la carte is available, Top Hat puts together set meals featuring nonya, Malacca Portuguese, traditional Malay, Thai, Western, and even vegetarian recipes. They're all brilliant. Desserts are huge and full of sin.

No. 7 Jalan Kia Peng. ⓒ 03/2141-8611. Reservations recommended. Main courses RM30–RM88 (US$7.90–US$23). Set meals RM37–RM123 (US$9.75–US$32). AE, DC, MC, V. Lunch Mon–Fri noon–2:30pm; dinner daily 6–10:30pm.

ATTRACTIONS

Most of Kuala Lumpur's historic sights are located in the area around the Merdeka Square/Jalan Hishamuddin area, while many of the gardens, parks, and museums are out at Lake Gardens. Taxi fare between the two areas will run you about RM5 (US$1.30).

Central Market ✦   The original Central Market, built in 1936, used to be a wet market, but the place is now a cultural center (air-conditioned!) for local artists and craftspeople selling antiques, crafts, and curios. It is a fantastic place for buying Malaysian crafts and souvenirs, with two floors of shops to chose from. The Central Market also stages evening performances (7:45pm on weekends) of Malay martial arts, Indian classical dance, or Chinese orchestra. Call the number above for performance information.

Jalan Benteng. ✆ **03/2274-6542**. Daily 10am–10pm. Shops until 8pm.

Islamic Arts Museum ✦✦   The seat of Islamic learning in Kuala Lumpur, the center has displays of Islamic texts, artifacts, porcelain, and weaponry.

Jalan Perdana. ✆ **03/2274-2020**. Admission RM8 (US$2.10). Tues–Sun 10am–6pm.

Istana Negara   Closed to the public, this is the official residence of the king. You can peek through the gates at the istana (palace) and its lovely grounds.

Jalan Negara. No phone.

Jame Mosque (Masjid Jame)   The first settlers landed in Kuala Lumpur at the spot where the Gombak and Klang rivers meet, and in 1909 a mosque was built here. Styled after an Indian Muslim design, it is one of the oldest mosques in the city.

Jalan Tun Terak. No phone.

Kuala Lumpur Lake Gardens (Taman Tasik Perdana)   Built around an artificial lake, the 91.6-hectare (229-acre) park has plenty of space for jogging and rowing, and has a playground for the kids. It's the most popular park in Kuala Lumpur. Inside the Lake Gardens, you'll find the Kuala Lumpur Orchid Garden (Jalan Perdana; weekend and public holiday admission RM1/US25¢ for adults and RM.50/US15¢ for children; weekdays free; daily 9am–6pm) with a collection of more than 800 orchid species from Malaysia and thousands of international varieties. The **Kuala Lumpur Bird Park** (Jalan Perdana; ✆ **03/2273-5423;** adults RM1/US$3.15, children RM6/US$1.60; daily 9am–6:30pm) is nestled in beautifully landscaped gardens, and has more than 2,000 birds within its 3.2 hectares (8 acres). The **Kuala Lumpur Butterfly Park** (Jalan Cenderasari; ✆ **03/2693-4799;** adults RM5/US$1.30, children RM1/US25¢; daily 9am–6pm) has more than 6,000 butterflies belonging to 120 species that make their home in this park, which has been landscaped with more than 15,000 plants to simulate the butterflies' natural rainforest environment. There are also other small animals and an insect museum.

Enter via Jalan Parliament. No phone. Free admission. Daily 9am–6pm.

Kuala Lumpur Railway Station   Built in 1910, the KL Railway Station is a beautiful example of Moorish architecture.

Jalan Sultan Hishamuddin. ✆ **03/2274-6542**. Daily 7:30am–10:30pm.

MATIC (Malaysia Tourist Information Complex)   At MATIC, you'll find an exhibit hall, tourist information services for Kuala Lumpur and Malaysia, and other travel-planning services. On Tuesday, Thursday, Saturday, and Sunday, there are cultural shows at 3pm, featuring Malaysian dance and music. Shows are RM5 (US$1.30) for adults and free for children.

Jalan Ampang. ✆ **03/2164-3929**. Daily 9am–6pm.

Menara Kuala Lumpur   Standing 421m (1,389 ft.) tall, this concrete structure is the third-tallest tower in the world, and the views from the top reach to
the far corners of the city and beyond. At the top, the glass windows are fashioned after the Shah Mosque in Isfahan, Iran.

Bukit Nanas. ✆ **03/2020-5448**. Adults RM8 (US$2.10); children RM3 (US80¢). Daily 9am–10pm.

Merdeka Square   Surrounded by colonial architecture with an exotic local
flair, the square is a large field that was once the site of British social and sporting events. These days, Malaysia holds its spectacular Independence Day celebrations on the field, which is home to the world's tallest flagpole, standing at
100m (330 ft.).

Jalan Raja. No phone.

National Art Gallery   The building that now houses the National Art
Gallery was built as the Majestic Hotel in 1932 and has been restored to display
contemporary works by Malaysian artists. There are international exhibits as well.

Jalan Sultan Hishamuddin. ✆ **03/4025-4990**. Free admission. Daily 10am–6pm.

National Mosque (Masjid Negara)   Built in a modern design, the most dis-
tinguishing features of the mosque are its 73m (243-ft.) minaret and the
umbrella-shape roof, which is said to symbolize a newly independent Malaysia's
aspirations for the future. Could be true: The place was built in 1965, the year
Singapore split from Malaysia.

Jalan Sultan Hishamuddin (near the KL Railway Station). No phone. Daily 9am–6pm.

National Museum (Muzim Negara) ★★   Located at Lake Gardens, the
museum has more than 1,000 items of historic, cultural, and traditional significance, including art, weapons, musical instruments, and costumes.

Jalan Damansara. ✆ **03/2282-6255**. Admission RM1 (US25¢), children under 12 free. Daily 9am–6pm.

National Planetarium *Kids*   The National Planetarium has a Space Hall with
touch-screen interactive computers and hands-on experiments, a Viewing Gallery
with binoculars for a panoramic view of the city, and an Ancient Observatory
Park with models of Chinese and Indian astronomy systems. The Space Theatre
has two different outer-space shows at 11am, 2pm, and 4pm for an extra charge
of RM6 (US$1.60) for adults and RM4 (US$1.05) for children.

Lake Gardens. ✆ **03/2273-5484**. Admission to exhibition hall RM3 (US80¢), children RM2 (US55¢).
Sat–Thurs 10am–4pm.

Parliament House   In the Lake Gardens area, the Parliament House is a
modern building housing the country's administrative offices, which were once
in the Sultan Abdul Samad Building at Merdeka Square.

Jalan Parliament. Parliament sessions are not open to the public. No phone.

Petaling Street ★   This is the center of KL's Chinatown district. By day,
stroll past hawker stalls, dim sum shops, wet markets, and all sorts of shops,
from pawn shops to coffin makers. At night, a crazy bazaar (which is terribly
crowded) pops up—look for designer knockoffs, fake watches, and pirate VCDs
(Video CDs) here.

Petronas Twin Towers ★   After 5 years of planning and building, Petronas
Twin Towers has been completed. Standing at a whopping 451.9m (1,482 ft.)
above street level, with 88 stories, the towers are the tallest buildings in the

world. From the outside, the structures are designed with the kind of geometric patterns common to Islamic architecture, and on levels 41 and 42, the two towers are linked by a bridge. Visitors are permitted on the sky bridge daily from 10am to 12:45pm and 3 to 4:45pm every day except Monday and public holidays.

Kuala Lumpur City Centre. No phone.

Sri Mahamariaman Temple   With a recent face-lift (Hindu temples must renovate every 12 years), this bright temple livens the gray street scene around it. It's a beautiful temple tucked away in a narrow street in KL's Chinatown area, which was built by Thambusamy Pillai, a pillar of old KL's Indian community.

Jalan Bandar. No phone.

Sultan Abdul Samad Building   In 1897, this exotic building was designed by Regent Alfred John Bidwell, a colonial architect responsible for many of the buildings in Singapore. He chose a style called Muhammadan or Neosaracenic, which combines Indian Muslim architecture with Gothic and other Western elements. Built to house government administrative offices, today it is the home of Malaysia's Supreme Court and High Court.

Jalan Raja. No phone.

GOLF GREENS FEES

People from all over Asia flock to Malaysia for its golf courses, many of which are excellent standard courses designed by pros. The **Bangi Golf Resort,** No. 1 Persiaran Bandar, Bandar Baru Bangi, 43650 Selangor (© **03/8925-3728;** fax 03/8925-3726), has 18 holes, at par 72. Designed by Ronald Fream, it has greens fees of RM100 (US$26) on weekdays and RM170 (US$45) on weekends and holidays. The **Mines Resort & Golf Club,** 101/5 mile, Jalan Sungei Besi, 43300 Seri Kembangan, Selangor (© **03/8943-2288**), features 18 holes at par 71. Designed by Robert Trent Jones Jr., it has greens fees of RM280 (US$74) on weekdays and RM350 (US$92) on weekends and holidays. **Suajana Golf & Country Club,** km 3, Jalan Lapangan Terbang Sultan Abdul Aziz Shah, 46783 Subang Selangor (© **03/7846-1466;** fax 03/7846-7818), has two 18-hole courses, each par 72, deigned by Robert Trent Jones Jr., with greens fees of RM170 (US$45) on weekdays and RM290 (US$76) on weekends and holidays.

SHOPPING

Kuala Lumpur is a truly great place to shop. In recent years, mall after mall has risen from city lots, filled with hundreds of retail outlets selling everything from haute couture to cheap chic clothing, electronic goods, jewelry, and arts and crafts. The **major shopping malls** are located in the area around Jalan Bukit Bintang and Jalan Sultan Ismail. There are also a few malls along Jalan Ampang. Suria KLCC, located just beneath the Petronas Twin Towers, has to be KL's best and brightest mall, and its largest. If you purchase electronics, make sure you get an international warranty.

Still the best place for Malaysian handicrafts, the huge **Central Market** on Jalan Benteng (© **03/2274-6542**) keeps any shopper saturated for hours. There you'll find a jumble of local artists and craftspeople selling their wares in the heart of town. It's also a good place to find Malaysian handicrafts from other regions of the country. One specific shop I like to recommend for Malaysian handicrafts is **Karyaneka,** Lot B, Kompleks Budaya Kraf (© **03/2164-4344**), with a warehouse selection of assorted goods from around the country, all of it fine quality.

Another favorite shopping haunt in KL is **Chinatown,** along Petaling Street. Day and night, it's a great place to wander and bargain for knockoff designer clothing and accessories, sunglasses, T-shirts, souvenirs, fake watches, and pirated videos.

Pasar malam (night markets) are very popular evening activities in KL. Whole blocks are taken up with these brightly lit and bustling markets packed with stalls selling everything you can dream of. They are likely to pop up anywhere in the city. Two good bets for catching one: Go to Jalan Haji Taib after dark until 10pm. On Saturday night, head for Jalan Tuanku Abdul Rahman.

NIGHTLIFE

There's nightlife to spare in KL, from fashionable lounges to sprawling discos, to pubs perfect for lounging. Basically, you can expect to pay about RM11 to RM20 (US$2.90–US$5.25) for a pint of beer, depending on what and where you order. While quite a few pubs are open for lunch, most clubs won't open until about 6 or 7pm. These places must all close by 1am, so don't plan on staying out too late. Nearly all have a happy hour, usually between 5 and 7pm, when drink discounts apply on draft beers and "house-pour" (lower-shelf) mixed drinks. Generally, you're expected to wear dress casual clothing for these places, but avoid old jeans, tennis shoes, and very revealing outfits.

While there are some very good places in Kuala Lumpur, the true nightlife spot is in a place called **Bangsar,** just outside the city limits. It's 2 or 3 blocks of bars, cafes, and restaurants that cater to a variety of tastes (in fact, so many expatriates hang out there that they call it Kweiloh Lumpur, "Foreigner Lumpur" in Mandarin). Every taxi driver knows where it is. Get in and ask to go to Jalan Telawi Tiga in Bangsar (fare should be no more than RM5 or RM6/US$1.30 or US$1.60); once there, it's very easy to catch a cab back to town. Begin at **The Roof** (2 Jalan Telawi 4; ℭ **03/2282-7168**), a three-story open-air cafe/bar that looks like a crazy Louisiana cathouse (you really can't miss it). From there you can try **La Bodega** (16 Jalan Telawi 2; ℭ **03/2287-8318**) for some funky dance music, or **Finnegan's** (ℭ **03/284-0187**), a very rowdy Irish bar. And that's only the beginning.

Back in Kuala Lumpur, there are some fun bars and pubs that I recommend. If you just want to hop around and see different places, I suggest heading for the corner of Jalan Sultan Ismail and Jalan P. Ramlee, and head down P. Ramlee to check out the colorful pubs, clubs, and tiki bars along this stretch. For a reliable Irish pub, **Delaney's,** on the ground floor of the Park Royal Hotel, Jalan Sultan Ismail (ℭ **03/2141-5195**), has a good selection of draft beers.

For a little live music with your drinks, the **Hard Rock Cafe,** Jalan Sultan Ismail next to Concorde Hotel (ℭ **03/2144-4062**), hosts the best of the regional bands, which play nightly for a crowd of locals, tourists, and expatriates who take their parties very seriously.

SIDE TRIPS FROM KUALA LUMPUR
TAMAN NEGARA NATIONAL PARK ★★★

Malaysia's most famous national park, **Taman Negara,** covers 434,300 hectares (1,085,750 acres) of primary rainforest estimated to be as old as 130 million years, and encompasses within its borders **Gunung Tahan,** peninsular Malaysia's highest peak, at 2,187m (2,392 ft.) above sea level.

Prepare to see lush vegetation and rare orchids, some 250 bird species, and maybe, if you're lucky, some barking deer, tapir, elephants, tigers, leopards, and rhinos. As for primates, there are long-tailed macaques, leaf monkeys, gibbons, and more. Malaysia has taken the preservation of this forest seriously since the early part of the century, so Taman Negara showcases efforts to keep this land in as pristine a state as possible while still allowing humans to appreciate the splendor.

There are outdoor activities for any level of adventurer. Short **jungle walks** to observe nature are lovely, but then so are the hardcore 9-day treks or climbs up Gunung Tahan. There are also overnight trips to night hides where you can observe animals up close. The jungle canopy walk is the longest in the world, and at 25m (83 ft.) above ground, the view is spectacular. There are also rivers for rafting and swimming, fishing spots, and a couple of caves.

If you plan your trip through one of the main resort operators, they can arrange, in addition to accommodations, all meals, treks, and a coach transfer to and from Kuala Lumpur. Prices vary wildly, depending on the time of season you plan your visit, your level of comfort desired, and the extent to which you want to explore the forests. The best time to visit the park is between the months of April to September; other times it will be a tad wet, and that's why it's called a rainforest.

Mutiara Taman Negara Resort ⟨⟩, well established in the business of hosting visitors to the park, is the best accommodation in the park in terms of comfort. It organizes trips for 3 days and 2 nights or for 4 days and 3 nights, as well as an a la carte deal where you pay for lodging (see above) and activities separately. Accommodations come in many styles: a bungalow suite for families, a chalet and chalet suite, both good for couples; standard guesthouse rooms in a motel-style longhouse; and dormitory hostels for budget travelers. Explorer visitors check into the chalets, which are air-conditioned with attached bathrooms, and enjoy a full itinerary of activities included in the package price. A la carte activities include a 3-hour jungle trek, a 1½-hour night jungle walk, the half-day Lata Berkoh river trip with swimming, a 2-hour cave exploration, and a trip down the rapids in a rubber raft (Kuala Tahan, Jerantut, 27000 Pahang; ⟨⟩ **09/266-3500;** fax 09/266-1500; Kuala Lumpur Sales Office 03/2721-8888; fax 03/2721-3388).

Nusa Camp will send you to the park; put you up in its own kampung house, chalet, or hostel accommodations; and guide your activities. Once there, you can embark on one of numerous guided trips out into the wilds: a night safari, a night walk, a trip to see an orang asli village, a tubing trip down rapids, overnight hikes, overnight river fishing trips, a trip to the canopy walkway, or an overnight trip to explore caves. This outfit is just slightly less expensive than Taman Negara Resort, above, but Taman Negara Resort is a better facility. Bookings are through the Kuala Lumpur Office: **Malaysia Tourist Information Centre (MATIC),** 109 Jalan Ampang (⟨⟩ **03/2162-7682;** fax 03/2162-7682).

GENTING HIGHLANDS

The "City of Entertainment," as Genting is known locally, serves as Malaysia's answer to Las Vegas, complete with bright lights (that can be seen from Kuala Lumpur) and gambling. And while most people come here for the casino, there's a wide range of other activities, although most of them seem to serve the purpose of entertaining the kids while you bet their college funds at the roulette wheel.

Genting has four hotels of varying prices within the resort. Rates vary depending on the season, so be prepared for higher rates during the winter holidays.

The **Genting Hotel** is a newer property in the resort complex and is linked directly to the casino. Promotional rates can be as low as RM97 (US$26) for low-period weekdays. The Highlands Hotel's main attraction is its direct link to the casino. You'll pay the highest rate here; promotional rates in this hotel are very rare. The **Resort Hotel** is comparable to the Theme Park Hotel below, but it's a little newer and the double-occupancy rooms all have two double beds and standing showers only. The **Theme Park Hotel** is a little less expensive than the others, primarily because it's a little older and you must walk outside to reach the casino. Promotional rates during the week can be as low as RM62 for up to three people in one room. All properties share the same address and contact numbers at Genting Highlands 69000, Pahang Darul Makmur (✆ **03/211-1118;** fax 03/211-1888).

The Resort casino is open 24 hours. Entry is a refundable deposit of RM200 (US$53) whether you're a guest at the resort or just visiting for the day. By the way, you must be at least 21 years old to enter the casino. Outside of the casino, there's also a pond, a bowling alley, and an indoor heated pool. The **Awana Golf and Country Club** (✆ **03/6101-3025;** fax 03/6101-3535) is the premier golf course in these hills. For children, there's the huge Genting Theme Park, covering 100,000 square feet and mostly filled with rides, plus many Western fast-food eating outlets, games, and other attractions. At night, Gentings dinner theaters stage pop concerts by international (mostly Asian) performers, and everything from lion dance competitions to Wild West and magic shows. For dining, the most highly recommended place is **The Peak Restaurant & Lounge,** Genting's fine-dining restaurant on the 17th floor of the Genting Hotel.

For buses from Kuala Lumpur, call **Genting Highlands Transport,** operating buses every half-hour from 6:30am to 9pm daily from the Pekeliling Bus Terminal on Jalan Ipoh. The cost for one way is RM2.60 (US70¢), and the trip takes 1 hour. The bus lets you off at the foot of the hill, where you take the cable car to the top for RM3 (US80¢). For bus information, call ✆ **03/4041-0173.**

You can also get there by hiring an outstation **taxi.** The cost is RM40 (US$11), and it can be arranged by calling the **Puduraya** outstation taxi stand at ✆ **03/2078-0213.**

The **Genting Highlands Resort** is owned and operated by Resorts World Berhad, who'll be glad to provide you with hotel reservations if you call ✆ **03/2162-3555** or fax 03/2161-6611. You can also visit the central office at Wisma Genting on Jalan Sultan Ismail in KL.

CAMERON HIGHLANDS

Located in the hills, this colonial-era resort town has a cool climate, which makes it the perfect place for weekend getaways by Malaysians and Singapore-ans who are sick of the heat. If you've been in the region a while, you might also appreciate the respite.

The climate is also very conducive to agriculture. After the area's discovery by British surveyor William Cameron in 1885, the major crop here became tea, which is still grown today. The area's lovely gardens supply cities throughout the region with vegetables, flowers, and fruit year-round. Among the favorites here are the strawberries, which can be eaten fresh or transformed into yummy desserts in the local restaurants. At the many commercial flower nurseries, you can see chrysanthemums, fuchsias, and roses growing on the terraces. Rose gardens are prominent here.

Ringlet is the first town you see as you make your way up the highlands and is the main agricultural center. Travel farther up the elevation to **Tanah Rata,** the major tourism town in the Highlands, where you'll find chalets, cottages, and bungalows. The town basically consists of shops along one side of the main street (Jalan Sultan Ahmad Shah), and food stalls and the bus terminal on the other. **Brinchang,** at 1,524m (5,029 ft.) above sea level, is the highest town, surrounding a market square where there are shops, Tudor inns, rose gardens, and a Buddhist temple.

Temperatures in the Cameron Highlands average 70°F (21°C) during the day and 50°F (10°C) at night. There are paths for treks though the countryside and to peaks of surrounding mountains. Two waterfalls, the Robinson Falls and Parit Falls, have pools at their feet where you can have a swim.

There are **no visitor information services** here. They've been closed for a very long time and have no immediate plans for reopening. Walking in each town is a snap because the places are so small, but the towns are far apart, so a walk between them could take up much time. There are local buses that ply at odd times between them for around RM3 (US80¢), or you could pick up one of the ancient, unmarked taxis and cruise between towns for RM4 (US$1.05). You'll find banks with ATMs and money-changing services along the main road in Tanah Rata.

The best choice for accommodations here is **The Smokehouse Hotel.** Situated between Tanah Rata and Brinchang, this picturesque Tudor mansion has pretty gardens outside and a charming old-world ambience inside. Built in 1937 as a country house in the heyday of colonial British getaways, the conversion into a hotel has kept the place happily in the 1930s. Guest suites have four-poster beds and antique furnishings, and are stocked with plush amenities. The hotel encourages guests to play golf at the neighboring course, sit for afternoon tea with strawberry confections, or trek along nearby paths (for which they'll provide a picnic basket). It's all a bizarre escape from Malaysia, but an extremely charming one (Tanah Rata, Cameron Highlands, Pahang Darul Makmur; ℂ **05/491-1215;** fax 05/491-1214; RM400–RM600/US$105–US$158 suite).

For a more economical place to stay, try **The Cool Point Hotel** (891 Persiaran Dayang Endah, 39000 Tanah Rata, Cameron Highlands, Pahang Darul Makmur; ℂ **05/491-4914;** fax 05/491-4070; RM125–RM180/US$33–US$47 double). Cool Point has an outstanding location, a 2-minute walk to Tanah Rata. Although the modern building has some Tudor-like styling on the outside, the rooms inside are pretty standard, but the place is very clean. Make sure you book your room early. This place is always a sellout.

Most of the sights can be seen in a day, but it's difficult to plan your time well. In Cameron Highlands, I recommend trying one of the sightseeing outfits in either Brinchang or Tanah Rata. **C. S. Travel & Tours,** 47 Main Rd., Tanah Rata (ℂ **05/491-1200;** fax 05/491-2390), is a highly reputable agency that will plan half-day tours for RM15 (US$3.95) or full days starting from RM80 (US$21). On your average tour, you'll see the Boh tea plantation and factory, flower nurseries, rose gardens, strawberry farms, butterfly farms, and the Sam Poh Buddhist Temple. You're required to pay admission to each attraction yourself. They also provide trekking and overnight camping tours in the surrounding hills with local trail guides. Treks are RM30 (US$7.90), and camping is RM150 (US$39) for 2 days and 1 night. Bookings are requested at least 1 day in advance. Also, pretty much every hotel can arrange these services for you.

If you want to hit around some balls, **Padang Golf,** Main Road between Tanah Rata and Brinchang (℡ 05/491-1126), has 18 holes at par 71, with greens fees around RM42 (US$11) on weekdays and RM63 (US$17) on weekends. They also provide club rentals, caddies, shoes, and carts.

To get to Cameron Highlands, the **Kurnia Bistari Express Bus** (℡ 05/491-2978) operates between Kuala Lumpur and Tanah Rata four times daily for RM10 (US$2.65) one-way. They don't accept bookings in Kuala Lumpur; just show up at the Puduraya bus terminal to buy your ticket, and board the next bus. The bus terminal is in the center of town along the main drag. Just next to it is the taxi stand. It's a two-horse town; you can't miss either of them. Outstation taxis from KL cost RM180 (US$47) for the trip. Call ℡ 03/2078-0213 for booking. For trips from Cameron Highlands, call ℡ 05/491-2355. Taxis are cheaper on the way back because they don't have to climb the mountains.

4 Johor Bahru

Johor Bahru, the capital of the state of Johor, is at the southern tip of the Malaysian peninsula, where Malaysia's north-south highway comes to its southern terminus. Because it's just over the causeway from Singapore, a very short jump by car, bus, or train, it's a popular point of entry to Malaysia. Johor Bahru, or JB, is not the most fascinating destination in Malaysia, but for a quick day visit from Singapore or as a stopover en route to other Malaysian destinations, it offers some good shopping, sightseeing, and dining.

VISITOR INFORMATION
The Malaysia Tourism Board office in Johor Bahru is at the **Johor Tourist Information Centre (JOTIC),** centrally located on Jalan Ayer Molek, on the second floor (℡ 07/222-4935). Information is available not only for Johor Bahru, but for the state of Johor as well.

GETTING THERE
BY CAR If you arrive by car via the causeway, you will clear the immigration checkpoint upon entering the Malaysia side.

BY BUS Buses to and from other parts of Malaysia are based at the Larkin Bus Terminal off Jalan Garuda in the northern part of the city. Taxis are available at the terminal to take you to the city. The easiest way to catch a bus from KL is at the old KL Railway Station. **Plusliner** (℡ 03/2274-9601) runs service 12 times daily for RM20 (US$5.25). The trip takes just under 6 hours. Most all other cities in Malaysia have service to Johor Bahru; consult each city section for bus terminal information. From Singapore, the **Singapore-Johor Express** (℡ 65/6292-8149) operates every 10 minutes between 6:30am and midnight from the Ban Sen Terminal at Queen Street near Arab Street, in Singapore. The cost for the half-hour trip is S$2.10 (US$1.20).

If you're looking to depart Johor Bahru via bus, contact one of the following companies at Larkin for route information: **Transnasional** (℡ 07/224-5182) or **Plusliner/NICE** (℡ 07/222-3317).

BY TRAIN The **Keretapi Tanah Melayu Berhad (KTM)** trains arrive and depart from the Johor Bahru Railway Station at Jalan Tun Abdul Razak, opposite Merlin Tower (℡ 07/223-4727). You can catch trains from **KL Sentral** (℡ 03/2730-2000) four times daily for a cost between RM14 and RM56 (US$3.60 and US$15), depending on the class you travel. From the **Singapore**

Railway Station (© 65/6222-5165), on Keppel Road in Tanjong Pagar, the short trip is between S$1.10 and S$4.20 (US65¢–US$2.50).

BY PLANE   The **Sultan Ismail Airport,** 30 to 40 minutes outside the city (© 07/599-4737), has regular flights to and from major cities in Malaysia and also from Singapore. The airport tax is RM20 (US$5.25) for international flights and RM5 (US$1.30) for domestic flights, but this is usually reflected in the price of the ticket. For reservations on **Malaysian Airlines** flights, call © 1300/88-3000 in Johor Bahru. A taxi from the airport to the city center will run you RM20 to RM25 (US$5.25–US$6.60) per person. There's also a **Hertz** counter, but to make your reservation, you must call the downtown office at © 07/223-7520. A RM4 (US$1.05) coach service runs between the airport and the JOTIC tourist information center in town. If you use this service for departures, make sure you catch the coach at least 2 hours before departure time. Call © 07/221-7481 for more information.

BY TAXI   Outstation taxis can bring you to Johor Bahru from any major city on the peninsula. From KL's **Puduraya Bus Terminal** (© 03/2078-0213 Outstation Taxi), the cost is about RM220 (US$58). For taxi stands in other cities, please refer to each city's section. For taxi hiring from **Johor Bahru,** call © 07/223-4494. The outstation taxi stand is located at Larkin Bus Terminal, but for an extra RM10 (US$2.65), they'll pick you up at your hotel.

GETTING AROUND
As in Kuala Lumpur, taxis charge a metered fare, RM2.05 (US55¢) for the first kilometer and an additional 10 sen for each 200m after that. Between midnight and 6am, you're charged an extra 50% of the total fare. For taxi pickup, there's an extra RM1 (US25¢) charge. Call **Citycab** at © 07/354-0007.

FAST FACTS: JOHOR BAHRU
The **American Express** office is located at **Overseas Express Travel & Tours,** Wisma Overseas Express, 29 Jalan Meldrum (© 07/224-6611). Major banks are located in the city center, and money-changers are at shopping malls and at JOTIC.

The main post office is on **Jalan Dato Onn** (© 07/223-2555), just around the corner from JOTIC. For Internet connection, I recommend the conveniently located Weblinks Connexions in the JOTIC center on Jalan Ayer Molek, L1-2 (© 07/225-1387). They charge RM2.50 (US65¢) per hour.

For more Fast Facts about Malaysia, see "Planning Your Trip to Malaysia," earlier in this chapter.

WHERE TO STAY
Several international chains have accommodations in JB. Most are intended for the business set, but holiday travelers will find the accommodations very comfortable.

The Hyatt Regency   The Hyatt is near the City Square, but it likes to fancy itself as a city resort, focusing on landscaped gardens and greenery around the premises—the private lagoon-style pool, with gardens seen from the glass windows of the main lobby, is surely spectacular. The deluxe rooms are located better than the others, with views of Singapore and fabulous sunsets. Rooms are bland, with typical amenities common to this type of international chain hotel. However, this is without a doubt the best accommodation in town in terms of comfort; its rival, Pan Pacific, has the better location, though.

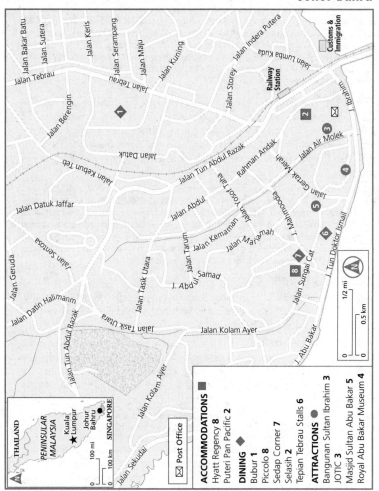

Jalan Sungai Chat, P.O. Box 222, 80720 Johor Bahru, Johor. ℂ **800/233-1234** or 07/222-1234. Fax 07/223-2718. 406 units. RM420–RM480 (US$111–US$126) double; RM500–RM600 (US$132–US$158) executive floor; from RM800 (US$211) suite. AE, DC, MC, V. **Amenities:** 3 restaurants (international, Japanese, Italian); lounge; outdoor lagoon-style pool on 2 levels; outdoor lighted tennis courts; fitness center; spa w/Jacuzzi, sauna, steam, and massage; concierge; limousine service; business center; 24-hr. room service; babysitting; same-day laundry service/dry cleaning; nonsmoking rooms; executive-level rooms. *In room:* A/C, TV w/satellite programming and in-house movie, minibar, coffee/tea-making facilities, hair dryer, safe.

Mutiara Hotel Johor Bahru   Formerly the Holiday Inn, this property has gotten a recent upgrade as the Mutiara, but that still does not compensate for its location—a bit far from the major attractions. Still, discounts here are good, so be sure to inquire. The big modern hotel block serves groups and conferences better than independent travelers. The handsome two-level lobby has polished marble floors and a domed ceiling supported by fat wood columns. Guest rooms are comfortable enough, with furniture in traditional fabrics and wood paneling details.

Jalan Dato Sulaiman, Century Garden, 80990 Johor Bahru, Johor. ✆ **07/332-3800**. Fax 07/331-8884. 330 units. RM370 (US$97) double; RM550 (US$145) suite. AE, DC, MC, V. **Amenities:** 4 restaurants (international, Szechuan, Italian, local); lobby lounge; outdoor pool; squash court; fitness center w/Jacuzzi, sauna, steam, and massage; concierge; business center; 24-hr. room service; same-day laundry service/dry cleaning; nonsmoking rooms; executive-level rooms. *In room:* A/C, TV w/satellite programming, minibar, coffee/tea-making facilities, hair dryer, safe.

The Puteri Pan Pacific   The good news about the Puteri is that it's located in the heart of the city, near attractions, shopping, dining, and entertainment. The bad news is it is a very busy hotel, and human traffic makes it noisy and somewhat on the rundown side. Nevertheless, little traditional touches to the decor make the Pan Pacific unique. Be sure to ask about special discounts, which can bring the price down by as much as half.

The Kotaraya, P.O. Box 293, 80730 Johor Bahru, Johor. ✆ **07/223-3333**. Fax 07/223-6622. 500 units. RM330–RM400 (US$87–US$105) double; RM450–RM2,000 (US$118–US$526) suite. AE, DC, MC, V. **Amenities:** 4 restaurants (international, local, Mediterranean, Chinese); lobby lounge; outdoor pool; outdoor lighted tennis court; squash court; well-managed popular fitness center w/Jacuzzi; sauna; steam; and massage; concierge; limousine service; business center; shopping arcade adjacent; 24-hr. room service; babysitting; same-day laundry service/dry cleaning; nonsmoking rooms; executive-level rooms. *In room:* A/C, TV w/satellite programming and in-house movies, minibar, coffee/tea-making facilities, hair dryer.

WHERE TO DINE

The majority of fine dining in Johor Bahru is in the hotels. Outside the hotels, you can sample some great local cuisine, both Malay and Chinese, and wonderful seafood from the city's hawker stalls.

Bubur TAIWAN CHINESE   For fast, inexpensive eats that you can even order for takeout, try this place. It's a family restaurant, so it can get pretty lively. The staff is quick and attentive without being imposing. The best dishes are the traditional braised pork in soy sauce and the grilled butterfish in black-bean sauce.

191 Jalan Harimau, Century Garden. ✆ **07/335-5891**. Reservations held for a half-hour only. Main courses RM7–RM12 (US$1.85–US$3.15). AE, MC, V. Daily 11am–5am except 4 days into the Chinese New Year.

Piccolo ITALIAN   Perhaps the most popular restaurant for the expatriate community in Johor Bahru, Piccolo has a lush lagoon-style poolside ambience with a very tropical and relaxed feel. Under the timber awning, the high ceiling and chic bamboo blinds make for romantic terrace dining. The antipasto is wonderful, as are dishes like chicken with shrimp and spinach. The grilled seafood is outstanding.

Hyatt Regency, Jalan Sungai Chat. ✆ **07/222-1234**. Main courses RM20–RM58 (US$5.25–US$15). AE, DC, MC, V. Daily 11:30am–2:30pm and 6:30–10:30pm.

Sedap Corner THAI/CHINESE/MALAY   Sedap Corner is very popular with the locals. It's dressed down in metal chairs and Formica-top tables, with a coffee shop feel. Local dishes like sambal sabah, otak-otak, and fish head curry are house specials, and you don't have to worry about them being too spicy.

11 Jalan Abdul Samad. ✆ **07/224-6566**. Reservations recommended. Main courses RM4.50–RM24 (US$1.20–US$6.30), though most dishes no more than RM6 (US$1.60). No credit cards. Daily 9am–9:45pm.

Selasih MALAY   For a broad-range sampling of Malaysian cuisine, try Selasih, which has a daily buffet spread of more than 70 items featuring regional dishes from all over the country. Each night, the dinner buffet is accompanied by traditional Malay music and dance performances. Children and seniors receive a 50% discount.

The Puteri Pan Pacific, The Kotaraya. ℂ 07/223-3333, ext. 3151. Reservations recommended. Buffet lunch RM28 (US$7.35); buffet dinner RM40 (US$11). AE, DC, MC, V. Daily 11:30am–2:30pm; Fri–Sat 6:30–10:30pm (no dinner on weekdays).

HAWKER CENTERS

The Tepian Tebrau Stalls in Jalan Skudai (along the seafront) and the stalls near the Central Market offer cheap local eats in hawker-center style. The dish that puts Johor Bahru on the map, ikan bakar (barbecued fish with chiles), is out of this world at the Tepian Tebrau stalls.

ATTRACTIONS

The sights in Johor Bahru are few, but there are some interesting museums and a beautiful istana and mosque. It's a fabulous place to stay for a day, especially if it's a day trip from Singapore, but to stay for longer might be stretching the point.

Bangunan Sultan Ibrahim (State Secretariat Building) The saracenic flavor of this building makes it feel older than it truly is. Built in 1940, today it houses the State Secretariat.

Jalan Abdul Ibrahim. No phone.

Masjid Sultan Abu Bakar This mosque was commissioned by Sultan Ibrahim in 1890 after the death of his father, Sultan Abu Bakar. It took 8 years and RM400,000 to build, and is one of the most beautiful mosques in Malaysia—at least from the outside. The inside? I can't tell you. I showed up in "good Muslim woman" clothing, took off my shoes, and crept up to the outer area (where I know women are allowed), and a Haji flew out of an office and shooed me off in a flurry. He asked if I was Muslim, I said no, and he said I wasn't allowed in. When I reported this to the tourism office at JOTIC, they thought I was nuts and said anyone with proper attire could enter the appropriate sections. Let me know if you get in.

Jalan Masjid. No phone.

Royal Abu Bakar Museum Also called the Istana Bakar, this gorgeous royal palace was built by Sultan Abu Bakar in 1866. Today it houses the royal collection of international treasures, costumes, historical documents, fine art from the family collection, and relics of the Sultanate.

Grand Palace, Johor. Jalan Tun Dr Ismail. ℂ 07/223-0555. Adults RM27 (US$7); children under 12 RM11 (US$3). Sat–Thurs 9am–4pm.

SPORTS & THE OUTDOORS

In addition to its cities and towns, Johor has some beautiful nature to take in, which is doubly good if you have only a short time to see Malaysia and can't afford to travel north to some of the larger national parks.

   Johor Endau Rompin National Park is about 488 sq. km (293 sq. miles) of lowland forest. There's jungle trekking through 26km (16 miles) of trails and over rivers to see diverse tropical plant species, colorful birds, and wild animals. Unfortunately, you'll have to be a camper to really enjoy the park because this is the only accommodation you'll get. Still, for those who love the great outdoors, first contact the National Parks (Johor) Corporation, JKR 475, Bukit Timbalan, Johor Bahru (ℂ 07/223-7471), for entry permission. You'll have to take an out-station taxi from Johor Bahru (cost: RM60/US$16); for booking, call ℂ 07/223-4494 to Kluang. The taxi driver will drop you at the shuttle to the park entrance. Take this shuttle (which you'll need to prearrange through the

National Parks Board) to the park entrance at Kahang. The 3-hour trip costs RM350 (US$92) for two people, and then you'll have to pay the RM20 (US$5.25) per-person entrance fee to the park. They can rent you all the gear you'll need, but you must bring your own food, and remember to boil your drinking water at least 10 minutes to get it into a potable condition.

The **Waterfalls at Lombong,** near Kota Tinggi, measuring about 34m (112 ft.) high, are about 56km (34 miles) northeast of Johor Bahru. You can cool off in the pools below the falls and enjoy the area's chalets, camping facilities, restaurant, and food stalls. An outstation taxi will also take you to the falls, which are a little off the track on your way east to Desaru. The cost is around RM60 (US$16).

Johor is a favorite destination for **golf** enthusiasts. The Royal Johor Country Club and Pulai Springs Country Club are just outside Johor Bahru and offer a range of country club facilities, while other courses require a bit more traveling time but offer resort-style accommodations. *One note of caution:* If you play in Johor, especially at the Royal Johor Country Club, don't wear yellow. It is the official color of the sultan and is worn only by him when he visits the courses.

The most famous course has to be the **Royal Johor Country Club,** 3211 Jalan Larkin, 80200 Johor Bahru, Johor (© **07/223-3322;** fax 07/224-0729). This 18-hole, par-72 course provides the favored game of the sultan of Johor, so they don't accept walk-ins. You must contact the club manager beforehand to obtain admission. Once you've received his okay, expect to pay RM105 (US$28) for weekday play and RM210 (US$55) for weekends. Other courses to try include the **Palm Resort Golf & Country Club,** Jalan Persiaran Golf, off Jalan Jumbo, 81250 Senai, Johor (© **07/599-6222;** fax 07/599-6001), with two 18-hole courses, par 72 and 74, and greens fees of RM150 (US$39) on weekdays and RM250 to RM325 (US$66–US$86) on weekends; the **Pulai Springs Country Club,** km 20 Jalan Pontian Lama, 81110 Pulai, Johor (© **07/521-2121;** fax 07/521-1818), with two 18-hole courses (both par 72) and greens fees of RM105 (US$28) on weekdays and RM210 (US$55) on weekends; or the **Ponderosa Golf & Country Club,** 10-C Jalan Bumi Hijau 3, Taman Molek, 81100 Johor Bahru, Johor (© **07/354-9999;** fax 07/355-7400), with 18 holes, par 72, and greens fees of RM80 (US$21) on weekdays and RM180 (US$47) on weekends.

SHOPPING

The **Johor Craftown Handicraft Centre,** 36 Jalan Skudai, off Jalan Abu Bakar (© **07/236-7346**), has, in addition to a collection of local crafts, demonstration performances of handicrafts techniques. **JOTIC,** 2 Jalan Ayer Molek (© **07/224-2000**), is a shopping mall with tourist information, cultural performances, exhibits, demonstrations of crafts, and restaurants.

5 Malacca

Whereas the destinations on the east coast are ideal for resort-style beach getaways, the cities on the west coast are perfect for vacations filled with culture and history, and Malacca is one of the best places to start. The attraction here is the city's cultural heritage, around which a substantial tourism industry has grown.

VISITOR INFORMATION

Surprisingly, there is no Malaysia Tourism Board office in Malacca, but there is a locally operated **Malacca Tourism Centre** in the town square (© **06/283-6538**).

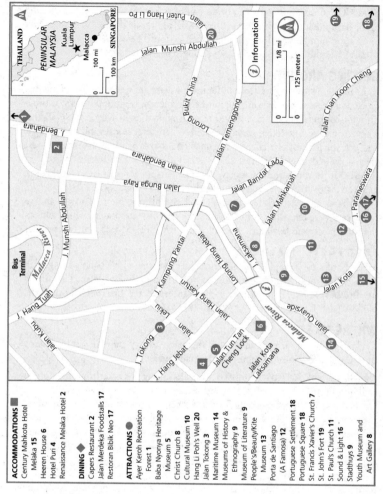

ACCOMMODATIONS
Century Mahkota Hotel Melaka 15
Heeren House 6
Hotel Puri 4
Renaissance Melaka Hotel 2

DINING
Capers Restaurant 2
Jalan Merdeka Foodstalls 17
Restoran Bibik Neo 17

ATTRACTIONS
Ayer Keroh Recreation Forest 1
Baba Nyonya Heritage Museum 5
Christ Church 8
Cultural Museum 10
Hang Li Poh's Well 20
Jalan Tokong 3
Maritime Museum 14
Museums of History & Ethnography 9
Museum of Literature 9
People's/Beauty/Kite Museum 13
Porta de Santiago (A Famosa) 12
Portuguese Settlement 18
Portuguese Square 18
St. Francis Xavier's Church 7
St. John's Fort 19
St. Paul's Church 11
Sound & Light 16
Stadthuys 9
Youth Museum and Art Gallery 8

GETTING THERE

Although there is an airport in Malacca, it's not open for any flights due to lack of demand. But although Malacca doesn't have a proper train station, the **KTM** stops at Tampin (☎ **06/441-1034**), 38km (23¾ miles) north of the city. It's not the most convenient way in and out of Malacca, but if you decide to stop en route between Kuala Lumpur and Johor Bahru, you can easily catch a waiting taxi to your hotel in town for RM35 to RM40 (US$9.20–US$11).

BY BUS From Singapore, contact **Malacca-Singapore Express** at ☎ **65/6293-5915.** Buses depart seven times daily for the 4½-hour trip (S$11/US$6.30). From **KL's Puduraya Bus Terminal** on Jalan Pudu, Transnasional (☎ **03/230-5044**) has hourly buses between 8am and 10pm for RM6.80 (US$1.80).

The bus station in Malacca is at Jalan Kilang, within the city. Taxis are easy to find from here.

BY TAXI   Outstation **taxis** can bring you here from any major city, including Johor Bahru (about RM120/US$32) and Kuala Lumpur (RM120/US$32). Taxi reservation numbers are listed in each city's section. The outstation taxi stand in Malacca is at the bus terminal on Jalan Kilang. There's no number for reservations.

GETTING AROUND

Most of the historic sights around the town square are well within walking distance. For other trips, **taxis** are the most convenient way around but are at times difficult to find. They're also not as clearly marked as in KL or Johor Bahru. They are also not metered, so be prepared to bargain. Basically, no matter what you do, you'll always be charged a higher rate than a local. Tourists are almost always quoted at RM10 (US$2.65) for local trips. Malaysians pay RM5 (US$1.30). If you're feeling sporty, you can bargain for a price somewhere in between. Trips to Ayer Keroh will cost about RM20 (US$5.25).

Trishaws (bicycle rickshaw) are all over the historic areas of town, and in Malacca they're renowned for being very, very garishly decorated (which adds to the fun). Negotiate for hourly rates of about RM20 (US$5.25) for two people.

FAST FACTS: MALACCA

Major **banks** are located in the historic center of town, with a couple along Jalan Putra. The most convenient post office location is on Jalan Laksamana (☎ **06/284-8440**). For centrally located **Internet,** try **Internet Booth Café,** No. 3A Jalan Kota Lakshamana (☎ **06/281-3266**).

WHERE TO STAY

Malacca is not very large, and most of the places to stay are well within walking distance of attractions, shopping, and restaurants.

Century Mahkota Hotel Melaka   Located along the waterfront, the hotel is walking distance from sightseeing, historical areas, shopping, and commercial centers. Rooms are more like holiday apartments, with minikitchens and up to three bedrooms for family living—a big hit with Malaysian and Singaporean families. Each apartment has a tiled main room with a clean cooking space at one end and simple rattan furnishings at the other—only bedrooms are air-conditioned. The views are of either the pools, the shopping mall across the street, or the muddy reclaimed seafront. The sprawling complex includes two outdoor pools and facilities for children, and is across from the largest shopping mall in Malacca. This place gets especially crowded during the school holidays in June and December.

Jalan Merdeka, 75000 Malacca. ☎ **06/281-2828.** Fax 06/281-2323. 617 units. RM198–RM428 (US$52–US$113) 1- to 3-bedroom apt. AE, DC, MC, V. **Amenities:** 3 restaurants (international, Asian, pizza); lounge and piano bar; 2 outdoor pools; outdoor lighted tennis courts; squash courts; fitness center w/sauna and massage; children's playground; game room; tour desk; car-rental desk; shuttle; business center; 24-hr. room service; babysitting; same-day laundry service/dry cleaning. *In room:* TV w/satellite programming, coffee/tea-making facilities, hair dryer.

Heeren House ★★   This is the place to stay in Malacca for a taste of the local culture. Started by a local family, the guesthouse is a renovated 100-year-old building furnished in traditional Peranakan and colonial style and located right in the heart of historical European Malacca. All the bedrooms have views of the Malacca River, and outside the front door of the hotel is a winding stretch of old buildings housing antiques shops. Just walk out and wander. The rooms on the higher floors are somewhat larger. Laundry service is available, and there's a cafe and gift shop on the premises. Reserve well in advance.

1 Jalan Tun Tan Cheng Lock, 75200 Malacca. ℭ **06/281-4241**. Fax 06/281-4239. 7 units. RM139 (US$37) double; RM299 (US$79) family suite. No credit cards. **Amenities:** Restaurant (local and international); same-day laundry service. *In room:* A/C, TV.

Hotel Puri 〈Value〉

In the olden days, Jalan Tun Tan Cheng Lock was known as "Millionaire Row" for all the wealthy families that lived here. This old "mansion" has been converted into a guesthouse, its tiled parlor has become a lobby, and the courtyard is where breakfast is served each morning. While Hotel Puri isn't big on space, it is big on value (discount rates can be pretty low). Rooms are very clean and, while not overly stylish, are comfortable enough for any weary traveler. Friendly and responsive staff add to the appeal.

118 Jalan Tun Tan Cheng Lock, 75200 Malacca. ℭ **06/282-5588**. Fax 06/281-5588. 50 units. RM110–RM200 (US$29–US$53) double; RM230 (US$61) triple; suites from RM305 (US$80). AE, MC, V. **Amenities:** Restaurant (international); tour desk; limited room service; babysitting; same-day laundry service. *In room:* A/C, TV w/satellite programming, fridge, coffee/tea-making facilities, hair dryer.

Renaissance Melaka Hotel 〈★〉

Renaissance is one of the most posh hotels in Malacca and, according to business travelers, is the most reliable place for quality accommodations—but aside from the pieces of Peranakan porcelain and art in the public areas, you could almost believe that you weren't in Malacca at all. The hotel is situated in a good location, though you'll still need a taxi to most of the sights. Renovations were completed 2 years ago to upgrade the guest rooms, which are fairly large and filled with Western comforts. Don't expect much from the views: The hotel is in a more business-minded part of the city—no historical landmarks to gaze upon here.

Jalan Bendahara, 75100 Malacca. ℭ **800/228-9898** in the U.S. and Canada, 800/251-259 in Australia, 800/441-035 in New Zealand, 800/181-737 in the U.K., or 06/284-8888. Fax 06/284-9269. 294 units. RM450–RM510 (US$118–US$134) double; from RM570 (US$150) suite. AE, MC, V. **Amenities:** 3 restaurants (international, Chinese, fusion cuisine); bar and lobby lounge; outdoor pool; golf nearby; squash courts; fitness center w/sauna, steam, and massage; concierge; tour desk; limousine service; business center; salon; 24-hr. room service; babysitting; same-day laundry service/dry cleaning; executive-level rooms. *In room:* A/C, TV w/satellite programming and in-house movies, minibar, coffee/tea-making facilities, safe.

WHERE TO DINE

In Malacca, you'll find the typical mix of authentic Malay and Chinese food. Because the city was the major settling place for the Peranakans in Malaysia, their unique style of food is featured in many of the local restaurants as well.

A good recommendation for a quick bite at lunch or dinner if you're strolling in the historical area is the long string of open-air food stalls along Jalan Merdeka, just between Mahkota Plaza Shopping and Warrior Square. Mama Fatso's is especially good for Chinese style seafood and Malay sambal curry. A good meal will run you about RM35 to RM40 (US$9.20–US$11) per person. And believe me, it's a good meal.

Capers Restaurant CONTINENTAL

This is the nicest fine-dining establishment in Malacca at the moment, which means it is quite formal and pricey compared to the rest. Warm lighting and crystal and silver flatware are only a few of the many details that add to the elegant and romantic atmosphere. The signature dishes, like grilled tenderloin, come from the charcoal grill. The pan-fried sea bass is served quite artfully in a ginger and dill sauce over bok choy and potatoes. The wine list is large and international (including Portuguese selections, in keeping with the Malacca theme).

Renaissance Melaka Hotel, Jalan Bendahara. ℭ **06/284-8888**. Reservations recommended. Main courses RM20–RM48 (US$5.25–US$13). AE, DC, MC, V. Mon–Sat 6:30–10:30pm.

Portuguese Settlement PORTUGUESE   For a taste of Portuguese Malacca, head down to the Portuguese Settlement, where open-air food stalls by the water sell an assortment of dishes inspired by these former colonial rulers, including many fresh seafood offerings. Saturday nights are best; at 8pm, there's a cultural show with music and dancing.

Jalan d'Albuquerque off Jalan Ujon Pasir. No phone. Dinner RM15–RM20 (US$3.95–US$5.25) per person. No credit cards. Open nightly from 6pm.

Restoran Bibik Neo PERANAKAN   For a taste of the local cuisine, the traditional Nyonya food here is delicious and very reasonably priced. And while the restaurant isn't exactly tops in terms of decor, be assured that the food here is excellent and authentic. Ikan assam with eggplant is a tasty mild fish curry that's very rich and tasty, but I always go for the otak-otak (pounded fish and spices baked in a banana leaf).

No. 6, ground floor, Jalan Merdeka, Taman Melaka Raya. ⓒ **06/281-7054.** Reservations recommended. Main courses RM5–RM15 (US$1.30–US$3.95). AE, DC, MC, V. Daily 11am–3pm and 6–10pm.

ATTRACTIONS

To really understand what you're seeing in Malacca, you have to understand a bit about the history, so be sure to read the introduction at the beginning of this section. Most of the really great historical places are on either side of the Malacca River. Start at Stadthuys (the old town hall), and you'll see most of Malacca pretty quickly.

MUSEUMS

Baba Nyonya Heritage Museum ⭐   Called Millionaire's Row, Jalan Tun Ten Cheng Lock is lined with row houses that were built by the Dutch and later bought by wealthy Peranakans; the architectural style reflects their East-meets-West lifestyle. The Baba Nyonya Heritage Museum sits at nos. 48 and 50 as a museum of Peranakan heritage. The entrance fee includes a guided tour.

48/50 Jalan Tun Tan Cheng Lock. ⓒ **06/283-1273.** Admission RM8 (US$2.10) adults, RM 4 (US$1.05) children. Daily 10am–12:30pm and 2–4:30pm.

The Cultural Museum (Muzium Budaya) ⭐   A replica of the former palace of Sultan Mansur Syah (1456–1477), this museum was rebuilt according to historical descriptions to house a fine collection of cultural artifacts such as clothing, weaponry, and royal items.

Kota Rd., next to Porta de Santiago. ⓒ **06/282-0769.** Admission RM1.50 (US40¢) adults, RM.50 (US15¢) children. Sat–Thurs 9am–6pm; Fri 9am–12:15pm and 2:45–6pm.

The Maritime Museum and the Royal Malaysian Navy Museum   These two museums are located across the street from one another but share admission fees. The Maritime Museum is in a restored 16th-century Portuguese ship, with exhibits dedicated to Malacca's history with the sea. The Navy Museum is a modern display of Malaysia's less pleasant relationship with the sea.

Quayside Rd. ⓒ **06/282-6526.** Admission RM2 (US55¢) adults, RM.50 (US15¢) children. Sat–Thurs 9am–6pm; Fri 9am–12:15pm and 2:45–6pm.

The People's Museum, the Museum of Beauty, the Kite Museum, and the Governor of Melaka's Gallery   This strange collection of displays is housed under one roof. The People's Museum is the story of development in Malacca. The Museum of Beauty is a look at cultural differences of beauty throughout time and around the world. The Kite Museum features the traditions of making and flying wau (kites) in Malaysia, and the governor's personal collection is on exhibit at the Governor's Gallery.

Kota Rd. ℭ **06/282-6526.** Admission RM2 (US55¢) adults, RM.50 (US15¢) children. Sat–Thurs 9am–6pm; Fri 9am–12:15pm and 2:45–6pm.

Stadthuys—The Museums of History & Ethnography and the Museum of Literature ♠ The Stadthuys Town Hall was built by the Dutch in 1650, and it's now home to the Malacca Ethnographical and Historical Museum. It displays customs and traditions of all the peoples of Malacca, and takes you through the rich history of this city. Behind Stadthuys, the Museum of Literature includes old historical accounts and local legends. Admission price is for both exhibits.

Located at the circle intersection of Jalan Quayside, Jalan Laksamana, and Jalan Chan Koon Cheng. ℭ **06/282-6526.** Admission RM2 (US55¢) adults, RM.50 (US15¢) children. Sat–Thurs 9am–6pm; Fri 9am–12:15pm and 2:45–6pm.

The Youth Museums and Art Gallery In the old General Post office are these displays dedicated to Malaysia's youth organizations and to the nation's finest artists. It's an unusual combination.

Laksamana Rd. ℭ **06/282-6526.** Admission RM1 (US25¢) adults, RM.50 (US15¢) children. Sat–Thurs 9am–6pm; Fri 9am–12:15pm and 2:45–6pm.

HISTORICAL SITES

Christ Church The Dutch built this place in 1753 as a Dutch Reform Church, and its architectural details include such wonders as ceiling beams cut from a single tree and a Last Supper glazed tile motif above the altar. It was later consecrated as an Anglican church, and mass is still performed today in English, Chinese, and Tamil.

Located on Jalan Laksamana. No phone.

Hang Li Poh's Well Also called "Sultan's Well," Hang Li Poh's Well was built in 1495 to commemorate the marriage of Chinese Princess Hang Li Poh to Sultan Mansor Shah. It is now a wishing well, and folks say that if you toss in a coin, you'll someday return to Malacca.

Located off Jalan Laksamana Cheng Ho (Jalan Panjang). No phone.

Jalan Tokong ♠ Not far from Jalan Tun Tan Cheng Lock is Jalan Tokong, called the "Street of Harmony" by the locals because it has three coexisting places of worship: the Kampong Kling Mosque, the Cheng Hoon Teng Temple, and the Sri Poyyatha Vinayar Moorthi Temple.

Porta de Santiago (A Famosa) ♠ Once the site of a Portuguese fortress called A Famosa, all that remains today of the fortress is the entrance gate, which was saved from demolition by Sir Stamford Raffles. When the British East India Company demolished the place, Raffles realized the arch's historical value and saved it. The fort was built in 1512, but the inscription above the arch, "Anno 1607," marks the date when the Dutch overthrew the Portuguese.

Located on Jalan Kota, at the intersection of Jalan Parameswara. No phone.

Portuguese Settlement and Portuguese Square The Portuguese Settlement is an enclave once designated for Portuguese settlers after they conquered Malacca in 1511. Some elements of their presence remain in the Lisbon-style architecture. Later, in 1920, the area was a Eurasian neighborhood. In the center of the settlement, Portuguese Square is a modern attraction with Portuguese restaurants, handicrafts, souvenirs, and cultural shows. It was built in 1985 in an architectural style to reflect the surrounding flavor of Portugal.

Located down Jalan d'Albuquerque off of Jalan Ujon Pasir in the southern part of the city.

St. Francis Xavier's Church   This church was built in 1849 and dedicated to St. Francis Xavier, a Jesuit who brought Catholicism to Malacca and other parts of Southeast Asia.

Located on Jalan Laksamana. No phone.

St. John's Fort   The fort, built by the Dutch in the late 18th century, sits on top of St. John's Hill. Funny how the cannons point inland, huh? At the time, threats to the city came from land. It was named after a Portuguese church to St. John the Baptist, which originally occupied the site.

Located off Lorong Bukit Senjuang. No phone.

St. Paul's Church   The church was built by the Portuguese in 1521, but when the Dutch came in, they made it part of A Famosa, converting the altar into a cannon mount. The open tomb inside was once the resting place of St. Francis Xavier, a missionary who spread Catholicism throughout Southeast Asia, and whose remains were later moved to Goa.

Located behind Porta de Santiago. No phone.

Sound & Light   The Museums Department has developed a sound-and-light show at the Warrior Square, the large field in the historical center of the city, which narrates the story of Malacca's early history, lighting up the historical buildings in the area for added punch. This is a good activity when you first arrive to help you get your historical bearings.

Warrior Sq., Jalan Kota. (✆ 06/282-6526. Admission RM5 (US$1.30) adults, RM3 (US80¢) children. Shows nightly at 9:30pm.

OTHER ATTRACTIONS

Outside of Malacca are the 202 hectares (500 acres) of forest that make up **Ayer Keroh Recreational Forest,** where many attractions have been built. A taxi from Malacca will run you about RM20 (US$5.25). See the **Reptile Park** (✆ 06/231-9136), admission RM4 (US$1.05) for adults and RM2 (US55¢) for children, open daily 9am to 6pm; the **Butterfly & Reptile Sanctuary** (✆ 06/232-0033), admission RM5 (US$1.30) for adults and RM3 (US80¢) for children, open daily 8:30am to 5:30pm; the **Malacca Zoo** (✆ 06/232-4053), admission RM3 (US80¢) for adults and RM1 (US25¢) for children, open daily 9am to 6pm; and the **Taman Mini Malaysia/Mini ASEAN** (✆ 06/231-6087), admission RM5 (US$1.30) for adults and RM2 (US55¢) for children, open 9am to 5pm daily.

SHOPPING

Antique hunting has been a major draw to Malacca for decades. Distinct Peranakan and teak furniture, porcelain, and household items fetch quite a price these days, due to a steady increase in demand for these rare treasures. The area down and around Jalan Tun Tan Cheng Lok, called **Jonker Walk,** sports many little antiques shops that are filled with as many gorgeous items as any local museum. Whether you're buying or just looking, it's a fun way to spend an afternoon.

Modern **shopping malls** are sprouting up in Malacca, the biggest being the Mahkota Parade on Jalan Merdeka, just south of the field (Warrior Square) in the historic district. Two hundred retail stores sell everything from books to clothing.

For crafts, start at **Karyaneka** (✆ **06/284-3270**), on Jalan Laksamana, close to the town square. If you travel down Laksamana, you'll find all sorts of small crafts and souvenir shops.

6 Penang

Penang is unique in Malaysia because, for all intents and purposes, Penang has it all. Malacca has historical sights and museums, but it doesn't have a good beach for miles. Similarly, while KL has shopping, nightlife, and attractions, it also has no beach resorts. Penang has all of it: beaches, history, diverse culture, shopping, food—you name it, it has it. If you have only a short time to visit Malaysia but want to take in as wide of an experience as you can, Penang is your place.

Since Malaysia's independence in 1957, Penang has had relatively good financial success. Today the state of Penang is made up of the island and a small strip of land on the Malaysian mainland. Georgetown is the seat of government for the state. Penang Island is 285 sq. km (171 sq. miles) and has a population of a little more than 1 million. Surprisingly, the population is mostly Chinese (59%), followed by Malays (32%) and Indians (7%).

VISITOR INFORMATION

The main **Malaysia Tourism Board (MTB)** office is located at no. 10 Jalan Tun Syed Sheh Barakbah (✆ **04/261-9067**), just across from the clock tower by Fort Cornwallis. There's another information center at **Penang International Airport** (✆ **04/643-0501**) and a branch on the third level at **KOMTAR (Kompleks Tun Abdul Razak)** on Jalan Penang (✆ **04/261-4461**).

GETTING THERE

BY PLANE   **Penang International Airport** (✆ **04/643-0811**) has direct flights from Singapore about seven times daily (**Singapore Airlines** toll-free in Singapore ✆ **800/223-8888**; **Malaysia Airlines** ✆ **65/336-6777**). From KL, Malaysia Airlines has two flights daily (✆ **1300/88-3000**). The airport is 20km (12 miles) from the city. To get into town, you must purchase fixed-rate coupons for taxis (RM23/US$6.05 to Georgetown; RM35/US$9.20 to Batu Feringgi). There's also the **Penang Yellow Bus Company** bus no. 83, which will take you to Weld Quay in Georgetown.

There are also car rentals at the airport. Talk to **Hertz** (✆ **04/643-0208**) or **Budget** (✆ **04/643-6025**).

BY TRAIN   By rail, the trip from KL to Butterworth takes 6 hours and costs RM59 (US$15) for first-class passage, RM25.40 (US$6.70) for second class, and RM14 (US$3.80) for third class. Three trains leave daily. Call **KL Sentral** (✆ **03/2730-2000**) for schedule information.

The train will let you off at the **Butterworth Railway Station** (✆ **04/323-7962**), on Jalan Bagan Dalam (near the ferry terminal) in Butterworth, on the Malaysian mainland. From there, you can take a taxi to the island or head for the ferry close by.

BY BUS   Many buses will bring you only to Butterworth, so if you want the trip to take you all the way onto the island, make sure you buy a ticket that specifically says Penang. These buses will let you out at **KOMTAR** on Jalan Gladstone across from the Shangri-La Hotel. If you're dropped in Butterworth at the bus terminal on Jalan Bagan Dalam (next to the ferry terminal), you'll need to grab a taxi or take the ferry to the island.

In KL, **Plusliner/NICE** (© 03/2722-2760) departs from the KL Train Station regularly. The NICE Executive Express coaches leave six times daily, costing RM50 (US$13). The trip takes about 4½ hours.

For buses back to KL call their counter at the **Garden Inn Hotel**, 41 Jalan Ansor (© **04/227-7370**).

BY FERRY   The ferry to Penang is nestled between the Butterworth Railway Station and the Butterworth bus terminal. It operates 24 hours a day and takes 20 minutes from pier to pier. From 6am to midnight, ferries leave every 10 minutes. From midnight to 1:20am, boats run every half-hour, and from 1:20 to 6am, they run hourly. Purchase your passage by dropping 60 sen (US15¢) in exact change in the turnstile (there's a change booth if you don't have it). Fare is paid only on the trip to Penang; the return is free. The ferry lets you off at **Pengalan Raja Tun Udah**, Weld Quay (© **04/210-2363**).

The ferry also takes cars for a fee of RM7 (US$1.85), which includes passenger fees.

BY TAXI   The outstation taxi stand is in Butterworth next to the bus terminal (© **04/323-2045**). Fares to Butterworth from KL are about RM240 (US$63).

BY CAR   If you're driving, you can cross over the 13.5km (8-mile) Penang Bridge, the longest bridge in Southeast Asia. All cars are charged RM7 (US$1.85) for the trip to Penang. It's free on the return.

GETTING AROUND

BY TAXI   Taxis are abundant, but be warned they do not use meters, so you must agree on the price before you ride. Most trips within the city are between RM3 and RM6 (US80¢–US$1.60). If you're staying out at the Batu Feringgi beach resort area, expect taxis to town to run RM20 (US$5.25), and RM30 (US$7.90) at night. The ride is about 15 or 20 minutes, but it can take 30 minutes during rush hour.

BY BUS   Buses also run all over the island and are well used by tourists who don't want to spring RM20 (US$5.25) every time they want to go to the beach. The most popular route is the **Hin Bus Co. (Blue Bus)** no. 93, which operates every 10 minutes between Pengkalan Weld (Weld Quay) in Georgetown and the beach resorts at Batu Feringgi. It makes stops at KOMTAR Shopping Plaza and also at the ferry terminal. Fare is RM1 (US25¢). Give your money to the nice ticket person on board.

CAR RENTAL   **Hertz** has an office in Georgetown at 38 Farquhar St. (© **04/263-5914**).

BY BICYCLE & MOTORCYCLE   Along Batu Feringgi there are bicycles and motorcycles available for rent.

BY TRISHAW   In Georgetown, it's possible to find some trishaw action for about RM20 (US$5.25) an hour. It's fun, and I recommend it for traveling between sights, at least for an hour or two.

ON FOOT   I think everyone should walk at least part of the time to see the sights of Georgetown because in between each landmark and exhibit there's so much more to see. A taxi, even a trishaw, will whisk you right by back alleys

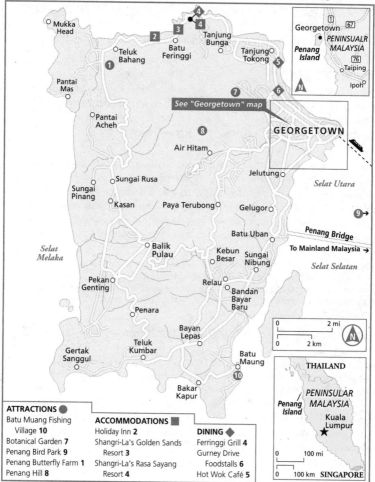

Penang Island

ATTRACTIONS ●
Batu Muang Fishing
Village **10**
Botanical Garden **7**
Penang Bird Park **9**
Penang Butterfly Farm **1**
Penang Hill **8**

ACCOMMODATIONS ■
Holiday Inn **2**
Shangri-La's Golden Sands
Resort **3**
Shangri-La's Rasa Sayang
Resort **4**

DINING ◆
Ferringgi Grill **4**
Gurney Drive
Foodstalls **6**
Hot Wok Café **5**

See "Georgetown" map

where elderly haircutters set up alfresco shops, bicycle repairmen sit fixing tubes
in front of their stores, and Chinese grannies fan themselves in the shade. The
streets of Georgetown are stimulating, with the sights of old trades still being
plied on these living streets, the noise of everyday life, and the exotic smells of
an old Southeast Asian port. Give yourself at least a day here.

FAST FACTS: PENANG

American Express has an office in Georgetown at **Mayflower Acme Tours,**
10th floor, Unit 10-05 MWE Plaza, No. 8 Lebuh Farquhar (℃ **04/262-8196**).
The **banking center** of Georgetown is in the downtown area (close to Ft.
Cornwallis) on Leboh Pantai, Leboh Union, and Leboh Downing. For **Internet**
service in town, try **STC Net Café,** 221 Chulia St. (℃ **04/264-3378**), which
charges RM6 (US$1.60) per hour. Out on Batu Feringgi, head for Cyber by the
Beach, **Golden Sands Resort** (℃ **04/881-2096**), with fees of RM5 (US$1.30)
per hour. The main post **office** in Georgetown is on Leboh Downing

(© **04/261-9222**). Another convenient location is out on Jalan Batu Feringgi (© **04/881-2555**).

For more Fast Facts about Malaysia, see "Planning Your Trip to Malaysia," earlier in this chapter.

WHERE TO STAY

While Georgetown has many hotels right in the city for convenient sightseeing, many visitors choose to stay at one of the beach resorts 30 minutes away at Batu Feringgi. Trips back and forth can be a bother (regardless of the resorts' free shuttle services), but if you're not staying in a resort, most of the finer beaches are off-limits.

The City Bayview Hotel, Penang   This city hotel is perfect for those who visit Penang for its cultural treasures rather than its beaches. A good budget choice, it has a number of fair dining venues, including a rooftop revolving restaurant with excellent views of the island. Choose from guest rooms in the new wing, completed in 1999, or those in the old wing, which have been recently refurbished. Either choice offers cool rooms in neutral tones, not as elegant as many, but comfortable and definitely value for money.

25-A Farquhar St., Georgetown, 10200 Penang. © **04/263-3161**. Fax 04/263-4124. 320 units. RM350–RM450 (US$92–US$118) double. AE, DC, MC, V. **Amenities:** 3 restaurants (international, Chinese); club w/live entertainment; lobby lounge; outdoor pool; concierge; limousine service; business center; 24-hr. room service; babysitting; same-day laundry service/dry cleaning; nonsmoking rooms. *In room:* A/C, TV w/in-house movie, minibar, coffee/tea-making facilities, hair dryer, safe.

Eastern & Oriental Hotel (E&O) ★★   E&O first opened in 1884, established by the same Sarkies brothers who were behind the Raffles Hotel in Singapore. Closed for many, many years (it was desperately in need of an overhaul), it reopened in April 2001. It is without a doubt the most atmospheric hotel in Penang, with its manicured lawns and tropical gardens flanking a white colonial-style mansion, with a lacelike facade and Moorish minarets. Accommodations are all suites, with little sitting areas and sleeping quarters separated with pocket sliding doors. You can expect molding details around every door and paned window, oriental carpets over polished plank floorboards, and Egyptian cotton linens dressing each poster bed. Dining along the hotel's many verandas is gorgeous. *One caveat:* There's no beach, but the pool in the seafront garden is very pretty.

10 Farquhar St., 10200 Penang. © **04/222-2000**. Fax 04/261-6333. www.e-o-hotel.com. 101 units. RM1635–RM33,440 (US$430–US$8800). AE, DC, MC, V. **Amenities:** 2 restaurants (Continental, Chinese); English-style pub; outdoor pool; small fitness center w/sauna; concierge; limousine service; 24-hr. room service; same-day laundry service/dry cleaning. *In room:* A/C, TV w/satellite programming, minibar, coffee/tea-making facilities.

Holiday Inn Resort Penang *(Kids)*   This is a recommended choice for families, but be warned that this resort has little appeal for vacationing couples or singles sans children. For families, it has everything—special KidSuites have a separate room for the wee ones, with TV, video, and PlayStation, some with bunk beds—choose from jungle, treasure island, or outer space themes. Holiday Inn also has a Kids Club, fully supervised day care with activities and games, and a lifeguard. Older kids can join in beach volleyball, water polo, bike tours, and an assortment of watersports arranged by the staff. Guest rooms are in two blocks: a low-rise structure near the beach and a high-rise tower along the hillside, connected by a second-story walkway. Naturally, the beachside rooms command the greater

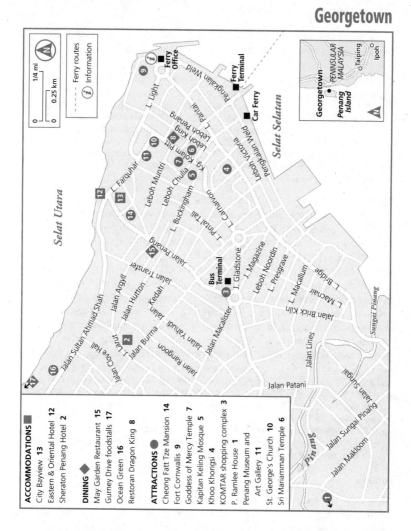

ACCOMMODATIONS
City Bayview **13**
Eastern & Oriental Hotel **12**
Sheraton Penang Hotel **2**

DINING
May Garden Restaurant **15**
Gurney Drive foodstalls **17**
Ocean Green **16**
Restoran Dragon King **8**

ATTRACTIONS
Cheong Fatt Tze Mansion **14**
Fort Cornwallis **9**
Goddess of Mercy Temple **7**
Kapitan Keling Mosque **5**
Khoo Khongsi **4**
KOMTAR shopping complex **3**
P. Ramlee House **1**
Penang Museum and Art Gallery **11**
St. George's Church **10**
Sri Mariamman Temple **6**

rate. Beachside rooms also have better ambience and slightly larger rooms, with wood floors and details, while tower rooms have less charm. The lack of dining options gets tiring.

72 Batu Ferringhi, 11100 Penang. © **04/881-1601.** Fax 04/881-1389. www.penang.holiday-inn.com 362 units. RM400–RM850 (US$105–US$224) double; RM700–RM750 (US$184–US$197) KidSuite; from RM1,400 (US$368) suite. AE, DC, MC, V. **Amenities:** Restaurant (international); lobby lounge; outdoor pool and children's pool; outdoor lighted tennis courts; fitness center; watersports equipment rentals; children's club; game room; concierge; tour desk; limousine service; 24-hr. room service; massage; babysitting; same-day laundry service/dry cleaning. *In room:* A/C, TV w/satellite programming and in-house movies, minibar, coffee/tea-making facilities, hair dryer, iron, safe.

Shangri-La's Golden Sands Resort ⊀ *Kids*   Rasa Sayang's little sister property is located just next door. A newer resort, it is priced lower than the Rasa Sayang, so it attracts more families. The beach, pool area, and public spaces fill up fast in the morning, and folks are occupied all day with beach sports like parasailing and jet-skiing, and pool games. For the younger set, a kids' club keeps small ones busy while Mom and Dad do "boring stuff." Rooms are large, with full amenities, and the higher-priced categories have views of the pool and the sea. Better still, guests here can use the facilities at Rasa Sayang.

Batu Feringgi Beach, 11100 Penang. ℂ 800/942-5050 in the U.S. and Canada, 800/222448 in Australia, 800/442179 in New Zealand, or 04/881-1911. Fax 04/881-1880. www.shangri-la.com. 395 units. RM415–RM590 (US$109–US$155) double; RM1,295 (US$341) suite. AE, DC, MC, V. **Amenities:** 3 restaurants (international, Italian, seafood); lobby lounge; 2 outdoor lagoon-style pools; outdoor lighted tennis courts; watersports equipment and activities; children's center; game room; concierge; tour desk; car-rental desk; limousine service; shuttle service to Shangri-La Hotel in Georgetown; business center; salon; 24-hr. room service; babysitting; same-day laundry service/dry cleaning; self-service launderette. *In room:* A/C, TV w/satellite programming and in-house movie, fridge, coffee/tea-making facilities, hair dryer, safe.

Shangri-La's Rasa Sayang Resort ★★★

Of all the beachfront resorts on Penang, Rasa Sayang is the finest. It has been here the longest, celebrating its 25-year anniversary in 1998, so it had the first pick of beachfront property and plenty of space to create lush gardens and pool areas. Get a room looking over the pool area, and your private balcony will be facing the picturesque palm-lined beach. The free-form pool is sprawled amid tropical landscaping and cafes, and the rest of the grounds have strolling gardens that are romantically illuminated in the evenings. The hotel is both elegant and relaxed, with Malay-style decor in the public areas and rooms. You'll also appreciate the good seafood restaurants nearby. Facilities include an outdoor pool, fitness center, small putting green, and table tennis. Guests have access to nearby tennis courts, sailing, boating, and water-skiing. Make sure to ask about the incredible bargain packages.

Batu Feringgi Beach, 11100 Penang. ℂ 800/942-5050 in the U.S. and Canada, 800/222448 in Australia, 800/442179 in New Zealand, or 04/881-1811. Fax 04/881-1984. www.shangri-la.com. 514 units. RM515–RM670 (US$136–US$176) double; RM750 (US$197) deluxe sea-facing double; from RM970 (US$255) suite. AE, DC, MC, V. **Amenities:** 5 restaurants (Continental grill, 2 international cafes, Chinese, Japanese); lobby lounge; beachfront bar; 4 outdoor pools, including 1 children's pool; outdoor lighted tennis courts; fitness center w/Jacuzzi, sauna, steam, and massage; watersports equipment and activities; children's center; game room; concierge; tour desk; car-rental desk; limousine service; shuttle service to Shangri-La Hotel in Georgetown; business center; salon; 24-hr. room service; babysitting; same-day laundry service/dry cleaning. *In room:* A/C, TV w/satellite programming and in-house movies, minibar, coffee/tea-making facilities, hair dryer, safe.

Sheraton Penang Hotel ★★

If you prefer to stay in town, Sheraton's Penang offering is hard to beat. Its 20-story high-rise is filled with elegance throughout, from the contemporary lobby and public rooms filled with modern art, to the discreet and professional service of its staff. Guest rooms are well appointed with stately furnishings of European design with local decorator touches. Many good views of the city and ocean are to be had. Marble bathrooms have a separate shower stall and bathtub plus fine toiletries. You can expect excellence from this hotel, which is used to catering to the demands of the international business traveler.

3 Jalan Larut, 10050 Georgetown, Penang. ℂ 04/226-7888; fax 04/226-6615. www.sheraton.com 237 units. RM460 (US$121) double; from RM575 (US$151) suite. AE, DC, MC, V. **Amenities:** 2 restaurants (international, Korean); bar and lobby lounge; outdoor pool; fitness center w/sauna and massage; concierge; tour desk; limousine service; 24-hr. business center; shopping arcade adjacent; 24-hr. room service; babysitting; same-day laundry service/dry cleaning; nonsmoking rooms; executive-level rooms. *In room:* A/C, TV w/satellite programming and in-house movies, minibar, coffee/tea-making facilities, hair dryer, iron, safe.

WHERE TO DINE

Feringgi Grill ★★ CONTINENTAL

The Feringgi Grill is comparable to any five-star hotel grill anywhere. From the dreamy lobster bisque to the carving cart of perfectly grilled top-quality meats flown in from all over the world, you'll be living the good life with each bite. A good wine selection will help revive you when you think you've died and gone to heaven. And don't even mention the desserts—the whole cart is a sore temptation sent straight from hell. Feringgi is perfect for a romantic dinner, or a change from all that char koay teow you've been eating in town.

Shangri-La's Rasa Sayang Resort, Batu Feringgi Beach. ✆ **04/881-1811**. Reservations recommended. Main courses RM50–RM68 (US$13–US$18). AE, DC, MC, V. Daily 7–10:30pm.

Hot Wok Café ⚜ PERANAKAN   This place is the no. 1 recommended Peranakan restaurant in the city, and small wonder: The food is great and the atmosphere is fabulous. Filled with local treasures such as wooden lattice work, wooden lanterns, carved Peranakan cabinets, tapestries, and carved wood panels, the decor will make you want to just sit back, relax, and take in sights you'd only ever see in a Peranakan home. The curry capitan, a famous local dish, is curry chicken stuffed with potatoes, with a thick, delicious coconut-based gravy. The house specialty is a mean perut ikan (fish intestine with roe and vegetable).

125-D Desa Tanjung, Jalan Tanjung. ✆ **04/899-0858**. Reservations recommended for weekends. Main courses RM9–RM15 (US$2.35–US$3.95). AE, DC, MC, V. Daily 11am–3pm and 6–11pm.

May Garden Restaurant CANTONESE   This is a top Cantonese restaurant in Georgetown, and while it's noisy and not too big on ambience, it has excellent food. But how many Chinese do you know who go to places for ambience? It's the food that counts! Outstanding dishes include the tofu and broccoli topped with sea snail slices or the fresh steamed live prawns. They also have suckling pig and Peking duck. Don't agree to all the daily specials, or you'll be paying a fortune.

70 Jalan Penang. ✆ **04/261-6806**. Reservations recommended. Main courses start at RM8 (US$2.10). Seafood is priced by weight in kilograms. AE, DC, MC, V. Daily noon–3pm and 6–10:30pm.

Ocean Green ⚜⚜ SEAFOOD   I can't rave enough about Ocean Green. If the beautiful sea view and ocean breezes don't make you weep with joy, the food certainly will. A long list of fresh seafood is prepared steamed or fried, with your choice of chile, black-bean, sweet-and-sour, or curry sauces. On the advice of a local food expert, I tried the lobster thermidor, expensive but divine, and the chicken wings stuffed with minced chicken, prawns, and gravy.

48F Jalan Sultan Ahmad Shah. ✆ **04/226-2681**. Reservations recommended. Main courses starting from RM12 (US$3.15); seafood priced according to market value. AE, MC, V. Daily 9am–11pm.

Restoran Dragon King PERANAKAN   Penang is famous around the world for delicious local Peranakan dishes, and Dragon King is a good place to sample the local cuisine at its finest. It was opened 20 years ago by a group of local teachers who wanted to revive the traditional dishes cooked by their mothers. In terms of decor, the place is nothing to shout about—just a coffee shop with tile floors and folding chairs—but all the curries are hand blended to perfection. Their curry capitan will make you weep with joy, it's so rich. But come early for the otak-otak, or it might sell out. While Dragon King is hopping at lunchtime, dinner is quiet.

99 Leboh Bishop. ✆ **04/261-8035**. Main courses RM8–RM20 (US$2.10–US$5.25). No credit cards. Daily 11am–3pm and 6–10pm.

FOOD STALL DINING

No section on Penang dining would be complete without full coverage of the local food stall scene, which is famous. Penang hawkers can make any dish you've had in Malaysia, Singapore, or even southern Thailand better. I had slimy char koay teow in Singapore and swore off the stuff forever. After being forced to try it in Penang (where the fried flat noodles and seafood are a specialty dish), I was completely addicted. Penang might be attractive for many things—history, culture, nature—but it is loved for its food.

Gurney Drive Foodstalls, toward the water just down from the intersection with Jalan Kelawai, is the biggest and most popular hawker center. It has all kinds of food, including local dishes with every influence: Chinese, Malay, Indian. In addition to the above-mentioned char koay teow, there's char bee hoon (a fried thin rice noodle), laksa (fish soup with noodles), murtabak (a sort of curry mutton burrito), oh chien (oyster omelette with chile dip), and rojak (a spicy fruit and seafood salad). After you've eaten your way through Gurney Drive, you can try the stalls on Jalan Burmah near the Lai Lai Supermarket.

ATTRACTIONS
IN GEORGETOWN

Cheong Fatt Tze Mansion ⍟   Cheong Fatt Tze (1840–1917), once dubbed "China's Rockefeller" by the *New York Times,* built a vast commercial empire in Southeast Asia, first in Indonesia and then in Singapore. He came to Penang in 1890 and continued his success, giving some of his spoils to build schools throughout the region. His mansion, where he lived with his eight wives, was built between 1896 and 1904. Inside are lavish adornments—stained glass, crown moldings, gilded wood carved doors, ceramic ornaments, and seven staircases.

Lebuhraya Leith. ✆ 04/261-0076. Admission RM10 (US$2.65) adults and children. Open for guided tours Mon, Wed, and Fri–Sat at 11am.

Fort Cornwallis   Fort Cornwallis is built on the site where Capt. Francis Light, founder of Penang, first landed in 1786. The fort was first built in 1793, but this site was an unlikely spot to defend the city from invasion. In 1810, it was rebuilt in an attempt to make up for initial strategic planning errors. In the shape of a star, the only actual buildings still standing are the outer walls, a gunpowder magazine, and a small Christian chapel. The magazine houses an exhibit of old photos and historical accounts of the old fort.

Lebuhraya Leith. ✆ 04/262-9461. Admission RM1 (US25¢) adults, RM.50 (US15¢) children. Daily 8am–7pm.

Goddess of Mercy Temple   Dedicated jointly to Kuan Yin, the goddess of mercy, and Ma Po Cho, the patron saint of sea travelers, this is the oldest Chinese temple in Penang. On the 19th of each second, sixth, and ninth month of the lunar calendar, Kuan Yin is celebrated with Chinese operas and puppet shows.

Leboh Pitt. No phone.

Kapitan Keling Mosque   Captain Light donated a large parcel of land on this spot for the settlement's sizable Indian Muslim community to build a mosque and graveyard. The leader of the community, known as Kapitan Keling (or Kling, which ironically was once a racial slur against Indians in the region), built a brick mosque here. Later, in 1801, he imported builders and materials from India for a new, brilliant mosque. Expansions in the 1900s topped the mosque with stunning domes and turrets, adding extensions and new roofs.

Jalan Masjid Kapitan Keling (Leboh Pitt). No phone.

Khoo Khongsi ✯   The Chinese who migrated to Southeast Asia created clan associations in their new homes. Based on common heritage, these social groups formed the core of Chinese life in the new homelands. The Khoo clan, which immigrated from Hokkien province in China, acquired this spot in 1851 and set to work building row houses, administrative buildings, and a clan temple around a large square. The temple here now was actually built in 1906 after a fire destroyed its predecessor. It was believed that the original was too ornate, provoking the wrath of the gods. One look at the current temple, a Chinese baroque masterpiece, and you'll wonder how that could possibly be. Come here in August for Chinese operas.

Leburaya Cannon. ✆ 04/261-4609. Free admission. Daily 9am–5pm.

P. Ramlee House   This is the house where legendary Malaysian actor, director, singer, composer, and prominent figurehead of the Malaysian film industry P. Ramlee (1928–73) was born and raised. A gallery of photos from his life and personal memorabilia offers a glimpse of local culture even those who've never heard of him can appreciate.

No phone. Free admission. Daily 9am–5pm.

Penang Museum and Art Gallery ✯✯   The historical society has put together this marvelous collection of ethnological and historical findings from Penang, tracing the port's history and diverse cultures through time. It's filled with paintings, photos, costumes, and antiques, among much more, all presented with fascinating facts and trivia. Upstairs is an art gallery. Originally the Penang Free School, the building was built in two phases, the first half in 1896 and the second in 1906. Only half of the building remains; the other was bombed to the ground in World War II. It's a favorite stop on a sightseeing itinerary because it's air-conditioned!

Leburaya Farquhar. ✆ 04/261-3144. Free admission. Sat–Thurs 9am–5pm.

St. George's Church   Built by Rev. R. S. Hutchins (who was also responsible for the Free School next door, home of the Penang Museum) and Capt. Robert N. Smith, whose paintings hang in the museum, this church was completed in 1818. While the outside is almost as it was then, the contents were completely looted during World War II. All that remains are the font and the bishop's chair.

Farquhar St. No phone.

Sri Mariamman Temple   This Hindu temple was built in 1833 by a Chettiar, a group of southern Indian Muslims, and received a major face-lift in 1978 with the help of Madras sculptors. The Hindu Navarithri festival is held here, whereby devotees parade Sri Mariamman, a Hindu goddess worshipped for her powers to cure disease, through the streets in a night procession. It is also the starting point of the Thaipusam Festival, which leads to a temple on Jalan Waterfall.

Leburaya Queen. No phone

OUTSIDE GEORGETOWN

Batu Muang Fishing Village   If you'd like to see a local fishing village, here's a good one. This village is special for its shrine to Admiral Cheng Ho, the early Chinese sea adventurer.

Southeast tip of Penang. No central phone.

Botanical Gardens Covering 30 hectares (70 acres) of landscaped grounds, this botanical garden was established by the British in 1884, with grounds that are perfect for a shady walk and a ton of fun if you love monkeys. They're crawling all over the place and will think nothing of stepping forward for a peanut (which you can buy beneath the DO NOT FEED THE MONKEYS sign). Also in the gardens is a jogging track and kiddie park.

About a 5- or 10-min. drive west of Georgetown. ✆ **04/228-6248**. Free admission. Daily 7am–7pm.

Penang Bird Park The Bird Park is not on Penang Island, but on the mainland part of Penang state. The 2-hectare (5-acre) park is home to some 200 bird species from Malaysia and around the world.

Jalan Teluk, Seberang Jaya. ✆ **04/399-1899**. Admission RM5 (US$1.30) adults, RM2 (US55¢) children. Daily 9am–7pm.

Penang Butterfly Farm The Penang Butterfly Farm, located toward the northwest corner of the island, is the largest in the world. On its 0.8-hectare (2-acre) landscaped grounds there are more than 4,000 flying butterflies from 120 species. At 10am and 3pm, there are informative butterfly shows. Don't forget the insect exhibit—there are about 2,000 bugs.

Jalan Teluk Bahang. ✆ **04/881-1253**. Admission RM5 (US$1.30) adults, RM2 (US55¢) children over 5; free for children under 4. Mon–Fri 9am–5pm; Sat–Sun 9am–6pm.

Penang Hill Covered with jungle growth and 20 nature trails, the hill is great for trekking. Or, you can go to Ayer Hitam, a town in the central part of Penang, and take the Keretapi Bukit Bendera funicular railway to the top. It sends trains up and down the hill every half-hour from 6:30am to 9:30pm weekdays and until midnight on weekends; it costs RM4 (US$1.05) for adults and RM2 (US55¢) for children. If you prefer to make the trek on foot, go to the Moon Gate at the entrance to the Botanical Garden for a 5.5km (9-mile), 3-hour hike to the summit.

A 20- to 30-min. drive southwest from Georgetown. The funicular station is on Jalan Stesen Keretapi Bukit.

SHOPPING

The first place anyone here will recommend that you go for shopping is **KOMTAR.** Short for Kompleks Tun Abdul Razak, it is the largest shopping complex in Penang, a full 65 stories of clothing shops, restaurants, and a couple of large department stores. There's a **duty-free shop** on the 57th floor. On the third floor is a **tourist information center.**

Good shopping finds in Penang are batik, pewter products, locally produced curios, paintings, antiques, pottery, and jewelry. If you care to walk around in search of finds, there are a few streets in Georgetown that are the hub of shopping activity. In the city center, the area around Jalan Penang, Leburhaya Campbell, Leburhaya Kapitan Keling, Lebuhraya Chulia, and Lebuhraya Pantai is near the Sri Mariamman Temple, the Penang Museum, the Kapitan Keling Mosque, and other sites of historic interest. Here you'll find everything from local crafts to souvenirs and fashion, and maybe even a bargain or two. Most of these shops are open from 10am to 10pm daily.

Out at Batu Feringgi, the main road turns into a fun **night bazaar** every evening just at dark. During the day, there are also some good shops for batik and souvenirs.

NIGHTLIFE

Clubs in Penang stay open a little later than in the rest of Malaysia, and some even stay open until 3am on the weekends.

If you're looking for a bar that's a little out of the ordinary, visit **20 Leith Street,** 11-A Lebuh Leith (© **04/261-8873**). Located in an old 1930s house, the place has seating areas fitted with traditional antique furniture in each room of the house. Possibly the most notorious bar in Penang is the **Hong Kong Bar,** 371 Lebuh Chulia (© **04/261-9796**), which opened in 1920 and was a regular hangout for military personnel based in Butterworth. It has an extraordinary archive of photos of the servicemen who have patronized the place throughout the years, plus a collection of medals, plaques, and buoys from ships.

For dancing, the resorts in Batu Feringgi have the better discos. **Zulu's Seaside Paradise,** Paradise Tanjung Bungah (© **04/890-8808**), is a world-beat dance club, spinning African, reggae, and other danceable international music.

Hard Life Café, 363 Lebuh Chulia (© **04/262-1740**), is an interesting alternative hangout. Decorated with Rastafarian paraphernalia, the place fills up with backpackers, who sometimes aren't as laid back as Mr. Marley would hope they'd be. Still, it's fun to check out the books where guests comment on their favorite (or least favorite) travel haunts in Southeast Asia.

7 Langkawi

Where the beautiful Andaman Sea meets the Strait of Malacca, Langkawi Island positions itself as one of the best emerging island paradise destinations in the region. Since 1990, the Malaysian Tourism Board has dedicated itself to promoting the island and developing it as an ideal travel spot. Now, after a decade of work, the island has proven itself as one of this country's holiday gems.

Its biggest competition comes from Phuket, Thailand's beach-lover fantasy to the north. But, day for day and dollar for dollar, I'd take Langkawi over Phuket hands down. Why? Well, despite being pumped up by government money and promotional campaigns, Langkawi remains relatively unheard of on the travel scene. So, while you get the same balmy weather, gorgeous beaches, fun water sports, and great seafood, you also avoid the horrible effects of tourism gone awry—inflated prices, annoying touts, and overcrowding. Besides, I've stayed in almost every luxury property on Phuket and can testify that Langkawi's finest resorts can compete with pride.

One final note: Malaysia has declared Langkawi a duty-free zone, so take a peek at some of the shopping in town, and enjoy RM4 (US$1.05) beers.

VISITOR INFORMATION

The MTB office is unfortunately situated in Kuah town on Jalan Persiaran Putra, so most travelers miss it completely, instead heading straight for the beach areas. If you'd like to pick up some of their information, ask your taxi driver to stop on the way to your resort. For specific queries, you can also call them at © **04/966-7789.** If you're arriving by plane, there's another MTB office at the airport (© **04/955-7155**).

GETTING THERE

BY PLANE   Malaysia Airways makes Langkawi very convenient from either mainland Malaysia or Singapore. From KL, two daily flights depart for

Langkawi's International Airport (© **04/955-1322**). Call Malaysia Airline's ticketing office in KL or Langkawi at © **1300/88-3000**. From Singapore, Malaysian Airlines flies direct daily but has numerous other flights with stops in either KL or Penang. For Singapore reservations call © **65/6336-6777.**

The best thing to do is prearrange a shuttle pickup from your resort; otherwise, you can just grab a taxi out in front of the airport. To Pantai Cenang or Pantai Tengah, the fare should be about RM25 (US$6.60), while to the farther resorts at Tanjung Rhu and Datai Bay, it will be as high as RM40 (US$11). To call for a pickup from the airport, dial © **04/955-1800.**

BY TRAIN Taking the train can be a bit of a hassle because the nearest stop (in Alor Setar) is quite far from the jetty to the island, requiring a cab transfer. Still, if you prefer rail, hop on the overnight train from KL (the only train), which will put you in to Alor Setar at around 6am. Just outside the train station, you can find the taxi stand, with cabs to take you to the Kuala Kedah jetty for RM10 (US$2.65). Call KL Sentral, at © **03/2730-2000,** or the Alor Setar Railway Station, at © **04/731-4045,** for further details.

BY BUS To be honest, I don't really recommend using this route. If you're coming from KL, the bus ride is long and uncomfortable, catching the taxi transfer to the jetty can be problematic, and by the time you reach the island, you'll need a vacation from your vacation. Fly or use the train. If you're coming from Penang, the direct ferry is wonderfully convenient.

BY FERRY From the jetty at Kuala Kedah, about five companies provide ferry service to the island (trip time: about 1 hr. and 45 min.; cost: RM15/US$3.95). Contact **LADA Holdings,** at © 04/762-3823 in Kuala Kedah or 04/966-8823 in Langkawi; Langkawi Ferry Services, at © 04/762-4524 in Kuala Kedah or 04/966-9439; or Nautica Ferries, at © 04/762-1201 in Kuala Kedah or 04/966-7868 in Langkawi. Ferries let you off at the main ferry terminal in Kuah, where you can hop a taxi to your resort for RM30 to RM40 (US$7.90–US$11).

If you're coming from Penang, the ferry is the way to go. **Bahagia Express** has a morning and afternoon speedboat from Weld Quay in Georgetown for RM35 (US$9.20). Call them in Penang at © **04/263-1943,** or visit their office across from the clock tower, just next to the main tourism board office. If you're heading from Langkawi to Penang, you can0 call Bahagia in Langkawi, at © **04/966-5784.**

GETTING AROUND

BY TAXI Taxis generally hang around at the airport, the main jetty, the taxi stand in Kuah, and at some major hotels. From anywhere in between, your best bet is to call the taxi stand for a pickup (© **04/966-5249**). Keep in mind that if you're going as far as one side of the island to the other, your fare can go as high as RM40 (US$11).

CAR & MOTORCYCLE RENTAL At the airport and from agents in the complex behind the main jetty, car rentals can be arranged starting at RM60 (US$16) per day. This is for the standard, no-frills model—actually, mine was more reminiscent of some of the junkers I drove throughout college, but it still got me around. Insurance policies are lax, as are rental regulations. My rental guys seemed more concerned with my passport documents than with my driver's license. If you're out on the beach at Cenang or Tengah, a few places rent Jeeps and motorcycles from RM80 (US$21) per day and RM30 (US$7.90) per day, respectively. Pick a good helmet.

Langkawi

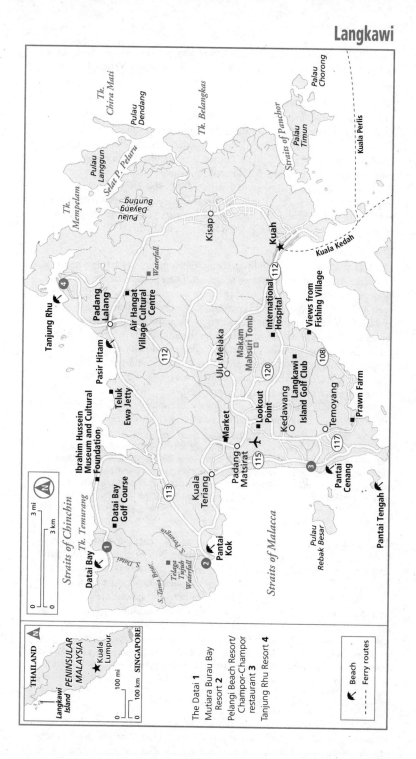

Straits of Chinchin
Tk. Temurang

Straits of Malacca

Straits of Panchor

Tk. Chira Mati

Tk. Belangkas

Tk. Mempelam

Pulau Langgun

Pulau Dendang

Pulau Chorong

Pulau Timun

Kuala Perlis

Selat P. Peluru

Pulau Dayang Bunting

Kisap

Kuah

Kuala Kedah

Tanjung Rhu

Padang Lalang

Air Hangat Village Cultural Centre

Waterfall

International Hospital

Views from Fishing Village

Pasir Hitam

112

Ulu Melaka

Makam Mahsuri Tomb

120

Langkawi Island Golf Club

108

Teluk Ewa Jetty

112

Kedawang

Temoyang

Prawn Farm

Ibrahim Hussein Museum and Cultural Foundation

Market

Lookout Point

117

Datai Bay Golf Course

Padang Matsirat

115

Pantai Cenang

113

Kuala Teriang

Pantai Tengah

Datai Bay

S. Datai

Pantai Kok

S. Tama Besar

Pulau Rebak Besar

S. Perumpa

Telaga Tujuh Waterfall

THAILAND

PENINSULAR MALAYSIA

Kuala Lumpur

SINGAPORE

Langkawi Island

100 mi

100 km

The Datai **1**
Mutiara Burau Bay Resort **2**
Pelangi Beach Resort/ Champor-Champor restaurant **3**
Tanjung Rhu Resort **4**

Beach
Ferry routes

3 mi

3 km

BY FOOT   The main beaches at Cenang and Tengah can be walked quite nicely; however, don't expect to be able to walk around to other parts of the island.

FAST FACTS: LANGKAWI

The only major **bank** branches seem sadly located far from the beach areas, in Kuah town, mostly around the blocks across the street from the Night Hawker Center (off Jalan Persiaran Putra). Money-exchangers keep long hours out at Pantai Cenang and Pantai Tengah, but for other resorts, you'll have to change your money at the resort itself. The main **post office** is in Kuah town at the LADA Kompleks on Jalan Persiaran Putra (© **04/966-7271**). Otherwise, use your resort's mail services. Along the Pantai Cenang and Pantai Tengah main road, you'll find at least a half dozen small **Internet** places. **The Shop,** a small convenience store along the strip, provides service for RM6 (US$1.60) per hour.

WHERE TO STAY

The Datai 👬👬👬   Aesthetically speaking, this is one of my favorite resorts in Southeast Asia, coming darn close to heaven. Datai is the epitome of sublime, its tropical resort design incorporating nature at every turn. Beyond the graceful open-air lobby, pass the lily pond courtyard to the Datai's brilliant lounge—you'll find a hillside veranda surrounded by lush jungle and suspended above a breathtaking bay. Rooms and villas, also built into the hillside, are expert in their studied Southeast Asian elegance. Minimalist in design, the color schemes stick close to nature, with rosewood tones, deep local tapestries, and regal celadon-color upholstery. Even lower-priced deluxe rooms have a quaint seating area with a view, plus an oversize bathroom with designer body-care products, a separate stall shower, and a long bathtub. Guest facilities, which include two pools, a spa, and golf course, show the same meticulous attention to luxury. This is a top pick.

Jalan Teluk Datai, Langkawi, Kedah. © **800/223-6800** in the U.S. and Canada, 800/181-123 in the U.K., or 04/959-2500. Fax 04/959-2600. RM1,325 (US$349) double; RM1,520–RM1,890 (US$400–US$497) villa; RM2,135–RM5,880 (US$562–US$1,547) suite. Prices jump about 50% Dec–Jan. AE, DC, MC, V. **Amenities:** 3 restaurants (international, Thai, Malaysian); lounge; 2 outdoor pools surrounded by jungle; golf course; 2 outdoor lighted tennis courts; fitness center w/Jacuzzi, sauna, steam, and massage; spa; watersports equipment; mountain bike rental; concierge; limousine service; limited room service; babysitting; same-day laundry service/dry cleaning; jungle trekking; library. *In room:* A/C, TV w/satellite programming and in-house movies, minibar, coffee/tea-making facilities, hair dryer, safe.

Mutiara Burau Bay Beach Resort   Burau offers beachside resort accommodations for less money than its upscale neighbors. Not nearly as ritzy, this place feels more like summer camp than a resort. All guest rooms are contained in cabanas, with simple decor that's a bit on the older side. For the price, though, they offer value for money. Burau also organizes golf, massage, Jeep treks, jungle treks, mountain biking, tennis, canoeing, catamaran sailing, jet skiing, scuba diving, snorkeling, fishing, water-skiing, windsurfing, and yachting.

Teluk Burau, 07000 Langkawi, Kedah. © **04/959-1061.** Fax 04/959-1172. 150 units. RM250 (US$66) garden-view chalet; RM280 (US$74) sea-view chalet; RM370 (US$97) family chalet; RM735 (US$193) royal chalet. AE, DC, MC, V. **Amenities:** 3 restaurants; beach bar; outdoor pool; outdoor lighted tennis courts; children's center; game room; concierge; activities desk; car-rental desk; shuttle service; business center; 24-hr. room service; massage; babysitting; same-day laundry service; nonsmoking rooms. *In room:* A/C, TV w/satellite programming and in-house movie, minibar, coffee/tea-making facilities.

Pelangi Beach Resort 👬   For those who prefer a more active vacation or are looking for a resort that's more family-oriented, I recommend Pelangi. A top-quality resort, this place stands out from neighboring five-star resorts for its sheer fun. A long list of organized sports and leisure pastimes make it especially attractive for families, but surprisingly, I never found children to be a distraction here. Pelangi's 51 ethnic wooden chalets are huge inside and are divided into either one, two, or four guest rooms. You'll be welcomed by vaulted ceilings, modern bathrooms, and large living spaces. But it's the little things you'll love— I didn't want to get out of bed and leave my squishy down pillows and snuggly bedding! In addition, Pelangi's location, near the central beach strip for island life, means you're not cloistered away from the rest of civilization.

Pantai Cenang, 07000 Langkawi, Kedah. ℭ **04/952-8888.** Fax 04/952-8899. 350 units. RM620–RM690 (US$163–US$182) double; from RM1,100 (US$289) suite. AE, DC, MC, V. **Amenities:** 3 restaurants (international, Thai, barbecue); 3 bars; 2 large outdoor pools w/swim-up bar; golf nearby; minigolf course; outdoor lighted tennis courts; squash courts; fitness center w/sauna, steam, and massage; Jacuzzi; watersports center w/equipment rental, boating excursions, concierge; tour desk car-rental desk; limousine service; shuttle service; business center; 24-hr. room service; babysitting; same-day laundry service/dry cleaning; jungle trekking. *In room:* A/C, TV w/satellite programming and in-house movies, minibar, coffee/tea-making facilities, hair dryer, safe.

Tanjung Rhu Resort 🌟🌟 Everyone on the island will agree that the beach at Tanjung Rhu wins first prize, no contest. It's a wide crescent of dazzlingly pure sand wrapped around a perfect crystal azure bay. Tree-lined karst islets jut up from the sea, dotting the horizon. It's just gorgeous. This resort claims 440 hectares (1,100 acres) of jungle in this part of the island, monopolizing the scene for extra privacy, but it has its pros and cons. The pros? Guest rooms are enormous and decorated with a sensitivity to the environment, from natural materials to toiletries wrapped in organic recycled paper. The cons? Make sure you don't book your vacation during the months of June or December, when Malaysia and Singapore celebrate school holidays, because the place draws families like flies. Still, during between-holiday downtime, I love this resort's friendly and casual atmosphere—and, of course, the beach.

Tanjung Rhu, Mukim Ayer Hangat, Langkawi, Kedah 07000. ℭ **04/959-1033.** Fax 04/959-1899. 138 units. RM980–RM1,950 (US$258–US$513) double. AE, DC, MC, V. **Amenities:** 3 restaurants; bar; 2 outdoor pools, 1 saltwater and 1 freshwater; golf nearby; outdoor lighted tennis courts; fitness and spa center w/Jacuzzi, sauna, steam, and massage; watersports (nonmotorized), trekking, and boat tours; concierge; activity desk; limousine service; shuttle service; 24-hr. room service; babysitting; same-day laundry service/dry cleaning; library. *In room:* A/C, TV w/satellite programming and in-room video w/movie library, minibar, coffee/tea-making facilities, hair dryer, safe, compact disc player.

WHERE TO DINE

If you're out at one of the more secluded resorts, chances are good that you'll stay there for most of your meals. However, if you're at Pantai Cenang or Pantai Tengah, I strongly recommend taking a stroll down to **Champor-Champor** 🌟, just across the road in the Pelangi Resort (ℭ **04/955-1449**), which serves magnificently creative dishes at lunch and dinner—a local roti canai served like a pizza, and local fish catches doused in sweet sauces. Everything is incredibly fresh, wildly delicious, and amazingly inexpensive. As for decor, the imaginative catchall beach shack atmosphere really relaxes. After dinner, hang around the bar for the best fun on the island. Because Langkawi is an official duty-free port, one beer costs a wee RM4 (US$1.05)! If you're in Kuah town looking for something good to eat, the best local dining experience can be found at the evening **hawker stalls** just along the waterfront near the taxi stand. A long row of hawkers cook up every kind of local favorite, including seafood dishes. You can't get any cheaper or more laid-back. After dinner, from here it's easy to flag down a taxi back to your resort.

Finally, I'm not one to bash places, but I got suckered by a glossy brochure for **Barn Thai,** a Thai restaurant on the eastern side of the island built deep inside a thick mangrove forest. Sound interesting? The food was terrible and over-priced, while the atmosphere was destroyed by busloads of tourists. Stay away.

ATTRACTIONS

Most visitors will come for the **beaches.** All resorts are pretty much self-con-tained units, planning numerous water-sports activities, trekking, sports, and tours.

For a fun day trip, I recommend taking one of the local boat trips to some of Langkawi's other islands. Most diving trips take you out to **Payar Marine Park** for two dives per day. Off Payar Island, a floating platform drifts above a stun-ning coral reef, where dive operators and snorkel gear rentals are available (there's also a glass-bottom boat, if you don't want to get wet). Day trips to other **sur-rounding islands,** such as Pulau Singa Besar, Pulau Langgun, Pulau Rebak, or Pulau Beras Basah, give you a day of peaceful sun-soaking and swimming. The full-day trip to Payar Island floating reef platform costs RM170 (US$45), but dives and rental of snorkel gear cost extra. If you want to hop around to nice secluded island beaches, the half-day island-hopping tour costs RM45 (US$12). The half-day **round-island tour** also stops at a few attractions, including the **Batik Art Village** (RM30/US$7.90). In Langkawi, call Asian Overland at ⓒ 04/955-2002, or talk to your hotel tour desk operator.

Perhaps one of the loveliest additions to Langkawi's attractions is the **Ibrahim Hussein Museum and Cultural Foundation,** Pasir Tengkorak, Jalan Datai (ⓒ 04/959-4669). The artistic devotion of the foundation's namesake fueled the creation of this enchanting modern space designed to showcase Malaysia's contribution to the international fine-arts scene. If you can pull yourself from the beach for any one activity in Langkawi, this is the one I recommend. Mr. Hussein has created a museum worthy of international attention—truly a gem. It's open daily from 10am to 5pm; admission is adults for RM7 (US$1.85), and children enter free.

SHOPPING

Langkawi's designated Duty Free Port status makes shopping here quite fun and very popular. In Kuah town, the **Sime Darby Duty Free Shop,** Langkawi Duty Free, 64 Persiaran Putra, Pekan Kuah (ⓒ 04/966-6052), carries the largest selection.

10

Bali (Indonesia)

updated by Charles Agar

Once known only as tourist paradise, our image of Bali is now defined by the events of October 12, 2002, on a night when, in the main tourist area of Kuta, bomb blasts rang out that would echo the world over and usher in a new wave of fear. Some 185 people, the majority Australian tourists, lost their lives. In an instant, the very soul of this island paradise, a land known for welcome and an island of tranquility in the tumultuous Indonesian archipelago, was shattered. For years Bali was synonymous with affordable, high-end resorts; vibrant culture; beautiful beaches; and a timeless allure that drew expatriate artists, writers, and escapists from all over the world. Warnings from the international community are still in place, and though the Indonesian government has taken important steps to update security on its tourist cash cow, many balk at the thought of returning to the scene of such carnage. It's important to know that the peaceful Balinese still welcome visitors warmly, now even more so, and a visit to Bali is still replete with kingly comforts at cost, fine dining, beautiful resorts, and immersion in an ancient culture on an island dreamscape.

In a land of volcanic peaks, bubbling springs, tropical jungle, and stunning beaches, Balinese people live in constant relation with nature and their faith in Agama Hindu Dharma, a blend of Hindu, Buddhist, Javanese, and indigenous beliefs. The beauty and harmony of this faith colors every aspect of life, from fresh flowers strewn in obeisance or the calm of morning prayer at temple. Daily ceremonies abound—tooth fillings, weddings, and cremations—drawing elaborately dressed women with ornate fruit offerings balanced on their heads, and men unselfconsciously adorned with colorful sarongs and traditional headdress. You're sure to catch the soothing music of the *gamelan,* the music of the island, and many find that the pleasures here are serendipitous, lucky meetings with friendly locals; an impromptu fete; or a beautiful sunset shared with the right person. Despite the horror of recent events, Bali is still the beautiful island paradise that has attracted so many for so long.

1 Getting to Know Bali

THE LAY OF THE LAND

Bali might be a small island, but it doesn't lack topographical variety. Located in the center of Indonesia's vast archipelago, the island has an area of 5,620 sq. km (roughly 3,485 sq. miles), only the size of a large metropolis. The land is divided in half east to west by a volcanic mountain chain and is scored lengthwise by deep river gorges. White sand beaches line the coast to the east, as well as near

Bali

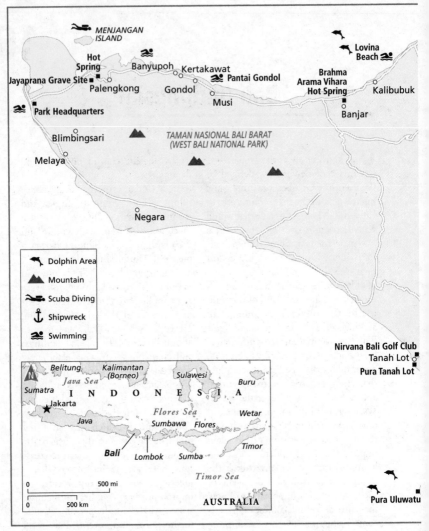

Kuta in the most populated area of wider lowlands to the south. Active volcanoes dot the island, including **Gunung Agung**, a dynamic peak and a power point of Balinese culture and belief. Central **Ubud** is one of the more beautiful spots, with mountainous scenery, lush vegetation, and the Bali's famed terraced rice farms. The far west is the least developed area of the island, with mountainous terrain mostly given over to national park land.

A LOOK AT THE PAST
As distinct as Balinese life is, its people and culture originated elsewhere. Evidence of settlement goes back to the Neolithic period of around 3000 B.C., but the culture flourished under Chinese and Indian influences, including the

introduction of Buddhism and Hinduism beginning in 800 B.C. Bali was ruled
periodically by the Javanese and, with the rise of Islam on the mainland, the last
Javanese Majapahit king fled the Jakarta for Bali in 1515, cementing the island's
Javanese influence and affecting a renaissance in art and culture that would survive years of Muslim incursion.

The first real Western presence was established in 1601 when a Dutch contingent came to set up formal relations and establish trade. Attempts to expand
relations were largely rebuffed—even as the Dutch East India Company
expanded throughout the area—but Balinese slaves were shipped to Dutch and
French merchants. In the era of Napoleon, Holland's East Indian holdings

passed first to the French and then to the British, who returned them to the Dutch in the peace agreement following Napoleon's Waterloo defeat in 1815.

The modern era of internationalism was initiated in the 1830s by Danish trader Mads Lange, who operated directly with the rajas and bypassed the Dutch completely. That didn't sit well with the Dutch, and after several years of tension and shows of force on both sides, the Balinese formally recognized Dutch sovereignty. For several decades, the Dutch rule was strong, but Balinese dissented and resisted the Dutch edict ending the practice of suttee, the ritual practice of widows immolating themselves on their husbands' funeral pyres.

Perhaps the most dramatic and tragic event in Balinese history came in 1906 when, in response to the looting of a wrecked Chinese trading vessel, Dutch troops landed at Sanur to take the island. Balinese troops lost any hope and, to the horror of the Dutch, marched directly into open fire in a mass suicide. A similar scene was repeated in 1908. Dutch control of Bali was complete by 1909.

Over the next couple of decades, a steady stream of European settlers and visitors came—doctors and teachers at first, followed by the first tourists, artists, and cultural explorers. By the 1930s, Bali's reputation as a magical paradise was spreading rapidly, and such figures as anthropologist Margaret Mead and artist Walter Spies frequented the island.

World War II saw an exodus of foreigners with the arrival of Japanese troops. For Indonesians, it was a time of both strain under the brief Japanese occupation and revelation in light of the withdrawal of Dutch control. Shortly after the end of the war in 1945, Nationalist Party founder **Sukarno,** a thorn in the side of the Dutch since the 1920s, announced a declaration of Indonesian independence and was named president. The Dutch withdrew under international pressure in 1949, allowing the creation of the Republic of Indonesia, a tentative federation.

Hindu Bali was suspect under the rule of Muslim Jakarta, and the island was hit very hard by economic collapse. In 1965, **Suharto** seized control in response to a staged communist coup, and bloody conflicts continued for several years. As many as 100,000 Balinese were killed as suspected communists or as ethnic Chinese.

Under Suharto, the military gained a far-reaching influence over national affairs. For the next 3 decades, until the major economic crisis of 1997, Indonesia enjoyed a period of prosperity in spite of Suharto's embezzling autocracy. During this time, and with government attention, Bali rose to prominence as a top tour destination in the region.

BALI & THE INDONESIAN CRISIS

In just the last half century, Bali has undergone remarkable change and weathered turmoil on the Indonesian mainland. The riots and protests that erupted in Indonesia in 1998 were the result of 3 decades of military rule and struggles to bring the world's fourth most populous country into the modern global economy. Chafing under the yoke of President Suharto, the Indonesians finally revolted, with demonstrations turning into riots that made headlines around the world. In June 1999, Indonesians witnessed their first free parliamentary election since 1955, ousting Suharto. But riots, bombings, and protests continue to plague the country, specifically in Aceh and Irian Jaya, where separatist movements have little support both locally and internationally. On May 20, 2002, East Timor was internationally recognized as an independent state after a protracted struggle. Now Indonesia is tentatively at peace under a provisional government headed by President Megawati, the daughter of Sukarno (predecessor to Suharto). Megawati inherits political instability and an economic crisis, but is hard at work to address corruption and the military's human rights record, and to carry this troubled land into the future. A big part of that involves shining up the now tarnished reputation of Indonesia's tourist gem, the sacred island of Bali, and the administration is taking every step to ensure security on the isle.

BALI TODAY

The bombings in October 2002 brought the world's problems to paradise, and Balinese are doing what they can to repair the damage literally and spiritually, stepping up security at sea and airports and encouraging tourists to return with bargain packages and, of course, that special Balinese hospitality.

As with any undiscovered paradise that isn't so undiscovered anymore, Bali buffs mourn the loss of the island's innocence. But Bali has always been a magnet for tourists and expats, and where there were no hotels or even electricity only a few decades ago, the island is now spotted with cybercafes, hotels, and pesky touts urging you to part with your money as quickly as you can. And yet, Balinese peaceful ways of life and worship endure.

CEREMONY & CELEBRATION: BALI'S PEOPLE & CULTURE
RELIGION

Over 90% of the population is **Hindu,** with the minority made up of Muslims, Buddhists, and Christians. Religious ritual plays into every facet of life.

Balinese Hindus believe in the ascending (and confusing) pantheon of Hindu gods, as well as dharma and adharma, order and disorder, and the need for balance between the two and rituals to that end. The importance of karma, or the consequence of individual actions, plays into the peaceful daily rhythms, and forms of "making merit" are as many as the people who practice them. Whether placing daily offerings of flowers on someone's car or enduring rigorous mountaintop pilgrimages, Balinese believe that, to achieve harmony, the forces of good must be saluted with offerings, while the forces of evil must be appeased.

With an estimated 20,000 temples and shrines, Bali is known as the "Island of the Gods," and every village has at least one temple with buildings dedicated to Vishnu, Brahma, and Shiva (the Creator, the Preserver, and the Destroyer).

CELEBRATIONS

Tooth filing is a rite of maturation, wherein the sharp front teeth, especially the canines, are filed down smooth (the idea being to differentiate humans from the animals). This can happen at any age, even after death, but is most often done to adolescents, who by that age have already been through the nearly dozen rituals that marked their first few days on the planet.

Weddings in Bali are unique, colorful affairs not to be missed, and surprisingly festive are **cremations.** Burning the body is the only way a soul can be freed of its earthly self and travel to its next incarnation (or to enlightenment), and death is a joyous occasion in Bali, full of floats and fanfare. Complicated towers (the higher the caste, the higher the tower) hold the body, carried aloft by cheering men who turn the tower in circles to send the spirit to heaven as they carry it to the burning ground. It's an extraordinary and wonderful event; there are even tours that will take you, or ask at any *losmen* (hostel) or at your hotel's front desk.

Compared to Western churchgoing, celebrations in Bali are very casual: Women gossip, children play, and dogs wander temple grounds freely, snacking on offerings. A priest chants, people pray and then get up, and others take their places. Ask before taking photos, and stay on your best behavior. Balinese are generally most welcoming and might even invite you for food or drinks.

MUSIC & DANCE

The sounds of the **gamelan**—the bright-sounding metal percussion ensembles that accompany just about every celebration and ceremony here—will first turn your head. Music is everywhere in Bali, from the raucous *dangdut*, or Indonesian pop pouring from restaurants and shops, as well as folk and the refined classical music that accompanies the many staged dance performances and temple worship.

If you have a chance, don't miss a performance of tradition dance, most commonly the **legong** and **barong dances,** intricate ballets that present scenes from the epic *Mahabarata* or *Ramayana*. It's a colorful, fun experience that you can see in most major hotels or in Ubud at the **Palace**—or, if you're lucky, you'll find a real, nontourist performance in outlying villages.

Wayang Kulit, or **shadow puppet plays,** are famed in Bali. Puppeteers use intricately cut leather figures to project images against a screen, again depicting tales from one of the Hindu epics with accompaniment by voice (often injecting news, gossip, and even crude jokes) and a small gamelan ensemble.

The other major example of "traditional" music is the **kecak,** a very dramatic and visual a cappella piece featuring as many as 100 men depicting a saga of a monkey king and his warriors.

ARTS & CRAFTS

Decoration and craft are as seamlessly woven into the fabric of life in Bali as are dance, music, and ritual. Fine carving and craftwork can be found adorning the most humble dwelling. Craftsmen are highly revered, and skilled wood and stone carvers turn out authentic works in street-side studios all over the island (concentrated in Ubud). Visitors are sure to walk away with some beautiful, original finds in wood and stone.

Masks used in traditional performance, many of the bug-eyed demoness Rangda, make fine souvenirs (but *beware:* tradition has it that even tourist copies can be inhabited). There's a lot of mass-produced clutter, and lots of these works have been "aged" by an artful banging around on the sidewalk; authentic antiques are rare, so be cynical of claims of authenticity—but the copies are quite good, though.

Ancient stylized **paintings** of deities and the delicately carved "lontar" palm frond books are both still produced on the island. Expatriates have had as much influence on modern Balinese art as the ancients. As guiding patrons, men such as **Rudolf Bonnet,** a Dutchman, and **Walter Spies,** whose home on the site of the Tjampuhan Hotel in Ubud became central to the arts in expat Mecca, influenced the local painters, opened societies, and brought the glory of Bali to the world at large. With a little searching, you can find some real masterpieces here.

LANGUAGE

The Balinese speak both Indonesian and Balinese—the former when out in public, the latter at home. Aside from the tendency toward seemingly jaw-breaking polysyllabic phrases, Indonesian is not that hard to learn—pronunciation is pretty straightforward, and spelling is mostly phonetic. Balinese is much more complicated, not least because there are actually three levels of it—high, middle, and low—used depending on the class and authority of the person to whom you are speaking.

English is spoken widely, and if you've learned a few words of Malay, you can give them a try here; the languages are quite similar.

2 Planning Your Trip to Bali

VISITOR INFORMATION

Many **Information Centers** are operated by the Department of Tourism: at **Ngurah Rai International Airport** (© **361/751011**); in **Ubud** at the crossroad of Monkey Forest Road and Jalan Raya Ubud; in **Kuta** at Jalan Benasari 36B, Legian (© **361/754090**); in **Denpasar** at Jalan Parman Niti Mandala (© **362/222387**); and in **Singaraja** at Jalan Veteran 23 (© **361/225141**). Better still is the efficient **Badung Government Tourist Office** in Kuta, Jalan Raya Kuta no. 2 (© **361/756176**).

Some good online sources include **Bali Paradise Online** (www.bali-paradise.com), **Bali Online** (www.indo.com), and **Bali Guide** (www.baliguide.com). **Bali Echo** (www.baliecho.com) is an informative art and culture magazine.

ENTRY REQUIREMENTS

Visitors from the U.S., Australia, and most of Europe, New Zealand, and Canada do not need visas. Sixty-day stamps are available on entry through Ngurah Rai Airport or the seaports of Padang Bai and Benoa. For stays of longer than 60 days, a tourist or business visa must be arranged *before* coming to Indonesia. Tourist visas are valid only for 4 weeks and cannot be extended; business visas can be extended for 6 months at Indonesian immigration offices.

⌒ Warning Health Concerns

No inoculations are required, but it's always a good idea to get shots for hepatitis A, tetanus, polio, and typhoid (ideally, you've already had some of these). You might consult your doctor or the CDC website (www.state.gov) if anything further is currently suggested. **Malaria** is a concern only if you plan to be out in remote villages near rice paddies after dark; it is not a concern in the tourist areas of Bali (indeed, the CDC has declared it malaria-free). The anxious can take malaria pills, but be aware that the prevention is sometimes almost as bad as the disease. You probably should not pet strange dogs—there are many stray dogs in Bali, and nearly all of them have some kind of mange, or possibly rabies.

You can't drink the water on Bali, but bottled water is cheap and readily available. Just about every hotel will supply you with a couple bottles or a jug of boiled water—to be extra cautious, use it to brush your teeth as well. Restaurants in tourist areas are used to supplying safe water, complete with ice made from boiled water, but if you want to be extra safe, ask for no ice and *air minum* (drinking water). Salads, too, are generally safe in tourist areas. As always, you can help avoid "Bali belly" (the Indonesian version of Montezuma's Revenge) by sticking to foods that have been peeled or well cooked. When in doubt, you can also get meat-free dishes.

⌐Tips Remember the Departure Tax

When you leave Bali, there will be an **airport departure tax** of Rp50,000 (about US$5).

CUSTOMS REGULATIONS

Customs allows you to bring in, duty-free, 200 cigarettes or 50 cigars and 2 pounds of tobacco; cameras and film; 2 liters of alcohol; and perfume clearly intended for personal use. Forbidden are guns, weapons, narcotics, pornography (leave it at home if you're unsure how it's defined), and printed matter with Chinese characters. Plants and fresh fruit might also be confiscated.

MONEY

The currency of Indonesia is the **rupiah,** from the Sanskrit word for wrought silver, *rupya.* Coins are available in denominations of Rp25, 50, 100, and even occasionally 5 and 10. Notes are Rp100, 500, 1,000, 5,000, 10,000, 20,000, 50,000, and 100,000.

   The following bills are no longer in circulation: the 1992 pink Rp10,000, the 1992 greenish Rp20,000 bill, and the blue Rp50,000 with ex-president Suharto's picture.

CURRENCY EXCHANGE & RATES   Rate of exchange has been marked by gross devaluation in recent years. The official exchange rate is 10,377 Indonesian rupiahs per US dollar.

   Most major hotels offer **exchange services** but offer less than favorable rates. Storefront exchange services line most streets and offer the best exchange, but it's important to be careful of scams such as counterfeit bills and damaged currency that won't be accepted anywhere. Ask first about commission, and be sure to count your bills before walking away. State-sponsored locations of **Wartel Telecommunications Service** are perhaps your best bet here.

   ATMs are becoming more common—there is at least one in most major tourist areas—and often give you a much better exchange rate. The same is true for **credit cards,** but their use is still mostly limited to the major hotels, restaurants, and shops.

WHEN TO GO

PEAK SEASON   The high tourist season is July and August, along with the weeks surrounding Christmas and New Year's, when prices are higher and tourist traffic is considerably increased. Try to avoid these times, as well as February and March (given the increased heat and humidity).

CLIMATE   Bali is just below the equator (so days are a consistent 12 hr.), and the temperatures always hover in the 80s Fahrenheit (upper 20s to low 30s Celsius). The rainy season lasts from October to April; rain usually comes in short, violent bursts that last an hour or so, and the humidity is at its crushing worst during this period. The hottest months are February, March, and April; remember that it gets a bit nippy at night up in the mountains, but a light sweater will certainly be enough.

PUBLIC HOLIDAYS   Public holidays are New Year's Day (Jan 1), Idul Fitri (celebration of the end of Ramadan, in late Feb), Nyepi (a major purification ritual and a time when Balinese are supposed to sit at home, silent, in late Mar), Good Friday and Easter Sunday (late Mar/early Apr), Muslim New Year (mid-May), Indonesia Independence Day (Aug 17), Ascension Day of Mohammed (early Dec), and Christmas (Dec 25).

GETTING THERE
BY PLANE
FROM THE U.S. & CANADA   Most visitors make a connection with Singapore, Bangkok, Taipei, or Japan via **China Air, Eva Air,** and **Garuda Indonesia** or **Singapore Air.** Check with travel agents for special deals; package rates, some with overnight connections through Bangkok, are affordable.

FROM THE U.K.   Bali is served from Europe by **Cathay Pacific** via Hong Kong; tickets can be purchased from **British Air, Singapore Air,** or **Air France.**

FROM AUSTRALIA & NEW ZEALAND   Flights from Australia and New Zealand can be booked through **Qantas** (www.qantas.com.au).

GETTING TO YOUR DESTINATION FROM THE AIRPORT
Ngurah Rai, Bali's airport, is considered part of Denpasar, but it's really 13km (8 miles) to the southwest. Few travelers stop in Denpasar; most connect directly with their destination of choice on the island.

With no public transport from the airport, most tourists either prearrange pick-up by their hotel (the rate is comparable to the official rates at the airport) or buy a ticket at the **official taxi counter** just outside of Customs and arrange a fixed rate ride to their destination. Avoid the temptation to go with unofficial cabs; you might get caught in a taxi scam that will leave you frustrated and likely overcharged and in the wrong place.

GETTING AROUND
BY CAR   Self-drive rentals are available but not advisable; roads are not clearly marked—if marked at all—and traffic is chaos. Given how cheap and easy it is to get a tourist shuttle to most of the areas, or to hire someone to drive you, it's best to avoid the headache. If you do decide to drive, remember that you will need an international driver's license or a locally issued tourist driving license. Traffic is on the left side, and it's "third-world rules" on the road, the more aggressively honking, larger vehicle goes first.

BY MOTORBIKE   Motorbikes are even more dangerous than cars. You will see your share of crashes. This is a nice way to see the island, though, and if you choose to ride, it's safer and more beautiful in remote areas. The same driving license requirements for cars apply to motorbikes and scooters.

Tips How to Obtain a Tourist Driver's License

If you don't come armed with an international driver's license, you'll need to get a tourist driver's license to rent cars and motorbikes. Contact the **Foreign License Service** (© **361/243-939**) at Jalan Agung Tresna no. 14 in Renon. Head to the service window for foreigners in the Pelayanan Samsat building, BPKB Section. To apply, you'll need photocopies of the photo and I.D. pages of your passport and the visa page, if applicable, plus Rp75,000 (US$7.30) in cash. The office is open Monday to Thursday and Saturday from 8:30am to 2:30pm, and Friday from 8:30am to 1pm. (Caught without a license, you'll need to bribe a few dollars or pay a fine.)

Tips A Note on Addresses & Phone Numbers

Street addresses can be as vague as "on the main street." Don't worry: Most places are easy to find. As for phone numbers, if no phone number is listed for an establishment, chances are good that there's no phone.

BY PUBLIC TRANSPORTATION   Blue and brown vans called *bemos* operate as buses in Bali. They have regular routes, but these aren't really written down. Just ask someone which bus and where to catch it. Prices are also similarly secretive, so ask around about how much the ride really should cost. Bemos are better for short hops (around town, for example) than long distances; metered taxis, if you can find them, are your best bet. Be sure that the driver turns on his meter (you might have to insist more than once).

BY PRIVATE TRANSPORTATION   There are two solid options for traveling around Bali, and both work quite well. Regular **tourist shuttles** run between all the major locales. These are reliable and cheap, and you can book them through a tourist office or your hotel. Also, many stores have signs advertising shuttle service.

BY BOAT   Several companies offer sometimes overlapping and competing service by sea to the nearby islands of Nusa Penida and Nusa Lembongan, and to Lombok. **Bounty Cruises** (© 361/733-3333) has daily hydrofoil service leaving at 9am from Bali's Benoa Harbor to Nusa Lembongan (30 min.; US$25), that continues on to Lombok's Sengiggi Beach (add 2½ hrs.; US$35) before arriving at Gili Meno (add 30 min.; US$40), one of the three islands in the small island group offshore of Lombok. Other popular operators include **Bali Hai Cruises** (© 361/720331), with day trips to Lembongan and Lombok; **Sail Sensations** (© 361/725864), with day sailing; and, for a luxury alternative, **Wakalouka** (© 361/484085), which transports you in style to its exclusive property on Nusa Lembongan. Most of these offer a **dinner sunset cruise** or **day trips** that make great outings.

TOUR GUIDES   Transport guides line the streets of all major towns and, often too eagerly, offer to arrange your itinerary. Be clear about the price, and be sure to write down your destination to avoid confusion. Even better, for about Rp1,000,000 (US$100), hire a private tour guide with a car and driver. It's an expensive option, but a guide can provide good insight into history and culture.

ACCOMMODATIONS

Bali hotels range from bungalows at Rp50,000 (US$5) a night (or less) to villas with your own retinue of servants for Rp9,300,000 (US$900). In the middle are an ever-increasing number of traditional bungalows that can only be described as sublime. Atmosphere is the rule here, and those who forgo Western chain-hotel comfort to stay in a **losmen** (traditional home stay) or find their own **rustic bungalow** (all more or less "roughin' it") often come away from Bali with fond memories of the tranquility of this island and the beauty of Balinese hospitality. That said, Bali's resorts and fine Western hotels cost a fraction of what luxury accommodation would elsewhere, and many come to enjoy the upgrade.

A NOTE ON PRICES   Promotional and Internet rates are available at all hotels in Bali. Paying the rack rate, or published rate, even in high season, is almost unheard of. Especially in the off season, it pays to shop around, and you can show up at the front desk of even the largest hotels and ask for the best rate. At the time of publication, Bali was struggling to recoup its losses after the tragic events of October 2002, and many hotels were practically giving away rooms to encourage tourists to come and to keep their doors open.

Important: Almost all the hotels charge a 21% government tax and service charge on top of the quoted rates. Some hotels tack on a charge in high season (the 2 or 3 weeks around Christmas and New Year's, and in July and Aug).

RESTAURANTS & DINING

The choices in Bali are many, but it's rare to find authentic Balinese or Indonesian on a menu for foreigners; for that, you'll have to go to a *warung,* a local cafe, and many visitors are dissuaded by the typical warung's run-down appearance. Most visitors surrender to the call of high-quality international spots sprouting up all over the island. Outside the more posh hotels, dining is affordable and varied, with great options for vegetarians. Caution should always be exercised about food consumption, and greater care is taken in all the tourist areas. Don't be put off by appearances: The food in warungs is authentic, good, and cheap.

Indonesian dishes that you are most likely to encounter include *nasi goreng* (fried rice, usually topped with an egg), *mie goreng* (fried noodles), *nasi campur* (a plate of boiled rice with sides of meat and veggies and a house specialty), *ayam goreng* (fried chicken), *gado gado* (salad with peanut sauce, served hot or cold), and *satay* (small chunks of meat on skewers served with peanut sauce). Padang food (sold in little cafes called *rumah makan* Padang) is spicy tidbits of fried fish, chicken, or veggies on a buffet; you pick what you want.

SHOPPING

The sheer quantity of arts and crafts available for purchase in Bali is overwhelming. There's something for all budgets, from tourist trinkets to fine art and antiques. It's a shopper's paradise of fabrics, clothing, wood and stone carvings, paintings, and doodads of varying quality. You get what you pay for generally—but with a bit of haggling, can get a lot more for what you pay. Shop around; the same item gets cheaper the more you look at it, and it's really the same stuff everywhere. Ask the price, offer half, smile, and go from there. Even at inflated prices, you'll still come out ahead of the game.

The real name of the buying game in Bali, in terms of quality for value, is to commission something. This can be anything from a wood carving to a garment. The latter doesn't take as long, but in either case, you must bring plenty of drawings or photos so that the creator will have a good blueprint to go by.

Tips On Shopping

Many of the big names in **sporting goods** crank out merchandise manufactured in Indonesia, translating to lower prices if you know where to look. There's a Nike shop in Kuta Square (see "Shopping," under "Kuta," later in this chapter), and Athletes Foot locations on Jalan Melasti in Legian and in the Galleria shopping center (see "Shopping," under "Nusa Dua," later in this chapter).

Telephone Dialing Info at a Glance

- **To place a call from your home country to Bali,** dial the international access code (011 in the U.S., 0011 in Australia, 0170 in New Zealand, and 00 in the U.K.), plus Indonesia's country code (62), plus the area code (361 for Kuta, Jimbaran, Nusa Dua, Sanur, and Ubud; 362 for Lovina; 363 for Candi Dasa; and 370 for Lombok), followed by the six-digit phone number (for example, from the U.S. to Lovina, you'd dial 011 + 62 + 362 + 000000).

- **To place a call within Indonesia,** you must use area codes if calling between states. Note that, for calls within the country, area codes are all preceded by a 0 (Lovina is 0362, Candi Dasa is 0363, Lombok is 0370, and so on).

- **To place a direct international call from Indonesia,** dial the international access code (001), plus the country code of the place you are dialing, plus the area code, plus the residential number of the other party.

- To reach the international operator, dial 102.

- **International country codes** are as follows: Australia 61, Burma 95, Cambodia 855, Canada 1, Hong Kong 852, Laos 856, Malaysia 60, New Zealand 64, the Philippines 63, Singapore 65, Thailand 66, U.K. 44, U.S. 1, Vietnam 84.

FAST FACTS: Bali

American Express There is a branch c/o Pacto Travel Agency in the Bali Beach Hotel in Sanur (© **361/288449**), and in Panin Bank at Jalan Legian 80X, Kuta (© **361/751058**).

Business Hours Most places keep "daylight hours," which on the equator pretty much means 6am to 6pm (or a little later).

Doctors & Dentists Ask your hotel for a referral—many have a doctor on call. In Kuta, try the **Bali International Medical Centre,** Jalan Bypass Ngurah Rai no. 100X (© **361/761263**). It's open daily from 8am to midnight and sometimes will send someone to your hotel. There is a general hospital in Denpasar, but for any serious problems, go home as soon as possible for treatment. For dentists, ask your hotel for a referral.

Drug Laws Though you might be offered hash and marijuana at every turn, Indonesia officially takes drug offenses very seriously. You run the risk of getting busted readily (because, as a tourist, they rather assume that you are using drugs) and languishing in jail for 9 or more years.

Electricity Currents can be either 110 volts (50 AC); or 220 to 240 volts (50 AC).

Embassies/Consulates **United States:** Jalan Hayam Wuruk no. 188, Denpasar (© **361/233605**). **Australia (Canada, New Zealand,** and **Great Britain** also have their representatives here):** Jalan Prof. Moch, Yamin 51, Denpasar

(© **361/235092**). Or, in Jakarta: **Canada:** Wisma Metropolitan I, 5th floor, Jalan Jen. Sudirman, Kav. 29, Jakarta (© **021/510709**). **Great Britain:** Jalan Thamrin 75, Jakarta (© **021/330904**).

Emergencies The number for the police is 110, ambulance is 118, and fire is 113.

Hospitals There is a main hospital in Denpasar, but for any serious ailment, evacuate to Hong Kong, Singapore, Kuala Lumpur, or Bangkok.

Internet/E-mail Internet cafes are springing up all over Bali, but the connections can still be painfully slow. Many hotels also will let you use their Internet connection to read e-mail.

Language The Balinese speak both Indonesian and Balinese—the former when out in public, the latter at home. English is widely spoken throughout Bali, particularly in the major tourist areas. While not everyone is fluent, most of the people you will be dealing with will speak enough English that you can communicate with them. (For more information, see "Language," earlier in this chapter.)

Liquor Laws You won't find liquor in any Muslim restaurant, but you will find it otherwise readily available throughout Bali, particularly the potent rice spirit *arak* and, of course, Bali Hai beer.

Police The phone number for the police is **110**.

Post Office/Mail Your hotel can send mail for you, or you can go to the post office in Denpasar, at Jalan Raya Puputan Renon (© **361/223568**). Other branches are in Kuta, Ubud, and Sanur. For big items, there are packing and shipping services in all major tourist areas.

Safety/Crime Bali is by and large a safe place to be, even after dark. Violent crime is rare. However, pickpockets are not, so you should exercise considerable caution by using a money belt, particularly in crowded tourist areas, and be careful not to flash large wads of cash. If you find yourself in need of assistance, contact the **Guardian Angels Tourist Police** (there are 265 of these angels dressed in blue) at © **361/763753** 24 hours a day.

Many hotels offer safety deposit boxes, and it is best to keep extra cash and other valuables in them. If nothing else, make sure your suitcase has a good lock on it. Even the best hotel can't always guarantee security for valuables left lying in plain sight.

Telephones Because many hotels charge a great deal even for using your calling card, you are better off using **Wartel's** privately owned public phones. There's one in every tourist center, though some work better than others. Some also have Internet services.

Time Bali is on Greenwich Mean Time plus 8 hours, except during daylight saving time, which it does not observe. That's 13 hours ahead of Eastern Standard Time in the U.S. and 16 hours ahead of Pacific Standard Time.

Tipping Tipping is not required and not even encouraged. Most restaurants include a service charge. Leave a small tip if you feel the need; more often than not, the recipient will be surprised.

Toilets Western-style toilets with seats are becoming more common than the Asian squat variety, though cheap losmen/home stays and some less touristic public places still have the latter. Always carry some toilet paper with you, or you might have to use your hand (the left one only, please) and the dip bucket available.

Water Avoid tap water in Bali unless properly boiled. Bottled water is available everywhere, and restaurants in tourist areas seem to use it as a matter of course, but you should always ask to be sure.

3 Kuta

A quick 10 minutes from the airport, you'll be in Kuta, Bali's most developed area, a popular spot for budget travelers and a longtime favorite for weekend vacationers from nearby Australian. It's also where Abu Sayef chose to attack the island on the night of October 12, 2002, so a somber pall still hangs over the town center.

Kuta is made up of narrow streets and alleys, and pedestrians share space with honking, mufflerless cars and motorbikes. You'll be harried by some of the most aggressive touts on the island, and the beaches are crowded and popular for toe-nail painting and massage in a scene reminiscent of the touristy beaches of Thailand. Unfortunately, the current makes swimming difficult and dangerous. The tourist rush means some of the best nightlife and dining on the island, though.

The best compromise of all, short of staying elsewhere on the island, is to hit the beaches just north of Kuta at Legian and Samniyak, which are actually quite nice and quiet.

GETTING THERE
Kuta is near the airport, and most hotels offer free airport pickup. Taxis for hire at the airport are best at the **official taxi counter,** where you'll pay a set fare.

GETTING AROUND
Kuta is a big rectangle. The two main north-south streets are oceanside Jalan Pantai Kuta and Jalan Legian, and are connected east-west by Jalan Benesari, Poppies Gang I, and many quaint alleys. You can easily **walk** all of this or take the reasonably priced blue and yellow **metered taxis.**

FAST FACTS: Kuta

Banks/Currency Exchange There is an ATM in the Kuta Square shopping mall (about halfway down on the left). Wartel outlets are found all around the main streets.

Internet/E-mail Internet cafes almost outnumber transport guides in Kuta and charge between Rp10,000 and Rp37,000 (US$1–US$3) per hour for reliable connection.

Post Office/Mail There is a main post office, but it's not conveniently located. There are also some postal agents, and your hotel can send mail for you.

Telephones The area code in Kuta is 361.

WHERE TO STAY

Kuta Beach, while still a booming resort, is quite noisy and busy really. We've listed the better choices in town and at nearby Legian and Seminyak to the north.

KUTA BEACH

Bounty Hotel ★★   The Bounty is clearly a party-down hotel, but at least one that feels like it is in Bali. The rooms are decidedly Western (with familiar comforts like hair dryers), but they have traditional wood floors and are decorated with Balinese fabric. Standard rooms are slightly smaller than deluxe, with the wash basin in the room. The complex, arranged around an attractive pool, features stone carvings and red tile ornamentation. The hotel (always a good place to grab a cab) is positioned equal walking distance between the beach and the shopping on Legian, and the same people own the **Bounty Bar & Restaurant,** a happening late-night spot. That fact and the fliers advertising various party spots give you an idea of the clientele.

Poppies Gang II, Jalan Segara Batu Bolong no. 18, Kuta, Bali. (*) **361/753030.** Fax 361/752121. 166 units. US$50–$60 double; US$95 deluxe. AE, DC, MV, V. **Amenities:** 2 restaurants; bar; 2 outdoor swimming pools; car rental; laundry; dry cleaning. *In room:* A/C, TV, minibar, fridge, IDD phone.

Hard Rock Hotel ★★   It's a bit much really, the Hard Rock Cafe's world domination, but you'll be disarmed by this hotel's fanciful design that, though entirely un-Balinese, is so much fun that you'll forget to care. The lobby is typical Hard Rock Cafe, lined with once-used guitars and gold records, and the decor throughout is bright with corridors done in varying rock themes. Rooms are light and airy, with photos of artists, and bathrooms are done in playful geometrics. The pool is the largest in Bali with slides and its own beach. There's an outdoor living room, an in-house radio station, and a recording studio where you can live out your own musician fantasies. Sure, rock blares 24/7 in the lobby, which has a popular bar, and in other public areas, but the fabulous kids' playroom—"Little Rock"—and that pool make it a great option for boomer families. You might forget that you're in Bali, but it's all good fun.

Jalan Pantai, Banjar Pande Mas, Kuta, Bali. (*) **361/761869.** Fax 361/761868. hardrockbali@bali-tourist.com. 418 units. US$170–US$180 double; US$350–US$550 suite. AE, DC, MC, V. **Amenities:** 3 restaurants; 3 bars; outdoor pool (w/swim-up bar); health club; spa, kids' club; concierge (can arrange rentals and tours); business center; shopping; salon; 24-hr. room service; massage; laundry; dry cleaning; meeting rooms; Internet service; rock and roll library. *In room:* A/C, satellite TV (on-demand movies), dataport, minibar, fridge, safe, IDD phone (specials such as video games and in-room Internet available upon request).

Hotel Restu Bali ★   Technically, this is in Legian, but it's on Kuta's main shopping drag of Jalan Raya, which means that you often end up wandering by here. It's about a 10-minute walk to the beach but is right in the middle of nighttime action. The hotel is a long, narrow rabbit's warren of different tropical nooks and crannies, and, for all the hustle and bustle outside, it's unbelievably serene. Standard rooms have wicker furniture and stark but nice baths. The Puri Deluxe are bungalow style, with thatched roofs and woven mats covering the walls and private patios. Bathrooms are the same, but the sink is in the room. Two very nice swimming pools spill into gurgling fountain pools that trickle all hours and can be heard from some rooms, a noise that's either soothing or distracting.

Jalan Raya Legian no. 113, Kuta, Bali. (*) **361/751251.** Fax 361/751252. restubali@denpasar.wasantara. net.id. 41 units. US$40–US$55 double (w/breakfast). AE, MC, V. **Amenities:** Restaurant; bar; 2 outdoor pools; Jacuzzi; 24-hr. room service; laundry; Internet service. *In room:* A/C, satellite TV, minibar (deluxe only), fridge, IDD phone.

Natour Kuta ✫   This is the only hotel in Kuta that is right on the beach—and at a spot on the beach that, while still not good for swimming, is nice for dipping up to your knees. Next to Kuta Square, this is the most convenient spot for downtown shopping. Pleasant also is the butterfly-shape pool, a nice beachside spot for viewing the sunset. All this means that you won't be spending too much time in the unimaginatively decorated long and narrow rooms—though try to get a third-floor standard, which has an ocean view. Skip the more costly bungalows in back, which provide little more than privacy or romance (even the bathrooms are the same size as in the standard room). The beach access and pool make this a good choice for families. Culture shows are held poolside in the evenings.

Jalan Pantai Kuta no. 1, Kuta, Bali. ✆ **361/751361.** Fax 361/751362 or 361/753-958. nkbh@denpasar. wasantara.net.id. 137 units. US$92–US$160 double; US$175–US$350 suites (seasonal rates available). AE, DC, MC, V. **Amenities:** Restaurant; 2 bars; outdoor pool; rentals; tour desk; shopping; salon; 24-hr. room service; laundry; dry cleaning; meeting rooms. *In room:* A/C, TV, IDD phone.

Poppies II Cottages ✫✫   This is by far the best midrange hotel in Kuta, with atmospheric thatched cottages set among gorgeous gardens abloom with a riot of bougainvillea. The small swimming pool, designed to look like a natural pond, is perhaps the prettiest in town and is surrounded by many nooks for lounging. The rooms, truth be told, aren't that special (despite a recent upgrade), but the open-air bathrooms are in marble, complete with small sunken tubs. An interesting touch is the Internet Cottage, where homesick guests can have their own e-mail address and website while in residence. The original Poppies Cottages, a short distance away, are less of a bargain and more drab but are comparable (and have a nice pool).

Poppies Lane I, Kuta, Bali. ✆ **361/751059.** Fax 361/752364. info@bali.poppies.net. 21 units (4 additional units at the older Poppies II). US$102 double (seasonal rates available). AE, DC, MC, V. **Amenities:** Restaurant; bar; outdoor pool; business center; shopping; room service; laundry; Internet service. *In room:* A/C, TV, IDD phone.

LEGIAN

Padma Hotel ✫   This sprawling complex has plenty of activities that make it attractive for families. Others might find it a bit out of the way from the heart of Kuta action (though there are shops and touts aplenty just outside the gate). Rooms have slightly better than average Bali furniture. Standard rooms, in a four-story high-rise, have a balcony, but only deluxe rooms have good views. Family rooms open onto a patio and central garden, but all baths are the same. The pool is large, and there is a nice grassy spot between the pool and the beach (no touts, and quiet). The beach here is still unswimmable. Many culturally geared activities, such as egg painting and instrument demonstrations, are offered, and the place is sufficiently self-contained and good for families.

Jalan Padma no. 1, Legian, Bali. ✆ **361/752-111.** Fax 361/752-140. 403 units. US$160 double; US$180 chalet; US$220–US$1,500 suite. AE, DC, MC, V. **Amenities:** 7 restaurants; 3 bars; outdoor pool; golf (nearby); game area w/Internet and PlayStation; tour desk; car rental; 24-hr. room service; babysitting; laundry. *In room:* A/C, satellite TV, minibar, fridge, safe, IDD phone.

Puri Tantra Bungalows ✫✫   Hidden behind a mahogany door connecting to a garden off the beach at Legian, this is one of the area's most intimate and peaceful choices. The six individual bungalows line a garden path that makes its way through the Yudana family's backyard, and if your luck holds out, you might find yourself romping with their big, fluffy dogs. The cottages consist of a main room and a dressing alcove, simple but sufficient. Outdoor bathrooms have sunken tubs in an interesting shell tile. Traditional gilded Balinese portals open onto a terrace or patio, some with bamboo furniture, or you can grab one of the garden lounges and relax on the lawn.

Jalan Padma Utara 50X, Legian, Bali (2km/1¼ miles W of Kuta). ℭ and fax **361/753195**. 6 units, all w/bathroom. US$40 bungalow. No credit cards. **Amenities:** Tour services and information; library. *In room:* kitchen area, fridge, safe, fan.

SEMINYAK

Legian ★★   This resort is a true Indonesian boutique. In fierce competition with Oberoi (below), it's actually amazing what wonderful things they can do with inlaid shell, coconut wood, and bamboo fibers. All rooms are suites, enormous and luxe, with terraces facing the sea and outdoor day beds that are almost too pretty to muss up. The building, though reminiscent of a pagoda, is concrete and a bit bland, but with the lawns and the pool facing the beach, it's easy to see how the planners justified sinking all of their investment into the rooms. Bikes are free to guests, solving the transportation problem for those with the lungs.

Jalan Laksmana, Seminyak, Kuta, Bali 80361. ℭ 361/730622. Fax 361/730623. 70 units. US$325–US$1,000 suite. AE, DC, MC, V. **Amenities:** Restaurant; 2 bars; 2-tiered pool; extensive spa; rentals available; tour desk; shopping; massage; laundry; dry cleaning; meeting rooms. *In room:* A/C, satellite TV (in-house movies), minibar, fridge, hair dryer, safe, tea and coffee.

Oberoi ★★   The first hotel in Seminyak and one of the leading hotels of the world, the Oberoi has attracted the likes of Henry Kissinger, Julia Roberts, and the British musician Donovan. The property is composed of individual *lanais*—native bungalows of coral stone with wood beams and thatch roofs. Rooms are somewhat bland, but the amenities are first class all the way: futon beds, glass and marble in the outdoor pools, sunken tubs, and goodies like slippers, robes, and flip-flops for the beach. Nine villas have their own private pool. Sadly, the beachfront grounds and poolside area are looking a little weatherworn. There's a mini outdoor amphitheater for the schedule of traditional dances.

Jalan Laksmana, Seminyak, Kuta, Bali 80361. ℭ **361/730361.** Fax 361/730791. www.oberoihotels.com. 75 units, all w/bathroom. US$240–US$700 garden-view cottage or villa; US$290–$800 ocean view. AE, DC, MC, V. **Amenities:** Restaurant; bar; outdoor pool; tennis court; fitness center; spa; sauna; tour desk; car rental; 24-hr. room service; massage; laundry; dry cleaning. *In room:* A/C, satellite TV (in-house movies), minibar, fridge, hair dryer, IDD phone.

Vila Lumbung Hotel ★   Vila Lumbung is a landscaped tropical garden with two- and three-story grass-roof villas designed in the manner of the Balinese lumbung—a building traditionally used for storing rice (a kind of upscale barn). Two-story bungalows consist of upstairs and downstairs units, offering a choice of either a private terrace or a balcony. Furniture is of coconut wood and teak, and the cool tile terrazzo floors are refreshing on your feet. The only potential drawback of the property is that it lies on the opposite side of the road from the sea, but the tiered pool—with a waterfall, cave, and bubble pool—is an oasis in itself.

Jalan Raya Petitenget no. 100X, Kuta, Bali. ℭ **361/-482220.** Fax 361/489970. www.HotelLumbung.com. 20 units. US$125–US$155 bungalow; US$355 deluxe villa (includes breakfast). MC, V. **Amenities:** Restaurant; 2 bars; outdoor pool; tour desk; rentals available; shopping; 24-hr. room service; laundry. *In room:* A/C, satellite TV, fridge, minibar, safe, IDD phone.

WHERE TO DINE

The international variety in Kuta is a result of homesick tourists; unfortunately, this translates into a variety of bad and mediocre copies of Western fare, but there *are* a couple of standouts, listed below. Besides these, if you absolutely must, there is always the **Hard Rock Cafe,** with its standard burgers and loud music.

KUTA BEACH

Kori Restaurant and Bar ✿✿ EUROPEAN/STEAKHOUSE   Valet parking in the narrow and chaotic Poppies Gang II? Finery uncharacteristic of Bali abounds at this chic dining venue. Choose to sit in the dining room, replete with linen and silver finery, or on one of the more romantic cushioned bamboo platforms that bridge the narrow garden oasis. The lunch menu is light, featuring dishes like *malai köfte,* spicy vegetarian fritters in a curry sauce, or the mouth-burning Bali chile burger (if you dare). The dinner menu has all the bells and whistles of a Western steakhouse. Try the mixed grill of U.S. beef loin, spare ribs, pork cutlet, and Nuerberger sausages, or order up the Singapore chile crab, savory and spicy fresh black Bali crabs served with a big ol'e bib. Topping the high end of the menu is the giant seafood grill, cooked and served on a hot lava stone. To finish off, there's a respectable stock of brandy and cognac.

Poppies Gang II, Kuta. ✆ 361/758-605. Main courses Rp30,000–Rp140,000 (US$3–US$14). AE, DC, MC, V. Daily 11:30am–11pm.

Made's Warung ✿ INDONESIAN   This is a long-time Kuta standby: a reliable, bustling, confusing open-air warung on a noisy street, whose popularity means possibly sharing a table. *Gado gado,* satay, and curries are all recommended, and the price is right (low). Fun surprises on the menu include bagel and smoked marlin, tofu burgers, Caesar salad, and Vegemite for an Aussie breakfast. Beverage choices range from iced coffee drinks to some very potent booze (be warned). There's another location in Seminyak.

Br. Pando Mas, Kuta. ✆ 316/755-297. Main courses Rp12,000–Rp30,000 (US$1.20–US$3). AE, MC, V. Daily 8am–midnight.

Mini Restaurant & Bar ✿✿ SEAFOOD   One of two restaurants right next to each other that serve fresh fish out of a tank, this is the larger of the two. At this cavernous, thatched-roof restaurant, you choose your fish from the tank and have it prepared as you like. A whole snapper runs about Rp62,000 (US$6) and easily serves two. Shellfish—enormous prawns and lobster—are delicious but come with a price tag. All dishes come with choice of sauce: butter garlic, sweet and sour, or soya. The menu offers many, many cocktails and some appealing frothy drinks. They do *babi guleng* combinations (with advance order) and also offer local, Chinese, and European dishes and even frog's legs.

Legian St., Kuta. ✆ 361/751651. Reservations not accepted. Main courses Rp15,000–Rp40,000 (US$1.45–US$3.85) (seafood by weight somewhat pricier). AE, MC, V. Daily 11am–11pm (bar open late).

Poppies Restaurant ✿ INDONESIAN/EUROPEAN   Poppies has a 25-year tradition of serving Indonesian and international specials on the busy beach. It's the place for your "Western" fix on the island and certainly is the prettiest restaurant in town: a garden setting with crawling vines overhead that keep the hot sun at bay, and babbling pools and waterfalls. Indonesian dishes include an outstanding *ikan pepes*—mashed fish cooked in a banana leaf with fine spices and very spicy local "pickles" (beware). The *mie goreng,* loaded with shrimp and vegetables, is also good. Service is slow, but this is a good place to dawdle.

Poppies Cottages, Poppies Lane I, Kuta. ✆ 361/751059. Reservations recommended. Men must wear shirts. Main courses Rp20,000–Rp50,000 (US$2–US$5). AE, MC, V. Daily 8am–11pm.

TJ's Restaurant ✿✿ MEXICAN   This is the best Mexican restaurant going and a real Bali original. Stop in if only for one of the famous frozen margaritas and to listen to some good tunes in this laid-back, open-air spot. Meals start with homemade corn chips, delicious dips, and an extensive menu of specials.

They advertise the "best burgers in town," but the jury is still out (they're good, though); everything from the quesadillas to the fish veracruz is delicious. Order up, kick back, and enjoy the vibe in this popular spot.

Poppies Lane, Kuta. ℂ **361/751093**. Main courses Rp20,000–Rp50,000 (US$2–US$5). MC, V. Daily 11am–11pm.

SEMINYAK

Kafe Warisan ★★★ FRENCH It's fine international dining in a Balinese setting here in this open courtyard of frangipani trees overlooking rich, green rice paddies. The standards, service, and menu are equally sophisticated, and with so many choices, you might have to come back for a few meals. Be sure to try the escargots here, stuffed into roasted mushrooms and topped with a pesto butter. Kafe Warisan serves the best steaks on the island, the finest cuts of meat imported from Australia, and even local venison. On the lighter side, try the grilled Tasmanian salmon, seafood fricassee, or grilled rosemary chicken breast. There's also an extensive wine list and a range of California wines by the glass. Stop by the nice boutique to peruse the collection of beaded dresses, silk sarongs, jewelry, antique batik, and other collectibles.

Jalan Kerobokan, (Kerobokan) Seminyak. ℂ **361/731175**. Reservations required. Main courses Rp77,000–Rp99,000 (US$7.40–US$10). AE, MC, V. Mon–Sat 11am–4pm and 7–11pm.

Ku De Ta ★★ BISTRO This is Kuta's "Europe meets Asia" international bistro aimed at an upscale clientele. With a daytime ambience dominated by the restaurant's beach proximity, at night, it's all about romantic lighting in the restaurant's open-air, minimalist decor. Add both an elegant bar and lounge area and a cigar lounge—complete with putting green—to the equation, and you've got an all-purpose evening out. Happily, what comes out of the kitchen makes you want to stay: Try the signature dish of slow-roasted, Asian-sauced duck with a star anise and pear essence; or the chile and sea-salted squid, with a mango and green papaya marmalade. The cigar lounge is open from 6pm until late.

Jalan Oberoi 9, Seminyak. ℂ **361/736969**. Reservations recommended. Main courses Rp30,000–Rp40,000 (US$3–US$4). AE, MC, V. Daily 7am–midnight (food service).

La Lucciola ★ ITALIAN If there's a see-and-be-seen spot among the Kuta crowd, it's La Lucciola. Even breakfast draws the beautiful people, and why not, with its prime beachfront location on this deserted stretch of Legian? With morning eye-poppers such as ricotta hot cakes and smoked salmon scrambled eggs on toasted focaccia, it's no wonder. The dinner menu is equally bewitching, with choice offerings such as lemongrass bok choy risotto with sesame ginger poached snapper; chicken and soba noodle salad with a soy sesame dressing; or a delectable loin of pork, chargrilled with apples and served with a pumpkin purée and onion relish. End with a bracing espresso and the white chocolate pra-line pannacotta for a fine evening.

Oberoi Rd., Kayu Aya Beach, Legian. ℂ **361/730838**. Main courses Rp20,000–Rp150,000 (US$2–US$15). AE, MC, V. Daily 8am–midnight.

OUTDOOR ACTIVITIES

Surfing is "gnarly" in Kuta (that means good), and enthusiasts from all over are drawn to its stupendous breakers, best between March and July. Surf shops line the main drags and can help with rentals or tide information, and **Cheyne Horan School of Surf** (ℂ 361/735-858) gives lessons. Beginners start just off at Kuta or Legian (with soft sand beach), but the legendary surf is at the low reef breaks and "barrels" of **Kuta Reef** at the southern end of the beach.

Unfortunately, the same surf makes recreational **swimming** virtually impossible. Even past the breakers, the current can be too strong. Pay close attention to swimming warnings and restrictions, and be very careful if you do swim. Tanning and splashing to cool off are about all that's left to do.

SHOPPING

With the touts constantly in your face, shopping in Kuta will seem mandatory. The streets (particularly Poppies Gang II) are lined with stalls offering tie-dyed sarongs, shorts, swimsuits, knock-off brand-name cologne, hats, and wristwatches. Given the hard sell, this might be the best place to hone your bargaining skills. **Kuta Square** is the place to go for Western-style shopping and could be called "Brand Name Row," with Nike, Polo, and Armani stores and fast food places such as McDonald's and KFC.

The **ABC Bookstore,** Jalan Pantai Kuta no. 41E (© 361/752745), offers used books with quite a few English-language selections.

KUTA AFTER DARK

Kuta is party central, going full-on from 11pm until dawn—every night. Clubs and bars abound, each with its own flavor, but all "same-same but different." Or, you could skip all that and do what the locals do: hang out by the food stalls on the beach on Friday and Saturday nights. Ask around; the scene changes daily.

CLUBS

Bounty Ship I, Jalan Legian (© 361/752-529, open daily 10pm–3am), is built to look like a galleon and has a lively dance floor and bar. It's cheesy but fun. The **Hard Rock Cafe,** Jalan Raya Kuta © 361/755661), is the most upscale in town and charges the occasional cover for live music. **Peanuts II,** Jalan Legian or Jalan Melasti, is surrounded by other bars and is a popular stop on pub crawls.

BARS

There are too many bars to mention, and many are pretty adolescent, but the **Hard Rock Hotel** (© 361/755-661) is classy in its own way. **Goa 2001,** Jalan Seminyak 1 (© 361/730-592, open daily 7pm–2am), is an old Kuta mainstay. **Kori Restaurant and Bar,** Poppies Gang II (© 361/758-605), is relaxed, cozy, and pricey, with a chic cigar salon, a pool table, and even valet parking.

Tee Off Over Tanah Lot

The **Nirwana Bali Golf Club,** Jalan Raya Tanah Lot, Tabanan (© 361/815970; fax 361/815962; www.nirwanabaligolf.com), is a sublime experience for golf junkies. The golf course sits on a 101-hectare (250-acre) tract of land only 30 minutes north of the airport that includes the 18-hole, par-72 championship course designed by Greg Norman; the five-star **Le Meridien Spa and Resort** (www.lemeridien-bali.com); and residential villas. It's exclusive, but it encourages visitors and tourists to use the facilities for a hefty price. Carts are required and are included in the green fee, along with an enchanting and well-trained caddy from the all-female caddy team. Green fees are available for 9 or 18 holes and differ for outside visitors and those staying at Le Meridien. Guests of the hotel pay US$72 for a full round (9 holes for US$52), while day-trippers pay a whopping US$125. Package rates are available.

4 Nusa Dua

In the 1970s, a French firm, commissioned by the Indonesian government, came up with the idea for a self-contained resort complex to "minimize the impact of tourism on the Balinese culture." It chose this 300-hectare tract of undeveloped land, devoid of any infrastructure, and basically transformed it into a theme park. Nusa Dua is now a roster of five-star, all-inclusive properties, all secluded and finely manicured. The beaches are clean and blissfully tout-free, but it can all seem a bit sterile. Still, it's suitable for families and business conventions.

GETTING THERE

Things couldn't be easier. Most hotels in Nusa Dua offer airport pickup, but you can find shuttles and cheap taxis at the airport and in Kuta. (Be sure to take only the official blue-and-yellow metered taxis in Kuta.) Bemos from Denpasar go to Nusa Dua by way of Kuta and Jimbaran.

GETTING AROUND

These big spreads make it so comfortable you won't want to or even have to leave the grounds—but even the most starry-eyed honeymooners might want a break from expensive hotel meals. Cabs are unreliable, and hotel transport, unless free, is at inflated prices. It's best to take a **local shuttle** with stops at all resorts.

WHERE TO STAY

Self-contained all, these behemoth estates can handle any eventuality, including transport, postage, and money changing.

VERY EXPENSIVE

Nusa Dua Beach Hotel and Spa *★★*   This fine resort has lot more local style than most and comes with all the top amenities. The bulk of the regular rooms, Superior standard, are smaller and more ordinary than the price warrants, but the Deluxe and Palace rooms are large, with Balinese fabric on the beds and, for the Palace rooms, DVD players and Jacuzzi tubs. Both swimming pools are picturesque and luxurious, but the best amenity is the exquisite spa with open-air, thatched massage pavilions and Bali-style beds set among fountains: romantic and relaxing. There is even a lap pool, if you have the strength. The gym, too, is well equipped, and the amenities throughout, including many choices for fine dining, are all top of the line.

P.O. Box 1028, Denpasar, Bali. © **361/771219** or 361/771210. Fax 361/772617. www.nusaduahotel.com. 380 units. US$150–US$230 double; US$300–US$2,800 suite. AE, DC, MC, V. **Amenities:** 5 restaurants; 4 bars; 2 outdoor pools; golf (nearby); spa; Jacuzzi; sauna; rentals available; kids' club; tour desk; business center; shopping; 24-hr. room service; massage; babysitting; laundry; dry cleaning; meeting facilities; Internet. *In room:* A/C, satellite TV, minibar, fridge, safe, IDD phone.

Sheraton Laguna Nusa Dua *★★*   There is something to be said for being able to step directly from your hotel room into the swimming pool. Here the pool is large and luxe, with its own sandy beach, the hotel's trump card. Even if the hotel is full to capacity, you'll find a slice of serenity poolside. The rooms are lavish but a bit flower-fussy, with a brash and brassy, vaguely tropical decor, but the huge wood and marble bathrooms make up for it. Additional luxury touches include in-room check-in, 24-hour butler service, and your own personalized stationery and business cards to use while in residence. The grounds are vast and manicured, but this can make getting to the beach an endeavor. Service is phenomenal, with nice touches such as a lit candle left by the turndown service.

P.O. Box 77, Nusa Dua Beach 80363, Bali. © 800/325-3535 or 361/771327. Fax 361/771326. www. sheraton.com. 276 units. US$285–US$400 double; US$490–US$1,200 suite. AE, DC, MC, V. **Amenities:** 3 restaurants; 4 bars; 3 outdoor pools (and kid's pool); golf (nearby); tennis court; fitness center; spa; Jacuzzi; watersports rentals; tour desk, car/motorbike rentals; shopping; salon; 24-hr. room service; massage; laundry; meeting room. *In room:* A/C, satellite TV (in-house movies), minibar, fridge; hair dryer, IDD phone.

Sheraton Nusa Indah ⚘ Short on character but long on Western creature comforts, the Nusa Indah makes for a most satisfying resort experience. The size is daunting—beginning with the airplane hangar–size lobby (air-conditioned, which is rare in Bali), big enough to accommodate the conference groups that make up the majority of its clientele. The thatched pavilion bar warmed at night by candlelight helps bring it down to size, as does the attentive staff. Rooms have dark wood paneling and smooth parquet floors, with colorful local fabric on beds. Large marble bathrooms have a separate area for the toilet, and sunken tubs. Views are either of the garden or of the pool, and some rooms on higher floors have ocean views. Between the giant pool and the beach are open-air pavilions (*bales*) with big cushions, perfect for serious all-day relaxing.

P.O. Box 36, Nusa Dua Beach 80363, Bali. © 800/325-3535 or 361/771906. Fax 361/771908. www. sheraton.com. 358 units. US$195–US$240 double. AE, DC, MC, V. **Amenities:** 3 restaurants; 2 bars; outdoor pool; fitness center; full spa; rentals available; tour desk; shopping; 24-hr. room service; laundry; meeting rooms. *In room:* A/C, satellite TV, hair dryer, IDD phone.

EXPENSIVE

Hotel Bualu ⚘ The Hotel Bualu was the first hotel to open in the Nusa Dua some 30 years ago, and the hotel has seen better days (and new rivals); the friendly staff and reasonable price tag make up for it, though. You don't get the bells and whistles of the big resorts here, but, then again, you might not want them—and you don't have to pay for them. The hotel has its own private beach across the street. Rooms are fairly standard rectangles, with terra cotta tile floors, carved wood trim, batik bedspreads on comfortable beds, and glass sliding doors to the garden veranda. Additions such as a lovely children's playground, carriage rides around town, and pony rides on the beach make this good for families on a budget.

P.O. Box 6, Nusa Dua, Bali. © 361/771310 or 361/771311. Fax 361/771313. 50 units. US$95 double; US$120 suite. AE, DC, MC, V. **Amenities:** 2 restaurants; bar; 2 swimming pools; tennis court; motorbike and bike rental; playground; tour desk; car rental; limited room service; babysitting; laundry; library. *In room:* A/C, TV, IDD phone.

Novotel ⚘⚘ This is what a Bali hotel beach resort should be: It's upscale and beautiful, but it feels like you're actually in Bali. The removed peninsular site means that you're away from the hassles but close to Benoa, an authentic fishing village. The resort straddles the main street: The oceanside is more expensive and has better beach access, while the "garden" side is quiet and secluded. Rooms are big, bright, and airy, decorated in coconut wood and in a minimalist Asian style that other hotels are beginning to copy. Better still, for the price, are the "Beach Cabanas," even bigger suites in semi-private bungalows (2 per pavilion), complete with outdoor stone tubs—most of them honeymoon-worthy. The three swimming pools all have their own flair, though none is very big. Lots of activities, including aerobics, soccer, a kid's club, and dance and cooking lessons, will keep you on the run, if you like. There's also a free shuttle to Nusa Dua, convenient for touring; but given that this is the best of both worlds—a terrific resort and authentic Bali—it's hard to see that you would need to. The ocean up this way is much deeper and better for swimming too.

Jalan Pratama Tanjung Benoa, P.O. Box 39, Nusa Dua 80361, Bali. ℂ 361/772239. Fax 361/772237. www. novotelbali.com. 192 units. US$186–US$210 double; US$332 beach cabana. AE, DC, MC, V. **Amenities:** 3 restaurants; 2 bars; 3 outdoor pools; tennis court; fitness center; spa; rentals; kid's club, tour desk, shuttle service; shopping; 24-hr. room service; massage; babysitting; laundry; dry cleaning; meeting room; library. *In room:* A/C, satellite TV, minibar, fridge, safe, IDD phone.

WHERE TO DINE

Nusa Dua has some fine dining, mostly at the hotels and priced accordingly. There are few other options short of the small warungs in town. This is a good place to splash out on a fine spread at the hotels; we mention just a few here: **The Amanusa** has a good Italian restaurant. **Kolak Restaurant** at the Bualu Hotel is another classy standby in Nusa Dua that serves fine, authentic Indonesian. **Raja's Table** at the Nusa Dua Beach Hotel has a nice menu of specialties from throughout the Asia-Pacific region and has fine panoramic views on the beachfront.

TOURS

To find a travel agent or guide, try either the busy **Tunas Indonesia Tours & Travel,** Jalan D. Tamblingan 107 (ℂ **361/288056**); or **Santa Bali Tours and Travel,** at the Grand Bali Hotel (ℂ **361/287628**).

OUTDOOR ACTIVITIES & WATERSPORTS

Unlike Kuta, the surf here is a considerable distance offshore, making swimming in the clear blue-green water most pleasant at high tide (only ankle-high at low tide). It's a popular surf, wind-surf, and jet-skiing spot. Dive excursions, all arranged by the hotels, will probably take you to areas closer to Sanur or to Amed and Tambulen in the northeast.

Golf enthusiasts will be thrilled with the 18-hole championship course at the **Bali Golf and Country Club** (ℂ **361/771791**), across from the Galleria and the Hyatt. The green fee is US$125, but the course is heavenly.

SHOPPING

Bualu, a nearby fishing village, has some outdoor stalls and persistent touts a la Kuta beach (though not quite as bad, and there are some good bargains to be had).

Nusa Dua's **Galleria** gives you both Western-style shopping and the ability to buy local crafts with little hassle, like an American outlet mall, and priced accordingly. There's also a Keris department store, with all the name brands, or the nearby **handicrafts center,** with souvenir items of better quality than what you find along the beaches. There's also a nice little supermarket.

NUSA DUA AFTER DARK

All of the hotels offer some kind of music at night and frequent Balinese dance and music programs, though these usually come as part of a costly buffet dinner package. Candle-light lounge-hopping should keep you busy for a few nights, but if you're looking for real nightlife, head to Kuta.

5 Ubud

For a dose of authentic culture and comfort, Ubud is the premier choice in Bali. Though there's no mistaking this tourist town for a rural or pastoral village, if your aim is to immerse yourself in the Balinese culture, there's no reason to go anywhere else. The town breathes atmosphere: You'll see ceremonies on every street corner, and the surrounding country is stunning. About the only thing it doesn't have is a beach, but they're all a short drive away.

Ubud is the cultural pulse of the island and the richest region in Bali for art production, which is possibly why so many expat artists have made their homes here. It's a town with nooks of true refinement, chic galleries, and some fine spas. Ubud's central location makes the whole island accessible by day trip, but the phosphorescent rice paddies, virgin jungle, gorges, and river valleys of this Shangri-La might keep you there for your whole trip.

VISITOR INFORMATION

Jalan Raya, on the south side of the main street, near the intersection with Monkey Forest Road (© **361/973-285**), is a good place to start. There are tourist agencies all over town, each offering competitive prices for day trips and shuttles to other tourist areas.

GETTING THERE

Many hotels in the area offer hotel pickup, and taxis will come here from the airport, about an hour away. Bemos drop you in the center of town, while the tourist shuttles have their own stops, usually on one of the two main drags.

GETTING AROUND

Transport touts in Ubud are quite aggressive and **minivans** are for hire on every corner for day trips or the short jaunt across town. Central Ubud is small enough to see **on foot,** and hotels away from the main action generally provide regular **shuttles** into town. The main street is Jalan Raya, which runs east-west; Monkey Forest Road runs perpendicular. Ubud is as good a place as any to **rent a motorbike** (about Rp50,000/US$5 per day) if you're an experienced rider. **Bicycles** are for hire at two or three street-side locations along Monkey Forest Road for about Rp10,000 (about US$1).

 FAST FACTS: Ubud

Banks/Currency Exchange There is an ATM next door to Casa Luna restaurant on Jalan Raya, as well as several on the main road on the way to Laplapan. Storefront money changers are everywhere.

Internet/E-mail It's impossible to take more than two steps without tripping over an Internet cafe in Ubud. Closer to the center of town is the Jineng Business Center (Jalan Hanoman, across from the Dirty Duck), open 8am to 10pm daily, with the most computers and fastest modems.

Post Office/Mail The post office is on the main road, but very far to the east. Major hotels offer postal service.

Telephone The area code in Ubud is 361.

WHERE TO STAY

In Ubud, no matter what your budget is, you'll find what you want, from sublime honeymoon compounds to the humblest *alang alang* (thatch-roof) cottage. Here we've listed an assortment, both in central Ubud and outside of town. Staying at the more rural properties might mean a long walk or ride, but the scenery is breathtaking. Many come, spend a few nights, and shop around for something new.

VERY EXPENSIVE

Amandari ✦✦✦   If you have ample disposable income, this exquisite hotel is an excellent place to part with it. It's also the place to rub elbows with the rich and famous for whom nothing but the Amandari and its pampering will do (Mick Jagger and Jerry Hall got married here). Laid out like the world's fanciest Balinese village, the rooms are all huge stone cottages roofed in thatch. Each suite is enclosed in its own walled compound and is full of delicate Balinese luxuries; some are even two-story and have their own private pool. Bathrooms are similarly ample in size, with fluffy towels, a large shower inside, and a tub outdoors. And the service—well, let's say you get what you pay for. It's all set on an eye-popping gorge, though the view is not as spectacular as the one over at the Kupu Kupu Barong hotel. However, its famous emerald green horizon pool, with water that spills over the far edge, mimics the exact color of the gorge and is marvelously engineered to blend seamlessly with the green beyond—the best. There is a free shuttle to Ubud (the hotel is about a 15-min. drive away), but it's hard to imagine wanting to leave very often. The one terrific restaurant has a bar and serves local and European favorites.

Kedewatan, Ubud, Bali. ✆ **361/975-333.** Fax 361/975-335. www.amandari.com. 29 units. US$600–$2,400 double; US$3,100 villa. AE, MC, V. **Amenities:** Restaurant; bar; outdoor pool; golf course; tennis course; health club; full spa; Jacuzzi; all rentals available; complimentary bicycles; concierge; tour desk; shopping; 24-hr. room service; massage; babysitting; laundry; dry cleaning. *In room:* A/C, minibar, fridge, hair dryer, safe, IDD phone.

Four Seasons Resort at Sayan ✦✦   The Four Seasons here is a masterpiece of planning that takes full advantage of its extraordinary setting right on the River Ayung. It's incredibly posh, though not intimidatingly so. You enter across a long bridge leading to a pond that, almost unbelievably, rests atop the central lobby, all in an immense crater of rice terraces. The design throughout is ultra-modern, but with good references to Balinese tradition. Rooms are either in two-story suites (bedroom below the sitting area), deluxe suites, or high-end villas with private plunge pools. Interiors are done in gleaming woods and natural fabrics, and are full of precious local art and artifacts. Expect luxurious bathrooms (2 to every suite/villa) with huge tubs, showers, and dressing areas, and more thick towels than a linen shop. Every room has views of the deep green gorge and/or the river, with in-room sound systems to further the vibe. The two-level horizon pool follows the serpentine shape of the river below. Pampering, of course, is at a maximum and includes "seamless" transfer between here and the resort at Jimbaran Bay; they take care of everything, including, if you wish, your packing. There is a regular shuttle to Ubud.

Sayan, Ubud, Gianyar Bali 80571. ✆ **361/977-577.** Fax 361/977-588. www.fourseasons.com. 46 units. US$450 suite; US$575–US$3,000 villa. AE, DC, MC, V. **Amenities:** 2 restaurants; bar; outdoor pool; health club; spa; all rentals available; tour desk; shopping; 24-hr. room service; laundry; dry cleaning; library w/games. *In room:* A/C, TV, minibar, fridge, safe, IDD phone.

Ibah ✦✦   On the comfy fringes of the main Ubud action, this is the most romantic hotel you'll find so close to town. It's a special marriage of Bali style and Western comfort. Large rooms here have spare, clean lines that employ lots of wood and natural fabrics. The four-poster canopy bed hung with mosquito netting is a nice touch. Good-size bathrooms have either outdoor or wood-floor showers. All rooms have spacious verandas or patios. The grounds make good use of the hilly terrain, and there are lots of secret nooks and crannies, even romantic alcoves in the hotel's heart-shape pool. Spa and massage are in lush wood and muslin-draped rooms, and there is a particularly luxe indoor Jacuzzi.

Campuhan, Ubud, P.O. Box 193, Bali. ℂ 361/974466. Fax 361/974467. www.ibahbali.com. 11 units. US$200–US$250 double; US$260–$315 suite; US$430–$500 villa. AE, MC, V. **Amenities:** Restaurant; bar; outdoor pool; health club; spa; Jacuzzi; all rentals; concierge; tour desk; salon; room service (6am–12pm); massage; babysitting; laundry; dry cleaning. *In room:* A/C, TV, minibar, fridge, hair dryer, safe, IDD phone.

Kupu Kupu Barong 🐦🐦 *(Finds)*   The selling point of this luxury boutique hotel is the view—so breathtaking, it's hard to tear yourself away. The hotel is set on a deep green gorge with a river rushing far below and palm trees rising above rice fields. Some rooms have better views than others, but even the least impressive are extraordinary. Wherever you end up will be comfortable and spacious, with a pleasing but plain decor. Bathrooms are in pieces—tub here, sink there, closet way over there—and this gives even more room but not much counter space. The two small pools are refreshing. The long distance into town is less noticeable with free shuttle service every hour until 11pm. The restaurant is tops.

Kedewatan, Ubud, Bali. ℂ 361/975478. Fax 361/975079. 19 units. US$335–US$405 double; US$699 suite. AE, DC, MC, V. **Amenities:** Restaurant; bar; outdoor pool; spa; free mountain bikes to borrow; tour desk; shopping; room service (6:30am–10:30pm); massage; laundry; dry cleaning. *In room:* A/C, TV, minibar, fridge, IDD phone.

EXPENSIVE

Bali Spirit Hotel and Spa 🐦   Located a fair jaunt from central Ubud in the village of Nyuh Kuning, this is a reasonable alternative to the really high-end luxury hotels such as the Amandari and Kupu Kupu Barong. The stunning hillside setting overlooks a river gorge and the rooms are not as luxurious, but you wouldn't know that unless you compared them in person. As it is, they are eye-poppers: comfortable, well-appointed, and bigger than average, some with thatched roofs and Bali fabrics. The pool is good-size, and there are traditional Balinese bathing pools in the holy river. There's also a fine spa with a full range of services. That and the free chauffeured car to take you wherever you want to go "at a moment's notice" make this a pampering experience.

P.O. Box 189, Nyuh Kuning Village, Ubud 80571, Bali. ℂ 361/974-013. Fax 361/974-012. www.balispirit hotel.com. 19 units. US$95–US$135 double; US$145 villa. Rates include breakfast. AE, MC, V. **Amenities:** Restaurant; bar; outdoor pool; full spa; tour desk; car rental; airport transfer; 24-hr. room service; massage; laundry; dry cleaning; Internet. *In room:* A/C, TV, minibar, fridge, IDD phone.

Komaneka Resort 🐦   Right on Monkey Forest Road, the Komaneka is clean and modern but still traditional Balinese, which is unique in central Ubud. It's also the only property where you can opt for a villa with a private pool this close to the action. Rooms are modern luxury without looking like a suburban condo. Tracing a long, narrow space, ending in a rectangular pool, guest buildings are well away from street noise, with views of gardens and rice paddies. The rooms are outfitted in lots of natural woods and fabrics, and the beds are hung with cheesecloth-like netting suspended from the thatched ceiling. Deluxe rooms have unique bathrooms that, while lacking in any real walls, are still arranged for privacy. Suites are bigger and have cushioned window seats, with well-stocked bathrooms featuring big marble baths and showers with wood floors.

Monkey Forest Rd. ℂ 361/976090. Fax 361/977140. www.komaneka.com. 20 units. US$135–US$190 double; US$210–US$344 garden and pool villa. AE, DC, MC, V. **Amenities:** Restaurant; outdoor pool; full spa; tour desk; car rental; shopping; 24-hr. room service; massage; laundry; library. *In room:* A/C, fridge, minibar, IDD phone.

MODERATE

Agung Raka Bungalows ⭐ You certainly won't have to sacrifice Balinese style here in these cozy bungalows. You'll be greeted by straw-hatted women whacking rice stalks; the bungalows are arranged around a series of working rice paddies. The property lies on the fringes of Ubud, and, thanks to the thriving village art community, you'll hardly know you've left. Lower-end bungalows are basic two-story wood-and-bamboo constructions with rudimentary outdoor bathrooms at the back and a staircase up to a cozy bedroom. Superior bungalows are single occupancy A-frames with teak and catay accents. The bathrooms here are large, modern courtyard facilities that include both a tile bathtub and a stone-floor shower. The suites are to die for: a dizzying spectacle of stone and marble, big enough for four but romantic enough for two—there's even an actual throne in one suite's bathroom garden, a toilet set in solitude under its own canopied hut. It's quirky, affordable luxury in Balinese style.

Pengosekan Village (2km/1¼ miles S of Ubud center). ☎ 361/975-757. Fax 361/975546. 22 bungalows, all w/bathroom. US$67 standard villa; US$73–US$137 bungalow; US$175–US$200 honeymoon suite. MC, V. **Amenities:** Restaurant; bar; outdoor pool; motorbike rental; tour desk; car rental; shuttle service; laundry. In room: A/C, TV, minibar, IDD phone.

Alam Sari ⭐⭐ This model hotel is the finest combination of comfort, social responsibility, setting, and low price. Everything the Alam Sari does is with a thought toward the local economy, ecology, and culture. Room decor, such as brightly dyed fabric and wood furniture, is locally made. The hotel employs, almost exclusively, villagers from neighboring Keliki, bolstering the local economy; it also follows environmentally friendly standards (solar water heaters, recycled paper, etc.). Rooms are lovely, with views of the gorge and looming volcano (as good as the one found at Kupu Kupu Barong, above, at a fraction of the price). The hotel is sufficiently self-contained, making the 20-minute ride to town an only occasional necessity. Traditional music is featured at night.

Keliki, Tromoi Pos 03, Kantor Pos Tegallalang, Gianyar 80561, Bali (9km/5½ miles N of Ubud). ☎ and fax **361/240308.** www.alamsari.com. 10 units. US$106 double; US$119 suite; US$198 family unit. AE, MC, V. **Amenities:** Restaurant; bar; bicycle hire; tour desk; car rental; laundry; library. In room: A/C, minibar, fridge, safe, IDD phone.

Ananda Cottages ⭐ Just north of Ubud proper, Ananda Cottages is far enough from the town center to discourage tourist hoards, yet atmospheric enough for the Balinese experience you're hoping for. The cottages and rooms are arranged around working rice terraces; rooms are connected by paths along terrace retaining walls, which, at night, are lit with miniature coal-fed, torch-like flames. The cottages are bi-level brick huts with bamboo pavilion roofs. Downstairs rooms are the better choice and have outdoor baths and patio living rooms. Upstairs rooms are nice, with modern baths and small verandas. The pool is small but on an interesting raised rice terrace.

Campuhan, Ubud. ☎ **361/975-376.** Fax 361/975-375. anandaubud@denpasar.wasantara.net.id. 54 units, all w/bathroom. US$40–US$50 double without A/C; US$60–US$70 double with A/C; US$175 suite villa. AE, MC, V. **Amenities:** Restaurant; bar; outdoor pool; shopping; 24-hr. room service; laundry. In room: A/C (some rooms), minibar, fridge, IDD phone.

Hotel Tjampuhan ⭐⭐ It's a tropical sanctuary with terraces that lead to a beautiful gorge, the Tjampuhan River, and the 900-year-old Gunung Lebah Temple. The hotel was built in 1928 for guests of the prince of Ubud and was chosen by Western artists Walter Spies and Rudolf Bonnet as headquarters for their art association, Pita Maha. All units have Balinese thatched roofs. Air-conditioned rooms are larger and have better views than fan rooms. Splurge for a Raja Room (or even Spies's own villa), with nice verandas overlooking the gorge. The grounds are in beautiful stonework, and immaculate gardens line the path down to the river. There are two very pretty pondlike pools and another with cold spring water, perfect for hot days.

Jalan Raya Campuhan, Ubud. © **361/975-368.** Fax 316/975-137. 64 units. US$70 double w/fan; US$115 double with A/C; US$175 Walter Spies villa. Includes breakfast. AE, MC, V. **Amenities:** 2 restaurants; 4 bars; outdoor pool; full spa; tour desk; car rental; shopping; massage; babysitting; laundry; dry cleaning; library. *In room:* A/C (some), minibar, fridge, IDD phone.

Pringga Juwita Water Garden Cottages ✿
This is a popular option, a small hotel heavy on the atmosphere, thanks to the nice, mossy stonework and the streams, lily ponds, and bubbling fountains that make the grounds more water than earth. Some rooms are a bit moldy, so check before checking in. Deluxe rooms are two stories. Downstairs is an open-air lounging area and marble bathroom; up some treacherous stairs is the bedroom, simple but for mahogany flooring and carved archways.

Jalan Bisma, Ubud 80571, Bali. © and fax **361/975734.** pringga@bali-travelnet.com. 25 units. US$65–$90 double. MC, V. **Amenities:** Restaurant; bar; outdoor pool; airport transfer; laundry. *In room:* A/C

INEXPENSIVE

Puri Garden Bungalows ✿
A bit more upscale than your average losmen, this is a good budget alternative. Rooms and bathrooms (all clean and big enough not to be claustrophobic) are larger than in an average losmen. Rooms have bamboo on the walls and rushes on the floor, while bathrooms are nicely tiled. There's no air-conditioning, only fans, but there is hot water. Second-story rooms have bathrooms down a steep flight of stairs, making middle-of-the-night calls of nature precarious. It's all arranged around a nice Buddha-adorned garden with fish ponds. Nearby Puri Garden II has 22 similarly appointed bungalows.

Monkey Forest Rd. © and fax **361/974-923.** bbainfo@bali-thepages.com. 8 units in Puri I and 22 units in Puri II. US$30 double w/fan; US$40–$50 with A/C. Rates include breakfast. MC, V. **Amenities:** Restaurant; bar; outdoor pool; tour desk; car rental; 24-hr. room service; laundry. *In room:* A/C (some rooms), TV, minibar, IDD phone.

LOSMEN

There are literally dozens of losmen (home-stay hotels) to chose from in Ubud. Just walk down Monkey Forest Road or the Jalan Hanoman; better still, turn down any little alley or side street that cuts across them. Try the following: **Esty's House,** Jalan Dewi Sita, Maruti Lane, Ubud, Bali (© **361/977679**), is clean and comfortable, with a nice patio sitting area out front. **Honeymoon Bakery Guesthouse,** Jalan Raya, Ubud, Bali (© **361/973283**), is a step up from typical losmen and is run by local restaurateurs, so the food is great. **Kajeng Homestay,** Jalan Kajeng 29, Ubud, Bali (© **361/975018**), doesn't look like much from the outside but is pretty out back, with a lily pond, valley views, and clean rooms. **Rice Paddy Bungalows,** off Monkey Forest Road, near the Puri Garden Hotel, is a nice garden complex; rooms have high ceilings, tiled floors, and Western bathrooms.

WHERE TO DINE

The tourist explosion in Ubud has brought with it some of the finest restaurants on the island. There's not much authentic local fare, but you'll find fine international choices. Many of the hotels, elsewhere serving mundane fare, are surprisingly good. Much of the fine dining here comes with a Western price tag.

Ary's Warung ☆☆ MODERN INDONESIAN   Ary's gourmet European and Indonesian specialties have fans from around the world. Stop in at least for one of their honey ginger lime drinks (with or without alcohol). Ary's is particularly nice at night, when it's lit by candles. You can sit on the second floor and watch the action in the busy street below, or see bats swooping to catch bugs near the streetlights. For appetizers, try the gazpacho, a generous bowl full of icy fresh flavor—perfect for a hot day—or the grilled goat cheese salad. Chicken crepes are tasty, stuffed with chicken, tomatoes, and leeks sautéed in garlic and white wine, with a creamy spinach sauce. Rendang Pedang is a West Sumatran beef dish simmered in coconut with local herbs—it's got a kick that sneaks up on you.

Main St. Main courses Rp25,500–Rp75,000 (US$2.45–US$7.25) (duck, lamb, and salmon much higher—up to Rp150,000/US$14). No credit cards. Daily 7:30am–1am.

Batan's Waru ☆☆ INDONESIAN/EUROPEAN   This is a new favorite in Ubud. Tucked away on a pleasant side street, it's particularly atmospheric at night, when the street entrance is lit with candles. The very ambitious menu has traditional dishes beyond the usual suspects and plenty of vegetarian options. For an appetizer, try *urap pakis,* wild fern tips with roasted coconut and spices; or the *lemper ayam,* chicken dumplings simmered in a banana leaf. "Uncle Karaman's Humus" is spicy and comes with grilled pepper flat bread and tomato mint relish, and everything is served with a dish of spicy hot condiments. Finish off with a perfect cup of decaf Illy-brand espresso. The restaurant also does smoked duck and a babi guleng feast, with a day's advance order, and there is a full menu of pasta, sandwiches, and light fare.

Jalan Dewi Sita, Ubud. ✆ 361/977528. Main courses Rp15,500–Rp43,000 (US$1.55–US$4.30). MC, V. Daily 8am–midnight.

Bebek Bengil (Dirty Duck Diner) ☆☆ INDONESIAN/EUROPEAN   Yes, they serve duck here—the famous house specialty is crispy duck stewed in Indonesian spices, and then deep fried and eaten with your fingers. Fans of this Ubud institution (including David Bowie) love that the duck here is not greasy. Other poultry includes stuffed chicken (with shiitake, sprouts, and spinach). The menu also lists salads and well-stuffed, crunchy sandwiches. Grilled tuna salad with lemon cumin vinaigrette is a light and healthful option that's not overly dressed. There are veggie options, including a mushroom cashew paté appetizer.

Padang Tegel (at the end of the street as it hooks into Monkey Forest Rd.), Ubud, Bali. ✆ 361/975-489. Main courses Rp12,500–Rp35,000 (US$1.25–US$3.50). MC, V. Daily 11am–11pm.

Cafe Lotus ☆ MODERN INDONESIAN/INTERNATIONAL   The food here isn't half bad, but the real reason to come to Cafe Lotus is for the chance to dine in the shadow of the Pura Saraswati temple (see attractions below). It's cozy in either the upscale dining room or the exotic bamboo platform seating above the lily pads in the evening breeze. It seems as if the menu is meant to tease, taking traditionally Western items like fettuccine and turning them into fiery dishes of hot chiles, black olives, and hearts of palm. The Balinese Satay Lilit, a mixed fish kabob with a hint of coconut, is served on skewers and presented on a plate the size of a boat. Not bad for the view.

Ubud Main Rd. ✆ 361/975-660. Main courses Rp25,000–Rp50,000 (US$2.50–US$5). No credit cards. Daily 9am–10pm.

Casa Luna 🌟🌟 INDONESIAN/BALINESE/CONTINENTAL   This innovative restaurant wouldn't be out of place in San Francisco; it has one of the widest menus in Ubud, with dazzling versions of local cuisine and nouvelle food from pumpkin ravioli to Mediterranean tofu. It's all imaginative, fresh, and beautifully prepared, from the Balinese paella to the satay. Big, healthful salads make Californians happy, as does the long list of frothy juice blends like pineapple, carrot, lemon and honey, or turmeric; you might also try an avocado shake. This restaurant is really bringing Indonesian food into the modern era, with uniquely prepared *nasi campur* or the *ikan Bali*. Save room for dessert; the Casa Luna bakery has decadent brownies with ice cream, lime tarts, and chocolate yogurt cake. Because you won't be able to try everything, I bet you will end up eating here more than once (all the expats sure do).

Main St. 📞 **361/973282.** Main courses Rp15,000–Rp50,000 (US$1.50–US$5). No credit cards. Daily 8am–1am.

Indus 🌟 ECLECTIC   This is the "must do" place just a short drive from the town center. Don't let that scare you away, but do admire the graceful marble work, the pillars, the carved wood furniture, and the view of Tjampuhan ridge. The airy setting and view alone make it worth the trip, but guests of the chic resorts up this way will be grateful for something this good so close by. Here you can sample beetroot and feta empanadas, grilled calamari tostada, or fine wraps and sandwiches—and don't overlook the fresh tuna and prawn crepes with lime leaves, coriander, and wasabi on the extensive tapas menu. Save room for the homemade ginger ice cream coconut crème caramel or a healthful fruit "smoothie."

Jalan Raya Sargingan, Campuhan, Ubud. 📞 **361/977684.** Dress "neat casual." Main courses Rp17,000–Rp50,000 (US$1.70–US$5). No credit cards. Daily 7:30am–11pm.

Satri's Warung 🌟🌟🌟 INDONESIAN/BALINESE   The house specialty of this funky, hidden courtyard is worth the hunt (and the wait). You need to order a day in advance for a feast of a whole chicken or duck marinated and glazed in a succulent sauce. Sounds simple, but it's great; the meat just falls off the bone, all artfully arranged and served with heaping plates of salad, cooked vegetables, and a large bowl of rice. Top it off with fresh-squeezed lemonade. Don't miss this restaurant, even if you don't have time for the chicken or duck; it's one of the finest warungs in all of Bali. The very friendly Satri serves her exceptionally good Indonesian food in generous portions, and warung also holds a twice-weekly cooking class so you can take some of the secrets home with you.

Monkey Forest Rd. (E side, 1-min. walk from Main Rd.—look for 2nd yellow beer sign). 📞 **361/973-279.** Main courses Rp14,000–Rp17,000 (US$1.40–US$1.70); banana chicken for 2 Rp125,000 (US$12.50); duck for 2 Rp150,000 (US$15). No credit cards. Daily 10am–10pm.

TeraZo 🌟🌟 MEDITERRANEAN   This new offshoot of the popular Batan Waru (also reviewed in this section) is Ubud's restaurant of the moment. The spacious interior is simple yet welcoming, with terraces behind a nice garden with decorative fountains. Considering the reach of the menu, the food is surprisingly good. The cool gazpacho made of ripe tomatoes is a welcome starter in the tropical heat, and the spring rolls are light and delicious. The eight-layer pie is a delicious pastry crust filled with smoked blue marlin, spinach, ricotta, and mushrooms; there's also a host of grilled items and fine pasta and gourmet Asian-influenced dishes, like the nasi kuning, yellow coconut rice with raisins, cashews, and strips of egg; or the kue tiaun, stir-fried rice noodles, chicken, and local greens. There's also a tempting breakfast menu with surprises like ricotta blintzes topped with honey and fresh yogurt.

Jalan Suweta, Ubud. © **361/978-941.** Main courses Rp24,000–Rp74,000 (US$2.40–US$7.40). AE, MC, V. Daily 8am–11pm.

Tutmak Warung Kopi ★★ INDONESIAN/EUROPEAN   Though it bills itself a warung, this would be called a cafe anywhere else, complete with nouvelle cuisine and modern art on the walls. "Warung Kopi" actually means coffeehouse, boasting the best coffee in Bali (it's darn good) and making this place a breakfast staple. Lunch and dinner menus emphasize European specials like rich pastas, chicken Dijonaisse, grilled sausages, and "organic salads." I love the spicy chicken sandwich on fat baguette bread, with a fresh salad on the side—not in the least Balinese, but a fine change of pace. Parents will be pleased with the kids' menu (this is about the only place that has one), including half sandwiches and similarly pint-size portions. Kids—and parents—can then fill up on fancy desserts like lime and mango mousse.

Jalan Dewi Sita. © **361/975-754.** Main courses Rp10,000–Rp30,000 (US$.95–US$2.90). No credit cards. Daily 9am–11pm.

ATTRACTIONS

Pura Saraswati ★★   The royal family commissioned this temple and water garden, dedicated to the Hindu goddess of art and learning, at the end of the 19th century. The main shrine is covered in fine carvings, and the bale houses (small pavilions) and giant *barong* masks are interesting. The restaurant Cafe Lotus is situated at the front, on the main street, so that diners can look out over the lovely grounds.

Jalan Raya Ubud, Ubud. Daily during daylight hours.

Puri Saren Agung, the Royal Palace ★   From the late 19th century to the mid-1940s, this was the seat for the local ruler. It's a series of elegant and well-preserved pavilions, many of them decorated incongruously with colonial-era European furniture. Visitors are welcome to stroll around, though there are no signs indicating what you are looking at, so it palls quickly. Evening dance performances are held in the courtyard, and it is by far the best and most dramatic setting for these in Ubud.

Jalan Raya, Ubud. Daily during daylight hours.

MUSEUMS

Starting with German-born Walter Spies in 1928, Ubud has enjoyed a long relationship with foreign artists. As a result, there are a few good museums in town and many galleries. All give you a good crash-course in authentic Balinese art, not to mention a welcome respite from souvenir stalls.

There are a number of small museums in town, including the **Seniwati Gallery of Art by Women,** Jalan Sriwedari 2B, Banjar Taman, Ubud (© **361/975-485;** free admission), featuring fine displays of painting and sculpture; and **Antonio Blanco's Gallery,** Jalan Campuhan, just past the bridge (© **361/975-502**). Admission costs Rp5,000 (US$.50); the gallery features works by this well-known Catalan expat, some fine nudes and inspired multimedia pieces.

Neka Museum ★★   Founded in 1982 by Suteja Neka, a former schoolteacher and art patron, this museum is a good introduction to the Balinese school. Housed in several pavilions, works are labeled in English and provide informed access to rural traditions and modern movements on the island or locally in Ubud. Don't miss the view of the Campuhan Gorge from the Smit Pavilion, and see what inspires local artists or get inspired yourself.

Jalan Raya Campuhan (about 10 min. N of central Ubud, near Ananda Cottages), Ubud. © 361/975074 or 361/975034. Admission Rp10,000 (US$.95). Daily 9am–5pm.

Puri Lukisan ✿ A major renovation has turned this formerly dilapidated display into something nearly on par with the Neka Museum. The gorgeous gardens of lily pond and rice paddy alone are worth a visit. Founded in 1956 by a prince of Ubud and a Dutch artist, there is an invaluable cross-section of styles to be seen here: paintings and sculptures that show the evolution of Balinese art, and one space dedicated to a revolving exhibit of up-and-coming local artists.

Jalan Raya Ubud, Ubud. © 361/975136. Admission Rp8,000 (US$.75). Daily 8am–4pm.

OUTDOOR ACTIVITIES

Monkey Forest ✿✿ Yes, there is a monkey forest at the southern end of Monkey Forest Road, and this is a popular day trip. Here, towering tree clusters are home to a troop of bad-tempered but photogenic primates who swing from branches, cannonball into pools of water, and do everything short of put on suits and pay taxes, all to the general delight of photo-snapping visitors. Signs warn you not to feed them, but locals stand under those very signs selling you bananas and nuts for precisely that purpose. Do so if you must, but do not tease the critters, who are grumpy enough as it is—just hand them the food. Make sure you have no other food on you: They will smell it. They're also known to snatch at dangling or glittering objects or gnaw on sandals. There's a small temple in the forest, and the track also leads to Nyuhkuning, a wood-carving village.

Monkey Forest Rd. Admission Rp3,000 (US28¢). Daily during daylight hours.

Elephant Safari Park ✿✿ The **Elephant Safari Park** is less safari and more elephant ride, and it's a real hoot. These native Sumatra elephants are well cared for and live in large, lush enclosures. The owners have worked carefully with locals from Taro Village, previously one of Bali's most remote and untouched villages, to make sure they leave little more than elephant tracks. A safari starts with Pachyderm 101, as knowledgeable guides tell about the animal's care and feeding, local ecology, threats to the native population, and preservation efforts. Then, along with a mahout (a guide), you'll have a galumphing trip through the jungle. Don't chicken out on the optional elephant bath. This entails mounting an elephant bareback, arms about a guide's waist, and riding along as the animal slowly walks into a deep river pool. At the handler's command, the elephant rears up and plunges onto its knees, submerging you up to your chin. Shampoo is optional. It's a fun day; wear your swimsuit and get ready for some good laughs.

Jalan Bypass Ngurah Rai, Pesanggaran. © 361/721480. Fax 361/721481. Park entrance (including transport) is US$48; US$68 w/elephant ride (kids are US$33 and US$48, and family rates are available). Reservations are recommended.

RAFTING & TREKKING

Just west of Ubud, the Ayung River has some good whitewater rafting and kayaking. The rapids aren't too impressive for experienced rafters, but the scenery along the way is, with rice paddies, deep gorges, and photo-op waterfalls. Two-hour trips include all equipment, hotel pickup, and lunch; most hotels can make the reservations. Contact **Sobek,** Jalan Tirta Ening 9, Bypass Ngurah Rai, Sanur (© **361/287059;** fax 361/289448).

WALKING

Ubud is surrounded by fascinating villages, scenic rice paddies, gorges, and rivers, and roads and paths lead to all of them. You can just wander, but I strongly urge you to buy a copy of the **Ubud Surroundings map,** available in all shops. Then head for the picturesque village of **Penestanan** or go on the rigorous **Campuhan Ridge walk.**

SHOPPING

Ubud is the shopper's paradise of Bali, with anything from tacky plastic do-hickies to priceless works that will have you thinking of selling the SUV.

Start at **Ubud Market** at the southeast corner of Monkey Forest Road and Jalan Raya Ubud (open during daylight hr.). It's a real market—great noisy fun, with dozens of stalls selling produce and livestock along with tourist kitsch.

All along **Monkey Forest Road, Jalan Raya Ubud,** and **Jalan Hanoman,** shop after shop is filled with gorgeous sarongs, wood carvings, mobiles, jewelry, incense, pottery, and gaily colored shirts, all geared to tourists, but not bad. Jewelry, housewares, and textiles can be found anywhere in town.

Several nearby crafts villages seem to be entirely devoted to some kind of commercial production. **Mas,** en route to Ubud from the south, is the most prominent wood-carving village, but there is also **Tegalalang** to the north. **Batubulan,** to the south, specializes in stone carving, while you'll find silver jewelry in **Celuk. Batuan** and **Keliki,** too, are major art centers. There are some great treasures to be had and going around by scooter or bemo makes for a fun day.

UBUD AFTER DARK

Ubud's nightlife scene is growing but still rather sedate. **Jazz Café,** Jalan Sukma 2, east of Monkey Forest Road (✆ **361/976594**), open 7:30 to 10:30pm, has good live jazz. **Sai Sai,** on Monkey Forest Road (✆ **361/976698**), open 7:30 to 11pm, gets pretty busy on Saturday night but is romantic on other nights, complete with gamelan music sometimes. The **Funkey Monkey** (✆ **361/903729**) open noon to 1am, is the cocktail bar for the cooler crowd; a live DJ spins the latest dance music.

PERFORMANCES

There are usually several dance, music, and shadow puppet performances to choose from every night in Ubud, both at the **Palace** and on other nearby stages. A *barong* performance at the Ubud Palace is your best and most stimulating choice (the kids will even like it). Touts sell tickets anywhere, but ask any front desk for a recommendation.

6 Candi Dasa

The best reason to camp out in Candi Dasa is to take advantage of the peace, relaxation, and historical riches of the eastern corner of the island. The beaches are eroded and it's overdeveloped, but you can find some of the island's finest accommodations here. Many choose to stay in nearby **Padangbai,** an atmospheric little fishing village with some basic accommodations.

GETTING THERE

There are shuttles from all major tourist areas to Candi Dasa, and most of the hotels offer airport pickup for a fee.

GETTING AROUND

There isn't much to the town of Candi Dasa itself—just one road, parallel to the beach—so your feet will do you just fine. Hotels just outside the center generally offer regular **shuttles** into town. **Motorbike** rental and **bemos** are available, too.

FAST FACTS: Candi Dasa

Banks/Currency Exchange Money changers are up and down the main street, offering competitive prices.

Car/Motorbike Rental Safari, on the main street (✆ **363-41707**), is a reliable and friendly tourist point, with a selection of cars, jeeps, and motorbikes.

Internet Safari, on the main street (✆ **363-41707**), has Internet service, as does Tarunga Beach Bungalows, also on the main street.

Post Office/Mail Asri Shop, on the main street, offers postal services.

Telephone Candi Dasa's area code is 363.

WHERE TO STAY

There is a range to satisfy everyone here. If you choose to stay in Padangbai, los-men are the only option. They're easy to find and pretty much all the same.

VERY EXPENSIVE

Amankila ★★   This is the seaside cousin of the Ubud Amandari, and it has breathtaking views (here of the ocean) and prices to match. The fact that they bring along pillows for you for the ride back in their SUV is always a good sign. The hotel is located on a bluff somewhat outside of Candi Dasa, but the distance doesn't seem to bother the clientele because the place is always booked. Large bungalows are dominated by a solid-wood four-poster canopy bed and have enormous dressing areas, luxe baths, and cushioned window seats. The high-end suites have better views and private pools. Service and amenities are luxe beyond belief. The Amankila has the only beach in Candi Dasa with sand, and perhaps the most striking feature is the breathtaking tiered pool, whose water matches the color of the ocean it seems to spill into. One restaurant serves breakfast and lunch; another serves dinner. There's a nice library with real leather-bound volumes.

Manggis. ✆ **361/771267** or 363-41333. Fax 361/771266. 35 units. US$600–US$1,200 suite. AE, MC, V. **Amenities:** 2 restaurants; bar; outdoor pool; tennis court; spa; watersports equipment rental; motorbike rental; tour desk; car rental; 24-hr. room service; massage; laundry; library. *In room:* A/C, satellite TV, minibar, fridge, coffeemaker, safe, IDD phone.

EXPENSIVE

Puri Bagus ★★   A lengthy but reasonable walk from the center of town, this is a compromise between the high-priced Amankila or Serai and the lesser hotels in Candi Dasa. Pretty and romantic, it's the best of its class. The grounds zigzag around the land jutting into the ocean, which laps right up to the edge, with steps down to the beach. Good-size bungalows are airy and light, thanks to many big windows, and Balinese music plays in them to greet you. Each has a small but clean and pretty sitting area; an open-air bath has hand-held showers (these are just a little frayed around the edges—probably weather-worn). The U-shape swimming pool has a very deep section for scuba practice and a large, shallow area for kids. There's an expensive but tasty restaurant with a fine ocean view and two bars. Dance programs and movies are offered at night, plus there's a full range of free daily activities.

P.O. Box 129, Candi Dasa, Karangasem 80801, Bali. ✆ **363-41131.** Fax 363-41290. www.bagus-discovery. com. 15 units. US$115–$160 double; US$235 2-bedroom villa. AE, DC, MC, V. **Amenities:** 2 restaurants; 2 bars; outdoor pool; tennis court (nearby); watersports equipment rentals; bike and scooter rentals; concierge; tour desk; car rental; shopping; room service (7am–midnight); massage; laundry. *In room:* A/C, minibar, fridge, IDD phone (better amenities, including fruit basket and sarong, in higher standards).

Serai ✿✿ From the outside, this comfortable, newish place looks more like a boxy, concrete apartment complex, but inside it is stark and chic. The staff is very friendly, and rooms are stylish, luxurious, and easy on the eyes, with nice touches like afternoon tea and treats on your patio. The large, lush central lawn and pool area is surrounded by teak lounges and leads to a large pebble beach. Getting to town is a bit of a haul, but regular shuttles make it convenient.

Buitan, Manggis, Karangasem, Bali 80871. ✆ **361/363-41011.** Fax 363-41015. www.ghmhotels.com. 58 units. US$180 standard; US$210 deluxe; US$310 suite. AE, DC, MC, V. **Amenities:** Restaurant; bar; rentals; tour services; shuttle bus; room service; babysitting; laundry; Internet. *In room:* A/C, satellite TV, minibar, fridge, IDD phone.

MODERATE

Watergarden ✿✿ One of the better-looking properties in Candi Dasa, the Watergarden has many repeat guests. The simple thatched, individual bungalows are not spectacular but are plenty comfortable; only some have air-conditioning, but each has a wide veranda overlooking one of the many lily ponds that give the hotel its name. The most private rooms are at the back, but they're also the farthest walk. For dining, don't miss Kafe TJ's (see "Where to Dine," below).

Main St., Candi Dasa. ✆ **363-41540.** Fax 363-41164. www.watergardenhotel.com. 14 units. US$70–US$85 double; US$160 2-bedroom suite. AE, MC, V. **Amenities:** Restaurant; bar (popular TJ's); outdoor pool; rentals available; games; tour desk; airport transfer; shopping; laundry; library. *In room:* A/C (some), TV, minibar, IDD phone.

INEXPENSIVE

Ashram Gandhi Candi Dasa Yes, this is a real ashram, and they are serious about it. It's a truly unique experience to stay here, and you are welcome to join in all daily activities, including prayer routines, yoga, meditation, and cleaning, though there are no obligations to participate. The vegetarian meals are quite good, and you can't beat the peaceful vibe; on the other hand, this is a commune—30 people live here full-time, amenities are minimal—cold water and fan only—and they do prohibit smoking, alcohol, and shared rooms by unmarried couples. Surrounding a lagoon, it's a nice location. There's a well-stocked reading room of spiritual literature, and the outside walls of the buildings feature quotes from Gandhi ("Learn to be your own judge and you will be happy.").

Main St., Candi Dasa. ✆ and fax **361/225-145.** 14 units. US$20–US$35 double. Only married couples can share rooms. Includes 3 vegetarian meals a day. 3-night minimum stay. **Amenities:** Restaurant; many classes; guides available.

Kubu Bali ✿ A great value for the price, the Kubu Bali is comfortable and atmospheric. Just off the main street in a ravine of rice terraces, it has grounds comprised of cobblestone gardens, statues, benches, aviaries, and pavilions on the terraced hillside. The handsomely decorated individual bungalows are simple, bright, and airy, with comfortable amenities. The bathrooms have nice porcelain tile and stone showers open to the sky. Each cottage has a porch and lounging couches, as well as its own sun deck. The immaculate grounds are crowned by an extremely pretty pool with views of the ocean.

Main St., Candi Dasa. ℭ **363-41532** or 363-41256. Fax 363-41531. 20 units. US$55 double; US$65 suite. MC, V. **Amenities:** Restaurant; outdoor pool; tour desk; car rental; shopping; room service (7am–10pm); massage; babysitting; laundry. *In room:* A/C, minibar, fridge, hair dryer, safe, IDD phone.

LOSMEN

There are a number of nice, atmospheric budget choices in and around town. Expect to pay between Rp100,000 and Rp200,000 (US$10–US$20), depending on beach proximity. Try **Ida's Homestay,** Main St., Candi Dasa (ℭ and fax **363-41096**); or **Kelapamas Homestay,** Main St., Candi Dasa, or P.O. Box 103, Amlapura 80801, Bali. (ℭ and fax **363-41947**). These are just two of many, and these are both closer to the beach and heavier on amenities than the many more bare-bones choices.

WHERE TO DINE

Kafe TJ's ✸✸ ASIAN/WESTERN   This is the best restaurant in Candi Dasa, hands down. The menu features good Western starters like guacamole, antipasto, and even potato skins, as well as fine Asian and Western dishes and entrees. The setting couldn't be nicer, and presentation is lovely. Try the satay served on little grills with actual glowing embers, or any of a number of Thai, Indian, and local curries, burgers, salads, and good sandwiches. The bar is one of the few nighttime hangouts in town, even if the atmosphere is a little less Bali and a little more Tahitian tropical island. You could just come for dessert; try the moist Wicked Chocolate Cake or tasty apple crumble with fine coffee.

In the Watergarden Hotel, Main St., Candi Dasa. ℭ **363-41540.** Main courses Rp15,000–Rp45,000 (US$1.50–US$4.50). AE, MC, V. Daily 7am–11pm.

Kubu Bali ✸ INDONESIAN/SEAFOOD   This is possibly the nicest looking restaurant in town, with pavilions bedecked with elaborate chandeliers, arranged among ponds, and set with large marble tables. The big, open kitchen (which helps ease fears about food sanitation) is at the entrance. It churns out a large menu, heavy on fish prepared all ways. You are better off having dessert at TJ's, however.

Kubu Bali Hotel. ℭ **363-41532.** Reservations not required. Main courses Rp12,500–Rp35,000 (US$1.20–US$3.40) (prawns higher). MC, V. Daily 9am–10pm.

Lotus Seaview ✸ INDONESIAN/SEAFOOD   Near the entrance to town and just a short walk from the center of things (the place offers shuttle service), this branch of the Lotus restaurants offers interesting variations on local fare (less fried). Fine choices include pastas, dishes "for meat lovers," or satay grilled at your table. Try the grilled fish satay or the *udang goreng,* sautéed shrimp with garlic, tomatoes, onions, and Balinese veggies. It's a good spot to drop in after snorkeling to enjoy the ocean view and have a fine fruit shake. Whatever you do, don't miss the *very* dense chocolate mousse—a barely whipped, pure chocolate concoction. Happy hours include a coffee and dessert special, and high tea is served.

Candi Dasa Beach. ℭ **363-41257.** Main courses Rp15,000–Rp45,000 (US$1.50–US$4.50). AE, MC, V. Daily 8am–10pm.

Warung Astawa ✸ INDONESIAN/CHINESE   It's hard to find good breakfast places around Candi Dasa, but this little warung earns kudos for its morning meal: Pancakes, fruit salad, and tomato-and-cheese omelets all get a thumbs up. At night, you can taste spring rolls and shrimp cocktails while watching Balinese dancers.

Main St., Candi Dasa. ℂ 363-41363. Main courses Rp6,000–Rp22,000 (US$0.60–US$2.20). Daily 8am–11pm.

OUTDOOR ACTIVITIES & WATERSPORTS

Watersports are the main reason for coming to Candi Dasa, with extremely healthy reefs and an array of marine life to explore with a snorkel or in full diving gear. Some spots are fit only for advanced divers, and you can even see the wreck of the WW II U.S.S. *Liberty* offshore at Tulamben.

Snorkeling and diving trips can be arranged through your hotel, with one of several operators along the main road (a couple are listed below).

As for swimming, the water between the "beach" and the seawalls is shallow but good for a dip; beyond the walls, it can be too rough.

SHOPPING

Shopping isn't much to write home about in Candi Dasa, but the absence of hard-selling touts can come as a relief. The **Asri Shop** (ℂ 363/41098), opposite the beach on the main street, is a catchall little spot not to be missed. There are a couple of bookstores in the area as well, and it's also worth checking out the authentic textiles in nearby Terganan.

CANDI DASA AFTER DARK

Candi Dasa is pretty low-key at night; most folks are up early for beach activities. The main beach road has several little bars and restaurants. **Warung Candi Agung,** on the main street (ℂ 363/41157), has dance performances, as does the nearby **Pandan Harum. TJ's** bar, in the Watergarden Hotel, is the most popular.

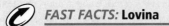

7 Lovina

Lovina attracts those looking to truly "get away from it all." Its real draw, though, are the dolphins that frolic off-shore every morning. It's also the logical jumping-off point for diving trips along the northern part of the island. This quiet stretch of beach is accessed only by rough mountain road, making this a mellow getaway. Though it is not as developed as the south of the island, there are some nice options.

GETTING AROUND

The main road runs parallel to the coast and is the locus of activity. You can get anywhere in town on foot, and **bemos** and shuttles connect with all locations.

ℂ FAST FACTS: Lovina

Banks/Currency Exchange Money changers are along the main road.

Internet/E-mail Spice Cyber (ℂ 362/41509), located in Spice Dive, a dive shop on Jalan Bina Ria, offers e-mail and fax service from 10am to 9pm daily for Rp30,000 (US.30¢) per hour.

Post Office/Mail There is no post office proper, but there are agents on the main road (or just hand your envelopes to your hotel to mail for you).

Telephone Find one on the main road west of Jalan Bina Ria. The area code for Lovina is 362.

WHERE TO STAY

Apart from a few luxury choices, accommodation here is basic but all beachside and affordable. It is a getaway, but the touts are here, too, of course.

VERY EXPENSIVE

Damai Lovina Hotel 🎐🎐   The motto of this hotel is "Hard to find, hard to leave," and it's a perfect little jewel of a place. Located high over Lovina, what you lose in beach access you gain in some of the finest accommodations in Bali. Rooms are all luxury villas done in teak and Balinese fabric, with four-poster beds draped in cheesecloth and large windows. Bathrooms have green-stone outdoor showers, wood sinks and vanities, and amenities in glass bottles. Deluxe villas have a bigger bathroom and an outdoor Jacuzzi spa tub. The grounds overlook a panorama of green hills, gorge, and blue ocean, with a small, lovely pool that seems to spill into the surroundings. For those worried about being so far (15–20 min.) from the ocean, there's regular shuttle service. It's comparable in luxury to the Amandari. The restaurant, Damai, is great (see below), though expensive, and guests can sign up for cooking courses.

P.O. Box 272. Jalan Damai, Kayuputih Lovina, Singaraja, Bali. 🕐 **362/41008.** Fax 362/41009. www.damai. com. 8 units. US$254–$285 double. Discount rates available. MC, V. **Amenities:** Restaurant; bar; saltwater swimming pool; all rentals; shuttle service; room service; laundry; library. *In room:* A/C, minibar, IDD phone.

EXPENSIVE

Puri Bagus Lovina 🎐🎐   This is a splendid place: high-end but affordable, and imaginative without going over the top. Rooms are all villas and simple but elegant and comfortable, with high, thatched ceilings and decorated in Bali fabric and local paintings. Prices vary according to the view (rice paddy, garden, or ocean). All rooms have verandas (some with sea view), and large bathrooms come with both indoor and outdoor showers. Suites will get you a private pool and even a kitchen. The landscaped grounds lead to a seawall: No sandy beach here, but there are nice *bales* (pavilions) overlooking the blue Java sea. The fine pool also has a good ocean view. There's a small seafood restaurant with outdoor kitchen, and another that serves fine Balinese fare. There's occasional evening entertainment.

P.O. Box 225, Lovina, Singaraja, Bali. 🕐 **362/21430.** Fax 362/22627. www.bagus-discovery.com. 40 units. US$125–US$150 double; US$350 suite. AE, DC, MC, V. **Amenities:** 2 restaurants; 2 bars; outdoor pool; spa; watersports rentals; motorbike rentals; tour desk; car rental; shuttle service; shopping; massage; laundry. *In room:* A/C, TV, minibar, IDD phone.

MODERATE

Hotel Aneka Lovina 🎐   This midrange accommodation is tidy but not memorable. Rooms are in thatched cottages set in a fine garden. Standard rooms are boring, with tiny, basic bathrooms, but second-story rooms offer nice views of green and thatch. Deluxe rooms are large, with carved wooden doors that lead to slightly less disappointing interiors—bamboo furniture and bigger bathrooms, some with tubs: a good deal. The small pool has a swim-up bar. There's occasional nighttime entertainment.

Jalan Rayan Lovina, North Bali. 🕐 **362/41121.** Fax 362/41827. www.aneka-hotels.com. 59 units. US$50–US$70 double. AE, MC, V. **Amenities:** 2 restaurants; 2 bars; outdoor pool; spa; watersports rentals; tour desk; room service (17 hr.); massage; laundry. *In room:* A/C, TV, IDD phone.

INEXPENSIVE

Rambutan Beach Cottages 🎐   This is by far the best budget option in Lovina. All rooms are in two-story red-and-white bungalows set in a pretty tropical garden. Budget rooms are better than others in this price range, but better still are standards and superiors, with plenty of nice Indonesian carved wood furniture and Bali fabrics. Rooms and bathrooms are large, in neat tile. Villas are furnished with classic teak furniture and come with a private garden and gazebo. The pool is an inviting little faux pond. The staff is friendly and speaks English, and can arrange any eventuality.

P.O. Box 195, Singaraja, Bali. © 362/41388. Fax 362/41057. Rambutan@indo.com. 33 units. US$15–US$55 double; US$85–US$180 villa. Rates include taxes and breakfast. MC, V. **Amenities:** Restaurant; bar; 2 outdoor pools (1 for kids); kids' playing area; all rentals; laundry. In room: A/C (higher standard), IDD phone.

LOSMEN

Bali's traditional budget accommodation is chock-a-block along the beaches and in the town of Lovina. All accept only cash and cost between Rp83,000 and Rp100,000 (US$8–US$10). Check out **Angsoka** (Jalan Bina Ria, Lovina Beach; © **362/41841**), a clean, comfortable choice; some rooms even have A/C, and there's a pool. **Astina Seaside Cottages** (500m or 1640 ft. from the main road; P.O. Box 141, Singaraja, Kalibukbuk, Lovina Beach; © **362/41187**) is a similar friendly standard, and **Bayu Kartika Beach Bungalows** (Jalan Ketapang, Kalibukbuk, Lovina Beach; © **362/41055**) is very popular with travelers.

WHERE TO DINE

With few exceptions, dining in Lovina is a pretty dull proposition, and the hotels are the best choices. Wander the main street, Jalan Bina Ria, and you're sure to stumble across something interesting. Here are a few:

Damai Restaurant ★★ NOUVELLE INDONESIAN   If you aren't staying here, do make the trip up the mountain to this luxe resort. You will pay more than you would for an average Bali meal, but the same standard might cost double back home. It's a limited specialties menu and thus focused on fresh ingredients (much of the produce comes from the hotel's organic farms). The presentation is modern, simple, and elegant, with small portions. The chicken satay, though more Chinese than Balinese, and the pan-fried fish in dill sauce are excellent. The wine list is extensive and priced accordingly.

Jalan Damai (in Hotel Damai), Kayuputih, Lovina. © **362/41008.** Reservations recommended. Lunch main courses Rp60,000–Rp88,000 (US$6–US$8.80); dinner set menu Rp400,000 (US$40). AE, MC, V. Daily 11am–3pm and 7–10pm.

Warung Kopi Bali ★ INDONESIAN/SEAFOOD   Better than the other tourist-oriented restaurants along Jalan Bina Ria, this place serves good, garlicky seafood kabobs, marinated shrimp, tuna, and veggies made with Balinese sauce all grilled together in a banana leaf. A large, delicious seafood basket combines more garlicky tuna, sweet-and-sour shrimp, deep-fried squid, fries, and vegetables. You get a free shot and garlic bread at happy hour.

Jalan Binara, Singaraja. © **362/41361.** Main courses Rp6,500–Rp20,000 (US$0.65–US$2). No credit cards. Daily 8am–11pm.

Warung Made Café ★ INDONESIAN   A bit noisy because it's on the busy main street, this warung has a nice menu of Balinese, vegetarian, and seafood items. It's also an ice-cream parlor serving great papaya and avocado shakes and the "Lovina Sunset" sundae. The friendly staff doesn't speak much English, but you might be speaking Malay after one of their lethal tropical cocktails, so it won't matter. A bulletin board has much information of interest to travelers, and at night there is live music or "bring your own tape or CD."

Jalan Main St. (right next to Aditya Hotel). ℂ 362/41239. Main courses Rp6,500–Rp20,000 (US$0.65–US$2). No credit cards. Daily 8am–11pm.

OUTDOOR ACTIVITIES & WATERSPORTS

The crystal-clear water at Lovina makes for some very fine **swimming,** and you can actually **snorkel** without a guide because coral begins rather close to shore. The reefs, a few hundred yards out, are best visited with a guide and by boat. Trips to nearby **Menjangan Island** (see "Sights near Lovina," below) to the west, or **Amed** and **Tulamben** to the east are some of the best diving in the region and can be booked at any hotel or dive shop in town.

Dolphin watching 🐾🐾 is what puts Lovina on the map, and trips leave early in the morning to view the beautiful creatures by boat. That moment when you're surrounded by leaping, laughing Flippers is certain to be memorable. Contact any hotel front desk or the folks at **Spice Dive,** Jalan Rina Bia (ℂ **362/ 41509**), or **Baruna,** Main Road, Kalibukbuk (ℂ **362/23775**), or any other shop.

8 Lombok

Lombok is what Bali was more than 20 years ago and a visit here is a flight into the rugged landscape of unspoiled Indonesia. Lombok is significantly dryer than Bali: Eastern regions are more characteristic of Australian geography, and in the south, many millions of years of volcanic runoff have sculpted a vast expanse of gently rolling hills that fans out from the island's lone looming volcano, **Gunung Rinjani.**

The people of Lombok are predominantly Muslim rather than Hindu, but, like the Balinese, many maintain animist traditions. Visitors to Lombok are drawn by the promise of unspoiled beaches, great **snorkeling and diving,** or the challenge of climbing **Mt. Rinjani** or visiting rural villages and waterfalls. The island's inhabitants are known for their artistry in decorative items, pottery, baskets, and woven textiles; a visit to the many villages specializing in these crafts will be a highlight of your trip.

Tourism is in its infancy here, and the touts are quite desperate for clients. Our advice is to spread the wealth; get that shoulder massage for Rp21,000 (US$2), tip someone to carry your bag, or make a few well-placed purchases, and you'll be much appreciated and keep the crowds at bay.

GETTING THERE

Any travel office on Bali can book your Lombok trip and arrange bus transfer packages, so inquire about this if your hotel does not offer shuttle service at the harbor (most do at the airport). We highly recommend the hydrofoil.

BY FERRY   The ferry (ℂ 361/721212) leaves Padang Bai (just south of Candi Dasa) twice a day and take 4 hours (Rp15,000/US$1.50).

BY HYDROFOIL   **Bounty Cruises** is your best bet, making the trip daily from Benoa Harbor (just north of Nusa Dua, ℂ 361/7333333), Bali at 9am and stopping at Senggigi Beach and the Gili Islands (2½ hr.; US$35). The Mabua Express (ℂ **361/721212**) departs from Benoa and arrives in Lempar about 2 hours later (US$25–US$30). Always check to confirm departure times.

BY PLANE   **Merpati** (ℂ 361/263918) and **Garuda National** (ℂ 361/ 227825) fly several times daily to Lombok's **Selaparang Airport** (20 min.;

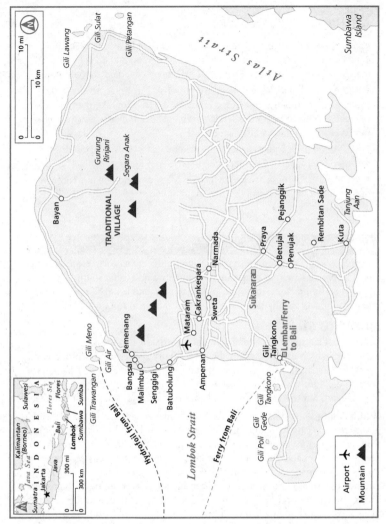

approximately US$30) from Bali and Jakarta, respectively. **Silkair** (© **370/ 628254;** fax 370/628292), the regional wing of Singapore Airlines, flies from Singapore daily. If you're planning on a quick hop over from Bali, note that frequent delays can turn a 20-minute flight into an infuriating several-hour ordeal, stranding you at the airport—this makes a relaxing 2½-hour boat ride seem all the more attractive. Be sure to double-check your return flight.

GETTING AROUND
Public transport is rattle-trap **bemos** or **horse-drawn carts,** so **renting a car or motorbike** is a good choice. Your hotel can set you up with a rental, or you can get one at the airport when you arrive. Hydrofoils connect with the Gili Islands.

> *FAST FACTS:* **Lombok**
>
> *Banks/Currency Exchange* There are two new ATM locations in Senggigi: Bank BDI (next to Silkair and the Pacific Supermarket) and Bank BCA (near the turnoff to the Senggigi Beach Hotel). Money-changers also abound.
>
> *Health/Safety* Lombok's monkeys are high-risk for rabies, so don't feed them, wear long pants and closed shoes, and don't provoke them. If bitten, you'll need to begin the series of rabies shots *immediately* (don't listen to anyone who says otherwise).
>
> *Internet/E-mail* Senggigi Beach has several cafes clustered along the southern end of Jalan Raya Senggigi (near Bayan Restaurant).
>
> *Post Office/Mail* There are post offices in Mataram and one in the center of Senggigi, but your hotel can also mail for you.

9 Senggigi

Senggigi, 12km (7½ miles) north of Mataram, is the main beach resort on Lombok. The beaches aren't as outstanding as those found farther south, but Senggigi has good tourist infrastructure, is close to sites, and is the best place for the causal visitor, particularly one planning only a short trip to Lombok.

WHERE TO STAY

Lombok has already come a long way since the days when shacks on the beach were your only overnight options. Five-star luxury properties are sprouting on the western coastline above Senggigi (the Oberoi, for one; ℂ **370/638444;** fax 370/632496; www.oberoihotels.com), attracting a more exclusive clientele to the island, but there are a few simple but comfortable atmospheric choices.

Alang Alang ℱ A few miles up the road from Senggigi Beach makes a world of difference. Alang Alang, meaning "thatched roof" in Indonesian, is that perfectly characteristic property you hoped to find at the end of your travels. It's small scale, affordable, beachfront, and far enough away from any real center of things to discourage touts. All but three of the bungalow units have "au naturel" outdoor bathrooms and showers, while inside are simple boutique rooms featuring carved platform beds, embroidered mosquito netting, and nice touches like soaps wrapped in dried coconut leaves. Get a bunch of friends together and rent the villa, a veritable Raja's palace with its own private beachfront swimming pool, kitchen, dining area, and two luxury outdoor bathrooms, both with the john out under the stars. There's also a romantic oceanfront restaurant.

Jalan Raya Mangsit, Senggigi, Lombok. ℂ **370/693518.** Fax 370/693194. www.alang-alang-villas.com. 19 units. US$90 standard room; US$125 deluxe bungalow; US$600 2-bedroom villa (capacity 6). MC, V. **Amenities:** Restaurant; bar; outdoor pool; bike and scooter rental; room service; massage; laundry; dry cleaning. *In room:* A/C, TV, kitchenette, minibar, fridge, hair dryer, safe, IDD phone.

Pool Villa Club at the Senggigi Beach Hotel ℱℱ Billed as a "hotel within a hotel," the Pool Villa Club ups the high-end ante on the nearby Sheraton. Villas are all duplexes, with separate living room, dining room, and upstairs bedroom with balcony. Rear terraces with teak lounges spill onto the lagoon pool that snakes through the property, and there are private sunken Jacuzzis. There are nice details throughout, like funky little crafts in banana leafs and fine bathroom amenities supplied by Bvlgari. Bathrooms are over the top, enormous and with large marble sunken tubs. It's become a popular honeymoon spot.

Jl. Pantai Senggigi, Mataram 83010, Lombok. © 370/693210. Fax 370/693200. villas@indo.net.id. 16 villas. US$380 villa. Rates include breakfast. AE, DC, MC, V. **Amenities:** Restaurant; bar; outdoor pool; golf course; tennis court; spa; Jacuzzi; rentals available; tour desk; 24-hr. room service; massage; laundry; dry cleaning. *In room:* A/C, satellite TV, minibar, fridge, coffeemaker, IDD phone.

Senggigi Beach Hotel ⭐   Down the a quiet dirt lane, this unassuming hotel is comfortable but not luxe, a la an American motel. Bungalows are slightly nicer, with bigger baths and nicer amenities. Each bungalow has two rooms with connecting doors, so this is a good option for families. Kids might also like running around the large grounds. The nondescript pool is a bit inland and provides relief from touts. There is a spa on-site, three restaurants (frequent evening theme dinners), and three bars.

Jalan Pantai Senggigi, Senggigi, P.O. Box 1001, Mataram 83010, Lombok. © 370/693210. Fax 370/693200. 149 units. US$130 double; US$160–US$250 bungalow. AE, DC, MC, V. **Amenities:** 3 restaurants; 3 bars; outdoor pool; tennis court; fitness center; rentals available; kids' club; tour desk; laundry. *In room:* A/C, TV, minibar, fridge, IDD phone.

Sheraton Senggigi ⭐⭐   The staff of this upscale gem is helpful, and all speak excellent English and can help with any eventuality. The newly redone lobby is tropical elegance, and the ocean-side garden at seaside is lush. Rooms, though done is tropical colors and tidy, are in uninspired chain decor. Bathrooms are large, and many rooms have great views. The pool is luxe, with a waterslide, and the nearby beach is free of vendors and touts. You might even be able to pet one of the tame deer grazing the compound. A recently completed beachfront spa pavilion is of the highest standard: ask the hotel's booking office about its fine vacation getaway packages. The three dining venues are all good choices, and there are some nice romantic getaways with views of the ocean on the grounds here.

Jalan Raya Senggigi km 8, Senggigi, P.O. Box 1154, Mataram 83015, Lombok. © 800/325-3535 or 370/693333. Fax 370/693140. www.sheraton.com. 156 units. US$170–US$190 double (deluxe); US$400–US$500 suite; US$1,100 beachfront villa. AE, DC, MC, V. **Amenities:** 3 restaurants; 2 bars; outdoor pool; tennis court; fitness center; Jacuzzi; sauna; rentals available; tour desk; 24-hr. room service; massage; babysitting; laundry. *In room:* A/C, satellite TV (in-house movies), minibar, fridge, hair dryer, safe, IDD phone.

WHERE TO DINE

Restaurants in Senggigi cluster around Jalan Raya Road, roughly in the center of Senggigi action, and there are just a few decent choices outside of the hotels. Try **Taman Senggigi,** Jalan Raya (© **370/693842**), which serves Indonesian and international dishes in a lush garden. **Gili Masak,** Jalan Raya (© **370/693105**), has a creative menu rich in Indonesian spices. Of the hotel restaurants, try **Alang Alang** (© **370/693518**), with its romantic atmosphere, or the Sheraton's **Kebun Anggrek** (© **370/693333**), which serves good international cuisine.

GILI ISLANDS

Just to the northwest of Lombok are three small islands that offer some of the best snorkeling and diving in the region. The reef is damaged and the currents can be rough, but the sea life is impressive. Snorkelers will be happy near the beaches to the north of **Gili Trawangan** and **Gili Meno,** but **Gili Trawangan** is renowned for great diving. Dive shops in Senggigi and the local hotels will arrange trips out to the islands. **Dream Divers** (© **370/693738;** www.dreamdivers.com) is one of the biggest and best organized.

Many tourists just make day diving trips here, but the islands do offer the most basic of overnight accommodations (mostly losmen). The biggest and most popular among the expat crowd is the **Villa Ombak** *, on Gili Trawangan (© **370/642336**).

10 Kuta

Not to be confused with the Bali Kuta, this Kuta is similarly popular as a surfing mecca but is little more than a wide spot in the road along this sweeping bay south of Mataram. There are some of the finest virgin white-sand beaches on the whole island, and Kuta is slated for development so now's the time to get here. Take care of your belongings, even when you think you're alone on a remote beach.

WHERE TO STAY

Matahari Inn * A laid-back, budget-friendly alternative to the Novotel, there are 25 very plain rooms and 6 luxe villas that are thatched Sasak-style bungalows and arranged around a small swimming pool and garden. The villas are plush, decorated with furnishings of inlaid wood or carved and gilded Balinese pieces. Bathrooms are comfortable and modern, with bathtubs in an outdoor garden. The Matahari staff is gracious and helpful, and can arrange excursions or activities like beach sports and horseback riding.

Kuta Beach, Lombok. © **370/655000.** Fax 370/654832. matahari@mataram.wasantara.net.id. 30 villas. US$15–$60 double. Rates include breakfast. No credit cards. **Amenities:** Restaurant; bar; outdoor pool; tour desk; laundry. *In room:* A/C (villas), IDD phone.

Novotel Lombok ** They say you either love or hate this off-the-beaten track gem. There's not much out here, but the hotel is self-sufficient and arranges good excursions. Standard rooms, in sandstone blocks, are arranged around bungalows constructed to look like the distinctive Sasak villages that you pass on the way to Kuta. Bungalows offer more space and have their own swimming pool. All rooms are done in all-natural fabrics and woods (even fun accents, like coconut-fiber telephones). The elevated pool is picturesque, with a series of lovely fountains. All of it overlooks the purest white beach and clear water, with surrounding hills and sky—a romantic, luxurious getaway. The staff is superb, all are genuinely friendly, and most speak excellent English. The Mandara Spa is the bee's knees.

Mandalika Resort Pantai Putri Nyale, Pujut Lombok Tengah, Nusa Tenggara Barat. © **370/653333.** Fax 370/653555. www.novotel-lombok.com. 108 units. US$130–US$150 double (deluxe); US$250 bungalow or villa. AE, DC, MC, V. **Amenities:** 2 restaurants; 2 bars; 3 outdoor pools; fitness center; fine spa; watersports rentals; kids' club; tour desk; car rental; shopping; massage; babysitting; laundry. *In room:* A/C, satellite TV, minibar, fridge, IDD phone.

WHERE TO DINE

Stick to the hotels here: Good bets are the Matahari Inn, the Kuta Indah Hotel and Restaurant, and, of course, the Novotel.

11

Cambodia

by Charles Agar

It wasn't long ago that travel guides about Cambodia weren't much more than protractive warnings and lists of safety precautions, and for good reason: Following years of war, the chaos and genocide of Pol Pot's Khmer Rouge, and a long period of civil and political instability, Cambodia was until recently an armed camp and was closed to foreign visitors (or open only to travelers of the danger-seeking variety). But Cambodia is healing, and, though this is a process that will take years, the country is enjoying a period of peace and prosperity under a stable coalition government. Cambodia offers travelers a host of experiences, from the legacy of ancient architecture to a growing urban capital and beautiful countryside. Even the shortest visit is a window into a vibrant ancient culture and a chance to meet with a very kind and resilient people.

What brings so many to this Buddhist land of smiles is **Angkor Wat,** the ancient capital and one of the man-made wonders of the world. The temple complex at Angkor is stunning, a pilgrimage point for temple aficionados and a place of spiritual significance to many. Most travelers limit their visit to a few days at the temples and the major sites in the growing capital, **Phnom Penh,** but travel in rural Cambodia, once unheard of, is now limited only by your tolerance for bumpy roads and rustic accommodation. Bouncing around the hinterlands of Cambodia still begs caution, though, and travelers should be aware of the mass amounts of UXO (unexploded mines), poor road conditions, and the absence of proper medical services. But dusty roads pay off when they connect hamlets rarely visited by outsiders or lead to unexplored rural ruins. Any of the larger tour operators are a good bet for arranging trips to the likes of mountainous **Rattanakiri,** in the northeast, the Thai border area, or rural riverside towns along the Mekong. The country's only port, **Sihanoukville,** is a little beach destination that's growing in popularity. Intrepid travelers commonly rent motorcycles or brave rattletrap buses.

Known for warm, beguiling smiles, smiles that have weathered great hardship, Khmer people are very friendly, approachable, and helpful; but be warned that the hard sell is on in Cambodia, and you're sure to be harried, especially by the persistent young sellers at Angkor Wat. Nevertheless, travelers here are sure to meet with great kindness.

For years, the lawlessness of Cambodia attracted some rather dubious foreign visitors who came in droves for budget drugs and prostitutions. Phnom Penh's expatriate community was notorious during years of instability, even the UN troops that arrived in 1992 were as much a part of the problem in their support of local vice as they were in maintaining order and ensuring fair elections. "Sexpats" and drug tourists are on the wane in Cambodia, but, sadly, there still is a contingent of folks who come to take advantage of Cambodia's seedier stock-in-trade. Only recently, Britain's Gary Glitter was given a *persona non grata* order by the Khmer government for his abhorrent behavior, and many others are being profiled and given one-way tickets out.

Tourism is growing in leaps and bounds, though, and there are many **non-government organizations (NGO's)** here to do their part to rebuild and support the growing nation. Their activities, centered in offices in Phnom Penh, are what keep social services and the infrastructure at subsistence levels. Volunteer opportunities abound, and the obligatory United Nations white Land Rovers seem to be the car of choice in most towns. The sum of these recent booms in tourism and the large expat community means finer services for visitors, and the hotels and restaurants in Siem Reap and Phnom Penh are on par with any in the region, although outside of these two centers it's sparse.

If only to see Angkor Wat, the trip is worth it. It is a beguiling land that is shaking off the shackles of a devastating recent history and is an exciting tourist destination.

1 Getting to Know Cambodia

THE LAY OF THE LAND

About the size of Missouri, some 181,035 sq. km (69,898 sq. miles), Cambodia's 20 provinces are bordered by Laos in the north, Vietnam in the east, Thailand to the west, and the Gulf of Thailand to the south. There is just one marine port in Cambodia: Sihanoukville, connected via a major American-built highway with the capital and largest city, Phnom Penh.

The mighty Mekong enters from Laos to the north and nearly bisects the country. The river divides into two main tributaries at Phnom Penh before it traces a route to the delta in Vietnam, and most areas of population density lie along the river valleys and fertile plains of this great river and its tributaries. Near Siem Reap, the Tonle Sap (Great Lake) is the largest lake in Southeast Asia. In the monsoon summer months, when the Mekong is swollen from the snows of Tibet, the river becomes choked with silt and backs up on the Mekong Delta. The result is an anomaly: The Tonle Sap river relieves the pressure by changing the direction of its flow and draining the Mekong Delta hundreds of miles in the opposite direction and into the Tonle Sap Lake.

The northeast of the country, Ratanakiri Province, and areas bordering Vietnam are quite mountainous and rugged, as are the Thai border areas defined by the Dangrek Mountains in the northwest and the Cardamom Mountains in the southwest. These jungle forest regions are a rich source for timber in the region, and steps toward preservation come slow.

A LOOK AT THE PAST

Some 2 millennia ago, a powerful people known as the Khmer ruled over much of present-day Southeast Asia, including parts of what is now eastern Thailand, southern Vietnam, and Laos. Theirs was a kingdom that seems to have been created in a dream, full of wondrous temples, magnificent cities rising from steamy jungles, and glorious gods.

The story of Khmer civilization is one of a slow decline from the zenith of the powerful Angkor Civilization of the 11th century. War and years of alternating occupation by neighboring Thailand to the west and Vietnam to the east, later by the French and Japanese, had Cambodia bouncing like a strategic ping-pong

ball, and the Khmer kingdom's size was chiseled away considerably. Remaining is what we know today as Cambodia, a tiny land half the size of Germany.

The name Cambodia is an Anglicized version of the French *Cambodge,* a bastardized name of the tribe of northern India from which the Khmer are said to descend. Citizens and language are alternately referred to as Khmer or Cambodian. Whatever the origins, the name Cambodia hardly evokes thoughts of ancient glory: To those of us born in the late 20th century, especially in the West, Cambodia suggests instead a history of oppression, civil war, genocide, drug running, and coups d'état. Constant political turbulence, armed citizenry, bandits, and war fallout, such as unexploded mines and bombs, have given the country a reputation as one of the world's most dangerous places to travel rather than a repository of man-made and natural wonders. It's important to have perspective on the country's troubled history in order to understand the present. Only then can we appreciate the present civil order and the fact that citizens have been or are being disarmed, and that Cambodia is making the slow push into this new century.

A TURBULENT POLITICAL PAST

Cambodia is populated by people of the **Mon-Khmer** ethnic group, who probably migrated from the north as far back as 1,000 B.C. It was part of the kingdom of Funan, a Southeast Asian empire that also extended into Laos and

Vietnam, to the 6th century, when it was briefly absorbed into a rebel nation called Chenla. It then evolved into its glorious Angkor period in the 8th century, from which sprung many of Cambodia's treasures, most notably the lost city of Angkor.

By the late 12th century, however, the Angkor kingdom began a decline, marked by internal rebellions. Angkor was lost to the Kingdom of Siam in 1431 and Vietnam jousted with Siam and also had a hand in controlling the kingdom, to some degree, beginning in the early 17th century. The French took over completely in 1863, followed by the Japanese and then the French again. Cambodia finally regained independence in 1953 under the leadership of **Prince Norodom Sihanouk.**

Vietnamese communist outposts in the country, however, drew Cambodia into the Vietnam Conflict. It was heavily bombed by American forces in the late 1960s. A U.S.–backed military coup followed in 1970, but in 1975 the infamous **Khmer Rouge,** led by the tyrannical **Pol Pot,** took over Cambodia, renamed it Kampuchea, and established a totalitarian regime in the name of communism. Opposition—even imaginary opposition—was brutally crushed, resulting in the death of over 2 million Cambodians. The civil and Vietnam wars decimated Cambodian infrastructure. It became, and still is, one of the world's poorest nations, with a mainly agrarian economy and a literacy rate of about 35%.

In response to Khmer Rouge infractions in its country, Vietnam invaded Cambodia in 1978 and occupied it with a small number of troops until 1989, installing a puppet regime led by Hun Sen as prime minister. When Vietnam departed, the United Nations stepped in and engineered a fragile coalition government between the Sihanouk and Hun Sen factions. There was never full agreement, however, and Hun Sen took over in a violent 1997 coup. The Khmer Rouge subsequently waned in power, and its former leader, Pol Pot, died in 1998.

In November 1998, a new coalition government was formed between the two leading parties, leading to relative political peace. Cambodia is now leaning toward a war crimes tribunal for Khmer Rouge perpetrators, but it still has not decided how to confront its vicious and bloody past and move forward.

THE PRESENT

These days, it looks as if Cambodia's assets might finally be able to get their due attention as tourists discover Cambodia's untapped beauty and rich history.

The ancient civilization of the Khmer is accessible and written large and in stone at **Angkor Wat.** The monumental Hindu temples are breathtaking in both beauty and historical significance, a lost city telling its story in crumbling roads, behemoth buildings, and ornate bas-reliefs covering crumbling temple walls. Then there is **Phnom Penh,** the capital, tatty but charming, with crumbling French colonial architecture and a splendid palace.

Cambodia is resplendent with natural gifts; the **Mekong River** is the country's lifeline and can be followed as it winds through the countryside. Cambodia's main highway connects with **Tonle Sap,** or Great Lake, Southeast Asia's largest lake, surrounded by fertile lowlands.

Cambodia's economy struggles, but now a member of ASEAN and under a peaceful coalition government headed by Hun Sen since 1998, the outlook is promising. Tourists know it and are coming in droves, many to rush into the countryside before the tour buses discover it. While Cambodia is not yet risk-free and a trip entails following safety precautions to the letter (see below), this land's marvels will be well worth your effort.

THE KHMER PEOPLE

Of the 11 million people in Cambodia, 90% are ethnic Khmer. The remaining 10% is a mix of ethnic Vietnamese, Chinese, hill tribes, and a small pocket of Cham Muslims. A look at the history of the nation shows a crisscrossing of invasion and the rise and fall of monarchies that make Cambodia the very definition of what the French aptly called Indochina; Cambodia is a geographic and cultural crossroads of the two powers, India and China, that shaped Southeast Asia. Khmer culture, like nearby Laos, is defined by Theravada Buddhism, but in other matters, one gets the distinct impression that Cambodia is still searching for its identity.

ETIQUETTE

Traditions and practices in Cambodia, like neighboring Thailand and Laos, are closely tied with Theravada Buddhism. Modest dress is expected of all visitors, and bare midriffs or short shorts are an offense to many and will cause a stir. Men and women should go easy on public displays of affection. As in all Buddhist countries, it is important to respect the space around any Buddhist monk; women especially should avoid touching and even speaking to the men in orange robes anywhere outside the temple.

In personal interaction, keep it light and friendly, especially when bargaining or handling any business affairs. If Khmer people are confused, misunderstand, or disagree, they do what many Westerners find inconceivable: smile, nod, and agree while whole in the knowledge that they will do something different. This is difficult to understand, but try to remember that if you're angry and lots of people around you are smiling, you're unlikely to have achieved your desired aim (in short, you're doomed). Direct discourse is certainly not standard procedure here, and many Western visitors can feel cheated by that misunderstanding. Be clear in what you expect from someone—whether a guide, a motorbike driver, or a business associate—and get firm affirmation of that fact.

On the line of cultural "no-no's," it's important to remember that the feet are considered dirty and that the head is sacred and pure. This means that even pointing the feet in the direction of another or stepping over someone, thus exposing the soles of the feet, is impolite. Touching someone's head, even tussling a child's hair, should be avoided.

Hospitality has its own elaborate rules, and, like in any culture, it is important to accept when possible, or comfortable, and say thank you, *Awk Koun*.

LANGUAGE

Like other languages in the region, Khmer belongs to the Mon-Khmer family and is a derivative of Sanskrit and Pali; but unlike in neighboring Thailand and Laos, the Khmer language is not tonal and is thus more merciful to the casual learner. Basic pronunciation is still frustrating and difficult, though. Khmer script is based on a south Indian model and is quite complex.

Referred to as Khmer or Cambodian interchangeably, the language embraces many loan words from French, Chinese, and now English, especially technical terms. Older Khmers still speak French, and young people are quite keen to learn and practice English. In the major tour centers, speaking slowly and clearly in basic English phrases will do the trick, but a few choice phrases in Khmer will get you far.

USEFUL KHMER PHRASES

Hello	**Soa s'day**
Good bye	**Lia haoy**
Thank you	**Awk koun**
Thank you very much	**Awk koun chelan**
How are you?	**Sohk sabai?**
I am fine.	**Sohk sabai.**
Yes (man)	**Baat**
Yes (woman)	**Jaa**
No	**Te**
I'm sorry	**Sohm To**
Do you have _____?	**Men awt men?**
	(lit. do you have
	or don't you?)
Water?	**Tuhk?**
Toilet?	**Bawngku uhn?**
How much?	**Th'lai pohnmaan?**
Can you make it	**Som joh th'lai.**
cheaper?	

2 Planning Your Trip to Cambodia

VISITOR INFORMATION

You'll find a wealth of information at www.gocambodia.com, or click on "Cambodia" at www.visit-mekong.com. The Cambodian Embassy to the U.S. sponsors www.embassy.org/cambodia.

- **In the U.S.:** 4500 16th St. NW, Washington, DC 20011 (© **202/726-7742;** fax 202/726-8381; www.embassy.org). **In NY:** 866 UN Plaza, Suite 420, New York, NY 10017 (© **212/421-7626;** fax 212/421-7743).
- **In Australia/New Zealand:** No. 5 Canterbury Crescent, Deakin, ACT 2600, Canberra (© **61-6/273-1259;** fax 61-6/273-1053; www.embassyof cambodia.org.nz/).
- **In Thailand:** No. 185 Rajdammri Rd, Lumpini Patumwan, Bangkok 10330, Thailand (© **662/254-6630;** fax 662/253-9859; recanbot@lox info.co.tlt).

WORKING WITH A TOUR OPERATOR

Many visitors choose to see Cambodia with the convenience of a guided tour, which is a good idea: It's not only safer and easier, but it also means that you won't miss the finer details of what you're seeing and can visit rural Cambodia in as much comfort as possible. Being part of a larger group tour is a good, affordable option. Even if you travel independently, you might want to sign up with a local tour operator (like Diethelm or Exotissimo, below) once you're there.

Recommended tour operators:

- **Abercrombie & Kent.** 1520 Kensington Rd., Suite 212, Oakbrook, IL 60523-2141 (© **800/323-7308;** fax 630/954-3324; www.aandktours. com).
- **Asia Transpacific Journeys.** 2995 Center Green Court, Boulder, CO 80301 (© **800/642-2742** or 303/443-6789; fax 303/443-7078; www.asia transpacific.com).

- **Diethelm Travel.** No. 65 St. 240, P.O. Box 99, Phnom Penh, Cambodia (© **023/219-151;** fax 023/219-150; www.diethelm-travel.com). **In Siem Reap:** House no. 4, Road no. 6, Krum no. 1, Sangkat no. 2, Phum Taphul, Siem Reap, Cambodia (© **63/963-524;** fax 63/963-694).
- **Exotissimo.** 46 Norodom Blvd. (© **023/218-948;** fax 023/426-586; www. exotissimo.com).

ENTRY REQUIREMENTS

All visitors are required to carry a passport and visa. A 1-month visa can be issued on arrival at the Phnom Penh or Siem Reap airports for about 80,000R (US$20), and an overland visa-upon-arrival is available from both Thailand and Vietnam. From Poi Pet (Thailand), a 1-month visa costs 1,000 Baht (about US$22); at the riverside checkpoint, when coming by boat from Chau Doc, a Vietnam visa costs US$22. Bring two passport photos for your application. For any other entry points, you must obtain your visa before arrival and specify your place of entry up front. There is no overland or water crossing between Laos and Cambodia, although some intrepid travelers report successfully bribing their way across the border.

Tourist visas can be extended three times for a total of 3 months. Any travel agent can perform the service for a small fee. Business visas, for just US$25 upon entry, can be extended indefinitely.

CUSTOMS REGULATIONS

For visitors 18 years or older, allowable amounts of goods when entering are as follows: 200 cigarettes or the equivalent quantity of tobacco, 1 opened bottle of liquor, and a reasonable amount of perfume for personal use. Currency in possession must be declared on arrival. Cambodian Customs on the whole is not stringent. With a long, sad history of theft from the Angkor temples, it is forbidden to carry antiques or Buddhist reliquary out of the country, but Buddhist statues and trinkets bought from souvenir stalls are fine.

MONEY

Cambodia's official currency is the Riel, but the Cambodian economy is tied to the fate of its de facto currency, the U.S. dollar. The exchange rate at the time of publication was **3,900 Riel = US$1.** It's important to have Riel for smaller purchases, but there is no point in exchanging large amounts of foreign currency into the local scrap. With that said, **we did not convert the U.S. dollar to Riel in this chapter.** The **Thai Bhat** is widely accepted in the western region of the country, and U.S. dollars are accepted everywhere. You'll commonly receive change for dollar payments in Riel, so it helps to be able to convert quickly (you can estimate by dividing Riel amounts by 4,000 or multiplying dollar quotes by 4,000). The Riel comes in denominations of 100, 200, 500, 1,000, 2,000, 5,000, 10,000, 50,000, and 100,000. Like the Vietnamese dong, you cannot change Cambodia's Riel outside the country, so anything you carry home is a souvenir.

CURRENCY EXCHANGE   You can change traveler's checks in banks in all major towns. Because the U.S. dollar is the de facto currency, it's not a bad idea to change traveler's checks to dollars for a 1% or 2% fee and make all purchases in U.S. cash.

TRAVELER'S CHECKS   Traveler's checks are accepted in most major banks for exchange, but not commonly at individual vendors, other than a few of the high-end hotels. American Express is a good bet and is represented by **Diethelm.**

ATMs   There are no ATMs with international capabilities in Cambodia.

CREDIT CARDS   Cambodia is very much a cash economy, but credit cards are becoming more widely accepted. Most large hotels and high-end restaurants accept the majors, but you'll want to carry cash for most transactions and certainly in the countryside. To report a lost or stolen card, see the "Fast Facts" section in chapter 3.

WHEN TO GO

CLIMATE   Cambodia's climate falls into the pattern of the southern monsoons that also hit neighboring Thailand and Vietnam from May to November. There is little seasonal temperature variation, meaning that it's always hot (a yearly mean of about 82°F/28°C), and the best time to go is in the dry season from December to April.

CLOTHING CONSIDERATIONS   Keep it light and loose; it's always hot, and you're sure to carry your own luggage at some time along the way. Loose, long-sleeve shirts and long pants are best. Cotton is the best choice, and long trousers are a better idea than shorts for two reasons: First, it's the best way to fend off mosquitoes. Second, culturally, shorts are worn by children, not adults (although long shorts are more accepted, especially for young men), and for women only rarely (with sporting events being the exception). A wide-brimmed hat is essential protection from the sun, and some even carry an umbrella to be used either as a parasol or as cover from sporadic rains. Sandals are acceptable in most arenas.

PUBLIC HOLIDAYS & EVENTS   **Independence Day** is November 9 (1953) and is celebrated throughout the country like the American July 4th. October 31 is **King Sihanouk's Birthday,** and **Khmer New Year** is in the middle of the month in April. There are water festivals and boat races at the end of November, and the **Angkor Festival** is held at the end of July.

SOME IMPORTANT SAFETY TIPS

- Though a far cry from the dangers of yore, it is still important to stay aware in rural areas because banditry remains a concern.
- Stay abreast of the political situation before and during your visit. Cambodia is enjoying one of the longest periods of political stability and growth, but the general elections scheduled for summer 2003 could bring regime change or coup d'état, as is the model, so stay informed.

(**Warning**   **Safety**

It is highly recommended that you check with your home country's overseas travel bureau or with the **United States Department of State** (click "Travel Warnings" at www.state.gov) to keep abreast of travel advisories and current affairs that could affect your trip.

The days of the Khmer Rouge taking backpackers hostage are long gone, and the general lawlessness and banditry that marked Cambodia as inaccessible and dangerous only a short time ago has abated. Gun-toting thugs, once a common site in any town, have been disarmed, but old habits die hard and, in general, travelers should take caution. Lack of infrastructure also means that rural travel is only for the adventurous.

Warning **Medical Safety & Evacuation Insurance**

The Cambodian medical system is rudimentary at best and nonexistent at worst. Make sure that you have medical coverage for overseas travel and that it includes emergency evacuation. For details on insurance, see chapter 3. There are a few clinics in Phnom Penh and Siem Reap, but for anything major, evacuation to Bangkok is the best option.

- Remember, too, that the police and military of Cambodia are not there to protect and serve. Any interaction with the constabulary usually results in frustration or your coming away short a few dollars. Contact your embassy for major problems, and call for police assistance only in cases of theft or extreme danger.
- Rural travel is really opening up, and you'll find a hearty welcome in even the most remote hamlet, but roads are rough and travel of any distance is best done in off-road conveyance with a sturdy suspension: Motorbike or four-wheel-drive trucks are best.
- Especially at night, travelers should stay aware, not unlike in any big city at night; purse snatching is not uncommon in Phnom Penh, and pickpockets are as proficient here as anywhere in the region, so take care.
- Land mines and unexploded ordnance can be found in rural areas in Cambodia, but especially in Battambang, Banteay Meanchey, Pursat, Siem Reap, and Kampong Thom provinces. Don't walk in heavily forested spots or in dry rice paddies without a local guide. Areas around small bridges on secondary roads are particularly dangerous.
- Domestic air travel has yet to pass international standards.

DRUGS

Cambodia is one of the world's biggest producers of cannabis—not to mention heroin, amphetamines, and other substances—and petty producers abound. You might be tempted to buy or sample substances offered, but if you're caught, you could face a lengthy jail sentence, which is guaranteed to be uncomfortable. Enough said.

HEALTH CONCERNS AND VACCINATIONS

In chapter 3, we outlined information about vaccinations and general issues that affect the region. Health considerations should comprise a good part of your trip planning for Cambodia, even if you're going for only a few weeks. You'll need to cover all the bases to protect yourself from tropical weather and illnesses, and you will need to get special vaccinations if rural areas are on your itinerary. You should begin your vaccinations as necessary at least weeks before your trip to give them time to take effect. If you follow the guidelines here and those of your doctor, however, there's no reason you can't have a safe and healthy trip.

Malaria is not a concern in Phnom Penh and any of the larger towns, but upcountry and even in and around Siem Reap and Angkor Wat, it's quite common. Many travelers take preventative medication. Check with the Center for Disease Control (CDC) at www.cdc.com for current information.

Other mosquito-borne ailments, such as **Japanese encephalitis** and **dengue fever,** are also prevalent. Your best protection is to wear light, loose-fitting clothes from wrist to neck and ankles, wear a bug repellent with DEET, and be particularly careful at sunset or when out and about early in the morning.

Hepatitis is a concern as anywhere (see chapter 3), and reliable statistics on **AIDs** are not out, but with rampant prostitution and drug abuse, Cambodia is certainly fertile ground for the disease. Recent efforts to educate needle users about the dangers of the substance and the importance of clean needles, as well as increased condom use, are positive signs.

FOREIGN EMBASSIES IN CAMBODIA

If you encounter problems during your visit, go to your embassy. Addresses for embassies in Phnom Penh are as follows: **U.S.:** #16 St. 228 between streets 51 and 63 (℃ **023/216-436;** check ww.usembassy.state.gov/cambodia/); **Canada:** No. 11, Senei Vanna Vaut Oum (St. 254; ℃ **023/213-470**); **Australia:** (Also serves New Zealanders) No. 11, Senei Vanna Vaut Oum (St. 254; ℃ **023/213-466**); and **U.K.:** No. 27–29 Botum Soriyavong (St. 75; ℃ **023/427-124**).

GETTING THERE

BY AIR   International flights, the most popular way to enter Cambodia, are many and affordable. Cambodia's two main hubs, Siem Reap Airport and Phnom Penh's Ponchentong Airport, are served by Dragonair, Malaysia Airlines, Silk Air (Singapore Airlines), Bangkok Airways, Lao Aviation, and Vietnam Airlines. You can fly directly from Bangkok and other major connections in Thailand, Hong Kong, Kuala Lumpur (Malaysia), Vientiane and Pakse (Laos), Ho Chi Minh City, and Singapore. There is a US$20 international departure tax from Phnom Penh and a US$15 tax from Siem Reap.

BY BUS   Pick-up trucks and limited bus service cover the connection with Poi Pet on the Thai border, and there's similar service from Vietnam's Moc Bai. In the summer monsoon, the road from Thailand can appear like the craters of the moon, and you'll come away from most bus rides dust-caked and exhausted, but service and roads are slowly improving. I highly recommend flying in or out of Phnom Penh or Siem Reap and connecting the two by internal flight or convenient boat connection.

BY BOAT   There are daily boats between Phnom Penh and Vietnam's border town, Chau Doc. From Vietnam, contact the Victoria Hotel in Chau Doc (℃ **076/865-010**) or one of the traveler cafes, such as **Sinh Café** (℃ **08/369-420**). In Phnom Penh, make arrangements through any hotel or travel agent (below).

GETTING AROUND

BY AIR   Connection between Phnom Penh and Siem Reap is frequent and regular on any number of carriers. There is a US$5 domestic departure tax in both Phnom Penh and Siem Reap.

BY BUS   Unlike neighboring Vietnam, you're free to hop local buses, but most travelers find it rough going in the extreme. Contact the folks at an old backpacker standby, the **Capitol Guesthouse** #14 AEO, Road 182, Sangkat Beng Prolitt (℃ **023/217-627**), for inexpensive seat-in-coach connections and tours throughout the country. Contact **Ho Wah Genting Transport Company** (℃ **023/210-859**) for inexpensive buses throughout Cambodia.

BY CAR/MOTORBIKE   Hiring a car with a driver, driving yourself, or going by rented motorbike is a great way to see Cambodia's rural highways and byways. Rough country roads mean that you'll need to hire the most durable of vehicles, with good suspension. Contact hotels and travel agents in their respective towns.

BY BOAT   Slow boats still connect Phnom Penh and Siem Reap along the Mekong and Tonle Sap rivers, but this is a trip only for the hearty. Go for the speedboat, which cuts the trip to about 5 hours, depending on the water level, and costs US$25. Any hotel can arrange a ticket; boats leave from the pier near the Japanese Bridge in the north end of town or connect with Siem Reap's Tonle Sap docks by taxi.

TIPS ON ACCOMMODATIONS

Be warned that accommodations often fill up in the winter high season, especially the finer hotels nearest Angkor Wat. Expect discounts in the low season, and don't forget that there is a 10% VAT at most hotels. The only quality accommodation that you'll find is in Phnom Penh and Siem Reap, but the standard is high and some budget properties are updating to rustic boutique properties.

TIPS ON DINING

It's heavy on the French cuisine here in their old colony, and it's mostly affordable and good. There's also good Thai, and tourist centers are choc-a-bloc with storefronts that lure backpackers with reasonable facsimiles of Western favorites.

TIPS ON SHOPPING

Limited to only a few small storefront antique stores and boutiques in the major tour centers, shopping for trinkets and memorabilia is best at the big markets: the Russian Market and Central Market in Phnom Pehn, and the Old Market in Siem Reap.

3 Phnom Penh

Founded in the mid–14th century by the Khmers as a monastery, Phnom Penh replaced Angkor Thom a century later as the country's capital and has long been a vital trading hub at the confluence of three rivers: the Mekong, Tonle Sap, and Bassac. Perhaps the city's most auspicious history was actually when it lay vacant; following an eviction order from Pol Pot, the city was deserted in a period of hours, and almost all of Phnom Penh's residents moved to the countryside in 1975, not to return until 1979 under the authority of Vietnamese troops.

It has been a long road to the peaceful and growing Phnom Penh of today. There were many years of frontier-style anarchy after the city was repopulated. Drugs and prostitution are still a big downtown commodity, but it's unlikely that you'll be caught in the crossfire, something you couldn't say 4 or 5 years ago. Today Phnom Penh enjoys its own kind of harmony of opposites and offers visitors peaceful moments of a sunset at riverside as well as dusty, motorbike-choked labyrinthine alleys. The city is an incongruous cluster of crumbling French colonials, and the central riverside area has a pace all its own that's great for wandering.

There's also much to see of historic interest in Phnom Penh. Its **Royal Palace** is a stone showpiece of classical Khmer architecture, and the **Silver Pagoda,** on the palace grounds, is a jewel-encrusted wonder. Throughout the city, you'll see the faded glory of aged **French colonial architecture.** There are also four notable wats, religious temples with resident monks.

Of more grisly interest is the **Tuol Sleng,** or Museum of Genocide, a schoolhouse-turned-prison where up to 20,000 victims of Pol Pot's excesses were tortured before being led to the **Cheoung Ek,** otherwise known as "The Killing Fields," about 16km (10 miles) from Phnom Penh. It's a town certainly worth exploring for a few days.

VISITOR INFORMATION AND TOURS

- **Diethelm Travel.** No. 65 St. 240, P.O. Box 99, Phnom Penh, Cambodia (© 023/219-151; fax 023/219-150; www.diethelm-travel.com). In Siem Reap: House no. 4, Road no. 6, Krum no. 1, Sangkat no. 2, Phum Taphul, Siem Reap, Cambodia (© 63/963-524; fax 63/963-694).
- **Exotissimo.** 46 Norodom Blvd. (© 023/218-948; fax 023/426-586; www. exotissimo.com).
- **Capitol Guesthouse Tours.** #14 AEO, Road 182, Sangkat Beng Prolitt (© 023/217-627). This is the town's budget travel cafe and a good place to arrange inexpensive rural and local tours and onward connections by bus and boat. Remember that you get what you pay for, but the services are convenient.

GETTING THERE

BY AIR   All major airlines in the region connect here. Pochentong Airport is just a 15 minute drive from the city center and a cab costs between US$5 and US$7.

BY BOAT   Speedboats connect with Siem Reap and leave every morning from the main dock on the north end of town. Tickets are available just about anywhere in town. The price is US$25 from most hotels or the Capitol Guesthouse (above).

BY BUS   Buses connect with neighboring Vietnam and points throughout the country. From Vietnam, contact **Saigontourist** (© 08/829-8914) or **Sinh Café** (© 08/369-420); for connections in-country, ask at any travel agent, hotel, or the Capitol Guesthouse (see above). A tourist bus to Siem Reap takes 6 to 7 hours and costs US$5. Ho Wah Genting Transport Company (© 023/210-859), with an office just west of the central market, sells tickets to all the major stops and minor hamlets in the country.

GETTING AROUND

Phnom Penh's downtown is accessible on foot, and it's easy to find your way because the streets are arranged in a grid and are numbered. For sites farther afield, like The Killing Fields or any temples, you'll need wheels. Metered taxis are everywhere in town, and any hotel can arrange daily car rental (with driver). Or, contact the folks at **Lucky! Lucky!,** at 413 Monivong Blvd. (© 023/212-788), who rent high quality motorbikes for rural touring (available for long-term rental) as well as jeeps and even luxury cars.

Motorcycle taxis, called **motodups,** can be hired anywhere and cost about 2,000 Riel (about US.50¢) for short trips in town. Bargain hard. These guys are everywhere, especially on the riverside, and the competition is in your favor. Then again, what the heck is US.50¢? Tip and you'll have a friend for life.

Ⓒ **FAST FACTS: Phnom Penh**

American Express For basic American Express services (reporting lost checks etc.) contact **Diethelm** at : No. 65 St. 240, P.O. Box 99, Phnom Penh, Cambodia (© 023/219-151; www.diethelm-travel.com).

Banks/Currency Exchange **Canadia Bank,** at #265 St. 110 (© 023/215-284); **Mekong Bank,** at 1 St. 114 (© 023/217-112); and **Cambodian Commercial**

Bank (CCB) at #26, Monivong Rd. (© 023/426-208) are just three of many in the downtown area that can cash traveler's checks and give cash advances. There is a **Western Union** office at Cambodia Asia Bank (© 023/210-900) in the Naga, a floating casino behind the Cambodiana Hotel.

Emergency For police, dial © 117; for fire, dial © 118; and for the expat hot line, dial © 023/724-793.

Clinics The International SOS Medical and Dental Clinic, at #161 St. 51 (© 023/216-911), is a good place for minor emergencies, as is the Naga Clinic, at #11 St. 254 (© 011/811-175). For any major emergency or injury, however, you'll want to arrange medical evacuation.

Internet/E-mail Internet outlets line the riverside Sisowath Street. Hourly access starts at US$1. Try **Penhcheth Web**, at #269 Sisowath, just one of many. Near the popular Capitol Guesthouse, **Friendly Web** has good access from its office at #199 EO, St. 107 (at the corner of Road 182; © 012/843-246). **KIDS** is an NGO where American owner Bill Herod brings Internet technology to Khmer students. They have good, inexpensive access in their offices at #17A St. 178 (© 023/218-452; kids@camnet.com.kh).

Post Office The post office is located in the north end of town on Street 13, east of Wat Phnom. It's open daily 6:30am to 5pm, and it makes standard deliveries and has an international phone. DHL has an office on #28, Monivong Rd. (© 023/427-726), and FedEx is at #701D, Monivong (© 023/216-712).

Telephone The local code for Phnom Penh is 023. International direct dialing is available in most hotels and at the post office. Storefront Internet cafes along Sisowath do inexpensive Internet calls or direct dialing. Cellphones are very popular in the city, and you'll find street-side stalls on wheels where you can make local and international calls for next to nothing, with a good cellular connection.

WHERE TO STAY

There are some choice hotels in town, from old, upscale gems to budget mini-hotels and even a few small boutique properties. I recommend spending a little more for bargain luxury because the midrange properties of Phnom Penh are rundown, at best. Always ask about seasonal rates. Some hotels charge a 10% VAT.

VERY EXPENSIVE

Hotel Inter-Continental Phnom Penh ★★ This is a true five-star property. For the high-end business traveler in Phnom Penh, the Inter-Continental is definitely the place to stay. This luxury behemoth has every amenity and every in-room convenience—even Internet connection (the only in town). You're just a short ride from the city center, but there's no reason to leave this self-contained, upscale gem. Rooms are done in tidy carpet, elegant dark wood furnishing, over-stuffed couches, floral curtains that match the spreads on the large king beds, and fine marble detailing in the entry. All is large and luxe, even the well-appointed bathrooms, and each room has an Art Deco oak desk and a floor-to-ceiling window with some of the best views in town. The large outdoor pool has a fun elephant fountain and elegant water-level bar, and the Clark Hatch fitness center is the best in town. Dining is fine Chinese and Western. The lobby is pure marble elegance, and the staff is superefficient and professional. Executive check-in comes with an addition of just US$18, and services in the fine executive lounge are certainly worth it. The regency suite is fit for kings, literally. Toto, I don't think we're in Cambodia anymore.

P.O. Box 2288, Regency Square, 296 Boulevard Mao Tse Toung. ✆ **023/424-888.** Fax 023/424-885. www. interconti.com. 354 units. US$170 single; US$200 double; US$300–US$1500 suite. AE, MC, V. **Amenities:** 2 restaurants; bar; 2 snack bars; outdoor pool; great fitness center; sauna; children's playroom; concierge; tour desk; car rental; business center; shopping; 24-hr. room service; massage; babysitting; laundry/dry cleaning; banquet facilities; Internet. *In room:* A/C, satellite TV, dataport, minibar, fridge, safe, IDD phone.

Raffles Hotel Le Royal ★★★   Built in 1929, this is Phnom Penh's best-loved grande dame, deluxe and atmospheric in quaint Art Deco and colonial themes. Reopened and expanded with a new wing in 1997, everything from the vaulted ceilings in the lobby to the classic original central stairs breathes history and charm like so many of the old hotels in the region. Rooms are no exception, with fine tiled entries, high ceilings, indirect lighting, a sitting area with inlaid furniture, and ornate touches like antique wall sconces and fine drapery. The scale is large but not imposing, and bathrooms are good-size and well appointed in decorative tile with marble counters. Landmark rooms, just one step above the standard, are a good choice in the older building and are larger, with nice appointments like claw-foot tubs. It's luxury with a price tag, but it's worth it. There are some interesting theme suites named for famous visitors; including Stamford Raffles. Even Jacqueline Kennedy has a room dedicated to photos and memorabilia of her 1967 visit. The central pool area is a tranquil oasis divided by a unique pavilion, and the amenities throughout, such as the fine massage facility, are luxe. The staff is very professional.

92 Rukhak Vithei Daun Penh (off Monivong Blvd.) Sangkat Wat Phnom. ✆ **023/981-888.** Fax 023/981-168. www.raffles.com. 208 units. US$260–US$290 single/double state room; US$300–US$320 single/double landmark room; US$300–US$2,000 suite. 10% service charge and 10% VAT. AE, MC, V. **Amenities:** 3 restaurants; 2 bars; 2 outdoor pools; health club; Jacuzzi; sauna; kids' club; concierge; tour desk; car rental; business center; shopping; 24-hr. room service; massage; babysitting; laundry/dry cleaning; Internet. *In room:* A/C, satellite TV, minibar, fridge, coffeemaker, hair dryer, safe, IDD phone.

EXPENSIVE

Hotel Cambodiana ★★   They've got it all at the Cambodiana. With a convenient location, atmosphere, and all the amenities, this is a good jumping-off point for the sites downtown. The building looks like a giant gilded wedding cake, and its vaulted Khmer-style roofs dominate the sky in the southern end of downtown. This is a very popular choice; the lobby is abuzz with activity, whether it's visiting dignitaries or disembarking tour buses, but the helpful staff seem to handle it all with grace. The large riverside pool is great, and there are some fine choices in international dining. An added bonus for some is the nearby Naga ship, the town's large riverside gambling venue. Rooms are priced according to their view of the river, and executive floors are a fine high standard. Everything's tidy but decorated in chain-hotel style in plain wood on carpet; it's a bit dull, and some floors reek of pungent deodorizers. Deluxe river-view rooms are the best bet; the high-end suites are richly decorated and unique. All rooms have picture windows and good views of town or the river.

313 Sisowath Quay. ✆ **023/426-288.** Fax 023/982-380. www.hotelcambodiana.com. 267 units. US$175–US$225 standard–deluxe; US$295–US$425 suite. AE, MC, V. **Amenities:** 4 restaurants; bar; outdoor pool; tennis court; small health club; Jacuzzi; sauna; concierge; car rental; business center; shopping; limited room service; massage; laundry/dry cleaning; executive-level rooms; banquet facilities; Internet. *In room:* A/C, satellite TV, minibar, fridge, safe, IDD phone.

Phnom Penh

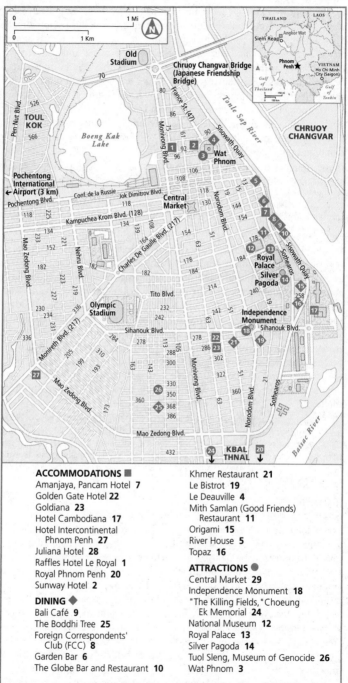

ACCOMMODATIONS ■
Amanjaya, Pancam Hotel **7**
Golden Gate Hotel **22**
Goldiana **23**
Hotel Cambodiana **17**
Hotel Intercontinental
　Phnom Penh **27**
Juliana Hotel **28**
Raffles Hotel Le Royal **1**
Royal Phnom Penh **20**
Sunway Hotel **2**

DINING ◆
Bali Café **9**
The Boddhi Tree **25**
Foreign Correspondents'
　Club (FCC) **8**
Garden Bar **6**
The Globe Bar and Restaurant **10**

Khmer Restaurant **21**
Le Bistrot **19**
Le Deauville **4**
Mith Samlan (Good Friends)
　Restaurant **11**
Origami **15**
River House **5**
Topaz **16**

ATTRACTIONS ●
Central Market **29**
Independence Monument **18**
"The Killing Fields," Choeung
　Ek Memorial **24**
National Museum **12**
Royal Palace **13**
Silver Pagoda **14**
Tuol Sleng, Museum of Genocide **26**
Wat Phnom **3**

Royal Phnom Penh ✿ A popular tourist hotel, the Royal is relaxed and atmospheric. Low buildings are arranged in harmony with lush surrounding gardens, and the amenities, like the large courtyard pool, gym, and massage facility, befit a larger, more expensive hotel. Rooms are carpeted and neatly trimmed in light wood, with overstuffed chairs, king beds with a grand wooden arc as a headboard, and Khmer statuary that's either a delightful local touch or gawdy and oppressive, depending on your luck. The Royal is sufficiently self-contained but far enough from the action in the town center that it has to be. The staff is professional and friendly. There are two restaurants to choose from and even a small lobby bakery counter. Suites are just larger versions of standard and deluxe rooms and not necessarily worth it.

Samdech Sothearos Blvd. Sangkat Tonle Bassac ✆ 023/982-673. Fax 023/982-661. www.royalphnompenh hotel.com. 75 units. US$125 double; US$165 deluxe double; US$195 minisuite; US$315 suite. AE, MC, V. **Amenities:** 2 restaurants; poolside bar; large outdoor pool w/kids' area; golf driving range and practice greens; 2 tennis courts; health club; spa; sauna; travel and business center; room service 7am–11pm; massage; laundry/dry cleaning; banquet facilities; Internet. *In room:* A/C, satellite TV, minibar, fridge, coffeemaker, IDD phone.

Sunway Hotel ✿✿ The Sunway is a very comfortable high-end choice. Just west of Wat Phnom in the north end of town, the facade and entry are majestic, and the wrought-iron chandelier suspended at mezzanine level in the cool marble of the lobby completes the elegant effect. The staff snaps to and is courteous even when busy. They cover all bases in amenities, with a good health club and large downstairs esthetic salon and massage area. The fine dining room and laid-back lobby lounge are stylish and inviting. Rooms are chain-hotel bland but are large, clean, and very comfortable. Done in a carpet of tight geometric design, white walls and ceiling are broken nicely by wooden valences, but the boring "hotel art" takes away from the semi-deluxe effect. Still, it's a very comfortable standard; bathrooms are large, with shower/tub combos and granite counters.

#1, St. 92, Sangkat Wat Phnom, PO Box 633. ✆ 023/430-333. Fax 023/430-339. asunway@bigpond. com.kh. 140 units. US$160 superior double; US$180 deluxe double; US$260 suite; US$850 presidential suite. AE, MC, V. **Amenities:** Restaurant and cafe; bar/lounge (live entertainment nightly); health club; Jacuzzi; sauna; steam room; concierge; tour desk; car rental; business center; shopping arcade; small book corner; 24-hr. room service; massage; babysitting; laundry/dry cleaning; Internet. *In room:* A/C, satellite TV, dataport, minibar, fridge, coffeemaker, safe, IDD phone.

MODERATE

Amanjaya, Pancam Hotel ✿✿ Riverside at Sisowath Quay, this three-story corner building is a true house of style. The porous laterite walls of the lobby, the same stone used in Angkor, and Buddhist statue throughout contribute to the cool boutique vibe of this place. Though sparse in terms of service and amenities, rooms are enormous, done in rich red silk hangings and bedspreads and dark wood trim and floors. All rooms have king beds. The suites are enormous and worth the extra outlay. All bathrooms are immaculate affairs done in wood and tile, with neat shower/tub units in standard rooms and separate shower and tub in suites, delineated by unique large-stone gravel paths in concrete. Rooms vary in size and shape, but be sure to ask about a corner suite with panoramic views of the river and busy street below. Noisy traffic is the only drawback.

#1 St. 154 Sisowath Quay. ✆ 023/214-747. Fax 023/219-545. 21 units. US$70 single; US$80 double; US$100–US$110 suite. MC, V. **Amenities:** Restaurant; limited room service; laundry/dry cleaning. *In room:* A/C, satellite TV, minibar, fridge, safe in suites only, IDD phone.

Juliana Hotel ⍟   Popular with large tour groups, the Juliana is located a good distance from the center of town, but rooms are situated around a luxuriant central pool shaded by palms and with a terrace and lounge chairs: a bright spot. The hotel is Thai-owned and managed, and also popular with businessmen. Standard rooms, the bread and butter for the large groups, aren't especially attractive and have aging red carpet and the nicks and scrapes of heavy use. That said, superior and deluxe rooms are large and well appointed in tidy carpet and light wood trim. Large beds are topped by regal headboards, and there are nice rattan furnishings throughout. Billing as a "city resort" kind of comes up short, but the Continental restaurant is inviting and the pool is a standout, even if rooms don't quite pass muster. The lobby and common areas try to be more than they are (i.e. luxurious) and come up short, but the staff is professional and helpful.

16 Juliana 152 Rd., Sangkhat Vealvong. ℭ 023/366-070-72 or 023/880-530-31. Fax 023/366-070-72. juliana@camnet.com.kh. 91 units. US$70 standard; US$120 superior; US$160 deluxe; US$240 suite. AE, MC, V. **Amenities:** 2 restaurants; small lobby bar; outdoor pool; small health club; sauna; car rental; business center; shopping; salon; room service 5am–11pm; large downstairs massage complex; babysitting; laundry; banquet facilities; Internet. *In room:* A/C, satellite TV, minibar, fridge, IDD phone.

INEXPENSIVE

Golden Gate Hotel ⍟   Standard US$15 rooms here are basic but clean and comparable to the Golden Bridge next door (below) and a few other budget options along Road 278 south of the town center. The Golden Gate also has nice deluxe rooms that are larger but just as plain. This is a popular spot for long-staying expatriates here on business, and the suites, with kitchenette and small living room, are more or less like your average one-room apartment. Everything's clean, though, and there's nice tile, clean carpet, and mismatched but tidy cloth and rattan furniture in all rooms. Go for a sizable deluxe room on a higher floor with a view. Standard rooms are crowded together in an older building and are accessible only by the stairs. Be sure to ask to see the room first.

#9, Rd. 278, Sangkat. ℭ 023/7211-161. Fax 023/721-005. goldengatehtls@hotmail.com. US$15/$30 Standard single/double; US$30 deluxe; US$40 suite. MC, V. **Amenities:** Restaurant; car rental; business center; limited room service; laundry; Internet. *In room:* A/C, satellite TV, minibar, fridge, IDD phone.

Goldiana ⍟⍟   A labyrinthine complex, the result of many construction phases, the Goldiana is one of the best budget choices in the Cambodian capital. South of the Victory Monument and a short ride from the main sites, it's low-luxe but squeaky clean; rooms are very large and have either carpet or wood flooring and clean white walls. The hotels maintenance, unlike many similar properties in the region, is meticulous. Although that new-car smell is long gone, it's low on the mildew and musty odors of similar standards in town. Bathrooms are smallish but comfortable, with a shower/tub combo and granite tile. The third-floor pool is a real bonus in this category. The lobby is a a mess of sparkly pomp and circumstance characterized by heavy curtains, large pottery with fake flowers, mirrors, and bright-colored carved wood, but there's a certain appeal to it all once it becomes familiar. The staff is kind and helpful and is used to the questions and concerns of long-staying patrons, tourists, and business clients. A stay of any length will feel like you're at home.

#10–12, St. 282, Sangkat Boeng Keng Kang 1. ℭ 023/219-558. Fax 023/219-490. www.goldiana.com. 157 units. US$35 single; US$45 double; US$55–US$95 suite. MC, V. **Amenities:** Restaurant; outdoor pool (rooftop); basic gym; car rental; courtesy car; business center; room service 6am–10pm; laundry/dry cleaning; Internet. *In room:* A/C, TV, minibar, fridge, IDD phone.

BUDGET

Affordable accommodation abounds in the Cambodian capital but can be rough around the edges. In and around Sisowath Street, the busy riverside boulevard, you'll find minihotels and budget lodging of all kinds starting at about US$10 per night. A few good choices in the south part of town iclude the **Golden Gate Hotel** (#9, Rd. 278, Sangkat; © **023/7211-161.** Fax 023/721-005. goldengate htls@hotmail.com) and the **Golden Bridge** next door (#7CD, Rd. 278, Sangkat Beng Keng Kang; © **023/721-396**); both offer rooms starting at US$15 and, though rather spartan, are comfortable choices with air-conditioning and satellite TV.

For rock-bottom budget, **Capitol Guesthouse** (in the town center at #14 AEO, Rd. 182, Sangkat Beng Prolitt; © **023/217-627**), the town's backpacker information center, manages a number of properties on or near Road 182. Very basic concrete rooms start at US$2, and it's a good place to meet other travelers and arrange cheap tours, but it's not especially comfortable.

Another good budget option is the **Last Home Guesthouse** (#47, St. 108, on the promenade south of Wat Phnom; © **023/724-917**), an old standby with concrete-block basic rooms above a popular little storefront eatery. Rooms are US$2 to US$8.

The eastern shore of the Boeung Kak Lake just north of town has grown in recent years into a cozy little backpacker ghetto. It's cheap sleep and eats, all ultrabasic, even downright grungy, but you're sure to meet some fellow travelers and spend little.

WHERE TO DINE

International cuisine abounds in the Cambodian capital, the remnants of French colonialism and the result of a recent influx of humanitarian aid workers. Some restaurants themselves are actually NGO (non-government organizations) projects designed to raise money for local causes or provide training. Ask Khmer folks where to eat, and you'll certainly be pointed to any of the street-side stalls or storefront Chinese noodle shops south of the Central Market, but good eats can be had from one of many options along riverside Sisowath or in among the lazy alleys of the town center.

For an interesting evening of local fun and frolic, cross the Cambodian-Japanese Friendship bridge on the Tonle Sap River in the north end of town and follow the main road a few short clicks to the town of **Prek Leap,** a grouping of large riverside eateries always crowded with locals on the weekend. Some of these places put on popular variety shows: It's the universal language of slapstick in play here and a good chance to eat, talk, and laugh with locals. All the restaurants serve similar good Khmer and Chinese fare. Go by taxi and pick the most crowded place; the more, the merrier.

EXPENSIVE

Chivit Thai ⭐⭐   You found it! Authentic Thai in an atmospheric, traditional wood house. The food is great, the price is low, and there's nice casual floor seating and a rustic but comfortable dining room, romantic in candlelight. Name your favorite Thai dish, and they do it here, and do it well. The Tom Yum (sweet, spicy Thai soup) is excellent, and they have good set menus comprised of many courses that are much finer than their low price tag. Enjoy!

House 129, Rd. no. 6 next to Angkor Hotel. © 012/830-761. Main courses US$2.50–US$5. Cash only. Daily 7am–10pm.

Dead Fish ✿ This place is a testament to Cambodia's loose zoning laws. Looking as much like a fanciful theater set or the rigging of a ship, the restaurant is a series of multitiered platforms centered on a large central bar. Seating is here-and-there, on floor cushions on this platform, on low chairs at another, and the multicolored lighting lends to the overall cinematic quality. They serve Thai, good Thai, for next to nothing. The bar is popular and kicks late into the evening.

Down a narrow corridor off Siwatha St., the N end. ℂ 012/630-6377. Main courses US$1–US$3. Cash only. Daily 8am–late.

Foreign Correspondents Club (FCC) ✿ CONTINENTAL With a long history as Phnom Penh's place to see and be seen, the FCC is as much a tour stop as a restaurant. Once the gathering place of the obligatory dust-caked, camera-toting, intrepid breed who came to chronicle the country's troubled times, the FCC is now a multifloor affair of restaurant, bar, and shops done in dark wood and terra-cotta. There are low reclining chairs in the cafe area, a fine dining room, and a dark bar as the stalwart centerpiece. The whole second floor is oriented to the fine views of the river and busy Sisowath below. Ceiling fans spin oblong patterns while dangled from the high, exposed tile roof, and geckos, as everywhere, chase along the walls. Come for a drink and a peek or to pretend you're here on assignment. The food is uninspired Western, but everything is good. They make fine pizza in their wood-fired oven and have good snacks like nachos and enchiladas, as well as treats like "Death by Chocolate," a fudge cake with mousse and ice cream. The upstairs bar is very popular in the evening, and the place is abuzz with activity day and night, whether power lunches or late night laughs. The building is now almost its own little shopping mall, with a small bookstore in the entry and an outlet for Diethelm Travel among other offices. It's a good place to pick up information on travel in the area.

#363 Sisowath St. ℂ 023/724-014. Main courses US$5–$18.50. MC, V. 7am–12pm.

Le Bistrot ✿✿ FRENCH For fine French in one of the most picturesque of the many colonials in town, this is romantic/atmospheric open-air dining at its best in Phnom Penh. Amid the murmur of voices and the clinking of glasses and silverware over a piece by Chopin, you might think you're in a quiet street off the Champs Elysée or a courtyard bistro in Soho. The menu is French, very French, and heavy on fine salads with fresh ingredients. You'll see a selection of the day's specials in a glass case at the entry, and the friendly staff can steer you toward what's good. I shared an order of the taboule as well as their special smoked herring with potato and light oil. The wine list has great depth, and Le Bistrot is a good place to come just for a drink and enjoy a candlelight evening on a romantic balcony that, like the rest of this stylish bistro, is like a flying carpet to another place.

#4D St. 29. ℂ 012/844-478. US$4–US$12. Cash only. Tues–Sun 12am–2pm and 6:30–10pm.

Origami ✿✿ Sushi in Cambodia? Go figure. There are a number of Japanese restaurants in town, in fact, but Origami serves fine sushi and all manner of good, authentic Japanese that'll have you saying "Oishi!" (ask there what it means). From tonkatsu, deep-fried pork over rice, to real Japanese Ramen (noodle soup), Ms. Kimura, the genial proprietor, covers all the bases. Essential ingredients are imported from Japan, and everything is priced accordingly. The sushi is the real deal, and the presentation and decor of this little park-side gem could have been lifted straight out of Tokyo. Popular for the many Japanese expats on humanitarian assignment, the restaurant is itself an NGO (non-government organization) offering Khmer kids training in Japanese language and culture.

#88 Sothearos St. (near the main downtown sites) ✆ 012/968-095. Main courses US$3–US$12; set menu US$10–US$20. Cash only. Mon–Sat 11am–2pm and 6–9:30pm.

River House ✿✿ FRENCH/CONTINENTAL One of many along the riverside, this bar and restaurant, like the nearby FCC (above), stands out by virtue of size and style. A classic corner colonial, its downstairs is an open-air bar area with quaint patio seating under canvas umbrellas; there's now an elegant air-conditioned dining room. Upstairs is a bass-thumping, dimly lit club with a dance floor that is a popular late-night haunt. Elegant rattan chairs, two stately (fully stocked) bars in wood and glass, and the fine linen and silver presentationare luxe far beyond the price tag. The food is excellent, characterized by fine French specials like duck done as you like, tournedos of beef, and coq au vin. Come for a romantic dinner and stay for dancing. They hold lots of special events, so ask around or call ahead to see what's going on.

#6 St. 110 (corner of Sisowath). ✆ 023/212-302. Main courses US$4–US$10. AE, MC, V. Daily 10:30am–12pm.

Topaz ✿✿ FRENCH/CONTINENTAL Good familiar food and atmosphere that's sophisticated but not stuffy are the hallmarks of Topaz, a 6-year-old French bistro. In air-conditioned comfort, diners can choose informal booth seating near the comfortable bar or sit at an elegant table in a formal dining room of pastel colors, fine linen, silver, and real stemwear. The dining room presentation is without rival in town. The staff is professional, and the menu features great steaks, pasta, and salad (the Caesar salad is noteworthy). Daily lunch sets are popular with the business crowd, and daily specials are contingent on the day's imports of fish or fine steaks. Wine racks line the dining room walls, with some great choices. Everything's good. Bon appetit!

#100 Sothearos Blvd. (near the downtown sites). ✆ 023/211-054. Main courses US$5–US$20. MC, V. Daily 11am–2pm and 6–11pm.

MODERATE

Bali Café ✿ INDONESIAN/WESTERN A similar setup to the popular FCC (above), this smart little second-floor cafe has a vaulted ceiling and open plan that faces busy Sisowath and the picturesque riverside: It's a good spot to relax and beat the heat. The unique Indonesian cuisine is heavy on curry of the sweet, coconut milk variety, but everything is good. I had the Gado Gado, a popular Indonesian dish of steamed mixed vegetables in peanut sauce. Come with friends and order up a table-covering repast for very little. Views from the window seats are good, but go for a spot in the raised central area where comfy chairs have the best high angle on the busy street below. It's a popular bar in the evening.

#379 Sisowath St. ✆ 023/982-211. Main courses US$3–US$5. Cash only. Daily 7am–10pm.

The Boddhi Tree ✿ ASIAN/KHMER Include lunch here with a trip to nearby Tuol Sleng Prison (see "Attractions" below), a site that doesn't inspire an appetite, really, but the Boddhi Tree is a peaceful oasis and not a bad spot to collect your thoughts after visiting vestiges of Cambodia's late troubles. Named for the tree under which the Buddha "saw the light," this verdant little garden courtyard and rough-hewn guesthouse has comfy balcony and courtyard seating, and seems to serve up as much calm as the coffee, tea, and light fare that makes it so popular. There are daily specials and often visiting chefs. All the curries are good, and they have great baguette sandwiches. Established in 1997 as a way to drum up funds and support to help Khmer kids and families in challenging circumstances, the folks here welcome your suggestions and invite visitors to get involved in their important work.

#50 St. 113, Beong Keng Kong (across from Tuol Sleng Museum). ℭ 011/854-430. www.boddhitree.com. Main courses US$2–US$3.75. Cash only. Daily 7am–9pm.

The Globe Bar and Restaurant ✦✦ CONTINENTAL   On the second floor of another of the town's classic riverside colonials, this cool cafe serves good, familiar fare and plays some great music, to boot (I heard a range from Hungarian folk to American bluegrass and even the Beach Boys). Staff is ultra-friendly, and the balcony views of the riverside are great. It's a good place just for drinks too. For food, start with the "Trio of Dips," including humus, balsamic tomato chutney, and baba ganoush, and be sure to ask about daily specials. It's a creative, ambitious mix of Thai and Western dishes, with anything from fettuccini to fresh fish and good Khmer dishes. The Thai masaman curry is excellent and well presented in fine local crockery. Other specials include a popular tofu clay pot, and the coconut milk soup comes highly recommended. This is relaxed fine dining that far exceeds the low price tag.

Above Air France at 389 Sisowath St. ℭ 023/215-923. Main courses US$2–US$6. V. Daily 11am–3pm and 5–10:30pm.

Le Deauville ✦ FRENCH   This open-air French bar and brasserie is a good, mellow choice. On the north end of the Wat Phnom roundabout, it serves fine, affordable French and Khmer dishes, and it's unpretentious and cozy. With a large open bar at center, tables are scattered in the street-side courtyard and shielded from the traffic by a wall of lush, potted greenery. Daily lunch set menus give you a choice of salad and entree, and you can choose from local specialties like filet of Mekong fish with lime or fine medallion de boeuf. The restaurant features good pizzas and spaghetti, and has a wine list that fits any taste and budget. Be sure to ask about Le Deauville II, the large dining barge that makes regular city cruises or can be chartered; aboard the ship, you can enjoy similar fine French cuisine as in this casual bistro. Le Deauville is a popular spot for a casual drink in the evening.

Kj St. 94 (just N of Wat Phnom). ℭ 012/843-204. Main courses US$2–US$6. V. Daily 7am–11pm.

INEXPENSIVE

Garden Bar CONTINENTAL/KHMER   There are so many little eateries lining the riverfront of Sisowath Road it's hard to pick. Here's one, an open-air corner bar with big, comfy rattan chairs with overstuffed cushions and in prime peoplewatching location. They serve good Western pub grub: burgers, steaks, and chicken dishes, as well as good pizzas and sandwiches. It's a great place to have a cold beer and a good meat-and-potatoes meal, or a groovy fruit shake and a simple salad or sandwich. The staff here couldn't be nicer; they're amenable to suggestions (burgers as you like, etc.) and will make you feel like a local from the get-go. The bar hops late into the evening.

Sisowath (corner of 148th). ℭ 012/852-907. Main courses US$3–US$6. Daily 8am–12pm.

Khmer Restaurant KHMER/WESTERN   Unpretentious and comfortable, this little street-side eatery is on a corner of Street 278, a neighborhood of many service apartments and budget lodging for long-staying foreigners. The menu and atmosphere cater to this fickle bunch, and it's a good place for surprisingly authentic Western-style "comfort foods," like lasagna, cheeseburgers, ample salads, and very good, very inexpensive Western breakfasts. Young salesmen out front will sell you that day's *Phnom Penh Post* or international newspaper for a small commission, and it's a comfy, open-air location. The staff speaks fluent Khmer and couldn't be nicer.

#6 St. 57 (corner of 278th) Sangkhat Boeuns Kang Kong. ☎ 023/216-336. Main courses US$1–US$5. Cash only. Daily 6:30am–10pm.

Mith Samlanh (Good Friends) Restaurant ★★ KHMER/INTERNA-TIONAL Not to be missed is this friendly little gem, an NGO (non-government organization) project where Khmer street kids are given shelter and taught useful skills for their reintegration into society: It's a unique opportunity to meet friendly mentors and young folks who've found a new lease on life. The food is great, mind you, an ever-changing tapas menu of local and international favorites like spring rolls, fried rice, good salads, and a host of desserts. I had sweet sticky rice with a nice mix of local fruit, and it was delicious. This is a great spot to cool off and have a light bite while touring the city center (right across from the "must-see" National Museum); the place is a cozy open-air colonial in a courtyard done up in primary-color murals of the kids' drawings. The name of the restaurant means "good friends"; in fact, you might find yourself giving English lessons, laughing, and smiling with these young survivors. The helpful mentoring staff members are happy to talk about their efforts with drug and AIDs education and planned 500-student vocational facility.

#215 St. 13 (across from the entrance to the National Museum). ☎ 012/802-072. Main courses US$1–US$3. Cash only. Daily 11am–2pm and 5–9pm.

SNACKS & CAFES
Java Café and Gallery, #56 E1 Preah Sihanouk Blvd (☎ 012/833-512), is a good spot in town to relax and escape the midday heat. Just south of the main sites (near the Independence Monument), this popular second-story oasis has casual seating on a large balcony and an open gallery interior. They serve real coffee, cappuccino, good cakes, and other baked goods; they sometimes feature live music in the evening. It's open 7am to 10pm.

The Shop is a nice little stop on popular Street 240 (☎ 023/986-964) that serves fine baked goods and great teas and coffees in a friendly and comfortable storefront. There are neat details, like butcher-block tables and fresh flowers, and they can arrange picnic lunches for day trips from Phnom Penh.

Pizza can be found at any number of storefronts on the crowded riverside; **Happy Pizza,** at 355 Sisowath (☎ 012/979-812), is among them. Beginning with the name, there are cute little codes in play here, so to cut through it all, say "Please don't put marijuana on my pizza" unless you want it. Same drill at **Ecstatic Pizza,** 193 Norodom (☎ 023/365-089); both are good and will deliver.

ATTRACTIONS
All sites in the city center can be reached on foot, but you'll want to hire a car with a driver or, for the brave, a motorcycle taxi to reach sites outside the city center. **Tuol Sleng** and **The Killing Fields** can be visited together, and arrangements can be made at any hotel lobby.

Wat Phnom ★★ This is Cambodia's "Church on the Hill." Legend has it that some time in the 14th century, a woman named Penh found sacred Buddhist objects in the nearby river and placed them here on the small hill that later became a temple. Well, the rest is history. *Phnom,* in fact, means "hill," so the name of the town translates to "Penh's Hill."

The temple itself is a standard Southeast Asian wat, with Naga snakes on the cornered peaks of the roof and didactic murals of the Buddha's life done in day-glow allegories along interior walls. Don't miss the central ceiling, which, unlike the bright walls, is yet to be restored and is gritty and authentic.

The hillside park around the temple was once a no-go zone peopled by armed dealers and pimps, and in the evening you should still be careful, but now it's a laid-back little park. You're sure to meet with some crafty young salesmen here who'll offer you the chance to show your Buddhist compassion by buying a caged bird for a dollar and letting it go; if you stick around long enough, you'll get to see the bird return to the comfort of the cage.

Royal Palace and Silver Pagoda ★★★   Don't miss this glittery downtown campus, the ostentatious jewel in the crown of Cambodia's monarchy. Built in the late 1860s under the reign of Norodom, the site is comprised of many elaborate gilded halls, all featuring steep tile roofs with stupa-shape cupolas and golden temple nagas denoting prosperity. Visitors can see the grand **Throne Hall,** the coronation site for Khmer kings and the largest gilded cathedral in the country. Don't miss the many royal busts and the gilded umbrella used to shade the king when in procession. The French built a small exhibition hall on the temple grounds, and visitors can see the many gifts given to the monarchy, among them cross-stitch portraits of the royal family. Just inside the door, don't miss an original by Cézanne that has suffered terrible water damage and hangs in a ratty frame like an unwanted diploma: a shame. The balcony of the exhibition hall is the best bird's eye view of the gilded temples. The facade of the neighboring **Royal Residence** is just as resplendent and is still the home of King Sihanouk.

The **Silver Pagoda** is just south of the palace and can be visited on the same entrance ticket. The floors of this grand temple are covered with 5,000 blocks of silver weighing more than 6 tons. The temple houses a 17th-century Buddha made of Baccarat crystal, and another made almost entirely of gold and decorated with almost 10,000 diamonds. That's not exactly what the Buddha had in mind perhaps, but it's quite beautiful. The temple courtyard is encircled by a covered walkway with a contiguous mural of Cambodia's history and mythology. On the southern end of the complex is a small hill covered in vegetation and said to model the sacred Mt. Meru; there's a large Buddha footprint and a small temple that seems to provoke very devout practice in Khmer visitors.

Between sts. 240 and 184 on Sothearos. The entrance is on the E side facing the river. Entrance fee is US$3 (US$5 w/still camera and US$8 w/video camera). Daily 7:30–11am and 2:30–5pm.

National Museum ★★★   What the British Museum is to the Elgin Marbles of Greece's Parthenon, the National Museum of Phnom Penh, opened in 1920 by King Sisowath, is to the statuary of Angkor Wat. This important storehouse holds artifacts and statuary from all over the country. The sad fact is that many pieces didn't make it here, but were plundered and smuggled out of the country. Nevertheless, this grand red sandstone edifice has a beautiful and informative collection of Khmer pieces. From the entrance, begin on your left with a room of small prehistorical artifacts. A clockwise loop around the central courtyard walks you through time, from static, stylized pieces of stiff-legged, standing Buddhas, to contra-posed and contorted forms in supplication. There are good accompanying descriptions in English, but this is not a bad place to have a knowledgeable guide (ask in the lobby). The central courtyard features a shiva lingum and large temple fragments.

Just N of the Royal Palace at St. 178, and a short walk from the river. Entrance fee US$3. Open daily 8–11am and 2–5:30pm.

Tuol Sleng, Museum of Genocide ★★ The grounds of this high-school-turned-prison-and-torture-chamber are like they were in 1979 at the end of Cambodia's bloody genocide. The whole impression of the atrocities committed at the site is visceral, too much for some visitors. From 1975 until 1979, an estimated 17,000 political prisoners, most just ordinary citizens, were torturedat Tuol Sleng and died, or were executed in the nearby Killing Fields. If you don't come with a guide, you'll certainly want to hire one at the entrance, although you're free to roam the grounds on your own. Local guides often have personal experience with the prison and are vital sources of oral history. They are open to questions, but go easy on any debate. Recrimination against the arbiters of these horrible events is an important issue here; just as Cambodians hope to move on into the future, they fear revisiting the past in international tribunals. The prison population of Tuol Sleng, also known as S-21, was carefully catalogued; in fact, the metal neck brace employed for holding subjects' heads in place for the admitting photograph is on display. There are some written accounts in English, paintings done by a survivor, and gory photos of the common torture practices in the prison, but perhaps what is most haunting is the fear in the eyes of the newly arrived; one wing of the buildings is dedicated to these very arrival photos. There was also an interesting exhibit of "Where are they now?" photo-essays and information about former guards, what they looked like then, what happened, and where they are now (only 7 prisoners survived). This site is a bit overwhelming for some, so be prepared.

S of town at the corner of sts. 350 and 113. Entrance fee US$2; guide fees vary (usually US$2 per person). Daily 8am–noon and 1–5pm.

"The Killing Fields," Choeung Ek Memorial Originally a Chinese cemetery before becoming the execution grounds for the Khmer Rouge during their maniacal reign under Pol Pot from 1975 to 1979, the site is a collection of mounds, mass graves, and a towering monument of catalogued human skulls. It's often visited in conjunction with a tour of Tuol Sleng (above).

15km (9¼ miles) S of Phnom Penh. Arrange a private car or motorcycle.

Central Market This Art Deco behemoth, built in 1937, is a city landmark and, on any given day, a veritable ant hill of activity. The building is a towering rotunda with busy wings extending in four directions. The eastern entrance is the best spot to find T-shirts, hats, and all manner of trinkets and souvenirs, as well as photocopy bootlegs of popular novels and books on Cambodia. Goldsmiths and watch repair and sales counters predominate in the main rotunda, and you can find some good deals. Spend some time wandering the nooks and crannies, though, and you're sure to come across something that strikes your fancy, whether that's a chaotic hardware shop, a cobbler hard at work with an awl, or just the cacophony and carnival-barker shouts of salesman and haggling shoppers. Be sure to bargain for any purchase. The **Russian Market** in the south end of town is comparable and equally worth a visit (it's a good stop on the return trip from The Killing Fields).

Between sts. 126 and 136 in the town center. Daily 5am–5pm.

Independence Monument   Built in the late 1950s to commemorate Cambo-dia's independence from the French on November 9, 1953, this towering obelisk is crowned with Khmer Nagas and is reminiscent of Angkor architecture and Hindu influence. As the fella' says, though, "It looks good from afar, but it's far from good." The area is at its most majestic at night, when lit in rainbow colors.
S of the town center at the intersection of Norodom and Sihanouk.

SHOPPING AND GALLERIES

The best shopping in town, for everything from souvenirs and trinkets to the obligatory kitchen sink, is at any of the large local markets. **The Central Market** (see "Attractions," above) shouldn't be missed, but the **Russian Market** between streets 440 and 450 in the far south of town is where the real deal on souvenirs can be had (go by cab). They'll see you comin' a mile away, and it requires some hard haggling to get the good deals on neat items like ancient-looking opium paraphernalia, carvings, and ceramic. It's all authentic-looking, even if made in China.

Shops and galleries are growing in number in the developing capital. Check out some good local work at the **Apsara Gallery,** #192 St. 178 (© **023/217-795**). All along Street 178, in fact, interesting little outlets are springing up and include a few affordable silk dealers like **Lotus Pond,** #57Eo St. 178 (© **012/833-149**), and **House Kravan,** #13Eo St. 178 (© **012/771-936**).

Take a stroll along Street 240, which is also developing its own cafe culture and has a few little hole-in-the-wall antique shops and boutiques like **Bliss,** #29 St. 240 (© **023/215-754**), which sells some unique beaded and embroidered cushions and quilts; or **Le Lezard Bleu** (© **012/767-417;** www.lizrdbleu.com), which features traditional and contemporary designs and accessories.

Bazar, at 28 Sihanouk Blvd, near the Independence Monument (© **012/866-178**), has a small but refined collection of Asian antiques and furniture.

For CDs, stop by **The Boom Boom Room,** on Street 93 in the backpacker area near Boeung Kok Lake.

For essentials and Western groceries, stop by the **Lucky Market,** #160 Sihanouk Blvd. (© **023/426-291**), and for fresh, organic produce and fine canned goods, **Veggy's** is at #23 St. 240 (© **023/211-534**).

Monument Books, at #111 Norodom Blvd. (© **023/217-617**), has a great selection of new books; it's a good spot to find books on the Khmer language and culture. At #51 St. 240, among new bistros and cafes, stop by **The London Book Centre** and exchange or buy new and used books; there's a good selection.

AFTER DARK

Phnom Penh is notorious for some of the seedier nightlife in all of Southeast Asia. There are some good, friendly bars in town, though many are the "hostess bar" variety. Most good romps start or end at the town's counterculture hub, **The Heart of Darkness,** #38 St. 51, Pasteur, open 7am to sunrise. Done in burgundy tones and cluttered with statuary and memorabilia, the Heart, as it's called, has had a face-lift in recent years and is not as seedy as its reputation of yore. It's where to go to find out what's on in town, and it's the only local venue with metal detectors.

The downtown area along the riverside is choc-a-bloc with small storefront bars and a few upscale spots. **The Rising Sun,** #20 St. 178 (© **023/986-270**), is one of the more comfy holes in the wall, a dark wooden stopover great for a few pints and a game of darts near the town center. **Tom's Irish Bar,** #170 St. 63 (near the Golden Gate Hotel; © **023/363-161**), is a comparable and friendly choice south of town, a long-time local and tourist favorite that has a classy wooden bar as well as comfy low-slung chairs in the roadside courtyard.

SPORTS

The **Clark Hatch Fitness Center** (℃ **023/424-888**), at the Hotel Inter-Continental, has got it all in the way of equipment. It invites daily visitors for a fee (US$8) that includes a pool and sauna. It's open weekdays from 6am to 10pm and weekends from 8am to 8pm.

DAY TRIPS FROM PHNOM PENH

OUDONG

Following defeat at Angkor by the Thais, the Khmer capital moved to Oudong, and kings ruled from there for more than 100 years until the power center shifted to nearby Phnom Penh in 1866. The area was a monastic center, and the 13th-century temples, like most others, pale in comparison to those of the Angkor complex. Still, the hills of Oudong offer breathtaking views. It's 1 hour west of Phnom Penh and is best reached by rented vehicle.

PHNOM CHISOR AND TONLE BATI

If you've been or are going to Angkor Wat, these temples will pale in compari-son, but the ride through the countryside and among rural villages makes for a good day. Tonle Bati (33km/20½ miles S) entrance US$3) is a small collection of Angkor-style temples. Entrance costs US$3. Nearby Phnom Chisor is a group of 10th-century ruins atop a picturesque hill. Phnom Penh travel agents can make all the arrangements.

SIHANOUKVILLE

Your only bet for a dip in the ocean and beachside R and R in Cambodia is in Sihanoukville some 230km (143mi.) south of Phnom Penh on the American-built highway. A popular summertime spot for Khmers, Sihanoukville is really a port town and though the beaches don't really stack-up to the likes of Thailand, they are not bad. Trips to outlying islands for scuba diving and snorkeling are attracting more and more Western tourists. To get there, contact **Capitol Guest-house** (℃ **023/217-627**) or **Ho Wa Genting Bus Co.** (℃ **023/210-859**), each with daily connections for the 3 to 4 hour ride (or rent a car from any travel agent in Phnom Penh). Accommodation is basic, but your best bet is the **Sea-side Hotel** on Ochhoeteal Beach (℃ **034/933-641**) on the southeast edge of town. There are a number of similar properties nearby but this is the best and boasts large tidy but basic rooms with air-conditioning for between US$25 and US$50. For tours to outlying island, contact the folks at **EcoAdventures South East Asia LTD.** (Samudera Market, Town Center, Sihanoukville ℃ **012/654-104;** www.EcoSea.com). They arrange great day tours with stops in remote coves where clients can snorkel or take a course in scuba.

4 Siem Reap and Angkor Wat

The ruins of the ancient city of **Angkor,** capital of the Khmer kingdom from 802 until 1295, are one of the world's marvels. The largest religious monument ever constructed, it's a vast and mysterious complex of hulking laterite and sand-stone blocks. Unknown to the world until French naturalist Henri Mouhot lit-erally stumbled onto it in 1861, the area of Angkor existed for centuries only as a myth—a wondrous city (or cities, to be exact), its exact location in the Cam-bodian jungle unknown.

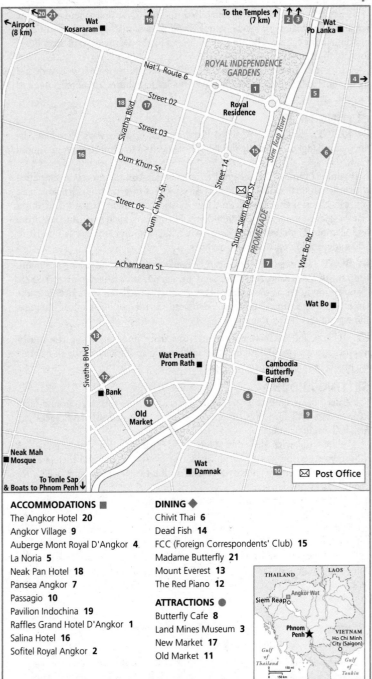

Siem Reap

Airport (8 km) ←

Wat Kosararam ■

To the Temples (7 km) ↑

Wat Po Lanka ■

ROYAL INDEPENDENCE GARDENS

Nat'l. Route 6

Street 02

Street 03

Royal Residence

Oum Khun St.

Street 05

Sivatha Blvd

Oum Chhay St.

Street 14

Stung Siem Reap St.

Siem Reap River

PROMENADE

Achamsean St.

Wat Bo Rd.

Wat Bo ■

Sivatha Blvd.

Wat Preath Prom Rath ■

Cambodia Butterfly Garden ■

■ Bank

Old Market

Wat Damnak ■

⊠ Post Office

Neak Mah Mosque ■

To Tonle Sap & Boats to Phnom Penh ↓

ACCOMMODATIONS ■
- The Angkor Hotel **20**
- Angkor Village **9**
- Auberge Mont Royal D'Angkor **4**
- La Noria **5**
- Neak Pan Hotel **18**
- Pansea Angkor **7**
- Passagio **10**
- Pavilion Indochina **19**
- Raffles Grand Hotel D'Angkor **1**
- Salina Hotel **16**
- Sofitel Royal Angkor **2**

DINING ◆
- Chivit Thai **6**
- Dead Fish **14**
- FCC (Foreign Correspondents' Club) **15**
- Madame Butterfly **21**
- Mount Everest **13**
- The Red Piano **12**

ATTRACTIONS ●
- Butterfly Cafe **8**
- Land Mines Museum **3**
- New Market **17**
- Old Market **11**

THAILAND

LAOS

Angkor Wat

Siem Reap

Phnom Penh ★

VIETNAM

Ho Chi Minh City (Saigon)

Gulf of Thailand

Gulf of Tonkin

0 ─── 150 mi
0 ─── 150 km

The temple complex covers some 96.6 sq. km (60 sq. miles) and carries the remains of passageways, moats, temples, and palaces that represent centuries of building in the capital. The temples are served by the nearby town of Siem Reap, some 6km (3½ miles) to the south.

A three- or four-day visit there will suffice (though many do it in fewer), and many come away with a newfound love for ancient cultures, Asian religions, and sunsets.

GETTING THERE

BY PLANE Siem Reap Airways, Royal Phnom Penh Airways, President Airlines, and Bangkok Air all fly the 1-hour connection to Siem Reap from Phnom Penh.

If you just want to see the great temples at Angkor, the process is simplified with international arrivals: Bangkok Airways flies directly from Bangkok, and you can check flights by Silk Air, Lao Aviation, Vietnam Airlines, and Royal Camboge Airline for other routes. *Note:* The international departure tax (from both Phnom Penh and Siem Reap) is US$20; the domestic tax is US$10 to US$4, depending on where you're flying.

BY BOAT Upriver speedboats can be booked just about anywhere in Phnom Penh (or in Siem Reap, for return) and are a good, affordable option at US$25. Contact any hotel or travel agent because they all sell the same tickets at the same price. The trip connects to Siem Reap via the great Tonle Sap lake, and some good scenery en route.

BY BUS Capitol Guesthouse tours runs daily minivans along the much-improved road between Phnom Penh and Siem Reap. Tickets for the all-day ride are just US$5. I recommend the boat.

GETTING AROUND

You'll need some kind of wheeled conveyance to make your way around Siem Reap and to and from the temples. Any hotel front desk or travel agent can make all arrangements.

A rented **car with driver** is about US$25 (double that with a guide). A **motorcycle taxi** is a good, cheap option for US$8 per day, and there are also motorbikes that pull small, **covered trailers for two** (kind of cute, really), for about US$11 per day.

Riding **your own motorbike** is a good option, but inexperienced riders should take heed of busy traffic. If you opt for your own bike, make sure you get a heavy chain lock; it's not a bad idea when parking near the temples to entrust your wheels to one of the ladies at the food stalls (they will all offer). The fee is an obligatory purchase of water or soda when you come back (ask the price before parking), and it avoids sticky little scams involving missing parts on the bike and your shelling out money to the very thief that did the deed. Welcome to Cambodia.

Warning **Airline Safety**

Be warned that no domestic air carrier in Cambodia has been checked against international airline safety codes. Though the political situation in-country is now stable, visitors should remember that, as recently as 1999, passengers aboard the fast boat faced armed robbers.

The temple roads are flat and well paved, and **bicycles** are becoming more popular. They can be rented for US$2 to US$3 per day from guesthouses and hotels; take care in the scorching midday heat.

VISITOR INFO AND TOURS

- **Diethelm.** No. 4, Airport Road No. 6, Siem Reap; ℂ **063/963-524;** fax 063/963-694; dtc@dtc.com.kh. All local and regional services.
- **Exotissimo.** No. 300, Airport Road No. 6, Siem Reap; ℂ **063/964-323;** fax 063/963-621; www.exotissimo.com; Cambodia@exotissimo.com. All local and regional services.
- **Amazing Cambodia.** Just north of the Old Market. P.O. Box 93027; ℂ **063/963-733;** amazingcambodia@yahoo.com. Offering many budget options, the folks here can arrange rentals, guides, and local tours, and provide lots of useful local information and sources. Stop by.

FAST FACTS: Siem Reap

Banks/Currency Exchange **Canadia Bank,** on the western side of the Old Market (ℂ **063/964-808**), is as good as any in town. You can change traveler's checks in some hotels and in any bank; **Cambodia Commercial Bank (CCB),** 130 Siwatha Blvd. (ℂ **063/380-154**), and **Mekong Bankb,** 43 Siwatha Blvd. (ℂ **063/964-420**), can do credit-card cash advances.

Emergency There is a tourist police station in the center of town (at the intersection of Rte. 6 and the main street, Siwatha Blvd.).

Internet/E-mail Small storefront offices aplenty surround the central market area. On the main street, though, try **Siem Reap Web,** #011 Siwatha Blvd. (ℂ **012/867-670**), an air-conditioned facility with the speediest dial-up service in town, for just over US$1 per hour.

Post Office The post office is located on Pokambor Avenue at riverside near the town center (next to the FCC, see "Where to Dine," below). It's open daily 7am to 5pm and can handle foreign and domestic regular and parcel post.

Telephone The code for Siem Reap is **63.** Most hotels have international direct dialing (IDD). Many of the Internet cafes around the Old Market have better rates and offer callback service for a small fee.

WHERE TO STAY

Cambodian tourism is in its infancy, but because Siem Reap has the longest history of recent visitors, it's rather developed. As the town grows, speculators continue to pour money into this cash cow. As a result, you have your pick of some of the finest upscale accommodations in the region.

For midrange hotels below US$100, there are lots of faceless tour-group choices, but smaller properties are sprucing themselves up to a more boutique standard, and on the budget end there are some atmospheric gems.

In the high season, high-end accommodation often fills up, so be sure to book ahead; In low season, be sure to ask for a discount. Most hotels levy a 10% VAT.

EXPENSIVE

Pansea Angkor ★★ The general impression at the Pansea Angkor is of a stylish, self-contained inner sanctum. Cross the small moat at the entry (it looks like a wall from the street) and into a steeply gabled lobby, cool in dark tones and grand Angkor-inspired reliefs. You've entered the oasis. The courtyard and central pool, a tranquil affair fed by the water of a newly constructed Shiva-lingum, is all palm trees and calm. There are fine gardens and the feel through-out, with Khmer roofs over finely crafted wooden building units, is serene. Rooms are large, well appointed, open, and elegant, with Apsara reliefs like a small shrine on one wall, cloth divans, and retro fixtures and local decor. The large bathroom connects with sleeping rooms by a unique bamboo sliding door, and another glass slider opens to a small private balcony with lounge chairs, most with a view of the cool courtyard. All is stately and comfortable, and if you're guarded from the cares of reality behind these walls, you're reminded of local culture in all the many fine details throughout. The lobby restaurant is a fine choice for a meal, and there are some great open sitting areas for drinks and a library with books, chess, and a conference table.

River Rd, Siem Reap. © **063/963-390.** Fax 063/963-391. www.pansea.com. 55 units. US$290 deluxe river view; US$310 deluxe pool view. AE, MC, V. **Amenities:** Restaurant; bar; outdoor pool; all rentals available; shopping; 24-hr. room service; laundry; dry cleaning; Internet; library area. *In room:* A/C, satellite TV, dataport, minibar, fridge, hair dryer, safe, IDD phone.

Raffles Grand Hotel D'Angkor ★★★ For luxury, atmosphere, and con-venience, there is no better choice in Siem Reap. Rebuilt in 1994 from the shell of a classic 1929 structure, it's authentic old Indochina that's neither museum piece nor overly stuffy. Right in the center of town, the imposing colonial facade gives way to a marble lobby, connected by neat black-and-white tile halls to the many rooms and fine services. There's an open metal elevator, an original period piece but functional. State rooms are large, with classic French doors and win-dows, neat black-and-white tile entries, fine furnishings, antique standing lamps, and an almost out-of-place high-tech entertainment module. It's very comfortable and atmospheric. Landmark rooms, the next higher standard, are similar but have four-poster beds, a balcony with rattan furniture, and nice touches like porcelain bathrooms and more antique detail. The central pool is magnificent, large and in a cool courtyard, and the nearby massage and health facilities are quite something. It's expensive, very expensive, but the price includes some of the finest service and a unique revisiting of old Indochina that you can't find anywhere else in town. There's an Apsara Dance show nightly.

1 Vithei Charles de Gaulle, Khum Svay Dang Kum, Siem Reap. © **063/963-888.** Fax 063/963-168. www. raffles.com. 131 units. US$360–US$390 double; US$390 landmark room; US$460–US$1,900. AE, MC, V. **Amenities:** 4 restaurants; 2 bars; outdoor pool; 2 tennis courts; health club; spa; Jacuzzi; sauna; steamroom; kids' club; concierge; tour desk; car rental; shopping; massage; laundry; dry cleaning. *In room:* A/C, satellite TV, dataport, minibar, fridge, coffeemaker, hair dryer, safe, IDD phone.

Sofitel Royal Angkor ★★ The answer is "Yes," and they probably have two of whatever you might need in this superluxe campus. Sofitel is famed in the region for bringing life back to classic hotels of old Indochina, but in Siem Reap, they started fresh in 2000, a project limited only by the designer's imag-ination. The lobby is an old-world Indochine replica with antique Khmer pagoda and a menagerie of overstuffed European furniture. Construction and decor throughout nicely marry Khmer and French architecture, with vaulted Naga roofs hanging high above the sculpted central garden and tranquil pond area. The courtyard pool is large and luxurious, with a short river meander crossed by a small bridge. The massage facility is tops, and the private massage areas are uniquely resplendent. Rooms are spacious, with dark wood floors and rich appointments like fine throw rugs and elegant built-in cabinetry. All bathrooms have tubs and are similarly large and comfortable in yellow patterned tile and granite counters. Spring for a superior room with a balcony and a view of the central courtyard: It's worth it. Not surprisingly, there's an Angkor theme throughout, but the statuary is not overdone and is quite pleasing in both common areas and sleeping quarters (unique in a town of gawdy reproductions of the sites). They have some great dining options and can help arrange any eventuality. If you stay for only a short time, be sure to take a moment, preferably near the magic hour of sunset (but any time will do) and take it all in from the island pagoda in the central pond.

(On the way to the temples, just N of the town center). Vithei Charles de Gaulle, Khum Svay Dang Kum, Siem Reap. © 063/964-600. Fax 063/964-610. www.accor.com. 238 units. US$280/US$320 superior single/double; US$300/US$340 deluxe single/double; US$320–US$1,500 suite. AE, MC, V. Amenities: 4 restaurants; 3 bars; large outdoor pool; health club; Jacuzzi; sauna; steamroom; rentals; concierge; tour desk; business center; shopping; 24-hr. room service; fine massage facility; laundry/dry cleaning; 1 nonsmoking floor; banquet facilities; Internet; small library. In room: A/C, satellite TV w/in-house movies, fax/dataport available (3 lines), minibar, fridge, coffeemaker, hair dryer, safe, IDD phone.

MODERATE

The Angkor Hotel ☆ Of the many bland choices along the airport road, Route 6, the Angkor Hotel is the best (and only slightly more expensive than the rest). Popular with group tours, the hotel is large and ostentatious, with high, Khmer-style roofs and large reproductions of temple statuary in the entry; nonetheless, everything is clean and comfortable, if a bit like a chain hotel. Rooms are bland but large, with crown molding, clean carpet, and good, familiar amenities like safes and a minibar. The bathrooms are a little small, though clean. This is a good, comfortable step down from the glitzier hotels in town, and the best choice if they're full. The lobby is always busy with tour groups heading in and out, but the staff seems to maintain a bit of equanimity through it all and is friendly and expedient. The hotel is sufficiently self-contained, with good basic amenities, an outdoor pool in the courtyard, a good restaurant, and all necessary services. The two caged bears in the hotel's garden are enough to make you cry, though.

Rte. 6, Phum Sala Kanseng. © 063/964-301. Fax 063/964-302. www.angkor-hotel-cambodia.com. 193 units. US$125 standard double; US$145 deluxe; US$190 suite (prices are net). V. Amenities: Restaurant; bar; outdoor pool; basic gym; tours; car rental; shopping; massage; laundry; Internet. In room: A/C, TV, minibar, fridge, hair dryer, safe, IDD phone.

Angkor Village ☆☆ Book early because the word is out that, for authentic rustic atmosphere and a bit of down-home comfort, Angkor Village is a boutique resort without rival in Siem Reap. Just across the river from the main market area, in a quiet neighborhood, this peaceful little hideaway is a unique maze of wood bungalows connected by covered boardwalks around a picturesque ivy-flanked pond in the center. Rooms are not particularly luxe (some are even a bit musty, really), but it's a good standard for the price and certainly makes up for any shortcomings in atmosphere. Varying in size and amenities, most rooms are rustic wooden affairs with high bamboo catay ceilings, beams, built-in cabinetry, comfortable beds, and decorative touches like traditional Khmer shadow puppets on the wall. Bathrooms are all large, with a shower/tub combo and large ceramic pots of water for bucket showers, authentic but just affectation. The central lobby is a series of platforms and private sitting areas, and the staff is very welcoming. The pool is small but quiet and picturesque in a verdant courtyard at the rear. The Auberge de Temples Restaurant is on a small island in the central pond and serves fine French and Khmer; the **Apsara Theater Restaurant,** just outside the gate, has Khmer-style banquet dining and gives a fine performance of beautiful Khmer Apsara dancing (nightly dinner at 7pm and show at 8pm costs US$20 dinner/theater; US$9 just theater).

Wat Bo Rd., Siem Reap. © **063/963-5613.** Fax 063/963-363. www.angkorvillage.com. 52 units. US$75–US$130. AE, MC, V. **Amenities:** Restaurant; bar; outdoor pool; rentals available; business center; shopping; limited room service; laundry; Internet; small library. *In room:* A/C, minibar, fridge, coffeemaker, safe, IDD phone.

Salina Hotel ⭐   This is one of the nicer tour-group facilities, but expect no more than basic utilitarian comfort. It's the low-cost that brings 'em in in droves to this unpretentious three-star; the staff is friendly and can help arrange any necessities, like guides and rentals. Rooms are large, comfortable, and basic, some with ratty red carpet, others with tile (or being tiled). Baths are small but tidy. This is an overall good value, but there's no atmosphere to speak of and the amenities are rather bare, though the restaurant isn't bad.

#125 Rd. no. 6, Siem Reap. © **063/380-221.** Fax 063/380-224. www.salinahotel.com. 64 units. US$45 single; US$55–$65 double; US$100 suite. AE, MC, V. **Amenities:** Restaurant; 2 bars; small gym; car rental; tour desk; business center; limited room service; laundry; Internet. *In room:* A/C, satellite TV, fridge, minibar, IDD phone.

INEXPENSIVE

The downtown area of Siem Reap, on either side of the main road, is brimming with budget accommodation. The **Red Piano,** a popular bar and restaurant near the Old Market, also has basic but comfortable rooms on the second floor starting at US$12.

Auberge Mont Royal D'Angkor ⭐⭐   Down a lazy lane just to the west of the town center, this quiet inn is a much better choice than the larger tourist hotels in this category. Canadian-owned and managed, it's cozy and comfortable. The staff is genial, the restaurant is inviting, and a standard rooms is like a boutique bungalow: There's character with a low price tag. Terra-cotta tile covers all open areas and rooms, and there are atmospheric touches like canvas lamps, carved wood beds, cushions, and traditional hangings, curtains, and bedspreads. The traditional decor is pleasant and inviting. Bathrooms are done in clean tile but aren't particularly large or luxe. Go for a spacious deluxe room with an open sitting area and large Khmer-style divans in curved wood: It's a great spot to lounge in style on a triangular Khmer pillow and rest from temple traipsing.

W of the town center. © **063/964-044.** www.auberge-mont-royal.com. 28 units. US$30 standard; US$50 deluxe double. AE, MC,, V. **Amenities:** Restaurant; bar; tour desk; car rental; laundry. *In room:* A/C, satellite TV, minibar, fridge, no phone.

La Noria ⭐⭐   With a similar sister property, Borann Auberge de Temples, La Noria is a mellow group of bungalows connected by a winding garden path. Near the town center, you wouldn't know it in the hush of this little laid-back spot. Rooms are basic but have nice local touches. Terra-cotta floors, wooden trim, and small balconies are all neat and tidy, and fine hangings and details like shadow puppets and authentic Khmer furniture round out a pleasing traditional decor. Bathrooms are small and basic but clean, with a guesthouse-style shower in-room setup. The place is light on amenities but has a small pool and makes up for any deficiency with gobs of charm. The open-air restaurant is a highlight, serving good Khmer and French. The hotel is affiliated with Krousar Thmey "New Family," a humanitarian group doing good work, and there is a helpful information board about rural travel and humanitarian projects.

Down a small lane off Rte. 6 to the NE of town. ✆ **063/964-242**. Fax 063/964-243. 28 units. US$29 w/fan; US$39 with A/C. Cash only. **Amenities:** Restaurant; outdoor pool; laundry. *In room:* A/C (optional).

Neak Pean Hotel ✦   It's an eclectic mix, the Neak Pean. The name itself means "wood house," and you'd do well to choose one of the higher standard wood bungalow rooms in the poolside area toward the back. Standard rooms are popular with tour groups and more or less concrete block travesties, musty and run down. In oversize wooden salas, deluxe rooms have a sort of rustic lodge appeal and are done in dark wood, with large double beds; most have balconies. Suites are larger versions of the same. Baths have granite counters and are tidy, with new fixtures and tile. The hotel entrance is on the main street, but it's a long walk through the main hotel to the nicer rooms out back. The pool is good-size and inviting, and the shade of the raised bungalows makes for a cool sitting area with comfy chairs. The restaurant is in its own pavilion at poolside, and service is basic but friendly here; they'll cover any necessity.

#53 Sivathat Rd., Siem Reap. ✆ 063/380-073. Fax 063/924-429. 105 units. US$40 double; US$90 deluxe double; US$120 suite. AE, MC, V. **Amenities:** Restaurant; outdoor pool; rentals available; tour desk; room service 6am–9pm; laundry; Internet. *In room:* A/C, satellite TV, fridge, phone.

Passagio ✦   New on the scene, this unpretentious little workhorse of a hotel is convenient to downtown and adjoins its own helpful travel agent, Lolei Travel. Rooms are large and tidy and not much more, but that's the beauty here: three floors that are something like a motel in the U.S. complete with tacky hotel art. The one suite has a bathtub; all others have just stand-up showers in bathrooms that are nondescript in plain tile but are neat and new. The friendly staff can arrange any detail and is eager to please.

Watdamanak Village (across the river to the E of town). ✆ 063/760-324. Fax 063/760-163. 17 units. US$25; US$55 1 suite. AE, MC, V. **Amenities:** Restaurant (breakfast only); travel agent; car rentals available; business center; laundry; Internet. *In room:* A/C, satellite TV, minibar, fridge, no phone.

Pavillon Indochina ✦✦   This converted traditional Khmer house and garden is the closest you'll get to the temples and is quite peaceful, even isolated, in a quite neighborhood. It's an upscale guesthouse really, charming and surprisingly self-contained, with a good restaurant and a friendly, knowledgeable French proprietor whose staff can help arrange any detail in the area. Just 2 years old, rooms are large, clean, and airy, in terra-cotta tile and wood trim, but they're not particularly luxe. There's a fine line between rustic atmosphere and necessary comforts, like hot water and air-conditioning (though many choose to go with a fan). The courtyard area is a picturesque garden dotted by quiet sitting areas with chairs or floor mats and comfy pillows. They have a good information corner where you can get the ins and outs on current happenings in town and at the temples. This is a good choice.

On the back road to the temples, Siem Reap. ✆ 012/804-952. www.pavillon-indochine.com. US$25–US$30. V. **Amenities:** Restaurant; tour desk; car rental; outdoor massage pavilion; laundry. *In room:* A/C, no phone.

WHERE TO DINE

Dining in Siem Reap is not a pricey affair. The major hotels all have fine upscale eateries, and below are a few of the better spots. The popular area around the

Old Market is a cluster of some nice storefront gems, most of little distinction from one another, but all are affordable and laid back.

MODERATE

Chivit Thai ★★ You found it! Authentic Thai in an atmospheric, traditional wood house. The food is great, the price is low, and there's casual floor seating and a rustic but comfortable dining room, romantic in candlelight. Name your favorite Thai dish, and they do it here, and do it well. The Tom Yum (sweet, spicy Thai soup) is excellent, and they have good set menus comprised of many courses that are much finer than their low price tag. Enjoy!

House 129, Rd. no. 6 next to Angkor Hotel. ✆ 012/830-761. Main courses US$2.50–US$5. Cash only. Daily 7am–10pm.

FCC (Foreign Correspondent's Club) ★★ New in town, the glowing white, modern cube of the FCC would be at home in a Nouveau Riche California suburb or a Jacques Tati film, but it is a bit jarring canal-side in the center of Siem Reap. The first floor is boutique shopping and the second floor is an elegant open space with high ceilings: a modern colonial. There is an Art Deco bar, low lounge chairs at the center, and standard dining space on the balcony. The main room is flanked on one end by an open kitchen. Newly opened, the place is already the town's runway and holds numerous functions and hosts live music. The menu is the same as the original FCC in Phnom Penh, with good soups, salads, and Western standards, like pasta, steaks, and good wood-fired pizzas. The staff still can't believe they work here, and service is hot and cold but very friendly. Even if just for drinks, you won't want to miss this place.

Pokambor Ave. (next to the Royal Residence). ✆ 012/900-123. Main courses US$4–US$12.50. MC, V. Daily 6am–12pm.

Madame Butterfly ★★ Serving the finest authentic Khmer- and Thai-influenced cuisine in town, the setting is very pleasant. In a converted traditional wooden home, seating is in low rattan chairs, and the decor is characterized by a tasteful collection of Buddhist and Khmer artifacts. Candlelight mingles with mellow indirect lighting, and the whole effect is casual and romantic. There are daily specials, and the menu reads like the short course in local cuisine and is heavy on good curries and hot-pot dishes; the helpful staff and French proprietor will gladly explain. I had a delicious dish of poached fish in coconut sauce with sticky-rice.

A short ride W on No. 6, airport road. ✆ 016/909-607. Main courses US$4–US$6. V. Daily 6am–10:30pm.

The Red Piano ★★ Ever since Angelina Jolie and cast and crew of the film *Tomb Raider II* made this their second home while filming at the temples, this atmospheric corner bar and restaurant has been "the place" to be in town. Imported steaks, spaghetti, sandwiches, salads, and international specialties like good Indian samosas or chicken cordon bleu round out a great menu of familiar fare. Everything is good, and this place is always hoppin' late into the evening; it's sometimes hard to get a seat at dinner time (no reservations are taken). The bar is inviting and the staff is friendly, even when taxed by the numbers of visitors. It's more laid back in the day and serves a delicious breakfast and lunch.

50m (164 ft.) NW of the Old Market. ✆ 063/963-240. Main courses US$2–US$9. Cash only. Daily 7am–12pm.

DINING AT THE TEMPLES

Across the busy parking lot closest to Angkor Wat, you're sure to spot the snazzy **Angkor Café** (② 012/826-346). This little gallery and souvenir shop serves, for a mint by Khmer standards, good coffee, tea, and sandwiches.

But for a very affordable and hearty meal while touring the temples, try **Sunrise Angkor** (② 012/946-595), one of many open-air eateries and the first one you'll see behind and to the left of Angkor Café. They have good breakfasts for very little.

In and among all the major temples, you'll see lots of small, bamboo-roofed eateries, and all will implore you to enter. The competition means that you have more leverage when haggling: "Are you sure this Coke is $2? Someone over there said it was. . . ." You get the picture.

SNACKS AND CAFES

For a good breakfast, real coffee and snacks (they also have a popular burger set), try **Blue Pumpkin,** a posh little cafe north of the market.

Butterfly Café ☆ is one not to miss. This netted enclosure is a butterfly farm and meticulous menagerie of local flora and fauna, including a pond filled with Japanese carp. There are detailed descriptions of all plants and some individual butterflies, but you're sure to meet the friendly U.K.– born owner, Ian, who's a great source of local information and will gladly explain or answer questions. They serve drinks and a limited lunch menu daily 8am to 5pm. It's just across the river and north of the market; entrance costs US$2.

ATTRACTIONS

Angkor Wat is the Disneyland of Buddhist Temples in Asia. The temple complex covers 96.6 sq. km (60 sq. miles) and requires at least a few busy days to get around the major sites thoroughly. Everyone has their favorite, but I've highlighted a few must-sees below. Be sure to plan carefully and catch a sunrise or sunset from one of temple's more prime spots; it's a photographer's dream. *Note:* The temples are magnificent in and of themselves, and days spent clambering around the templesare inherently interesting, but be careful not to come away from a visit to ancient Angkor with a memory of an oversized rock collection or jungle-gym. There's much to learn about Buddhism, Hinduism, architecture, and Khmer history; it's useful to hire a well-informed guide or join a tour group. There are also subtleties to temple touring, and a good guide is your best chance to beat the crowd and catch the intricacies or be in the right place for the magic moments of the day. Contact any hotel front desk or the out-bound tour agencies listed above. **Exotissimo** offers inexpensive tours to the main sites at just US$10 for a half day and US$17 for a full day with a guide and a vehicle (not including the temple entrance fee).

THE TEMPLES   Entrance fees for Angkor Wat are as follows: A 1-day ticket is US$20, a 3-day ticket is US$40, and a 1-week ticket is US$60. All tickets include all the sites within the temple compound, as well as Banteay Srei, to the north, and the outlying temples of the Roluos Group.

Angkor Thom ☆☆☆   The temple name means "the great city" in Khmer and is famed for its fantastic 45m (148-ft.) central temple, **Bayon.** The vast area of Angkor Thom, over a mile on one side, is dotted with many temples and features; don't miss the elaborate reliefs of the **Terrace of the Leper King** and the **Terrace of Elephants.**

The **Bayon** is a Buddhist temple built under a later king, Jayavarman VII (1190), but the temple nevertheless adheres to Hindu cosmology and can be read as a metaphor for the natural world. It has four huge stone faces, with one facing out and keeping watch at each compass point. The curious smiling image, thought by many to be a depiction of Jayavarman himself, is considered by many to be the enigmatic Mona Lisa of Southeast Asia. Bayon is also surrounded by two long walls with bas-relief scenes of legendary and historical events, probably painted and gilded originally. There are 51 smaller towers surrounding Bayon, each with 4 faces of its own.

Just north of the Bayon is the stalwart form of the **Baphuon,** a temple built in 1066 that is in the process of being put back together in a protractive effort that gives visitors an idea of what original temple construction might've been like.

Angkor Wat ★★★   The symbol of Cambodia, the four spires of the main temple of Angkor are known the world over. In fact, this is the most resplendent of the Angkor sites, one certainly not to miss even in the most perfunctory of tours.

Built under the reign of Suryavarman II in the 12th century, this temple, along with Bayon and Baphuon, is the pinnacle of Khmer architecture. From base to tip of the highest tower, it's 213m (669 ft.) of awe-inspiring stone in the definitive, elaborate Khmer style.

The famous bas-reliefs encircling the temple on the first level depict the mythical "Churning of the Ocean of Milk," a legend in which Hindu deities stir

---

⎛Moments   The Magic Hours at Angkor Wat

Visitors take away varied impressions of these amazing temples. Some gain insight into Buddhism or archaeology, and some relate their experience as connecting with the spiritual energy of the temples. The one common thread, though, is the visitors' impressions of sunrise and sunset. The skies over Angkor always put on a show; if you time it right, you can see the dawn or the day's afterglow framed in temple spires or glowing off the main wat. Photographers swoon. Here are a few hints for catching the magic hours at the temples.

The sunrise and sunset views from the upper terraces of **Angkor Wat** itself are some of the best, though it's a tough climb for some. Ignore half-hearted entreaties by staff to leave after the first clears of the horizon at sunset; stay for the afterglow.

Okay, so it's a bit crowded, but the views from **Phnom Bakeng (Bakeng Hill),** just a short drive past the entrance to Angkor Wat, is stunning at both sunrise and sunset. It's a good little climb up the hill, and those so inclined can go by elephant.

The open area on the eastern side of **Banteay Kdey** (see map) looks over one of Angkor's many reservoirs, this one full and a great reflective pool for the rising glow at sunrise.

For the best view of the temples, hands down, contact **Helicopters Cambodia Ltd.** ✈, at ⓒ **023/213-706.** For a hefty fee, you can see the sites from any angle you choose.

vast oceans in order to extract the elixir of immortality. This churning produced the Apsaras, Hindu celestial dancers, that can be seen on many temples.

The most measured and studied of all the sites, Angkor Wat is the subject of much speculation: It's thought to represent Mt. Meru, home of Hindu gods and a land of creation and destruction. Researchers measuring the site in *hat,* ancient Khmer units of measure, deduce that the symmetry of the building corresponds with the timeline of the Hindu ages, as a map or calendar of the universe, if you will. The approach from the main road crosses the baray (or reservoir) and is an ascending progression of three levels to the inner sanctum. The T-shirt hawkers are relentless, and the tricky steps and temple height are a challenge to those with vertigo, but the short trip is awe inspiring and the views from the top are breathtaking. *Note:* there is a guide rope on the southern face (and often a long line up).

Ta Prohm ★★★   The jungle foliage still has its hold on this dynamic temple, the only that was left in such a ruinous state when early archaeologists started freeing the temples from the jungle. Ta Prohm is a favorite for many; in fact, those very ruinous vines appeal to most. As large around as your average oak tree, the vines cleave massive stones in two or give way and grow over the top of temple ramparts. It's quite dynamic, and there are a few popular photo spots where the collision of temple and vine are most impressive. Sadly, Ta Prohm was looted quite heavily in recent years, and many of its stone reliquaries are lost.

ATTRACTIONS FARTHER AFIELD

Banteay Srei ★★   True temple buffs won't want to miss this distinct complex. Located some 32km (23½ miles) north of the main temples, the 10th-century buildings of Banteay Srei are done in a style unique to the high spires of Angkor. The site is a collection of low walls surrounding low-rise peaked structures of deep red sandstone. Translated as "The Citadel of Women," it has well-preserved relief carvings on the squat central buildings and intricate tellings of ancient Hindu tales. Go with a guide who can explain the finer details of temple inscriptions.

Kabal Spean *Finds*   Known as the "River of a Thousand Linga" (a linga is a phallic symbol representing the Hindu god Shiva), Kbal Spean lay undiscovered by Westerners until a French researcher stumbled across it only recently. Dating from the early 11th century, the relief carvings that line the stream beds are said to purify the water before it fills the reservoirs (called *barays*) of Angkor. It's the journey here that's really interesting, some rough roads through rural villages north of Banteay Srei, and there's a fun little forest hike of about 30 minutes to the first waterfall. Khmer folks come to picnic, and it's a good spot to swim or follow the path that trips along at brook-side; from there, you can view the many carvings in relief on the banks and creek bed.

5km (3½ miles) N of Banteay Srei. Entry fee US$3.

Land Mines Museum   You won't find signs leading you to this seemingly impromptu museum; Cambodian officials prefer their own rhetoric to that of the owner and curator, Mr. Akira. The museum itself is just a corrugated-roof area stacked high with disarmed ordnance and detailed data about the use, effects, and statistics about UXO (unexploded ordinance) in the country. Most interesting is the small grove out back, an exhibit of how mines are placed in a real jungle setting. The museum is a call to action for demining in the country. Resist any temptation to volunteer (unless properly trained), but you're sure to have a chance to chat with Mr. Akira, peruse his recent book on the subject, and sign a petition (he's hoping to achieve NGO status). It's an interesting visit.

On the main road to the temples, just before the checkpoint and a few clicks E. Go by motorbike or taxi. Open daily 7am–5pm.

Roluos Group   About 13km (8 miles) east of the town center, these three are best viewed in context of Angkor architecture's progression, as the forefathers of the more dynamic of Angkor's main temples. A visit to these temples is included in the temple ticket but will cost you a bit extra for transport.

SHOPPING

The Old Market, in the center of Siem Reap, is still the best place to find all kinds of good Buddhist trinkets and souvenirs like T-shirts and even good books on the temples. And in the area around the Old Market, some small storefront boutiques are popping up. For souvenirs and local handicraft, try **Sala,** near the Red Piano (see "Where to Dine," above; © **012/959-066**); or **Senteurs d'Angkor,** just across from the Old Market (© **063/964-801**); or **Timbrez,** near the Red Piano (© **012/952-716**).

Large, mall-style souvenir venues line the road just north of town on the way to the temples and are a good stop for the obligatory collector's minispoon or plastic replica of the temples.

The Lazy Mango Bookshop, 1 block west of the Old Market (lazymango books@yahoo.com), is where you can exchange that novel you've been dragging around or pick up a new one and talk with Don, the kind American owner.

AFTER DARK

Siem Reap is a town where most visitors are up with the sun and out visiting the temple sites, but there are a few good options of an evening.

Apsara Dance is an ancient art in Cambodia. Dancers in traditional gilded costume practice their slow art, characterized elegant contortions of a dancer's wrists. Combined with a fine buffet dinner in the traditional indoor banquet-house theater, contact the folks at the **Angkor Village** (© **063/963-5613**) to make reservations for the nightly show. Dinner begins at 7pm, and the show starts at 7:30pm (tickets cost US$20).

The Raffles Grand Hotel D'Angkor has a similar show in an open pavilion on the lawn at the front of the hotel. Call © **063/963-888** (same time and price).

Dr. Beat (Beatocello) Richner plays the works of Bach and some of his own comic pieces between stories and vignettes about his work as director of the **Kanth Bopha Foundation,** a humanitarian hospital just north of the town center. Admission is free, but donations are accepted in support of their valiant efforts to serve a steady stream of destitute patients, mostly children, who suffer from treatable diseases such as tuberculosis. Dr. Richner is as passionate about his music as he is about his cause. You're in for an enjoyable, informative evening. Performances are every Saturday at 7:15pm just north of the town center on the road to the temples.

There are a few popular bars near the Old Market in Siem Reap. The **Angkor What?** (1 block west of the Old Market) seems to be where it's at, and sometimes the black-lit, funky **Laundry** (on a side-street to the north of the Old Market) has good special events. Ask around.

12

The Philippines

updated by Charles Agar

The Philippines has a marketing problem, and, in the wake of recent events, foreign tourism here has dissolved to a trickle. Lacking the mystery of Malaysia or Indonesia; the rugged allure of Vietnam, Laos, and Cambodia; and the tourist mecca atmosphere that is Thailand, the Philippines have a difficult time convincing travelers that they should actually go. A long history of political and economic instability and recent insurgency movements and terrorism in the southwestern islands further relegates travel to those on business, those connected with an embassy, and those traveling on behalf of a mission or simply there by accident. In this chapter, we offer some historical and cultural information, a listing of the essentials in Manilla, the capital, and a few of the resort destinations that dot the magnificent coastline of this vast archipelago. Independent rural travel is left to the very hearty, and safety should be one of your primary concerns when making a trip to this troubled land. There is but little infrastructure outside of the larger cities.

1 Getting to Know the Philippines

THE LAY OF THE LAND

The Philippines are southeast of Hong Kong and northeast of Indonesia, bordered on the west by the South China Sea and on the east by the Pacific Ocean, and by Borneo just 24km (15 miles) from the country's southernmost point. The 7,107 islands that make up the Philippine archipelago form a land mass about the same size as Italy, but with some 17,742km (11,000 miles) of coastline. The country is divided into three main island groups: **Luzon,** the largest and northernmost group, includes the capital Manilla and the islands of Midoro and Palawan. **The Visayas,** the second largest, form the nation's center. **Mindanao,** to the south is a tropical wonderland that is now far too dangerous for foreign visitors.

A LOOK AT THE PAST

The first inhabitants of the Philippines arrived as early as 300,000 years ago, probably migrating over a land bridge from the Asian mainland with further migratory influence of the Negrito people and, in 1380, the Islamic Makdum group. When **Ferdinand Magellan** arrived in 1521, he claimed the archipelago for Spain (only to die shortly thereafter); in 1565, the Spanish established dominance that, though challenged by the Dutch, among others, lasted some 400 years. In 1898, following the Spanish-American War, the islands were ceded to the U.S. for US$20 million and remained under America sway until, in 1935, Manuel L. Quezon was sworn in as the first president of the Philippine Commonwealth. In 1942, Japan invaded the country, brutally interrupting the

> **⌒ Warning Travel Warning: The Philippines**
>
> Visitors should not travel to **Mindanao** or any of the remote beach resorts in the far south. After a recent rash of kidnapping and violence, U.S. State Department sources, among others, say that the threat of terrorism in the Philippines remains high. As recently as March 4, 2003, bombs targeted foreign visitors in the international airport on Mindanao, and extremist groups like Abu Sayef and the New People's Army (a Communist insurgency movement) are active. Even central Manila has been a target of smaller bombs. Embassy advice for visitors is to avoid crowded public spots frequented by foreigners, such as nightclubs, bars, and shopping malls. Kidnappers operate throughout the country and are known to extort funds from prominent local and foreign figures. Consult the U.S. State Department's travel warnings (travel.state.gov.) before travel.

process of transition from colony to independent nation. Filipino and American troops, under the direction of **General Douglas MacArthur,** resisted Japan's advance until MacArthur was ordered by President Roosevelt to retreat. "I shall return," was MacArthur's famous promise, and after years of oppression under Japanese rule, MacArthur did return and seized control once again, in 1944. The Philippines achieved full independence again in 1946.

Ferdinand Marcos was elected president in 1965, and hopes for democracy and economic growth were dashed in 1972 when he declared martial law and ruled as a dictator until 1986, when, under the threat of revolution, a snap election gave rule to **Corazon Aquino,** widow of a prominent opposition figure. Cory Aquino initiated a program of nonviolent civil unrest that resulted in Marcos and his beauty-queen wife, Imelda, fleeing the country to Hawaii (he died in 1989).

Aquino re-established the democratic institutions of the country but failed to tackle economic problems or win over the military or the powerful Filipino elite. U.S. influence, long on the wane, ended in 1992 with the closure of its last military base; in the same year, Aquino, who survived many coup attempts, was succeeded by **Fidel Ramos,** an economic reformer and peace broker with southern Muslims. 1998 elections saw the rise of former actor **Joseph Estrada,** who was deposed in upheavals in 2000, as the result of payoff scandals; the highest post passed to **Gloria Macapagal-Arroyo,** the vice president.

THE PHILIPPINES TODAY

To date, **President Arroyo** has garnered the support of the country on a platform of combating flagrant corruption, cronyism, and immorality in government. The country still suffers under terrorism and insurgency in the southern island province of Mindanao, where the long-active Moro movement and Muslim separatist factions flare regularly. Abu Sayef, an avowed terror organization, is based in the southwest; its large-scale campaign of kidnappings and bombings are fueled by the movement's desire for a separate Islamic state and have drawn world attention and an influx of American advisors to train the Philippine military in counterterrorism.

The Philippines

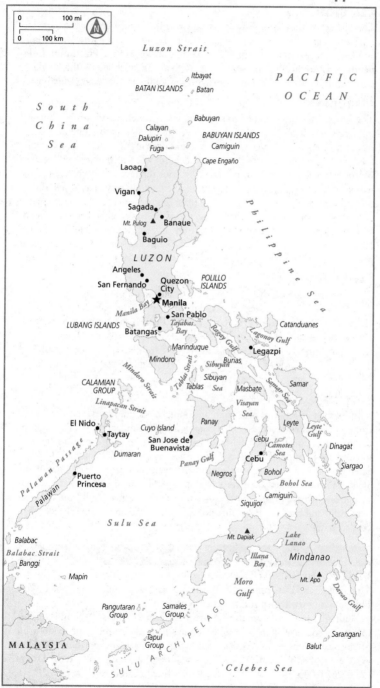

RELIGION

The Spanish missionaries came, they saw, and they surely conquered, converting more than 90% of the population to Christianity; 80% are **Roman Catholic** and 6% are **Protestant.** About 4% of Filipinos belong to the **Philippine Independent Church,** also known as the Aglipay, an offshoot of the Anglican church. About 5% of Filipinos, mostly in the south, are practicing **Muslims.**

ETIQUETTE

The Philippines is a unique crossroads in Asia, a melding of ancient Spanish influence and island tradition. Life moves at its own pace, adhering to the mantra of *bahala na* ("come what may") and mirroring Spanish passions for life, food, and fiestas more Latin than Asian. Seldom will you find a people who so welcome foreign visitors, but be careful in your interactions: A volatile combination of Latin pride and Asian "saving face" come into play here. *A few tips:* It is customary to leave some food on the plate to show you've had enough. Arrive at least 30 minutes late for social engagements (in business, however, punctuality is the rule). It also is customary to take off your shoes before entering a home. It's important to know that Filipinos don't like to say "no," so a "yes" is often just obligatory lip-service. "No" is spoken (or unspoken) in subtle hesitations.

LANGUAGE

Although there are nearly 2,000 regional languages on the Philippine archipelago, 90% of the populace speaks one of eight major languages (Tagalog, Cebuano, Hiligaynon/Ilonggo, Waray, Bicol, Ilocano, Kapampangan, Pangasinan) or one of their subgroups. **Tagalog** is the national language. English is still the lingua franca, and most official matters are conducted in both English and Tagalog, a few words of which will go far: Try "Sah-*lah*-maht" (thank you) or "Mah-gahn-*dahng* oo-*mah*-gah" (good morning).

CUISINE

Filipino food is a fusion of foreign and indigenous influences, mostly derived from the Spanish kitchen. Rice is the staple at every meal, and fresh seafood tops the list of regional delights. Island specialties are too numerous to list and include the likes of Chinese-style bird's nest soup, *balut,* a semifertilized egg eaten raw; and *buko pie,* a sweet, creamy pie made of coconut meat. Local **fruits** are as delicious as they are diverse in this tropical paradise, and anything from mango and papaya to the notoriously stinky durian seems to fall from the trees here. Rum and beer are the island's popular drinks and often come cheaper than bottled water.

2 Planning Your Trip to the Philippines

VISITOR INFORMATION

The Philippine Department of Tourism manages a useful site called Wow Philippines (**www.wowphilippines.com.ph**.)

With some of the most diverse marine life in Southeast Asia and a cache of world-class dive spots, the underwater aficionado might want to do a bit of advance planning. In Manila, contact any of the following: **Dive Buddies** (© **02/899-0838;** fax 02/899-7393; www.divephil.com) or **Whitetip Divers** (© **02/521-0433;** fax 02/522-1165; www.whitetip.com).

Outbound (in-country) **tour operators** are hit or miss. Most resorts can help arrange in-country travel specifics or offer all-inclusive packages.

ENTRY REQUIREMENTS

Visas are not required for visits up to 21 days, provided that you have a valid passport and a return ticket. Longer stays are possible but are best arranged directly with your country's Philippine embassy or consulate.

PHILIPPINE EMBASSY LOCATION

- **In the United States:** 1600 Massachusetts Ave. NW, Washington, DC 20036 (☎ 202/467-9300; www.embassyonline.com); also, Philippine Consulate, 56 Fifth Ave., 3rd floor, New York, NY 10036 (☎ 212/575-7915).
- **In Canada:** 130 Albert St., Ottawa, Ontario K104G5 (☎ 613/233-1121; www.philembassyca.org).
- **In Australia:** 1 Moonah Place, Yarralumla, ACT 2600 Canberra (☎ 06/273-2535; www.philembassy.au.com/).
- **In New Zealand:** 50 Hobson St., Thurndon, Wellington (☎ 04/472-9921).
- **In the United Kingdom:** 9A Palace Green London W8 4QE (☎ 207/937-1600; fax 207/937-2925; www.Philemb.Demon.Co.Uk/).

CUSTOMS REGULATIONS

Any amount over US$3,000 brought into the country must be declared. You are allowed to bring in 400 cigarettes or 2 tins of tobacco, and 2 bottles of alcoholic beverages, not to exceed 1 liter each. If you are returning to the U.S., you may take back US$400 worth of goods purchased in the Philippines. Duty-free items include 200 cigarettes or 100 cigars (no Cuban cigars) and a liter of alcohol. Shells, coral, animals, or produce are not allowed.

MONEY

The Philippine currency is the **peso.** It's divided into 100 centavos. Coins come in denominations of 1, 5, 10, and 25 centavos, and 1 and 5 pesos. Banknotes are in denominations of 5, 10, 20, 50, 100, 500, and 1,000 pesos.

CURRENCY EXCHANGE & RATES   The official rate as of this printing was **54.800 Philippine pesos per U.S. dollar.** Currency exchange is available at banks and hotels, but for a more favorable rate, try one of the money changers in all major city centers and at the airport. All major currencies are accepted, but you will have better luck with U.S. dollars. Rural areas run on cash, and carrying U.S. dollars in small denominations is best.

ATMs abound in cities: **Unionbank,** located in most of the big cities, is affiliated with PLUS. Most **major credit cards** (Amex, MasterCard, Visa) are accepted at more upscale venues, and cash-advance service is widely available. You can get cash or traveler's checks with your American Express card at the **American Express Bank** in Manila, 6750 Ayala Ave., Makati (☎ 2/818-6731).

WHEN TO GO

High season corresponds to the scorching dry season from March through May, but many prefer the Philippines during the warm, sunny days and balmy nights that last from November to February. Temperatures range from 68°F to 82°F (20°C–28°C). The southwest monsoon brings heavy rain from June to October. July and August are the wettest months and should be avoided.

PUBLIC HOLIDAYS   Businesses, banks, and government offices are closed on New Year's Day (Jan 1), Good Friday (the Fri before Easter), Araw ng Kagitingan (Apr 19), Labor Day (May 1), Independence Day (June 12), National

Hero's Day (Aug 30), Bonifacio Day (Nov 30), Christmas Day (Dec 25), and Rizal Day (Dec 31). All Saints Day (Nov 1) and Christmas Eve (Dec 24) are not official holidays but are usually treated as such. Christmas is a big holiday and combines with local festivals to make this a busy time to visit.

HEALTH CONCERNS

Consult the "Health & Safety" section in chapter 3. No special vaccinations are required, but updated **tetanus** is recommended, especially for divers. The two biggest threats to your health in the Philippines are the heat and mosquitoes. Stay hydrated and be careful of heat stroke and dehydration, and stay covered in clothes and bug spray in the countryside, especially at dawn or dusk.

Malaria is a consideration only if you're headed to rural areas; in this case, you might need a malarial prophylaxis. Consult the U.S. Center for Disease Control (www.cdc.gov) before rural travel.

Public facilities are below par here, so ask about the nearest private hospital, and be prepared to pay the bill in full.

No tap water is drinkable. Stick to affordable bottled water.

GETTING THERE
BY PLANE

Air travel is the only sure bet to get to the Philippines. There are no regular passenger ships to the country. A few cruise ships stop here, but not long enough to allow passengers much time to explore the country.

Manila's **Ninoy Aquino International Airport** is the main port of entry, and there are frequent regional connections via Bangkok, Hong Kong, and Singapore, as well as the U.S. and Canada, some 14 to 18 hours from the West Coast. **Philippine Airlines (PAL)** (© 800/435-9725), **Cathay Pacific** (© 800/233-2742), **Continental** (© 800/231-0856), **Japan Airlines** (© 800/525-3663), **Korean Air** (© 671/649-3301), **Northwest** (© 800/225-2525), and **United** (© 800/241-6522) all make regular flights to and from Manila or make the international connection through Hong Kong. From the U.K., try **British Airways** (© 0845/773-3377). From Australia, **PAL** (© 612/9079-2020) offers direct service to Manila from Sydney. **Qantas Airlines** (© 131313; www.qantas.com) flies from Melbourne, Adelaide, Brisbane, and Sydney. **Air Niugini** (© 612/92901544) flies to Manila, with a stopover in Port Moresby. **STA** (© 02/92121255 in Sydney) is one of the best discount agencies, with offices in Sydney, Perth, Melbourne, Adelaide, Canberra, Brisbane, and Hobart.

GETTING AROUND
BY PLANE

Domestic airlines are reliable, connecting all major cities. **Philippine Airlines (PAL)** (© 2/855-8888) has the greatest number of flights to the largest number of destinations, with **Air Philippines** (© 2/843-7001) running a close second. A number of small carriers connect with small towns.

You also are required to pay a "terminal fee" at the airports; it's P500 (about US$10) for international flights and P100 (about US$2) for domestic flights.

BY BUS/TRAIN

Buses crisscross all islands but are rough, at best, and beg endless caution. **Victory Liner** (© 2/361-1506) is one of the most dependable, comfortable, and safe companies. Many roads are unpaved and prone to washouts, especially in the north. There are trains; no one rides them. We recommend internal flights.

BY CAR

All the major car rental companies are here, and self-drive rental is an option, but the traffic in Manila is maddening and rural roads are rough and tumble. You must have an international driver's license or a valid license from your home country. We highly recommend hiring a driver to negotiate local traffic (and traffic police); experienced drivers are often a valuable source of information. In Manila, call: **Avis** (℃ **2/734-5851**), **Budget** (℃ **2/818-7363**), **Dollar** (℃ **2/844-3120**), or **Nissan Rent-a-Car** (desk at the airport; ℃ **2/816-1808**) for the closest location.

BY BOAT

The islands are all connected by every form of floating conveyance, from small motorized outriggers to luxury ships. Manila is the jumping-off point to all destinations. Shipping Lines, such as **WG&A,** Pier 14 (℃ **2/894-3211**), and **Asuncion Shipping Lines,** Pier 2, North Harbor (℃ **2/204024**), provide regular service, but it's rather basic, at best. You can book tickets through any travel agent. **Ferry boats** to smaller islands have a dubious safety record, and we recommend great caution. *Warning:* You will be hassled and harried at all ports and piers by swarms of touts and sellers. Guard your belongings.

TIPS ON ACCOMMODATIONS

Always ask for seasonal discounts, especially if you're traveling during the low season or are staying for more than a few days. Prices are quoted in U.S. dollars.

TIPS ON DINING

Dining takes on the flavors and styles of the various cultures that migrated or dominated the archipelago. While exploring the familiar Italian or French cuisines, do venture toward local delicacies like lapu-lapu fish; you might even find yourself at a local *turo-turo* (roadside pots where you just point and pray). Not all street stalls are to be avoided—stick to the ones where the food is hot, and ask for a glass of hot water to dip your utensils; the locals do.

Extreme care should be exercised when eating anywhere in-country. Lack of funds for maintenance have blurred the lines between the "in" and "out" pipes on water systems, and the lack of hot water prevents any reasonable attempt at hygiene. Absolutely **don't drink the water,** and be wary of any raw ingredients.

Ⓒ **FAST FACTS:** The Philippines

American Express In Manila, the office is located in the Ace Building, at the corner of Rada and de la Rosa streets, Legazpi Village, Makati, Manila. It's open from 8:30am to 5pm on weekdays, and 8:30am to noon on Saturday. The direct line for travel services is ℃ **2/814-4770. Thomas Cook** has an office in the Skyland Plaza Building, in Manila (℃ **2/816-3701**).

Bookstores In Manila, the **National Book Center** in Robinson's Mall, Ermita, has a good selection of novels and magazines.

Business Hours Private and government offices are usually open from 8am or 9am to 5pm Monday through Friday; banks are open until just 3pm.

Cameras & Film Manila has many camera equipment shops.

Doctors & Hospitals Most of the top hotels have a doctor on the premises available 24 hours a day. Otherwise, if you need emergency medical treatment, go to **Makati Medical Center** (© 2/815-9911).

Drug Laws Penalties are extremely strict for possession, use, or trafficking of illegal drugs in the Philippines. Convicted offenders can expect jail sentences, fines, or even the death penalty.

Earthquakes The Philippines is rocked by tremors and earthquakes quite often. If it's a big one, seek cover under tables, beds, or door frames to protect yourself from falling debris, or head to solid open ground.

Electricity The country's electric power is set at 220 to 240 volts AC, but some hotels come equipped with outlets for 110 to 120 volts. Power failures, called "brownouts," are very common in the Philippines, even in Manila. Pack a flashlight and maybe a candle or two.

Embassies The **U.S. Embassy** is located at 1201 Roxas Blvd., Manila (© 2/523-1001; fax 2/522-4361; http://usembassy.state.gov/manila/). The **Canadian Embassy** is at Allied Bank Center, Ayala Avenue, Makati, Manila (© 2/810-8861). The **Australian Embassy** is at Salustiana Ty Tower, 2nd floor, 104 Paseo de Roxas, Makati, Manila (© 2/817-7911 or 2/750-2840). The **New Zealand Embassy** is in the Gammon Center Building, Alfaro St. Salcedo Village, Makati, Manila (© 2/818-0916). The **Embassy of the U.K.** is in the LV Locsin Building, Ayala Avenue, Makati, Manila (© 2/810-8861).

Emergencies For police, dial **166**. For other emergencies, dial **7575**.

Internet/E-mail Internet cafes can be found throughout the Philippines, even in some pretty remote places. Wherever there are phone lines, you can bet someone is connected, but the connection is often slow. Most of the bigger hotels in Manila and Cebu offer Internet access in their business centers.

Language Tagalog is the most predominant of the many native languages, but English is spoken widely.

Liquor Laws The legal age for alcohol purchase and consumption is 18 years, although IDs are rarely checked. Bars and clubs don't stick to any official closing time, but it's generally 2 to 4am.

Post Offices/Mail Most tourist hotels offer postal services at the front counter. Post offices are open Monday to Friday from 8am to 5pm. Airmail letters to North America and Europe cost P11 (US22¢), and to Australia and New Zealand they cost P10 (US20¢). Postcards cost P8 (US16¢), regardless of the destination. All delivery is very slow. Courier companies in Manila include **DHL** (© 2/895-0511), **Federal Express** (© 2/833-3604), and **UPS** (© 2/832-1516).

Police The emergency services are reliable in Manila. For police emergencies, dial **166**.

Safety/Crime We strongly advise staying away from **Mindanao** and the southern islands of **Basilan, Sulu, Tawi-Tawi,** and **Jolo,** which are inhabited by rebels and pirates. Be aware in crowded public spaces; avoid demonstrations or protests and stay abreast of current issues. Theft and assaults on tourists are not uncommon but can probably be avoided with a little common sense and foresight. Be careful not to flaunt cash, wear expensive jewelry, or leave hotel doors open or unlocked. It is best to keep valuables and excess cash in your hotel's safe-deposit box until you need them. When traveling, keep your money and passport in a money belt. **Take a taxi in Manila,** especially at night.

Taxes The official taxes are 0.75% in hotels, 10% in restaurants, and 1% for sales or VAT (Value Added Tax).

Telephone & Faxes Phone service is good in the Philippines, and reception is incredibly clear. Hotels charge exorbitant rates, but prepaid phone cards are affordable. Dial ✆ **114** for directory assistance.

Time Philippine Standard Time is 8 hours ahead of Greenwich Mean Time (GMT). That's 13 hours from New York and 8 hours from London.

Tipping Tipping in restaurants and hotels is optional but always appreciated. Some restaurants tack on a service charge.

Toilets Public bathrooms are called "comfort rooms," or the "CR," but sadly, more often than not, they're not and can be shockingly unsanitary. It's a good idea to carry your own stash of toilet paper. Dispose used paper in the bin provided, not the basin, and flush with a few ladles of water from a barrel of standing water (or use only hotel toilets).

Water Confine your water consumption to *sealed* bottled water.

 Telephone Dialing Info at a Glance

- **To place a call from your home country to the Philippines,** dial the international access code (011 in the U.S., 0011 in Australia, 0170 in New Zealand, or 00 in the U.K.), the country code **(63)**, the city or area code (see below), and then the seven-digit phone number.

- **To place a call within the Philippines,** use the area code of the city you are trying to call, and then simply dial the seven-digit number. In some cases, you will find only five-digit numbers. These old numbers still work but will soon be replaced. Some area codes are: Manila: 2; Cebu: 32; Bohol: 38; Baguio: 74; Batangas: 43; Puerto Princesa: 48; Boracay: 36; and Puerto Galera: 912.

- **To place a direct international call from the Philippines,** dial the international country code (U.S. and Canada: 01; Australia: 61; New Zealand: 64; and U.K.: 44), then the area or city code, and then the number (for example, 01 + 212/999-9999).

---

3 Manila

Business travelers and cultural sojourners alike are sure to make the obligatory stop in Manila. To some, it's a wasteland of urban blight, but Manila has some interesting nooks and crannies. From an early history as a vital port, the town has flown the flags of many conquering forces, and there are a few good sites. Though congested and polluted, there are some great hotels with all the amenities, and this is a good place to splurge and find a bit of comfort in the busy city.

Manila

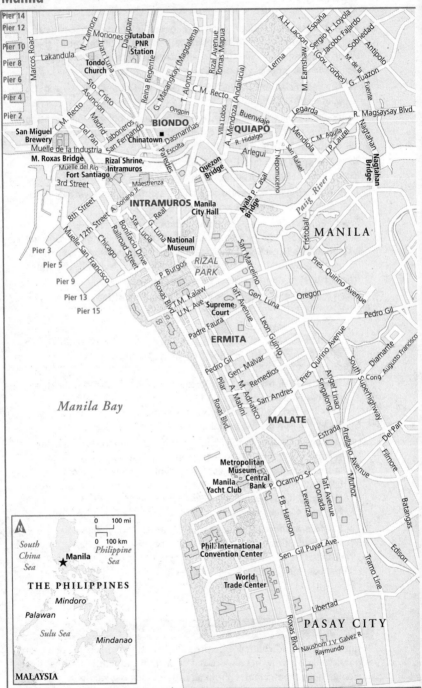

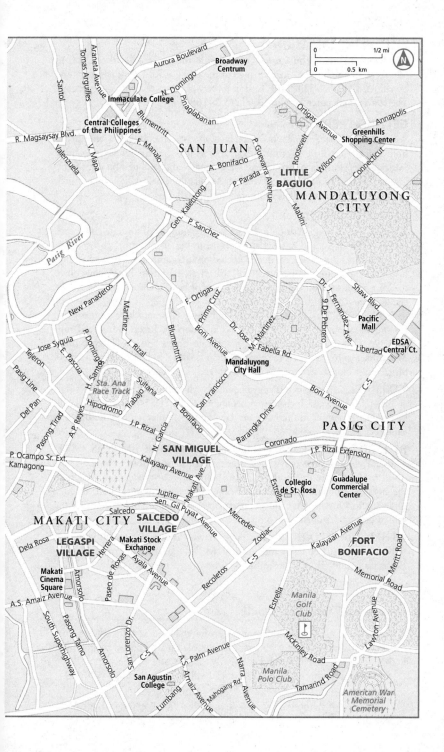

VISITOR INFORMATION
The **Department of Tourism** (DOT) has information desks at the airport in Manila or Cebu City. The main branch of the DOT at Rizal Park has maps and brochures. Call ℂ **2/523-8411,** or stop by between 8am and 5pm on weekdays. The **tourist assistance hot line** is ℂ **2/524-1660.**

GETTING THERE
See "Getting There," above, because you'll almost certainly be arriving by air from abroad. You'll be swarmed at the arrivals gate by representatives touting "official rates" for metro taxis. There are few metered taxis, but a bit of bargaining will get you to Makati or downtown Manila for US$2–US$3. Most hotels offer airport pickup at inflated rates (about US$10).

GETTING AROUND
Manila is a sprawling metropolis that's actually a number of separate cities, each with its own mayor and municipal government, but all a seeming chaos. South of the river, the oldest part of Manila, including **Intramuros,** is where you'll find historical and cultural hotspots. **Rizal Park,** stretching from Taft Avenue down to Roxas Boulevard on the bay, lies just south of here in what might be termed the main city center.

South of Rizal Park, **Ermita, Malate,** and **Pasay City** are where tourists come for the many hotels, restaurants, cafes, and shopping. **Roxas Boulevard** runs along Manila Bay and is home to many fine hotels and the **Metropolitan Museum.** Just to the east is the cosmopolitan financial hub of **Makati,** home to office tower blocks, ritzy condos, and high-end shopping and hotels.

TAXIS Taxis are cheap and convenient, though traffic is chaotic. Meters start at P20 (US$50¢) and inch up by increments of P1 (US$3¢). Carry small bills because drivers often don't have any change (or so they say). A small tip is expected; 5% or so should do.

BY LIGHT RAIL TRANSIT (LRT) & METROSTAR EXPRESS (MRT)
The LRT elevated railway system speeds through stations from Caloocan in the north to Baclaran in the south, while the brand-new *air-conditioned* MRT hugs the city's eastern perimeter from Taft Avenue (just north of the airport) through Ortigas and Quezon City. Buy a token for a flat rate of P11.50 (US23¢) at staffed booths. It's open from 5:30am to 9:30pm.

OTHER TRANSPORT *Calesas,* horse-drawn carriages for two (for tourists only), operate in Manila's Chinatown, Rizal Park, and Intramuros, and along Roxas Boulevard. Tricycle pedicabs can also be hired in most areas.

FAST FACTS: Manila

Banks/Currency Exchange Currency can be changed at banks (Mon–Fri 9am–3pm) and hotels, but for a more favorable rate, try one of the money changers scattered throughout the city centers and at the airport. All major currencies are accepted, but you will have more luck with U.S. dollars.

Post Office Most hotels offer mail service. Rizal Park Post Office is located near the Manila Hotel in Ermita and in the Makati Central Post Office at

Gil Puyat Avenue, Makati. Post offices are open Monday to Friday 8am to 5pm, and Saturday 8am to noon.
Telephone The area code for Manila is **2**.

WHERE TO STAY
It's no small relief to put a crisp, shiny lobby between you and the chaos of this city. Fortunately, fine properties abound in Ermita, Malate, and Makati.

ERMITA/MALATE
Very Expensive
Manila Hotel ✿✿✿   Without a doubt, this is Manila's most historic grand dame. Since its opening in 1912, the hotel, nestled between the walled city of Intramuros and the famed Manila Bay, has hosted everyone from Ernest Hemingway to John F. Kennedy, and the Beatles to Michael Jackson. Rooms exude a turn-of-the-century charm, with four-poster beds, fine fabrics, and ceiling fans. Rooms in the 18-story wing, added in 1970, are less expensive—and less charming—than rooms in the original building. All the first-class amenities that you would expect are here, and the penthouse and presidential suites are the height of luxury, complete with helipads. While poking around the lobby, ask the concierge for a look at the Archive Room, a cluttered history of the hotel's 88 years. There's even a MacArthur theme suite, a re-creation of the room where the general lived for 6 years. Dining options include fine Japanese and Italian restaurants.

One Rizal Park, 1099 Manila. ✆ 2/527-0011. Fax 2/527-0022 to 24. www.manila-hotel.com.ph. 500 units. US$250–US$300 double; US$325–US$2,500 suite. AE, DC, MC, V. **Amenities:** 3 restaurants; 3 bars; outdoor pool; tennis and squash courts; fitness center; whirlpool; sauna; tour desk; car rental; airport transfer; shopping; salon; 24-hr. room service; massage; babysitting; laundry; dry cleaning; meeting rooms. *In room:* A/C, satellite TV, minibar, fridge, safe, IDD phone.

Expensive
The Pan Pacific ✿✿   The only true luxury hotel in the Malate/Ermita area, the Pan Pacific strives for the perfection of the Peninsula, and details like bathtub TVs are certainly there to impress. It's famous as the first butler hotel in Manila, a reputation maintained in grand style. Double doors lead to the mirrors and marble of the fine bathrooms, and nice touches like bath salts and a personal loofah sponge anticipate every desire. The elegant down comforter and sea of pillows are a nice touch on the large beds. Spacious and technologically advanced, every room has dual phone lines (IDD/NDD Internet-ready), personal computers, and fax/printers.

M. Adriatico and Gen. Malvar St., Malate, Manila. ✆ 800/327-8585 in North America or, 2/536-0788 in Manila. Fax 2/526-6503. www.panpac.com. 240 units. US$190–US$230 double; US$250–US$1,250 suite. AE, DC, MC, V. **Amenities:** 2 restaurants; 2 bars; outdoor pool; fitness center; spa; Jacuzzi; tour desk; car rental; business center; shopping; 24-hr. room service; massage; laundry; dry cleaning; meeting facilities. *In room:* A/C, satellite TV, fax, minibar, fridge, coffeemaker, hair dryer, safe, IDD phone, butler service.

Moderate
Bayview Park Hotel ✿   Quality and value are why the Bayview is popular, and the combination is achieved without compromising luxury. Its location across from the U.S. Embassy is prime, overlooking the bay and within easy walking distance of attractions, but you don't pay sky-high prices. The hotel

offers a range of corporate, bay-view, and executive suites; you'll enjoy the best views from the junior suite's corner room. All standard and superior rooms are equipped with gadgets like individual bedside panel control, coffeemakers, and deposit boxes, and many rooms are interconnected for a large family or business gathering. The tranquil rooftop garden and pool rival anything you'd see at the Peninsula, and the modest fitness center offers massage service.

1118 Roxas Blvd., Ermita, Manila (corner of United Nations Ave.). (C) 2/526-1555. Fax 2/522-3040. www. bayviewparkhotel.com. 285 units. US$80–US$140 double; US$140 suite. AE, DC, MC, V. **Amenities:** 2 restaurants; bar; outdoor pool; fitness center; tour desk; car rental; airport transfer; business center; salon; shopping; laundry; dry cleaning; meeting rooms. *In room:* A/C, satellite TV, minibar, fridge, coffeemaker, hair dryer, safe, IDD phone.

MAKATI
Very Expensive
Mandarin Oriental ★★★   Service puts this glittering gem above Manila's five-star competitors and attracts a loyal business clientele for its high-quality, personalized attention. Employees warmly welcome you and lead you along the red carpet here. The rooms are soothing, in muted tones with huge desks that make it easy to spread out your laptop and files. Bathrooms are sleek, in all marble and porcelain. All suites come with fax machines, which in standard rooms are available on request. For dining, there's a dizzying array of international options to please every palate.

Paseo de Roxas and Makati Ave., Makati, Manila. (C) 2/750-8888. Fax 2/817-2472. www.mandarin-oriental. com. 464 units. US$290–US$440 double; US$490–US$870 suite. AE, DC, MC, V. **Amenities:** 3 restaurants (1 deli); 2 bars; outdoor swimming pool; fitness center; full spa; Jacuzzi; sauna; business center; shopping; 24-hr. room service; massage; laundry; meeting rooms; Internet. *In room:* A/C, satellite TV w/in-house movies, minibar, fridge, hair dryer, safe, IDD phone.

The Peninsula ★★★   The Peninsula is one of the most elegant hotels in the region. It certainly has the best lobby in town, with enormous tapestries and bright natural light filtering through gracefully arched glass windows. A grand curving staircase takes center stage, and live piano in the lobby lounge is cool and soothing. Rooms are airy and come equipped with fax machines and a handsome wooden entertainment center with a large TV. The comfortable bathrooms have separate shower, tub, and toilet areas. For dining, try palate pleasers like the hotel's Old Manila with fine Asian cuisines, or stop by The Lobby, a hot spot for politicians and the social elite, for 24-hour food and live music. There's also an Italian restaurant, a bar, and an a la carte buffet.

1226 Makati City, Manila (corner of Ayala and Makati aves.). (C) 2/810-3456. Fax 2/815-4825. www. peninsula.com. 500 units. US$295–US$355 double; US$430–US$2,700 suite. AE, DC, MC, V. **Amenities:** 3 restaurants (1 coffee shop and deli); 3 bars; outdoor pool; fitness center; full spa; Jacuzzi; sauna; rentals; tour desk; business center; shopping; salon; massage; laundry; dry cleaning; meeting facilities; Internet. *In room:* A/C, satellite TV /in-house movies, fax, minibar, fridge, hair dryer, safe, IDD phone.

Shangri-La Hotel ★★   Straighten your tie: This fine property caters to the international business executive. The design is as varied as the eccentric corporate moguls who stay here. Kind of a decorative mutt—it's *Gone with the Wind* meets Malaysia in the decor department, but in terms of service, the Shangri-La is second to none and upholds this upscale chain's reputation. The Makati location is perfect for shopping and business dealings. The rooms are spacious and appointed with a convenient push-button control panel by the bed, a separate shower stall in the marble bathroom, and even coffeemakers. The suites are huge and luxurious, each with a timeless ambience: You feel like royalty.

P.O. Box 4191, MCPO 1281, Makati, Manila (corner of Ayala and Makati aves). © **800/942-5050** in the U.S. and Canada, 800/222-448 in Australia, 0800/442-5050 in New Zealand, 44 181/747-8485 in the U.K., or 2/813-8888. Fax 2/813-5499. www.Shangri-La.com. 703 units. US$300 deluxe; US$315–US$390 executive; US$390–US$495 horizon; US$1,355–US$2,900 presidential suite. AE, DC, MC, V. **Amenities:** 3 restaurants; 2 bars; outdoor pool; fitness center; full spa; tour desk; car rental; airport transfer; business center; shopping; salon; 24-hr. room service; massage; laundry; dry cleaning; nonsmoking rooms; conference facilities; Internet. *In room:* A/C, satellite TV w/in-house movies, fax, minibar, fridge, coffeemaker, hair dryer, safe, IDD phone.

Moderate

Tiara Oriental ⭐   This moderately priced hotel is perfect for businesspeople who want a four-star boutique environment without all the fuss or expense. The Tiara Oriental is glittery all over, from the crisp marble lobby to gold accents in simple but elegant rooms. The hotel's smaller size doesn't compromise on the necessary amenities; there's a business center with secretarial services and Internet access, and other services such as messengers, freight, and travel arrangements. And it's the only gig in town with in-room instructions on what to do during an earthquake (this is good). The hotel provides shuttle service to the Makati Shopping Center, so you're not entirely reliant on the basic hotel cafe for all your meals (which, incidentally, served me only those breakfast Danishes I had picked out of the basket the previous morning).

7248 Malugay St., Makati City (near Makati Medical Center). © **2/729-7888**. Fax 2/729-4916. www. Tiara.com.ph. 114 units, all w/bathroom. US$95–US$100 double; US$120–US$220 suite. AE, DC, MC, V. **Amenities:** Restaurant; bar; rentals; tour desk; business center; limited room service; laundry; dry cleaning; Internet. *In room:* A/C, satellite TV, minibar, fridge, safe, IDD phone.

Inexpensive

YMCA ⭐   Tucked away down a residential back street of Makati, the YMCA is pretty much what you would expect, with rooms in need of a paint job and the familiar odor of a dorm room. The Spanish-influenced building, a cement pillared construction with a triangular pediment and wrought-iron posts, makes it a bit less institutional, and it *is* a great place to meet other travelers. They also offer cheap, dormitory-style accommodations, although it can be quite noisy and hard to sleep.

7 Sacred Heart Plaza St. (off Dao St.), San Antonio Village, Makati (near Makati Central Post Office). © **2/899-6101**. Fax 2/899-6097. 30 units. US$23–US$25double; US$44–US$52 suite for 3–6 persons. AE, DC, MC, V. **Amenities:** Restaurant; pool; tennis court; small fitness center; basketball court; laundry. *In room:* A/C, TV, tea and coffee, IDD phone.

WHERE TO DINE

If you crave it, Manila's got it. There's every variety of that familiar, salty, greasy, American fast food, a sad legacy of the country's later colonial years. The local **Aristocrat** chain is an old BBQ chicken standby since 1936 and pretty tasty, but the very brave will venture over to the fairly reliable **turo-turos** along Muralla in the Intramuros. In Makati, good eats are best in the many malls.

ERMITA/MALATE

Try **Café Havana** (1903 M. Adriatico at Remedios St., Malate; © **2/521-8097**), a popular hacienda with festive decor that serves good Spanish and Cuban fare. It's a popular business lunch spot with a chic cigar lounge. **Kamayan** (523 Padre Faura cor. M. Adriatico, Ermita, Manila; © **2/528-1723**) is a real hands-on experience, meaning that you'll tackle great Filipino food like the popular shellfish specials with only your hands (though you can use silverware); all is priced by weight. At **Kashmir** (Padre Faura, Ermita; © **2/524-6851**), you can sample authentic Indian and Malaysian food, like fine curries and tandoori, and follow it up with a sweet yogurt lassi. Its dark and plain interior keeps the focus on the good grub here. Don't miss the fine seafood at the **Seafood Market** (Ambassador Hotel, Mabini St., Malate; ℭ **2/524-7756**) or **Zamboanga** (1619 Macario Adriatico St., Ermita, Manila; ℭ **2/525-7638**), where the gifts of the sea are similarly appreciated.

MAKATI
Cabalen (Glorietta Park, Ayala Center Mall, Makati; ℭ **2/893-5915**) is a casual restaurant with an all-you-can-eat buffet of authentic Filipino entrees. **Le Souffle** (2nd Floor, Josephine Building, Makati Ave. at West Dr., Ayala Center, Makati; ℭ **2/812-3287**) is where to go for real French, along with decadent dishes like pan-fried goose liver or rack of lamb top off a menu of familiar favorites; this is a great place to just linger during an afternoon.

ATTRACTIONS
There are just a few sites of note in the city center, and plenty of guided city tours are available through most hotels. If you go alone, stick to taxis.

ERMITA/MALATE
Coconut Palace ⍟   Built for the Pope in anticipation of his visit to Manila in 1978, this stately palace is constructed of coconut lumber, fronds, and other indigenous materials. Commonly used for wedding receptions, the grounds house a beautiful **Orchidarium** and butterfly garden.

CCP/Cultural Center of the Philippines. ℭ **2/832-0223**. Admission P100 (US$2). Tues–Sun 9am–4:30pm.

Intramuros ⍟⍟   Realizing the strategic advantages of Manila Bay, Spanish colonists moved the capital from southern Cebu in 1571 and constructed this walled city. Historic Intramuros is the most popular sightseeing destination and is an oasis of calm in chaotic Manila. The complex covers some 64 hectares (158 acres), and many visitors here avail themselves of a horse and buggy (haggle, but expect to pay P600, about US$12, for the long circuit). You can poke around the garrison and chapel at your own pace or relax on the overgrown ramparts. **Fort Santiago,** within the compound walls, houses a crumbling prison and an exhibit commemorating the internment of Philippine national hero Jose Rizal. **San Agustin Church and Museum,** on the northwest corner of the complex, offers a unique glimpse of monastery quarters and a famed baroque church. The museum houses the Ayala Chapel and the tomb of the city's founder, Miguel Lopez de Lagazpi, and some fine art and artifacts. Don't miss **Casa Manila,** a collection of Spanish colonials just across the street from the entrance to the compound.

North of Rizal Park. Admission P50 (US$1). Daily 8am–6pm.

The National Museum Annex ⍟   With exhibits ranging from the prehistoric findings on Palawan to ethnological displays and tribal artifacts from throughout the ancient archipelago, a visit here is instructive. Check out the museum's Maritime Heritage Gallery, with craft from 890 and 710 B.C. and recovered items from the *San Diego,* a Dutch ship sunk in 1600.

Padres Burgos St. (a short walk from Rizal Park). ℭ **2/494-450**. Admission P100 (US$2). Mon–Sat 8:30am–noon and 1–5pm.

Rizal Park ⍟   Rizal Park honors the nationalist hero who was executed here at dawn by the Spanish on December 30, 1898. There is a bronze statue of the man, as well as Japanese gardens and Sunday concerts. It's a nice place to stroll.

Roxas Blvd. and United Nations Ave. (just outside the walls of Intramuros).

Where to Tee off on Luzon

If you are interested in getting in a few rounds of golf, Manila and the surrounding area have plenty of courses to choose from. Some are for members only, but the following are open to tourists: **Aguinaldo Golf Club,** Quezon City (© 2/911-8142); **Fort Bonifacio Golf Club,** Fort Bonifacio, Makati (© 2/812-7521); **Philippine Navy Gold Club,** BNS Fort Bonifacio, Makati (© 2/819-2780); and **Calatagan Golf Club,** Calatagan, Batangas (© 42/818-6961).

OUTSIDE THE CITY CENTER

Don't miss a trip to the picturesque **Chinatown** in the old districts of San Nicolas and Binondo. Not for the faint of heart, Manila's Chinatown is as authentically unkempt as they come, with unique shopping at Chinese herbalists, jewelers, and ceramicists. **The Chinese Cemetery,** north of Santa Cruz, along Aurora Ave, is manicured and spotted with huge tombs. Go with a guide to hear some of the fascinating tales of the departed. **The American Cemetery** (Fort Bonifacio in Makati, best by taxi) is a major draw for veterans and war buffs. The largest American burial ground outside the U.S., covering some 52 hectares (128 acres), the cemetery is the final resting place for the 17,000 soldiers who died in the Philippines and the Pacific during World War II. Maps done in tiled mosaic adorn the stark, circular memorial building.

SHOPPING

Don't miss the malls of Manila: They are the cultural heartbeat of the city. **SM Megamall** (along Edsa Ave., near the Hotel Inter-Continental) is just one of many in the downtown area where you can find some great deals.

No trip to Manila is complete without venturing to the open markets where local artists, weavers, sculptors, and the like spread out their livelihood for all to see. You will need to bargain hard—anything less, and you'll be overcharged. **The Central Market,** in Santa Cruz by Quezon Avenue, is a good place to go for fabrics and clothing, and **Baclaran,** just off Roxas Boulevard, has a small handicrafts market. Most interesting is the neighborhood market of **Quiapo.**

MANILA AFTER DARK

At first glance, it might appear that karaoke rules the Filipino night, but you'll be surprised at the variety of nightlife the city has to offer. Manila's many popular malls are chock-a-block with theme pubs like the Hard Rock Cafe and TGI Fridays. The **Heckle & Jeckle Café & Bar** (ground floor, Villa Bldg., Jupiter St., Makati; © 2/890-6904) and the **Prince of Wales Pub** (New Plaza Building, near Greenbelt Center, Makati; © 2/815-4274) are just a few of many popular bars in the busy downtown. **Manila Bay Sunset Cruises** (ask any concierge) are popular at dusk and offer great views of the busy harbor.

4 Excursions from Manila

The provincial roads leading south out of Metro Manila will take you out of the seething city and into greener pastures. Most destinations are within 3 hours of the city, and you can book an inexpensive tour through your hotel or a travel agency in Manila. Try **Baron Travel** (© 2/817-4926) or any local tour service.

Mount Pinatubo ★★   After 600 years of silence, on June 15, 1991, 1,759m (5,770-ft.) Mt. Pinatubo blew its top, blasting sulfur dioxide 40km (25 miles) high and forming a cloud that encircled the globe within 21 days. Nine hundred lives were lost and 42,000 homes were destroyed. Treks to the crater are popular but very rigorous, with two overnights. A good portion of the hike is on sandy ash, which requires more effort, but the reward for your troubles is a hard-to-beat swim in the stunning crater lake. **Swagman Travel** (© 2/524-5816) arranges tours, as do most travel agents in Manila.

Corregidor ★   Of vital strategic importance in World War II was the tadpole-shape island of Corregidor, standing guard at the entrance to the Bay of Manila 42km (26 miles) west of the capital and just offshore of the Bataan Peninsula to the north. From 1902 to 1922, Corregidor island was fortified by the American military as part of the Harbor Defenses of Manila and Subic Bay, but construction was halted with the Washington Disarmament Treaty of 1922, which bound the U.S. to cease improvements on existing fortifications in colonies west of the International Dateline. Day trips here offer good views of island scenery and some historical insight. **Sun Cruises** (© 2/635-5099, fax 2/635-6699) operates package tours from Manila. Boarding is at 7:30am.

5 Boracay Island

Ah, Boracay. Everything they say is true and more. Owing its existence to deposits of the finest sand, the beaches of Boracay are the stuff of legend. Just 9km (6 miles) at its widest point, the island was discovered in the 1980s by intrepid backpackers and Boracay is now a laid-back beach bum paradise with high-end resorts backed up against clusters of budget bungalows.

VISITOR INFORMATION
The Tourist Center (© 36/288-3704) is located near boat station no. 2 and is helpful with transport and tours; you can change money there or at **Allied Bank** (© 36/288-3026; near boat station 3). There are Internet cafes in town, as well as postal service (try resort front desks for convenience). The phone code is 36, and international calls are available at most hotels and resorts.

GETTING THERE
BY PLANE   Boracay is served by two airports: **SEAIR** and **Asian Spirit** have regular flights to **Caticlan Airport,** just a short boat ride away from the island; Air Philippines flies to **Kalibo Airport,** a 2-hour bus ride to the resort. Arrange transport through your hotel or resort, to keep it simple.

GETTING AROUND
The popular beach areas on the island can be easily traversed on foot, and there are pleasant walks along the white sands, but taxis and motorized tricycles are available anywhere. It's a good place to rent a bike or motorcycle.

WHERE TO STAY
Accommodations on White Beach range from the rustic and basic to high-end native-style cottages or resorts, mostly in the north end. Prices vary seasonally.

Boracay Regency Beach Resort ★★   The newest and largest of the big resorts, the Regency has many features that set it one step above others. It's the only place with a pool on the front beach, using fresh water from a natural underground spring on the property. All rooms are nicely lit and furnished with

dark wood and bamboo; deluxe rooms are a bit bigger than the standard superiors and have bathtubs. All terraces face the pool. Services include island-hop-
ping, boat tours, and ticket confirmations.

Balabag, Boracay. ℂ **36/288-6111.** Fax 36/288-6777. 43 units. US$106 superior; US$119 deluxe; US$154
family room; US$155–US$300 suite. AE, DC, MC, V. **Amenities:** 2 restaurants; bar; outdoor pool; tour desk;
transport rental; salon; limited room service; laundry; meeting rooms. *In room:* A/C, satellite TV, minibar, IDD
phone.

Friday's Resort ★★
Friday's cottages are situated on the finest part of the
talcum powder white-sand beach. Simple and traditional, bungalows have bamboo catay walls, thatched roofs, and wooden floors. Baths are plain, large, and
done in tidy tile. Verandahs overlook the beach, face the freshwater pool, or are
nestled among the treetops. Loads of leisure activities, including paddleboating,
windsurfing, jet-skiing, volleyball, and mountain biking, as well as indoor treats
like billiards, darts, and ping-pong, keeps the kids (of any age) busy and happy.
The restaurant is one of the best on Boracay.

Far N end of White Beach. Bookings: 8741 Paseo De Roxas, Makati, Manila. ℂ **2/750-4488.** Fax 2/750-8457.
www.fridaysboracay.com. 35 units. US$120–US$145 deluxe; US$145–US$170 premier. AE, DC, MC, V. **Amenities:** Restaurant; 2 bars; outdoor pool; diving school; tour desk; shopping; laundry. *In room:* A/C, satellite TV,
minibar, fridge, IDD phone.

La Reserve Resort and Hotel ★
Some of these French-owned creatively
painted bungalows are duplexes; each can fit up to three people, making this an
ideal place for a small family. There are nice oil paintings throughout, and even
the wallpaper is hand-painted. The hotel is near boat station no. 1 and right in
the beachside action. La Reserve is also considered to have the best restaurant
on the island.

Akland, Boracay. ℂ **36/288-3020.** Fax 36/288-3017. 7 units. June–Nov US$80–US$110. AE, DC, MC, V.
Amenities: Restaurant; 2 bars; outdoor pool; Jacuzzi; tour desk; limited room service; laundry. *In room:* A/C
(some), satellite TV, minibar, fridge, IDD phone.

Lorenzo Resorts: Main, South, and Grand Villas ★★
Each of the three
Lorenzo properties offers guests comfortable accommodations, and no matter
which one you choose, you can use any of the resorts' facilities. **Lorenzo Main,**
located in the heart of White Beach, has a garden; rooms are wooden cottages
with *nipa* roofing, all quite clean and traditionally decorated. **Lorenzo Grand
Villas,** the newest of the family, is situated at the far south end of the island on
a cliff that commands beautiful views of the passage between Boracay and Panay.
It's bright and designed with fanciful landscaping around the central pool and
quaint ponds. This is the best place for families, although access to the beach
involves steep stairs. **Lorenzo South** is probably the most convenient; it is not
as loud as Lorenzo Main and not as far away as Lorenzo Villas. The beachfront
here is secluded, and the snorkeling is excellent. All rooms have a balcony facing
the beach, and the suite has a Jacuzzi.

Bookings: Quezon City, Manila. ℂ **2/928-0719.** Fax 62/926-1726. Room rates vary, from US$40 for a dou-
ble w/fan to US$220 for a villa. AE, DC, MC, V. **Amenities:** Restaurant; bar; 3 outdoor pools; spa; sport rentals;
game room; massage; laundry; meeting rooms. *In room:* A/C, satellite TV, minibar, fridge, IDD phone.

Pearl of the Pacific Beach Resort ★★
The well-appointed rooms of this
contemporary resort blend naturally with the sprawling hills and slopes along
White Beach. The design is the most original of all the resorts here and features
neutral colors and unique textures. Choose from beach-level rooms or hillside
cottages connected to the main pavilion by a funky zigzag industrial-metal

bridge. The cottages were recently renovated, but the suites are also very nice, with seaward views. Each suite is two levels; the beds and bathroom are on the top level, and a few steps down take you to the living room with a sitting area. The rod-iron poster beds are plush and comfortable, and the bathrooms are large, with separate shower and tub and unfinished wooden wardrobes with sliding doors. If you find yourself on the hillside feeling a little lazy, a van can escort you down to the beach. There's fun and sports galore here, as with most resorts in the area; just inquire at the desk. At the Princesa Rita Restaurant, you can enjoy the international cuisine and beach views in an alfresco whitewashed space with soft wood lighting and piped-in music.

Balabag, White Beach. © **36/288-3962.** Fax 36/288-3220. Manila office, © 2/924-4480; fax 2/924-4482. 56 units. US$110 standard; US$125 deluxe; US$140–US$295 suite. AE, DC, MC, V. **Amenities:** Restaurant; bar; outdoor pool; spa; sauna; watersports rentals; tour desk; car rental; airport transfer; business center; massage; laundry; meeting rooms. *In room:* A/C, satellite TV, minibar, IDD phone.

Waling Waling Beach Hotel ⚓   What stands out about this place is that every room's private terrace looks out onto White Beach. Unlike the traditional nipa cottage style of so many other resorts here, the Mediterranean-style facade and interior will make you feel at home, with large, spacious rooms; thick mattresses; dresser drawers; and large TVs. The wooden lounge chairs and side tables are perfect for sunbathing or sipping a mango shake. Be sure to inquire about special promo rates—they're excellent bargains.

Balabag, White Beach. © **36/288-5555** or 36/288-5560. Fax 36/288-4555. Manila office, 2/724-2089; fax 2/721-4927. 23 units. US$100 standard; US$140–US$180 deluxe; US$240 suite. AE, DC, MC, V. **Amenities:** Restaurant; bar; outdoor pool; spa; watersports rentals; tour desk; shopping; room service; massage; laundry. *In room:* A/C, satellite TV, minibar, fridge, hair dryer, IDD phone.

Willy's Beach Resort ⚓⚓   Right across from Boracay's most photographed landmark, Willy's Rock, is Willy's Beach Resort, an impressive Mediterranean-style villa shaded by lofty coconut and palm trees. Willy's has amenities and services comparable to its neighbors, only at a better value. The decor is basic, with foam mattresses, but all rooms have hot showers and French doors that open onto terraces overlooking a sandy, shaded courtyard and restaurant. The palm-thatched roof means that rooms are a bit dark for some. The popular beach bar offers happy hour between 5 and 7pm. There are also room service, turndown twice daily, laundry, arranged tours, and complimentary transport to the airport.

Balabag, White Beach. © **36/288-3151.** Fax 36/288-3016. 40 units. US$74 double; US$78–US$84 suite. AE, DC, MC, V. **Amenities:** Restaurant; bar; outdoor pool; spa; watersports rental; tour desk; airport transfer; room service; laundry. *In room:* A/C, satellite TV, minibar, IDD phone.

MARINE SPORTS

In the clear sea off Boracay, you can see up to 30m (100 ft.) toward the bottom, and sea life is more abundant than we can list. There are a numerous **dive sites,** but the variety will appeal to snorkelers and divers of all levels. There are some 20 scuba schools on the island, so consult any resort front desk. Popular **snorkeling** sites include Ilig-Iligan, Crocodile Island, and Yapak; those same dive shops can rent or arrange any trips. **Windsurfing** is also very popular on the east end of the island along Bulabog Beach.

GOLF

Fairways and Bluewater Resort Golf and Country Club (© **36/288-3191**), north of White Beach, has an 18-hole, par-72 Graham Marsh–designed golf course. Check with your resort for details.

BORACAY AFTER DARK

Life on Boracay is mercifully mellow, but the southern half of White Beach does come alive at night. Any number of discos and bars are open late, especially in the high season. Try **Beachcomber** or **Moondogs,** near boat station no. 1, or just stroll along the beachside and see what's hoppin'.

6 Palawan

Palawan has been described by naturalists as "the last frontier," a virgin, untamed island. It's characterized by rich biodiversity, lush jungle, and rare fauna that are only now falling under tentative environmental protection measures. There are some fine resorts and beautiful scenery in Bacuit Bay, but you're sure to want to get underwater to see the real show along the island's reefs. Tourists will head straight for Puerto Princesa or El Nido.

VISITOR INFORMATION

There's a **City Tourism Office** (✆ 48/433-2983) in the airport. Banks and money-changers abound, but most visitors rely on their hotel or resort for any eventuality (including onward travel). The area code for Puerto Princesa is 48. International calls can be made.

GETTING THERE

BY PLANE Air Philippines (✆ 2/843-7770) and **Philippine Airlines** (✆ 2/816-6691) have daily flights to Puerot Prince, and the private charter **A. Soriano** (✆ 2/804-0408) has regular service from Manila to its private airstrip in **El Nido** for P4,600 (US$92) one-way.

BY BOAT WG&A Ferry (✆ 2/894-3211) makes two trips a week to **Puerto Princesa** from Manila. The trip takes about 24 hours. We recommend flying.

PUERTO PRINCESA

Puerto can best be described as just another Filipino backwater, a gateway to the resorts on the island, really. For an interesting day trip, don't miss the **St. Paul Subterranean River National Park,** a unique underwater river and a fascinating natural resource worth the trouble. However, it's a very rugged and a long day trip.

WHERE TO STAY

Dos Palmas Resort ✶✶ The 50 units of this fine, high-end resort are all large and luxe, and the whole place has an eye to the environment, both conservation and appreciation. There are ample opportunities to get out on the ocean, snorkel, dive, or kayak.

Arreceffi Island, Honda Bay, Puerto Princesa. ✆ 48/434-3118. www.dospalmas.com.ph. US$280–US$360. MC, V. **Amenities:** Restaurant; bar; outdoor pool; tennis, Jacuzzi; dive shop; marine sports rentals; recreation center (ping-pong, billiards); small business center; gift shop; laundry; library. *In room:* A/C, satellite TV, minibar, IDD phone.

Legend Hotel ✶✶ A gorgeous swimming pool, all the amenities, impeccable services, and luxury rooms characterize this fine property. It makes for a nice stay.

Malvar St., Puerto Princesa. ✆ 48/433-9076. US$55–US$75 double; US$92–US$117 suite. AE, DC, MC, V. **Amenities:** Restaurant; bar; airport transfer; business center; laundry. *In room:* A/C, satellite TV, minibar, hair dryer, IDD phone.

Hotel Fleuris (⋆)   Rooms are crisp and clean in this boutique hotel. The staff is friendly and helpful and can help you navigate the island.

Lacao St., Puerto Princesa. (℃) **48/434-4338.** US$40–US$60. AE, MC, V. **Amenities:** Restaurant; bar; coffee shop; 24-hr. room service. *In room:* A/C, satellite TV, minibar, fridge, coffee and tea, IDD phone.

EL NIDO

This tropical cluster of limestone islets is truly paradise and attracts honeymooners, beach bums, and dive enthusiasts. Up until the 1980s, it was nothing but a malarial backwater. Then Japanese divers appeared on the scene and started buying up islands. Development followed shortly thereafter, with simple diving camps at first and now a few proper resorts. Bacuit Bay has been declared a protected area, though, and development is limited.

All of the resorts and many independent outfitters in town organize daily excursions, kayak trips, or snorkeling and diving.

RESORTS

Miniloc Island Resort and Lagen Island Resort (El Nido; (℃) **2/894-5644;** fax 2/810-3620; www.elnidoresorts.com) sits on its own private cove, protected at the rear by a sheer limestone cliff. Miniloc attracts young, active romantics; the luxurious Lagen Island is more comfy and upscale.

Health nuts and nature lovers will enjoy the ecoconsciousness and wellness programs at the **Malapacao Island** (fax 48/433-4892; www.malapacao.com),

The **Dolarog Resort** (El Nido 5313, Palawan; fax **48/433-4892**) is a secret just waiting to be discovered, secluded and picturesque.

There are a number of budget and home-stay accommodations in El Nido: Try **Lally & Abet Cottages** (far end of Quezon St.; (℃) **48/715-3890**).

Finds **Amanpulo Resort**

Throughout the archipelago, anyone in the know speaks of Amanpulo in hushed tones. It's the best of the best, no less sublime than any of the other Aman Resorts around the world. A paradise retreat for the rich and famous, the sophisticated Amanpulo, meaning "peaceful island," gives its guests so much serenity and privacy that you wouldn't even know it if Robert de Niro was next door. (Rumor has it that he is a regular.) The cottages, called *casitas,* are spaciously arranged on the beach, perched on hillsides, or set between treetops. Fresh flowers are placed throughout your casita daily. The beauty of this paradise will take your breath away, and it won't be easy to go back to the real world.

Flights from Manila will take you to the resort's private airstrip daily at 1:30pm. This is the only way to get here. A round-trip on **A. Soriano Aviation Charter Flights** ((℃) **2/834-0371**) will cost you US$275 per adult. Be sure to call the resort for reservations and any schedule changes.

Contact the resort for more information: P.O. Box 456 Pasay Tramo Post Office, Pasay City, Manila; (℃) **2/532-4040;** fax 2/532-4044; manila sales@amanresorts.com.

DIVING & SNORKELING   The area is known for some of the best diving in the country, although, sadly, the reefs are badly scarred by dynamite and cyanide fishing. All resorts can arrange trips, and there are a few dive shops on Calle Hama Road.

7 Cebu and the South

Called the "Manila of the South" by many, Cebu is the gateway to this troubled, tropical region of the country. Recent violence on Mindanao has the area under a general warning, and there is little reason to venture this far from Manila. There are some fine hotels in metropolitan Cebu, though, if you find yourself stuck here (it's the main air hub in the south). Try **The Cebu Plaza** (Nivel Hills, Lahug; ✆ **32/231-1231;** fax 32/231-2071; Manila reservations: ✆ 2/634-7505; fax 2/634-7509; Cphres@cebu.webling.com) or the **Cebu City Marriott** (Cebu Business Park, Cebu City; ✆ **800/888-2233** or 32/232-6100; fax 32/232-6101; Ccmhotel@mozcom.com). Both are fine international choices.

13

Myanmar (Burma)

by Charles Agar

In preparing this guide, we were confronted with problematic political realities in Myanmar—realities that made us question the advisability of sending readers there. The political unfairness of the government of Myanmar has influenced the international community to post sanctions against the country. This chapter introduces you to Myanmar; provides some background on history, culture, and the political situation; and suggests resources and tour operators that the intrepid traveler can contact for aid in planning a trip to this dazzling yet troubled land.

1 Getting to Know Myanmar

Now that the whole world is mapped and our very definition of a "frontier" involves rocket fuel or swims in a scientist's petri dish, there are few places where you can make proverbial first tracks in a pair of hiking boots. Many previously unspoiled destinations disappoint travelers who show up to find Coca-Cola billboards being erected near picturesque beaches, or local people trading colorful traditional attire for American Levi's. Quaint towns, especially in Asia, are rapidly being replaced by steel-and-glass cityscapes, and nothing is more disheartening to a seeker than to get into the back of beyond only to greet a busload of gawking tourists.

Not so in Myanmar (formerly Burma), which seduces travelers with the promise of adventure and beauty unspoiled by the trampling hordes of Western feet. **Yangon** (Rangoon), the nation's capital, still resembles a postcard from the 1950s. Ancient and serene temples rise from the morning mist, uncluttered by souvenir tents and idling tour buses. Local people still stop and gaze curiously at strangers passing through. Adventure lurks in the forests and hills.

Like neighboring countries in Indochina, Myanmar constantly reminds you of its ancient Buddhist heritage. The temples are obvious, but it's the little things that stand out: small, merit-making kindnesses; folks in three-piece suits practicing impromptu ablutions when crossing paths with a mendicant monk; worshippers at small roadside altars; and such idiosyncrasies as the Burmese always handing things to one another, especially money, with two hands (stemming from temple procedure). There's much to learn and see here, and its customs, such as the practice of men wearing *longyis* (cloth wrappings), are long gone in neighboring countries in the region. Burma is a snapshot of the past.

Unfortunately, preservation of this pristine portrait has cost the Burmese people dearly. Since 1962, Myanmar has been under the strangling grip of a military junta whose "Burmese Way of Socialism" closed the country to the outside world and grounded its economy to near collapse. The Burmese people struggle to survive amid poverty and political oppression.

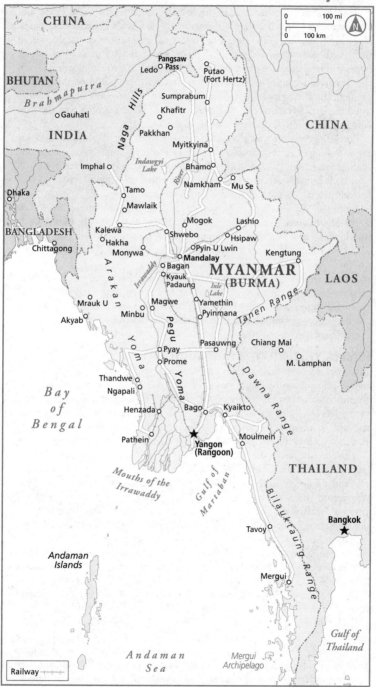

Myanmar

So what's an interested traveler to do? On one side, the **State Peace and Development Council (SPDC)** (formerly the State Law and Order Restoration Council or SLORC), the ruling elite, opens its arms to foreign visitors, luring them with smiles and welcoming them to spend foreign money—money it hopes will help mask the problems of a nation that it has so sadly neglected. On the other side, nongovernment organizations that support Myanmar's prodemocracy movement are raising the call to world travelers, urging them to avoid travel to Myanmar and thus prevent the SPDC from obtaining the hard currency and global legitimacy it needs to survive.

Burmese people are friendly, even if worried about repercussions for interacting with foreign visitors. You'll at least be greeted with smiles here; even young soldiers wave from passing trucks and women working in the blazing sun will wipe their brows, wave, and smile, the moon-shape splotches of *Tanaka,* a natural sunscreen, like great clownish dimples on their cheeks.

Almost all visitors arrive in **Yangon** and visit the city's amazing temples such as the **Shwedagon.** Typical itineraries include a connection with **Mandalay,** a simple flight, and side trips to **Bagan,** an ancient temple city, or **Inle Lake,** a picturesque natural wonder. Many return to Yanogon from Mandalay by a luxury (or budget) trip on the wide, slow Irrawaddy.

If you yearn for an adventurous travel experience, Myanmar can satisfy your expectations. With the proper preparations, you can enjoy this hidden corner of the world with relative security, and with current and accurate information, you can minimize your contributions to the damages caused by the current regime. Please travel wisely.

BURMA YESTERDAY, MYANMAR TODAY

Myanmar is a name derived from the Burmese language and reputedly is a closer transcription than the older moniker "Burma." The name change was only recently imposed on the country by the ruling elite in effort to further distance themselves from colonial rule, but because the junta has no mandate, the international community has yet to officially recognize the change. Myanmar and Burma can be used interchangeably (depending on whom you're speaking with).

The country lies in the northwest corner of Southeast Asia, sharing borders with Thailand, Laos, China, Tibet, India, and Bangladesh. The northern regions rise and plunge with the foothills of the Himalayan mountain range. Here streams originate, converging in low-lying plains to form the Ayeyarwady (Irrawaddy) River. The river bisects the country before branching out into deltas, flowing southward through Myanmar's tropical southern landscape to the Andaman Sea.

The people are divided into over 67 unique ethnic groups. Descended from people who migrated in waves from central Asia, Tibet, and southern China, the many races that developed over the centuries battled each other constantly— and, in some cases, still do so today. The majority of the population is **Bamar,** the race of the ruling elite. Most of the other races are divisions of hill tribe peoples who share similar cultures with the people of northern Thailand and Southern China.

Theravada Buddhism is the country's ruling religion, having drifted there from its origins in Sri Lanka. Before Buddhism, the people of Burma practiced as many different forms of animism—the worship of spirit and nature gods called *Nats*—as there were tribes. Today, although a profound majority of the population is Buddhist, animism is still alive and well in the northern regions, and you'll find shrines honoring local Nats anywhere from high on mountain-tops to busy alleyways.

Buddhism has a far-reaching influence on the people of Myanmar. Theravada, the most orthodox of Buddhist tracts, follows strictly the teachings of the Lord Buddha. Many men and boys enter the monkshood (if only for a short time); life is conservative, and the artistic tradition of Sri Lankan Buddhism abounds, from Myanmar's many breathtaking temples to a multitude of fascinating Buddha images.

Myanmar is rich in natural resources, including rubies and other gemstones mined in the north and teak trees, desirable for their fine hardwood lumber. Its fertile soils yield bountiful rice crops, but, unfortunately, Myanmar's biggest claim to agricultural fame is the opium poppy. As the world's largest producer of illicit opium, Myanmar's hill-tribe farmers in the north depend on poppies for survival because their sale brings more money than other subsistence crops. Farmers sell the crops to manufacturers who produce and distribute the opium and heroin derivatives globally. Much of the true wealth gained by the sale is diverted to tribal rebel groups for the purchase of weapons in the fight for independence from Myanmar's ruling military junta.

HISTORY & POLITICAL TURBULENCE

Before the Anglo-Burmese wars, which ended in 1886, Burma had been a monarchy since the 11th century. British colonialism put the country on the world map but failed to protect it from the invading Japanese in World War II. In 1946, following the Japanese surrender, Burma became an independent state, and a fledgling democracy began under the courageous leadership of **Aung San,** an independence hero who was able to unite Burma's many ethnic groups to form a single nation. Unfortunately, the following year, Aung San was killed in a coup. To this day, he remains a national hero, with his image plastered on almost every wall in the country.

The following 15 years were wrought with domestic chaos until General Ne Win took hold of the reins. He filled government positions with high-ranking military officials, which gave rise to the all-powerful Revolutionary Council. Under a socialist decree, privatization was banished, the military ruled all affairs (including those social and economic), and the country was virtually closed to the outside world.

Since then, there have been many challenges to Ne Win's government, most of which were initiated by the country's many different ethnic minority groups. The most threatening challenge came in 1988, following a brief and rare period of relative political openness, when people began to collect and speak openly about their human rights and democracy. In September of that year, the army retaliated with a brutal sweep, killing as many as 10,000 people. This massacre drove the government to form the **State Law and Order Restoration Council (SLORC),** and it inspired a young intellectual, **Aung San Suu Kyi,** daughter of independence leader Aung San, to become head of the opposition party, the prodemocracy National League for Democracy (NLD).

General elections were held in 1990, and despite the political imprisonment of Ms. Suu Kyi, the NLD won 82% of the votes. The SLORC chose to ignore the expressed wishes of the Burmese people and remained in power, imprisoning many NLD figures.

Today Ms. Suu Kyi remains under house arrest in Myanmar's capital. She is recognized globally as the voice of democracy for the people of Burma, who suffer under strict SLORC oppression policies. In early 1999, the International Labour Organization (ILO) pointed a finger at the SLORC as a leading abuser of basic labor rights. Shortly afterward, a report to the United Nations Human Rights Commission (UNHCR) stated that human rights violations were on the rise, with the government intimidating citizens and preventing them from exercising fundamental rights.

In March 1999, when Aung San Suu Kyi's husband, Michael Aris, who was residing in the United Kingdom, fell critically ill with cancer, the Myanmar government refused him a visa to enter the country. Instead, the Myanmar government tried to convince Ms. Suu Kyi to leave, promising her that she'd be allowed to return. In fear of permanent exile, she remained in Myanmar; sadly, her husband died shortly afterward. The global press has accepted this as proof of the cruel manner in which the SLORC regards its people, and the people of Myanmar see the incident as yet another reason to hold Ms. Suu Kyi in the highest of esteem as the true soul of the nation.

THE SLORC & TOURISM: TO GO OR NOT TO GO

The State Law and Order Restoration Committee (SLORC) opened the country to tourism in the early 1990s, and a flood of overseas hotel investors, travel agencies, and tour operators rushed in. However, alongside reports of the country's vast wealth of cultural beauty came reports of government projects that conscripted labor to complete infrastructure and tourism projects. Such labor projects increased dramatically when the SLORC declared 1996 as "Visit Myanmar Year." Sources reported cruel labor practices during the restoration of the Royal Palace in Mandalay in preparation for 1996.

The SLORC's hopes of attracting foreign money through tourism were crushed when Aung San Suu Kyi publicly urged tourists to refrain from visiting Myanmar until a legitimate government had been established. By the mid-1990s, travel agents had begun to drop Myanmar packages like a bad habit. In November 1997, the junta renamed itself the **State Peace and Development Council (SPDC),** in a vain attempt to improve its international profile.

However, over the past couple of years, a new side to the argument has developed. Does boycotting tourism in Myanmar help the Burmese people? Some say no, pointing to the jobs created by the tourism industry and the access that tourism gives local people to the outside world and to increased international awareness of issues in the country. Many NGOs have suggested that maybe it's time for the world to see Burma, and to expose the country to the world at large.

As visitors to Burma, like it or not, we join the debate and vote with our tourist dollars. The military junta's response to foreign pressure has been to further silence internal dissent through imprisonment, torture, and murder. Burmese press is nothing more than the clanging mouthpiece of the generals, and foreign journalists are routinely denied entry or have their film and notes confiscated. The junta's economic policy serves no other purpose than to line its own pockets. This means that Myanmar, junta at the wheel, has become the world's leading producer of opium and its byproduct, heroin, in a time of increased domestic and global addiction (60% of U.S. heroin reportedly comes from Burma). Widespread intravenous drug use fuels an AIDS epidemic that has gone unchecked and is expected to reach outbreak proportions unrivaled in the region. Exploitation of natural resources is without limit as fragile rainforests' timber is harvested with impunity and is done with conscripted indigenous labor. The realities of this military junta are hard to face and, with the

Burmese policy of isolation, go almost unobserved by the foreign press. The question is, should we go to Burma? Do we bring the country into humanitarian perspective for ourselves and, by meeting Burmese and putting a face on some of the more glowing injustices, do we raise the world's consciousness? Or is our contribution of at least US$200 just another way to support a rogue regime? Food for thought.

2 Planning Your Trip to Myanmar

VISITOR INFORMATION

Ethical issue or no, many travelers choose to visit Myanmar. While planned tours are unarguably the most convenient way to see the country, nongovernmental organizations are suggesting a "backpacker" route for those who are really interested in seeing "the true Burma." They urge foreign visitors to patronize family-run guesthouses and restaurants, and use transportation that supports local people to ensure that your money stays out of the hands of the government and finds its way to the people who truly need it. **The Burma Project at the Open Society Institute,** 400 W. 59th St., 4th Floor, New York, NY 10019 (© **212/548-0632;** fax 212/548-4655; www.soros.org/burma), is a leading NGO in the struggle for democracy. Its website provides extensive links to facts and articles about Myanmar and its political situation.

WORKING WITH A TOUR OPERATOR

- **Abercrombie & Kent:** 1520 Kensington Rd., Suite 212, Oakbrook, IL 60523-2141 (© **800/323-7308;** fax 630/954-3324; www.aandktours. com). This premier operator does a fabulous job with tours in Myanmar, booking you into the best hotels and transportation options available.
- **Diethelm Travel:** 1 Inya Rd., Kamayut Township (© **951/527-110** or 951/527-117; fax 951/527-135; www.diethelm-travel.com). This is a large, reputable tour operator with offices throughout Southeast Asia. You can plan all or part of your trip through this company.
- **Exotissimo:** #0303 Sakura Tower, 339 Bogyoke Aung San St., Kyauktada Township, Yangon, Myanmar. (© **951/255-427** or 951/255-388; fax 951/255-428; myanmar@exotissimo.com). A great choice, the folks at Exotissimo can customize any of its programs and has good eco-tour options.

ENTRY REQUIREMENTS

Myanmar consulates issue visas for stays of up to 28 days. The cost is US$25; three passport photos are required. An extension of up to 14 days can be granted within the country. Arrangements can be made with any travel agent in Thailand and require at least 2 working days.

MONEY

At an airport checkpoint, tourists are required to exchange US$200 into what are called Foreign Exchange Certificates (FEC), a kind of tourist monopoly money whose value corresponds to the dollar (US$1 = 1FEC, though the actual value fluctuates) and comes in denominations of 1, 5, 10 and 20 FEC. The policy ensures that at least part of the money you spend will fill government coffers. However, some travelers report bribing their way around the money exchange and thus carrying U.S. cash to be exchanged on the black market (gold vendors and on the street); this way your money goes directly to Burmese people. Regardless, FEC are required to pay for tourist hotels (though larger properties accept credit cards). Any amount over your original exchange of US$200 can be exchanged back to US dollars before leaving. The policy is subject to change without notice.

GETTING THERE & GETTING AROUND

Travelers to Myanmar can enter only by plane. International carriers servicing Myanmar include **Myanmar Airways International** (www.maiair.com), **Thai Airways International,** and **Silk Air** (Singapore Airlines), among others, with direct access from Bangkok, Singapore, and Hong Kong. **Air Mandalay** connects Thailand's Chiang Mai with Mandalay and Yangon.

Once in Myanmar, the most convenient public transportation between cities is flying **Air Mandalay** (www.air-mandalay.com) or **Yangon Airways** (www.yangonair.com), which operate between most major cities. **Myanmar Railways** will take you from Yangon to Mandalay and beyond. Buses connect all major sites, as well as riverboats for stunning tours of the Ayeyerwady and its sights.

The most famous and luxurious mode of travel is to book passage aboard the **Eastern & Oriental's Road to Mandalay,** a grand river cruiser that moves between Mandalay and Bagan, with trips down to Yangon as well. Visit its website at www.orient-express.com, or call ℂ 800/524-2420 **in the U.S.,** ℂ 020/7805-5100 **in the U.K.,** ℂ 1800/000-395 **in Australia,** or ℂ 09/379-3708 in **New Zealand.**

Remember that there is a US$10 airport departure tax when leaving Myanmar.

MYANMAR EMBASSY LOCATIONS

- **In the U.S.:** Myanmar Embassy, 2300 S St. NW, Washington, DC 20008 (ℂ 202/332-9045). Permanent Mission of Myanmar to the United Nations, 10 E. 77th St., New York, NY 10021 (ℂ 212/535-1310).
- **In the U.K.:** 19A Charles St., London W1X 8ER (ℂ **0171/629-6966**).
- **In Australia:** 22 Arkana St., Yarralumla, Canberra A.C.T. 2600 (ℂ **6102/ 627-33811**).
- **In Canada:** 85 Range Rd., Suite 902–903, Sandringhan, Ottawa, Ontario (ℂ **613/232-6434**).
- There is no Myanmar representation in **New Zealand.**

⟨*Warning* Safety

It is highly recommended that you check with your home country's overseas travel departments or with the United States Department of State (visit travel.state.gov, or call the "travel hot line" at ℂ **202/647-5225**) to be warned of travel advisories and current affairs that might affect your trip.

Medical safety and evacuation insurance is highly recommended. You should obtain emergency evacuation insurance coverage for the length of your stay, in addition to your health insurance policy. A good evacuation plan will get you out of the country in situations that pose political danger, will help you secure adequate legal assistance if you are unfortunate enough to need it, and will transport you to the nearest reputable medical facility (in Bangkok) in the event of a health emergency.

FOREIGN EMBASSIES IN MYANMAR

Many countries strongly urge that you keep in touch with your native consulate within Myanmar upon arrival and throughout your stay. In the event of an emergency, you'll be thankful that it has your travel itinerary on hand. International representatives in Myanmar are as follows: **U.S.,** 581 Merchant Rd. (© **951/282-055**); **U.K.,** 80 Strand Rd. (© **951/821-700**); and **Australia,** 88 Strand Rd. (© **951/251-809**). There is no presence for New Zealand or Canada in Myanmar at this time.

3 Yangon

Yangon, formerly Rangoon, is a city with a pace all its own. It's a unique cross-roads of Burmese, Indian, Bangladeshi, and indigenous populations and is worth taking some time to explore. The most famous and exquisite sight, and a must-see, is the **Shwedagaon Pagoda.** The construction of the pagoda remains a mystery, hidden in many local legends; however, recorded history suggests that it predates the 11th century. The huge Sri Lankan–influenced, bell-shape pagoda rises over 100m (300 ft.) above the cityscape, a vision of glistening gold—8,688 precious solid gold plates, bejeweled in a huge fortune of diamonds, rubies, sapphires, and other gems. Inside, the *stupa* enshrines eight hairs from the Lord Buddha; outside, within the temple walls, is a small city of pagodas, temples, shrines, and astrological pillars, all crowded with the devout.

Yangon also retains the charm of an exotic British outpost. A walk down city streets is a sensory assault of exotic city planning, with tropical colonial architecture interlaced with Burmese temples and shops. Don't miss the sprawling **Scott Market,** a great place to wander and buy yourself a *longyi,* the cotton skirt worn by men (a similar version is worn by women). Have it sewn on the spot, and get a lesson in how to tie it properly. Wear a longyi in Burma, and you'll be all the rage (they're not laughing at you, just near you).

WHERE TO STAY

Yangon has a few top-quality places to stay, the most famous of which is **The Strand Hotel** (92 Strand Rd.; © **951/243-377;** fax 951/289-880; reservations@strandhotel.com.mm). Built at the turn of the 19th century, the Strand is a gorgeous monument to British colonial opulence. The **Pan Sea Yangon** (35 Taw Win Rd.; © **951/229-860;** fax 951/228-26; www.pansea.com) is typical of Pan Sea properties in the region: refined, but not isolated from culture or nature; the rooms are plush and stylish. You'll also find good accommodations at **Traders Hotel Yangon** (223 Sule Pagoda Rd.; © **951/242-828;** fax 951/242-800; thyn@shangri-la.com), a business hotel (operated by the Shangri-La hotel corporation) in a great location. For beautiful accommodations on Inya Lake, try the **Renaissance Lake Hotel–Yangon** (37 Kabah Aye Pagoda Rd.; © **951/662-866;** fax 951/665-537; renaissanceinyalake@mptmail.net.mm).

4 Mandalay

Mandalay is the most visited city in Myanmar next to Yangon. The main attraction is the **Royal Palace,** a perfect square enclosed in walls over 2km (1¼ miles) in length on each side. Surrounded by a moat, the walled palace is open to the public through special guided tours that visit only the Lion's Room, where the royal throne was located, and the palace museum. **Mandalay Hill** has a nice little temple (it seems that every hilltop in Burma has a temple or stupa), and climbing it falls into the paradigm of merit-making pilgrim travel (going by car doesn't count). The views of the town, palace, and river make it worth the climb.

5 Bagan

Bagan, a riverside city of more than 2,000 pagodas, is located just to the south of Mandalay. Comparable with Cambodia's Angkor Wat, these 11th-century temples stretch as far as the eye can see and are stunning images of ancient Buddhist expression and testimonies to the wealth of a once mighty kingdom. Visit the temples by bicycle, or arrange a private car or even a horse cart. It's a big, dusty plain, so be sure to bring (and drink) lots of water. Bagan's temples at sunset find rival only at Angkor; the temples are like an elaborate canvas upon which the sun paints broad strokes in orange, red, and purple.

Index

See also Accommodations index, below.
Key to Abbreviations: (B) Myanmar (Burma); (C) Cambodia; (H) Hong Kong; (I) Bali (Indonesia); (L) Laos; (M) Malaysia; (P) the Philippines; (S) Singapore; (T) Thailand; (V) Vietnam.

GENERAL INDEX

Abdul Gafoor Mosque (S), 491
Abercrombie & Kent, 66, 630, 691
Abhisek Dusit Throne Hall (Bangkok, T), 150
Absolute Asia, 67
Accommodations. *See also* Accommodations Index
best hotel bargains, 18–19
best resorts and luxury hotels, 17–18
shopping online for, 56–57
AIDS, in Thailand, 116
Airfares, 62–63
shopping online for, 56
Airlines, 60–61, 68
bankruptcy and, 63
staying comfortable in long-haul flights, 63–64
Airport security, 61–62
Akha tribe (T), 221
Al-Abrar Mosque (S), 490
Alcazar (Pattaya, T), 172
Alexandre Yersin Museum (Nha Trang, V), 330
Alibi Bar and Brasserie (H), 101
Aljunied Brothers (S), 511
Allez Boo (Ho Chi Minh City, V), 368
All Lao Services (L), 408
Amanpulo Resort (P), 684
Amed (I), 620
The American Cemetery (Manila, P), 679
Ana Mandara (Nha Trang, V), 331
Ancient Gallery (Ho Chi Minh City, V), 368
Angkor, temples at (C), 650
restaurants, 659
sightseeing, 659–661
traveling to, 652
Angkor Thom (C), 659
Angkor Wat (C), 10, 14, 625, 660–661

Ang Mo Kio (S), 431
Ann's Tours (Hanoi, V), 268, 289
Ann Tours (Ho Chi Minh City, V), 350, 369
An Phu Tourism (Danang, V), 305
An Phu Tourist (Hoi An, V), 310
Antiques
Malaysia
Kuala Lumpur, 546
Malacca, 564
Singapore, 509, 511
Thailand, 21, 155, 156, 216
Antonio Blanco's Gallery (Ubud, I), 611
Anusarn Night Market (Chiang Mai, T), 236
Anywhere Music Pub (S), 514
Ao Phrao (Paradise Beach; Ko Samet, T), 176
Apocalypse Now (Hanoi, V), 287
Apocalypse Now (Ho Chi Minh City, V), 369
Apricot Gallery (Hanoi, V), 286
Arab Street (S), 21, 430
shopping, 510–511
sights and attractions, 492–493
Armenian Church (S), 481
Army Museum (Hanoi, V), 281
Asian Civilisations Museum (S), 481
Asia Transpacific Journeys, 67, 630
Asri Shop (Candi Dasa, I), 617
ATMs (automated teller machines), 43
"Au Co" Traditional Troupe (Ho Chi Minh City, V), 369
Authentique Interiors (Ho Chi Minh City, V), 367
Awana Golf and Country Club (Genting, M), 551

Axolotl Village (Ko Samui, T), 198
Ayer Keroh Recreational Forest (Malacca, M), 564
Ayutthaya (T), 13

Baan Khily Gallery (Luang Prabang, L), 421
Baba Nyonya Heritage Museum (Malacca, M), 562
Bac Ha Market (Sapa, V), 293
Baci ceremonies (L), 7, 376, 419
Backroads, 67
Bagan (B), 694
The Balcony (Bangkok, T), 158
Bali Golf and Country Club (Nusa Dua, I), 603
Bali, 581–624
accommodations, 590–591
American Express, 592
brief description of, 27–28
business hours, 592
climate, 588
consulates, 592–593
cultural traditions and practices, 33–34, 585–587
currency and currency exchange, 42
customs regulations, 588
dentists and doctors, 592
drug laws, 592
electricity, 592
emergencies, 593
entry requirements, 38, 587
health concerns, 587
history and politics, 582–585
holidays, 588–589
language, 586–587, 593
lay of the land, 581–582
money matters, 588
planning your trip to, 587–591
restaurants and dining, 591
safety/crime, 593
seasons, 588

Bali *(cont.)*
  shopping, 591
  telephones, 592, 593
  time zone, 593
  tipping, 593
  toilets, 593–594
  transportation, 589–590
  traveling to, 589
  visitor information, 587
  water, 594
  what's new, 4
Bamboo Bar at the Oriental Hotel (Bangkok, T), 157
Bamboo Bar (Cha-Am, T), 184
Banana Club (Phuket, T), 217
Ban Boran Antiques (Phuket, T), 216
Bangi Golf Resort (Kuala Lumpur, M), 548
Bangkok (T), 124–160
  accommodations, 129–140
  banks, 129
  cultural pursuits, 153–155
  Internet/e-mail, 129
  layout of, 125
  massage parlors ("modern" or "physical"), 159
  motorcycle taxis, 128
  nightlife, 22, 156–160
  performing arts, 156
  restaurants, 140–146
  sex scene, 157–160
  shopping, 155–156
  sights and attractions, 146–155
  taxis, 127–128
  telephone, 126
  temples and wats, 151–153
  transportation, 126–129
  traveling to, 61, 125–126
  visitor information, 125
  waterways, 146
  what's new, 1–3
Bangrak Market (Bangkok, T), 155
Bangsar (M), 549
Bangunan Sultan Ibrahim (Johor Bahru, M), 557
Banks
  Cambodia
    Phnom Penh, 636–637
    Siem Reap, 653
  Laos
    Luang Prabang, 410
    Vientiane, 394
  Thailand, 121
    Bangkok, 129
    Ko Samui, 191
    Phuket, 203

Vietnam
  Dalat, 333
  Danang, 305
  Hanoi, 269
  Ho Chi Minh City, 350
  Hoi An, 310
  Hue, 297
  Nha Trang, 324
Ban Puen Palace (Phetchaburi, T), 187
Banteay Srei (C), 661
Banyan Tree Club & Laguna (Bang Tao Bay, T), 214
Bao Dai's Palace (Dalat, V), 338–339
Bao Dai Villa's (Nha Trang, V), 331
Bao Khanh Street (Hanoi, V), 287
Baphuon (C), 660
The Barbican (Bangkok, T), 158
Bargaining, 36
Bar Gelateria Bellavista (S), 489
Bar None (S), 517
Batu Muang Fishing Village (Penang, M), 573
Bayon (C), 659–660
Beaches
  best, 11
  Langkawi (M), 580
  Singapore, 506
    Sentosa, 504
  Thailand
    Ao Phrao (Paradise Beach; Ko Samet), 176
    Pattaya Beach, 169–171
    Similan archipelago, 218
  Vietnam, 3
    China Beach (My Khe), 304
    Hoi An, 320
    Mui Ne Beach, 345–346
Beaujolais (S), 518
Bicycling, in Singapore, 506–507
Binh Tay Market (Ho Chi Minh City, V), 367
The Black Stupa (That Dam; Vientiane, L), 404
Black travelers, 54
Blue Canyon Country Club (Phuket, T), 214
Blue House (Luang Prabang, L), 421

Blue Stars Sea Kayaking (Ko Samui, T), 196
Blue Water Anglers (Phuket, T), 212
Boat Quay (S), 488–489
Boat trips and tours, 69. *See also* Ferries
  Bali, 590
  Cambodia, 634, 635
  Langkawi (M), 580
  Laos, 385, 386–387
    Luang Prabang, 408, 410
  Nha Trang (V), 324, 331
  the Philippines, 669
  Thailand, 241
    Bangkok, 128, 146
Bobby Chin's (Hanoi, V), 288
Bodycare Spa at Poppies (Chaweng Beach, T), 198
Boom Boom Room (S), 518
Boracay Island, 680–683
Botanical Gardens (Penang, M), 574
Boun Ok Phansa (L), 383
Bounty Ship I (Kuta, I), 600
Brewerkz (S), 516
Brinchang (M), 552
Brix (S), 514
Bruahaus Bangkok (T), 159
Bualu (I), 603
Buddha Park (Vientiane, L), 403
Buddhism, 30–31
Buddhist Lent (L), 383
Buffalo Tours (Hanoi, V), 269, 289
Bugis Street/Bugis Junction (S), 430, 481
Bukit Timah Nature Reserve (S), 494
The Bull's Head (Bangkok, T), 159
Bun Song Heua (Dragon Boat Races, L), 16, 383
Burma. *See* Myanmar
Business etiquette, 71
Bus travel, 69
Butterfly & Reptile Sanctuary (Malacca, M), 564
Butterfly Garden (near Laem Din, T), 197
Butterfly Park and Insect Kingdom Museum of Singapore, 504
Buu Dien (General Post Office) (Ho Chi Minh City, V), 364

California (H), 101–102
Calypso Cabaret (Bangkok, T), 157
Camacrafts (Vientiane, L), 405
Cambodia, 625–662. *See also specific cities*
accommodations, 635
brief description of, 28
climate, 632
clothing considerations, 632
cultural traditions and practices, 31–32
currency and currency exchange, 41
customs regulations, 631
drugs, 633
entry requirements, 38, 631
etiquette, 629
foreign embassies in, 634
health concerns and vaccinations, 633–634
history of, 626–629
language, 629–630
lay of the land, 626
money matters, 631–632
people of, 629
planning your trip to, 630–631
public holidays and events, 632
restaurants, 635
safety tips, 632–633
shopping, 635
transportation, 634–635
traveling to, 634
visitor information, 630
what's new, 5
Camel Fishing Game (Lamai, T), 196
Cameron Highlands (M), 551–553
Candi Dasa (I), 613–617
Can Tho (V), 369
Cantonese Assembly Hall (Quang Trieu/Guangzhou Assembly Hall; Hoi An, V), 318
Cao Dai Holy See (Tay Ninh, V), 13
Cape Mui Ne (V), 345
Carnegie's (S), 514
Carol Cassidy: Lao Textiles (Vientiane, L), 405
Car rentals, shopping online for, 57
Caruso (Vientiane, L), 405
Catamaran sailing (Ko Samui, T), 196

Cat-Cat Village (Sapa, V), 293
Cathedral of the Good Shepherd (S), 481
Cau Lac Bo Nhac Jazz Club (Hanoi, V), 288
C Club (H), 100
Cebu (P), 685
Cellphones, 58–60
Central Circus (Hanoi, V), 287
Central Market (Hoi An, V), 319–320
Central Market (Kuala Lumpur, M), 21, 546, 548
Central Market (Phnom Penh, C), 21, 648
Central Plain (T), 106
Cha-Am (T). *See* Hua Hin/Cha-Am
Cham Islands (V), 320
Cham Museum (Danang, V), 14–15, 304, 306–307
ChamPa (Hoi An, V), 321
Cham Tower (near Phan Thiet, V), 345
Changi Chapel and Museum (S), 500–501
Changi Golf Club (S), 507
Changi International Airport (S), 439
Changi Point (S), 506
Chasers (H), 101
Chatuchak Park (Bangkok, T), 156
Chatuchak Weekend Market (Bangkok, T), 20
Chau Doc (V), 369, 370–371
Chaweng Bay (Ko Samui, T), accommodations, 192–194
Chaweng Beach (T), 11
Chaweng Noi Bay (Ko Samui, T), accommodations, 192–194
Cheong Fatt Tze Mansion (Penang, M), 572
Chettiar's Hindu Temple (aka the Tank Road Temple, S), 489
Chiang Mai National Museum (T), 232
Chiang Mai (T), 222–237
accommodations, 226–229
bookstores, 225
consulates, 225–226
exploring, 232–236
exploring outside, 234–236
Internet and e-mail access, 226
nightlife, 236–237
post office, 226
restaurants, 229–232

shopping, 236
transportation, 224–225
traveling to, 222–224
visitor information, 222
Chiang Rai Handicrafts Center (T), 242
Chiang Rai (T), 237–242
Chiang Saen Buddha (Chiang Mai, T), 234
Chiang Saen National Museum (T), 244
Chiang Saen (T), 10, 242–245
CHIJMES (Convent of the Holy Infant Jesus, S), 481
China Beach (My Khe; Danang, V), 304
China Jump Bar & Grill (S), 517
Chinatown (Kuala Lumpur, M), 536
shopping, 549
Chinatown (Manila, P), 679
Chinatown (S), 428
accommodations, 456–457
restaurants, 471–473
shopping, 509–511
sights and attractions, 490
Chinatown Seal Carving Souvenir (S), 510
Chinese Assembly Hall (Hoi An, V), 319
Chinese Cemetery (Manila, P), 679
Chinese Garden (S), 494–495
Chinese New Year, 15
Cholon District 5 (Ho Chi Minh City, V), 366–367
Christ Church (Malacca, M), 563
Christy's Cabaret (Ko Samui, T), 199
The Citadel & Imperial City (Hue, V), 301
City Hall (Ho Chi Minh City, V), 364
City Hall (Municipal Building, S), 484
Clarke Quay (S), 489
Clark Hatch Fitness Center (Hanoi, V), 285
Clark Hatch Fitness Center (Phnom Penh, C), 650
Clothing, 35–36
packing tips, 45
Club 97 (H), 102
Cockfighting (Bangkok, T), 154
Coconut Palace (Manila, P), 678
The Colonnade (Bangkok, T), 157

Concept CM2 (Bangkok, T), 158
Cooking classes, Thailand
  Bangkok, 154
  Ko Samui, 197
  Phuket, 215
Coral Divers (Hua Hin, T), 184
Corregidor (P), 680
The Crazy Elephant (S), 514
Crazy Kim Bar (Nha Trang, V), 331–332
Credit cards, 44
Cremations, in Bali, 10
C. R. Harbour (Chiang Rai, T), 241
Crystal Cave Disco at Empress Hotel (Chiang Mai, T), 237
Cua Dai beach (Hoi An, V), 320
Cua Ngo Mon (The Noon Gate; Hue, V), 301–302
Cuc Phuong National Park (V), 288
Cuisine
  the Philippines, 666
  Singapore, 466–447
  Thailand, 112–113
  Vietnam, 251
The Cultural Museum (Malacca, M), 562
Cultural no-nos, 16–17
Cultural traditions and practices, 29–36
  Bali, 33–34, 585–587
  Cambodia, 31–32
  Hong Kong, 29
  Laos, 31–32
  Malaysia, 33, 521–522
  Myanmar, 31–33
  the Philippines, 34
  Singapore, 33
  Thailand, 29–31
  Vietnam, 31–32, 251
Currency and currency exchange, 41
Curve (H), 102
Customs regulations, 39–40. See also specific countries

Dalat Market (Cho Da Lat, V), 338
Dalat Palace Golf Club (V), 341
Dalat Railway Station (Cremaillaire Railway; Dalat, V), 340
Dalattourist (Dalat, V), 332–333

Dalat (V), 321, 332–341
  accommodations, 334–336
  attractions, 338–341
  cafes, 338
  restaurants, 337–338
  sports and outdoor activities, 341
  transportation, 333
  traveling to, 332
  visitor information and tours, 332–333
Danang (V), 304–308
Dance Fever (Bangkok, T), 159
Delaney's (H), 101
Delaney's (Kuala Lumpur, M), 549
DeltaDeco (Hanoi, V), 286
Diarrhea, 48
Dien Bien Phu (V), 289
Dietary precautions, 48–49
Diethelm Travel
  Cambodia, 631
  Laos, 67, 379, 382, 385, 388, 391, 406, 407, 424
  Myanmar, 691
Disabilities, travelers with, 51–52
Diseases, tropical, 48
Diva Café (Hanoi, V), 288
Dive Master's EcoDive 2000 (Phuket, T), 213
Doi Inthanon National Park (T), 234
Dole Thailand pineapple factory, 184
Dolphin Diving Center (Pattaya, T), 170
Dolphin watching (Lovina, I), 620
Dragon Boat Races (Bun Song Heua, L), 383
Dragon Trail Nature Walk (S), 504
Dublin Jack (H), 102
Dusk til Dawn (H), 102–103

East Coast Park (S), 501, 506, 507
Eastern & Oriental Express, 117–118
Eastern Seaboard (T), 160–161
Easy Divers (Ko Samui, T), 196
EcoAdventures South East Asia LTD. (Sihanoukville, C), 650
Eco-tourism (L), 4

Electricity, 70. See also specific countries
Elephant Safari Park (Ubud, I), 612
Elephant trekking, 214
El Nido (P), 684
E-mail. See Internet and e-mail access
Emperor Jade Pagoda (Phuoc Harbour Island; Ho Chi Minh City, V), 365
Empress Place Building (S), 484
Entry requirements, 38–39. See also specific countries
Erawan Shrine (Bangkok, T), 156
Escorted tours, 65–67
Esplanade Park (S), 489
Etiquette and customs, 16–17, 34–36, 70–71. See also Cultural traditions and practices
  business, 71
  Cambodia, 629
  Laos, 376–377
  Thailand, 110, 112
  Vietnam, 252
Europa Sailing Club (S), 508
Exotissimo Travel
  Cambodia, 631
  in France, 67
  Laos, 379, 391, 407–408
  Myanmar, 691
  Vietnam
    Danang, 305
    Hanoi, 269
    Ho Chi Minh City (Saigon), 67, 350

Fabrics (textiles)
  Bangkok (T), 155
  Laos, 21
Fairways and Bluewater Resort Golf and Country Club (Boracay, P), 682
Families with children, information and resources, 53
Fantasea Divers (Phuket, T), 213
Far East Plaza (S), 509
The Fat Frog Café (S), 514–515
Feng shui, 35
Ferries. See also Boat trips and tours
  Hong Kong, 79, 80
  Malaysia
    Langkawi, 576
    Penang, 566

Sentosa Island (S), 503
Thailand
Ko Samet, 174
Ko Samui, 190
Phuket, 217–218
Festivals and celebrations, 46
best, 15–16
Festivals of Singapore, 505
Fire Cat (Bangkok, T), 158
Fishing (Ko Samui, T), 196
The Flag Tower (Hue, V), 301
**The Forbidden Purple City
(Hue, V), 302**
**Fort Canning Park (S), 430,
484–485**
**Fort Cornwallis (Penang, M),
572**
Fort Siloso (S), 504–505
Fountain Gardens (S), 504
**The French Quarter (Dalat,
V), 339–340**
Frommers.com, 57
**Fukian Assembly Hall (Phuc
Kien; Hoi An, V), 318–319**
**Funkey Monkey (Ubud, I),
613**
**Funky Monkey
(Hanoi, V), 287**

Galleria (Nusa Dua, I),
603
Gay and lesbian travelers
information and
resources, 52
Singapore, 518
Gecko Bar (Hanoi, V), 287
Gem Travel (T), 235
**General Post Office (Buu
Dien; Ho Chi Minh City, V),
364**
**Genting Highlands (M),
550–551**
**Genting Highlands Resort
(M), 551**
**Georgetown (Penang, M),
7, 565.** *See also* Penang
sights and attractions,
572–573
**Giac Lam Pagoda (Ho Chi
Minh City, V), 366**
Giai Dieu (Hanoi, V), 286
Gili Islands, 623–624
Goa 2001 (Kuta, I), 600
**Goddess of Mercy Temple
(Penang, M), 572**
**Golden Triangle (Kuala
Lumpur, M), 536**
**Golden Triangle (T),
218, 242, 245**
**Golden Triangle Tours
(Chiang Rai, T), 241**

Golf
Bali, 600, 603
Malaysia
Cameron Highlands,
553
Genting, 551
Johor Bahru, 558
Kuala Lumpur, 548
the Philippines
Boracay, 682
Manila, 679
Singapore, 507
Thailand
Hua Hin/Cha-Am, 184
Pattaya, 170
Phuket, 214
Vietnam
Dalat, 341
Ho Chi Minh City, 367
Phan Thiet, 346
**Governor of Melaka's
Gallery (Malacca, M),
562–563**
**The Grand Palace (Bangkok,
T), 13, 147**
Greetings, 34
Gulliver's (Bangkok, T), 159
Gunung Agung (I), 12
Gunung Kawi (I), 14
Gunung Tahan (M), 549

Hadjee Textiles (S), 510
**Had Nai Yang National Park
(T), 213**
Haggling, 36
**Hainan Assembly Hall (Hoi
An, V), 319**
**Hai's Scout Café (Hoi An, V),
320**
**Hajjah Fatimah Mosque (S),
492**
Halong Bay (V), 12, 288
**Handicrafts, best
bargains, 21**
**Handspan Adventure Travel
(Hanoi, V), 269, 289**
**Hang Li Poh's Well (Malacca,
M), 563**
**Hang Nga Guest House and
Art Gallery (Dalat, V), 339**
**Hanoi Hilton (Hoa Lo Prison,
V), 284**
**Hanoi Opera House (V),
284, 287**
Hanoi Tourism (V), 269
**Hanoi Traditional Opera
(V), 287**
Hanoi (V), 264–289
accommodations, 270–275
activities, 285

banks/currency exchange,
269
ecotourism, 288
excursions from, 288–289
Internet and e-mail access,
269
nightlife, 287–288
post office/mail, 269
restaurants, 275–281
shopping, 285–286
sights and attractions,
281–285
telephone, 269
dialing information,
265
tourist cafes, 269
tours, 268–269
transportation, 268
traveling to, 265
**Hard Life Café (Penang, M),
575**
**Hard Rock Café (Bangkok, T),
158**
**Hard Rock Cafe (Kuala
Lumpur, M), 549**
Hard Rock Cafe (Kuta, I), 600
Hard Rock Cafe (S), 515
**Hard Rock Hotel (Kuta, I),
600**
**Harry's Quayside Bar &
Upstairs at Harry's Wine
Bar (S), 516**
**Hat Sai Kaeo (Ko Samet, T),
173**
**Haw Par Villa (Tiger Balm
Gardens, S), 495**
HDB New Towns (S), 431
**Health care, general avail-
ability of, 47–48**
Health concerns, 2, 47–50.
See also specific countries
Health insurance, 47, 50
**Health Oasis Resort (Ko
Samui, T), 198**
**The Heart of Darkness
(Phnom Penh, C), 649**
Heat exhaustion, 49–50
**Heritage (Ho Chi Minh City,
V), 367**
**The Hideaway Spa (Phuket,
T), 198**
**Hien Minh (Ho Chi Minh City,
V), 368**
Hiking
Bali, 12
Dalat (V), 341
Hill tribes
Laos, 7
Thailand, 220–221, 235,
241
Vietnam, 289

Hin Yaay & Hin Ta (Ko Samui, T), 197
Hmong tribe, 220
Hoa Lo Prison (Hanoi Hilton, V), 284
Hoa Lu (V), 288–289
Hoan Kiem Lake (Hanoi, V), 285
Ho Chi Minh, 250
  Mausoleum (Hanoi, V), 281
  Museum (Hanoi, V), 281
  Residence (Hanoi, V), 281–282
Ho Chi Minh City (Saigon, V), 346–369
  accommodations, 351–359
  attractions, 364–367
  banks/currency exchange, 350
  consulates, 350
  districts of, 351
  emergencies, 350
  Internet and e-mail access, 350–351
  nightlife, 22, 368–369
  post office/mail, 351
  restaurants, 359–364
  safety, 351
  scam alert, 347
  shopping, 367–368
  snacks and cafes, 363–364
  sports and outdoor activities, 367
  transportation, 347
  traveling to, 346–347
  visitor information and tours, 347, 350
Ho Chi Minh Fine Arts Museum (Ho Chi Minh City, V), 367–368
Ho Chi Minh Municipal Theater (Saigon Opera House, V), 364
Hoi An Central Market (V), 20
Hoi An Tourist Guiding Office (V), 310
Hoi An Tourist Service Company (V), 310
Hoi An (V), 10, 308–321
  attractions, 316–320
  beaches, 320
  map, 309
  nightlife, 320–321
  restaurants, 314–316
  shopping, 320
  transportation, 308, 310
  traveling to, 308
  visitor information and tours, 310
Holidays, 46
Hollywood (Bangkok, T), 159

Hong Hoa (Hanoi, V), 286
Hong Kong, 6, 74–103
  accommodations, 82–91
  American Express, 80
  bars, 101–103
  brief description of, 24–25
  business hours, 81
  climate, 78
  consulates, 81
  cultural traditions and practices, 29
  currency and currency exchange, 42, 78
  customs regulations, 75
  dentists and doctors, 81
  departure tax, 78
  electricity, 81
  emergencies, 81
  entry requirements, 38, 75
  health concerns, 79
  hospitals, 81
  layout of, 74–75
  money matters, 78
  museums, 97–99
  newspapers, 81
  nightlife, 100–103
  planning your trip to, 75
  police, 81
  post offices, 81–82
  public holidays, 78–79
  restaurants, 91–95
  safety, 82
  shopping, 100
  sights and attractions, 96–100
  taxes, 82
  taxis, 80
  telephone, 82
  temples, 99–100
  time zone, 82
  tipping, 82
  transportation, 79–80
  traveling to, 60–61, 79
Hong Kong Bar (Penang, M), 575
Hong Kong Heritage Museum, 97
Hong Kong International Airport, 79
  accommodations near, 90–91
Hong Kong Museum of Art, 97
Hong Kong Museum of History, 97–98
Hong Kong Museum of Medical Sciences, 98
Hong Kong Science Museum, 98
Hong Kong Space Museum, 98
Hon Mieu Island (V), 331

Hopf Brewery (Pattaya, T), 172
Ho Phra Keo (Vientiane, L), 403
Ho Than Tho (Lake of Sighs; Dalat, V), 341
House of Hoi An Traditional Handicraft (V), 319
House of Opium (Sob Ruak, T), 245
Hua Hin/Cha-Am (T), 176–185
  accommodations, 179–182
  banks, 178
  nightlife, 184–185
  restaurants, 182–183
  shopping, 184
  side trip to Phetchaburi, 185, 187
  transportation, 178
  traveling to, 177–178
  visitor information, 177
Hua Hin Tourist Information Center (T), 177, 185
Hue (V), 294–304
  accommodations, 297–299
  attractions, 301–303
  cafes, bars, and nightlife, 301
  restaurants, 299–301
  shopping, 301
Hun Tiep Lake and the Downed B-52 (Hanoi, V), 282
Huong Giang Company (Hue, V), 296

I brahim Hussein Museum and Cultural Foundation (Langkawi, M), 580
Ikho 2 (Vientiane, L), 405
Images of Singapore (Sentosa Island, S), 15, 505
Imaginative Traveler, 67
Imperial City (Hue, V), 301–303
Imperial Mae Ping Hotel (Chiang Mai, T), Elvis festival at, 237
Imperial Samui Hotel (Ko Samui, T), 198
The Imperial Tombs (Hue, V), 303
Independence Monument (Phnom Penh, C), 649
Indonesia. See Bali
Inherited Arts & Crafts (S), 510
Insect Kingdom Museum of Singapore, 504
Insomnia (H), 102

Insurance, 46–47
Inter-Lao Tourism (L), 380, 391, 408, 424
Internet and e-mail access, 57–58, 165
　Bali
　　Candi Dasa, 614
　　Kuta, 594
　　Lovina, 617
　　Ubud, 604
　Cambodia
　　Phnom Penh, 637
　　Siem Reap, 653
　Laos, 388
　　Luang Prabang, 410
　　Vientiane, 394
　Malaysia, 534
　　Penang, 567
　the Philippines, 670
　Singapore, 445
　Thailand
　　Bangkok, 129
　　Chiang Mai, 226
　　Chiang Rai, 238
　　Ko Samui, 191
　　Phuket, 203
　Vietnam, 262–263
　　Dalat, 333
　　Hanoi, 269
　　Ho Chi Minh City, 350–351
　　Hue, 297
Intimex (Hanoi, V), 286
Intramuros (Manila, P), 678
Intrepid, 67
Isaan, 106
Islamic Arts Museum (Kuala Lumpur, M), 546
Island Safari Adventure Company (Chalong, T), 214
The Istana and Sri Temasek (S), 493
Istana Kampong Glam (S), 492–493
Istana Negara (Kuala Lumpur, M), 546
Itineraries, suggested, 69–70

J alan Tokong (Malacca, M), 14, 563
Jamae Mosque (S), 490
Jame Mosque (Masjid Jame; Kuala Lumpur, M), 14, 546
Japanese Covered Bridge (Hoi An, V), 319
Japanese Garden (S), 494–495
Jazz Café (Ubud, I), 613
J Central Beach (S), 504
Jeep Pub (Cha-Am, T), 184
Jet lag, 64

Jewelry (M), 21
Jim Thompson's House (Bangkok, T), 147
JJ Mahoney (S), 515
JJ's (H), 103
Joe Bananas (H), 100
Johor Bahru (M), 535, 553–558
Johor Craftown Handicraft Centre (Johor Bahru, M), 558
Johor Endau Rompin National Park (M), 557–558
Jonker Walk (Malacca, M), 564
Juara Bay (Tioman Island, M), 11
Jurong BirdPark (S), 495
Jurong Country Club (S), 507
Jurong Reptile Park (S), 495–496

K abal Spean (C), 661
KAF Traditional Sculptures and Art Accessories (Hanoi, V), 286
Kalare Food & Shopping Center (Chiang Mai, T), 236
Kallang Riverside Park (S), 508
Kampong Glam (S), 430
Kapitan Keling Mosque (Penang, M), 572
Karen tribe (T), 220
Karon (T), accommodations, 205–208
Karyaneka (Malacca, M), 565
Kata (T), accommodations, 205–208
Kayaking, 407
　Laos, 12
　　Luang Namtha, 422
　Thailand
　　Ko Samui, 196
　　Phuket, 212–213
　Vietnam, 12
　　Hanoi, 288
Kenly Silk (Ho Chi Minh City, V), 367
Khai Dinh's Tomb (Hue, V), 13, 303
Khai Silk (Hanoi, V), 286
Khao Laem Ya–Samet National Park (T), 172–173
Khao Luang Cave (Phetch-aburi, T), 185
Khao Phra Thaew National Park (T), 213–214

Khao Sam Roi Yot National Park (T), 184
Khao San Road (Bangkok, T), 158–159
Khmer people, 629
Khoo Khongsi (Penang, M), 573
King's Castle (Bangkok, T), 158
Kin Lee & Co. (S), 511
Kite-fighting, Bangkok (T), 154
Kite Museum (Malacca, M), 562–563
KOMTAR (Penang, M), 574
Kong Meng San Phor Kark See Temple (S), 497
Kori Restaurant and Bar (Kuta, I), 600
Ko Samet (T), 161, 172–176
Ko Samui (T), 176, 187–199
　car rentals, 190–191
　nightlife, 198–199
　restaurants, 195–196
　sights and activities, 196–198
　transportation, 190–191
　traveling to, 188, 190
　visitor information, 188
Kosila Bookshop (Vientiane, L), 405
Kowloon (H)
　accommodations, 82–88
　bars, 101
　restaurants, 91–93
Kranji War Memorial (S), 497
Kuala Lumpur Bird Park (M), 546
Kuala Lumpur Butterfly Park (M), 546
Kuala Lumpur International Airport (KLIA, M), 536
Kuala Lumpur Lake Gardens (Taman Tasik Perdana, M), 546
Kuala Lumpur (M), 535–553
　accommodations, 540–544
　nightlife, 549
　restaurants, 544–545
　shopping, 548–549
　side trips from, 549–553
　sights and attractions, 545–548
　taxis, 538
　transportation, 538–539
　traveling to, 536, 538
　visitor information, 536
Kuala Lumpur Railway Station (M), 546
Kuala Terengganu (M), 10
Kuan Yin Thong Hood Cho Temple (S), 485

Kuta (I), 594–600, 624
Kuta Beach (I)
  accommodations, 595–596
  restaurants, 598–599
Kwong Chen Beverage Trading (S), 509

L a Belle Collection (S), 510
Lac Hong Art Gallery (Ho Chi Minh City, V), 368
Lahu people (T), 221
Lai Kham wihaan (Chiang Mai, T), 233
Lake Gardens (Kuala Lumpur, M), 536
Lake of Sighs (Ho Than Tho; Dalat, V), 341
Lamai Bay (T), accommodations, 194–195
Lam Ty Ni Pagoda (Dalat, V), 339
Lan Anh International Tennis Court (Ho Chi Minh City, V), 367
Land Mines Museum (C), 661–662
Lane Xang Travel (L), 391
Langkawi (M), 575–580
Lao Cai (V), 293
Lao National Museum (Vientiane, L), 403
Laos, 372–426
  American Express, 388
  brief description of, 26
  business hours, 388
  climate, 382
  cultural traditions and practices, 31–32
  currency and currency exchange, 42
  customs regulations, 381
  dentists and doctors, 388
  drug laws, 388
  electricity, 388
  embassies in, 388
  embassy locations overseas, 381
  emergencies, 388
  entry requirements, 38, 380
  etiquette and customs, 376–377
  health concerns, 383
  holidays, 382–383
  Internet and e-mail access, 388
  Vientiane, 394
  language, 377–378, 389
  lay of the land, 374
  money matters, 381–382
  organized tours and travel agents, 379–380
  peak season, 382
  people and culture, 374, 376
  post offices/mail, 389
  safety, 389
  telephone, 389
  telephone dialing info, 391
  time zone, 389
  tipping, 389
  tips on accommodations, dining, and shopping, 387–388
  toilets, 390
  transportation, 385–387
  travel advisory, 373
  traveling to, 383–385
  visitor information, 378–379
  water, 390
  what's new, 3–4
Lao Tourism (L), 380, 391
Lau Pa Sat Festival Pavilion (S), 490
Lau Pa Set Festival Village (S), 480
Legends (Bangkok, T), 158
Le Meridien Spa and Resort (I), 600
Les Epices (Ho Chi Minh City, V), 367
Letranger: Books and Tea (Luang Prabang, L), 421
Linh Phuoc Pagoda (Dalat, V), 340
Liquid Room (S), 517
Liquor laws, 71
Lisu people (T), 221
Little India (Kuala Lumpur, M), 536
Little India (S), 430, 480
  restaurants, 473
  shopping, 511
  sights and attractions, 491–492
The Loft (Phuket, T), 216
Lombok (I), 11, 620–622
Long Bar (Raffles Hotel, S), 7, 449, 515
Long Son Pagoda (Nha Trang, V), 330
Lost-luggage insurance, 47
Lovina (I), 617–620
Luang Namtha (L), 421–423
Luang Prabang Boat Races (L), 383
Luang Prabang (L), 10, 407–421
  accommodations, 410–415
  attractions, 419–420
  nightlife, 421
  restaurants, 415–418
  shopping, 420–421
  snacks and cafes, 418
  transportation, 410
  traveling to, 408
  visitor information and tours, 407–408
Lucifer's (Bangkok, T), 158
Lucky Plaza (S), 509
Lucky Sea Tours (Hua Hin, T), 184
Lumphini Staduim (Bangkok, T), 153

M acRitchie Nature Trail (S), 498
Madame Tussaud's (H), 96
MadDogs (H), 102
Mae Kok River (T), 237
  boat tours, 241
Maesalong Tours (Chiang Rai, T), 241
Mai Chau (V), 289
Malacca (M), 558–565
Malacca Zoo (M), 564
Malapacao Island (P), 684
Malaysia, 520–580
  accommodations, 531
  brief description of, 27
  business hours, 533
  climate, 526
  clothing considerations, 526
  cultural traditions and practices, 33
  currency and currency exchange, 42, 524–525
  customs regulations, 524
  dentists and doctors, 533
  drug laws, 533
  electricity, 533
  entry requirements, 38, 524
  health and insurance, 527
  Internet and e-mail access, 534
  language, 534
  lay of the land, 521
  liquor laws, 534
  money matters, 524–526
  people, etiquette, and customs, 521–522
  planning your trip to, 522, 524–533
  postal services, 534
  public holidays and events, 526–527
  restaurants, 531–532
  safety/crime, 527
  seasons, 526

shopping, 532–533
suggested itineraries, 533
taxes, 534
telephone, 534
television, 535
time zone, 535
toilets, 535
transportation, 529–531
traveling to, 527–529
visitor information,
    522, 524
water, 527, 535
what's new, 4
Malay Village (S), 501
Mambo (Bangkok, T), 157
Mambo Beach Club (Phuket,
    T), 217
Mandai Orchid Gardens (S),
    498
Mandalay (B), 693–694
Manila (P), 671–680
Man Mo Temple (H), 99
The Marble Mountains
    (Danang, V), 307
The Maritime Museum
    (Malacca, M), 562
The Maritime Museum (S),
    505
Markets
    Bangkok (T), 155
    best, 20–21
    Chiang Mai (T), 236
    Kuala Lumpur (M), 549
    Singapore, 511
    Vientiane (L), 403
Masjid Negara (National
    Mosque; Kuala Lumpur,
    M), 547
Masjid Sultan Abu Bakar
    (Johor Bahru, M), 557
MATIC (Malaysia Tourist
    Information Complex;
    Kuala Lumpur, M), 546
Maya's (Ho Chi Minh City, V),
    368
Mayleck Pub (Luang
    Prabang, L), 421
MC Decoration (Ho Chi Minh
    City, V), 367
Medical insurance, 47, 50
Mekong Delta (V), 248,
    369–370
Menara Kuala Lumpur (M),
    547
Menjangan Island (I), 620
Merdeka Square (Kuala
    Lumpur, M), 535–536, 547
Merlion Park (S), 489–490
The Merlion (S), 505
Mid-Autumn Festival (V), 15
Mien people (T), 221

The Mieu Temple (Hue, V),
    302
Mines Resort & Golf Club
    (Kuala Lumpur, M), 548
Ming Village (S), 496
Minh Mang, Tomb of (Hue,
    V), 303
Mini Siam (Pattaya, T),
    170–171
The Mission Church (Sapa,
    V), 294
Mondial Hotel (Ho Chi Minh
    City, V), 369
Money matters, 41–44
Monkey Forest (Ubud, I), 612
Morning Market (Talaat Sao;
    Vientiane, L), 20–21, 403
Mosques
    etiquette at, 36
    Malaysia
        Johor Bahru, 557
        Kuala Lumpur, 547
        Penang, 572
    Singapore, 490–492
Mosquitoes, 48, 49
Mountain biking
    Dalat (V), 341
    Thailand, 235
Mount Phu Si (Phousi; Luang
    Prabang, L), 419
Muaythai (Thai boxing), 153,
    171, 198, 217
Muddy Murphys (S), 515
Mui Ne Beach (V), 345–346
Mui Ne Sailing Club (Phan
    Thiet, V), 346
Museum of Beauty
    (Malacca, M), 562–563
Museum of History and
    Culture (Hoi An, V), 317
Museum of Trade Ceramics
    (Hoi An, V), 317
Museums, best, 14
Mutiara Taman Negara
    Resort (M), 550
Muzim Negara (National
    Museum; Kuala Lumpur,
    M), 547
Muzium Budaya (Malacca,
    M), 562
Myanmar (Burma), 686–694
    brief description of, 28–29
    cultural traditions and
        practices, 31–33
    currency and currency
        exchange, 42
    embassies in foreign
        countries, 692
    entry requirements,
        38, 691
    foreign embassies in, 693

history of, 688–690
money matters, 691–692
safety, 692
traveling to, 692
visitor information, 691
My Son (near Danang, V),
    307–308
My Tho (V), 369

Na Dan (Ko Samet, T),
    173
Nagore Durgha Shrine (S),
    490
Nam Ha Biodiversity Conser-
    vation Area (L), 422
NamHa Trekking (Luang
    Namtha, L), 422
Nam Lik River (L), 407
Nam Son (Hanoi, V), 286
Na Muang Falls (T), 197
Nana Plaza (Bangkok, T), 159
National Art Gallery (Kuala
    Lumpur, M), 547
National Mosque (Masjid
    Negara; Kuala Lumpur, M),
    547
The National Museum Annex
    (Manila, P), 678
The National Museum
    (Bangkok, T), 14, 147
National Museum (Muzim
    Negara; Kuala Lumpur, M),
    547
National Museum of Viet-
    namese History (Hanoi, V),
    284
National Museum (Phnom
    Penh, C), 15, 647–648
National Orchid Garden (S),
    496
National Planetarium (Kuala
    Lumpur, M), 547
National Theater (Bangkok,
    T), 156
National University (Hanoi,
    V), 283–284
Ned Kelly's Last Stand
    (H), 101
Neka Museum (Ubud, I),
    611–612
The New Century (Hanoi, V),
    288
Newton (S), 480
The Next Page (S), 516
Nha Trang Sailing Club (V),
    331
Nha Trang (V), 321–332
    accommodations, 324–328
    crime, 322
    nightlife, 331

Nha Trang *(cont.)*
   restaurants, 328–330
   sports and outdoor
      activities, 331
   transportation, 322
   traveling to, 322
   visitor information and
      tours, 322, 324
Night Bazaar (Chiang Mai,
   T), 20
Nightlife, hottest spots, 22
Night Market (Chiang Mai,
   T), 236
Night Market (Chiang Rai, T),
   242
Night Safari (S), 498
Nine Dynastic Urns (Hue, V),
   302
Nirwana Bali Golf Club
   (Tabanan, I), 600
Nong Nooch (Pattaya, T),
   171
The Noon Gate (Cua Ngo
   Mon; Hue, V), 301–302
Northern Thailand, 106,
   218–222
No. 5 (S), 516
Notre Dame Cathedral (Ho
   Chi Minh City, V), 364
Novotel Siam (Bangkok, T),
   158
Nusa Camp (M), 550
Nusa Dua (I), 601–603

O'Briens (Ho Chi Minh
   City, V), 368
Ocean Dunes Golf Course
   (Phan Thiet, V), 346
OckPopTok (Luang Prabang,
   L), 421
Octopus Diving (Nha Trang,
   V), 324, 331
Old Chiang Mai Cultural
   Center (T), 236
The Old House of Phun Hung
   (Hoi An, V), 318
The Old House of Tan Ky (Hoi
   An, V), 318
Old Quarter (Hanoi, V), 285
101 Catinat (Ho Chi Minh
   City, V), 368
One-Pillar Pagoda (Hanoi, V),
   282
Oot-Ni (Vientiane, L), 405
Orang Laut, 215
Orchard Road area (S), 480
   accommodations, 457–463
   restaurants, 473–477
   shopping, 508–509
   sights and attractions, 493

O'Reilly's Irish Pub
   (Bangkok, T), 158
Oriental House
   (Hanoi, V), 286

Package tours, 64–65
Packing tips, 45
Padangbai (I), 613
The Padang (S), 485
PaddleAsia Co. Ltd. (Phuket,
   T), 213
Pagodas. *See* Temples, wats,
   and pagodas
Pala-U waterfall (T), 184
Palawan (P), 683–685
Palladium (Pattaya, T), 171
Palm Resort Golf & Country
   Club (Johor Bahru, M), 558
Paradise Beach (Ao Phrao;
   Ko Samet, T), 176
Parasailing, 212
Parliament House (Kuala
   Lumpur, M), 547
Parliament House (S),
   485–486
Particular Art Gallery (Ho
   Chi Minh City, V), 368
Passports, 39, 72–73
Pasteur Institute (Nha Trang,
   V), 321
Patong (T)
   accommodations, 208–211
   restaurants, 211–212
Patpong (Bangkok, T),
   nightlife, 157–158
Pattaya Beach (T), 169–171
Pattaya Elephant Village (T),
   171
Pattaya Go-Kart (T), 171
Pattaya (T), 161, 162–172
   accommodations, 165–168
   nightlife, 171–172
   restaurants, 168–169
   transportation, 164
   traveling to, 162, 164
   visitor information, 162
Patuxay (Victory Monument;
   Vientiane, L), 403–404
Payar Marine Park
   (Langkawi, M), 580
Peak Explorer (H), 96
Peak Tower (H), 96
Peak tram (H), 96
Peanuts II (Kuta, I), 600
Pearls (Ko Samui, T), 198
Penang Bird Park (M), 574
Penang Butterfly Farm (M),
   574
Penang Hill (M), 574

Penang (M), 565–575
   accommodations, 568–570
   nightlife, 575
   restaurants, 570–572
   shopping, 574
   sights and attractions,
      572–574
   transportation, 566–567
   traveling to, 565–566
   visitor information, 565
Penang Museum and Art
   Gallery (M), 573
Penestanan (I), 613
The People's Museum
   (Malacca, M), 562–563
Peranakan Place (S), 493
Perfume River (V), 294, 296
Petaling Street (Kuala
   Lumpur, M), 547
Petronas Twin Towers (Kuala
   Lumpur, M), 547–548
Pewter, 21
Phang-Nga Bay National
   Park (T), 212
Phang-nga Bay (T), 11–12
Phan Thiet Market (V), 345
Phan Thiet (V), 11, 341–346
Phat Tire Ventures (Dalat, V),
   333, 341
Phetchaburi (T), 185
The Philippines, 663–685
   accommodations, 669
   brief description of, 28
   cuisine, 666
   cultural traditions and
      practices, 34
   customs regulations, 667
   embassies in foreign
      countries, 667
   embassies of foreign
      countries in, 670
   entry requirements, 667
   etiquette, 666
   health concerns, 668
   history of, 663–664
   holidays, 667–668
   Internet and e-mail access,
      670
   languages, 666
   lay of the land, 663
   money matters, 667
   planning a trip to, 666–668
   post offices/mail, 670
   religion, 666
   restaurants, 669
   safety/crime, 670–671
   seasons, 667
   telephone, 671
   transportation, 668
   traveling to, 668
   visitor information, 666

Phim-phone Minimart
(Vientiane, L), 405
Phi Phi Don (T), 217, 218
Phi Phi Le (T), 217, 218
Phnom Chisor (C), 650
Phnom Penh (C), 11, 625,
635–650
accommodations, 5,
637–642
banks/currency exchange,
636–637
day trips from, 650
emergencies, 637
Internet and e-mail access,
637
nightlife, 22, 649
post office, 637
restaurants, 642–646
shopping and galleries, 649
sights and attractions, 646
telephone, 637
transportation, 636
traveling to, 636
visitor information and
tours, 636
Phonsavan (L), 423–425
Phra Bang (Luang Prabang,
L), 419
Phra Kaen Chan (Chiang
Mai, T), 233
Phra Nakhorn Khiri (Phetchaburi, T), 185
Phra Ram Raja Nivesana
(Phetchaburi, T), 187
Phra Singh (Chiang Mai, T),
233
Phra That Chomtong (Wat
Doi Tong; Chiang Rai, T),
240–241
Phra That Luang (Vientiane,
L), 404
Phuc Kien (Fukian Assembly
Hall; Hoi An, V), 318–319
Phuket Country Club (T), 214
Phuket FantaSea (Phuket, T),
216–217
Phuket (T), 199–218
American Express, 203
banks, 203
hospitals, 203
Internet and e-mail
access, 203
nightlife, 216–217
shopping, 215–216
side trips from, 217–218
sights and activities,
212–215
transportation, 202–203
traveling to, 200, 202
visitor information, 200
Phuket Town (T), accommo-
dations, 203–204

Phung Hiep (V), 369
Phuoc Hai (Emperor Jade
Pagoda; Ho Chi Minh City,
V), 365–366
Phu Si, Mount (Luang
Prabang, L), 419
Pinatubo, Mount (P), 680
Pizzadelic (Patong, T), 208
Plain of Jars (Xieng
Khouang, L), 13–14,
425–426
Polite Pub (Hanoi, V), 287
Ponderosa Golf & Country
Club (Johor Bahru, M), 558
Po Ngar Cham Towers (Nha
Trang, V), 330
Porta de Santiago (A
Famosa; Malacca, M), 563
Portuguese Settlement and
Portuguese Square
(Malacca, M), 563–564
P. Ramlee House (Penang,
M), 573
Pratunam Market (Bangkok,
T), 155
Prenn Falls (Dalat, V), 341
Press Club (Hanoi, V), 288
Propaganda (H), 101
Puerto Princesa (P), 683–684
Pulai Springs Country Club
(Johor Bahru, M), 558
Pulau Ubin (S), 506, 507
Pura Saraswati (Ubud, I),
611
Puri Lukisan (Ubud, I), 612
Puri Saren Agung, the Royal
Palace (Ubud, I), 611

Q Bar (Bangkok, T), 159
Q Bar (Ho Chi Minh City, V),
369
Quang's Ceramics (Hanoi, V),
286
Quang Trieu/Guangzhou
Assembly Hall (Hoi An, V),
318
Quan Kong Temple (Hoi An,
V), 319
Quan Su Pagoda
(Hanoi, V), 285
Quan Thanh Temple (Hanoi,
V), 283
Que Pasa (S), 519

R abies, 49
Raffles Bar & Billiards (S),
516–517
Raffles City Shopping Centre
(S), 509
Raffles Hotel (S), 486

Raffles Hotel Shopping
Arcade (S), 509
Raffles Landing Site (S), 486
Rainbow Diver (Nha Trang,
V), 324
Ratchadamnoen Stadium
(Bangkok, T), 153
Ratchadaphisek Road
(Bangkok, T), nightlife, 159
Rattanakiri (C), 625
Raya Island (T), 213
Redang Marine Park (M), 12
Red Cross of Luang Prabang
(L), 421
Red Cross Snake Farm
(Bangkok, T), 153–154
The Red Dunes (Mui Ne, V),
345
The Reggae Pub (Ko Samui,
T), 199
Reptile Park (Malacca, M),
564
Restaurants, best, 19–20
Restrooms, 73
Reunification Palace (Ho Chi
Minh City, V), 365
Revolutionary Museum (Ho
Chi Minh City, V), 365
Rex Hotel (Ho Chi Minh City,
V), 369
Ringlet (M), 552
Ripley's Believe It or Not!
Odditorium (H), 96
Ripley's Believe It or Not
(Pattaya, T), 171
The Rising Sun (Phnom Penh,
C), 649
Riva's (Bangkok, T), 159
River City shopping mall
(Bangkok, T), 156
River House (S), 489
River rafting
Laos
Luang Namtha, 422
Vang Vieng, 407
Thailand, 236
Ubud (I), 612
The Riverside Restaurant &
Bar (Chiang Mai, T), 237
Rizal Park (Manila, P), 678
Roluos Group (C), 662
Royal Abu Bakar Museum
(Johor Bahru, M), 557
Royal Hua Hin Golf Course
(T), 184
Royal Johor Country Club
(Johor Bahru, M), 558
Royal Malaysian Navy
Museum (Malacca, M), 562
Royal Palace Museum (Luang
Prabang, L), 419

Royal Palace (Phnom Penh, C), 647
The Royal Princess Hotel's Casablanca Room (Chiang Mai, T), 236–237
Royal Theater (Hue, V), 302
Russian Market (Phnom Penh, C), 648, 649

Safety, 2, 50–51
The Sa Huynh Culture Museum (Hoi An, V), 317
Saigon Duty Free Shop (Ho Chi Minh City, V), 367
Saigon Opera House (Ho Chi Minh Municipal Theater, V), 364
Saigon Saigon (Ho Chi Minh City, V), 368
Saigontourist (Ho Chi Minh City, V), 350
Saigon (V). See Ho Chi Minh City
Sailing
    Singapore, 508
    Thailand
        Ko Samui, 196
        Phuket, 212
    Vietnam, 6–7, 331
St. Andrew's Cathedral (S), 486–487
St. Francis Xavier's Church (Malacca, M), 564
St. George's Church (Penang, M), 573
St. John's Fort (Malacca, M), 564
St. Paul's Church (Malacca, M), 564
Sai Sai (Ubud, I), 613
Sakya Muni Buddha Gaya (Temple of a Thousand Lights, S), 491–492
Same Same Not Different Café (Hoi An, V), 320–321
Sam Mountain (V), 371
Sam Tung Uk Museum (H), 99
Samui Institute of Thai Culinary Arts (SITCA) (Ko Samui, T), 197
Samui Monkey Theater (near Bophut, T), 197
Sandalwood Buddha (Chiang Mai, T), 233
Santiburi Dusit Resort (Ko Samui, T), 198
Sapa (V), 12, 289–294
SARS (Severe Acute Respiratory Syndrome), 2
Sasanaransi Buddhist Temple (S), 498

Satri Lao Silk (Vientiane, L), 405
Savanh Banhao Tourism (L), 408
Saxophone Pub and Restaurant (Bangkok, T), 158
Scuba diving
    Bali
        Candi Dasa, 617
        Gili Islands, 623–624
    Nha Trang (V), 324, 331
    the Philippines
        Boracay, 682
        Palawan, 685
    Singapore, 507
    Thailand
        Hua Hin/Cha-Am, 184
        Ko Samui, 196
        Pattaya, 170
        Phuket, 213
Sea Bees Diving (Phuket, T), 213
Sea Canoe (Phuket, T), 212
Sea Gypsies (T), 215
Sea kayaking. See Kayaking
Seasons, 44–46
Seatran Travel (T), 218
The Secret Garden Pub (Ko Samui, T), 199
Seletar Base Golf Course (S), 507
Senggigi (I), 622–624
Senior travel, 52–53
Seniwati Gallery of Art by Women (Ubud, I), 611
Sensations (Bangkok, T), 158
Sentosa Golf Club (S), 507
Sentosa Island (S), 15, 502–507
Shenanigan's (Bangkok, T), 158
Shenanigan's (Pattaya, T), 171
Shenton Way (S), 430–431
Sheridan's (Ho Chi Minh City, V), 368
Shopping. See also Markets
    bargaining, 36
    best bargains, 21–22
Siam Discovery Center (Bangkok, T), 158
Siam Safari Nature Tours (Chalong, T), 214
Siam Square (Bangkok, T), 158
Siem Reap (C), 651–662
    accommodations, 653–657
    Internet and e-mail access, 653
    nightlife, 662
    restaurants, 657–659

    shopping, 662
    sights and attractions, 659–662
    transportation, 652–653
    traveling to, 652
    visitor info and tours, 653
Sighing Buddha (Chiang Mai, T), 233
Sihanoukville (C), 625, 650
Silori WonderGolf Sentosa (S), 505
Siloso Beach (S), 504
Silver Lake (Mui Ne, V), 345
Silver Pagoda (Phnom Penh, C), 647
Sime Darby Duty Free Shop (Langkawi, M), 580
Similan archipelago (T), 218
Simon Cabaret (Phuket, T), 217
Singapore, 427–519
    accommodations, 448–463
        busy season, 448–449
        reservations, 449
        taxes and service charges, 448
    American Express, 444
    bars and clubs, 513–518
    brief description of, 26–27
    business hours, 444
    car rentals, 443–444
    car travel, 443
    climate, 436–437
    cultural traditions and practices, 33
    currency and currency exchange, 42, 435
    customs regulations, 434–435
    departure tax, 434–435
    drugstores, 444
    electricity, 444–445
    entry requirements, 38–39, 434
    gay nightspots, 518
    hawker centers, 479–480
    health concerns, 437
    Internet and e-mail access, 445
    language, 445
    layout of, 427–428, 430–431
    liquor laws, 445
    mail, 445–446
    money matters, 435–436
    newspapers and magazines, 446
    nightlife, 22, 512–519
    planning your trip to, 431–444
    police, 446

public holidays and events,
   437
restaurants, 463–480
   costs, 467–468
   cuisines, 466–467
   tips on, 467
   wine with dinner, 467
seasons, 436
shopping, 508–511
sights and attractions,
   480–506
smoking, 446
taxes, 446
taxis, 442–443
telephones, 446–447
time zone, 447
tipping, 447
Tourist Refund Scheme,
   435
transportation, 439–444
   Sentosa Island,
      502–504
traveling to, 438–439
visitor information, 431
what's new, 4
Singapore Art Museum, 487
Singapore Botanic Gardens,
   496
Singapore Chinese
   Orchestra, 513
The Singapore Crocodilarium,
   501–502
Singapore Discovery Centre,
   496–497
Singapore Handicraft Center,
   510
Singapore History Museum,
   487
Singapore Lyric Opera, 513
Singapore Philatelic
   Museum, 487
Singapore River (S), 428
Singapore River, sights and
   attractions along, 488–490
Singapore Symphony
   Orchestra, 513
Singapore Zoological
   Gardens, 499
Single travelers, 55–56
Sinh Café (Dalat, V), 333
Sinh Café (Ho Chi Minh City,
   V), 350
The Sinh Café IV (Hoi An, V),
   310
The Sinh Café V (Hue, V), 297
Siong Lim Temple (S), 499
Sky Lounge (H), 101
Smoking, 73
Snake farms (Ko Samui, T),
   197

Snorkeling
   Bali
      Candi Dasa, 617
      Lombok, 620
      Lovina, 620
   the Philippines
      Boracay, 682
      Palawan, 685
   Thailand
      Ko Samui, 196
      Pattaya, 170
      Phuket, 213
Sodetour (L), 379, 391,
   408, 424
Soi Cowboy (Bangkok, T),
   159
Somerset's Bar (S), 517
Songkran (T), 15
Songserm (T), 217, 218
Sound & Light (Malacca, M),
   564
Sousath Travel (Phonsavan,
   L), 424
South China Sea (V), 6–7
Southeast Coast (T), 106
Southern Peninsula (T),
   106, 176
The Spa Resort (Ko Samui,
   T), 198
Sparks (Bangkok, T), 159
Spasso (Bangkok, T), 158
The Spotted Cow (Hanoi, V),
   287
Springfield Royal Country
   Club (Cha-Am, T), 184
Sri Mahamariaman Temple
   (Kuala Lumpur, M), 548
Sri Mariamman Hindu
   Temple (S), 490–491
Sri Mariamman Temple
   (Penang, M), 573
Sri Perumal Temple (S), 492
Sri Veerama Kaliamman
   Temple (S), 492
Stadthuys—The Museums of
   History & Ethnography
   and the Museum of Litera-
   ture (Malacca, M), 563
Stanley (H), 20
Stanley Market (H), 100
Star Ferry (H), 6, 80
Statue of Raffles (S),
   487–488
Student travel, 54–55
Suajana Golf & Country Club
   (Kuala Lumpur, M), 548
Sukhumvit Road (Bangkok,
   T), nightlife, 159
Sultan Abdul Samad Build-
   ing (Kuala Lumpur, M), 548
Sultan Mosque (S), 493

Sun, exposure to the, 49
Sungei Buloh Wetland
   Reserve (S), 500
Suntec City (S), 431
Sun Yat-sen Nanyang Memo-
   rial Hall (S), 500
Supreme Court (S), 488
Surfing (I), 599

Talaat Sao (Morning
   Market; Vientiane, L), 403
Taman Mini Malaysia/Mini
   ASEAN (Malacca, M), 564
Taman Negara (M), 549–550
Taman Negara National Park
   (M), 12, 520, 521, 533,
   549–550
Taman Tasik Perdana (Kuala
   Lumpur Lake Gardens, M),
   546
Tamarind Springs (Lamai, T),
   198
Tanah Rata (M), 552
Tanglin Shopping Centre (S),
   509
Tanglin Sports Centre (S),
   507
Tanjong Beach (S), 504
Tanjong Pagar (S), 428
Tanjung Rhu (M), 11
Tank Road Temple (Chettiar's
   Hindu Temple, S), 489
Tan My (Hanoi, V), 286
Ta Prohm (C), 661
Taurus Brew House
   (Bangkok, T), 159
Tavanh Tour (L), 391
Tavanh (V), 293–294
Telephone Bar
   (Bangkok, T), 158
Temple of a Thousand Lights
   (Sakya Muni Buddha Gaya,
   S), 491–492
Temple of Literature and
   National University (Hanoi,
   V), 283–284
Temples, wats, and pagodas
   Cambodia, Phnom Penh,
      646–647
   etiquette at, 36
   Hong Kong, 99–100
   Laos
      Luang Prabang,
         419–420
      Vientiane, 404–405
   Malaysia
      Kuala Lumpur, 548
      Penang, 572, 573
   Myanmar, 693, 694

Temples, wats, and pagodas
(cont.)
  Singapore, 490–492,
    497–499
  Thailand
    Bangkok, 151–153
    Chiang Mai, 232–234
    Chiang Rai, 240–241
    Chiang Saen, 244
    Ko Samui, 197
    Phetchaburi, 185, 187
    Phuket, 215
  types of, 111
  Vietnam
    Dalat, 339, 340
    Hanoi, 282–285
    Ho Chi Minh City,
      365–366
    Hoi An, 319
    Hue, 302–303
    My Son, 307–308
    Nha Trang, 330
Temple Street Night Market
  (H), 20
Tennis
  Ho Chi Minh City (V), 367
  Singapore, 507
Thai Binh Reading Pavilion
  (Hue, V), 302
Thai boxing (Muaythai),
  153, 171, 198, 217
Thai Hoa Palace (Hue, V), 302
Thailand, 104–245. *See also*
  specific cities and resort
  areas
    accommodations, 120
    American Express, 120
    ATM networks, 120
    banks, 121
    brief description of, 25
    business hours, 121
    car rentals, 119
    climate, 115–116
    cuisine, 112–113
    cultural traditions and
      practices, 29–31
    currency and currency
      exchange, 42
    customs regulations, 114
    electricity, 121
    embassies and consulates,
      121
    entry requirements, 39, 114
    etiquette and customs,
      110, 112
    history of, 106–110
    holidays, 116–117
    languages, 113
    lay of the land, 104, 106
    mail, 122
    money matters, 115

  newspapers and maga-
    zines, 122
  people and culture, 110
  planning your trip to, 114
  police, 122
  radio and TV, 122–123
  regions in brief, 106–107
  religion, 110
  restaurants, 120
  restrooms, 123
  safety, 123
  shopping, 120
  taxes and service charges,
    123
  telephone, telex, and fax,
    123–124
  time zone, 124
  tipping, 124
  transportation, 118–119
  traveling to, 117–118
  useful phrases, 113–114
  water, 124
  what's new, 1–3
Thailand Cultural Center
  (Bangkok, T), 156–157
Thai Marine Leisure (Phuket,
  T), 212
Thai massage, 154
Thaipusam, 16
Thai Style Antique and
  Décor (Phuket, T), 216
Tha-lang National Museum
  (Phuket, T), 214–215
Thang Long (Hanoi, V), 286
Thang Long Water Puppet
  Theater (Hanoi, V), 287
Thanh Ha Silk (Hanoi, V),
  286
Thanh Mai (Hanoi, V), 286
That Chomsi Stupa (Luang
  Prabang, L), 419
That Dam (the Black Stupa;
  Vientiane, L), 404
That Luang Festival (Vien-
  tiane, L), 15–16, 383
That Makmo (Luang
  Prabang, L), 420
"The Killing Fields," Choe-
  ung Ek Memorial (Phnom
  Penh, C), 648
Thewet Market (Bangkok, T),
  156
Thian Hock Keng Temple (S),
  14, 491
Thien Mu Pagoda (Hue, V),
  302–303
Thien Vuong Pagoda (Dalat,
  V), 340
Thompson, Jim, House
  (Bangkok, T), 147

Throne Hall (Phnom Penh, C),
  647
Tiger Balm Gardens (Haw
  Par Villa, S), 495
Tioman Island (M), 12
TM Brothers (Dalat, V), 333
TM Brothers (Ho Chi Minh
  City, V), 350
Toa Payoh (S), 431
Tomb of Minh Mang (Hue,
  V), 303
Tomb of Tun Duc (Hue, V),
  303
Tom's Irish Bar (Phnom Penh,
  C), 649–650
Tonkinese Alps (V), 289
Tonle Bat I (C), 650
Top Ten (S), 517–518
Tours
  escorted, 65–67
  package, 64–65
Tours of Peace (TOP), 254
Tradewinds Resort in
  Chaweng (T), 196
Train travel, 68–69
The Tran Family Home and
  Chapel (Hoi An, V),
  317–318
Tran Quoc (Hanoi, V), 282
Traveler's checks, 43–44
Travel insurance, 46–47
Treat's Same Same Café (Hoi
  An, V), 320
Trekking
  Thailand, 213–214,
    234–235
  Ubud (I), 612
Tribal Museum (Chiang Mai,
  T), 232
Trip-cancellation insurance,
  46–47
Tropical diseases, 48
Truc Lam (Bamboo Forest)
  Zen Monastery
  (Dalat, V), 340
T'shop Lai Gallery (Vientiane,
  L), 405
Tsim Sha Tsui (H), 100
Tuk-tuk (Bangkok, T), 128
Tulamben (I), 620
Tun Duc, Tomb of (Hue, V),
  303
Tuol Sleng, Museum of
  Genocide (Phnom Penh, C),
  648
Tuol Sleng S-21 Prison
  Museum (Phnom Penh,
  C), 15
20 Leith Street (Penang, M),
  575

Ubud (I), 10–11, 603–613
  accommodations, 604–608
  nightlife, 613
  outdoor activities, 612–613
  restaurants, 608–611
  shopping, 613
  sights and attractions,
    611–612
  transportation, 604
  traveling to, 604
  visitor information, 604
Underwater World (S), 506

Valley of Love (Dalat, V),
  340–341
Vang Vieng (L), 12, 406–407
Van Mieu–Quoc Tu Giam
  (Hanoi, V), 283–284
Vasco's Bar (Ho Chi Minh
  City, V), 368
Vegas Thai Boxing (Phuket,
  T), 217
Vegetarian Festival (Phuket,
  T), 214
Victoria Peak (H), 6, 96–97
Victoria Theatre and Concert
  Hall (S), 488
Victory Monument (Patuxay;
  Vientiane, L), 403–404
Vientiane Boat Race Festival
  (L), 383
Vientiane Book Center (L),
  405
Vientiane (L), 390–405
  accommodations, 395–398
  attractions, 402–405
  emergencies, 395
  nightlife, 405
  post office/mail, 395
  restaurants, 4, 398–402
  shopping, 405
  snacks and cafes, 402
  telephone/fax, 395
  transportation, 394
  traveling to, 394
  visitor information, 391
Vietnam, 246–371
  accommodations, 260–261
  art forms, 251–252
  brief description of, 25–26
  central coast, 294
  climate, 256
  crime, 262
  cuisine, 251
  cultural traditions and
    practices, 31–32, 251
  currency and currency
    exchange, 42–43,
    255–256
  customs regulations, 255

dentists and doctors, 262
dietary precautions, 257
dress codes, 258
electricity, 262
embassies in, 262
embassy locations, 255
emergencies, 262
entry requirements,
  39, 253
etiquette, 252
health concerns, 257–258
history of, 248, 250–251
holidays, 257
hospitals, 262
Internet and e-mail access,
  262–263
language, 252–253, 263
lay of the land, 247
liquor laws, 263
Mekong Delta, 369–370
money matters, 255–256
north and northwest high-
  land regions, 289
peak season, 256
planning your trip to,
  253–261
police, 263
post offices/mail, 263
regions in brief, 247–248
religion, 252
restaurants, 261
safety, 263
shopping, 261
smoking in, 261
south central, 321
taxes, 263
telephone and fax,
  263–264
time zone, 264
tipping, 264
toilets, 264
tours for Vietnam
  veterans, 254
transportation, 259–260
traveling to, 258–259
useful phrases, 253
water, 264
what's new, 3
Vietnam Ethnology Museum
  (Hanoi, V), 285
Vietnam Fine Arts Museum
  (Hanoi, V), 14, 282
Vietnam Golf and Country
  Club (Ho Chi Minh City, V),
  367
Vietnam History Museum
  (Ho Chi Minh City, V), 365
Vietnamtourism Danang (V),
  304
Viet Silk (Ho Chi Minh City,
  V), 367

Vimanmek Mansion Museum
  (Bangkok, T), 150
VolcanoLand (S), 506

Wak Hai Cheng Bio
  Temple (S), 491
War Remnants Museum (Ho
  Chi Minh City, V), 366
Warung Candi Agung (Candi
  Dasa, I), 617
Wat Arun (Temple of Dawn;
  Bangkok, T), 151
Wat Benchamabophit (the
  Marble Wat; Bangkok, T),
  151–152
Wat Chalong (Phuket, T), 215
Wat Chedi Luang (Chiang
  Mai, T), 232
Wat Chet Yot (Chiang Mai,
  T), 233
Wat Chiang Man (Chiang
  Mai, T), 233
Wat Doi Tong (Phra That
  Chomtong; Chiang Rai, T),
  240–241
Water, drinking, 48
  Thailand, 124
Waterfalls
  Lombong (M), 558
  Prenn Falls (Dalat, V), 341
  Thailand
    Na Muang Falls, 197
    Pala-U, 184
Water-skiing, Singapore,
  507–508
Watersports, Patong Beach
  (T), 212
Wat Kamphaeng Laeng
  (Phetchaburi, T), 187
Wat Khao Phra Yai (Pattaya,
  T), 170
Wat Ko Keo Suttharam
  (Phetchaburi, T), 187
Wat Mahathat (Temple of
  the Great Relic; Bangkok,
  T), 151, 155
Wat Mai (Luang Prabang, L),
  419
Wat Mung Muang (Chiang
  Saen, T), 244
Wat Ong Teu (Vientiane, L),
  404
Wat Pa Sak (Chiang Saen, T),
  244
Wat Pha Kao Pan (Chiang
  Saen, T), 244
Wat Phan Tao (Chiang Mai,
  T), 232
Wat Phnom (Phnom Penh, C),
  646–647

Wat Phra Bat Nua (Luang Prabang, L), 419
Wat Phra Bouj (Chiang Saen, T), 244
Wat Phra Chedi Luang (Chiang Saen, T), 244
Wat Phra Kaeo (Bangkok, T), 13, 150
Wat Phra Kaeo (Chiang Rai, T), 241
Wat Phra Singh (Chiang Mai, T), 233
Wat Phra Singh (Chiang Rai, T), 241
Wat Phra That (near Chiang Mai, T), 234
Wat Po (Bangkok, T), 151, 154
Wat Pra Nahng Sahng (Phuket, T), 215
Wat Pra Tong (Phuket, T), 215
Wats. See Temples, wats, and pagodas
Wat Saket (The Golden Mount; Bangkok, T), 152
Wat Sangakaeo Don Tan (Chiang Saen, T), 244
Wat Si Muang (Vientiane, L), 404
Wat Si Saket (Vientiane, L), 404–405
Wat Suan Dok (Chiang Mai, T), 234
Wat Suthat and the Giant Swing (Bangkok, T), 152
Wat Tham Phousi (Luang Prabang, L), 419
Wat Traimit (The Golden Buddha; Bangkok, T), 152–153
Wat Wisunalat/Visounarath (Luang Prabang, L), 419–420
Wat Xieng Thong (Luang Prabang, L), 13, 420
Wat Yai Suwannaram (Phetchaburi, T), 185
Websites, travel-planning and booking, 56–57
Western Canned Foods (Hanoi, V), 286
Western Thailand (T), 106
Western Tours (Hua Hin, T), 184, 185
West Lake (Hanoi, V), 282
White-water rafting. See River rafting
Wild Planet (T), 235
Wildside Eco Group (L), 4, 380, 391, 406, 407, 422

Windsurfing
    Ko Samet (T), 176
    Patong Beach (T), 212
    Singapore, 508
Wiring emergency funds, (T), 115
Women travelers, 53–54
Wonderful Rocks (Ko Samui, T), 197
Wong Tai Sin (H), 99–100
Woodcarvings, 21–22

X ieng Khouang, 423–426
Xuan Huong Lake (Dalat, V), 338

Y angon (B), 693
The Yellow Star Café (Hoi An, V), 321
The Youth Museums and Art Gallery (Malacca, M), 563
Yue Hwa (S), 510

Z ouk/Phuture/Velvet Underground (S), 518
Zulu's Seaside Paradise (Penang, M), 575

ACCOMMODATIONS

Agung Raka Bungalows (Ubud, I), 607
Alam Sari (Ubud, I), 607
Alang Alang (Senggigi, I), 622
Albert Court Hotel (S), 455–456
Amandari (Ubud, I), 605
Amanjaya, Pancam Hotel (Phnom Penh, C), 640
Amankila (Candi Dasa, I), 614
Amari Boulevard Hotel (Bangkok, T), 137–138
Amari Coral Beach Resort (Patong, T), 209
Ana Mandara Resort (Nha Trang, V), 324–325
Ananda Cottages (Ubud, I), 607
Andaman Resortel (Patong, T), 210–211
The Angkor Hotel (Siem Reap, C), 655
Angkor Village (Siem Reap, C), 655
Angsoka (Lovina, I), 619

Anou Hotel (Vientiane, L), 397
Ao Pai Hut (Ko Samet, T), 175
Army Hotel (Hanoi, V), 272–273
Ashram Gandhi Candi Dasa (I), 615
Astina Seaside Cottages (Lovina, I), 619
Auberge de la Plaine des Jarres (Phonsavan, L), 425
Auberge Mont Royal D'Angkor (Siem Reap, C), 656
Bali Spirit Hotel and Spa (Ubud, I), 606
Bamboo Green Hotel (Danang, V), 305–306
Bamboo Green (Sapa, V), 291
Bangkok Marriott Resort & Spa (T), 133
Bangkok YWCA (T), 136–137
Bao Dai Hotel (Bao Dai's Villas; Nha Trang, V), 325–326
Bayu Kartika Beach Bungalows (Lovina, I), 619
Bayview Park Hotel (Manila, P), 675–676
Berjaya Hotel, Duxton Road (S), 457
Best Western Rosedale on the Park (H), 89–90
Bien Xanh Blue Ocean Resort (Phan Thiet, V), 343
Bishop Lei International House (H), 89
The Boat Landing (Luang Namtha, L), 423
Bong Sen Hotel Annex (Ho Chi Minh City, V), 358
Booth Lodge (H), 86
Boracay Regency Beach Resort (P), 680–681
Bossotel Inn (Bangkok, T), 134
Bounty Hotel (Kuta, I), 595
BP International House (H), 84–85
Bungalow Thavansouk and Sunset Restaurant (Vang Vieng, L), 406
Capitol Guesthouse (Phnom Penh, C), 642
Caravelle Hotel (Ho Chi Minh City, V), 352
Carlton Hotel Singapore, 452–453
Cat Cat Guesthouse (Sapa, V), 291–292

Cebu City Marriott (P), 685

The Cebu Plaza (P), 685

Century Mahkota Hotel Melaka (Malacca, M), 560

The Century Riverside Hotel (Hue, V), 297–298

Chau Long Sapa Hotel (V), 292

Chaweng Resort (Ko Samui, T), 192

Chiang Inn Hotel (Chiang Mai, T), 227

Chinatown Hotel (Bangkok, T), 134

Chinatown Hotel (S), 457

The City Bayview Hotel, Penang (M), 568

City Lodge (Bangkok, T), 139–140

Coco Beach (Phan Thiet, V), 343–344

Concorde Hotel Kuala Lumpur (M), 542

The Cool Point Hotel (Cameron Highlands, M), 552

Cua Dai (Hoi An, V), 313

Damai Lovina Hotel (I), 618

Dan Chu Hotel (Hanoi, V), 273

The Datai (Langkawi, M), 578

Day Inn Hotel (Vientiane, L), 397

De Syloia (Hanoi, V), 272

Diamond Cliff Resort (Patong, T), 209

Dolarog Resort (El Nido, P), 684

Dong Loi Hotel (Hue, V), 299

Dong Phuong Hotel (Nha Trang, V), 327–328

Dos Palmas Resort (Puerto Princesa, P), 683

Douang Deuane Hotel (Vientiane, L), 398

Dusit Island Resort Hotel (Chiang Rai, T), 239

The Dusit Thani (Bangkok, T), 135–136

Eastern & Oriental Hotel (E&O; Penang, M), 568

Eaton Hotel (H), 85

Eden Hotel (Hanoi, V), 273

The Empress Hotel (Chiang Mai, T), 227–228

Empress Hotel (Dalat, V), 335

Esty's House (Ubud, I), 608

Four Seasons Hotel Singapore, 457–458

Four Seasons Resort at Sayan (Ubud, I), 605

Friday's Resort (Boracay, P), 681

The Fullerton Singapore, 449

Full Moon Beach (Phan Thiet, V), 344–345

Furama Resort Danang (V), 305

Galaxy Hotel (Hanoi, V), 273–274

Genting Hotel (M), 551

Golden Bridge (Phnom Penh, C), 642

Golden Gate Hotel (Phnom Penh, C), 641, 642

Golden Sand Inn (Karon, T), 207

The Golden Triangle Inn (Chiang Rai, T), 239–240

Goldiana (Phnom Penh, C), 641

Golf III Hotel (Dalat, V), 335

Goodwood Park Hotel (S), 458–459

Grand Hotel (Ho Chi Minh City, V), 354–355

Grand Hyatt Erawan (Bangkok, T), 137

Grand Hyatt Hong Kong, 89

Grand Hyatt Singapore, 459

The Grand Luang Prabang (Xieng Keo, L), 411

Grand Plaza Parkroyal (S), 454

Guoman Hotel (Hanoi, V), 272

Hai Yen Hotel (Nha Trang, V), 326

Hai Yen (Sea Swallow Hotel; Hoi An, V), 312

Ha Long Hotel (Hanoi, V), 274

Hang Nga Guest House (Dalat, V), 335–336

Hanoi Daewoo Hotel (V), 270

Harbour View International House (H), 90

Hard Rock Hotel (Kuta, I), 595

Heeren House (Malacca, M), 560–561

Hilton Hanoi Opera (V), 270–271

Hilton International Bangkok at Nai Lert Park (T), 138

Hilton International Singapore, 460

Hoa Binh Hotel (Hanoi, V), 274

Hoa Hong Hotel (Hue, V), 298–299

Hoang Cuong Hotel (Hanoi, V), 274–275

Hoi An Beach Resort (V), 311–312

Hoi An Hotel (V), 312

Hoi An Riverside Resort (V), 311

Holiday Inn Crowne Plaza (Bangkok, T), 136

Holiday Inn Resort Penang (M), 568–569

Holiday Inn Resort Phuket (Patong, T), 209–210

Honeymoon Bakery Guesthouse (Ubud, I), 608

Hong Hoa Hotel (Ho Chi Minh City, V), 358–359

Hong Ngoc Hotel (Hanoi, V), 275

Hotel Aneka Lovina (I), 618

Hotel Bualu (Nusa Dua, I), 602

Hotel Cambodiana (Phnom Penh, C), 638

Hotel Continental (Ho Chi Minh City, V), 355

Hotel Dai Loi (Fortune Hotel; Dalat, V), 336

Hotel Fleuris (Puerto Princesa, P), 684

Hotel Inter-Continental Hong Kong, 82, 84

Hotel Inter-Continental Phnom Penh (C), 637–638

Hotel Inter-Continental Singapore, 453

Hotel Istana (Kuala Lumpur, M), 540–541

Hotel Majestic (Ho Chi Minh City, V), 352–353

Hotel Nam Song (Vang Vieng, L), 406

Hotel New Otani Singapore, 454–455

Hotel Puri (Malacca, M), 561

Hotel Restu Bali, 595

Hotel Saigon Morin (Hue, V), 298

Hotel Tjampuhan (Ubud, I), 607–608

Huong Giang Hotel (Hue, V), 298

Huong Sen Hotel (Ho Chi Minh City, V), 356

Huy Hoang Mini Hotel (Hoi An, V), 313

The Hyatt Regency (Johor Bahru, M), 554–555

Ibah (Ubud, I), 605–606

Ida's Homestay (Candi Dasa, I), 616

The Imperial Golden Triangle Resort (Chiang Saen, T), 243

The Imperial Mae Ping Hotel (Chiang Mai, T), 226–227

Imperial Samui Hotel (Ko Samui, T), 192

Island Shangri-La Hong Kong, 88

Juliana Hotel (Phnom Penh, C), 641

JW Marriott Hotel Kuala Lumpur (M), 541

Kajeng Homestay (Ubud, I), 608

Kata Beach Resort (T), 205

Katanoi Bay Inn (Kata Noi, T), 207

Kata Thani Hotel (T), 205

Kelapamas Homestay (Candi Dasa, I), 616

Kim Do Royal City Hotel (Ho Chi Minh City, V), 356–357

King's Garden Resort (Ko Samui, T), 193–194

Komaneka Resort (Ubud, I), 606

Kowloon Hotel (H), 85

Kubu Bali (Candi Dasa, I), 615–616

Kupu Kupu Barong (Ubud, I), 606

Lane-Xang Hotel (Vientiane, L), 398

La Noria (Siem Reap, C), 656–657

Lao-Paris Hotel (Vientiane, L), 398

The Lao Plaza Hotel (Vientiane, L), 395

La Reserve Resort and Hotel (Boracay, P), 681

Last Home Guesthouse (Phnom Penh, C), 642

Le Calao (Luang Prabang, L), 413

The Legend Hotel (Kuala Lumpur, M), 542

Legend Hotel (Puerto Princesa, P), 683

Legian (Kuta, I), 597

Le Meridien Baan Boran Hotel (Chiang Saen, T), 243–244

Le Meridien President (Bangkok, T), 137

Le Royal Meridien (Bangkok, T), 137

L'hotel Souvannaphoum (Luang Prabang, L), 413

Lorenzo Resorts: Main, South, and Grand Villas (Boracay, P), 681

Malibu Garden Resort (Ko Samet, T), 175

Maly Hotel (Phonsavan, L), 425

Mandarin Oriental (H), 88

Mandarin Oriental (Manila, P), 676

Mandarin Singapore, 460

Manichan Guesthouse (Luang Namtha, L), 423

Manila Hotel (P), 675

Manoluk Hotel (Luang Prabang, L), 413

Marina Mandarin Singapore, 453–454

Marina Phuket (Karon, T), 207

Matahari Inn (Kuta Beach, Lombok, I), 624

Melia Hotel (Hanoi, V), 271

Meliá Kuala Lumpur (M), 542–543

Miniloc Island Resort and Lagen Island Resort (El Nido, P), 684

Mom Tri's Boathouse & Villa Resort (Kata, T), 205

Montien Hotel (Bangkok, T), 136

Mouang Luang Hotel (Luang Prabang, L), 413–414

Muang Kulaypan Hotel (Ko Samui, T), 192–193

Mui Ne Sailing Club (Phan Thiet, V), 344

Mutiara Burau Bay Beach Resort (Langkawi, M), 578

Mutiara Hotel Johor Bahru (M), 555–556

Natour Kuta (I), 596

Neak Pean Hotel (Siem Reap, C), 657

New Luang Prabang Hotel (Luang Prabang, L), 414

New Merry V. Guesthouse (Bangkok, T), 135

New Star Bungalow (Ko Samui, T), 193

New World Hotel Saigon (Ho Chi Minh City, V), 353

Ngoc Lan Hotel (Dalat, V), 336

Nha Trang Lodge Hotel (V), 326

Norfolk Hotel (Ho Chi Minh City, V), 355–356

Novotel Bangkok (T), 139

Novotel Coralia Ocean Dunes Phan Thiet (V), 342–343

Novotel Dalat Hotel (V), 334

Novotel Hotel Vientiane (L), 395–396

Novotel Lombok (Kuta Beach, I), 624

Novotel (Nusa Dua, I), 602–603

Nusa Dua Beach Hotel and Spa (I), 601

Oberoi (Kuta, I), 597

OK Post Hotel (Nha Trang, V), 327

Omni Saigon Hotel (Ho Chi Minh City, V), 353–354

Orchard Parade Hotel (S), 461–462

Orchid Guesthouse (Vientiane, L), 398

The Oriental (Bangkok, T), 132

Padma Hotel (Kuta, I), 596

Palace Hotel (Ho Chi Minh City, V), 357

The Pan Pacific Hotel Kuala Lumpur (M), 541

The Pan Pacific (Manila, P), 675

Pansea Angkor (Siem Reap, C), 654

Pan Sea Hotel (Luang Prabang, L), 411–412

Pan Sea Yangon (B), 693

Passagio (Siem Reap, C), 657

Patong Merlin (T), 210

The Pavilion Resort (Lamai, T), 194–195

Pavillon Indochina (Siem Reap, C), 657–659

Pearl of the Pacific Beach Resort (Boracay, P), 681–682

Pelangi Beach Resort (Langkawi, M), 578–579

The Peninsula Bangkok (T), 132–133

Peninsula Excelsior Hotel (S), 455

The Peninsula Hotel (H), 84

The Peninsula (Manila, P), 676

Phousi Hotel (Luang Prabang, L), 414

Phuc Loi (Hanoi, V), 275

Phuket Arcadia Hotel (Karon, T), 206

Phuket Cabana Resort (Patong, T), 210

Phuket Club Mediterranee (Kata, T), 206

Phu Quy (Nha Trang, V), 328

Pool Villa Club at the Senggigi Beach Hotel (I),
622–623

Poppies II Cottages (Kuta, I),
596

P.P. Princess Resort (Phi Phi
Don, T), 218

The Princess Village (Ko
Samui, T), 193

Pringga Juwita Water Gar-
den Cottages (Ubud, I),
608

Puri Bagus (Candi Dasa, I),
614

Puri Bagus Lovina (I), 618

Puri Garden Bungalows
(Ubud, I), 608

Puri Tantra Bungalows (Kuta,
I), 596–597

The Puteri Pan Pacific (Johor
Bahru, M), 556

Que Huong Hotel (Nha
Trang, V), 327

Raffles Grand Hotel
D'Angkor (Siem Reap, C),
654

Raffles Hotel Le Royal
(Phnom Penh, C), 638

Raffles Hotel (S), 449, 452

Raffles the Plaza (S), 454

Rama Hotel (Luang Prabang,
L), 414

Rambutan Beach Cottages
(Lovina, I), 618–619

Red Piano (Siem Reap, C),
656

Regal Airport Hotel (H),
90–91

Regalis Court (S), 463

The Regent (Bangkok, T),
138–139

The Regent Kuala Lumpur
(M), 540

RELC International Hotel (S),
463

Renaissance Kuala Lumpur
Hotel (M), 540

Renaissance Lake Hotel–
Yangon (B), 693

Renaissance Melaka Hotel
(Malacca, M), 561

Renaissance Riverside Hotel
Saigon (Ho Chi Minh City,
V), 354

Resort Hotel (Genting, M),
551

Rex Hotel (Ho Chi Minh City,
V), 357

Rice Paddy Bungalows
(Ubud, I), 608

Rimkok Resort Hotel
(Chiang Rai, T), 239

The Ritz-Carlton, Millenia
Singapore, 452

River Ping Palace (Chiang
Mai, T), 228

River View Lodge (Chiang
Mai, T), 228

Royal Dokmaideng Hotel
(Vientiane, L), 396–397

Royal Hotel (Sapa, V), 292

Royal Palm Resortel (Patong,
T), 211

Royal Phnom Penh (C), 640

Royal Phuket City Hotel (T),
203–204

Royal Princess (Bangkok, T),
134

Royal Princess Hotel (Chiang
Mai, T), 227

Saigon Mui Ne Resort (Phan
Thiet, V), 344

Saigon Prince Hotel, a Duxton Hotel (Ho Chi Minh
City, V), 356

Saigon Tourane Hotel
(Danang, V), 306

Salina Hotel (Siem Reap, C),
656

The Salisbury YMCA (H), 86

Samui Yacht Club (Lamai, T),
195

Sandy Inn (Karon, T), 208

Say Nam Khan Guest House
(Luang Prabang, L),
414–415

Sayo Guesthouse (Luang
Prabang, L), 415

Seaside Hotel
(Sihanoukville, C), 650

Senggigi Beach Hotel (I),
623

Serai (Candi Dasa, I), 615

Settha Palace Hotel (Vientiane, L), 396

Shangri-La Hotel (Bangkok,
T), 133

The Shangri-La Hotel Kuala
Lumpur (M), 541–542

Shangri-La Hotel (Manila, P),
676–677

Shangri-La Hotel (S),
459–460

Shangri-La's Golden Sands
Resort (Penang, M),
569–570

Shangri-La's Rasa Sayang
Resort (Penang, M), 570

Sheraton Laguna Nusa Dua
(I), 601–602

Sheraton Nusa Indah (I), 602

Sheraton Penang Hotel (M),
570

Sheraton Senggigi (I), 623

Sheraton Towers Singapore,
461

Siam Inter-Continental Hotel
(Bangkok, T), 139

Singapore Marriott Hotel,
461

The Smokehouse Hotel
(Cameron Highlands, M),
552

Sofitel Dalat Palace (V), 334

Sofitel Metropole Hanoi (V),
271–272

Sofitel Plaza Saigon (Ho Chi
Minh City, V), 354

Sofitel Royal Angkor (Siem
Reap, C), 654–655

The Spa Resort (Lamai, T),
195

Spring Hotel (Mua Xuan; Ho
Chi Minh City, V), 358

Stanford Hillview Hotel (H),
86, 88

Stanford Hotel (Kuala
Lumpur, M), 543

Strand Hotel (S), 456

The Strand Hotel (Yangon,
B), 693

Suk 11 Guesthouse
(Bangkok, T), 140

The Sukhothai (Bangkok, T),
135

Sunway Hotel (Phnom Penh,
C), 640

Suriwongse Hotel (Chiang
Mai, T), 228

Swiss-Garden Hotel (M), 543

Swiss-Inn (Kuala Lumpur, M),
543–544

Swissôtel Merchant Court
(S), 456

Swissôtel Stamford (S), 455

Tai-Pan Hotel (Vientiane, L),
397

Tanjung Rhu Resort
(Langkawi, M), 579

The Tavorn Hotel
(Phuket, T), 204

Thanh Bin II Hotel (Hoi An,
V), 313

Thanh Tra Hotel (Chau Doc,
V), 370

Thavorn Palm Beach Hotel
(Karon, T), 206–207

Theme Park Hotel (Genting,
M), 551

Tiara Oriental (Manila, P),
677

Top North Guest House
Chiang Mai, T), 229

Traders Hotel Singapore, 462

Traders Hotel Yangon (B),
693

Tradewinds (Ko Samui, T), 193

Truc Linh Villa Hotel and Restaurant (Nha Trang, V), 328

Trung Cang Hotel (Dalat, V), 336

Tum-Tum Cheng (Luang Prabang, L), 415

Victoria Chau Doc (V), 370

Victoria Hoi An Resort (V), 310–311

Victoria Phan Thiet Resort (V), 343

Victoria Sapa (V), 291

Vien Dong Hotel (Nha Trang, V), 326–327

Vila Lumbung Hotel (Kuta, I), 597

Villa Santi Hotel (Luang Prabang, L), 412

Villa Santi Resort (Luang Prabang, L), 412

Vinh Hung I and II (Hoi An, V), 313

Vong Deaun Resort (Ko Samet, T), 175

Vongduern Villas (Ko Samet, T), 175–176

Waling Waling Beach Hotel (Boracay, P), 682

Wangcome Hotel (Chiang Rai, T), 239

Watergarden (Candi Dasa, I), 615

Willy's Beach Resort (Boracay, P), 682

Windsor Hotel (Ho Chi Minh City, V), 357–358

Yasaka Saigon-Nhatrang Hotel (Nha Trang, V), 325

YMCA (Manila, P), 677

York Hotel Singapore, 462–463

Frommer's
Portable Guides
Complete Guides for the
Short-Term Traveler

FROMMER'S® COMPLETE TRAVEL GUIDES

Alaska
Alaska Cruises & Ports of Call
Amsterdam
Argentina & Chile
Arizona
Atlanta
Australia
Austria
Bahamas
Barcelona, Madrid & Seville
Beijing
Belgium, Holland & Luxembourg
Bermuda
Boston
Brazil
British Columbia & the Canadian
   Rockies
Brussels & Bruges
Budapest & the Best of Hungary
California
Canada
Cancún, Cozumel & the Yucatán
Cape Cod, Nantucket & Martha's
   Vineyard
Caribbean
Caribbean Cruises & Ports of Call
Caribbean Ports of Call
Carolinas & Georgia
Chicago
China
Colorado
Costa Rica
Cuba
Denmark
Denver, Boulder & Colorado Springs
England
Europe
European Cruises & Ports of Call

Florida
France
Germany
Great Britain
Greece
Greek Islands
Hawaii
Hong Kong
Honolulu, Waikiki & Oahu
Ireland
Israel
Italy
Jamaica
Japan
Las Vegas
London
Los Angeles
Maryland & Delaware
Maui
Mexico
Montana & Wyoming
Montréal & Québec City
Munich & the Bavarian Alps
Nashville & Memphis
New England
New Mexico
New Orleans
New York City
New Zealand
Northern Italy
Norway
Nova Scotia, New Brunswick &
   Prince Edward Island
Oregon
Paris
Peru
Philadelphia & the Amish Country
Portugal

Prague & the Best of the Czech
   Republic
Provence & the Riviera
Puerto Rico
Rome
San Antonio & Austin
San Diego
San Francisco
Santa Fe, Taos & Albuquerque
Scandinavia
Scotland
Seattle & Portland
Shanghai
Sicily
Singapore & Malaysia
South Africa
South America
South Florida
South Pacific
Southeast Asia
Spain
Sweden
Switzerland
Texas
Thailand
Tokyo
Toronto
Tuscany & Umbria
USA
Utah
Vancouver & Victoria
Vermont, New Hampshire & Maine
Vienna & the Danube Valley
Virgin Islands
Virginia
Walt Disney World® & Orlando
Washington, D.C.
Washington State

FROMMER'S® DOLLAR-A-DAY GUIDES

Australia from $50 a Day
California from $70 a Day
England from $75 a Day
Europe from $70 a Day
Florida from $70 a Day
Hawaii from $80 a Day

Ireland from $60 a Day
Italy from $70 a Day
London from $85 a Day
New York from $90 a Day
Paris from $80 a Day

San Francisco from $70 a Day
Washington, D.C. from $80 a Day
Portable London from $85 a Day
Portable New York City from $90
   a Day

FROMMER'S® PORTABLE GUIDES

Acapulco, Ixtapa & Zihuatanejo
Amsterdam
Aruba
Australia's Great Barrier Reef
Bahamas
Berlin
Big Island of Hawaii
Boston
California Wine Country
Cancún
Cayman Islands
Charleston
Chicago
Disneyland®
Dublin
Florence

Frankfurt
Hong Kong
Houston
Las Vegas
Las Vegas for Non-Gamblers
London
Los Angeles
Los Cabos & Baja
Maine Coast
Maui
Miami
Nantucket & Martha's Vineyard
New Orleans
New York City
Paris
Phoenix & Scottsdale

Portland
Puerto Rico
Puerto Vallarta, Manzanillo &
   Guadalajara
Rio de Janeiro
San Diego
San Francisco
Savannah
Seattle
Sydney
Tampa & St. Petersburg
Vancouver
Venice
Virgin Islands
Washington, D.C.

FROMMER'S® NATIONAL PARK GUIDES

Banff & Jasper
Family Vacations in the National
   Parks

Grand Canyon
National Parks of the American West
Rocky Mountain

Yellowstone & Grand Teton
Yosemite & Sequoia/Kings Canyon
Zion & Bryce Canyon

FROMMER'S® MEMORABLE WALKS

Chicago	New York	San Francisco
London	Paris	

FROMMER'S® WITH KIDS GUIDES

Chicago	Ottawa	Vancouver
Las Vegas	San Francisco	Washington, D.C.
New York City	Toronto	

SUZY GERSHMAN'S BORN TO SHOP GUIDES

Born to Shop: France	Born to Shop: Italy	Born to Shop: New York
Born to Shop: Hong Kong, Shanghai & Beijing	Born to Shop: London	Born to Shop: Paris

FROMMER'S® IRREVERENT GUIDES

Amsterdam	Los Angeles	San Francisco
Boston	Manhattan	Seattle & Portland
Chicago	New Orleans	Vancouver
Las Vegas	Paris	Walt Disney World®
London	Rome	Washington, D.C.

FROMMER'S® BEST-LOVED DRIVING TOURS

Britain	Germany	Northern Italy
California	Ireland	Scotland
Florida	Italy	Spain
France	New England	Tuscany & Umbria

HANGING OUT™ GUIDES

Hanging Out in England	Hanging Out in France	Hanging Out in Italy
Hanging Out in Europe	Hanging Out in Ireland	Hanging Out in Spain

THE UNOFFICIAL GUIDES®

Bed & Breakfasts and Country Inns in:	Southwest & South Central Plains	Mexio's Best Beach Resorts
California	U.S.A.	Mid-Atlantic with Kids
Great Lakes States	Beyond Disney	Mini Las Vegas
Mid-Atlantic	Branson, Missouri	Mini-Mickey
New England	California with Kids	New England & New York with Kids
Northwest	Central Italy	New Orleans
Rockies	Chicago	New York City
Southeast	Cruises	Paris
Southwest	Disneyland®	San Francisco
Best RV & Tent Campgrounds in:	Florida with Kids	Skiing & Snowboarding in the West
California & the West	Golf Vacations in the Eastern U.S.	Southeast with Kids
Florida & the Southeast	Great Smoky & Blue Ridge Region	Walt Disney World®
Great Lakes States	Inside Disney	Walt Disney World® for Grown-ups
Mid-Atlantic	Hawaii	Walt Disney World® with Kids
Northeast	Las Vegas	Washington, D.C.
Northwest & Central Plains	London	World's Best Diving Vacations
	Maui	

SPECIAL-INTEREST TITLES

Frommer's Adventure Guide to Australia & New Zealand	Frommer's France's Best Bed & Breakfasts and Country Inns
Frommer's Adventure Guide to Central America	Frommer's Gay & Lesbian Europe
Frommer's Adventure Guide to India & Pakistan	Frommer's Italy's Best Bed & Breakfasts and Country Inns
Frommer's Adventure Guide to South America	Frommer's Road Atlas Britain
Frommer's Adventure Guide to Southeast Asia	Frommer's Road Atlas Europe
Frommer's Adventure Guide to Southern Africa	Frommer's Road Atlas France
Frommer's Britain's Best Bed & Breakfasts and Country Inns	The New York Times' Guide to Unforgettable Weekends
Frommer's Caribbean Hideaways	Places Rated Almanac
Frommer's Exploring America by RV	Retirement Places Rated
Frommer's Fly Safe, Fly Smart	Rome Past & Present

Booked aisle seat.

Reserved room with a view.

With a queen – no, make that a king-size bed.